# Benchmark Papers in Electrical Engineering and Computer Science

**Series Editor: John B. Thomas**
**Princeton University**

**PUBLISHED VOLUMES**

SYSTEM SENSITIVITY ANALYSIS
*J. B. Cruz, Jr.*
RANDOM PROCESSES, PART I: Multiplicity Theory and Canonical Decompositions
*Anthony Ephremides and John B. Thomas*
ALGEBRAIC CODING THEORY: History and Development
*Ian F. Blake*
PATTERN RECOGNITION: Introduction and Foundations
*Jack Sklansky*
COMPUTER-AIDED CIRCUIT DESIGN: Simulation and Optimization
*S. W. Director*
ENVIRONMENTAL MODELING: Analysis and Management
*Douglas Daetz and Richard H. Pantell*
AUTOMATIC CONTROL: Classical Linear Theory
*George J. Thaler*
CIRCUIT THEORY: Foundations and Classical Contributions
*M. E. Van Valkenburg*
DATA COMMUNICATION: Fundamentals of Baseband Transmission
*L. E. Franks*
NONLINEAR SYSTEMS: Processing of Random Signals—Classical Analysis
*A. H. Haddad*
RANDOM PROCESSES, PART II: Poisson and Jump-Point Processes
*Anthony Ephremides*
DIGITAL FILTERS AND THE FAST FOURIER TRANSFORM
*Bede Liu*
DETECTION AND ESTIMATION: Applications to Radar
*Simon S. Haykin*
DATA COMPRESSION
*Lee D. Davisson and Robert M. Gray*

Additional volumes in preparation

Benchmark Papers
in Electrical Engineering
and Computer Science / 14

A BENCHMARK® Books Series

# DATA COMPRESSION


Edited by

**LEE D. DAVISSON**
University of Southern California

**and ROBERT M. GRAY**
Stanford University



Dowden, Hutchinson & Ross, Inc.
STROUDSBURG, PENNSYLVANIA

Distributed by
HALSTED PRESS
A Division of
John Wiley & Sons, Inc.

Benchmark Papers in Electrical Engineering and Computer Science, Volume 14
Library of Congress Catalog Card Number: 76-3629
ISBN: 0-87933-089-9



78 77 76 1 2 3 4 5
Manufactured in the United States of America

LIBRARY OF CONGRESS CATALOGING IN PUBLICATION DATA

Main entry under title:
Data compression
(Benchmark papers in electrical engineering and computer science / 14)
Includes indexes.
1. Data compression (Telecommunication) 2. Coding theory.
I. Davisson, Lee D. II. Gray, Robert M., 1943–
TK5102.5.D335 1976 621.38 76-3629
ISBN 0-470-15053-X
ISBN: 0-87933-089-9



Exclusive Distributor: **Halsted Press**
A Division of John Wiley & Sons, Inc.
ISBN: 0-470-15053-X

# PERMISSIONS

The following papers have been reprinted with the permission of the authors and copyright holders.

ACADEMIC PRESS, INC.—*Information and Control*
On the Quantization of Finite Dimensional Messages

ACOUSTICAL SOCIETY OF AMERICA—*The Journal of the Acoustical Society of America*
Speech Analysis and Synthesis by Linear Prediction of the Speech Wave

AMERICAN TELEPHONE & TELEGRAPH COMPANY—*Bell System Technical Journal*
Adaptive Redundancy Removal in Data Transmission

INSTITUTE OF ELECTRICAL AND ELECTRONICS ENGINEERS, INC.
*IEEE Transactions on Communication Technology*
A Comparison of Orthogonal Transformations for Digital Speech Processing
Image Coding by Linear Transformation and Block Quantization
A Variable Step-Size Robust Delta Modulator
*IEEE Transactions on Information Theory*
Analog Source Digitization: A Comparison of Theory and Practice
Asymptotically Efficient Quantizing
Buffer Overflow in Variable Length Coding of Fixed Rate Sources
Computation of Channel Capacity and Rate-Distortion Functions
Data Compression Using Straight Line Interpolation
Enumerative Source Encoding
A Geometric Treatment of the Source Encoding of a Gaussian Random Variable
Information Rates in Sampling and Quantization
Instrumentable Tree Encoding of Information Sources
Nonlinear Estimation with Quantized Measurements—PCM, Predictive Quantization, and Data Compression
On Optimum Quantization
On Variable-Length-to-Block Coding
Optimum Quantizers and Permutation Codes
Properties of an Optimum Digital System and Applications
Quantizing for Minimum Distortion
Source Coding Theorems Without the Ergodic Assumption
Theoretical Limitations on the Transmission of Data from Analog Sources
Tree Encoding of Gaussian Sources
Tree Encoding of Speech
Trellis Encoding of Memoryless Discrete-Time Sources with a Fidelity Criterion
Universal Noiseless Coding
*IRE Transactions of the Professional Group on Circuit Theory*
A Study of Rough Amplitude Quantization by Means of Nyquist Sampling Theory
*IRE Transactions on Information Theory*
Predictive Coding
Quantizing for Minimum Distortion

## *Permissions*

*IRE Transactions on Space Electronics and Telemetry*
Message Compression
*Proceedings of the IEEE*
Analysis of Some Redundancy Removal Bandwidth Compression Techniques
Comments on "Sequence Time Coding for Data Compression"
Information Rates of Gaussian Signals Under Criteria Constraining the Error Spectrum
Linear and Adaptive Delta Modulation
Sequence Time Coding for Data Compression
Statistical Delta Modulation
The Theoretical Analysis of Data Compression Systems
Visual Fidelity Criterion and Modeling
*Proceedings of the IRE*
A Method for the Construction of Minimum Redundancy Codes
Quantizing Distortion in Pulse-Count Modulation with Nonuniform Spacing of Levels
*Proceedings of the Mervin J. Kelly Communications Conference*
A Comparison of Digital Image Transforms
*Proceedings of the National Telemetry Conference*
An Adaptive Nonlinear Data Predictor
*Proceedings of the 1974 International Conference on Communications*
A Mathematical Theory of Data Compression?

WESTERN PERIODICALS COMPANY—*Proceedings of the Seventh Hawaii International Conference on System Sciences*
Joint Source and Channel Coding

# SERIES EDITOR'S PREFACE

This Benchmark Series in Electrical Engineering and Computer Science is aimed at sifting, organizing, and making readily accessible to the reader the vast literature that has accumulated. Although the series is not intended as a complete substitute for a study of this literature, it will serve at least three major critical purposes. In the first place, it provides a practical point of entry into a given area of research. Each volume offers an expert's selection of the critical papers on a given topic as well as his views on its structure, development, and present status. In the second place, the series provides a convenient and time-saving means for study in areas related to but not contiguous with one's principal interests. Last, but by no means least, the series allows the collection, in a particularly compact and convenient form, of the major works on which present research activities and interests are based.

Each volume in the series has been collected, organized, and edited by an authority in the area to which it pertains. In order to present a unified view of the area, the volume editor has prepared an introduction to the subject, has included his comments on each article, and has provided a subject index to facilitate access to the papers.

We believe that this series will provide a manageable working library of the most important technical articles in electrical engineering and computer science. We hope that it will be equally valuable to students, teachers, and researchers.

This volume, *Data Compression,* has been edited jointly by L. D. Davisson of the University of Southern California and by R. M. Gray of Stanford University. It contains forty-six papers developing the theory and practice of data compression. Most of the papers are of relatively recent origin, reflecting not only the comparative youth of the field but also its growing importance. Both editors are heavily involved in research in this area and both are well known for their contributions to this and related areas.

JOHN B. THOMAS

# PREFACE

*Simplicity is the great friend of Nature.*—Stern

*Nothing is more noble, nothing more venerable than fidelity.*—Cicero

Data compression is the science and/or art of processing information so as to obtain a simple representation with at most a tolerable loss of fidelity. Such simplification may be necessitated by storage constraints, bandwidth limitations, or communications channel capacity. Fidelity of the eventual reproduction of the information based on the simplified or compressed representation is measured by mathematical distortion measures such as error power or by purely subjective methods based on psychophysical tests.

In spite of the importance of data compression to modern communications and signal processing, there does not exist at this writing a unified text devoted to the subject. In this collection we attempt to partially fill this gap by presenting in pedagogical order a variety of papers on the various theoretical and practical aspects of data compression, along with an editorial commentary that places the diverse results within a common framework of information and communications theory. In particular, the mathematical and practical tradeoffs between simplicity or compression on one hand and fidelity on the other provide a common focus for comparing and contrasting all the ideal and ad hoc data compression systems described herein.

LEE D. DAVISSON
ROBERT M. GRAY

# CONTENTS

# CONTENTS BY AUTHOR

# DATA COMPRESSION

# INTRODUCTION

Data compression is the science and/or art of massaging data from a given information source in such a way as to obtain a simplified or ''compressed'' version of the source data with at most some tolerable loss of fidelity. Such data reduction may be required because of storage constraints, limited bandwidth, limited capacity on a communications link, or simply by the desire to ''sift'' the data for important attributes. Common applications of data compression are found in systems for communications, speech and image processing, pattern recognition, information retrieval, storage, and cryptography.

The theory and practice of data compression began with W. F. Sheppards's study of the ''rounding off'' of real numbers to a fixed number of decimal places—the first use of uniform quantization [''On the Calculation of the Most Probable Values of Frequency Constants for Data Arranged According to Equidistant Divisions of a Scale,'' *Proc. London Math. Soc.,* **24,** Pt. 2, 353–380 (1898)]. The history of the development of data compression has usually proceeded along two fairly distinct lines: the more mathematical engineers, on one hand, have tried to develop mathematical models of sources and data compression systems and the figures of merit and optimal performance bounds with which to compare such systems; the more pragmatic engineers, on the other hand, have developed largely ad hoc and often ingenious systems to accomplish data compression and the analyzing or simulating of such particular systems to establish their performance. In recent years, these separate paths have begun to remerge, with sophisticated techniques from information theory and estimation theory being applied to compress real data and with physical insight into practical compression systems that spawn new abstract mathematical theories for the approximation of random processes.

In this collection we present both generally acknowledged classic papers on data compression and some perhaps less well known papers, which in the editors' opinion fill some historical, technical, or pedagogical gap. The papers are drawn from both the theoretical and the more practical sides of the literature, and reflect a variety of systems, approaches, and results. Some very recent developments on the mathematical side, however, are currently in a state of flux and require a highly mathematical background; these are deferred to a later, more mathematical volume in this Benchmark series, tentatively entitled *Ergodic and Information Theory*. Papers in the latter volume relevant to data compression are briefly referred to in the editors' comments and in the papers included here.

A collection such as this provides the editors with an opportunity to present the diverse areas of and approaches to data compression in a unified framework by classifying and comparing the various theories and data-compression schemes. Toward this end, we now present a brief discussion of some basic concepts underlying most such systems and classify the various compression algorithms.

A general model for a communications system is presented in Figure 1. The source is usually assumed to produce a discrete-time random process $\{X_n\}_{n=-\infty}^{\infty}$, that is, a sequence of random variables. Although many physical processes of interest are continuous-time processes, the discrete-time model is commonly adopted for any or all of the following reasons: (1) digital and therefore discrete-time communications links are becoming increasingly common; (2) a continuous-time process can be modeled as a discrete-time process by sampling, by performing expansions such as the Karhunen–Loève expansion, or by segmentation, that is, by viewing consecutive waveforms as individual "letters" in a complicated alphabet; and (3) simplicity. Of interest in the various papers will be the regularity conditions imposed on the source, such as stationarity, ergodicity, and independence. The source is characterized by its alphabet $A$, that is, the set of values that $X_n$ can assume, and its probabilistic description. The alphabet $A$ might be the set of real numbers, a finite set, a collection of waveforms, a collection of two-dimensional intensity distributions, and so on. The probabilistic description, often represented by $\mu$, is typically a family of $n$-dimensional probability density, distribu-

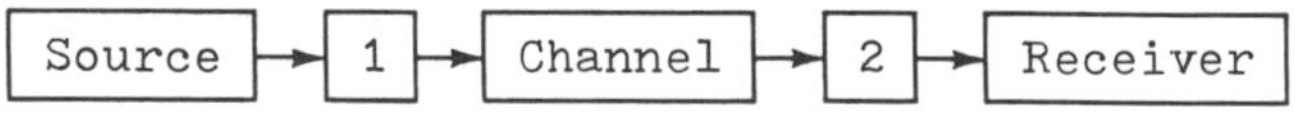


**Figure 1**

tion, or mass functions. We assume that the source produces one symbol in $A$ each $\tau_s$ seconds and therefore has a symboling rate of $R_s = 1/\tau_s$ symbols per second. This is called a fixed-rate source.

The channel is assumed to be a fixed-rate digital communications link, that is, a discrete-time, finite-alphabet device that accepts and transmits to the receiver one symbol in a finite alphabet $B$ each $\tau_c$ seconds. The alphabet $B$ has $||B||$ letters and is often taken to be binary; that is, $B = \{0, 1\}$. Information theory guarantees that this assumption entails essentially no loss of generality. The transmission rate of the channel is defined as $R_c = 1/\tau_c$ symbols per second (or bits per second if $B = \{0, 1\}$). Denote the channel input process by $\{Y_n\}$ and the channel output process by $\{\hat{Y}_n\}$. The channel may or may not be noisy; that is, in general $\hat{Y}_n$ need not equal $Y_n$. A noiseless channel sends symbols without error, in which case $\hat{Y}_n = Y_n$.

Box 1 of Figure 1 incorporates all operations that process the source data to prepare it for channel transmission, for example, coding, analog-to-digital conversion, and modulation. We refer to this box simply as an *encoder*. Similarly, box 2 processes the received data into the form desired by the receiver. This box is called the *decoder*. To ensure a compatible throughput rate for the system, we require that integers $K$ and $L$ exist such that $K\tau_s = L\tau_c \triangleq T$; that is, the channel transmits $L$ channel symbols in the same time that the source produces $K$ symbols. This guarantees that the received sequence $\{\hat{X}_n\}$ will have the same received symbol rate (although there will usually be some delay). Within boxes 1 and 2 may be variable-length devices, filters, block coders, buffers, and the like.

The symbol compression coefficient $\eta$ of a code is defined as the number of channel symbols sent per source symbol; $\eta = L/K = \tau_s/\tau_c = R_c/R_s$. The quantity $1/\eta = R_s/R_c$ is sometimes called the *coding rate*, especially in error-correcting applications.

Say that we have a measure of the distortion or cost $\rho_n(X_1, \ldots, X_n; \hat{X}_1, \ldots, \hat{X}_n)$ of reproducing $X_1, \ldots, X_n$ at the receiver as $\hat{X}_1, \ldots, \hat{X}_n$. Common examples of such distortion measures are average squared error $n^{-1} \Sigma (X_i - \hat{X}_i)^2$ and Hamming distance $n^{-1} \Sigma d(X_i, \hat{X}_i)$, where $d(X_i, \hat{X}_i)$ is zero if $X_i = \hat{X}_i$ and one otherwise. The mean distortion $E_\mu \rho_n(X_1, \ldots, X_n; \hat{X}_1, \ldots, \hat{X}_n)$, where $E_\mu$ denotes expectation over the source probabilities, provides a figure of merit with which to compare data-compression systems.

The basic theoretical goal of data compression is the following: given an allowed class $F_E$ of encoders and an allowed class $F_D$ of decoders, what is the optimal performance theoretically attainable (OPTA) using devices of the given type? The classes of allowed encoders–decoders are often specified by constraints on their complexity or demands on the compression; typical classes are all quantizers with $N$ levels, all block codes of fixed length and size, or all time-invariant filters of a given type with constrained output entropy. "Optimal" is taken to mean the minimum average distortion. Thus the basic quantities of interest are the OPTA functions of a source $\{X_n\}$, distortion measure $\rho_n$, and classes of devices $(F_E, F_D)$ defined by

$$\delta_X^{(n)}(F_E, F_D) = \inf_{(F_E, F_D)} E\rho_n(X_1, \ldots, X_n; \hat{X}_1, \ldots, \hat{X}_n),$$

where the infimum is over all encoders and decoders within the class. The infimum is required to be mathematically precise since a minimum may not exist; that is, there may not be devices actually yielding $\delta_X^{(n)}(F_E, F_D)$, even though performance quite close to $\delta_X^{(n)}$ can be achieved.

In some applications one is interested in $\delta_X^{(n)}$ for a fixed $n$ and in others the best $n$ is desired, which motivates another OPTA function $\delta_X(F_E, F_D)$, defined as

$$\delta_X(F_E, F_D) = \inf_n \delta_X^{(n)}(F_E, F_D).$$

Many of the papers in this collection will be concerned either with the evaluation of OPTA functions or in the comparison of particular algorithms with an appropriate OPTA. Thus the comparisons given in the editorial comments will usually classify the papers according to assumptions on the source $\{X_n\}$, the distortion measure $\rho_n$, and the allowed device classes $F_E$ and $F_D$.

The information transmission theorem of information theory states that the encoding operation can be factored into two separate steps: (1) *source coding* or data compression, the mapping of the original sequence into the information required at the receiver, and (2) *channel coding* or reliable communication, the use of error correction to send the desired information reliably to the receiver. Similarly, the decoding can be factored into channel decoding and source decoding. Because of this important result, studies of data compression often lump the channel encoder and channel decoder with the communications link to obtain a new noiseless or almost noiseless channel with a fixed, finite alphabet. This allows one to focus on the problem of source coding without the added complications of channel coding and is the reason why most of the papers presented here assume (with theoretical justification) that channel errors contribute a negligible amount to overall performance. Some papers, however, do consider more general systems that incorporate channel coding, modulation–demodulation, and filtering.

The class of coding devices ($F_E$, $F_D$) can be broken up into basically two types. *Block codes* involve the processing of consecutive nonoverlapping blocks of data to produce consecutive nonoverlapping blocks of coded data; the lengths of the blocks may be fixed or may vary as a function of the data. Such systems essentially begin anew with each new data block and have been the principal structure used in information theory research. *Nonblock structures* are essentially nonlinear filters possessing memory and delay so that each new code symbol produced depends possibly both on past and future data. Such systems may still process consecutive blocks, but they overlap and therefore affect the processing of past and future blocks. These schemes have generally arisen in the communications literature, such as predictive quantizing and delta modulation. The most common constraints placed on both structures are a given alphabet size or output entropy.

In any collection of this sort, there is the risk of omitting appropriate papers. Constraints on length preclude presenting all relevant works, and those included necessarily reflect the biases of the editors and their colleagues. Many papers peripheral to the topic of data compression or more appropriate to other collections are not included, but are instead described briefly and referred to in the editorial comments or in the papers contained in this volume. In particular, the classical papers of C. E. Shannon on the information theory approach to source coding (rate-distortion theory) may be found in an excellent collection, *Key Papers in the Development of Information Theory,* D. Slepian (ed.), IEEE Press, New York, 1973; the relevant parts are summarized in the editorial discussions and in the more intuitive or applied papers included. We have also chosen to omit most of the appendixes of the papers to allow the inclusion of more papers since we feel the more mathematical appendixes are peripheral to the main results. We apologize for omissions of any important papers, but this collection can represent only a small sample of the many diverse areas, approaches, techniques, and theories of an exciting and important subject.

# Part I

# OVERVIEWS OF DATA COMPRESSION

# Editors' Comments on Papers 1 and 2

1 **BLASBALG and Van BLERKOM**
*Message Compression*

2 **GRAY and DAVISSON**
*A Mathematical Theory of Data Compression?*

Papers 1 and 2, published 12 years apart, each attempt to describe in tutorial terms the general goals, approaches, techniques, and results of data compression. Paper 1 is primarily engineering oriented, yet it provided hints of the future directions of the theory. Primary contributions were the realizations that (1) source coding could be factored into the separate operations of entropy compression and noiseless coding, and (2) that source probabilistic descriptions are rarely known precisely and any real system must be built accordingly.

*Entropy compression* is an irreversible operation such as quantization that maps a source into an approximation of itself with a lower entropy rate; it is therefore capable of reliable transmission over a channel of reduced capacity (by Shannon's channel-coding theorem). *Noiseless coding* (or exact coding, entropy coding, information preserving coding, or distortion-free redundancy removal) is an invertible operation of the approximation into the appropriate channel language, for example, a nearly memoryless equiprobable process with the appropriate alphabet. A memoryless equiprobable channel input process is theoretically desirable since this assures that the channel input entropy rate $H(Y)$ equals log $||B||$ bits per symbol. Since the noiseless coding operation is invertible, the entropy rates of $\{\hat{X}_n\}$ and $\{Y_n\}$ in bits per second must be equal. Hence $KH(\hat{X}) = LH(Y)$ and therefore $\eta = L/K = H(\hat{X})/\log ||B||$, the minimum possible value (maximal possible compression) for reliable transmission of $\{\hat{X}_n\}$ by Shannon's noiseless coding theorem.

The term "redundancy removal" is used in the literature to mean both noiseless coding and combined entropy compression—noiseless coding operations such as a predictive-quantization scheme. Because of this possible confusion, we shall not use the term. Furthermore, "redundancy removal" is not always an appropriate name even for noiseless coding, for we may begin with a memoryless source, but still wish to encode it into another memoryless source utilizing the channel alphabet; that is, noiseless coding may be required even if there is no source redundancy to remove.

The second observation of Blasbalg and Van Blerkom, that, as source statistics are rarely known precisely, practical systems should be built accordingly, led to their notion of adaptive coding. This is the underlying idea of the universal coding techniques developed some years later.

Paper 2 is a more modern tutorial of a more mathematical bent. The primary focus is on block compression systems; the OPTA, coding theorems, drawbacks of the Shannon approach, and several recent results are outlined. Universal block coding is discussed and some recent nonblock results are briefly described. Paper 2 is concerned entirely with the problem of entropy compression. In such block systems the noiseless coding is simply accomplished by sending the $||B||$-ary index of the reproduction block within a code instead of the block itself over the channel (or by using any other noiseless coding scheme on the entropy-compressed sequence).

Reprinted from *IRE Trans. Space Electron. Telemetry,* **8,** 228–238 (Sept. 1962)

# Message Compression*

H. BLASBALG†, SENIOR MEMBER, IRE, AND R. VAN BLERKOM†

***Summary***—**Two general classes of operations for the purpose of compressing the output of a message source are considered: (1) Entropy-reducing (ER) transformation, and (2) Information-preserving (IP) transformation (redundancy removal). The type (1) transformation, when acceptable, can yield substantial compression gains in telemetry applications while the type (2) transformation can yield substantial gains for certain types of source statistics.**

**A new concept, adaptive coding, is introduced. It is shown that for quasi-stationary source statistics it is possible to obtain estimates of the statistics and to use these subsequently for efficient coding. A general statistical measure for monitoring the efficiency of the adaptive procedure is presented and a decision rule, based on this statistic, for updating the coding is defined. It is shown that the statistical estimates need not be precise since the coding efficiency remains reasonably insensitive to small errors; hence, only violent changes in the source statistics must be detected.**

**A number of configurations for performing adaptive and non-adaptive compression are discussed in detail. Some of these procedures, such as predictive coding, are well known while others are new. In particular, a practical configuration is presented for compressing the output of many sensors which have the statistical structure; no changes in the signal for relatively long time intervals and very rapid changes for relatively short time intervals. It is concluded that this approach has the advantage over variable rate commutation procedures in that short message bursts can always be detected without increasing the communications channel capacity.**

**The problem of buffer overflow is considered in general and specifically, in the multiple sensor compression system configuration. Here it is shown that buffer overflow can be controlled simply by degrading the fidelity of the sensor outputs gradually and under control. In general, it is concluded that the buffer design problem is just another difficult problem in designing an efficient telemetry system. It is, however, a poor excuse for eliminating compression from telemetry system design without giving it proper consideration. In short, compression is a possible trade-off among the theoretical channel parameters and practical considerations which can influence the over-all system performance and which deserves consideration.**

## Introduction

To COMPRESS a message is to extract or transform those properties of the message that are significant to an observer. Considered here are two types of transformations of the message:

1) Entropy-reducing (ER) transformations.
2) Information-preserving (IP) transformations (redundancy removal).

### *Entropy-Reducing (ER) Transformations*

The entropy-reducing transformation is an irreversible operation on the message which results in an "acceptable" reduction in fidelity. The vocoder (a device for compressing speech) technique[1] is an example of message degradation at the sending end which preserves speech intelligibility. The major emphasis in picture compression today is concerned with ER transformations. In both the vocoder and TV, the human observer generally determines the acceptable degree of message fidelity. In general, the ER transformations depend on the properties of the message source and its receiver. That is, an ER operation acceptable in one application can be unacceptable in another. Since the human sensors of speech and pictures are significantly different, one expects that the useful ER transformations for each case will be, and in fact are, significantly different.

### *Information-Preserving (IP) Transformations (Exact Coding)*

The IP transformations are used for mapping an input set of message sequences into a corresponding output set that contains fewer binary digits. The mapping is reversible. Hence, given the output set of sequences, the input can always be reconstructed exactly. To realize the mapping (or coding), it is essential to know the source statistics. The stronger the correlations within the message sequences, the greater the redundancy within the message and, of course, the information generated by the source is less. The mapping of the input sequences results in an output sequence which ideally is completely random. Thus, IP transformations remove message redundancy. Whereas IP transformations have received much attention since the advent of information theory, ER transformations have received little attention except in the two important areas of speech and TV. The study of ER transformations with respect to the important area of space sensors is presently gaining momentum. ER transformations have received less attention in the past since, as previously mentioned, the operations are sensor-oriented and their effect must almost always be studied empirically.

### *Adaptive Coding*

In many cases of practical interest, the sensor output statistics are initially unknown to the designer, therefore making efficient coding impossible; that is, the entire message is transmitted. This procedure is valid in the absence of prior information, since it assumes that the message is generated by a maximum entropy source.

* Received June 4, 1962. Part of this work was presented at the Northeast Electronics Research and Engineering Meeting, Boston, Mass., November 14, 1961, and to the IRE Professional Group on Space Electronics and Telemetry, Washington, D. C.; October 24, 1961.

† Communications Systems Center, IBM Federal Systems Division, Rockville, Md.

[1] "Proc. Seminar on Speech Compression and Processing," AF Cambridge Res. Ctr., L. G. Hanscom Field, Bedford, Mass., vol. 1, Rept. No. TR-59-198.

Most telemetry or communications systems do, in fact, operate in this maximum entropy mode. If statistics are postulated *a priori* and in fact do not match those of the source, it is possible that the coding will lead to a bit rate which exceeds the maximum entropy of the source (*i.e.*, message expansion results, precisely shown later in this paper). The standard methods of straight transmission of the source output guard against this situation.

Adaptive coding is a message-compression procedure which is a compromise between the most efficient coding (when the source statistics are completely known) and maximum entropy coding (straight transmission, when the source statistics are unknown). In an adaptive coding procedure, past statistical measurements are used for coding future measurements. The coding procedure is continuously monitored to determine its efficiency and whether a change in the procedure is required. For this procedure to be efficient, the sensor output statistics must be quasistationary. Hence, in order to code adaptively, it is essential to define a decision rule of adaptation which depends on past measurements and which will be useful for future measurements. As long as the decision rule is known at the transmitter and receiver, and as long as it is defined on past measurements, the receiver will always know when the sender has switched the coding. This important concept will be examined in more detail in subsequent sections.

*Operations on Message Source (Block Diagram)*

Fig. 1 represents ER and IP operations on the source at the receiver and transmitter. The message source M is mapped by the ER transformation F into an output FM. The operation F is irreversible; one can, therefore, never recover the precise message M from FM. The IP transformation R operates on the message FM, which results in an output RFM. The operator R is reversible; hence FM can be recovered. In fact, the output FM can be considered as the "effective" message source ($M_e$ = FM) as far as the exact coding operator R is concerned. So as to combat channel disturbances, it is essential to reinsert some redundancy. Without redundancy an error can cause a rapid degradation of message, since the errors propagate. However, the redundancy can be reinserted efficiently and effectively for the particular disturbance encountered.

At the receiver the transmitted signal waveform is correctly detected and the message RFM is generated. The result of the inverse mapping $R^{-1}$ gives the effective message FM. The receiver, depending on the particular application, may increase the entropy of the received message FM by the operation GFM. For example, in the vocoder the received short-time spectral intensity of the speech signal is properly combined with both periodic and random sources in order to reproduce an intelligible acoustic waveform. The resultant waveform

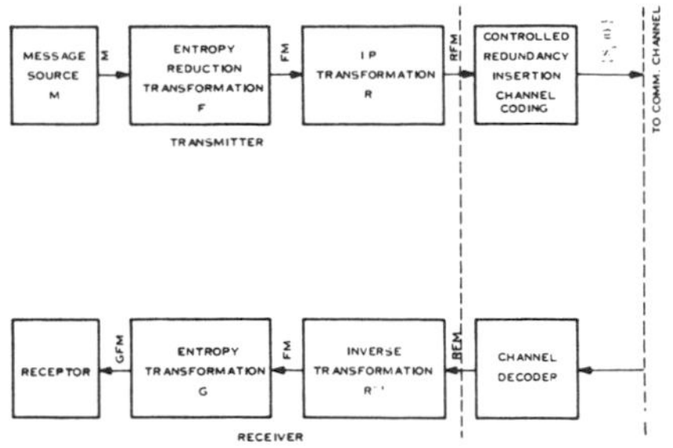


Fig. 1—Operations on message source at transmitter and receiver.

has a greater entropy than the received signal FM. In TV one finds a similar situation in the case of pictures whose intensity is quantized to, say, two levels. For the case of human faces, black and white pictures are quite unacceptable. However, adding the correct amount of thermal noise renders the resultant picture more pleasing to the eye. In space sensor applications, one generally accepts the data in the form FM.

## ER Transformations Applied to Sensor Outputs That are Inherently Statistical

*Compression by Measuring Signal Statistics*

Let us consider a sensor output which can be represented by a finite set of coordinates $S_i = \{C_{ij}\}, j = 1, 2, \cdots, K$. The coordinates can be orthogonal coefficients, sample values, or any set of $K$ measurable properties of the output. If each coordinate is quantized to $N$ values, then the number of possible signal configurations which can be sensed is $D = N^K$, and hence, at most, $\log_2 D = K \log_2 N$ bits per configuration must be specified so as to describe the output. Note that the number $D$ can be extremely large, so large it can be stated with reasonable credibility that an extremely large number of the possible configurations will never occur. In fact, if $\{P_i\}, i = 1, 2, \cdots, D$ represents the probability of occurrence of each configuration, then it is possible to identify each configuration by $\log_2 1/P_i$ bits, then the average number of bits per configuration is

$$H = -\sum_{i=1}^{D} P_i \log_2 P_i. \tag{1}$$

If $P_i = 1/D$ for all $i$, for example, all configurations are equally probable (or there is an absence of redundancy), it is well known that

$$H = H_{max} = \log_2 D = K \log_2 N. \tag{2}$$

The compression ratio is defined as

$$C_R = \frac{H_{max}}{H} = \frac{K \log_2 N}{-\sum_{i=1}^{D} P_i \log_2 P_i} \geq 1. \tag{3}$$

The relative redundancy is defined as

$$R = \frac{H_{max} - H}{H_{max}} = 1 - \frac{1}{R}$$

or,

$$C_R = \frac{1}{1 - R}. \tag{4}$$

From (2) it is clear that the maximum entropy is directly proportional to the dimensionality $K$ of the signal space and only logarithmically proportional to the number of quantum levels per coordinate. By reducing the dimensionality of the signal space, we can immediately reduce the maximum entropy of the message. Thus, when a signal is transmitted through a narrower low-pass filter, its maximum entropy is reduced since the number of coordinates required for specifying it is reduced. This is an example of a commonly used ER transformation.

Assume now, that a measurement of $K$ properties of a statistical phenomenon is made simultaneously on a single realization. (Fig. 2 represents this situation.) One can assume that the properties are statistically independent (although this is not a limitation on our discussion). At the output of each branch in the diagram is a binary counter of $\log_2 S$ bits. This configuration is now a discrete probability density analyzer which permits a measurement of the distribution of properties $\{C_i\}$ from $S$ realizations. In Fig. 3 the possible results of such a measurement are shown. It is clear from this model that, in order to specify this measurement from $S$ realizations, we need at most

$$H_D = KN \log_2 S(N) \text{ bits/measurement.} \tag{5}$$

The number of realizations $S(N)$ depends upon the number of quantum levels per measured property and, for statistical stability, it is essential that $S(N) \gg N$. This measurement can be considered as an ER transformation, since the original signal cannot be reconstructed from this data. In fact, the ER transformation in this case is such that all permutations of the measurement will yield the same data, *i.e.*, the order in which the data occurred is not preserved. The compression ratio $C_E$ in this case is

$$\begin{aligned} C_E &= \frac{S(N)K \log_2 N}{KN \log_2 S(N)}; \qquad S(N) \gg N \\ &= \frac{S(N) \log_2 N}{N \log_2 S(N)}. \end{aligned} \tag{6}$$

The quantity $S(N)/N$ represents the number of samples per quantum level and is related to the stability of the estimates of the discrete probability density. It should be clear from (6) that statistical phenomena can require significantly fewer bits for specification than the transmission of the exact sensor output, particularly where accurate probability estimates are required (*i.e.*, $S(N) \gg N$). Once again the transformation is ER since the order of the events is not preserved.

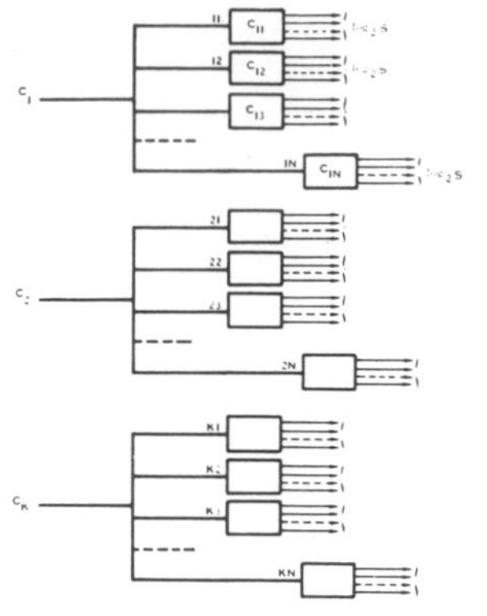

Fig. 2—State diagram of signal.

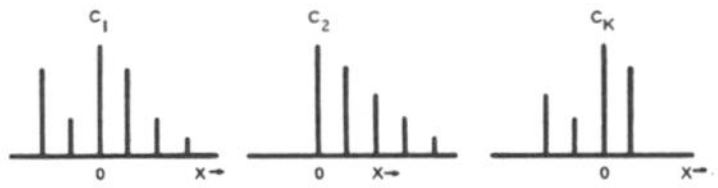

Fig. 3—Dimensionality reducing transformation.

*Compressor for Statistical Phenomena (Nonadaptive Case)*

Assume that theoretical considerations lead to the conclusion that the measurement of a certain property of an atomic particle experiment will have a statistical law $\{P_i\}$. For example, the $\{P_i\}$ can represent the probability distribution of the observed particles. The results of measurement must be transmitted only when the expected statistical law is violated. Let $\{X_i\}$, $i = 1, 2, \cdots, N$ be the energy states of the particles which the measurement apparatus can resolve, and let $\{P_i\}$ be the expected statistical law. An efficient and extremely important statistic for testing the validity of the law is

$$\Delta H(S) = S \sum_{i=1}^{N} \lambda_i \log \frac{\lambda_i}{P_i} \tag{7}$$

$$\sum_{i=1}^{N} P_i = 1,$$

$$\sum_{i=1}^{N} \lambda_i = 1,$$

and where $\{\lambda_i\}$ are the empirical probabilities of the energy states measured from $S$ observations. If

$$\Delta H(S) \begin{cases} \le H_0 \rightarrow \text{expected law is confirmed,} \\ > H_0 \rightarrow \text{expected law is violated.} \end{cases}$$

An important property of $\Delta H(S)$ is that for reasonably large $S$ it has a chi-square distribution with $K - 1$ degrees of freedom.[2] Thus, the parameters of the distribution

[2] M. Kupperman, "Further Applications of Information Theory to Multivariate Analysis and Statistical Inference," Ph.D. dissertation, George Washington University, Washington, D. C.; 1957.

$(S, K)$ depend only on the experimental apparatus and, hence, are known *a priori*, permitting the construction of confidence intervals and confidence levels. It is quite clear, that in this method of compression, information is transmitted only when a significant change in the expected statistical law occurs.

Fig. 4 diagrams an apparatus for performing this measurement. The states $\{X_i\}$ are detected by a probability distribution analyzer which counts the frequency of occurrence of each. This information is then fed into an entropy computer which measures the information in the experiment. Each time a given state occurs, it contributes an amount of information $(-\log P_i)$, the total sum of which is stored in the accumulator. The output of the accumulator and the entropy computer is then fed into a digital subtractor (*i.e.*, a reversible shift register), and the validity of the expected law is tested in the decision device. If the law is confirmed, data is not transmitted. If the law is violated, the new probability estimates are transmitted. Extremely large compression gains can be achieved by this technique if the initial hypothesis is satisfied.

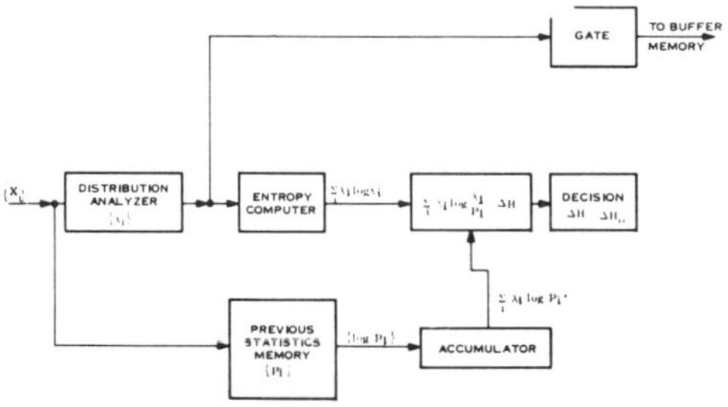


Fig. 4—Statistical data compressor.

*Compression of Statistical Phenomena (Adaptive Case)*

Conceptually, Fig. 4 can be easily extended to adaptive compression if the statistics are known to be quasi-stationary. In this case, when the expected law is not satisfied, the new observed statistical law is transmitted to the receiver and also stored in the previous statistics memory, thus replacing the old statistics. Subsequent measurements $\{\lambda_i\}$ are now compared to the new law, and the same procedure for sending is used.

Other adaptive procedures are also possible, although these become exceedingly more difficult to instrument both in circuit logic complexity and in memory storage capacity. For example, when a new set of statistics is observed this set can be stored at transmitter and receiver. When a match occurs, the code number of the match is transmitted. If the same match reoccurs, then we can send the length of the run for which the same occurs. When a new set of statistics is observed, it can be transmitted and can also become a member of the now known class. We will now briefly formulate this more general adaptive compression procedure.

Let $\{P_{ij}\}$, $j = 1, 2, \cdots, K$ be $K$ distributions which have been measured and stored. Then

$$\sum_{i=1}^{N} P_{ij} = 1. \tag{9}$$

Let $\{\lambda_i\}$ be a set of empirical distributions which have just been measured. Then we form the information statistic

$$\Delta H_j = \sum_{i=1}^{N} \lambda_i \log \frac{\lambda_i}{P_{ij}}. \tag{10}$$

If

$$\begin{aligned} \min\{\Delta H_1, \Delta H_2, \cdots, \Delta H_j, \cdots, \Delta H_k; \Delta H_x\} \\ &= \Delta H_j; \quad \text{the } j\text{th law is true,} \\ &= \Delta H_x; \quad \text{new law is observed.} \end{aligned} \tag{11}$$

That is, we obtain the best match and then decide whether the best match is sufficiently good. If it is, the code identifying the $j$th law is transmitted. If the match is not sufficiently good, then the new statistics are stored at the transmitter and also at the receiver. One can go even further by counting the number of times that each statistical law is satisfied. When the statistics are ergodic, the adaptive system can evolve into an optimum one by learning all of the statistical laws.

It should be clear from these examples that adaptive compressors require memory, preferably of the random access type, since past measurements must be stored and must be accessible for future use. The more complex the adaptive process, the greater the storage requirements. In the case where the measured phenomenon is ergodic, adaptivity can be extremely effective. The same is true for the case of quasistationarity, provided the process is stable over the interval of stationarity.

## IP Transformations

## (Redundancy Removal or Exact Coding)

*Predictive Transformations (Mappings)*

A message has redundancy if there is a certain degree of predictability among the sequences which constitute the message. A predictive transformation represents an operation on the input message sequences for the purpose of producing a set of output sequences that exhibit a prescribed structure. In many cases, this mapping is cascaded with another IP transformation called run-length coding[3] so as to achieve compression. That is, the output of the run-length coder is a compressed version of the input message. Run-length coding, a mapping, can be instrumented easily and, hence, is of practical interest. Thus, given the input message and given that

[3] P. Elias, "Predictive coding—Part I," IRE Trans. on Information Theory, vol. IT-1, pp. 16–33; March, 1955.

the output transformation is run-length coded, a predictive transformation for which the run-length coding is efficient must then be found. Most often, intuition has been used to find this transformation very simply. Previous sequence prediction is a predictive transformation which, because of its simplicity, has been used in conjunction with run-length coding in TV applications and has resulted in compression ratios of approximately two (Fig. 5(a) shows such a compressor and Fig. 5(b) shows an expander).

If the probability of obtaining long consecutive runs of the same sequence is high, then the output of the mod-2 adder will contain long strings of zeros; hence, large compression gains can be achieved. The output of the run-length coder is a number proportional to the logarithm of the consecutive string of zeros plus a flag which identifies the end of the run. There are many transformations which fall into this class. Fig. 6 represents predictive transformations that include a decision device. The output of the decision device is a "one" or "zero," depending on whether the prediction is correct or incorrect. In this manner, by properly manipulating the predictive procedure, the sequence of decisions generates a Shannon-Fano code.[4] (We show only the compressor here.)

The elements of the prediction function are stored in a memory. A previous sequence $\{X_i\}$ selects a set of elements $\{Y_i\}$ as a prediction. The decision unit decides if the next input sequence $X_i$ is an element of the predicted set. If it is an element, a zero is generated indicating that the element $X_i$ is contained in the predicted set. The next prediction set is selected as a subset of $\{Y_i\}$. The process is continued until the measured sequence $X_i$ matches one of the elements in $\{Y_i\}$. If $X_i$ is not an element of the set $\{Y_i\}$ then a new set $\{Y_j\}$ is selected as a prediction which contains no elements of the previous set. The length of the code is proportional to the number of binary decisions required to classify the element of the set. The interesting and important fact is that the output binary sequence uniquely identifies the element, although the code is variable length.

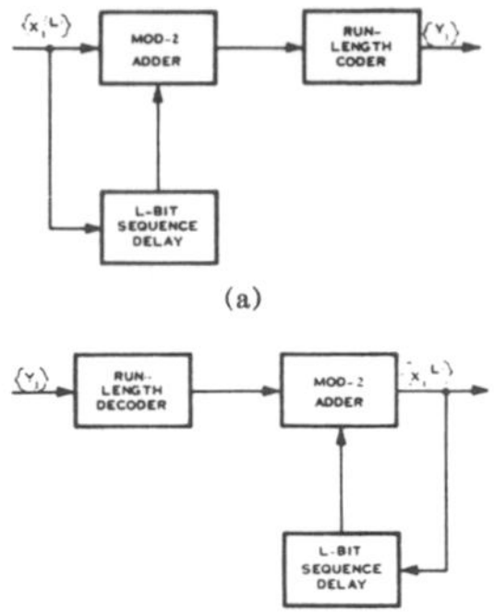


Fig. 5—(a) Previous sequence compressor. (b) Previous sequence expander.

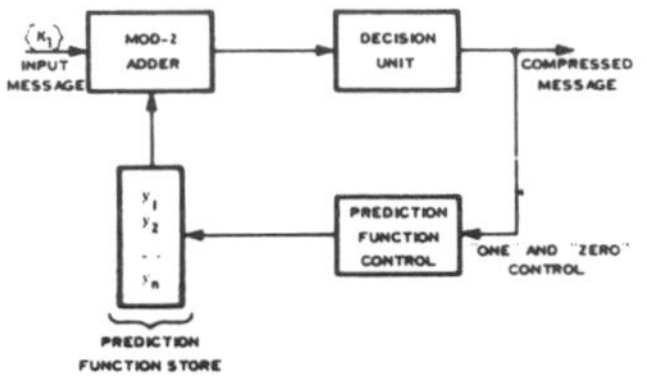


Fig. 6—Shannon-Fano compressor.

### *The Cascade of IP Compressors*

An important property of IP mappings is that the transformations can be cascaded without loss of information. A set of serial transformations permits the use of compression techniques which are intuitively clear, and when intuition fails, we can resort to theory and more sophisticated methods.

Since compressors require memory, it is possible to save memory by using simple compression techniques and then cascading the simple operations with more complex ones requiring less memory. For example, to remove frame-to-frame redundancy in TV, it is necessary to store a frame. If a simple redundancy-removal operation can lead to 3:1 compression, then storage capacity has been reduced by 66 per cent for the frame-to-frame redundancy remover. Fig. 7 indicates a simple cascaded predictor which removes sample-to-sample correlations by previous value prediction and then uses previous line prediction on the remainder. The result is transformed to a run-length code.

If there are $K$ bits per sample, then the output of the first mode-2 is a comparison of the previous sample with the present one. The delay line is $K$ bits long. The second stage stores an entire line and, hence, is $LK$ bits long, where $L$ is the number of samples per line. The second mod-2 compares the previous line with the present and sends out an encoded correction sequence. (Note that previous sample prediction can be considered as a simple example of adaptive coding. It is an updating procedure in which the previous sequence is always predicted for the present.) A rectangular type of structure is exhibited in Fig. 8.

By using previous value prediction horizontally, we remove horizontal correlation; and by using previous line prediction, we remove vertical correlations. Fig. 8(c) can be compressed by run-length coding.

## Adaptive IP Transformations

### *Measure of Coding Efficiency*

The adaptive coding process requires a measure of the efficiency of a particular coding procedure which can then

[4] R. M. Fano, "Transmission of Information," John Wiley and Sons, Inc., New York, N. Y.; 1961.

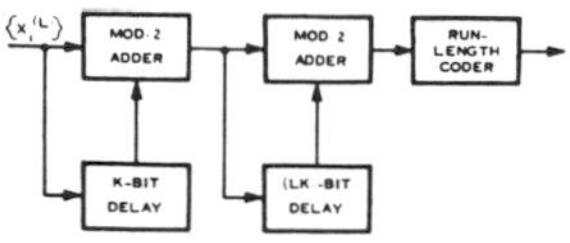


Fig. 7—Cascaded previous sequence and previous line compressor for TV.

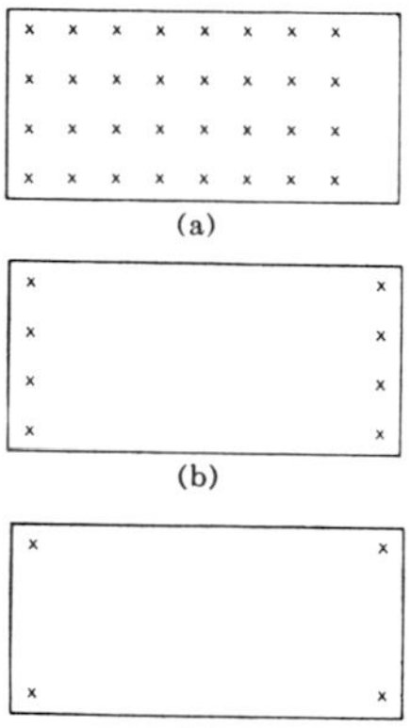

Fig. 8—Examples of cascaded prediction. (a) Picture exhibiting rectangular symmetry. (b) Horizontal correlations removed by previous sample prediction. (c) Vertical correlation removed by previous line prediction.

be used for the purpose of determining when a new procedure is to be adopted. The statistical estimates used to determine a change in the coding procedure should preferably be useful for the purpose of generating the new code. (This property should actually be required of all adaptive processes.) Such a measure, which is important in coding as well as in decision processes, exists.

Let $\{p_i\}$ be the true probabilities of occurrence of sequences $\{X_i\}$ and let $\{q_i\}$ be the probabilities of occurrences of sequences $\{Y_i\}$. If the $\{Y_i\}$ do occur and a code is used whose symbol lengths are proportional to $(-\log p_i)$, the optimum code for the $\{X_i\}$, then the excess number of bits required for the $i$th sequence is simply

$$\delta_i = \log_2 q_i - \log_2 pi = \log_2 \frac{q_i}{p_i}. \qquad (12)$$

The average number of bits per sequence in excess is simply

$$\Delta H = \sum_{i=1}^{N} q_i \, \delta_i = \sum_{i=1}^{N} q_i \log_2 \frac{q_i}{p_i} \geq 0. \qquad (13)$$

In the case where the statistics are unknown *a priori*, straight transmission can be used. This is a case of maximum entropy; that is, $p_i = 1/N$ for all $i$. After the measurement of $S$ realizations, it is decided that the best estimates of the $\{q_i\}$ is $\lambda_i(S) = [n_i(S)/S]$, where $n_i$ is the number of occurrences of the $i$th sequence out of the number of measurements $S$. Then, the initial excess is simply

$$\Delta H_1 = \sum_{i=1}^{N} \lambda_i \log_2 \lambda_i N$$
$$= \log_2 N + \sum_{i=1}^{N} \lambda_i \log \lambda_i. \qquad (14)$$

If $\Delta H_1 \geq \Delta H_0$, the coding used (*i.e.*, straight transmission) is inefficient and we now code according to $p_i = \lambda_i$. If $\Delta H_1 < \Delta H_0$, we continue with straight transmission. The new measurement is then

$$\Delta H_2 = \sum_{i=1}^{N} \lambda_i \log \frac{\lambda_i}{p_i} \geq \Delta H_0. \qquad (15)$$

For samples of reasonable size $S$, it can be shown that $\Delta H$ has a chi-square distribution of $N - 1$ degrees of freedom for the null hypothesis and noncentral chi-square for neighboring distributions where the noncentrality is the excess.[2] This permits a simple calculation for the specification of confidence intervals and confidence levels.

For quasistationary processes it is essential to investigate the sensitivity of the excess measure $\Delta H$. In Fig. 9 this is shown for the binary case when

$$\Delta H = \log \frac{\lambda}{p} + (1 - \lambda) \log \frac{1 - \lambda}{1 - p}. \qquad (16)$$

Note that zero excess always occurs when the coding matches the statistics. Also note that for $\lambda = 0.5$, the case of maximum entropy (or straight transmission) for all values of $p > 0.5$ or $p < 0.5$, there is an expansion in the coding in excess of that required for straight transmission. Also note that the excess curves are fairly flat in the neighborhood of the minimum. Hence, precise knowledge of the statistics is not essential to achieve reasonably optimum efficiency. Thus, the statistical estimates $\{\lambda_i\}$ need not be precise and can therefore be measured from a sample of relatively small size. We can, therefore, conclude that an adaptive system should guard only against violent changes in the statistics, since the coding is not critical for relatively small ones. This conclusion should hold for the multistate case as well, since as seen from (12), $\{\delta_i\}$ can take on positive and negative values and, hence, the average can be small. (Note, however, that this average is always positive.)

### *Optimum Adaptive Coder for Quasistationary Messages*

It is now possible to combine the nonadaptive coder, Fig. 6, with the statistical data compressor of Fig. 4 to achieve the optimum adaptive compressor shown in Fig. 10.

The message source generates sequences $\{X_i\}$ whose probabilities are measured by the distribution analyzer. These are the stored $\{P_i\}$ statistics. The prediction function generator generates a sequence classification, in the manner required for the stored Shannon-Fano coding. The input $X_i$ is compared with the predictions $\{Y_i\}$

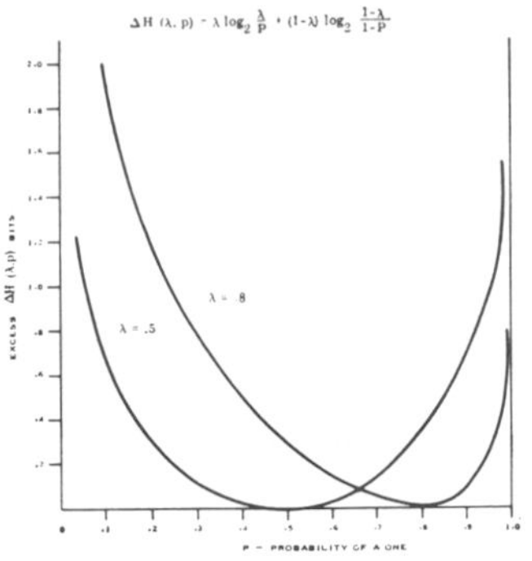


Fig. 9—Excess bits when code is derived from probabilities $P$ and the true probabilities are $\lambda$.

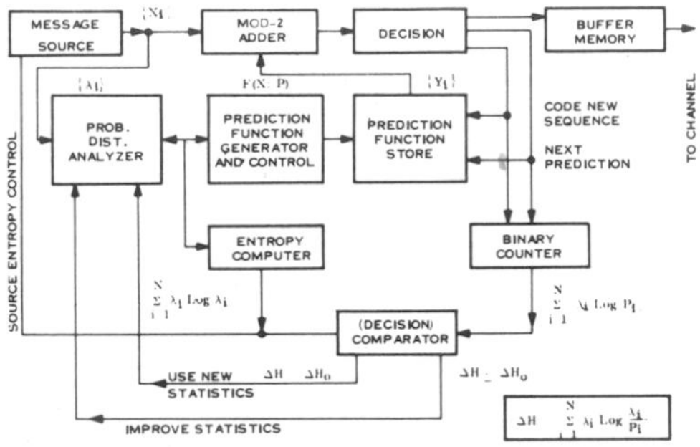


Fig. 10—Functional block diagram of adaptive coder for quasi-stationary messages.

according to the rules previously described. The number of decisions required to classify $X_i$ represents the code length.

While the generated code is based on the $\{P_i\}$ statistics, the entropy in the measured statistics $\{\lambda_i\}$ is computed, along with the average number of decisions that represents the average code length. After $S$ observations the excess $\Delta H$ is measured. If $\Delta H$ is less than a preassigned threshold, $\Delta H_0$, the $\{\lambda_i\}$ are averaged into the earlier statistics, $\{P_i'\}$ resulting in a better estimate of the measured statistics; consequently, coding even closer to the true source rate can be achieved. (If the process is ergodic, this coding procedure will evolve into the optimum procedure; for example, as when the message statistics are known *a priori*.) If the excess exceeds $\Delta H_0$, the presence of a new set of statistics is indicated. In this case the $\{\lambda_i\}$ statistics become the new $\{P_i\}$ statistics now used for code generation.

A control line, which adjusts the source entropy in accordance with channel load conditions, is also shown, since an overloaded channel can lead to rapid and serious degradation of the message. To prevent the arbitrary loss of message, an acceptable fidelity control should be introduced in case of overload. This is easily done by reducing the number of quantum levels in the measured analog quantity, as will now be shown.

Let $\{X_i^{(L)}\}$ be binary sequences which are $L$ bits long. Thus, each sequence represents a measurement corresponding to one of $2^L$ levels. By neglecting the least significant bit, we now have sequences of $2^{L-1}$ quantum levels, or the accuracy in the measurement is halved. Under overload conditions, this process can be continued progressively until the overload condition is removed. With this procedure, the fidelity is controlled in accordance with the short-time information rate. The slower the source rate, the better the fidelity of reproducing the analog output. As long as the fidelity control criterion is defined on past data also known to the receiver, it is unnecessary for the transmitter to send information concerning how and when to vary fidelity.

The best fidelity criteria must be determined separately for each specific problem. A decision theory approach could be used to determine the optimum fidelity criteria from a set of possible criteria. Here the loss function would be determined by the difference in usefulness of the original information and the degraded information. In many cases the optimum, or near optimum, criteria will be obvious to the experimenter. When it is not, the problem is generally too complicated for an analytic solution.

### *A Binary Adaptive Compressor*

Assume that we are dealing with binary sequences $\{X_i^{(L)}\}$ of length $L$ and that we are given a set of conditional probabilities $\{P[0;\, X_i^{(L)}],\ P[1;\, X_i^{(L)}]\}$ such that $P[0;\, X_i^{(L)}]$ = probability that a zero will follow the $i$th sequence, $[P\ 1;\, X_i^{(L)}]$ = probability that a one will follow the $i$th sequence,

and

$$P[0;\, X_i^{(L)}] + P[1;\, X_i^{(L)}] = 1; \quad \text{for all } i. \qquad (17)$$

Also $\{\xi_i\};\ i = 1, 2, \cdots, M$ represents the *a priori* probabilities of the sequences $\{X_i^{(L)}\},\ i = 1, 2, \cdots, M$ such that

$$\sum_{i=1}^{M} \xi_i = 1. \qquad (18)$$

Fig. 11 illustrates such a process, in which a given state $X_i^{(L)}$ can be followed by one of two other states $X_j^{(L)}$ of $X_n^{(L)}$ one bit later; that is, the sequence $X_i^{(L)}$ has $(L-1)$ bits in common with the sequences $[X_j^{(L)},\, X_n^{(L)}]$. Only the last bit differs. The states of such a system are highly constrained in that a given sequence, one bit later, cannot be followed by all other sequences. This type of process can be illustrated with the following example.

Consider sequences for $L = 2$ bits. The possible binary numbers are 00, 01, 10, and 11. Each two-bit sequence is used to predict the next bit. The resulting two-bit sequence is then used to predict the next bit, etc. Such a process is simply illustrated in Fig. 12. The transition probabilities $\{P[0;\, X_i^{(L)}],\ P[1;\, X_i^{(L)}]\}$ are assigned to each branch (not shown in the diagram). A particular flow graph structure is time invariant, although the transition probabilities can be time dependent. For a quasistationary process, we assume that the transition probabilities can be measured and that they are useful for some future time for coding purposes.

Fig. 13 shows an adaptive binary compressor whose statistics are changed on each measurement. The binary decoding matrix generates an output pulse on one of $2^L$ lines corresponding to a given $L$-bit binary sequence. At the output of each line is a zero and one gate and corresponding binary counter stages. When a sequence $X_i$ is applied to the matrix, the $j$th output line is selected. If the following bit is a one, the corresponding circuit gates through this number to the one's counter, $BC_1$. If the following bit is a zero, the number one passes through gate zero and is stored on $BC_0$; in this manner the statistics $\{P[0; X_i^{(L)}], P[1; X_i^{(L)}]\}$ are generated. The prediction of a one or a zero following a sequence $X_i^{(L)}$ is based on whether the one's or zero's counter in the $i$th channel has a larger number stored. In this case the prediction is based on the most probable value.

In the diagram shown, correct and wrong predictions (guesses) are weighted the same. Hence, if a prediction

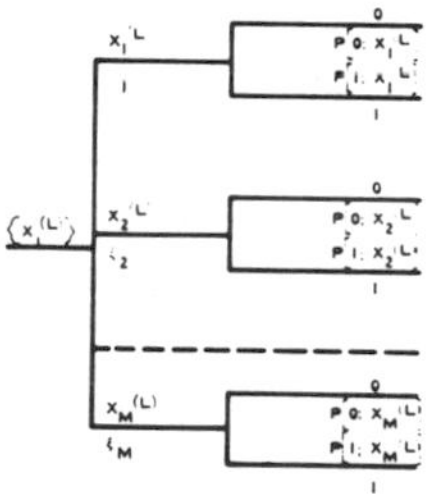

Fig. 11—True diagram of binary process.

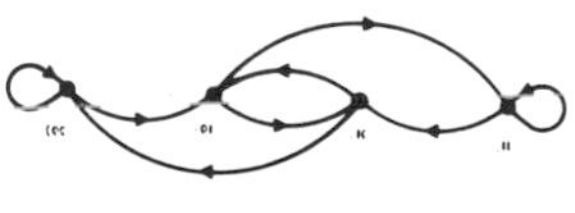

Fig. 12—Flow graph for simple binary compressor.

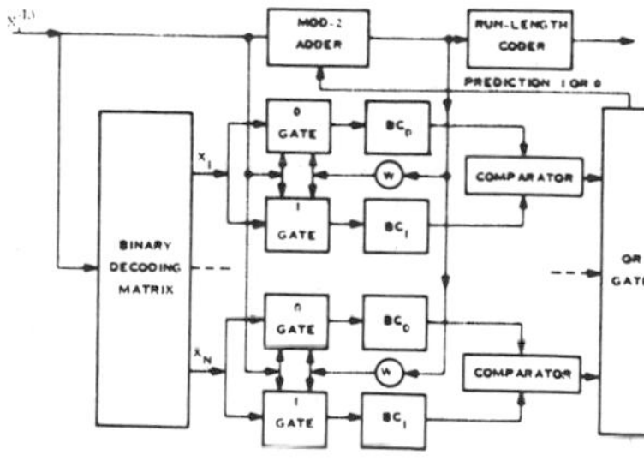


Fig. 13—Adaptive binary predictive compressor.

of, say, a zero is correct, the number $W$ is added to the zero's counter and subtracted from the one's counter. The reverse is true for the case when a zero is incorrectly predicted. When both counters have the same number stored, a one or a zero can be predicted in a random manner.

It is, perhaps, best to consider a single reversible binary counter in each channel, preset to a number $N/2$ where $\log_2 N$ is the capacity of the counter. The problem is now a random-walk problem, in which a correct prediction of one, for example, feeds the number $W$ in the forward count direction and an incorrect decision of a one feeds the number $W$ in the reverse count direction. A similar procedure is used for correct and incorrect predictions of zero. When the number in the counter is $n > N/2$, a one is predicted, and when $n < N/2$ a zero is predicted. For the special case $n = N/2$, a random selection of one or zero is made for the prediction. There is still the problem of finding a suitable approach for the case when the counter is at the barriers $n = 0$, $n = N$. If we wish, the counter can remain in this position until the wrong prediction is made, at which time $W$ counts are subtracted or added. For this special case, there is no gain in a correct decision, but there is a loss for an incorrect decision. (This result may not be unreasonable, since this is a state of certainty and hence contributes no information. For example, a rational observer does not bet against a sure thing.)

Of course, other modes of operation are also possible. For example, the barriers at $n = 0$, $n = N$ can be reflecting barriers. That is, whenever the end is reached, the counter is set back to a different state. In any case, in the problem considered here, it is expected that the adaptivity will not be too sensitive to the mode of operation at $n = 0$ and $n = N$. It was shown previously that the adaptive process is sensitive only to large changes in the statistics. When a large change does occur, particularly for $P$ very close to unity and $P$ very close to zero, the procedure outlined will adapt very rapidly to this case. Hence, we conclude that any reasonable procedure at the barriers $n = 0$, $n = N$ will suffice for reasonably efficient coding. (The procedure outlined can be useful for black and white pictorial messages; for compressing on most significant bits, etc.)

### *A Compressor for Multiple Sensor Outputs*

In certain applications (in which many sensors are used for monitoring a space vehicle's performance or in certain scientific experiments), the sensor signals exhibit a time structure which is constant for relatively long periods of time and which changes rapidly for substantially shorter periods of time. In order to detect the short, rapid changes with the required fidelity, sample speeds twice as high as the expected frequency of the signal are needed. The type of signal described is quasistationary; that is, the statistics are all concentrated at a single value for large portions of the time and are dispersive for shorter periods.

Fig. 14 shows a relatively simple, multichannel compressor, efficient for the case in which the number of channels is large and in which the sensor behavior is as previously described. The output of a conventional PCM multiplexer is fed into a mod-2 adder and into a delay line equal to the frame delay. The present and previous frames are compared in the mod-2 adder, and a change between the present and previous samples is sensed. A channel code (or address) $Y$ is also generated, along with a frame code word. When a change is detected, the code $XY$ is gated through, identifying the sensor value as well as the sensor itself. When a change does not occur, there is complete absence of a symbol. At the end of a frame a code $F$ is generated.

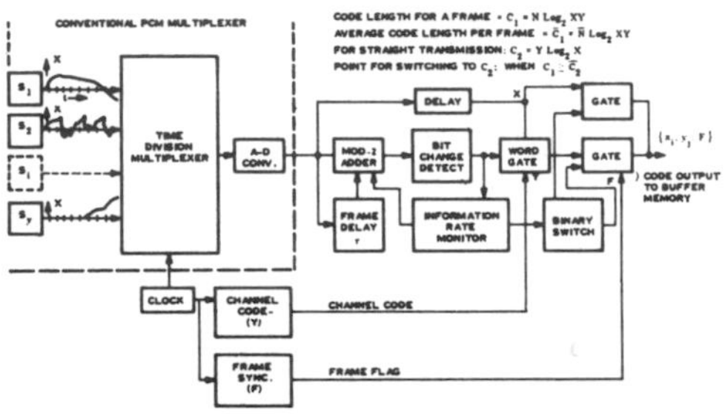


Fig. 14—Adaptive multichannel compressor with fidelity control.

*Buffer Considerations*

A buffer is an essential part of any exact coder; for the codes used are of variable length, whereas the source output and the channel communication rate are uniform. The buffer must, therefore, takeup the fluctuations about the mean source rate. If the statistics of the code lengths are known, a buffer can be designed so that the probability of overflow is small. Since the buffer output is matched to the channel information-handling rate, one cannot exceed this rate without paying the penality of rapid message degradation. This type of degradation is essentially the same as when the buffer overflows; that is, a portion of the message is lost. This, of course, introduces an error with a certain probability of occurrence. However, the communications problem in general is a statistical one with a predetermined error probability of detection built into the system. When we examine the over-all problem of communications (which includes message coding), we simply realize that there is another source of error that depends on the message statistics alone (rather than on channel statistics). We must accept this error factor if efficient communications is to be achieved, on the average, and if certain physically realizable conditions (buffer size) are to be met.

Rather than design the buffer for a given probability of overflow, it may be more desirable, particularly in an adaptive system, to regulate the information input to the buffer. This regulation would prevent overflow by controlling the fidelity of the source. In this case, errors in the sensor outputs are introduced in a controlled manner and according to practical criteria. (An example of fidelity control is shown in Fig. 14.) The information-rate monitor measures the relative number of sensors whose outputs change during successive frames. This number is proportional to the information flow rate into the buffer. If a condition of overflow is predicted, a signal is fed to the mod-2 adder which removes the least significant bit from the comparison procedure. That is, all sensors that change only in the least significant bit are treated as if no change had occurred, and a code is not transmitted. For example, a code number 1010 is assumed the same as 1011. Hence, an uncertainty is introduced in the least significant bit. If the information flow is not reduced sufficiently, then the two least significant bits can be removed from the comparison. This is one important example of fidelity control. The receiver need not be notified of the changes in fidelity, since it can detect this procedure by monitoring the past output.

*Multiple Sensor Decoder*

Fig. 15 shows the receiver portion of the multiplexed decoder. The purpose of the logic is to reconstruct at the receiver the multiplexed signal which existed prior to coding. Beyond this point, a standard PCM demultiplexer can be used to channelize the messages.

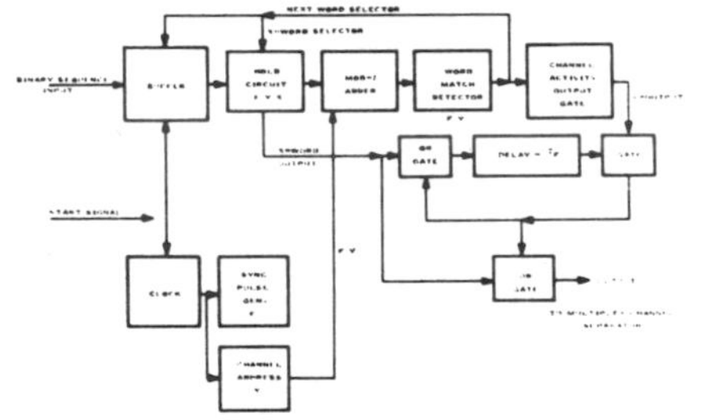

Fig. 15—Multiple sensor decoder.

The received messages are fed into a buffer the same as at the transmitter. A clock at the receiver generates the synchronizing code $F$ as well as the channel address $Y$. (Note that the synchronizing code can be considered as another channel address.) A start signal initiates the clock and reads out of memory the synchronizing information stored in a hold circuit. This code is compared in the mod-2 adder with the locally generated sync and channel address information. Since a comparison exists, it is detected by the word-match detector. The detector then selects the next code word $YX$. If a match exists, the word $X$ is gated to the output line and the next $YX$ word is read from memory. If a match does not occur, the word is left in the hold circuit until a match does occur, at which time the previously described feedback procedure is initiated. The output of the line contains, on a multiplexed oasis, the values of the sensors in binary at their proper position in time sequence. When there is no output at some of the channels, it indicates that a change has not occurred. Thus, at this point we reconstruct the multiplexed signal that enters the buffer at the transmitter. It is now necessary only to reconstruct the multiplexed signal at the output of the $A$-$D$ converter at the transmitter.

The output of the word-match detector generates a gate whose time position with respect to the sync pulse indicates which channel is active. The $X$-word output line contains the channel values and coincides in time with the $Y$ output. For example, the $Y$ gates have a duration equal to the duration of the $X$ words. The $X$ words are fed into an OR gate and also into a recirculating delay line whose length is equal to a frame. Whenever a channel is active during a frame (indicating that a new word $X$ is present), the stored word is gated out at the delay line output end. When a channel activity pulse is absent, the previous word $X$ is recirculated, and subsequently applied to the OR gate. Hence, the $X$ input line to the OR gate represents the channel values that have changed in the proper time sequence, while the delay line output represents the sample values that have not changed. Thus, the combination represents the frame output. At this point, the time-multiplexed PCM is fed into a standard demultiplexer.

*Calculations of Compression Ratio for the Case Where the Relative Number of Sensors That Change is Small*

We will now calculate the compression ratio for the type of system just considered. For $Y$ channels where each sample value is represented by $\log_2 X$ bits, we have for straight transmission (maximum entropy case) $Y \log_2 X$ bits per frame. If $n$ channels out of $kY$ are active, where $k \gg 1$, then we have $n \log_2 XY$ bits using the channel address type of coding. If, on the average, $\bar{n}$ channels are active, we obtain a compression ratio

$$C = \frac{kY \log_2 X}{\bar{n} \log_2 XY} = \frac{1}{\left(\frac{\bar{n}}{kY}\right)} \frac{1}{1 + \frac{\log_2 Y}{\log_2 X}} = \frac{1}{d\left(1 + \frac{\log_2 Y}{\log_2 X}\right)} \approx \frac{1}{2d}; \quad \text{when } \frac{\log_2 Y}{\log_2 X} \approx 1. \tag{19}$$

Thus, without adapting, the compression ratio is half the reciprocal of the mean duty factor.

In a two-state adaptive system using either code

$$c_1 = \log_2 XY \tag{20}$$

or

$$c_2 = Y \log_2 X,$$

we switch to $c_2$ if

$$n_0 \log_2 XY > kY \log_2 X$$

or

$$d_0 > \frac{1}{1 + \frac{\log_2 Y}{\log_2 X}} \approx \frac{1}{2}, \tag{21}$$

when more than 50 per cent of the channels change on the average. If $\alpha$ is the percentage time when $c_1$ is used (assuming that during this time $d < \frac{1}{2}$ channels are active) and $(1 - \alpha)$ is the percentage time that $c_2$ is in use, then the compression ratio is

$$C = \frac{kY \log_2 X}{\bar{n}\alpha \log_2 XY + (1 - \alpha)kY \log_2 X} = \frac{1}{2\alpha\, d + (1 - \alpha)}; \quad \text{when } \frac{\log_2 X}{\log_2 Y} \approx 1 \geq 1. \tag{22}$$

It is clear that the adaptive system is bounded by the straight transmission case, while the nonadaptive system can require a 100 per cent increase in channel over the straight transmission case. It should also be clear that the significant factor affecting the compression is the duty ratio. For significant compression ratios, this number must be small. Furthermore, for significant compression ratios, the percentage of time $\alpha$ for which code $c_1$ is used must be close to unity. The adaptive mode might still be useful if it can be achieved cheaply, as in this problem.

We will now consider an important example for which the compression system will be useful. Consider $Y$ channels, each of which generates information at the rate of $W_0$ cps for some mean-time $T_0$ and which generate information at the rate of $mW_0$ ($m \gg 1$), for some time $\Delta T$ where $1/mW_0 \ll T \ll T_0$. It is essential to detect the very rapid changing information in its entirety, although the times of occurrence of the information burst are unknown. The communication channel bandwidth is $BW_0$ when $Y < B \ll mY$. To reproduce the information burst, each channel must be sampled at the rate of $2\,mW_0$ samples per second. Without compression a bandwidth of approximately $2\,mYW_0$ is required. We further assume that the probability of a burst $b \ll 1/Y$. Hence, there is a very small probability of obtaining even one burst of data each frame. Note that, when the channels are varying slowly, $m$ times as many samples are taken as required. Thus, a compression of approximately $m$ can be achieved by using run-length coding on the changes. (For the purpose of this calculation we can assume that the functions are approximately constant over these periods.) In fact, the information at the output of the compressor can be sent through the bandwidth $W_0$. If there is a sufficient number of samples in the burst to adapt, then we can feed the burst of data into the buffer uncoded. If the buffer stores $W_0T_0$ samples per channel, and if a single burst occurs with a probability $b < 1/W_0T_0$ and if $W_0T_0 \approx mW_0\, \Delta T$, then we require approximately a bandwidth $2W_0$ to transmit the required data as compared to $mW_0$. The important point to notice from this example is that large compression ratios can be realized with simple equipment for the important example considered here. It should also be recognized that procedures which do not sample the experiment at the maximum rate can lead to a loss of an information burst that may be the essential information in the experiment.

## Conclusions

Major gains in message compression can be achieved by first reducing entropy in the sensors and then applying exact coding to the result. The entropy-reducing operations can be used to remove the information which is clearly of no value, while exact coding can be used to remove any residual redundancy. Operations for reducing entropy must be defined by the experimenter; he must decide whether the results of these operations are useful. From the communications point of view the source combined with the entropy-reducing operations is now the effective source. The exact coding operations (since these are information preserving) can become part of the communications system. That is, the over-all purpose of the communications system is to transmit the effective source information so that it will be received at distant points with the required fidelity. Exact coding is simply an information-preserving transformation in the communications system to permit more efficient use of the facilities.

Some investigators have tried to separate the information source from the communications channel, but an efficient telemetry system for scientific purposes, or otherwise, can be realized only by considering the entire system, source and link together. Although it is quite natural and logical to insert redundancy in the experimental design, it is quite unnatural and illogical to think that this redundancy will be efficient for the purpose of achieving immunity against channel disturbances. It is logical, how ever, to remove the source redundancy and then to reinsert the necessary amount and type of redundancy intelligently so as to achieve realiability. This procedure can lead to more measurements and to even more reliability.

Since, in most applications, the source statistics are unknown, it is essential to use adaptive coding. For ergodic processes, the adaptive system can approach ideal coding. In the case of quasistationary processes, it is essential to detect only violent nonstationarities: for example, significant changes in the message statistics (as defined mathematically) since coding procedures seem to be quite insensitive for "neighboring" source statistics. This is, however, quite desirable, for it permits rapid detection of changes in the statistics and, therefore, allows rapid adaptation to coding these changes.

In space applications, the compressor must be relatively simple, realiable, etc., particularly if it is to be spaceborne. It is, however, unfair and unrealistic to consider the compressor as an added luxury to the communications and telemetry system. There are certain penalties for not removing redundancy from the message source, penalties which influence the entire communications system or mission. For example, we may be forced to make fewer experiments, to use more power, and more bandwidth, to tolerate larger errors, etc. Compression is, therefore, not a luxury but an essential part of any space communications system and must be considered in the same light that power, bandwidth, noise, errors, weight, reliability, etc., are considered. We have shown that the addition of simple circuitry to a conventional PCM coder can lead to the efficient transmission of bursts of information, which might require very large bandwidths to accurately detect and to transmit these bursts.

In applications of an extremely reliable link from earth to the space vehicle and a weak link from space to earth, and where the "distance" to the vehicles is of the order of many milliseconds of round trip time, feedback can be used to improve the efficiency of communications from space to earth. That is, the optimum code based on past data can be computed in real time on the ground, and the most efficient code to be used can be transmitted to the vehicle for use. This is an application in which the feedback channel is used for compressing the forward channel and, hence reducing the bandwidth, power, error rates, etc. In this application, compression may very well compete with feedback error detection schemes. Here, with compression, for the same power, we can transmit more energy per symbol and can reduce the error probability so as to make it negligible. (For a white Gaussian channel, it can be shown that the error probability falls off exponentially with compression ratio.) This is another example to show that the use of compression is part of the over-all systems problem.

Finally, the buffer is an essential part of the bandwidth compression technique. Since there is always the probability that the buffer will overflow and introduce errors, there is justified concern about it. However, in the absence of compression, there is also the chance that by not using this property we are not observing the very important phenomena we might otherwise observe and, consequently, information is lost. We seem to be adjusted to accepting errors in transmission introduced by channel disturbances, yet are unwilling to accept errors introduced by overflow of the buffer. Furthermore, we have shown that buffer overflow can be minimized by reducing the fidelity in a controlled manner. Is this procedure worse than arbitrarily cutting out possible useful information at the outset by being grossly inefficient in the use of the communications facilities? We doubt it! The standard approach to this problem is, however, much simpler conceptually, especially since we have become accustomed to this type of inefficiency. It is, moreover, accepted as the proper approach to the design of telemetry systems. From our point of view, the design of the buffer is just another difficult statistical problem in trying to optimize a communications channel. It can be avoided by refusing to face the possibility of using redundancy removal operations, but such neglect does not necessarily come cheaply. It does, however, come easily.

The authors wish to acknowledge contributions to this work by F. Ellersick, particularly the section dealing with the compression of multiple sensor outputs.

# 2



Reprinted from *Proc. 1974 Intern. Conf. Commun.*, 1974, pp. 40A-1–40A-5

# A MATHEMATICAL THEORY OF DATA COMPRESSION?

**Robert M. Gray**
*Stanford University*

**Lee D. Davisson**
*University of Southern California*

ABSTRACT

Mathematical approaches to data compression have been of limited use in practical systems largely because the standard mathematical assumptions are usually physically unrealistic. In this tutorial we briefly describe the Shannon approach to data compression, its shortcomings, and several recent results and conjectures that suggest that the answer to the implied title question is now a hopeful "maybe."

## INTRODUCTION

Data compression has historically proceeded along two nearly disjoint paths. On one hand were the data compressors, those who designed essentially ad hoc algorithms to "compress" data such as images and speech by reducing the data rate with at most a tolerable loss in fidelity. On the other hand were the theoreticians attempting a mathematical formulation of such systems and hopefully mathematical solutions in terms of figures of merit with which to compare compression systems and bounds on the optimal attainable performance given certain system constraints. Such results allow the comparison of compression systems with each other and with an an absolute "yardstick" of optimal performance.

One of the initially most promising such theories was Shannon's rate-distortion theory which applied the techniques and insights of information theory to the problem of data compression[1,2,3,4,5]. Shannon's basic approach and results can be summarized as follows: Let $\{X_n\}_{n=-\infty}^{\infty}$ denote a discrete-time source with alphabet $A$, that is, $\{X_n\}$ is a sequence of random variables taking values in some set $A$. Let $\mu$ denote the probabilistic description of the random variables. The alphabet $A$ can be binary, real numbers, or even two-dimensional intensity distributors (images). A source is also denoted by $[A,\mu]$ to emphasize the alphabet and statistical description.

Shannon considered only block compression systems, i.e., systems that map consecutive source blocks $X_k^N \triangleq (X_k, X_{k+1}, \ldots, X_{k+N-1})$ ; $k = 1,2,\ldots$, into consecutive encoded reproduction blocks $\hat{X}_k^N$. The allowed set of reproduction blocks is much smaller than the possible number of source blocks and hence "compression" is achieved, i.e., it takes fewer bits to specify the reproduction block than the original source block. Let $\hat{A}$ be the available reproduction alphabet, that is, the set of allowable reproduction letters. These may be determined by available transmission equipment, receiver demands, storage media, quantization levels, etc.

Shannon assumed the existence of a mathematical distortion measure, $\rho_N(X^N,Y^N)$, to measure the distortion or cost or loss resulting if a source block $X^N$ is reproduced as $Y^N$. For simplicity it is usually assumed that the measure is single-letter, i.e., there is a per-letter measure $\rho(X^1,Y^1)$ $\rho_N(X^N,Y^N) = N^{-1}\sum_{i=0}^{N-1}\rho(X_i,Y_i)$. Examples of such measure are squared-error and Hamming distance.

Block compression schemes are idealized as follows: given any integer blocklength $N$, a codebook $C_N$ is a collection of some finite number $\|C_N\|$ of reproduction blocks called codewords. Given a codebook $C_N$, a source block $X^N$ is encoded into the best possible codeword in the $\rho_N$ sense, i.e., $X^N$ is mapped into the codeword $y^N$ in $C_N$ minimizing $\rho_N(X^N,y^N)$. The resulting codeword is denoted $\hat{x}(X^N)$.

The interesting parameters of a code are its average distortion $\rho_\mu(C_N) \triangleq E_\mu\left(\rho(X^N,x(X^N))\right)$, where $E_\mu$ denotes expectation or statistical average over the source statistics $\mu$, and its rate $R(C_N) \triangleq N^{-1}\log\|C_N\|$. The rate of a code reflects its size or complexity and gives the required channel capacity for reliable communication of the reproduction. Mathematically, "compression" corresponds to reducing the rate. Actual transmission rate compression can be attained by noiseless encoding of the reproduction sequence produced by block compression.

The primary goal of the theory is to determine the optimal attainable performance given the above formulation. There are two approaches possible here:

1) The rate-distortion approach wherein the maximal allowable average distortion is constrained (possibly due to customer demands) and the required rate (and hence channel capacity) is minimized. The minimal attainable rate subject to an average distortion constraint is defined as $r_\mu(d) = \inf_N r_\mu(d,N)$ where

$$r_\mu(d,N) = \inf_{C_N:\rho_\mu(C_N)\leq d} R(C_N)$$

is the minimal attainable rate using blocklength $N$ codes and the infimums are used as the minimums may not exist.

2) The distortion-rate approach wherein the rate is constrained (possibly due to capacity constraints, transmission equipment, available quantization levels, etc.) and the resulting average distortion is minimized. Define $\delta_\mu(R) = \inf_N \delta_\mu(R,N)$ where

$$\delta_\mu(R,N) = \inf_{C_N:R(C_N)\leq R} \rho_\mu(C_N)$$

We shall focus on the distortion-rate approach since in most communications systems the rate constraints are well-defined while average distortion requirements are rarely precisely known.

The well-defined functions $\delta_\mu$ and $r_\mu$ provide the desired performance bounds, but unfortunately they are usually impossible to evaluate even with a computer as the class of all codebooks is too large and the computations are difficult. Here is where information theory enters: Shannon[1,2] showed that under certain conditions $\delta_\mu$ and $r_\mu$ are equal to well-defined information theoretic minimizations that are susceptable to fast computer evaluation using convex programming techniques[6]. In particular, Shannon and others[1,2,3,4] showed that there is a function $R_\mu(d)$, called the rate-distortion function, and its inverse $D_\mu(R)$, called the distortion-rate function, such that if the source is stationary and ergodic and some additional technical assumptions are made, then $\delta_\mu(R) = D_\mu(R)$ and $r_\mu(d) = R_\mu(D)$. The functions $R_\mu$ and $D_\mu$ are studied in detail in (1,2,3,4) and computation algorithms are given in (6).

Stationarity means that the statistical description $\mu$ does not change in time. Ergodicity means roughly that all actual source sequences are "typical" in that relative frequencies converge to the appropriate probabilities and sample averages converge to the corresponding expectations.

Taken at face value, the previous formulation and theorem appear to provide the desired figures of merit and bounds on optimal performance as well as a method of evaluating these quantities. These results have, indeed, provided some useful bounds and insights in certain special situations [7;4,Ch.5]. Unfortunately, however, the theory has several serious drawbacks that have limited its potential usefulness. These problems with the formulation enter at so basic a level that real-world data compressors have often been discouraged from spending the time to learn this potentially useful theory. In short, the required assumptions are almost never met in practice. In particular:

1) One rarely has precise knowledge of the probabilities $\mu$ governing a source. These are often unknown and at best approximate, yet the original Shannon theory includes no measure of the "mismatch" between possibly inaccurate mathematical models and "real" sources nor figures of merit and performance bounds in such unknown or inaccurately specified statistical environments.

2) Real processes such as speech usually violate the required statistical regularity requirements of stationarity and ergodicity . Since ergodicity is required to relate probabilistic or ensemble averages to the corresponding time averages, the entire usefulness of statistical methods is in doubt in nonergodic situations.

3) Block codes do not include many useful data compression schemes (such as predictive and interpolative schemes[8]) and hence the theory does not apply to such nonblock schemes. In addition, in many situations block codes require such great complexity that they are virtually impossible to implement, yet there is no comparable theory for nonblock structures.

4) One rarely has tractable, subjectively meaningful criteria, e.g., weighted-mean-squared-error is a notoriously poor measure of subjective quality of images[9].

We next briefly describe recent results and conjectures to each of these problems. Details may be found in the references indicated and an expanded version of this paper is available as a U.S.C. Technical Report [29].

## UNKNOWN STATISTICS

The problem of unknown, incomplete, or inaccurate statistics can be formalized as follows: Instead of building a system for a single source $[A,\mu]$, we assume instead that there is a class of sources $\{[A,\mu_\theta];\ \theta\in\Lambda\}$ and that nature will choose one member of the class at random. The class reflects our knowledge (or lack thereof) of the possible source probabilities. The data compressor must build a system without knowledge of the $\theta$ chosen by nature that hopefully works "well" regardless of $\theta$. Such a compression scheme is called "universal." The first approach to universal coding was essentially a "worst case" approach of building a code of sufficiently large rate to ensure that the average distortion constraint is satisfied for all sources in the class [10;11;4,Ch.6]. If nature is not malevolent, however, and the true source is not the "worst" one, this approach leads to requiring much more rate than necessary to meet the fidelity constraint, or, equivalently, much more average distortion than necessary for the given rate. Ziv[12] first demonstrated for a weak definition of "universal" that for a fixed rate (possibly chosen to ensure as above that the worst source has a specified average distortion), one can construct "universal codes" such that the resulting average distortion is almost as small as the minimum attainable average distortion for the "true" but unknown source. Since Ziv's original work, many alternative definitions of "universal codes" and many techniques for proving the appropriate theorems have been introduced [13,14,15,16].

We here mention only the strongest form of universality as it is physically the most interesting, and we consider only the topological approach as it is both the simplest and most powerful. Since the object of data compression is to approximate a given source by a simpler one, a useful tool is the following distance measure between random processes. Let $[A,\mu]$ or $\{X_n\}$ denote a given stationary source and let $[B,\nu]$ or $\{Y_n\}$ be a stationary process with alphabet B, e.g., if B = A this is another source and if $B = \hat{A}$ it is a reproduction process. Let $[A\times B,p]$ or $\{X_n,Y_n\}$ denote any stationary process producing pairs, i.e., the output at each time is a pair consisting of $X_n \in A$, $Y_n \in B$, and the individual coordinates $\{X_n\}$ and $\{Y_n\}$ are as described by $[A,\mu]$ and $[B,\nu]$, respectively. Thus any $[A\times B,p]$ can be thought of as a "supersource" that produces both $\{X_n\}$ and $\{Y_n\}$ , but stochastically links them in a stationary way. The process or $\bar{\rho}$ distance between $[A,\mu]$ and $[B,\nu]$ is defined as

$$\bar{\rho}([A,\mu],[B,\nu]) \triangleq \inf_{[A\times B,p]} E_p\{\rho(X_0,Y_0)\},$$

that is, $\bar{\rho}$ measures how well two processes can be "matched up" at a particular time in an average distortion sense if the two processes are connected in a stationary random manner. The process distance provides a measure of the "mismatch" between sources in a data compression sense as made precise in the following theorem:

<u>Mismatch Theorem</u>[14,15]: Given any block code $C_N$, and any two stationary sources $[A,\mu_\varphi]$ and $[A,\mu_\varphi]$ , then

$$|\rho_{\mu_\theta}(C_N) - \rho_{\mu_\varphi}(C_N)| \le \bar{\rho}([A,\mu_\theta],[A,\mu_\varphi])$$

$$|\delta_{\mu_\theta}(R) - \delta_{\mu_\varphi}(R)| \le \bar{\rho}([A,\mu_\theta],[A,\mu_\varphi])$$

and, if the sources are ergodic,

$$|D_{\mu_\theta}(R) - D_{\mu_\varphi}(R)| \le \bar{\rho}([A,\mu_\theta],[A,\mu_\varphi])$$

The Mismatch Theorem shows that the process distance between two sources gives the maximal performance loss when applying a code built for one source to another (mismatch of actual codes) and the maximal difference in optimal performance of the two sources (mismatch of theoretical performance bounds). Using the Mismatch Theorem and the $\bar{\rho}$ distance to "carve up" the class of sources, the following theorem results:

<u>Universal Coding Theorem</u>[14,15]: Given a class of stationary sources $\{[A,\mu_\theta];\ \theta\in\Lambda\}$ such that for any $\epsilon > 0$ there exists a partition of the class into a finite number $K(\epsilon)$ of subclasses of maximal $\bar{\rho}$ diameter $\epsilon$ (any two sources in a subclass are within $\bar{\rho}$ distance $\epsilon$ of each other), then for sufficiently long blocklength N there exists a code $C_N$ such that

$$\rho_{\mu_\theta}(C_N) \le \delta_{\mu_\theta}(R) + \epsilon \qquad \text{all } \theta \in \Lambda$$

$$R(C_N) \le R + \epsilon$$

In words, the code $C_N$ has rate nearly R and average distortion nearly optimal for the true but unknown source regardless of which source in the class is chosen by nature! Classes satisfying the assumptions of the theorem are basically classes for which the alphabet is not too large and the memory eventually dies out (15,17).

Even though the theorem is an existence theorem rather than constructive, the proofs are simple and lend insight into the design of systems that is reflected in existing schemes such as the Rice Machine(18). Most importantly, however, it demonstrates that the Shannon figures of merit and performance bounds extend in a meaningful way to unknown statistical environments and that one is not doomed to a "worst case" approach.

## NONERGODIC AND NONSTATIONARY SOURCES

A source that is stationary but not ergodic can under quite general assumptions be modeled as a class of ergodic processes with a prior, i.e., Nature chooses an ergodic member of the class at the beginning of time and sends that source forever(13,19). This is known as the ergodic decomposition of a stationary process and allows immediate application of results for classes of processes such as the previous to individual stationary but nonergodic sources. Furthermore, the ergodic decomposition implies that the stationary subsources of the previous section can be considered to be ergodic without loss of generality. In other words, a class of stationary subsources can be made into a "finer" class of ergodic subsources by decomposing each stationary member of the class into a subclass consisting of its ergodic decomposition. Stationary but nonergodic sources are therefore easily included into the previous analysis.

The problem of nonstationary sources is considerably more difficult. The universal coding viewpoint suggests a possible approach to analyzing a particular class of nonstationary sources that inherit the desirable properties of stationary sources and provide a model for "locally stationary" sources such as speech.

The previously discussed universal results can be viewed as follows: Nature has a class of ergodic sources. At the beginning of time she switches to one of the sources randomly and then solders the switch closed so that that source is sent forever. This model is similar to composite sources as described by Berger [4, Chap. 6] where the subsources are all independent, identically distributed (white) random processes and the switch position is itself a sequence of independent, identically distributed random variables. Combining the more general subsources considered here with the concept of the moveable switch suggests the following model of switched sources: We are given a class of ergodic sources $\{[A,\mu_\theta];\ \theta \in \Lambda\}$ and a time varying switch sequence $\{S_n;\ n = \ldots,-1,0,1,\ldots\}$. If at time n the switch has value $S_n = \theta$, then the output of the switched process at that time is the $n^{th}$ output of the $\theta^{th}$ subsource. The sequence of switch positions may itself be a random process or a deterministic but unknown sequence. Note that a sample function of the switched source is a concatenation of pieces of sample functions of the ergodic subsources and hence will retain some of the statistical regularity of ergodic sources even though the output of the switched source is extremely nonstationary. Thus a switched source is locally ergodic in the well defined sense that we are always observing the output of an ergodic source, but the source being observed may change with time. If the subsources are required only to be stationary then the resulting switched or composite source is similarly locally stationary. This model appears to be a natural one for speech as implied in the modern linear predictive compression schemes that assume that for short periods of time speech appears as the output of a linear filter driven by stationary noise or periodic impulses. As deterministic waveforms can be included in the subsources, the switched source intuitively well describes this model by having the various subsources specified by the impulse responses of the linear filter and the driving noise or impulse train. Transients due to switching may be included in this model, but we here assume perfect switching for simplicity. Note that switched sources can also model "evolving" locally stationary sources such as processes with a drifting mean or slowly time-varying covariance.

If the switch position is constrained to vary slowly (at least with high probability), then the fixed switch universal approach generalizes immediately to time varying switched sources provided only that the blocklength is short in comparison to the average switching time. Investigation of such models is only beginning, but they appear to provide a rigorous yet intuitive model allowing the extension of the Shannon theory to nonstationary environments.

## NONBLOCK DATA COMPRESSION

Consider the following simple data compression system: Given three binary numbers x,y, and z, define maj(x,y,z) as 0 if the majority of x,y, and z is 0 and one otherwise, e.g., maj(0,1,0) = 0.

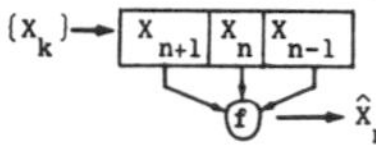


$$\hat{X}_n = \text{maj}(X_{n+1}, X_n, X_{n-1})$$

Assume the source is an independent equiprobable binary sequence, and let the per-letter distortion be $\rho(X,\hat{X}) = 0$ if $X = \hat{X}$ and 1 if $X \ne \hat{X}$ (Hamming distance). Each time unit a new source digit is shifted in and a new reproduction digit equal to the majority of the past, current, and future source digits is shifted out. Compression is achieved in that the source entropy rate of one bit per symbol is reduced to a reproduction entropy rate shown by computer evaluation to be less than .8 bit per symbol. The resulting average distortion is $E\rho(X_0,\hat{X}_2) = 1/4$. Although this simple scheme does not work very well (a rate 1/2 blocklength 2 block code of {0,0},{1,1} does equally well). It demonstrates, however, that a nonblock structure involving a time invariant nonlinear discrete-time filter can be used to obtain entropy compression. We generalize this notion as follows: Given a source $\{X_n\}$ (or $[A,\mu]$) and any integer N, a sliding-block source encoder of blocklength 2N + 1 is any function $f^{(N)}$ mapping source blocks of length 2N+1 into a single reproduction letter. The reproduction sequence $\{\hat{X}_n\}$ is given by $\hat{X}_n = f^{(N)}(X_{n-N},\ldots,X_n,\ldots,X_{n+N})$. Thus at each unit of time a single reproduction letter is put out depending on the corresponding source ouput and its finite "past" and "future". A sliding block code $f^{(N)}$ has average distortion $\rho_\mu(f^{(N)}) \triangleq E_\mu\{(X_0, f^{(N)}(X_{-N},\ldots,X_N))\}$, where the distortion need only be measured at a single time since $\{\hat{X}_n\}$ is stationary, and entropy rate $H_\mu(f^{(N)}) \triangleq H(\hat{X})$, where $H(\hat{X})$ denotes the entropy rate of the resulting reproduction process. Analagous to the block coding systems we define the minimal attainable average distortion using fixed rate sliding block codes as follows:

$$\delta_\mu{}^*(R) = \inf_N \delta_\mu(R,N) \qquad \text{where}$$

$$\delta_\mu{}^*(R,N) = \inf_{f^{(N)}:H_\mu(f^{(N)}) \le R} \rho(f^{(N)})$$

Sliding-Block Coding Theorem (20): Given a stationary source $[A,\mu]$ that is not periodic, then

$$\delta_\mu^*(R) = \inf_{[\hat{A},\nu]:H_\nu \leq R} \bar{\rho}([A,\mu], [\hat{A},\nu])$$

If the source is also ergodic, then

$$\delta_\mu^*(R) = D_\mu(R)$$

The second part of the theorem states that in the ergodic case, sliding block codes can do as well (and no better) than block codes. These coding structures can be easily modified to include feedback and feed-forward, and the theorem remains unchanged[20,21]. The first part of the theorem holds more generally and can be interpreted as stating that the minimal average distortion attainable using fixed rate deterministic codes equals the smallest process distance between the given source and any reproduction process with the correct entropy rate.

## FIDELITY MEASURES

As pointed out by Budrikis[9] in his survey paper on fidelity measures for images quantifying a subjective fidelity measure in a tractable form is an exceedingly complicated and perhaps impossible task. For example, the weighted-mean-squared-error is known to be woefully inadequate yet is often used as it appears to have some relation to visual processing and is the only tractable measure available[22]. Budrikis points out that any subjectively meaningful fidelity measure must reflect to some extent the biological receiver processing. A one-dimensional fidelity measure is inadequate to describe quality if the receiver processes the data by decomposing it, separately and independently processing individual pieces, and finally reconstructing the desired representation. Any such separate channel processing will likely have several simultaneous fidelity demands, e.g., each piece must be reproduced well for the final reproduction to be good. To model such situations vector-valued fidelity measures are required. Choose, say, $J$ fidelity measures $\rho_j(x,y)$, $j=1,\ldots,J$, to hopefully measure the separate important features. Unfortunately, a vector-valued distortion measure does not fit easily into the distortion-rate formulation as we cannot minimize a vector valued average distortion for a given rate, i.e., we must choose which features are the most important and hence deserving of rate. A vector-valued distortion measure is easily included in the rate-distortion view[23], but, as we have seen, this view is usually less natural. Furthermore, one still has the problem of weighting the importance of the separate channels when one demands a vector-valued fidelity.

To adapt simultaneous fidelity requirements to the distortion-rate approach, let $\alpha_j$, $j = 1,\ldots,J$ be relative importance weightings of the separate channels and define a measure of the form $\rho(x,y) = \max \alpha_j\rho_j(x,y)$. This measure is small only if all of the $\alpha_j\rho_j$ are small and large if any of the $\alpha_j\rho_j$ are large. This fidelity measure thus reflects the demand for simultaneous satisfaction of several separate fidelity requirements.

Recent psychophysical testing results indicate that the eye behaves in the manner described above[24,25,26,27].

If the eye does process images via independent channels, the failure of the traditional weighted-mean-squared-error is not surprising. Given a noisy picture with low mean-square-error averaged over the entire spatial frequency domain, all of the error energy might concentrate in a particular channel and destroy the picture. Conversely, a slightly subthreshold error in each channel could add up to a large average error, yet the picture would appear undistorted.

Let the alphabet $A$ consist of all real-valued, nonnegative two dimensional intensity distributions $\{I(x,y)\ ;\ (x,y) \in [0,L]^2\}$. The eye is known to be sensitive to $U(f,g) = \mathcal{F}(\log I(x,y))$, where $\mathcal{F}$ denotes the two-dimensional spatial Fourier transform. This sensitivity was the motivation for the traditional measure

$$\rho_1'(I_X,I_Y) = \left(\iint df\, dg\ |U_X(f,g) - U_Y(f,g)|^2 W(f,g)\right)^{1/2}$$

where $W$ is some frequency weighting reflecting the approximately linear processing of the eye. The preceding discussion suggests the following alternative class of measures: Carve the spatial frequency domain into $J$ disjoint regions $F_j$, $j = 1,\ldots,J$, and let $\alpha_j$, $j = 1,\ldots,J$ be nonnegative weights. As the eye does appear to filter locally for spatial frequency channels define

$$\rho_j(I_X,I_Y) = \left(\iint_{F_j} df\, dg\ |U_X(f,g) - U_Y(f,g)|^2\right)^{1/2}$$

and the resulting per-letter distortion measure

$$\rho(I_X,I_Y) = \max_j \alpha_j\rho_j(I_X,I_Y)$$

Discussion:

1) The $F_j$ are assumed small enough so that (i) any weighting $W(f,g)$ due to prefiltering is fairly constant over $F_j$ and hence can be included in the $\alpha_j$ (which can also include differing thresholds), and (ii) the channels $F_j$ can be combined to well model most human channels.

2) The measure $\rho$ preserves much of the simplicity of the traditional measure and can be shown to be a metric. This measure therefore satisfies the requirements of the universal coding theory and easily fits into the framework of the preceding sections. Although explicit evaluations of the appropriate distortion-rate functions may not be possible for this measure (they rarely are for any measures), it seems amenable to fast computer evaluation using available techniques[8].

3) The above measure overcomes at least intuitively the faults of the traditional measure and seems at least an appropriate candidate for extensive psychophysical testing to hopefully determine fairly universal $J$, $F_j$ and $\alpha_j$ for classes of images.

4) A potential drawback of the proposed distortion measure is that it does not incorporate the possibility that a normally unimportant channel can become important if it is highly active, i.e., the $\alpha_j$ may depend on the picture. Hopefully, however, the weightings are fairly constant over the classes of images. This observation should be included in any phychophysical studies of the proposed measure.

5) Another potential drawback is the failure to include temporal processing by the eye due to the single-letter assumption. As this would add tremendous complexity to the measure before its fundamental properties have been tested, we feel studies of such a more general measure are not now appropriate.

6) The proposed measure lies between the traditional average extreme on one hand and the pointwise extreme of the sup norm on the other, i.e., the measure

$$\rho^*(I_X,I_Y) = \sup_{f,g} W(f,g)\ |U_X(f,g) - U_Y(f,g)|$$

This is also a candidate distortion measure, but we feel it is likely too strong and too complicated to be generally useful. It may be useful, however, when dealing with discrete raster image models (small finite arrays).

7) Other two-dimensional spatial transforms could also be used for simplicity.

In summary, the above approach is theoretically sound, is likely an improvement over the traditional measure, and is an intuitively satisfying candidate for a subjectively meaningful fidelity measure. In addition, a similar approach might be applicable to speech compression by considering temporal frequency channels or time domain channels and a similar measure.

We realize that our conjectures above are totally outside our own fields. We hope, however, that such conjectures will be taken as intended-- as some plausible candidates suggested by and consistent with the theory (and hopefully not blatantly inaccurate).

REFERENCES


(1) C.E. Shannon, "A Mathematical Theory of Communication," Bell Syst. Tech. Journal, vol. 27, 379-424, 623-656, 1948.

(2) C.E. Shannon, "Coding Theorems for a Discrete Source with a Fidelity Criterion," IRE Nat'l. Conv. Rec., part 4, 142-163, 1959.

(3) R.G. Gallager, Information Theory and Reliable Communication, Chap. 9, Wiley, New York, 1968.

(4) Toby Berger, Rate-Distortion Theory, Prentice-Hall, Englewood Cliffs, New Jersey, 1971.

(5) L.D. Davisson, "Rate-distortion theory and application," Proc. of the IEEE, 60, 800-808, 1972.

(6) R. Blahut, "Computation of Channel Capacity and Rate-Distortion Functions," IEEE Trans. IT, 18, 460-473, 1972.

(7) T. Goblick and J. Holsinger, "Analog source digitization: A comparison of theory and practice," IEEE T-IT, 13, 323-326, 1967.

(8) L.D. Davisson, "The Theoretical Analysis of Data Compression Systems," Proc. of the IEEE, vol. 56, 176-186, 1968.

(9) Z.L. Budrikis, "Visual Fidelity Criterion and Modeling," IEEE Proc., 60, 771-778, 1972.

(10) D.J. Sakrison, "The rate-distortion function for a class of sources," Inform. and Control, 15, 165-195, 1969.

(11) D.J. Sakrison, "The Rate of a Class of Random Processess," IEEE T-IT, 16, 10-16, 1970.

(12) J. Ziv, "Coding of Sources with unknown statistics-Part II; Distortion relative to a fidelity criterion," IEEE T-IT, 18, 389-394 , 1972.

(13) R.M. Gray and L.D. Davisson, The Ergodic Decomposition of Discrete Stationary Sources," to appear in IEEE T - IT, 1974.

(14) R.M. Gray, D. Neuhoff, and P.C. Shields, "A Generalization of Ornstein's $\bar{d}$ Distance with Applications to Information Theory," to appear in Annals of Probability, 1974.

(15) D. Neuhoff, R.M. Gray, and L.D. Davisson, "Fixed Rate Universal Source Coding with a Fidelity Criterion," to be submitted to IEEE T - IT.

16. M.B. Pursley, "Coding Theorems for Non-Ergodic Sources and Sources with Unknown Parameters," USC EE Report, 466, Jan. 1974.

17. P.C. Shields, "Separability of the Space of Markov Chains in the $\bar{d}$-Metric," submitted to Annals of Probability.

18. R.F. Rice and J.P. Plaunt, "Adaptive Variable-Length Coding for Efficient Compression of Spacecraft Television Data," IEEE Com. Tech., 19, 889-897, 1971.

19. R.M. Gray and L.D. Davisson, "Source Coding Without the Ergodic Assumption," to appear in IEEE T-IT, July, 1974.

20. R.M. Gray, D.L. Neuhoff, and D.S. Ornstein, "Nonblock Source Coding with a Fidelity Criterion," submitted to IEEE T-IT, 1974.

21. R.M. Gray and D.L. Neuhoff, "Process Definitions of Distortion-Rate Functions, Stochastic Codes, and the Information Transmission Theorem," submitted to IEEE T-IT, 1974.

22. T.G. Stocham, Jr., "Image Processing in the Context of a Visual Model," Proc. of the IEEE, 60, 828-841, 1972.

23. R.M. Gray, "A New Class of Lower Bounds to Information Rates of Stationary Sources via Conditional Rate-Distortion Functions," IEEE T-IT, 19, 480-489, 1973.

24. M.B. Sachs, J. Nachimias, and J.G. Robson, "Spatial-Frequency Channels in Human Vision," Jour. of the Optical Society of America, 61, 1176-1186, 1971.

25. C.F. Stromeyer, III, and B. Julesz, "Spatial-Frequency Masking in Vision: Critical Bands and Spread of Masking," Jour. of the Optical Society of America, 62, 1221-1232, 1972.

26. L. Harmon, "Masking in Visual Recognition: Effects of Two-Dimensional Filtered Noise," Science, 180, 1194-1197, 1973.

27. J.L. Mannos and D.J. Sakrison, "The Effects of a Visual Fidelity Criterion on the Encoding of Images," submitted for publication.

28. L.D. Davisson and R.M. Gray, "Advances in Data Compression," in Advances in Communications, edited by Balakrishnan and Viterbi, 1974.

29. R.M. Gray and L.D. Davisson, "A Mathematical Theory of Data Compression?," USC EE Tech. Rep., 1974.



ACKNOWLEDGEMENT

The research here subscribed has been supported by NSF Grants GK31630 and GK14190, NASA Grant NGL 05-018-118, and the JSEP at Stanford under U.S. Navy Contract N00014-67-A-0112-0044.

# Part II

# NOISELESS SOURCE CODING

# Editors' Comments on Papers 3 Through 11



In this group of papers we focus on the noiseless aspect of source coding—the operation of mapping a discrete-alphabet source into a possibly different alphabet (usually assumed to be binary) in such a way that the encoded process is nearly memoryless and the original process can be recovered perfectly (or nearly so). We begin here since this was the facet of source coding first considered in depth by Shannon, and since the many theoretical and practical considerations are usually simpler and more completely understood than their entropy-compression counterparts.

In noiseless source coding we require an average distortion of zero (or an arbitrarily small amount) and wish to find codes that achieve this. Even though we require the receiver to be able to reconstruct source symbols at the original source rate, the actual encoding operation usually involves the mapping of fixed- or variable-length blocks of source data into fixed- or variable-length blocks of encoded data. The decoder reverses the procedure and, assuming idealized infinite buffers, has an output of the appropriate rate.

Shannon's classic paper ["The Mathematical Theory of Communication," *Bell System Tech. J.*, **27,** 379–423 (1948); also, in book form, University of Illinois Press, Urbana, Ill. (1949)] first introduced the entropy concept as a measure of the complexity of an information source, and laid the groundwork for the statistical methods used in data compression. If $H(X)$ is the entropy of the source in bits per source symbol and $C = \log \|B\|$ is the capacity of an alphabet $B$ noiseless channel in bits per channel symbol, Shannon showed that there exist noiseless source encoding–decoding operations for ergodic sources if $\tau_s^{-1}H(X) < \tau_c^{-1}C$ [or $H(X) < (L/K)\log \|B\|$ or $\eta > H(X)/\log \|B\|$] and only if $\eta \geqslant H(X)/\log \|B\|$. Thus the OPTA for ergodic sources is zero only if $(F_E, F_D)$ includes source encoders–decoders for which $\eta > H(X)/\log \|B\|$.

Shannon proved his existence theorem using both fixed- and variable-length block coding structures. In addition, he suggested a particular construction (also discovered independently by R. M. Fano) for fixed-length block to variable-length block encoding. In Paper 3, Huffman provided a simple scheme for optimal encoding–decoding using fixed-length block to variable-length block encoders. This scheme has proved practical as well as clever and is in common use today. Elias (Paper 4) studied redundancy removal using prediction theory by viewing the nonredundant information as the difference between a source sample and its predicted value based on previous outputs. This provides a link with the Wiener theory of communications, leads to the notion of run length coding (also a commonly used practical scheme), and provides a philosophical basis for some entropy-compression systems to be considered later. Similar approaches are considered in the papers by Oliver, Kretzmer, and Harrison referred to by Lucky in Part VI.

Huffman coding requires long, possibly infinite buffers to maintain a constant throughput rate. For example, if a Huffman code maps source blocks of fixed length $k$ into variable-length code words of maximal length $M$ (possibly infinite), a finite-length buffer connecting the encoder and channel will overflow eventually unless $R_c/R_s \geqslant N/k$. If the buffer overflows, symbols may be lost, and a catastrophic loss of synchronization may occur. In Paper 5, Jelinek presents modifications of Huffman coding that are viable with finite-length buffers and considers problems of both overflow and underflow.

Jelinek and Schneider (Paper 6) develop a generalization of run length coding that involves mapping source blocks of variable length into code blocks of fixed length. Note that this encoder structure is the same as the Huffman decoder. Buffer problems are again considered.

In Paper 7, Hellman presents a scheme that simultaneously performs noiseless source coding and channel coding. For a noiseless channel, this demonstrates that a completely nonblock structure—a channel convolutional encoder—can be used to noiseless source encode, with a channel sequential decoder (tree-search algorithm) used as a decoder. This nonblock approach to source coding is currently an active area of theoretical research and will be considered in depth in our forthcoming Benchmark volume *Ergodic and Information Theory*.

All the theory and codes described so far assume a complete and accurate knowledge of the source statistics, a requirement rarely met in practice. Lynch (Paper 8), Davisson (Papers 9 and 11), and Cover (Paper 10) present both theoretical and practical approaches to the problem of building good codes for unknown sources. These schemes use fixed-length block to variable-length block encoders.

As previously noted, the problem of unknown source statistics was studied much earlier by Blasbalg and Van Blerkom. It should also be noted that much of the pioneering work in this area was published in the Russian literature by Kolmogorov, Fitingof, Shtarkov, and Babkin; their results are referred to in Papers 10 and 11.

# 3



Reprinted from *Proc. IRE,* **40**(9), 1098–1101 (1952)

# A Method for the Construction of Minimum-Redundancy Codes*

DAVID A. HUFFMAN†, ASSOCIATE, IRE

***Summary*—An optimum method of coding an ensemble of messages consisting of a finite number of members is developed. A minimum-redundancy code is one constructed in such a way that the average number of coding digits per message is minimized.**

## Introduction

One important method of transmitting messages is to transmit in their place sequences of symbols. If there are more messages which might be sent than there are kinds of symbols available, then some of the messages must use more than one symbol. If it is assumed that each symbol requires the same time for transmission, then the time for transmission (length) of a message is directly proportional to the number of symbols associated with it. In this paper, the symbol or sequence of symbols associated with a given message will be called the "message code." The entire number of messages which might be transmitted will be called the "message ensemble." The mutual agreement between the transmitter and the receiver about the meaning of the code for each message of the ensemble will be called the "ensemble code."

Probably the most familiar ensemble code was stated in the phrase "one if by land and two if by sea." In this case, the message ensemble consisted of the two individual messages "by land" and "by sea", and the message codes were "one" and "two."

In order to formalize the requirements of an ensemble code, the coding symbols will be represented by numbers. Thus, if there are $D$ different types of symbols to be used in coding, they will be represented by the digits $0, 1, 2, \cdots, (D-1)$. For example, a ternary code will be constructed using the three digits 0, 1, and 2 as coding symbols.

The number of messages in the ensemble will be called $N$. Let $P(i)$ be the probability of the $i$th message. Then

$$\sum_{i=1}^{N} P(i) = 1. \tag{1}$$

The length of a message, $L(i)$, is the number of coding digits assigned to it. Therefore, the average message length is

$$L_{av} = \sum_{i=1}^{N} P(i)L(i). \tag{2}$$

The term "redundancy" has been defined by Shannon[1] as a property of codes. A "minimum-redundancy code" will be defined here as an ensemble code which, for a message ensemble consisting of a finite number of members, $N$, and for a given number of coding digits, $D$, yields the lowest possible average message length. In order to avoid the use of the lengthy term "minimum-redundancy," this term will be replaced here by "optimum." It will be understood then that, in this paper, "optimum code" means "minimum-redundancy code."

The following basic restrictions will be imposed on an ensemble code:

(a) No two messages will consist of identical arrangements of coding digits.

(b) The message codes will be constructed in such a way that no additional indication is necessary to specify where a message code begins and ends once the starting point of a sequence of messages is known.

Restriction (b) necessitates that no message be coded in such a way that its code appears, digit for digit, as the first part of any message code of greater length. Thus, 01, 102, 111, and 202 are valid message codes for an ensemble of four members. For instance, a sequence of these messages 1111022020101111102 can be broken up into the individual messages 111-102-202-01-01-111-102. All the receiver need know is the ensemble code. However, if the ensemble has individual message codes including 11, 111, 102, and 02, then when a message sequence starts with the digits 11, it is not immediately certain whether the message 11 has been received or whether it is only the first two digits of the message 111. Moreover, even if the sequence turns out to be 11102, it is still not certain whether 111-02 or 11-102 was transmitted. In this example, change of one of the two message codes 111 or 11 is indicated.

C. E. Shannon[1] and R. M. Fano[2] have developed ensemble coding procedures for the purpose of proving that the average number of binary digits required per message approaches from above the average amount of information per message. Their coding procedures are not optimum, but approach the optimum behavior when $N$ approaches infinity. Some work has been done by Kraft[3] toward deriving a coding method which gives an average code length as close as possible to the ideal when the ensemble contains a finite number of members. However, up to the present time, no definite procedure has been suggested for the construction of such a code

* Decimal classification: R531.1. Original manuscript received by the Institute, December 6, 1951.

† Massachusetts Institute of Technology, Cambridge, Mass.

[1] C. E. Shannon, "A mathematical theory of communication," *Bell Sys. Tech. Jour.*, vol. 27, pp. 398–403; July, 1948.

[2] R. M. Fano, "The Transmission of Information," Technical Report No. 65, Research Laboratory of Electronics, M.I.T., Cambridge, Mass.; 1949.

[3] L. G. Kraft, "A Device for Quantizing, Grouping, and Coding Amplitude-modulated Pulses," Electrical Engineering Thesis, M.I.T., Cambridge, Mass.; 1949.

to the knowledge of the author. It is the purpose of this paper to derive such a procedure.

## Derived Coding Requirements

For an optimum code, the length of a given message code can never be less than the length of a more probable message code. If this requirement were not met, then a reduction in average message length could be obtained by interchanging the codes for the two messages in question in such a way that the shorter code becomes associated with the more probable message. Also, if there are several messages with the same probability, then it is possible that the codes for these messages may differ in length. However, the codes for these messages may be interchanged in any way without affecting the average code length for the message ensemble. Therefore, it may be assumed that the messages in the ensemble have been ordered in a fashion such that

$$P(1) \geqq P(2) \geqq \cdots \geqq P(N-1) \geqq P(N) \qquad (3)$$

and that, in addition, for an optimum code, the condition

$$L(1) \leqq L(2) \leqq \cdots \leqq L(N-1) \leqq L(N) \qquad (4)$$

holds. This requirement is assumed to be satisfied throughout the following discussion.

It might be imagined that an ensemble code could assign $q$ more digits to the $N$th message than to the $(N-1)$st message. However, the first $L(N-1)$ digits of the $N$th message must not be used as the code for any other message. Thus the additional $q$ digits would serve no useful purpose and would unnecessarily increase $L_{av}$. Therefore, for an optimum code it is necessary that $L(N)$ be equal to $L(N-1)$.

The $k$th prefix of a message code will be defined as the first $k$ digits of that message code. Basic restriction (b) could then be restated as: No message shall be coded in such a way that its code is a prefix of any other message, or that any of its prefixes are used elsewhere as a message code.

Imagine an optimum code in which no two of the messages coded with length $L(N)$ have identical prefixes of order $L(N)-1$. Since an optimum code has been assumed, then none of these messages of length $L(N)$ can have codes or prefixes of any order which correspond to other codes. It would then be possible to drop the last digit of all of this group of messages and thereby reduce the value of $L_{av}$. Therefore, in an optimum code, it is necessary that at least two (and no more than $D$) of the codes with length $L(N)$ have identical prefixes of order $L(N)-1$.

One additional requirement can be made for an optimum code. Assume that there exists a combination of the $D$ different types of coding digits which is less than $L(N)$ digits in length and which is not used as a message code or which is not a prefix of a message code. Then this combination of digits could be used to replace the code for the $N$th message with a consequent reduction of $L_{av}$. Therefore, all possible sequences of $L(N)-1$ digits must be used either as message codes, or must have one of their prefixes used as message codes.

The derived restrictions for an optimum code are summarized in condensed form below and considered in addition to restrictions (a) and (b) given in the first part of this paper:

$$\text{(c)} \quad L(1) \leqq L(2) \leqq \cdots \leqq L(N-1) = L(N). \qquad (5)$$

(d) At least two and not more than $D$ of the messages with code length $L(N)$ have codes which are alike except for their final digits.

(e) Each possible sequence of $L(N)-1$ digits must be used either as a message code or must have one of its prefixes used as a message code.

## Optimum Binary Code

For ease of development of the optimum coding procedure, let us now restrict ourselves to the problem of binary coding. Later this procedure will be extended to the general case of $D$ digits.

Restriction (c) makes it necessary that the two least probable messages have codes of equal length. Restriction (d) places the requirement that, for $D$ equal to two, there be only two of the messages with coded length $L(N)$ which are identical except for their last digits. The final digits of these two codes will be one of the two binary digits, 0 and 1. It will be necessary to assign these two message codes to the $N$th and the $(N-1)$st messages since at this point it is not known whether or not other codes of length $L(N)$ exist. Once this has been done, these two messages are equivalent to a single composite message. Its code (as yet undetermined) will be the common prefixes of order $L(N)-1$ of these two messages. Its probability will be the sum of the probabilities of the two messages from which it was created. The ensemble containing this composite message in the place of its two component messages will be called the first auxiliary message ensemble.

This newly created ensemble contains one less message than the original. Its members should be rearranged if necessary so that the messages are again ordered according to their probabilities. It may be considered exactly as the original ensemble was. The codes for each of the two least probable messages in this new ensemble are required to be identical except in their final digits; 0 and 1 are assigned as these digits, one for each of the two messages. Each new auxiliary ensemble contains one less message than the preceding ensemble. Each auxiliary ensemble represents the original ensemble with full use made of the accumulated necessary coding requirements.

The procedure is applied again and again until the number of members in the most recently formed auxiliary message ensemble is reduced to two. One of each of the binary digits is assigned to each of these two composite messages. These messages are then combined to form a single composite message with probability unity, and the coding is complete.

TABLE I

OPTIMUM BINARY CODING PROCEDURE

| Message Probabilities | | | | | | | | | | | | |
|---|---|---|---|---|---|---|---|---|---|---|---|---|
| *Original Message Ensemble* | *Auxiliary Message Ensembles* 1 | 2 | 3 | 4 | 5 | 6 | 7 | 8 | 9 | 10 | 11 | 12 |
| | | | | | | | | | | | | →1.00 |
| | | | | | | | | | | | →0.60 | |
| | | | | | | | | | | →0.40 | 0.40 | |
| | | | | | | | | | →0.36 | 0.36 | | |
| | | | | | | | | →0.24 | 0.24 | 0.24 | | |
| 0.20 | 0.20 | 0.20 | 0.20 | 0.20 | 0.20 | 0.20 | 0.20 | 0.20 | 0.20 | | | |
| | | | | | | | →0.20 | 0.20 | 0.20 | | | |
| 0.18 | 0.18 | 0.18 | 0.18 | 0.18 | 0.18 | 0.18 | 0.18 | 0.18 | | | | |
| | | | | | | →0.18 | 0.18 | 0.18 | | | | |
| | | | | | →0.14 | 0.14 | 0.14 | | | | | |
| 0.10 | 0.10 | 0.10 | 0.10 | 0.10 | 0.10 | 0.10 | 0.10 | | | | | |
| 0.10 | 0.10 | 0.10 | 0.10 | 0.10 | 0.10 | 0.10 | | | | | | |
| 0.10 | 0.10 | 0.10 | 0.10 | 0.10 | 0.10 | 0.10 | | | | | | |
| | | | | →0.10 | 0.10 | | | | | | | |
| | | →0.08 | 0.08 | 0.08 | 0.08 | | | | | | | |
| | | | →0.08 | 0.08 | | | | | | | | |
| 0.06 | 0.06 | 0.06 | 0.06 | 0.06 | | | | | | | | |
| 0.06 | 0.06 | 0.06 | 0.06 | | | | | | | | | |
| 0.04 | 0.04 | 0.04 | 0.04 | | | | | | | | | |
| *0.04 | 0.04 | 0.04 | | | | | | | | | | |
| 0.04 | 0.04 | 0.04 | | | | | | | | | | |
| 0.04 | 0.04 | | | | | | | | | | | |
| | →0.04 | | | | | | | | | | | |
| 0.03 | | | | | | | | | | | | |
| 0.01 | | | | | | | | | | | | |

Now let us examine Table I. The left-hand column contains the ordered message probabilities of the ensemble to be coded. $N$ is equal to 13. Since each combination of two messages (indicated by a bracket) is accompanied by the assigning of a new digit to each, then the total number of digits which should be assigned to each original message is the same as the number of combinations indicated for that message. For example, the message marked *, or a composite of which it is a part, is combined with others five times, and therefore should be assigned a code length of five digits.

When there is no alternative in choosing the two least probable messages, then it is clear that the requirements, established as necessary, are also sufficient for deriving an optimum code. There may arise situations in which a choice may be made between two or more groupings of least likely messages. Such a case arises, for example, in the fourth auxiliary ensemble of Table I. Either of the messages of probability 0.08 could have been combined with that of probability 0.06. However, it is possible to rearrange codes in any manner among equally likely messages without affecting the average code length, and so a choice of either of the alternatives could have been made. Therefore, the procedure given is always sufficient to establish an optimum binary code.

The lengths of all the encoded messages derived from Table I are given in Table II.

Having now determined proper lengths of code for each message, the problem of specifying the actual digits remains. Many alternatives exist. Since the combining of messages into their composites is similar to the successive confluences of trickles, rivulets, brooks, and creeks into a final large river, the procedure thus far described might be considered analogous to the placing of signs by a water-borne insect at each of these junctions as he journeys downstream. It should be remembered that the code which we desire is that one which the insect must remember in order to work his way back upstream. Since the placing of the signs need not follow the same rule, such as "zero-right-returning," at each junction, it can be seen that there are at least $2^{12}$ different ways of assigning code digits for our example.

TABLE II

RESULTS OF OPTIMUM BINARY CODING PROCEDURE

| $i$ | $P(i)$ | $L(i)$ | $P(i)L(i)$ | *Code* |
|---|---|---|---|---|
| 1 | 0.20 | 2 | 0.40 | 10 |
| 2 | 0.18 | 3 | 0.54 | 000 |
| 3 | 0.10 | 3 | 0.30 | 011 |
| 4 | 0.10 | 3 | 0.30 | 110 |
| 5 | 0.10 | 3 | 0.30 | 111 |
| 6 | 0.06 | 4 | 0.24 | 0101 |
| 7 | 0.06 | 5 | 0.30 | 00100 |
| 8 | 0.04 | 5 | 0.20 | 00101 |
| 9 | 0.04 | 5 | 0.20 | 01000 |
| 10 | 0.04 | 5 | 0.20 | 01001 |
| 11 | 0.04 | 5 | 0.20 | 00110 |
| 12 | 0.03 | 6 | 0.18 | 001110 |
| 13 | 0.01 | 6 | 0.06 | 001111 |
| | | | $L_{av}=3.42$ | |

The code in Table II was obtained by using the digit 0 for the upper message and the digit 1 for the lower message of any bracket. It is important to note in Table I that coding restriction (e) is automatically met as long as two messages (and not one) are placed in each bracket.

### GENERALIZATION OF THE METHOD

Optimum coding of an ensemble of messages using three or more types of digits is similar to the binary coding procedure. A table of auxiliary message ensembles similar to Table I will be used. Brackets indicating messages combined to form composite messages will be used in the same way as was done in Table I. However, in order to satisfy restriction (e), it will be required that all these brackets, with the possible exception of one combining the least probable messages of the original ensemble, always combine a number of messages equal to $D$.

It will be noted that the terminating auxiliary ensemble always has one unity probability message. Each preceding ensemble is increased in number by $D-1$ until the first auxiliary ensemble is reached. Therefore, if $N_1$ is the number of messages in the first auxiliary ensemble, then $(N_1-1)/(D-1)$ must be an integer. However $N_1=N-n_0+1$, where $n_0$ is the number of the least probable messages combined in a bracket in the original ensemble. Therefore, $n_0$ (which, of course, is at least two and no more than $D$) must be of such a value that $(N-n_0)/(D-1)$ is an integer.

In Table III an example is considered using an ensemble of eight messages which is to be coded with four digits; $n_0$ is found to be 2. The code listed in the table is obtained by assigning the four digits 0, 1, 2, and 3, in order, to each of the brackets.

TABLE III
OPTIMUM CODING PROCEDURE FOR $D=4$

| Message Probabilities | | | | | |
|---|---|---|---|---|---|
| *Original Message Ensemble* | *Auxiliary Ensembles* | | | $L(i)$ | *Code* |
| | | | →1.00 | | |
| | | →0.40 | | | |
| 0.22 | 0.22 | 0.22 | | 1 | 1 |
| 0.20 | 0.20 | 0.20 | | 1 | 2 |
| 0.18 | 0.18 | 0.18 | | 1 | 3 |
| 0.15 | 0.15 | | | 2 | 00 |
| 0.10 | 0.10 | | | 2 | 01 |
| 0.08 | 0.08 | | | 2 | 02 |
| | →0.07 | | | | |
| 0.05 | | | | 3 | 030 |
| 0.02 | | | | 3 | 031 |

### ACKNOWLEDGMENTS

The author is indebted to Dr. W. K. Linvill and Dr. R. M. Fano, both of the Massachusetts Institute of Technology, for their helpful criticism of this paper.

# 4



Reprinted from *IRE Trans. Inform. Theory,* **IT-1**(1), 16–23, 30–33 (1955)

# Predictive Coding—Part I

PETER ELIAS†

*Summary*—**Predictive coding is a procedure for transmitting messages which are sequences of magnitudes. In this coding method, the transmitter and the receiver store past message terms, and from them estimate the value of the next message term. The transmitter transmits, not the message term, but the difference between it and its predicted value. At the receiver this error term is added to the receiver prediction to reproduce the message term. This procedure is defined and messages, prediction, entropy, and ideal coding are discussed to provide a basis for Part II, which will give the mathematical criterion for the best predictor for use in the predictive coding of particular messages, will give examples of such messages, and will show that the error term which is transmitted in predictive coding may always be coded efficiently.**

## Introduction

TWO MAJOR contributions have been made within the past few years to the mathematical theory of communication. One of these is Wiener's work on the prediction and filtering of random, stationary time series, and the other is Shannon's work, defining the information content of a message which is such a time series, and relating this quantity to the bandwidth and time required for the transmission of the message.[1] This paper makes use of the point of view suggested by Wiener's work on prediction to attack a problem in Shannon's field: prediction is used to make possible the efficient coding of a class of messages of considerable physical interest.

Consider a message which is a time series, a function $m_i$ which is defined for all integer $i$, positive or negative. Such a series might be derived from the sampling used in a pulse-code modulation system.[2] From a knowledge of the statistics of the set of messages to be transmitted, we may find a predictor which operates on all the past values of the function, $m_j$ with $j$ less than $i$, and produces a prediction $p_i$ of the value which $m$ will next assume. Now consider the error $e_i$, which is defined as the difference between the message and its predicted value:

$$e_i = m_i - p_i . \tag{1}$$

All of the information generated by the source in selecting the term $m_i$ is given just as well by $e_i$; the error term may be transmitted, and will enable the receiver to reconstruct the original message, for the portion of the message that is not transmitted, $p_i$, may be considered as information about the *past* of the message and not about its present; indeed, since $p_i$ is a quite determinate mathematical function, it contains no information at all by Shannon's definition of this quantity.[3]

The communications procedure which will be discussed is illustrated in Fig. 1. There is a message-generating source that feeds into a memory at the transmitter. The transmitter has a predictor, which operates on the past of the message as stored in the memory to produce an estimate of its future. The subtractor subtracts the prediction from the message term and produces an error term $e_i$, which is applied as an input to the coder. The coder codes the error term, and this coded term is sent to the receiver. In the receiver the transmitting process is reversed. The receiver also has a memory and an identical predictor, and has predicted the same value $p_i$ for the message as did the predictor at the transmitter. When the coded correction term is received, it is decoded to reproduce the error term $e_i$. This is added to the predicted value $p_i$ and the message term $m_i$ is reproduced. The message term is then presented to the observer at the receiver, and is also stored in the receiver memory to permit the prediction of the following values of the message.

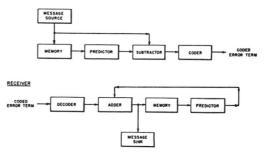

Fig. 1—Predicting coding and decoding procedure.

This procedure is essentially a coding scheme, and will be called *predictive coding.* The memory, predictor, subtractor, and coder at the transmitter, and the memory, predictor, adder, and decoder at the receiver may be considered as complex coding and decoding devices. Predictive coding may then be compared with the ideal coding methods given by Shannon and Fano.[4] In general,

† Elec. Engrg. Dept. and Res. Lab. Elec., Mass. Inst. Tech., Cambridge, Mass.

[1] For historical remarks on the origin of modern information theory see C. E. Shannon and W. Weaver, "The Mathematical Theory of Communication," Univ. of Illinois Press, Urbana, Ill., p. 52 (footnote) and p. 95 (footnote); 1949.

[2] B. M. Oliver, J. R. Pierce, and C. E. Shannon, "The philosophy of PCM," Proc. I.R.E., vol. 36, pp. 1324–1331; November, 1948; also, W. R. Bennett, "Spectra of quantized signals," *Bell Sys. Tech. Jour.*, vol. 27, pp. 446–472; July, 1948.

[3] Shannon and Weaver, *op. cit.*, p. 31.

[4] Shannon and Weaver, *op. cit.*, p. 30; also R. M. Fano, Tech. Rep. No. 65, Res. Lab. Elect., M.I.T., Cambridge, Mass.; 1949.

predictive coding cannot take less channel space for the transmission of a message at a given rate than does an ideal coding scheme, and it will often take more. However, there is a large class of message-generating processes which are at present coded in a highly inefficient way, and for which the use of large codebook memories, such as are required for the ideal coding methods, is impractical. Time series which are obtained by sampling a smoothly varying function of time are examples in this class. For many such processes predictive coding can give an efficient code, using a reasonable amount of apparatus at the transmitter and the receiver.

It should be noted that in the transmission scheme of Fig. 1 errors accumulate. That is, any noise which is introduced after the transmitter memory, or at the receiver, or in transmission, will be perpetuated as an error in all future values of the message, as will any discrepancy between the operation of the two memories, or the two predictors. This means that eventually errors will accumulate to such an extent that the message will disappear in the noise. If, therefore, continuous messages, i.e., time series each member of which is selected from a continuum of magnitudes, are to be transmitted, it will be necessary periodically to clear the memories of both the receiver and the transmitter and start afresh. This is undesirable, since after each such clearing there will be no remembered values on which to base a prediction, and more information transmission will be required for a period following each such clearing, until enough remembered values have accumulated to permit good prediction once more.

A more satisfactory alternative is the use of some pulse-code transmission system in which only quantized magnitudes of input are accepted. Such a system may be made virtually error-free.[5] A system of this kind has the further advantage that the only very reliable memory units now available or in immediate prospect are of a quantized nature, most of them being capable only of storing binary digits. The use of a quantized system requires that the predicted values be selected from the permissible quantized set of message values. Strictly interpreted, this severely limits the permissible predictors; if by a choice of scale the permissible quantized levels are made equal to the integers, then the restriction on $p(m_{i-1} \cdots m_{i-n})$ is that it take integer values for all sets of integer arguments. Actually the ordinary extrapolation formulas have this property, and may be used as predictors. But it is not necessary to limit the choice of predictors so severely. The problem may be evaded by using any function as a predictor and computing its value to a predetermined number of places by digital computing techniques, the prediction then being taken to be the function rounded off to the nearest integer. If the predictor as originally computed was optimum in some well-defined sense, then the rounded predictor will presumably be less good in that sense, but in cases where predictive coding may be expected to be useful the difference will usually be small.

[5] Oliver, Pierce, and Shannon, *loc. cit.*

It is necessary to define precisely what is meant by an optimum predictor for use in predictive coding—i.e., to define some quantity, which depends upon the choice of the predictor, and define as optimum a predictor which minimizes this quantity. Wiener's work uses as a criterion the minimization of the mean square error term $\overline{e^2}$. Wiener has pointed out that other criteria are possible, but that the mathematical work is made simpler by the mean square choice.[6] Minimizing the mean square error corresponds to minimizing the power of the error term, and if no further coding is to be done, this is a reasonable criterion for predictive coding purposes. However, in the system illustrated in Fig. 1, the error term is coded before it is transmitted, and its power may be radically altered in the coding process. What we are really interested in minimizing is the channel space which the system will require for the transmission of the error term. This leads to the following criterion which will be justified in Part II of this paper: *That predictor is best which leads to an average error-term distribution having minimum entropy.*

The coder of Fig. 1 also requires some consideration. Predictive coding eliminates the codebook requirement by using prediction. To take advantage of the resultant savings in equipment, it is necessary to show that the coder itself will not require a large codebook. This reduces to the problem of showing that a message whose terms are assumed independent of one another may always be coded efficiently by a process with a small memory requirement. It will be shown that this is true. It is necessary to use two kinds of coding processes: one for cases in which the entropy of the distribution from which the successive terms are chosen is large compared to unity, and another for cases in which the entropy is small compared to unity.

The following sections of the present paper are devoted to a discussion of messages, prediction, entropy, and ideal coding. Part II will discuss the predictor criterion given above, the classes of messages for which a predictor that is optimum by this criterion may be found, and other classes of messages for which predictive coding may be of use. Mathematically defined examples of message-generating processes which belong to these classes will be given, and the problem of coding the error term so as to take advantage of the minimal entropy of its average distribution will be examined.

## Characterization of Messages

A necessary preliminary to a discussion of messages is a precise definition of what "message" is taken to mean.[7] Since a communication system is designed to transmit many messages, what is actually of interest is the

[6] N. Wiener, "The Extrapolation, Interpolation and Smoothing of Stationary Time Series with Engineering Applications," published in 1942 as an NDRC report, and in 1949 as a book, by the Mass. Inst. Tech. Press, Cambridge, Mass., and John Wiley & Sons, Inc., New York, N. Y., especially p. 13.

[7] Such definitions are given by Wiener, *ibid.*, and Wiener, "Cybernetics," Mass. Inst. Tech. Press, and John Wiley & Sons, Inc., 1948; also by Shannon and Weaver, *loc. cit.* Our discussion starts with a definition like Wiener's and ends with one like Shannon's.

characterization of the ensemble from which the transmitted messages are chosen, or the stochastic process by which they are generated. As a preliminary definition, we may say that a message is a single-valued real function of time, chosen from an ensemble of such functions. It will be denoted by $m(a, t)$, where $a$ is a real number between zero and one which labels the particular message chosen from the ensemble, and $m(a, t)$ is defined, for each such $a$, for all values of $t$ from $-\infty$ to $\infty$. This definition must be restricted in several respects, in part to take into account the physical requirements of transmitting systems and in part for mathematical convenience.

First, it is assumed that the ensemble from which the messages are chosen is ergodic. This means that any one message of the ensemble, except for a set whose measure in $a$ is zero, is typical of the ensemble in the following sense: let $Q(a)$ be the probability distribution of the parameter of distribution $a$. Then with probability one, for any function $f[m(a, t)]$ and almost any $a_1$,

$$\lim_{T\to\infty} \frac{1}{2T} \int_{-T}^{T} f[m(a_1, t)]\, dt = \int_0^1 f[m(a, t)]\, dQ(a). \tag{2}$$

I.e., any function of $m$ has the same average value when averaged over time as a function of a single message, as when averaged over the ensemble of all possible messages. We can thus find out all possible statistical information about the ensemble by observing a single message over its entire history. The ergodic requirement implies that the ensemble is stationary: i.e., that the statistics do not change with time. Its practical importance is that it permits us to speak indifferently of the message or the ensemble, and makes it unnecessary to specify the sense in which we speak of an average. In particular, it permits the substitution of measurable time averages for experimentally awkward ensemble averages.

Second, it is assumed that the average square of the message [in either sense of (2)] is finite. The message will be represented in physical systems by a voltage or a current, or the displacement of a membrane, or the pressure in a gas, or by several such physical variables, as it proceeds from its origin to its destination. All of these representations require power; in particular, representation as a voltage or a current between two points separated by a fixed impedance, which is a necessary intermediate representation in any presently used electrical communication method, requires a power proportional to the square of the message. Since only a finite amount of power may be supplied to a physical transmitter, it is obviously required that the average message power be bounded.

Third, it is assumed that the spectrum of the message vanishes for frequencies greater than some fixed frequency $f_0$. This will not in general be true for the radio-frequency spectrum of the messages as they are generated by a source, and it has been shown that a function with an infinitely extended spectrum cannot be reduced to a function with a spectrum of finite range by any physically realizable filter; the transfer characteristic of a filter can be zero only for a set of frequencies of total measure zero.[8] However, this is no practical problem. For since the message has a finite total power distributed over the spectrum, there will always be an $f_0$ so high that a negligible fraction of the total power will be located beyond it in the power spectrum.

The reason for this assumption is that, as Shannon has pointed out, any function of time that is band-limited may be replaced by a time series, which gives the values of the function at times separated by an interval $1/2f_0$.[9] For any band-limited function we have the following identity:

$$m(t) = \sum_{i=-\infty}^{\infty} m(i/2f_0)\left\{\frac{\sin \pi(2f_0t - i)}{\pi(2f_0t - i)}\right\}. \tag{3}$$

The values of the function at the sampling points $t = i/2f_0$, which are the coefficients of this series, thus completely determine the function. If the function is not initially band-limited, the expansion will give a function which passes through the same values at the sampling points, but which is band-limited. As we assume band-limited messages, for our purpose the series and the function are equivalent, and since the series is easier to deal with in the sequel, it is desirable to change the definition of the message. Henceforth the message will be defined as the series of coefficients in the expansion (3). By choice of the unit of time, the sampling interval is made unity, and the message is then $m_i(a)$, defined for all (positive and negative) integer values of the index $i$.

A message is thus a time series drawn from an ergodic ensemble of such series, and each term in any one message is drawn from a probability distribution whose form is determined by the preceding terms of that message. For the reasons indicated in the first section, we will be interested primarily in quantized messages, for which this probability distribution will be discrete. However, it will at times be more convenient in the analysis and the examples to deal with continuous distributions, it being understood that quantization will ultimately be used. In the discrete case, the message term $m_i$ will be selected from a discrete probability distribution $M_k$, where $M_k(m_{i-1} \cdots m_{i-j} \cdots)$ is the conditional distribution giving the probability that, for a particular set of past values $m_{i-1} \cdots m_{i-j} \cdots$, the message term $m_i$ will take the integer value $k$. In the continuous case, the message term $m_i$ will be chosen from a continuous conditional distribution $M(m_i : m_{i-1} \cdots m_{i-j} \cdots)$. Both of these distributions are dependent on the set of values of the preceding message terms $m_{i-1} \cdots m_{i-j} \cdots$, but are of course independent of the value of the index $i$, by the stationary nature of the ensemble.

[8] Wiener, "The Extrapolation, Interpolation and Smoothing of Stationary Time Series with Engineering Applications," NDRC Report, Mass. Inst. Tech. Press, Cambridge, Mass., p. 37; 1942.

[9] C. E. Shannon, "Communication in the presence of noise," Proc. I.R.E., vol. 37, pp. 10–21; January, 1949.

Stochastic processes of this sort are known as Markoff processes and have an extensive mathematical literature.[10] An $n$th order Markoff process is one in which the distribution from which each term is chosen depends on the set of values of the $n$ preceding terms only; a process in which each term is chosen from a single unconditional probability distribution may be called a Markoff process of order zero. It should be noted that, while any Markoff process yielding a message with a finite second moment is included in this definition, we will expect most of the messages to be Markoff processes of a rather special kind. The messages have been derived by the time-sampling of a continuously varying physical quantity. The sampling rate must be high enough so that the sampling does not suppress significant variations in the message—i.e., the $f_0$ must be above the bulk of the spectral power of the message. Now for most such messages, the average rate of variation with time is much lower than the highest rate that the system must be capable of transmitting. Consequently, it is to be expected that on the average, successive message values will be near to one another. This means, in particular, that in the discrete case the index $k$ is not just an arbitrary labeling of a particular symbol—as it is, for example, in Shannon's finite-order Markoff approximations to English[11]—but may be expected to give a genuine metric: message values with indexes near to one another may be expected to have probabilities near to one another, and the conditional distributions mentioned above may be expected to be unimodal. This is not a restriction on what kinds of series will be considered to be messages, but is rather a specification of the class of messages for which predictive coding may be expected to be of use, as will be discussed in detail in Part II of this paper.

For a message ensemble for which the conditional distributions are not given *a priori*, it is necessary to determine them by the observation of a number of messages, or of a single message for a long time. It is obviously impossible to do this on the assumption that the distribution from which a particular message term is chosen depends on the infinite set of past message values. What can, in fact, be measured are the zeroth order approximation, in which each term is treated as if it were drawn from the same distribution, giving $M(m_i)$, an unconditional distribution; the first order conditional distribution $M(m_i : m_{i-1})$, and so on to the $n$th order conditional distribution for some finite $n$. A communications system which is designed to transmit this approximation will be inefficient: the approximating process itself would generate messages with a greater information content than the messages which are actually being transmitted, and a system designed for the approximation will waste time or power or bandwidth when transmitting the real message. This will be discussed more fully later.

[10] Shannon and Weaver, *op. cit.*, p. 15; also, M. Frechet, cited there, and P. Levy, "Processus Stochastique et Mouvement Brownien," Gauthier-Villars, 1948, which give further references.

[11] Shannon and Weaver, *op. cit.*, pp. 9–15.

## Prediction

Norbert Wiener has developed a very general method for finding the linear predictor for a given ensemble of messages which minimizes the root mean square error of prediction. His method was developed for the difficult case of nonband-limited messages, i.e., continuous functions of time which cannot be reduced to time series. However, he has also solved the much simpler problem of the prediction of time series, such as the messages which were defined above. The details of this work are thoroughly covered in the literature,[12] and this section will merely define some terms, note some results, and discuss the prediction problem from a point of view which is weighted towards probability considerations and not towards Fourier transform considerations.

From a time series, a linear prediction $p_i$ of the value of a message term $m_i$ is a linear combination of the previous message values

$$p_i = \sum_{j=1}^{\infty} a_j m_{i-j} .$$

The error $e$, is defined as

$$e_i = p_i - m_i .$$

The predictor itself may be considered to be the set of coefficients $a_j$. The best linear predictor, in the rms sense, is the set of coefficients which, on the average, minimizes $e^2$. Wiener has shown that this predictor is determined, not by the message ensemble directly, but by the autocorrelation function of the ensemble. In general, there will be many ensembles with the same autocorrelation function, and the same linear predictor will be the best in the rms sense for all of them.

The autocorrelation function for a time series is defined by

$$c_k = \lim_{N\to\infty} \frac{1}{2N+1} \sum_{i=-N}^{N} m_i m_{i-k} .$$

Devices for rapidly obtaining approximate autocorrelation functions have been constructed.[13] These devices accept the message directly as an input, and graph or tabulate the function. By the use of such devices, or by a statistical examination of the message, or in some cases by an *a priori* knowledge of the message-generating process, it is possible to determine the autocorrelation function. The best linear predictor in the rms sense may then be determined. But it should be noted that there may be nonlinear predictors which are very much better.

Indeed, given a complete knowledge of the stochastic definition of the message, i.e., a complete knowledge of

[12] Wiener, *op. cit.* Also H. W. Bode and C. E. Shannon, "A simplified derivation of linear least square smoothing and prediction theory," Proc. IRE, vol. 38, pp. 417–425; April, 1950.

[13] T. P. Cheatham, Jr., Tech. Rep. No. 122, Res. Lab. Elect., M. I. T. (to be published). See also, Y. W. Lee, T. P. Cheatham, Jr., and J. B. Wiesner, "The Application of Correlation Functions in the Detection of Small Signals in Noise," Tech. Rep. No. 141, Res. Lab. Elect., M. I. T.; 1949.

the conditional probability distributions $M(m_i : m_{i-1} \cdots m_{i-j} \cdots)$ or $M_k(m_{i-1} \cdots m_{i-j} \cdots)$ the *best* rms predictor, with no restriction as to linearity, is directly available. Obviously the best rms predictor for a message term $m_i$ defined in this way is the mean of the distribution from which it is chosen, which is determined by the past message history: i.e., the best rms predictor, $p^*$, is

$$p^* = \bar{m}_i = \sum_{k=-\infty}^{\infty} kM_k(m_{i-1} \cdots m_{i-j} \cdots)$$

or

$$= \int_{-\infty}^{\infty} m_i M(m_i : m_{i-1} \cdots m_{i-j} \cdots)\, dm_i$$

in the discrete and continuous cases respectively. For the mean of a distribution is that point about which its second moment is a minimum. Of course, the mean need not be a linear function of the past message values. However, it is some determinate function of these values unless the message values are completely uncorrelated—i.e., unless the Markoff process is of order zero. In this case, it is just the constant which is the mean of the zero-order distribution. We therefore have as the unconditionally best rms predictor the function $p^*(m_{i-1} \cdots m_{i-j} \cdots)$.

From this same general statistical viewpoint the best predictor on a mean-absolute error basis is the prediction of the median of the conditional distribution, since the median is that point about which the first absolute moment is a minimum. Like the mean, the median is defined by the conditional distribution $M$ as a function of the past history of the message. This definition may not be unique: if there is a region of zero probability density between the two halves of a probability distribution, any point in the region is a median. However, the definition may be made unique by selecting a point within this range, for those sets of past message values for which the ambiguity arises. We will denote the best predictor in the mean-absolute sense by $p^{**}$, it being understood that the definition has been made unique in some suitable way if the ensemble is such as to require this.

Finally, it may be desired to predict in such a way that in the discrete case, the probability of no error is a maximum, and in the continuous case the probability density has the maximum possible value at zero error. This requires modal prediction. The mode of the conditional distribution will not be unique if there are several equal probabilities which are each larger than any other probability in the discrete case, or if the continuous distribution attains its maximum value at more than one point. The difficulty may again be removed by a suitable choice, and $p^{***}$ will signify the best modal predictor.

In any of these cases, and indeed for any other prediction criterion which yields a determinate value of the prediction as a function of the past history of the message, the error term $e_i$ is drawn from a distribution $E(e_i : m_{i-1} \cdots m_{i-j} \cdots)$ or $E_k(m_{i-1} \cdots m_{i-j} \cdots)$ which is of exactly the same form as the original distribution of the message term, but which has been shifted along the axis by the amount of the prediction. If it is desired to limit predictions to the possible quantized values of a discrete probability distribution, it is only necessary to make $p^{**}$ and $p^{***}$ unique in a way which does this in the cases of ambiguity; where the median and mode are uniquely defined, they will always coincide with one of the possible values of the message. For rms prediction it is necessary to take the quantized value that is nearest to the computed mean of the distribution as the value of $p^*$.

As an example of a predictable function, consider

$$M(m_i : m_{i-1}) = \frac{1}{\sigma\sqrt{2\pi}} \exp\left[-(m_i - am_{i-1})^2/2\sigma^2\right]. \quad (4)$$

The unconditional distribution of $m_i$ may be found by using the reproductive property of the normal distribution. $\overline{M}(m_i)$ will be normal, with a standard deviation $\sigma'$, and $am_{i-1}$ will have a normal distribution with standard deviation $a\sigma'$ : then,

$$\sigma^2 + a^2\sigma'^2 = \sigma'^2; \qquad \sigma' = \frac{\sigma}{\sqrt{1 - a^2}} \quad (5)$$

and

$$\overline{M}(m_i) = \frac{1}{\sigma'\sqrt{2\pi}} \exp\left[-m_i^2/2\sigma'^2\right]. \quad (6)$$

The zero-order approximation to this first-order Markoff process has, then, a message term distribution of the same form as the original conditional distribution, but a standard deviation which is larger by a factor $1/\sqrt{1 - a^2}$. By our definition in a previous section the process will generate messages only if $a < 1$: otherwise the standard deviation will be infinite, and the message will require infinite power for transmission. A more general example in complete analogy to (4) is:

$$M(m_i : m_{i-1} \cdots m_{i-j} \cdots)$$
$$= \frac{1}{\sigma\sqrt{2\pi}} \exp\left[-\left(m_i - \sum_{j=1}^{\infty} m_{i-j}a_j\right)^2 \Big/ 2^2\right]. \quad (7)$$

Wiener's prediction procedure is designed for functions of the form (7), in which each term of the time series is drawn from a normal distribution with constant $\sigma$, with a mean which is a linear combination of past values, the permissible combinations being limited by the requirement that the resultant average distribution have a finite second moment. The linear combination of past values which is the mean of the conditional distribution is also the best linear rms predictor, and is indeed *the* best rms predictor $p^*$, as noted above. Wiener's method is then a procedure for finding this linear combination in terms of the autocorrelation function of the message.

The combination of past terms in the exponent may be rewritten as a sum of differences, less a constant times the message value $m_i$. The stochastic function determined by the conditional distribution will then be as approximation to the solution of the difference equation obtained by setting the exponent in (7) equal to zero. In the limit $\sigma \to 0$, the stochastic function will become precisely the function which is a solution to this equation, as determined by the set of past message values (initial conditions): as $\sigma$ grows, the function will wander about in the neighborhood of this solution, diverging from it more and more as $i$ increases. In (4) above, the equation obtained is just $m_i - am_{i-1} = 0$, and the solution, $m_i = am_{i-1}$, gives a geometric approach to the origin.

In the case of continuous functions of time, taking appropriate limits gives a normal distribution about a linear function of the past which may include integral or differential operators on the past. The bulk of Wiener's analysis is devoted to this case. Although the method was designed with functions like (7) in mind, it is clearly not limited to them. In the case of time series it is possible to use a distribution which is not normal, with a standard deviation (or other parameter or parameters) which is not constant, but is also determined by the past values of the message. So long as the *mean* of the distribution is still a linear combination of past values, the predictor derived from the autocorrelation function will still give the best rms predictor. If the mean is a nonlinear function of the past values, the predictor obtained from the autocorrelation function will be the best linear approximation to this nonlinear function in the rms sense.

Where the best predictor is indeed linear, or is well approximated by a linear combination of past values, the great practical superiority of Wiener's method over the use of the conditional distribution should be clear. For in this method only the autocorrelation function, a function of a single variable, needs to be measured; the predictor can then be computed no matter what the order of the Markoff process may be. Using the conditional probability distribution directly, an $n$th order Markoff process will require the observational determination of a function of $n + 1$ variables. This becomes a task of fantastic proportions when $n$ is as large as four or five: it is practical for small $n$ only for a quantized system with very few possible quantized levels.

The direct use of the conditional distribution may, however, be quite valuable if the best rms predictor is a highly nonlinear function of only a few past values, particularly in a quantized system. Nonlinearity is no more difficult to treat than is the linear case as far as analysis by this method is concerned. For the synthesis problem the lack of suitable nonlinear elements for the physical construction of nonlinear operators on the past is confined to the case of continuous functions of time; in the case of time series with quantized terms, digital computer techniques can provide any desired nonlinear function of any number of variables—at, of course, an expense in equipment which may become very large for large $n$.

When the conditional distribution always has a point of symmetry, we may note that the best rms predictor $p^*$ is equal to the best mean absolute predictor $p^{**}$. If the distribution is also always unimodal, then the best modal predictor $p^{***}$ will also be the same as $p^*$. In particular, this will be the case for the examples (4) and (7), but it does not, of course, depend on the linearity of the predictor.

## Entropy, Averaging, and Ideal Coding

The entropy $H$ of a probability distribution $M$ has been defined as[14]

$$H = -\sum_{k=-\infty}^{\infty} M_k \log M_k$$

and

$$H = -\int_{-\infty}^{\infty} M(m_i) \log M(m_i)\, dm_i \tag{8}$$

in the discrete and continuous cases, respectively. The entropy of a probability distribution may be used as a measure of the information content of a symbol or message value $m_i$ chosen from this distribution. The choice of the logarithmic base corresponds to the choice of a unit of entropy: when logarithms are taken to the base two, as is convenient in many discrete cases, the unit of entropy is the "bit," a contraction for binary digit, since in a two-symbol system with the two symbols equiprobable, the entropy per symbol is one bit for this choice of base. In the continuous case computations are often made simpler by the use of natural logarithms. The resultant unit of entropy is called by Shannon the natural unit. We have one natural unit $= \log_2 e$ bits.

Wiener, Shannon, and Fano[14] give a number of reasons for the use of this function as a measure of information per symbol, and the arguments are plausible and satisfying, but as Shannon remarks, the ultimate justification of the definition is in the implications and applications of entropy as a measure of information.[15] For the analysis of communications systems, the definition is completely justified by theorems which prove that it is possible to code any message with entropy $H$ bits per symbol in a binary code which uses an average of $H + \epsilon$ binary digits per message symbol, where $\epsilon$ is a positive quantity which may be made as small as desired, and by equivalent theorems in the case of the discrete channel with noise —i.e., where there is a finite probability that a symbol

[14] This is the definition given by Shannon (Shannon and Weaver, *op. cit.*) and Fano (R. M. Fano, "The Transmission of Information", Tech. Rep. No. 65, Res. Lab. Elec., M. I. T.; 1949) Wienes ("Cybernetics", *op. cit.*, p. 76) gives a definition with the opposite sign. There is no real conflict here, however, for Wiener is talking about a different measure. Wiener asks, how much information we are given about a message term, whose exact value will never be known, when we are given the probability distribution from which it is chosen. The answer is that we know a good deal when the distribution is narrow, and very little when the distribution is broad. Correspondingly, entropy as Wiener defines it has a large positive value for very narrow distributions and a large negative value for very broad distributions. This measure is useful in determining how much information has been transmitted when a message term which is contaminated by noise with a known distribution is received; we can use Bayes' theorem and find the probability distribution of the original message, and measure information transmitted by measuring the entropy of this distribution. Shannon, on the other hand, asks how much information is transmitted by the precise transmission of a message symbol, when we know *a priori* the probability distribution from which it was selected. In this case, if the distribution is very narrow, the message term tells us very little when it arrives; we knew what it would be before we received it. If the distribution is broad, however, then the arrival of the term tells us a good deal. This requires the use of the opposite sign for entropy. Shannon's definition will be used through this paper; it is the more appropriate one for the kind of problem with which we are concerned.

[15] Shannon and Weaver, *op. cit.*, p. 19.

transmitted at one quantized level will be received at a different level, and in the case of the continuous channel with noise—in which the message term is chosen from a continuous distribution, and is received mixed with noise, so that each received term is the sum of a signal term and a noise term, and reception is always approximate.

For messages as defined in a previous section, we have, in general, that the entropy of the distribution from which any single message term is chosen is a function of the message history: in both the continuous and discrete cases we are concerned with conditional distributions, whose form depends on the set of values of the terms $m_{i-1} \cdots m_{i-j} \cdots$ which prcede the message term $m_i$ whose entropy is defined in (8). For such cases—i.e., Markoff processes of order one or greater—the entropy is defined in terms of the probability, not of each message term, but of a sequence of $N$ message terms, the limit being taken as $N$ approaches infinity. Following Shannon,[16] we define $G_N$ in the discrete and the continuous cases as

$$G_N = -(1/N) \int_{-\infty}^{\infty} \cdots \int_{-\infty}^{\infty} M(m_i, \cdots m_{i-N}) \cdot \log M(m_i, \cdots m_{i-N})\, dm_i \cdots dm_{i-N}$$

$$= -(1/N) \sum_{m_i=-\infty}^{\infty} \cdots \sum_{m_{i-N}=-\infty}^{\infty} M(m_i, \cdots m_{i-N}) \cdot \log M(m_i, \cdots m_{i-N}). \quad (9)$$

Then the entropy per symbol of the process is defined as

$$H = \lim_{N\to\infty} G_N. \quad (10)$$

The distribution $M(m_i, \cdots m_{i-N})$ in (9) is not a conditional but a joint distribution: the distribution which determines the probability of getting a given set of $N$ values for the $N + 1$ message terms $m_{i-N}$ to $m_i$. Now the joint probability distribution of order $N + 1$ is related to the conditional probability distribution and the joint distribution of order $N$ by

$$M(m_i, \cdots m_{i-N}) = M(m_i : m_{i-1} \cdots m_{i-N})M(m_{i-1}, \cdots m_{i-N}). \quad (11)$$

Using the relation (11) in the expression (9), for a message generating process which is a Markoff process of finite order $k$, and taking the limit (10), we have

$$H = \int_{-\infty}^{\infty} \cdots \int_{-\infty}^{\infty} M(m_{i-1}, \cdots m_{i-k})\, dm_{i-1} \cdots dm_{i-k} \cdot \left\{\int_{-\infty}^{\infty} M(m_i : m_{i-1} \cdots m_{i-k}) \cdot \log M(m_i : m_{i-1} \cdots m_{i-k})\, dm_i\right\} \quad (12)$$

with a similar relation for the discrete case, in which the integrals are replaced by sums. In words, what (12) states is that the entropy for the process as a whole is just the average over-all past histories of the entropy of the conditional distribution of order $k$ which defines the process: the information content per symbol of a message generated by such a stochastic process is the average of the entropies of the distribution from which the successive message terms are chosen.

[16] Shannon and Weaver, *op. cit.*, p. 25.

It was noted that only a finite order Markoff process can, in general, be used as a model of a message source, and that, in general, the use of such an approximation is inefficient. We may now state this more exactly. If a $k$th order Markoff process is approximated by a process of order less than $k$, then the entropy of the approximating process will be greater than or equal to the entropy of the original process, with the equality holding only if the original process is actually of order less than $k$: i.e., only if the $k$th order conditional distribution can be expressed in terms of conditional distributions of lower order. The result holds also for suitably convergent processes of infinite order. It is a direct consequence of the following more general theorem.

*Averaging Theorem I*

Let $P(x: y)$ be a probability density distribution of $x$, for each value of the parameter $y$: i.e., for all $y$,

$$\int_{-\infty}^{\infty} P(x: y)\, dx = 1,$$

and

$$P(x: y) \geq 0$$

for all $x$ and $y$. Let $Q(y)$ be a probability density distribution of $y$:

$$\int_{-\infty}^{\infty} Q(y)\, dy = 1$$

$$Q(y) \geq 0.$$

Let $R(x)$ be the distribution $P(x: y)$ averaged over the parameter $y$, and let $H'$ be its entropy:

$$R(x) = \int_{-\infty}^{\infty} Q(y)P(x: y)\, dy$$

$$H' = -\int_{-\infty}^{\infty} R(x) \log R(x)\, dx. \quad (13)$$

Let $H(y)$ be the entropy of the distribution $P(x: y)$ as a function of the parameter $y$, and let $H$ be its average value:

$$H(y) = -\int_{-\infty}^{\infty} P(x: y) \log P(x: y)\, dx$$

$$H = \int_{-\infty}^{\infty} Q(y)H(y)\, dy.$$

Then we always have $H' \geq H$, and the equality holds only when the $y$ dependence of $P(x: y)$ is fictitious. In words, the entropy of the average distribution is always greater than the average of the entropy of the distribution.

The proof is given in the appendix.[17] The theorem remains true for discrete distributions, and the statement is unchanged except for the uniform substitution of the summation indexes $i$ and $j$ for the continuous variables $x$ and $y$ and the replacement of integrations by sums. By successive application of the proof it is also obvious that the result holds for a distribution which is a function of $n$ parameters $y_1$ to $y_n$. The application to Markoff processes is direct, for a conditional distribution of order $k - 1$ may be expressed as an integral of the form $R(x)$ in (13), where $P(x: y)$ is the conditional distribution of order $k$ and $y$ is the term $m_{i-k}$.

The theorem is also applicable to cases in which the dependence of the distribution on past history is not explicit. If the dependence of the distribution $M(m_i : m_{i-1} \cdots m_{i-k})$ on the set of past message values is through a dependence on one or several parameters (e.g., the mean and the standard deviation of a distribution are functions of the set of past message values but the distribution is always normal), the conclusion still holds: the entropy of the average distribution, averaged over the distribution of the parameters, is always greater than the average over the parameters of the entropy. This is illustrated by the example of (4). The average message term distribution of the process is a normal distribution with a standard deviation $\sigma/\sqrt{1 - a^2}$, with an entropy which may easily be computed[18] as

$$H_0 = \log \sigma \sqrt{2\pi e} + \log (1/\sqrt{1 - a^2}),$$

but each message term has a normal distribution with standard deviation, with entropy just

$$H = \log \sigma \sqrt{2\pi e},$$

which is thus the average entropy of the process as a whole. The difference between these two entropies may be made as large as we like by letting $a$ approach one.

A second averaging theorem which will be useful later deals with averages over a single distribution.

*Averaging Theorem II*

Let $P(x)$ be a probability distribution with entropy $H$:

$$\int_{-\infty}^{\infty} P(x)\,dx = 1, \qquad P(x) \geq 0 \qquad \text{for all } x,$$

$$H = -\int_{-\infty}^{\infty} P(x) \log P(x)\,dx.$$

Let $Q(x, y)$ be a weighting function:

$$\int_{-\infty}^{\infty} Q(x, y)\,dx = \int_{-\infty}^{\infty} Q(x, y)\,dy = 1,$$

$$Q(x, y) \geq 0 \qquad \text{for all } x \text{ and } y.$$

Let $R(x)$ be the averaged distribution with entropy $H'$:

$$R(x) = \int_{-\infty}^{\infty} P(y)Q(x, y)\,dy$$

$$H' = -\int_{-\infty}^{\infty} R(x) \log R(x)\,dx.$$

Then we always have $H' \geq H$, and the equality holds only when the weighting function is a Dirac delta function.

This theorem is given by Shannon.[19] It is also true in the discrete case: the equality then holds only if the average distribution $R(x)$, or $R_i$ in the discrete case, is a mere permutation of the distribution $P(x)$, or $P_i$.

At the beginning of this section it was stated that it is possible to code a message with entropy $H$ bits per symbol by a coding method which uses $H + \epsilon$ binary output symbols per input symbol, on an average. Such a coding scheme will be called an *ideal code*. Shannon has given two such coding procedures, and Fano has given one which is quite similar to one of Shannon's.[20] We will call coding by means of Shannon's second procedure, or by means of Fano's method, *Shannon-Fano coding*. Both are procedures for giving short codes to common messages and long codes to rare messages. They are given in the references. We will here only note the important result. Coding a group of $N$ message terms at once, the average number $H_1$ of output binary symbols per input message symbol is bounded:

$$G_N \leq H_1 \leq G_N + 1/N. \qquad (14)$$

Here $G_N$ is the quantity defined in (9). As $N$ increases $G_N$ approaches $H$, the true entropy of the process, so $H_1$ also approaches $H$. For a discrete process, an *efficient* code may be defined as one for which the ratio $H/H_1$ is near one. It is clear that there are two reasons why a Shannon-Fano code for small $N$ may be inefficient: first, if $G_N$ is small, the ratio $G_N/H_1$ may be small, if $H_1$ is near its upper bound in (14). Second, for small $N$, $G_N$ may be a poor approximation to $H$.

It should be noted that it is *not* reasonable to define an efficiency measure for continuous distributions as a ratio of entropies. For a process which is ultimately to be quantized, the entropy of a continuous distribution does not approximate the entropy of the discrete distribution which is obtained by quantization, unless the scale of the variable in the continuous distribution is so chosen as to make the interval between quantized levels unity. Using a different choice of scale adds a constant to the entropy of the distribution, so that the ratio which defines efficiency is changed. For this reason, until a quantizing level spacing is chosen, it is possible to speak only of the differences between the entropies of continuous distributions, and not of their ratios.

[17] The content of this theorem is implied by the derivations leading up to Shannon's fundamental theorem, Shannon and Weaver, *op. cit.*, p. 28. However, the theorem can be stated and proved as a property of entropy as a functional of a probability distribution, with no reference to sequences of message terms, and the proof is so straightforward and simple that the theorem deserves an independent statement.

[18] Shannon and Weaver, *op. cit.*, p. 56.

[19] Shannon and Weaver, *op. cit.*, p. 21, property 4 for the discrete case; p. 55, property 3 for the continuous case.

[20] Shannon and Weaver, *op. cit.*, p. 29; Fano, *op. cit.* Shannon's procedure is simpler to handle mathematically; Fano's is perhaps somewhat simpler to grasp. Fano's method is not quite completely determinate. In cases in which the two methods do not agree, Fano's provides a more efficient code than Shannon's.

# Predictive Coding—Part II

[*Editors' Note:* Material has been omitted at this point.]

CODING METHODS FOR INDEPENDENT MESSAGE TERMS

Predictive coding treats successive error terms as if they were uncorrelated: i.e., as if the only correlation between successive message terms were due to changes in the mean, and not in the form, of the message term distribution. As we have seen in the preceding examples, this procedure is sometimes ideal and often efficient. That is, it leads to an average error term distribution which, in many cases of interest, may be expected to have only slightly more entropy than the true entropy per symbol of the original message-generating process. This leads us to a consideration of the general problem of the efficient coding of a message having uncorrelated terms. The discussion will be restricted to quantized messages. For practical purposes, we are interested in coding methods which either are non-nmemonic or required only small codebook memories. It turns out that the problem can be solved in one or another of two ways, depending on the distribution from which the uncorrelated message terms are chosen.

*Case I: $H > 1$*

If $H$, the entropy of the message term distribution, is large compared to one bit, then Shannon-Fano coding of each message term will be efficient. For from (14) in Part I, we have

$$H \leq H_1 \leq H + 1, \tag{28}$$

since $G_N = H$ for a message with uncorrelated terms. This gives an efficiency $R \geq H/(1 + H)$ which is near one for $H \gg 1$. Since we are coding only one message term at a time, the codebook memory has only $M$ entries for the $M$ possible quantized values of the message, and may conveniently be realized by such devices as the binary coding tube[22]. Eq. (28) implies that for $H = 1$ it is possible to have an efficiency as low as 50 per cent, but actually it can be shown that this is not the case, and that for $H$ even somewhat smaller than 1, an efficiency of 66-2/3 per cent can always be obtained. For most applications this efficiency will be high compared to other inefficiencies in the system; thus Shannon-Fano coding of individual error terms solves problem for $H \geq 1$.

*Coding Rare and Random Events* The next category that must be considered is message term distributions having an entropy $H < 1$. For this kind of message, Shannon-Fano coding of single message terms will not be useful, since each message term cannot be coded with less than one output binary digit, giving an $H_1 \geq 1$, which will be highly inefficient for small $H$. Indeed, it is clear that no method of coding single message terms into binary digits can be efficient. It is necessary to code a large number of terms at one time to obtain an output of much less than one binary digit per symbol. To avoid a large codebook memory, the coding must be non-nmemonic. That this is possible is due to the fact that a low-entropy discrete distribution must have one high-probability term. Indeed, even for $H = \frac{1}{2}$, the largest probability must be $\geq 0.89$.[25] Low-entropy messages with uncorrelated message terms will then always consist of long runs of a single high-probability symbol, interrupted by occasional low-probability symbols. We will first consider coding methods for the simplest process of this type, in which there are only two symbols, and will then show that the general low-entropy distribution may be coded efficiently by a combination of these methods and Shannon-Fano coding.

Consider a sequence of zeros and ones. We assume that the successive values of the sequence are statistically independent. Let the probability of a zero be $p$, and the probability of a one, $1 - p = \epsilon$. We will define a run of $k$ zeros as a segment of $100 \cdots 00$ of the sequence consisting of a one, which indicates the start of the run, followed by $k$ zeros and a second one, which terminates the run. The second one is not counted as a part of the run, since it will be counted as the first symbol of the next run. Note that by this definition a succession of $j$ ones is counted as $j - 1$ successive runs of zeros, each of length zero; followed by a run of zeros of some greater length.

To find the distribution of runs of zeros, we note that, given that a segment of the sequence *is* a run, we know that it starts with a one, and the probability that it has just $k$ zeros is the probability that it has $k$ zeros followed by a one. The distribution function for runs of zeros is thus

$$S(k) = (1 - p)p^k. \tag{29}$$

We may check that this is a reasonable probability distribution:

$$\sum_{k=0}^{\infty} S(k) = (1 - p) \sum_{k=0}^{\infty} p^k = 1$$

and find the mean number of zeros per run:

$$\sum_{k=0}^{\infty} kS(k) = (1 - p) \sum_{k=0} kp^k = p/(1 - p). \tag{30}$$

To code the sequence we describe each run by giving a binary number that indicates the number of zeros in the

[25] A two-term distribution with one probability $P_o = 0.89$ has an entropy $H = \frac{1}{2}$. Any distribution with more than two terms and with the largest probability $P_o < 0.89$ will have more entropy than this, by averaging Theorem II, Part I, since it can be obtained by an averaging operation on the two-term distribution. Therefore, if any distribution is to have $H = \frac{1}{2}$, it must have $P_o \geq 0.89$.

run.[26] The code number for a run of $k$ zeros is obtained by omitting the first digit of the binary number $k + 1$.[27] The code for the sequence

$$1000000001000000100000001000001000000000$$

is thus the sequence

$$,001,11,000,10,010. \tag{31}$$

The coded version is shorter than the uncoded version, and this discrepancy will evidently increase with the average run length. And the difference in length would be even greater if it were not for the commas in the coded sequence. This is not a trivial matter—the commas, or some equivalent for them, are necessary, since we must know how the sequence of zeros and ones in the coded output is split up into code numbers describing individual run lengths. Because of the commas, the output is in a ternary, not a binary code, and each comma counts as one ternary output digit.

To find the average number of coded output digits for a run of zeros, note that it takes one comma for each run, no additional digits for a run of length zero, one additional digit for a run of length one or two; in general

$$C(k) = n + 1 \tag{32}$$

digits for a run of length $k$, where

$$\sum_{j=0}^{n-1} 2^j \leq k \leq \sum_{j=1}^{n} 2^j.$$

Now

$$\sum_{j=0}^{n-1} 2^j = 2^n - 1; \qquad \sum_{j=1}^{n} 2^j = 2^{n+1} - 2. \tag{33}$$

Using (29), (32), and (33) we can find $\bar{C}$, the average number of coded output digits per run,

$$\begin{aligned}\bar{C} &= \sum_{k=0}^{\infty} C(k)S(k)\\ &= 1 + [(1-p)/p]\Big[0p + 1\sum_{2}^{3} + \cdots\\ &\qquad\qquad + n\sum_{2^n}^{2^{n+1}-1} p^k + \cdots\Big]\\ &= 1 + [(1-p)/p][0/(1-p) + p^2/(1-p) + \cdots\\ &\qquad\qquad + p^{2^n}/(1-p) + \cdots]\end{aligned}$$

$$\bar{C} = 1 + (1/p)\sum_{n=1}^{\infty} p^{2^n}. \tag{34}$$

$\bar{C}$ is the number of ternary output digits per run. The equivalent number of binary digits per run is

$$\bar{C}\log_2 3. \tag{35}$$

From (30) the average number of zeros per run is $p/(1-p)$. There is a one at the start of each run, so the average number of input binary digits per run is

$$1 + p/(1-p) = 1/(1-p) \tag{36}$$

and the entropy per symbol of the input is, by definition,

$$p\log_2(1/p) + (1-p)\log_2[1/(1-p)]. \tag{37}$$

Thus the input entropy per run is the product of (36) and (37), and dividing this by (35) gives the efficiency or relative entropy $R$ of the coding process

$$R = \frac{p\log_2(1/p) + (1-p)\log_2[1/(1-p)]}{(1-p)\bar{C}\log_2 3}. \tag{38}$$

This coding process is the second of a family of similar processes. The $m$th such process uses $m$ symbols to code the lengths of runs of zeros in an $m$-ary code, the $(m+1)$st symbol being reserved for the commas in the coded message (31). For $m = 1$, the coding process reproduces the input signal. For $m = 3$, the coded output may be pairs of binary symbols, with the pair 00 being used for the commas. Larger values of $m$ yield codes that are more efficient for very small $\epsilon = 1 - p$. Using the summation formulas

$$\sum_{j=0}^{n-1} m^j = (m^n - 1)/(m-1);$$

$$\sum_{j=1}^{n} m^j = (m^{n+1} - 1)/(m-1) - 1$$

in place of (32), a derivation like (33) gives the relations

$$\bar{C}(m, p) = 1 + (1/q)\sum_{n=1}^{\infty} q^{m^n}, \text{ with } q = p^{1/(m-1)} \tag{39}$$

$$R(m, p) = \frac{p\log_2(1/p) + (1-p)\log_2 1/(1-p)}{(1-p)\bar{C}(m,p)\log_2(m+1)} \tag{40}$$

of which (34) and (38) are the special cases $m = 2$. It is shown in the Appendix that

$$\lim_{p\to 1} R(m, p) = \log m/\log(m+1). \tag{41}$$

Therefore an $m$ may be chosen to give as high an asymptotic efficiency as may be desired. As in the case of $m = 3$, some of the higher $m$ values may conveniently be obtained by using combinations of binary or ternary digits to make up the necessary $m + 1$ message symbols: $m = 7$ is the next highest value realizable directly in binary digits.[28]

[26] Shannon (Shannon and Weaver, *op. cit.*, p. 33) discusses the problem of coding rare and random events as an example for discrete coding. He suggests sending a special code, such as a sequence of zeros, for the rare event, and using as a run-length code the number of zeros in the run, expressed in a modified binary number system that skips all numbers in which the special sequence occurs. He remarks that the procedure is asymptotically ideal for $p$ near 1, i.e., as the rare event becomes rarer, providing that the length of the special sequence is properly adjusted. The modification used here is simpler to deal with analytically, and simpler to realize physically in a coding circuit. It also has the property of asymptotic ideality, as do a number of variants.

[27] The first digit on the left of a binary number is always a one, and supplies only positional information. This information is supplied by the comma in the sequence (31). It is necessary to add one to the number before removing the first digit in order to provide a representation for a run of length zero. In this code, such a run is indicated by two successive commas.

[28] $m$-ary digits with $m \neq 2^n - 1$ may, of course, be recoded into binary digits. This takes an amount of codebook memory and gives an efficiency of translation, which are as usual inversely related.

In Fig. 4, $R(m, p)$ is plotted against the logarithm to the base two of the average run length, $\log_2 [1/(1-p)]$, for $m$ values of 1, 2, and 3. Each curve has a broad maximum, which moves to the right as $m$ increases, the maximum being located approximately at the point where $\overline{C}(m, p) = m + 1$. This is to be expected, since at this point the frequency of the special symbol that indicates the start of a run will be equal to the average frequency of the other symbols. From the maximum, each curve approaches its asymptotic efficiency from above. The expression (41) for the asymptotic efficiency is the obvious statement that for $p$ very near 1, the $(m + 1)$st symbol which indicates the start of a run contributes very little information, since the runs are long and the symbol occurs very seldom. Note that for any value of $p$, one of the three codes shown will have an efficiency $R \geq 79$ per cent.

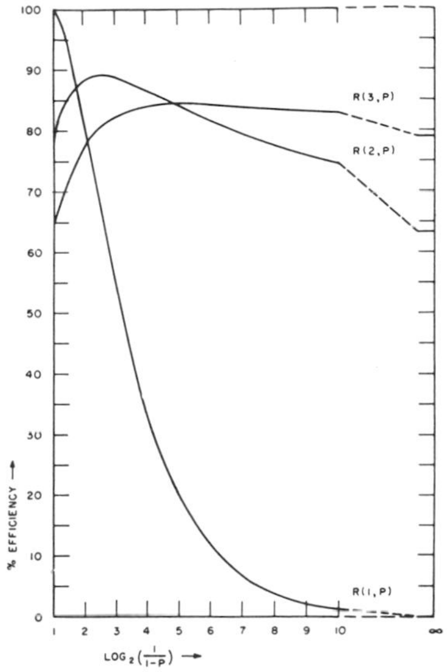


Fig. 4—Efficiency of non-nmemonic coding.

*Case II: $H < 1$*

Returning to the general low-entropy distribution, let the message terms be so labelled that $M_0$ is the term with high probability, and the rare terms are $M_k$, $1 \leq k \leq n$. Then define

$$\epsilon = \sum_{j=1}^{n} M_j$$

$$P_k = M_k/\epsilon.$$

The message may then be divided into two messages: one is a two-state process, with probabilities $p = 1 - \epsilon$ and $\epsilon$, and the other is an $n$-state process with probability distribution $P_k$. The two-state process may be coded by the method described above, using $m$ symbols to code lengths of runs of the common event and an $(m + 1)$st symbol to indicate that a rare event has occurred, ending one run and starting the next. "The" rare event here is actually a signal that one of the low-probability symbols has occurred, and a term of a Shannon-Fano code for the probability distribution $P_k$ follows the special symbol, to indicate which term of this distribution ended the run. Note that the Shannon-Fano coding need not be in the $m$-ary system used for the run-length codes. If an $m$ value of 1 or 3 (or any other $m = 2^i - 1$) is used, and the $m + 1$ symbols used are actually combinations of binary digits, then the Shannon-Fano code may be in ordinary binary notation. Since in Shannon-Fano coding the end of each coded term can be located by inspection, there will be no possibility of confusion.

The entropy of any low-entropy process is divisible into two terms that represent the two processes given above. We have

$$\begin{aligned} H &= -\sum_{i=0}^{n} M_i \log M_i \\ &= -M_0 \log M_0 - \sum_{i=1}^{n} (\epsilon P_i) \log (\epsilon P_i) \\ &= -M_0 \log M_0 - \epsilon \log \epsilon - \epsilon \sum_{i=1}^{n} P_i \log P_i \\ &= -(1-\epsilon) \log (1-\epsilon) - \epsilon \log \epsilon - \sum_{i=1}^{n} P_i \log P_i \\ &= H_2 + \epsilon H_n, \end{aligned} \qquad (42)$$

where $H_2$ is the entropy of the two symbol process and $H_n$ is the entropy of the distribution $P_k$. From (28) we have for $H_n'$, the average number of binary digits per symbol in the Shannon-Fano code of the $n$-state process,

$$H_n' \leq H_n + 1. \qquad (43)$$

For the two-state process, we have by the definition of $R$ in Part II,

$$H_2' = H_2/R(m, p).$$

Using these two bounds and (42), the over-all efficiency of the combined coding is thus

$$R' = \frac{H_2 + \epsilon H_n}{H_2' + \epsilon H_n'} \geq \frac{H_2 + \epsilon H_n}{H_2/R(m, p) + \epsilon(1 + H_n)}, \qquad (44)$$

and finally, since $R(m, p) < 1$ and all the terms are positive,

$$R' \geq \frac{H_2}{H_2/R(m, p) + \epsilon}. \qquad (45)$$

Using only $m = 1$ and $m = 3$, taking the higher efficiency of the two,[29] and noting that $H_2$ is determined by $\epsilon$,

$$H_2 = -\epsilon \log_2 \epsilon - (1-\epsilon) \log_2 (1-\epsilon), \qquad (46)$$

[29] We are restricted to the use of a coding scheme that gives binary digits directly in evaluating (44) and (45), for the expression (43) is valid only for coding into binary digits. In the general case, coding into $m$-ary digits, the equivalent relation is $H_n' \leq H_n + \log_2 m$ bits.

we have that $R' = 66.7$ per cent at $\epsilon = \frac{1}{2}$. For smaller $\epsilon$, $R'$ never goes below about 65 per cent, and as $\epsilon \to 0$ $(p \to 1)$, $R'$ approaches the asymptotic efficiency of the two-state coding scheme. This may be seen by noting that in the limit of small $\epsilon$, (46) becomes[26]

$$H_2 \doteq \epsilon \log_2 (e/\epsilon). \tag{47}$$

Substituting this in (45),

$$R' \geq \frac{\log_2 (e/\epsilon) R(m, p)}{\log_2 (e/\epsilon) + R(m, p)}$$

and

$$\lim_{\epsilon \to 0} R' = \lim_{\epsilon \to 0} R(m, p) = \log m / \log (m + 1), \tag{48}$$

where the right side of (48) is given by (41). This is an asymptotic efficiency of 79 per cent for $m = 3$, and can, of course, be made as high as is desired by choice of sufficiently large $m$. For $\epsilon = \frac{1}{2}$, the entropy per symbol of the process $H_2 \geq 1$, by an argument like that in footnote 5, so we have a coding method with an efficiency $R' \geq 65$ per cent for all messages with successive message terms independently selected and with entropy $H \leq 1$.

## Appendix

### *Asymptotic Efficiency of Run-Length Coding*

Expressions for $\overline{C}(m, p)$ and $R(m, p)$ for $p$ near one may be found by means of the exponential integral

$$EI(x) = \int_x^\infty (e^{-x}/x)\, dx.$$

First, for $q$ less than one, $q^{m^x}$ is a monotonic decreasing function of $x$, so we have the upper and lower bounds

$$U = \int_0^\infty q^{m^x}\, dx > \sum_{n=1}^{\infty} q^{m^n} > \int_1^\infty q^{m^x}\, dx = L. \tag{49}$$

Making the substitution $z = m^x \log(1/q)$, using natural logarithms, gives

$$U = (1/\log m) EI[\log (1/q)]$$
$$L = (1/\log m) EI[m \log (1/q)]. \tag{50}$$

Now from (39), for $p$ near one,

$$q = p^{1/(m-1)} = (1 - \epsilon)^{1/(m-1)} = 1 - (1 - p)/(m - 1).$$

Using this in (50) gives:

$$U = (1/\log m) EI[(1 - p)/(m - 1)]$$
$$L = (1/\log m) EI[m(1 - p)/(m - 1)].$$

Using the series expansion of $EI$ and keeping the first two terms,[30]

[30] Franklin, "Treatise on Advanced Calculus," John Wiley & Sons, Inc., New York, N. Y., p. 572; 1940.

$$U = \frac{-\gamma + \log (m - 1) + \log [1/(1 - p)]}{\log m}$$
$$L = U - 1,$$

where $\gamma$ is Euler's constant, $\gamma = 0.5772\cdots$.

From (39) and (50) we thus have, for $p$ near one,

$$U + 1 > \overline{C}(m, p) > L + 1 = U. \tag{51}$$

From (36) and (37) we have the input entropy per run, converting to natural logarithms:

$$H/(1 - p) = 1/(1 - p)[(1 - p) \log 1/(1 - p) + p \log (1/p)].$$

For $p$ near one, this becomes

$$H/(1 - p) \doteq \log [e/(1 - p)].$$

Recalling that each output digit is $(m + 1)$-ary, and is equivalent to $\log(m + 1)$ natural units, we have, for the efficiency $R(m, p)$ for $p$ near one,

$$\frac{\log [e/(1 - p)]}{U \log (m + 1)} > R(m, p) > \frac{\log [e/(1 - p)]}{(U + 1) \log (m + 1)}.$$

Taking the limit gives the same result for each of the bounds so

$$\lim_{p \to 1} R(m, p) = \log m/\log (m + 1)$$

which is (41), the relation to be proved.

## Acknowledgment

This paper presents results obtained in a thesis entitled "Predictive Coding," submitted in 1950 to the Faculty of Arts and Sciences of Harvard University in partial fulfillment of the requirements for the Ph.D. degree. The author would like to thank Profs. Le Corbeiller, Brillouin, and Mimno of Harvard for their interest and encouragement; also Prof. Wiener of the Massachusetts Institute of Technology, and R. L. Dietzold of Bell Telephone Laboratories, for some interesting discussions.

Some of this material was presented by the author at the 1952 I.R.E. National Convention. At the same session papers were given by Oliver, Kretzmer, and Harrison, on television problems.[31] In particular, the paper by Harrison discusses *linear* predictive coding, but it makes use of a power, rather than an information, criterion for prediction. A note by the author[32] is also relevant to the linear predictive coding problem.

[31] B. M. Oliver, "Efficient coding," *Bell Sys. Tech. Jour.*, vol. 31, pp. 724–750; 1952.
E. R. Kretzmer, "Statistics of television signals," *Bell Sys. Tech. Jour.*, vol. 31, pp. 751–763; 1952.
C. W. Harrison, "Experiments with linear prediction in television," *Bell Sys. Tech. Jour.*, vol. 31, pp. 764–783; 1952.

[32] P. Elias, "A note on autocorrelation and entropy," Proc. I.R.E., vol. 39, p. 839; July, 1951.

# 5



Reprinted from *IEEE Trans. Inform. Theory,* **IT-14**(3), 490–501 (1968)

# Buffer Overflow in Variable Length Coding of Fixed Rate Sources

FREDERICK JELINEK, MEMBER, IEEE

***Abstract*—In this paper, we develop and analyze an easily instrumentable scheme for variable length encoding of discrete memoryless fixed-rate sources in which buffer overflows result in code-word erasures at locations that are perfectly specified to the user. Thus, no loss of synchronism ever occurs. We find optimal (i.e., minimizing the probability of buffer overflow) code-word length requirements under the Kraft inequality constraint, relative to various constant transmission rates *R*, and show that these do not result in the minimal average code-word length. The corresponding bounds on the probability of buffer overflow provide a linkup between source coding and Rényi's generalized source entropy. We show, further, that codes having optimal word lengths can be constructed by the method of Elias, and we develop corresponding sequentially instrumented encoders and decoders. We show that the complexity of these encoders and decoders grows only linearly with the encoded message block length *k*, provided the size *d* of the coder alphabet is a power of 2, and otherwise grows no worse than quadratically with *k*.**

Manuscript received October 15, 1966; revised December 12, 1967. This work was supported in part by the National Science Foundation under Grant GP 3010 and by NASA Contract NSR 33-010-026.

The author is with the School of Elec. Engrg. and Center for Radiophysics and Space Research, Cornell University, Ithaca, N. Y. 14850

## I. Introduction

VARIABLE length source coding of discrete information sources was introduced by Shannon[1] who showed that there are errorless codes of ergodic sources having an average word length per source output symbol that approaches arbitrarily closely the source entropy expressed in $d$-nary units (where $d$ is the size of the coding alphabet), provided the encoded blocks of information symbols are sufficiently large.

*Definition 1*: A *fixed rate* discrete source is one that generates successive output symbols at regular time intervals.

In applying variable length encoding to fixed rate sources, one runs into the problem of buffer *overflow* and *exhaust*. Namely, suppose that the source is discrete, stationary, and memoryless, that it generates one symbol per second, that the channel transmits $r$ symbols per second, and that the encoder maps sequences of length $k$ of source output symbols into code words $\phi$ of channel input symbols. Let $N^*$ and $N_*$ be the lengths of the longest and shortest code words $\phi$, respectively. Then, any finite storage buffer interconnecting the encoder with the channel will eventually overflow unless $r \geq N^*/k$. The consequent loss of symbols, if not properly handled, will result in a catastrophic garbling of the message. Moreover, as long as $r > N_*/k$, the interconnecting buffer will sometimes become empty, which is also undesirable since the consequent idleness of the transmitter can knock the receiver out of its synchronism with the encoder.

In this paper, we shall develop and analyze an easily instrumentable scheme for variable length encoding of discrete memoryless fixed-rate sources. We shall find optimal (i.e., minimizing the probability of buffer overflow) code-word length requirements under the Kraft[2]–McMillan[3] inequality constraint ($d$ is the code alphabet size, $m_i$ are the code-word lengths)

$$\sum_{i=1}^{s} d^{-m_i} \leq 1$$

relative to various transmission speeds $r$, and show that these do not result in the minimal average code-word length. We shall further show that codes of optimal word lengths can be constructed by the method of Elias,[5] and we shall develop corresponding sequentially instrumented encoders and decoders. Assuming the present binary arithmetic computer technology, we shall show that the complexity of these encoders and decoders grows only linearly with the encoded message block length $k$ provided the size $d$ of the coder alphabet is a power of 2, and otherwise grows no worse than quadratically with $k$.

Suppose the following.

1) The fixed rate discrete memoryless source generates one symbol $z$ per second, where $z \in \{0, 1, \cdots, c-1\}$. The source is governed by a probability distribution $Q(\ )$ such that

$$Q(0) \geq Q(1) \geq \cdots \geq Q(c-1) > 0, \quad \text{and} \quad Q(0) > \frac{1}{c}.$$

2) The encoder outputs are denoted by $s$ and are taken from the alphabet $\{0, 1, \cdots, d-1\}$.

3) $z_i$ and $s_i$ denote the $i$th symbols put out by the source and encoder, respectively. Sequences of length $k$ starting at time 1 are denoted by a boldface letter with superscript $k$. Thus,

$$\mathbf{z}^k \triangleq (z_1, \cdots, z_k)$$

$$\mathbf{s}^l \triangleq (s_1, \cdots, s_l);$$

$\mathbf{z}_m^k \triangleq (z_1^m, \cdots, z_k^m)$ denotes the $m$th sequence of a set of source output sequences of length $k$.

4) A code is specified by a code function $\phi$. The code word corresponding to $\mathbf{z}^k$ is denoted by $\phi(\mathbf{z}^k)$ and its length by $m(\mathbf{z}^k)$. Thus,

$$\phi(\mathbf{z}^k) = (s_1, s_2, \cdots, s_{m(\mathbf{z}^k)})$$

for some specific sequence $s_i = s_i(\mathbf{z}^k) \in \{0, \cdots, d-1\}$.

Our results will also provide a theoretical linkup between coding and Rényi's generalized entropy (of the source) of order $\gamma$[12]

$$I_\gamma(Q) \triangleq \begin{cases} \dfrac{1}{1-\gamma} \log_d \left( \sum_{z=0}^{c-1} Q(z)^\gamma \right) & \gamma \neq 1, \gamma > 0 \\ \lim_{\eta \uparrow 1} I_\eta(Q) = -\sum_z Q(z) \log_d Q(z) & \gamma = 1. \end{cases} \tag{1}$$

Namely, let $P(k, B)$ be the probability that a source output sequence of length $k$ cannot be identified by the decoder (because of buffer overflow) when the buffer length is $B$. Then, we shall show that ($g$ is some constant)

$$P(k, B) \leq gB \exp_d \left[ -\frac{1-\gamma}{\gamma} B \right]$$

provided the coding rate $R$ satisfies

$$R \geq I_\gamma(Q) + f(k)$$

where $f(k) \to 0$ as $k \to \infty$. Thus, Rényi's entropy $I_\gamma(Q)$ determines the limiting encoding rate for a given reliability $(1-\gamma)/\gamma$, the latter approaching zero as the rate approaches the (ordinary) source entropy $H(Z) = I_1(Q)$.

Finally, we shall compare the error performance of variable length encoding with that of block coding[9] and conclude that the former is always better at rates sufficiently close to (ordinary) source entropy, and that for most sources it is better at all rates.

Before describing the operation of the suggested coding system, let us introduce some additional notation and a definition.

5) All logarithms denoted by "log" will be understood to have the base $d$. The entropy $H(Z)$ of the source will also be understood to involve logarithms to the base $d$.

6) The expression $[x]^-$ will denote the greatest integer less than or equal to $x$.

*Definition 2*: A code is called *instantaneous*[4] if the position of the last code-word symbol can be found by the decoder without reference to any subsequent symbols.

Prefix codes and block codes are instantaneous, but the code $\{(1, 0), (1, 0, 0)\}$ is not, although it is uniquely decipherable.

## II. The Buffer Instrumented Encoder System

A schematic diagram of the suggested *buffer instrumented encoder system* is shown in Fig. 1. It consists of four basic components. 1) An *instantaneous word encoder* (IWE) that implements some instantaneous code by generating the words $\phi(\mathbf{z}^k)$ that correspond to the source sequences $\mathbf{z}^k$ fed into it. 2) An *encoder buffer* (EB) of length $B + m$ (this is the left buffer in Fig. 1) into whose empty stages are fed either the code words generated by the IWE (one $d$-nary code-word symbol per stage) or some bookkeeping $d$-nary symbols by means of which the decoder can keep track of erasures due to buffer overflow and of insertions due to buffer exhaustion

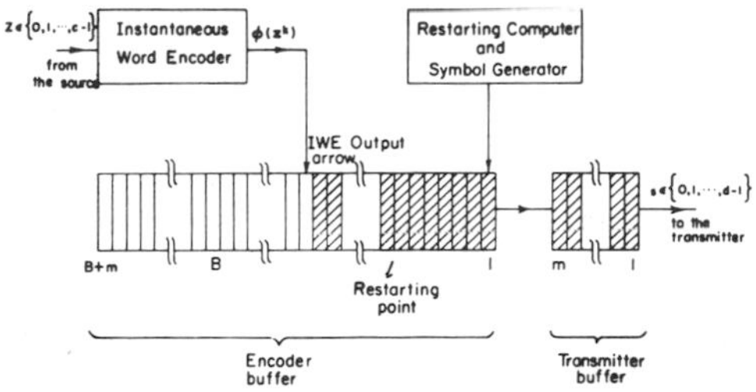


Fig. 1. Buffer instrumented variable length encoder system. Transmitter buffer shifts to right $m$ times in every cycle. Block of $m$ digits is transferred from encoder buffer to transmitter buffer at the beginning of each cycle. A cycle takes $k$ source intervals (seconds).

(for precise definition of these events, see 4). 3) A *transmitter buffer* (TB) of length $m$ (this is the right buffer in Fig. 1) which shifts its contents one stage to the right once every $k/m$ seconds, releasing to the transmitter the $d$-nary symbol located in the right-most stage. The TB is thus emptied once every $k$ seconds (i.e., once every time interval it takes the IWE to generate a code word) at which time it is filled by an instantaneous transfer into it of the contents of the $m$ right-most stages of the EB. 4) A *restarting computer and symbol generator* (RCSG) that assures code-word insertion from the IWE into the appropriate empty stages of the EB, keeps track of the number of complete code words in the EB and of their stage location, supplies the EB after a buffer exhaust with a bookkeeping sequence that will permit an uninterrupted release of symbols by the TE to the transmitter, assures erasure of the appropriate EB stages when a buffer overflow takes place, and supplies the EB with a bookkeeping sequence from which the decoder can conclude that an overflow took place and can determine the number of code words erased as a consequence. The character of both the exhaust and overflow bookkeeping sequences is such that their beginning and end is identifiable so that the decoder shall not confuse them with code words generated by the IWE.

The reason for two buffers (EB and TB) is to simplify the following analysis (a practical system may use only one buffer). In Fig. 1, the $l$th stage of EB is identified as a *restarting point*. The bookkeeping sequences inserted by the RCSG are such that the first code word inserted into the EB right after buffer exhaust or overflow will have its beginning symbol located in the $l$th stage. This restarting strategy assures that the overflow–exhaust process is *recurrent* (see Feller,[6] Definition 1, p. 282) and thus provides the means for overbounding of the average number of erased code words.

We are now ready to specify in detail the operation of the system of Fig. 1. At the start, the first $l + m - 1$ stages of the EB are filled with zeros and the IWE *output arrow* is pointed at EB stage number $t_0 = l$ (in general, $t_i$ denotes the position of the output arrow after the $i$th cycle). Whatever its contents and regardless of all considerations, the TB will shift one stage to the right once every $1/R \triangleq k/m$ seconds, always releasing its right-most symbol to the transmitter. We will now describe the manner in which the TB is kept supplied with the proper symbols. The $i$th ($i = 1, 2, \cdots$) EB operating cycle of duration $k$ seconds (the time it takes the IWE to generate a code word) starts with a shift of the EB by $m$ stages to the right. The $m$ released symbols are fed in sequence into the TB, filling the latter. Next, if the system is not in an *extended overflow mode* (see below), the $m(\mathbf{z}_i^k)$ symbols of $\phi(\mathbf{z}_i^k)$ are fed into the empty stages of the EB, the first symbol into the $t_{i-1}$th stage. The RCSG then computes the (tentative) next IWE output arrow location $t_i = t_{i-1} + m(\mathbf{z}_i^k) - m$. Depending on the value of $t_i$, the cycle will be completed in one of three modes.

*Case 1*: If $1 \leq t_i \leq B + 1$, the system enters the *regular mode*. The IWE output arrow is relocated to stage $t_i$, and the EB remains unchanged until the beginning of the next cycle.

*Case 2*: If $t_i < 1$, a *terminal event* is said to have taken place, and the system enters the *exhaust mode*. To be able to handle terminal events, we insist that no code word $\phi(\mathbf{z}^k)$ can start with the symbol 0, and that the restarting position $l \geq 2$. Now, if an exhaust occurs at time $i$, the RCSG sets $t_i = l$ and inserts after the code word $\phi(\mathbf{z}_i^k)$ the *exhaust character* (0, 0) followed by a sequence of 0's of length $m_e = [l - 2] - [t_{i-1} + m(\mathbf{z}_i^k) - m]$ (since $l \geq 2$, then $m_e \geq 0$). Finally, the IWE output arrow is relocated to stage $t_i = l$ (which, because of the insertion of the zero sequence of length $m_e + 2$ will be the right-most "empty" stage after the next $m$ shift of EB) and the EB remains unchanged until the start of the next cycle. Since the instantaneous nature of the code allows the decoder to identify the end of a code word, and since no code word can start with a 0, the decoder will be able to find the point at which message transmission resumes (it is the first nonzero symbol following the (0, 0) exhaust character).

*Case 3*: If $t_i > B + 1$, a terminal event is said to have taken place and the system enters the *overflow mode*. If an overflow occurs at time $i$, the RCSG first eliminates from the EB all parts of the code word $\phi(\mathbf{z}_i^k)$ plus all the complete code words $\phi(\mathbf{z}_{i-j}^k)$, $j = 0, 1, \cdots, \lambda$ (this means that $\lambda$ is such that the first symbol of $\phi(\mathbf{z}_{i-\lambda-1}^k)$ is not in any stage of EB and that its last symbol is either in the EB, or in the $m$th stage of the TB). Behind the last symbol of $\phi(\mathbf{z}_{i-\lambda-1}^k)$, the RCSG inserts the *overflow character* (0, 1) followed by the sequence $(s_1(\lambda), s_2(\lambda), \cdots, s_\omega(\lambda))$, which is the $d$-nary expansion of $\lambda$, the number of complete code words eliminated from the buffer (i.e., $\lambda = s_1(\lambda) + s_2(\lambda)\, d + \cdots + s_\omega(\lambda)\, d^{\omega-1}$). The value of $\omega$ is chosen to equal the minimum integer such that $(d^\omega - 1)$ is greater than or equal to the maximum number of code words that can be eliminated

TABLE I
LIST OF SYMBOLS FOR FIG. 1

| | |
|---|---|
| $\lambda$ | = the number of complete code words currently in the buffer |
| $l$ | = the EB restarting position |
| $\nu$ | = the number of code words not accepted from the instantaneous encoder during overflow |
| $b$ | = the EB stage following the last symbol of the incomplete (partly transmitted) code word |
| $t_i$ | = the EB stage following the last occupied symbol in the EB |
| $i, j$ | = time indices |
| $B + m$ | = EB size |
| $m$ | = shift size = TB size |
| $m_e$ | = number of dummy 0's inserted after current exhaust |
| $m_0$ | = number of dummy 0's inserted after current overflow |
| $(s_1(\lambda), s_2(\lambda), \cdots, s_\omega(\lambda))$ | = bookkeeping code word that specifies the number of code words eliminated from the EB after overflow |
| $\omega$ | = length of the above sequence |

(clearly, $(d^\omega - 1) \leq B/[\min_{z^k}\{m(\mathbf{z}^k)\}]$). Let $b$ be the buffer position following the last symbol of the code word $\phi(\mathbf{z}^k_{i-\lambda-1})$ at time $i$. There are two possibilities. 1) If $b + 2 + \omega \leq l$, then the RCSG follows the sequence $(s_1(\lambda), \cdots, s_\omega(\lambda))$ by $m_0 = l - 2 - b - \omega$ zeros, sets $t_i = l$, and relocates the IWE output arrow to stage $t_i$. The EB remains unchanged until the start of the next cycle. 2) If $b + 2 + \omega > 1$, the system enters the *extended overflow mode* referred to earlier. It will take $\nu = -[(l - b - 2 - \omega)/m]^- m$ shifts of the EB before the symbol $s_\omega(\lambda)$ appears for the first time to the right of the $l$th EB stage. The system will remain in the extended overflow mode for $\nu$ cycles, at the beginning of each of which an $m$ shift takes place and the code word put out by the IWE is dumped (thus a total of $\lambda + \nu + 1$ code words are eliminated). In the last of these cycles, the system leaves the extended overflow mode and the RCSG inserts $m_0 = l - (b + 2 + \omega - \nu m)$ additional 0's behind the symbol $s_\omega(\lambda)$ and sets $t_{i+\nu} = l$. The output arrow is then relocated to the $t_{i+\nu}$th stage and the EB remains unchanged until the start of the $(i + \nu + 1)$th cycle. Since the decoder can keep track of the position $b$ in the EB (this is, in fact, the position of the 0 in the overflow character (0, 1)), it can compute the value of $\nu$. Since the value of $\lambda$ is supplied through the sequence $(S_1(\lambda), \cdots, s_\omega(\lambda))$, our strategy allows the decoder to stay synchronized with the encoder system at all times. Table I provides an explanatory list of the symbols just defined. The operation of the buffer instrumented encoder system is described by the flow chart of Fig. 2. There the order "shift" refers to the shift of $m$ symbols from EB to TB. The $R$ shifts per second of the TB are not represented.

## III. PERFORMANCE CHARACTERISTICS OF THE BUFFER INSTRUMENTED ENCODER

We will now evaluate the performance of our source encoder.

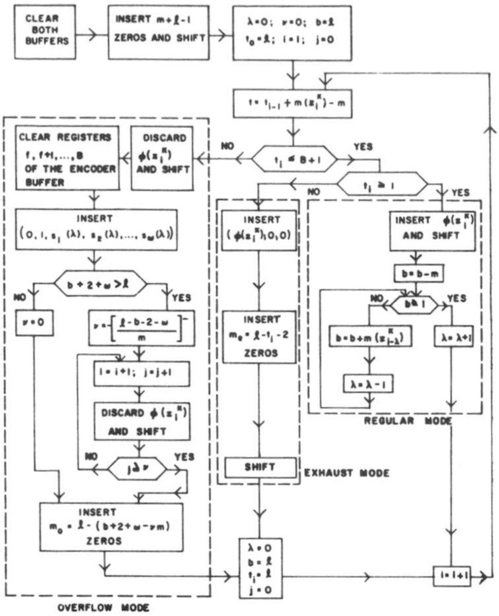


Fig. 2. Flow chart of the restarting computer and symbol generator. The order *shift* refers to a shift of the encoder buffer by $m$ stages to the right. The order *insert* refers to an insertion of symbols into the encoder buffer. The regular shifts of the transmitter buffer are not represented.

*Lemma 1*

Let a discrete memoryless source, generating sequences $\mathbf{z}^k$ with probabilities $P(\mathbf{z}^k)$ be given. If the code words $\phi(\mathbf{z}^k)$ of the instantaneous word encoder are of length $m(\mathbf{z}^k)$ and the transmitter buffer length $m$ satisfies

$$\bar{m} \triangleq \sum_{\mathbf{z}^k} P(\mathbf{z}^k)m(\mathbf{z}^k) < m < \max_{\mathbf{z}^k} \{m(\mathbf{z}^k)\}, \tag{2}$$

then the probability $F_l$ that the buffer instrumented encoder overflows before it exhausts is bounded by

$$F_l < \frac{d^{-\rho_0(B+2-l)}}{1 - d^{-\rho_0(B+2-\alpha)}}; \qquad l = 1, 2, \cdots, B + 1 \tag{3}$$

where $B + m$ is the encoder buffer size. In (3),

$$\alpha \triangleq -m + \min_{\mathbf{z}^k} \{m(\mathbf{z}^k)\} \tag{4}$$

and $\rho_0 > 0$ is the unique real solution of

$$\frac{1}{\rho} \log \left(\sum_{\mathbf{z}^k} P(\mathbf{z}^k) d^{\rho(m(\mathbf{z}^k) - m)}\right) = 0. \tag{5}$$

*Proof*: Define

$$M(\mathbf{z}^k) \triangleq m(\mathbf{z}^k) - m. \tag{6}$$

Let $F_n$, $n = 1, 2, \cdots, B+1$ be the probability that an overflow takes place before exhaustion if the restarting point of the encoder buffer (see Fig. 1) is located at $l = n$. Then, for all $n$,

$$F_n = \sum_{j=-n+1}^{B+1-n} P\{M(\mathbf{z}_1^k) = j\} F_{n+j} + \sum_{t=1}^{\infty} P\{M(\mathbf{z}_1^k) = B + 1 - n + t\} \quad (7)$$

where the first term on the right is the probability that an overflow takes place before exhaustion after more than one code word has been inserted, and the second term is the probability that an overflow takes place after the insertion of the first code word. The problem is to solve (7) for the unknowns $F_n$. This can be done by direct application of a method presented in Feller,[6] Sec. 14.8. It turns out that[1]

$$F_l \leq \frac{d^{\rho_0 l} - d^{\rho_0 \alpha}}{d^{\rho_0 (B+2)} - d^{\rho_0 \alpha}} \qquad l = 1, 2, \cdots, B+1 \quad (8)$$

where $\rho_0 > 0$ is the unique real solution of (5). The existence of the solution is assured by the fact that the left-hand side of (5) is a semi-invariant function and that $m$ has a value satisfying (2). The lemma is now proved, since (8) implies (3). Q.E.D.

We are now in a position to find an upper bound on $\bar{N}$, the average number of code words per input sequence $\mathbf{z}^k$ erased (eliminated) by the buffer instrumented encoder system operating under the algorithm of Fig. 2. Let $\mathcal{A}_n$ denote the occurrence of a terminal event (i.e., either exhaustion or overflow) during the $n$th encoder cycle (i.e., subsequent to an attempted insertion of the $n$th code word $\phi(\mathbf{z}_n^k)$ into the encoder buffer), let $\mathcal{E}_n$ denote the occurrence of an overflow during the $n$th cycle, and let $K_n$ be the number of code words erased during the $n$th cycle ($K_n = 0$ if no overflow takes place during the $n$th cycle, otherwise $K_n = \nu + \lambda + 1$, with $\nu$ and $\lambda$ as defined in Section II). Then,

$$\bar{N} \triangleq \lim_{n\to\infty} P\{\mathcal{E}_n\} \mathbf{E}[K_n/\mathcal{E}_n]. \quad (9)$$

Now $\lambda$, the number of complete code words in the buffer, can never exceed $B/(\alpha + m)$ (see (4)). Thus $\omega$, the length of the bookkeeping sequence $(s_1(\lambda), \cdots, s_\omega(\lambda))$, is bounded by

$$\omega \leq \log \left[\frac{B}{\alpha + m}\right] + 1 \triangleq \omega_M. \quad (10)$$

Since $b$, the buffer position following the last symbol of the incomplete (partially transmitted) code word left in the buffer after an overflow, cannot exceed $B - m$, then,

$$\nu \leq \frac{b + \omega + 2 - l}{m} + 1 \leq \frac{B - m + 3 + \omega_m - l}{m} + 1 \triangleq \nu_M \quad (11)$$

and

$$\mathbf{E}[K_n/\mathcal{E}_n] \leq \frac{B}{\alpha + m} + \nu_M + 1 \triangleq K(B). \quad (12)$$

Since the restarting point $l$ is kept constant for all times, terminal events are *recurrent* (see Feller,[6] Definition 1, p. 282). It follows, therefore, that (see Feller,[6] Theorem 3, p. 286)

$$\lim_{n\to\infty} P\{\mathcal{E}_n\} = F_l \lim_{n\to\infty} P\{\alpha_n\} = \frac{F_l}{\mathbf{E}[T]} \quad (13)$$

where $F_l$ was defined in Lemma 1, and $\mathbf{E}[T]$ is the expected number of encoder cycles elapsed before the first terminal event takes place (the random variable $T$ is commonly called the stopping time of the recurrent process).

It is easy to see that the output arrow of the instantaneous word encoder (see Fig. 1) performs a random walk on the first $B$ stages of the buffer during the time between any two successive terminal events. It makes one step each cycle, the step length being equal to $M(\mathbf{z}^k)$ (see (6)) when $\phi(\mathbf{z}^k)$ was inserted. Hence, by a famous theorem of Wald (for proof see Blackwell and Girshick,[16] p. 271),

$$\frac{1}{\mathbf{E}[T]} = \frac{-\mathbf{E}[M(\mathbf{z}^k)]}{-\mathbf{E}\left[\sum_{i=1}^{T} M(\mathbf{z}_i^k)\right]}. \quad (14)$$

It should be kept in mind that in the expectation of the denominator of the right-hand expression in (14), the upper limit $T$ is a random variable. Now,

$$-\mathbf{E}\left[\sum_{i=1}^{T} M(\mathbf{z}_i^k)\right] \geq -(B + 1 - l + \max\{M(\mathbf{z}^k)\}) \times P\{\text{overflow before exhaust}\} - (-l)P\{\text{exhaust before overflow}\}, \quad (15)$$

since $(B + 1 - l + \max\{M(\mathbf{z}^k)\})$ is the largest positive distance walked before an overflow took place, and $(-l)$ is the smallest negative distance before an exhaust. Defining

$$\beta \triangleq \max_{\mathbf{z}^k} \{m(\mathbf{z}^k)\} - m, \quad (16)$$

we get from (15) that

$$-\mathbf{E}\left[\sum_{i=1}^{T} M(\mathbf{z}_i^k)\right] \geq -(B + 1 - l + \beta)F_l + l(1 - F_l) = (B + 1 + \beta)F_l + l. \quad (17)$$

[1] A detailed proof of this lemma can be found in Jelinek,[9] Sec. A.2.

Furthermore,

$$-\mathbf{E}[M(\mathbf{z}^k)] = -\sum_{\mathbf{z}^k} P(\mathbf{z}^k)m(\mathbf{z}^k) + m = m - \bar{m} \tag{18}$$

and, therefore, from (9), (12) through (14), (17) and (18),

$$\bar{N} \leq K(B)(m - \bar{m}) \frac{F_l}{l - (B + 1 + \beta)F_l}$$

$$= \frac{K(B)(m - \bar{m})}{(l/F_l) - (B + 1 + \beta)} \tag{19}$$

provided the denominator is positive. (Wald proved that if (18) is positive, then so is the left-hand side of (17)). To minimize the right-hand side of (19), we seek that value of $l$ that will maximize $l/F_l$. But, by (3),

$$l/F_l \geq l d^{-\rho_0 l} d^{\rho_0(B+2)}(1 - d^{-\rho_0(B+2-\alpha)})$$

$$\text{for} \quad l = 2, 3, \cdots, B + 1. \tag{20}$$

The function $x\, d^{-\rho_0 x}$ is maximized by $x = 1/(\rho_0 \ln d)$, as can be checked by differentiation. Noting that the allowable range of $l$ is restricted, it can be checked that the choice

$$l = \begin{cases} 2 & \text{for} \quad \rho_0 \geq \dfrac{1}{2 \ln d} \\ \left[\dfrac{1}{\rho_0} + 1\right]^- & \text{for} \quad 0 < \rho_0 < \dfrac{1}{2 \ln d} \end{cases} \tag{21}$$

is almost optimal.

We summarize the result in the following theorem.

*Theorem 1*

Given a discrete memoryless source generating sequences $\mathbf{z}^k$ with probabilities $P(\mathbf{z}^k)$, if the code words $\phi(\mathbf{z}^k)$ of the instantaneous word encoder are of length $m(\mathbf{z}^k)$, the transmitter buffer length $m$ satisfies (2), $\rho_0 > 0$ is the unique solution of (5), and the restarting position $l$ is selected by the rule (21), then $\bar{N}$, the average number of code words per input sequence $\mathbf{z}^k$ erased by the buffer instrumented encoder is bounded by

$$\bar{N} \leq \begin{cases} \left[\dfrac{K(B)(m - \bar{m})}{2 - [B + 1 + \beta + 2d^{-\rho_0(2-\alpha)}]d^{-\rho_0 B}}\right] d^{-\rho_0 B}; & \text{if} \quad \rho_0 \geq \dfrac{1}{2 \ln d} \\ \left[\dfrac{K(B)(m - \bar{m})e\rho_0 \ln d}{1 - [(B + 1 + \beta)e\rho_0 \ln d + d^{-\rho_0(1-\alpha)}]d^{-\rho_0(B+1)}}\right] d^{-\rho_0(B+1)}; & \text{if} \quad 0 < \rho_0 < \dfrac{1}{2 \ln d} \end{cases} \tag{22}$$

provided the buffer size $B$ is sufficiently large to make the denominators in (22) positive. In (22), the parameters $\alpha$ and $\beta$ are defined by (4) and (16), and

$$K(B) \triangleq \frac{B}{\alpha + m} + \frac{\log B - \log(\alpha + m) + B + 2}{m} + 1.$$

*Remark*: Ordinarily, $B \geq \beta + 1$. Then the denominator of the top bound of (22) exceeds $2(1 - (B + 1)e^{-1/2B})$ and is, thus, positive for $B \geq 3$. Under the same assumption, the denominator of the bottom bound exceeds $(1 - (2Be\rho_0 \ln d + 1)\, d^{-\rho_0 B})$ and is, therefore, positive for $B \geq 3/(\rho_0 \ln d)$. In any case, if the denominator is positive, then it follows from (22) and the definition of $K(B)$ that the bound has the form

$$\bar{N} \leq (g_1 B + g_2 \log B)\, d^{-\rho_0 B}. \tag{23}$$

## IV. Quasi-Optimal Prefix Codes and their Buffer Instrumented Performance

We would now like to specify that class of prefix codes for which the general bound (22) on $\bar{N}$ would be minimal. It is obvious from the asymptotic form (23) that our aim must be to maximize the unique root $\rho_0$ of equation (5) subject to the constraint of the Kraft inequality (25). The basic result is the following theorem.

*Theorem 2*

Let a discrete memoryless source of entropy $H(Z)$, generating sequences $\mathbf{z}^k$ with probabilities $P(\mathbf{z}^k) = \prod_{i=1}^{k} Q(z_i)$, $z_i \in \{0, \cdots, c - 1\}$, and a transmitter buffer length $m$ satisfying

$$kH(Z) < m < k \log c \tag{24}$$

be given. The set of values $\{m(\mathbf{z}^k)\}$ that simultaneously satisfies the Kraft inequality

$$\sum_{\mathbf{z}^k} d^{-m(\mathbf{z}^k)} \leq 1 \tag{25}$$

and maximizes the root $\rho$ of (5) is specified by

$$m(\mathbf{z}^k) = -\log \frac{P(\mathbf{z}^k)^{1/(1+\rho_0)}}{\sum_{\mathbf{z}^k} P(\mathbf{z}^k)^{1/(1+\rho_0)}} \tag{26}$$

where $\rho_0$ is the unique solution of the equation

$$\frac{m}{k} = \frac{1}{\rho} \log \left( \sum_{z=0}^{c-1} Q(z)^{1/(1+\rho)} \right)^{1+\rho} \triangleq \frac{1}{\rho} E_s(\rho). \tag{27}$$

The assignment (26) will satisfy the inequality (2)

$$\sum_{\mathbf{z}^k} P(\mathbf{z}^k)m(\mathbf{z}^k) < m < \max_{\mathbf{z}^k} \{m(\mathbf{z}^k)\}. \tag{2}$$

*Remark*: $\rho_0$ is also the unique solution of (5) when $m(\mathbf{z}^k)$ has the maximizing value (26) for all $\mathbf{z}^k$; it is positive and monotonically increasing with $m$ in the interval (24). As $m$ approaches the left and right limits of the interval (24), $\rho_0$ approaches 0 and $\infty$, respectively.

*Proof*: The relation (5) is equivalent to

$$\left(\sum_{\mathbf{z}^k} P(\mathbf{z}^k) d^{\rho m(\mathbf{z}^k)}\right)^{1/\rho} = d^m. \tag{28}$$

The solution $\rho_0$ of (28) is a monotonically increasing function of $m$, since the left-hand side of (28) is a monotonically increasing function of $\rho$. (It can be written as $d^{(1/\rho)\gamma_{X'}(\rho)}$ where $\gamma_{X'}(\ )$ is the semi-invariant function of the random variable $X' = m(\ )$.) Maximizing $\rho$ for a given $m$ is, then, the same as minimizing $m$ for a given $\rho$. Thus, the aim is to find for all $\rho > 0$ that set $\{m(\mathbf{z}^k)\}$ that will minimize the left-hand side of (28) under the constraint (25). This problem is solved by applying the well-known Kuhn–Tucker theorem.[8] The unique solution is given by

$$m^0(\mathbf{z}^k) = -\log \frac{P(\mathbf{z}^k)^{1/(1+\rho)}}{\sum_{\mathbf{z}^k} P(\mathbf{z}^k)^{1/(1+\rho)}}. \qquad (29)$$

If

$$\lim_{\rho \downarrow 0} \frac{k}{\rho} E_s(\rho) < m < \lim_{\rho \downarrow \infty} E_s(\rho) \qquad (30)$$

is satisfied, then (27) will have a unique solution $\rho_0$ that will be positive. But the limits in (30) and (24) can easily be shown to be equal. It remains to prove that the assignment (26) satisfies (2). But, since $\rho_0 > 0$ satisfies (5), then

$$\begin{aligned}\sum_{\mathbf{z}^k} P(\mathbf{z}^k)m(\mathbf{z}^k) - m &= \frac{1}{\rho_0} \sum_{\mathbf{z}^k} P(\mathbf{z}^k)[\rho m(\mathbf{z}^k) - \log \sum_{\mathbf{z}^k} P(\mathbf{z}^k) d^{\rho m(\mathbf{z}^k)}] \\ &= \frac{1}{\rho_0} \sum_{\mathbf{z}^k} P(\mathbf{z}^k) \log \frac{d^{m(\mathbf{z}^k)}}{\sum_{\mathbf{z}^k} P(\mathbf{z}^k) d^{m(\mathbf{z}^k)}} \\ &\le \frac{1}{\rho_0} \sum_{\mathbf{z}^k} P(\mathbf{z}^k)\left[\frac{d^{\rho m(\mathbf{z}^k)}}{\sum_{\mathbf{z}^k} P(\mathbf{z}^k) d^{m(\mathbf{z}^k)}} - 1\right] \log e = 0\end{aligned}$$

with equality only if $d^{\rho m(\mathbf{z}^k)} = \sum_{\mathbf{z}^k} P(\mathbf{z}^k)\, d^{\rho m(\mathbf{z}^k)}$ for all $\mathbf{z}^k$. The last condition can be satisfied only if $m(\mathbf{z}^k)$ is constant for all $\mathbf{z}^k$, and this, with (26), implies that $P(\mathbf{z}^k) = c^{-k}$ for all $\mathbf{z}^k$. But the last condition would make the left- and right-hand sides of (24) equal, which is contrary to the assumption. Thus, the first inequality in (2) holds. Next, if $m \ge \max_{\mathbf{z}^k} \{m(\mathbf{z}^k)\}$, then for $\rho_0 > 0$

$$\sum_{\mathbf{z}^k} P(\mathbf{z}^k) d^{\rho_0 (m(\mathbf{z}^k) - m)} \le 1 \qquad (31)$$

with equality if and only if $m(\mathbf{z}^k) = m$ for all $\mathbf{z}^k$. We have shown that this violates (26). On the other hand, an inequality in (31) would violate the assumption that $\rho_0$ satisfies (5). We may thus conclude that the right-hand inequality of (2) holds as well. Q.E.D.

The numbers (26) are not necessarily integers, so they cannot be used directly as code-word lengths. Thus, the natural quasi-optimal assignment that satisfies (25) and guarantees the existence of a prefix code suitable for buffer encoder instrumentation is

$$m(\mathbf{z}^k) = -\left[\log \frac{P(\mathbf{z}^k)^{1/(1+\rho)}}{\sum_{\mathbf{z}^k} P(\mathbf{z}^k)^{1/(1+\rho)}}\right]^- + 1 \qquad (32)$$

where the 1 is added to accommodate the requirement that no code word start with a 0 (actually the 1 could be replaced by adding the number $\log(1 - d^{-1})$ to the logarithm inside the $[\ ]^-$ sign). Since $P(\mathbf{z}^k) = \prod_{i=1}^k Q(z_i)$ for a discrete memoryless channel, we obtain (see (32))

$$\frac{1}{\rho} \log \left(\sum_{\mathbf{z}^k} P(\mathbf{z}^k) d^{\rho m(\mathbf{z}^k)}\right) \le \frac{k}{\rho} \log \left[\sum_{z} Q(z)^{1/(1+\rho)}\right]^{1+\rho} + 2 \qquad (33)$$

so that $\rho_0$ pertaining to the bound (22) will be at least as large as the solution $\rho_1$ of (see (27))

$$\frac{1}{\rho} E_s(\rho) = \frac{m-2}{k} \qquad (34)$$

which is unique, positive, and finite, provided

$$H(Z) < \frac{m-2}{k} < \log c. \qquad (35)$$

Relations (32) and (35) will also ensure the satisfaction of (2).

It should be noted from (32) that for $\rho = 0$, the quasi-optimal lengths $m(\mathbf{z}^k)$ are those that minimize the average

$$\bar{m} = \sum_{\mathbf{z}^k} P(\mathbf{z}^k) m(\mathbf{z}^k).$$

As $\rho$ and, therefore, rate $R = m/k$ increase, the longer code words are getting shorter, and the shorter are getting longer, until at $\rho = \infty$ all the code words have the same length, i.e., $m(\mathbf{z}^k) = k \log c$. At larger rates, the optimal average is being sacrified for a smaller variance, thus reducing the overflow probability.

Comparing the definition (27) of $(1/\rho)E_s(\rho)$ with definition (1) of Rényi's generalized entropy[12] $I_\gamma(Q)$, we see that

$$\frac{1}{\rho} E_s(\rho) = I_{(1-\rho)/\rho}(Q).$$

Thus, we may conclude from Theorems 1 and 2 that for $B$ sufficiently large, $\bar{N}$ can be bounded by (see (23))

$$\bar{N} \le (g_1 B + g_2 \log B)\, d^{-\rho B}$$

provided the instantaneous word encoder in Fig. 1 is designed to instrument a quasi-optimal code of word length $k$ and rate

$$R \ge I_{(1-\rho)/\rho}(Q) + 2/k.$$

This result constitutes the first operational (from a coding point of view) justification[2] of the concept of Rényi's entropy.

[2] For previous attempts to link coding with Rényi's entropy, see the work of Campbell.[14],[15]

## V. Construction of an Easily Instrumentable Quasi-Optimal Instantaneous Code

Since the buffer strategy given in the flow chart of Fig. 2 is simple to carry out, the suggested source coding scheme will be practically useful if a method can be found that generates some easily encodable and decodable quasi-optimal instantaneous code. In this section, we will display encoders and decoders corresponding to the Elias[5] source coding scheme. In Section VI, their complexity will be shown to grow linearly with the encoded message block length $k$ if the encoder alphabet size $d$ is a power of 2, and to grow, at worst quadratically with $k$ otherwise.

Define the auxiliary probability distribution

$$Q_\rho^*(z) \triangleq \frac{Q(z)^{1/(1+\rho)}}{\sum_z Q(z')^{1/(1+\rho)}}; \qquad z \in \{0, 1, \cdots, c-1\} \tag{36}$$

and note that if $\rho \geq 0$ and $Q(0) \geq Q(1) \geq \cdots \geq Q(c-1)$, then $Q_\rho^*(0) \geq Q_\rho^*(1) \geq \cdots \geq Q_\rho^*(c-1)$. If the source is constant, discrete, and memoryless, then

$$\frac{P(\mathbf{z}^k)^{1/(1+\rho)}}{\sum_{\mathbf{z}_0^k} P(\mathbf{z}_0^k)^{1/(1+\rho)}} = \frac{\prod_{i=1}^k Q(z_i)^{1/(1+\rho)}}{\sum_{\mathbf{z}_0^k} \prod_{i=1}^k Q(z_i^0)^{1/(1+\rho)}} = \prod_{i=1}^k Q_\rho^*(z_i). \tag{37}$$

Thus, a code will be quasi-optimal relative to $\rho$ if its word lengths are given by

$$m(\mathbf{z}^k) = -\left[\sum_{i=1}^k \log Q_\rho^*(z_i)\right]^- + 1. \tag{38}$$

With the above observation in mind, we are ready to state our version of Elias' sequential encoding algorithm.[3]

1) Defining $Q_\rho^*(-1) \triangleq 0$, compute

$$\pi(\mathbf{z}^k) \triangleq \sum_{i=-1}^{z_1-1} Q_\rho^*(i) + Q_\rho^*(z_1) \sum_{i=-1}^{z_2-1} Q_\rho^*(i) + \cdots + Q_\rho^*(z_{k-1}) \cdots Q_\rho^*(z_1) \sum_{i=-1}^{z_k-1} Q_\rho^*(i) + Q_\rho^*(z_k) Q_\rho^*(z_{k-1}) \cdots Q_\rho^*(z_1) \tag{39}$$

and

$$P_\rho^*(\mathbf{z}^k) = Q_\rho^*(z_k) Q_\rho^*(z_{k-1}) \cdots Q_\rho^*(z_1). \tag{40}$$

2) Express $\pi(\mathbf{z}^k)$ as an infinite, but unique, $d$-nary fraction

$$\pi(\mathbf{z}^k) = s_1(\mathbf{z}^k)d^{-1} + s_2(\mathbf{z}^k)d^{-2} + \cdots + s_l(\mathbf{z}^k)d^{-l} + \cdots \qquad s_i(\mathbf{z}^k) \in \{0, 1, \cdots, d-1\} \tag{41}$$

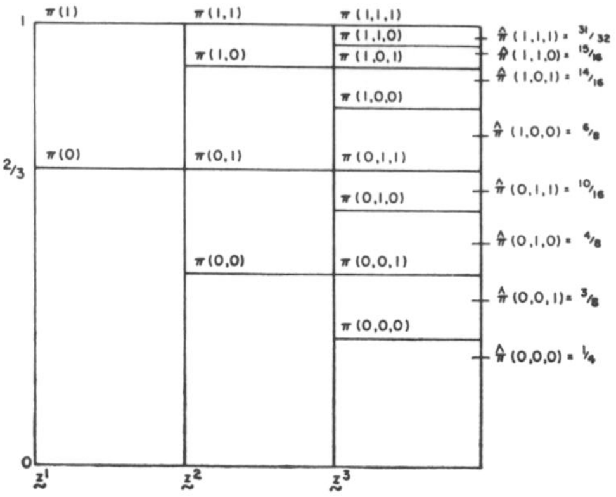


Fig. 3. Location of points $\pi(\mathbf{z}^k)$, $k = 1, 2, 3$, and $\hat{\pi}(\mathbf{z}^3)$ in the interval [0, 1], as determined by the sequential encoding algorithm for $c = d = 2$, $Q_\rho^*(0) = \frac{2}{3}$, $Q_\rho^*(1) = \frac{1}{3}$.

by choosing $s_i(\mathbf{z}^k)$ so that

$$0 \leq \left[\pi(\mathbf{z}^k) - \sum_{j=1}^{i} s_j(\mathbf{z}^k)d^{-j}\right] < d^{-i} \qquad \text{for all } i = 1, 2, \cdots.$$

3) Let the code word $\phi(\mathbf{z}^k)$ be the sequence

$$\phi(\mathbf{z}^k) = (s_1(\mathbf{z}^k), \cdots, s_{m(\mathbf{z}^k)}(\mathbf{z}^k)) \tag{42}$$

where

$$m(\mathbf{z}^k) = [-\log P_\rho^*(\mathbf{z}^k) + 1]^- \tag{43}$$

and $[\ ]^-$ stands for "integral part of."

A graphical illustration of the operation of the above algorithm in terms of successive subdivision of the unit interval is shown in Fig. 3. It is the one-to-one correspondence[4] between the points $\pi(\mathbf{z}^k)$ (see (41)) and the numerical equivalents

$$\hat{\pi}(\mathbf{z}^k) \triangleq s_1(\mathbf{z}^k)d^{-1} + \cdots + s_{m(\mathbf{z}^k)}(\mathbf{z}^k)d^{-m(\mathbf{z}^k)} \tag{44}$$

of the code words $\phi(\mathbf{z}^k)$ (see (42)) that assures unique decipherability provided the decoder can determine boundaries between successive code words. (For an example, see Fig. 3.) This can be done in either of two ways. One can precede each code word by a prefix that specifies the word length, or one can reserve a particular sequence of encoder symbols and use it as a comma between succeeding code words. Adopting the first straetgy, we change step 3) of the Elias sequential encoding algorithm as follows.

[3] A heuristic description of this algorithm is given in Abramson,[4] p. 61.

[4] For a detailed proof of this fact as well as for a more thorough exposition of the Elias scheme, see Jelinek,[9] Sec. A.4.

3′) Let code word $\phi_1(\mathbf{z}^k)$ be the sequence

$$\phi_1(\mathbf{z}^k) = (s_1^*(m(\mathbf{z}^k)), \cdots, s_n^*(m(\mathbf{z}^k)), s_1(\mathbf{z}^k), \cdots, s_{m(\mathbf{z}^k)}(\mathbf{z}^k)) \tag{45}$$

where $m(\mathbf{z}^k) = [-\log P_\rho(\mathbf{z}^k) + 1]^-$, and $s_i^*(m(\mathbf{z}^k))$, $i = 1, \cdots, n$ are $d$-nary symbols such that

$$m(\mathbf{z}^k) - \min_{\mathbf{z}_0^k} \{m(\mathbf{z}_0^k)\} = s_n^*(m(\mathbf{z}^k)) + s_{n-1}^*(m(\mathbf{z}^k))d^1 + \cdots + s_1^*(m(\mathbf{z}^k))d^{n-1}.$$

Since

$$\min_{\mathbf{z}_0^k} \{m(\mathbf{z}_0^k)\} \geq -k \log Q_\rho^*(0);$$

$$\max_{\mathbf{z}_0^k} \{m(\mathbf{z}_0^k)\} \leq -k \log Q_\rho^*(c-1) + 1,$$

it is sufficient if the prefix size $n$ satisfies

$$(d^n - 1) \geq k \log \frac{Q_\rho^*(0)}{Q_\rho^*(c-1)} + 1,$$

i.e., if

$$n(k) = \left[\log k + 1 + \log\left(\log \frac{Q_\rho^*(0)}{Q_\rho^*(c-1)} + \frac{2}{k}\right)\right]^-. \tag{46}$$

A simple flow chart of the sequential prefix encoding algorithm is given in Fig. 4. Each code word $\phi_1(\mathbf{z}^k)$ is preceded by the symbol 1 to make the outputs compatible with the buffer encoding strategy that prohibits the use of a 0 as an initial code word symbol. It should be noted that the algorithm does not store the symbols of the sequence $\mathbf{z}^k$, and that it generates outputs sequentially and in the right order.

The second method of making the Elias sequential code instantaneous requires, first, a selection of the comma character length $n$. With this number fixed, the steps 1, 2, and 3, of the original algorithm are carried out with an encoder alphabet of size $d_2 = d^n - 1$, the computations being governed by the probabilities $Q_{\rho_2}^*(z)$, $z \in \{0, 1, \cdots, c-1\}$, where $\rho_2 = \rho[\ln d^n/\ln (d^n - 1)]$. Each obtained symbol is then converted into a $d$-nary sequence of length $n$, and the code word is completed by appending the $n$ symbol "comma" $(d-1, d-1, \cdots, d-1)$. We will omit the analysis of this comma method and just state the following.

*Corollary 1 to Theorem 1*

Let a discrete memoryless channel of entropy $H(Z)$ governed by the probabilities $Q(0) \geq Q(1) \geq \cdots \geq Q(c-1)$ be given. If the transmitter rate $R = m/k$ satisfies

$$H(Z) < R - \frac{1}{k} n(k) < \log c \tag{47}$$

where $n(k)$ is given in (46), then (see (27))

$$\frac{1}{\rho} E_s(\rho) = R - \frac{1}{k} n(k) \tag{48}$$

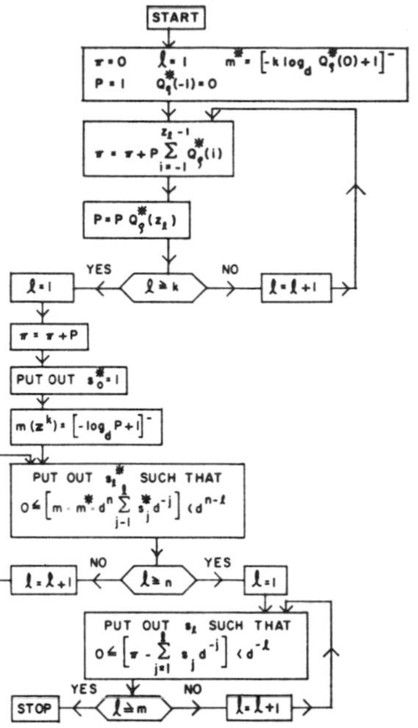


Fig. 4. Flow chart of the sequential encoding algorithm suitable, for use with a buffer instrumented encoder system. The algorithm uses given source probabilities $Q_\rho^*(\ )$ to encode sequences $\mathbf{z}^k$ into code words $\phi(\mathbf{z}^k)$. The definition $Q_\rho^*(-1) \triangleq 0$ is being used.

has a unique positive solution $\rho_0$. If the prefix version (i.e., steps 1, 2, 3′) of the sequential algorithm is used to realize the instantaneous encoder component of the buffer instrumented encoder system, then the latter's error performance will satisfy (22), provided the restarting position is determined by the rule (21). The above conclusion also holds for the comma version of the sequential algorithm if $n(k)$ is given by

$$n(k) = 2 \log \frac{Rk}{2} + 3 + \frac{2}{\ln d}\left(1 + \frac{2}{Rk}\left[\log \frac{Rk}{2} + 1\right]\right) \tag{49}$$

and $\log (Rk/2) + 1 \leq Rk/4$ is satisfied.

We have not yet considered the decoding of our sequential code. How to find the length $m(\mathbf{z}^k)$ from either the initial subsequence $(s_1^*, \cdots, s_n^*)$, or from the location of the comma character $(d-1, \cdots, d-1)$ is trivial and need not be discussed. Once $m(\mathbf{z}^k)$ is known, the problem is to compute $\mathbf{z}^k$ from $(s_1, \cdots, s_{m(\mathbf{z}^k)})$. It is shown in Jelinek,[9] Sec A.4, that this can be done recursively and without error. A flow chart of a decoder of the sequential prefix code (corresponding to the encoder of

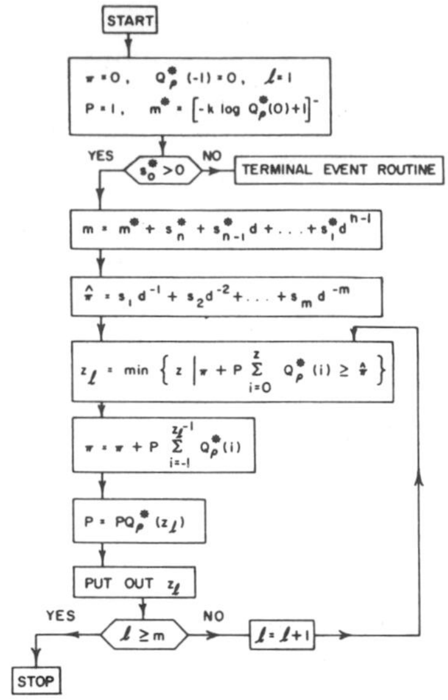


Fig. 5. Flow chart of the sequential decoding algorithm corresponding to a buffer instrumented encoder system. The algorithm uses given source probabilities $Q_\rho^*(\ )$ to decode code words $(\mathbf{s}^{*n}, \mathbf{s}^m)$, where $m = f(\mathbf{s}^{*n})$, into source sequences $\mathbf{z}^k$. The definition $Q_\rho^*(-1) \triangleq 0$ is being used.

Fig. 4) is provided in Fig. 5. The required modification that would result in a sequential comma decoder is trivial.

In conclusion, we remark that the minimal error probability encoding for a rate $R = m/k \geq H(Z) + 1/k$ would be achieved by solving the equation

$$R - \frac{1}{k} = \frac{1}{\rho_0} E_s(\rho_0)$$

for $\rho_0$, and then constructing the code words by the Huffman[13] procedure corresponding to the probabilities $Q_{\rho_0}^*(z)$. It is, of course, the difficulty of instrumenting this encoding scheme that necessitates the compromise involved in Elias' encoding.

## VI. Coder Complexity and Conclusions

To assess the effectiveness of buffer instrumented variable length coding, we must compare its error performance with that of block coding, and find the rate of growth of complexity with increasing message block size $k$.

It is shown in Jelinek,[9] Ch. 5, that $P_a$, the probability of ambiguity of an optimal block code that encodes message sequences of length $k$ into code words of length $m = Rk$, is bounded by

$$d^{-k\alpha_L(R,k)} \leq P_a \leq d^{-k\alpha_U(R)} \tag{50}$$

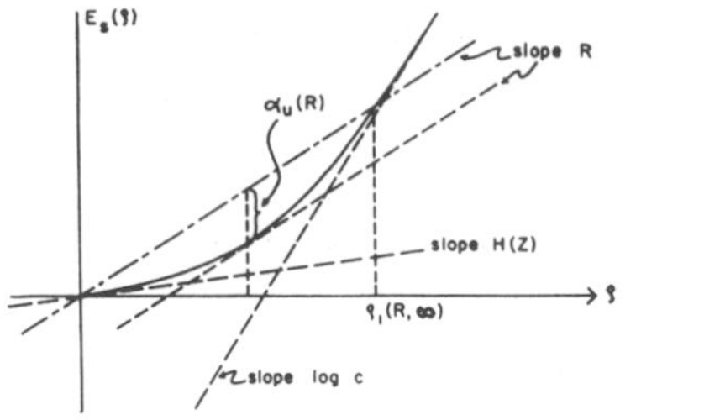


Fig. 6. Relation between the optimal block coding exponent $\alpha_U(R)$ and the limiting buffer instrumented variable length encoding exponent $\rho_1(R, \infty)$.

where

$$\lim_{k\to\infty} \alpha_L(R, k) = \alpha_U(R). \tag{51}$$

The exponent $\alpha_U(R)$ is given by the parametric relation (see (27))

$$\alpha_U(R) = \delta E_s'(\delta) - E_s(\delta) \tag{52}$$

where $\delta$ is the unique solution of

$$R = E_s'(\delta). \tag{53}$$

$\alpha_U(R)$ is positive and finite for

$$H(Z) < R < \log c \tag{54}$$

and is infinite for $R \geq \log c$.

On the other hand, from the relation (23) that follows the statement of Theorem 1 and from Corollary 1, we see that the bound on $\bar{N}$, corresponding to the buffer instrumented code with the instantaneous encoder component (see Fig. 1) realized by either of the two varieties of the sequential algorithm, is given asymptotically by (24)

$$\bar{N} \leq (g_1 B + g_2 \log B)\, d^{-\rho_0(R,k)B} \tag{24}$$

where $\rho(R, k)$ is a unique solution of (48) that is positive and finite if (47) is satisfied.

Since $\lim_{k\to\infty} (1/k)n(k) = 0$, it is easy to compare the exponents $\alpha_U(R)$ and $\rho_0(R, \infty)$. This is done in Fig. 6. It is seen there that if $H(Z)$ is very small and $\log c$ is very large, then at least for some rates $R$, $\rho_0(R, \infty) < \alpha_U(R)$. In general, the relation would seem to be the opposite one. A large $\log c$ coupled with a small $H(Z)$ indicates that some outputs are very probable and most are very improbable. Hence, it is only reasonable that, in this case, block coding, which effectively ignores the improbable source outputs, would be more efficient. However, it should be kept in mind that the bounds (50) are valid only for optimal block codes that are difficult to instrument. The modification of the Elias sequential algorithm required to obtain a practical block encoding scheme leads to considerably worse exponents than $\alpha_U(R)$, and these become infinite only for rates $R > -\log Q(c - 1)$ (see Jelinek,[9] Sec. 5.3). For best results, one ought to combine the good features of the block and the variable length coding methods. In such a scheme, some set $\mathfrak{I}^c$ of improbable source output sequences would be provided with a single code word, and the remaining sequences would get their own separate code words. However, these code words would be of nonuniform length. One would then optimize the overall probability of error by varying the size of the ambiguous set $\mathfrak{I}^c$. The possibilities of this approach are being investigated at Cornell University.

It is interesting to note that the same relation between $\rho_0(R, \infty)$ and $\alpha_U(R)$ holds also between the error-determining parameters corresponding to sequential and block channel coding. The block coding exponent $E_U(R)$ is based on a function $E_2(\delta)$ through relationships (52) and (53), and the Pareto parameter[10],[11] $\gamma(R)$ that determines the probability of buffer overflow in sequential decoding is the solution of

$$R = \frac{E_2(\gamma)}{\gamma}.$$

Let us now turn to the discussion of the encoder's complexity. From the flow chart of Fig. 2, it follows that the complexity of the restarting computer is independent of the message block length $k$, and depends on the buffer size $B$ through the size of the registers needed to store the variables listed in Table I, and through the computation effort expended during overflow to convert $\lambda$ (the number of code words erased from the buffer) into the bookkeeping code word $s_1(\lambda), \cdots, s_\omega(\lambda)$. It is obvious that the register size grows linearly with $B$, and it will be seen that the conversion effort grows, at worse, as $\omega^2$. But $\omega \sim \log B$, so the infrequently required conversion process presents no problems. The decoder's device corresponding to the restarting computer is, at worse, as complicated as the latter.

The encoder and decoder of Figs. 4 and 5, respectively, operate independently of the buffer size $B$. The structure of these algorithms does not depend on the block length $k$ at all. Hence, their complexity is a function of the accuracy required to compute the numbers $P_\rho^*(\mathbf{z}^k)$ and $\pi(\mathbf{z}^k)$, and of the computation effort required to determine $m(\mathbf{z}^k)$ and the code word $\phi(\mathbf{z}^k)$.

In any actual situation, the numbers $Q_\rho^*(z)$, $z \in \{0, 1, \cdots, c-1\}$ available to the decoder and encoder can, at best, be good estimates of the corresponding intrinsic parameters of the information source. There exists, therefore, some integer $\lambda > 0$ such that it is satisfactory to express all probabilities $Q_\rho^*(z)$ by

$$Q_\rho^*(z) = q(z)\, d^{-\lambda} \tag{55}$$

where $q(z) < d^\lambda$ is a positive integer for all $z \in \{0, 1, \cdots, c-1\}$. The product $P_\rho^*(\mathbf{z}^k)$ is then given by

$$P_\rho^*(\mathbf{z}^k) = Q_\rho^*(z_k)Q_\rho^*(z_{k-1}) \cdots Q_\rho^*(z_1) = q(z_k)q(z_{k-1}) \cdots q(z_1)d^{-k\lambda} \tag{56}$$

and all the other terms in the sum (39) are also integral multiples of $d^{-k\lambda}$. Since computers perform binary arithmetic, all computations would involve binary representations of $\pi(\mathbf{z}^k)\, d^{k\lambda}$ and $P(\mathbf{z}^k)\, d^{k\lambda}$ (instead of $\pi(\mathbf{z}^k)$ and $P(\mathbf{z}^k)$) and would thus be carried out by manipulation of the integers $g(z)$. Since both $P(\mathbf{z}^k)$ and $\pi(\mathbf{z}^k)$ are points in the interval $[d^{-k\lambda}, 1]$, they can be accurately determined with the help of binary registers containing no more than $[k\lambda \log d + 2]^-$ stages. It follows from (39) and (56) that the consequent computing effort would grow linearly with $k$.

Let us next analyze the problem of accurate computation of $m(\mathbf{z}^k)$. Given any $\mathbf{z}^k$, $P_\rho^*(\mathbf{z}^k)$ will be uniquely expressible as a $d$-nary fraction

$$P_\rho^*(\mathbf{z}^k) = \alpha_0\, d^{-r} + \alpha_1\, d^{-(r+1)} + \cdots \tag{57}$$

where $\alpha_0$ is a member of the set $\{1, 2, \cdots, d-1\}$, $\alpha_i \in \{0, 1, \cdots, d-1\}$, $i > 0$, and for at least one $i \geq 0$, $\alpha_i < (c-1)$. Then,

$$-\log_d P_\rho^*(\mathbf{z}^k) = r + \log_d (\alpha_0 + \alpha_1 d^{-1} + \cdots) < r + 1 = m(\mathbf{z}^k)$$

where the last equality follows from (43). Thus, the problem is reduced to one of finding the order of the highest nonzero coefficient in the $d$-nary expansion of $P_\rho^*(\mathbf{z}^k)$, or rather of $P_\rho^*(\mathbf{z}^k)\, d^{k\lambda}$, which is actually available in the computer. It can easily be shown (see Jelinek,[9] Sec. A.4) that the corresponding computational effort grows quadratically with $k$ if $d$ is not a power of 2, and otherwise grows linearlv with $k$.

The determination of the code word $\phi(\mathbf{z}^k)$ requires a conversion of $\pi(\mathbf{z}^k)\, d^k$ from a binary to a $d$-nary representation that can again be accomplished with an effort that grows quadratically with block size $k$ for $d$ not a power of 2, and linearly with $k$ otherwise.

The preceding conclusions should be kept in mind when trying to decide whether the prefix or the comma variety of the Elias sequential algorithm should be used. The comma variety has the advantage that an error in a code-word symbol causes only an error in the decoding of the corresponding message block $\mathbf{z}^k$, and, at worst, an error in the next block as well (if the symbol error occurred in the comma part of the code word). A symbol error in a code word of a prefix code may cause decoding errors in all the succeeding message blocks. Since it follows from (46), (48), and (49) that the error performance of the comma code is only slightly inferior, this code seems preferable. On the other hand, for comma codes the encoding and decoding is done with the alphabet $d_2 = d^n - 1$ which, except for $d = 3$, $n = 2$, is never a power of 2. Thus, the encoders and decoders of comma codes grow necessarily as the square of the message block length $k$, and this is their major disadvantage.

ACKNOWLEDGMENT

The author is indebted to P. Elias for allowing the publication of the sequential encoding algorithm, and to I. G. Stiglitz for calling the author's attention to the algorithm in another context.

REFERENCES

[1] C. E. Shannon, "A mathematical theory of communication," C. E. Shannon and W. Weaver, *The Mathematical Theory of Communication.* Urbana, Ill.: University of Illinois Press, 1949.

[2] L. G. Kraft, "A device for quantizing, grouping, and coding amplitude modulated pulses," M.S. thesis, Dept. of Elec. Engrg., Massachusetts Institute of Technology, Cambridge, Mass., 1949.

[3] B. McMillan, "Two inequalities implied by unique decipherability," *IRE Trans. Information Theory,* vol. IT-2, pp. 115–116, December 1956.

[4] N. Abramson, *Information Theory and Coding.* New York: McGraw-Hill, 1963.

[5] P. Elias, unpublished result.

[6] W. Feller, *An Introduction to Probability Theory and its Applications.* vol. 1, 2nd ed. New York: Wiley, 1957.

[7] ——, *An Introduction to Probability Theory and its Applications.* vol. 2. New York: Wiley, 1966.

[8] H. W. Kuhn and A. W. Tucker, "Nonlinear programming," *Proc. 2nd Berkeley Symp. on Math. Statistics and Probability,* Berkeley, Calif.: University of California Press, 1951, pp. 481–492.

[9] F. Jelinek, *Probabilistic Information Theory.* New York: McGraw-Hill, 1968.

[10] J. E. Savage, "Sequential decoding—the computation problem," *Bell Sys. Tech. J.*, vol. 45, January 1966.

[11] I. M. Jacobs and E. Berlekamp, "A lower bound to the distribution for sequential decoding," *IEEE Trans. Information Theory,* vol. IT-13, April 1967.

[12] A. Rényi, "On measures of entropy and information," *Proc. 4th Berkeley Symp. on Mathematical Statistics and Probability,* vol. 1. Berkeley, Calif.: University of California Press, 1961, pp. 561–574.

[13] D. A. Huffman, "A method of construction of minimum redundancy codes," *Proc. IRE,* vol. 40, September 1952.

[14] L. L. Campbell, "A coding theorem and Rényi's entropy," *Information and Control,* vol. 8, August 1965.

[15] L. L. Campbell, "Definition of entropy by means of a coding problem," *Z. Wahrscheinlichkeitstheorie verw. Geb.* vol. 6, pp. 113–118, 1966.

[16] D. Blackwell and M. A. Girshick, *Theory of Games and Statistical Decisions.* New York: Wiley, 1954.

# 6



Reprinted from *IEEE Trans. Inform. Theory,* **IT-18**(6), 765–774 (1972)

# On Variable-Length-to-Block Coding

FREDERICK JELINEK, SENIOR MEMBER, IEEE, AND KENNETH S. SCHNEIDER, MEMBER, IEEE

***Abstract*—Variable-length-to-block codes are a generalization of run-length codes. A coding theorem is first proved. When the codes are used to transmit information from fixed-rate sources through fixed-rate noiseless channels, buffer overflow results. The latter phenomenon is an important consideration in the retrieval of compressed data from storage. The probability of buffer overflow decreases exponentially with buffer length and we determine the relation between rate and exponent size for memoryless sources. We obtain codes that maximize the overflow exponent for any given transmission rate exceeding the source entropy and present asymptotically optimal coding algorithms whose complexity grows linearly with codeword length. It turns out that the optimum error exponents of variable-length-to-block coding are identical with those of block-to-variable-length coding and are related in an interesting way to Renyi's generalized entropy function.**

## I. Introduction

ENCODING of variable-length sequences of source outputs into codewords of constant length is called *variable-length-to-block coding*. It can be considered a generalization of run-length encoding [3] and is a technique of data compression that seems especially attractive for a skew source (where the frequency of some output letters very much exceeds that of others) or for retrieval situations that require block formatting of data. Variable-length-to-block coding was recently considered by Tunstall [7] who described an encoding construction and proved it optimal in a certain sense (see Section III).

In this paper we will apply variable-length-to-block coding to fixed-rate sources and channels. We will be concerned with the problems analyzed by Jelinek [2] for block-to-variable-length encoding: buffer overflow, construction of optimal codeword sets, and coding theorems. The overflow problem is important in real-time transmission of quantized data that are then encoded to minimize the overall rate. Gish and Pierce [9] have shown that when this approach is applied to Gaussian data, its performance is close to the rate-distortion optimum.

It will be shown in the Appendix that the fixed-rate source and channel concept can also serve as a model of an important problem in fast retrieval from storage of encoded (compressed) data. Thus, the applicability of buffer overflow results is not limited to communication situations.

Let us begin by considering Fig. 1, which consists of three objects; a constant memoryless source (henceforth abbreviated CMS), a fixed-rate noiseless channel (henceforth abbreviated FRC), and a user. The CMS emits digits $z$ in the $c$-ary alphabet $J_c = (0,1,\cdots, c-1)$ at the rate of one every second. These are independent and identically distributed random variables under the common probability distribution $\{Q(z)\}$. (The convention will be adopted that $Q(0) \leq Q(1) \leq \cdots \leq Q(c-1)$.) The FRC can accept digits in the $d$-ary alphabet $J_d = (0,1,\cdots, d-1)$ at its input and transmit them to its output without error. However, the channel can only accept digits for transmission at the rate of one every $(\log d)/R$ seconds. The parameter $R$ is called the channel rate. Finally, the user is interested in learning the outputs of the CMS.

The task of the communication engineer is to employ the FRC as a link by which the user may learn the outputs of

Manuscript received September 15, 1970; revised February 6, 1972. This work was supported in part by NASA Contract NAS 2-5643.
F. Jelinek is with the School of Electrical Engineering, Cornell University, Ithaca, N.Y. 14850.
K. Schneider was with the School of Electrical Engineering, Cornell University, Ithaca, N.Y. 14850. He is now with the M.I.T. Lincoln Laboratory, Lexington, Mass.

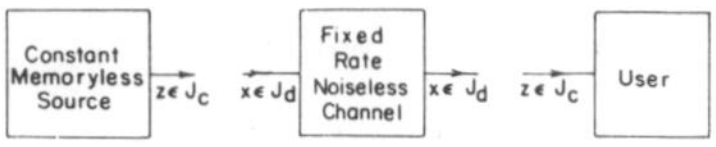

Fig. 1. Given information transmission entities.

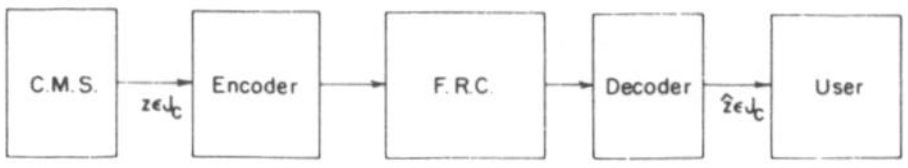

Fig. 2. Transmission system.

the CMS to within some tolerance of error. To this end, two devices called an encoder and decoder are introduced (see Fig. 2). The encoder accepts letters in the $c$-ary alphabet that cause it to generate outputs in the $d$-ary channel alphabet. The decoder accepts $d$-ary letters as its inputs and generates outputs $\hat{z}$ in the $c$-ary source alphabet.

Since source sequences of variable length (called *source words*) are assigned codewords of constant length and since the source generates letters at a constant rate, the encoder generates outputs at a variable rate. Since the channel accepts letters also at a constant rate, the encoder outputs must be fed into a buffer that will tend to fill when a succession of short sourcewords is generated, and it will tend to empty when a succession of long sourcewords is generated. This presents the problem of buffer overflow and exhaust whose consequence is that the user will on occasion not be able to receive perfectly the digits put out by the source.

In this paper we will first derive a variable-to-block coding version of Shannon's first coding theorem proving that perfect decoding is possible at all rates exceeding the source entropy, provided that sufficiently large codeword sets are used (Section III). We then introduce a specific scheme for variable-length-to-block encoding of fixed-rate source information for transmission through fixed-rate channels (Section IV). Such coding necessitates occasional buffer overflow, and we bound the consequent probability of error $P(e)$ as a function of varying rate (Section V) and obtain the sourceword assignments that minimize the former (Section VI). In fact, we shall show that

$$(1/B) \log_d P(e) \approx -\rho,$$

where $B$ is the buffer length and $\rho$ is positive provided that $R$ exceeds $H(Z)$, the entropy of the source. In Section VII we derive for every source distribution $\{Q(z)\}$ an expression for $R^*(\rho)$, the rate above which the error exponent $\rho$ is achievable with a word set of sufficiently large size. In Section VIII we provide a variable-length-to-block coding and decoding algorithm whose complexity grows linearly with block-length $M$ and which, for $M$ sufficiently large, achieves the exponent $\rho$ at all rates $R > R^*(\rho)$. It turns out that $R^*(\rho)$ is identical to the minimal rate at which block-to-variable-length encoding achieves exponent size $\rho$ [2].

## II. Terminology

Before describing the actual variable-length-to-block coding model it will be convenient to introduce some of the terminology that will be used.

Let us begin by considering $w$, an arbitrary sequence of $c$-ary letters

$$w = z_1 z_2 \cdots z_{L(w)}, \tag{1}$$

where $L(w)$ is the length of the sequence.

Let $W(T)$ denote a $T$-element set of words $w$,

$$W(T) = \{w_i: 1 \leq i \leq T\}.$$

Let $w^*$ be an arbitrary $c$-ary sequence and let $z$ be an element of $J_c$. A new $c$-ary sequence $w = w^*z$ may be formed by appending $z$ to $w^*$ as a suffix. Definitions 1 and 2 describe two special properties that $W(T)$ may have.

*Definition 1:* Let $w_i$ and $w_j$ be elements of $W(T)$. If for every $i$ and $j$ $(i \neq j)$ $w_i$ is not a prefix of $w_j$, then $W(T)$ is called proper.

*Definition 2:* If every infinite length $c$-ary string has a prefix that is a word in $W(T)$, then $W(T)$ is called complete.

An example of a word set that is both complete and proper is $W(3) = (0,10,11)$.

The following lemmas concerning complete and proper word sets will now be stated. Their proofs are given by Schneider [4].

*Lemma 1:* $W(c) = J_c$ is complete and proper and it is the only complete and proper word set of size $c$.

*Lemma 2:* If $W(T)$ is a complete and proper word set of size $T$ and $w^*$ is an element of $W(T)$, then

$$W(T + c - 1) = \left\{(W(T) - w^*) \bigcup_{z \in J_c} w^*z\right\}$$

is a complete and proper word set of size $T + c - 1$. In this case $W(T + c - 1)$ is said to be an extension of $W(T)$ and $w^*$ is called the extending word.

*Lemma 3:* Let $W(T)$ be a complete and proper word set of size $T$. There exists a sequence $\{W_n\}$ with $W_n$ a complete and proper word set of size $c + (n - 1)(c - 1)$, $W_1 = J_c$, $W_{n+1}$ an extension of $W_n$, and $W(T)$ a member of the sequence.

*Lemma 4:* If $W(T)$ is a complete and proper word set of size $T$, then

$$T = c + n(c - 1)$$

for some integer $n \geq 0$.

From now on we will restrict our attention to complete and proper word sets $W(T)$ relative to a CMS. Any infinite output sequence of a CMS can be segmented into elements of $W(T)$ by the completeness property. The properness of $W(T)$ implies that only one partition of a realization into elements of $W(T)$ is possible. Thus, one may think of any source output sequence not only as an infinite string of $z$, but also of $w$. In this manner the constant memoryless $c$-ary information source may also be thought of as a $T$-ary information source, one putting out letters in the alphabet $W(T)$, although not at a constant rate.[1]

The $w$ that are emitted by the $T$-ary source are independent and identically distributed random variables. The distribution $\{Q(z)\}$ generates the following distribution on the alphabet $W(T)$. If $w = z_1 \cdots z_{L(w)}$ then

$$P(w) = \prod_{i=1}^{L(w)} Q(z_i). \tag{2}$$

Consider $w_i \in W(T)$. Let us assign a $d$-ary sequence $\Phi(w_i)$ to $w_i$ with the following properties. $\Phi(w_i)$ has length $M = 2 + \lfloor \log_d T \rfloor$ (the symbol $\lfloor y \rfloor$ will stand for "greatest integral value less than or equal to $y$"). The first letter of $\Phi(w_i)$ will be the digit "1" (the purpose of this tag will become apparent in Section IV). The remaining $1 + \lfloor \log_d T \rfloor$ digits will be the expansion to base $d$ of $i$, the index of $w_i$. The collection of $c$-ary source words and $d$-ary sequences, $\{w_i, \Phi(w_i)\}$, will be called a variable-length-to-block code defined on $W(T)$. $\Phi(w_i)$ will be called the codeword of $w_i$.

## III. A Source-Coding Theorem

A measure of the effectiveness of a variable-to-block coding scheme is the compression ratio

$$\frac{M \log d}{E[L(w)]}.$$

It is proportional to the average number of code digits per source output. Tunstall [7] proved that the following algorithm obtains for every admissible size $T = c + (n-1) \cdot (c-1)$ the complete and proper word set $W(T)$ minimizing the compression ratio.

*Algorithm 1:* Let $W^*(c) = J_c$; this is a complete and proper word set of size $c$.

Let $W^*(c + c - 1)$ be the complete and proper word set of size $(c + c - 1)$, which is formed from $W^*(c)$ by extending the most probable word in $W^*(c)$.

Let $W^*(c + 2(c-1))$ be the complete and proper word set of size $(c + 2(c-1))$, which is formed from $W^*(c + (c-1))$ by extending the most probable word in $W^*(c + c - 1)$.

Continue this procedure, forming $W^*(c + n(c-1))$ by extending the most probable word in $W^*(c + (n-1) \cdot (c-1))$, for $n = 1,2,\cdots$.

We will denote the minimal compression ratio by

$$R_{\min}(T) = \min_{W(T)} \frac{M \log d}{E[L(w)]}$$

and show that $R_{\min}(T)$ converges to the source entropy $H(Z)$ as $T \to \infty$.

*Lemma 5:* Consider a constant memoryless source. Let $W(T)$ be a complete and proper word set of size $T$ defined on $J_c$, the source alphabet. Let $\{P(w)\}$ be the distribution on $W(T)$ generated by $\{Q(z)\}$, the source statistics, and define

$$E(L(w)) = \sum_{w \in W(T)} P(w)L(w)$$

$$H(W) = -\sum_{w \in W(T)} P(w) \log P(w)$$

then,

$$H(W) = E(L(w))H(Z). \tag{3}$$

*Proof:* For $W(T)$ let $\{W_n\}$ be the sequence of Lemma 3 and define

$$E_n = \sum_{w \in W_n} P(w)L(w)$$

$$H_n = -\sum_{w \in W_n} P(w) \log P(w).$$

The lemma is obviously true for $W_1 = J_c$, so we only need to prove it for $W_{n+1}$ assuming it true for $W_n$. Let $w^*$ be the word that extends $W_n$ to $W_{n+1}$, i.e.,

$$W_{n+1} = \left\{(W_n - w^*) \bigcup_{z \in J_c} w^*z\right\}.$$

Then by the inductive hypothesis

$$\begin{aligned} H_{n+1} &= H_n + P(w^*) \log P(w^*) - \sum_{z \in J_c} P(w^*)Q(z) \\ &\quad \cdot \log P(w^*)Q(z) \\ &= H_n + P(w^*)H(Z) = [E_n + P(w^*)]H(Z). \end{aligned}$$

But

$$\begin{aligned} E_{n+1} &= E_n - P(w^*)L(w^*) + \sum_{z \in J_c} P(w^*)Q(z)[L(w^*) + 1] \\ &= E_n + P(w^*) \end{aligned}$$

Q.E.D.

Consider $W^*(a)$, the word set formed by Algorithm 1 that has size $a$. Define

$$\max(a) = \max_{w \in W^*(a)} P(w)$$

$$\min(a) = \min_{w \in W^*(a)} P(w) \tag{4}$$

and assume that the source-output letters are so ordered that

$$Q(0) \leq Q(1) \leq \cdots \leq Q(c-1). \tag{5}$$

*Lemma 6:*

$$\frac{\max(a)}{\min(a)} \leq \frac{1}{Q(0)}. \tag{6}$$

*Proof:* $W^*(a)$ was obtained from $W^*(a - (c-1))$ by extending the most probable codeword of the latter. Let $w^*$ be that codeword. Let us first assume that the least probable codeword of $W^*(a)$ is an extension of $w^*$, i.e.,

$$\min(a) = P(w^*)Q(0).$$

The most probable codeword has probability $\max(a) \leq$

[1] The properness requirement is a restriction that is not necessary for unique encoding and decoding. The word set (000,001,010,01,10,1) is not proper but could be used as a basis of a variable-length-to-block code based on the rule: "parse source output sequence into the longest sourcewords found in the set." Under such a rule $1110011\cdots$ would be parsed unambiguously as (1),(1),(10),(01),$(1\cdots)$. The properness restriction avoids many complications in analysis. In particular it allows a straightforward assignment of probability to sourcewords.

$P(w^*)$ so

$$\frac{\max(a)}{\min(a)} \le \frac{P(w^*)}{P(w^*)Q(0)} = \frac{1}{Q(0)}.$$

If, on the other hand, the least probable codeword of $W^*(a)$ was already a codeword of $W^*(a-(c-1))$, then

$$\frac{\max(a)}{\min(a)} \le \frac{P(w^*)}{\min(a-(c-1))} = \frac{\max(a-(c-1))}{\min(a-(c-1))}.$$

Hence, the lemma holds for $W^*(a)$ if it held for $W^*(a-(c-1))$. Since it clearly holds for $W^*(c)$, the lemma is proven by induction. Q.E.D.

*Theorem 1 (Source Coding):* For optimal variable-to-block word sets,

$$\lim_{T\to\infty} R_{\min}(T) = H(Z). \tag{7}$$

*Proof:* By our previous definition,

$$R_{\min}(T) = \frac{M \log d}{E(L(w))}$$

the expectation being with respect to the measure $P(w)$ induced by $W^*(T)$. If $H(Z) = 0$, then the source has only one possible output, so the theorem holds. Otherwise, since $M = 2 + \lfloor \log_d T \rfloor$ (see last paragraph of Section II), we get from Lemma 5 that

$$R_{\min}(T) = \frac{(2 + \lfloor \log_d T \rfloor) \log d}{H(W)} H(Z)$$

$$\ge \frac{\log d + \log T}{\log T} H(Z). \tag{8}$$

On the other hand, using (6)

$$H(W) \ge -\log \max(T) \ge \log Q(0) - \log \min(T)$$

$$\ge \log Q(0) + \log T$$

so that by Lemma 5

$$R_{\min}(T) \le \frac{2 \log d + \log T}{\log Q(0) + \log T} H(Z). \tag{9}$$

Q.E.D.

Theorem 1 constitutes a variable-length-to-block coding proof of the direct part of Shannon's first coding theorem.

## IV. Transmission of Variable-Length-to-Block Coded Information

The remainder of the paper is concerned with the use of variable-length-to-block coding for transmitting information from a fixed-rate source through a fixed-rate channel. The proposed system is shown in Fig. 3 and will be referred to as the "variable-length-to-block coding model." It consists of two codebooks, three buffers, and an object called a restart computer. The two codebooks $\Phi_e$ and $\Phi_d$ are based on $W(T)$, a complete and proper word set with the variable-length-to-block code defined upon it. The buffers called source buffer, encoder buffer, and transmitter buffer, are, respectively, $D$, $B + 2$, and $D$ stages long, where

$$M = 2 + \lfloor \log_d T \rfloor = \text{codeword length} \tag{10}$$

$$D = L(w_1). \tag{11}$$

The encoder buffer length $B + 1$ is assumed to be an integral multiple of $M$. The $l$th stage of the encoder buffer will be called the *restart position.*

An encoder buffer stage will be considered one stage-unit wide, overflow and exhaust barriers will be a fixed distance of $B$ stage units apart, the latter being locatable anywhere within the first stage unit. The encoder buffer pointer (EBP) will be capable of pointing at any buffer position. The read and write heads of the transmitter buffer move continuously clockwise, the former at a steady rate of $R/\log d$ stage units per second. Whenever the read head crosses a stage boundary, it reads the contents of that stage and inserts it into the fixed-rate channel.

Initially, the source buffer is empty, while the transmitter buffer and the first $l$ stages of the encoder buffer are filled with 0's. The read and write heads point at the first boundary of stage 1, the exhaust barrier is at the right boundary of stage 1, and the EBP points at the right boundary of stage $l$. At time zero everything is turned on simultaneously (i.e., the read head starts moving and reading, and the source puts out its first letter). The source buffer fills up with digits as they are being emitted by the CMS. It continues to do this until they constitute a word $W$ in $W(T)$. This must eventually take place because $W(T)$ is complete. When this word has been formed, the source buffer supplies it to $\Phi_e$, which has stored within it the variable-length-to-block code $\{w_i, \Phi(w_i)\}$. $\Phi_e$ inserts the codeword corresponding to the sourceword that has been supplied to it into the $M$ rightmost available stages of the encoder buffer (i.e., into stages $l, l+1, \cdots, l+r-1$). At this moment the read head is located exactly $L(w)R/\log d$ stage units past the write head. Let $\lambda$ be the number of empty transmitter buffer stages (here $\lambda = \lceil L(w)R/\log d \rceil$ where $\lceil a \rceil$ denotes the least integer that is greater than or equal to $a$). Then the encoder buffer shifts $\lambda$ stages to the right, the outshifted digits being written by the write head into the empty stages of the transmitter buffer. The write head is then moved up to the read head position and the EBP is moved $M - (L(w)R/\log d)$ stage units left (thus the EBP again points to the first empty stage, although not necessarily to its right boundary). $\Phi_e$ then erases the source buffer. This buffer then begins filling up with source digits again until a word in $W(T)$ is formed, and the operation continues as before. The source and transmitter buffers are of length $D$. Thus, the first never overflows and the second never exhausts.

This operation of the encoder continues (the EBP moving $M - L(w)R/\log d$ stage units left whenever a codeword corresponding to some sourceword $W$ is inserted) until the encoder buffer either overflows or exhausts.

An exhaust occurs if the EBP moves to the right of the exhaust barrier, which happens whenever the write head

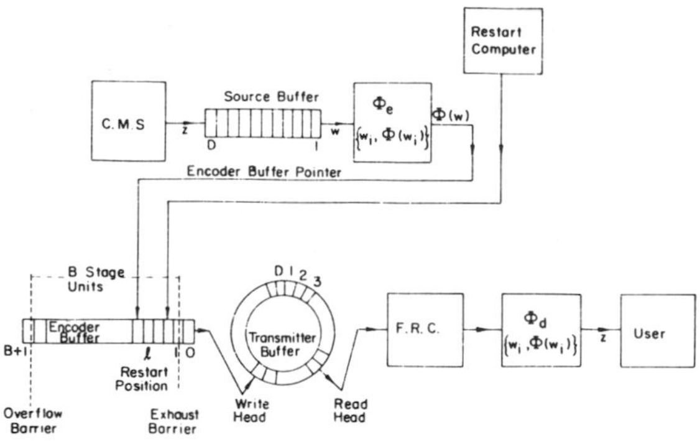


Fig. 3. Variable-length-to-block coding model.

cannot be supplied with all the digits it requires. If at this moment the read head is located $a$ units from the nearest preceding stage boundary, the EBP is moved $a$ units to the left of the right boundary of the $l$th stage. The exhaust barrier is moved to a position $a$ units to the left of the right boundary of the first stage. The restart computer then inserts a codeword that tells the user that an exhaust took place and follows it by as many dummy 0 digits as are needed to fill the remaining empty stages of the transmitter buffer and the first $l$ stages of the encoder buffer. The write head is pulled up to the read head. Thus the EBP will restart under conditions that are identical with initial conditions.

An overflow occurs if the attempted insertion of a codeword would place the EBP to the left of the overflow barrier. The restart computer then erases the entire encoder buffer except for any part of the rightmost stored codeword and inserts a codeword telling the user that an overflow took place and how many codewords were lost. Insertion of an appropriate number of dummy digits and an appropriate positioning of the EBP and of the overflow and exhaust barriers then allows restarting of the encoder buffer under conditions identical with the initial conditions.

We omit any discussion of the decoder beyond assuring the reader that it can be so arranged that except for overflowed codewords, the user will always know exactly what was put out by the source. When an overflow occurs, the overflow codeword will tell the user how many source digits were lost. The devices of Fig. 3 and their operation are quite similar to those of Jelinek [2, Fig. 1]. A detailed description was given there, and with its help an interested reader can develop a complete model for the present system.

It may be useful to point out that the EBP performs a random walk on the encoder buffer that will be crucial to our analysis. At each restart, the EBP is exactly $l$ stage units to the left of the exhaust barrier and $B - l$ stage units to the right of the overflow barrier.

In analyzing the performance of the variable length-to-block coding model we will be interested in the average per digit probability of error, defined as

$$\bar{P}(e) = \lim_{n \to \infty} \frac{1}{n} \sum_{i=1}^{n} P(e_i), \tag{12}$$

where

$$P(e_i) = \Pr \left\{ \begin{matrix} \text{user does not learn the identity} \\ \text{of the } i\text{th digit out of the CMS} \end{matrix} \right\}. \tag{13}$$

Upper and lower bounds to $\bar{P}(e)$ will be derived.

## V. Bounds on $\bar{P}(e)$

Define

$$E_i = \left\{ \begin{matrix} \text{event of an overflow on} \\ \text{the } i\text{th step of the EBP} \end{matrix} \right\} \tag{14}$$

$$A_i = \left\{ \begin{matrix} \text{a terminal event (an overflow or} \\ \text{exhaust) on the } i\text{th step of the EBP} \end{matrix} \right\} \tag{15}$$

$h_i$ = number of source letters lost on the $i$th step of the EBP. Of course $h_i$ equals 0 if overflow does not occur on the $i$th EBP step. If

$$N' = \lim_{i \to \infty} E[h_i], \tag{16}$$

then it can be shown that (see Schneider [4, pp. 298–300])

$$\frac{R}{M \log d} N' \le \bar{P}(e) \le 2N'. \tag{17}$$

Therefore, we will develop bounds on $N'$. If overflow occurs on a step of the EBP then at least one and at most $BL^*/M$ digits will be lost due to erasure, where $L^* = \max L(w)$. Hence

$$P(E_i) \le E[h_i \mid E_i]P(E_i) = E[h_i] \le (BL^*/M)P(E_i).$$

Define

$$F(x) = \Pr \left( \begin{matrix} \text{encoder buffer overflows before it exhausts} \\ \text{if the restart position of EBP is } x \text{ units to} \\ \text{the left of the exhaust barrier} \end{matrix} \right). \tag{18}$$

At each restart of the variable-length-to-block coding model the conditions on the CMS and buffers are identical. Thus, terminal events and overflows are recurrent. For definition see Feller [5]. This immediately implies that

$$\lim_{i\to\infty} P(E_i) = F(l) \lim_{i\to\infty} P(A_i) = \frac{1}{E[T']} F(l), \tag{19}$$

where $T'$ is the number of EBP steps before the first terminal event. Therefore,

$$\bar{P}(e) \begin{cases} \leq 2 \dfrac{BL^*}{M} F(l) \\ \geq \dfrac{R}{M \log d} \dfrac{F(l)}{E[T']}. \end{cases} \tag{20}$$

Let

$$s(w) = M - L(w)R/\log d \tag{21}$$

be the size of the EBP step when the codeword corresponding to sourceword $w$ is inserted into the encoder buffer. Then it follows from standard random walk theory (see Kemperman [10, p. 64]) that if $E[s(w)] < 0$ then

$$F(l) \begin{cases} \leq K_1 e^{-(B-l)r} \\ \geq K_2 e^{-(B-l)r}, \end{cases} \tag{22}$$

where $r$ is the unique positive root of the equation

$$E[e^{rs(w)}] = 1. \tag{23}$$

It remains to upper bound $E[T']$. Define $w^i$ as the $i$th $w$ emitted by the CMS and *dist* as the net distance traveled by the EBP from the time the variable-length-to-block coding model is started until the first terminal event. Then

$$E[\text{dist}] = E\left\{\sum_{i=1}^{T'} \left(M - \frac{L(w^i)R}{\log d}\right)\right\}$$
$$\leq (B + L^* - l)F(l) - l(1 - F(l)). \tag{25}$$

Applying Wald's lemma to (25), we get

$$E[T'] \leq \frac{l - (B + L^*)F(l)}{E\{(L(w^i)R/\log d) - M\}} \tag{26}$$

and using (22), the right-hand side is surely positive for $B$ sufficiently large. We can now combine (20), (22), and (26) into the following theorem.

*Theorem 2:* The probability of error of transmission through a fixed-rate channel of variable-length-to-block coded information (using a complete and proper word set $W(T)$) generated by a constant memoryless fixed-rate source is bounded by

$$K_3 d^{-\nu_0 B \log d/R} \leq \bar{P}(e) \leq K_4 d^{-\nu_0 B \log d/R}, \tag{27}$$

where $B$ is the buffer length, $R$ is the transmission rate, $d$ is the channel alphabet, and $\nu_0$ is the largest nonnegative solution of

$$\log_d \left[\sum_{w\in W(T)} P(w)\, d^{\nu((M \log d/R) - L(w))}\right] = 0. \tag{28}$$

$\nu_0$ will be positive (and thus the bound (27) nontrivial) provided

$$R > \frac{M \log d}{E(L(w))}.$$

*Remark:* Detailed formulas for the constants $K_3$ and $K_4$ can be found on [4, pp. 133 and 145].

Since by Theorem 1 the codes produced by Algorithm 1 are such that $R_{\min}(T) \to H(Z)$, we can conclude the following.

*Corollary:* For size $T$ sufficiently large, Algorithm 1 produces word sets $W(T)$ for which $\nu_0 > 0$ whenever the coding rate $R$ exceeds the entropy $H(Z)$.

## VI. The Optimal Word Set

It would be desirable to specify an algorithm that would construct a complete and proper word set $W(T)$ maximizing the exponent $\nu_0$ for any given transmission rate $R$ (Algorithm 1 does not do this!). By the end of the next section we will be able to do just that, but for the time being we are forced to proceed in the opposite direction: given $\nu_0 > 0$, we will find the word set $W_{\nu_0}(T)$ maximizing

$$-\log_d \sum_{w\in W(T)} P(w)\, d^{-\nu_0 L(w)}. \tag{30}$$

The root $R$ called $R(\nu_0,T)$ (see Fig. 4) of

$$\frac{\nu_0 M \log d}{R} = -\log_d \sum_{w\in W_{\nu_0}(T)} P(w)\, d^{-\nu_0 L(w)} \tag{31}$$

will then have the following significance (since (28) and (31) impose the same condition).

i) For any complete and proper word set $W(T)$ ($T$ fixed) and any transmission rate $R < R(\nu_0,T)$, the error exponent will be less than $\nu_0$.

ii) For rates $R \geq R(\nu_0,T)$ the exponent $\nu_0$ will be achievable with the word set $W_{\nu_0}(T)$.

In the next section we will obtain an asymptotic formula $R(\nu)$ for $R(\nu,T)$. Then given a desired transmission rate $R$, we will be able to find the root $\nu_0$ of $R = R(\nu)$ and use the word set $W_{\nu_0}(T)$ to achieve approximately the exponent $\nu_0$, the approximation being tighter with increasing word set size $T$.

*Algorithm 2:* $W_{\nu_0}(T)$ is constructed in the following way. Begin with $W_{\nu_0}(c) = J_c$. Form $W_{\nu_0}(c + (c - 1))$ by extending that word in $W_{\nu_0}(c)$ that has $P(w)d^{-\nu_0 L(w)}$ largest. Form $W_{\nu_0}(c + 2(c - 1))$ by extending that word in $W_{\nu_0}(c + (c - 1))$ that has $P(w)d^{-\nu_0 L(w)}$ largest. Continue this procedure until a word set of size $T$ is formed.

*Theorem 3:* The word set $W_{\nu_0}(T)$ maximizes the quantity (30).

Let $W(T)$ be some complete and proper word set and let $\lambda$ denote the empty word. Let $\lambda, w_1, \cdots, w_n$ denote the nodes in the tree corresponding to $W(T)$ that have been extended (cf. Lemma 3) and let the indexing be such that

$$1 = P(\lambda) \geq P(w_1)\, d^{-\nu_0 L(w_1)} \geq P(w_2)\, d^{-\nu_0 L(w_2)} \geq \cdots$$
$$\geq P(w_n)\, d^{-\nu_0 L(w_n)}. \tag{32}$$

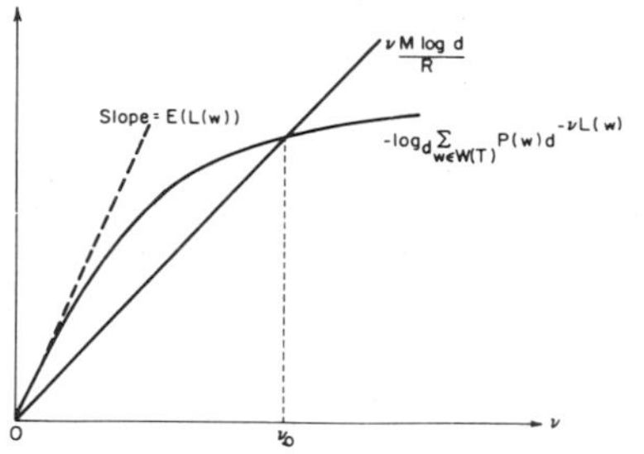


Fig. 4. $\nu_0$-defining curves.

It is easy to see that if $i < j$ then $w_i$ cannot be an extension of $w_j$. The words $\{w_i\}$ define a sequence of complete and proper word sets $\{W_i\}$ such that $W_i$ is an extension $W_{i-1}$ and $W_n = W(T)$. Then

$$\begin{aligned}\sum_{W(T)} P(w)\, d^{-\nu_0 L(w)} &= \sum_{W_{n-1}-w_n} P(w)\, d^{-\nu_0 L(w)} + P(w_n) \sum_z P(z/w_n)\, d^{-\nu_0 [L(w_n)+1]} \\ &= \sum_{W_{n-1}} P(w)\, d^{-\nu_0 L(w)} - P(w_n)\, d^{-\nu_0 L(w_n)} (1 - d^{-\nu_0}).\end{aligned}$$

It follows from above by recursion that

$$\sum_{W(T)} P(w)\, d^{-\nu_0 L(w)} = d^{-\nu_0} - (1 - d^{-\nu_0}) \cdot \sum_{i=1}^{n} P(w_i)\, d^{-\nu_0 L(w_i)}.$$

We wish to prove that Algorithm 2 minimizes the above expression, or equivalently that it maximizes the quantity

$$\sum_{i=1}^{n} P(w_i)\, d^{-\nu_0 L(w_i)}. \tag{33}$$

It is only necessary to show that the set $W(T)$ that maximizes (33) is obtainable by extending the optimal word set $W(T - (c - 1))$ through the word $w^* \in W(T - (c - 1))$ that maximizes $P(w) d^{-\nu_0 L(w)}$. This statement is clearly true for $T = c$. We must show that it holds for $T = c + n(c - 1)$ when it holds for $T = c + k(c - 1)$, $k = 1,2,\cdots,n - 1$.

Let $\lambda, w_1, \cdots, w_n$ be the extension words of the optimal $W(T)$, let $\lambda_1, w_1', \cdots, w_{n-1}'$ be the extension words of the optimal $W(T - (c - 1))$, and let $w_n'$ be the word that Algorithm 2 would use to extend $W(T - (c - 1))$. Of course, the indexing satisfies (32).

Let $j$ be the least integer such that $w_j \neq w_j'$. Then since $W(T - (c - 1))$ is obtained by Algorithm 2,

$$P(w_j')\, d^{-\nu_0 L(w_j')} > P(w_j)\, d^{-\nu_0 L(w_j)} \cdots$$

Now $w_j$ is either one of the words $w_{j+1}', \cdots, w_n'$, or

$$P(w_j)\, d^{-\nu_0 L(w_j)} < P(w_n')\, d^{-\nu_0 L(w_n')}.$$

In the latter case, because of the index rule (32), $W(T)$ could not be optimal.

Let us then assume that $w_j = w_l'$ where $l \in \{j + 1, \cdots, n\}$. Now $w_{j+1}$ is a direct extension of one of the words $\lambda, w_1, \cdots, w_j$. It must therefore be either identical with one of the words $w_{l+1}', \cdots, w_n'$, or it must be different from all the words $\lambda, w_1', \cdots, w_n'$. In the latter case it is an extension of one of the words $\lambda, w_1', \cdots, w_{j-1}', w_l'$ that Algorithm 2 never extended, and therefore

$$P(w_{j+1})\, d^{-\nu_0 L(w_{j+1})} < P(w_n')\, d^{-\nu_0 L(w_n')}$$

so $W(T)$ cannot be optimal. Therefore $w_{j+1} = w_{l+k}'$ for some $k \geq 1$. Continuing in this manner we see that eventually for some $m \in \{j + 1, \cdots, n\}$,

$$P(w_m)\, d^{-\nu_0 L(w_m)} < P(w_n')\, d^{-\nu_0 L(w_n')}$$

and at the same time

$$P(w_{j+k})\, d^{-\nu_0 L(w_{j+k})} \leq P(w_{l+k})\, d^{-\nu_0 L(w_{l+k})}$$

so that the quantity (33) is for $W(T)$ smaller than it would be for the best extension of $W(T - (c - 1))$. This contradicts our assumption that $w_j \neq w_j'$ for some $j$. Hence $W(T)$ is the best extension of $W(T - (c - 1))$. Q.E.D.

Unfortunately, the complexity of instrumentation of any code produced by Algorithm 2 grows linearly with $T$, i.e., exponentially with the codeword length. We will treat this problem in the last section.

It is interesting to note that the preceding proof of the theorem does not involve any use of the memoryless character of the source. The algorithm is optimal for all sources.

## VII. The Rate Above Which the Exponent $\nu_0$ is Achievable With a Word Set of Sufficiently Large Size $T$

As defined in the preceding sections, $R(\nu_0,T)$ is the transmission rate for which (and not below which) there exists a complete and proper word set of size $T$ that when used will result in a probability of error $\bar{P}(e)$ whose exponent is $\nu_0$. We would like to relate $R(\nu_0,T)$ to the probability distribution $Q(z)$ of the source. We shall only succeed in the limit of large $T$. Our result is summarized in the following theorem.

*Theorem 4:* For $\nu_0 > 0$ and $H(Z) > 0$,

$$R(\nu_0) = \lim_{T\to\infty} R(\nu_0, T) = \nu_0 \log d/(r - 1), \tag{34}$$

where $r$ is the unique positive root of

$$\sum_{z \in J_c} (Q(z) d^{-\nu_0})^{1/r} = 1. \tag{35}$$

*Proof:* By (31) and the definition of codeword length $M$,

$$R(\nu_0,T) = \frac{\nu_0 (\log d)(2 + \lfloor \log_d T \rfloor)}{-\log_d \sum_{W_{\nu_0}(T)} P(w) d^{-\nu_0 L(w)}}. \tag{36}$$

Applying the argument of Lemma 6 to the word sets $W_{\nu_0}(T)$, we get

$$f(T) \triangleq \max_{w \in W_{v_0}(T)} P(w)d^{-v_0 L(w)}$$
$$\leq \frac{d^{v_0}}{Q(0)} \min_{w \in W_{v_0}(T)} P(w)d^{-v_0 L(w)} \quad (37)$$

and, therefore,

$$R(v_0) = \lim_{T\to\infty} R(v_0,T) = v_0 \log d \left[ \lim_{T\to\infty} \frac{\log_d T}{-\log_d Tf(T)} \right] \quad (38)$$

so that our problem is to estimate the function $f(T)$. Let $\{W_n\}$ be the extension sequence of word sets whose member is $W_{v_0}(T)$ (see Lemma 3). Then for all $n$ and any $r \neq 0$ [cf. (33)]

$$\sum_{W_{n+1}} [P(w)d^{-v_0 L(w)}]^{1/r}$$
$$= \sum_{W_n} [P(w)d^{-v_0 L(w)}]^{1/r} - [P(w^*)d^{-v_0 L(w^*)}]^{1/r} \cdot \left\{1 - \sum_{J_c} [Q(z)d^{-v_0}]^{1/r}\right\}, \quad (39)$$

where $W_{n+1} = \{W_n - w^*\} \cup \{w^*z : z \in J_c\}$. Hence if $r$ satisfies (35), the left-hand side of (39) is invariant to $n$ so that

$$\sum_{W_{v_0}(T)} [P(w)d^{-v_0 L(w)}]^{1/r} = \sum_{W_1} [P(w)d^{-v_0 L(w)}]^{1/r}$$
$$= \sum_{z} [Q(z)d^{-v_0}]^{1/r} = 1. \quad (40)$$

It follows directly from (40) and (37) that

$$TQ(0)d^{-v_0}f(T)^{1/r} \leq 1 \leq Tf(T)^{1/r}$$

and hence that

$$\lim_{T\to\infty} \frac{\log T}{-\log Tf(T)} = \frac{1}{r-1}. \quad (41)$$

Equation (41) combined with (38) then gives (34). Standard convexity arguments establish that (35) indeed has a unique positive root. Q.E.D.

*Remark:* The original lengthy proof of this theorem can be found in [4, pp. 162–176]. Its merit is that it is constructive, i.e., the fact that $\sum P(w)d^{-v_0 L(w)} \approx T^{1-r}$ follows from direct consideration of Algorithm 2, which forces (35) to hold. A crucial lemma in that derivation is due to Kesten [8]. The observation that the invariance property (40) leads to a considerable shortening of the proof was made by Forney.

The form of Theorem 4 is inconvenient in that it gives $R(v_0)$ in terms of the parameter $r$. Let us try to eliminate this deficiency by fixing $r$ and solving for $v_0$. From (35),

$$v_0 \log d = r \log \sum_{z \in J_c} Q(z)^{1/r} \quad (42a)$$

so that [see (34)]

$$R(v_0) = \frac{r}{r-1} \log \sum_{z \in J_c} Q(z)^{1/r} \quad (42b)$$

is the rate at which [see (27)]

$$\lim_{B\to\infty} \frac{1}{B} \log_d \bar{P}(e) = -v_0 \log d / R(v_0).$$

Substituting (42a) and (42b) into the above equation we conclude that exponent $(r - 1)$ is achievable at all rates exceeding the right-hand side of (42b). Making the change of variable

$$\rho = r - 1$$

we get the following theorem.

*Theorem 5*[2]*:* As the word-set size $T \to \infty$, the error probability satisfies

$$\lim_{B\to\infty} -\frac{1}{B} \log_d \bar{P}(e) \geq \rho.$$

at all rates $R$ exceeding the limiting rate

$$R^*(\rho) = \frac{1}{\rho} \log \left[ \sum_{z \in J_c} Q(z)^{1/(1+\rho)} \right]^{1+\rho}.$$

Comparing Theorem 5 with Theorem 2 of [2] we can conclude that for any given rate $R$ the marginal limiting buffer overflow exponents $\rho$ obtainable for variable-length-to-block and block-to-variable-length encodings are the same! Furthermore, $R^*(\rho)$ is the Renyi entropy of order $1/(1 + \rho)$ and the present theorem confirms the fundamental nature of that quantity. Of course, $\lim_{\rho\to 0} R^*(\rho) = H(Z)$, as expected.

The function $R^*(\rho)$ also determines the error exponent of block-to-block coding that maps blocks of length $K$ of some digits into uniform-length codewords. In Jelinek [1] it is shown that the optimum block-coding scheme has its performance characterized by

$$\lim_{K\to\infty} -(1/K) \log P_{AMB} = \alpha_u(R)$$

where

$$\alpha_u(R) = \max_{\rho} \rho[R - R^*(\rho)]$$

$P_{AMB}$ = Pr (a block codeword cannot be correctly decoded).

It is interesting to speculate what are the consequences of this equivalence between variable-length-to-block and block-to-variable-length coding. First, one would tend to conjecture that removing the unnecessary requirement that source words satisfy the prefix condition will leave the $R^*(\rho)$ function unchanged and will therefore not have any asymptotic consequences on buffer overflow performance. Secondly, the completely general variable-length-to-variable-length encoding will also not affect the $R^*(\rho)$ curve.

Theorem 5 allows us to determine the limiting transmission rate $R^*(\rho)$ at which exponent $\rho$ is achievable provided the optimal code of the preceding section is used. The more

[2] This simplification of Theorem 4 was discovered by Jelinek while lecturing at the 1972 summer program of the International Center for Mechanical Sciences, Udine, Italy. Stimulating discussions with I. Csiszar, which led to this advance, are gratefully acknowledged.

usual case is that a rate $R > H(Z)$ is given, and it is desired to construct a code whose exponent $\rho$ is maximal. Algorithm 2 requires knowledge of $v_0$ specified by (42a). By Theorem 5 one simply solves $R = R^*(\rho)$ and obtains $v_0$ via (42a):

$$v_0 = \log \left[ \sum_{z \in J_c} Q(z)^{1/(1+\rho)} \right]^{1+\rho}$$

## VIII. Instrumentable Quasi-Optimal Coding

In this section we will describe an instrumentable encoder–decoder pair that will allow the fixed-rate system of Fig. 3 to achieve any exponent $v_0 > 0$ at transmission rates $R$ arbitrarily close to $R(v_0)$. The coder will simultaneously parse the source output sequence $z_1, z_2, \cdots$ into a sequence of variable length subsequences $w^1, w^2, \cdots$, and will generate the appropriate codewords $\Phi(w^i)$ of block length $M$ corresponding to the latter. The decoder will recover from the sequence $\Phi(w^1), \Phi(w^2), \cdots$, the source output sequence $z_1, z_2, \cdots$.

For a fixed $\rho > 0$

$$Q^*(z) = \frac{Q(z)^{1/(1+\rho)}}{\sum_z Q(z)^{1(1+\rho)}}, \qquad z \in J_c, Q^*(-1) \triangleq 0. \quad (43)$$

Because of (5), $Q^*(i) \geq Q^*(i-1)$. Our encoding algorithm is a modification of the Elias scheme (see Jelinek [1, pp. 92–97]) and utilizes a parameter $\tau$ that also helps to define the block length $M$ as the smallest integer satisfying

$$M \geq \log_d \tau - \log_d Q^*(0) + 1. \quad (44)$$

*Algorithm 3:*

1) Set $P_0 \leftarrow 1, \pi_0 \leftarrow 0, j \leftarrow 0.$

2) Set $j \leftarrow j + 1$

$$\pi_j \leftarrow \pi_{j-1} + P_{j-1} \sum_{i=-1}^{z_j - 1} Q^*(i)$$

$$P_j \leftarrow P_{j-1} Q^*(z_j).$$

3) If $P_j > \tau^{-1}$ go to 2, otherwise continue.

4)

$$w = z_1, z_2, \cdots, z_j; \qquad \pi(w) = \pi_j; \qquad P^*(w) = P_j.$$

5) Express $\pi(w)$ uniquely as a $d$-ary fraction

$$\pi(w) = s_1 d^{-1} + s_2 d^{-2} + \cdots + s_{M-1} d^{-M+1} + \cdots \quad s_i \in J_d.$$

6) The codeword is

$$\Phi(w) = 1, s_1, s_2, \cdots, s_{M-1}.$$

The above algorithm is certainly simple to carry out. However, we must show that $\pi(w) \in (0,1)$ as implied by step 5, and that to each codeword $\Phi(w)$ there corresponds at most one sequence $w$. Note first that if $w = z_1, z_2, \cdots, z_n$ then

$$\pi(w) = \sum_{i=-1}^{z_1 - 1} Q^*(i) + Q^*(z_1) \sum_{i=-1}^{z_2 - 1} Q^*(i) + \cdots + Q^*(z_1) Q^*(z_2) \cdots Q^*(z_{n-1}) \sum_{i=-1}^{z_n - 1} Q^*(i).$$

The points $\pi(w)$ are arranged lexicographically. In fact, let $w = z_1, \cdots, z_{i-1}, z_i, \cdots, z_n$, and $w' = z_1, \cdots, z_{i-1}, z_i', \cdots, z_m'$ where $z_i' < z_i$. Then

$$\begin{aligned} \pi(w) - \pi(w') &\geq Q^*(z_1) \cdots Q^*(z_{i-1}) Q^*(z_i') \left[ 1 - \sum_{i=-1}^{z_{i+1}'-1} Q^*_{(i)}(i) - \cdots - Q^*(z_{i+1}') \cdots Q^*(z_{m-1}') \sum_{i=-1}^{z_m'-1} Q^*(i) \right] \\ &\geq Q^*(z_1) \cdots Q^*(z_{i-1}) Q^*(z_i') Q^*(c-1)^{m-i} \geq P^*(w'). \end{aligned} \quad (45)$$

Thus $\min \pi(w) = 0$ and $\max \pi(w) = 1 - Q^*(c-1)^n$ where $n$ is the length of the sequence $w$ that consists only of the letters $z = c - 1$. It follows that $\pi(w) \in (0,1)$ as implied in (5).

To prove that the codewords are distinct, note that the encoding rule maps $\pi(w)$ onto the point

$$\hat{\pi}(w) = s_1 d^{-1} + s_2 d^{-2} + \cdots + s_{m-1} d^{-m+1} \quad (46)$$

so that the codewords will be distinct if $\pi(w') < \hat{\pi}(w)$ whenever $\pi(w') < \pi(w)$. By (45) this will be satisfied if for all $w'$,

$$P^*(w') \geq d^{-M+1}. \quad (47)$$

Because of the stopping rule 3,

$$P^*(w')/Q^*(0) > \tau^{-1}$$

so codewords will be distinct if (44) holds.

We next turn to the design of the decoder. Since (45) and (47) are assumed to hold, we need only to find the largest point $\pi(w)$ satisfying

$$\pi(w) < s_1 d^{-1} + s_2 d^{-2} + \cdots + (s_{M-1} + 1) d^{M-1} = \hat{\pi}^*.$$

This is done as follows.

*Algorithm 4:*

1) Set $P_0 \leftarrow 1, \pi_0 \leftarrow 0, j \leftarrow 0.$

2) Set $j \leftarrow j + 1$

$$z_j \leftarrow \min \left[ z : \pi_{j-1} + P_{j-1} \sum_{i=0}^{z} Q^*(i) \geq \hat{\pi}^* \right]$$

$$\pi_j \leftarrow \pi_{j-1} + P_{j-1} \sum_{i=-1}^{z_j - 1} Q^*(i)$$

$$P_j \leftarrow P_{j-1} Q^*(z_j).$$

3) If $P_j > \tau^{-1}$ go to 2, otherwise continue.

4) The source sequence is $w = z_1, z_2, \cdots, z_j$.

Our last task is to prove Theorem 6.

*Theorem 6:* Let the transmission rate $R$ of the encoder system of Fig. 3 be such that $R > R^*(\rho)$ for some $\rho > 0$. If the code of the present section is used with $\tau$ sufficiently large, then

$$\overline{P(e)} \leq K d^{-\rho B}. \quad (48)$$

*Proof:* Let $r = \rho - 1$ and define $v_0$ by (42a). By Theorem 2, the bound (48) holds provided

$$\frac{v_0 M \log d}{R} \leq -\log_d \sum_{W(T)} P(w) d^{-v_0 L(w)} = -\log_d \sum_{W(T)} P^*(w)^r. \tag{49}$$

Because of step 3 of the encoding algorithm, the right-hand side of (49) exceeds $-\log_d T\tau^{-r}$. Let $q^*(w)$ denote the $Q^*$-probability of the last digit of $w$. By (36), (43), and step 3,

$$1 = \sum_{W(T)} P^*(w) \geq \sum_{W(T)} \frac{P^*(w)}{q^*(w)} Q^*(0) \geq Q^*(w)\tau^{-1}T.$$

Therefore (49) will hold whenever

$$(v_0 M \log d)/R \leq (r - 1) \log_d \tau + \log_d Q^*(0).$$

Since $M$ is the smallest integer satisfying (44), we may conclude that (48) will hold provided

$$R \geq \frac{v_0 \log d[\log_d \tau - \log_d Q^*(0) + 2]}{(r - 1) \log_d \tau + \log_d Q^*(0)}. \tag{50}$$

Since the right-hand side of (50) converges to $R(v_0)$ as $\tau \to \infty$, the theorem is proved. Q.E.D.

*Remark:* A crucial step in the preceding proof was inequality (44), which guarantees distinctness of codewords provided (45) holds. But this is so only if $Q^*(c - 1) = \max Q^*(z)$. So the $Q^*$-ordering of source outputs is vital to the success of our encoding algorithm.

### Acknowledgment

The authors wish to thank Prof. H. Kesten of Cornell University who provided a crucial step in the original proof of Theorem 4.

## Appendix

### Retrieval of Compressed Data and the Fixed-Rate Model

In this Appendix we wish to indicate why buffer overflow results are of interest in applications involving retrieval of compressed data. We will treat the case of variable-length-to-block coding but the same problems arise also in block-to-variable-length coding.

Suppose variable-length-to-block encoded data are stored on tape, disk, or in core. In a typical retrieval situation one might wish to obtain data starting with the $k$th and ending with the $(k + m - 1)$th source output. Suppose encoding is done according to the rules of Section IV, corresponding to rate $R$ and buffer size $B$, i.e., the exhaust strategy of insertion of dummy letters is being followed. Then on the average, the $k$th source output will be encoded in the $t(k)$th codeword, where

$$t(k) = \left\lfloor \frac{R}{M \log d} k \right\rfloor + 1. \tag{A1}$$

Furthermore, the probability $P(K,B)$ that the $k$th source output is encoded into one of the codewords

$$\{t(k), t(k + 1), \cdots, t(k) + (B/M) - 1\} \tag{A2}$$

will be equal to the probability that in the transmission situation buffer overflow would not take place before the $k$th digit was put out of the source.

The knowledge that the $k$th source output was encoded into one of the codewords of (A1) is not sufficient for the decoder to identify the former without first decoding all the preceding codewords. This difficulty may be eliminated in many ways, one of which is as follows.

The recorded information is encoded in sequence from the beginning of the tape until the first $B$-buffer overflow takes place. When it does, the tape location of the codeword that caused the overflow (i.e., did not fit into the buffer) is noted and so is the sequence order of the first source letter it represents. The overflowing codeword is then relocated to the restart location of the buffer, and the recording of information continues until the next overflow takes place, etc. At the end of recording an overflow table is created of sequence orders $k$ of first source letters of overflowing codewords and of the tape addresses $A(k)$ of the latter. To make retrieval faster one additional refinement is introduced. After every $N$ codewords, a special marker codeword is entered that states the difference between the actual and expected sequential order of the first source letter encoded by the next codeword. (The expected order is one that the letter would have if exactly $E[L(w)]$ source letters were encoded into each codeword.)

The retrieval of the $k$th source output would proceed as follows. The computer finds the largest entry $l$ not exceeding $k$ in the overflow table and its tape address $A(l)$. It then goes to the tape address $A(l) + t(k - l)$ and backs up from there to the nearest preceding marker codeword. It then determines the sequential order of the first source letter of the codeword following the marker codeword, and starts to decode beginning with that codeword until it finds the desired information. The latter is located at worst in the $(N + B/M)$th codeword decoded.

It is obvious that if the probability of buffer overflow is small, the overflow table will be short and so will the search for the desired information. Ordinarily, the overflow table would be stored at the beginning of the tape and would be transferred into core whenever the tape was to be used extensively.

### References

[1] F. Jelinek, *Probabilistic Information Theory.* New York: McGraw-Hill, 1968.
[2] F. Jelinek, "Buffer overflow in variable length coding of fixed rate sources," *IEEE Trans. Inform. Theory*, vol. IT-14, pp. 490–501, May 1968.
[3] S. W. Golomb, "Run-length encodings," *IEEE Trans. Inform. Theory* (Corresp.), vol. IT-12, pp. 399–401, July 1966.
[4] K. S. Schneider, "Reliable data compression of constant rate Markov sources for fixed rate channels," Ph.D. dissertation, Cornell University, Ithaca, N.Y., June 1970.
[5] W. Feller, *An Introduction to Probability Theory and Its Applications*, 2nd ed., vol. 1. New York: Wiley, 1957.
[6] A. L. Johns, "A proof of Wald's lemma on cumulative sums," *Ann. Math. Statist.*, vol. 30, p. 1245, 1959.
[7] B. P. Tunstall, "Synthesis of noiseless compression codes," Ph.D. dissertation, Georgia Inst. Technol., Atlanta, 1968.
[8] H. Kesten, personal communication.
[9] H. Gish and J. N. Pierce, "Asymptotically efficient quantizing," *IEEE Trans. Inform. Theory*, vol. IT-14, pp. 676–683, Sept. 1968.
[10] J. H. B. Kemperman, *The Passage Problem for a Stationary Markov Chain.* Chicago: Univ. Chicago Press, 1961.

# 7



Reprinted from *Proc. Seventh Hawaii Intern. Conf. System Sci.*, 1974, pp. 46–48

# JOINT SOURCE AND CHANNEL ENCODING

**Martin E. Hellman**

*Stanford University*

Abstract

In certain communication problems, such as remote telemetry, it is important that any operations performed at the transmitter be of a simple nature, while operations performed at the receiver can be orders of magnitude more complex. Channel coding is well matched to such situations, while conventional source coding is not. In this paper we propose a joint or one-step source and channel coding scheme which is well matched to this asymmetric complexity requirement. The encoder is a convolutional encoder and the decoder is a type of sequential decoder. If the channel is noiseless, this system reduces to an optimal noiseless source encoder which is simpler than any other known to date.

## 1. INTRODUCTION

The purpose of noiseless source coding is to remove redundancy from data prior to transmission. The purpose of channel coding is to add redundancy to the data in order to allow correction of most errors which occur in transmission. If source coding removes redundancy and channel coding adds it back in, why not dispense with both operations and use the natural redundancy of the source for error correction? A simple example shows why this cannot be done. Suppose the message "I AM NOT ABLE TO PROVIDE SUPPORT." is transmitted directly and a single character is received in error: "I AM NOW ABLE TO PROVIDE SUPPORT." is received. Not only is the error overlooked, but the meaning of the message has been reversed. This is in spite of the fact that the amount of redundancy is more than sufficient to correct single errors. Although the redundancy is large it is not evenly distributed.

## 2. ERROR PROPAGATING CODES

We have developed a very simple device to transform the redundancy of the source into a usable form. This joint source and channel encoder is a convolutional encoder. It consists of a shift register and a number of mod-2 adders. A typical rate one encoder with sixteen stages is shown in Figure 1 at the end of this paper. Usually 10-100 stages will be more than adequate. The output bits are transmitted over the noisy channel and placed through the decoder which performs the inverse operation of the encoder (see Figure 2 at end of paper). It is seen that because of the feedback in the decoder, even a single transmission error will cause many errors in the decoded information. If there are enough stages in the encoder then the output following an error is complete gibberish. For example a single character error in the message used above can cause the output: "I AM NOWJ.MXAAVWM,E WTROVBGZ, RI." It is easily seen that the characters most likely to be in error are the W and the J of NOWJ... . A first attempt would be to change the J of NOWJ... to a blank, making the text "I AM NOW...". This puts two errors in the decoder, the first being due to the channel, the second being due to our attempted correction. Thus the output is again gibberish: "I AM NOW HU.CVKIWXRORBHUWTZHUIGK*" When we try correcting the W we find the output is meaningless except when the proper correction to a T is tried. This example used a 5 bit code with star = 00000, A = 00001,... Z = 11010, blank = 11011, period = 11100, comma = 11101, quote = 11110, question mark = 11111. Low order bits were encoded first. This code has lower redundancy than most codes in common use (e.g., ASCII) and therefore even greater correction capabilities exist with these other codes.

Note the simplicity of both the encoder and the feedback decoder, each consisting of a shift register and several exclusive OR gates. The only complexity involved is in recognizing what is and what is not a meaningful message and in deciding which errors are most likely. It is the necessity of having such a capability which makes the receiver more complex than the transmitter. This requirement can be met by having a sequential decoder at the receiver. The sequential decoder need not have a complete description of the source characteristics, but of course a less complete description doesn't allow as great an error correction capability.

## 3. SEQUENTIAL DECODER

The sequential decoder is very similar to the usual sequential decoder used for channel decoding. However the metric is now modified to include the source statistics. For a discrete memoryless source with probability distribution $q(u)$, and a discrete memoryless channel with transition matrix $p(y|x)$ the metric increment is

$$m = \ln[q(u)p(y|x)/p(y)].$$

Using arguments from the theory of brahcing random walks it can be shown that reliable decoding takes place so long as the rate of the source is less than the capacity of the channel.

Thus far we have only seen a rate one code. Rate 1/n codes are obtained in the usual way. Rate k codes are obtained by shifting k bits into the encoder at once and only making one transmission. Rate k/n codes are obtained by the obvious extension. Note that what is usually referred to as a rate one half source code corresponds to a rate two channel code.

Koshelev [IEEE Trans. Info. Th., IT-19, 340-343, 1973] independently realized the applicability of convolutional codes to joint source and channel coding and investigated the computational requirements of the sequential decoder.

## 4. DISCUSSION

It is interesting to note that these codes do not require knowledge of the source statistics for encoding, this information being required only by the sequential decoder for metric evaluation. Again this is well matched to the asymmetric complexity requirements of remote telemetry.

If a rate one code is used and the sequential decoder is not used then the output of the feedback decoder can be used for error detection provided the recipient of the decoded information can distinguish between meaningful and meaningless source sequences. Very little additional hardware is required to implement this; there is no loss in rate, and yet significant error detection is obtained.

Figure 1

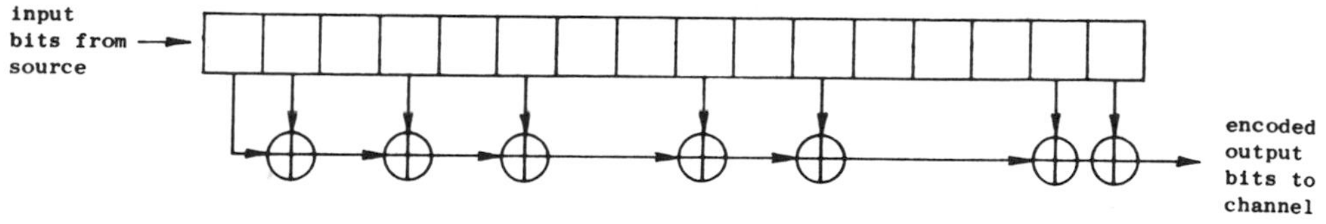


Figure 2

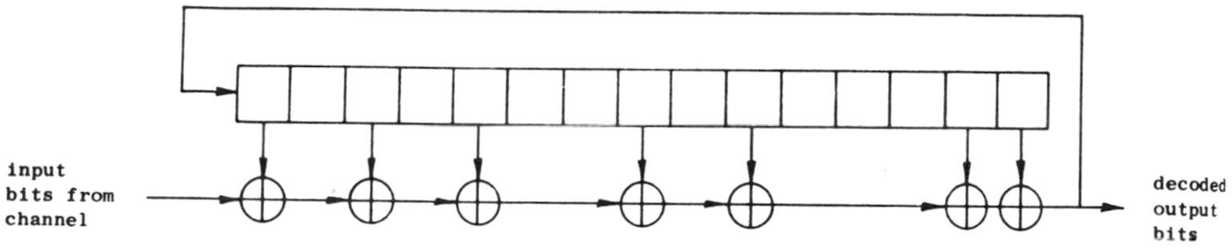

# 8



Reprinted from *Proc. IEEE,* **54**(10), 1490–1491 (1966)

# SEQUENCE TIME CODING FOR DATA COMPRESSION

In the type of data compression operation which removes data samples that are considered redundant by a given compression algorithm [1], it is necessary to send information about the time of occurrence of the remaining nonredundant samples. If a time word is sent periodically, then the *relative* times of occurrence of nonredundant samples in the interval between periodic time words may be considered a strictly monotonic sequence with a fixed maximum length.

This sequence may be encoded and decoded by means of the following procedure.

Consider a total of $m$ sample time intervals between periodic time words. Then there are a maximum of $m-1$ samples to be compressed, and assume that in a given situation $q$ of the $m-1$ samples are left for transmission. These $q$ samples can form a total of $N_q$ strictly increasing sequences, where by the combinatorial formula

$$N_q = \binom{m-1}{q}. \qquad (1)$$

The matter of actually encoding and decoding these sequences can be examined by slightly modifying a method developed by Gordon [2] for nondecreasing monotonic sources. In Gordon's method, a *path-count matrix* is constructed from which a *coding matrix* is derived, which is used for both encoding and decoding. The same general procedure is used here; however, the resulting matrices are different from those of the nondecreasing monotonic source.

The various $q$-length sequences out of $m-1$ elements may be represented as a matrix of points as shown in Fig. 1(a). This figure is drawn for an actual case of $m=9$ and $q=6$. This is obviously not a good example of worthwhile compression, but these numbers are used for convenience in illustrating the techniques involved. The first periodic time word is represented by the *start* point, where all paths start. Likewise, the second periodic time word is represented by the *end* point, where all paths end. The strictly increasing monotonicity of the sequences sets two parallel lines at an angle of 45 degrees passing through the *start* and *end* points as upper and lower boundaries for the possible paths. At each point in the matrix the number of *different* paths from the start point up to that point is shown on the figure as a *path count.* The total number of paths can be obtained by adding the path counts at the points immediately *before* the end point. In the example in Fig. 1(a) this is calculated as

$$N_q = 21 + 6 + 1 = 28 = \binom{8}{6} = \binom{m-1}{q}.$$

The coding technique consists of encoding each sequence as the sum of a set of numbers corresponding to each path. These numbers are obtained from the *coding* matrix, which matrix is otbained from the *path-count* matrix as follows.

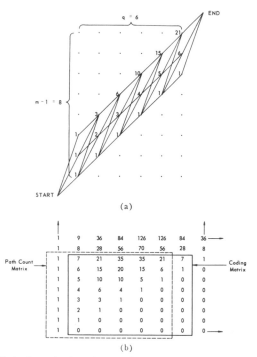

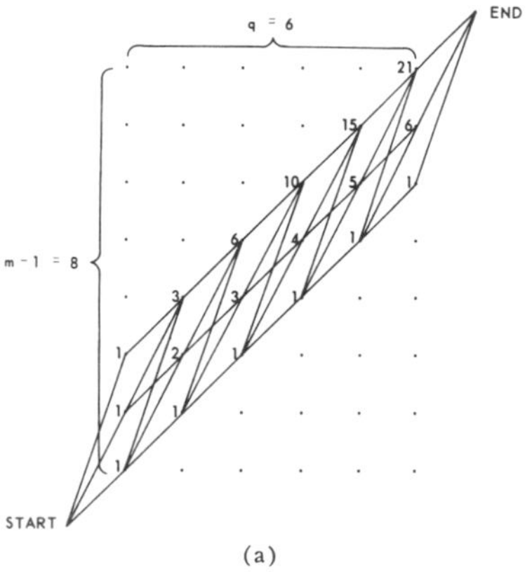


(a)

Path Count Matrix (inner dashed box) / Coding Matrix (outer solid box)

| | | | | | | | |
|---|---|---|---|---|---|---|---|
| 1 | 9 | 36 | 84 | 126 | 126 | 84 | 36 |
| 1 | 8 | 28 | 56 | 70 | 56 | 28 | 8 |
| 1 | 7 | 21 | 35 | 35 | 21 | 7 | 1 |
| 1 | 6 | 15 | 20 | 15 | 6 | 1 | 0 |
| 1 | 5 | 10 | 10 | 5 | 1 | 0 | 0 |
| 1 | 4 | 6 | 4 | 1 | 0 | 0 | 0 |
| 1 | 3 | 3 | 1 | 0 | 0 | 0 | 0 |
| 1 | 2 | 1 | 0 | 0 | 0 | 0 | 0 |
| 1 | 1 | 0 | 0 | 0 | 0 | 0 | 0 |
| 1 | 0 | 0 | 0 | 0 | 0 | 0 | 0 |

(b)

Fig. 1. Construction of a coding matrix from a path-count matrix for a strictly increasing monotonic sequence. (a) Graphical construction of a path count matrix. (b) Path count and coding matrices.

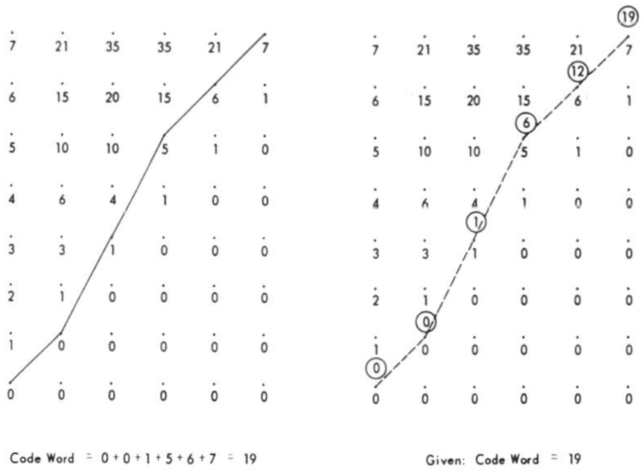


(a) (b)

Fig. 2. An example of sequence encoding and decoding.
(a) Encoding. (b) Decoding.

*Transformation from path-count matrix to coding matrix:* Shift over one column to the right in the path-count matrix to obtain the coding matrix. In other words, use the second column of the path-count matrix as the first-column in the coding matrix, and so on, until the $(q+1)$th column of the path-count matrix becomes the $q$th column of the coding matrix. The row numbering remains the same, except that each row is modified in accordance with the above column shifting. This transformation is illustrated in Fig. 1(b) for the same case of $m=9$, $q=6$.

It should be noted that in Fig. 1(b), the general path-count matrix has been written for any $q$ and any $m$ with extension directions indicated by the arrows. The extension of this matrix is carried out by observing the following rules.

1) The leftmost column has unity elements.
2) The diagonal rising from the lower left-hand corner has unity elements.
3) All elements below this diagonal are zero.
4) If the rows are numbered in an increasing direction from the bottom to the top, and the columns from left to right, then the value of the element $a_{i,j}$ is computed by the formula

$$a_{i,j} = a_{i-1,j} + a_{i-1,j-1}. \quad (2)$$

It should also be noted that the coding matrix indicated in Fig. 1(b) would again be limited to the boundaries imposed by the two diagonals from the *start* and *end* corners. In this case ($m=9$, $q=6$) these are: the all-zero diagonal below the unity diagonal, and the diagonal just above the unity diagonal with elements 2, 3, 4, 5, 6, 7.

To encode a sequence, draw the path on the coding matrix and add the elements touched by the path. This sum provides a unique code word $w$ whose value ranges from 0 to $N_q-1$, inclusive.

To decode a received code word $w$, start at the element $a_{i,q}$ in the rightmost column of the coding matrix which satisfies the inequality

$$a_{i,q} \leq w < a_{i+1,q}.$$

Now $a_{i,q}$ is on the sequence path. To find the neot point qn the sequence path, use $w_{-1} = w - a_{i,q}$ and find $a_{i,\,q-1}$ such that

$$a_{i,q-1} \leq w_{-1} < a_{i+1,q-1}.$$

Now $a_{i,q-1}$ is on the sequence path. Continue this procedure until a point on the path in the first column has been found. Then the sequence is given by the set of values corresponding to the row numbers of the elements in the $q$ columns, starting at the leftmost column.

This encoding and decoding procedure is illustrated in Fig. 2 for the case of $m=9$, $q=6$, and a particular sequence.

*Note*: It has recently come to the attention of the author that an encoding and decoding scheme similar to that given above has been independently developed by Prof. L. D. Davisson, Princeton University, Princeton, N. J. [3].

Thomas J. Lynch
Goddard Space Flight Center
National Aeronautics and
Space Administration
Greenbelt, Md.

References

[1] J. E. Medlin, "Sampled data prediction for telemetry bandwidth compression," *IEEE Trans. on Space Electronics and Telemetry*, vol. SET-11, pp. 29–36, March 1965.
[2] G. A. Gordon, "An algorithmic code for monotonic sources," Final Report of GSFC Summer Workshop 1965, Greenbelt, Md., NASA GSFC X-100-65-407, pp. A57–A69.
[3] Private communication.

# 9



Reprinted from *Proc. IEEE,* **54**(12), 2010 (1966)

# COMMENTS ON "SEQUENCE TIME CODING FOR DATA COMPRESSION"

In a recent letter,[1] Lynch presents a method of encoding the times of occurrence of transmitted (nonredundant) samples for compressed data. The purpose of this letter is to present some further results for the method of coding.

Suppose a block of $m-1$ samples is compressed to $q$ transmitted samples. Then there are a total of

$$\binom{m-1}{q}$$

possible spacings of these $q$ samples within the block. Lynch finds the encoded and decoded words by constructing a coding matrix. The coding technique has a simpler analytic basis. It can be verified that if $\{n_i; i=1, \cdots, q\}$ are the times of occurrence of the samples from the beginning of the block then the code word is:

$$T(\{n_i\}) = \sum_{i=1}^{q} \binom{n_i - 1}{j}.$$

Similarly, the sequential decoding procedure can be given by noting that

$$n_q \text{ satisfies } \begin{cases} T(\{n_i\}) - \binom{n_q - 1}{q} \geq 0, \\ T(\{n_i\}) - \binom{n_q}{q} < 0 \end{cases}$$

$$n_{q-1} \text{ satisfies } \begin{cases} T(\{n_i\}) - \binom{n_q - 1}{q} - \binom{n_{q-1} - 1}{q-1} \geq 0, \\ T(\{n_i\}) - \binom{n_q - 1}{q} - \binom{n_{q-1}}{q-1} < 0 \end{cases}$$

and so on.

Suppose the average length of the transmitted samples is $\bar{L}$ bits. Then one possible application of this technique would be to transmit the data in a format similar to the following:

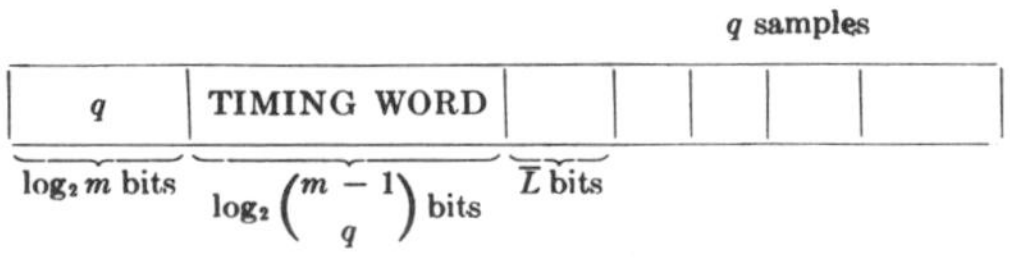


It is of interest to consider the average transmission rate per sample for this method of coding:

$$B(m) = \frac{1}{m}\left[\log_2 m + \log_2 \binom{m-1}{q} + q\bar{L}\right].$$

For large $m$:

$$\binom{m-1}{q} \cong \sqrt{\frac{m}{(m-q)q2\pi}} \left(\frac{m}{m-q}\right)^m \left(\frac{m-q}{q}\right)^q.$$

In the limit as $m \to \infty$, the ratio $m/q$ in general converges in probability to the average run length between samples. Supposing these run lengths to be geometric with probability $p$, this average run length is $1/(1-p)$. Then as $m \to \infty$, the average transmission rate is

$$\begin{aligned} B &= p \lim_{m \to \infty} B(m) \\ &= p \lim_{m \to \infty} \left[\log_2 \frac{m}{m-q} + \frac{q}{m} \log_2 \frac{m-q}{q} + \frac{q}{m} \bar{L}\right] \\ &= -p \log_2 p - (1-p) \log_2 (1-p) + (1-p)\bar{L} \end{aligned}$$

which is 100 percent efficient. However, it may take a large block to approach the maximum efficiency and in addition it is questionable whether a significant advantage is gained over a simple run length coding scheme. For example, if the data are transmitted as a level word of average length $L$ and a timing word of fixed length $T$ bits, then the transmission rate can be shown to be

$$(\bar{L} + T) \frac{1-p}{1-p^{2T}} \text{ bits per sample.}$$

For $p=0.8$, $\bar{L}=T=4$ bits, this is 92.5 percent efficient and is readily implemented.

L. D. Davisson
Princeton University
Princeton, N. J.

# 10



Reprinted from *IEEE Trans. Inform. Theory,* **IT-19**(1), 73–77 (1973)

# Enumerative Source Encoding

THOMAS M. COVER

***Abstract*—Let $S$ be a given subset of binary $n$-sequences. We provide an explicit scheme for calculating the index of any sequence in $S$ according to its position in the lexicographic ordering of $S$. A simple inverse algorithm is also given. Particularly nice formulas arise when $S$ is the set of all $n$-sequences of weight $k$ and also when $S$ is the set of all sequences having a given empirical Markov property. Schalkwijk and Lynch have investigated the former case. The envisioned use of this indexing scheme is to transmit or store the index rather than the sequence, thus resulting in a data compression of $(\log|S|)/n$.**

Manuscript received October 21, 1971; revised June 1, 1972. This work was supported in part by AFOSR Contract F44620-69-C-0101 and by NSF Contract GK-34363.

The author was on leave at the Massachusetts Institute of Technology, Cambridge, Mass., and Harvard University, Cambridge, Mass. He is now with the Department of Electrical Engineering and Statistics, Stanford University, Stanford, Calif.

## I. Introduction

LET $\{0,1\}^n$ denote the set of binary $n$-sequences and let $x = (x_1,x_2,\cdots,x_n)$ denote a generic element of this set. Let $S$ be a subset of $\{0,1\}^n$. Define $n_S$ to be the number of elements in $S$ and let $n_S(x_1,x_2,\cdots,x_k)$ denote the number of elements in $S$ for which the first $k$ coordinates are given by $(x_1,x_2,\cdots,x_k)$.

By lexicographic ordering we mean the ordinary dictionary ordering under the interpretation that $0 < 1$. More formally, $x < y$ if $x_k < y_k$ for the least index $k$ such that $x_k \neq y_k$. For example, $00101 < 00110$.

The following formula provides the desired $1-1$ lexicographic mapping $S \rightarrow \{0,1,2,\cdots, |S| - 1\}$.

*Proposition 1:* The lexicographic index of $x \in S$ is given by

$$i_S(x) = \sum_{j=1}^{n} x_j n_S(x_1,x_2,\cdots,x_{j-1},0). \tag{1}$$

*Proof:* Words with prefix $(x_1,x_2,\cdots,x_{j-1},0)$ lexicographically precede words with prefix $(x_1,x_2,\cdots,x_{j-1},1)$. For each $j$ such that $x_j = 1$, we simply count the number of elements of $S$, given by $n_S(x_1,x_2,\cdots,x_{j-1},0)$, which first differ from $x$ in the $j$th term and therefore have lower lexicographic index. By adding these numbers for $j = 1,2,\cdots,n$, we eventually count all the elements in $S$ of lower index than $x$.

The extension of these results to arbitrary finite alphabet sizes is immediate. The formula is as follows.

*Proposition 2:* The lexicographic index of $x \in S \subseteq \{1,2,3,\cdots,M\}^n$ is given by

$$i_S(x) = \sum_{j=1}^{n} \sum_{m=1}^{x_j-1} n_S(x_1,x_2,\cdots,x_{j-1},m).$$

The inverse function is also easily calculated.

Here is the inverse for Proposition 1.

*Inverse Algorithm:* Let $i$ and $S$ be given. The following algorithm finds $x$ such that $i_S(x) = i$.

*Step 1:* If $i > n_S(0)$ set $x_1 = 1$ and set $i = i - n_S(0)$; otherwise set $x_1 = 0$.

*Step 2:* For $k = 2,\cdots,n$, if $i > n_S(x_1,x_2,\cdots,x_{k-1},0)$ set $x_k = 1$ and set $i = i - n_S(x_1,x_2,\cdots,x_{k-1},0)$; otherwise set $x_k = 0$.

## II. Some Applications

*Example 1—Enumeration of All Binary n-Sequences:*

$$S = \{0,1\}^n.$$

Then $n_S(x_1,x_2,\cdots,x_k) = 2^{n-k}$, and

$$i_S(x) = \sum_{i=1}^{n} x_i 2^{n-i}. \tag{2}$$

The inverse function of $i$ is the standard base-two expansion $x_1x_2\cdots x_n$ of the integer $i$. There is nothing new here.

*Example 2—Enumeration of Sequences of Weight w:*

$$S = \left\{x \in \{0,1\}^n: \sum_{j=1}^{n} x_j = w\right\}.$$

Here

$$n_S(x_1,x_2,\cdots,x_{k-1},0) = \binom{n-k}{n(w,k)}$$

where

$$n(w,k) = w - \sum_{j=1}^{k-1} x_j$$

since there are only this number of ways of placing the last $n(w,k)$ 1's in the last $n-k$ terms of the sequence. Therefore,

$$i_S(x) = \sum_{k=1}^{n} x_k \binom{n-k}{n(w,k)}. \tag{4}$$

For example, for $w = 3$, $n = 7$,

$$i(1000101) = \binom{6}{3} + \binom{2}{2} + \binom{0}{1} = 20 + 1 + 0 = 21$$

$$i(1110000) = \binom{6}{3} + \binom{5}{2} + \binom{4}{1} = 20 + 10 + 4 = 34,$$

which is in agreement with

$$n_S - 1 = \binom{7}{3} - 1 = 34.$$

This function is quite simple to compute, as is its inverse. The resulting data compression is approximately $H(w/n)$, where $H$ is the entropy function.

Suppose that even this encoding scheme is considered too complex by virtue of the complexity of the calculation of $\binom{n}{i}$, or in the general case, the calculation of $n_S(x_1,x_2,\cdots,x_k,0)$. The obvious answer is to approximate $\binom{n}{i}$ or $n_S(x_1,x_2,\cdots,x_k,0)$ by suitable functions of low complexity. Any integer upper bound will do, but sufficiently loose bounds will diminish the compression, although the mapping will still be invertible and no information will be lost.

The indexing scheme for sequences of length $n$ and weight $w$ is well known in the combinatorial literature (see, e.g., Lehmer [1]). The author does not know whether the general scheme of Proposition 2 has been previously published, although the idea seems to be implicit in any lexicographic indexing scheme. The derivation of the mapping of Example 2 for data compression has been given by Lynch [2] and Schalkwijk [3] (see also Davisson [4]). Schalkwijk's interesting paper provided the impetus for the generalized applications we are presenting here. The following application is not found elsewhere.

*Example 3:*

$$S = \left\{x \in \{0,1\}^n: \left|\sum_{i=1}^{n} x_i - w\right| \le m\right\}.$$

Here we wish to enumerate (in order) all the sequences for which the number of 1's lies in the interval $[w-m, w+m]$. The application to the compression of a Bernoulli source with parameter $p$ is obvious: simply setting $w = np$ and $m = (w(n-w)/n)^{1/2}\alpha$ guarantees $\Pr\{S\} \approx 2(1-\Phi(\alpha))$. Thus a compression $H(p)$ can be achieved with probability approximately one by an appropriate moderately large choice of $\alpha$.

In this example

$$n_S(x_1,x_2,\cdots,x_{k-1},0) = \sum_{t=w-m}^{w+m} \binom{n-k}{n(t,k)}. \tag{5}$$

Thus the index of $x$ is given by

$$i_S(x) = \sum_{k=0}^{n} \sum_{t=w-m}^{w+m} x_k \binom{n-k}{n(t,k)}. \tag{6}$$

Thus, for $w = 3$, $m = 1$, $i_S(11000110) = \binom{7}{2} + \binom{7}{3} + \binom{7}{4} + \binom{6}{1} + \binom{6}{2} + \binom{6}{3} + \binom{2}{1} + \binom{1}{0} = 115$.

*Example 4—Enumeration of Permutations:* Let $S$ be the set of all permutations of the integers $\{1,2,\cdots,n\}$. Suppose that we wish to enumerate the $n!$ elements of $S$ lexicographically. Thus, for example, $i(1,2,\cdots,n) = 0$, and $i(n, n-1,\cdots, 1) = n! - 1$. Given the permutation $(x_1, x_2,\cdots,x_n)$, let $r_i$ equal the number of elements $x_j$, $j = i+1, i+2,\cdots, n$, such that $x_j < x_i$. Then by Proposition 2,

$$i(x_1,x_2,\cdots,x_n) = \sum_{i=1}^{n} r_i(n-i)!.$$

This is precisely Lehmer's [1] enumeration formula for permutations.

*Example 5—Enumeration of Monotone Functions:* This problem was suggested by the recent work of Elias [5] on simple encodings for monotone functions. Elias' encodings are only slightly less efficient in the length of the encoding than the optimal encoding given here and are recommended for certain practical applications.

Let $F$: $\{0,1,2,\cdots,m\} \to \{0,1,2,\cdots,n\}$ be an integer-valued function. We shall say that $F$ is *monotone nondecreasing* if $F(i) \le F(i+1)$, $i = 0,1,\cdots, m-1$; and we shall say that $F$ is *strictly monotone* if $F(i) < F(i+1)$, $i = 0,1,\cdots, m-1$. Finally, $F$ will be said to be a *distribution function* if $F(m) = n$. We consider the following four separate enumeration problems:

$$\mathscr{F}_1 = \{F\colon F \text{ monotone nondecreasing}\}$$

$$\mathscr{F}_2 = \{F\colon F \text{ monotone nondecreasing distribution function}\}$$

$$\mathscr{F}_3 = \{F\colon F \text{ strictly monotone}\}$$

$$\mathscr{F}_4 = \{F\colon F \text{ strictly monotone distribution function}\}.$$

Clearly $\mathscr{F}_4 \subseteq \mathscr{F}_2 \subseteq \mathscr{F}_1$ and $\mathscr{F}_4 \subseteq \mathscr{F}_3 \subseteq \mathscr{F}_1$.

Now let $C_k(m,n)$ denote the number of elements in $\mathscr{F}_k$, where the functions $F$ have domain $\{0,1,\cdots,m\}$ and range $\{0,1,\cdots,n\}$. To determine $C_k(m,n)$, define the jumps $n_i = F(i) - F(i-1)$, $i = 1,2,\cdots,m$, and define $n_{m+1} = n - F(m)$. Note that $n_{m+1} = 0$ if $F$ is a distribution function and also that $n_i \ge 0$ and $n_i \ge 1$ imply weak and strict monotonicity, respectively. It can be seen that $C_k(m,n)$ is the number of integer solutions of

$$(k=1)\colon \quad \sum_{j=1}^{m+1} n_j = n, \qquad n_j \ge 0$$

$$(k=2)\colon \quad \sum_{j=1}^{m} n_j = n, \qquad n_j \ge 0$$

$$(k=3)\colon \quad \sum_{j=1}^{m+1} n_j = n+1, \qquad n_j \ge 1$$

$$(k=4)\colon \quad \sum_{j=1}^{m} n_j = n, \qquad n_j \ge 1.$$

The number of solutions of these equations is simply the number of ways of placing a given number of balls in a given number of cells and can be found by an argument in Feller [6, pp. 38, 39] to be

$$C_1(m,n) = \binom{n+m+1}{m+1}$$

$$C_2(m,n) = \binom{n+m}{m}$$

$$C_3(m,n) = \binom{n+1}{m+1}$$

$$C_4(m,n) = \binom{n}{m}.$$

To define a lexicographic ordering on $\mathscr{F}$ we shall say $F_1 < F_2$ if $\exists k \in \{0,1,2,\cdots, m-1\}$ such that $F_1(i) = F_2(i)$, $i \le k$, $F_1(k+1) < F_2(k+1)$. The key observation is that the number of monotone functions for which $F(0),F(1),\cdots,F(k-1)$ are fixed and $F(k) > r$ is simply $C_i(m-k, n-r-1)$; i.e., the number of monotone functions with domain $\{0,1,\cdots, m-k\}$ and range $\{0,1,\cdots, n-r\}$. We apply Proposition 2 to count the number of functions having a *higher* index than $F$ and then subtract this from the total number of functions in $\mathscr{F}_k$ to obtain the following expression for the index of $F$ in $\mathscr{F}_k$:

$$i_k(F) = C_k(m,n) - 1 - \sum_{i=0}^{m} C_k(m-i, n-F(i)-1), \qquad k = 1,2,3,4.$$

Thus, for example, there are $\binom{4}{3} = 4$ strictly monotone functions and $\binom{6}{3} = 20$ weakly monotone functions from $\{0,1,2\}$ to $\{0,1,2,3\}$; and $i_3(0,1,2) = i_1(0,0,0) = 0$.

*Example 6—Enumeration of Convex Functions $F$: $\{0,1,\cdots,m\} \to \{0,1,\cdots,n\}$:* The local nature of the definition of convex functions yields a nice application of Proposition 2. The results, found with Bolour, will not be given here.

Many other examples can be given, but we shall proceed to one last example in which there is some empirical dependence among the terms of the sequence.

## III. Application to Markov Processes

The following application is given because of its utility in encoding Markov processes and not because of its ease of derivation. We envisage the use as follows. Let $\mathbf{v}$ denote the sequence statistics given in (7). First an encoding of $\mathbf{v} = (\nu_{01},\nu_{10},\nu_{00},\nu_{11})$ (requiring at most $4 \log n$ bits) will be given, followed by an encoding of $\mathbf{x} \in S_{\mathbf{v}}$. This will result in a compression of $\mathbf{x}$ that is arbitrarily close to the optimal compression of a first-order stationary Markov source having statistics corresponding to $\mathbf{v}$. The difference comes from the asymptotically negligible $(4 \log n)/n$ bits per symbol necessary to encode $\mathbf{v}$. If $\mathbf{v}$ is known *a priori*, there is no loss whatsoever. The encoding of the *statistics* $\mathbf{v}$ of the sequence is similar to the idea of universal codes in Babkin [7] and Shtarkov and Babkin [8].

Define the number of 01, 10, 00, and 11 blocks in $\boldsymbol{x}$ by

$$\begin{aligned} \nu_{01} &= \sum_{i=1}^{n-1} \bar{x}_i x_{i+1} \\ \nu_{10} &= \sum_{i=1}^{n-1} x_i \bar{x}_{i+1} \\ \nu_{00} &= \sum_{i=1}^{n-1} \bar{x}_i \bar{x}_{i+1} \\ \nu_{11} &= \sum_{i=1}^{n-1} x_i x_{i+1}. \end{aligned} \tag{7}$$

Let

$$\boldsymbol{\nu} = (\nu_{01},\nu_{10},\nu_{00},\nu_{11}). \tag{8}$$

Let $S = S_{\nu}$ denote the set of all $\boldsymbol{x} \in \{0,1\}^n$ satisfying (7).

*Remark:* By definition we see that $\nu_{01} + \nu_{10} + \nu_{00} + \nu_{11} = n - 1$. Note also that a 2-state stationary Markov process, with transition probabilities $P_{ij}$, has

$$\begin{aligned} E\{\nu_{01}\} &= (n-1)p_{01}p_{10}/(p_{01}+p_{10}) \\ E\{\nu_{10}\} &= (n-1)p_{10}p_{01}/(p_{01}+p_{10}) \\ E\{\nu_{00}\} &= (n-1)p_{00}p_{10}/(p_{01}+p_{10}) \\ E\{\nu_{11}\} &= (n-1)p_{11}p_{01}/(p_{01}+p_{10}). \end{aligned} \tag{9}$$

From this it can be seen that the statistics $p_{ij}$ of the process are completely recoverable from $E\{\boldsymbol{\nu}\}$. Finally, for ergodic processes ($p_{00} \neq 1$, $p_{11} \neq 1$), $\boldsymbol{\nu} \to E\{\boldsymbol{\nu}\}$ with probability one. Thus almost all sample functions $\boldsymbol{x} = (x_1,x_2,\cdots,x_n)$ will have $\boldsymbol{\nu}(\boldsymbol{x})$ near $E\{\boldsymbol{\nu}\}$. This is made explicit in the Shannon–MacMillan theorem (Ash [9, p. 197]).

We shall introduce the definition

$$g(\boldsymbol{\nu}) = \text{number of sequences } \boldsymbol{x} \text{ satisfying (7) for which } x_1 = 0. \tag{10}$$

Thus $g(\boldsymbol{\nu}) = n_{S_{\nu}}(0)$ in the previous notation.

The critical calculation of $g$ is given by the following lemma.

*Lemma 1:*

$$g(\nu_{01},\nu_{10},\nu_{00},\nu_{11}) = \begin{cases} \dbinom{\nu_{00}+\nu_{10}}{\nu_{10}}\dbinom{\nu_{11}+\nu_{01}-1}{\nu_{01}-1}, & \nu_{01} = \nu_{10} \text{ or } \nu_{01} = \nu_{10}+1 \\ 0, & \text{otherwise.} \end{cases} \tag{11}$$

*Proof:* $\boldsymbol{\nu}(\boldsymbol{x}) = \boldsymbol{\nu}$, $x_1 = 0$, implies there are $\nu_{10} + 1$ runs of 0's and $\nu_{01}$ runs of 1's; and also that there are a total of $\nu_{10} + \nu_{00} + 1$ 0's and $\nu_{01} + \nu_{11}$ 1's. Since the runs of 0's and 1's alternate, beginning with a run of 0's, we have $g = 0$ unless $\nu_{01} = \nu_{10}$ or $\nu_{01} = \nu_{10} + 1$.

Now from Feller [6, pp. 36–37] we know that there are $\binom{r-1}{m-1}$ positive integer solutions to $r_1 + r_2 + \cdots + r_m = r$. Thus there are $\binom{\nu_{10}+\nu_{00}}{\nu_{10}}$ ways to choose the (nonzero) run lengths of the 0's and $\binom{\nu_{10}+\nu_{11}-1}{\nu_{01}-1}$ ways to choose the run lengths of the 1's. The choices can be made independently, and they completely characterize the sequence $\boldsymbol{x}$. Then (11) results and the lemma is established.

Finally, applying the fundamental counting result of Proposition 1 in Section I, we have the following calculation of the index of $\boldsymbol{x}$ in the set $S = S_{\nu}$ of all sequences with Markov property $\boldsymbol{\nu}$.

*Proposition 3:*

$$i_S(\boldsymbol{x}) = \sum_{k=1}^{n} x_k g(\boldsymbol{\nu} - \boldsymbol{\nu}(x_1,x_2,\cdots,x_{k-1},\bar{x}_k)),$$

where $\bar{x}_k = 1 - x_k$.

*Proof:* We observe from (7) that $\boldsymbol{\nu} = \boldsymbol{\nu}(x_1,\cdots,x_n) = \boldsymbol{\nu}(x_1,\cdots,x_k) + \boldsymbol{\nu}(x_k,\cdots,x_n)$. Thus a sequence $(\bar{x}_k,z_{k+1},\cdots,z_n)$ will be an acceptable termination of $(x_1,x_2,\cdots,\bar{x}_k)$ (i.e., $\boldsymbol{\nu}(x_1,\cdots,\bar{x}_k,z_{k+1},\cdots,z_n) = \boldsymbol{\nu}$ and hence $(x_1,\cdots,\bar{x}_k,z_{k+1},\cdots,z_n) \in S_{\nu}$) if and only if $\boldsymbol{\nu}(\bar{x}_k,z_{k+1},\cdots,z_n) = \boldsymbol{\nu} - \boldsymbol{\nu}(x_1,x_2,\cdots,\bar{x}_k)$. Since $g$ counts the number of continuations for a given $\boldsymbol{\nu}$ for which the first term is zero, and since $x_k g = 0$ unless $\bar{x}_k = 0$, the proposition follows.

*Proposition 4:* The number of elements in $S_{\nu}$ is given by $g(\nu_{01},\nu_{10},\nu_{00},\nu_{11}) + g(\nu_{10},\nu_{01},\nu_{11},\nu_{00})$.

*Proof:* The number of sequences with initial term 1 and property $\boldsymbol{\nu}$ is simply the number of sequences with initial term 0 and property $\tilde{\boldsymbol{\nu}} = (\nu_{10},\nu_{01},\nu_{11},\nu_{00})$; as is easily seen by complementing all the 0's and 1's. Thus $g(\boldsymbol{\nu})$ counts the elements in $S_{\nu}$ with initial term 0, and $g(\tilde{\boldsymbol{\nu}})$ counts the elements in $S_{\nu}$ with initial term 1.

*Comment:* The inverse function $i \to \boldsymbol{x}$ is easily calculated by the recurrence algorithm in Section I.

*Example:* Consider the sequence $\boldsymbol{x} = (0,1,1,0,0,1,1,0)$. Here $\boldsymbol{\nu}(\boldsymbol{x}) = (\nu_{01},\nu_{10},\nu_{00},\nu_{11}) = (2,2,1,2)$. The equivalence class $S_{\nu}$ has $g(2,2,1,2) + g(2,2,2,1) = \binom{3}{2}\binom{3}{1} + \binom{4}{2}\binom{2}{1} = 9 + 12 = 21$ elements. The index of $\boldsymbol{x}$ in $S_{\nu}$ is given by

$$\begin{aligned} i(\boldsymbol{x}) &= x_2 g(2,2,0,2) + x_3 g(1,1,1,2) + x_6 g(1,1,-1,1) + x_7 g(0,0,0,1) \\ &= \binom{2}{2}\binom{3}{1} + \binom{2}{1}\binom{2}{0} + 0 + 0 \\ &= 3 + 2 = 5. \end{aligned}$$

Thus there are 5 sequences in $S_{\nu}$ that are lexicographically less than $\boldsymbol{x}$. We verify the calculation by exhibiting the first few elements in $S_{\nu}$.

$\boldsymbol{\nu} = (\nu_{01},\nu_{10},\nu_{00},\nu_{11}) = (2,2,1,2)$:

| | | | | | | | | | |
|---|---|---|---|---|---|---|---|---|---|
| | 0 | 0 | 1 | 0 | 1 | 1 | 1 | 0 | $i = 0$ |
| | 0 | 0 | 1 | 1 | 0 | 1 | 1 | 0 | $i = 1$ |
| | 0 | 0 | 1 | 1 | 1 | 0 | 1 | 0 | $i = 2$ |
| | 0 | 1 | 0 | 0 | 1 | 1 | 1 | 0 | $i = 3$ |
| | 0 | 1 | 0 | 1 | 1 | 1 | 0 | 0 | $i = 4$ |
| $\boldsymbol{x} =$ | 0 | 1 | 1 | 0 | 0 | 1 | 1 | 0 | $i = 5$ |
| | 0 | 1 | 1 | 0 | 1 | 1 | 0 | 0 | $i = 6$ |
| | 0 | 1 | 1 | 1 | 0 | 0 | 1 | 0 | $i = 7$ |
| | … | … | … | … | … | … | … | … | … |
| | … | … | … | … | … | … | … | … | … |
| | 1 | 1 | 1 | 0 | 1 | 0 | 0 | 1 | $i = 20.$ |

Hence, since an arbitrary integer in $\{0,1,\cdots,20\}$ can be expressed with 5 binary digits, we can compress the sequences in $S_\nu$ from length 8 to length 5. By using Stirling's approximation on (11) and counting the elements of $S_\nu$ using Proposition 4, we obtain an approximate compression ratio of $1/n[(\nu_{00} + \nu_{10})H(\nu_{10}/(\nu_{00} + \nu_{10})) + (\nu_{11} + \nu_{01})H(\nu_{01}/(\nu_{00} + \nu_{10}))]$, the same as would be obtained from a Markov process with corresponding statistics.

## References


[1] D. H. Lehmer, "Teaching combinatorial tricks to a computer," in *Proc. Symp. Applied Mathematics*, vol. 10: *Combinatorial Analysis.* Providence, R.I.: Amer. Math. Soc., 1960.

[2] T. J. Lynch, "Sequence time coding for data compression," *Proc. IEEE* (Lett.), vol. 54, pp. 1490–1491, Oct. 1966.

[3] J. P. M. Schalkwijk, "An algorithm for source coding," *IEEE Trans. Inform. Theory*, vol. IT-18, pp. 395–399, May 1972.

[4] L. D. Davisson, "Comments on 'Sequence time coding for data compression'," *Proc. IEEE* (Lett.), vol. 54, p. 2010, Dec. 1966.

[5] P. Elias, "On binary representations of monotone sequences," in *Proc. 6th Princeton Conf. Systems Theory*, Apr. 1972.

[6] W. Feller, *An Introduction to Probability Theory and Its Applications*, vol. 1. New York: Wiley, 1957.

[7] V. F. Babkin, "Method of universal coding for a source of independent messages with non-exponential complexity of calculations" (in Russian), *Probl. Inform. Transmiss.*, vol. 7, No. 4, 1971.

[8] Yu. M. Shtarkov and V. F. Babkin, "Combinatorial method of universal coding for discrete stationary sources" (in Russian), *Probl. Contr. Inform. Transmiss.*, to be published.

[9] R. Ash, *Information Theory.* New York: Wiley, 1965.

# 11



Reprinted from *IEEE Trans. Inform. Theory,* **IT-19**(6), 783–795 (1973)

# Universal Noiseless Coding

LEE D. DAVISSON

**Abstract—Universal coding is any asymptotically optimum method of block-to-block memoryless source coding for sources with unknown parameters. This paper considers noiseless coding for such sources, primarily in terms of variable-length coding, with performance measured as a function of the coding redundancy relative to the per-letter conditional source entropy given the unknown parameter. It is found that universal (i.e., zero redundancy) coding in a weighted sense is possible if and only if the per-letter average mutual information between the parameter space and the message space is zero. Universal coding is possible in a maximin sense if and only if the channel capacity between the two spaces is zero. Universal coding is possible in a minimax sense if and only if a probability mass function exists, independent of the unknown parameter, for which the relative entropy of the known conditional-probability mass-function is zero. Several examples are given to illustrate the ideas. Particular attention is given to sources that are stationary and ergodic for any fixed parameter although the whole ensemble is not. For such sources, weighted universal codes always exist if the alphabet is finite, or more generally if the entropy is finite. Minimax universal codes result if an additional entropy stability constraint is applied. A discussion of fixed-rate universal coding is also given briefly with performance measured by a probability of error.**

## I. Introduction

We start with a general discussion. More precise definitions will appear subsequently. Suppose we are given a discrete-time and discrete-alphabet source that we wish to block encode without error to minimize the average codeword length, where the code is not allowed to depend on some unknown parameters of the source message probabilities. The unknown parameter could be something as simple as, say, the probability of a one in a binary independent-letter source or as general as the complete set of message probabilities for the source. Such sources are called *composite* (see, e.g., Berger [1]).

In some cases, although not usually, the unknown parameter may have a known prior distribution so that all *ensemble* message probabilities are known. As has been frequently stated, however, there is no reason to suppose that coding for the whole ensemble will be efficient for the actual parameter in effect. One of the important results of this paper is to establish that coding for the whole ensemble does, under certain circumstances, have a very important meaning in an asymptotic sense. For example, suppose we have a composite binary source in which the probability $\theta$ of a "one" is chosen by "nature" randomly according to the uniform probability law on [0,1] and then fixed for all time. The user is not told $\theta$, however. Subsequently the source produces independent-letter outputs with the chosen, but unknown, probability. The probability, given $\theta$, that any message block of length $N$ contains $n$ ones in any given pattern is then

$$\theta^n(1-\theta)^{N-n}. \tag{1}$$

If $\theta$ were known, a per-letter average codeword length at least equal to the entropy of

$$-\theta \log_2 \theta - (1-\theta)\log_2(1-\theta) \quad \text{b} \tag{2}$$

would be required (and could be approached arbitrarily closely) to block encode the source. Although $\theta$ is unknown, the *composite* source output probabilities are known. In fact the probability of any given message containing $n$ ones in $N$ outputs is simply

$$\int_0^1 \theta^n(1-\theta)^{N-n}\,d\theta = \frac{1}{N+1}\binom{N}{n}^{-1}. \tag{3}$$

(Note that the *composite* source does not produce independent letters. This is due to the fact that past observations provide information about the value of $\theta$ in effect. The composite source is stationary but not ergodic.)

There is no reason to suppose that the use of the probabilities of (3) to design a variable-length code will do well for any $\theta$ that comes along in the sense of approaching (2). One of the surprising results, which will be shown subsequently, is that the probabilities of (3) provide codes as good asymptotically as the probabilities of (1) with $\theta$ known exactly.

This example has illustrated an interesting and important point of problem definition. Does one regard such a source as a stationary ergodic source with unknown message probabilities, or does one state simply that the source is not ergodic? While it is important that a precise statement be made in this regard to adequately define the coding problem, such precise statements typically have not been made in the literature. In this paper we will regard such sources to be *conditionally* stationary ergodic in the sense precisely defined in Definition 2 appearing in Section III. Roughly what is meant is that a source ensemble characterized by any possible value of the unknown parameter is stationary ergodic. We now turn to a definition.

*Definition 1: Universal coding* is any method of block encoding for composite sources where the following holds. a) The encoding depends only on the observed source message block encoded and not past or future outputs, i.e., it is blockwise memoryless. b) Some performance measure(s) is attained arbitrarily closely as the block length goes to infinity.

Any type of coding, in the sense of mapping the source message blocks into code blocks, is allowed provided that the mapping depends only on the message block to be encoded and not past and future blocks. This excludes what is loosely called "adaptive coding" where past statistical

Manuscript received November 28, 1972; revised May 15, 1973. This work was supported by the National Science Foundation under Grant GK 14190 and by the Advanced Research Projects Agency of the Department of Defense monitored by the Air Force Eastern Test Range under Contract F08606-72-C-0008.

The author is with the Department of Electrical Engineering, University of Southern California, Los Angeles, Calif. 90007.

source message information is used to affect the coding. (The real reason for not using past information, of course, is uncertainty about stationarity; that is, statistics from past blocks may be an unreliable measure of current conditions.)

The performance measure to be used in any application could include, for example, the average codeword length, a distortion measure on the receiver output, and encoding complexity. In this paper, however, we consider noiseless coding only and complexity is either ignored or given brief mention. Variable-length coding is considered for the most part, without length constraints, so that functions of the coding redundancy are used to measure performance. Several functions will be proposed.

All previously known universal coding methods are constructive and do roughly the same thing: the message block is divided into two parts. The second part contains an encoding of the block in the usual sense and the first part tells how the encoding is done. As the block length goes to infinity, the first part takes up a vanishingly small fraction of the whole codeword while the average length of the second part converges to the minimum. In this paper it is shown that constructive methods need not be employed explicitly. However, interesting code constructions based upon maximum-likelihood estimation, sufficient statistics, and histograms can be made and will be discussed.

The paper was originally intended to be a tutorial review of universal coding, but the temptation and ease of extension to new directions could not be resisted. Therefore, both old and new results (mostly the latter) will be found with appropriate credits where applicable. In contrast with earlier work, which relies heavily on constructions, the viewpoint of this paper is primarily information-theoretic. An attempt is made to make new precise definitions of various forms of redundancy and universal coding with respect to these forms of redundancy. The insight gained through mutual information and extensions to infinite alphabets is entirely new, as is the explicit application of maximum-likelihood estimation and sufficient statistics to universal coding. The section on histogram encoding is only partially new, as are some of the specific examples used.

To put things in proper perspective, Section II presents a general history of universal coding. Section III presents the necessary terminology and fundamentals to be used in the paper. Section IV defines several performance measures for universal coding, finds necessary and sufficient conditions for universal coding, and demonstrates a number of constructive coding methods. Briefly, it is found that universal coding with respect to a prior probability distribution on the unknown parameter is possible if and only if the per-letter average mutual information between the source message space and the parameter space tends to zero as the block size goes to infinity. This always happens for conditionally stationary-ergodic finite-entropy sources. In a stronger maximin sense, universal coding is possible if and only if the per-letter channel capacity between the parameter space and the source message space is zero. Finally, universal coding is possible in a *weakly* minimax sense if and only if a mixture probability mass function exists for which the relative entropy of the conditional probability mass function tends to zero for every value in the parameter space. If the convergence is uniform in the parameter, then minimax universal codes result. With some mild constraints on the parameter space, this happens for conditionally ergodic sources. Section V presents histogram constructions. Section VI discusses some implications of the work to fixed length codes and finally, Section VII proposes some open problems.

## II. A History of Universal Coding

Kolmogorov [2] introduced the term universal coding, although he gave it only brief mention and suggested the possibility of such coding in the sense described in Section I. The general approach proposed was combinatoric rather than probabilistic as was traditional in coding problems. Fitingof [3], [4] exploited this approach in greater detail using mixed combinatoric-probabilistic methods. Codes based on his ideas are described in Section V.

At approximately the same time, Lynch [5], [6] and Davisson [7] presented a (somewhat practical) technique for encoding time-discrete conditionally stationary ergodic binary sources. The universality of the scheme in the sense of attaining the per-letter entropy is demonstrated in [7]. Cover [8] has also presented specific enumeration techniques. Shtarkov and Babkin [9] demonstrated the same thing for any stationary finite-order, finite-alphabet Markov source, showing in particular that the increased per-letter average code length is of the order of log (block length)/ block length. Results for arbitrary stationary finite-alphabet sources are also included in [9]. Babkin [10] considered the complexity of a scheme for an independent-letter source and estimated the coding redundancy.

All the preceding was derived for variable-length coding. Ziv [11] took a different approach by using fixed-rate codes with performance measured by the probability of error. He showed that the error probability can be made arbitrarily small with a large enough block size provided that the message entropy is less than the coding rate. In contrast to [1]–[10], this can result in a chosen rate, which is much greater than the actual (unknown) message entropy. Although the term universal was not used, the same type of idea is involved in the research of Berger [1] on a composite source with a distortion measure. Universal coding with a distortion measure has also been considered by Ziv [11].

An application of what might be called universal coding to "real" data is provided by the Rice [12] technique, whereby successive blocks of video data are examined; the best code for each block is chosen from among a set number of code books, and the code book designation is encoded along with the actual codeword. Another example is the analysis–synthesis technique [17] for speech waveforms, where adaptive predictor parameters are measured on each block and sent along as part of the block codeword.

The interested reader is also referred to [13]–[16] which present related adaptive methods where statistical information from past blocks is used in the coding.

## III. Notation and Preliminaries

Throughout, capital letters will be used for random variables with lower-case letters used for specific values of the random variables. Let $(\Omega,\mathscr{F},\mathscr{P})$ be a probability space. We will be concerned with two functions defined on this probability space: the source message stochastic process $X = \{X_i \mid i = 0, \pm 1, \pm 2,\cdots\}$, which is observed and is to be encoded and a random variable $\Theta$, which is unknown to the encoder and decoder whose value, if known, would be used to improve the coding (e.g., the probability of a "one" in Section I). The random variable $X_i: \Omega \to A$ has a countable range space, the alphabet space $A = \{a_1,a_2,\cdots,a_L\}$, which without loss of generality is taken to be the non-negative integers, i.e., $a_i = i - 1$, where $L$ is the size of the alphabet. Unless specifically stated, $L = \infty$ is allowed. Coding is done with specific reference to the message block $X_N = (X_1,X_2,\cdots,X_N)$ of length $N$ with values $x_N = (x_1,x_2,\cdots,x_N)$ defined on the range product alphabet space $A^N$. Only noiseless coding will be considered (mostly variable length, but also fixed length with vanishing probability of error). For simplicity the coding alphabet is taken to be binary with 2 the base of all logarithms so that entropies and codeword lengths are in bits.

The unknown parameter $\Theta$ takes values in the measurable space $(\Lambda,\mathscr{B})$ and is $(\mathscr{F},\mathscr{B})$-measurable (i.e., the inverse image of any $B \in \mathscr{B}$ belongs to $\mathscr{F}$). Let $\Omega_\theta \in \mathscr{F}$ be the inverse image of any given value $\theta$ with conditional probability measure $\mathscr{P}_\theta$, i.e., $\mathscr{P}_\theta(\mathscr{A}) \equiv 0$ for any $\mathscr{A} \in \mathscr{F}$ such that $\mathscr{A} \cap \Omega_\theta = 0$.

*Definition 2:* A source is *conditionally stationary ergodic* if for every $\theta \in \Lambda$ the message ensemble defined on $(\Omega,\mathscr{F},\mathscr{P}_\theta)$ is stationary ergodic.

As noted in the introduction this definition makes it possible to discriminate between sources that would be ergodic if some parameter were known and the ensemble of all source message sequences. In general, however, conditional stationarity and ergodicity are not assumed but are only required when certain limits are needed to exist.

The measure $\mathscr{P}$ may or may not be known. It is assumed, however, that the measure $\mathscr{P}_\theta$ is known for all $\theta \in \Lambda$ so that the (measurable) block conditional message probability mass function, $p(x_N \mid \theta)$, is known for all $N$.

The common notational abuse of distinguishing probabilities, entropies, etc., by their arguments will be employed. For example, $p(\cdot)$ will be a generic notation for probability mass function.

With respect to a probability measure $w(\cdot)$ defined on $\Lambda$, the mixture probability mass function of $X_N$ is

$$p(x_N) = \int_\Lambda p(x_N \mid \theta)\, dw(\theta). \tag{4}$$

The probability measure $w$ may or may not be known and may or may not represent the "true" prior probability measure (induced by $\mathscr{P}$ of the probability space) of the unknown parameter $\Theta$. One might not be willing to accept the concept of a prior probability at all or, as will be seen, might not like the weighting it implies because, at any one time, the coder sees only one member of the nonergodic ensemble. The $w$ might actually be a preference weighting or it might be *a priori* chosen to be "least favorable" as will be discussed. The space of all such probability measures on $\Lambda$ will be denoted $W$.

The conditional entropy $H(X_N \mid \theta)$ defined pointwise on $\theta \in \Lambda$ and the average conditional entropy $H(X_N \mid \Theta)$ are defined in the usual fashion as are the entropies $H(X_N)$ and $H(\Theta)$, the average mutual information $I(X_N;\Theta)$, the conditional average of the mutual information $I(X_N;\theta)$, and the average conditional mutual information $I(X_N;\Theta \mid X_{N-1})$.

Given an arbitrary probability mass function $q(x_N)$, not necessarily in the convex hull of $p(x_N \mid \theta)$, i.e., not necessarily satisfying (4) for any $w \in W$, the relative entropy of $p(x_N \mid \theta)$ with respect to $q(x_N)$ is defined as

$$H(p\colon q) = \sum_{A^N} p(x_N \mid \theta) \log \frac{p(x_N \mid \theta)}{q(x_N)}. \tag{5}$$

If, in addition, $q(x_N)$ satisfies (4) for some $w \in W$, $p(\cdot)$ will be used notationally rather than $q(\cdot)$, and (5) is then the conditional average (for the prior probability measure on $\Theta$) of the mutual information between $X_N$ and $\theta$, $I(X_N;\theta)$.

In subsequent proofs there will be need for the well-known *Kraft inequality*. Let $l(x_N)$ be the code length in bits for message block $x_N$ of any *uniquely decipherable prefix* code defined on $A^N$. Then

$$\sum_{A^N} 2^{-l(x_N)} \le 1. \tag{6}$$

The following theorem, which is a consequence of (6), will be used frequently.

*Variable Length Source Coding Theorem:* Given a probability mass function $q(x_N)$ with corresponding entropy

$$H(X_N) = -\sum_{A^N} q(x_N) \log q(x_N) < \infty \tag{7}$$

it is possible to construct a uniquely decipherable code on block $x_N$ of length $l(x_N)$ satisfying

$$l(x_N) < -\log q(x_N) + 1 \tag{8}$$

so that the expected length $\bar{l}(X_N)$ satisfies

$$\bar{l}(X_N) = \sum_{A^N} q(x_N) l(x_N)$$

$$H(X_N) \le \bar{l}(X_N) < H(X_N) + 1. \tag{9}$$

No uniquely decipherable code exists with $\bar{l}(X_N) < H(X_N)$. The minimum average codeword length is attained by Huffman coding if $L < \infty$.

In the subsequent material reference to a code will mean a set of uniquely decipherable codewords on a source output block of length $N$. The code will be specified by its length function, $l(x_N)$, which satisfies (6). The space of all such length functions is denoted $C_N$. The space of all code sequences is denoted

$$C = \mathop{\times}_{N=1}^{\infty} C_N.$$

A *universal code*, in conformance with Definition 1, will mean a *sequence* of codes in $C$ approaching optimum in the sense of some performance measure as $N \to \infty$.

## IV. Universal Coding

Suppose that the source $N$-block conditional probability function is known as in Section III except for a fixed but unknown parameter $\Theta \in \Lambda$. That is,

$$p(\mathbf{x}_N \mid \theta) = \Pr[\mathbf{X}_N = \mathbf{x}_N \mid \Theta = \theta] \tag{10}$$

is a known (measurable) function of $\mathbf{x}_N$, $N$, and $\theta$. $\mathbf{X}_N$ is observed but $\Theta$ is not. The source may or may not be conditionally stationary ergodic. We give several examples, which will be referred to frequently throughout the balance of the paper.

*Example 1:* As in the example of Section I the source is a binary independent-letter source with $\Lambda = [0,1]$

$$p(\mathbf{x}_N \mid \theta) = \theta^n(1-\theta)^{N-n} \tag{11a}$$

where

$$n = \sum_{i=1}^{N} x_i. \tag{11b}$$

*Example 2:* The source is one of $M < \infty$ distinct types, $\Lambda = \{1,2,\cdots,M\}$, such possible sources are the following. 1) The source is independent-letter exponential with parameter (0.5). 2) The source is independent-letter Poisson with parameter (5.6). 3) The source is Markov with a given transition matrix, etc.

*Example 3:* The source is binary, $\Lambda = [0,1]$, and $\mathbf{X}_N$ is with probability one equal to the first $N$ digits of the binary expansion of $\theta$. That is, let

$$\theta = \sum_{i=1}^{\infty} \theta_i 2^{-i} \qquad \theta_i \in \{0,1\} \tag{12}$$

where, for uniqueness, no expansion using an infinite string of zeros is used except for $\theta = 0$. Then

$$p(\mathbf{x}_N \mid \boldsymbol{\theta}) = \begin{cases} 1, & \text{if } \mathbf{x}_N = (\theta_1,\theta_2,\cdots,\theta_N) \\ 0, & \text{otherwise.} \end{cases} \tag{13}$$

*Example 4:* The source is independent-letter Poisson with parameter $\Theta \in \Lambda = [0,\infty)$

$$p(\mathbf{x}_N \mid \theta) = \frac{\theta^{\Sigma x_i} e^{-N\theta}}{\pi(x_i!)}. \tag{14}$$

*Example 5:* The source is conditionally stationary ergodic and entropy stable in the sense that the per-letter conditional entropy satisfies

$$\frac{H(\mathbf{X}_k \mid \theta)}{k} - \lim_{N\to\infty} \frac{H(\mathbf{X}_N \mid \theta)}{N} \le \varepsilon_k$$

$$\lim_{k\to\infty} \varepsilon_k = 0 \tag{15}$$

with $\{\varepsilon_k\}$ a known sequence. $\Lambda$ is the set of all $\{\varepsilon_k\}$-uniform entropy-converging stationary-ergodic source probabilities.

The problem is to design an encoder for a source such as those in Examples 1–5 that performs well in some as yet undefined sense without knowing $\theta$. Since coding is to be noiseless, variable-length coding performance can be measured relative to the source entropy conditioned on $\theta$. (How meaningful the conditional entropy is, of course, depends upon how well the source has been parametrized. For conditionally stationary-ergodic sources it is obviously the most meaningful quantity.)

If a code assigns a word of length $l(\mathbf{x}_N)$ to source message block $\mathbf{x}_N$, the conditional average length is

$$\bar{l}(\mathbf{X}_N \mid \theta) = \sum_{A^N} l(\mathbf{x}_N) p(\mathbf{x}_N \mid \theta) \ge H(\mathbf{X}_N \mid \theta) \tag{16}$$

the lower bound following from (9). If $H(X_N \mid \theta) = \infty$, the conditional redundancy is defined as zero since any code is equally effective. For simplicity it will be assumed subsequently that $\Lambda$ is redefined, if necessary, so that $H(H_N \mid \theta) < \infty$ for all $N < \infty$, $\theta \in \Lambda$. We would like, of course, to minimize this for all possible $\theta$ (i.e., approach the entropy $H(\mathbf{X}_N \mid \theta)$). It is not possible to do this pointwise because this would require $\theta$ to be known. That is, $l(\mathbf{x}_N)$ can depend only on what is observed, the source message block, and not the unknown parameter $\theta$. We will define the following.

*Definition 3:* The conditional redundancy of a code for $H(\mathbf{X}_N \mid \theta) < \infty$ is

$$r_N(l,\theta) = \frac{1}{N}[\bar{l}(\mathbf{X}_N \mid \theta) - H(\mathbf{X}_N \mid \theta)]. \tag{17}$$

We know $r_N(l,\theta) \ge 0$ by the variable-length source coding theorem and (16). The average codeword length with respect to $w(\theta)$ is

$$\bar{l}(\mathbf{X}_N) = \int_\Lambda l(\mathbf{X}_N \mid \theta)\, dw(\theta)$$

$$= \int_\Lambda \sum_{A^N} l(\mathbf{x}_N) p(\mathbf{x}_N \mid \theta)\, dw(\theta) \ge H(\mathbf{X}_N \mid \Theta) \tag{18}$$

the lower bound following from (16).

### *Two Examples of Universal Coding*

Before proceeding to a more formal definition of the problem, two examples will be presented to demonstrate the *possibility* of coding a source with conditional redundancy arbitrarily close to zero for all $\theta \in \Lambda$. In Example 1, an $N$-block of $N$–$n$ zeros and $n$ ones is observed. If $\theta$ were known each letter would be independent with $p(\mathbf{x}_N \mid \theta)$ given by (1)

$$p(\mathbf{x}_N \mid \theta) = (1-\theta)^N \left(\frac{\theta}{1-\theta}\right)^n. \tag{19}$$

Consider the following encoding procedure. It is seen from (19) that all sequences with the same number of ones are equally probable. Send the message in two parts. Part one consists of a fixed-length code for the number of ones using at most $\log(N+1) + 1$ b. Part two is a code indicating the location of the ones within the block, one of $\binom{N}{n}$ possibilities. Using a fixed codeword length (given $n$) for each of the possibilities, at most $\log\binom{N}{n} + 1$ b, a variable length that depends on the number of ones is required for this information. The per-letter coding rate is then

$$\leq \frac{1}{N}\left[(\log (N+1)+2)+\log \binom{N}{n}\right]. \tag{20}$$

The first part goes to zero as $N \to \infty$. The expected value of the second part must converge to the per-letter entropy of (2) because the coding rate cannot be below the source entropy, and, at the same time, the second part of the code is optimal, all messages conditioned on the first part being equally likely, independent of $\Theta$

$$n = \sum_{i=1}^{N} x_i$$

is a sufficient statistic for $\Theta$, an idea which will be used more generally later). This will in fact be demonstrated quantitatively later in the section (see also [7]). This method of coding was first presented in [5]–[7]. Note that a comparison of (20) and (3) shows that coding with respect to the whole ensemble with $\Theta$ uniform on [0,1] is asymptotically optimum for this example.

Turning to Example 2, generate a uniquely decipherable code for each of the $M$ possible source distributions using words of length at most $-\log p(\boldsymbol{x}_N \mid \theta) + 1$ by (8). Upon observing a source block $\boldsymbol{x}_N$ to be encoded, send the message in two parts. First go through all $M$ codes and find the minimum-length codeword for $\boldsymbol{x}_N$. As the first part of the message, send the *number* $\theta'$ of the code book of the minimum-length codeword, requiring at most $\log(M) + 1$ b. For the second part of the message, send the corresponding codeword for $\boldsymbol{x}_N$. The average coding rate for any $\theta$ is then

$$\leq \frac{\log (M)+1}{N} + \frac{1}{N}\sum_{A^N} p(\boldsymbol{x}_N \mid \theta)(\min_{\theta'} \{-\log p(\boldsymbol{x}_N \mid \theta')\} + 1)$$

$$\leq \frac{\log M}{N} + \frac{H(\boldsymbol{X}_N \mid \theta)}{N} + \frac{2}{N}. \tag{21}$$

As $N \to \infty$, $M$ remains fixed, so that the minimum coding rate for known $\theta$ is achieved.

A decision-theoretic interpretation of the preceding procedure would be that it is equivalent to making a maximum-likelihood decision as to the true state $\Theta$ of the source at the encoder and then conveying both the decision and the corresponding codeword to the receiver.

### *Formulation of the Universal Coding Problem*

Several measures of optimal universal coding effectiveness will now be proposed. All involve differences between the coding rate and the conditional entropy per block symbol; i.e., all are functions of the conditional redundancy. In each case the infimum is taken over the class $C_N$ of uniquely decipherable codes of block length $N$ or sequences of such codes in $C$, the infinite product space of the $C_N$. Quantities defined as limits are meaningful only if the limit exists. The quantities defined are directly analogous to Bayes', maximin, and minimax risk in decision theory.

*Definition 5:* a) The average redundancy of a code $l \in C_N$ is

$$\mathscr{R}_N(w,l) = \int_{\Lambda} r_N(l,\theta)\, dw(\theta). \tag{22}$$

b) The minimum $N$th-order average redundancy of $w$ is

$$\mathscr{R}_N^*(w) = \inf_{l \in C_N} \mathscr{R}_N(w,C_N). \tag{23}$$

c) The minimum average redundancy of $w$ is (if it exists)

$$\mathscr{R}^*(w) = \lim_{N\to\infty} \mathscr{R}_N^*(w). \tag{24}$$

d) If $\mathscr{R}^*(w) = 0$, a sequence of codes that attains the limit is called *weighted universal.*

Note that the integrand of (22) is nonnegative. Therefore, the conditional redundancy of a weighted universal code converges in probability to zero; i.e.,

$$\lim_{N\to\infty} \Pr\,[r_N(l,\theta) > \varepsilon] = 0. \tag{25}$$

The limit may not be uniform in $\theta$. However, by the Riesz theorem there exists a subsequence of codes which converges almost surely.

*Definition 6:* a) The $N$th-order maximin redundancy of $W$ is

$$\mathscr{R}_N^- = \sup_{w \in W} \mathscr{R}_N^*(w). \tag{26}$$

b) The maximin redundancy of $W$ (if it exists) is

$$\mathscr{R}^- = \lim_{N\to\infty} \mathscr{R}_N^-. \tag{27}$$

If $\mathscr{R}^+ = 0$, a sequence of codes that attains the limit is called *maximin universal.* If there is a $w_* \in W$ which achieves the supremum (as a function of $N$) it is *least favorable.* Equation (25) holds for $w_*$ also, if it exists, of course.

*Definition 7:* a) The $N$th-order minimax redundancy of $\Lambda$ [13], [16] is

$$\mathscr{R}_N^+ = \inf_{C_N} \sup_{\theta\in\Lambda} [r_N(l,\theta)]. \tag{28}$$

b) The minimax redundancy of $\Lambda$ (if it exists) is

$$\mathscr{R}^+ = \lim_{N\to\infty} \mathscr{R}_N^+. \tag{29}$$

If the minimax redundancy $\mathscr{R}^+$ is zero, then the user can transmit the source output at a rate per symbol arbitrarily close to the source entropy rate *uniformly* over all values $\theta \in \Lambda$ (unlike (25)) by taking $N$ large enough. $\mathscr{R}^+ = 0$ is the strongest and most desirable condition to be proposed and can in some cases be achieved, as in the two examples already given. It will be seen, however, that in some cases it is too much to desire. If $\mathscr{R}^+ = 0$, a sequence of codes which attains the limit is called *minimax-universal.*

Although (29) is the form of primary interest, there will be occasion to refer to a weaker form of minimax universal codes.

*Definition 8:* The weak minimax redundancy of $\Lambda$ is

$$\tilde{\mathscr{R}} = \inf_{C} \sup_{\theta\in\Lambda} \lim_{N\to\infty} r_N(l,\theta) \tag{30}$$

where the infinum is over code *sequences.* If $\bar{\mathscr{R}} = 0$, a code sequence which attains the limit is called *weakly minimax universal.* If a code is weakly minimax universal but not minimax universal, it means that the redundancy cannot be bounded uniformly in $N$ over $\Lambda$. Therefore, in practice we would not know how large $N$ should be to insure that the redundancy is below a desired level. This is, however, slightly stronger than (25).

Now the following will be shown.

*Theorem 1:*

a) $\mathscr{R}_N^+ \geq \mathscr{R}_N^- \geq \mathscr{R}_N^*(w)$, for every $N = 1,2,\cdots$.

If the limits exist,

b) $\mathscr{R}^+ \geq \mathscr{R}^- \geq \mathscr{R}^*(w)$.

c) $\mathscr{R}^+ \geq \bar{\mathscr{R}} \geq \mathscr{R}^*(w)$.

*Proof:* $\mathscr{R}_N^- \geq \mathscr{R}_N^*(w)$ by definition. Now let $l'(x_N)$ and $l''(x_N)$ be two arbitrary codes in $C_N$. Consider

$$\inf_{l'(x_N) \in C_N} \int_\Lambda r_N(l',\theta)\, dw(\theta) \leq \int_\Lambda r_N(l'',\theta)\, dw(\theta) \leq \sup_{\theta \in \Lambda} r_N(l'',\theta).$$

Taking the supremum over $w \in W$ of the left side and the infimum over the codes $l''(x_N)$ on the right side retains the inequality. Therefore,

$$\mathscr{R}_N^- \leq \mathscr{R}_N^+.$$

Part b) of the theorem follows by taking limits (when they exist). Part c) follows by first noting that for any sequence of codes in $C$,

$$\mathscr{R}^*(w) \leq \lim_{N\to\infty} \mathscr{R}_N(w,l) \leq \sup_{\theta\in\Lambda} \lim_{N\to\infty} r_N(l,\theta)$$
$$\Rightarrow \mathscr{R}^*(w) \leq \bar{\mathscr{R}}.$$

Second, for any $\varepsilon > 0$, there exists a sequence of codes such that for all $\theta \in \Lambda$, from (29)

$$\lim_{N\to\infty} r_N(l,\theta) \leq \mathscr{R}^+ + \varepsilon.$$

Therefore from (30)

$$\bar{\mathscr{R}} \leq \sup_{\theta\in\Lambda} \lim_{N\to\infty} r_N(l,\theta) \leq \mathscr{R}^+ + \varepsilon.$$

Since this is true for all $\varepsilon > 0$

$$\bar{\mathscr{R}} \leq \mathscr{R}^+.$$

*Minimum Redundancy Codes*

Coding with respect to a measure $w \in W$ is considered first. By Definition 5, (17), and (22),

$$\mathscr{R}_N^*(w) = \inf_{C_N} \frac{\int_\Lambda [\bar{l}(X_N \mid \theta) - H(X_N \mid \theta)]\, dw(\theta)}{N}$$
$$= \inf_{C_N} \frac{1}{N} \int_\Lambda \left[\sum_{A^N} p(x_N \mid \theta) l(x_N) - H(X_N \mid \theta)\right] dw(\theta)$$
$$= \inf_{C_N} \frac{1}{N} \left[\sum_{A^N} p(x_N) l(x_N) - H(X_N \mid \Theta)\right].$$

By the source coding theorem the sum is minimized by encoding with respect to the mixture probability mass function so that from (9)

$$\frac{1}{N}\{H(X_N) - H(X_N \mid \Theta)\} \leq \mathscr{R}_N^*(w) < \frac{1}{N}\{H(X_N) + 1 - H(X_N \mid \Theta)\}$$

or

$$\frac{1}{N} I(X_N;\Theta) \leq \mathscr{R}_N^*(w) < \frac{1}{N} I(X_N;\Theta) + \frac{1}{N} \tag{31}$$

$$\mathscr{R}^*(w) = \lim_{N\to\infty} \frac{1}{N} I(X_N;\Theta).$$

The preceding assumes $H(X_N \mid \Theta) < \infty$. If this is not so, the same conclusion can be reached by expanding $l(x_N)$ before integrating as $l(x_N) = [lx_N + \log p(x_N)] - [\log p(x_N)]$. The latter factor yields $I(X_N,\theta)$ inside the integral and then (31) follows. Hence we have the following theorem.

*Theorem 2:* The minimum average $N$th-order redundancy of $w$ is bounded as in (31). For a finite-alphabet source, the minimum is achieved by Huffman coding with respect to the mixture probability mass function. The necessary and sufficient condition for the existence of weighted universal codes is that the per-letter average mutual information between $X_N$ and $\Theta$ tend to zero.

Note that for a conditionally stationary-ergodic source, in terms of the conditional mutual information

$$\mathscr{R}^*(w) = \lim_{N\to\infty} \frac{1}{N} I(X_N;\Theta) = \lim_{N\to\infty} I(X_N;\Theta \mid X_{N-1}) \tag{32}$$

if the latter is termwise finite, so that weighted universal codes exist if and only if $X_N$ and $\Theta$ have finite conditional average mutual information for all $N$ and are asymptotically independent (in the preceding sense) conditioned on the past $N-1$ message values. It will be seen in Section V that this is always the case if $H(X_1) < \infty$.

Furthermore, we can obtain a theorem for maximin universal codes by using (26), (27), and (31) to get

$$\sup_{w\in W} \frac{1}{N} I(X_N;\Theta) \leq \mathscr{R}_N^- < \sup_{w\in W} \left[\frac{1}{N} I(X_N;\Theta) + \frac{1}{N}\right] \tag{33}$$

$$\mathscr{R}^- = \lim_{N\to\infty} \sup_{w\in W} \frac{1}{N} I(X_N;\Theta). \tag{34}$$

Therefore we have the following theorem.

*Theorem 3:* The $N$th-order maximin redundancy is bounded as in (33). The minimum is achieved for finite alphabets by Huffman coding with respect to the mixture probability mass function determined by the least favorable measure $w^*$ if it exists. The maximin redundancy is given by (34). The necessary and sufficient condition for the existence of maximin universal codes is that the capacity $\mathscr{R}^-$ of the channel between $\Lambda$ and $A$ be zero.

Finding a necessary and sufficient condition for minimax universal codes takes a little more work. Suppose we take an arbitrary probability mass function $q(x_N)$. Then there exists a code with word lengths satisfying (8), therefore, from (28)

$$\mathscr{R}_N^+ \leq \sup_{\theta \in \Lambda} \frac{\sum_{A^N} p(x_N \mid \theta)[-\log q(x_N) + 1 + \log p(x_N \mid \theta)]}{N}$$

$$= \sup_{\theta \in \Lambda} \frac{1}{N} H(p:q) + \frac{1}{N}. \tag{35}$$

Therefore, a sufficient condition for minimax universal coding is that there exist a sequence of probability mass functions for $X_N$ for which the relative entropy vanishes uniformly over $\theta \in \Lambda$ with $N$. Obviously a sufficient condition for *weak* minimax coding is that the relative entropy vanish only pointwise. That the vanishing of relative entropy is also necessary follows from (6). Suppose there is a sequence of $l(x_N)$ for which $\mathscr{R}^+ = 0$. Then define

$$Q_N = \sum_{A^N} 2^{-l(x_N)}$$

where, by the Kraft inequality (6)

$$Q_N \leq 1.$$

Let

$$q(x_N) = \frac{2^{-l(x_N)}}{Q_N} \tag{36}$$

so that

$$\sum_{A^N} q(x_N) = 1. \tag{37}$$

Since $\mathscr{R}^+ = 0$, from (29)

$$0 = \lim_{N \to \infty} \sup_{\theta \in \Lambda} \left\{ \frac{\sum_{A^N} p(x_N \mid \theta)[l(x_N) + \log p(x_N \mid \theta)]}{N} \right\}$$

$$= \lim_{N \to \infty} \sup_{\theta \in \Lambda} \left\{ \frac{\sum_{A^N} p(x_N \mid \theta)[-\log q(x_N) + \log p(x_N \mid \theta)] - \log Q_N}{N} \right\} \geq \lim_{N \to \infty} \frac{1}{N} \sup_{\theta \in \Lambda} H(p:q) \geq 0. \tag{38}$$

Similarly the necessary condition for *weak* minimax coding is the pointwise vanishing of the relative entropy.

To summarize we have the following theorem.

*Theorem 4:* The necessary and sufficient condition for the existence of minimax universal codes is that there exist a sequence of probability mass functions $q(x_N)$ for which the per-letter relative entropy of $p(x_N \mid \theta)$ is zero uniformly in $\theta$, i.e.,

$$\mathscr{R}^+ = \lim_{N \to \infty} \frac{1}{N} \sup_{\theta \in \Lambda} H(p:q) = 0. \tag{39}$$

The necessary and sufficient condition for the existence of weakly minimax codes is that the convergence to zero be only pointwise in $\theta$. A sufficient condition for the existence of minimax universal codes is that there exist a *mixture* probability mass function for which the conditional average of the mutual information be zero, i.e., $q(\cdot)$ satisfies (4) for some $w \in W$ so that (39) becomes

$$\lim_{N \to \infty} \frac{1}{N} \sup_{\theta \in \Lambda} I(X_N, \theta) = 0. \tag{40}$$

A sufficient condition for the existence of a weakly universal codes is that the convergence to zero be only pointwise in $\theta$.

The determination of maximin and minimax codes is most easily made by searching the class of minimum average redundancy codes. This is analogous to decision theory where Bayes' rules are sometimes more easily found than minimax rules, so that minimax rules are constructed by searching the class of admissible Bayes' rules or by finding the Bayes' rule with respect to a "best guess" least favorable prior. (For $\Lambda$ finite, minimum average redundancy codes have in fact been called Bayes [18].)

Rather than calculate the mutual information directly it is frequently easier to construct a code which has zero redundancy. We will consider now several examples where the mutual information can be shown to vanish (directly, though), and then turn to constructive techniques. Suppose with $w$-measure one $\Theta$ takes on only a denumerable number, $M$, of values $\{\theta_k\}$ with probabilities $\{w_k\}$. Then

$$\frac{1}{N} I(X_N, \Theta) = \frac{1}{N} [H(\Theta) - H(\Theta \mid X_N)]$$

$$\leq \frac{1}{N} H(\Theta) \leq \frac{\log M}{N}. \tag{41}$$

Or from (31), (40) we have the following.

*Corollary:* If $\Theta$ takes on at most a denumerable number of values with $w$-measure one, weighted universal codes exist if $H(\Theta) < \infty$. (It is possible to construct infinite-entropy discrete random variables, e.g., $w_k \sim (k \log^{1+\delta} k)^{-1}$, $\delta > 0$.) If $\Theta$ takes on only a finite $M < \infty$ number of values, minimax universal codes exist. This was already shown by construction in (21) for Example 2.

Returning now to Example 1 with $\Theta$ uniform and using (1) and (3) the conditional average of the mutual information is

$$\frac{1}{N} I(X_N; \theta) = \frac{1}{N} \sum_{n=0}^{N} \binom{N}{n} \theta^n (1-\theta)^{N-n}$$

$$\cdot \log \left[ (N+1) \binom{N}{n} \theta^n (1-\theta)^{N-n} \right]$$

$$= \frac{\log (N+1)}{N} - \frac{1}{N} \times \begin{bmatrix} \text{entropy of a binomial} \\ \text{random variable with} \\ \text{parameter } \theta \end{bmatrix}$$

$$\leq \frac{\log (N+1)}{N} \xrightarrow[N \to \infty]{} 0. \tag{42}$$

Hence the code constructed by taking $\Theta$ uniform results in a minimax universal code (although *not* necessarily minimax for $N < \infty$) and hence, through Theorem 1, a maximin and weighted universal code for any $w \in W$.

It is clear that the minimax property depends upon the choice of $w$. If, in this example, there is an interval in [0,1] given zero weight, then coding with the mixture probability mass function is not minimax universal.

The existence of weighted universal codes can depend upon the choice of $w$ as well. In Example 3, take $\Theta$ to be uniform. Then

$$H(X_N \mid \theta) = 0, \qquad \text{all } \theta \in \Lambda$$
$$H(X_N) = N \tag{43}$$

so that the minimum average redundancy is

$$\mathscr{R}^*(w) = \lim_{N\to\infty} \frac{1}{N} I(X_N;\Theta) = 1. \tag{44}$$

This is fairly obvious because the "randomness" is in the $\Theta$ rather than $X_N$ and $\mathscr{R}^*(w) > 0$ is a consequence of the artificiality of the problem setup. $\mathscr{R}^*(w) > 0$ can in fact be demonstrated in this example for any distribution on $\Theta$ with a nonconstant absolutely continuous component on [0,1]. On the other hand, from the corollary, if $\Theta$ takes on only a denumerable number of values with $H(\Theta) < \infty$, weighted universal coding is possible.

Example 4 provides us with an infinite-alphabet example. It should be clear that if the Poisson parameter can take on "too many" values, universal coding may not be possible. Suppose we let

$$dw(\theta) = \alpha e^{-\alpha\theta}\, d\theta, \qquad \theta \ge 0, \tag{45}$$

where $\alpha$ is some constant. Then the mixture probability mass function is

$$p(x_N) = \int_0^\infty \frac{\theta^n e^{-N\theta}}{\prod_{i=1}^N (x_i!)} \alpha e^{-\alpha\theta}\, d\theta \tag{46}$$

$$= \frac{\alpha n!}{(N+\alpha)^{n+1} \prod_{i=1}^N (x_i!)} \tag{47}$$

where

$$n = \sum_{i=1}^N x_i.$$

The average mutual information is

$$\frac{1}{N} I(X_N;\Theta) = \frac{1}{N}\int_0^\infty \sum_{n=0}^\infty \frac{(N\theta)^n e^{-N\theta}}{n!} \cdot \log\left[\left(\frac{N+\alpha}{N}\right)^{n+1}\left(\frac{N}{\alpha}\right)\frac{(N\theta)^n e^{-N\theta}}{n!}\right] \alpha e^{-\alpha\theta}\, d\theta$$
$$= \int_0^\infty \left\{\frac{1}{N}\left[(N\theta+1)\log\frac{N+\alpha}{N} + \log\frac{N}{\alpha} - \begin{pmatrix}\text{entropy of a Poisson}\\ \text{random variable with}\\ \text{parameter } N\theta\end{pmatrix}\right]\right\} \alpha e^{-\alpha\theta}\, d\theta$$
$$\le \frac{\left(1+\frac{N}{\alpha}\right)\log\left(1+\frac{\alpha}{N}\right) + \log\frac{N}{\alpha}}{N} \xrightarrow[N\to\infty]{} 0. \tag{48}$$

On the other hand, it can be shown that for any $N < \infty$ and any $\varepsilon > 0$ there is an $\alpha > 0$ such that

$$\frac{1}{N} I(X_N;\Theta) > \varepsilon. \tag{49}$$

Therefore, no maximin (or minimax by Theorem 1) universal coding is possible by Theorem 1. However, *weakly* minimax universal coding is possible, as can be seen by taking the limit of the integrand in (48) for every $\theta$. It also can be shown that minimax universal codes exist if $\Lambda$ is defined as a finite rather than an infinite interval.

We now turn to universal coding based upon constructive methods.

### *A Sufficient Condition for the Existence of Universal Codes*

Theorem 2 provides a necessary and sufficient condition for the existence of weighted universal codes. The calculations involved cannot always be easily done and, in addition, no particular insight as to practical implementation can be gained in many instances. The theorem presented here provides some help in that direction. The theorem applies to the coding scheme where code books are developed and enumerated for many "representative" values of $\theta$. For any given $x_N$, the identity of the code book with the shortest codeword plus the codeword itself is transmitted in the way presented for Example 2 earlier in this section.

*Theorem 6—Code Book Theorem:* Suppose there exists a sequence of partitions of $A^N$ into sets $\{\Gamma_j^{(N)}; j = 1,2,\cdots, J(N)\}$, $J(N)$ possibly infinite, with $x_N \in \Gamma_{j(x_N)}^{(N)}$, where for some set $\{\theta_j; j = 1,2,\cdots,J(N)\}$, and some sequence of vanishing positive numbers $\varepsilon(N)$

$$E\left[\frac{1}{N}\log\frac{p(X_N \mid \Theta)}{p(X_N \mid \theta_{j(X_N)})}\right] \le \varepsilon(N). \tag{50}$$

Let

$$\mu_j^{(N)} = \Pr[\Gamma_j^{(N)}] = \int_\Lambda \sum_{\Gamma_j^{(N)}} p(x_N \mid \theta)\, dw(\theta). \tag{51}$$

a) If

$$\lim_{N\to\infty} \frac{1}{N} E[-\log \mu_{j(X_N)}^{(N)}] = 0 \tag{52}$$

then weighted universal codes exist.

b) If (50) and (52) hold pointwise in $\theta$, i.e., for some sequence of vanishing numbers $\varepsilon(N,\theta)$

$$\frac{1}{N} E\left[\log\frac{p(X_N \mid \theta)}{p(X_N \mid \theta_{j(X_N)})} \,\middle|\, \theta\right] \le \varepsilon(N,\theta) \tag{53}$$

and for some set of probabilities, not necessarily satisfying (51) for any $w \in W$,

$$\lim_{N\to\infty} \frac{1}{N} E[-\log \mu_{j(X_N)}^{(N)} \mid \theta] = 0 \tag{54}$$

then weakly minimax universal codes exist.

c) If (53) and (54) hold uniformly in $\theta$, i.e., $\varepsilon(N,\theta) \le \varepsilon(N)$ in (53) and $\lim_N \sup_\theta$ can replace $\lim_N$ in (54), minimax universal codes exist.

*Comment 1:* (54) is obviously satisfied, in particular if

$$\lim_{N\to\infty} \frac{\log J(N)}{N} = 0. \tag{55}$$

*Comment 2:* The sequence $\{\theta_j\}$ is a sequence of asymptotically maximum-likelihood estimates of $\Theta$ for the source output observations $\{x_N\}$. It is seen that the theorem is useful if a set of these estimates can be found involving a many-to-one mapping of $A^N$ into $\Lambda$. Several examples will be given after the theorem proof.

*Proof:* Part a) will be proven by showing that the conditions of the theorem imply vanishing per-letter mutual information

$$\frac{1}{N} I(X_N;\Theta) = E\left[\frac{1}{N}\log\frac{p(X_N \mid \Theta)}{p(X_N)}\right]$$
$$\le E\left[\frac{1}{N}\log\frac{p(X_N \mid \theta_{j(x_N)})}{p(X_N)}\right] + \varepsilon(N).$$

$\theta_{j(x_N)}$ is a deterministic mapping. Therefore, $p(X_N)$ can be factored trivially to give

$$\frac{1}{N} I(X_N;\Theta) \le E\left[\frac{1}{N}\log\frac{p(X_N \mid \theta_{j(x_N)})}{p(X_N \mid \theta_{j(x_N)})p(\theta_{j(x_N)})}\right] + \varepsilon(N)$$
$$= \frac{1}{N} E[-\log \mu_{j(x_N)}] + \varepsilon(N) \underset{N\to\infty}{\longrightarrow} 0. \tag{56}$$

Parts b) and c) of the theorem follow by considering relative entropy with

$$q(x_N) = p(x_N \mid \theta_{j(x_N)})\mu_{j(x_N)} \tag{57}$$

and proceeding as in (56).

A code construction based upon $J(N)$ code books, one for each of the "representative" values $\theta_j$, is suggested by (50)–(57).

Find a code book for the set $\{\theta_j\}$ with words of length

$$m_j \le -\log \mu_j^{(N)} + 1. \tag{58}$$

For each $\theta_j$ find a code book for every $x_N \in A^N$ with words of length

$$n_j(x_N) \le -\log p(x_N \mid \theta_j) + 1. \tag{59}$$

The codeword corresponding to each $x_N$ is then composed of two parts: the code book $j(x_N)$ to which $x_N$ belongs and the codeword in that code book; thus from (58) and (59)

$$l(x_N) = m_{j(x_N)} + n_{j(x_N)}(x_N)$$
$$\le -\log \mu_{j(x_N)}^{(N)} - \log p(x_N \mid \theta_{j(x_N)}) + 2.$$

It follows immediately that this code is universal in the appropriate sense. Examples 1–5 can all be handled by the code book theorem. Example 5 will be considered in the next section. In Example 2, $\{\theta_j\}$ are possible values of $\Theta$. In Example 1, the values $\theta_j$ are $j/(N+1)$, $j = 0,1,\cdots,N$, corresponding to the relative frequency of ones observed at the source output. This is a particular example of a sufficient statistic. More generally, if $\theta_s(x_N)$ is a sufficient statistic for $\Theta$, by the factorization theorem

$$p(x_N \mid \theta) = p(x_N \mid \theta_s(x_N))p(\theta_s(x_N) \mid \theta). \tag{60}$$

Therefore, the values $\{\theta_j\}$ are maximizing values of $p(\theta_s(x_N) \mid \theta_j)$, which is a great simplification in many cases (e.g., Example 1). As a special but important case, let $\{\theta_{sj};\ j = 1,2,\cdots,J(N) \le \infty\}$ be an enumeration of the values of a sufficient statistic for $\theta$ and let $\{\theta_k\}$ be the corresponding maximum-likelihood estimates, which are assumed to exist, i.e.,

$$p(\theta_{sj} \mid \theta_j) = \sup_{\theta\in\Lambda} p(\theta_{sj} \mid \theta). \tag{61}$$

Then

$$\mu_j^{(N)} = \sum_{x_N:\,\theta_s(x_N)=\theta_{sj}} \int_\Lambda p(x_N \mid \theta)\,dw(\theta)$$
$$= \sum_{x_N:\,\theta_s(x_N)=\theta_{sj}} p(x_N \mid \theta_s(x_N)) \int_\Lambda p(\theta_s(x_N) \mid \theta)\,dw(\theta)$$
$$= \int_\Lambda p(\theta_{sj} \mid \theta)\,dw(\theta)$$
$$= p(\theta_s(x_N) = \theta_{sj}). \tag{62}$$

Then in the code book theorem we can take $\varepsilon(N) = \varepsilon(N,\theta) = 0$. We have the following.

*Corollary 1:* A sufficient condition for weighted universal codes to exist is that a sufficient statistic for $\Theta$ have entropy satisfying

$$\lim_{N\to\infty} -\frac{1}{N}\sum_{j=1}^{J(N)} p(\theta_{sj})\log p(\theta_{sj}) = 0.$$

*Corollary 2:* A sufficient condition for weakly minimax universal codes to exist is that the sequence of probability mass functions for the sufficient statistic is such that

$$\lim_{N\to\infty}\frac{1}{N} E[-\log p(\theta_s(x_N)) \mid \theta] = 0 \tag{63}$$

for every $\theta \in \Lambda$. Minimax universal codes exist if this convergence to zero is uniform in $\theta$.

In Example 4, the sum of the letter outputs in the block is a sufficient statistic for $\Theta$. As previously noted, minimax universal codes do not exist for $\Lambda = [0,\infty)$. It is now seen that this can be interpreted as being due to the sufficient statistic taking on arbitrarily large values with nonvanishing probability. We *can* construct a weakly minimax universal code as follows. For the first part of the code, send

$$n = \sum_{i=1}^{N} x_i$$

using a two-part subcode. Let $M$ be the integer satisfying

$$\log_2(n+1) \le M < \log_2(n+1) + 1. \tag{64}$$

Send $M$ zeros followed by a 1. Then send the natural binary codeword of length $M$ for $n$. The per-letter code length contributed by the sufficient statistic is then

$$\le \frac{2[\log_2(n+1) + 1]}{N}. \tag{65}$$

By the convexity of $\log x$, for any value of $\theta$

$$E\left[\frac{2[\log(n+1)+1]}{N}\,\middle|\,\theta\right] \le \frac{2\log(E[n \mid \theta]+1)+1}{N} = \frac{2\log(N\theta+1)+1}{N} \xrightarrow[N\to\infty]{} 0. \tag{66}$$

Note that this code construction is only weakly minimax since (66) is unbounded in $\theta$ for $N < \infty$.

The second part of the code consists of course of the message sequence conditioned on the sufficient statistic. This coding can be done optimally.

## V. Histogram Encoding

We now consider code constructions of great generality for use when very little is known of the source. In terms of Section IV, the $\Theta$ parameter could represent all possible source probabilities in a class, e.g., Example 5. Essentially the idea is to measure the block conditional histogram on subblocks, encoding both the histogram and the codeword constructed according to the histogram. Obviously the latter portion must do at least as well as the code constructed using the actual subblock conditional probabilities. In fact, if it is known that the source is conditionally stationary ergodic and $k$th-order Markov where $k < \infty$, then the histogram of that order is a sufficient statistic for $\Theta$ and the corollaries to the code book theorem apply. If the alphabet size is finite, the number of values of the sufficient statistic in (55) satisfies $\log J(N) < L^{k+1} \log(N+1)$, and it is seen immediately that a minimax universal code results. If $L = \infty$ and/or if the source is not Markov, then one must be satisfied with weaker forms of universal codes.

If the source is finite-alphabet and conditionally stationary ergodic, the conditional probabilities converge and the values of $\theta_i$ in the code book theorem can be taken as those conditional probabilities, which are $k$th-order Markov and which coincide with the possible values of the $k$th-order relative frequencies for each $N$. We then let $k \to \infty$ with $N$, so that (55) is satisfied. Because of the convergence of conditional probabilities, (53) is satisfied and thus the sequence is weakly minimax. Without further restriction, the codes are not minimax.

If the source is infinite-alphabet and conditionally stationary ergodic, (53) is satisfied by the histograms as in the last paragraph, but $J(N) = \infty$ and conditions of the form of (52) or (54) must be added for universal coding in the appropriate sense. Because of the importance of this type of coding we will describe the particular construction in greater detail. The essential constructive idea for these codes is due to Fitingof [3], [4] with improvement and information-theoretic interpretation by Shtarkov and Babkin [9].

*Theorem 7:* Let $\Lambda$ be the space of all stationary-ergodic processes indexed by $\theta$ with finite alphabet size, i.e., $L < \infty$. Then weakly minimax (and hence weighted) universal codes exist. If in addition the probabilities are entropy-stable in the sense of satisfying (15), minimax universal codes exist.

Two constructive methods will be presented for proof of the theorem.

*Proof:* Both are based on histograms on subblocks of length $k$ (called $k$-grams by Fitingof [3]), where for simplicity in the second method it is assumed that $N/k$ is an integer. In the proof, as $N \to \infty$ we will let $k \to \infty$ in such a way that the per-letter "overhead" information $\to 0$. The reason for this is that we want certain source probability information to require a vanishing portion of the codeword while increasing the allowed dimensionality of the probability information.

The first construction uses conditional histograms. Encode the first $k$ values using a fixed-length code of at most $\log(L^k) + 1$ b. Follow this by an encoding of the *conditional* histogram of each of the $L$ source letters, where the conditioning is on each of the $L^k$ possible immediate past sequences of length $k$. Using a fixed-length code, this requires at most

$$\begin{aligned} &\{(\text{number of histograms}) \\ &\quad \times (\text{number of cells in the histogram}) \\ &\quad \times \log_2(\text{number of possible values in each cell})\} + 1 \\ &= L^k \times L \times \log_2(N+1) + 1 \\ &= L^{k+1} \log_2(N+1) + 1 \quad \text{b}. \end{aligned} \tag{67}$$

Finally this is followed by a codeword for the remaining $N - k$ letters following the first $k$ (which are already encoded). The length of the codeword will be chosen in proportion to the log of the conditional histogram for each value. To be more precise, let the histogram by denoted as follows:

$$q_k(x_{n+k+1} \mid x_{n+1}, \cdots, x_{n+k}). \tag{68}$$

Then the codeword will be at most of length

$$-\log_2 \prod_{n=0}^{N-k-1} q_k(x_{n+k+1} \mid x_{n+1}, \cdots, x_{n+k}) + 1. \tag{69}$$

Then the total per-letter codeword length is, from (67)–(69),

$$\begin{aligned} \frac{1}{N} l(X_N) \le \frac{1}{N} \log L^k + \frac{1}{N} L^{k+1} \log_2(N+1) \\ - \frac{1}{N} \sum_{n=0}^{N-k-1} \log_2 q_k(x_{n+k+1} \mid x_{n+1}, \cdots, x_{n+k}) \\ + \frac{3}{N}. \end{aligned} \tag{70}$$

Letting $N, k \to \infty$ so that $k/\log N \to 0$ eliminates all terms but the sum, which requires greater scrutiny. By definition of the histogram, the sum can be written as the following:

$$-\frac{1}{N}\sum_{n=0}^{N-k-1}\log_2 q_k(x_{n+k+1}\mid x_{n+1},\cdots,x_{n+k})$$

$$= -\frac{1}{N}\sum_{x_{k+1}\in A^{k+1}}(\text{number of times } x_{k+1} \text{ follows } x_k)$$

$$\cdot \log_2 q_k(x_{k+1}\mid x_k)$$

$$= -\frac{N-k}{N}\sum_{x_{k+1}\in A^{k+1}}\frac{(\text{number of times } x_{k+1} \text{ follows } x_k)}{(\text{number of times } x_k \text{ appears})}$$

$$\cdot\frac{(\text{number of times } x_k \text{ appears})}{N-k}\cdot\log_2 q_k(x_{k+1}\mid x_k)$$

$$= -\frac{N-k}{N}\sum_{x_{k+1}\in A^k} q_k(x_{k+1}\mid x_k)q_k(x_k)\log_2 q_k(x_{k+1}\mid x_k). \quad (71)$$

Note that the quantity in (71) (called quasi-entropy [3]) represents the absolute minimum average codeword length for the given histogram and, hence, for the observed block when the $k$-length constraint is applied. If the average of (71) is now taken over the ensemble (i.e., average with respect to $p(x_N \mid \theta)$), it is bounded above by $((N-k)/N)\, H(X_k \mid X_{k-1}, \theta)$ through convexity of $-x\log x$. The weak minimax redundancy is bounded by letting $k \to \infty$ with $N$ so that $k/\log N \to 0$, and by using (70) and (71) we have

$$\mathscr{R} \le \sup_\theta \lim_{N\to\infty}\left\{\frac{N-k}{N}H(X_{k+1}\mid X_k,\theta) - \frac{1}{N}H(X_N\mid\theta)\right\}$$

$$\le \lim_{N\to\infty}\left(\frac{H(X_{k+1}\mid\theta)}{k+1} - \lim_{N\to\infty}\frac{H(X_N\mid\theta)}{N}\right) = 0 \quad (72)$$

the latter statement following from the stationary ergodic property. By Theorem 1, weighted universal codes also exist. If in addition (15) holds, then

$$\mathscr{R}^+ \le \lim_{k\to\infty}\varepsilon_k = 0.$$

The second constructive proof is based upon a histogram of the possible values of the $k$-grams. Use a fixed-length code for the histogram as in (68), requiring at most

$$(\text{number of cells}) \times \log_2(\text{number of possible values/cell})$$
$$= L^k\log_2(N+1) + 1 \quad \text{b.} \quad (73)$$

as before. Call the histogram itself $q_k(x_k)$ as in (71). Encode each of the $k$-grams using at most $-\log_2 q_k(\cdot) + 1$ b. The per-letter codeword length is then

$$\frac{1}{N}l(X_N) \le \frac{1}{N}L^k\log_2(N+1) + \frac{1}{N} - \frac{1}{k}$$

$$\cdot\sum_{A^k} q_k(x_k)\log q_k(x_k) + \frac{1}{k}. \quad (74)$$

Taking the expected value of (74), we obtain

$$\frac{1}{N}\bar{l}(X_N\mid\theta) \le \frac{1}{N}L^k\log(N+1) + \frac{1}{N} + \frac{1}{k}H(X_k\mid\theta) + \frac{1}{k}. \quad (75)$$

Letting $k$, $N \to \infty$, $k/\log N \to 0$,

$$\mathscr{R} \le \sup_\theta \lim_{N\to\infty}\left[\frac{1}{k}H(X_k\mid\theta) - \frac{1}{N}H(X_N\mid\theta)\right] = 0 \quad (76)$$

and if (15) applies

$$\mathscr{R}^+ \le \lim_{k\to\infty}\varepsilon_k = 0.$$

The theorem is established. Note that convergence will be slower with $k$ in the second method than in the first since $k$-grams are encoded independently.

The theorem can be extended to infinite-alphabet sources as follows.

*Theorem 8:* Let $\Lambda$ be the space of all stationary-ergodic processes indexed by $\theta$ as in Theorem 7 with finite entropy $H(X_1) < \infty$. Weighted universal codes for such sources exist. If there exists a probability mass function $p(x_1)$ such that

$$E[-\log p(X_1)\mid\theta] < \infty \quad (77)$$

for all $\theta\in\Lambda$, then weakly minimax universal codes exist. If (77) is a bounded function of $\theta$ and (15) holds, minimax universal codes exist.

*Remark:* (77) is a very weak restriction. The existence of $E[\log X_1 \mid \theta]$ is sufficient for example.

*Proof:* The proof is by construction in a manner similar to the last. All values in the block of length $N$ are limited in value to $\log(N+1)$, taken to be an integer for simplicity, and the result encoded by either of the code constructions of the last theorem with truncated alphabet size $L = \log(N+1)$. Additional information is added to the end of the block for those values $\ge \log(N+1)$ on a letter-by-letter basis in order of their appearance using a codeword of length $\le -\log p(x_1) + 1$. Using the second construction of the last theorem, to be specific, and noting that the limiting operation decreases entropy, the average codeword length is bounded in (75) with $L = \log N$ plus the additional information for the extreme values

$$\frac{1}{N}\bar{l}(X_N\mid\theta) \le \frac{1}{N}(\log N+1)^k + \frac{1}{N} + \frac{1}{k}H(X_k\mid\theta) + \frac{1}{k}$$

$$+ \sum_{x_1=\log(N+1)}^{\infty} p(x_1\mid\theta)[-\log p(x_1) + 1].$$

The last term goes to zero with $N\to\infty$ in the weighted sense since $H(X_1) < \infty$, and in the minimax sense if (77) holds. The other terms are handled as in the last theorem with $k$, $N\to\infty$ so that $(\log N+1)^k/N \to 0$.

This completes the proof of Theorem 8. Note that Theorems 2, 7, and 8 imply that the mutual information between the parameter space and the observation space goes to zero for *all* finite-entropy conditionally stationary-ergodic sources. Thus for all stationary-ergodic sources it is not necessary to know the source probabilities to encode in an asymptotically optimal fashion. Of course, the less one knows of the source probabilities, the larger the block size must be for a given average redundancy level.

The vanishing of the mutual information can in fact be shown directly through the convergence of conditional probabilities and the code book theorem.

The idea of quasi-entropic encoding [3], [9], [11] can be extended to arbitrary nonstationary, nonergodic sources. Here the performance measure could be taken as the minimum average length code over the block which is fixed on $k$-grams. It is obvious from (71) and (74) that quasi-entropic encoding does the best that can be done in this regard.

## VI. Fixed-Rate Coding

We suppose now that fixed rather than variable-length coding is to be employed blockwise. Let $R$ be the coding rate in bits per source letter so that each block is encoded into $RN$ b. We can define error probabilities in analogy to the redundancies of Section IV. Here a *code* will mean an assignment of $x_N$ to one of the distinct $2^{RN}$ codewords or a random assignment, in which case an error is made. $C_N(R)$ is now the space of all such assignments. For a particular code let

$$\delta(x_N) = \begin{cases} 0, & \text{if } x_N \text{ has a distinct codeword} \\ 1, & \text{otherwise} \end{cases}$$

so that the conditional error probability is

$$P_{eN}(R,\theta) = \sum_{A^N} \delta(x_N) p(x_N \mid \theta). \quad (79)$$

*Definition 9:* The average error probability of $w$ is given by

$$P_e^*(R,w) = \lim_{N\to\infty} \inf_{C_N(R)} \int_\Lambda P_{eN}(R,\theta)\, dw(\theta). \quad (80)$$

*Definition 10:* The maximin error probability of $W$ is given by

$$P_e^-(R) = \lim_{N\to\infty} \sup_{w\in W} \inf_{C_N(R)} \int_\Lambda P_{eN}(R,\theta)\, dw(\theta). \quad (81)$$

*Definition 11:* The minimax error probability of $\Lambda$ is given by

$$P_e^+(R) = \lim_{N\to\infty} \inf_{C_N(R)} \sup_{\theta\in\Lambda} P_{eN}(R,\theta). \quad (82)$$

*Definition 12:* The weakly minimax error probability of $\Lambda$ is given by

$$\tilde{P}_e = \inf_{C(R)} \sup_{\theta\in\Lambda} \lim_{N\to\infty} P_{eN}(R,\theta). \quad (83)$$

A code sequence for which zero error probability is attained will be called a universal code in the various senses that were defined for variable-length codes in Section IV. Theorems for performance as in (83) have been considered by Ziv [11].

General theorems can be developed for universal fixed-rate coding in analogy with Section IV. It is apparent, for example, that the $\inf_{C_N(R)}$ in (80), (81) is taken by assigning distinct codewords to the most probable $x_N$ vectors with respect to the mixture probability mass function. Let $\delta(x_N)$ satisfy the equation

$$\delta(x_N) = \begin{cases} 0, & \text{if } p(x_N) > T_N \\ 1, & \text{if } p(x_N) \le T_N \end{cases} \quad (84)$$

where $T_N$ is determined parametrically as the smallest value for which

$$\sum_{A^N} (1 - \delta(x_N)) \le 2^{RN}. \quad (85)$$

Obviously a necessary and sufficient condition for weighted fixed-rate universal coding is that $R$ be large enough so that

$$\lim_{N\to\infty} \sum_{A^N} \delta(x_N)p(x_N) = 0. \quad (86)$$

A similar procedure holds for (81). The integrands are nonnegative in (80) and (81); therefore, zero error probability implies almost-everywhere zero error probability with respect to $w$. Therefore, we need only find a mixture which yields $P_e^+(R) = 0$ in (82) to get a minimax code, if one exists.

We will not develop the general theorems, however. We will only consider a theorem for finite-alphabet conditionally stationary-ergodic sources that follows immediately from Theorem 7 and the McMillan asymptotic equipartition property.

*Theorem 9:* Let $\Lambda$ be the space of all stationary-ergodic processes indexed by $\theta$ with finite alphabet $L < \infty$. Then for any rate $R$ such that

$$R > \lim_{N\to\infty} N^{-1} \sup_\theta H(X_N \mid \theta) \quad (87)$$

weakly minimax (and hence weighted) fixed-rate universal codes exist in the sense of (83).

*Proof:* We use either of the codes in Theorem 7 with zeros added on the end if $l(x_N) < RN$ and truncation if $l(x_N) > RN$, in which case an error occurs. By the stationary-ergodic property (for the first code) for any $k_0$,

$$\Pr\left[\lim_{N\to\infty} \frac{l(X_N)}{N} = H(X_{k_0+1} \mid X_{k_0}, \theta) \mid \theta\right]$$
$$= \Pr\left[\lim_{N\to\infty} \frac{1}{N}\sum_{n=0}^{N-k} -\log q_{k_0}(x_{n+k} \mid x_{n+1},\cdots,x_{n+k_0-1})\right.$$
$$\left. = H(X_{k_0+1} \mid X_{k_0}, \theta) \mid \theta\right] = 1. \quad (88)$$

Therefore, we can find a sequence of values $k$ and $N$, depending on $k$, such that for every $\theta \varepsilon \Lambda$

$$\lim_{k,N\to\infty} \Pr\left[\frac{l(X_N)}{N} > R \mid \theta\right] = 0. \quad (89)$$

Another construction due to Ziv [11] is based upon the $k$-gram histogram of Theorem 7. Find the most frequently occurring $k$-grams in the block of $N$ and assign each of these a fixed-length code of length

$$\le \log J + 1. \quad (90)$$

Send the list of $Jk$-grams first. Then follow this by $N/k$ fixed-length codewords for the observed $k$-gram sequence.

The per-letter codeword length is

$$\frac{l(x_N)}{N} = \frac{l(X_N)}{N} \le \frac{1}{N}\left[J(\log L^k + 1) + \frac{N}{k}(\log I + 1)\right] \quad \text{b.} \tag{91}$$

Choose $J$, $k$, and $N$ so that the result is less than $R$. To be specific, pick some $\varepsilon$ such that

$$0 < \varepsilon < R - \lim_{k\to\infty} k^{-1} \sup_\theta H(X_k \mid \theta)$$

$$2^{k(R-\varepsilon)} \le J < 2^{k(R-\varepsilon)} + 1 \tag{92}$$

resulting in

$$\frac{l(X_N)}{N} \le \frac{k2^{k(R-\varepsilon)}}{N} \log_2 L + R - \varepsilon + \frac{k}{N}\log_2 L + \frac{1 + 2^{-k(R-\varepsilon)}}{k}. \tag{93}$$

Now let $k, N \to \infty$ so that

$$\frac{k2^{k(R-\varepsilon)}}{N} \to 0. \tag{94}$$

For sufficiently large $N$,

$$\frac{l(X_N)}{N} \le R.$$

To achieve $R$ exactly the balance of the block if any is filled with zeros.

Note that the first part of the codeword, the codeword list, requires a vanishingly small portion of the message, as usual. For the balance of the message we are coding as well as can possibly be done with a code fixed on $k$-grams. From (92) and a statement similar to (88) and (89) we conclude immediately that

$$\lim_{N\to\infty} P_{eN}(l,\theta) = 0 \tag{95}$$

because for large enough $k$ we have

$$J > 2^{H(X_k \mid \theta)}$$

distinct codewords for every $\theta \in \Lambda$ for our conditionally stationary source. The codes constructed are also seen to be minimax if (89) can be bounded uniformly in $\boldsymbol{\theta}$. They are only weighted universal if (87) holds only almost everywhere with respect to $w$.

For more general sources, we have done the best we can; we could in fact define the entropy as the minimum rate for which (95) holds [11].

## VII. Some Open Problems

1) Show, if possible, by counterexample that the stronger condition of (40) is not necessary for minimax universal coding; i.e., the conditional average of the mutual information can be nonzero for all prior probability measures $w(\boldsymbol{\theta})$, while the relative entropy of (39) is zero for some probability mass function.

2) Give an interpretation to the vanishing of per-letter mutual information for conditionally stationary-ergodic sources. Determine whether finite entropy is necessary and, if not, extend to nondiscrete sources.

3) Investigate the effect of length constraints on the variable-length codes.

4) Establish theorems for fixed-rate coding as in Section VI. In particular find a condition on the source for which the integrand of (89) can be bounded *uniformly* in $\theta$ to get minimax and maximin fixed-rate universal codes.

5) Find minimax universal codes for finite $N$.

6) Apply universal codes to practical sources.

7) Apply the methods defined here to coding with distortion.

## Acknowledgment

The author wishes to acknowledge the many helpful suggestions of M. B. Pursley of the University of Southern California and of Prof. Robert M. Gray of Stanford University, who noted in particular the asymptotic conditional independence of (32) for conditionally stationary-ergodic sources.

## References

[1] T. Berger, *Rate Distortion Theory—A Mathematical Basis for Data Compression.* Englewood Cliffs, N.J.: Prentice-Hall, 1971.
[2] A. N. Kolmogorov, "Three approaches to the quantitative definition of information," *Probl. Inform. Transm.*, vol. 1, no. 1, pp. 3–11 (in Russian), pp. 1–7 (English Transl.), 1965.
[3] B. M. Fitingof, "Optimal coding in the case of unknown and changing message statistics," *Probl. Inform. Transm.*, vol. 2, no. 2, pp. 3–11 (in Russian), pp. 1–7 (English Transl.), 1966.
[4] ——, "The compression of discrete information," *Probl. Inform. Transm.*, vol. 3, no. 3, pp. 28–36 (in Russian), pp. 22–29 (English Transl.), 1967.
[5] T. J. Lynch, "Sequence time coding for data compression," *Proc. IEEE* (Corresp.), vol. 54, pp. 1490–1491, Oct. 1966.
[6] ——, "Data compression with error-control coding for space telemetry," Ph.D. dissertation, Univ. Maryland, College Park, May 1966.
[7] L. D. Davisson, "Comments on 'Sequence time coding for data compression'," *Proc. IEEE* (Corresp.), vol. 54, p. 2010, Dec. 1966.
[8] T. Cover, "Enumerative source coding," *IEEE Trans. Inform. Theory*, vol. IT-19, pp. 73–76, Jan. 1973.
[9] Y. M. Shtarkov and V. F. Babkin, "Combinatorial method of universal coding for discrete stationary sources," presented at the 2nd Int. Information Theory Symp., Tsahkadsor, USSR, Sept. 1971; also *Probl. Contr. Inform. Transm.*, to be published (in Russian).
[10] V. F. Babkin, "Method of universal coding for an independent message source with non-exponential computational complexity," *Probl. Inform. Transm.*, vol. 7, no. 4, 1971.
[11] J. Ziv, "Coding of sources with unknown statistics—Part I: Probability of encoding error; Part II: Distortion relative to a fidelity criterion," *IEEE Trans. Inform. Theory*, vol. IT-18, pp. 384–394, May 1972.
[12] R. F. Rice and J. R. Plaunt, "Adaptive variable-length coding for efficient compression of spacecraft television data," *IEEE Trans. Commun. Technol.*, vol. COM-19, pp. 889–897, Dec. 1971.
[13] Y. M. Shtarkov, "Adaptive coding for discrete sources," presented at the Int. Information Theory Symp., Pacific Grove, Calif., Jan. 1972.
[14] Y. M. Shtarkov and N. E. Ryb'eva, "Adaptive coding of Poisson sources," presented at the Int. Information Theory Symp., Pacific Grove, Calif., Jan. 1972.
[15] H. Blasbalg and R. Van Blerkom, "Message compression," *IRE Trans. Space Electron. Telem.*, vol. SET-8, pp. 228–238, Sept. 1962.
[16] R. E. Krichevskii, "The relation between redundancy coding and the reliability of information from a source," *Probl. Inform. Transm.*, vol. 4, no. 3, pp. 48–57 (in Russian), pp. 37–45 (English Transl.), 1968.
[17] B. S. Atal and S. L. Hanauer, "Speech analysis and synthesis by linear prediction of the speech wave," *J. Acoust. Soc. Am.*, vol. 50, no. 2, pp. 637–655, 1971.
[18] T. M. Cover, "Admissibility properties of Gilbert's encoding for unknown source probabilities," *IEEE Trans. Inform. Theory* (Corresp.), vol. IT-18, pp. 216–217, Jan. 1972.

Part III

# DISTORTION-RATE THEORY

# Editors' Comments on Papers 12 Through 18



In Part III, we trace the development of several aspects of Shannon's information theory approach to data compression: rate-distortion or distortion-rate theory. Shannon ["Coding Theorems for a Discrete Source with a Fidelity Criterion," *IRE Natl. Conv. Record, Part 4,* 142–163 (1959); also in *Information and Decision Processes,* R. E. Machol (ed.), McGraw-Hill, New York, 1960] considered fixed-rate coding systems and showed that the OPTA function, an intractable quantity in general, was equal to a well-defined information-theorety quantity, the distortion-rate function (DRF) (or inverse rate-distortion function) for ergodic sources. The DRF is a well-defined minimization problem, and Shannon used standard Lagrange multiplier techniques to evaluate several examples. The basic coding theorem relating the OPTA to the DRF was proved using random coding arguments. (Excellent detailed developments may be found in R. G. Gallager, *Information Theory and Reliable Communication,* Wiley, New York, 1968, and chap. 9, T. Berger, *Rate-Distortion Theory,* Prentice-Hall, Englewood Cliffs, N.J., 1971).

In Paper 12, Sakrison presents an intuitively pleasing geometric development of the Shannon theory of source coding. He adopts the standard rate-distortion view of minimizing the rate subject to a fidelity constraint. In Paper 13, Gray and Davisson present the distortion-rate view (discussed in the introduction) of minimizing the distortion subject to a code rate constraint. In this paper the most general discrete-time coding theorem is presented, and the results for entropy compression in unknown statistical environments are presented and compared to related results of Ziv and Sakrison.

Goblick and Holsinger (Papers 14 and 15) used rate-distortion concepts to obtain the OPTA for specific communications systems for analog sources; they used the squared-error criterion and compared these bounds with several practical systems such as amplitude modulation, angle modulation, digital communications, and quantization. The topics of analog-to-digital conversion and quantization are central to the study of data compression; many further results along this line are presented in the next section.

Since Shannon's original work, one primary concern of the theory has been the evaluation and bounding of rate-distortion or distortion-rate functions. An example of an exact analytic evaluation of the rate-distortion function for the common Gaussian model and a complex distortion measure is provided by McDonald and Schultheiss (Paper 16), and Blahut (Paper 17) presents a fast and efficient algorithm for numerically obtaining rate-distortion functions based on the Kuhn–Tucker algorithm described by Gallager. An alternative approach is to develop analytic bounds to rate-distortion functions. [A summary of such bounds may be found in R. M. Gray, " A New Class of Lower Bounds to Information Rates of Stationary Sources via Conditional Rate-Distortion Functions," *IEEE Trans. Inform. Theory,* **19,** 480–489 (1973).]

In Paper 18, Budrikis considers one of the basic problems of the theory, the finding of a tractable yet subjectively meaningful fidelity criterion. The specific application considered is image compression, but the problems described and the caution urged are typical of many applications.

# 12



Reprinted from *IEEE Trans. Inform. Theory*, **IT-14**(3), 481–486 (1968)

# A Geometric Treatment of the Source Encoding of a Gaussian Random Variable

DAVID J. SAKRISON, MEMBER, IEEE

*Abstract*—**This paper gives a geometric treatment of the source encoding of a Gaussian random variable for minimum mean-square error. The first section is expository, giving a geometric derivation of Shannon's classic result[1] which explicitly shows the steps in source encoding and the properties that a near optimum code must possess. The second section makes use of the geometric insight gained in the first section to bound the performance that can be obtained with a finite block length of $L$ random variables. It is shown that a code can be found whose performance approaches that of the rate distortion function as $1/L$ in mean-square error and $(\ln L)/L$ in rate.**

## Introduction

In this paper we give a geometric discussion of the problem of source encoding a Gaussian random variable so that its value can be transmitted over a noiseless channel with a minimum rate for a fixed level of mean-square error distortion. Section I gives a geometric derivation of Shannon's classical formula[1] for the rate-distortion function of a Gaussian random variable. Since the result is well known, the intention of the treatment is expository. The method of proof makes explicit how the encoding is accomplished and what properties a near-optimum encoding or "quantization" method should possess. Section II makes use of the insight gained by the geometric formulation to investigate the rate at which the performance of a code can approach the rate-distortion function as a function of the block length of the code. This result is new and depends on a list-encoding scheme used by Pinkston[2] for a digital source. Our result is similar to a result obtained independently by Wyner[3] (his theorem 1) who also used a geometric approach. Wyner in addition considers the effect of probability of error in transmission over a noisy channel.

## I. A Geometric Derivation of the Rate-Distortion Function for a Gaussian Random Variable

In this section we present a geometric derivation of the rate-distortion function for a Gaussian random variable with a mean-square error distortion measure. The result is hardly new, being a consequence of Shannon's early work;[1] however, the geometric proof has definite expository value in providing insight into the process of source encoding. The geometric derivation makes explicit the manner in which encoding is accomplished and those properties which a near-optimum method of source coding must possess. The price paid for this additional insight is that our geometric derivation is restricted to the Gaussian source with mean-square error distortion measure. Further, our proof of the negative side of the proof cannot be made tight in the sense that it applies *only* in the case of long block length.

We thus consider a situation in which we wish to transmit a sequence of identically distributed, statistically independent Gaussian random variables of zero mean and variance $\sigma^2$ over a channel which allows error-free transmission at an average rate of $R$ bits per random variable. Our goal is to derive by geometric methods the minimum mean-square error with which these random variables can be so transmitted.

Let us start by grouping $L$ of these random variables together into a block; this block will then be described by a word of $LR$ bits which can be transmitted in an error-free manner to the user. We will regard this block of $L$ random variables, $X_1, X_2, \cdots, X_L$, as a vector-valued $L$-dimensional random vector $\mathbf{X}$:

$$\mathbf{X} = (X_1, X_2, \cdots, X_L) \tag{1}$$

and assume that $L$ is large. Our problem can now be stated as follows. We can pick $Q = 2^{RL}$ code vectors or representation vectors $\mathbf{x}_1, \mathbf{x}_2, \cdots, \mathbf{x}_Q$, in the space representing the possible values of $\mathbf{X}$. The $L$-dimensional space is then partitioned into $Q$ representation regions, the $j$th representation region consisting of all those values of $\mathbf{x}$ lying at a Euclidean distance closer to $\mathbf{x}_j$ than to any other representation vector (equidistant points being arbitrarily assigned to one representation region or the other). When the random variable $\mathbf{X}$ takes on the value $\mathbf{x}$, we will transmit in an error-free manner the index $j$ of the representation vector $\mathbf{x}_j$ which lies closest to $\mathbf{x}$; that is, the index of the representation region containing $\mathbf{x}$. The receiver then uses $\mathbf{x}_j$ as an approximation to the value $\mathbf{x}$ assumed by $\mathbf{X}$. If we take the inner product in the Euclidean $L$ space occupied by our observations of $\mathbf{x}$ to be

$$(\mathbf{x}, \mathbf{y}) = \frac{1}{L} \sum_{k=1}^{L} x_k y_k \tag{2}$$

then the distance

$$||\mathbf{x} - \mathbf{x}_j||^2 = \frac{1}{L} \sum_{k=1}^{L} (x_k^j - x_k)^2 \tag{3}$$

Manuscript received June 26, 1967; revised December 1, 1967. The research reported in this paper was supported wholly by the National Aeronautics and Space Administration under Grant NGR 05-003-143.

The author is with the Department of Electrical Engineering and Computer Sciences and Space Science Laboratory, University of California, Berkeley, Calif. 94720

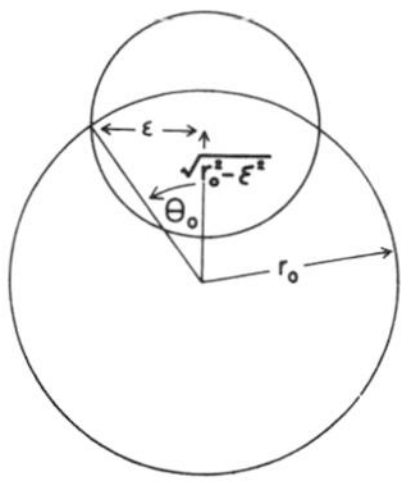


Fig. 1. Optimum positioning of the representation sphere of radius $\mathcal{E}$ relative to the message sphere of radius $r_0$.

represents the average error per component when $\mathbf{X}$ takes on the value $\mathbf{x} = (x_1, x_2, \cdots, x_L)$ and the vector $\mathbf{x}_i = (x_1^i, x_2^i, \cdots, x_L^i)$ is used to approximate $\mathbf{x}$. Our goal, then, is to study the minimum potential expected value of such approximation error when the dimension $L$ is large and the $Q = 2^{RL}$ representation vectors are judiciously chosen.

Let us now make some observations upon the probable location of the vector $\mathbf{X}$. The random variable $L\,||\mathbf{X}||^2$ is chi squared with $L$ degrees of freedom. From the known density function[4] for $||\mathbf{X}||$, it is easily shown that

$$E\{||\mathbf{X}||\} = \sigma\sqrt{\frac{2}{L}}\,\Gamma(L/2 + 1/2)/\Gamma(L/2) \tag{4}$$

and

$$E\{||\mathbf{X}||^2\} = \sigma^2 \tag{5}$$

and hence

$$\text{var}\,\{||\mathbf{X}||\} = \sigma^2[1 - (2/L)\Gamma^2(L/2 + 1/2)/\Gamma^2(L/2)]. \tag{6}$$

By using the expansion for ln $\Gamma$ with remainder,[5] this term can be bounded by

$$\text{var}\,\{||\mathbf{X}||\} \leqq \sigma^2/1.2L. \tag{7}$$

For large values of $L$, the value of $||\mathbf{X}||$ is thus very close in the mean-square sense to its expected value. For this reason, we define the vector-valued random variable $\mathbf{X}_p$ to be

$$\mathbf{X}_p = \mathbf{X}\,\frac{E\{||\mathbf{X}||\}}{||\mathbf{X}||} \tag{8}$$

so that the length of $\mathbf{X}_p$ is given by

$$||\mathbf{X}_p|| \equiv E\{||\mathbf{X}||\}.$$

Since

$$E\{||\mathbf{X} - \mathbf{X}_p||^2\} = \text{var}\,\{||\mathbf{X}||\} \leqq \sigma^2/1.2L \tag{9}$$

we introduce little mean-square error for large $L$ by approximating $\mathbf{X}$ by $\mathbf{X}_p$. Further, if we quantize $\mathbf{X}_p$ to the closest representation point $\mathbf{x}_i$, then the total mean-square error at the receiver is the sum of the quantization error and var $\{||\mathbf{X}||\}$:

$$\begin{aligned} D &= E\{||\mathbf{X} - \mathbf{x}_i||^2\} = E\{||\mathbf{X} - \mathbf{X}_p + \mathbf{X}_p - \mathbf{x}_i||^2\} \\ &= E\{||\mathbf{X}_p - \mathbf{x}_i||^2\} + \text{var}\,\{||\mathbf{X}||\}, \end{aligned} \tag{10}$$

the cross term being zero, which is easily shown by evaluating the expected value of the cross term for a fixed value of $\mathbf{X}_p$. Since we can make var $\{||\mathbf{X}||\}$ as small as we please by making $L$ sufficiently large, we lose nothing in our encoding or "quantizing" process by first projecting $X$ onto the sphere of radius $E\{||\mathbf{X}||\}$. The advantage of doing this is that $\mathbf{X}_p$ is uniformly distributed on the surface of an $L$-dimensional sphere of radius $E\{||\mathbf{X}||\}$.

Shannon's rate-distortion theory[1],[6] has the following implication for transmission of a Gaussian random variable of variance $\sigma^2$ using a noiseless channel of capacity $R$ bits per random variable. It is not possible by any means to achieve such transmission with a mean-square error of less than

$$D(R) = \sigma^2 2^{-2R}, \tag{11}$$

but by encoding the random variables into suitably long blocks (suitably large $L$), transmission with a mean-square error arbitrarily close to $D(R)$ can be achieved. With the above remarks in mind concerning the distribution of $\mathbf{X}_p$ and var $\{||\mathbf{X}||\}$, we are in a position to give a geometric proof of the above statement. The proof will omit some of the $\epsilon - \delta$ arguments required to make it rigorous (although these could be added without difficulty) in order that the essential steps not be obscured.

Let us start by first proving the positive side of this statement using a random coding argument. This involves selecting a set of representation vectors at random and showing that the probability of a given point $\mathbf{X}$ not lying within a distance $\mathcal{E}$ of one of the $Q = 2^{RL}$ representation vectors is negligible as long as $\mathcal{E}$ is greater than $\sqrt{D(R)}$.

Consider the situation shown in the cross-sectional representation of Fig. 1. All of the projected message vectors lie on the sphere of radius $r_0 \triangleq E\{||\mathbf{X}||\} \sim \sigma$. It is easily seen that a sphere of radius $\mathcal{E}$ subtends the largest surface area of this message sphere if it is centered so that its diameter is a chord of the message sphere joining the points where the cross sections of the two spheres intersect. The center of the sphere of radius $\mathcal{E}$ will lie in this case at a distance of $\sqrt{r_0^2 - \mathcal{E}^2}$ from the center of the message sphere.

We will therefore pick all our $Q = 2^{RL}$ representation points $\mathbf{x}_1, \mathbf{x}_2, \cdots, \mathbf{x}_Q$, to lie on the surface of a sphere of radius $\sqrt{r_0^2 - \mathcal{E}^2}$ by choosing the points independently according to a uniform .probability distribution on the surface of this sphere.

Now consider an arbitrary projected message point $\mathbf{x}_p$. We wish to find the probability that there will not be any representation point lying on the surface of the sphere of radius $\sqrt{r_0^2 - \mathcal{E}^2}$ that is within distance $\mathcal{E}$ of $\mathbf{x}_p$. Let us denote this probability by $P_{\mathcal{E}}$. Note that if no one of the representation points lies within distance $\mathcal{E}$ of $\mathbf{x}_p$, the closest representation point must still be withi

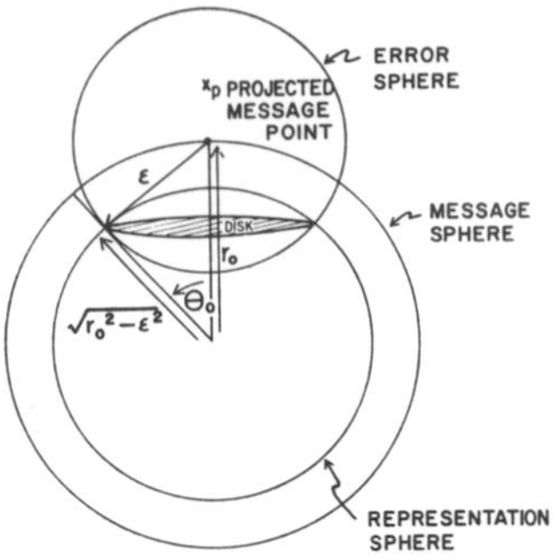


Fig. 2. Figure illustrating situation used for calculating $P_\epsilon$.

distance $2r_0$ of $\mathbf{x}_p$. Thus the error may be bounded by

$$E\{||\mathbf{X}_p - \mathbf{x}_i||^2\} \leqq (1 - P_\varepsilon)\varepsilon^2 + P_\varepsilon(2r_0)^2.$$

For convenience in what follows, we shall use the notation

$V_L$ = volume of an $L$-dimensional sphere of unit radius.

$A_L$ = surface area ($L - 1$ dimensional volume) of an $L$-dimensional sphere of unit radius.

$AC_L(\theta)$ = surface area ($L - 1$ dimensional volume) of an $L$-dimensional polar cap of unit radius and polar angle $\theta$.

Thus

$$AC_L(\pi/2) = (1/2)A_L.$$

Fig. 2 shows the positioning of an arbitrary projected message point surrounded by a sphere of radius $\varepsilon$. From this figure, our distribution for picking the representation points, and the fact that the ratio of the areas involved is independent of the radius of the sphere, we have

$$P_\varepsilon = \left[1 - \frac{AC_L(\theta_0)}{A_L}\right]^Q \tag{12}$$

in which

$$\theta_0 = \tan^{-1}(\varepsilon/\sqrt{r_0^2 - \varepsilon^2}) \quad \text{and} \quad Q = 2^{RL}. \tag{13}$$

Now from Fig. 2 we can see that the area of a spherical cap of unit radius and polar angle $\theta_0$ is

$$\begin{aligned} AC_L(\theta_0) &\geqq \text{area } (L-1)\text{-dimensional disk of radius } \sin\theta_0 \\ &= V_{L-1}(\sin\theta_0)^{L-1} \\ &= V_{L-1}\left(\frac{\varepsilon}{r_0}\right)^{L-1}. \end{aligned} \tag{14}$$

However,

$$V_n = \int_0^1 A_n r^{n-1}\,dr = \frac{1}{n}A_n. \tag{15}$$

Combining (12) and (15) and inequality (14) yields

$$P_\varepsilon \leqq \left[1 - \frac{A_{L-1}\left[\dfrac{\varepsilon}{r_0}\right]^{L-1}}{(L-1)A_L}\right]^Q. \tag{16}$$

But from (15) and the well-known expression[7] for $V_L$ we have

$$\frac{A_{L-1}}{(L-1)A_L} = \frac{1}{\sqrt{\pi}} \frac{\Gamma\left(\frac{L}{2}+1\right)}{L\Gamma\left(\frac{L-1}{2}+1\right)}.$$

For large values of $L$, Stirling's approximation shows this quantity to be approximately

$$\frac{A_{L-1}}{(L-1)A_L} \approx \frac{1}{\sqrt{2\pi L}}. \tag{17}$$

Combining inequality (16) with (13) and (17) yields

$$P_\varepsilon \leqq \left[1 - \frac{1}{\sqrt{2\pi L}}\left(\frac{\varepsilon}{r_0}\right)^{L-1}\right]^{2^{LR}}. \tag{18}$$

We now take the radius of the error sphere to be $(1 + \delta)$ times the value $\sqrt{D(R)}$ given by (11)

$$\varepsilon = (1 + \delta)\sigma 2^{-R}, \qquad \delta > 0. \tag{19}$$

Let us note that $r_0$ is asymptotic to $\sigma$; making this substitution and that given by (19) into (18) yields

$$P_\varepsilon \approx \left[1 - \frac{1}{\sqrt{2\pi L}} 2^{-R(L-1)}(1+\delta)^{L-1}\right]^{2^{RL}}, \tag{20}$$

which, for large $L$, is approximately

$$P_\varepsilon \approx \exp\left[-\frac{(1+\delta)^L}{\sqrt{2\pi L}} \frac{2^R}{1+\delta}\right]. \tag{21}$$

Thus the probability of an arbitrary point on the message sphere not being within $\varepsilon$ of some representation point becomes zero for $\varepsilon$ given by (19) with $\delta > 0$.

We now consider the negative side of the source encoding theorem: that it is not possible to transmit with an error less than that given by (11) using only $R$ bits per random variable. As opposed to Shannon's proof[6] using inequalities on mutual information which holds independently of $L$, our proof holds only in the limit as $L$ becomes large. Its value is thus limited; however it is of interest in demonstrating that the geometric arguments used in the positive part were tight. We proceed in three steps.

First we note that since var $\{||\mathbf{X}||\}$ approaches zero as $1/L$, we have not lost anything asymptotically by our operation of projecting $\mathbf{X}$ onto the sphere of radius $r_0$.

Secondly, we ask what is the most efficient possible shape for a representation region. In proving the positive side of the statement, this point was treated only summarily. At this point we wish to recognize that since $\mathbf{X}_p$ is uniformly distributed on the surface of the message sphere of radius $r_0$, the optimum shape for a representation region is the one that minimizes $\epsilon^2$ for a fixed value of $A$, where

$A$ = area of message sphere intersected by the representation region,

$\epsilon^2$ = moment of inertia of the above area about the representation vector

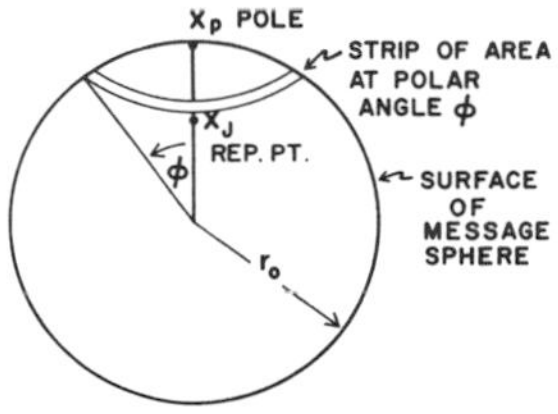


Fig. 3. Geometry indicating the shape of the optimum representation region.

= mean-square error resulting in quantizing vectors projected into the representation region to the representation vector.

It is easy to see what the optimum representation region is. Let the position of the representation vector $\mathbf{x}_i$ be arbitrary and let $\mathbf{x}_p$ denote the intersection with the message surface of a straight line from the center of the message sphere through $\mathbf{x}_i$. This situation is shown in cross section in Fig. 3. The point $\mathbf{x}_p$ is obviously closer to $\mathbf{x}_i$ than any other point on the surface of the message sphere. Moreover, taking $\mathbf{x}_p$ to be the pole of the message sphere, all points at the same polar angle $\phi$ are the same distance from $\mathbf{x}_i$ and this distance increases monotonically with $\phi$. Thus in placing a fixed amount of area on the surface of the representation sphere, the moment of inertia about $\mathbf{x}_i$ is minimized if all of this area is placed as close to the pole as possible. The representation region of optimum shape is then a polar cap on the message sphere. When the dimension $L$ is large, virtually all of the $(L-1)$ dimensional volume of the polar cap is at its edge, so that for the optimum decision region

$\mathcal{E}^2$ = square of the distance from $\mathbf{x}_i$ to the edge of the polar cap.

This is minimized relative to the radial position of $\mathbf{x}_i$ (recall that the polar cap was optimum independently of the radial distance of $\mathbf{x}_i$) by locating $\mathbf{x}_i$ at a radius $\sqrt{r_0^2 - \mathcal{E}^2}$. The optimum representation region is thus exactly that which we assumed earlier in the discussion pertinent to Fig. 1, namely, a sphere of radius $\mathcal{E}$ about a representation point at a distance $\sqrt{r_0^2 - \mathcal{E}^2}$ from the origin.

Third, given representation regions all of which are the optimum shape, what is the minimum number that we require? Since $\mathbf{X}_p$ is uniformly distributed on the surface of the message sphere, no non-negligible fraction of the area of this sphere can be left uncovered. Thus $Q$, the number of representation regions required, is bounded below by the inequality

$$A_L r_0^{L-1} = \text{area of the message sphere}$$
$$\leqq Q[\text{area of polar cap of chord length } 2\mathcal{E}], \qquad (22)$$

in which $Q$ is $2^{RL}$. Now since the area of the polar cap in question is certainly smaller than the area of a sphere of diameter $2\mathcal{E}$, (22) can be weakened to the inequality

$$A_L r_0^{L-1} \leqq Q A_L \mathcal{E}^{L-1} = 2^{RL} A_L \mathcal{E}^{L-1}. \qquad (23)$$

After simple manipulation and noting that $r_0$ is asymptotic to $\sigma$, this inequality becomes

$$\mathcal{E}/\sigma \geqq [2^{-R}]^{L/L-1}$$

and for $L$ arbitrarily large, this implies

$$\mathcal{E}/\sigma \geqq 2^{-R}, \qquad (24)$$

which is the negative part of the statement we wished to prove.

Let us now note to what extent we have made use of the Gaussian assumption. In proving the negative statement, we made use of the spherical symmetry of the distribution of $\mathbf{X}$, and hence the Gaussian assumption was crucial. However, in proving the positive statement, the only thing we made use of was the fact that we could ignore the mean-square error introduced by first projecting a message vector onto a sphere of radius $r_0$. Thus, the positive statement required only the property expressed by (9).

When the distribution of $X$ is not Gaussian, (10) can be replaced by the bound

$$D \leq E\{\|\mathbf{X}_p - \mathbf{x}_i\|^2\} + V + 2r_0 V^{1/2}$$

in which

$$V = E\{(\|\mathbf{X}\| - r_0)^2\}$$

and $r_0$ is still the mean of $\|\mathbf{X}\|$ under the Gaussian distribution. Thus the contribution to the mean-square error due to projecting $\mathbf{X}$ onto the surface of a sphere of radius $r_0$ can be neglected whenever $V$ approaches 0 as $L$ becomes large. It can be shown that this holds whenever the variance of $X$ is finite (this was shown just prior to proof and is not proven here).

We can thus make the following positive statement for any random variable of finite variance.

Let a random variable have a variance $\sigma^2$. Consider transmitting a long block of statistically independent variables from this distribution

$$\mathbf{X} = (X_1, X_2, \cdots, X_L).$$

Then by making $L$ sufficiently large the block can be transmitted using a rate no greater than $R$ bits per random variable with a mean-square error arbitrarily close to $\sigma^2 2^{-2R}$.

Of those distributions of finite $\sigma$ the Gaussian distribution is thus the "worst case" in the sense that the rate distortion function of the Gaussian random variable is an upper bound (in rate) for the rate distortion function of any distribution of finite $\sigma$. This is because the Gaussian distribution is spherically symmetric.

## II. Approach of the Performance to $D(R)$ with Block Length

In Section I asymptotic expressions were used freely, and no attempt was made to discover how performance approached that given by $R(D)$ (or $D(R)$) as a function of the block length $L$. In this section we find an upper bound in performance (in both rate $R$ and mean-square error $D$) as a function of $L$. The method of list encoding used in obtaining the bound was suggested to the author by Pinkston,[2] who used the technique in the study of digital sources.

We proceed as in Section I by collecting $L$ successive independent Gaussian random variables of variance $\sigma^2$ into a block which we denote by the vector $\mathbf{X}$, and then projecting $\mathbf{X}$ onto the sphere of radius $E\{||\mathbf{X}||\} \triangleq r_0$ to obtain $\mathbf{X}_p$. The vector $\mathbf{X}_p$ is now quantized as follows. An ensemble of lists of code vectors is generated by picking successive vectors in each list independently from a distribution that assigns uniform mass to the surface of the $L$-dimensional sphere of radius $\sqrt{r_0^2 - \varepsilon^2}$. The value of $\varepsilon$ is free to be chosen, $0 < \varepsilon < r_0$, and the number of words in each list is infinite. A given encoder or quantizer uses a given list of code vectors. Given a generated value of $\mathbf{X}_p$, say $\mathbf{x}_p$, the encoder goes down the list and finds the first vector in the list, say $\mathbf{x}_j$, such that $||\mathbf{x}_p - \mathbf{x}_j|| < \varepsilon$. The encoder then transmits the index $j$ in an error-free manner, and the receiver uses $\mathbf{x}_j$ as an approximation to the quantized source vector. From (9) and (10) the total mean-square error in such transmission is bounded by

$$D = E\{||\mathbf{X} - \mathbf{x}_j||^2\} \leqq \varepsilon^2 + \sigma^2/1.2L. \tag{25}$$

We now consider the rate of this source. The entropy of a given encoder using a particular code list is

$$H(\text{list}) = -\sum_{k=1}^{\infty} P(j \mid \text{list}) \log_2 P(j \mid \text{list}) \tag{26}$$

in which $P(j \mid \text{list})$ is the probability over the distribution generated by $\mathbf{X}$ that the $j$th word in the list is transmitted. Because the entropy is a convex function of the probabilities $P(j \mid \text{list})$, $j = 1, 2, \cdots$, it follows that in the ensemble of code lists there is at least one list with entropy less than or equal to

$$H = -\sum_{j=1}^{\infty} P(j) \log_2 P(j), \tag{27}$$

in which

$$P(j) = \int P(j \mid \text{list})\, dP\,(\text{list}) \tag{28}$$

is the average of the $P(j \mid \text{list})$ over the ensemble of code lists. Since this ensemble was generated by picking the vectors independently with uniform distribution on the surface of the sphere of radius $\sqrt{r_0^2 - \varepsilon^2}$,

$$P(j) = q^{j-1}p \tag{29}$$

in which

$p = P\,\{$vector chosen at random on surface of a sphere of radius $\sqrt{r_0^2 - \varepsilon^2}$ is within distance $\varepsilon$ of point at radius $r_0\}$ (30)

and

$$q = 1 - p. \tag{31}$$

Substituting for (29) and (31) in (27) results in

$$H = \frac{-q \log_2 q - p \log_2 p}{p} = \frac{-(1-p)\log_2(1-p)}{p} - \log_2 p. \tag{32}$$

If we write the series expansion for $-[\log(1-p)]/p$ and bound this series by the geometric series, we obtain

$$H \leqq \frac{1}{\ln 2}[1 - \ln p]. \tag{33}$$

Let us now return to (30). From the geometry of the situation, $p$ is equal to the ratio of two areas. The first area is that portion of the surface area of a sphere of radius $\sqrt{r_0^2 - \varepsilon^2}$ contained within a sphere of radius $\varepsilon$ at a distance of $r_0$ from the center of the first sphere. The second area is simply the surface area of a sphere of radius $\sqrt{r_0^2 - \varepsilon^2}$. From Fig. 2 and (14), (15), and the expression for $A_{L-1}/(L-1)A_L$, we see that $p$ can be bounded by

$$p \geqq \frac{[A_{L-1}/(L-1)]\left[\frac{\varepsilon}{r_0}\sqrt{r_0^2 - \varepsilon^2}\right]^{L-1}}{A_L(\sqrt{r_0^2 - \varepsilon^2})^{L-1}} = \frac{\Gamma\left(\frac{L+1}{2} + \frac{1}{2}\right)}{\pi L \Gamma\left(\frac{L+1}{2}\right)}\left(\frac{\varepsilon}{r_0}\right)^{L-1}. \tag{34}$$

Substituting from inequality (34) into inequality (33) weakens the resulting inequality to

$$H \leqq \frac{1}{\ln 2}(L-1)\ln\left(\frac{r_0}{\varepsilon}\right) + \ln(\pi L) + 1 - \ln\left[\Gamma\left(\frac{L+1}{2} + \frac{1}{2}\right)\Big/\Gamma\left(\frac{L+1}{2}\right)\right]. \tag{35}$$

Using Stirling's expansion with remainder[5] to bound the logarithm of the gamma function weakens inequality (35) to

$$H \leqq \frac{1}{\ln 2}\left\{(L-1)\ln\left(\frac{r_0}{\varepsilon}\right) + (\tfrac{1}{2})\ln L + \tfrac{1}{2} + \ln 2\pi + 5/[12(L+1)]\right\}. \tag{36}$$

We now turn to the value of $r_0 = E\{||\mathbf{X}||\}$. From (4) we have

$$\ln\left(\frac{r_0}{\varepsilon}\right) \leqq \ln\left(\frac{\sigma}{\varepsilon}\right) + \frac{1}{6(L+1)} \leqq \ln\left(\frac{\sigma}{\varepsilon}\right) + \frac{1}{6(L-1)}. \tag{37}$$

Substituting from inequality (37) into inequality (36) results in

$$H \leqq \frac{1}{\ln 2}\left\{(L-1)\ln\left(\frac{\sigma}{\varepsilon}\right) + (\tfrac{1}{2})\ln L + (\tfrac{2}{3} + \ln 2\pi) + 5/[12(L+1)]\right\}. \tag{38}$$

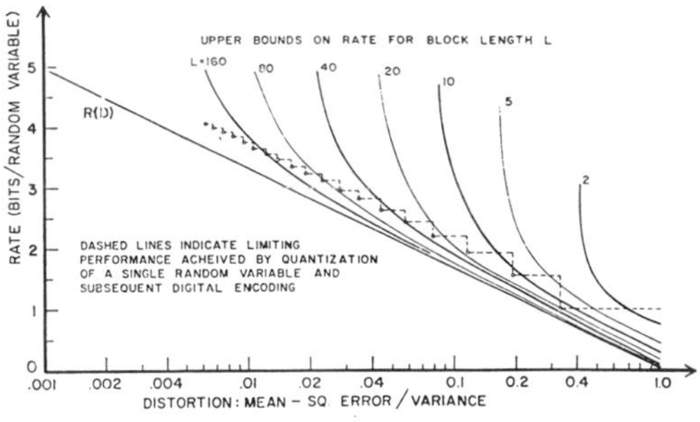


Fig. 4. Bounds on performance for different block lengths.

Lastly, we recognize that $\ln(\sigma/\mathcal{E})/\ln 2$ equals $R(\mathcal{E}^2)$, the rate distortion function; further, a Huffman code or other digital source code can be used to encode the quantized vectors with a rate no greater than

$$R = (H + 1)/L \leqq \left(\frac{L-1}{L}\right) R(\mathcal{E}^2) + \frac{\{\frac{1}{2} \ln L + (\frac{2}{3} + \ln 4\pi) + 5/[12(L+1)]\}}{L \ln 2} \tag{39}$$

bits per random variable.[8]

Equations (25) and (39) upper bound the manner in which the mean-square error and transmission rate approach the performance given by the rate distortion function. The approach is as $1/L$ in mean-square error and $(\ln L)/L$ in rate. The reader should note that although $R(\mathcal{E}^2)(L-1)/L$ appears in (39), this cannot result in performance better than that given by the rate distortion function because of the presence of the $\sigma^2/1.2L$ term in the mean-square error. Equation (39) could be rewritten in terms of $R(D)$ for $D$ given by (25) so that we consider only the approach in rate for fixed $D$, but the result does not seem as meaningful to interpret.

The bounds of (25) and (39) are plotted in Fig. 4 along with the rate distortion function and the performance that could be achieved by quantizing each random variable individually and then using a digital (e.g., Huffman) code to encode a long block of quantized random variables. This performance is plotted directly from the work of Max,[9] who has calculated the minimum mean-square quantization error that results from quantizing a single Gaussian random variable into a variable number of quantization levels of optimum spacing. Max has also calculated the entropy of the corresponding quantized distribution. The dashed curve is a plot of this entropy versus the quantization error, the jumps occurring at the points at which the number of quantization levels change. As can be seen from this figure, the performance that can be obtained by quantizing random variables individually is not substantially inferior to that of the curves for optimum encoding, which requires simultaneous quantization of a block of $L$ random variables. For a fixed distortion level, a code that quantizes random variables individually requires only a slightly higher rate than can be achieved with arbitrarily long block length (the rate given by the $R(D)$ curve). Indeed, this difference in performance is so small and the implementation of simultaneous quantization so difficult, that simultaneous quantization may never be used in practice. However, the curves are of interest in that they specify just what one can achieve by implementations of various degrees of complexity. It is not known whether the asymptotic rate of approach to $R(D)$ given by (25) and (39) ($1/L$ in $D$ and $(\ln L)/L$ in $R$) is the tightest possible, although the author conjectures that it is.

## Acknowledgment

The author gratefully acknowledges stimulating conversations with J. Pinkston, Prof. W. L. Root, and B. Haskell.

## References

[1] C. E. Shannon, "A mathematical theory of communication," *Bell Sys. Tech. J.*, vol. 17, pp. 623–656, October 1948. (See especially pt. 5.)

[2] J. Pinkston, private communication. Use of the list-encoding procedure to bound the performance of encoding an independent-letter binary source is to appear in Pinkston's Ph.D. dissertation, Massachusetts Institute of Technology, Cambridge, 1967.

[3] A. D. Wyner , "Communication of analog data from a Gaussian source over a noisy channel," preprint, Bell Telephone Labs., Murray Hill, N. J., October 1967.

[4] H. Cramér, *Mathematical Methods of Statistics*, Princeton, N. J.: Princeton University Press, 1946, p. 233.

[5] E. T. Whittaker and G. N. Watson, *Modern Analysis*, 4th ed., London: Cambridge University Press, 1950, pp. 251–253.

[6] C. E. Shannon, "Coding theorems for a discrete source with a fidelity criterion," in *Information and Decision Processes*, R. E. Machol, Ed. New York: McGraw-Hill, 1960, pp. 93–126.

[7] R. Courant, *Differential and Integral Calculus*, vol. 2. New York: Interscience, 1936, pp. 298–304.

[8] R. Fano, *Transmission of Information*. New York: Wiley, 1961, ch. 3.

[9] J. Max, "Quantizing for minimum distortion," *IRE Trans. Information Theory*, vol. IT-6, pp. 7–12, March 1960.

# 13



Reprinted from *IEEE Trans. Inform. Theory,* **IT-20**(4), 502–509, 516 (1974)

# Source Coding Theorems Without the Ergodic Assumption

ROBERT M. GRAY, MEMBER, IEEE, AND LEE D. DAVISSON, MEMBER, IEEE

***Abstract*—Source coding theorems are proved for discrete-time stationary processes subject to a fidelity criterion. The alphabet of the process is assumed to be a separable metric space, but the process is not assumed to be ergodic. When the process is not ergodic, the minimum average distortion for a fixed-rate code is not given by the distortion-rate function of the source as usually defined. It is given instead by a weighted average of the distortion-rate functions of ergodic subsources comprising the ergodic decomposition of the source. Potential applications to universal source coding with a fidelity criterion are discussed.**

## I. INTRODUCTION

ALMOST all theorems extant on source coding subject to a fidelity requirement make the assumption that the source involved is both stationary and ergodic [1, ch. 7], [3, ch. 9]. In this paper we show that in the finite-alphabet case considered by Gallager [3, theorem 9.8.3], the ergodic assumption can be dropped entirely, and that in the abstract case considered by Berger [1, theorem 7.2.4], if we assume that the alphabet of the source is a separable metric space, then the ergodic assumption can again be dropped. Although we show that it is only stationarity that is required to prove source coding theorems, the concept of ergodicity is crucial in the proofs and fundamental in the relevant description of stationary sources. Perhaps surprisingly, the solution is not in terms of the rate-distortion or the distortion-rate function (DRF) of the source as usually defined, but is given by a closely related information, theoretic minimization.

Manuscript received April 16, 1973; revised December 14, 1973. This work was supported in part by the National Science Foundation under Grants GK-31630 and GK-14190, and in part by the Joint Service Program at Stanford Electronics Laboratory under U.S. Navy Contract N00014-67-A-0112-0044.

R. M. Gray is with the Department of Electrical Engineering, Stanford University, Stanford, Calif.
L. D. Davisson is with the Department of Electrical Engineering, University of Southern California, Los Angeles, Calif.

In this section we somewhat loosely outline the problem and the known solution for the stationary ergodic case. We then consider a simple special case of a stationary nonergodic source for which the generalization of the source coding theorem is trivial, yet which contains one of the fundamental concepts involved in this paper. The section is then completed by outlining the results and giving a brief sketch of the basic steps involved in their proof.

Unfortunately, a good deal of measure theory is required even in the finite-alphabet case (unlike Gallager [3]), and hence Section II is devoted to summarizing required definitions and theorems. Every attempt has been made to match our notation to Berger's measure-theoretic treatment of the stationary ergodic source coding theorem [1, ch. 7]. Details omitted herein may be found in Berger [1].

Say we have a discrete-time source with individual output letters drawn from some alphabet $A_0$ and a reproducing alphabet $\hat{A}_0$. A block-length $N$ code $C_N$ is simply a collection of $M$ $N$-tuples $y_i^N = (y_{i_0}, \cdots, y_{i_{N-1}})$, $i = 0, \cdots, M-1$, where each letter of each $N$-tuple is drawn from $\hat{A}_0$ so that $y_i^N \in \hat{A}^N$, the $N$-fold Cartesian product of $\hat{A}_0$. We assume we have a nonnegative single-letter distortion measure $\rho_N$ defined on $A^N \times \hat{A}^N$, i.e.,

$$\rho_N(x^N, y^N) = N^{-1} \sum_{i=0}^{N-1} \rho_1(x_i, y_i)$$

where $\rho_1$ is called the per-letter distortion measure. A source is encoded by looking at a source $N$-tuple $x^N$ and mapping it into the codeword $y^N \in C_N$ such that $\rho_N(x^N, y^N)$

is minimized. We denote the resulting codeword by $\hat{x}^N(x^N)$ and write

$$\rho_N(x^N \mid C_N) = \rho_N(x^N, \hat{x}^N(x^N)) = \min_{y^N \in C_N} \rho_N(x^N, y^N).$$

The rate $R$ of a code $C_N$ is defined by $R = N^{-1} \ln M$, and the average distortion of a code $\rho(C_N)$ is given by

$$\rho(C_N) = E\{\rho_N(X^N \mid C_N)\}$$

where $X^N$ denotes a random source vector and the expectation is over the source ensemble.

There are two approaches to studying the "optimum" performance obtainable in source coding systems. The first and by far the most common is the rate-distortion approach, wherein we fix the desired average distortion and find the minimum rate for which there exists a code meeting the fidelity constraint; i.e., one studies the function $r(D)$, where

$$r(D) = \inf_N \inf_{C_N: \rho(C_N) \leq D} N^{-1} \ln M(C_N)$$

where $M(C_N)$ is the number of words in the code $C_N$. It is well known that for stationary ergodic sources $r(D)$ can be given in terms of the rate-distortion function $R(D)$, which is defined as an information-theoretic minimization. Specifically,

$$r(D) \geq R(D)$$

and for arbitrary $\varepsilon > 0$, there exists a sufficiently large $N$ and a code $C_N$ having

$$N^{-1} \ln M(C_N) \leq R(D) + \varepsilon$$

$$\rho(C_N) \leq D + \varepsilon.$$

An alternative approach is to specify a fixed rate and find the minimum possible average distortion attainable. This is the distortion-rate approach and is the more natural when one begins with a capacity constraint or a fixed number of quantization levels as opposed to an average fidelity constraint. In this case we are interested in the optimum performance theoretically obtainable (OPTA) $\delta(R)$ defined by

$$\delta(R) = \inf_N \inf_{C_N: N^{-1} \ln M(C_N) \leq R} \rho(C_N)$$

and the answer for stationary ergodic sources is given in terms of the DRF (inverse rate-distortion function) $D(R)$

$$\delta(R) \geq D(R)$$

and for arbitrary $\varepsilon > 0$, there exists an $N$ and a code $C_N$ such that

$$N^{-1} \ln M(C_N) \leq R + \varepsilon$$

$$\rho(C_N) \leq D(R) + \varepsilon.$$

For the usual stationary ergodic case the two views are entirely equivalent (although one may be more natural for a particular problem) and the functions are evaluated via identical parametric equations [1, ch. 2]. We shall see that this equivalence no longer holds, however, for fixed-rate source coding of stationary nonergodic sources. This nonequivalence is implicit in Ziv [8], as will be discussed.

Ergodicity is crucial in proving coding theorems since the law of large numbers or more general ergodic theorems provide a crucial step in random coding arguments. Roughly speaking, an ergodic source is a stationary source for which all doubly infinite output sequences are "typical," so that relative frequencies of functions of a finite number of letters of the process converge with probability one to their expectation. As an example, if one considers a Bernoulli process consisting of a sequence of independent identically distributed (i.i.d.) binary random variables with $\Pr(1) = p$, $\Pr(0) = 1 - p$, then the relative frequency of ones in a block of length $N$ converges to $p$ with probability one as $N \to \infty$. Now suppose instead that at time $-\infty$, Nature flips a fair coin and chooses either $p = p_1$ or $p = p_2$, $p_1 \neq p_2$, and then sends a Bernoulli random process with the chosen parameter. The resulting source is a mixture source, and the probability of $k$ ones in a block of length $N$ is given by

$$\tfrac{1}{2}p_1^k(1 - p_1)^{N-k} + \tfrac{1}{2}p_2^k(1 - p_2)^{N-k}$$

so that the resulting mixture source is stationary, but it is no longer i.i.d. and no longer ergodic. It is not ergodic since any doubly infinite sequence (string) is not typical of the mixture source, but rather is typical of one or the other of the subsources comprising the mixture; i.e., the relative frequency of ones approaches either $p_1$ or $p_2$, but not $\frac{1}{2}(p_1 + p_2)$. Similarly, if Nature spins a fair wheel to determine $p$ so that $p$ is a uniform [0,1] random variable, we would have a stationary nonergodic source consisting of a mixture of an uncountable number of stationary ergodic subsources [9]. As shall be discussed in the next section, Rohlin's ergodic decomposition theorem states that any stationary source having an alphabet with a separable $\sigma$-algebra can be considered as a unique mixture of a possibly uncountable number of stationary ergodic subsources, so that the preceding Bernoulli example is in a sense typical.

Consider now the case of a source that is a mixture of a finite number, say $K$, of stationary ergodic subsources with prior probabilities $w_k$, $k = 0,\cdots,K - 1$. This can also be viewed as a composite source with memory, where the particular subsource is chosen at $-\infty$ and fixed for all time [1, sec. 6.1]. We build a code book for the mixture as follows. For each of the subsources we can build a rate $R + \varepsilon/2$ code $C_N(k)$, such that for $N$ sufficiently large,

$$\rho(C_N(k) \mid k) \leq D_k(R) + \varepsilon \tag{1.1}$$

where $\rho(C_N(k) \mid k)$ is the average distortion of a code $C_N(k)$ if the $k$th subsource is the "true" source chosen by Nature. We choose $N$ large enough so that a $C_N(k)$ satisfying (1.1) can be found for each $k = 0,1,\cdots,K - 1$. We then form a supercode book

$$C_N = \bigcup_{k=0}^{K-1} C_N(k)$$

consisting of all of the words in each of the subcodes. The source encoder still finds the best word in $C_N$ for whatever source $N$-tuple it sees. Thus $C_N$ has average distortion

$$\begin{aligned}\rho(C_N) &= \sum_{k=0}^{K-1} \rho(C_N \mid k)w_k \\ &\leq \sum_{k=0}^{K-1} \rho(C_N(k) \mid k)w_k \\ &\leq \sum_{k=0}^{K-1} D_k(R)w_k + \varepsilon\end{aligned}$$

and the number of codewords $M(C_N)$ contained in $C_N$ is

$$\begin{aligned}M(C_N) &= \sum_{k=0}^{K-1} M(C_N(k)) \leq K \cdot \exp\,(N(R + \varepsilon/2)) \\ &= \exp\,\{N(R + \varepsilon/2 + N^{-1} \ln K)\}\end{aligned}$$

so that by choosing $N$ large enough, $C_N$ has rate $\leq R + \varepsilon$. If the $k$th subsource is present, we have from the usual theory that $\rho(C_N \mid k) \geq D_k(R)$. Thus we have that for arbitrarily small $\varepsilon$

$$\sum_{k=0}^{K-1} D_k(R)w_k \leq \delta(R) \leq \sum_{k=0}^{K-1} D_k(R)w_k + \varepsilon. \qquad (1.2)$$

It is the weighted average of the DRF's of the individual ergodic components that yields $\delta(R)$, and not the usual DRF of the mixture source.

In fact, more than (1.2) is true. Given a code $C_N$ satisfying (1.2), we might ask how well this code would perform for a specific subsource as opposed to its performance for the mixture. Specifically, what is the average distortion $\rho(C_N \mid k)$ if the $k$th subsource is in effect?

We have

$$\rho(C_N \mid k) \leq \rho(C_N(k) \mid k) \leq D_k(R) + \varepsilon. \qquad (1.3)$$

Thus we have the surprising result that when the ergodic decomposition is finite, there exists a single code $C_N$ of rate approximately $R$ such that the average distortion obtained under any subsource is the best possible, ignoring second-order terms; i.e., it is just as small as if we knew in advance which subsource would be chosen by nature. In this sense the code $C_N$ is "universal" [9].

The preceding simple construction would not have worked in general if we had used the rate-distortion approach. Specifically, if the subcodes each had average distortion $D^*$ and the minimum rate possible $R_k(D^*)$, then the union code would have had the correct average distortion, but the rate would have been approximately $\sup_k R_k(D^*)$, as in Sakrison [7]. For the "worst" (i.e., maximum rate) subsource, the performance would be identical to that of the previous construction, but for any other subsource we would obtain an average distortion $D^* \cong D_k(R_k(D^*)) \geq D_k\,(\sup_j R_j(D^*))$, the average distortion obtainable for the $k$th subsource under the fixed-rate scheme with rate $\sup_k R_k(D^*)$. Thus fixing the rate allows each subsource to be encoded as efficiently as possible even though we do not know which subsource is actually in effect, i.e., if the $k$th subsource is in effect, then the average distortion is approximately $D_k(\sup_j R_j(D^*))$, the best obtainable for that rate. On the other hand, fixing the average distortion forces us to signal at the rate required for the worst subsource and thereby lose efficiency if another subsource is chosen by Nature (as long as we are constrained to fixed-length coding). The advantages of the distortion-rate approach over the rate-distortion approach when coding a class of sources (here induced by a single stationary source and its ergodic decomposition) was first observed by Ziv [8]. Our results will be compared and contrasted with Ziv's in the next section.

This trivial special case yields one of the fundamental ideas involved in the general theorems to come. Roughly speaking, we first decompose stationary sources into a possibly uncountable mixture of ergodic subsources. Let them be indexed by a parameter $\phi$ taking values in some space $\Lambda$, let them have a prior distribution $W(\phi)$, and let $D_\phi(R)$ be the DRF of the $\phi$th ergodic subsource. We then use the ergodic decomposition plus a modification of a scheme of Blackwell *et al.* [10] and Sakrison [7] to obtain a finite decomposition of the source into "quasi-ergodic subsources," sources for which laws of large numbers "almost hold" and for which we can prove coding theorems in a familiar manner by combining the techniques of Gallager [3], Berger [1], and Sakrison [7] with a few new tricks developed here. Our basic result is that, for discrete-time stationary sources with separable alphabets,

$$\delta(R) = \int_\Lambda dW(\phi)D_\phi(R).$$

In the general case, (1.3) is no longer true, but it shall be seen that a similar relation does hold for most of the subsources in the decomposition.

## II. Preliminaries and Prerequisites

Our notation follows Berger [1, ch. 7]. The reader is referred to Berger for additional motivation and details. The measure-theoretic details not in Berger may be found in [4], for example.

Let $A_0$ and $\hat{A}_0$ be two nonempty abstract spaces, called the source alphabet and the available reproducing alphabet, respectively. Let $\mathscr{A}_0$ and $\hat{\mathscr{A}}_0$ be $\sigma$-algebras of subsets of $A_0$ and $\hat{A}_0$, respectively. Define the measurable space

$$(A,\mathscr{A}) = \mathop{\times}_{k=-\infty}^{\infty} (A_k,\mathscr{A}_k)$$

of exemplars $(A_k,\mathscr{A}_k)$ of the measurable space $(A_0,\mathscr{A}_0)$; i.e., $A$ is the set of doubly infinite sequences (strings) with elements in $A_0$, and $\mathscr{A}$ is the smallest $\sigma$-algebra containing the cylinder sets [1, p. 266], [2, ch. 1]. Similarly, define $(\hat{A},\hat{\mathscr{A}})$. Let $\mu$ be a probability measure on $\mathscr{A}$, and call the probability space $(A,\mathscr{A},\mu)$ a discrete-time source. A source is usually abbreviated by $[A,\mu]$. Strings in $A$ are usually denoted by $x$ or $\theta$, and the projection of $x$ onto $A_k$ is denoted by $x_k$.

Define the shift transformation $T$: $A \to A$ by

$$(Tx)_n = x_{n+1}.$$

$T$ is an invertible transformation. We assume the source $[\mathscr{A},\mu]$ is stationary: i.e., $T$ is measure preserving,

$$\mu(TE) = \mu(E), \qquad E \in \mathscr{A}$$

where

$$TE = \{Tx: x \in E\}.$$

A set $E \in \mathscr{A}$ is invariant if $TE = E$. The source $[A,\mu]$ is said to be ergodic if every measurable invariant subset has measure zero or one. Berger's results hold for sources that are both stationary and ergodic. The aim of this paper is to drop the requirement of ergodicity, with only a quite general additional constraint on the alphabet $A_0$. We define the general problem and then give Berger's theorem for stationary ergodic sources for reference.

Define $(A^n,\mathscr{A}^n) = \times_{k=0}^{n-1} (A_k,\mathscr{A}_k)$. The restriction of $\mu$ to $\mathscr{A}^n$ is denoted by $\mu^n$, and elements of $A^n$ are denoted by $x^n = (x_0,\cdots,x_{n-1})$. The superscript will be suppressed when it is clear from context, i.e., when the $n$ elsewhere in an expression prevent confusion with an element of $A$.

A code book $C_N$ is a collection of $M = \|C_N\|$ $N$-tuples $\{y_i^N\}_{i \in I_M}$, where $I_M \triangleq \{0,1,\cdots,M-1\}$, drawn from the available reproducing alphabet $\hat{A}^N = \times_{k=0}^{N-1} \hat{A}_k$. A source $N$-tuple $x^N$ is encoded into the codeword $y^N \in C_N$ that minimizes a single-letter nonnegative distortion measure

$$\rho_N(x^N,y^N) = N^{-1} \sum_{i=0}^{N-1} \rho_1(x_i,y_i).$$

The resulting codeword is denoted by $\hat{x}^N(x^N)$. Define

$$\begin{aligned}\rho_N(x \mid C_N) &= \min_{y^N \in C_N} \rho_N(x^N,y^N)\\ &= \rho_N[x,\hat{x}(x)].\end{aligned}$$

The rate $R$ of a code book $C_N$ is defined by $R = N^{-1} \ln M$. Let $\mathscr{C}(N,R)$ denote the set of all block-length $N$ code books having rate $R$ or less.

The average distortion of a code book $C_N$ is

$$\begin{aligned}\rho(C_N) &\triangleq \int_{A^N} \rho_N(x \mid C_N)\, d\mu^N(x)\\ &\triangleq E_\mu[\rho_N(X^N \mid C_N)].\end{aligned}$$

Since we will eventually be concerned with numerous measures, all expectations are subscripted with the appropriate measure (superscripts on the measures may be dropped if clear). Capital letters refer to random variables or vectors.

Define the OPTA's

$$\begin{aligned}\delta(R,N) &= \inf_{C_N \in \mathscr{C}(N,R)} \rho(C_N)\\ \delta(R) &= \lim_{N\to\infty} \delta(R,N).\end{aligned}$$

It can easily be shown that for stationary sources the limit exists and that $\delta(R) = \inf_N \delta(R,N)$. If the source is ergodic, then $\delta(R)$ can be evaluated as an information-theoretic minimization as follows (see Berger [1, ch. 7] for details). Let $q^n$ be a conditional probability measure on $\hat{\mathscr{A}}^n$, given events in $A^n$. Let $p^n$ denote the joint measure on $\mathscr{A}^n \times \hat{\mathscr{A}}^n$ induced by $\mu^n$ and $q^n$. Let $I(\mu^n,q^n)$ be the average mutual information of the joint probability space $(A^n \times \hat{A}^n, \mathscr{A}^n \times \hat{\mathscr{A}}^n, p^n)$ as defined in [1, p. 269, eq. (7.1.18)]. Define for each $R \in (0,\infty)$ and each $n = 1,2,\cdots$ the following set of conditional measures

$$Q_n(R,\mu) = \{q^n: n^{-1}I(\mu^n,q^n) \le R\}$$

and define

$$E_{\mu,q}[\rho_n(X^n,\hat{X}^n)] = \int_{A^n\times\hat{A}^n} \rho_n(x^n,\hat{x}^n)\, dp^n(x^n,\hat{x}^n).$$

The $n$th-order DRF of $[A,\mu]$ is given by

$$D_n(R) = \inf_{q^n \in Q_n(R,\mu)} E_{\mu,q}[\rho_n(X^n,\hat{X}^n)]$$

and the DRF of the source $[A,\mu]$ is defined as

$$D(R) = \lim_{n\to\infty} D_n(R).$$

Berger [1, ch. 7] has shown that, for stationary and ergodic sources, $\delta(R) = D(R)$. More precisely, the following theorem holds.

*Theorem 1 (Berger):* Assume a stationary ergodic discrete-time source $[A,\mu]$ with DRF $D(R)$ with respect to a single-letter fidelity criterion. Assume a letter $\hat{x}^*$ exists for which

$$E[\rho_1(X,\hat{x}^*)] \le \rho^* < \infty.$$

Then we have the following.

1) (Negative): For any positive interger $N$ and any code $C_N \in \mathscr{C}(N,R)$,

$$\rho(C_N) \ge D_N(R) \ge D(R). \tag{2.1}$$

2) (Positive): For any $\varepsilon > 0$ and any $\infty > R \ge 0$, there exists for sufficiently large $N$ a code book $C_N$ having rate less than $R + \varepsilon$ and average distortion satisfying

$$\rho(C_N) \le D(R) + \varepsilon. \tag{2.2}$$

If the source is stationary but not ergodic, then the negative coding theorem (2.1) is still valid. To see this, recall that for any code $C_N$ of size $M$ and a deterministic encoding rule $\hat{x}^N(\cdot)$ we have, defining $\hat{X}^N = \hat{x}^N(X^N)$, that $H(\hat{X}^N \mid X^N) = 0$, and hence

$$\begin{aligned}R &= N^{-1} \ln M \ge N^{-1}H(\hat{X}^N)\\ &= N^{-1}I(\mu^N,q^N)\end{aligned}$$

where

$$q^N(\hat{x}^N \mid x^N) = \begin{cases}1, & \hat{x}^N = \hat{x}^N(x^N)\\ 0, & \text{otherwise.}\end{cases}$$

If the average distortion for this code is $\rho(C_N)$, we can only improve things by considering all possible random encoders satisfying the above rate constraint, i.e.,

$$\begin{aligned}\rho(C_N) &= E_\mu[\rho_N(X^N,\hat{x}^N(X^N))]\\ &\ge \inf_{q^N \in Q_N(R,\mu)} E_{\mu,q}[\rho_N(X^N,\hat{X}^N)] = D_N(R).\end{aligned}$$

The proof of (2.2), however, depends quite strongly on the ergodicity. We shall show that in general (2.2) does *not* hold for nonergodic sources, but that $\delta(R)$ can be found in terms of a closely related information-theoretic minimization.

A fundamental tool of this derivation is Rohlin's ergodic decomposition theorem [4], [5], [6], [17]. This powerful theorem states roughly that any stationary source having a separable alphabet can be considered to be an essentially unique mixture of stationary ergodic subsources. Equivalently, we can view the stationary source as a composition of stationary ergodic sources, where nature randomly chooses one of the subsources at time $-\infty$. This corresponds to the "fixed switch position" composite source (with memory) discussed by Berger [1, p. 194]. We collect here the required definitions and state a version of Rohlin's theorem incorporating all of the required properties.

The $\sigma$-algebra $\mathscr{A}$ is said to be separable if there exists a countable system of sets $\mathscr{G}$ which generates the $\sigma$-algebra $\mathscr{A}$ and separates the points; i.e., $\mathscr{A}$ is the smallest complete $\sigma$-algebra containing all the sets in $\mathscr{G}$, and if $x,y \in A$, then there exist $\mathscr{B}_1,\mathscr{B}_2 \in \mathscr{G}$ such that $\mathscr{B}_1 \cap \mathscr{B}_2 = \Phi$ and $x \in \mathscr{B}_1$, $y \in \mathscr{B}_2$. If $\mathscr{A}_0$ is separable, then so is $\times_{k=-\infty}^{\infty} \mathscr{A}_k = \mathscr{A}$. After stating the Rohlin theorem, we will consider the two cases of most interest, in which $\mathscr{A}_0$ and hence $\mathscr{A}$ are separable.

*Theorem 2 (Rohlin):* Let $[A,\mu] = (A,\mathscr{A},\mu)$ be a stationary discrete-time source having a separable $\sigma$-algebra $\mathscr{A}$. Then there exists 1) a collection of measurable invariant sets $\{A_\theta\}_{\theta \in \Omega}$, where the $A_\theta$ are either coincident or disjoint; 2) a conditional probability measure $\mu_\theta(C) = \mu(C \mid \mathscr{I}_1)_\theta$ relative to $\mathscr{I}_1$, the $\sigma$-algebra of invariant subsets; i.e., if $B \in \mathscr{I}_1$ and $C \in \mathscr{A}$, then $\mu_\theta$ is $\mathscr{I}_1$-measurable and

$$\mu(C \cap B) = \int_B \mu_\theta(C)\, d\mu(\theta) = \int_B \mu(C \mid \mathscr{I}_1)\, d\mu$$

3) $\mu_\theta(A_\theta) = 1$ and the measures $\mu_\theta$ either coincide or are mutually singular; and 4) the source $[A,\mu_\theta]$ is stationary and ergodic.

We denote the decomposition by $[A,\mu] = \langle A,\mu_\theta \rangle$. We shall use this notation even when the individual subsources are not ergodic. Note that the decomposition is "unique" in the sense that any two versions of a conditional probability are almost everywhere (a.e.) equal.

Since the sources $[A,\mu_\theta]$ are ergodic, we have from the ergodic theorem [2] that for any $C \in \mathscr{A}$,

$$\lim_{n\to\infty} n^{-1} \sum_{k=0}^{n-1} I_C(T^{-k}\omega) = \mu_\theta(C_1), \qquad \mu_\theta\text{—a.e.}$$

where $I_C$ is the indicator function of the set $C$. Since $\mathscr{A}$ is separable, it has a countable basis, say $\{C_i; i = 1,2,\cdots\}$. Let $\mathscr{G}$ contain all the $C_i$ and possibly any other countable number of sets in $\mathscr{A}$. Since countable intersections of null sets are null sets, we have that

$$\lim_{n\to\infty} n^{-1} \sum_{k=0}^{n-1} I_C(T^{-k}\omega) = \mu_\theta(C), \qquad \text{all } C \in \mathscr{G}, \quad \mu_\theta\text{—a.e.} \tag{2.3}$$

A string $\omega$ satisfying (2.3) is said to be $\theta$-representative, since relative frequencies of all generators (and possibly some additional sets) in $\omega$ converge to the appropriate probability. Equation (2.3) states that $A_\theta$ may be taken as the set of all $\theta$-representative strings. In particular, if $\omega$ is $\theta$-representative, then $\mu_\omega = \mu_\theta$ (since the two measures agree on generators and therefore are identical), and $A_\omega = A_\theta$.

The preceding form of the decomposition theorem in terms of the sample functions of $[A,\mu]$ and the measure $\mu$ is the most useful for proving the theorems herein. The alternative form implied in the introduction is intuitively more pleasing and will be used in some of the theorem statements.

By collecting together all sample functions $\theta$ producing the same measures $\mu_\theta$, reindexing the measures, using the fact that separable metric spaces are isomorphic to the unit interval, and finally defining the appropriate $\sigma$-algebra, we obtain the following alternative statement. There exists 1) a partition of $A$ consisting of disjoint measurable invariant sets $\{A_\phi\}$, where $\phi$ takes on values in some subset $\Lambda$ of the real line; 2) a canonical system of probability measures $\mu_\phi$, $\phi \in \Lambda$, and a prior $W(\phi)$ such that

$$\mu_\phi(A_\phi) = 1 \qquad \mu(E) = \int_\Lambda \mu_\phi(E)\, dW(\phi)$$

and 3) the source $[A,\mu_\theta]$ is stationary and ergodic.

The preceding version simply collects all identical subsources together under one index and provides a mod-0 unique partition, where mod-0 means unique except for sets whose union has measure zero. Note that in general $\Lambda$ has an uncountable number of elements.

In the next section we consider two cases where $\mathscr{A}_0$ is separable. The major case of interest is that of a finite alphabet $A_0$, in which case $\mathscr{A}_0$ is finite and $\mathscr{A}$ trivially separable. This special case is then used to prove the coding theorem under the following more general assumptions. We assume that the distortion measure $\rho_1$ is a finite-valued (but possibly unbounded) metric defined on $(A_0 \cup \hat{A}_0) \times (A_0 \cup \hat{A}_0)$. Thus for any $x,y \in A_0 \cup \hat{A}_0$,

$$\rho_1(x,y) = 0 \Leftrightarrow x = y$$

$$\rho(_1x,y) < \infty.$$

The metric $\rho_1$ induces a topology on $A_0$ making $A_0$ a topological space; i.e., define the sphere $V_x(r) = \{y: \rho_1(x,y) < r\}$, $r > 0$, and define a set $\mathscr{B} \in A_0$ to be open if $x \in \mathscr{B}$ implies there is a sphere $V_x(r) \in \mathscr{B}$. The class of open sets is a topology on $A_0$, and $A_0$ is called a metric space.

We assume that $A_0$ is a *separable* metric space; i.e., $A_0$ has a countable base of open sets such that every open set in $A_0$ is a union of open sets in the countable base (this is equivalent to the usual definition requiring that $A_0$ have a countable dense subset).

Virtually all cases of interest are covered by this formulation, e.g.,

1) any denumerable metric space;
2) $\mathscr{L}_2[a,b]$ and $l_2$ (with the corresponding norms);
3) $C[a,b]$;
4) any finite- or infinite-dimensional Euclidean space.

We note that none of these is entirely included under Ziv's assumptions [8].

The measurable space $(A_0,\mathscr{A}_0)$ is defined by generating the $\sigma$-algebra $\mathscr{A}_0$ from the countable basis of open sets of $A_0$. Thus $\mathscr{A}_0$ is separable and the space $(A_0,\mathscr{A}_0)$ is called a measurable topological space. Generating $\mathscr{A}_0$ in this way causes it to be also a Borel $\sigma$-algebra; that is, every open set in $A_0$ is contained in $\mathscr{A}_0$ (since it can be written as a countable union of the generating sets). Thus all open sets determined by $\rho_1$ are by definition measurable.

Since $\mathscr{A}_0$ is separable, so is $\times_{k=-\infty}^{\infty} \mathscr{A}_k$, so that if the source $[A,\mu]$ is such that the single-letter alphabet $A_0$ is a separable metric space, then the ergodic decomposition theorem holds.

As a final observation of this section, we note that the distortion measure can be generalized somewhat, e.g., by having any nonnegative monotonic function of a metric as in [8], or possibly by having a more abstract distortion measure as considered by Berger [1, ch. 7]. This would only add additional work, however, and it is felt the definition used here is sufficiently general.

## III. Source Coding Theorems

In this section we present and discuss the basic coding theorems and a related corollary. The positive theorems are proved in the Appendix; the negative coding theorems and the corollaries are easy to establish and are proved in this section.

*Theorem 3:* Let $[A,\mu]$ be a stationary discrete-time source with a finite alphabet $A_0$, a finite reproducing alphabet $\hat{A}_0$, and a bounded single-letter distortion measure. Let $\langle A,\mu_\theta\rangle$ be the ergodic decomposition of $[A,\mu]$, and assume that $D_{n,\theta}(R)$, $n = 1,2,\cdots$, and $D_\theta(R)$ are $\mu$-measurable. Then

$$\delta(R) \geq \int_\Omega d\mu(\theta) D_\theta(R) \tag{3.1}$$

and for any $\varepsilon > 0$ and any finite $R > 0$, there exists for sufficiently large $N$ a code book $C_N$ having rate less than $R + \varepsilon$ and average distortion

$$\rho(C_N) \leq \int_\Omega D_\theta(R)\, d\mu(\theta) + \varepsilon. \tag{3.2}$$

It can be shown that the $\mu$-measurability of $D_{n,\theta}(R)$ and $D_\theta(R)$ need not be assumed since it follows from the $\mu$-measurability of $\mu_\theta$ [16].

The negative side of the coding theorem (3.1) follows immediately from Theorem 1, since if $[A,\mu_\theta]$ is in effect, then

$$E_{\mu_\theta}\{\rho(X^N \mid C_N)\} = \rho(C_N \mid \theta) \geq D_\theta(R). \tag{3.3}$$

Integrating (3.3) yields (3.1). The positive coding theorem (3.2) requires a lengthy argument (as briefly summarized in Section I), which is presented in the Appendix.

Theorem 3 is a direct generalization of Gallager [3, theorem 9.8.3, p. 500] for the case of single-letter distortion measures. As in Gallager's case, the assumption that the distortion measure is bounded can be removed, as is done in the next theorem by extending and applying certain techniques of Sakrison [7].

*Theorem 4:* Let $[A,\mu]$ be a stationary discrete-time source with alphabet $A_0$, a separable metric space with metric $\rho_1$, the per-letter distortion measure. Let $\langle A,\mu_\theta\rangle$ be the ergodic decomposition of $[A,\mu]$. Assume that

1) $\hat{A}_0$ is a totally bounded metric space with metric $\rho_1$;
2) $\rho_1$ is finite (but not necessarily bounded), i.e.,

$$\rho_1(x,y) < \infty, \qquad \text{for } x,y \in A_0 \quad \text{or} \quad x,y \in \hat{A}_0$$

3) there exists an $\tilde{x}^* \in A_0$ and an integrable function $\rho^*(\theta)$ such that

$$E_{\mu_\theta}[\rho_1(x,\tilde{x}^*)] < \infty, \qquad \mu\text{—a.e. } \theta$$

$$E_\mu[\rho_1(x,\tilde{x}^*)] = \rho^* < \infty.$$

Let $D_\theta(R)$ be the DRF of $[A,\mu_\theta]$. We have

$$\delta(R) \geq \int_\Omega d\mu(\theta) D_\theta(R)$$

and for arbitrary $\varepsilon > 0$ and finite $R > 0$, there exists for sufficiently large $N$ a code $C_N$ having rate less than $R + \varepsilon$ and average distortion

$$\rho(C_N) \leq \int_\Omega d\mu(\theta) D_\theta(R) + \varepsilon.$$

Thus we have

$$\delta(R) = \int_\Omega d\mu(\theta) D_\theta(R) = \int_\Lambda dW(\phi) D_\phi(R)$$

so that the minimum average distortion obtainable from a fixed-rate code applied to a stationary source is not given by the DRF of the source, but by the weighted average of the DRF's of the individual ergodic components of the stationary source. Thus the ergodic subsources provide the crucial building blocks of stationary sources with separable alphabets.

The negative coding theorem follows as in the previous theorem.

We note that Neuhoff [18] has shown that assumption 1) can be weakened to the assumption that every bounded subset of $\hat{A}_0$ is totally bounded.

The information transmission theorem holds for $\delta(R)$. That is, for any $\varepsilon > 0$, average distortion arbitrarily close to $\delta(C - \varepsilon)$ can be achieved over any channel of capacity $C$ using a code of rate $R = C - \varepsilon$. The converse to the information transmission theorem does *not* hold in general, however, for $\delta(R)$. The converse holds for $D(R)$, $D(R)$ being achieved by the channel which is "matched" to the source, i.e., the channel identical to the test channel yielding $D(R)$.

Since, as noted, the converse for the usual DRF remains valid, and since a positive coding theorem can be proved for the weighted average DRF, we have

$$\int_\Omega d\mu(\theta) D_\theta(R) \geq D(R).$$

Hence for the nonergodic case $\delta(R)$ may be larger than the DRF as usually defined. This inequality does not appear to follow directly from convexity arguments and hence requires the previous coding theorem for its proof. As an example of a case where the preceding inequality is strict, consider the equiprobable mixture of two i.i.d. Gaussian sources with variances $\sigma_1^2$ and $\sigma_2^2$ (the appropriate coding theorem was proved in Section I). From Berger [1, p. 101] we have that, for a source with variance $\sigma^2$, the mean-squared-error DRF $D_\sigma(R)$ satisfies

$$D_\sigma(R) \le \sigma^2 e^{-2R} \tag{3.4}$$

with equality if the source is Gaussian. Since the mixture source has variance $(\sigma_1^2 + \sigma_2^2)/2$ but is *not* Gaussian,

$$\begin{aligned}\int d\mu(\theta) D_\theta(R) &= \sum w_k D_k(R)\\ &= \tfrac{1}{2}D_{\sigma_1}(R) + \tfrac{1}{2}D_{\sigma_2}(R)\\ &= \tfrac{1}{2}(\sigma_1^2 + \sigma_2^2)\exp(-2R) > D_1(R)\\ &\ge D(R)\end{aligned}$$

where $D_1(R)$ is the first-order DRF of the mixture source.

The definition of $\delta(R)$ involving an expectation over the source probabilities $\mu$ is the traditional quantity used to define the "optimum performance" attainable by fixed-rate coding a stationary source $[A,\mu]$. For example, Ziv defines the optimal average distortion of an individual stationary source in essentially this manner [8]. In the light of the ergodic decomposition, however, potential objections arise to this definition. Specifically, if observing a stationary source really means we are observing some unknown stationary ergodic subsource $[A,\mu_\theta]$, then it is really

$$E_{\mu_\theta}\{\rho_N(X^N \mid C_N)\} = \rho_N(C_N \mid \theta)$$

we should be concerned about, and not

$$\rho(C_N) = \int_\Omega d\mu(\theta)\rho(C_N \mid \theta).$$

Specifically, the best of all possible situations would arise if for sufficiently large $N$ there existed a code $C_N$ such that

$$\rho(C_N \mid \theta) \le D_\theta(R) + \varepsilon, \qquad \text{for all } \theta. \tag{3.5}$$

Although (3.5) is true in the trivial finite case discussed in Section I, it may not be true in general. To see this, consider the following argument. In the Appendix it is shown that Theorem 4 can be restated as saying that there exists a sequence of codes $C_N, N = 1,2,3,\cdots$, having rate $R$ and average distortion satisfying

$$\lim_{N\to\infty} \rho(C_N) = \int_\Omega d\mu(\theta)D_\theta(R) = \int_\Lambda dW(\phi)D_\phi(R). \tag{3.6}$$

Since $\rho(C_N \mid \theta) \ge D_\theta(R)$, we can rewrite (3.6) as

$$\lim_{N\to\infty} \int_\Lambda dW(\phi)|\rho(C_N \mid \phi) - D_\phi(R)| = 0 \tag{3.7}$$

so that $\rho(C_N \mid \phi)$ converges in mean to $D_\phi(R)$ [4, p. 86], [11, p. 103]. This does not imply the uniform convergence required for (3.5). It does, however, imply convergence in measure [11, p. 103]; i.e., for arbitrary $\varepsilon > 0$ we have that

$$\lim_{N\to\infty} W\{\phi: |\rho(C_N \mid \phi) - D_\phi(R)| \ge \varepsilon\} = 0. \tag{3.8}$$

Convergence in measure in turn implies that there is a subsequence $C_{N_k}$ of the sequence of codes $C_N$ obtained in the theorem such that

$$\lim_{k\to\infty} \rho(C_{N_k} \mid \phi) = D_\phi(R), \qquad W\text{—a.e.}$$

Lemma A of the Appendix can then be invoked to obtain a full sequence of codes having this property; i.e., there exists a sequence of codes $C_N$, $N = 1,2,\cdots$, such that

$$\lim_{N\to\infty} \rho(C_N \mid \phi) = D_\phi(R), \qquad W\text{—a.e.} \tag{3.9a}$$

or

$$\lim_{N\to\infty} \rho(C_N \mid \theta) = D_\theta(R), \qquad \mu\text{—a.e.} \tag{3.9b}$$

Thus asymptotically the sequence of codes $C_N$ has average distortion close to the best attainable even if one knew the subsource in effect for almost all $\theta$ or $\phi$. Of more interest from an implementation standpoint is the fact that convergence a.e. of the sequence $C_N$ implies almost uniform convergence; i.e., given $\varepsilon > 0$, there exists a $W$-measurable set $\Lambda_0 \le \Lambda$ such that $W(\Lambda_0) \le \varepsilon$, and $\rho(C_N \mid \phi)$ converges uniformly to $D_\theta(R)$ on $\Lambda - \Lambda_0$. Thus we have the following corollary.

*Corollary:* Given the assumptions of Theorem 4 and arbitrary $\varepsilon_1,\varepsilon_2 > 0$, for sufficiently large $N$ there exists a rate $R + \varepsilon_1$ code book $C_N$ such that for all $\theta$ except for some set $\Lambda_0$ of $W$-measure less than $\varepsilon_2$ we have

$$\rho(C_N \mid \phi) \le D_\phi(R) + \varepsilon_1, \qquad \phi \in \Lambda - \Lambda_0. \tag{3.10}$$

The corollary has the following rather surprising consequence. There exists for sufficiently large block length a single code $C_N$ such that the average distortion when the subsource $[A,\mu_\phi]$ is in effect is arbitrarily close to the best possible attainable for that subsource for all but a collection of subsources having arbitrarily small probability. This is true even though the code book and encoding rule are chosen without knowledge of which subsource is in effect. Thus the code $C_N$ is universal, in a sense, for all possible subsources in the ergodic decomposition.

The problem of universal coding is quite similar to the one considered here. Given a class of subsources, usually without a prior, one attempts to build a single code that "works" regardless of which subsource is present [i.e., such that (3.10) holds for all $\phi$ if the subsources are ergodic]. Universal coding theorems usually involve a constructive approach [8], [9], which in effect first estimates which subsource is present and then sends a code for that subsource. Notable exceptions are Sakrison's approach [7], which involves random coding arguments, i.e., existence proofs, and Davisson's approach [9], which involves existence proofs for noiseless universal source coding. All of the aforementioned approaches involve stronger assumptions either on the alphabet [8] or on the sources [7] than were required for Theorem 4. We here have combined methods of Gallager [3], Berger [1], and Sakrison [7] to obtain results similar to those of Ziv [8]. It might appear that in return for stronger assumptions on the alphabet, Ziv obtains results that are stronger than our corollary (if the class is treated as a mixture and the corollary viewed as a universal coding theorem), since he shows that, given a class of stationary subsources, one can find a code such that asymptotically the average distortion for the actual subsource chosen by Nature is the smallest possible for *all* subsources, rather than "almost all" as in (3.9). He does not, however, state what the smallest possible average distortion for an individual stationary subsource is. In fact, it is given precisely by Theorem 4 (under more general alphabet assumptions) and the corollary, and hence Ziv's results implicitly contain the "almost everywhere" condition of (3.9) when one realizes that his stationary subsources are themselves mixtures of stationary ergodic subsources. His results are stronger if all of his subsources are ergodic.

In Neuhoff *et al.* [12], these analogies with universal coding are pursued by extending several definitions of universal coding for the noiseless case that were used in Davisson [9]. The results of this paper and several other techniques are there used to study the existence of universal codes subject to a fidelity criterion. In Gray and Davisson [17], a relatively simple and intuitive derivation of the ergodic decomposition theorem is presented, along with information- and estimation-theoretic interpretations and applications to universal coding.

## Acknowledgment

The authors wish to thank Prof. T. Kailath of Stanford University for first suggesting the use of the ergodic decomposition theorem; Prof. D. Ornstein and Prof. P. Shields of Stanford University for helping us understand the implications of the Rohlin theorem and for kindling our interest in ergodic theory; and M. Pursley of the University of Southern California, Prof. D. Sakrison of the University of California at Berkeley, and D. Neuhoff of Stanford University for their participation in numerous helpful and enjoyable discussions on the subjects treated herein.

## References

[1] T. Berger, *Rate Distortion Theory*. Englewood Cliffs, N.J.: Prentice-Hall, 1971, ch. 7.
[2] P. Billingsley, *Ergodic Theory and Information*. New York: Wiley, 1965.
[3] R. G. Gallager, *Information Theory and Reliable Communication*. New York: Wiley, 1968, especially ch. 9.
[4] Yu. Rozanov, *Stationary Random Processes*. San Francisco: Holden-Day, 1967.
[5] V. A. Rohlin, "On the fundamental ideas of measure theory," *Amer. Math. Soc. Translation*, no. 71, 1952.
[6] ——, "Lectures on the entropy theory of measure-preserving transformations," *Russian Math. Surveys*, vol. 22, no. 5, pp. 1–52, 1967.
[7] D. J. Sakrison, "The rate distortion function for a class of sources," *Inform. Contr.*, vol. 15, pp. 165–195, 1969.
[8] J. Ziv, "Coding of sources with unknown statistics—Part II: Distortion relative to a fidelity criterion," *IEEE Trans. Inform. Theory*, vol. IT-18, pp. 389–394, May 1972.
[9] L. D. Davisson, "Universal noiseless coding," *IEEE Trans. Information Theory*, vol. IT-19, pp. 783–795, Nov. 1973.
[10] D. Blackwell, L. Breiman, and A. Thomasian, "The capacity of a class of channels," *Ann. Math. Stat.*, vol. 30, pp. 1229–1241, 1959.
[11] P. R. Halmos, *Measure Theory*. New York: Van Nostrand, 1950.
[12] D. Neuhoff, R. M. Gray, and L. D. Davisson, "Fixed-rate universal coding with a fidelity criterion," submitted for publication to *IEEE Trans. Inform. Theory*.
[13] J. Nedoma, "On the ergodicity and $r$-ergodicity of stationary probability measures," *Z. Wahrscheinlichkeitstheorie*, vol. 2, pp. 90–97, 1963.
[14] S. Berberian, *Measure and Integration*. New York: Chelsea, 1965.
[15] W. Rudin, *Real and Complex Analysis*. New York: McGraw-Hill, 1966.
[16] M. Pursley, L. Davisson, and R. Gray, "Variable-rate coding for non-ergodic sources subject to a fidelity constraint," in preparation.
[17] R. M. Gray and L. Davisson, "The Ergodic decomposition of stationary discrete random processes," *IEEE Trans. Inform. Theory*, to be published.
[18] D. Neuhoff, Stanford Univ., Stanford, Calif., 1973, unpublished.

[*Editors' Note:* Appendix A has been omitted.]

# 14



Reprinted from *IEEE Trans. Inform. Theory,* **IT-11**(4), 558–567 (1965)

# Theoretical Limitations on the Transmission of Data From Analog Sources

THOMAS J. GOBLICK, JR., MEMBER, IEEE

***Abstract*—Fundamental limitations on the performance of any type of communication system transmitting data from an analog source may be obtained by application of a theorem in Shannon's original paper on information theory. In order to transmit the output of an analog source to a sink with mean-squared error $\epsilon$ or less, it is necessary to transmit information from source to sink at rates greater than some minimal rate $R(\epsilon)$ bits per second. If a channel of capacity $C$ bits per second is used, then in order for any communication system to be able to achieve $\epsilon$ mean-squared error or less with this channel it is necessary that $R(\epsilon) \leq C$. This inequality can be used to determine the minimum mean-squared error obtainable for a given source-channel pair without discussing any particular communication system. As an example, the minimum mean-squared error is calculated for cases in which the analog source and additive channel noise are stationary, Gaussian processes. The performance of amplitude and angle modulation systems is compared to the theoretically ideal performance obtainable in some of these cases.**

## I. Introduction

An analog waveform $a(t)$ is usually sent over a noisy channel in one of two different ways. In an analog modulation system $a(t)$ is used to modulate a carrier signal to form the signal $s[t; a(t)]$ to be transmitted over the channel. The receiver then attempts to determine $a(t)$ by operating on the noisy signal it receives. If $a(t)$ were selected from only a finite set of distinct waveforms $\{a_i(t)\}$, $i = 1, \cdots, M$, the receiver would simply test $M$ statistical hypotheses concerning all the possible transmitted signals. However, we are concerned here with the case in which $a(t)$ is selected from an infinite set. It is convenient to view the job of the receiver in this case to be that of forming a statistical estimate $\hat{a}(t)$ of the modulating waveform $a(t)$. The optimum receiver, in a mean-squared error sense, is that receiver which minimizes

$$\epsilon = E[a(t) - \hat{a}(t)]^2$$

where $E$ denotes statistical expectation. The minimum mean-squared error that can be achieved in any case clearly depends on both the statistical properties of $a(t)$ and the particular communication channel that is used, as well as the form of $s[t; a(t)]$, i.e., the modulation system.

In another type of system the waveform $a(t)$ may be processed and converted to binary digits (perhaps by filtering, sampling, and quantizing) which are in turn transmitted over the channel by a digital communication system. When $a(t)$ is drawn from an infinite set, it is impossible to represent $a(t)$ exactly in some interval of time with a finite number of binary digits. This implies that every possible waveform $a(t)$ does not have a unique digital representation. The receiver, in general, then, cannot recover exactly the original waveform from the digits it receives and hence distortions result between $a(t)$ and the final receiver output even in the digital system.

Information theory has been very valuable in illuminating the fundamental theoretical limitations in a variety of practical communication problems. The transmission of analog waveforms described is no exception. The purpose of this paper is to point out the implications of a theorem in Shannon's original paper [1] on information theory to the transmission of analog data. The interpretation of this theorem allows us to determine the minimum mean-squared error $\epsilon_{\min}$ obtainable by any communication system, analog or digital, in terms of the rate-distortion function of the $a(t)$ random process and the information capacity of the available channel. As an example of the utility of this approach we calculate $\epsilon_{\min}$ for various cases in which $a(t)$ and the channel noise are stationary Gaussian processes.

## II. General Theory

### A. Analog Channels

Consider a noisy channel with analog waveforms $u(t)$ and $v(t)$ as input and output, respectively. We wish to review the steps in finding the information capacity of such a channel[1] under an average power constraint on the transmitted signals, i.e., $\langle u^2(t)\rangle \leq S$, where $\langle\ \rangle$ denotes time averaging. First denote the waveforms $u_T(t)$ and $v_T(t)$ which are equal to $u(t)$ and $v(t)$, respectively, in the interval $0 \leq t \leq T$, and zero everywhere else. We next obtain an approximate representation for $u_T$ and $v_T$ in terms of finite dimensional vectors by expanding these waveforms in the truncated orthonormal expansions

$$u_{TN}(t) = \sum_{i=1}^{N} u_i\varphi_i(t), \qquad 0 \leq t \leq T,$$

$$v_{TN}(t) = \sum_{i=1}^{N} v_i\varphi_i(t), \qquad 0 \leq t \leq T,$$

and where

$$\int_0^T \varphi_i(t)\varphi_j(t)\, dt = \begin{cases} 1 & \text{if } i = j \\ 0 & \text{if } i \neq j \end{cases}.$$

Manuscript received December 30, 1964; revised July 1, 1965.
The author is with Lincoln Lab., Massachusetts Institute of Technology, Lexington, Mass. (Operated with support from the U. S. Army, Navy, and Air Force.)

[1] See Fano [2], ch. 5, for a detailed discussion.

Now the sets of coefficients in these expansions may be regarded as $N$-dimensional vectors

$$\bar{u}_{TN} = (u_1, u_2, \cdots, u_N)$$

$$\bar{v}_{TN} = (v_1, v_2, \cdots, v_N).$$

For a particular probability density $p(\bar{u}_{TN})$ of the channel input vector $\bar{u}_{TN}$, the average mutual information between $u_{TN}(t)$ and $v_{TN}(t)$ is defined as

$$I(u_{TN}; v_{TN}) = \int d\bar{u}_{TN} \int d\bar{v}_{TN} p(\bar{u}_{TN}, \bar{v}_{TN}) \log \frac{p(\bar{u}_{TN}, \bar{v}_{TN})}{p(\bar{u}_{TN})p(\bar{v}_{TN})} \quad (1)$$

where the two integrals in this expression are volume integrals over $N$-dimensional spaces involving the various probability densities of $\bar{u}_{TN}$ and $v_{TN}$. Now if the set of orthonormal functions $\{\varphi_i(t)\}$ is a complete set, then as $N \to \infty$, we expect that

$$u_{TN}(t) \to u_T(t)$$

$$v_{TN}(t) \to v_T(t).$$

We now define the average mutual information between input and output of an analog channel in the interval $0 \leq t \leq T$ as

$$I(u_T; v_T) = \lim_{N \to \infty} I(u_{TN}; v_{TN}). \quad (2)$$

The maximum average rate of transmission of information (per second) over the channel when used independently in intervals $T$ seconds long is thus

$$C_T(S) = \max_{p(\bar{u}T)} \frac{I(u_T; v_T)}{T} \quad (3)$$

where the maximization in this equation is carried out over all possible probability densities $p(\bar{u}_T)$ subject to the constraint that

$$E \frac{1}{T} \int_0^T u^2(t)\, dt \leq S. \quad (4)$$

If the channel noise is stationary, the foregoing expressions apply to any interval $T$ seconds long. The channel capacity (per second) is

$$C(S) = \text{l.u.b.}_T\, C_T(S). \quad (5)$$

The definition of channel capacity implies that it is impossible to transmit information at a rate greater than $C$ information units per second over a channel of capacity $C$.

### *B. Analog Information Sources*

We now turn our attention to an analogous development of definitions for information sources. Suppose that the analog waveform $a(t)$ is a continuous parameter, stationary random process and that we wish to send to a receiving point a facsimile or reasonable approximation of $a(t)$ in the interval $0 \leq t \leq T$. Call this facsimile $b(t)$: $0 \leq t \leq T$. It is well known that in order to build a communication system which would result in $b(t) = a(t)$, $0 \leq t \leq T$, an infinite amount of information would have to be transmitted to the receiver. We thus relax our fidelity criterion to require only

$$E \frac{1}{T} \int_0^T (a(t) - b(t))^2\, dt \leq \epsilon, \qquad \epsilon > 0. \quad (6)$$

This constraint generally requires that only a finite amount of information be transmitted from source to receiver in this interval. Stationarity of the $a(t)$ process and channel noise again implies that any communication system satisfying the fidelity requirement of (6) would satisfy this same criterion in any interval $T$ seconds long.

Any communication system that provides a facsmile $b(t)$ at a receiving point may be visualized as a concatenation of deterministic and random devices. We would expect to see such deterministic or nonrandom devices as filters, amplifiers, samplers, nonlinearities, etc., in the system. The noisy communication channel is a random device. Whatever the particular form that the communication system takes, it may be regarded simply as a mapping of the function $a(t)$ into $b(t)$ in an interval of $T$ seconds, and this mapping will be random in some sense due to the random channel perturbations or the errors in digitization of $a(t)$. Thus for any such communication system having $a(t)$ as its input we can evaluate (at least formally) the average mutual information $I(a_T; b_T)$ between $a(t)$ and $b(t)$ in an interval of $T$ seconds. We define the quantity $R_T(\epsilon)$ as

$$R_T(\epsilon) = \min \frac{I(a_T; b_T)}{T} \quad (7)$$

where the minimization in (7) is carried out over all possible communication systems (including all possible noisy channels) subject only to the constraint that

$$E \frac{1}{T} \int_0^T (a(t) - b(t))^2\, dt \leq \epsilon. \quad (8)$$

The quantity $R_T(\epsilon)$ may be interpreted as the minimum required information capacity (per second) necessary to provide a receiver output $b(t)$ satisfying (8) when the source output is operated upon independently in successive intervals $T$ seconds long.

This minimum required information capacity may be lower bounded by defining the function

$$R(\epsilon) = \text{g.l.b.}_T\, R_T(\epsilon). \quad (9)$$

The function $R(\epsilon)$ is precisely the rate-distortion function of a source with a fidelity criterion defined by Shannon [1], [3]. The fidelity criterion is fundamental to the definition of the rate of generating information for a continuous parameter source. It was applied also to discrete sources for which nonexact transmission of the source output is acceptable [3]. For a given $\epsilon > 0$, the quantity $R(\epsilon)$ is the minimum rate (per second) of transmission of information necessary to achieve a mean-squared error $\epsilon$ or less between facsmile and actual source output, and thus $R(\epsilon)$ may be interpreted as the information rate of the source under this fidelity criterion.

Thus any communication system that transmits $a(t)$ to a receiving point with $\epsilon$ or less mean-squared error must have an average mutual information $I'_{T'}$ in any interval $T'$ between input and final output that satisfies the inequality

$$\frac{I'_{T'}}{T'} \geq \underset{T}{\text{g.l.b.}}\, R_T(\epsilon) = R(\epsilon) \tag{10}$$

since, if this were not so, the definition of $R(\epsilon)$ would be contradicted. We therefore can conclude that a communication system with input $a(t)$ and which is *not* capable of transmitting at least $R(\epsilon)$ units of information (per second) then cannot provide a receiver output $b(t)$ such that

$$E(a(t) - b(t))^2 \leq \epsilon. \tag{11}$$

### *C. Source-Channel Combinations*

Since it is well known that the information capacity of a cascade of devices must be equal to, or less than, that of any of the individual devices, the capacity of any communication system must be equal to, or less than, the capacity of the noisy channel which is one of the links in the system.[2] We thus conclude that we must send at least $R(\epsilon)$ units of information per second in order to satisfy (8), while the noisy channel will not permit us to send any more than $C$ units per second. Therefore, we can state the following theorem.

*Theorem*

A necessary condition for transmitting the waveform $a(t)$ to a receiving point via a noisy channel with capacity $C$ (per second) with mean-squared error $\epsilon$ or less is

$$R(\epsilon) \leq C. \tag{12}$$

This theorem was stated by Shannon.[3]

There is strong motivation for using the average mutual information function to order all possible communication systems in order to prove the theorem. Shannon has demonstrated the uniqueness of the mutual information function by proving a converse statement to the theorem. In fact, $R(\epsilon) < C$ has been shown to be both a necessary and sufficient condition to achieve $\epsilon$ mean-squared error for several interesting classes of sources. The sufficiency proofs are more involved and will not be discussed here. Any function of the source and channel parameters other than average mutual information would have led to meaningless results since a sufficiency statement would be impossible to prove.

The definition of the function $R(\epsilon)$ guarantees that this function is continuous and monotone decreasing with $\epsilon$. Therefore, if $0<\epsilon_1<\epsilon_2$, then $R(\epsilon_2) \leq R(\epsilon_1)$. The smallest value of $\epsilon$ for which the condition $R(\epsilon) \leq C$ is satisfied is the condition defining $\epsilon_{min}$. The monotonicity of $R(\epsilon)$ implies that this minimum value of $\epsilon$ corresponds to the maximum information rate $R$ for which $R(\epsilon) \leq C$ still holds, or

$$R(\epsilon_{min}) = C. \tag{13}$$

[2] This statement is proved for discrete, memoryless channels in [2], ch. 6.

[3] See Shannon, [1], part of Theorem 21.

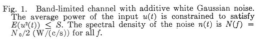

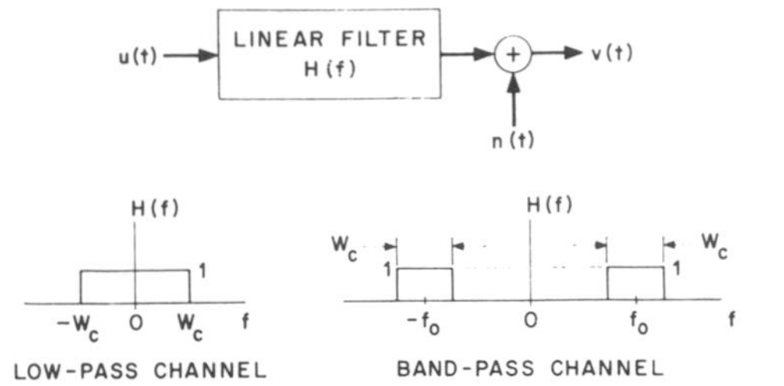


Fig. 1. Band-limited channel with additive white Gaussian noise. The average power of the input $u(t)$ is constrained to satisfy $E(u^2(t)) \leq S$. The spectral density of the noise $n(t)$ is $N(f) = N_0/2$ (W/(c/s)) for all $f$.

Continuity of $R(\epsilon)$ implies that there is a value of $\epsilon_{min}$ which satisfies (13). This is the relation we seek; it defines $\epsilon_{min}$ in terms of functions of the statistical characteristics of the source and channel and independent of any particular communication system. However, in order to apply this result we must be able to compute the rate-distortion function $R(\epsilon)$ for the given source (for a mean-squared error fidelity criterion) and the information capacity of the given channel.

Of course, the aforementioned conclusions also hold for discrete, finite sources (providing outputs that can have only a finite number of different values at discrete, regularly spaced times). In this case, even if we require $\epsilon = 0$, a discrete, noiseless channel with input and output alphabets of the same size as the source alphabet (thus having finite capacity) can be used in (7) or (9) to demonstrate a finite upper bound on $R(0)$. In fact, since $\epsilon \to 0$ implies a vanishing number of errors in transmission of the source output, we can conclude that $R(0)$ is equal to the entropy $H(A)$ of the discrete source [2]. Equation (12) thus reduces to the well-known result

$$H(A) \leq C$$

pertaining to the necessary condition for exact transmission of the output of a discrete, finite source.

In the following section we will illustrate the use of (13) to determine $\epsilon_{min}$ for several examples in which $a(t)$ is a stationary Gaussian process. The available channel is always taken to be the one shown in Fig. 1, the band-limited, white Gaussian channel with average transmitted signal power $S$ and noise power density $N_0/2$ (W/(c/s)).[4] The capacity of this channel is given by the famous equation [1], [2]

$$C = W_c \log_2\left(1 + \frac{S}{N_0 W_c}\right)\text{(bits/second)}. \tag{14}$$

It is well known that $C$ approaches a finite limit with increasing bandwidth $W_c$. The capacity of the infinite bandwidth, white Gaussian channel is

$$C_\infty = \frac{1}{\ln 2}\frac{S}{N_0}\text{ (bits/second)}. \tag{15}$$

[4] A double-sided noise power density spectrum is used in this work.

## III. Gaussian Sources

The computation of channel capacity has thus far received much more attention than the computation of rate-distortion functions. But $R(\epsilon)$ has been derived for at least one interesting class of analog information sources, namely, when $a(t)$ is a stationary Gaussian process.

Shannon has derived $R(\epsilon)$ very elegantly for the time-discrete, Gaussian source (producing statistically independent outputs) under a mean-squared error fidelity criterion [3]. Use of the sampling theorem for band-limited functions with this result then gives $R(\epsilon)$ for the band-limited, white Gaussian source.

The rate-distortion function (mean-squared error fidelity criterion) for a Gaussian process with arbitrary power density spectrum $S_a(f)$ was first published by Kolmogorov in 1956 [4] but no derivation of the results appears. The same result was derived independently by Jordan, in December 1962, and Holsinger, in August 1963.[5] In April 1964, McDonald and Schultheiss [7] published results (without derivation) for stationary Gaussian sources which were extended to include a frequency-weighted mean-squared error fidelity criterion.

### A. Band-Limited Source

First consider the stationary Gaussian process $a(t)$ with zero mean and power density spectrum

$$S_a(f) = \begin{cases} \dfrac{A}{2W_s}, & |f| \leq W_s \\ 0, & \text{elsewhere.} \end{cases} \tag{16}$$

Since $a(t)$ is a band-limited function, it can be exactly represented by a sequence of samples taken $1/2W_s$ seconds apart. Furthermore, these samples would be statistically independent Gaussian random variables with zero mean and variance $E(a^2(t))$ given by

$$E(a^2(t)) = \int_{-\infty}^{\infty} S_a(f)\, df = A. \tag{17}$$

Shannon has derived the rate-distortion function for the source which produces statistically independent, Gaussian distributed samples with zero mean and variance $\sigma^2$. The fidelity criterion between source samples $\{a_i\}$ and the received facsimile samples $\{b_i\}$ was taken as

$$\epsilon = E(a_i - b_i)^2. \tag{18}$$

For this source and fidelity criterion the information rate per sample (expressed in bits) is

$$R_1(\epsilon) = \begin{cases} \frac{1}{2}\log_2 \dfrac{\sigma^2}{\epsilon}, & 0 < \epsilon \leq \sigma^2 \\ 0, & \epsilon > \sigma^2. \end{cases} \tag{19}$$

Considering the sequences of samples $\{a_i\}$ and $\{b_i\}$ to be samples of $a(t)$ and $b(t)$, the fidelity criterion of (18) on sampled waveforms is exactly the same as the mean-squared error criterion for the waveforms $a(t)$ and $b(t)$, given in (11). Since the sampled representation of $a(t)$ requires $2W_s$ samples per second, the rate-distortion function for the white, band-limited Gaussian source with mean-squared error as fidelity criterion is

$$R(\epsilon) = W_s \log_2 \frac{A}{\epsilon} \text{ (bits/second)}, \qquad 0 < \epsilon \leq A. \tag{20}$$

Now consider the problem of transmitting the output of a band-limited, white Gaussian source to a receiving point via the channel shown in Fig. 1. We may use any communication system for which the transmitted signal has average power $S$ and is band-limited to $W_c$ c/s. The minimum mean-squared error that can be achieved by any such system can be found by combining (13), (14), and (20), resulting in

$$\frac{A}{\epsilon} \leq \frac{A}{\epsilon_{\min}} = \left(1 + \frac{S}{N_0 W_c}\right)^{W_c/W_s} = \left(1 + \frac{W_s}{W_c}\frac{S}{N_0 W_s}\right)^{W_c/W_s}. \tag{21}$$

The quantity $\epsilon_{\min}/A$ is the minimum normalized mean-squared error, or alternately, it may be more convenient to use as a parameter $A/\epsilon_{\min}$, which may be interpreted as the maximum signal-to-noise power ratio at the receiver output, if one regards the difference between $a(t)$ and the facsimile $b(t)$ as a kind of noise. Thus we have the maximum output SNR achievable by any communication system for this particular source and channel expressed only in terms of the two quantities $S/N_0W_s$ and $W_c/W_s$. The SNR $S/N_0W_s$ involves the transmitted signal power and the channel noise in a bandwidth equal to the source bandwidth. The ratio $W_c/W_s$ may be interpreted as a kind of modulation system bandwidth expansion factor or bandspreading index allowed by this source-channel combination.

If the available channel has infinite bandwidth, we use (15) in place of (14), resulting in[6]

$$\frac{A}{\epsilon_{\min}} = e^{S/N_0 W_s}. \tag{22}$$

### B. Discussion

To study (21) and (22) more closely, we define the quantities

$$\rho_c = 10 \log_{10} \frac{S}{N_0 W_s}$$
$$\rho_0 = 10 \log_{10} \frac{A}{\epsilon_{\min}} \tag{23}$$

which are simply the SNRs in the channel and final output expressed in decibels.

Suppose $W_c/W_s$ is finite and fixed. Then for $S/N_0W_s \gg$

[5] Both Jordan and Holsinger have written memoranda [5], [6] which rigorously derive this result, but neither one has been published to date.

[6] A reviewer pointed out that (21) and (22) were derived by Lawton in a report that the author was not aware of, namely, "Investigation of analog and digital communication systems," Rome Air Dev. Ctr., N. Y., Final Rept. (Phase 3 Rept.), Tech. Doc. Rept. RADC-TDR-63-147, ch. IV, pp. 100–105, May 1963.

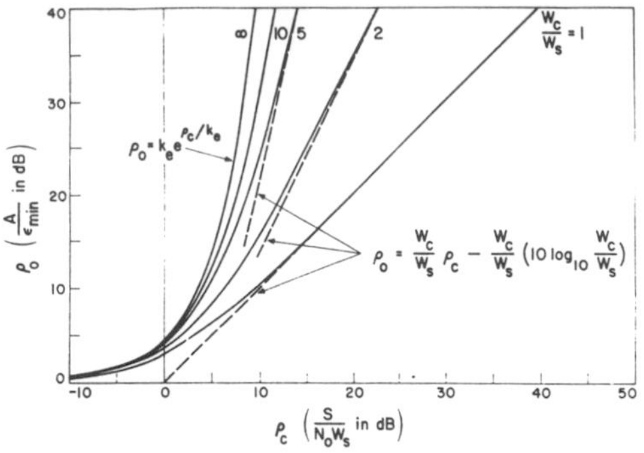

Fig. 2. Graph of $A/\epsilon_{min}$ vs. $S/N_0W_s$ for a band-limited, white source spectrum, and the band-limited, white Gaussian channel shown in Fig. 1. $W_c/W_s$ is the ratio of channel bandwidth to source bandwidth.

$W_c/W_s$, we have from (21)

$$\rho_0 \approx \frac{W_c}{W_s}\rho_c - \frac{W_c}{W_s} 10 \log_{10} \frac{W_c}{W_s} \tag{24}$$

On the other hand, for $S/N_0W_s \ll W_c/W_s$, we can write

$$\rho_0 \approx K_e e^{\rho_c/K_e} \tag{25}$$

where

$$K_e = 10 \log_{10} e .$$

In Fig. 2 we plot $\rho_0$ vs $\rho_c$ for several values of $W_c/W_s$, including $W_c/W_s \rightarrow \infty$. We also include the asymptotes given by (24) and (25) for several of these curves. We see that as $\rho_c \rightarrow +\infty$, $\rho_0$ approaches from above the straight line asymptote given by (24). As $\rho_c \rightarrow -\infty$, $\rho_0$ approaches the $\rho_c$ axis ($\rho_0 \rightarrow 0$) from above while being bounded above by the exponential curve of (25). Even though there is a rather smooth transition between these radically different limiting forms of (21), we may take the breakpoints of these curves at the usual place, namely, at the intersection of the two straight line asymptotes. The value of $\rho_c$ at this breakpoint is given by

$$\rho_c^* = 10 \log_{10} \frac{W_c}{W_s} \tag{26}$$

which is merely the bandwidth expansion factor expressed in decibels.

For $\rho_c < 0$, ($S/N_0W_s < 1$) we see that it is impossible to improve $\rho_0$ by using a bandwidth expanding communication system since $\rho_0$ is essentially independent of $W_c/W_s$ in this region. Under these conditions the prime concern in improving $\rho_0$ should be in somehow increasing $\rho_c$. On the other hand, for $\rho_c > \rho_c^*$ we see that each decible increase in $\rho_c$ implies a theoretically possible increase of $W_c/W_s$ decibels in $\rho_0$. In this domain, a large channel bandwidth can be put to good use in improving $\rho_0$ while keeping $\rho_s$ to a minimum. It may thus be useful to use (22) as a means of determining combinations of $\rho_c$ and $W_c/W_s$ in order to achieve a prescribed output SNR $\rho_0$. Although there is no clearly defined break-point in the curve corresponding to $W_c/W_s \rightarrow \infty$, the same conclusion holds for $\rho_c < 0$, namely, that the prime concern in improving $\rho_0$ here should be focused on increasing $\rho_c$.

Note that in the curves of Fig. 2, $\rho_0$ is never negative, as indeed it never should be. This is true because an output SNR of unity (0 dB) can always be achieved at the receiver if the receiver output is simply a constant equal to the mean value of $a(t)$. Since no channel is needed to achieve this level of performance, this corresponds to the achievable output SNR with zero information capacity between source and receiver.

### *C. Arbitrary Source Spectrum*

Consider now the stationary Gaussian process $a(t)$ with power density spectrum denoted by $S_a(f)$. First define the set of frequencies $F$ as

$$F(\Phi) = \{f: S_a(f) \geq \Phi\} \tag{27}$$

Next define the power density spectrum $N(f)$ as

$$N(f) = \begin{cases} \Phi & \text{for } f \in F(\Phi) \\ S_a(f) & \text{otherwise.} \end{cases} \tag{28}$$

The rate-distortion function for the $a(t)$ process for a mean-squared error fidelity criterion is given parametrically in terms of $\Phi$ as [4]–[7]

$$R(\Phi) = \int_0^\infty df \log_2 \frac{S_a(f)}{N(f)} \text{ (bits/second)}$$
$$= \int_F df \log_2 \frac{S_a(f)}{\Phi}$$
$$\epsilon(\Phi) = \int_{-\infty}^\infty df\, N(f) . \tag{29}$$

From the preceeding we see that $N(f)$ may be interpreted as the power density spectrum of the error $a(t) - b(t)$. In the case of a power density spectrum $S_a(f)$ which is monotone decreasing for increasing $f \geq 0$, $N(f)$ becomes

$$N(f) = \begin{cases} S_a(f), & |f| > \varphi \\ S_a(\varphi), & |f| \leq \varphi \end{cases} \tag{30}$$

where $S_a(\varphi) = \Phi$ and the rate-distortion function is expressed parametrically in $\varphi$ as

$$R(\varphi) = \int_0^\varphi \log_2 \frac{S_a(f)}{S_a(\varphi)} df$$
$$\epsilon(\varphi) = 2\varphi S_a(\varphi) + 2 \int_\varphi^\infty S_a(f)\, df, \qquad \varphi \geq 0. \tag{31}$$

### *D. Butterworth Source Spectra*

The rate-distortion function for the Gaussian random process with first-order Butterworth power spectrum

$$S_a(f) = \frac{1}{1 + \left(\frac{f}{W_s}\right)^2} \tag{32}$$

can be derived explicitly using (31)[7] as

$$R(\varphi) = \frac{2W_s}{\ln 2}(\varphi - \tan^{-1}\varphi) \quad \text{(bits/second)}$$

$$\frac{\epsilon(\varphi)}{A} = 1 + \frac{2}{\pi}\left(\frac{\varphi}{1+\varphi^2} - \tan^{-1}\varphi\right), \quad \varphi \geq 0 \tag{33}$$

where, in this case, the average power output of the source is

$$A = 2\int_0^\infty S_a(f)\,df = \pi W_s.$$

Large values of $\varphi$ correspond to small $\epsilon/A$ and, therefore, large information rates $R(\varphi)$.

These results can be combined with (13) and (14) to obtain the maximum achievable output SNR for any communication system which must transmit a Gaussian random process with spectrum given by (32) via the channel of Fig. 1. In this case, the combination of (14) and (33) was done by plotting both the rate-distortion function $R(\varphi)/W_s$ vs. $\epsilon(\varphi)/A$ and the channel capacity $C/W_c$ [14] vs. $S/N_0W_s$ for some fixed value of $W_c/W_s$ on the same graph. Pairs of values of $(A/\epsilon_{\min}, S/N_0W_s)$ for which $R(\varphi) = C$ are then easily found graphically. Our choice of parameters is a natural one since the $A/\epsilon_{\min}$ clearly depends only on the parameters $S/N_0W_s$ and $W_c/W_s$.

In Fig. 3, curves of $\rho_0$ vs $\rho_c$ are plotted for various values of $W_c/W_s$ for the first order Butterworth source spectrum. These curves are very different in character from those of Fig. 2 for the band-limited source. The behavior of the curves in Fig. 3 as $\rho_c \to \infty$ may be studied by expanding (33) in an asymptotic series for large $\varphi$. We have for $\varphi \gg 1$

$$R(\varphi) = \frac{2W_s}{\ln 2}\left[\varphi - \frac{\pi}{2} + \left(\frac{1}{\varphi} - \frac{1}{3\varphi^3} + \frac{1}{5\varphi^5} - \cdots\right)\right]$$

(bits/second)

$$\frac{\epsilon(\varphi)}{A} = \frac{2}{\pi}\left[\left(\frac{1}{\varphi} - \frac{1}{\varphi^3} + \frac{1}{\varphi^5}\cdots\right) + \left(\frac{1}{\varphi} - \frac{1}{3\varphi^3} + \frac{1}{5\varphi^5} - \cdots\right)\right]$$

$$= \frac{2}{\pi}\left(\frac{2}{\varphi} - \frac{2}{3\varphi^3} + \frac{6}{5\varphi^5} - \cdots\right). \tag{34}$$

We can thus write for $\varphi \to \infty$, which implies $A/\epsilon \to \infty$,

$$R(\epsilon) \approx \frac{W_s}{\ln 2}\left(\frac{8}{\pi}\frac{A}{\epsilon} - \pi\right) \quad \text{(bits/second)}. \tag{35}$$

This asymptotic form for $R(\epsilon)$ is quite accurate for $A/\epsilon > 10$.

[7] The parameter $\varphi$ in this equation is not exactly the same as the $\varphi$ in (31) due to a simple substitution of variables.

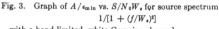

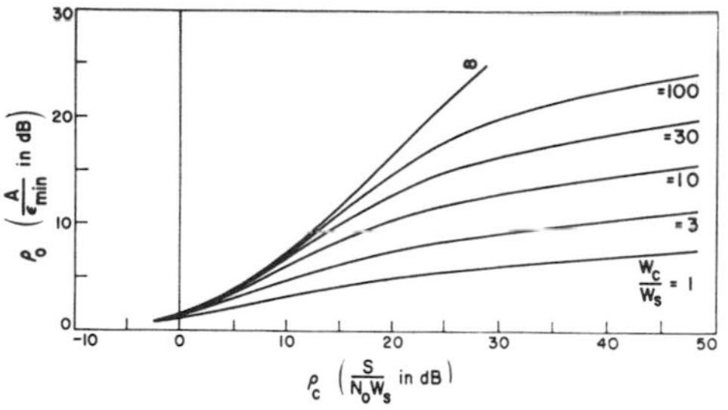


Fig. 3. Graph of $A/\epsilon_{\min}$ vs. $S/N_0W_s$ for source spectrum $1/[1 + (f/W_s)^2]$ with a band-limited, white Gaussian channel.

Since large $A/\epsilon$ implies large $R(\epsilon)$, and large channel capacity implies large $S/N_0W_s$, we can combine (35) with (14) for large $S/N_0W_s$ to arrive at the asymptotic relation between $\rho_0$ and $\rho_c$ as

$$\rho_0(\text{dB}) \approx 10\log_{10}\frac{W_c}{W_s} + 10\log_{10}\rho_c + 10\log_{10}\frac{\pi}{8K_s}. \tag{36}$$

We see that $\rho_0$ depends on the logarithm of $\rho_c$, which is itself expressed in decibels. This is consistent with the shape of the curves of Fig. 3. These curves thus do not approach straight line asymptotes for large $\rho_c$, as do the curves of Fig. 2.

For large $\rho_c$, combining (15) and (35) results in the limits of performance with the infinite bandwidth channel as

$$\rho_0 \approx \rho_c + 10\log_{10}\frac{\pi}{8} \tag{37}$$

showing a linear dependence of $\rho_0$ on $\rho_c$ in this case. However, comparison of this result with the corresponding result for the band-limited source [(22) or (25)] shows a radical difference between the two.

### *E. Higher Order Butterworth Spectra*

Equation (31) was used to calculate the rate distortion functions for the Butterworth source spectra given by

$$S_a^{(n)}(f) = \frac{1}{1 + \left(\frac{f}{W_s}\right)^{2n}} \tag{38}$$

for values of $n = 1, 2, 3, 5, 10,$ and $20$. These computations were performed on a digital computer since explicit expression for $R(\varphi)$ and $\epsilon(\varphi)$ for these functions would be tedious, if not impossible, to find. These curves are plotted in Fig. 4. If we allow $n \to \infty$ in (38), we approach the band-limited spectrum of (16). We also include in Fig. 4 the band-limited source and also the source with Gaussian spectrum

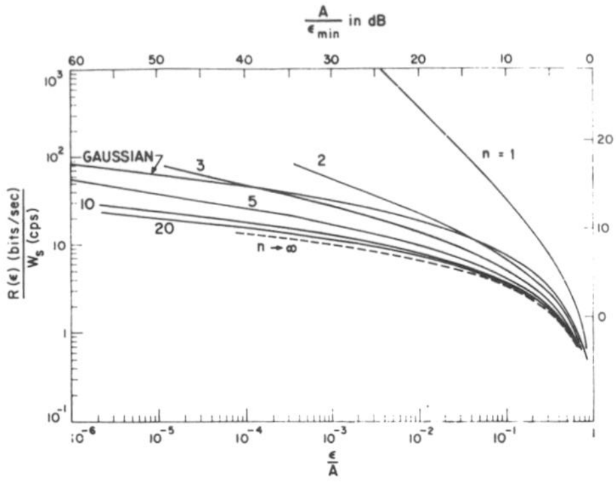


Fig. 4. The rate distortion functions $R(\epsilon)/W_s$ vs. $\epsilon/A$ for Butterworth spectra $1/[1 + (f/W_s)^{2n}]$ for various $n$ and the Gaussian spectrum $\exp[-\frac{1}{2}(f/W_s)^2]$. The curves may also be interpreted as $A/\epsilon_{\min}$ vs. $S/N_0W_s$ for the various spectra when used with the infinite bandwidth, white Gaussian channel.

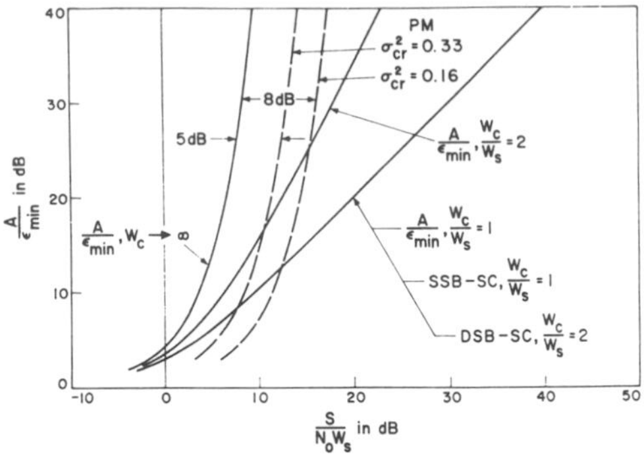


Fig. 5. Comparison of theoretical limits with actual performance of various analog modulation systems transmitting the output of a white, band-limited source.

$$S_a(f) = \exp\left[-\frac{1}{2}\left(\frac{f}{W_s}\right)^2\right]. \tag{39}$$

Having $R(\epsilon)/W_s$ for many different source spectra in Fig. 4, we may now determine $\epsilon_{\min}/A$ for each of these spectra when the available channel is the infinite bandwidth, white Gaussian channel with capacity given by (15). In using (13) we equate the information rate of the source with $C_\infty$. The curves in Fig. 4 of $R(\epsilon)/W_s$ vs. $\epsilon/A$ may thus be re-labeled as

$$C_\infty/W_s = \frac{1}{\ln 2}\frac{S}{N_0W_s} \text{ vs. } \epsilon_{\min}/A,$$

or more simply as $S/N_0W_s$ vs. $\epsilon_{\min}/A$, giving us curves similar to those of Figs. 2 and 3. Fig. 4 thus is labeled as curves of $R(\epsilon)/W_s$ vs. $\epsilon/A$ pertaining to the sources alone, and curves $A/\epsilon_{\min}$ vs. $S/N_0W_s$ pertaining to communication systems using an infinite bandwidth, white Gaussian channel.

## IV. Comparison of Theory with Practice

There is an endless variety of communication systems which could be used to transmit the output of a Gaussian source over an additive, white Gaussian channel. We consider only three different systems here: amplitude and angle analog modulation, and a simple digital communication system.

### A. Amplitude Modulation

In a double-sideband, suppressed carrier system (DSB-SC) the transmitted signal is

$$s[t; a(t)] = \sqrt{\frac{2S}{A}}\, a(t) \cos 2\pi f_0 t.$$

The receiver first multiplies the incoming signal plus channel noise by $\cos 2\pi f_0 t$ and low-pass filters to obtain the low-pass signal

$$G[a(t) + n_c(t)]$$

where $G$ is a gain factor and $n_c(t)$ is the residual channel noise out of the low-pass filter. Since $n_c(t)$ is Gaussian when the channel noise is Gaussian, the optimum receiver in a mean-squared error sense merely performs an optimum linear filtering of the low-pass signal plus noise. In fact, we will assume that the optimum unrealizable filter is used to recover $a(t)$ at the receiver since this can be approximately realized with delayed output and the delay is not important in our problem. Van Trees [8] gives a detailed discussion of this type of modulation system.

For the white, band-limited source of (16), the result is

$$\frac{A}{\epsilon} = 1 + \frac{S}{N_0W_s}. \tag{40}$$

For this source, a channel in which $W_c/W_s = 2$ is necessary. Therefore the theoretical limit on $A/\epsilon$ in this case is obtained from (21) as

$$\frac{A}{\epsilon} = \left(1 + \frac{1}{2}\frac{S}{N_0W_s}\right)^2 = 1 + \frac{S}{N_0W_s} + \left(\frac{S}{2N_0W_s}\right)^2.$$

An ideal single-sideband, suppressed carrier system (SSB-SC) would send only the positive frequency part of $S_a(f)$ in a positive frequency RF band and correspondingly handle negative frequencies in a negative frequency RF band. An SSB-SC signal can be derived from the DSB-SC signal given before by using ideal band-pass filters to remove the lower sidebands. The same mixing and filtering operations at the receiver would bring together both halves of the original signal spectrum. Although these operations are difficult to accomplish in practice, we compare the performance of such an ideal SSB-SC system to our theoretical limits.

In this ideal system it is clear that the source-spectrum splitting and recovery is not significant in a mean-squared error sense and the receiver again must simply perform an optimum linear filtering of $a(t) + n_c(t)$. The performance of this ideal system is therefore given by (40). However, it is clear that the SSB-SC system requires a channel in

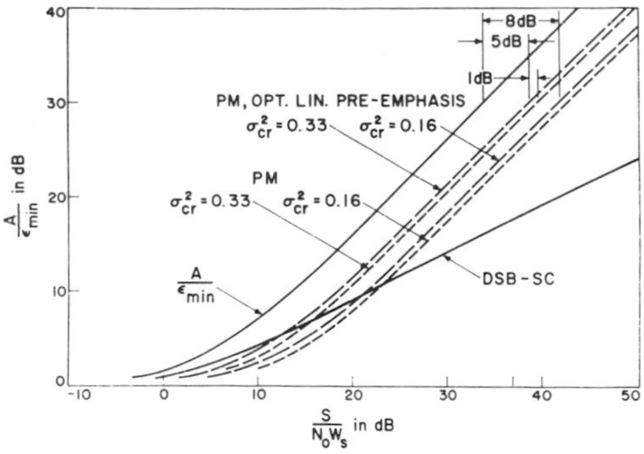


Fig. 6. Comparison of theoretical limits with actual performance of various analog modulation systems transmitting the output of a first-order Butterworth source.

which $W_c/W_s = 1$. We can see from (21) with $W_c/W_s = 1$ that this ideal SSB–SC system with a white, band-limited source achieves the theoretically ideal performance (again assuming the receiver approximately realizes the optimum realizable filter with delay). Moreover, we can conclude that this band-limited channel is the one which minimizes the average mutual information between a white, band-limited source and sink subject to the mean-squared error constraint of (8).

Using Van Trees' results, for a DSB–SC system with the Butterworth source spectrum of (32), we get

$$\frac{A}{\epsilon} = \left(1 + \frac{2}{\pi}\frac{S}{N_0 W_s}\right)^{1/2} \tag{41}$$

and the channel bandwidth that is used is infinite (in the strict sense). These results for AM systems are plotted along with the theoretical limits in Figs. 5 and 6.

*B. Angle Modulation*

Under angle modulation systems we include phase-modulation (PM), with and without optimum linear pre-emphasis. Here we again rely completely on the work of Van Trees [8] and Van Trees and Boardman [9] for the performance of the optimum receivers for these systems. The transmitted signal in a PM system is

$$s[t; a(t)] = \sqrt{2S} \cos [2\pi f_0 t + x(t)]$$

where

$$x(t) = \begin{cases} \beta a(t), & \text{for no pre-emphasis} \\ \int_{-\infty}^{\infty} h(t-u)a(u)\,du, & \text{for linear pre-emphasis} \end{cases}$$

and $\beta$ is the modulation index. The optimum receiver for PM has been shown to be a phase-locked loop whose performance in a mean-squared error sense has been analyzed for high SNR's $S/N_0W_s$ for which the loop may be linearized. As $S/N_0W_s$ decreases the loop becomes increasingly nonlinear and eventually unlocks. Receiver performance in this nonlinear or threshold region is very difficult to calculate. We use only results for linearized loops in this paper.

The linearity of a phase-lock loop may be assured by contraining the mean-squared phase error between the incoming signal and the tracking signal generated by the receiver. In Van Trees' notation [8], [9] this mean-squared phase error is denoted $\sigma_{cr}^2$ for optimum receivers which use only realizable filters within the loop, and an unrealizable post-loop filter (formally realized with delay). As $S/N_0W_s$ increases, $\sigma_{cr}^2$ decreases, of course, and $A/\epsilon$ increases, but not as rapidly as is theoretically possible [for fixed $\beta$ or pre-emphasis filter $h(t)$]. The performance of angle modulation systems is closest to ideal when these systems are operating close to threshold. We will therefore plot $A/\epsilon$ in terms of $S/N_0W_s$ for fixed values of $\sigma_{cr}^2$ (radians$^2$) which guarantee that the loop is linear [implying $\beta$ or $h(t)$ varies].

For the white, band-limited source, linear pre-emphasis does not improve the performance of PM. The relation between $A/\epsilon$, $S/N_0W_s$, and $\sigma_{cr}^2$ in this case is [8], [9]

$$\frac{A}{\epsilon} = \exp\left(\frac{S}{N_0 W_s}\cdot\sigma_{cr}^2\right)$$

and the strict channel bandwidth used by this system is infinite. This result was derived by linearizing the receiver and thus holds only for values of $\sigma_{cr}^2$ less than some threshold value for which the linear approximations are valid. Note that this result differs from $A/\epsilon_{\min}$ only by the factor $\sigma_{cr}^2$ in the exponent. Thus a SNR $1/\sigma_{cr}^2$ larger than ideal is required to achieve a certain $A/\epsilon$.

For the Butterworth source, PM with optimum linear pre-emphasis [8], [9] is also identical to that given in Fig. 3 with $W_c \to \infty$ except that $\sigma_{cr}^2$ again multiplies $S/N_0W_s$. Thus the margin of difference between the theoretical limits and the practically achievable values of $S/N_0W_s$ is a factor of $1/\sigma_{cr}^2$.[8] For PM with no pre-emphasis the result is

$$\frac{A}{\epsilon} = \frac{1}{\pi}\frac{S}{N_0 W_s}\sigma_{cr}^2 + 1 \tag{42}$$

and this represents only a 1 dB difference from PM with optimum pre-emphasis.

It is clear that the comparison of angle modulation with the theory is very much a function of our choice of $\sigma_{cr}^2$. It appears that large $\sigma_{cr}^2$ increases $A/\epsilon$. In fact, for $\sigma_{cr}^2 > 0.5$ radians$^2$, angle modulation systems appear to perform within 3 dB of ideal. But phase-locked receivers are not really linear for these values of $\sigma_{cr}^2$ and performance is therefore not given by the preceeding equations. ($\sigma_{cr}^2 = 0.5$ radians$^2$ corresponds to $\sigma_{cr} \approx 40°$.) Unfortunately there is no clearly defined value of $\sigma_{cr}^2$ beyond which the above performance equations no longer hold. If we adopted a value of $\sigma_{cr}^2 = 0.16$ rad$^2$ ($\sigma_{cr} \approx 23°$), almost everyone would agree that phase-locked receivers are essentially linear in this region and our formulas for performance certainly hold. On the other hand, a

[8] This is discussed in some detail in [10].

value of $\sigma_{cr}^2 = 0.33$ rad$^2$ ($\sigma_{cr} \approx 33°$) results in significant nonlinear effects. For our comparison of angle modulation with theory we adopt for $\sigma_{cr}^2$ the range of values between 0.33 rad$^2$ (optimistic) and 0.16 rad$^2$ (conservative). These values would put PM with optimum pre-emphasis about 5 to 8 dB in $S/N_0W_s$ from the theoretical limits, but with the same general form of behavior with $S/N_0W_s$. These results are plotted in Figs. 5 and 6 as dashed lines. The values of $\sigma_{cr}^2$ adopted for this comparison represent to the author optimistic and conservative limits, and there most certainly are people who would not choose this same range of values. Since $\sigma_{cr}^2$ always appears multiplying $S/N_0W_s$ in the preceding equations, varying $\sigma_{cr}^2$ has the effect of merely sliding the performance curves along the $S/N_0W_s$ axis. The performance of angle modulation is thus simple to obtain for any choice of $\sigma_{cr}^2$ from Figs. 5 and 6.

### C. A Digital System (Orthogonal Signals)

Consider a system in which $a(t)$ is first converted into a sequence of binary digits which are then transmitted over the channel essentially without error. Then the only distortion between $a(t)$ and the final receiver output $b(t)$ is due to the inability of the receiver to exactly reconstruct $a(t)$ from the exact sequence of digits produced by the A–D converter. If a digital data rate of $R^*$ binary digits per second is required to achieve a mean-squared error of $\epsilon$ or less in such a system, then we must have $R^* \geq R(\epsilon)$. If this were not true, then a communication system incorporating a discrete noiseless channel with capacity $R^* < R(\epsilon)$ would be capable of achieving $\epsilon$ mean-squared error, a contradiction of the definition of $R(\epsilon)$.

Suppose a digital communication system transmitting one of $M$ equi-energy, orthogonal waveforms of duration $T$ is used to transmit the digital representation of $a(t)$ over the channel. The data rate for the system is

$$R^* = \frac{1}{T} \log_2 M \quad \text{(bits/second)}.$$

The error rate of this system for incoherent detection when the channel noise is additive, white Gaussian noise is bounded quite accurately as

$$P_e \leq \frac{M}{2} \exp\left(-\frac{1}{2}\frac{ST}{N_0}\right) = \exp(-\alpha)$$

where

$$\alpha = -\ln P_e = \frac{1}{2}\frac{ST}{N_0} - \ln\frac{M}{2}.$$

If a certain error rate $P_e^* \leq e^{-\alpha^*}$ is required to keep the distortion of $a(t)$ due to channel errors negligible, we may use the preceding equations to obtain the constraint on the SNR $S/N_0W_s$ as

$$\frac{C_\infty}{W_s} = \frac{1}{\ln 2}\frac{S}{N_0W_s} \geq 2\frac{R^*}{W_s}\left[1 + \frac{\log \frac{1}{2P_e^*}}{\log M}\right]. \quad (43)$$

This inequality indicates that we must digitize $a(t)$ in a way which keeps $R^*$ down to a minimum for a given $\epsilon$. The most efficient digitization would result in $R^* \equiv R(\epsilon)$. The factor in parentheses is a function of the error rate $P_e^*$ and the number of orthogonal signals employed. If modest error rates such as $10^{-2}$ to $10^{-3}$ would suffice, the factor in parentheses could be reduced to 2 for $M$ of 50 to 500, which would be about the practical limit. This would result in

$$\frac{1}{\ln 2}\frac{S}{N_0W_s} \geq 4\frac{R(\epsilon)}{W_s}$$

even if $R^* = R(\epsilon)$. This digital system thus requires $S/N_0W_s$ to be at least 4 times (6 dB) larger than ideal for a given $\epsilon/A$. It is reasonable to expect $R^* \approx 2R(\epsilon)$ for simple digitization schemes such as filtering, sampling and quantizing, resulting in a 6 to 9 dB margin in $S/N_0W_s$ for this system relative to the ideal performance. This compares favorably with the results for angle modulation. However, the complexity of the digital system for $M$ of 50 to 500 is probably significantly greater than the analog system.

## V. Summary

We have illustrated how one of Shannon's original theorems may be interpreted and used to derive bounds on the performance of communication systems transmitting data from analog sources. Given a particular information source, i.e., a random process generating a waveform $a(t)$, and a particular channel, there is a minimum obtainable mean-squared error, $\epsilon_{min}$, between final receiver output and $a(t)$ that is independent of the type of communication system employed. In order to calculate $\epsilon_{min}$ for a particular source-channel combination, we need to calculate only the rate-distortion function of the $a(t)$ random process (for a mean-squared error fidelity criterion) and the information capacity of the given channel.

The rate-distortion function can be calculated for stationary Gaussian random processes which are frequently used to model analog information sources. We therefore treat in detail several examples of Gaussian sources in combination with band-limited, white Gaussian channels. These examples indicate clearly that modulation systems which expand bandwidth cannot be used to good advantage unless the SNR $S/N_0W_s$ is adequate. It is also clear from the radical difference between Figs. 2 and 3 that the potential effectiveness of bandwidth expansion systems depends sensitively on the statistical properties of the source output.

The performance of several types of practical communication systems was compared to theoretical limits for two source spectra. The margins in $S/N_0W_s$ required by these systems over and above the ideal performance represent the potential payoff of all efforts to develop more efficient techniques to transmit data from Gaussian sources over channels with additive Gaussian noise.

## References

[1] C. E. Shannon, "A mathematical theory of communication," *Bell Sys. Tech. J.*, vol. 27, pp. 379 and 623, 1948.
[2] R. M. Fano, *Transmission of Information*. New York: M.I.T. Press-Wiley, 1961.
[3] C. E. Shannon, "Coding theorems for a discrete source with a fidelity criterion," *1959 IRE Nat'l Convention Record*, pt. 4, p. 142.
[4] A. N. Kolmogorov, "On the Shannon theory of information transmission in the case of continuous signals," *IRE Trans. on Information Theory*, vol. IT-2, pp. 102–108, December 1956.
[5] K. L. Jordan, unpublished memo., M.I.T. Lincoln Lab., Lexington, Mass., December 1962.
[6] J. L. Holsinger, unpublished memo., M.I.T. Lincoln Lab., Lexington, Mass., August 1963.
[7] R. A. McDonald and P. M. Schultheiss, "Information rates of Gaussian signals under criteria constraining the error spectrum," *Proc. IEEE*, vol. 52, pp. 415–416, April 1964.
[8] H. L. Van Trees, "Analog modulation theory and continuous estimation," presented at M.I.T., Cambridge, Mass., July 1964.
[9] H. L. Van Trees and C. J. Boardman, "Optimum angle modulation," to be published in *IEEE Trans. on Communication Technology*,
[10] H. L. Van Trees, "A comparison of optimum angle modulation on systems and rate-distortion bounds," submitted to *Proc. IEEE* (*Corres.*).

# 15



Reprinted from *IEEE Trans. Inform. Theory,* **IT-13**(2), 323–326 (1967)

# ANALOG SOURCE DIGITIZATION: A COMPARISON OF THEORY AND PRACTICE

## I. Introduction

We consider the transmission of an analog waveform $u(t)$ to a sink (final destination of the source output) by first converting this waveform to a digital representation, which is in turn transmitted over the channel by a digital communication system. Since it is impossible to represent the set of all possible waveforms $u(t)$ in some interval of time with a finite number of binary digits, the receiver then cannot infer the exact source output from the digits it receives, and hence distortions result between $u(t)$ and the final receiver output even if the digits are transmitted over the channel without error.

Throughout this correspondence we will assume that the digital representation of $u(t)$ is transmitted over the channel *without error.* This assumption is consistent with situations in which a coded digital communication system is used to transmit reliably over a noisy channel. This work also applies to the storage of analog waveforms in digital memories with no errors in read-in and read-out. We model an analog source as a stationary Gaussian process with zero mean and known power density spectrum $S(f)$. We use as a fidelity criterion the mean-squared error between source output and the reconstructed waveform at the final output of the receiver. This fidelity criterion is mathematically tractable and is meaningful in many applications. The fundamental limitations on minimizing the number of binary digits in the digital representation of $u(t)$ for a fixed mean-squared error are presented. Some simple digitization schemes are also compared to the theoretical limits for several different source spectra.

## II. Quantizers

Perhaps the most common method of converting analog data samples to digital form is a simple amplitude quantizer. Consider a time-discrete Gaussian source producing $1/T_0$ independent samples per second and consider converting (encoding) these samples into digital form with a quantizer having $M$ uniformly spaced output levels $\{v_i\}$, $i = 1, \cdots M$, (a uniform, $M$ level quantizer in our terminology). Suppose further that a sample $u$ is mapped by the quantizer into the nearest output level (in a euclidian distance sense) (see Fig. 1), and that the set of output levels is centered about the mean of the samples (which is always taken to be zero in this work). The mean-squared error $\epsilon^2$ between quantizer inputs and outputs is now a function only of $M$, the number of output levels, and $v_{max}$, the maximum output level. The number of binary digits needed to represent the set of quantizer output levels is $r$, where $r$ is the smallest integer satisfying

$$M \leq 2^r.$$

This is one method of converting analog samples to binary digits.

A second method of digitizing an analog quantity would be to represent quantizer outputs by symbols from an $M$-symbol alphabet by simply numbering the output levels from 1 to $M$. A trivial sort of block coding could be used to convert sequences of such $M$-ary symbols to sequences of binary digits, requiring a minimum of $\log_2 M$ bits per $M$-ary symbol, and hence $\log_2 M$ bits per sample.

A third and more complex digitization scheme is as follows. The quantizer outputs will not be equiprobable in the case of Gaussian samples, and so the entropy $H_Q(V)$ of these outputs satisfies

$$H_Q(V) = -\sum_{i=1}^{M} p_i \log_2 p_i < \log_2 M \text{ bits per sample}$$

where $p_i$, the probability of the output level $v_i$, is easy to calculate for a uniform quantizer. The quantizer outputs, regarded as outputs of a discrete memoryless source, could theoretically be coded to require a minimum of only $H_Q(V)$ bits per sample to be transmitted to the sink to achieve vanishing probability of erroneous reconstruction of the sequence of quantizer outputs from the coded version.[1,2] We will refer henceforth to such coding as "entropy coding" of the quantizer outputs.

The point to be made is that the data rate required to send the quantizer outputs to the receiver depends on the amount of processing that the quantizer outputs undergo. If each quantizer output is expressed directly in binary digits, the required data rate is $r$ bits per sample where $M \leq 2^r$. If sequences of the $M$-ary quantizer outputs are mapped into sequences of binary digits,[3] the data rate can be reduced to $\log_2 M$ bits per sample. If the quantizer outputs are entropy coded, a data rate of $H_Q(V)$ bits per sample is required. It remains to optimize performance for each of these methods of transmitting the quantizer outputs to the receiver.

The information rate of a source producing independent Gaussian samples has been derived by Shannon for the fidelity criterion of $\epsilon^2$ mean-squared error between the source output and its facsimile at the sink as[1,4]

$$R(\epsilon^2) = \tfrac{1}{2} \log_2 \frac{A}{\epsilon^2} \text{ bits per sample}$$

where $A$ is the variance of the source samples. Part of the significance of the information rate of a source with a fidelity criterion is as

[1] C. E. Shannon, "A mathematical theory of communication," *Bell Sys. Tech. J.*, vol. 37, pp. 379–623, 1948.

[2] R. M. Fano, *Transmission of Information.* Cambridge, Mass.: M.I.T. Press, and New York: Wiley, 1961.

[3] This is clearly not necessary when $M$ is a power of 2.

[4] C. E. Shannon, "Coding theorems for a discrete source with a fidelity criterion," *IRE Nat'l Conv. Rec.*, pt. 4, pp. 142–163, 1959.

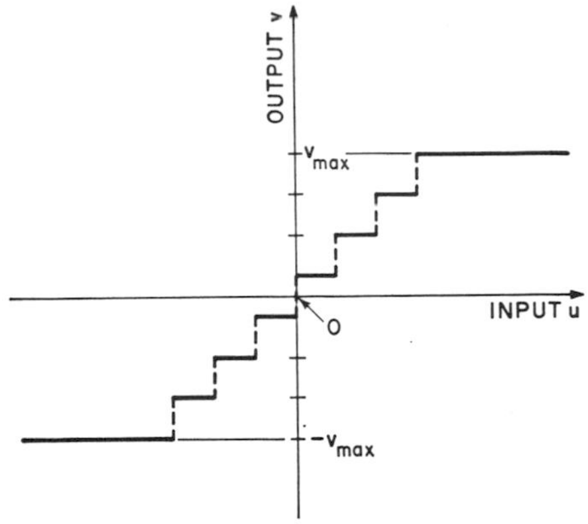


Fig. 1. Input-output relationship for a uniform quantizer with $M = 8$ output levels.

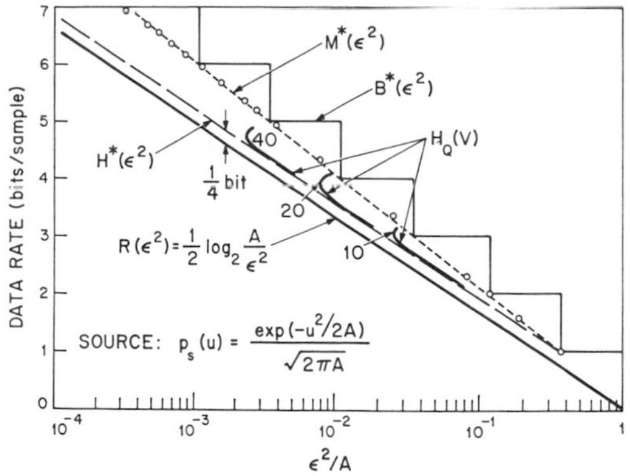


Fig. 2. Data rates required to send uniform quantizer outputs to a receiver as a function of $\epsilon^2/A$. Also shown are curves of quantizer output entropy $H_Q(V)$ vs. $\epsilon^2/A$ as $v_{max}$ is varied for $M = 10, 20, 40$.

follows. It is impossible to satisfy the fidelity criterion ($\epsilon^2$ mean-squared error, in our case) by transmitting over a channel of capacity $C < R(\epsilon^2)$ between source and sink. If we consider using a noiseless binary channel between source and sink, the capacity of this channel must be at least $R(\epsilon^2)$ bits per source sample to achieve $\epsilon^2$ mean-squared error. That is, no fewer than $R(\epsilon^2)$ bits transmitted per source sample could achieve $\epsilon^2$ mean-squared error. This statement holds for any source encoder which translates the source samples to binary digits, whether it is a uniform quantizer or a device which maps blocks of source samples into sequences of binary digits. $R(\epsilon^2)$ thus gives the limiting performance that one could expect for any scheme which transmits the source output to the sink in the form of binary digits.

In Fig. 2 we show several curves of $H_Q(V)$ vs. $\epsilon^2/A$ (where $A = E(u^2)$) as $v_{max}$ is varied for quantizers having 10, 20, and 40 output levels. For values of $\epsilon^2/A$ less than 0.5, the lower envelope of such curves for $M$ ranging from 2 to 140 is fitted quite accurately by the function

$$H^*(\epsilon^2) = \tfrac{1}{4} + \tfrac{1}{2}\log_2 \frac{A}{\epsilon^2} \text{ bits per sample.}$$

The curve of $H^*(\epsilon^2)$ vs. $\epsilon^2/A$ represents the best obtainable performance for uniform quantizers used with Gaussian samples, and this performance would be achievable only by entropy coding of the quantizer levels.

In Fig. 2 we also plot $R(\epsilon^2)$ for independent Gaussian samples. It is quite striking that the uniform quantizer with entropy coding requires only about $\frac{1}{4}$ bits per sample more than the minimum data rate achievable by *any* digitization scheme. It is also worth noting that the adjustment of quantizer parameters is not sensitive in that the curves of $H_Q(V)$ vs. $\epsilon^2/A$ for a given $M$ are very close to the $H^*(\epsilon^2)$ curve over a wide range of $\epsilon^2/A$.

When sequences of $M$-ary quantizer outputs are expressed in binary digits, the data rate ($\log_2 M$ bits per sample) is independent of the quantizer level spacing, and performance is optimized by simply minimizing the mean-squared error. The circles in Fig. 2 represent values of $\log_2 M$ plotted against the minimum mean-squared error obtainable by a uniform quantizer with $M$ output levels. These points are fitted closely by the function

$$M^*(\epsilon^2) = 0.125 + 0.6 \log \frac{A}{\epsilon^2} \text{ bits per sample.}$$

Thus $M^*(\epsilon^2)$ represents the achievable data rate (bits per sample) if each of the quantizer outputs is converted directly to an $M$-ary digit. It may not be surprising that $M^*(\epsilon^2)$ diverges from $R(\epsilon^2)$ as $\epsilon^2/A$ decreases, but even this simple digitization scheme performs respectably relative to theoretical limits over a useful range of $\epsilon^2/A$. The staircase curve in Fig. 2 is denoted $B^*(\epsilon^2)$ and represents the required data rate when each of the quantizer outputs is converted directly to binary digits with no further coding.

The circled points in Fig. 2 were computed by J. Max[5] for uniform quantizers for Gaussian samples. He also minimized the mean-squared error by optimizing the choice of the $M$ output levels and the range of input amplitudes mapped into each level. He gave the entropy of the $M$ output levels for the quantizers so optimized, as well as for quantizers with uniform output level spacing. In contrast to this, we have minimized the mean-squared error for a *fixed output entropy*, or from another viewpoint, minimized the output entropy for a fixed mean-squared error for uniform quantizers. The difference between our work on uniform quantizers and Max's is mainly a philosophical one, but an important one. We have obtained a curve $H^*(\epsilon^2)$ which gives the trade-off between output entropy and mean-squared error for uniform quantizers. Our results indicate that this trade-off for uniform quantizers is very close to the ideal relationship for Gaussian samples.

## III. Gaussian Processes

A more general class of analog sources for which the information rate is known (under a mean-squared error fidelity criterion) is the class of stationary Gaussian processes.[6] Therefore, we are in a position to compare theory with practice in digitization of this class of sources. The information rate $R(\epsilon^2)$ for a Gaussian process with power spectrum $S(f)$ is given by the parametric relations

$$R(\varphi) = \int_{\mathfrak{F}} \log_2 \frac{S(f)}{\varphi}\, df \text{ bits per second}^7$$

$$\epsilon^2(\varphi) = 2\varphi \int_{\mathfrak{F}} df + 2 \int_{\bar{\mathfrak{F}}} S(f)\, df$$

[5] J. Max, "Quantizing for minimum distortion," *IRE Trans. on Information Theory*, vol. IT-6, pp. 7–12, March 1960.

[6] T. J. Goblick, Jr., "Theoretical limitations on the transmission of data from analog sources," *IEEE Trans. on Information Theory*, vol. IT-11, pp. 558–567, October 1965. References on this development are given; note that $\epsilon$ is used to denote the mean-squared error, while $\epsilon^2$ is used here.

[7] Henceforth, we will abbreviate bits per second as bps.

and

$$\mathfrak{F} = \{f \geq 0 \text{ such that } S(f) \geq \varphi\}$$
$$\bar{\mathfrak{F}} = \{f \geq 0 \text{ such that } S(f) < \varphi\}, \qquad \varphi > 0.$$

In the case of a bandlimited white Gaussian source of bandwidth $W_s$, the output can be represented by (independent) samples spaced $1/2W_s$ seconds apart, and from $R(\epsilon^2)$ for the time-discrete source we have in this case

$$R(\epsilon^2) = W_s \log_2 \frac{A}{\epsilon^2} \text{ bps}$$

where

$$A = \int_{-\infty}^{\infty} S(f)\, df.$$

Suppose the output waveform $u(t)$ of a white bandlimited Gaussian source is digitized by sampling and quantizing with a uniform quantizer, and that entropy coding is done on the quantizer outputs to reduce the average number of bits necessary to specify these levels to the receiver. The minimum data rate necessary to achieve $\epsilon^2$ mean-squared error with this digitization system is gotten from the results of the previous section as

$$H(\epsilon^2) = 2W_s H^*(\epsilon^2) \text{ bps}.$$

If the quantizer outputs are not coded, but directly expressed in $M$-ary digits, the data rate becomes

$$M(\epsilon^2) = 2W_s M^*(\epsilon^2) \text{ bps}.$$

Likewise, if the quantizer outputs are each mapped into binary digits, the data rate is

$$B(\epsilon^2) = 2W_s B^*(\epsilon^2) \text{ bps}.$$

The digitization systems described above can clearly be used with the same results with any Gaussian process strictly bandlimited to $W_s$ Hz and with average power $A$. The samples for such sources will be correlated in general, but the above systems achieve their stated performance while ignoring these correlations between samples. Of course, this is not the best obtainable performance for an arbitrary band limited Gaussian process because we have ignored these correlations, and this costs something in performance.

A stationary Gaussian process with an arbitrary power density spectrum $S(f)$ could be digitized by the above system provided that it was first bandlimited by an ideal lowpass filter with cutoff frequency $W_F$ Hz. Since the waveform $v(t)$ reconstructed from the quantized samples of $u(t)$ will be bandlimited to $W_F$ Hz, the spectrum of the error $e(t) = u(t) - v(t)$ will be equal to $S(f)$ for $|f| > W_F$. Therefore, the bandlimiting filter introduces a mean-squared error of

$$\epsilon_F^2 = 2 \int_{W_F}^{\infty} S(f)\, df.$$

If the samples of $u(t)$ are quantized to yield a mean-squared error of $\epsilon_Q^2$, the total mean-squared error is

$$\epsilon^2 = \epsilon_F^2 + \epsilon_Q^2$$

and the resulting data rate is

$$H(\epsilon^2) = 2W_F H^*(\epsilon_Q^2) \text{ bps},$$
$$M(\epsilon^2) = 2W_F M^*(\epsilon_Q^2) \text{ bps},$$

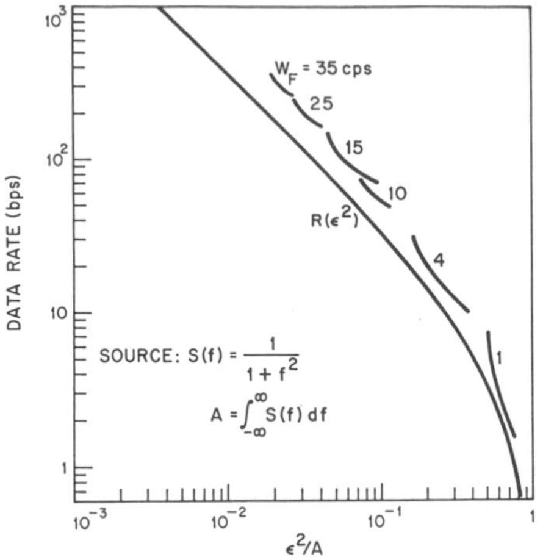


Fig. 3. Data rate $H(\epsilon^2)$ vs. $\epsilon^2/A$ for the BSQC encoder corresponding to several values of filter bandwidth $W_F$ for a Gaussian process.

or

$$B(\epsilon^2) = 2W_F B^*(\epsilon_Q^2) \text{ bps},$$

depending upon whether the quantizer outputs are entropy coded, expressed in $M$-ary symbols, or binary digits, respectively.

The above data rates are clearly functions of both $W_F$ and $\epsilon_Q^2$. If $W_F$ is first fixed and $\epsilon_Q^2$ varied, a curve of $H(\epsilon^2)$ vs. $\epsilon^2$ will result. An example of such curves is shown for various values of $W_F$ in Fig. 3 which were computed for the nonbandlimited source power spectrum

$$S(f) = \frac{1}{1 + f^2}.$$

The lower envelope of these curves, denoted $H_L(\epsilon^2)$, is clearly significant in characterizing the digitization system consisting of the 1) bandlimiting filter, 2) sampler, 3) uniform quantizer, and 4) entropy encoder (abbreviated as the BSQC encoder or digitizer). $H_L(\epsilon^2)$ represents the lowest data rate (in bps) necessary to achieve $\epsilon^2$ mean-squared error with the BSQC encoder.

In Fig. 4 we show curves of $R(\epsilon^2)/W_s$ (solid lines) and $H_L(\epsilon^2)/W$ (dashed lines) vs. $\epsilon^2/A$ for sources with power spectra given by

$$S(f) = \frac{1}{1 + \left(\frac{f}{W_s}\right)^{2n}}$$

where

$$A = \int_{-\infty}^{\infty} S(f)\, df.$$

For the range of $\epsilon^2/A$ included in this figure, $H_L(\epsilon^2)$ is no more than 2 times $R(\epsilon^2)$ for the source corresponding to $n = 1$, and this margin between $H_L(\epsilon^2)$ and $R(\epsilon^2)$ decreases significantly as $n$ increases. The circles in the figure represent values of $B(\epsilon^2)$ resulting from the variation of $W_F$ and $\epsilon_Q^2$ that were closest to the $R(\epsilon^2)$ curve. These points represent performance achievable by mapping each quantizer output directly into binary digits (termed the BSQB encoder in Fig. 4). A significant saving in data rate is seen to be attributable

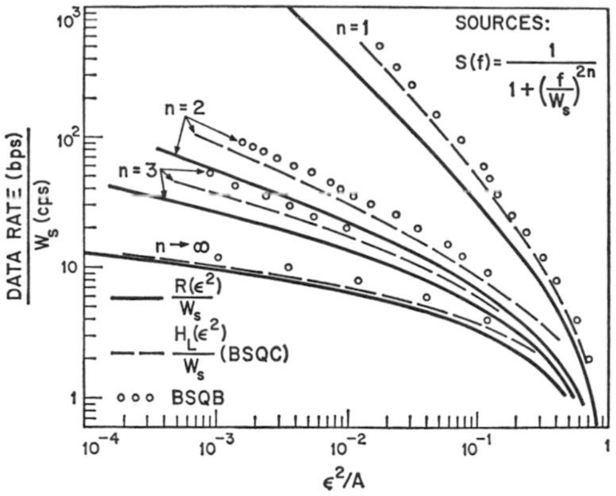


Fig. 4. Normalized data rates vs. $\epsilon^2/A$ for BSQC and BSQB encoders for several different Gaussian source spectra.

to the coding of quantizer outputs, as compared to merely converting them directly to binary digits. The values of $M(\epsilon^2)$ are not significantly different from the values of $B(\epsilon^2)$ and are not shown in the figure.

It can be shown that if the output of the ideal lowpass filter is "whitened" prior to sampling and quantizing, with "recoloring" done by a filter following the interpolation of the quantized samples, the performance of both encoders is unchanged. This is, of course, due to the fact mentioned earlier that the results of sampling and quantizing a bandlimited source are independent of the source spectrum.

## V. Summary

1) The information rate of a time-discrete, amplitude continuous source relative to a fidelity criterion provides a bound on the performance of any kind of quantizer.
2) The information rate of an analog source relative to a fidelity criterion provides a lower bound to the digital data rate achievable by *any* digitization scheme that satisfies the fidelity criterion.
3) In the case of the Gaussian processes studied here, simple filtering, sampling, and quantizing schemes are compared to the theoretically ideal performance to give a feeling for the gap between theory and practice.

Thus if we know the information rate of a source, we are in a position to compare the data rates of existing digitization systems with the theoretical minimum corresponding to a certain level of fidelity. Such a comparison not only provides a measure of the worth of existing systems, but large gaps between theoretical and practical data rates would provide legitimate motivation for further research into new digitization techniques.

## Acknowledgment

The authors are deeply indebted to Mrs. M. Simon for writing many computer programs to obtain the numerical data used in the figures.

T. J. Goblick, Jr.
M.I.T. Lincoln Laboratory[8]
Cambridge, Mass.
J. L. Holsinger
Defense Research Corp.
Santa Barbara, Calif.

[8] Operated with support from the U. S. Air Force.

# 16



Reprinted from *Proc. IEEE,* **52**(4), 415–416 (1964)

## Information Rates of Gaussian Signals Under Criteria Constraining the Error Spectrum

Shannon[1] introduced the concept of information rate under a specified fidelity criterion and obtained explicit results for the case of Gaussian white noise under a mean square error criterion. The information rate of a general Gaussian signal under a mean square error criterion was computed by Kolmogorov.[2] By taking an approach somewhat different from that chosen by Kolmogorov, it is a simple matter to obtain results for the case where not only the total mean square error but also some of its spectral properties are prescribed.

Consider a stationary Gaussian signal $x(t)$ with power spectral density $S_x(f)$. Suppose $x(t)$ is applied to an idealized set of band-pass filters $F_i$, with adjacent but non-overlapping passbands, each of width $\Delta f$ and free of frequency and phase distortion. In other words, the postulated filters divide $x(t)$ into a series of components $g_i(t)$ which are statistically independent and, if $\Delta f$ is taken small enough, have essentially flat power spectra. Thus Shannon's results for information rate under a mean square error criterion become applicable to each component. If the mean square error allowed in the $i$th band is $N_i$, the information rate of $g_i(t)$ is

$$r_i \approx \begin{cases} \Delta f \log \dfrac{\Delta f\, S_x(f_i)}{N_i}, & N_i \le \Delta f\, S_x(f_i) \\ 0, & N_i > \Delta f\, S_x(f_i) \end{cases} \quad (1)$$

Eq. (1) becomes exact when $\Delta f \to 0$. If, instead of fixing the maximum mean square errors $N_i$, one prescribes the maximum value of the error spectrum $N(f)$, then (for sufficiently small $\Delta f$) $N_i \approx N(f_i)\Delta f$. Because of the independence of the various $g_i(t)$, the total information rate under the specified restraint on the error spectrum is simply the sum of the various $r_i$. Thus (1) leads to

$$R = \lim_{\Delta f \to 0} \sum_{i=0}^{\infty} r_i = \int_0^\infty df \log \frac{S_x(f)}{N_1(f)} \quad (2)$$

where

$$N_1(f) = \begin{cases} N(f) \text{ where } N(f) \le S_x(f) \\ S_x(f) \text{ where } N(f) > S_x(f) \end{cases} \quad (3)$$

Note that the integrand in (2) is non-negative and that it vanishes in frequency ranges where allowed error spectrum exceeds the signal spectrum.

Formal justification of the limiting operations implied in the above argument is somewhat tedious, but involves no conceptual difficulties.[3]

If average properties of the error spectrum rather than its complete frequency structure are specified, one can proceed simply by minimizing (2) over the range of the allowed error spectra. Thus the rate under a mean square error criterion is simply

$$R_1 = \min_{N(f)} \{R\} = \min_{N(f)} \left\{ \int_0^\infty df \log \frac{S_x(f)}{N_1(f)} \right\} \quad (4)$$

under the constraint

$$\int_0^\infty df\, N(f) \le E. \quad (5)$$

$E$ is the allowed mean square error.

Since the results of this particular computation are not new, the formal minimization is not presented here. It is, in any case, quite straightforward.[3] However, a graphical interpretation of the conclusion may be of some interest. The positive frequency axis may be divided into two sets, $\alpha$ and $\beta$, such that

$$f \in \alpha \text{ if } S_x(f) < A$$

and

$$f \in \beta \text{ if } S_x(f) \ge A \quad (6)$$

where $A$ is a number so chosen that

$$\int_0^\infty df\, N(f) = E = A\mu(\beta) + \int_{f\in\alpha} df\, S_x(f) \quad (7)$$

and $\mu(\beta)$ is the Lebesque measure of the set $\beta$.[4]

In other words, the total area $E$ of the noise spectrum "fills up" part of the area under the signal spectrum much as a liquid fills an irregular container. This is illustrated in Fig. 1. Frequency ranges which are completely "filled up" make no contribution to the information rate. The desired rate $R_1$ is given by

$$R_1 = \int_{f\in\beta} df \log \frac{S_x(f)}{A} \quad (8)$$

which is, of course, equivalent to the expression previously given by Kolmogorov.[2]

A case of some practical interest is the calculation of information rates under a frequency weighted mean square error criterion. If $L(f)$ is a non-negative weighting function on the error spectrum and the allowable weighted mean square error is $T$, the desired rate $R_2$ is given by

$$R_2 = \min_{N(f)} \left\{ \int_0^\infty df \log \frac{S_x(f)}{N_1(f)} \right\}$$

$$= \min_{L(f)N(f)} \left\{ \int_0^\infty df \log \frac{L(f)\, S_x(f)}{L(f)\, N_1(f)} \right\} \quad (9)$$

under the constraint

$$\int_0^\infty df\, L(f)N(f) \le T. \quad (10)$$

It is clear that the minimization problem defined by (9) and (10) is identical to the one defined by (4) and (5), if in the latter one replaces signal and noise spectra with their weighted versions, $L(f)S_x(f)$ and $L(f)N(f)$, respectively. The results given by (6)–(8) therefore remain applicable with the same modifications. It is interesting to note that the minimizing error spectrum is, in this case

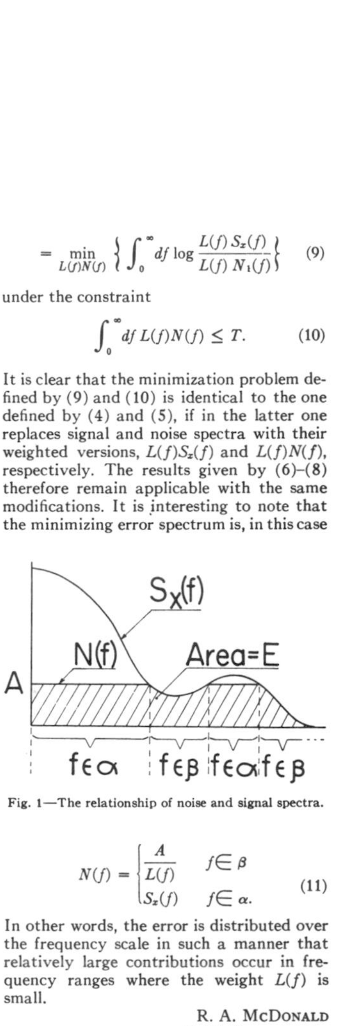


Fig. 1—The relationship of noise and signal spectra.

$$N(f) = \begin{cases} \dfrac{A}{L(f)} & f \in \beta \\ S_x(f) & f \in \alpha. \end{cases} \quad (11)$$

In other words, the error is distributed over the frequency scale in such a manner that relatively large contributions occur in frequency ranges where the weight $L(f)$ is small.

R. A. McDonald
P. M. Schultheiss
Dept. of Engrg. and Appl. Science
Yale University
New Haven, Conn.

Manuscript received October 30, 1963. The work reported here was performed at Yale University, New Haven, Conn., and was supported by a contract between Yale University and Bell Telephone Laboratories, Murray Hill, N. J.

[1] C. E. Shannon, "The Mathematical Theory of Communication," University of Illinois Press, Urbana, Ill.; 1949.

[2] A. N. Kolmogorov, "On the Shannon theory of information transmission in the case of continuous signals," IRE Trans. on Information Theory, vol. 2, pp. 102–108; December, 1956.

[3] R. A. McDonald, "Information Rates . . . ," D. Engr. thesis, School of Engineering, Yale University, New Haven, Conn.; 1961.

[4] If $\int_0^\infty S_x(f)\, df \ge E$. Otherwise $R_1$ is clearly zero.

# 17



Reprinted from *IEEE Trans. Inform. Theory,* **IT-18**(4), 460–473 (1972)

# Computation of Channel Capacity and Rate-Distortion Functions

RICHARD E. BLAHUT, MEMBER, IEEE

***Abstract*—By defining mutual information as a maximum over an appropriate space, channel capacities can be defined as double maxima and rate-distortion functions as double minima. This approach yields valuable new insights regarding the computation of channel capacities and rate-distortion functions. In particular, it suggests a simple algorithm for computing channel capacity that consists of a mapping from the set of channel input probability vectors into itself such that the sequence of probability vectors generated by successive applications of the mapping converges to the vector that achieves the capacity of the given channel. Analogous algorithms then are provided for computing rate-distortion functions and constrained channel capacities. The algorithms apply both to discrete and to continuous alphabet channels or sources. In addition, a formalization of the theory of channel capacity in the presence of constraints is included. Among the examples is the calculation of close upper and lower bounds to the rate-distortion function of a binary symmetric Markov source.**

## I. Introduction

Channel capacity, a fundamental concept in information theory, was introduced by Shannon [1] to specify the asymptotic limit on the maximum rate at which information can be conveyed reliably over a channel. The rate-distortion function, also introduced by Shannon [1], [2], serves an analogous function in the area of data compression coding for sources. These two basic concepts are discussed in detail in Gallager [3], Jelinek [4], and Berger [5].

Evaluation of a channel capacity $C$ or a rate-distortion function $R(D)$ involves the solution of a convex programming problem. In most cases analytic solutions cannot be found. Programmed computer search techniques have proved to be tedious even for small alphabet sizes and to be impractical for the larger alphabet sizes.

This paper reformulates the problems of computing $C$ and $R(D)$ from a new and slightly broader perspective, based on the observation that average mutual information $I(p,Q)$ can be written in either of the two following forms:

$$I(p,Q) = \max_{P} \Sigma_j \Sigma_k p_j Q_{k|j} \log \frac{P_{j|k}}{p_j}$$

$$I(p,Q) = \min_{q} \Sigma_j \Sigma_k p_j Q_{k|j} \log \frac{Q_{k|j}}{q_k},$$

where $P$ is an arbitrary transition matrix from the channel output alphabet to the channel input alphabet and $q$ is an arbitrary probability distribution on the output alphabet.

Manuscript received April 22, 1971; revised July 29, 1971. This work was supported in part by the IBM Resident Study Program. It was part of the author's doctoral dissertation, Department of Electrical Engineering, Cornell University, Ithaca, N.Y.

The author is with the IBM Corporation, Owego, N.Y., and the Department of Electrical Engineering, Cornell University, Ithaca, N.Y.

Arimoto [13] used the first of the preceding expressions in an investigation of $C$, thereby obtaining Theorems 1 and 3 as well as Corollary 2 of this paper.[1]

This approach places the existing theory of $C$ and $R(D)$ in a more transparent setting and suggests several new results. In particular, the approach in question results in algorithms for determining $C$ and $R(D)$ by means of mappings from probability vectors to probability vectors. Under the first of these mappings, the sequence of average mutual informations associated with the successive channel input probability vectors increases monotonically to $C$. The other mapping produces a sequence of (information, distortion) pairs $(I,D)$ that converges to a point on the $R(D)$ curve; the convergence is monotonic in the $(I,D)$ plane in the direction perpendicular to the slope of $R(D)$ at the limiting point.

## II. Capacity of Unconstrained Discrete Channels

For the purposes of information theory, a discrete channel is described by a probability transition matrix $Q = [Q_{k|j}]$ where $Q_{k|j}$ is the probability of receiving the $k$th output letter given that the $j$th input letter was transmitted. In general, $Q$ is not square. The capacity of the channel is defined as

$$C = \max_{p \in P^n} I(p,Q) = \max_{p \in P^n} \Sigma_j \Sigma_k p_j Q_{k|j} \log \frac{Q_{k|j}}{\Sigma_j p_j Q_{k|j}},$$

where

$$P^n = \{p \in R^n : p_j \geq 0 \;\forall j;\; \Sigma_j p_j = 1\}$$

is the set of all probability distributions on the channel input, and $I(p,Q)$ is known as the mutual information between the channel input and channel output. The choice of logarithm base affects $C$ only by a scale factor. It is usually convenient in applications to take base 2 so that $C$ is expressed in terms of bits-per-channel use; for theoretical work, natural logs are more convenient.

The utility of the concept of capacity is widely discussed in the literature. Intuitively, the capacity of a channel expresses the maximum rate at which information can be reliably conveyed by the channel. Any coding scheme that superficially appears to operate at a rate higher than $C$ will cause enough data to be lost because of uncorrectable channel errors so that the actual information rate is not to be greater than $C$.

Our concern in this section is with the calculation of capacity. The approach is to broaden the definition of

[1] The author is indebted to the editor for pointing out the prior existence of the Arimoto paper.

capacity to a larger maximization problem, which allows greater flexibility. This is done in the following theorem. Here, and in the sequel, maxima or minima are understood to be over the appropriate space of probability vectors or probability transition matrices (unless the domain is explicitly stated).

*Theorem 1:* Suppose the channel transition matrix $Q$ is $n \times m$. For any $m \times n$ transition matrix $P$, let

$$J(p,Q,P) = \Sigma_j \Sigma_k p_j Q_{k|j} \log \frac{P_{j|k}}{p_j}$$

Then the following is true.

a) $$C = \max_p \max_P J(p,Q,P).$$

b) For fixed $p$, $J(p,Q,P)$ is maximized by

$$P_{j|k} = \frac{p_j Q_{k|j}}{\Sigma_j p_j Q_{k|j}}.$$

c) For fixed $P$, $J(p,Q,P)$ is maximized by

$$p_j = \frac{\exp\,(\Sigma_k Q_{k|j} \log P_{j|k})}{\Sigma_j \exp\,(\Sigma_k Q_{k|j} \log P_{j|k})}.$$

*Proof:*

a) It suffices to show that

$$I(p,Q) = \max_P \Sigma_j \Sigma_k p_j Q_{k|j} \log \frac{P_{j|k}}{p_j}.$$

Let

$$P^*_{j|k} = \frac{p_j Q_{k|j}}{\Sigma_j p_j Q_{k|j}}$$

and

$$q_k = \Sigma_j p_j Q_{k|j}$$

so that

$$I(p,Q) = \Sigma_j \Sigma_k q_k P^*_{j|k} \log \frac{P^*_{j|k}}{p_j}.$$

Then

$$\begin{aligned} I(p,Q) - \Sigma_j \Sigma_k p_j Q_{k|j} \log \frac{P_{j|k}}{p_j} &= \Sigma_j \Sigma_k q_k P^*_{j|k} \log \frac{P^*_{j|k}}{P_{j|k}} \\ &\geq \Sigma_j \Sigma_k q_k P^*_{j|k} - \Sigma_j \Sigma_k q_k P_{j|k} \\ &= 0 \end{aligned}$$

with equality[2] iff $P_{j|k} = P^*_{j|k}$.

b) This fact is an immediate consequence of the equality condition of part a).

c) If for some $k$, $P_{j|k} = 0$, then $p_j$ should be set equal to zero in order to maximize $J$ as it is. Such a $j$ can be deleted from the sum and dropped from further consideration. $J(p,Q,P)$ can now be maximized over $p$ by temporarily ignoring the constraint $p_j \geq 0$, and using a Lagrange multiplier to constrain

$$\Sigma_j p_j = 1.$$

$$\frac{\partial}{\partial p_j} \left\{ \Sigma_j \Sigma_k p_j Q_{k|j} \log \frac{P_{j|k}}{p_j} + \lambda(\Sigma_j p_j - 1) \right\} = 0$$

$$-\log p_j - 1 + \Sigma_k Q_{k|j} \log P_{j|k} + \lambda = 0.$$

Hence,

$$p_j = \frac{\exp \Sigma_k Q_{k|j} \log P_{j|k}}{\Sigma_j \exp \Sigma_k Q_{k|j} \log P_{j|k}},$$

where $\lambda$ is selected so that

$$\Sigma_j p_j = 1.$$

Notice that this $p_j$ is always positive so that the inequality constraint $p_j \geq 0$ is not operative.

[2] The inequality used here is the well-known $\log x \geq 1 - (1/x)$ with equality iff $x = 1$. This inequality will be used in the sequel without further comment.

The following corollary states a familiar condition on the solution of the basic problem. It is stated here both because it follows immediately from Theorem 1 and because the particular form that arises motivates the remainder of this section.

*Corollary 1:* If $p$ achieves capacity, then

$$p_j = \frac{p_j \exp \Sigma_k Q_{k|j} \log \dfrac{Q_{k|j}}{\Sigma_j p_j Q_{k|j}}}{\Sigma_j p_j \exp \Sigma_k Q_{k|j} \log \dfrac{Q_{k|j}}{\Sigma_j p_j Q_{k|j}}}.$$

*Proof:* This is just the simultaneous satisfaction of parts b) and c) of the theorem.

The form of the equation in Corollary 1 is meant to suggest that any $p$ can be used in the right-hand side in order to generate a new $p$ on the left. Under appropriate conditions, this new $p$ gives a better estimate of capacity as proved in Theorem 3.

*Corollary 2:*

$$C = \max_p \log \Sigma_j \exp\,(\Sigma_k Q_{k|j} \log P_{j|k}).$$

*Proof:* This follows from substituting part c) into part a).

The following specialization of the Kuhn–Tucker theorem will be used in the proof of Theorem 3.

*Theorem 2:* A vector $p \in \boldsymbol{P}^n$ achieves capacity for the channel with transition matrix $Q$ if and only if there exists a number $C$ such that

$$\Sigma_k Q_{k|j} \log \frac{Q_{k|j}}{\Sigma_j p_j Q_{k|j}} = C, \qquad p_j \neq 0$$

$$\Sigma_k Q_{k|j} \log \frac{Q_{k|j}}{\Sigma_j p_j Q_{k|j}} \leq C, \qquad p_j = 0.$$

For a proof, see Gallager or Jelinek. The conditions are sometimes called the Kuhn–Tucker conditions. The number $C$ is then the channel capacity. It proves convenient to restate Theorem 2 as follows.

*Corollary 3:* A vector $p \in \boldsymbol{P}^n$ achieves capacity for the channel with transition matrix $Q$ if and only if there exists a number $C$ such that

$$\exp(-C)\exp \Sigma_k Q_{k|j} \log \frac{Q_{k|j}}{\Sigma_j p_j Q_{k|j}} = 1, \qquad p_j \neq 0$$

$$\exp(-C)\exp \Sigma_k Q_{k|j} \log \frac{Q_{k|j}}{\Sigma_j p_j Q_{k|j}} \leq 1, \qquad p_j = 0.$$

*Theorem 3:* For any $p \in \boldsymbol{P}^n$, let

$$c_j(p) = \exp \Sigma_k Q_{k|j} \log \frac{Q_{k|j}}{\Sigma p_j Q_{k|j}}.$$

Then, if $p^0$ is any element of $\boldsymbol{P}^n$ with all components strictly positive, the sequence of probability vectors defined by

$$p_j^{r+1} = p_j^r \frac{c_j^r}{\Sigma_j p_j^r c_j^r}$$

is such that $I(p^r,Q) \rightarrow C$ as $r \rightarrow \infty$.

*Proof:* Given any $p^r$, we increase $J(p,Q,P)$ by using Theorem 1-b) to pick $P_{j|k}$ and then, with $P_{j|k}$ fixed, using Theorem 1-c) to pick a new $p$ vector. The composition of these two operations is just the operation that appears in the theorem. Hence, the algorithm in question increases mutual information. It also follows easily that the mutual information is strictly increasing unless Corollary 1 is satisfied by $p^r$, which in turn implies satisfaction of the first condition of Corollary 3. Thus, $I(p,Q)$ is stable only for those $p$ for which the first of the Kuhn–Tucker conditions is satisfied. We shall show that $I^r$ can converge only to values of $I(p,Q)$ that are stable in this way, and furthermore, that convergence is impossible unless the second of the Kuhn–Tucker conditions also is satisfied at the limit point.

Since $I(p^r,Q)$ is increasing and is bounded by $C$, $I^r$ must converge to some number $I^\infty \leq C$. Let $V(p^r) = I(p^{r+1},Q) - I(p^r,Q)$. Then $V(p^r) \rightarrow 0$ since $I^r$ converges. By the Bolzano–Weierstrass Theorem, the sequence $(p^r)$ has a limit point $p^*$ and a subsequence $(p^r)$ converging to $p^*$. Therefore, by continuity of $V$, $V(p^r) \rightarrow V(p^*)$. But $V(p^r) \rightarrow 0$. Therefore, $V(p^*) = 0$ and hence $p^*$ satisfies the first of the Kuhn–Tucker conditions.

Now suppose $p^*$ does not achieve capacity. Then by the sufficiency condition of Corollary 3,

$$\frac{c_j^*}{\Sigma_j p_j^* c_j^*} > 1$$

for some $j$, where $c_j^* = c_j(p^*)$.

Since some subsequence $\{p^{r_k}\}$ converges to $p^*$, then by continuity $\{c_j^{r_k}\}$ converges to $c_j^*$ for all $j$. But,

$$p_j^r = p_j^0 \prod_{n=0}^{r} b_j^n$$

where

$$b_j^n = \frac{c_j^n}{\Sigma_j p_j^n c_j^n}$$

and $\{b_j^n\}$ has a subsequence converging to a number greater than 1. Therefore, the sequence of partial products does not converge and $p_j^r$ does not converge, which is a contradiction.

Therefore, $p^*$ achieves capacity and $I^\infty = C$. This completes the proof of the theorem.

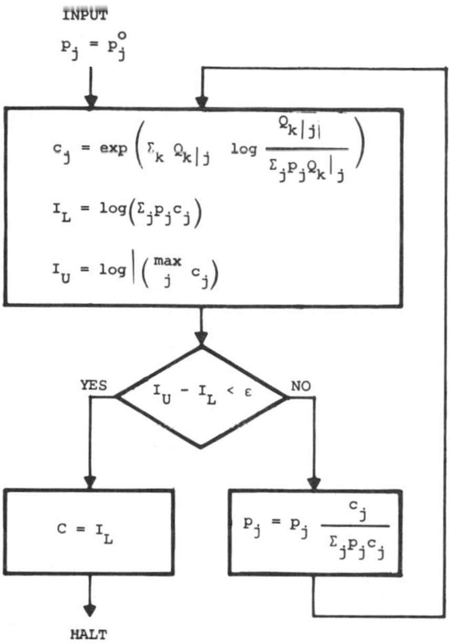


Fig. 1. Capacity algorithm.

The application of Theorem 3 to the computation of channel capacity is illustrated in Fig. 1. The termination is based on the fact that for any probability assignment $p$ the following holds

a)

$$C \geq \log \Sigma_j p_j c_j$$

b

$$C \leq \log (\max_j c_j),$$

where

$$c_j = \exp \Sigma_k Q_{k|j} \log \frac{Q_{k|j}}{\Sigma_j p_j Q_{k|j}}.$$

Part a) is a simple consequence of Corollary 2 and part b) appears as a problem in Gallager [3, p. 524].

## III. Rate-Distortion Functions for Discrete Sources

A discrete-alphabet memoryless source, which produces the $j$th letter with probability $p_j$, is to be reproduced in terms of a second alphabet that need not be of the same size, although often it is identical to the source alphabet. A distortion matrix with elements $\rho_{jk}$ specifies the distortion associated with reproducing the $j$th source letter by the $k$th reproducing letter ($0 \leq j \leq m-1$, $0 \leq k \leq n$ 1). Without loss of generality, it can be assumed that for each source letter, there is at least one reproducing letter such that the resulting distortion equals zero.

Rate-distortion theory is concerned with the average amount of information about the source output that must be preserved by any data compression scheme such that the reproduction can be subsequently generated from the compressed data with average distortion less than or equal to some specified $D$. The rate-distortion function is defined as

$$R(D) = \min_{Q \in Q_D} \Sigma_j \Sigma_k p_j Q_{k|j} \log \frac{Q_{k|j}}{\Sigma_j p_j Q_{k|j}} = \min_{Q \in Q_D} I(p,Q),$$

where

$$Q_D = \{Q \in R^m \times R^n : \Sigma_k Q_{k|j} = 1, Q_{k|j} \geq 0, d(Q) \leq D\}$$

and

$$d(Q) = \Sigma_j \Sigma_k p_j Q_{k|j} \rho_{jk}.$$

The definition of rate-distortion functions is justified by source compression theorems, which are widely reported [3]–[5]. Intuitively, if average distortion $D$ is specified, then any compression must retain an average of at least $R(D)$ bits per source letter, and conversely, compression to a level arbitrarily close to $R(D)$ is possible by appropriate selection of the compression scheme.

The investigation of rate-distortion functions is usually carried out parametrically in terms of a parameter $s$, which is introduced as a Lagrange multiplier. This parameter turns out to be equal to the slope of the rate-distortion curve at the point it parameterizes [5]. These facts will be assumed in the following and the discussion will begin with the following parametric expression for $R(D)$.

$$R(D) = \min_{Q} \left[ \Sigma_j \Sigma_k p_j Q_{k|j} \log \frac{Q_{k|j}}{\Sigma_j p_j Q_{k|j}} - s(\Sigma_j \Sigma_k p_j Q_{k|j} \rho_{jk} - D) \right],$$

where

$$D = \Sigma_j \Sigma_k p_j Q^*_{k|j} \rho_{jk}$$

and $Q^*$ is the point that achieves the above minimum.

The minimization is now over all transition matrices $Q$. The value of $D$, however, is no longer an input to the computation; rather, a value of $s$ is specified whereupon both $D$ and $R(D)$ are generated for the point on the $R(D)$ curve that has slope $s$.

*Theorem 4:* Let

$$F(p,Q,q) = \Sigma_j \Sigma_k p_j Q_{k|j} \log \frac{Q_{k|j}}{q_k} - s \Sigma_j \Sigma_k p_j Q_{k|j} \rho_{jk}.$$

Then

a)

$$R(D) = sD + \min_q \min_Q F(p,Q,q),$$

where

$$D = \Sigma_j \Sigma_k p_j Q^*_{k|j} \rho_{jk}$$

and $Q^*$ achieves the above minimum.

b) For fixed $Q_{k|j}$, $F(p,Q,q)$ is minimized by

$$q_k = \Sigma_j p_j Q_{k|j}.$$

c) For fixed $q$, $F(p,Q,q)$ is minimized by

$$Q_{k|j} = \frac{q_k \exp(s\rho_{jk})}{\Sigma_k q_k \exp(s\rho_{jk})}.$$

*Proof:*

a) It suffices to prove that $I(p,Q) = \min_q F(p,Q,q)$.

$$\begin{aligned}\Sigma_j \Sigma_k p_j Q_{k|j} \log \frac{Q_{k|j}}{q_k} - I(p,Q) &= \Sigma_j \Sigma_k p_j Q_{k|j} \log \frac{Q_{k|j}}{q_k} - \Sigma_j \Sigma_k p_j Q_{k|j} \log \frac{Q_{k|j}}{\Sigma_j p_j Q_{k|j}} \\ &= \Sigma_j \Sigma_k p_j Q_{k|j} \log \frac{\Sigma_j p_j Q_{k|j}}{q_k} \\ &\geq \Sigma_j \Sigma_k p_j Q_{k|j} - \Sigma_k q_k = 0\end{aligned}$$

with equality if and only if

$$q_k = \Sigma_j p_j Q_{k|j}.$$

b) This follows immediately from the equality condition of part a).

c) Temporarily ignore the inequality constraint $Q_{k|j} \geq 0$ and introduce a Lagrange multiplier to constrain $\Sigma_k Q_{k|j} = 1$.

$$\frac{\partial}{\partial Q_{k|j}} \left[ \Sigma_j \Sigma_k p_j Q_{k|j} \log \frac{Q_{k|j}}{q_k} - s \Sigma_j \Sigma_k p_j Q_{k|j} \rho_{jk} + \Sigma_j \lambda_j \Sigma_k Q_{k|j} \right] = 0$$

$$p_j \log Q_{k|j} - p_j \log q_k + p_j - s p_j \rho_{jk} + \lambda_j = 0.$$

Hence

$$Q_{k|j} = \frac{q_k \exp(s\rho_{jk})}{\Sigma_k q_k \exp(s\rho_{jk})},$$

where $\lambda_j$ has been selected as that

$$\Sigma_k Q_{k|j} = 1.$$

Notice that this is always nonnegative so that the inequality constraint $Q_{k|j} \geq 0$ is satisfied.

A familiar condition on the minimizing $Q$ is the following.

*Corollary 4:* If $Q$ achieves a point on the $R(D)$ curve parameterized by $s$, then

$$Q_{k|j} = \frac{q_k \exp(s\rho_{jk})}{\Sigma_k q_k \exp(s\rho_{jk})},$$

where

$$q_k = \Sigma_j p_j Q_{k|j} = q_k \Sigma_j p_j \frac{\exp(s\rho_{jk})}{\Sigma_k q_k \exp(s\rho_{jk})}.$$

*Proof:* This is just the simultaneous satisfaction of parts b) and c). The first equation of Corollary 4 defines a transition matrix $Q(q)$ given any $q$. This will form the basis for the algorithm of Theorem 6.

*Corollary 5:* In terms of the parameter $s$,

$$R(D_s) = sD_s + \min_q \left[ -\Sigma_j p_j \log \Sigma_k q_k \exp(s\rho_{jk}) \right]$$

$$D_s = \Sigma_j p_j \frac{q_k^* \exp(s\rho_{jk})}{\Sigma_k q_k^* \exp(s\rho_{jk})} \rho_{jk},$$

where $q_k^*$ achieves $R(D_s)$.

*Proof:* This follows immediately by substituting part c) of the theorem into part a).

Corollary 5 expresses the substance of a theorem by Haskell [6]. The following variation is also useful.

*Corollary 6:*

$$R(D) = \max_{s \in [-\infty, 0]} \min_{q} \left[sD - \Sigma_j p_j \log \Sigma_k q_k \exp(s\rho_{jk})\right].$$

*Proof:* Let $Q$ achieve $R(D)$ and let $D_s$ be the average distortion value parameterized by $s$. Then

$$\begin{aligned} R(D) &- \min_q \left[sD - \Sigma_j p_j \log \Sigma_k \exp(s\rho_{jk}) q_k\right] \\ &= R(D) - sD - \min_q \left[sD_s - \Sigma_j p_j \log \Sigma_k q_k \exp(s\rho_{jk})\right] + sD_s \\ &= R(D) - sD - R(D_s) + sD_s \\ &= \Sigma_j \Sigma_k p_j Q_{k|j} \log \frac{Q_{k|j} \exp(s\rho_{jk})}{\Sigma_j p_j Q_{k|j}} \\ &\quad - \min_Q \Sigma_j \Sigma_k p_j Q_{k|j} \log \frac{Q_{k|j} \exp(s\rho_{jk})}{\Sigma_j p_j Q_{k|j}}. \\ &\geq 0. \end{aligned}$$

The content of this corollary can be expressed in a pleasant form if

$$\Sigma_j \exp(s\rho_{jk})$$

is independent of $k$. We digress further to illustrate this in a special case.

*Corollary 7:* Suppose the alphabet consists of binary $n$-tuples and the distortion is Hamming distance. Then

$$R(D) = \max_{\rho \in [0, \frac{1}{2}]} \min_q \left[D \log \rho + (1 - D) \log (1 - \rho) + \Sigma_j p_j \log \Sigma_k A_{jk}(\rho) q_k\right],$$

where $A_{jk}(\rho)$ is the $n$-tuple transition matrix of a binary symmetric channel of transition probability $\rho$. In particular, if

$$\Sigma_j A_{jk}^{-1}(D) p_j \geq 0 \ \forall k$$

then

$$R(D) = D \log D + (1 - D) \log (1 - D) - \Sigma_j p_j \log p_j.$$

*Proof:* Let the superscript $n$ denote the block length and notice that the matrix $\exp(s\rho_{jk}^{n})$ can be expressed inductively by

$$\exp(s\rho_{jk}^{n}) = \begin{vmatrix} \exp(s\rho_{jk}^{n-1}) & \exp(s) \exp(s\rho_{jk}^{n-1}) \\ \exp(s) \exp(s\rho_{jk}^{n-1}) & \exp(s\rho_{jk}^{n-1}) \end{vmatrix}.$$

Define $\rho$ by $\exp(s) = \rho/(\rho - 1)$. The result then follows from the previous corollary.

The analog of Theorem 2 is the following.

*Theorem 5:* A necessary and sufficient condition on an output probability assignment $q$ to yield a point on the $R(D)$ curve via the transition matrix

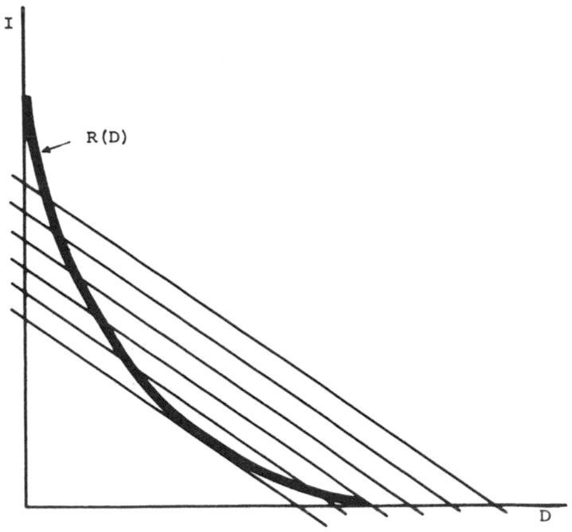


Fig. 2. *I-D* plane.

$$Q_{k|j} = \frac{q_k \exp(s\rho_{jk})}{\Sigma_k q_k \exp(s\rho_{jk})}$$

is that $q$ satisfy

$$c_k = \Sigma_j p_j \frac{\exp(s\rho_{jk})}{\Sigma_k q_k \exp(s\rho_{jk})} = 1, \qquad q_k \neq 0$$

$$c_k = \Sigma_j p_j \frac{\exp(s\rho_{jk})}{\Sigma_k q_k \exp(s\rho_{jk})} \leq 1, \qquad q_k = 0.$$

For a proof, see Berger or Gallager.

The major theorem of this section is the following.

*Theorem 6:* Let the parameter $s < 0$ be given. Let $q^0$ be any probability vector such that all components are nonzero. Let $q^{r+1}$ be given in terms of $q^r$ by

$$q_k^{r+1} = q_k^r \Sigma_j \frac{p_j A_{jk}}{\Sigma_k A_{jk} q_k^r},$$

where $A_{jk} = \exp(s\rho_{jk})$. Then,

$$D(Q(q^r)) \to D_s, \qquad \text{as } r \to \infty$$

$$I(p, Q(q^r)) \to R(D_s), \qquad \text{as } r \to \infty,$$

where $(D_s, R(D_s))$ is a point on the $R(D)$ curve parameterized by $s$.

*Proof:* Theorem 4 can be used to provide the first part of the proof. The following proof will, however, bring out the geometrical role of the parameter $s$.

For any probability vector $q$, recall that $Q(q)$ is given by

$$Q_{k|j}(q) = \frac{A_{jk} q_k}{\Sigma_k A_{jk} q_k}.$$

Consider the *I-D* plane of Fig. 2. For any probability vector $q$, let $V(q) = I(q) - sD(q)$, where $I(q) = I(p, Q(q))$. Then $V(q)$ is the value at which a line of slope $s$ through the point $(I(q), D(q))$ intercepts the $I$ axis. The point in the $R(D)$ curve parameterized by $s$ has a tangent that is parallel to every such line of slope $s$, and lies beneath them. We will show that the sequential values $V(q^r)$ are strictly decreasing unless $(I(q), D(q))$ is a point on the $R(D)$ curve in which case $V(q)$ is stationary.

Let

$$Q^{r+1} = Q(q^r).$$

Then

$$Q^{r+1}_{k|j} = \frac{A_{jk}q_k^r}{\Sigma_k A_{jk}q_k^r}$$

and

$$q_k^{r+1} = \Sigma_j p_j Q^{r+1}_{k|j}.$$

Then

$$\begin{aligned} V(q^{r+1}) &= \Sigma_j\Sigma_k p_j Q^{r+1}_{k|j} \log \frac{Q^{r+1}_{k|j}}{q_k^{r+1}} - s\Sigma_j\Sigma_k p_j Q^{r+1}_{k|j}\rho_{jk} \\ &= \Sigma_j\Sigma_k p_j Q^{r+1}_{k|j} \log \frac{A_{jk}q_k^r}{q_k^{r+1}\Sigma_k A_{jk}q_k^r} - \Sigma_j\Sigma_k p_j Q^{r+1}_{k|j} \log A_{jk} \\ &= -\Sigma_j\Sigma_k p_j Q^{r+1}_{k|j} \log \Sigma_k A_{jk}q_k^r + \Sigma_j\Sigma_k p_j Q^{r+1}_{k|j} \log \frac{q_k^r}{q_k^{r+1}} \\ &= -\Sigma_j\Sigma_k p_j Q^r_{k|j} \log \Sigma_k A_{jk}q_k^r + \Sigma_k q_k^{r+1} \log \frac{q_k^r}{q_k^{r+1}}. \end{aligned}$$

Now let

$$W(q^r) = V(q^r) - V(q^{r+1})$$

so that

$$\begin{aligned} W(q^r) &= \Sigma_j\Sigma_k p_j Q^r_{k|j} \log \frac{Q^r_{k|j}\Sigma_k A_{jk}q_k^r}{q_k^r A_{jk}} + \Sigma_k q_k^{r+1} \log \frac{q_k^{r+1}}{q_k^r} \\ &\geq \Sigma_j\Sigma_k p_j Q^r_{k|j}\left[1 - \frac{q_k^r A_{jk}}{Q^r_{k|j}\Sigma_k A_{jk}q_k^r}\right] \\ &\quad + \Sigma_k q_k^{r+1}\left[1 - \frac{q_k^r}{q_k^{r+1}}\right] = 0 + 0 = 0 \end{aligned}$$

with strict inequality unless $q_k^r = q_k^{r+1}\ \forall k$.

Thus, $V(q^r)$ is nonincreasing and is strictly decreasing unless

$$q_k^r = q_k^r \Sigma_j p_j \frac{A_{jk}}{\Sigma_k q_k^r A_{jk}},$$

which is just the first condition of Theorem 5. Since $V(q^r)$ is decreasing and is bounded below by $R(D) - sD$, it must converge to some number $V^\infty$. We now argue as in the proof of Theorem 3 to show that $V^\infty = R(D) - sD$. That is, by the Bolzano–Weierstrass Theorem, the sequence $q^r$ has a limit point $q^*$ and by continuity of $V(q)$ this limit point satisfies

$$q_k^* = q_k^* \Sigma_j p_j \frac{A_{jk}}{\Sigma_k A_{jk} q_k^*}.$$

In addition, this limit point must satisfy the second of the Kuhn–Tucker conditions since otherwise convergence could not occur. This completes the proof of the theorem.

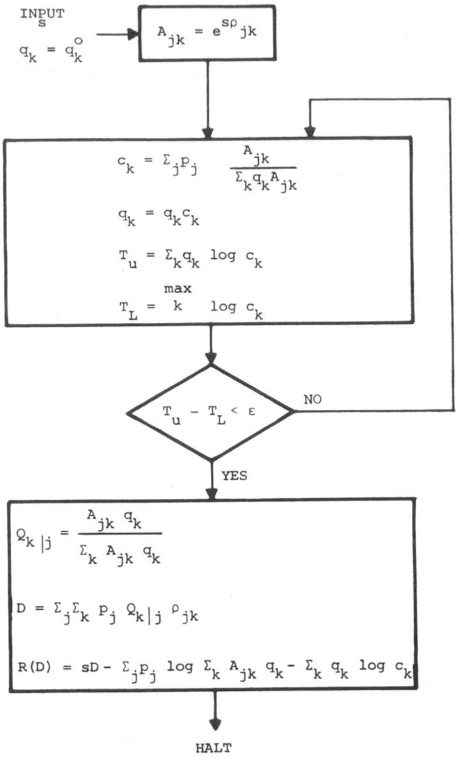


Fig. 3. Rate-distortion algorithm.

The application of this theorem to the numerical computation of rate-distortion functions is illustrated in Fig. 3. In order to estimate the accuracy after any finite number of steps, the following theorem is employed.

*Theorem 7:* Let the parameter $s \leq 0$ be given and let $A_{jk} = \exp(s\rho_{jk})$. Suppose $q$ is any output probability vector and let

$$c_k = \Sigma_j p_j \frac{A_{jk}}{\Sigma_k A_{jk}q_k}.$$

Then at the point

$$D = \Sigma_j\Sigma_k p_j \frac{A_{jk}q_k}{\Sigma_k A_{jk}q_k}\rho_{jk}$$

we have

a)

$$R(D) \leq sD - \Sigma_j p_j \log \Sigma_k A_{jk}q_k - \Sigma_k q_k c_k \log c_k$$

b)

$$R(D) \geq sD - \Sigma_j p_j \log \Sigma_k A_{jk}q_k - \max_k \log c_k$$

*Proof:*

a)

$$Q_{k|j} = \frac{A_{jk}q_k}{\Sigma_k A_{jk}q_k}$$

is a transition matrix giving distortion $D$. Hence

$$R(D) \le I(p,Q) = \Sigma_j\Sigma_k p_j Q_{k|j} \log \frac{Q_{k|j}}{\Sigma_j p_j Q_{k|j}}$$

$$= \Sigma_j\Sigma_k p_j Q_{k|j} \log \frac{A_{jk}q_k}{(\Sigma_k A_{jk}q_k)(\Sigma_j p_j Q_{k|j})}$$

$$= sD - \Sigma_j p_j \log \Sigma_k A_{jk}q_k - \Sigma_k q_k c_k \log c_k.$$

b) A lower bound theorem for rate-distortion functions states that

$$R(D) \ge sD + \Sigma_j p_j \log \lambda_j,$$

where $\lambda_j$ is any vector such that

$$\Sigma_j p_j \lambda_j A_{jk} < 1$$

(see Berger or Gallager). Let

$$c_{\max} = \max_k \Sigma_j p_j \frac{A_{jk}}{\Sigma_k A_{jk}q_k}$$

and let

$$\lambda_j = (c_{\max} \Sigma_k A_{jk}q_k)^{-1}.$$

Then

$$\Sigma_j p_j \lambda_j A_{jk} \le 1$$

and

$$R(D) \ge sD - \Sigma_j p_j \log \Sigma_k A_{jk}q_k - \max_k \log c_k.$$

## IV. Capacity of Constrained Discrete Channels

Many channels have an associated expense of using each channel letter. A common example is the power associated with each output symbol. A constrained discrete channel is a discrete channel with the requirement that the average expense be less than or equal to some specified number $E$.

Although capacity at an expense $E$ has been investigated in the past, and occasionally the function $C(E)$ has been determined, there does not seem to have been developed any formalization of the theory of $C(E)$ functions. This formalization is straightforward and is provided in the Appendix.

A vector $e_j$ is specified, where $e_j$ is called the expense of using the $j$th input letter. The capacity at expense $E$ is then defined as

$$C(E) = \max_{p \in P_E} \Sigma_j\Sigma_k p_j Q_{k|j} \log \frac{Q_{k|j}}{\Sigma_j p_j Q_{k|j}} = \max_{p \in P_E} I(p,Q),$$

where

$$P_E = \{p \in P^n : \Sigma_j p_j e_j \le E\}.$$

As discussed in the Appendix, this can be rewritten parametrically as

$$C(E) = \max_p \left[\Sigma_j\Sigma_k p_j Q_{k|j} \log \frac{Q_{k|j}}{\Sigma_j p_j Q_{k|j}} - s(\Sigma_j p_j e_j - E)\right],$$

where

$$E = \Sigma_j p_j^* e_j$$

and $p^*$ achieves the above maximum.

The maximization is now over all input probability vectors $p$. The generalization of Theorem 1 is the following.

*Theorem 8:* Let

$$J(p,Q,P) = \Sigma_j\Sigma_k p_j Q_{k|j} \log \frac{P_{j|k}}{p_j} - s\Sigma_j p_j e_j.$$

Then

a)

$$C(E) = sE + \max_P \max_p J(p,Q,P),$$

where

$$E = \Sigma p_j^* e_j$$

and $p^*$ achieves the above maximum.

b) For fixed $p$, $J(p,Q,P)$ is maximized by

$$P_{j|k} = \frac{p_j Q_{k|j}}{\Sigma_j p_j Q_{k|j}}.$$

c) For fixed $P$, $J(p,Q,P)$ is maximized by

$$p_j = \frac{\exp(\Sigma_k Q_{k|j} \log P_{j|k} - se_j)}{\Sigma_j \exp(\Sigma_k Q_{k|j} \log P_{j|k} - se_j)}.$$

*Proof:* The proof is essentially the same as that of Theorem 1.

*Corollary 8:* If $p$ achieves capacity at expense $E$, then for some $s \in [0,\infty]$

$$p_j = \frac{p_j \exp\left(\Sigma_k Q_{k|j} \log \frac{Q_{k|j}}{\Sigma_j p_j Q_{k|j}} - se_j\right)}{\Sigma_j p_j \exp\left(\Sigma_k Q_{k|j} \log \frac{Q_{k|j}}{\Sigma_j p_j Q_{k|j}} - se_j\right)}.$$

*Proof:* This is just the simultaneous satisfaction of parts b) and c).

*Corollary 9:* A parametric solution in terms of $s$ is

$$C(E_s) = sE_s + \max_P [\log \Sigma_j \exp(\Sigma_k Q_{k|j} \log P_{j|k} - se_j)]$$

$$E_s = \Sigma_j e_j \frac{\exp(\Sigma_k Q_{k|j} \log P^*_{j|k} - se_j)}{\Sigma_j \exp(\Sigma_k Q_{k|j} \log P^*_{j|k} - se_j)},$$

where $P^*$ achieves the maximum.

*Corollary 10:*

$$C(E) = \min_{s \in [0,\infty]} \max_P \cdot [sE + \log \Sigma_j \exp(\Sigma_k Q_{k|j} \log P_{j|k} - se_j)].$$

*Proof:* Let $p^*$ achieve $C(E)$ and let $E_s$ be the expense parameterized by $s$. Then

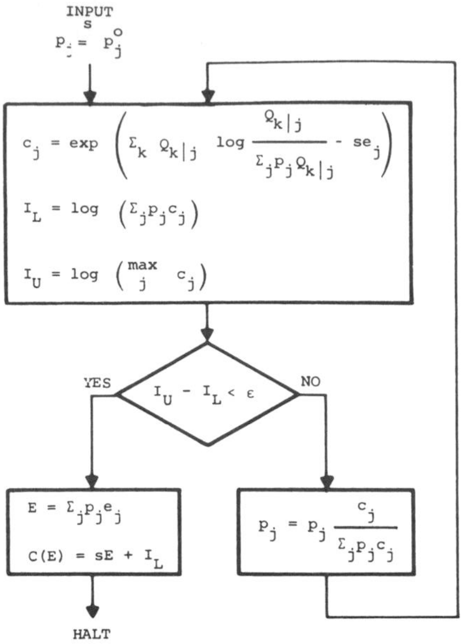


Fig. 4. Constrained capacity algorithm.

$$C(E) - \max_{p} \left[sE + \log \Sigma_j \exp\left(\Sigma_k Q_{k|j} \log P_{j|k} - se_j\right)\right]$$

$$= C(E) - sE - \max_{p} \left[sE_s + \log \Sigma_j \exp\left(\Sigma_k Q_{k|j} \log P_{j|k} - se_j\right)\right] + sE_s$$

$$= C(E) - sE + C(E_s) + sE_s$$

$$= \Sigma_{jk} p_j^* Q_{k|j} \log \frac{Q_{k|j} \exp(-se_j)}{\Sigma_j p_j^* Q_{k|j}} - \max_{p} \Sigma_{jk} p_j Q_{k|j} \log \frac{Q_{k|j} \exp(-se_j)}{\Sigma_j p_j Q_{k|j}}$$

$$\leq 0.$$

*Theorem 9:* A vector $p \in \boldsymbol{P}^n$ achieves capacity at some expense $E_s$ parameterized by $s$ for the channel with transition matrix $Q$ and expense vector $e$ if and only if there exists a number $V$ such that

$$\Sigma_k Q_{k|j} \log \frac{Q_{k|j}}{\Sigma_j p_j Q_{k|j}} - se_j = V, \qquad p_j \neq 0$$

$$\Sigma_k Q_{k|j} \log \frac{Q_{k|j}}{\Sigma_j p_j Q_{k|j}} - se_j \leq V, \qquad p_j = 0.$$

*Proof:* The proof is lengthy but only trivially different from the proof of Theorem 2. The reader can readily modify any published proof of Theorem 2.

*Theorem 10:* Let $s \in [0,\infty]$ be given, and for any $p \in \boldsymbol{P}^n$ let

$$c_j(p) = \exp\left(\Sigma_k Q_{k|j} \log \frac{Q_{k|j}}{\Sigma_j p_j Q_{k|j}} - se_j\right).$$

Then if $p^0$ is any element of $\boldsymbol{P}^n$ with all components strictly positive, the sequence of probability vectors defined by

$$p_j^{r+1} = p_j^r \frac{c_j^r}{\Sigma_j p_j^r c_j^r}$$

is such that

$$I(p^r, Q) \to C(E_s), \qquad \text{as } r \to \infty$$

$$e(p^r) \to E_s, \qquad \text{as } r \to \infty,$$

where $E_s$ is the expense of the point parameterized by $s$.

*Proof:* Let

$$V(p) = I(p) - se(p) = \Sigma_j p_j \log c_j$$

and show that $V(p)$ is increasing. Let

$$W(p) = V(p^{r+1}) - V(p^r)$$

$$= \Sigma_j p_j^r \frac{c_j^r}{\Sigma_j p_j^r c_j^r} \log c_j^{r+1} - \Sigma_i p_i^r \log c_i^r$$

$$= \frac{1}{\Sigma_j p_j^r c_j^r} \left[\Sigma_i \Sigma_j p_i^r p_j^r c_j^r \log c_j^{r+1} - \Sigma_i \Sigma_j p_i^r p_j^r c_j^r \log c_i^r\right]$$

$$= \frac{1}{\Sigma_j p_j^r c_j^r} \left[\Sigma_i p_i^r \Sigma_j p_j^r c_j^r \log \frac{c_j^{r+1}}{c_i^r}\right]$$

$$\geq 1 - \Sigma_j p_j^r \frac{c_j^r}{c_j^{r+1}}$$

with equality iff

$$c_j^{r+1}/c_i^r = 1 \;\forall\; i, j \ni p_i \neq 0 \neq p_j.$$

We now substitute the defining equation for $c_j$ and apply Jensen's inequality.

$$W(p^r) \geq 1 - \Sigma_j p_j^r \exp \Sigma_k Q_{k|j} \log \frac{\Sigma_j p_j^{r+1} Q_{k|j}}{\Sigma_j p_j^r Q_{k|j}}$$

$$\geq 1 - \Sigma_j p_j^r \Sigma_k Q_{k|j} \exp \log \frac{\Sigma_j p_j^{r+1} Q_{k|j}}{\Sigma_j p_j^r Q_{k|j}}.$$

Therefore

$$W(p^r) \geq 1 - \Sigma_k \Sigma_j p_j^{r+1} Q_{k|j} = 0.$$

Thus, $V(p)$ is increasing; moreover, $V(p)$ is strictly increasing unless

$$c_j^{r+1} = c_i^r, \qquad \forall i, j \ni p_i \neq 0 \neq p_j,$$

which condition reduces to the first condition of Theorem 9. We now argue as in the proof of Theorem 3 to show that $V(p)$ converges to $C(E) - sE$. That is, by the Bolzano–Weierstrass Theorem, $\{p^r\}$ has a limit point and by continuity it must satisfy the above Kuhn–Tucker condition. In addition, this limit point must satisfy the second of the Kuhn–Tucker conditions since otherwise convergence could not occur.

A flow diagram for the algorithm of Theorem 10 is shown in Fig. 4.

The following theorem provides a termination for this algorithm.

*Theorem 11:* Let the parameter $s$ be given. Suppose $p$ is any probability vector, and let

$$c_j = \exp\left(\Sigma_k Q_{k|j} \log \frac{Q_{k|j}}{\Sigma_j p_j Q_{k|j}} - s e_j\right).$$

Then, at the point

$$E = \Sigma_j p_j c_j$$

a)
$$C(E) \geq sE + \log \Sigma_j p_j c_j$$

b)
$$C(E) \leq sE + \log \max_j c_j.$$

*Proof:*

a) $p$ is a probability vector giving expense $E$. Hence

$$C(E) \geq I(p,Q) = \Sigma_j p_j \Sigma_k Q_{k|j} \log \frac{Q_{k|j}}{\Sigma_j p_j Q_{k|j}}$$
$$= \Sigma_j p_j \log c_j + s e_j = sE + \Sigma_j p_j \log c_j.$$

b) Suppose $p^*$ achieves capacity at expense parameterized by $s$. Then by Corollary 10,

$$C(E) \leq sE + \log \Sigma_j p_j^* \exp\left(\Sigma_k Q_{k|j} \log \frac{Q_{k|j}}{\Sigma_j p_j^* Q_{k|j}} - s e_j\right).$$

Hence

$$C(E) - (sE + \max_j c_j)$$
$$\leq \log \Sigma_j p_j^* \exp\left(\Sigma_k Q_{k|j} \log \frac{Q_{k|j}}{\Sigma_j p_i^* Q_{k|i}} - s e_j - \max_j \log c_j\right)$$
$$\leq \log \Sigma_j p_j^* \exp\left(\Sigma_k Q_{k|j} \log \frac{Q_{k|j}}{\Sigma_j p_j^* Q_{k|j}} - s e_j - \log c_j\right).$$

We now use

$$\log c_j + s e_j = \Sigma_k Q_{k|j} \log \frac{Q_{k|j}}{\Sigma_j p_j Q_{k|j}}$$

so that

$$C(E) - (sE + \max_j c_j)$$
$$\leq \log \Sigma_j p_j^* \exp \Sigma_k Q_{k|j} \log \frac{\Sigma_j p_j Q_{k|j}}{\Sigma_j p_j^* Q_{k|j}}$$
$$\leq \log \Sigma_j p_j^* \Sigma_k Q_{k|j} \exp \log \frac{\Sigma_j p_j Q_{k|j}}{\Sigma_j p_j^* Q_{k|j}}$$

(Jensen's inequality)

$$= \log \Sigma_k \Sigma_j p_j Q_{k|j} = 0.$$

## V. Continuous Channel and Source Alphabets

The discussion of the preceding sections has been confined to discrete channels and sources. If we turn attention to channels or sources that are described by probability densities, then the earlier discussion can be mimicked in order to provide the analogous theory for continuous probability distributions.

We shall not develop this continuous distribution theory in detail here, both because this would be largely a repetition of the discrete case and because a detailed treatment is available elsewhere [12]. However, several comments will be made to indicate the necessary modifications.

Suppose for any input $x$, $Q(y/x)$ is a probability density function describing the channel. Capacity is defined as

$$C(E) = \sup_{p(x) \in \boldsymbol{P}_E} \iint p(x) Q(y/x) \log \frac{Q(y/x)}{\int Q(y/x) p(x)\, dx}\, dx\, dy,$$

where

$$\boldsymbol{P}_E = \left\{ p: \boldsymbol{R} \to \boldsymbol{R} \middle| \int p(x)\, dx = 1,\ p(x) \geq 0, \int p(x) e(x)\, dx \leq E \right\}.$$

Rate-distortion functions are similarly defined as an infimum of a mutual information over a space of conditional probability distributions.

The use of the supremum and infimum suggest that, in general, these are not actually achieved by any continuous probability distribution (e.g., convergence is to a discrete distribution) so that Kuhn–Tucker-like conditions on the extremizing probability distribution may be vacuously true. However, these conditions can nonetheless be stated and are useful for recognizing points that do not achieve the solution.

The search for extremizing probability distributions is now a problem in the calculus of variations with constraints, but otherwise closely follows the discrete case. The continuous versions of Theorems 6 and 10 can be stated. However, since the extremum might not be achieved, the proof cannot assert the existence of a limiting distribution. The proof must be modified to show that any point below the supremum (respectively above the infimum) cannot be a limit point.

## VI. Multiple Constraints

Some channels may have more than one constraint specified simultaneously. The most common example is a continuous channel that is constrained both in peak power and in average power. It is straightforward to generalize capacity-expense theory to handle this situation. The basic definition for the discrete channel is as follows

$$C(E^1, E^2) = \max_{p \in \boldsymbol{P}_{E^1 E^2}} \Sigma_j \Sigma_k p_j Q_{k|j} \log \frac{Q_{k|j}}{\Sigma_j p_j Q_{k|j}},$$

where

$$\boldsymbol{P}_{E^1 E^2} = \{p \in \boldsymbol{P}^n : \Sigma_j p_j e_j^1 \leq E^1 \text{ and } \Sigma_j p_j e_j^2 \leq E^2\}.$$

The generalization of Theorem 10 is the following.

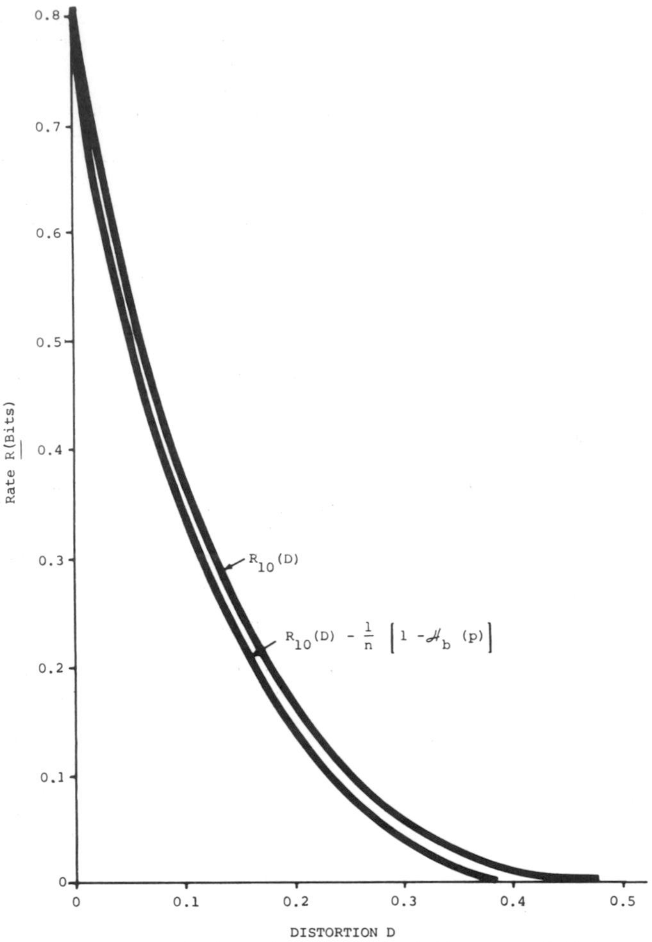


Fig. 5. Upper and lower bounds for the rate-distortion function of a binary symmetric Markov source $p = 0.25$.

*Theorem 13:* Let $(s_1,s_2) \in [0,\infty] \times [0,\infty]$ be given and for any $p \in \boldsymbol{P}^n$ let

$$c_j(p) = \exp\left(\Sigma_k Q_{k|j} \log \frac{Q_{k|j}}{\Sigma p_j Q_{k|j}} - s_1 e_j^{\,1} - s_2 e_j^{\,2}\right).$$

Then, if $p^0$ is any element of $\boldsymbol{P}^n$ with all components strictly positive, the sequence of probability vectors defined by

$$p_j^{r+1} = p_j^{\,r} \frac{c_j^{\,r}}{\Sigma p_j^{\,r} c_j^{\,r}}$$

is such that

$$I(p^r,Q) \rightarrow C(E_{s_1}{}^1,E_{s_2}{}^2), \quad \text{as } r \rightarrow \infty$$
$$e^1(p^r) \rightarrow E_{s_1}{}^1, \quad \text{as } r \rightarrow \infty$$
$$e^2(p^r) \rightarrow E_{s_2}{}^2, \quad \text{as } r \rightarrow \infty,$$

where $C(E_{s_1}{}^1,E_{s_2}{}^2)$ is a point on the capacity-expense surface parameterized by $(s_1,s_2)$.

This theorem is offered without proof.

The analogous situation for rate-distortion functions can be considered. Thus, it may be desired that two (or more) separate definitions of distortion be satisfied [8]. One situation where this would occur is if the reproduced data is to be made available to two different users with different

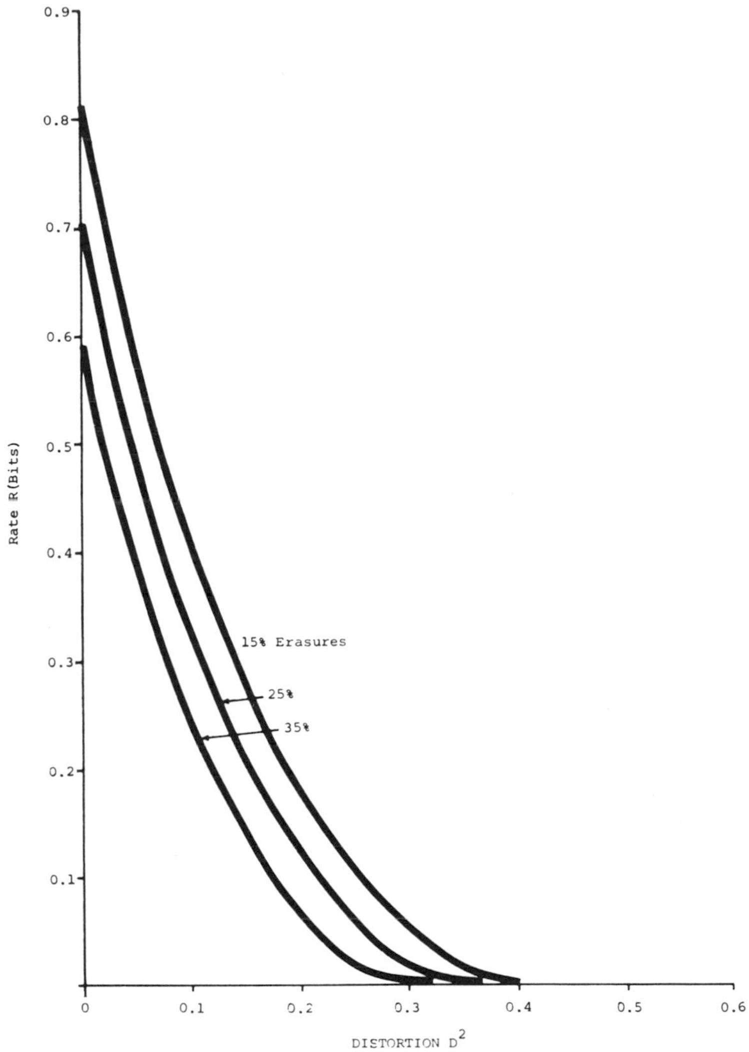


Fig. 6. Rate-distortion function of binary symmetric source with erasure option.

applications in mind. The appropriate definition is as follows

$$R(D^1, D^2) = \min_{Q \in Q_{D^1 D^2}} \Sigma_j \Sigma_k p_j Q_{k|j} \log \frac{Q_{k|j}}{\Sigma_j p_j Q_{k|j}}$$

where

$$Q_{D^1 D^2} = \{Q : d^1(Q) \le D^1, d^2(Q) \le D^2\}$$

$$d^1(Q) = \Sigma_j \Sigma_k p_j Q_{k|j} \rho_{jk}^1$$

$$d^2(Q) = \Sigma_j \Sigma_k p_j Q_{k|j} \rho_{jk}^2.$$

The generalization of Theorem 6 is the following.

*Theorem 14:* Let $s_1 \le 0$, $s_2 \le 0$ be given. Let $q^0$ be any output probability vector such that all components are nonzero. Let $q^{r+1}$ be given in terms of $q^r$ by

$$q_k^{r+1} = q_k^r \Sigma_j \frac{p_j A_{jk}}{\Sigma_k A_{jk} q_k^r}$$

where

$$A_{jk} = \exp (s_1 \rho_{jk}^1 + s_2 \rho_{jk}^2).$$

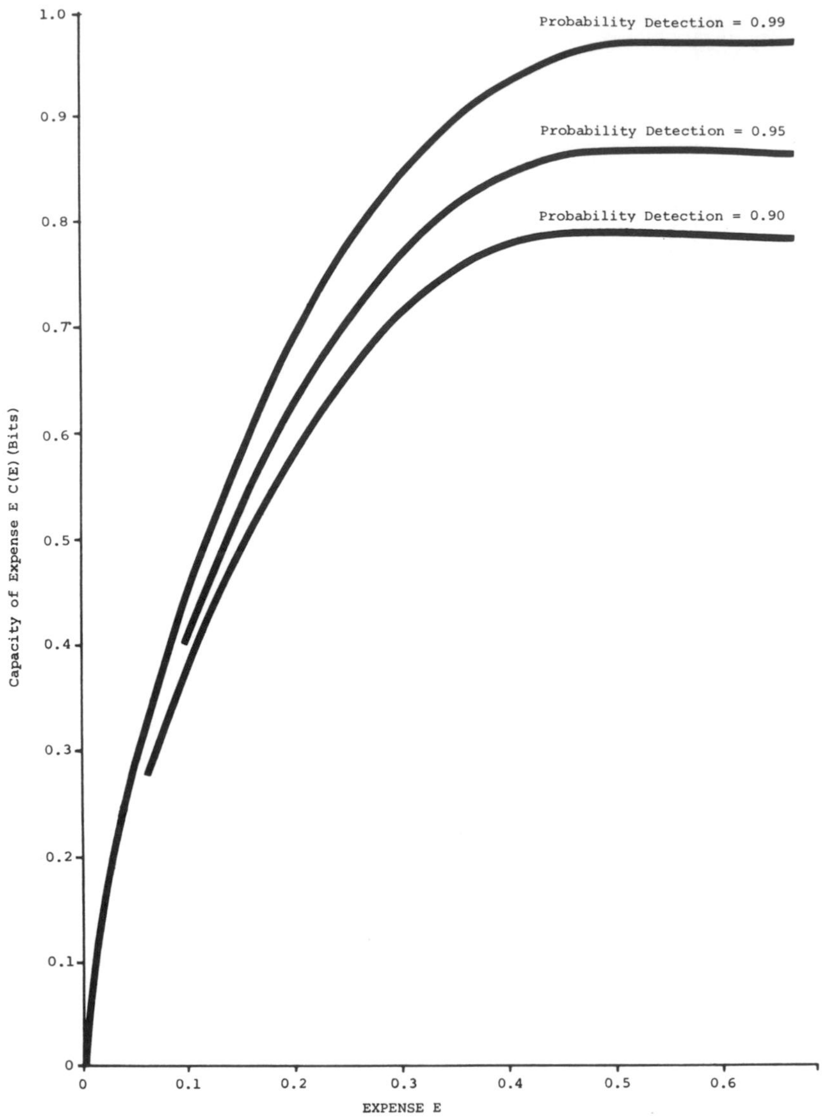


Fig. 7. Capacity-expense function for binary asymmetric channel with expense equal to percent of ones transmitted. False-alarm probability = 0.001.

Then

$$d^1(q^r) \to D_{s_1}{}^1, \qquad \text{as } r \to \infty$$

$$d^2(q^r) \to D_{s_2}{}^2, \qquad \text{as } r \to \infty$$

$$I(q^r) \to R(D_{s_1}{}^1, D_{s_2}{}^2), \qquad \text{as } r \to \infty.$$

This theorem is offered without proof.

## VII. Examples

A long-standing problem in information theory is the determination of the rate-distortion function for a binary symmetric Markov source [7]–[9]. Gray [10] has recently solved this problem for a range of small $D$, but the problem for arbitrary $D$ is unsolved. The rate-distortion function for a source with memory is defined as

$$R(D) = \liminf R_n(D),$$

where $R_n(D)$ is the rate-distortion function of a source whose alphabet is the set of words of length $n$ with probabilities assigned to these words by the Markov source starting in an equiprobable state.

The algorithm of Theorem 6 has been used to calculate $R_{10}(D)$ as shown in Fig. 5. Also shown is a lower bound to $R(D)$ based on a recent theorem of Wyner and Ziv [11]. This theorem states that

$$R(D) \geq R_n(D) + H - \frac{1}{n} H(p_n),$$

where $H$ is the source entropy rate and $H(p_n)$ is the entropy of the set of $n$-words. For the binary symmetric Markov case, this becomes

$$R(D) \geq R_n(D) - \frac{1}{n}[p \log p + (1-p)\log(1-p) + 1],$$

where $p$ is the transition probability.

Tighter bounds can be obtained by calculating $R_n(D)$ for $n > 10$. However, the tightness is improving as $1/n$ while the computations increase exponentially. Computation to an accuracy of $10^{-3}$ bits of all $R_n(D)$ curves from $n = 2$ to $n = 10$ by taking 9 points per curve required 12 min of execution time on the IBM 360 model 65.

The second example is a multiple-distortion problem. A memoryless source produces equiprobable i.i.d. outputs from a binary alphabet. In order to facilitate compression, a user agrees to allow a certain percentage $D_1$ of erasures. Of the unerased data, he requires at most a percentage $D_2$ be in error. Thus, the relevant distortion matrices are

$$\rho_{jk}^1 = \begin{vmatrix} 0 & 0 & 1 \\ 0 & 0 & 1 \end{vmatrix} \qquad \rho_{jk}^2 = \begin{vmatrix} 0 & 1 & 0 \\ 1 & 0 & 0 \end{vmatrix}.$$

The numerical solution of the problem is shown in Fig. 6. These curves were prepared by computing $R(D^1, D^2)$ for 1600 different values of $(D^1, D^2)$ to an accuracy of $10^{-3}$ bits. This required 83 s of computation time on an IBM 360 model 65.

The final example postulates the existence of a noisy binary channel, which transmits a one by the presence of a pulse and a zero by the absence of a pulse. The receiver is characterized by a probability of detection and by a probability of false alarm. The only design option available to the user is to conserve power by minimizing the percentage of ones used in a message. Fig. 7 shows the capacity-expense functions. These were computed by generating 300 points to an accuracy of $10^{-3}$ bits, which required 5 s of computation time on an IBM 360 model 65.

## Acknowledgment

The author wishes to acknowledge the advice and criticism of Prof. T. Berger of Cornell University.

## Appendix

## Capacity–Expense Functions

*Definition:* An *expense schedule* for a channel $Q$ is a vector $e$ whose $j$th component $e_j$ is called the expense of using the $j$th channel input letter.

*Definition:* The *capacity at expense* $E$ is

$$C(E) = \max_{p \in P_E} \Sigma_{jk} p_j Q_{k|j} \log \frac{Q_{k|j}}{\Sigma_j p_j Q_{k|j}} = \max_{p \in P_E} I(p,Q),$$

where

$$P_E = \{p \in P^n : \Sigma_j p_j e_j \leq E\}.$$

This is well defined if $P_E$ is nonempty since $P_E$ is compact and hence $I(p,Q)$ attains its maximum on $P_E$.

*Remark:* Without loss of generality, we can assume that $E_{\min} = 0$ and $C(E)$ exists for all $E \geq E_{\min}$. This is equivalent to assuming $\min e_j = 0$, which can be obtained by adding an appropriate constant to all $e_j$, thereby performing a simple horizontal translation of the $C(E)$ graph.

*Remark:* If $E' > E$ then $P_{E'} \subset P_E$ and hence $C(E)$ is a monotonic nondecreasing function.

*Theorem:* $C(E)$ is a convex upward function. That is, given $E'$, $E''$, and $\lambda \in [0,1]$, then $C(\lambda E' + (1-\lambda)E'') \geq \lambda C(E') + (1-\lambda)C(E'')$.

*Proof:* Let $p', p''$ achieve $(E', C(E')), (E'', C(E''))$, respectively. Let $p^* = \lambda p' + \bar{\lambda} p''$, where $\bar{\lambda} = (1-\lambda)$. Then

$$e(p^*) = \Sigma_j(\lambda p_j' + \bar{\lambda} p_j'')e_j = \lambda E' + \bar{\lambda} E''.$$

Hence $p^* \in P_{\lambda E' + \bar{\lambda} E''}$ so that

$$C(\lambda E' + \bar{\lambda} E'') \geq I(p^*, Q)$$

$$\begin{aligned} C(\lambda E' + \bar{\lambda}E'') &- \lambda C(E') - \bar{\lambda} C(E'') \\ &\geq I(p^*,Q) - \lambda I(p',Q) - \bar{\lambda} I(p'',Q) \\ &= \lambda \Sigma_j \Sigma_k p_j' Q_{k|j} \log \frac{\Sigma_j p_j' Q_{k|j}}{\Sigma_j p_j^* Q_{k|j}} + \bar{\lambda} \Sigma_j \Sigma_k p_j'' Q_{k|j} \log \frac{\Sigma_j p_j'' Q_{k|j}}{\Sigma_j p_j^* Q_{k|j}} \\ &\geq \lambda(\Sigma_{jk} p_j' Q_{k|j} - \Sigma_{jk} p_j^* Q_{k|j}) + \bar{\lambda}(\Sigma_{jk} p_j'' Q_{k|j} - \Sigma_{jk} p_j^* Q_{k|j}) \\ &= 0. \end{aligned}$$

*Corollary:* $C(E)$ is continuous except possibly at $E = 0$.

*Proof:* $C(E)$ is convex and monotonic.

*Corollary:*

$$\lim_{E \to E_{\max}} C(E) = C,$$

where $C$ is the channel capacity,

$$E_{\max} = \Sigma_j p_j^* e_j$$

and $p^*$ achieves $C$.

*Proof:* $C(E)$ is continuous.

*Corollary:* $C(E)$ is strictly increasing in $E < E_{\max}$.

*Proof:* $C(E)$ is convex.

*Corollary:* If $E \leq E_{\max}$ then $(E, C(E))$ is achieved by some $P$ such that

$$e(P) = \Sigma_j p_j e_j = E.$$

*Proof:* $C(E)$ is strictly increasing if $E < E_{\max}$.

*Theorem:* If $p', p''$ both achieve the point $(E, C(E))$, then so does

$$p = \lambda p' + \bar{\lambda} p'', \qquad \forall \lambda \in [0,1].$$

*Proof:*

$$e(p) = \Sigma_j(\lambda p_j' + \bar{\lambda} p_j'')e_j = \lambda E + \bar{\lambda} E = E.$$

Therefore, $p \in P_E$ so that

$$C(E) \geq I(p,Q) \geq \lambda I(p',Q) + \bar{\lambda} I(p'',Q) = C(E).$$

*Theorem:* Suppose $0 \leq E \leq E_{\max}$. Then $C(E)$ can be expressed parametrically in terms of a parameter $s \in [0,\infty]$ by

$$C(E_s) = sE_s + V_s$$

$$E_s = \Sigma_j p_j^* e_j,$$

where

$$V_s = \max_{p \in P} \Sigma_j p_j Q_{k|j} \log \frac{Q_{k|j}}{\Sigma_j p_j Q_{k|j}} - s\Sigma_j p_j e_j$$

and $p^*$ achieves this maximum.

*Proof:* Any such point $(E_s, C(E_s))$ is clearly on the $C(E)$ curve. It is only necessary to prove that every point on the $C(E)$ curve can be so generated.

Since $C(E)$ is concave, it has a derivative everywhere except possibly at a countable set of points and it has a left and a right derivative everywhere. Given the point $E$, let $s$ be the left derivative of $C(E)$ at $E$. Then for any $E'$, by convexity of $C(E)$,

$$C(E') \leq C(E) + s(E' - E).$$

Now, the parameter $s$ generates some point on $C(E)$. Let $(E_s, C(E_s))$ be this point. Then

$$C(E_s) = \max_{p \in P} \Sigma_j \Sigma_k p_j Q_{k|j} \log \frac{Q_{k|j}}{\Sigma_j p_j Q_{k|j}} - s\Sigma_j p_j e_j + sE_s$$

$$\geq \max_{p \in \{p: \Sigma_j p_j e_j = E\}} \left[ \Sigma_j \Sigma_k p_j Q_{k|j} \log \frac{Q_{k|j}}{\Sigma_j p_j Q_{k|j}} - s\Sigma_j p_j e_j + sE_s \right]$$

$$C(E_s) \geq C(E) - sE + sE_s.$$

Therefore, $C(E_s) = C(E) + s(E_s - E)$ so that either $E = E_s$ or they are connected by a straight line of slope $s$. In the latter case, the convexity of $C(E)$ assures that every intermediate point on this straight line is also a point of $C(E)$ and it is straightforward to verify that every point on this connecting line satisfies the parametric equation of the theorem.

*Corollary:* If $C(E)$ is strictly concave in the neighborhood of some point, then the value of $s$ that generates this point generates only this point.

*Corollary:* If $s_1, s_2$ are the left and right derivatives at a point $E$, then $s$ generates $(E, C(E))$ if and only if $s \in [s_1, s_2]$.

## REFERENCES


[1] C. Shannon, "A mathematical theory of communication," *Bell Syst. Tech. J.*, vol. 27, pp. 379–423, 623–656, 1948.

[2] C. Shannon, "Coding theorems for a discrete source with a fidelity criterion," in *1959 IRE Nat. Conv. Rec.*, pt. 4, pp. 142–163.

[3] R. G. Gallager, *Information Theory and Reliable Communication.* New York: Wiley, 1968.

[4] F. Jelinek, *Probabilistic Information Theory.* New York: McGraw-Hill, 1968.

[5] T. Berger, *Rate Distortion Theory: A Mathematical Basis for Data Compression.* Englewood Cliffs, N.J.: Prentice-Hall, 1971.

[6] B. G. Haskell, "The computation and bounding of rate-distortion functions," *IEEE Trans. Inform. Theory*, vol. IT-15, pp. 525–531, Sept. 1969.

[7] R. L. Dobrushin, "Mathematical problems in the Shannon theory of optimal coding of information," in *Proc. 4th Berkeley Symp. Mathematical Statistics and Probability*, vol. 1. Berkeley and Los Angeles: Univ. California Press, 1962, pp. 211–252.

[8] T. J. Goblick, Jr., "Coding for a discrete information source with a distortion measure," Ph.D. dissertation, Dep. Elec. Eng., M.I.T., Cambridge, Mass, 1962.

[9] T. Berger, "Nyquist's problem in data transmission," Ph.D. dissertation, Harvard Univ., Cambridge, Mass, 1965.

[10] R. M. Gray, "Information rates of autoregressive sources," Ph.D. dissertation, Univ. Southern California, Los Angeles.

[11] A. D. Wyner and J. Ziv, "Bounds on the rate-distortion function for stationary sources with memory," *IEEE Trans Inform. Theory*, vol. IT-17, pp. 508–513, Sept. 1971.

[12] R. E. Blahut, "Computation of information measures," Ph.D. dissertation, Cornell Univ., Ithaca, N.Y., 1972.

[13] S. Arimoto, "An algorithm for computing the capacity of arbitrary discrete memoryless channels," *IEEE Trans. Inform. Theory*, vol. IT-18, pp. 14–20, Jan. 1972.

# 18



Reprinted from *Proc. IEEE,* **60**(7), 771–779 (1972)

# Visual Fidelity Criterion and Modeling

ZIGMANTAS L. BUDRIKIS

***Abstract*—Fidelity measures and criteria for visual communications are discussed. It is recognized that the basis of visual fidelity assessment is subjective judgement of reproduced pictures. However, in design and elsewhere there is also need for explicit evaluation of visual communication waveforms. The rate distortion theory model for such evaluations is brought out and two existing evaluations of limited scope, viz., weighted noise measurement and $K$ rating, are reviewed in relation to that theory.**

**It is suggested that video distortion can largely be identified with visibility of errors in reproduction. Relevant findings on luminance vision are examined. It is found that a comprehensive model of visibility would incorporate excitation, inhibition, and masking, and that considerable quantitative knowledge of these factors already exists. Looking ahead, a block schematic is given of a meter which might measure distortion produced by quantization noise in a video feed back quantizer.**

## I. Introduction

TRANSMISSION fidelity is central in the complex of communications. A communication problem is only fully defined when it includes the receiver's fidelity requirement. So as to admit the most favorable solutions, that requirement should be as true as possible to the nature of the communication. This is especially so with visual communications, the area of interest for the present paper, which are well known for their large demands on channel capacity [1]–[3].

The ultimate destination of visual messages is man and, therefore, the receiver of interest is man's sense of vision. To understand his fidelity requirements one needs to know properties of the visual sense. We will restrict ourselves to monochrome television and hence our interest need not extend beyond luminance vision.

One way of approaching our subject would be to launch immediately into a review of all that is known about luminance vision. But our purpose will be served better if we first determine what it is that we want to know. To this end we will first examine the practical view of visual fidelity and how it is assessed. We will find that the basis for it is an overall subjective evaluation of achievement within an agreed context.

In the established practice of analog transmission there are routine measurements and tests which involve waveforms and have criterion values. We will call this type of evaluation ***explicit*** so as to distinguish it from the more fundamental evaluation of subjective testing which gives only implicit judgements on waveforms. We would like to have explicit fidelity evaluations which would be applicable also to digital transmission and, if possible, more generally still.

To see what is expected from a completely general explicit evaluation of fidelity, or its qualitative inverse which is distortion, we will look at rate distortion theory [4], [5]. Then we will examine two of the existing evaluation routines, namely, weighted random-noise measurement [6], [7], and Lewis' $K$ rating [8], paying particular attention to what restricts them and what visual properties they might be based on.

We will come to the conclusion that in visual communication systems which function adequately, and particularly in those meant for entertainment, defects brought about by quantization and/or transmission are barely visible. We can then say that the defects are at, or near, threshold and that distortion can be identified with abundance of such defects, weighted in relation to visibility. We will, therefore, review psychophysics of vision with emphasis on visual threshold data and models which unify such data.

We will see that, in accordance with best current indications, quantitatively the weighting should consist of filtering of the error waveform followed by a variable attenuation. The filtering should have a bandpass characteristic both spatially and in time. Physiologically, the characteristic is deemed to come about by an interplay of two distinct mechanisms, one excitation and the other inhibition. The control signal for the attenuation should be obtained nonlinearly from a similar filtering operation, but now on the signal rather than error waveform. It would account for masking, or the reduction in the ability to discriminate, which occurs on, or in the neighborhoods of, changes, both within a picture and from one picture to the next.

In assessing distortion by additive random noise only excitation needs to be taken into account. This is so because masking is of no real interest when the noise is signal-independent anyway, and inhibition is effective only in a low spatial/temporal frequency region where random noise would have negligible spectral components. But all three factors would have to enter an evaluation of quantizing noise.

Even with some gaps still existing in quantitative knowledge, it will be possible to look to a likely form of a meter capable of evaluating distortion by many kinds of quantizing noise. The meter would need to weight and sum at the site of each picture element contributions by noise and signal from several picture frames and hence would need to be a computing device with a multimegabit memory.

Despite its complexity, the evaluation would still not meet all requirements of rate distortion theory, since it would not take account of receiver tolerances to geometric distortions, picture shading, nonlinear gray-scale changes, and the like. This must surely disappoint those who would want to make theoretical prognosis on what achievement is possible, or impossible, in the field of video source encoding. But the meter could still prove a boon to designers of video quantizers.

## II. The Nature of Fidelity in Visual Communications

Television is an extension of man's eyes. If it has a utilitarian purpose as, for instance, traffic control, then the required quality of picture transmission could be determined

Manuscript received September 14, 1971; revised April 3, 1972. This work was supported by the Radio Research Board of Australia.

The author is with the Bell Telephone Laboratories, Inc., Holmdel, N. J. 07733, on leave of absence from the Department of Electrical Engineering, University of Western Australia, Nedlands 6009, W.A., Australia.

from the demands of the given task. But if it is used for entertainment then there is almost no limit to how good one might want to make the system. The limitation is an economical one.

According to Seyler [9] the objective of entertainment television is to produce "as accurately as practicable a realistic replica of the natural environment shown, i.e., (to create) in the viewer's mind the illusion of direct communication." We subscribe to this principle. But since our concern is with transmission rather than with optoelectrical transducer design or with setting of new scanning raster standards, we will accept the view that existing systems properly achieve Seyler's objective. This means that we regard as the original visual image any display on a studio quality monitor by uncorrupted video waveforms which themselves conform to some recognized set of standards, be it for broadcast television [10] or phone television. Similarly, we accept the quality requirements for transmission and reproduction as stipulated by such given standards, but not necessarily in terms of the given wording. Since we do not wish to restrict ourselves to analog transmission we only accept the requirements in what they imply with regard to reproduced images but not in what they ask on analog waveform quality in terms of response and signal-to-noise ratio.

Implicit evaluation of fidelity by comparing reproduced, or impaired, pictures with their originals is a matter for subjective testing. Such testing has a comparatively long tradition and is, in fact, the usual avenue by which new standards are set and new proposals accepted.

Probably the first full documentation of subjective test procedures, together with psychometric evaluations, applied to television, is by Mertz, Fowler, and Christopher [11]. They described two techniques. The first was to compare the impaired television picture with a defocused lantern slide projection of the same subject matter. They then used the amount of defocus required for equivalence as an indicator of subjective impairment. The other technique was to present only the impaired picture and to let the viewer express his opinion by one of seven preworded comments which ranged from "impairment not perceptible" to picture "not usable." Mertz *et al.* [11] studied impairment by additive noise and by echoes using both techniques with a common preference evaluation procedure. They found that the techniques gave substantially the same results.

The technique of presenting only the impaired picture and asking for a preworded comment has been used by many subsequent investigators (e.g., [12], [13]). Since no reference picture is given in such tests, it might be thought that here the fidelity assessment is in some absolute sense. However all viewers, both skilled and laymen, have an acquired knowledge of what good quality pictures within the given standards look like, and this would certainly be reflected in their choice of comment. Indeed, the difference in response from the two groups largely reflects the difference in their remembered standards.

Probably the biggest contribution to variation in results from one laboratory to another is from variations in viewing conditions. The factors which are important are the type and level of ambient lighting, size of screen and type of surround, the peak and lowest luminance on the screen, the voltage-to-luminance transfer characteristic, and the viewing distance. A plea for standardization made by Prosser *et al.* [13] has, to some extent, been heeded. Viewing conditions used by them for testing with the European 625-line system are shown in Table I.

TABLE I
VIEWING CONDITIONS USED IN [13] FOR SUBJECTIVE TESTING WITH EUROPEAN 625-LINE SYSTEM

| | |
|---|---|
| General lighting | diffuse, approx. 3 lx |
| Screen size | 0.53-m tube or larger |
| Surroundings | unspecified |
| Peak screen luminance | 5.5 cd/m² |
| Lowest screen luminance | 0.35 cd/m² |
| Voltage-to-luminance transfer characteristic | unspecified |
| Viewing distance | six times picture height |

## III. RATE DISTORTION THEORY

Although evaluation by subjective testing is, and will remain, the ultimate touchstone of quality in visual communications, there is, of course, also need for explicit evaluations performed on waveforms. The most general framework for explicit fidelity evaluations was created by Shannon [4], [14]. We will sketch the thoughts and their context for the case of waveforms which are continuous at the source.

When a continuous waveform is transmitted, it is neither possible nor necessary to recover it exactly. It is only necessary to maintain a prescribed fidelity, or, more precisely, not to allow the distortion to exceed a specified criterion value. Hence distortion needs to be defined.

Assume that a typical waveform $x(t)$ at the transmitter is specified on the finite interval $(0, T)$ and is at least approximately limited in bandwidth. It can be represented with arbitrarily high precision by a finite-dimensional vector $\boldsymbol{x}$ [15]. Similarly, the received waveform $y(t)$ can be represented by $\boldsymbol{y}$. The transmission process is described by $p_{\boldsymbol{x}}(\boldsymbol{y})$, the conditional probability density of $\boldsymbol{y}$, given $\boldsymbol{x}$, and the complete system is described by the joint density

$$p(\boldsymbol{x}, \boldsymbol{y}) = p(\boldsymbol{x})p_{\boldsymbol{x}}(\boldsymbol{y}).$$

The amount of distortion in the particular transmission, $\boldsymbol{x} \rightarrow \boldsymbol{y}$, must be a function of the two vectors, say $d_T(\boldsymbol{x}, \boldsymbol{y})$, and the distortion during $(0, T)$, averaged over all transmitted and received signals is

$$D_T(p(\boldsymbol{x}, \boldsymbol{y})) = \int \cdots \int d_T(\boldsymbol{x}, \boldsymbol{y}) p(\boldsymbol{x}, \boldsymbol{y}) d\boldsymbol{x} d\boldsymbol{y}. \quad (1)$$

As time averages, the distortion in the particular transmission will be $d = d_T/T$, and evaluated over all transmissions, $D = D_T/T$.

If the source and transmission are ergodic, and if $T$ is large enough, then, almost certainly, $D$ will equal $d$.

For a given source, and hence fixed $p(\boldsymbol{x})$, $D$ can only be altered by altering $p_{\boldsymbol{x}}(\boldsymbol{y})$. Doing this will also alter the mutual information $I_T(X; Y)$, which is defined by

$$I_T(X; Y) = \int \cdots \int p(\boldsymbol{x}, \boldsymbol{y}) \log \frac{p(\boldsymbol{x}, \boldsymbol{y})}{p(\boldsymbol{x})p(\boldsymbol{y})} d\boldsymbol{x} d\boldsymbol{y}. \quad (2)$$

The rate of a continuous source is then defined as the smallest mutual information per unit time, where the minimization is achieved by altering $p_{\boldsymbol{x}}(\boldsymbol{y})$ without thereby allowing the average distortion to exceed a specified criterion value

$D^*$, i.e.,

$$R(D^*) = \min_{p_x(y)} \left( \frac{I_T(X; Y)}{T} \right)$$

given $D \leq D^*$.

Similar definitions, with only minor changes, hold for discrete sources and, not surprisingly, result in inherently simpler situations. This was exploited by Shannon in his later work [14], when he demonstrated several properties of $R(D^*)$, explored it's significance to source coding, and then generalized the new results to the continuous case.

To encode the vector $\boldsymbol{x}$ means to represent it by a vector from a finite set $\boldsymbol{y}_i$ ($i = 1, 2, \cdots, l$). The conditional density $p_x(\boldsymbol{y})$, which before could have been called the transmission law, now becomes the encoding law and, using Dirac delta functions, can be written as

$$p_x(\boldsymbol{y}) = \sum_i P(\boldsymbol{y}_i/\boldsymbol{x})\delta(\boldsymbol{y} - \boldsymbol{y}_i)$$

where $P(\boldsymbol{y}_i/\boldsymbol{x})$ is the probability that $\boldsymbol{x}$ would be represented by $\boldsymbol{y}_i$.

It is possible to make the encoding more restricted. Thus the space of $\boldsymbol{x}$ could be divided into nonoverlapping subsets $\boldsymbol{X}_j$ and the encoding probabilities made to depend only on which subset the given $x$ belongs to

$$p_{x \in X_j}(\boldsymbol{y}) = \sum_i P_j(\boldsymbol{y}_i)\delta(\boldsymbol{y} - \boldsymbol{y}_i).$$

Even further, the encoding law could be made deterministic by dividing the space of $\boldsymbol{x}$ into exactly $l$ subsets and then putting

$$P_j(\boldsymbol{y}_i) = \begin{cases} 1, & \text{when } i = j \\ 0, & \text{when } i \neq j. \end{cases}$$

Whatever the restrictions on the encoding law, the evaluations of distortion and mutual information still are in accordance with (1) and (2). The minimization for determining the rate is also the same, except that $p_x(\boldsymbol{y})$ may only be taken over the restricted class. It is obvious that, with increasing severity of restriction, the rate, for a given distortion, can only go up.

Our particular interest is in the distortion function $d_T$. It goes without saying that, no matter what the transmission or coding law and what the restriction on it, the theoretical function $d_T$ for a given source is always the same. Yet from a practical viewpoint this can bear stressing, for it is conceivable that a distortion function which is inferred from experiments would be blind to any but the particular kinds of distortions which were present in the experiments. By progressively widening the scope of observations, or by gaining a better insight into the underlying basis of the evaluation, one might arrive at distortion measures with less and less restriction. The $d_T$ of the theory is there already.

## IV. Explicit Evaluations of Analog Television Links

Results of subjective tests of the kind discussed in Section II and general experience have led to direct evaluations of certain types of impairments sustained in analog transmission of television signals. These include cross talk, echoes, random noise, and single-frequency interference [16]. We will review

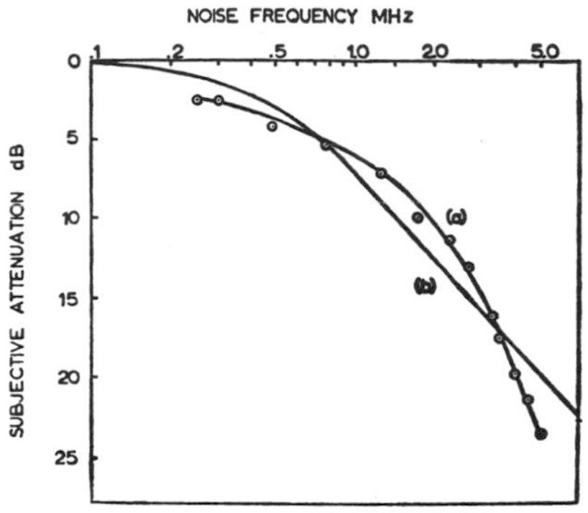


Fig. 1. Noise weighting characteristics in 625-line television system. (a) Measured curve at four times picture height from Müller and Demus [21]. (b) Standard CMTT curve.

measurement of random noise as one that has the most possible relevance to digital transmission. Also we look at an evaluation of a somewhat different kind, namely the $K$-rating scheme of linear distortion on the basis of test signal results [17].

### A. Evaluation of Additive Random Noise

Luminance noise is unavoidable in visual communications. Pictures produced on a monitor by uncorrupted video waveforms, taken straight from the source, will already have some randomly fluctuating granularity. Typically, the peak-to-peak signal to rms noise ratio in waveforms from a good quality 625-line flying spot scanner is of the order of 40 dB.

The noise at the source is, to all intents, Gaussian. Its power may be independent of the amplitude of the signal, as in the vidicon camera, or it may go up with increasing level, as in the flying-spot scanner [18]. Noise added by an analog channel in transmission will generally also be Gaussian, differing from the source noise only in spectral characteristics. The power density spectrum of the noise at the source will generally rise almost linearly over the passband, while on the channel it will be flat or rising, depending on modulation employed.

Noise at a low power level is innocuous, but with increasing level it becomes plainly visible and reduces the visibility of genuine picture material. The distortion caused by noise can, especially at moderate levels, be identified with its visibility.

Many investigators have studied the visibility of noise and the variation of this with different factors [6], [7], [18]–[23]. It is found that, given noise of fixed power, it is less visible when it is spectrally biased towards higher frequencies, and more visible when in the mid-grays of the luminance range. Its visibility is lowest with increasing picture content. It is less for moving pictures than for stills.

The precise variation of visibility, as function of spectral distribution, depends on the viewing distance, because a change in distance alters the ratio of lines per millimeter on the viewer's retina to cycles per second in the scanned waveform. A typical spectral noise visibility curve, with experimental points borrowed from Müller and Demus [21], is shown in Fig. 1. These points were determined for the 625-line system at a viewing distance of four times picture height. The noise was added, successively in different spectral bands, to a monoscope test pattern.

Quantitative data have also been obtained on the variation of visibility of noise with some of the other factors, including effects of grey level and picture content [7], [20], [24]. However, none of these need to be taken into account when evaluating distortion by channel noise. This is so because channel noise is independent of the signal and, if one were to take a statistical average in accordance with (1), i.e., average it over all picture material, all noise would fare equally in respect of picture-dependent variations.

The fact that there are variations with luminance level, picture content, and movement shows, however, that in television the distortion measure $d_T$ is essentially a function of both $\boldsymbol{x}$ and $\boldsymbol{y}$. But it can be simplified to one which is a function only of $(\boldsymbol{x}-\boldsymbol{y})$ when, as in the case of channel noise, $(\boldsymbol{x}-\boldsymbol{y})$ is independent of $\boldsymbol{x}$. Clearly, this forebodes much greater complexity for the case of quantization when the noise is, in fact, picture-dependent. But all that is necessary to evaluate channel noise is to pass it through a spectral weighting filter which would imitate the eye's weighting, and measure its average power.

The weighting characteristic adopted by the CMTT for the 625-line system is shown as curve (b) in Fig. 1. It is the characteristic of a single-stage low-pass filter which has a time constant of 0.33 $\mu$s and a 6-dB/octave asymptotic slope. Similar characteristics, with appropriately altered time constants, are standard for the other television systems.

A comment is perhaps warranted on the particular shape of the adopted weighting characteristic. It is obvious that the data of Müller and Demus would be more closely approximated by a filter which has a 12-dB/octave asymptotic slope. A steeper slope can also be argued theoretically [25]. The filtering action has its origins in a circular visual point spread function which, when referred to the television raster, results in a two-sided impulse response, symmetrical about the time of the impulse. A one-sided impulse response already gives an asymptotic slope of not less than 6 dB/octave [26], so that the symmetrical two-sided response must give a slope which is not less than 12 dB/octave.

Reasoning along the same lines also shows that the characteristic of Fig. 1 is but an envelope of the true function which must have a microstructure with maxima at intervals of frame frequency and clustered around line frequency harmonics [19], [25]. But in measuring random noise which has zero correlation from line to line and from frame to frame, the microstructure is of no consequence. Again, however, the situation is different with quantizing noise.

### B. Linear Distortion and K Rating

Linear response errors are just as unavoidable during transmission over an analog channel as is the addition of random noise. But, while noise is independent of the signal, the linear transmission errors are deterministically related to it. Given a linear channel and absence of noise, the waveform at the receiver will be

$$y(t) = \int_0^t h(\tau)x(t-\tau)d\tau, \qquad 0 < t < T$$

where $h$ is the impulse response of the channel. Or, reverting to vector notation,

$$\boldsymbol{y} = H\boldsymbol{x}$$

where $H$ is a matrix whose elements come from the vector $\boldsymbol{h}$, a sufficiently precise representation of $h(t)$.

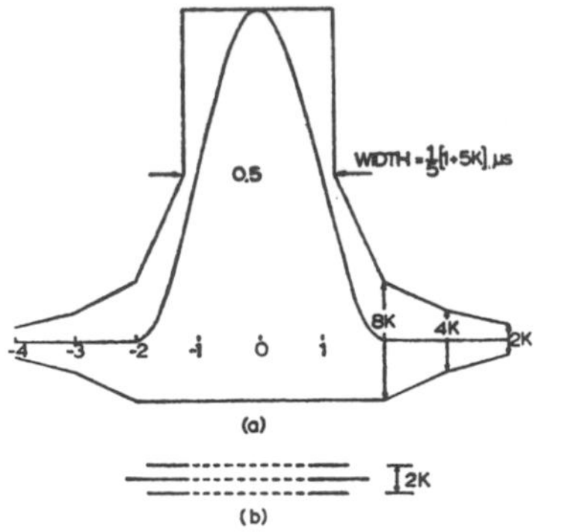

Fig. 2. Pulse and bar test with tolerances expressed as multiples of $K$. (a) Sine-squared pulse inside tolerance window. (b) Tolerance limits on amplitude along top of bar.

Given no other disturbances, the distortion function would then be $d_T(\boldsymbol{x}, H\boldsymbol{x})$, i.e., a function of the source waveform and the channel impulse response. If we may assume that the video process is ergodic, and if a sufficiently large $T$ is chosen in the first place, then $d_T/T$ would be the average distortion.

Although our real difficulty is of a different kind, a remark on ergodicity may be useful at this point. Since we are interested in the video waveforms for their pictorial content, any definition of an ensemble of such waveforms must have its time origin tied to a definite point on the scanning raster [27]. This gives then a nonstationary ensemble, and without stationariness, there is no ergodicity in the usual sense [28]. But sequences of samples taken from the same location in successive frames, i.e., $x(t)$, $x(t-T_p)$, $x(t-2T_p)$, $\cdots$, will be stationary. The same can be said about such sequences of sets of samples and, indeed, of sequences of pictures. The distortion evaluation would necessarily be over such stationary sequences and therefore would not preclude ergodicity in a widened sense.

Our real difficulty is, of course, that we do not know the function $d_T$ and, as yet, not even a simplified version which would be at least adequate to evaluate distortion by linear filtering. What is then done in practice? Apart from implicit evaluation by subjective response to received test patterns and more general pictures, the channel is tested with fixed waveforms [8], [29].

Test waveforms are chosen for their similarity to parts of actual picture signals [30]. Of the small catalog of test waveforms in general use, the most interesting, from our point of view, are the pulse and bar because there is a numerical channel evaluation procedure associated with them. The pulse is shown inside a tolerance window in Fig. 2(a). It has sine-squared shape and a half-amplitude width of $1/B$, where $B$ is the system bandwidth. The "bar" is a rectangular pulse, some 25 $\mu$s in duration, and shaped by the same network [31].

However, the interest in the bar is in its flat top which tests how well the channel can keep to a constant value over a good part of a scanning line. The quality of the channel's response to rapid changes is tested by the pulse.

To establish the rating of a television facility its pulse and bar response is checked against tolerance windows. These are shown in Fig. 2(a) and (b) with all dimensions expressed as multiples of the single number $K$. The smallest value of $K$ for both windows, which will still accommodate the responses, is then quoted as the rating. Typically, a television link might have a $K$ rating of 0.03.

Lewis proposed the particular evaluation on the basis of his experience in judging the quality of received pictures and relating it to responses to the test waveforms [8]. Others have found it reasonable. Accepting it as successful, we may look upon it as a distortion evaluation in miniature. The pulse and bar waveforms stand in for the ensemble of video signals and $d_T$ is then a selection of the largest weighted deviation of response from input, with the weights determined by the input. Where the input is held constant the weight is highest, where it has the greatest rate of change the weight is lowest. No doubt, the weights are meant to be inverses of the relative visibilities of errors in reproduction and the distortion function is then to be equated to the most visible error.

## V. Psychophysics of Vision

It is clear from the preceding sections that visibility of defects plays an important role in the assessment of television facilities. Emotion may well influence the pronouncement on a very poor facility, but an adequately functioning system will be judged by the extent to which errors can be seen. When only the reproduction is presented to the viewer then, of course, not all objectively definable errors will be subjectively identifiable, since clues to identification will only be given by the context. Therefore, identification and, from there, picture semantics also play a role, but much would already be helped if the visibility of objectivity defined departures could be correctly assessed, and even if only in most cases.

Visibility is closely related in concept to visual threshold and visual detection. When a visual stimulus is presented to a subject, chances are that it will not always be seen by him on every presentation. We can associate with that stimulus, in the given circumstances of presentation, a probability of detection. As the size of the stimulus is varied so the probability of detection is changed. The curve of probability versus stimulus size is the visibility function. The stimulus size for which the probability is 0.5 is usually known as the visual threshold.

In a very extensive study of visual thresholds Blackwell [32] found that in all cases the probability of detection could be approximated well by a normal curve when plotted against a linear scale of stimulus increment. This suggested two things to Blackwell [33]; one, that the neural events on which the detection is based are normally distributed and, two, that there is a linear transformation from external stimulus to the neural events. Actually, thoughts differ considerably on the visual detection mechanism (see [33] and, say, [34]), but Blackwell's reading of the evidence will be sufficient for our purposes.

Much about the visual mechanism is nonlinear. Thus visual properties vary appreciably as the level of illumination, to which the eye is allowed to adapt, is changed [35], and the curve along which the steady state varies is highly nonlinear [36]. Also, at any given adaptation luminance, the differential threshold, expressed as a percentage, is higher at luminances both above and below the adaptation level and this variation is nonlinear (e.g., [2]).

But, on the other hand, there is also much that obeys superposition. Thus the level to which the eye adapts is, according to Holladay's principle, identifiable with a single luminance which itself is obtained as a weighted linear sum of all the luminances in the visual field [37]. Linear additivity is brought out by threshold data when thresholds are measured as functions both of stimulus area and of stimulus duration (see, e.g., [25]). Again, when an intermittent light is high enough in frequency to be perceived as constant, the perceived brightness corresponds to the average of the time-varying luminance (Talbot–Plateau law [10]). Similarly, a black and white grating also becomes a gray, corresponding to average, when it is too fine to be resolved.

From all this it is clear that before luminance is changed into sensory perception, or before detection takes place, the input distribution is subjected to spatial and temporal filtering which is at least largely linear [25], [33], [38], [39]. Both the spatial and the temporal filter characteristics show bandpass resonances [40]–[43]. However, just as the visibility of random noise in television, so a multiplicity of data on detection of stimuli on plain backgrounds can be explained by a filter with only low-pass characteristics. We will see probable reasons for the discrepancy shortly, but for now let us define the model more fully.

Let $L(x, y, t)$ be the luminance distribution in the visual field of the observer and referred to coordinates which are fixed to his visual axis. This is convolved with a response $S(\xi, \eta, \tau)$, which, one assumes, can be separated into a point spread function $U(\xi, \eta)$ and an impulse response $V(\tau)$, to give an output $C(x, y, t)$ on which detection, and perception, are more immediately based.

$$C(x, y, t) = \int_{-\infty}^{\infty}\int_{-\infty}^{\infty}\int_{-\infty}^{\infty} U(\xi, \eta)V(\tau) \cdot L(x - \xi, y - \eta, t - \tau)d\xi d\eta d\tau. \quad (3)$$

With subjective test results being necessarily as imprecise as they are the exact shapes for $U$ and $V$ are unimportant, so long as the space and time constants are of the right size [44]. Gaussian, inverse square, negative exponential, and other point spreads and impulse responses have been used [25], [33], [45], [46]. The constants decrease somewhat with adaptation luminance but in the range of interest in television, i.e., from, say, 1 to 300 cd/m², one can well assume a single pair of constants which, with exponential spread and impulse responses, would be 3.2′ for the radial space constant and 120 ms for the time constant [25].

Given a linear system, an obvious approach is to test it with sinusoidal inputs. This has also been done with the visual mechanism, showing it as having the resonant, or bandpass, characteristics already referred to. But much more was revealed, including at least part of the reason why a low-pass model suits many situations, when Robson [47] tested

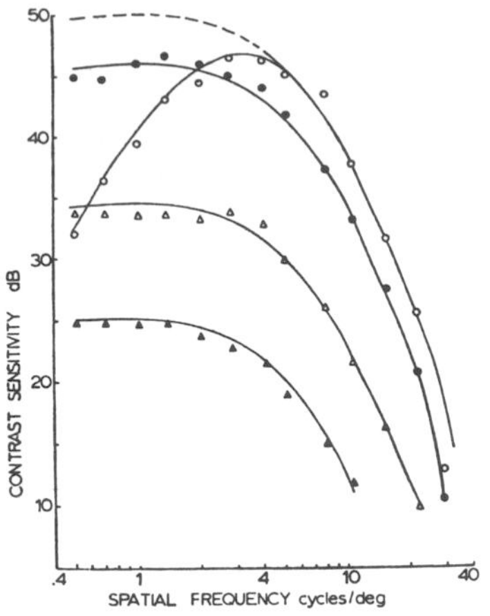


Fig. 3. Spatial frequency response curves measured by Robson [47] for different temporal frequencies. ○ 1 Hz, ● 6 Hz, △ 16 Hz, and ▲ 22 Hz. The broken line would apply when all curves were to be generated from a single low-pass curve by shifts on the vertical direction only.

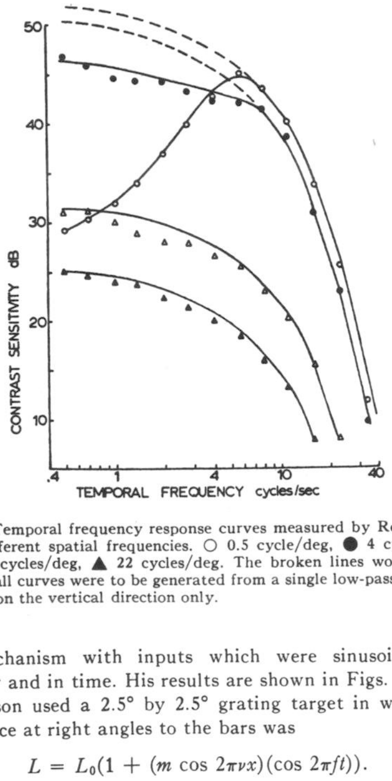


Fig. 4. Temporal frequency response curves measured by Robson [47] for different spatial frequencies. ○ 0.5 cycle/deg, ● 4 cycles/deg, △ 16 cycles/deg, ▲ 22 cycles/deg. The broken lines would apply when all curves were to be generated from a single low-pass curve by shifts on the vertical direction only.

the mechanism with inputs which were sinusoids both spatially and in time. His results are shown in Figs. 3 and 4.

Robson used a 2.5° by 2.5° grating target in which the luminance at right angles to the bars was

$$L = L_0(1 + (m \cos 2\pi\nu x)(\cos 2\pi f t)).$$

$L_0$ was kept constant at 20 cd/m$^2$ and the value of $m$ at subjective disappearance of bars was measured for different frequencies, $\nu$ and $f$. The inverse of that $m$ value was defined as the contrast sensitivity.

A reasonable assumption is that at threshold the modulation of the internal output $C(x, y, t)$ was always the same. Figs. 3 and 4 then represent measured cross sections in the frequency domain of the response $S(\xi, \eta, \tau)$. If this response were truly separable, as assumed in (3), then within either family the curves should differ from each other only by constant factors or, in the logarithmic plots, by constant displacements in the vertical direction. The actual curves drawn obey this restriction, except at very low frequencies where they would need to follow the dotted lines. Whenever the characteristics conform to the single shape, they are purely low-pass and it can be seen that this holds for the spatial frequency characteristics when the temporal frequency is some 6 Hz or larger, and for the temporal frequency characteristics when the spatial frequency is some 16 cycles/deg or larger. Below these limits the respective characteristics take on bandpass properties. It thus must depend on circumstances whether an experiment will reveal a low-pass or a bandpass response.

It is meaningful physiologically [45] to say that the low-frequency decline in sensitivity is caused by inhibition and to speak of the overall response as excitation suffering inhibitory reduction. In accordance with this the excitatory response is given by the low-pass curves in Figs. 3 and 4, including the broken-line sections at the very low frequencies.

One might combine excitation and inhibition by dividing one by the other in the frequency domain. However, a more convincing approach has been suggested by Sperling [45]. His arguments stem from physiological evidence and come to the specific conclusion that the internal output $C(x, y, t)$ be obtained by solving the differential equation

$$\frac{dC}{dt} + (a + bI)C = H \tag{4}$$

where $a$ and $b$ are constants, and $I(x, y, t)$ and $H(x, y, t)$ are inhibition and excitation, respectively. These two functions are to be determined by convolution integrals such as (3), but, of course, using new response functions $U_I$, $V_I$, $U_H$, and $V_H$ which would satisfy experimental findings such as Robson's and, at the same time, the restriction imposed by (4).

Combined with assumptions on detection, such as Blackwell's theory [33], calculated internal outputs can be used to predict visibilities, and, more commonly, comparative visibilities, of stimuli. However, with the present limited understanding of detection [34], predictions on visibility as such can only be made for stimuli which are presented on a uniform background. Predictions on comparative visibility of different stimuli presented in turn under identical conditions will, no doubt, be as good for nonuniform as for uniform backgrounds. But the reduction in visibility produced by background nonuniformities appears not to have been grasped as yet theoretically.

The reduction in visibility by background nonuniformity is a manifestation of masking, defined as the reduction in visibility of one stimulus by another [48]. Sometimes masking is confused with inhibition but the two are quite distinct. In fact, masking is severest where and when the effects of inhibition are the lowest, namely, at the edges of uniform luminance areas and at onsets of luminances. If anything, masking can be related to the total output $C(x, y, t)$ produced by the background.

The time course of masking has been investigated much more than its spatial variations [44], [48], [49]. A typical result for the time course of masking has been taken from Crawford [50] and is shown in Fig. 5.

Masking is of especial interest in television-signal quantization because it furnishes possibilities for varying the accuracy of representation, some of which already have been utilized. Limb [44] recognized that the differential quantizer with unequal quantum steps [51] relies on masking of errors by spatial transitions in luminance. The variation of visibility of a vertical line, one television element wide, as function of distance from a dark-to-light transition, measured by Limb [44], is shown in Fig. 6. Clearly, the variation of tolerance with distance from pulse center in the $K$-rating window (Fig. 2) is also based on this type of masking.

A somewhat different phenomenon but also probably due to masking, only this time by temporal changes and, therefore, of potential application in interframe coding, was found by Seyler and Budrikis [52], [53]. This was that a viewer is unable to notice initial bluriness of a new scene. In fact, at changeover the new scene can have a spatial resolution only one-tenth of normal but this will not be seen so long as full resolution is restored gradually within about half a second.

## VI. Prospects for Visual Fidelity Algorithms

Potentially one of the most rewarding areas to which predictions on visibility could be applied is the design of quantization procedures for television signals. Calculations based only on excitation have already proved useful in selecting dither waveforms [46]. Another example would be the design of a block vocabulary for block DPCM encoding [54] where, however, masking and inhibition would also need to be taken into account.

We may think of the computer routines which would perform such calculations as error evaluating meters, not unlike the weighted noise meter used in analog applications. Just as in the noise meter, errors would be attenuated selectively before being measured on, say, a time-average basis. Going by the evidence from psychophysics, the preferred measurement would be of the mean absolute, but not much would be altered if the mean square would be measured instead [46].

Often a debate on fidelity criteria tends to revolve around the sole issue of whether one should use the mean square, mean absolute, or the mean of some other function of error. But, from what we have seen, in visual communications a much more important consideration is the processing of errors, their filtering, and signal-dependent attenuation before measurement. We may also remark that suitability of a scale can depend as much on signal properties as on the ultimate receiver which it is intended to imitate. Thus the weighted noise meter for analog channels measures average power. But since the noise, which that meter is intended to measure, is Gaussian, it could measure, with equal effect, the average of any one from a very large class of nonlinear functions of deviation.

As yet the least quantitatively defined factor in visibility is, as we saw, the phenomenon of masking. For the rest, there are model constructs for which most parameter values could be deduced from already existing data. But, altogether, we already know enough that we may at least speculate on the form of a meter which would adequately assess the visibility of quantization noise. Fig. 7 is a block diagram for one designed to assess the errors produced by a video feedback quantizer.

The quantization error, produced by subtracting the reconstruction in the feedback quantizer from an equally

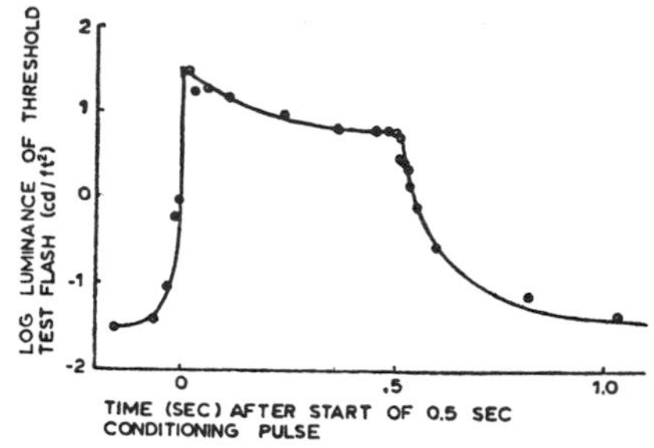


Fig. 5. Threshold luminance of brief flashes at different time instants with respect to a 0.5-s 10-cd/ft² conditioning light pulse on dark-adapted eye measured by Crawford [50].

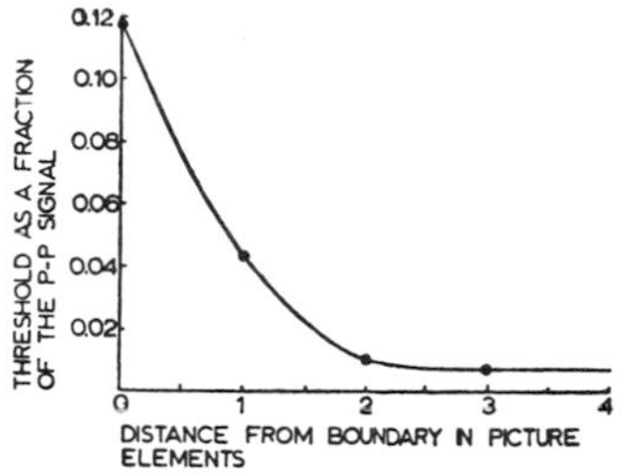


Fig. 6. Threshold of line next to light–dark boundary as a function of the separation between line and boundary, measured by Limb [44].

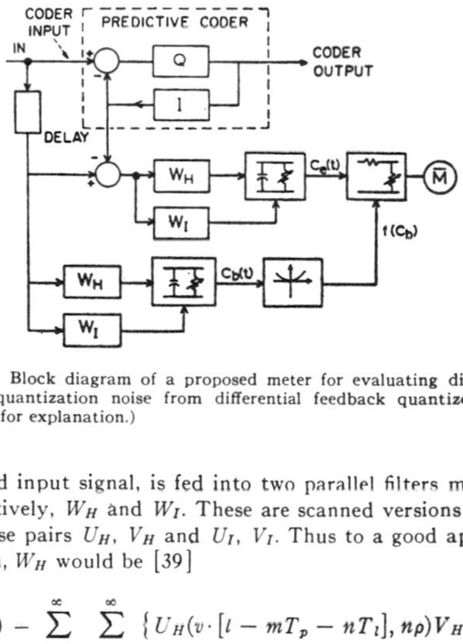


Fig. 7. Block diagram of a proposed meter for evaluating distortion by quantization noise from differential feedback quantizer. (See text for explanation.)

delayed input signal, is fed into two parallel filters marked, respectively, $W_H$ and $W_I$. These are scanned versions of the response pairs $U_H$, $V_H$ and $U_I$, $V_I$. Thus to a good approximation, $W_H$ would be [39]

$$W_H(t) = \sum_{m=0}^{\infty} \sum_{n=-\infty}^{\infty} \{U_H(v\cdot[t - mT_p - nT_l], n\rho)V_H(mT_p) + U_H(v\cdot[t - (m + 1/2)T_p - (n + 1/2)T_l], \cdot(n + 1/2)\rho)V_H((m + 1/2)T_p)\}$$

where $v$ is the speed of the spot on the screen, $T_p$ the frame period, $T_l$ the line period, and $\rho$ the distance between adjacent lines in a field. The expression accounts for interlace and relies on the fact that the point spread function $U_H$ is limited in its spatial extent.

The outputs of these filters are then combined in a network which obeys (4) and so give $C_e(t)$, the scanned version of $C(x, y, t)$ due to error. $C_e(t)$ is attenuated in a variable attenuator and then measured in a long time constant rectifying or power meter. The control signal for the attenuator is shown as derived from $C_b(t)$, the scanned version of $C(x, y, t)$ due to background. This is merely a tenative acceptance of the suggestion that masking could be related to the total internal output. But the function $f$, shown in the block schematic of Fig. 7, is not yet known.

In keeping with what one expects, the meter would be more severe on errors which are correlated from line to line and repeated from frame to frame than on those which are not. Also it would be more severe on errors which occur in empty places than those which occur near changes in luminance, both spatial and temporal. To be at all useful, it would have to sort, in correct order of subjective merit, at least all feedback quantizers. It would have to show, for instance, that addition of random or pseudorandom noise to the unquantized signal can improve the subjective performance of some quantizers [46], even if it increases the objective noise power.

The meter might be successful in sorting quantizers in a larger class. But it could not be expected to evaluate correctly all errors. For instance, it would not cope at all with such gross forms of error as picture shading, gamma changes, or geometrical distortion.

This point brings us to a final comment and that is on rate calculations for the video source. Such calculations presuppose, as we saw in Section III, a distortion measure which would be unrestricted as to the errors which it could assess. From what we have seen, we are still nowhere near such an unrestricted measure. Also, rate calculations are only manageable when the measure is a function only of $(\boldsymbol{x}-\boldsymbol{y})$ and only possible when the criterion value $D^*$ is specified. The measure for the video case certainly depends on $\boldsymbol{x}$ *and* $\boldsymbol{y}$, and the criterion value is not known. From this it does not seem reasonable that one could set any bound on how far down the source rate could actually be taken by encoding. The most that seems possible are soft bounds.

## VII. Conclusion

Fidelity assessment in visual communications has been reviewed and is seen as being of two kinds: implicit evaluation by subjective testing and explicit assessment by an indicating meter or by calculation. Subjective testing is accepted as the more binding form of evaluation, while explicit measures are seen as a very useful adjunct to routine operation and to the design of new, and particularly digital, systems.

Rate distortion theory has been reviewed in order to determine desirable properties of an explicit measure. It is seen that, ideally, the measure should not be restricted at all as to type of error that it would evaluate. Two practical evaluation procedures have been discussed, namely, measurement of additive random noise and rating of analog facilities by their response to testing waveforms. New light has been thrown on both procedures by comparing them with the evaluation which is envisaged in rate distortion theory.

It is recognized that visual distortion in systems of acceptable quality can largely be identified with visibility of subjectively small errors. For this reason a selected review has been made of psychophysics of vision, with emphasis on visual thresholds. The important factors are seen to be excitation, inhibition, and masking, each originating with the luminance distribution on the retina and modified by spatial and temporal filtering. Data have been sought out from the literature which go some way towards specifying these processes quantitatively. The largest gap in understanding is found to exist with regard to masking.

The outlook for effective practical evaluation of fidelity of television quantizers has been considered. Full evaluations are as yet impossible but seem very likely for the foreseeable future, although probably entailing considerable computational tasks. However, the outlook for an unrestricted distortion function to suit rate distortion theory is found to be less optimistic.

## Acknowledgment

The author wishes to thank both A. J. Seyler and J. O Limb for their help in pointing out current directions of thinking on visual fidelity. The author's awareness of psychophysics of vision was enhanced by participation in psychology seminars, organized by J. Ross and in part conducted by G. Sperling.

## References

[1] A. J. Seyler, "The coding of visual signals to reduce channel-capacity requirements," *Proc. Inst. Elec. Eng.*, vol. 109, pt. C, pp. 676–684.
[2] W. F. Schreiber, "Picture coding," *Proc. IEEE (Special Issue on Redundancy Reduction)*, vol. 55, pp. 320–330, Mar. 1967.
[3] J. O. Limb, "Source-receiver encoding of television signals," *Proc. IEEE (Special Issue on Redundancy Reduction)*, vol. 55, pp. 364–379, Mar. 1967.
[4] C. E. Shannon, "A mathematical theory of communication," *Bell Syst. Tech. J.*, vol. 27, pp. 646–656, 1948.
[5] R. G. Gallager, *Information Theory and Reliable Communication*. New York: Wiley, 1968, pp. 442–502.
[6] J. M. Barstow and H. N. Christopher, "The measurement of random monochrome video interference," *AIEE Trans. (Commun. Electron.)*, vol. 72, pp. 735–741, Jan. 1954.
[7] Y. Yamaguchi, "The visibility of monochrome television random interferences and its measurement," *NHK Tech. Mono.* 11 (Japan Broadcasting Corp.), Feb. 1968.
[8] N. W. Lewis, "Waveform responses of television links," *Proc. Inst. Elec. Engr.*, vol. 101, pt. III, pp. 258–270, July 1954.
[9] A. J. Seyler, "Visual communication and psychophysics of vision," *Proc. IRE* (Australia), vol. 23, pp. 291–304, Mar. 1962.
[10] D. G. Fink, *Television Engineering Handbook*. New York: McGraw-Hill, 1957, ch. 2.
[11] P. Mertz, A. D. Fowler, and H. N. Christopher, "Quality rating of television images," *Proc. IRE*, vol. 38, pp. 1269–1283, Nov. 1950.
[12] G. L. Fredendall and W. L. Behrend, "Picture quality—Procedure for evaluating subjective effects of interference," *Proc. IRE*, vol. 48, pp. 1030–1034, June 1960. (See also other papers in same special issue on TASO.)
[13] R. D. Prosser, J. W. Allnatt, and N. W. Lewis, "Quality grading ot imparied television pictures," *Proc. Inst. Elec. Eng.*, vol. 111, pp. 491–502, Mar. 1964.
[14] C. E. Shannon, "Coding theorems for a discrete source with a fidelity criterion," in *Information and Decision Processes*, R. E. Machol, Ed. New York: McGraw-Hill, 1960, pp. 93–126.
[15] J. M. Wozencraft and I. M. Jacobs, *Principles of Communication Engineering*. New York: Wiley, 1965, p. 294.
[16] Members of the Technical Staff, Bell Telephone Laboratories, *Transmission Systems for Communications*, 3rd ed., 1965, pp. 372–395.
[17] *CCIR Study Group XI* Rep. 84 (Warsaw Green Book), vol. 1, pp. 419–439, Sept. 1956.
[18] R. D. A. Maurice, M. Gilbert, G. F. Newell, and J. G. Spencer, "The visibility of noise in television," in *BBC Engineering Monograph 3*, Oct. 1955.
[19] R. C. Brainard, "Low-resolution TV: Subjective effects of noise added to a signal," *Bell Syst. Tech. J.*, vol. 46, pp. 233–260, Jan. 1967.
[20] G. F. Newell and W. K. E. Geddes, "Visibility of small luminance perturbations in television displays," *Proc. Inst. Elec. Eng.*, vol. 110, pp. 1979–1984, Nov. 1963.
[21] J. Müller and E. Demus, "Ermittlung eines Rauschbewertungsfilters für das Fernsehen," *Nachrichtentech. Z.*, vol. 12, pp. 181–186, Apr. 1959.

[22] R. Fatechand, "Theoretical and experimental characteristics of random noise in TV," *J. Brit. IRE*, vol. 19, pp. 335–344, June 1959.

[23] T. S. Huang, "The subjective effect of two-dimensional pictorial noise," *IEEE Trans. Inform. Theory*, vol. IT-11, pp. 43–53, Jan. 1965.

[24] CCIR, Japan, "Weighting curves for random monochrome noise against noise frequency and video amplitude," in *CCIR Doc. 41*, Los Angeles, Calif., Jan. 1959.

[25] Z. L. Budrikis, "Visual thresholds and the visibility of random noise in TV," *Proc. IRE* (Australia), vol. 22, pp. 751–759, Dec. 1961.

[26] E. A. Guillemin, *Synthesis of Passive Networks*. New York: Wiley, 1957, p. 294.

[27] L. E. Franks, "A model for the random video process," *Bell Syst. Tech. J.*, vol. 45, pp. 609–630, Apr. 1966.

[28] Y. W. Lee, *Statistical Theory of Communication*. New York: Wiley, 1960, p. 209.

[29] J. Müller, "Anforderungen und Messungen an Fernseh-Weitverbindungen," *Nachrichtertech. Z.*, vol. 13, pp. 327–334, July 1960.

[30] A. J. Seyler and J. B. Potter, "Waveform testing of television transmission facilities," *Proc. IRE* (Australia), vol. 21, pp. 470–478, July 1960.

[31] W. E. Thomson, "The synthesis of a network to have a sine-squared impulse response," *Proc. Inst. Elec. Eng.*, vol. 99, pt. III, pp. 373–376, Nov. 1952.

[32] H. R. Blackwell, "Contrast threshold of the human eye," *J. Opt. Soc. Amer.*, vol. 36, pp. 624–643, 1946.

[33] H. R. Blackwell, "Neural theories of simple visual discrimination," *J. Opt. Soc. Amer.*, vol. 53, pp. 129–159, Jan. 1963.

[34] *Signal Detection and Recognition by Human Observers: Contemporary Readings*, J. A. Swets, Ed. New York: Wiley, 1964.

[35] G. S. Brindley, *Physiology of the Retina and Visual Pathway*. London, England: Arnold, 1960, p. 144 ff.

[36] J. C. Stevens and S. S. Stevens, "Brightness function: Effects of adaptation," *J. Opt. Soc. Amer.*, vol. 53, pp. 375–385, Mar. 1963.

[37] P. Moon and D. E. Spencer, "The visual effect of nonuniform surrounds," *J. Opt. Soc. Amer.*, vol. 35, pp. 233–248, Mar. 1945.

[38] D. H. Kelly, "Frequency doubling in visual responses," *J. Opt. Soc. Amer.*, vol. 56, pp. 1628–1633, Nov. 1966.

[39] Z. L. Budrikis, "Visual smoothing with application to television," Ph.D. dissertation, University of Western Australia, Nedlands, Australia, 1969.

[40] O. H. Schade, "Optical and photoelectric analog of the eye," *J. Opt. Soc. Amer.*, vol. 46, pp. 721–739, Sept. 1956.

[41] F. W. Campbell and J. G. Robson, "Application of Fourier analysis to the visibility of gratings," *J. Physiol.* (London), vol. 197, pp. 551–566, 1968.

[42] H. deLange, "Research into the dynamic nature of the human fovea-cortex systems with intermittent and modulated light," *J. Opt. Soc. Amer.*, vol. 48, pp. 777–798, 1958.

[43] D. H. Kelly, "Visual responses to time-dependent stimuli," *J. Opt. Soc. Amer.*, vol. 51, pp. 422–429, Apr. 1961.

[44] J. O. Limb, "Vision oriented coding of visual signals," Ph.D. dissertation, University of Western Australia, Nedlands, Australia, 1966.

[45] G. Sperling, "Model of visual adaptation and contrast detection," *Perception Psychophys.*, vol. 8, pp. 143–157, March 1970.

[46] J. O. Limb, "Design of dither waveforms for quantized visual signals," *Bell Syst. Tech. J.*, vol. 48, pp. 2555–2582, Sept. 1969.

[47] J. G. Robson, "Spatial and temporal contrast—Sensitivity functions of the visual system," *J. Opt. Soc. Amer.*, vol. 56, pp. 1141–1142, Aug. 1966.

[48] G. Sperling, "Temporal and spatial masking, 1. Masking by impulse flashes," *J. Opt. Soc. Amer.*, vol. 55, pp. 541–559, May 1965.

[49] H. D. Baker, "Initial stages of dark and light adaptation," *J. Opt. Soc. Amer.*, vol. 53, pp. 98–103, Jan. 1963.

[50] B. H. Crawford, "Visual adaptation in relation to brief conditioning stimuli," *Proc. Roy. Soc.* (London), vol. 134B, pp. 283–302, 1947.

[51] J. O. Limb and F. W. Mounts, "Digital differential quantizer for television," *Bell Syst. Tech. J.*, vol. 48, pp. 2583–2599, Sept. 1969.

[52] A. J. Seyler and Z. L. Budrikis, "Measurements of temporal adaptation to detail vision," *Nature*, vol. 184, pp. 1215–1217, 1959.

[53] A. J. Seyler and Z. L. Budrikis, "Detail perception after scene changes in television image presentations," *IEEE Trans. Inform. Theory*, vol. IT-11, pp. 31–43, Jan. 1965.

[54] J. L. Hullett and Z. L. Budrikis, "Block DPCM encoding of TV phone picture signals," to be published.

# Part IV
# QUANTIZATION

# Editors' Comments on Papers 19 Through 25



Quantization is both the oldest and the simplest form of data compression; it is by far the most popular means of converting analog signals to digital format. It is a special case of block techniques (block length 1) and nonblock techniques (constraint length 1) and is considered separately because of its importance. Given a real alphabet $A$, a (one-dimensional) quantizer consists of a collection of levels or representative values $\hat{A} = \{a_1, \ldots, a_N\}, a_i \in A$, and a set of crossover values $-\infty = r_1 < a_1 \leq r_2 < a_2 \leq r_3 \ldots a_{N-1} \leq r_N < a_N < r_{N+1} = \infty$. The quantizer $q(x)$ maps $x \in A$ into the level $a_j$ if $x \in (r_j, r_{j+1}]$. The quantizer is the source encoder and the decoder is the identity transformation if we consider only the entropy-compression aspect of source coding.

The literature on quantization considers primarily two OPTA functions for quantizers. Define the average distortion of a quantizer $q$ on a source $\{X_n\}$ by

$$\rho_X(q) = E\rho(X, q(X)),$$

where the expectation is over the source probabilities. Define $Q(N)$ as the class of all quantizers with $N$ levels, and define

$$\delta_X{}^*(N) = \inf_{q \in Q(N)} \rho_X(q)$$

as the OPTA over all quantizers having $N$ levels. Define $Q(R)$ as the class of all quantizers such that, when used on the source $X$, the quantized source $\{\hat{X}_n\}$, where $\hat{X}_n = q(X_n)$, has entropy less than $R$. Define the entropy-constrained OPTA as

$$\delta_X(R) = \inf_{q \in Q(R)} \rho_X(q).$$

The two OPTA simply put different constraints on the allowable quantizers, that is, define "compression" in different ways. The fixed-level OPTA $\delta_X{}^*(N)$ is the most relevant quantity when further noiseless coding is not done, and $\delta_X(R)$ is more relevant when noiseless coding is to follow quantization. In addition, $\delta_X(R)$ provides easy comparison with the OPTA over all rate $R$ source codes; that is, since $H(\hat{X}) \leqslant \log N$, we have, for fixed $R$, that

$$\delta_X{}^*(2^R) \geqslant \delta_X(R) \geqslant D_X(R)$$

or

$$\delta_X{}^*(N) \geqslant \delta_X(\log N) \geqslant D_X(\log N),$$

where $D_X(R)$ is the distortion-rate function.

In Paper 19, Panter and Dite consider quantizing a finite interval $(-V, V)$ of the real line with $\rho(z, y) = (z - y)^2$, a squared-error distortion measure. Using an approximation valid for "smooth" source probability densities, they derive conditions on $\{a_i\}$ and $\{r_i\}$ to achieve $\delta_X{}^*(N)$. For example, they show that, for optimal performance, crossover levels should be midway between output levels; that is, $r_k = (a_k + a_{k+1})/2$.

Widrow (Paper 20) models the effects of uniform quantization as that of an independent additive noise, and uses the model to evaluate the squared-error performance of sampling and uniform quantizing of continuous-time random processes. Max (Paper 21) uses differential calculus to derive the relations between $\{a_i\}$ and $\{r_i\}$ for $\delta_X{}^*(N)$ for several distortion measures $\rho$. He demonstrates that optimal performance requires $r_k = (a_k + a_{k+1})/2$ for a variety of $\rho$, and uses numerical techniques to determine the detailed relations of $\{a_i\}$ and $\{r_i\}$ for Gaussian processes and squared-error distortion measure. Much of Max's work was independently derived by S. P. Lloyd in an unpublished work.

An efficient computer algorithm utilizing dynamic programming techniques to find optimal $\{a_i\}$ and $\{r_i\}$ for quite general distortion measures may be found in Bruce ["On the Optimum Quantization of Stationary Signals," *1964 IEEE Intern. Conv. Record, Part 1,* 118–124 (1964)].

An alternative to the numerical evaluations of Max, Lloyd, and Bruce of the properties of optimum (fixed-level) quantizers is the use of approximations, as in Paper 19, to obtain slightly suboptimal quantizers. In Paper 22, Roe presents approximations for the more general $\nu^{\text{th}}$ law distortion measure $\rho(z, y) = (z - y)^\nu$. Wood (Paper 23) also uses approximations, but is the first to also consider the output entropy. He shows that for moderately large $N$ the uniform quantizer $q$ yielding $\rho_X(q) = \delta_X{}^*(N)$ has smaller output entropy than the optimal nonuniform $N$-level quantizer. If quantization is to be followed by buffering and noiseless coding, output entropy is more important than alphabet size, and simple uniform quantization becomes more appropriate than fixed-level OPTA. This motivated Wood to define the constrained-entropy OPTA $\delta_X(C)$ for a noiseless channel as being the more appropriate OPTA in such systems. Wood was the first to define $\delta_X(R)$ and the first to note that, in the Gaussian MSE case, the uniform quantizer very nearly yields the fixed-rate OPTA.

Gish and Pierce (Paper 24) obtain quite general results along Wood's line; they show that uniform quantization nearly yields $\delta_X(R)$ and compares the quantizer fixed-rate OPTA with the appropriate rate-distortion functions. They also consider the performance of block ($n$-dimensional) quantizers.

In Paper 25, Kellog considers overall PCM systems rather than just the quantizer and shows that, with nearly optimal filters and quantizers, performance quite near the rate-distortion OPTA is possible. Kellog focused on Gaussian sources and squared-error distortion, and used primarily numerical techniques.

# 19



Reprinted from *Proc. IRE,* **39,** 44–48 (Jan. 1951)

# Quantization Distortion in Pulse-Count Modulation with Nonuniform Spacing of Levels*

P. F. PANTER†, SENIOR MEMBER, IRE, AND W. DITE†

***Summary***—**It is shown that the distortion introduced in a pulse-count-modulation system due to quantization can be minimized by nonuniform spacing of levels. Equations are derived for an arrangement of nonuniform level spacing that produces minimum distortion. It is also shown that minimum distortion is significantly less than distortion resulting from uniform quantization when the crest factor of the signal is greater than four.**

## I. Introduction

It has been shown in a previous paper[1] that the process of quantization in a pulse-count-modulation system introduces distortion. In that paper, equations were derived for the special case of equal-level spacing. This paper studies the effect of non-uniform-level spacing with the view of obtaining minimum distortion.

It is shown that by taking the statistical properties of the signal into consideration, the distortion can be minimized by a proper level distribution, which is a function of the probability density of the signal. In practice, nonuniform quantization is realized by compression followed by uniform quantization. The most common form of compression is the so-called logarithmic one, where the levels are crowded near the origin and spaced farther apart near the peaks. It is shown that with logarithmic compression the distortion is largely independent of the statistical properties of the signal.

## II. Distortion for Nonuniform Spacing

Consider a quantized signal $y(t)$ as shown in Fig. 1. Let the levels be symmetrically disposed about zero voltage level, but otherwise placed in an arbitrary manner in the interval $(-V, V)$. The problem of minimizing the distortion of the quantized signal by properly spacing the levels will be considered now. Denote the levels by $y_{-n}, y_{-n+1}, \cdots, y_0, y_1, \cdots y_{n-1}, y_n$, where $y_k = -y_{-k}$ and $y_0 = 0$. Further, assume that a signal value of $y$ which satisfies

$$y_{k-1/2} < y < y_{k+1/2} \qquad (1)$$

is transmitted as level $y_k$. The $y$'s with fractional subscripts are the crossover values.

The measure of distortion that is adopted is the mean-square-distortion voltage defined as

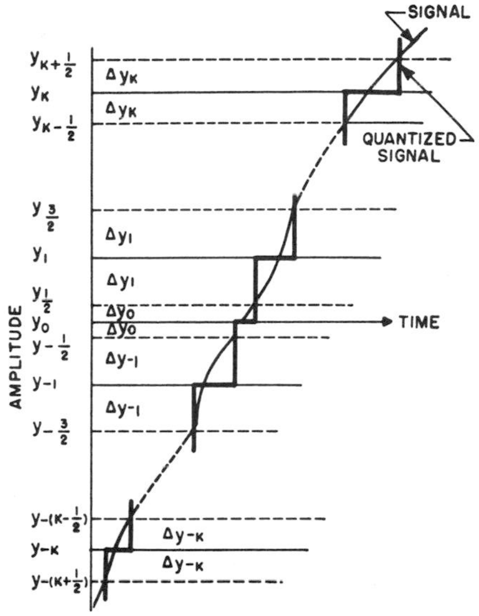


Fig. 1—Nonuniform quantization.

$$\sigma_k = \int_{y_{k-1/2}}^{y_{k+1/2}} (y - y_k)^2 P(y) dy, \qquad (2)$$

where $\sigma_k$ is the distortion in the $k$th level. The error of the transmitted signal is $(y - y_k)$ and $P(y)$ the probability density of the signal $y$.

First, derive a relation between the various $y$'s in (2) so that $\sigma_k$ in the $k$th level is a minimum.

Suppose that the levels are so close that $P(y)$ may be considered as nearly constant over the region of integration and equal to $P(y_{av})$
where

$$y_{av} = \frac{y_{k+1/2} + y_{k-1/2}}{2};$$

$$\sigma_k = \frac{P(y_{av})}{3}\left[(y_{k+1/2} - y_k)^3 + (y_k - y_{k-1/2})^3\right]. \qquad (3)$$

Differentiating $\sigma_k$ with respect to $y_k$ gives

$$\frac{d\sigma_k}{dy_k} = P(y_{av})\left[-(y_{k+1/2} - y_k)^2 + (y_k - y_{k-1/2})^2\right] = 0$$

or

$$y_k = \frac{y_{k+1/2} + y_{k-1/2}}{2} = y_{av}. \qquad (4)$$

* Decimal classification: R148.6. Original manuscript received by the Institute, June 16, 1949; revised manuscript received, December 22, 1949. Presented, 1949 IRE National Convention, March 7, 1949, New York, N. Y. The work described in this paper was done under the sponsorship of the Signal Corps Engineering Laboratories, Fort Monmouth, N. J.

† Federal Telecommunication Laboratories, Inc., Nutley, N. J.

[1] A. G. Clavier, P. F. Panter, and D. D. Grieg, "PCM distortion analysis," *Elec. Eng.*, vol. 66, pp. 1110–1122; November, 1947.

Thus, the condition for making $\sigma_k$ a minimum is that $y_k$ lie half-way between $y_{k+1/2}$ and $y_{k-1/2}$.

$$\left.\begin{aligned} y_{k+1/2} &= y_k + \Delta y_k, \\ y_{k-1/2} &= y_k - \Delta y_k. \end{aligned}\right\} \tag{5}$$

Substituting these values in (3), it follows

$$\sigma_k = \frac{2}{3} P(y_k)\Delta y_k^3. \tag{6}$$

The total mean-square-distortion voltage is found by summing over all levels, giving

$$\sigma_d = \frac{2}{3} \sum_{-n}^{n} P(y_k)\Delta y_k^3. \tag{7}$$

Now, it will be proved that the mean-square-distortion $\sigma_d$ is a minimum when $\sigma_k$ is constant, independent of the $k$th level.

By the definition of an integral, we may write

$$2\sum_{-n}^{n} P^{1/3}(y_k)\Delta y_k = \int_{-V}^{V} P^{1/3}(y)dy = 2K, \tag{8}$$

where $K$ is a constant, since the integral is a function of only its limits. Let $\mu_k = P^{1/3}(y_k)\Delta y_k$; then (7) and (8) become, respectively,

$$\sigma_d = \frac{2}{3} \sum_{-n}^{n} \mu_k^3, \tag{9}$$

and

$$K = \sum_{-n}^{n} \mu_k. \tag{10}$$

The problem is now reduced to minimizing the sum of cubes subject to the condition that the sum of the variables is a constant.

From Lagrange's method of undetermined multipliers, it follows that (9) is a minimum when

$$\mu_{-n} = \mu_{-n+1} = \cdots = \mu_{n-1} = \mu_n = \frac{K}{2\mu + 1}. \tag{11}$$

From this, it follows

$$P^{1/3}(y_k)\Delta y_k = \frac{K}{2n+1} \tag{12}$$

or

$$\sigma_k = \frac{2}{3} \frac{K^3}{(2n+1)^3}.$$

The total minimum distortion power

$$\sigma_m = \frac{2}{3} \frac{K^3}{(2n+1)^2}$$
$$= \frac{1}{12(2n+1)^2}\left(\int_{-V}^{V} P^{1/3}(y)dy\right)^3. \tag{13}$$

Since $P(y)$ is an even function and letting $N = 2n+1$ be the total number of steps,

$$\sigma_m = \frac{2}{3N^2}\left(\int_0^V P^{1/3}(y)dy\right)^3. \tag{14}$$

The ratio of the mean-square-distortion voltage to the mean-square-signal voltage is

$$D_m^2 = \frac{\sigma_m}{\sigma} = \frac{2}{3N^2} \frac{\left[\int_0^V P^{1/3}(y)dy\right]^3}{\int_0^V y^2 P(y)dy}, \tag{15}$$

Equation (15) gives the minimum distortion resulting with optimum level spacing.[2]

An approximate method of obtaining levels may be obtained by writing (where $k$ is positive)

$$\begin{aligned} y_k &= \Delta y_0 + 2\Delta y_1 + \cdots + 2\Delta y_{k-1} + \Delta y_k \\ &= \frac{K}{N}\left[\frac{1}{P^{1/3}(y_0)} + \frac{2}{P^{1/3}(y_1)} + \cdots \right. \\ &\qquad \left. + \frac{2}{P^{1/3}(y_{k-1})} + \frac{1}{P(y_k)}\right] \\ &= \frac{K}{2V}\left[\frac{1}{P^{1/3}(y_0)} + \frac{2}{P^{1/3}(y_1)} + \cdots \right. \\ &\qquad \left. + \frac{2}{P^{1/3}(y_{k-1})} + \frac{1}{P(y_k)}\right]\frac{2V}{N}. \end{aligned} \tag{16}$$

The series may be approximated by an integral

$$y = A\int_0^z \frac{1}{P^{1/3}(z)} dz, \tag{17}$$

where we have changed the variable on the right to $z$ to avoid confusion. $A$ is a constant of proportionality so chosen that when $z = V$; $y = V$. Hence

$$y = V \frac{\int_0^z \frac{1}{P^{1/3}(z)} dz}{\int_0^V \frac{1}{P^{1/3}(z)} dz}. \tag{18}$$

By letting $z$ vary from 0 to $V$, $y$ will describe a curve as shown in Fig. 2. As $z$ takes on the values of $z_0 = 0$, $z_1 = 2V/N \cdots z_k = 2kV/N \cdots z_n = 2nV/N$, we get the point $y_0 = 0, y_1 \cdots y_k \cdots y_n$.

While approximate, this derivation has the advantage that the levels are obtained quickly. The relation (12) may be used to make spot checks since

$$\begin{aligned} y_{k+1} &= y_k + \Delta y_k + \Delta y_{k+1} \\ &= y_k + \frac{K}{N}\left(\frac{1}{P^{1/3}(y_k)} + \frac{1}{P^{1/3}(y_{k+1})}\right). \end{aligned} \tag{19}$$

[2] This equation was first derived by P. R. Aigrain using a slightly different method.

From Fig. 2, it may be seen that the uniform spacing along the $z$ axis is transformed into a nonuniform spacing along the $y$ axis. The compressed output $z$ is then subjected to uniform quantization. To recapitulate, nonuniform spacing of levels may be realized by passing the signal through a compressor with a given characteristic and applying uniform quantization to its output. Obviously, this also implies that a corresponding expansion is incorporated in the receiver.

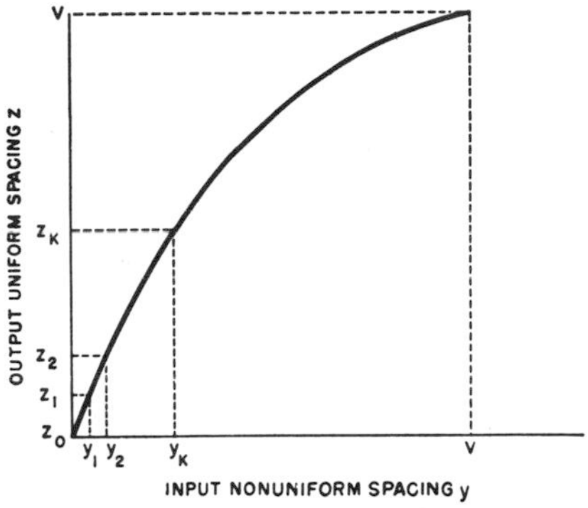


Fig. 2—Compression curve for nonuniform-level spacing.

$$y_k = \Delta y_0 + 2\Delta y_1 + \cdots + 2\Delta y_{k-1} + \Delta y_k$$

$$= \frac{K}{2V}\left[\frac{1}{P^{1/3}(y_0)} + \frac{2}{P^{1/3}(y_1)} + \cdots + \frac{2}{P^{1/3}(y_{k-1})} + \frac{1}{P(y_k)}\right]\frac{2V}{N},$$

$$\therefore\ y \doteq A\int_0^z \frac{1}{P^{1/3}(z)}\,dz$$

$$= \frac{\int_0^z \frac{1}{P^{1/3}(z)}\,dz}{\int_0^V \frac{1}{P^{1/3}(z)}\,dz},$$

where

$z = V$ and $y = V$.

## III. Logarithmic Compression

A compression curve that is relatively easy to obtain and has been used in practice is the so-called logarithmic compression curve. The positive half of the compression characteristic is given by

$$v_2 = k \log\left(1 + \frac{\mu v_1}{V}\right), \tag{20}$$

where

- $\mu$ = compression parameter
- $v_1$ = input voltage
- $v_2$ = output voltage
- $V$ = maximum input voltage
- $k$ = an undetermined constant.

To find $k$, let $v_2 = V$ when $v_1 = V$, so that the maximum values of the input and compressed waves are equal. This gives

$$v_2 = \frac{V}{\log(1+\mu)}\log\left(1 + \frac{\mu v_1}{V}\right). \tag{21}$$

The parameter $\mu$ controls the degree of compression and may be chosen so that large changes in the input produce relatively small changes in the output. As shown in Fig. 3 for $\mu = 1{,}000$, a 60-db change in the input will cause only a 20-db change in the output. When $\mu$ is large, the levels are crowded about zero, $\mu = 0$ corresponds to uniform spacing.

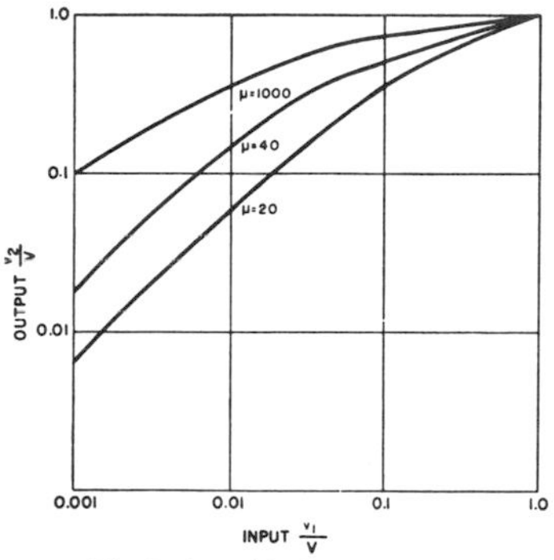


Fig. 3—Logarithmic compression.

$$v_2 = \frac{V}{\log(1+\mu)}\log\left(1 + \frac{\mu v_1}{V}\right).$$

Differentiating, (21) yields

$$dv_2 = \frac{\mu}{\log(1+\mu)}\,\frac{V}{V + \mu v_1}\,dv_1. \tag{22}$$

As the compressed signal is divided into $N$ uniformly spaced levels, $\Delta v_2 = 2V/N$. This gives

$$\Delta v_1 = \frac{2\log(1+\mu)}{\mu N}(V + \mu v_1). \tag{23}$$

In the notation of the previous section, $\Delta y_k \doteq \Delta v_1/2$ so that

$$\Delta y_k = \frac{\log(1+\mu)}{\mu N}(V + \mu y_k) = \alpha(V + \mu y_k), \tag{24}$$

where

$$\alpha = \frac{\log(1+\mu)}{\mu N}. \tag{25}$$

From (23), it follows that the ratio of the largest to the smallest level is given approximately by

$$\frac{\Delta y_n}{\Delta y_0} \doteq 1 + \mu. \tag{26}$$

It is interesting to note that

$$\frac{(dv_2/dv_1)_{v_1=0}}{(dv_2/dv_1)_{v_1=V}} \text{ is also equal to } 1 + \mu.$$

This ratio, when expressed in decibels, is often referred to as the compression of the system.

The distortion power is given approximately by (7) when the number of levels is large

$$\sigma_d = \frac{2}{3}\sum_{-n}^{n} P(y_k)\Delta y_k^3$$
$$= \frac{2\alpha^2}{3}\sum_{-n}^{n} (V + \mu y_k)^2 P(y_k)\Delta y_k$$
$$= \frac{2\alpha^2}{3}\sum_{-n}^{n} [V^2P(y_k) + 2V\mu y_k P(y_k) + \mu^2 y_k^2 P(y_k)]\Delta y_k. \quad (27)$$

Since $P(y_k)$ is an even function and $y_k = -y_k$, the second term in the summation vanishes. Thus,

$$\sigma_d = \frac{2\alpha^2}{3}\sum_{-n}^{n} [V^2P(y_k) + \mu^2 y_k^2 P(y_k)]\Delta y_k.$$

Converting this into an integral with $2\Delta y_k = dy$ and using (41) and (46) of the Appendix yields

$$\sigma_d = \frac{\alpha^2V^2}{3}\int_{-V}^{V} P(y)dy + \frac{\alpha^2\mu^2}{3}\int_{-V}^{V} y^2P(y)dy$$
$$= \frac{\alpha^2V^2}{3} + \frac{\alpha^2\mu^2\sigma}{3}, \quad (28)$$

where $\sigma$ is the mean-square-voltage and $V$ is the peak value of the signal. Hence, the distortion is given by

$$D = \left(\frac{\sigma_d}{\sigma}\right)^{1/2} = \frac{\log(1+\mu)}{3^{1/2}\mu N}(C^2 + \mu^2)^{1/2}, \quad (29)$$

when $C$ is the ratio of peak to root-mean-square value of signal. For a given $C$, the distortion is a function of $\mu$ only and will be a minimum for optimum $\mu$ as shown in Fig. 4.

When $\mu$ is large compared to $C$, this becomes

$$D = \frac{\log(1+\mu)}{3^{1/2}N}. \quad (30)$$

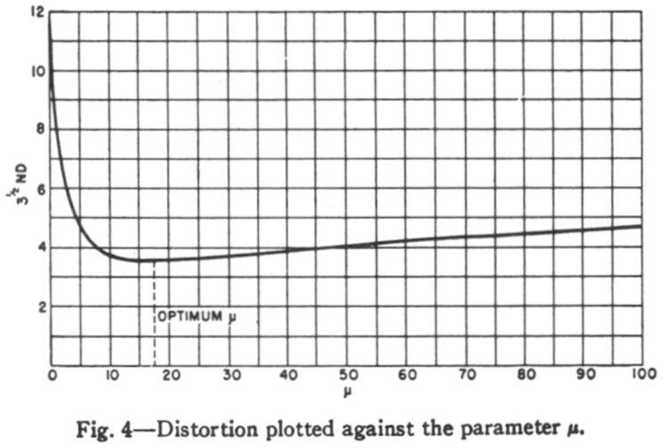


**Fig. 4—Distortion plotted against the parameter $\mu$.**

$$C = 12 \quad \text{and} \quad 3^{1/2}ND = \log(1+\mu)\left(1 + \frac{C^2}{\mu^2}\right)^{1/2}$$

Hence, when $\mu$ is large, the distortion is largely independent of the signal.

The distortion for uniform quantization may be obtained by letting $\mu$ become zero in (29).

$$D = C/3^{1/2}N. \quad (31)$$

For a sine wave,

$$C = 2^{1/2}$$

and

$$D = \frac{2^{1/2}}{3^{1/2}N} = \frac{2}{6^{1/2}N}.$$

When a signal is uniformly quantized, the distortion depends on the ratio of the peak to the root-mean-square value. This is illustrated in curve 1 of Fig. 5; curve 2 gives the minimum distortion for optimum logarithmic compression when the compression parameter $\mu$ is selected by curve 3.

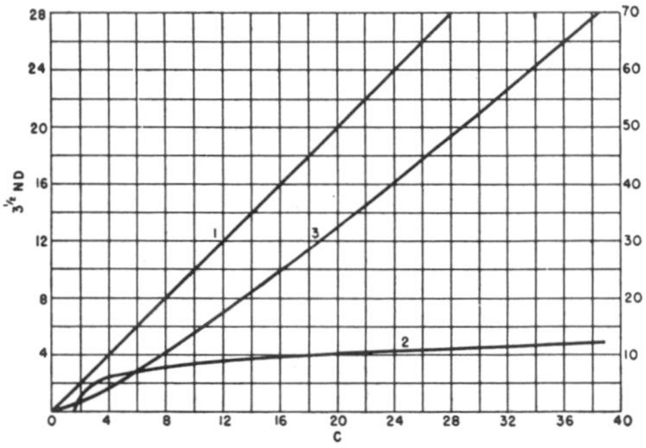


Fig. 5—Distortion characteristics. Curve 1 is for uniform quantization $3^{1/2}ND = C$. Curve 2 is for optimum logarithmic compression.

$$3^{1/2}ND = \log(1+\mu)\left(1 + \frac{C^2}{\mu^2}\right)^{1/2}.$$

Curve 3 is for the case where

$$C = \left[\frac{\mu^2}{\frac{1+\mu}{\mu}\log(1+\mu) - 1}\right]^{1/2}.$$

## IV. Application to Specific Signals

To illustrate the various points involved, let the preceding results be applied to the class of signals specified by the probability density given by

$$P(y) = \frac{1}{(3+2\lambda)^{1/2}\sigma^{1/2}\beta(1/2, \lambda+1)}\left(1 - \frac{y^2}{(3+2\lambda)\sigma}\right)^{\lambda}, \quad (32)$$

which is discussed in the Appendix. Here $\lambda$ is a parameter that determines the ratio of the peak value to the root-mean-square value. For $-1 < \lambda < 0$, the signal is relatively flat, while for $0<\lambda<\infty$, the signal has sharp peaks. When $\lambda=0$, all values are equally probable. If we let

$$A = \frac{1}{\sigma^{1/2}(3+2\lambda)^{1/2}\beta(1/2, \lambda+1)},$$

$$a = \sigma^{1/2}(\beta+2\lambda)^{1/2},$$

we find that the minimum distortion is given by

$$D_m^2(\lambda) = \frac{2A}{3N^2\sigma}\left[\int_0^a \left(\frac{1-y^2}{a^2}\right)^{\lambda/3} dy\right]^3$$

$$= \frac{Aa^3}{12N^2\sigma}\left[B\left(1/2, 1+\frac{\lambda}{3}\right)\right]^3$$

$$= \frac{2\lambda+3}{12N^2}\,\frac{B^3(1/2, 1+\lambda/3)}{B(1/2, 1+\lambda)}. \qquad (33)$$

In this case

$$C = (2\lambda+3)^{1/2}. \qquad (34)$$

The distortion for uniform-level spacing is from (31)

$$D = \frac{1}{3^{1/2}N}(3+2\lambda)^{1/2}. \qquad (35)$$

The quantity $ND$ is plotted versus $C$ in Fig. 6. It is seen that for small values of $C$, there is little advantage in using the minimum spacing. It is not until the crest factor is above 6 that the difference between the two distortion figures is 6 db. The distortion for optimum spacing attains a final value of about $1.65/N$. Thus, the chief advantage of the optimum spacing occurs when the crest factor of the signal is high.

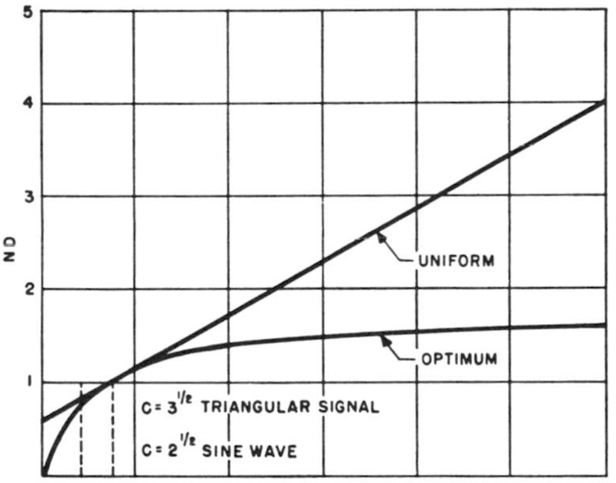


Fig. 6—Distortion plotted against crest factor for the Pearson distribution.

## V. Appendix, Statistical Properties of the Signal

### Pearson Distribution

The probability density given by

$$P(y) = \frac{1}{(3+2\lambda)^{1/2}\sigma^{1/2}B(1/2, \lambda+1)}\left(1-\frac{y^2}{(3+2\lambda)\sigma}\right)^{\lambda} \qquad (36)$$

is known as the Pearson distribution. In (36), $\sigma$ is power and $\lambda$ is a parameter satisfying $-1<\lambda<\infty$. Further, the variable $y$ is restricted to the interval

$$-[(3+2\lambda)\sigma]^{1/2} \leqq y \leqq +[(3+2\lambda)\sigma]^{1/2}.$$

Finally, $B(m, n)$ is the beta function.

For special values of $\lambda$, $P(y)$ reduces to simple forms. We have for $\lambda=0$

$$P(y) = \frac{1}{2(3\sigma)^{1/2}}, \qquad -(3\sigma)^{1/2} < y < (3\sigma)^{1/2},$$

which is a rectangular distribution with a peak-to-peak amplitude of $2\,(3\sigma)^{1/2}$. The case $\lambda=-1/2$ reduces to the distribution function of a sine wave whose maximum value is $A=(2\sigma)^{1/2}$. If $\lambda=-1$, we find that

$$P(y) = \infty$$

when $y=\pm\sigma^{1/2}$,

$$P(y) = 0$$

elsewhere.

The distribution consists of impulses at $y=\pm\sigma^{1/2}$ of strength 1/2; the signal is a square wave. When $\lambda\rightarrow\infty$, the probability density reduces to the normal distribution.

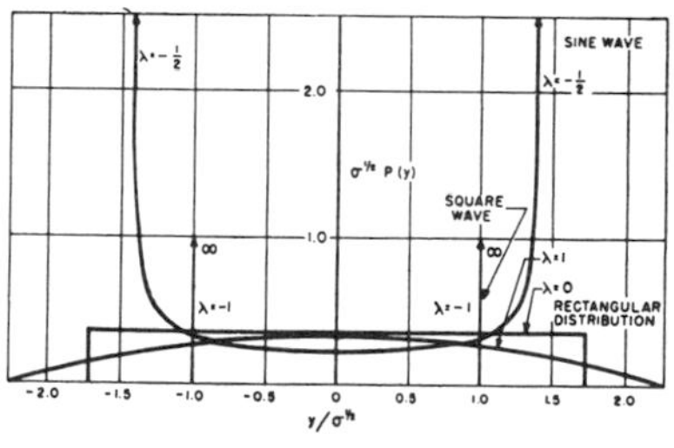


Fig. 7—Pearson distribution curves of $\sigma^{1/2}P(y)$ plotted against $y/\sigma^{1/2}$.

The probability density (36) is plotted in Fig. 7 for several values of $\lambda$ with constant power. Actually $\sigma^{1/2}P(y)$ is plotted against $y/\sigma^{1/2}$ to get a set of curves applicable to all values of $\sigma$. From these curves, it is seen that $\lambda=0$ is the dividing line between two classes of signal. If $\lambda$ is negative, the signals tend to concentrate near the maximum value. For $\lambda$ positive, values near zero are emphasized.

# 20



Reprinted from *IRE Trans. Circuit Theory,* **CT-3**(4), 266–276 (1956)

# A Study of Rough Amplitude Quantization by Means of Nyquist Sampling Theory*

BERNARD WIDROW†

IN MANY system and signal analysis problems, it is convenient to work with the probability density distributions of signals rather than with the signals themselves. Thus, the new "signals" are these probability densities, and the results of analyses are statistical.

This approach has been helpful in providing an understanding of the process of amplitude quantization. Quantization or round-off is a nonlinear operation that is effected whenever a physical quantity is represented numerically. The value of a measurement is designated by an integer corresponding to the nearest number of units contained in the measured physical quantity. Incorporation of such a process within a system makes the entire system nonlinear and difficult to deal with by any direct analytical procedure. The statistical approach greatly reduces complexity by giving average results which are very often adequate for system evaluation and design. Statistical descriptions of quantization turn out

* Manuscript received by the PGCT, August 8, 1956. The research reported in this paper was supported jointly by the U. S. Army, Navy, and Air Force, under contract with Mass. Instit. Tech., Cambridge, Mass. This paper is an abstraction of a dissertation submitted in partial fulfillment of the requirements for the degree of doctor of science.

† Dept. Elec. Eng., M. I. T.

to be fairly easy to get because the quantizer output probability density distribution is obtained by a linear sampling process upon the input distribution density.

### The Quantizer

A rounding-off process may be represented symbolically as in Fig. 1. For purposes of analysis, it has been found convenient to define the quantizer as a nonlinear operator having the input-output relation of Fig. 1. Its output $X'$ is a single-valued function of the input $X$, and it has an "average gain" of unity. An input lying somewhere within a quantization "box" of width $q$ will yield an output corresponding to the center of that box (*i.e.*, the input is rounded to the center of the box). More general quantizers such as those in Fig. 2 (a) and (b) could be obtained by preceeding and following the quantizer of Fig. 1 with instantaneous linear amplifiers (multiplying factors) and adding dc levels to the quantizer input and output (tailoring averages).

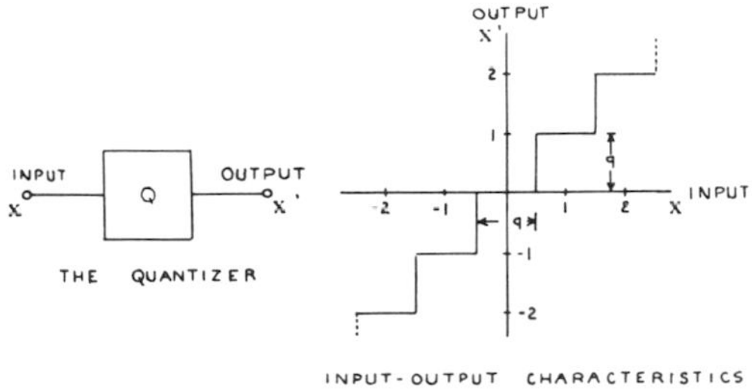


Fig. 1—The quantizer; input-output characteristics.

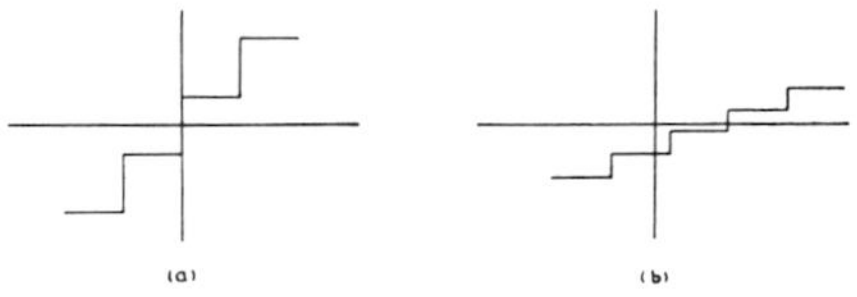


Fig. 2—More general quantizers.

A quantizer may be defined to process continuous data or sampled data. In this paper, the inputs to quantizers will be sampled. Many of the conclusions drawn carry over to the quantization of continuous data, however.

### A Statistical Description of the Quantization Process

#### *First-Order Statistics*

If the samples of some continuous variable are random and statistically independent of each other, a first-order probability density $W(X)$ completely describes this process. The characteristic function of $W(X)$ is its Fourier transform:

$$F_x(\xi) = \int_{-\infty}^{\infty} W(X)\, e^{-jx\xi}\, dX. \qquad (1)$$

A quantizer input variable may take on a continuum of magnitudes, while the output variable can assume only discrete states. The probability density of the output $W'(X')$ consists of a series of impulses that are uniformly spaced along the amplitude axis, each one centered in a quantization box.

Fig. 3 shows how the output distribution is derived from that of the input. Since any event occurring within a quantization box is always "reported" as at the center of that box, each impulse has a magnitude equal to the area under the probability density $W(X)$ within the bounds of the box. The impulse distribution $W'(X')$ has a periodic characteristic function, being the Fourier transform of a series of impulses having uniform spacing $q$. The point of view developed by W. K. Linvill for the study of amplitude sampling as an amplitude-modulation process with an impulse carrier has been found to be most useful in the derivation of $W'(X')$ and its more general counterparts. The necessary aspects of Linvill's ideas will be developed next.

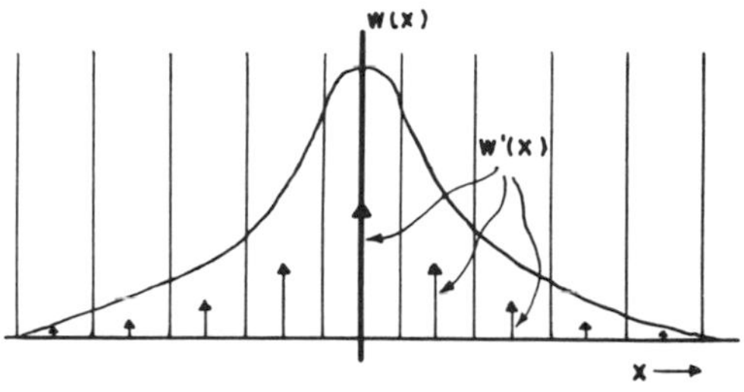


Fig. 3—Area sampling used in the derivation of $W'(X)$.

*Amplitude Sampling Treated as Linear Impulse Modulation*: The process of periodically sampling a function $f(t)$ is the same as multiplying it by a series of impulses of unit area which are spaced uniformly. The impulse carrier of fundamental frequency $\Omega = 2\pi/T$ may be represented by the Fourier series in (2).

$$f^*(t) = [f(t)][\text{impulse carrier}] = [f(t)][(1/T)] \sum_{-\infty}^{\infty} e^{jn\Omega t}. \qquad (2)$$

It is the sum of an infinite number of sinusoidal carriers with uniform frequency spacing $\Omega$ which, when modulated by $f(t)$, develop identical "sidebands" about each frequency $n\Omega$. The pattern of these sidebands is the same as that of the Fourier transform of $f(t)$. $F^*(j\omega)$, the Fourier spectrum of the series of impulses $f^*(t)$, is the sum of a periodic array of sections, separated by the frequency $\Omega$, where the typical repeated section is the same as $(1/T)F(j\omega)$, the spectrum of the envelope of the pulses. If it were possible to separate the zeroth section of $F^*(j\omega)$ from the rest, it would be possible to recover an envelope from its samples. This can be done with an "ideal low-pass filter" if the sections are distinct and do not overlap. The gain as a function of frequency for such a filter together with $F^*(j\omega)$ are shown in Fig. 4. If $F^*(t)$ is applied to the input of the low-pass filter of Fig. 4, the output will be $f(t)$. Since the impulse response of the ideal low-pass filter is $[\sin(\pi t/T)]/(\pi t/T)$, it follows by linearity that the envelope of the impulses is a sum of these, properly weighed and spaced in time, as shown in Fig. 5.

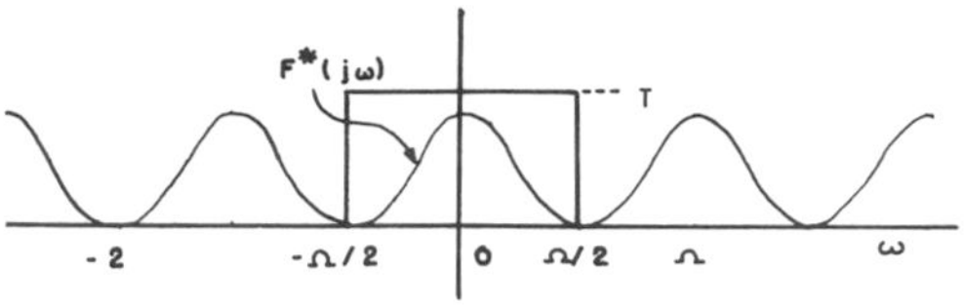


Fig. 4—Recovery of envelope from samples in the frequency domain.

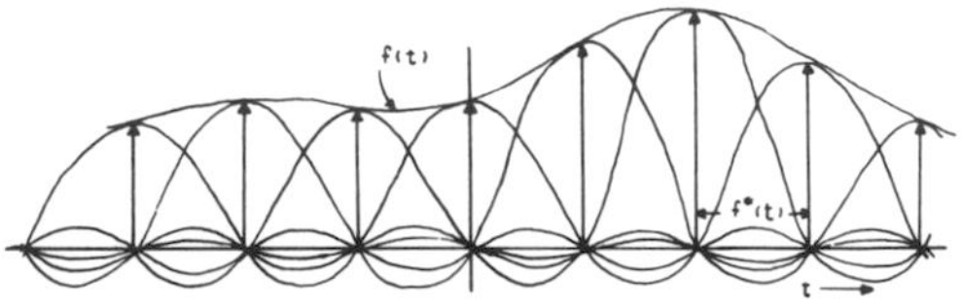


Fig. 5—Recovery of envelope from samples in the time domain

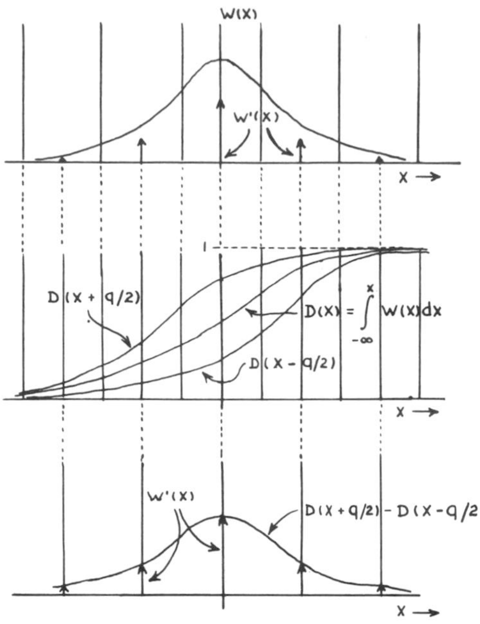


Fig. 6—Construction of area samples.

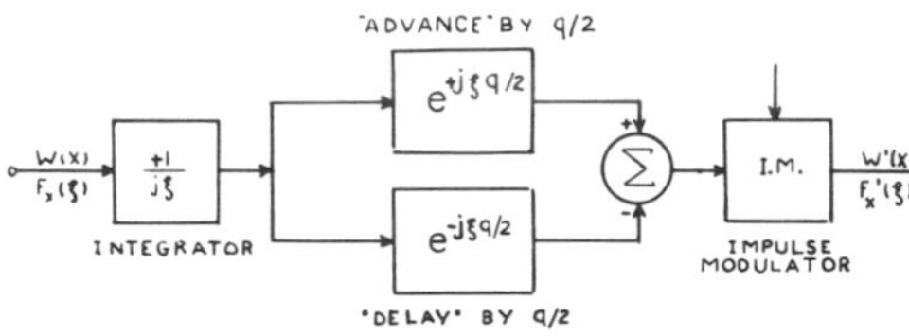


Fig. 7—Block diagram of the area sampling of Fig. 8.

The low-pass filter is an interpolater that yields $f(t)$ as long as $f(t)$ has no significant harmonic content at higher frequency than $\Omega/2$. This is the Nyquist bandwidth restriction on $f(t)$.

*Derivation of the First-Order Probability Density of a Quantized Variable*: The distribution of a quantizer output $W'(X')$ consists of "area samples" of the input distribution density $W(X)$. The quantizer may be thought of as an area sampler acting upon the "signal," the probability density $W(X)$. Fig. 6 shows how $W'(X')$ may be constructed by sampling the difference $D(x + q/2) - D(x - q/2)$, where $D(x)$ is the distribution, the integral of the distribution density. Fig. 7 is a block schematic diagram of this process, showing how $W(X)$ is first modified by a linear filter of "gain" $[\sin(q\xi/2)]/(q\xi/2)$ and then sampled to give $W'(X')$.

When the radian "fineness" $\phi$, $2\pi$ times the reciprocal of the box width, is twice as high as the radian "frequency" of the highest "frequency" component contained in the shape of $W(X)$, it is possible to recover $W(X)$ from the quantized distribution $W'(X')$ by inverse transforming the quotient of a typical section of $F_{x'}(\xi)$ and $[\sin(q\xi/2)]/(q\xi/2)$.

The characteristic function of the distribution density of the sum of two random independent variables is the product of the individual cf's. Fig. 8 shows the distribution $Q(n)$ and its characteristic function. $Q(n)$ will be shown to be the distribution of quantization noise. Its cf is $F_n(\xi) = [\sin(\pi\xi/\phi)]/(\pi\xi/\phi) = [\sin(q\xi/2)]/(q\xi/2)$. If purely random independent noise of distribution $Q(n)$ were added to a signal of distribution $W(X)$, their sum would have a cf $F_x(\xi)[\sin(\pi\xi/\phi)]/(\pi\xi/\phi)$, which is identical with the typical section of $F_{x'}(\xi)$. The derivatives of a cf at the origin determine moments. It follows that the moments of a quantized signal are the same as if the quantizer were a source of independent random additive noise of distribution $Q(n)$ provided that Nyquist's restriction on $W(X)$ is met. If the moments of $W(X)$ are $m_1, m_2, \cdots$, and the moments of $W'(X')$ are $\mu_1, \mu_2, \cdots$, they may be expressed in terms of each other and the box size $q$ as in (3). Advantage is taken of the facts that $Q(n)$ has a second moment of $1/12\, q^2$ and a fourth moment of $1/80\, q^4$.

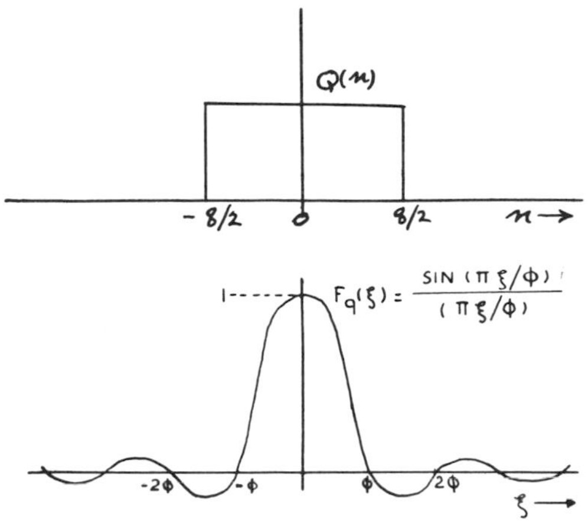


Fig. 8—The distribution of quantization noise and its characteristic function.

$$
\begin{aligned}
m_1 - \mu_1 &= 0 \\
m_2 - \mu_2 &= -\tfrac{1}{12}q^2 \qquad (3)\\
m_3 - \mu_3 &= -\tfrac{1}{4}\mu_1 q^2 \\
m_4 - \mu_4 &= -\tfrac{1}{2}\mu_2 q^2 + \tfrac{7}{240}q^4. \\
&\cdot \\
&\cdot \\
&\cdot
\end{aligned}
$$

The right-hand sides are the well known Sheppard corrections for grouping.

It is now possible to derive $W'(X')$ from $W(X)$. The understanding of the quantizer would be complete if it were true that the quantization noise (the difference between input and output) were independent of the quantizer input. This is not true, however. Not only is the quantization noise statistically related to the input, but it is also causally related. Since the output of a quantizer is a single-valued function of the input, any given input yields a definite output and a definite noise.

The *distribution* density of the noise itself will be shown to be $Q(n)$, independent of the *distribution* density of the quantizer input (as long as the Nyquist restriction is satisfied). Their causal tie will show up later when joint input-output distribution densities are derived.

*Derivation of the Probability Density of Quantization Noise*: Quantization noise is always the difference between an input variable and the value of the box to which it has been assigned. The distribution of quantization noise resulting from events assigned to the zeroth box may be constructed by plotting $W(-X)$ between $-q/2 < X < q/2$. Likewise, the noise distribution resulting from events in the first box may be obtained by considering $W(-X)$ for values $-3q/2 < X < -q/2$, recentered to the origin. Events taking place in the various boxes are exclusive of each other. The probability of a given noise magnitude arising is the sum of the probabilities of that noise from each box. Fig. 9 shows how the distribution of quantization noise is constructed from $W(-X)$.

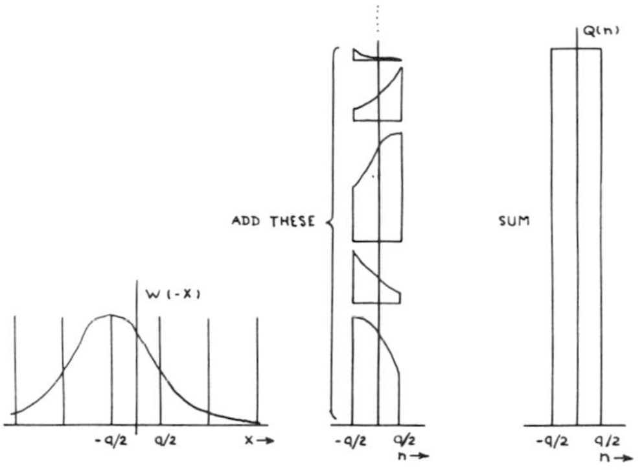


Fig. 9—Construction of distribution of quantization noise.

Since the development of the distribution of quantization noise (Fig. 9) is an additive linear process, the quantization noise distribution is the sum of the distributions of noise corresponding to constituents that are added to get $W(X)$. All that needs be considered is the quantization of the basic form $(\sin(\pi X/q))/(\pi X/q)$. The strips as in Fig. 9 are added to give the quantization noise distribution which turns out to be precisely flat-topped.

An arbitrary distribution satisfying the Nyquist condition is the sum of a series of $(\sin(\pi X/q))/(\pi X/q)$'s, where each gives a flat-topped distribution of quantization noise. The sum of flat-topped distributions is flat-topped. If the distribution density of a signal being quantized is $W(X)$, and the quantization grain is fine enough to satisfy the Nyquist restriction, the distribution of the noise introduced by the quantizer will be flat-topped. This distribution is $Q(n)$, shown in Fig. 8.

*Derivation of the Joint Probability Density of the Quantizer Input and Output*: A most general statistical description of a device having a random stationary output is the joint distribution between input and output. From this, the output distribution, input distribution, the difference (between input and output) distribution, and the joint distribution between input and difference may be determined. Any one of the joint distributions will determine all the rest, but at least one joint distribution need be known for a complete statistical picture. Infinite numbers of joint distributions could give the same input, output, and difference distribution densities, so that the latter are not sufficient for a complete understanding.

A study of Fig. 10 shows how a joint in-out distribution

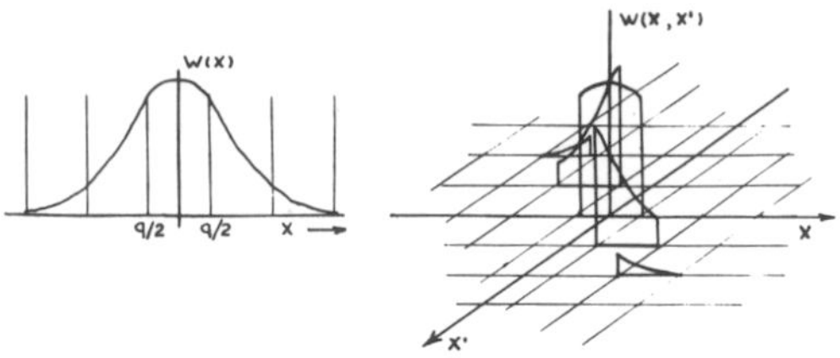


Fig. 10—Formation of joint in-out distribution from quantizer imput distribution.

$W(X, X')$ is derived from a given input distribution $W(X)$. The strips of $W(X)$ are placed at the values of $X'$ to which they correspond. Consider next the situation shown in Fig. 11. For every value of $X$, all values of noise are possible between $\pm q/2$ because the noise is independent of $X$. The joint distribution (Fig. 12) between $X$ and $(X + n)$ shows this, whereas any plane parallel to the $(X + n)$ and $w$ axes cuts a flat-topped section from the surface of joint probability $w(X, X + \text{noise})$. The surface of joint probability is everywhere parallel to the $X + n$ axis. The projection of the surface on the $X - w$ plane has the same shape as $W(X)$ and has an area of $1/q$. The total volume under the surface is unity.

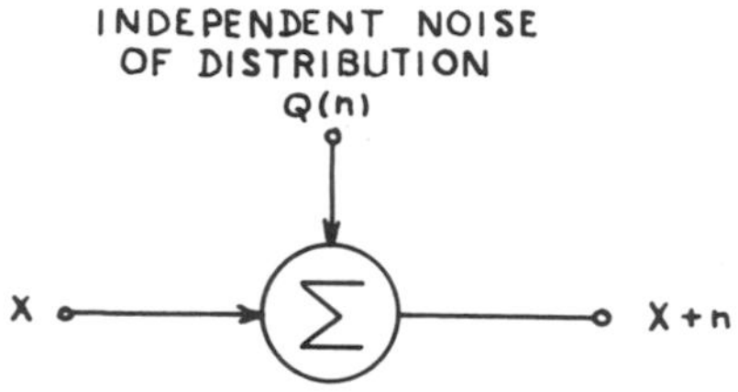


Fig. 11—Addition of independent quantization noise.

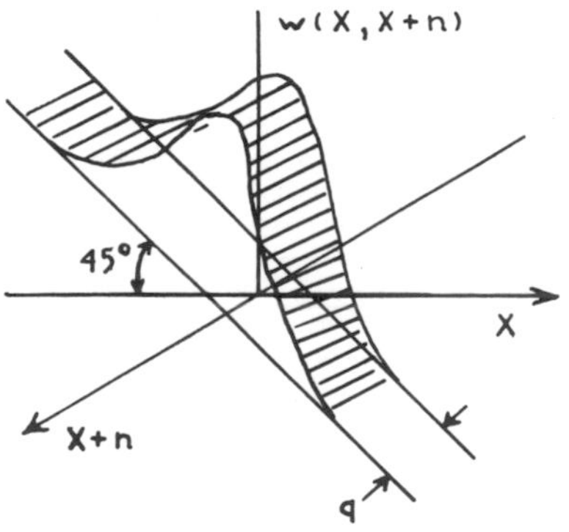


Fig. 12—Joint in-out distribution for a quantizer and for a source of additive independent quantization noise.

A study of Figs. 10 and 12 shows that the strips of Fig. 10 are sections of the three-dimensional surface of Fig. 12 (if first multiplied in amplitude by $q$) cut by a series of planes parallel to the $W$ and $X$ axes with spacing $q$ along the $X + n$ axis. The strips of Fig. 10 are thus the results of the amplitude modulation of a periodic carrier, which is a series of uniformly-spaced impulse sheets, by an envelope which is the joint probability surface. It should be possible to deduce the joint characteristic function of the distribution $W(X, X')$ from that of $w(X, X + n)$. At the same time, the ways in which quantization is akin to the addition of random independent noise as in Fig. 11 should be detected.

The methods of amplitude sampling may readily be generalized to handle sampling by impulse sheets. Each sheet extends to infinity in both directions, and has a unit volume per unit length. The Fourier series for the amplitude sheets $Z(X, X')$ is

$$Z(X,X') = \sum_{n=-\infty}^{\infty} 1/q \, e^{-jn\phi x'}. \quad (4)$$

$Z$ appears to be one-dimensional, because there is no variation with $X$. If $\xi_a$ is the variable that $X$ transforms into, and $\xi_b$ is the variable that $X'$ transforms into, the two-dimensional spectrum of $Z(X, X')$ is a string of impulses having the spacing $\phi$ along the $\xi_b$ axis. Each impulse has the amplitude $1/q$. When a carrier having this spectrum is modulated by an envelope $w(X, X + n)$, the resulting spectrum is periodic along $\xi_b$, and aperiodic along $\xi_a$. The shape of a typical section is the same as the spectrum of $w(X, X + n)$. The whole series of sections results from the convolution of the two two-dimensional spectra. Since the sections of $w(X, X + n)$ are to be first multiplied by $q$, the factor $1/q$ is compensated for and the value of $F_{x,x'}(\xi_a, \xi_b)$ is 1 at the origin. All characteristic functions must have the value 1 at their origins in order that the total volume under their probability densities be unity.

It is of interest to derive the typical section of $F_{x,x'}(\xi_a, \xi_b)$, the Fourier transform of $w(X, X + n)$ which is the joint distribution between the input and the input plus an independent noise of distribution $Q(n)$ as in Fig. 11. A joint cf of two variables may be deduced from the characteristic functions resulting from sums of various proportions of the two variables. A block diagram illustrating this technique is given in Fig. 13. Formally

$$F_{x,x+n}(\xi_a, \xi_b) = \iint_{-\infty}^{\infty} w(X, X + n) \, e^{j[X\xi_a + (X+n)\xi_b]} \, dX \, d(X + n) \quad (5)$$

also,

$$F_{\Sigma}(\xi) = \iint_{-\infty}^{\infty} w(X, X + n) e^{j[k_1 \xi X + k_2 \xi (X+n)]} \, dX \, d(X + n). \quad (6)$$

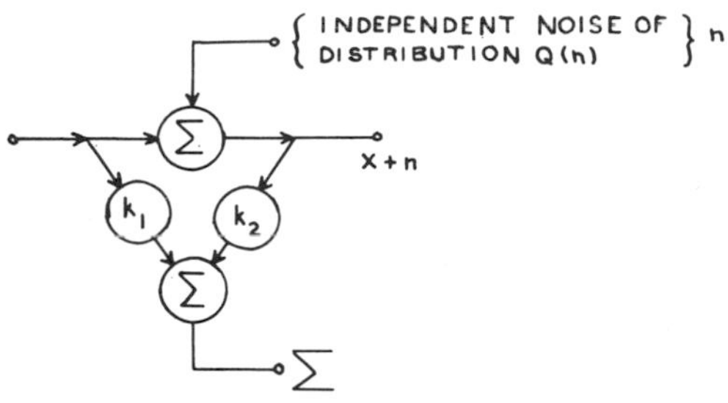


Fig. 13—Flow diagram useful in calculation of $F_{x,x+n}(\xi_a, \xi_b)$.

$F_\Sigma(\xi)$ can be readily evaluated and leads to $F_{x,x+n}(\xi_a, \xi_b)$ if the substitution is made, $k_1\xi = \xi_a$, $k_2\xi = \xi_b$. Any $\xi_a$, $\xi_b$ can be obtained by choice of $k_1$, $k_2$, and $\xi$. The sum $\Sigma$ equals $(k_1 + k_2) X + k_2 n$. The cf of $X$ is $F_x(\xi)$, and the cf of the independent noise is $F_n(\xi)$.

$$\therefore F_\Sigma(\xi) = F_x[(k_1 + k_2)\xi]F_n(k_2\xi)$$

whence

$$F_{x,x+n}(\xi_a, \xi_b) = F_x(\xi_a + \xi_b)F_n(\xi_b)$$

$$= F_x(\xi_a + \xi_b)\frac{\sin(\pi\xi_b/\phi)}{(\pi\xi_b/\phi)}. \quad (7)$$

$F_{x,x'}(\xi_a, \xi_b)$, the joint cf of the input and output of a quantizer is now expressible in terms of the cf of the quantizer input, $F_x(\xi)$.

$$F_{x,x'}(\xi_a, \xi_b) = \sum_{n=-\infty}^{\infty} F_x(\xi_a + \xi_b + n\phi)\frac{\sin[\pi(\xi_b + n\phi)/\phi]}{[\pi(\xi_b + n\phi)/\phi]}$$

$$= \sum_{n=-\infty}^{\infty} F_x(\xi_a + \xi_b + n\phi)\frac{\sin(\pi\xi_b/\phi + n\pi)}{(\pi\xi_b/\phi + n\pi)}. \quad (8)$$

This is a complete statistical description of the quantizer for first-order (uncorrelated) statistics. Fig. 14 is a sketch of the joint cf $F_{x,x'}(\xi_a, \xi_b)$ which is the Fourier transform of the joint input-output distribution shown in Fig. 10.

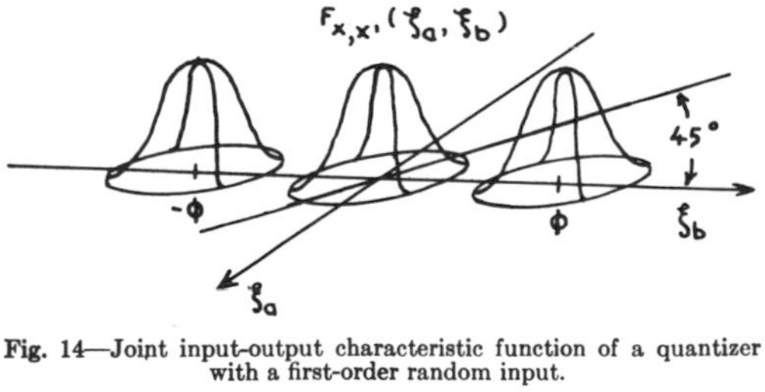


Fig. 14—Joint input-output characteristic function of a quantizer with a first-order random input.

The joint and self moments depend only upon the slopes (partial derivatives) of $F_{x,x'}(\xi_a, \xi_b)$ at the origin, and are unaffected by the periodicity of that function as long as there is no overlap. It may be concluded that with respect to all detectable moments, quantization is the same as addition of random independent noise of distribution $Q(n)$, as long as the Nyquist restriction on $W(X)$ is satisfied.

The impulse distribution of the quantizer output, and the distribution of the quantizer noise $Q(n)$ may be rederived readily from $F_{x,x'}(\xi_a, \xi_b)$. A plane perpendicular to the $\xi_a$, $\xi_b$ plane through the $\xi_b$ axis intersects the joint input-output cf $F_{x,x'}(\xi_a, \xi_b)$, giving a section which is $F_{x'}(\xi_b)$, the cf of the output (see Fig. 14). As determined previously, the cf $F_{x'}(\xi_b)$ is periodic of frequency $\phi$ where each section is identical with the cf of the sum of the quantizer input and independent quantization noise. Likewise, a plane perpendicular to the $\xi_a$, $\xi_b$ plane through the $\xi_a$ axis gives an intersection which is $F_x(\xi_a)$, the cf of the quantizer input.

A section of $F_{x,x'}(\xi_a, \xi_b)$ through the $F$ axis and a 45° line in the $\xi_a - \xi_b$ plane as shown in Fig. 14, when projected either upon the $F - \xi_a$ plane or upon the $F - \xi_b$ plane gives the cf of the distribution of quantization noise (the distribution of $X' - X$). That the cut is at 45° insures the periodicity of the joint cf to have no effect upon the distribution of quantizer noise. This distribution is therefore the same as the distribution of added noise in Figs. 11 and 13, being $Q(n)$, as shown previously.

The description of the quantizer response to first order statistics is complete and useful in itself. However, in order to understand the behavior of the quantizer is systems, particularly in feedback systems, it is necessary to consider how the quantizer reacts to correlated (high-order) input samples. The methods already developed will be extended to handle multidimensional input distributions. It has been shown that, in many respects, quantization is the same as addition of a random independent noise. Conditions will be shown under which quantization of corelated samples will be very much like addition of random independent uncorrelated noise of distribution $Q(n)$.

### *Higher Order Statistical Inputs*

If the random quantizer input variable $X$ is second order, (the simplest Markov process), a joint distribution density $W(X_1, X_2)$ is required to completely describe its statistics. $X_1$ and $X_2$ are an adjacent sample pair. The distribution of the output is $W'(X_1', X_2')$. The joint distribution between output and input is $W(X_1, X_1', X_2, X_2')$, having cf $F_{x_1x_1'x_2x_2'}(\xi_{1a}, \xi_{2a}, \xi_{1b}, \xi_{2b})$. In order to sketch the joint distribution, five dimensions are needed. Some other way to illustrate its significant features will be sought.

$W(X_1, X_2)$ may be resolved into a two-dimensional sum of a series of sin $X/X$'s (which is analogous to the previous one-dimensional case) provided a two-dimensional Nyquist restriction is satisfied. The cf of $W(X_1X_2)$ is a sum of the separate components because of the linearity of the

Fourier transform. The quantization process is a linear operation upon probability distributions and characteristic functions. As a matter of fact, any situation in which a stationary random signal, even though the operation upon the signals may be nonlinear and have memory, has the characteristic that a linear operation is performed upon the input distribution to give the output distribution. The output and joint distribution of a quantizer are the sums of the corresponding distributions that could result from each component of the input distribution acting separately. It is necessary here to consider nonphysical distribution densities that not only have areas and volumes different from unity, but also have regions of negative density.

The Fourier transform of $W(X_1, X_2)$ is (9).

$$F_{x_1x_2}(\xi_1, \xi_2) = \iint_{-\infty}^{\infty} W(X_1, X_2)e^{j(X_1\xi_1 + X_2\xi_2)}\, dX_1\, dX_2. \quad (9)$$

If this cf is negligible outside the range $-\phi/2 < \xi_1, \xi_2 < \phi/2$ where $\phi = 2\pi/q$, a two-dimensional Nyquist restriction is satisfied. $W(X_1X_2)$ may be thought of as a sum (10) where each coefficient $A_{kl}$ is the value (amplitude sample) of $W(X_1, X_2)$ at $X_1 = kq$ and $X_2 = lq$.

$$W(X_1, X_2) = \sum_{k=-\infty}^{\infty} \sum_{l=-\infty}^{\infty} A_{kl} \frac{\sin \pi(X_1/q + k)}{\pi(X_1/q + k)} \cdot \frac{\sin \pi(X_2/q + l)}{\pi(X_2/q + l)}. \quad (10)$$

All that needs be considered to be perfectly general is how the quantizer acts upon an input distribution such as the $k, l$ term of the above sum.

Start with a special case, the 0, 0 term, a two-dimensional "(sin $X/X$)" centered at the origin. Such a distribution is a degenerate second order, clearly that of first-order statistics, and already examined completely. The adjacent samples $X_1$ and $X_2$ are statistically independent of each other, and so are their quantization noises. Periodicities of "frequency" $\phi$ in the joint input-output cf must exist along the output variable axes $\xi_{1b}$ and $\xi_{2b}$. There is no periodic variation of this joint cf with the input variables $\xi_{1a}$ and $\xi_{2a}$. The quantization noise, which is first order, is also expressed here as being degenerate second order.

The more general problem, that of quantization of the two-dimensional "(sin $X/X$)" distribution component centered at $X_1 = kq$ and $X_2 = lq$ presents no new difficulties. This situation cannot be distinguished from that of quantizing (with identical quantizers) two first-order jointly-related variables $X_1$ and $X_2$ as shown in Fig. 15, except that the possibility of having different averages for $X_1$ and $X_2$ is included. This could not arise in physical stationary processes where $X_1$ and $X_2$ are adjacent samples of the same random process. It should be noticed that $X_1$ and $X_2$ are actually statistically independent of each other since their joint distribution is factorable. It

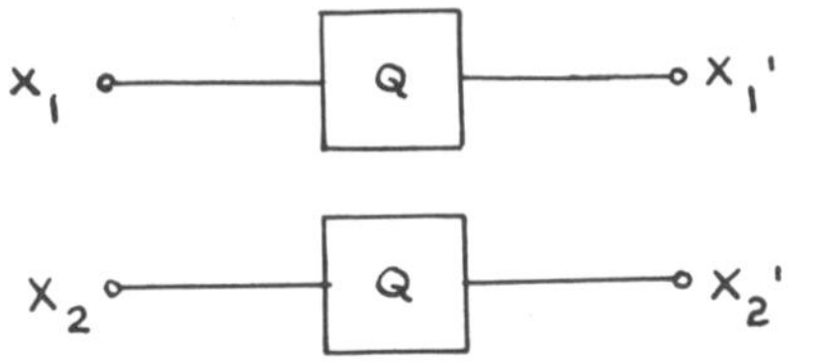

Fig. 15—Representation of the quantization of a second-order signal as the separate quantization of two jointly-related first-order signals.

is no surprise then that the quantization noise due to the $k, l$ component turns out to be first order. The quantization process is the same as for the 0, 0 component because $X_1$ and $X_2$ are shifted by integral numbers of quantization boxes. Any such shift signifying an integral increment to the average of the quantizer input is always accompanied by an identical shift in the quantizer output. It follows that the joint input-output cf due to the $k, l$ component has a typical section that is identical with that which would result singularly if the quantizer were replaced by a source of first order quantization noise. Linearity of the quantization process insures that the joint input-output cf for any second-order input distribution density quantized sufficiently fine to satisfy the Nyquist condition will have a typical section which is the same as the cf resulting if the quantizer were replaced by purely random quantization noise.

Fig. 15 may be modified to include 3 or more jointly-related first-order signals to represent higher-order processes. By arguments similar to those of the second-order process, a most general result may be induced: If the probability density distribution of an $n$-th order quantizer input has an $n$-dimensional cf that is negligible outside the range $-\phi/2 < \xi_{1a} \cdots \xi_{na} < \phi/2$, the joint cf between the quantizer output and input, a function of $2n$ variables $\xi_{1a}, \xi_{1b} \cdots \xi_{na}\xi_{nb}$, is periodic of radian fineness $\phi$ along the axes $\xi_{1b}, \xi_{2b}, \cdots \xi_{nb}$ and aperiodic along the axes $\xi_{1a}, \xi_{2a}, \cdots \xi_{na}$, having a typical repeated section which is the same as the joint cf between the quantizer input signal and that input plus independent first-order noise of distribution $Q(n)$. A sketch of this for a first-order quantizer input is already shown in Fig. 14. When the multi-dimensional Nyquist restriction is met, all self and joint moments are unaffected if the quantizer is replaced by a source of first-order independent noise of distribution $Q(n)$. These moments, being determined by derivatives of the cf at its origin, are not affected by the periodicities when there is no appreciable overlap. The periodicities in the cf domain correspond to the regularly-spaced impulses in the quantizer output distribution density.

## Applications

### *Sensitivity of the Nyquist Test to Distribution Properties*

To what extent the Nyquist condition is met as a function of the quantization fineness is a question that naturally arises. This will be answered for several cases of Gaussian statistics which are important in quantizer system analysis and which will show qualitatively what is to be expected for other kinds of smooth distributions.

Consideration of the first-order Gaussian cf shows that $F_x(\xi)$ will not go to zero outside of any finite band about its origin. However, it acquires negligible proportions very rapidly, going down with $e^{-\xi^2\sigma^2/2}$. $\sigma$ is the root mean square of the Gaussian signal $X$. If we let the quantization box size $q = \sigma$, then the error made by assuming that the cf obeys the Nyquist restriction may be estimated from consideration of Fig. 16 where the cf of quantized first-order Gaussian statistics is shown. Each section, repeated with radian fineness $\phi = 2\pi/q = 2\pi/\sigma$, is of the form $e^{-\xi^2\sigma^2/2}$ $[\sin(\pi\xi/\phi)]/(\pi\xi/\phi)$. The errors in the moments of the quantized statistics when evaluated by assuming that the quantization noise is independent and of the distribution $Q(n)$ are due to the contributions of the overlap to the derivatives of the typical section at the origin. Because $X$ was chosen with zero average, the typical repeated cf section is even (symmetrical), causing the contributions to the odd derivatives to cancel, while the contributions to the even derivatives reinforce. The theoretical errors in all odd moments are zero. The errors in mean square and in mean fourth that result have been calculated for several box sizes.

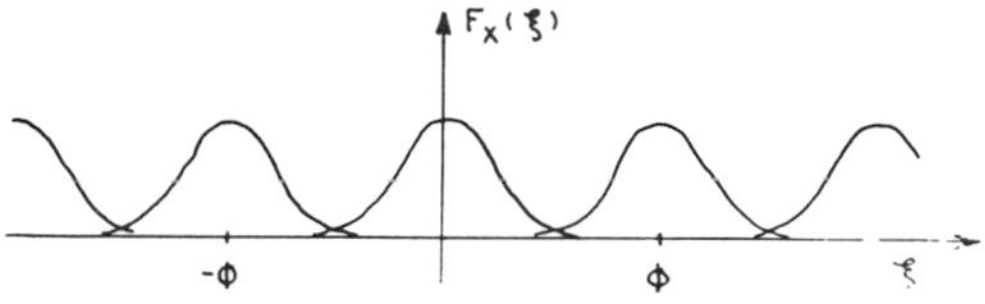


Fig. 16—Characteristic function of first-order Gaussian distribution after quantization.

Errors in analysis are extremely small when $q = \sigma$. They remain moderately small when the quantization is as rough as $q = 2\sigma$, but increase rapidly as the roughness increases further. When $q = \sigma$, the error in the mean square is $10^{-6}$ per cent of the mean square of the input, and about $10^{-5}$ per cent of the mean square of the quantization noise. These percentages climb to 3 and 9 per cent respectively when $q$ is increased to $2\sigma$. Such errors are very tolerable, being suprisingly small for quantization that rough. The error in mean fourth is $3(10)^{-5}$ per cent of the mean fourth of the quantizer input, $6(10)^{-2}$ per cent of the mean fourth of $Q(n)$ when $q = \sigma$. The error in mean fourth becomes large for $q = 2\sigma$, being 17 per cent of the mean fourth of the input and 250 per cent of the mean fourth of $Q(n)$.

The accuracy of this description of first-order statistics as reflected in the accuracy of the moments of the quantizer output for Gaussian input is sufficiently great until the box size is as big as two standard deviations. From there on, the Nyquist restriction breaks down rapidly.

It was held that quantization noise is first order and uncorrelated although the quantizer input may be highly correlated, for fine quantization. Just how fine this has to be as a function of the correlation coefficient of a second-order Gaussian input will give a general indication of the sensitivity of the statistical independence of quantization noise to quantization box size.

The general $k$, $l$ moment of a second-order process is given by (11).

$$\overline{X_1^k X_2^l} = \frac{1}{(-j)^{(k+l)}} \frac{\partial^{(k+l)}}{\partial \xi_1^k \, \partial \xi_2^l} F_{x_1 x_2}(\xi_1, \xi_2) \Big|_{\xi_1 = \xi_2 = 0}. \quad (11)$$

Its errors when calculated (as above) are due to the contributions of overlap to this derivative at the origin. Of interest is the error in the corelation $\overline{(X_1X_2)}$, the 1, 1 moment. This error is equal in magnitude to the correlation in the quantization noise. A plot of the normalized correlation of quantization noise (the ratio of the joint first moment to the mean square) as a function of the normalized correlation coefficient of the second-order Gaussian distribution of the input (the ratio of the correlation coefficient $\overline{(X_1X_2)} \equiv \sigma_{12}$ to the mean square $\sigma^2$) is shown in Fig. 17. A good approximation for the correlation of quantization noise is (12).

$$(\text{normalized correlation}) \approx e^{-4\pi^2\sigma^2/q^2(1-\sigma_{12}/\sigma^2)}. \quad (12)$$

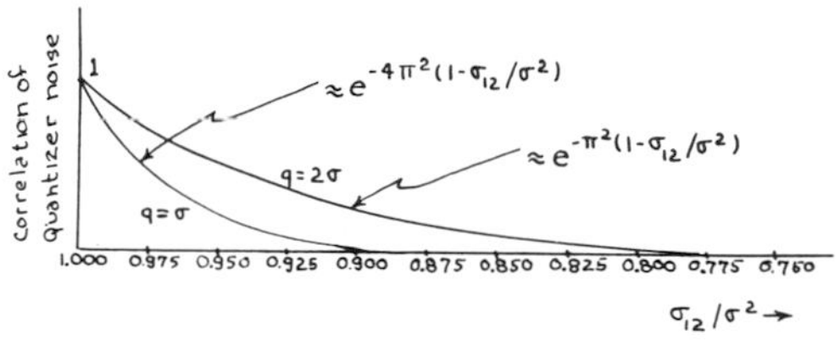


Fig. 17—Correlation of quantization noise vs correlation of quantizer input signals.

It can be seen that quantization noise is practically uncorrelated until the box size is one standard deviation and the input correlation is 95 per cent, or until the box size is two standard deviations and the input correlation is 80 per cent. A box size of two standard deviations corresponds to extremely rough quantization. The dynamic range of an input variable is practically three quantization levels. This is almost in the realm of switching circuits.

It can now be qualitatively stated that if the dynamic range of a variable being quantized extends over several boxes, the quantization noise will be uniformly distributed and will be a first order process. All moments will be the same as if the quantizer were a source of random independent noise.

*Gathering and Processing Grouped Statistical Data*

Statistical information is usually obtained by averaging the values of recorded numerical measurements. An approximate first-order distribution density may be had in the form of a histogram whose groups have width corresponding to the granularity of the data. Multi-dimensional histograms may be constructed from the same kind of data for higher-order processes. It is usually desirable to have some means of arriving at the original ungrouped distribution densities, particularly when the quantization is rough. This is perfectly possible when the Nyquist condition is satisfied. When the most significant part of the dynamic range of a smoothly-distributed variable covers about four or more quantization levels, the ungrouped distribution may be obtained with very small error in moments, as was shown above for the Gaussian statistics use. The "bars" of the histogram are "compressed" into impulses in the center of each group, tnen a minimum "bandwidth" envelope is passed through the impulse samples ["(sin $X/X$)" interpolation], and what results is the true ungrouped distribution convolved with $Q(n)$. Another way of acquring the ungrouped distribution density having an analytic cf is to calculate its moments, which may be accomplished by means of Sheppard's corrections for first-order distributions. These corrections may be generalized for higher-order cases by treating the quantizer as a source of independent first-order noise distributed according to $Q(n)$.

An example of how properties of higher-order distributions are able to be obtained from roughly-quantized experimental data is the calculation of an autocorrelation function. Since the autocorrelation is a joint first moment, quantization is again equivalent to the addition of random independent noise. A two-bit autocorrelator could be used when the full dynamic range of a random variable is broken up into four quantization levels. Only negligible error will be made in a point on the autocorrelation curve as long as the correlation coefficient before quantization is less than 0.8. The quantization noise is uncorrelated. The only change necessary is the subtraction of $1/12\ q^2$ from the mean square point. Mean squares of independent random waves add, and the mean square of quantization noise, the second moment of $Q(n)$, is one-twelfth of the square of the box size. Autocorrelations of data deliberately made crude have been calculated by the M.I.T. Whirlwind computer. All results show that autocorrelations obtained from rough data (2-bit accuracy) are equivalent to those taken from fine-grained data.

*System Applications—Error Analysis*

Two examples of closed-loop quantizer systems are shown in Fig. 18(a) and (b). The former has a quantizer in the feedforward section, while the latter has quantized feedback. The symbol "D" represents a linear sampled-data filter, one whose present output sample is a linear combination of past and present input samples. Any sampled-data system having a single quantizer and a feedback path about it can be reduced to either form. These systems could represent situations ranging from crude contactor servos to very precise numerical difference-equation solution.

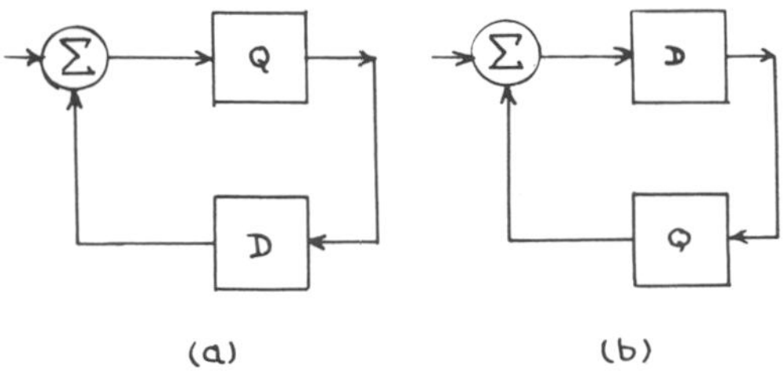


Fig. 18—Quantizer sample-data feedback systems.

The first problem to be considered when making a statistical analysis of these systems is that of testing the signal at the quantizer input for the satisfaction of the Nyquist condition. Elaborate and conservative methods have been devised for this, but the whole question practically reduces to whether or not the signal input to the quantizer has a dynamic range covering at least several quantization boxes.

Actual probability density distributions of the outputs of quantizers and quantizer systems are obtainable with varying degrees of difficulty depending on the natures of the systems and the statistics of their input signals. These include the effects of the causality of quantization noise. For example, the probability density of the output signal in Fig. 18(b) is continuous if appropriate Nyquist conditions are satisfied at both the input and output of the quantizer. The distribution of the system output is identical with that which would result if the quantizer were replaced by a source of random independent noise. On the other hand, the output distribution of Fig 18(a) is discrete, having a minimum bandwidth envelope corresponding to the distribution would result if again the quantizer were replaced by a source of random noise.

The moments of these distributions are far more readily obtainable because they depend only upon the moments of the signal and of the quantization noise. This was shown for the quantizer alone, and can be shown to apply generally to "linear" quantizer systems and certain nonlinear ones. Thus, the moments of signal plus noise are obtainable by treating quantization as addition of independent random noise having the distribution density $Q(n)$.

In most situations, the quantization noise alone is of interest. The causal tie between noise and signal is of secondary importance. The distribution of the noise component in a system output is usually easy to calculate, and once acquired, characterizes the effects of quantization in the system for the large class of input signals that allow satisfaction of the Nyquist condition at the quantizer input.

Once a quantizer is driven with an input that satisfies the Nyquist restriction, addition of another independent signal cannot change this situation. When their respective cf's are multiplied to give the cf of the sum, the result can be no wider than the narrower cf of the two constituents. In general, it will be even narrower than this and the restriction will be met more easily. In the amplitude domain, a quantizer having a sufficiently great dynamic range (extending over several quantization boxes) can only have this range increased by the addition of another independent input. Since the output of a quantizer is the same as the input plus an additive noise of fixed distribution $Q(n)$, the quantizer is "linearized" by any input component satisfying the Nyquist restriction. The same effects are realized with statistically related input components except where the addition of a component signal reduces the dynamic range already existing to one so small that the restriction is no longer met.

The system consequences of the "linearization" of a quantizer are similar to those for the quantizer alone. Here, the entire system is "linearized." For two input components, the quantizer output consists of the sum of three parts. Two of them are the respective output components of the linear equivalent system when driven by the two inputs. The third is due to quantization noise. It has a different waveform in time after the addition of the second input component, but has the same statistical characteristics as before.

According to the Central Limit Theorem, the addition of a good number of independent random quantities of arbitrary distribution yields a random process that becomes closer and closer to Gaussian as the number of included variables is increased. The output of a sampled-data filter at a given sample time is a weighed sum of past inputs that are often of a first-order process, so that statistical outputs of "long-memory" sampled-data systems are almost Gaussian. In particular, if the impulse response from a quantizer point to the output contains a half-dozen samples or more, a given noise output, the sum of that many independent past noises is nearly Gaussian. All that is needed to specify the first order distribution of the system output component due to quantization noise, then, is its mean square. Since the original quantization noise samples are independent, mean squares add. The mean square system noise is then $1/12\ q^2$ times the sum of the squares of the impulse magnitudes of the response at the output to a unit impulse applied at the quantizer position.

As an example of a simple approach to an error analysis problem, consider the numerical solution of the homogeneous first-order nonlinear differential equation with its initial conditions:

$$\frac{dy}{dt} + y^2 = 0, \qquad y(0) = 1.12. \tag{13}$$

An associated difference equation with a sampling interval of 1/10 is (14).

$$y_{k+1} = y_k - \frac{1}{10} y_k^2, \qquad y_0 = 1.12. \tag{14}$$

The numerical point-by-point solution of this difference equation is given in Fig. 19. Notice that rounding after squaring greatly simplified the calculations and maintained the length of the numbers within three decimal digits. A block diagram showing the numerical solution scheme (including quantization) is Fig. 20(a). Fig. 20(b) gives the "small signal" response in $y_k$ due to a unit impulse applied at the quantizer position. The "gain" of the squaring device is $2y_k$ which is taken to be approximately 2.

| $K$ | $Y_K$ | $Y_K^2$ | $Y_K^2$ (rounded) | $Y_{K+1} = Y_K - \frac{1}{10} Y_K^2$ (rounded) |
|---|---|---|---|---|
| 0 | 1.12 | 1.2544 | 1.3 | $Y_1$ = 1.12 - 0.13 = 0.99 |
| 1 | 0.99 | 0.9801 | 1.0 | $Y_2$ = 0.99 - 0.10 = 0.89 |
| 2 | 0.89 | 0.7921 | 0.8 | $Y_3$ = 0.89 - 0.08 = 0.81 |
| 3 | 0.81 | 0.6561 | 0.7 | $Y_4$ = 0.81 - 0.07 = 0.74 |
| 4 | 0.74 | 0.5476 | 0.5 | $Y_5$ = 0.73 - 0.05 = 0.68 |

Fig. 19—Point-by-point solution to (14).

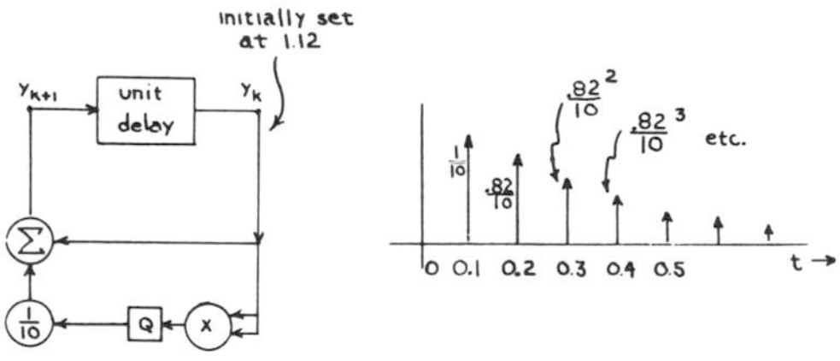


Fig. 20—(a) Block diagram of numerical solution. (b) "Small signal" unit impulse response from quantizer point to output.

The error to be expected in such a solution due to round-off may be predicted by replacing the quantizer of Fig. 20(a) by an independent noise source whose mean square is 1/1200. The variance of the error in the fourth-output sample, for example, is

$$\frac{1}{1200}\left[\left(\frac{1}{10}\right)^2 + \left(\frac{0.82}{10}\right)^2 + \left(\frac{0.82^2}{10}\right)^2 + \left(\frac{0.82^3}{10}\right)^2\right] = 20(10)^{-6}.$$

Thus the root mean square error in the fourth-output sample when averaged over several initial conditions in the vicinity of 1.12 will be less than 1 per cent of this sample.

## Conclusion

A numerical abstraction or description of a continuous function of an independent variable may be made by plotting the function on graph paper, as in Fig. 21.

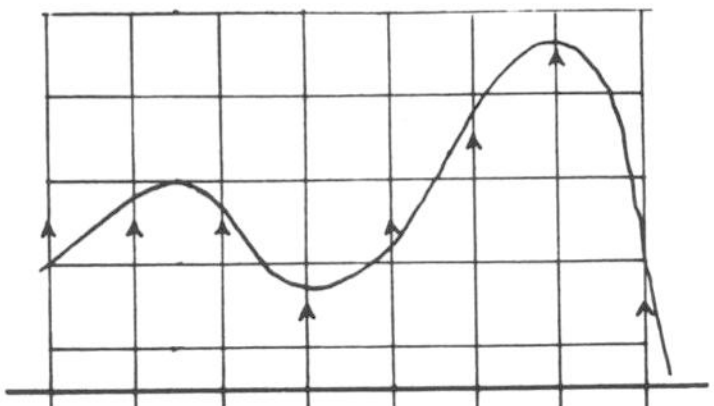

Fig. 21—Sampling and quantization.

Shown are the quantized samples of the function, a series of numerical values. This plot suggests that quantization should be like sampling in amplitude, which is indeed the case. Quantization is a sampling process that acts not upon the function itself but upon its probability density distribution. A Nyquist sampling theorem for quantization exists such that if the quantization is sufficiently fine, statistics are recoverable, whereas in conventional sampling, the Nyquist sampling restriction when satisfied insures that the function is recoverable.

Whenever the statistics are recoverable, the noise generated by the quantizer is well understood. This knowledge allows one to answer questions such as, would it be better to sample less often and quantize finer, making use of the same amount of effort and equipment. When quantization takes place in a system, it is possible to predict the quality of performance in terms of the equipments used in achieving it.

## Acknowledgment

The author wishes to thank Prof. W. K. Linvill for his assistance in this research. During the past several years, he has served as a combination of supervisor and father confessor. His method of approach to problems has had a most positive influence on the course of this thesis. The author also wishes to acknowledge the help of Profs. E. A. Guillemin and J. B. Wiesner who served as readers.

## Bibliography

[1] Linvill, W. K. Class Notes for 6.54 (Pulsed-Data Systems). Massachusetts Institute of Technology, 1953.
[2] Kochenburger, R. J. *Analysis and Synthesis of Contactor Servomechanisms.* D. Sc. dissertation, Massachusetts Institute of Technology, 1949.
[3] Middleton, D. Class Notes for AM 215-216 (Applied Mathematics). Harvard University.
[4] Linvill, W. K., and Sittler, R. W. *Design of Sampled-Data Systems by Extension of Conventional Techniques.* Massachusetts Institute of Technology Lincoln Laboratory Division 6, Report #R-222, July, 1953.
[5] Cramer, H. *Mathematical Methods of Statistics.* Princeton N. J.: Princeton University Press, 1946.
[6] Sheppard, W. F. "On the Calculation of the most Probable Values of Frequency-Constants, for Data arranged according to Equidistant Divisions of a Scale," *Proceedings of the London Mathematical Society*, vol. 29 (1898), p. 353-357.
[7] Bowley, A. L. *Elements of Statistics.* London: P. S. King and Son, Ltd., 1937.
[8] Bennett, W. R. "Spectra of Quantized Signals," *Bell System Technical Journal*, vol. 27 (July, 1948) p. 446-472.

# 21



Reprinted from *IRE Trans. Inform. Theory*, **6,** 7–12 (1960)

# Quantizing for Minimum Distortion*

JOEL MAX†

*Summary*—**This paper discusses the problem of the minimization of the distortion of a signal by a quantizer when the number of output levels of the quantizer is fixed. The distortion is defined as the expected value of some function of the error between the input and the output of the quantizer. Equations are derived for the parameters of a quantizer with minimum distortion. The equations are not soluble without recourse to numerical methods, so an algorithm is developed to simplify their numerical solution. The case of an input signal with normally distributed amplitude and an expected squared error distortion measure is explicitly computed and values of the optimum quantizer parameters are tabulated. The optimization of a quantizer subject to the restriction that both input and output levels be equally spaced is also treated, and appropriate parameters are tabulated for the same case as above.**

* Manuscript received by the PGIT, September 25, 1959. This work was performed by the Lincoln Lab., Mass. Inst. Tech., Lexington, Mass., with the joint support of the U. S. Army, Navy, and Air Force.

† Lincoln Lab., Mass. Inst. Tech., Lexington, Mass.

IN MANY data-transmission systems, analog input signals are first converted to digital form at the transmitter, transmitted in digital form, and finally reconstituted at the receiver as analog signals. The resulting output normally resembles the input signal but is not precisely the same since the quantizer at the transmitter produces the same digits for all input amplitudes which lie in each of a finite number of amplitude ranges. The receiver must assign to each combination of digits a single value which will be the amplitude of the reconstituted signal for an original input anywhere within the quantized range. The difference between input and output signals, assuming errorless transmission of the digits, is the quantization error. Since the digital transmission rate of any system is finite, one has to use a quantizer which sorts the input into a finite number of ranges, $N$. For a given $N$, the system is described by specifying the end points, $x_k$, of the $N$ input ranges, and an output level, $y_k$, corresponding to each input range. If the amplitude probability density of the signal which is the quantizer input is given, then the quantizer output is a quantity whose amplitude probability density may easily be determined as a function of the $x_k$'s and $y_k$'s. Often it is appropriate to define a distortion measure for the quantization process, which will be some statistic of the quantization error. Then one would like to choose the $N$ $y_k$'s and the associated $x_k$'s so as to minimize the distortion. If we define the distortion, $D$, as the expected value of $f(\epsilon)$, where $f$ is some function (differentiable), and $\epsilon$ is the quantization error, and call the input amplitude probability density $p(x)$, then

$$D = E[f(s_{\text{in}} - s_{\text{out}})]$$
$$= \sum_{i=1}^{N} \int_{x_i}^{x_{i+1}} f(x - y_i)p(x)\, dx$$

where $x_{N+1} = \infty$, $x_1 = -\infty$, and the convention is that an input between $x_i$ and $x_{i+1}$ has a corresponding output $y_i$.

If we wish to minimize $D$ for fixed $N$, we get necessary conditions by differentiating $D$ with respect to the $x_i$'s and $y_i$'s and setting derivatives equal to zero:

$$\frac{\partial D}{\partial x_j} = f(x_j - y_{j-1})p(x_j) - f(x_j - y_j)p(x_j) = 0 \qquad j = 2, \cdots, N \qquad (1)$$

$$\frac{\partial D}{\partial y_j} = -\int_{x_j}^{x_{j+1}} f'(x - y_j)p(x)\, dx = 0 \qquad j = 1, \cdots, N \qquad (2)$$

(1) becomes (for $p(x_j) \neq 0$)

$$f(x_j - y_{j-1}) = f(x_j - y_j) \qquad j = 2, \cdots, N \qquad (3)$$

(2) becomes

$$\int_{x_j}^{x_{j+1}} f'(x - y_j)p(x)\, dx = 0 \qquad j = 1, \cdots, N. \qquad (4)$$

We may ask when these are sufficient conditions. The best answer one can manage in a general case is that if all the second partial derivatives of $D$ with respect to the $x_i$'s and $y_i$'s exist, then the critical point determined by conditions (3) and (4) is a minimum if the matrix whose $i$th row and $j$th column element is

$$\left.\frac{\partial^2 D}{\partial p_i\, \partial p_j}\right|_{\text{critical point}},$$

where the $p$'s are the $x$'s and $y$'s, is positive definite. In a specific case, one may determine whether or not the matrix is positive definite or one may simply find all the critical points (*i.e.*, those satisfying necessary conditions) and evaluate $D$ at each. The absolute minimum must be at one of the critical points since "end points" can be easily ruled out.

The sort of $f$ one would want to use would be a good metric function, *i.e.*, $f(x)$ is monotonically nondecreasing

$$f(0) = 0$$
$$f(x) = f(-x).$$

If we require that $f(x)$ be *monotonically increasing* (with $x$) then (1) implies

$$|x_j - y_{j-1}| = |x_j - y_j| \qquad j = 2, \cdots, N$$

which implies (since $y_{j-1}$ and $y_j$ should not coincide) that

$$x_j = (y_j + y_{j-1})/2 \qquad j = 2, \cdots, N$$

($x_j$ is halfway between $y_j$ and $y_{j-1}$).

We now take a specific example of $f(x)$ to further illuminate the situation.

Let $f(x) = x^2$

(3) implies

$$x_j = (y_j + y_{j-1})/2 \quad \text{or} \quad y_j = 2x_j - y_{j-1} \qquad j = 2, \cdots, N, \qquad (5)$$

(4) implies

$$\int_{x_j}^{x_{j+1}} (x - y_j)p(x)\, dx = 0 \qquad j = 1, \cdots, N. \qquad (6)$$

That is, $y_j$ is the centroid of the area of $p(x)$ between $x_j$ and $x_{j+1}$.

Because of the complicated functional relationships which are likely to be induced by $p(x)$ in (6), this is not a set of simultaneous equations we can hope to solve with any ease. Note, however, that if we choose $y_1$ correctly we can generate the succeeding $x_i$'s and $y_i$'s by (5) and (6), the latter being an implicit equation for $x_{j+1}$ in terms of $x_j$ and $y_j$.

A method of solving (5) and (6) is to pick $y_1$, calculate the succeeding $x_i$'s and $y_i$'s by (5) and (6) and then if $y_N$ is the centroid of the area of $p(x)$ between $x_N$ and $\infty$, $y_1$ was chosen correctly. (Of course, a different choice is appropriate to each value of $N$.) If $y_N$ is not the appropriate centroid, then of course $y_1$ must be chosen again. This search may be systematized so that it can be performed on a computer in quite a short time.[1]

This procedure has been carried out numerically on the IBM 709 for the distribution $p(x) = 1/\sqrt{2\pi}\, e^{-x^2/2}$, under the restriction that $x_{N/2+1} = 0$ for $N$ even, and $y_{(N+1)/2} = 0$ for $N$ odd. This procedure gives symmetric results, *i.e.*,

[1] Obtaining *explicit* solutions to the quantizer problem for a nontrivial $p(x)$ is easily the most difficult part of the problem. The problem may be solved analytically where $p(x) = 1/\sqrt{2\pi}\, e^{-x^2/2}$ only for $N = 1$, $N = 2$. For $N = 1$, $x_1 = -\infty$, $y_1 = 0$, $x_2 = +\infty$. For $N = 2$, $x_1 = -\infty$, $y_1 = -\sqrt{2/\pi}$, $x_2 = 0$, $y_2 = \sqrt{2/\pi}$, $x_3 = +\infty$, ($\sqrt{2/\pi}$ is the centroid of the portion of $1/\sqrt{2\pi}\, e^{-x^2/2}$ between the origin and $+\infty$.) For $N \geqq 3$, some sort of numerical estimation is required. A somewhat different approach, which yields results somewhat short of the optimum, is to be found in V. A. Gamash, "Quantization of signals with non-uniform steps," *Electrosvyaz*, vol. 10, pp. 11–13; October, 1957.

if a signal amplitude $x$ is quantized as $y_k$, then $-x$ is quantized as $-y_k$. The answers appear in Table I on page 11.

An attempt has been made to determine the functional dependence of the distortion on the number of output levels. A log-log plot of the distortion vs the number of output levels is in Fig. 1. The curve is not a straight line. The tangent to the curve at $N = 4$ has the equation $D = 1.32\ N^{-1.74}$ and the tangent at $N = 36$ has the equation $D = 2.21\ x^{-1.96}$. One would expect this sort of behavior for large $N$. When $N$ is large, the amplitude probability density does not vary appreciably from one end of a single input range to another, except for very large amplitudes, which are sufficiently improbable so that their influence is slight. Hence, most of the output levels are very near to being the means of the end points of the corresponding input ranges. Now, the best way of quantizing a uniformly distributed input signal is to space the output levels uniformly and to put the end points of the input ranges halfway between the output levels, as in Fig. 2, shown for $N = 1$. The best way of producing a quantizer with $2N$ output levels for this distribution is to divide each input range in half and put the new output levels at the midpoints of these ranges, as in Fig. 3. It is easy to see that the distortion in the second case is $\frac{1}{4}$ that in the first. Hence, $D = kN^{-2}$ where $k$ is some constant. In fact, $k$ is the variance of the distribution.

If this sort of equal division process is performed on each input range of the optimum quantizer for a normally distributed signal with $N$ output levels where $N$ is large then again a reduction in distortion by a factor of 4 is expected. Asymptotically then, the equation for the tangent to the curve of distortion vs the number of output levels should be $D = kN^{-2}$ where $k$ is some constant.

Commercial high-speed analog-to-digital conversion equipment is at present limited to transforming equal input ranges to outputs midway between the ends of the input ranges. In many applications one would like to know the best interval length to use, *i.e.*, the one yielding minimum distortion for a given number of output levels, $N$. This is an easier problem than the first, since it is only two-dimensional (for $N \geqq 2$), *i.e.*, $D$ is a function of the common length $r$ of the intervals and of any particular output level, $y_k$. If the input has a symmetric distribution and a symmetric answer is desired, the problem becomes one dimensional. If $p(x)$ is the input amplitude probability density and $f(x)$ is the function such that the distortion $D$ is $E[f(s_{out} - s_{in})]$, then, for an even number $2N$ of outputs,

$$D = 2 \sum_{i=1}^{N-1} \int_{(i-1)r}^{ir} f\left(x - \left[\frac{2i-1}{2}\right]r\right)p(x)\,dx + 2\int_{(N-1)r}^{\infty} f\left(x - \left[\frac{2N-1}{2}\right]r\right)p(x)\,dx. \tag{7}$$

For a minimum we require

$$\frac{dD}{dr} = -\sum_{i=1}^{N-1}(2i-1)\int_{(i-1)r}^{ir} f'\left(x - \left[\frac{2i-1}{2}\right]r\right)p(x)\,dx - (2N-1)\int_{(N-1)r}^{\infty} f'\left(x - \left[\frac{2N-1}{2}\right]r\right)p(x)\,dx = 0. \tag{8}$$

A similar expression exists for the case of an odd number of output levels. In either case the problem is quite susceptible to machine computation when $f(x)$, $p(x)$ and $N$ are specified. Results have been obtained for $f(x) = x^2$, $p(x) = 1/\sqrt{2\pi}\, e^{-x^2/2}$, $N = 2$ to 36. They are indicated in Table II on page 12.

A log-log plot of distortion vs number of output levels appears in Fig. 1. This curve is not a straight line. The tangent to the curve at $N = 36$ has the equation $D = 1.47\ N^{-1.74}$. A log-log plot of output level spacing vs number of outputs for the equal spacing which yields lowest distortion is shown in Fig. 4. This curve is also not a straight line. Lastly, a plot of the ratio of the distortion for the optimum quantizer to that for the optimum equally spaced level quantizer can be seen in Fig. 5.

## Key to the Tables

The numbering system for the table of output levels, $y_i$, and input interval end points, $x_i$, for the minimum mean-squared error quantization scheme for inputs with a normal amplitude probability density with standard deviation unity and mean zero is as follows:

> For the number of output levels, $N$, even, $x_1$ is the first end point of an input range to the right of the origin. An input between $x_i$ and $x_{i+1}$ produces an output $y_i$.
>
> For the number of output levels, $N$, odd, $y_1$ is the smallest non-negative output. An input between $x_{i-1}$ and $x_i$ produces an output $y_i$.

This description, illustrated in Fig. 6, is sufficient because of the symmetry of the quantizer. The expected squared error of the quantization process and informational entropy of the output of the quantizer are also tabulated for the optimal quantizers calculated.[2] (If $p_k$ is the probability of the $k$th output, then the informational entropy is defined as $-\sum_{k=1}^{N} p_k \log_2 p_k$.)

Table II also pertains to a normally distributed input with standard deviation equal to unity. The meaning of the entries is self-explanatory.

[2] The values of informational entropy given show the minimum average number of binary digits required to code the quantizer output. It can be seen from the tables that this number is always a rather large fraction of $\log_2 N$, and in most cases quite near 0.9 $\log_2 N$. In the cases where $N = 2^n$, $n$ an integer, a simple $n$ binary digit code for the outputs of the quantizer makes near optimum use of the digital transmission capacity of the system.

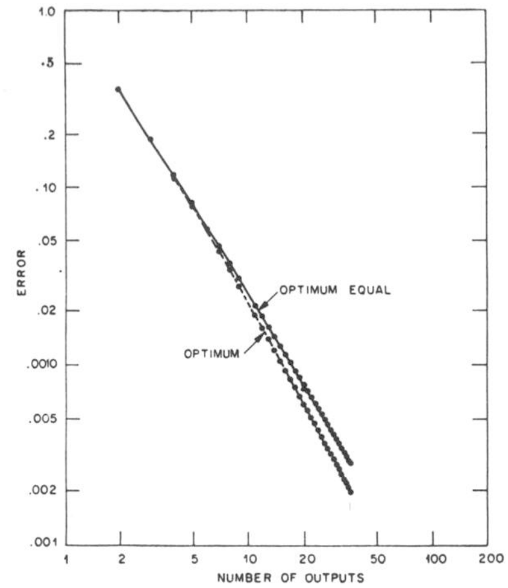


Fig. 1—Mean squared error vs number of outputs for optimum quantizer and optimum equally spaced level quantizer. (Minimum mean squared error for normally distributed input with $\sigma = 1$.)

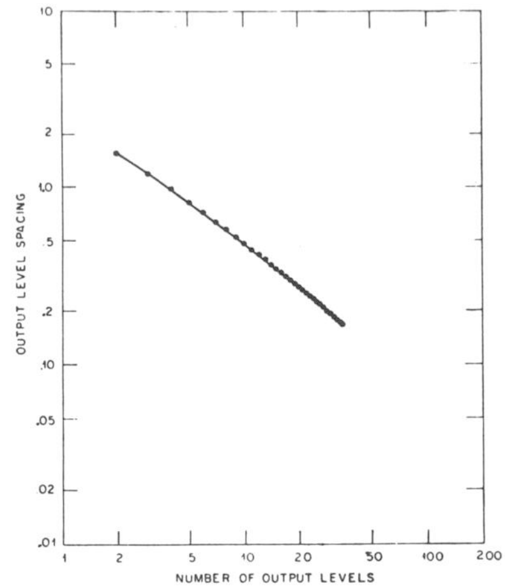


Fig. 4—Output level spacing vs number of output levels for equal optimum case. (Minimum mean squared error for normally distributed input with $\sigma = 1$.)

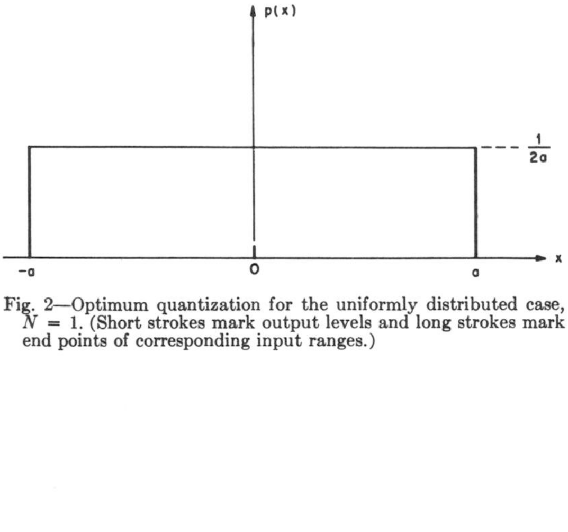


Fig. 2—Optimum quantization for the uniformly distributed case, $N = 1$. (Short strokes mark output levels and long strokes mark end points of corresponding input ranges.)

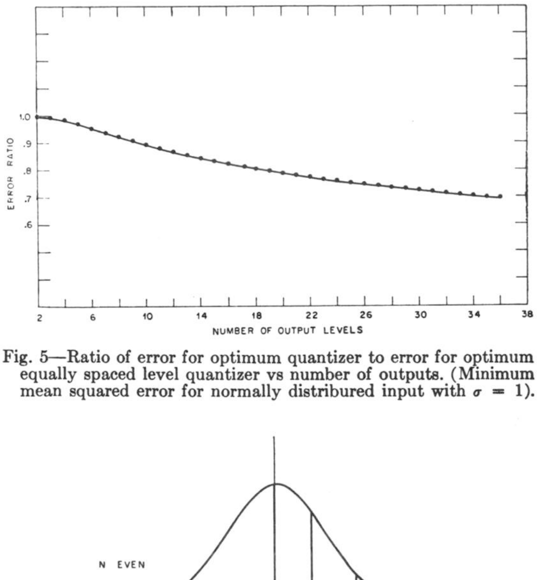


Fig. 5—Ratio of error for optimum quantizer to error for optimum equally spaced level quantizer vs number of outputs. (Minimum mean squared error for normally distribured input with $\sigma = 1$).

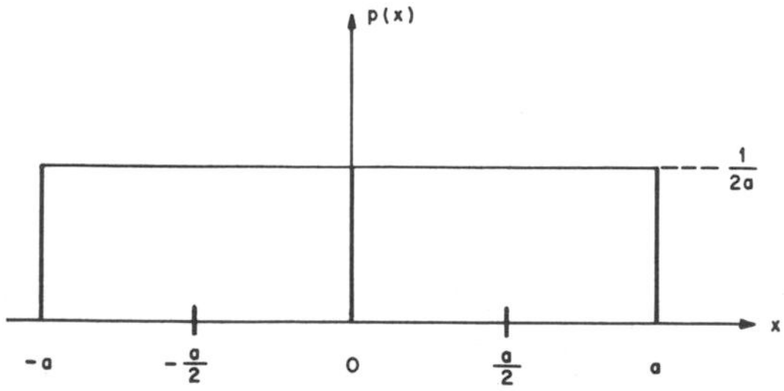


Fig. 3—Optimum quantization for the uniformly distributed case, $N = 2$. (Short strokes mark output levels and long strokes mark end points of corresponding input ranges.)

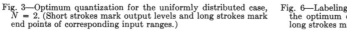

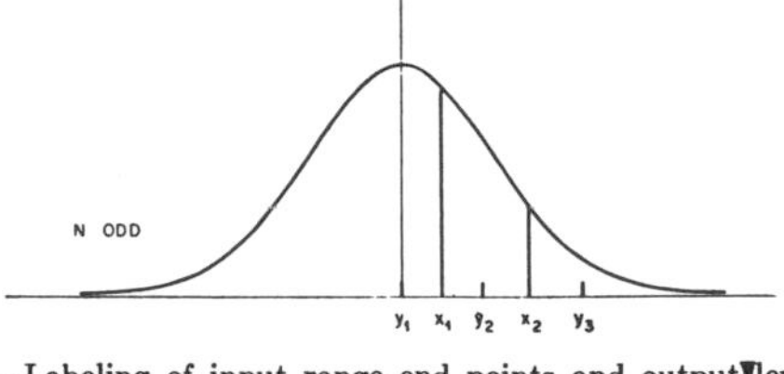

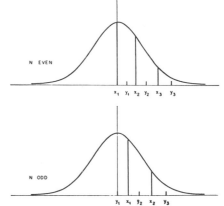

Fig. 6—Labeling of input range end points and output levels for the optimum quantizer. (Short strokes mark output levels and long strokes mark input range end points.)

TABLE I

Parameters for the Optimum Quantizer

| | N = 1 | | N = 2 | | N = 3 | |
|---|---|---|---|---|---|---|
| | $x_i$ | $y_i$ | $x_i$ | $y_i$ | $x_i$ | $y_i$ |
| j = 1 | — | 0.0 | 0.0 | 0.7980 | 0.0 | 1.224 |
| 2 | | | | | 0.6120 | |
| Error | 1.000 | | 0.3634 | | 0.1902 | |
| Entropy | 0.0 | | 1.000 | | 1.536 | |

| | N = 4 | | N = 5 | | N = 6 | |
|---|---|---|---|---|---|---|
| | $x_i$ | $y_i$ | $x_i$ | $y_i$ | $x_i$ | $y_i$ |
| j = 1 | 0.0 | 0.4528 | 0.3823 | 0.0 | 0.0 | 0.3177 |
| 2 | 0.9816 | 1.510 | 1.244 | 0.7646 | 0.6589 | 1.000 |
| 3 | | | | 1.724 | 1.447 | 1.894 |
| Error | 0.1175 | | 0.07994 | | 0.05798 | |
| Entropy | 1.911 | | 2.203 | | 2.443 | |

| | N = 7 | | N = 8 | | N = 9 | |
|---|---|---|---|---|---|---|
| | $x_i$ | $y_i$ | $x_i$ | $y_i$ | $x_i$ | $y_i$ |
| j = 1 | 0.2803 | 0.0 | 0.0 | 0.2451 | 0.2218 | 0.0 |
| 2 | 0.8744 | 0.5606 | 0.5006 | 0.7560 | 0.6812 | 0.4436 |
| 3 | 1.611 | 1.188 | 1.050 | 1.344 | 1.198 | 0.9188 |
| 4 | | 2.033 | 1.748 | 2.152 | 1.866 | 1.476 |
| 5 | | | | | | 2.255 |
| Error | 0.04400 | | 0.03454 | | 0.02785 | |
| Entropy | 2.647 | | 2.825 | | 2.983 | |

| | N = 10 | | N = 11 | | N = 12 | |
|---|---|---|---|---|---|---|
| | $x_i$ | $y_i$ | $x_i$ | $y_i$ | $x_i$ | $y_i$ |
| j = 1 | 0.0 | 0.1996 | 0.1837 | 0.0 | 0.0 | 0.1684 |
| 2 | 0.4047 | 0.6099 | 0.5599 | 0.3675 | 0.3401 | 0.5119 |
| 3 | 0.8339 | 1.058 | 0.9656 | 0.7524 | 0.6943 | 0.8768 |
| 4 | 1.325 | 1.591 | 1.436 | 1.179 | 1.081 | 1.286 |
| 5 | 1.968 | 2.345 | 2.059 | 1.693 | 1.534 | 1.783 |
| 6 | | | | 2.426 | 2.141 | 2.499 |
| Error | 0.02293 | | 0.01922 | | 0.01634 | |
| Entropy | 3.125 | | 3.253 | | 3.372 | |

| | N = 13 | | N = 14 | | N = 15 | |
|---|---|---|---|---|---|---|
| | $x_i$ | $y_i$ | $x_i$ | $y_i$ | $x_i$ | $y_i$ |
| j = 1 | 0.1569 | 0.0 | 0.0 | 0.1457 | 0.1369 | 0.0 |
| 2 | 0.4760 | 0.3138 | 0.2935 | 0.4413 | 0.4143 | 0.2739 |
| 3 | 0.8126 | 0.6383 | 0.5959 | 0.7505 | 0.7030 | 0.5548 |
| 4 | 1.184 | 0.9870 | 0.9181 | 1.086 | 1.013 | 0.8512 |
| 5 | 1.623 | 1.381 | 1.277 | 1.468 | 1.361 | 1.175 |
| 6 | 2.215 | 1.865 | 1.703 | 1.939 | 1.776 | 1.546 |
| 7 | | 2.565 | 2.282 | 2.625 | 2.344 | 2.007 |
| 8 | | | | | | 2.681 |
| Error | 0.01406 | | 0.01223 | | 0.01073 | |
| Entropy | 3.481 | | 3.582 | | 3.677 | |

| | N = 16 | | N = 17 | | N = 18 | |
|---|---|---|---|---|---|---|
| | $x_i$ | $y_i$ | $x_i$ | $y_i$ | $x_i$ | $y_i$ |
| j = 1 | 0.0 | 0.1284 | 0.1215 | 0.0 | 0.0 | 0.1148 |
| 2 | 0.2582 | 0.3881 | 0.3670 | 0.2430 | 0.2306 | 0.3464 |
| 3 | 0.5224 | 0.6568 | 0.6201 | 0.4909 | 0.4653 | 0.5843 |
| 4 | 0.7996 | 0.9424 | 0.8875 | 0.7493 | 0.7091 | 0.8339 |
| 5 | 1.099 | 1.256 | 1.178 | 1.026 | 0.9680 | 1.102 |
| 6 | 1.437 | 1.618 | 1.508 | 1.331 | 1.251 | 1.400 |
| 7 | 1.844 | 2.069 | 1.906 | 1.685 | 1.573 | 1.746 |
| 8 | 2.401 | 2.733 | 2.454 | 2.127 | 1.964 | 2.181 |
| 9 | | | | 2.781 | 2.504 | 2.826 |
| Error | 0.009497 | | 0.008463 | | 0.007589 | |
| Entropy | 3.765 | | 3.849 | | 3.928 | |

| | N = 19 | | N = 20 | | N = 21 | |
|---|---|---|---|---|---|---|
| | $x_i$ | $y_i$ | $x_i$ | $y_i$ | $x_i$ | $y_i$ |
| j = 1 | 0.1092 | 0.0 | 0.0 | 0.1038 | 0.09918 | 0.0 |
| 2 | 0.3294 | 0.2184 | 0.2083 | 0.3128 | 0.2989 | 0.1984 |
| 3 | 0.5551 | 0.4404 | 0.4197 | 0.5265 | 0.5027 | 0.3994 |
| 4 | 0.7908 | 0.6698 | 0.6375 | 0.7486 | 0.7137 | 0.6059 |
| 5 | 1.042 | 0.9117 | 0.8661 | 0.9837 | 0.9361 | 0.8215 |
| 6 | 1.318 | 1.173 | 1.111 | 1.239 | 1.175 | 1.051 |
| 7 | 1.634 | 1.464 | 1.381 | 1.524 | 1.440 | 1.300 |
| 8 | 2.018 | 1.803 | 1.690 | 1.857 | 1.743 | 1.579 |
| 9 | 2.550 | 2.232 | 2.068 | 2.279 | 2.116 | 1.908 |
| 10 | | 2.869 | 2.594 | 2.908 | 2.635 | 2.324 |
| 11 | | | | | | 2.946 |
| Error | 0.006844 | | 0.006203 | | 0.005648 | |
| Entropy | 4.002 | | 4.074 | | 4.141 | |

| | N = 22 | | N = 23 | | N = 24 | |
|---|---|---|---|---|---|---|
| | $x_i$ | $y_i$ | $x_i$ | $y_i$ | $x_i$ | $y_i$ |
| j = 1 | 0.0 | 0.09469 | 0.09085 | 0.0 | 0.0 | 0.08708 |
| 2 | 0.1900 | 0.2852 | 0.2736 | 0.1817 | 0.1746 | 0.2621 |
| 3 | 0.3822 | 0.4793 | 0.4594 | 0.3654 | 0.3510 | 0.4399 |
| 4 | 0.5794 | 0.6795 | 0.6507 | 0.5534 | 0.5312 | 0.6224 |
| 5 | 0.7844 | 0.8893 | 0.8504 | 0.7481 | 0.7173 | 0.8122 |
| 6 | 1.001 | 1.113 | 1.062 | 0.9527 | 0.9122 | 1.012 |
| 7 | 1.235 | 1.357 | 1.291 | 1.179 | 1.110 | 1.227 |
| 8 | 1.495 | 1.632 | 1.546 | 1.411 | 1.344 | 1.462 |
| 9 | 1.793 | 1.955 | 1.841 | 1.681 | 1.595 | 1.728 |
| 10 | 2.160 | 2.366 | 2.203 | 2.000 | 1.885 | 2.042 |
| 11 | 2.674 | 2.982 | 2.711 | 2.406 | 2.243 | 2.444 |
| 12 | | | | 3.016 | 2.746 | 3.048 |
| Error | 0.005165 | | 0.004741 | | 0.004367 | |
| Entropy | 4.206 | | 4.268 | | 4.327 | |

| | N = 25 | | N = 26 | | N = 27 | |
|---|---|---|---|---|---|---|
| | $x_i$ | $y_i$ | $x_i$ | $y_i$ | $x_i$ | $y_i$ |
| j = 1 | 0.08381 | 0.0 | 0.0 | 0.08060 | 0.07779 | 0.0 |
| 2 | 0.2522 | 0.1676 | 0.1616 | 0.2425 | 0.2340 | 0.1556 |
| 3 | 0.4231 | 0.3368 | 0.3245 | 0.4066 | 0.3921 | 0.3124 |
| 4 | 0.5982 | 0.5093 | 0.4905 | 0.5743 | 0.5537 | 0.4719 |
| 5 | 0.7797 | 0.6870 | 0.6610 | 0.7477 | 0.7202 | 0.6354 |
| 6 | 0.9702 | 0.8723 | 0.8383 | 0.9289 | 0.8936 | 0.8049 |
| 7 | 1.173 | 1.068 | 1.025 | 1.121 | 1.077 | 0.9824 |
| 8 | 1.394 | 1.279 | 1.224 | 1.328 | 1.273 | 1.171 |
| 9 | 1.641 | 1.510 | 1.442 | 1.556 | 1.487 | 1.374 |
| 10 | 1.927 | 1.772 | 1.685 | 1.814 | 1.727 | 1.599 |
| 11 | 2.281 | 2.083 | 1.968 | 2.121 | 2.006 | 1.854 |
| 12 | 2.779 | 2.480 | 2.318 | 2.514 | 2.352 | 2.158 |
| 13 | | 3.079 | 2.811 | 3.109 | 2.842 | 2.547 |
| 14 | | | | | | 3.137 |
| Error | 0.004036 | | 0.003741 | | 0.003477 | |
| Entropy | 4.384 | | 4.439 | | 4.491 | |

| | N = 28 | | N = 29 | | N = 30 | |
|---|---|---|---|---|---|---|
| | $x_i$ | $y_i$ | $x_i$ | $y_i$ | $x_i$ | $y_i$ |
| j = 1 | 0.0 | 0.07502 | 0.07257 | 0.0 | 0.0 | 0.07016 |
| 2 | 0.1503 | 0.2256 | 0.2182 | 0.1451 | 0.1406 | 0.2110 |
| 3 | 0.3018 | 0.3780 | 0.3655 | 0.2913 | 0.2821 | 0.3532 |
| 4 | 0.4556 | 0.5333 | 0.5154 | 0.4396 | 0.4255 | 0.4978 |
| 5 | 0.6132 | 0.6930 | 0.6693 | 0.5912 | 0.5719 | 0.6460 |
| 6 | 0.7760 | 0.8580 | 0.8287 | 0.7475 | 0.7225 | 0.7000 |
| 7 | 0.9460 | 1.033 | 0.9956 | 0.9100 | 0.8788 | 0.9586 |
| 8 | 1.126 | 1.218 | 1.172 | 1.081 | 1.043 | 1.127 |
| 9 | 1.319 | 1.419 | 1.362 | 1.263 | 1.217 | 1.306 |
| 10 | 1.529 | 1.640 | 1.570 | 1.461 | 1.404 | 1.501 |
| 11 | 1.766 | 1.892 | 1.804 | 1.680 | 1.609 | 1.717 |
| 12 | 2.042 | 2.193 | 2.077 | 1.929 | 1.840 | 1.964 |
| 13 | 2.385 | 2.578 | 2.417 | 2.226 | 2.111 | 2.258 |
| 14 | 2.871 | 3.164 | 2.899 | 2.609 | 2.448 | 2.638 |
| 15 | | | | 3.190 | 2.926 | 3.215 |
| Error | 0.003240 | | 0.003027 | | 0.002834 | |
| Entropy | 4.542 | | 4.591 | | 4.639 | |

*Cont'd next page*

TABLE I, *Cont'd*

|  | $N = 31$ | | $N = 32$ | | $N = 33$ | |
|---|---|---|---|---|---|---|
|  | $x_j$ | $y_j$ | $x_j$ | $y_j$ | $x_j$ | $y_j$ |
| $j = 1$ | 0.06802 | 0.0 | 0.0 | 0.06590 | 0.06400 | 0.0 |
| 2 | 0.2045 | 0.1360 | 0.1320 | 0.1981 | 0.1924 | 0.1280 |
| 3 | 0.3422 | 0.2729 | 0.2648 | 0.3314 | 0.3218 | 0.2567 |
| 4 | 0.4822 | 0.4115 | 0.3991 | 0.4668 | 0.4530 | 0.3868 |
| 5 | 0.6254 | 0.5528 | 0.5359 | 0.6050 | 0.5869 | 0.5192 |
| 6 | 0.7730 | 0.6979 | 0.6761 | 0.7473 | 0.7245 | 0.6547 |
| 7 | 0.9265 | 0.8481 | 0.8210 | 0.8947 | 0.8667 | 0.7943 |
| 8 | 1.088 | 1.005 | 0.9718 | 1.049 | 1.015 | 0.9392 |
| 9 | 1.259 | 1.170 | 1.130 | 1.212 | 1.171 | 1.091 |
| 10 | 1.444 | 1.347 | 1.299 | 1.387 | 1.338 | 1.252 |
| 11 | 1.646 | 1.540 | 1.482 | 1.577 | 1.518 | 1.424 |
| 12 | 1.875 | 1.753 | 1.682 | 1.788 | 1.716 | 1.612 |
| 13 | 2.143 | 1.997 | 1.908 | 2.029 | 1.940 | 1.821 |
| 14 | 2.477 | 2.289 | 2.174 | 2.319 | 2.204 | 2.060 |
| 15 | 2.952 | 2.665 | 2.505 | 2.692 | 2.533 | 2.347 |
| 16 |  | 3.239 | 2.977 | 3.263 | 3.002 | 2.718 |
| 17 |  |  |  |  |  | 3.285 |
| Error | 0.002658 | | 0.002499 | | 0.002354 | |
| Entropy | 4.685 | | 4.730 | | 4.773 | |

|  | $N = 34$ | | $N = 35$ | | $N = 36$ | |
|---|---|---|---|---|---|---|
|  | $x_j$ | $y_j$ | $x_j$ | $y_j$ | $x_j$ | $y_j$ |
| $j = 1$ | 0.0 | 0.06212 | 0.06043 | 0.0 | 0.0 | 0.05876 |
| 2 | 0.1244 | 0.1867 | 0.1816 | 0.1209 | 0.1177 | 0.1765 |
| 3 | 0.2495 | 0.3122 | 0.3036 | 0.2423 | 0.2359 | 0.2952 |
| 4 | 0.3758 | 0.4394 | 0.4272 | 0.3650 | 0.3552 | 0.4152 |
| 5 | 0.5043 | 0.5691 | 0.5530 | 0.4895 | 0.4762 | 0.5372 |
| 6 | 0.6355 | 0.7020 | 0.6819 | 0.6166 | 0.5996 | 0.6620 |
| 7 | 0.7705 | 0.8391 | 0.8146 | 0.7471 | 0.7261 | 0.7903 |
| 8 | 0.9104 | 0.9818 | 0.9523 | 0.8820 | 0.8567 | 0.9231 |
| 9 | 1.057 | 1.131 | 1.096 | 1.023 | 0.9923 | 1.062 |
| 10 | 1.211 | 1.290 | 1.248 | 1.170 | 1.134 | 1.207 |
| 11 | 1.375 | 1.460 | 1.411 | 1.327 | 1.285 | 1.362 |
| 12 | 1.553 | 1.646 | 1.587 | 1.495 | 1.445 | 1.528 |
| 13 | 1.749 | 1.853 | 1.781 | 1.679 | 1.619 | 1.710 |
| 14 | 1.971 | 2.090 | 2.001 | 1.883 | 1.812 | 1.913 |
| 15 | 2.232 | 2.375 | 2.260 | 2.119 | 2.030 | 2.146 |
| 16 | 2.559 | 2.743 | 2.584 | 2.401 | 2.287 | 2.427 |
| 17 | 3.025 | 3.307 | 3.048 | 2.767 | 2.609 | 2.791 |
| 18 |  |  |  | 3.328 | 3.070 | 3.349 |
| Error | 0.002220 | | 0.002097 | | 0.001985 | |
| Entropy | 4.815 | | 4.856 | | 4.895 | |

TABLE II

PARAMETERS FOR THE OPTIMUM EQUALLY SPACED LEVEL QUANTIZER

| Number Output Levels | Output Level Spacing | Mean Squared Error | Informational Entropy |
|---|---|---|---|
| 1 | — | 1.000 | 0.0 |
| 2 | 1.596 | 0.3634 | 1.000 |
| 3 | 1.224 | 0.1902 | 1.536 |
| 4 | 0.9957 | 0.1188 | 1.904 |
| 5 | 0.8430 | 0.08218 | 2.183 |
| 6 | 0.7334 | 0.06065 | 2.409 |
| 7 | 0.6508 | 0.04686 | 2.598 |
| 8 | 0.5860 | 0.03744 | 2.761 |
| 9 | 0.5338 | 0.03069 | 2.904 |
| 10 | 0.4908 | 0.02568 | 3.032 |
| 11 | 0.4546 | 0.02185 | 3.148 |
| 12 | 0.4238 | 0.01885 | 3.253 |
| 13 | 0.3972 | 0.01645 | 3.350 |
| 14 | 0.3739 | 0.01450 | 3.440 |
| 15 | 0.3534 | 0.01289 | 3.524 |
| 16 | 0.3352 | 0.01154 | 3.602 |
| 17 | 0.3189 | 0.01040 | 3.676 |
| 18 | 0.3042 | 0.009430 | 3.746 |
| 19 | 0.2909 | 0.008594 | 3.811 |
| 20 | 0.2788 | 0.007869 | 3.874 |
| 21 | 0.2678 | 0.007235 | 3.933 |
| 22 | 0.2576 | 0.006678 | 3.990 |
| 23 | 0.2482 | 0.006185 | 4.045 |
| 24 | 0.2396 | 0.005747 | 4.097 |
| 25 | 0.2315 | 0.005355 | 4.146 |
| 26 | 0.2240 | 0.005004 | 4.194 |
| 27 | 0.2171 | 0.004687 | 4.241 |
| 28 | 0.2105 | 0.004401 | 4.285 |
| 29 | 0.2044 | 0.004141 | 4.328 |
| 30 | 0.1987 | 0.003905 | 4.370 |
| 31 | 0.1932 | 0.003688 | 4.410 |
| 32 | 0.1881 | 0.003490 | 4.449 |
| 33 | 0.1833 | 0.003308 | 4.487 |
| 34 | 0.1787 | 0.003141 | 4.524 |
| 35 | 0.1744 | 0.002986 | 4.560 |
| 36 | 0.1703 | 0.002843 | 4.594 |

# 22



Reprinted from *IEEE Trans. Inform. Theory,* **IT-10**(4), 384–385 (1964)

# QUANTIZING FOR MINIMUM DISTORTION


SUMMARY

It is shown that the interval points, $x_K$, which minimize the distortion error

$$D = \sum_{k=0}^{N-1} \int_{xk}^{xk_{+1}} P(x)\,|x - y_k|^\theta\,dx$$

for a continuous, differentiable density function, $P(x)$, are given approximately by

$$\int_0^{x_n} [P(x)]^{1/(\theta+1)}\,dx \cong 2C_1 n + C_2$$

where $C_1$ and $C_2$ are constants.


In a paper with the above title, Max[1] has given a number of computed values for the range end points $x_k$ and the output levels $y_k$ of an optimum quantizer which minimizes a distortion error $D$ defined by

$$D = \sum_{k=0}^{N-1} \int_{x_k}^{x_{k+1}} P(x)\,|x - y_k|^\theta\,dx. \tag{1}$$

The specific cases treated by Max had $\theta = 2$ and a normal probability density function $P(x) = (2\pi)^{-1/2} \exp(-\frac{1}{2}x^2)$ for the input signal level. Explicit and quite accurate expressions for the required $x_k$ and $y_k$ may be obtained for more general $P(x)$ by the following approximation procedure.

The extreme range limits, $x_0$ and $x_N$, are presumed given. The other $x_k$ and the $y_k$ are to be adjusted so that $\partial D/\partial x_k = \partial D/\partial y_k = 0$. If $\epsilon_k$ $\Delta_k$ are defined by

$$\epsilon_k = x_{k+1} - x_k \tag{2}$$

$$\Delta_k = y_k - x_k \tag{3}$$

then the above two conditions may be written

$$\epsilon_k = \Delta_{k+1} + \Delta_k \tag{4}$$

$$\int_0^{\Delta_k} P(x_k + r)(\Delta_k - r)^{\theta-1}\,dr = \int_{\Delta_k}^{\epsilon_k} P(x_k + r)(r - \Delta_k)^{\theta-1}\,dr. \tag{5}$$

For $P(x)$ sufficiently differentiable, $P(x_k + r)$ can be expanded in a Taylor's series about $x_k$, and (5) becomes

$$\begin{aligned} 0 = {} & [P(x_k) + \Delta_k P'(x_k) + \tfrac{1}{2}\Delta_k^2 P''(x_k) + \cdots]\,\frac{1}{\theta}\,(\Delta_{k+1}^\theta - \Delta_k^\theta) \\ & + [P'(x_k) + \Delta_k P''(x_k) + \tfrac{1}{2}\Delta_k^2 P'''(x_k) + \cdots] \cdot \frac{1}{\theta+1}\,(\Delta_{k+1}^{\theta+1} + \Delta_k^{\theta+1}) \\ & + [\tfrac{1}{2}P''(x_k) + \tfrac{1}{6}\Delta_k P'''(x_k) + \cdots]\,\frac{1}{\theta+2}\,(\Delta_{k+1}^{\theta+2} - \Delta_k^{\theta+2}) \\ & + [\tfrac{1}{6}P'''(x_k) + \cdots]\,\frac{1}{\theta+3}\,(\Delta_{k+1}^{\theta+3} + \Delta_k^{\theta+3}) + \cdots. \end{aligned}$$

Now suppose that $N$ is large enough so that

$$P(x_k) \gg \Delta_k P'(x_k) \gg \Delta_k^2 P''(x_k) \gg \cdots,$$

then only the first two lines are important, and

$$-\frac{1}{\theta+1}\,\frac{P'(x_k)}{P(x_k)} \cong \frac{1}{\theta}\,\frac{\Delta_{k+1}^\theta - \Delta_k^\theta}{\Delta_{k+1}^{\theta+1} + \Delta_k^{\theta+1}}.$$

With $\Delta_{k+1} - \Delta_k \cong d\Delta_k \to 0$ and $\epsilon_k \cong dx_k \to 0$, this becomes

$$-\frac{1}{\theta+1}\,\frac{P'(x_k)}{P(x_k)} \cong \frac{d\Delta_k}{\Delta_k x_k}$$

which integrates to

$$[P(x_k)]^{1/\theta+1}\Delta_k \cong C_1 = \text{constant}. \tag{6}$$

Since

$$\Delta_k \cong \tfrac{1}{2}\epsilon_k \cong \tfrac{1}{2}\,dx_k,$$

this can be integrated again, yielding

$$\int_0^{x_n} [P(x)]^{1/(\theta+1)}\,dx \cong 2C_1 n + C_2. \tag{7}$$

The integration constants, $C_1$ and $C_2$, can be adjusted to give the required fit to the extreme range limits $x_0$ and $x_N$.

For the case treated by Max, with $\theta = 2$ and a normal $P(x)$, (7) becomes

$$x_n = \sqrt{6}\,\operatorname{erf}^{-1}\left(\frac{2n - N}{N + \alpha}\right) \tag{8}$$

where $\operatorname{erf}^{-1}$ is the inverse error function. If $\alpha$ were set equal to zero, this would yield the correct values $x_0 = -\infty$, $x_N = +\infty$. However, the assumptions made in deriving (7) are not valid for the last interval, which must have $\epsilon_{N-1} = \infty$, and it is more accurate to keep $\alpha$ finite and restrict (8) to the range $1 \leqq n \leqq N - 1$. The constant $\alpha$ may now be adjusted so that the $x_n$ given by the approximation (8) satisfy certain known limiting properties of the exact solution.

For a normal frequency function and $\theta = 2$, (5) becomes

$$\int_0^{\epsilon_n} (r - \Delta_n) e^{-x_n r - r^2/2}\,dr = 0.$$

For $x_n$ very large, but $x_n\epsilon_n$ and $\Delta_n x_n$ not necessarily either large or small, this reduces to

$$x_n\Delta_n \cong 1 - \frac{x_n\epsilon_n}{e^{x_n\epsilon_n} - 1}. \tag{9}$$

From this result and the relations (2), (3), and (4) it follows that

$$\lim_{N\to\infty} x_{N-1}\Delta_{N-1} = 1 \tag{10}$$

$$\lim_{N\to\infty} x_{N-2}\epsilon_{N-2} = L, \tag{11}$$

where $L = 1.5936$ is the root of

$$L + \frac{L}{e^L - 1} = 2.$$

In order to have the approximation (8) satisfy the limit property (11) it is necessary to set

$$\alpha = \frac{2}{e^{L/3} - 1} - 2 = 0.8532. \tag{12}$$

Manuscript received February 4, 1964.

[1] J. Max, "Quantizing for Minimum Distortion," IEEE Trans. on Information Theory, vol. IT-6, pp. 7–12; January, 1960.

Although the approximation (8) was derived on the assumption that $N$ was large, it is remarkably accurate even for small $N$. For the case $N = 6$, Max[1] computes a minimum $D = 0.05798$. The $x_n$ given by (8) lead to a value $D = 0.05806$, and the individual values of the $x_n$ are within 3 per cent of the correct values. For $N = 36$, all of $x_n$ given by (8) are correct to better than one-half per cent, and the resulting distortion error is indistinguishable from Max's value. Considerably larger deviations of the $x_n$ from the optimum values could be permitted without making any important change in the distortion error. It is convenient and sufficiently accurate to obtain the output levels, $y_n$, by computing (8) for both integral and half-integral values of $n$ and setting $y_n = x_{n+(1/2)}$.

As was pointed out by Max,[1] practical limitations in equipment may require that all the input intervals be equal in size, and that the output levels bisect these intervals. In terms of the notation used above, this requirement is $\epsilon_n = 2\Delta_n = r =$ constant. For this case also, it is possible to get an accurate functional relationship between $r$ and $N$ by using the Euler-McClaurin summation formula to evaluate the sum which appears in (8) of the paper by Max.[1] The algebra is straightforward, but rather long, and only the final result will be quoted here.

Suppose that $P(x)$ is a symmetric function and define

$$F_0(z) = \int_z^{zN} P(x)\,dx$$

$$F_1(z) = \int_z^{zN} xP(x)\,dx$$

$$R = \tfrac{1}{2}Nr$$

$$A \equiv A(R) = 4F_1(R) - 4RF_0(R)$$

$$B \equiv B(R) = 2RF_0(R) - F_1(R)$$

$$C \equiv C(R) = R^2P(R) - 2RF_0(R).$$

Then, for large $N$, $D$ will be minimized if $R$ is a root of

$$N^2A + 4NB - \tfrac{2}{3}R + \tfrac{4}{3}C = 0$$

or

$$N = \frac{2}{A}\left(-B + \sqrt{\tfrac{1}{6}RA + B^2 - \tfrac{1}{3}AC}\right). \qquad (13)$$

In general, the right-hand side is a rapidly varying function of $R$, so it is easy to plot $R$ as a slowly varying function of $N$, and from $R$ compute $r = 2R/N$.

For the particular case where $P(x)$ is the normal distribution, the results based on (13) can be compared with the values of $r$ computed by Max.[1]

| $N$ | $r$ (from (13) | $r$ (from Max) |
|---|---|---|
| 4 | 0.99513 | 0.9957 |
| 36 | 0.17030 | 0.1703 |

Evidently, the accuracy of (13) is more than adequate even for small $N$.

Acknowledgment

I am indebted to James D. Bruce for arousing my interest in this problem.

Glenn M. Roe
GE Research Lab.
Schenectady, N. Y.

# 23



Reprinted from *IEEE Trans. Inform. Theory,* **IT-15**(2), 248–252 (1969)

# On Optimum Quantization

ROGER C. WOOD, MEMBER, IEEE

***Abstract*—The problem of minimizing mean-square quantization error is considered and simple closed form approximations based on the work of Max and Roe are derived for the quantization error and entropy of signals quantized by the optimum fixed-*N* quantizer. These approximations are then used to show that, when *N* is moderately large, it is better to use equi-interval quantizing than the optimum fixed-*N* quantizer if the signal is to be subsequently buffered and transmitted at a fixed bit rate. Finally, the problem of optimum quantizing in the presence of buffering is examined, and the numerical results presented for Gaussian signals indicate that equilevel quantizing yields nearly optimum results.**

THE REDUCTION of quantization error by tailoring the structure of the quantizer to the signal to be processed has received considerable theoretical attention in the past. We shall consider this concept for the special case of stochastic signals whose samples are independently and identically distributed. This problem of quantizing for minimum distortion for a signal of known probability density $p(x)$ was first considered in detail by Max [1] in 1961. By assuming the number of levels $N$ to be fixed, Max derived equations for the optimum intervals $(y_{k-1}, y_k)$ and levels $x_k$. When the criterion is minimum mean-square error, the appropriate equations are

$$x_k = \frac{\int_{y_{k-1}}^{y_k} xp(x)\,dx}{\int_{y_{k-1}}^{y_k} p(x)\,dx} \equiv \mu(y_{k-1}, y_k) \tag{1}$$

and

$$y_k = \tfrac{1}{2}(x_k + x_{k+1}). \tag{2}$$

Hence, the representative levels are the conditional means on the given intervals, and the interval boundaries are halfway between the levels. The analytical solution of these equations is impossible for all but trivial cases, but a numerical solution is straightforward. Moreover, Roe [2] has derived excellent approximate formulas based on Max's results.

The above equations will, in general, require an iteration technique for their solution. One such technique is given by Max, and many others are also feasible.

The purpose of this paper is to derive a simple estimate of the error saving to be obtained by Max's quantizer, which shall be labeled the optimum fixed-$N$ quantizer; to examine the effect on signal entropy of such quantizing, and finally to examine the problem of optimum quantization in the presence of buffering (i.e., for fixed transmission rate and, therefore, fixed entropy).

Manuscript received November 17, 1967; revised August 9, 1968. This research was supported in part by the National Science Foundation under Grant GK 144 and by NASA under Research Grant G237-62.

The author is with the Department of Electrical Engineering, University of California, Santa Barbara, Calif. 93106.

### A Convenient Approximation

Since all forms of the optimizing equations depend on the conditional mean $\mu(\eta_1, \eta_2)$, we shall generate an approximation for that function. To do so, we note that if $p(x)$ is sufficiently well behaved[1] on the interval $(\xi - \Delta/2, \xi + \Delta/2)$ we can generate Taylor's series expansions about $\xi$ for both the numerator and denominator, and therefore, formally, we can write

$$\mu\left(\xi - \frac{\Delta}{2}, \xi + \frac{\Delta}{2}\right) \cong \frac{\xi p(\xi) + \frac{\Delta^2}{24}[\xi p''(\xi) + 2p'(\xi)]}{p(\xi) + \frac{\Delta^2}{24}p''(\xi)} \tag{3}$$

$$= \xi + \frac{\frac{\Delta^2}{12}p'(\xi)}{p(\xi) + \frac{\Delta^2}{24}p''(\xi)} \tag{4}$$

$$\cong \xi + \frac{\Delta^2}{12}\frac{p'(\xi)}{p(\xi)} \tag{5}$$

for $\Delta$ small enough.

Thus we have derived, for small intervals, an approximate expression for the conditional mean in terms of the midpoint and length of the given interval.

### The Second-Order Moments of the Quantized Distribution

We can give a considerable amount of information about the behavior of the first two moments of the quantized variable. In particular we have the following theorem.

*Theorem 1*

When the optimum fixed-$N$ quantizer is employed, the first moment of the quantized variable is given by $\mu$, and the second moment can be approximated by

$$V(x^*) \cong \sigma^2 - \sum_k \frac{\Delta_k^3}{12} p(\xi_k)$$

[1] Since in all cases we truncate the Taylor's series after several terms, it will suffice for our purposes that the first few (at most, five) derivatives exist and are continuous. Moreover, for the approximation which will be developed to be close, the number of $N$ levels must be large enough (i.e., the interval lengths $\Delta$ small enough) so that

$$p(x) >> \Delta p'(x) >> \Delta^2 p''(x) >> \cdots .$$

Thus the critical interval size, for application of the approximations, is seen to depend closely upon the nature of the probability density $p(x)$.

where $\Delta_k$ is the length and $\xi_k$ the midpoint of the $k$th quantizer interval.

*Proof:* For the first moment, $E(x^*) = E[E(x \mid y_{k-1} < x < y_k)] = \mu$ so that the quantized variable has the same mean as the original continuous variable. Considering the second moment of $x^*$, we note first that we can write

$$E(x^2) \equiv \int_{-\infty}^{\infty} x^2 p(x)\, dx = \sum_k \int_{\xi_k - 1/2\Delta_k}^{\xi_k + 1/2\Delta_k} x^2 p(x)\, dx. \tag{6}$$

Expanding $x^2p(x)$ about $x = \xi$ yields, after integrating over the intervals $(\xi_k - \frac{1}{2}\Delta_k, \xi_k + \frac{1}{2}\Delta_k)$,

$$E(x^2) = \sum_k \left(\Delta_k \xi_k^2 p(\xi_k) + \frac{\Delta_k^3}{4\cdot 3!}[\xi_k^2 p''(\xi_k) + 4\xi_k p'(\xi_k) + 2p(\xi_k)] + O(\Delta_k^5)\right). \tag{7}$$

Therefore, letting $\mu_k = E[x \mid y_{k-1} < x < y_k]$ and $p_k = P[y_{k-1} < x < y_k]$, we can write

$$\begin{aligned} E[(x^*)^2] &= \sum_k \mu_k^2 p_k \\ &\cong \sum_k \left\{\left[\xi_k + \frac{\frac{\Delta_k^2}{12}p'(\xi_k)}{p(\xi_k) + \frac{\Delta_k^2}{24}p''(\xi_k)}\right] \cdot \left[\Delta_k \xi_k p(\xi_k) + \frac{\Delta_k^3 \xi_k p''(\xi_k)}{24} + \frac{2\Delta_k^3 p'(\xi_k)}{24}\right]\right\} \\ &\cong \sum_k \left(\Delta_k \xi_k^2 p(\xi_k) + \frac{\Delta_k^3}{24}[4\xi_k p'(\xi_k) + \xi_k^2 p''(\xi_k)]\right) \\ &\cong E(x^2) - \tfrac{1}{12}\sum_k \Delta_k^3 p(\xi_k), \end{aligned} \tag{8}$$

for $\Delta_k$ small enough. Hence, the variance of the quantized variable is less than that of the continuous variable and is given by

$$V(x^*) = \sigma^2 - \tfrac{1}{12}\sum \Delta_k^3 p(\xi_k) + O(\Delta_k^5) \tag{9}$$

which completes the proof.

The significance of this result is that the variance of the quantized variable is less than that of the original signal. Hence, the signal and noise are dependent and no pseudo-independence of the sort considered by Widrow [3] is possible. Thus, the common additive noise model is not appropriate for the case of optimum fixed-$N$ quantizing.

## Closed Form Approximations for the Mean-Square Error and the Entropy of the Quantized Signal

Although the correction term for the second moment derived above did not possess a convenient closed form, it enabled us to demonstrate the lack of independence between signal and noise. We now develop a general technique for deriving a closed form approximation to the error, and therefore also the correction term for signals with well-behaved probability density functions. In addition, we derive an approximation to the entropy of the quantized sample.

For a mean-square error criterion, Roe has shown that the interval points for the optimum fixed-$N$ quantizer can be approximated by

$$\int_0^{y_k} [p(x)]^{1/3}\, dx \cong 2C_1 k + C_2 \tag{10}$$

where $C_1$ and $C_2$ are constants, provided only that, in the sense described previously, $N$ is large and $p(x)$ sufficiently differentiable. Clearly, if $(y_o, y_N)$ spans the domain of definition of $p(x)$, the quantity

$$\int_0^{y_N} [p(x)]^{1/3}\, dx - \int_0^{y_o} [p(x)]^{1/3}\, dx$$

depends only on $p(x)$ and $C_1 = O(1/N)$.

*Theorem 2*

For any signal with probability distribution $p(x)$ well enough behaved for Roe's approximations (10) to be applicable, the mean-square quantization error of the optimum fixed-$N$ quantizer can be approximated, for large $N$ ($\Delta$ small), by

$$\epsilon^2 = \tfrac{1}{12}(2C_1)^3 N \tag{11}$$

where $C_1$ is given by evaluating (10) and is of the order $N^{-1}$.

*Proof:* For any $p(x)$ well enough behaved

$$\int_0^{y_k} [p(x)]^{1/3}\, dx \cong 2C_1 k + C_2 .$$

If we now define $z(x)$ to be

$$z = \int_0^x [p(t)]^{1/3}\, dt,$$

$$\frac{dx}{dz} = \frac{1}{\frac{dz}{dx}} = [p(x)]^{-1/3}$$

and

$$\Delta_k = [z(y_k) - z(y_{k-1})]\left.\frac{dx}{dz}\right|_{(x=\xi_k)} = 2C_1[p(\xi_k)]^{-1/3}.$$

Hence, we can write

$$\begin{aligned} \epsilon^2 &\cong \tfrac{1}{12}(2C_1)^2 \int_{y_o}^{y_N} [[p(x)]^{-1/3}]^2 p(x)\, dx \\ &= \tfrac{1}{12}(2C_1)^2 \int_{y_o}^{y_N} [p(x)]^{1/3}\, dx \\ &= \tfrac{1}{12}(2C_1)^2[2C_1 N + C_2 - 2C_1\cdot O - C_2] \\ &= \tfrac{1}{12}(2C_1)^3 N \end{aligned}$$

which concludes the proof.

For the case of a Gaussian signal, this procedure yields

$$\epsilon^2 = \frac{2.73N}{(N + 0.853)^3} \tag{12}$$

since $C_1 = 1.6/(N + 0.853)$ (see [2]).

TABLE I
COMPARISON OF EXACT AND APPROXIMATE VALUES FOR MEAN-SQUARE ERROR AND ENTROPY FOR TWO QUANTIZATION METHODS

| | Optimum Fixed $N$ | | | | Equilevel | | | |
|---|---|---|---|---|---|---|---|---|
| | Mean-Square Error | | Entropy | | Mean-Square Error | | Entropy | |
| $N$ | Exact | Approximate | Exact | Approximate | Exact | Approximate | Exact | Approximate |
| 5 | 0.0799 | 0.0797 | 2.20 | 2.24 | 0.176 | 0.213 | 1.50 | 1.37 |
| 10 | 0.0229 | 0.0232 | 3.13 | 3.12 | 0.0507 | 0.0533 | 2.40 | 2.37 |
| 15 | 0.0107 | 0.0109 | 3.68 | 3.67 | 0.0240 | 0.0237 | 2.97 | 2.95 |
| 20 | 0.00620 | 0.00628 | 4.07 | 4.07 | 0.0132 | 0.0133 | 3.37 | 3.36 |
| 25 | 0.00404 | 0.00408 | 4.38 | 4.38 | 0.00847 | 0.00852 | 3.69 | 3.69 |
| 30 | 0.00283 | 0.00287 | 4.64 | 4.64 | 0.00590 | 0.00592 | 3.95 | 3.95 |
| 35 | 0.00210 | 0.00212 | 4.86 | 4.86 | 0.00434 | 0.00435 | 4.17 | 4.17 |

We now derive asymptotic expressions for the entropy of the quantized signal that depend only upon the properties of the probability density $p(x)$, for both the optimum fixed $N$ and the equilevel quantizer.

*Theorem 3*

For signals of finite range $R$ and such that the entropy $H(x)$ of the continuous signal is finite, the entropy of the quantized signal, when the optimum fixed-$N$ quantizer is employed, can be approximated by

$$H(x_o^*) \cong \tfrac{2}{3}H(x) - \tfrac{1}{3}\log\left(\frac{12\epsilon^2}{N}\right) \tag{13}$$

for large $N$.

If equilevel quantizing is performed, the entropy of the quantized signal approaches

$$H(x_e^*) = H(x) - \tfrac{1}{2}\log\left(\frac{12\epsilon^2}{N}\right) - \tfrac{1}{2}\log R \tag{14}$$

*Proof:* We note that

$$p_k \log p_k = p(\xi_k)\,\Delta_k[\log p(\xi_k) + \log \Delta_k]$$

so that

$$\begin{aligned}
H(x_o^*) &= -\sum_k p_k \log p_k \\
&\cong -\Big(\sum_k p(\xi_k)\log p(\xi_k)\,\Delta_k + \sum_k (\log \Delta_k) p(\xi_k)\,\Delta_k\Big) \\
&\cong H(x) - \sum_k (\log \Delta_k) p(\xi_k)\,\Delta_k \qquad \text{for small } \Delta_k \\
&\cong H(x) - \sum_k (\log [2C_1(p(\xi_k))^{-1/3}])p(\xi_k)\,\Delta_k \\
&\cong H(x) - \log 2C_1 + \frac{1}{3}\int_{v_0}^{v_N} p(\xi)\log p(\xi)\,d\xi \\
&= \tfrac{2}{3}H(x) - \log 2C_1 \\
&\cong \tfrac{2}{3}H(x) - \tfrac{1}{3}\log\left(\frac{12\epsilon^2}{N}\right),
\end{aligned}$$

since

$$\epsilon^2 \cong \frac{(2C_1)^3}{12} N,$$

and

$$2C_1 \cong \left(\frac{12\epsilon^2}{N}\right)^{1/3}.$$

Thus, we have derived an expression for the entropy of the quantized signal, which depends only on the properties of the probability density $p(x)$. We can, in a similar fashion, derive an expression for $H(x^*)$ when equi-interval quantizing is employed. To do this, we note that

$$\begin{aligned}
H(x_e^*) &= -\sum_k p_k \log p_k \\
&\cong -\sum_k p(\xi_k)\,\Delta[\log p(\xi_k) + \log \Delta] \\
&\cong H(x) - \log \Delta \\
&\cong H(x) - \tfrac{1}{2}\log\frac{12\epsilon^2}{N} - \tfrac{1}{2}\log R
\end{aligned}$$

since $\Delta = R/N$ and $\epsilon^2 = \frac{1}{12}\Delta^2$ for $N$ large enough.

The rapid convergence of these approximations, for the case of Gaussian signals, is readily apparent from the data of Table I, which contains exact and approximate computations of entropy and mean-square error for equilevel and optimum fixed-$N$ quantization. In performing the equilevel computations, $R$ was taken to be 8 in the design of the quantizer and the approximations. The exact results, however, are based on the true (infinite) range.

## THE APPLICATION OF BUFFERING AND ENCODING TO THE QUANTIZED SIGNAL

In the previous paragraphs, we derived expressions for the mean-square error and the entropy of the quantized signal for both the optimum fixed-$N$ quantizer and for simple equi-interval quantizing. Those estimates are now employed to evaluate the effect of encoding the quantized signals and buffering so that the average bit rate is fixed. We assume, for purposes of comparison, that the mean-square error is fixed, and examine the difference in entropy between signals quantized by the above two devices. For this case, again under the assumption that the probability density $p(x)$ is well behaved, we are able to prove a quite startling and significant theorem about the relative asymptotic behavior of the two types of quantizers.

*Theorem 4*

Within the limits of our approximation, and therefore asymptotically for large $N$ (given $p(x)$ well behaved and $H(x)$ finite) the output of the optimum fixed-$N$ quantizer has entropy greater than or equal to that of the output of an equilevel quantizer yielding the same mean-square error, provided the range can be assumed to be finite. Therefore, assuming $N$ is large, it is always better[2] to quantize with an equilevel quantizer than with an optimum fixed-$N$ quantizer, if the output signal is to be encoded and transmitted at a fixed average bit rate.

*Proof:* We note that from (13) and (14), we can write

$$H(x_o^*) - H(x_e^*) \cong \tfrac{1}{3}\log R - \tfrac{1}{3}H(x) + \tfrac{1}{3}\log(N_o/N_e) \quad (15)$$

where the subscripts $o$ and $e$ represent optimum fixed $N$ and equilevel quantizers, respectively. Since the errors are assumed to be equal

$$\frac{(2C_1)^3}{12}N_o = \frac{R^2}{12N_e^2}. \quad (16)$$

Now applying (10) for $y_N$ and $y_o$ we can write

$$2C_1 = \int_0^{y_N} [p(x)]^{1/3}\,dx/N_o\,. \quad (17)$$

Thus, by combining (16) and (17), we can solve for the ratio $N_o/N_e$ and (15) becomes

$$\begin{aligned} H(x_o^*) &- H(x_e^*) \\ &\cong \tfrac{1}{3}H(x) + \tfrac{1}{2}\log\left[\int_{y_o}^{y_N}[p(x)]^{1/3}\,dx\right] \\ &= \frac{1}{2}\left[\frac{2}{3}\int_{y_o}^{y_N} p(x)\log p(x)\,dx + \log\left(\int_{y_o}^{y_N}[p(x)]^{1/3}\right)\right] \\ &= \tfrac{1}{2}[E(\log[p(x)]^{2/3}) + \log E([p(x)]^{-2/3})] \\ &\geqq \tfrac{1}{2}E[\log[p(x)]^{2/3} + \log[p(x)]^{-2/3}] = 0, \end{aligned} \quad (18)$$

since log $x$ is a concave function. Moreover, equality is achieved if and only if $[p(x)]^{2/3}$ is a constant, that is, for the uniform distribution. For this case, however, there is no difference between the two devices, for the optimum fixed-$N$ quantizer is, in fact, equi-interval. Thus we conclude that for fixed mean-square error, the entropy of a signal quantized by the optimum quantizer is not less than that which obtains if the same signal is quantized by an equi-interval device, at least to the order of our approximation. Since a signal can, by means of encoding, be transmitted at an average bit rate approaching the signal entropy, this implies that an optimum fixed-$N$ quantizer should never by employed if encoding is also to be performed, and the theorem is proved.

To illustrate more fully the significance of these remarks, we will consider the case of unit-variance Gaussian signals in detail. For this case,

$$H(x) = \tfrac{1}{2}\log 2\pi e$$

and

$$H(x_o^*) = -0.3115 + \log(N + 0.853). \quad (19)$$

If the range is taken to be 8 (i.e., $\pm 4\sigma$), we have for the equi-interval case

$$H(x_e^*) \cong -0.953 + \log N. \quad (20)$$

[2] From the viewpoint of minimum error. The practical questions of implementation are discussed later.

The mean-square error for each case is

$$\epsilon_o^2 \cong \frac{2.73}{(N + 0.853)^2} \quad (21)$$

for the optimum fixed-$N$ quantizer and

$$\epsilon_e^2 \cong 5.33/N^2 \quad (22)$$

for the equi-interval quantizer. If the entropies of the two methods are equated, i.e., if a transmission rate is fixed,

$$-0.3115 + \log(N_o + 0.853) \cong 0.953 + \log N_e$$

so that as $N_o$, $N_e$ become large

$$0.64 + \log N_o \cong \log N_e$$

and $N_e \cong 1.559\, N_o$.

Thus, expressing the mean-square errors for each case in terms of $N_o$, we have

$$\epsilon_o^2 \cong \frac{2.73}{(N_o + 0.853)^2} \quad (23)$$

and

$$\epsilon_e^2 \cong \frac{5.33}{(1.559N_o)^2} = \frac{2.19}{N_o^2}. \quad (24)$$

Hence, for $N_o$ moderately large, the error using equi-interval quantizing is less than that using the optimum fixed-$N$ quantizer, if the signals are to be subsequently encoded and transmitted at a fixed bit rate. The reason for this apparent anomaly is that, for a given $N$, the entropy of the equi-interval quantized signal is considerably less than that of the optimum fixed-$N$ quantized signal; and by employing more levels, this smaller entropy can be converted into lower mean-square error. Thus it is apparent that the optimum fixed-$N$ quantizer loses more in terms of increased entropy than it gains in reduction of mean-square error, if encoding is to be practiced. It should be pointed out that it is necessary to use a buffer to achieve an advantage from any encoding scheme which involves words of variable length. There is therefore an apparent tradeoff between fixing $N$ and using the more complex optimum quantizer but no buffer, and using a ordinary quantizer with a buffer.

It should be noted that as $N$ becomes very large, so also does the quantized entropy. Thus, the indicated difference may be trivial compared to $H(x^*)$. However, for the case of Gaussian signals, (treated as an example in the following sections), there does exist a wide range of values over which the difference is appreciable.

## The Optimizing Equations for the Case of Encoded Signals

It was shown in the previous section that if the quantized signal is to be encoded, buffered, and transmitted at a fixed average bit rate, the use of the optimum fixed-$N$ quantizer yields suboptimum results; results which are worse, in fact, than for a simple equilevel quantizer. We derive, in this section, conditions upon the optimum quantizer subject to the constraint of fixed average bit rate rather than fixed $N$. For simplicity, we assume that the encoding will be performed efficiently enough so that the entropy of the quantized signal is an adequate measure of the the average output bit rate. We again take the mean-square error as our optimization criterion, although other criteria might be more desirable for certain applications.[3] Under these assumptions, our optimization problem is to find the values of $y_k$, $x_k$, and $N$ that minimize the mean-square quantization error

$$\epsilon^2 = \sum_{k=1}^{N} \int_{y_{k-1}}^{y_k} (x - x_k)^2 p(x)\, dx \tag{25}$$

subject to

$$\sum_{k=1}^{N} p_k \log p_k = C, \tag{26}$$

where

$$p_k = \int_{y_{k-1}}^{y_k} p(x)\, dx,$$

i.e., so that the entropy of $x^*$ is constant.

It is easily shown that the $x_k$ must be given by

$$x_k = \mu(y_{k-1}, y_k),$$

so that the problem is expressible solely in terms of the $y_k$ and $N$.

As was the case for the optimum fixed-$N$ quantizer, an analytic solution to these equations can be found only for trivial cases. Therefore, for the particular case of Gaussian signals, the optimizing equations were converted to steepest-descent equations, which were implemented and solved on the System Development Corporation Q-32 computer under the control of the TSS time-sharing system. The correctness of the computer program was checked by suppressing the entropy constraint, which gave results that agreed with Max's. Next, the entropy term was made dominant and the constraint set to that for maximum entropy. The results again agreed with the theoretical (i.e., equal $p_k$).

The convergence of the steepest-descent equations is very slow, demonstrating that, as is also true for the fixed-$N$ optimum, the mean-square quantization error is very insensitive to moderately small deviations from the optimum interval structure.

The numerical results for Gaussian signals are rather surprising, in that the optimum fixed-entropy quantizer yields an error rate almost negligibly different from that of simple equilevel quantizing, except for very small $N$. These results are displayed in Fig. 1, from which we can see that the optimum fixed-entropy quantizer displays a marked improvement over the optimum fixed-$N$ quantizer, but not over equilevel quantizing. In fact, the equilevel quantizer suffers in the comparison given because the range was assumed to be 8. For very small $N$, this

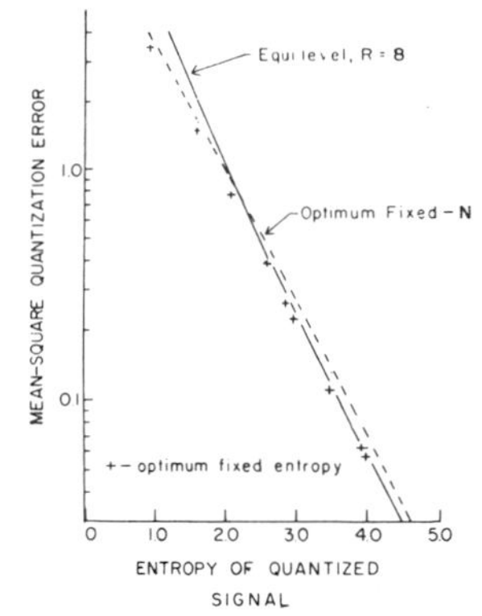


Fig. 1. Comparison of entropy versus mean-square error for equilevel, optimum fixed-$N$ and optimum fixed entropy quantization.

obviously gives a poor choice of levels, and a better measure for comparison would be the optimum equilevel quantizer [1].

Thus, equilevel quantizing, currently employed because of its ease of implementation, is superior to optimum fixed-$N$ quantizing if the output signal is to be buffered, for all but very small values of $N$. Moreover, because of the insensitivity of the mean-square quantization error to moderate changes in interval structure, equilevel quantizing gives nearly optimum results for the special case of Gaussian signals.[4]

### References


[1] J. Max, "Quantizing for minimum distortion," *IRE Trans. Information Theory*, vol. IT-6, pp. 7–12, March 1960.
[2] G. M. Roe, "Quantizing for minimum distortion," *IEEE Trans. Information Theory*, vol. IT-10, pp. 384–385, October 1964.
[3] B. Widrow, "A study of rough amplitude quantization by means of Nyquist sampling theory," *IRE Trans. Circuit Theory*, vol. CT-3, pp. 266–276, December 1956.
[4] R. C. Wood, "Optimum quantizing in hybrid computation," Ph.D. dissertation, Dept. of Engrg., University of California, Los Angeles, August 1966.


[3] Prof. Leo Breiman, of the University of California, Los Angeles, has suggested as an alternative formulation that the mutual information $I(x, x^*)$ be maximized subject to $H(x^*) = C$.

[4] It has been brought to my attention by Dr. G. M. Roe, in private communication, that it is possible to obtain an analytical derivation of these computer based conclusions, and to extend them to well-behaved density functions other than the Gaussian. Specifically, for the fixed-entropy quantizer discussed above, the optimum level spacing approaches the equal-interval case, with

$$\frac{d}{dk}(y_k) \cong \sqrt{\lambda}\left\{1 + \frac{\lambda}{24}\left[\left(\frac{p'}{p}\right)^2 - \frac{4}{5}\frac{p''}{p}\right] + O(\lambda^2)\right\}$$

with $\lambda$ (a Lagrange multiplier) given by

$$\lambda = e^{2(H_1 - H_0)}$$

$$H_1 = \int_{y_0}^{y_N} p(x) \log p(x)\, dx$$

$$H_0 = \sum_{k=1}^{N} p_k \log p_k$$

and

$$\epsilon^2 \cong \tfrac{1}{12}\lambda$$

# 24



Reprinted from *IEEE Trans. Inform. Theory,* **IT-14**(5), 676–681, 683 (1968)

# Asymptotically Efficient Quantizing

HERBERT GISH, MEMBER, IEEE, AND JOHN N. PIERCE, SENIOR MEMBER, IEEE

***Abstract*—It is shown, under weak assumptions on the density function of a random variable and under weak assumptions on the error criterion, that uniform quantizing yields an output entropy which asymptotically is smaller than that for any other quantizer, independent of the density function or the error criterion. The asymptotic behavior of the rate distortion function is determined for the class of $\nu$th law loss functions, and the entropy of the uniform quantizer is compared with the rate distortion function for this class of loss functions. The extension of these results to the quantizing of sequences is also given. It is shown that the discrepancy between the entropy of the uniform quantizer and the rate distortion function apparently lies with the inability of the optimal quantizing shapes to cover large dimensional spaces without overlap. A comparison of the entropies of the uniform quantizer and of the minimum-alphabet quantizer is also given.**

## Introduction

THE ENTROPY $H$ of the output of a quantizer is the minimum amount of information which must be transmitted in order to be able to determine the quantizer output with an arbitrarily small error. If we establish some mean error criterion $E$ (e.g., mean square, mean absolute) between the quantizer input and output as a measure of quantizer reproduction fidelity, various types of quantizers can be ranked by comparisons of their $H(E)$ curves. In addition, the merits of quantization as opposed to other means of source encoding can be ascertained by comparing $H(E)$ to Shannon's [1], [2] rate distortion function $R(E)$. The function $R(E)$, which depends only on the distribution of the variable being transmitted, specifies the minimum amount of information which must be transmitted in order to reconstruct the variable with a mean error $E$.

In the following we investigate the relation between the entropy of the output of a quantizer and its mean error. In particular, we look at the asymptotic relation between the two quantities as the mean error is required to become very small and show that for a specified error uniform quantization yields minimum entropy. The result is shown to be valid under rather weak assumptions about the density function of the variable being quantized and the mean error criterion being used. The performance of the asymptotically optimum quantizer is compared to bounds on the rate distortion function.

Manuscript received June 23, 1967; revised February 5, 1968.
H. Gish is with SIGNATRON, Inc., Lexington, Mass. 02173
J. N. Pierce is with the AF Cambridge Research Laboratories, Bedford, Mass. 01730

## Asymptotic Optimality of Uniform Quantizing

Let $X$ be the random variable at the quantizer input we will assume that the density function $f(x)$ is reasonably smooth. The quantizer divides the range of $X$ into a possibly infinite number of adjacent intervals $I_n$

$$I_n = (g_n, g_{n+1}) \tag{1}$$

and maps $X$ into the discrete-valued random variable $Y$

$$Y = Y_n \quad \text{if} \quad X \in I_n. \tag{2}$$

The entropy of $Y$ is

$$H = -\sum p_n \log p_n \tag{3a}$$

where

$$p_n = P(X \in I_n) = \int_{I_n} dx\, f(x). \tag{3b}$$

The mean-square error will be written as $E$; we will investigate more general loss functions subsequently. The value of $E$ is

$$E = \sum \int_{I_n} dx\, f(x)(x - Y_n)^2. \tag{4}$$

If the lengths of all of the intervals are reasonably small, then $f(x)$ will be approximately constant over each interval, and we can write

$$p_n \approx f(g_n)(g_{n+1} - g_n). \tag{5}$$

Furthermore, under this condition, putting $Y_n$ at the midpoints of the intervals will lead to approximately the minimum mean-square error for the prescribed set of intervals

$$Y_n = (g_n + g_{n+1})/2, \tag{6}$$

$$E \approx \sum f(g_n)(g_{n+1} - g_n)^3/12. \tag{7}$$

Suppose now that we define the mesh points $g_n$ by

$$g_n = g(n\delta) \tag{8}$$

where $g(t)$ is some suitably smooth monotone increasing function. Then we can inquire as to what choice of $g$ leads to the slowest increase of $H$ with decreasing $E$ as $\delta$ is allowed to become small.

We first note that for small $\delta$

$$g_{n+1} - g_n \approx \delta g'(n\delta) \tag{9}$$

where the prime indicates derivative, so that, from (3a) and (5)

$$H \approx -\sum \delta g'(n\delta) f(g(n\delta)) \log (\delta g'(n\delta) f(g(n\delta)))$$

which, as $\delta$ becomes arbitrarily small, goes over into the integral form

$$H \approx -\int dt\, g'(t) f(g(t)) \log (\delta g'(t) f(g(t))). \tag{10}$$

Similarly,

$$E \approx \sum f(g(n\delta))(\delta g'(n\delta))^3/12$$

approaches

$$E \approx \int dt\, g'(t) f(g(t)) (\delta g'(t))^2/12. \tag{11}$$

Making the obvious substitution

$$s = g(t)$$

in these integrals then leads to

$$H \approx -\int ds\, f(s) \log (\delta f(s) g'(g^{-1}(s))) \tag{12}$$

and

$$E \approx (\delta^2/12) \int ds\, f(s)(g'(g^{-1}(s)))^2. \tag{13}$$

If we define $H_0$ to be the entropy of the continuous distribution

$$H_0 = -\int ds\, f(s) \log (f(s)) \tag{14}$$

and temporarily define

$$\gamma(s) = g'(g^{-1}(s)) \tag{15}$$

we then have

$$E \approx (\delta^2/12) \int ds\, f(s)(\gamma(s))^2 \tag{16}$$

and

$$H \approx H_0 - \log \delta - \int ds\, f(s) \log (\gamma(s)). \tag{17}$$

It is readily verified that for fixed $\delta$ and $E$, $H$ is a minimum when $\gamma(s)$ is a constant, or equivalently, when $g'(t)$ is independent of $t$. We may conveniently take this constant to be unity and set

$$g(t) = t \tag{18}$$

which then leads to[1]

$$E \approx \delta^2/12 \tag{19}$$

$$H_{\min} \approx H_0 - \log \delta. \tag{20}$$

From this pair of equations we can write the equation relating $H$ to $E$

$$H_{\min} \approx H_0 - (\tfrac{1}{2}) \log (12E) \quad \text{as} \quad E \to 0. \tag{21}$$

If we define $V_0$ to be entropy variance corresponding to $H_0$,[2] that is, the variance of a Gaussian distribution having the same entropy $H_0$, we have

$$H_0 = (\tfrac{1}{2}) \log (2\pi e V_0) \tag{22}$$

so that (21) can be rewritten as

$$H_{\min} \approx (\tfrac{1}{2}) \log (V_0/E) + (\tfrac{1}{2}) \log (2\pi e/12)$$

or as

$$H_{\min} \approx (\tfrac{1}{2}) \log_2 (V_0/E) + 0.255 \tag{23}$$

as $E \to 0$, in bits.

We now note that the result can be generalized somewhat. Suppose that in place of (4) we define an average error by

$$E_L = \sum \int_{I_n} dx\, f(x) L(x - Y_n) \tag{4'}$$

where

a) $L(0) = 0$.
b) $L$ is an increasing function of the magnitude of its argument.
c) The function $M(x)$ defined from $L(x)$ by (7'b) below satisfies: $xM'(x)$ is monotone.

Then (7) becomes

$$E_L \approx \sum f(g_n) \int_{-(g_{n+1}-g_n)/2}^{(g_{n+1}-g_n)/2} du\, L(u)$$

which we rewrite in the form

$$E_L \approx \sum f(g_n)(g_{n+1} - g_n) M(g_{n+1} - g_n) \tag{7'a}$$

where the function $M$ is defined by

$$M(v) = (1/v) \int_{-v/2}^{v/2} du\, L(u). \tag{7'b}$$

Then (11) is replaced by

$$E_L \approx \int dt\, g'(t) f(g(t)) M(\delta g'(t)) \tag{11'}$$

[1] Refer to Appendix I, for conditions on $f(x)$ which establish the validity of (19) and (20). Also, see Appendix II for the outline of a more rigorous but less intuitive approach to the derivation of (21).

[2] Analogous to the entropy power of a continuous process.

(13) is replaced by

$$E_L \approx \int ds\, f(s) M(g'(g^{-1}(s))) \tag{13'}$$

and, finally, the variational pair (16) and (17) is replaced by

$$E_L \approx \int ds\, f(s) M(\delta\gamma(s)) \tag{16'}$$

$$H \approx H_0 - \int ds\, f(s) \log (\delta\gamma(s)). \tag{17'}$$

The stationary solutions of the Euler–Lagrange equation for the system of (16') and (17') must satisfy

$$\gamma(s) M'(\gamma(s)) = \text{constant}. \tag{18'a}$$

The condition c) after (4') guarantees that $\gamma(s) = \text{constant}$ is the unique solution of the variational problem from which we are again led to the solution

$$g(t) = t \tag{18'b}$$

implying uniform quantizing and the relations

$$E_L \approx M(\delta) \tag{19'}$$

$$H_{\min} \approx H_0 - \log \delta. \tag{20'}$$

Finally, we arrive at the relation between $H_{\min}$ and $E_L$:

$$H_{\min} \approx H_0 - \log (M^{-1}(E_L)). \tag{21'}$$

We have thus shown that under rather weak assumptions about the density function of the random variable and about the error criterion, the uniform quantizer is asymptotically optimum.

## Comparison with Rate Distortion Function

When $E$ is mean-square error, it is well known[3] that the rate distortion satisfies

$$(\tfrac{1}{2}) \log (V_0/E) \leq R(E) \leq (\tfrac{1}{2}) \log (V/E) \tag{24}$$

where $V$ and $V_0$ are the variance and entropy variance, respectively. Equation (23) shows that the uniform quantizer can always attain a performance asymptotically within approximately $\frac{1}{4}$ bit of the rate distortion lower bound.

When we use the more general error measure given by (4'), a lower bound on $R(E_L)$, which we will write as $r(E_L)$, is given by Shannon[4]

$$r(E_L) = H_0 - \phi(E_L) \tag{25}$$

where

$$\phi(E_L) = \sup_{\{p(u)\}} \left( -\int du\, p(u) \log (p(u)) \right) \tag{26}$$

subject to the constraints that $p(u)$ be a density and that

$$E_L = \int du\, L(u) p(u). \tag{27}$$

[3] See Shannon [1], p. 80.
[4] See Shannon [2], p. 120.

The solution of the variational problem specified by (26) and (27) is given by

$$p(u) = A \exp (-\lambda L(u)) \tag{28a}$$

where the constants $A$ and $\lambda$ are determined by the constraints. The corresponding value of $\phi(E_L)$ is

$$\phi(E_L) = -\log (A) - \lambda E_L \log (e). \tag{28b}$$

If we assume a loss function of the form

$$L(u) = |u|^a \tag{29a}$$

the corresponding value of $\phi$ is

$$\phi(E_L) = (1/a) \log (e \cdot a \cdot E_L) + \log (2\Gamma(1 + 1/a)). \tag{29b}$$

The same loss function substituted in (7'), (19'), and (21') gives

$$H_{\min} \approx H_0 - (1/a) \log ((1 + a)E_L) - \log (2), \quad \text{as } E_L \to 0. \tag{30}$$

The asymptotic entropy of the uniform quantizer thus exceeds the lower bound on the rate distortion function by

$$H_{\min} - r(E_L) \approx (1/a) \log (a \cdot e/(1 + a)) + \log (\Gamma(1 + 1/a)). \tag{31}$$

Table I gives the value of the right-hand side of (31) for a few values of the loss exponent $a$. The last line of Table I indicates that for arbitrarily large loss exponents, the uniform quantizer achieves the rate distortion bound. This can be viewed as a verification of the intuitively satisfying notion of the optimality of uniform quantizing under a bounded error requirement.

We will now show that any difference between $H_{\min}$ and $r(E_L)$ is due to a limitation imposed by the quantization process rather than any inherent weakness in the lower bound $r(E_L)$. In fact, for a loss function which is positive and a monotonically increasing function of the magnitude of its argument, we will show

$$\lim_{E_L \to 0} [R(E_L) - r(E_L)] = 0. \tag{32}$$

First note that if $X$ is the variable to be transmitted and $Y$ its reconstruction, then by definition

$$R(E_L) = \min_{\{p(y \mid x)\}} \left[ \iint dx dy\, p(x, y) \log \frac{p(x, y)}{p(x)p(y)} \right] \tag{33}$$

where the expression in brackets is the mutual information between $X$ and $Y$, and where the minimization is performed subject to the constraint

$$E_L = \iint dx dy\, L(x - y) p(x, y). \tag{34}$$

Thus, if we select some conditional density for which (34) is satisfied, the resulting mutual information between $X$ and $Y$ will provide an upper bound on $R(E_L)$.

As a specific choice for the conditional density, consider

$$p(y \mid x) = e^{-\lambda L(y - x)} \Big/ \int dv\, e^{-\lambda L(v)} \tag{35}$$

TABLE I

| $a$ | $H_{min} - r(E_L)$ (in bits) |
|---|---|
| 0 | $\infty$ |
| 1/20 | 2.085 |
| 1/10 | 1.624 |
| 1/5 | 1.196 |
| 1/4 | 1.068 |
| 1/3 | 0.913 |
| 1/2 | 0.715 |
| 1 | 0.443 |
| 2 | 0.255 |
| 3 | 0.179 |
| 4 | 0.138 |
| 5 | 0.113 |
| 10 | 0.059 |
| 20 | 0.030 |
| $\infty$ | 0 |

where $\lambda$ is determined by (34) and is not dependent on $p_1(x)$, the probability density of $X$. Letting $R_b(E_L)$ denote the mutual information between $X$ and $Y$, we obtain

$$R_b(E_L) = -\int dy \log (p_2(y))p_2(y) - \phi(E_L) \geq R(E_L) \quad (36)$$

where $p_2$ is the density of $y$ and is given by

$$p_2(y) = \left[\int dx\, e^{-\lambda L(y-x)}p_1(x)\right] \Big/ \int dv\, e^{-\lambda L(v)}. \quad (37)$$

Now as $E_L \to 0$, we have

$$p_2(y) \to p_1(y)$$

since $p(y \mid x)$ approaches a delta function (for as $E_L \to 0$, $\lambda \to \infty$). Hence, for $p_1(y)$ sufficiently well behaved

$$\lim_{E_L \to 0} R_b(E_L)$$

$$= \lim_{E_L \to 0} \left[-\int dy \log (p_2(y))p_2(y) - \phi(E_L)\right] \quad (38a)$$

$$= H_0(x) - \phi(E_L) = r(E_L) \quad (38b)$$

which establishes (32).[5]

## Comparison with Minimum-Alphabet Quantizer

As a practical matter, it may be desirable to place a restriction on the number of quantizer output levels (particularly when uniform quantizing implies an infinite number of levels) even though this may be reflected in increased entropy. Now, for any specified average error there is a minimum number of quantizer levels which can yield an error that small. We will refer to such a quantizer as a minimum-alphabet quantizer. Its output entropy provides an upper bound on the minimum entropy attainable with consistent simultaneous constraints on average error and alphabet size.

We will restrict our attention here to the case of mean-square error, and compare the entropies of the minimum-alphabet and minimum-entropy quantizers.

[5] This is a generalization of the result of Gerrish and Schultheiss [3], who considered the case where $L(u) = u^2$.

Let $N$ be the number of quantizer output levels, and let $(A, B)$ be the range of the density function. Then from (8) we can take

$$g(0) = A, \quad g(N\delta) = B$$

or

$$N = (g^{-1}(B) - g^{-1}(A))/\delta.$$

By writing this as

$$N = (1/\delta) \int_{g^{-1}(A)}^{g^{-1}(B)} dt$$

and making the substitution $s = g(t)$, we get

$$N = (1/\delta) \int_A^B ds/g'(g^{-1}(s))$$

or, from (15),

$$N = (1/\delta) \int_A^B ds/\gamma(s). \quad (39)$$

The minimization of $N$ subject to the constraint that $E$ is fixed and given by (16) leads to the known results [4] that

$$\gamma(s) = (f(s))^{-1/3} \int dt(f(t))^{1/3} \quad (40a)$$

$$E \approx (\delta^2/12)\left(\int dt(f(t))^{1/3}\right)^3. \quad (40b)$$

Substitution of (40a) in (17) then gives the asymptotic entropy of the minimum-alphabet quantizer, which we will denote by $H_{maq}$

$$H_{maq} \approx H_0 - \log(\delta) + (\tfrac{1}{3}) \int dt\, f(t) \log (f(t)) - \log\left(\int dt(f(t))^{1/3}\right). \quad (40c)$$

Finally, expressing the entropy in terms of the ms error,

$$H_{maq} \approx H_0 - (\tfrac{1}{2}) \log (12E) + (\tfrac{3}{2}) \log \left(\int dt(f(t))^{1/3}\right) + (\tfrac{1}{3}) \int dt\, f(t) \log (f(t)), \quad \text{as } E \to 0.$$

The increase in entropy relative to the uniform quantizer can then be written as

$$2(H_{maq} - H_{min}) \approx \log \left(\int dt\, f(t)(f(t))^{-2/3}\right) - \int dt\, f(t) \log ((f(t))^{-2/3}). \quad (41)$$

(The somewhat awkward way of writing (41) was chosen to emphasize the positivity of the difference, which follows immediately from the convexity of the logarithm.) Table II gives the value of $H_{maq} - H_{min}$ for a few common distributions. (Strictly speaking, the values for distributions defined on the entire line or half-line should be assumed to refer to distributions approximately equal to the

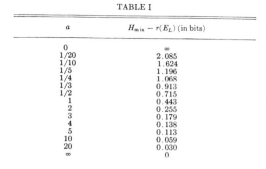

TABLE II

| $f(x)$ | Range | $\Delta = H_{maq} - H_{min}$ (in bits) |
|---|---|---|
| $1$ | (0,1) | 0 |
| $2x$ | (0,1) | 0.052 |
| $(n+1)x^n$, $n$ large | (0,1) | 0.312 |
| $\log(1/x)$ | (0,1) | 0.122 |
| $(2\pi)^{-1/2}\exp(-x^2/2)$ | $(-\infty, \infty)$ | 0.156 |
| $\exp(-x)$ | $(0, \infty)$ | 0.312 |
| $3x^{-4}$ | $(1, \infty)$ | 0.944 |
| $\alpha \exp(-x^\alpha)/\Gamma(1/\alpha)$ | $(0, \infty)$ | $0.312/\alpha$ |
| $(2+\alpha)x^{-(3+\alpha)}$ ($\alpha$ very small) | $(1, \infty)$ | $0.571 + (0.5)\log_2(1/\alpha)$ |
| $\alpha x^{\alpha-1}$ ($\alpha$ very small) | (0,1) | $0.292 + 0.481/\alpha - 0.5\log_2(1/\alpha)$ |

tabulated ones, but truncated at some large absolute value, since the variational procedure which leads to (40) is based on boundedness of the random variable.) It can be seen that except for "peculiar" distributions, like the last three in Table II, or for distributions with infinite variance and finite entropy, the entropy of the minimum-alphabet quantizer is not strikingly larger than that of the uniform quantizer.

For completeness we include the asymptotic dependence of $\log N$ on $E$

$$\log N \approx (\tfrac{3}{2}) \log \left( \int ds (f(s))^{1/3} \right) - (\tfrac{1}{2}) \log (12E) \qquad (42a)$$

which can be found by substituting (40a) in (39). This relation indicates the transmitted digit rate required when entropy-reducing coding is not used. It can be verified by comparison with (41) that

$$\log N - H_{min} = 3(H_{maq} - H_{min}). \qquad (42b)$$

## Quantizing of Sequences

Suppose that a stationary random process $X(t)$ is sampled every $\tau$ seconds to produce the finite sequence $X_1, X_2, \cdots, X_D$ with

$$X_n = X(n\tau) \qquad n = 1, \cdots, D. \qquad (43)$$

Then if each of these samples is quantized uniformly with step size $\delta$, the average error is again

$$E_L \approx M(\delta) \qquad (44)$$

(ignoring any error introduced by the finite sampling frequency), whereas the average entropy per sample is now

$$H \approx -\log(\delta) + H_0/D \qquad (45)$$

where $H_0$ is the continuous entropy of the joint distribution of $D$ consecutive samples

$$H_0 = -\int \cdots \int dx_1 \cdots dx_D f(\mathbf{x}) \log (f(\mathbf{x})). \qquad (46)$$

(We indicate vector-valued quantities here by bold-face notation.) For the case of independent samples, as from a band-limited, flat-spectrum Gaussian process sampled at twice its highest frequency, (45) of course yields the same entropy per sample as (20').

We next observe that the uniform quantizing of the individual samples is equivalent to quantizing the $D$-dimensional vectors consisting of $D$ consecutive samples by dividing $D$-space into $D$-cubes with sides of length $\delta$ parallel to the coordinate axes. A natural question to ask is whether any more efficient quantizing of $D$-space can be found. The answer to this question is yes, in general, but the concomitant problem of finding the optimum shapes in which to quantize $D$-space appears to be very difficult to solve.

Suppose that for the loss function we again adopt one which depends only on the pairwise coordinate differences; specifically, let

$$\Lambda(\mathbf{X} - \mathbf{Y}) = (1/D) \sum_{i=1}^{D} L(X_i - Y_i) \qquad (47)$$

be the error per coordinate incurred when the sequence $\mathbf{Y}$ is substituted for the sequence $\mathbf{X}$; correspondingly, $E_L$ will be the expected value of $\Lambda(\mathbf{X} - \mathbf{Y})$. Then, if $D$-space is partitioned into translates of a region of shape $S$ and volume $V$, it is easy to show, by the analog of the earlier derivation, that

$$H \approx H_0/D - \log(V)/D \quad \text{(entropy/coordinate)} \qquad (48)$$

and

$$E_L \approx M_S(V) \qquad (49a)$$

where

$$M_S(V) = (1/V) \int_S dx_1 \cdots dx_D \Lambda(\mathbf{x} - \mathbf{x}^0) \qquad (49b)$$

with $\mathbf{x}^0$ being that value which minimizes the integral. Using (49), the nonoptimality of $D$-cubes parallel to the coordinate axes can be verified for certain loss functions. For example, with the quadratic loss function $L(u) = u^2$, a covering of 2-space by hexagons is slightly better than a covering by squares. For another example, with the absolute loss function $L(u) = |u|$, a covering of 2-space by squares with diagonals parallel to the coordinate axes is slightly better than a covering with normally-oriented squares.

The effectiveness of quantizing with $D$-cubes can be gauged, in a manner analogous to the one-dimensional case, by making a comparison with the lower bound on the rate distortion function for the $D$-dimensional sequence $\mathbf{X}$. The lower bound for the loss function $\Lambda(\mathbf{X} - \mathbf{Y})$ parallels the one-dimensional case and is given by

$$r(E_L) = H_0/D - \phi(E_L) \quad \text{(entropy/coordinate)} \qquad (50)$$

where $\phi(E_L)$ is given by (26). Thus, if we let $H_C(E_L)$ denote the entropy of the $D$-cube quantizer output and take $L(u) = |u|^a$, then the difference $H_C(E_L) - r(E_L)$ is asymptotically equal to the right-hand side of (31), and the calculations of Table I apply.

We should further note, by an extension of the arguments used previously, that in $D$-space

$$\lim_{E_L \to 0} [R(E_L) - r(E_L)] = 0. \qquad (51)$$

In general, the shape which minimizes $M_S(V)$ for a fixed volume $V$ is the shape

$$S = \{\mathbf{x}: \Lambda(\mathbf{x}) \leq b\} \tag{52a}$$

with the constant $b$ chosen to yield the specified volume $V$; however, in most cases it is impossible to cover $D$-space with such shapes without overlap. For the loss function $L(u) = |u|^{1/c}$, the volume of the shape in (52a) is[a]

$$V = (2b^c D^c \Gamma(1 + c))^D / \Gamma(1 + cD) \tag{52b}$$

and the normalized loss is

$$M_S(V) = bcD/(1 + cD) \tag{52c}$$

so that substituting in (48) and (49) we have

$$H \approx H_0/D - \log (2\Gamma(1 + c)) - c \log (E_L) - c \log (D)$$
$$- c \log (1 + 1/cD) + (1/D) \log (\Gamma(1 + cD)) \tag{52d}$$

which, when $D$ is large, approaches

$$H \approx H_0/D - \log (2\Gamma(1 + c)) + c \log (c/eE_L). \tag{52e}$$

If we let $c = 1/a$ and compare (52e) with (29b), we see that the two expressions are identical. Thus, for this loss function the discrepancy between the entropy with quantizing and the rate distortion bound rests entirely on the inability of the optimum shapes to cover spaces of large dimensionality.

[*Editors' Note:* Material has been omitted at this point.]

## References


[1] C. E. Shannon and W. Weaver, *The Mathematical Theory of Communication.* Urbana, Ill.: University of Illinois Press, 1959.
[2] C. E. Shannon, "Coding theorems for a discrete source with a fidelity criterion," in *Information and Decision Processes*, R. E. Machol, Ed. New York: McGraw-Hill, 1960.
[3] A. M. Gerrish and P. M. Schultheiss, "Information rates of non-Gaussian processes," *IEEE Trans. Information Theory*, vol. IT-10, pp. 265–271, October 1964.
[4] J. Max, "Quantizing for minimum distortion," *IRE Trans. Information Theory*, vol. IT-6, pp. 7–12, March 1960.
[5] P. F. Panter and W. Dite, "Quantization distortion in pulse-count modulation with nonuniform spacing of levels," *Proc. IRE*, vol. 39, pp. 44–48, January 1951.
[6] T. J. Goblick, Jr. and J. L. Holsinger, "Analog source digitization: A comparison of theory and practice," *IEEE Trans. Information Theory (Correspondence)*, vol. IT-13, pp. 323–326, April 1967.
[7] J. T. Pinkston, III, "Encoding independent sample information sources," Ph.D. dissertation, Massachusetts Institute of Technology, Cambridge, September 1967.
[8] F. Jelinek, "Evaluation of distortion rate functions for low distortions," *Proc. IEEE*, vol. 55, pp. 2067–2068, November 1967.

# 25



Reprinted from *IEEE Trans. Inform. Theory,* **IT-13**(3), 506–511 (1967)

# Information Rates in Sampling and Quantization

WILLIS C. KELLOGG, MEMBER, IEEE

***Abstract*—A computer-aided analysis of a digital communications system has been conducted. Salient results compare the performance of approximately optimum PCM systems with the rate-distortion function, under the assumptions of Gaussian inputs and mean-square-error distortion measure. The calculated distortion is greater than the theoretical minimum by two or three decibels in most cases. The results presented also illuminate the tradeoff between sampling rate and number of quantization levels in a channel of fixed capacity.**

**The presampling and reconstruction filters are represented in the computer by their impulse responses; that is, filtering of signals is accomplished by evaluating the convolution integrals numerically. Impulse responses with durations of 20 sample times or fewer are long enough to model most known results in optimum filtering of sampled stationary random functions.**

**Procedures are described for computing the autocorrelation function of the quantizer output, and the cross correlation between the quantizer output and a signal correlated with the input. The procedure adopted is the naive one of integrating numerically the appropriate bivariate normal distribution.**

## I. Introduction

COMPUTED RESULTS are given in this paper for the performance of the system of Fig. 1, and these results are compared with theoretical bounds obtained from information theory. The performance of this digital communication system with an optimum zero-memory quantizer is shown to come within a few decibels (often three or fewer) of the theoretical optimum predicted by the rate-distortion function. When designing for a channel of fixed capacity, one must pick both the sampling rate and the number of quantization levels in an optimal way. The data presented here illuminate the tradeoff between sampling rate and number of quantization levels.

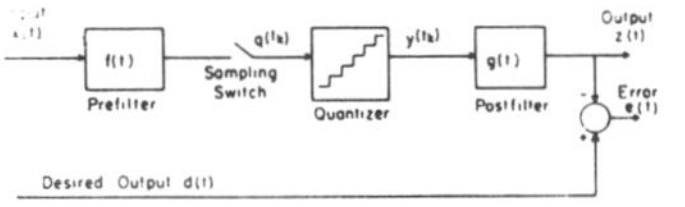


Fig. 1. System model.

In Fig. 1, an input random function $x(t)$ is passed through a prefilter, sampler, quantizer, and postfilter, to produce some output $z(t)$. The filters and the quantizer are to be chosen so as to make $z(t)$ approximate $d(t)$, the desired output, which is correlated with $x(t)$. In cases in which $d(t) = x(t)$, Fig. 1 models a PCM communication system in which the digital information is transmitted without error to the reconstruction filter. In other cases $x(t)$ may be a noisy version of some random function arising in the course of a measurement or observation, from which $d(t)$ is to be obtained by a linear operation. Then the system becomes a data processing system, and the prefilter, sampler, and quantizer constitute an analog-to-digital converter. In such cases, the postfilter might well be a digital computer program.

This paper is concerned with the optimization and evaluation of the system of Fig. 1 in its role as a PCM system. The role as a data-processing system is emphasized in previous papers by this author.[1],[2] Furthermore, we consider only distortion due to sampling and quantization, and neglect errors in transmission of the digital symbols.

The performance criterion by which we judge the system is the mean-square distortion measure $D$, given by

$$D = \frac{1}{T} \int_0^T E\{[e(t)]^2\}\, dt \tag{1}$$

where $e(t)$ is the error signal of Fig. 1, $T$ is the sampling period, and $E\{\ \}$ denotes an ensemble average or expected value.

Several authors, most notably Brown[3] and Robbins,[4] have considered joint optimization of the prefilter and postfilter without quantization, using frequency-domain arguments. More recently Tufts and Johnson[5] have considered post-sampling filters constrained to have impulse responses which vanish outside a finite interval, so that the postfilter must reconstruct from a finite number of samples. Under these constraints the optimum impulse response can be obtained by matrix methods on a digital computer. The present work makes use of these matrix techniques to optimize the prefilters and postfilters in the time domain. Ruchkin[6] has discussed the optimum postfiltering of sampled and quantized random functions, and has examined the tradeoff between sampling rate and number of quantization levels for Gaussian processes on the assumption that a channel of limited capacity must be used to transmit the quantized samples. The present work differs from Ruchkin's in that: a) prefiltering is considered; b) optimum quantization is used; c) an improved method is used for computing the autocorrelation function of the quantizer output; and d) results are compared with Shannon's rate-distortion function.[7]

It has not been possible to optimize the prefilter, quantizer, and postfilter jointly. Therefore, the strategy

Manuscript received August 18, 1966; revised March 31, 1967. The research reported here was made possible through support extended to Cruft Lab., Harvard University, Cambridge, Mass., by the U. S. Army Research Office, the U. S. Air Force Office of Scientific Research, and the U. S. Office of Naval Research under the Joint Services Electronics Program by Contract Nonr-1866(16). During the course of this research the author was supported in part by a Mitre Corporation Staff Scholarship.

The author is with M.I.T. Lincoln Lab., Lexington, Mass. (Operated with support of the U. S. Air Force.) He was formerly with the Division of Engineering and Applied Physics, Harvard University, Cambridge, Mass.

to be used is to obtain a jointly optimum of prefilter and postfilter for the case in which no quantizer is present; follow the prefilter of this pair by a sampler and the zero-memory quantizer which is optimum for a single sample; and optimize the postfilter for the prefilter and quantizer so obtained. Various parts of the optimization can be performed with varying degrees of generality. The optimization of the prefilters and postfilters in the absence of quantization requires a knowledge only of the autocorrelation function of the input and the cross correlation between the input and the desired output. The procedure described in Section III for the quantizer optimization requires that each sample have a probability density, and the optimization has in fact been performed only for the case of Gaussian samples. In optimizing the post-quantization filter we require a knowledge of the correlations of the quantized samples and their cross correlation with the desired output, and these correlations have been obtained only for Gaussian inputs.

Thus, while the filter and quantizer design algorithms applied here are general, the quantitative results of Figs. 5, 6, and 7 are correct only for Gaussian inputs with the specified autocorrelation functions.

## II. Optimization of the Prefilters and Postfilters

The PCM system of Fig. 1 requires a postfilter to reconstruct the continuous output function from the quantized samples which have been transmitted to it. The prefilter has a less fundamental role to play, but its use results in reduced distortion. In this section we discuss the optimization of the prefilter and postfilter in the time domain, under the constraint that their impulse responses vanish outside finite time intervals. The optimum filters are of interest in themselves because they demonstrate the feasibility of convolution-sum representations of digital filters, and the quality of performance that can be achieved with small numbers of samples.

The optimum postfilter for a given input, prefilter, and quantizer can be specified in terms of $R_y(t)$, the autocorrelation function of the $y$-process, and $R_{dy}(t)$, the cross-correlation function between the desired output and the $y$-process. An argument is given in a previous paper[1] which involves minimizing the distortion measure of (1) by varying the postfilter $g(t)$ over the set of allowed functions. The optimum postfilter is specified by the equation

$$R_{dy}(t - kT) = \sum_{m=M(t)}^{N(t)} R_y(kT - mT)g_0(t - mT), \qquad M(t) \leq k \leq N(t) \tag{2}$$

where $g_0(t)$ is the impulse response of the optimum postfilter, $T$ is the sampling period, and the limits are

$$\begin{aligned} M(t) &= [t/T] - N_{b_g} + 1 \\ N(t) &= [t/T] + N_{f_g} \end{aligned} \tag{3}$$

where $[t/T]$ is the integer such that $[t/T] \leq t/T < [t/T] + 1$. The significance of (3) is that $g_0(t) = 0$ unless $-N_{f_g}T \leq t < N_{b_g}T$. One solves (2) by fixing $t$ at some interesting value and allowing $k$ to take on integral values in the specified range. There results a system of $(N_{f_g}+N_{b_g})$ equations in the $(N_{f_g} + N_{b_g})$ unknowns $g_0(t - mT)$, $M(t) \leq m \leq N(t)$. The finite time-span bounds are necessary if $g_0(t)$ is to be realized as a digital computer program. However, by fixing $N_{f_g} = 0$ and making $N_{b_g}$ very large, one can approximate the optimum realizable postfilter of Robbins[4] et al. If both $N_{f_g}$ and $N_{b_g}$ are made large, one obtains postfilters resembling nonrealizable or infinite-lag filters. In previous papers[1],[2] several examples are given of postfilters with $N_{b_g} = N_{f_g} = 10$, so that, for each $t$, $z(t)$ is reconstructed from ten past and ten future samples. In most cases, such filters approximate closely the performance of the optimum nonrealizable or infinite-lag filters.

When one uses the optimal reconstruction filter given by (2), the distortion is given by

$$D = R_d(0) - \frac{1}{T}\int_{-N_{f_g}T}^{N_{b_g}T} R_{dy}(t)g_0(t)\,dt. \tag{4}$$

It is not possible to write an equation like (2) specifying the optimum prefilter for a given quantizer and postfilter, because the quantization noise depends in a complicated way on the prefilter. The approach taken in this work will be to use the prefilter of a prefilter-postfilter pair which is jointly optimum in the absence of quantization. In this case $q(kT) = y(kT)$. A variational argument given in a previous paper[1] shows that the impulse response $f_0(t)$ of the optimum prefilter is specified by the integral equation

$$h(t) = \int_{-N_{b_f}T}^{N_{f_f}T} f_0(-u)K(t - u)\,du. \tag{5}$$

In terms of the known functions $g(t)$, $R_{dx}(t)$, and $R_x(t)$, the inhomogeneous part is

$$h(t) = \int_{-M_kT}^{N_kT} g(\tau)R_{dx}(\tau - t)\,d\tau. \tag{6}$$

The kernel function is given by

$$K(t - u) = \sum_{k=-K_0}^{K_1} g_k R_x(t - u + kT) \tag{7}$$

where

$$g_k = \int_{M_kT}^{N_kT} g(t)g(t - kT)\,dt. \tag{8}$$

The limits in (6), (7), and (8) reflect the time-span bounds on $g(t)$:

$$\begin{aligned} M_k &= \text{Max}\,(-N_{f_g}, k - N_{f_g}) \\ N_k &= \text{Min}\,(N_{b_g}, k + N_{b_g}) \end{aligned} \tag{9}$$

$$\begin{aligned} K_0 &= (N_{f_g} + N_{b_g}) \\ K_1 &= N_{f_g} + N_{b_g} - 1. \end{aligned} \tag{10}$$

If $g(t)$ is understood to vanish outside the allowed region all these limits may be replaced with $\pm\infty$, but they are included here to emphasize that the summations and integrations in (6), (7), and (8) have finite ranges and can readily be approximated numerically. The limits of integration in (5) arise because $f_0(t)$ is constrained to vanish unless $-N_{ff}T \leq t \leq N_{bf}T$. By fixing $N_{ff} = 0$ and letting $N_{bf}$ become large one can approximate realizable prefiltering; and by letting both $N_{ff}$ and $N_{bf}$ become large, one can approximate nonrealizable or infinite lag prefiltering.

Numerical solutions of (5) have been obtained by substituting a numerical integration formula for the integral, whereupon (5) becomes a matrix equation of the same form as (2). This is a hazardous procedure since well-behaved kernels give rise to ill-conditioned matrices. Fair success is had with a step size $T/4$ and time-span bounds $N_{bf} + N_{ff} \leq 20$, so that matrices of size 81 by 81 or smaller result. In particular, a previous paper[1] contains several examples in which $N_{bf} = N_{ff} = 10$, so that each sample value is affected by behavior of the input for ten sample periods in the past, and ten sample periods in the future. With these time-span bounds the prefilter performance comes close to that of nonrealizable or infinite-lag prefilters.

Brown[3] has given a frequency-domain development of jointly optimum nonrealizable prefilters and postfilters for sampled-data systems without quantizers. His argument applies to filters whose impulse responses may be nonzero for all past and future times. Let $F_0(j\omega)$ and $G_0(j\omega)$ be the transfer functions of the optimum prefilter and postfilter, $S_x(j\omega)$ be the power spectral density[1] of the input $x(t)$, and $S_{dx}(j\omega)$ be the cross-power spectrum between $x(t)$ and the desired output $d(t)$. Brown's result implies that both the prefilter and the postfilter are ideal lowpass or bandpass filters with the same passband. Outside the passband, $F_0(j\omega) = G_0(j\omega) = 0$. Inside the passband they obey the relation

$$F_0(j\omega)G_0(j\omega) = T\,\frac{S_{dx}(j\omega)}{S_x(j\omega)}. \tag{11}$$

For the examples considered here, in which $S_x(j\omega)$ has its maximum at $\omega = 0$, the passband is simply the interval $-\pi/T \leq \omega \leq \pi/T$.

A simple consequence of Brown's work is developed in a previous paper.[1] Suppose the desired output is the same as the input, so that $x(t) = d(t)$. Then there exists a nonrealizable postfilter which will, when used with no prefilter at all, yield a distortion exactly twice that produced by the jointly optimum prefilter-postfilter combination. In other words, when the input is the same as the desired output, and the samples are not quantized, the maximum improvement to be obtained with prefiltering is to halve the distortion.

[1] In this paper we mean by $S_x(j\omega)$ the two-sided spectral density:

$$S_x(j\omega) = \int_{-\infty}^{\infty} R_x(t)e^{-j\omega t}\,dt, \qquad -\infty < \omega < \infty$$

$S_{dx}(j\omega)$ is similarly two-sided.

## III. Quantizer Design and Evaluation

In this section we discuss the design of the quantizer in Fig. 1. The resulting quantizer is truly optimum only if successive samples $q(t_k)$ are independent for different values of $k$. This limitation is accepted because it makes the analysis tractable and because it corresponds to the practice of using fixed quantizers in real systems.

The quantizer of Fig. 1 is a zero-memory nonlinear device whose output $y$ assumes the value $y_k$ whenever its input $q$ falls within the interval $q_{k-1} \leq q < q_k$, $k = 1, 2, \cdots, N$. In order that the set of input intervals cover the real line we must have $q_0 = -\infty$, $q_N = \infty$. The $2N - 1$ parameters $q_1, \cdots, q_{N-1}, y_1, \cdots, y_N$ are at the disposal of the designer, who seeks to minimize the quantity $E\{(q - y)^2\}$.

Max[8] and others have considered how to choose these parameters in an optimal way. It is not difficult to see that the interval endpoints $q_k$ must satisfy

$$q_k = \frac{y_k + y_{k+1}}{2}, \qquad k = 1, 2, \cdots, N - 1. \tag{12}$$

Let each sample of the quantizer input $q$ be identically distributed with density $p(q)$. Then the least-mean-square performance criterion requires that the quantizer output levels $y_k$ must satisfy

$$y_k = \frac{\int_{q_{k-1}}^{q_k} qp(q)\,dq}{\int_{q_{k-1}}^{q_k} p(q)\,dq}. \tag{13}$$

From (12) we see that $q_k$ can be given in terms of $y_k$ and $y_{k+1}$, so that (13) specifies for each $k$ a relation between $y_{k-1}$, $y_k$, and $y_{k+1}$. The system is readily solved numerically by means of a multivariate Newton–Raphson iteration. Such a solution is detailed in a previous paper[1] (Appendix E), for the case in which $p(q)$ is a Gaussian density. The results presented in Section IV of this paper were obtained with quantizers designed by this procedure.

Although this paper is concerned primarily with a digital system for transmission and reconstruction of continuous parameter random functions, it is useful to compare the performance of the optimum zero-memory quantizer with Shannon's rate-distortion function. The rate-distortion function $R(D)$ is defined for a particular source as the minimum mutual information $R$ between the source and a receiver in order that the receiver can reconstruct the messages produced by the source with average distortion $D$ or less. Shannon[7] has shown that, when the message is a single Gaussian random variable, the channel realizing the rate-distortion function is one that adds an uncorrelated Gaussian noise random variable to the message.

Figure 2 compares the performance of a quantizer with that of the ideal channel for a single Gaussian random variable of unit variance. In Fig. 2 the quantizer points

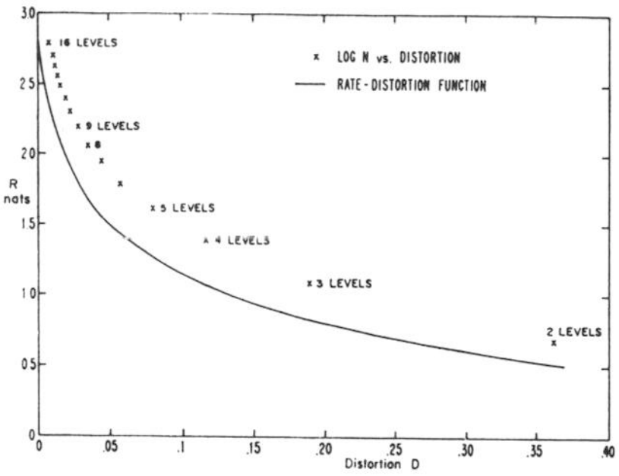


Fig. 2. Quantizer performance versus rate-distortion function.

have been plotted against $\log_e N$, where $N$ is the number of levels. This convention is unfair to the quantizer, since the actual rate is less; but it corresponds to the practice in PCM of representing all quantization levels with bit strings of the same length, as though all quantizer output levels were equiprobable.

Figure 2 shows, for example, that a least-mean-square four-level quantizer operating on a unit-variance Gaussian random variable has a mean distortion of about 0.12, and uses the channel capacity at about 1.4 nats per sample. The optimal channel which realizes the rate-distortion function for this source is one which adds Gaussian noise; operating at the same rate, it would produce a mean distortion of only about 0.06. Alternatively, it would achieve the distortion of 0.12 while using up only 1.1 nats of channel capacity.

Before we pass on to the specific examples of Section IV, we need to make two more calculations concerning the quantizer. In Section II, eq. (2), the optimal postfilter to follow the quantizer is specified in terms of $R_y(kT)$ and $R_{dy}(t)$. The former quantity is the autocorrelation function of the quantizer output $y$, evaluated at the sample times; the latter is the cross correlation between the quantizer output and the desired system output.

To simplify notation, we assume that the gain factors of the prefilter and postfilter have been adjusted so that $q(t)$, the prefilter output, is a unit-variance Gaussian random function.

The cross-correlation function $R_{dy}(t)$ can be obtained from a result of Bussgang[9]:

$$R_{dy}(t) = CR_{dq}(t) \tag{14}$$

where the constant $C$ is given by,

$$C = \sum_{k=1}^{N} \frac{y_k}{\sqrt{2\pi}} \left[ \exp\left(\frac{q_{k-1}^2}{2}\right) - \exp\left(\frac{q_k^2}{2}\right) \right]. \tag{15}$$

In computing $R_y(kT)$ it is convenient to make the substitution $\rho = R_q(kT)$. According to the assumption that $q(t)$ is a unit-variance Gaussian random function, $q(mT)$ and $q(mT + kT)$ are unit-variance Gaussian random variables with cross covariance $\rho = R_q(kT)$. Thus we have

$$R_y(kT) = E\{y(mT)y(mT + kT)\}$$

$$= \sum_{i=1}^{N} \sum_{j=1}^{N} \frac{y_i y_j}{2\pi\sqrt{1 - \rho^2}} \cdot \int_{q_{i-1}}^{q_i} \int_{q_{j-1}}^{q_j} \exp\left[ -\frac{\xi^2 - 2\rho\xi\eta + \eta^2}{2(1 - \rho^2)} \right] d\eta \, d\xi$$

$$= \sum_{i=1}^{N} \sum_{j=1}^{N} \frac{y_i y_j}{2\sqrt{2\pi}} \int_{q_{i-1}}^{q_i} \exp\left[ -\frac{\eta^2}{2} \right] \cdot \left[ \operatorname{erf}\left( \frac{q_j - \rho\eta}{\sqrt{2(1 - \rho^2)}} \right) - \operatorname{erf}\left( \frac{q_{j-1} - \rho\eta}{\sqrt{2(1 - \rho^2)}} \right) \right] d\eta \tag{16}$$

where

$$\operatorname{erf}(x) = \frac{2}{\sqrt{\pi}} \int_0^x e^{-t^2} \, dt.$$

We can simplify (16) by defining a function

$$\psi(\rho, \eta) = \sum_{j=1}^{N} \frac{y_j}{2} \left[ \operatorname{erf}\left( \frac{q_j - \rho\eta}{\sqrt{2(1 - \rho^2)}} \right) - \operatorname{erf}\left( \frac{q_{j-1} - \rho\eta}{\sqrt{2(1 - \rho^2)}} \right) \right]. \tag{17}$$

This function is the conditional mean of the quantizer output at time $(m + k)T$ given that its input at time $mT$ is $\eta$. The time dependence is buried in the quantity $\rho = R_q(kT)$. The conditional mean is defined in terms of the tabulated function erf $(x)$ and is easy to compute with any computer for which an erf $(x)$ subroutine is available. The function $\psi(\rho, \eta)$, is plotted in Fig. 3 for a symmetrical four-level quantizer.

In terms of $\psi(\rho, \eta)$, (15) becomes

$$R_y(kT) = \sum_{i=1}^{N} \frac{y_i}{\sqrt{2\pi}} \int_{q_{i-1}}^{q_i} \psi(\rho, \eta) \exp\left[ -\frac{\eta^2}{2} \right] d\eta. \tag{18}$$

$R_y(kT)$ depends upon the properties of the quantizer being used, but depends upon the input process $q(t)$ only through its autocorrelation function $\rho = R_q(kT)$. $R_y(kT)$ is plotted against $\rho$ in Fig. 4 for symmetrical two- and four-level quantizers. The two-level curve is an arc sine curve, as was found by Van Vleck and Middleton.[11]

The curves have infinite slopes at the point $\rho = 1$. One can show that this behavior will always occur. The exact symmetry of the curves, and in particular the infinite slopes at the point $\rho = -1$, are obtained only in the case of symmetrical quantizers.

Ruchkin[6] has expressed the integral of (16) as a series of Hermite polynomials. While his development leads to certain insights, notably the facts about infinite slopes in the curves of Fig. 4, it is plagued by slow convergence of the series. The most direct path to numerical results seems to be numerical integration of (18).

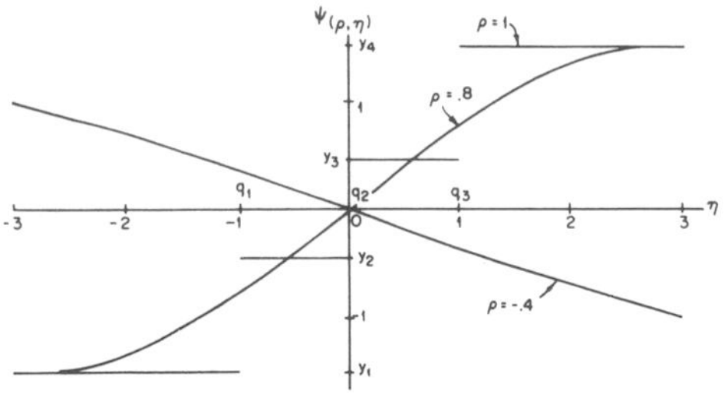


Fig. 3. The function $\psi(\rho, \eta)$ for a symmetrical four-level quantizer.

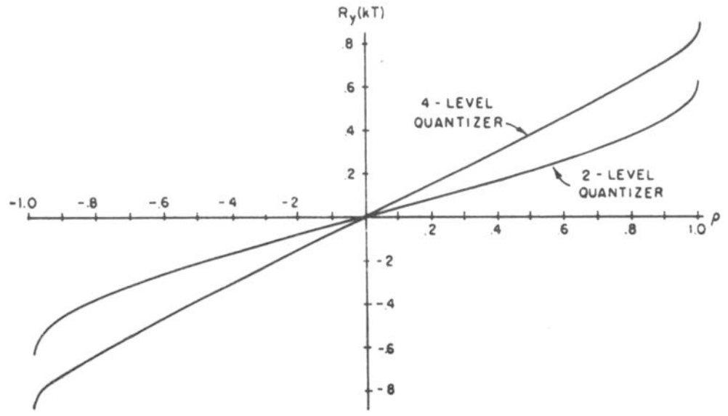


Fig. 4. $R_y(kT)$ vs. $\rho$ for symmetrical two- and four-level quantizers.

## IV. The Sampled-Data System and the Rate-Distortion Function

In this section we assemble the components discussed in Sections II and III and, considering only Gaussian inputs, compare the performance of the assembled system with Shannon's rate-distortion function.[7] McDonald and Schultheiss[10] have considered the rate-distortion function for a Gaussian random function $x(t)$ with power spectral density $S_x(j\omega)$. The function can best be described in terms of a positive parameter $N_0$. Let $\Omega$ be the set on the $\omega$-axis such that

$$N_0 \leq S_x(j\omega), \qquad \omega \in \Omega \tag{19}$$

and let $\Omega'$ be the complement of $\Omega$ on the $\omega$-axis. For any value of $N_0$ the distortion $D$ is given by

$$D = \frac{1}{2\pi} \int_{\Omega'} S_x(j\omega)\, d\omega + \frac{N_0}{2\pi} \int_{\Omega} d\omega \tag{20}$$

and the corresponding rate $R$ by

$$R = \frac{1}{4\pi} \int_{\Omega} \log \frac{S_x(j\omega)}{N_0}\, d\omega. \tag{21}$$

There is a simple channel having the distortion of (20) and the information rate of (21). It consists of an ideal bandpass filter with passband $\Omega$ and additive Gaussian noise of spectral density $N_0$ added in the passband, where $N_0$ and $\Omega$ are related as in (19).

According to the argument of Brown[3] referred to in Section II, a sampled-data system with optimal infinite-lag prefilter and postfilter is an ideal bandpass system. For the "lowpass" spectra to be considered in the following examples, the set $\Omega$ is a single interval centered at $\omega = 0$. Let us pick the sampling period $T$ so that the length of this interval is $2\pi/T$. Then the passband of the sampled data system with the optimal prefilters and postfilters is the interval $\Omega$. Let us use the freedom implied in (11) to pick $G_0(j\omega) = T, \; -\pi/T < \omega < \pi/T$. Then, if an independent Gaussian random variable of variance $N_0/T$ is added to each sample, the sampled-data system will have exactly the distortion of (20) and the average mutual information of (21). In other words, a sampled-data system can realize the rate-distortion function exactly for a Gaussian input. However, a given sampling rate is suitable for only one value of distortion. If one wishes to achieve the minimum distortion for various information rates, one must select both the sampling rate (i.e., measure of the set $\Omega$) and the additive noise variance $N_0/T$ in the optimal way, as indicated in (19).

For this idealized sampled-data system, the first term on the right of (20) is the distortion due to sampling, and arises from the finite bandwidth of the system. The second term in (20) is distortion due to noise added in the passband.

Figure 2 shows that the quantization noise for an optimum zero-memory quantizer of 16 levels or fewer is less than twice the additive Gaussian noise for the same information rate. One might hope that a carefully designed PCM system using such a least-mean-square quantizer would come similarly close to the rate-distortion curve.

Comparisons of PCM systems with the rate-distortion function are presented in Figs. 5, 6, and 7 for Gaussian inputs with different spectra. For each sampling rate, the points for various numbers of quantization levels lie along a curve which has a vertical asymptote at the value of distortion due to sampling alone. At some larger value of distortion, corresponding to a finite number of quantization levels, this curve crosses the one below it and becomes the curve closest to the rate-distortion curve.

In Fig. 5 the spectrum is broad and most of the distortion is due to the first term of (20). The PCM system points approach the $R(D)$ curve most closely at a point corresponding to a sampling rate about 2.5 times that for the PCM system. In Fig. 6, with a narrower spectrum, points on the $R(D)$ curve correspond to sampling rates about 2 times those of the nearest PCM system curves, because more of the distortion is due to quantization noise and less to the limited bandwidth. In Fig. 7, with an exponentially decaying spectrum, the corresponding factor is about 1.4. These figures illuminate the tradeoff between sampling rate and number of quantization levels. Decreasing the sampling rate in order to reduce quantization noise is more useful when the input spectrum has gently sloping tails.

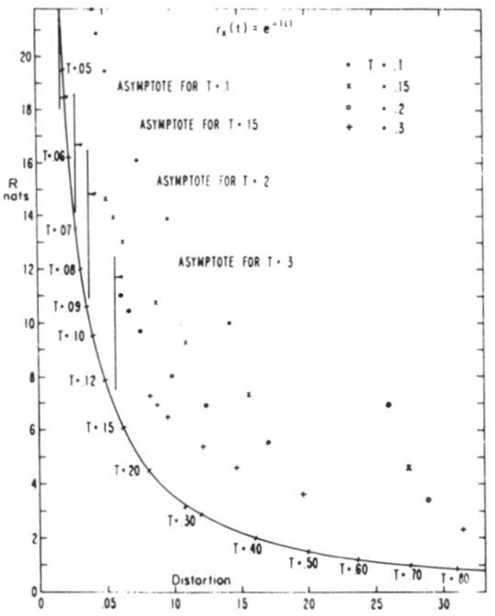


Fig. 5. PCM system performance versus rate-distortion function.

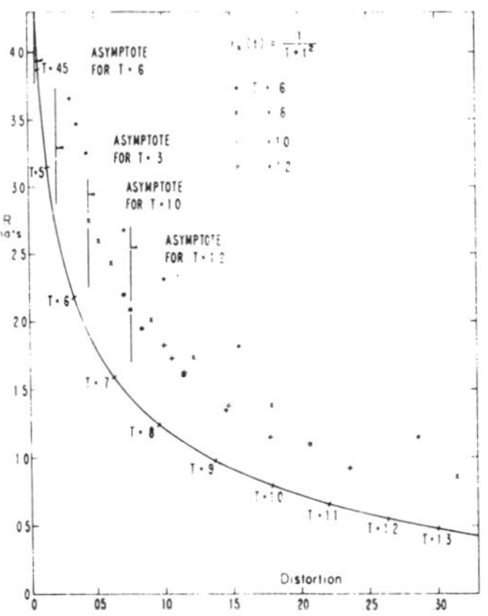


Fig. 7. PCM system performance versus rate-distortion function.

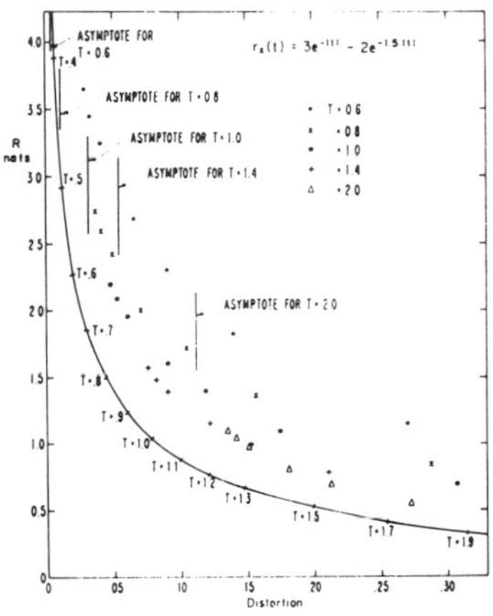


Fig. 6. PCM system performance versus rate-distortion function.

## V. Conclusions

The central results of the present work are those contained in Figs. 5, 6, and 7. They result from the fusion of three threads: the work on optimum filtering of Brown[3] and Robbins,[4] as extended by Tufts and Johnson,[5] and Kellogg[1] to finite numbers of samples; the work of Max[8] and others in design of minimum mean-square-error quantizers; and the work of Shannon[7] and McDonald and Schultheiss[10] on theoretical bounds on information rates.

The PCM system of Fig. 1 can come reasonably close to theoretically optimum performance, but only if the number of quantization levels and the sampling rate are carefully chosen, and if a presampling filter is used. In general, the optimization procedure will assign more of the total error to spectral truncation in the case of a spectrum with gently sloping tails, and more to quantization in the case of a spectrum which cuts off sharply.

The prefilters and postfilters used to obtain Figs. 5, 6, and 7 were modeled as digital filters, whose impulse responses vanished outside the interval of $\pm 10$ sample times. It is interesting that filters with impulse responses of such short duration can approximate the optimum infinite-duration filters obtained by Brown[3] and Robbins[4] in the frequency domain.

## References

[1] W. C. Kellogg, "Numerical operations on random functions," Ph.D. dissertation, Div. of Engrg. and Appl. Physics, Harvard University, Cambridge, Mass., February 1966.

[2] W. C. Kellogg, "Numerical operations on random functions," Div. of Engrg. and Appl. Physics, Harvard University, Tech. Rept. 496, April 1966.

[3] W. M. Brown, "Optimum prefiltering of sampled data," *IRE Trans. Information Theory (Correspondence)*, vol. IT-7, pp. 269–270, October 1961.

[4] H. M. Robbins, "An extension of Wiener filter theory to partly sampled systems," *IRE Trans. Circuit Theory*, vol. CT-6, pp. 362–370, December 1959.

[5] D. W. Tufts and N. Johnson, "Methods for recovering a random waveform from a finite number of samples," *IEEE Trans. Circuit Theory*, vol. CT-12, pp. 32–39, March 1965.

[6] D. S. Ruchkin, "Linear reconstruction of quantized and sampled random signals," *IRE Trans. Communications Systems*, vol. CS-9, pp. 350–355, December 1961.

[7] C. E. Shannon, "Coding theorems for a discrete source with a fidelity criterion," in *Information and Decision Processes*, R. E. Machol, Ed. New York: McGraw-Hill, 1960, p. 93.

[8] J. Max, "Quantizing for minimum distortion," *IRE Trans. Information Theory*, vol. IT-6, pp. 7–12, March 1960.

[9] J. J. Bussgang, "Cross-correlation functions of amplitude-distorted Gaussian signals," M.I.T. Research Lab. of Electronics, Cambridge, Tech. Rept. 216, March 26, 1952.

[10] R. A. McDonald and P. M. Schultheiss, "Information rates of Gaussian signals under criteria constraining the error spectrum," *Proc. IEEE (Correspondence)*, vol. 52, pp. 415–416, Arpil 1964.

[11] J. H. Van Vleck and D. Middleton, "The spectrum of clipped noise," Radio Research Lab., Harvard University, Rept. 21, July 21, 1943; also, *Proc. IEEE*, vol. 54, pp. 2–19, January 1966.

# Part V
# BLOCK DATA COMPRESSION

# Editors' Comments on Papers 26 Through 35



Perhaps the most natural generalization of a quantizer is a block quantizer, that is, a system mapping successive fixed-length blocks of data into a finite number of allowed reproduction blocks, also of fixed length. As it contains the one-dimensional quantizers described in Part IV, such a class can only provide improved performance. Unfortunately, however, the cost of such improvement can be a significantly increased equipment complexity. This difficulty led both to permutation codes and to another class of fixed-length block coding schemes that first perform some transformation on a block of data, possibly to "whiten" it, and then perform one-dimensional quantization on the coordinates of the transformed data. These schemes that map fixed-length blocks into fixed-length blocks have the advantage of being synchronous and therefore of not having the buffer problems of variable-length techniques.

In Paper 26, Schützenberger considered block quantizers and compared average distortion with output entropy. In particular, he showed that, for block length $n$, $N$ $n$-dimensional quantization levels, and $\rho(z, y) = (z - y)^{\alpha}$, and a general class of sources, $E\rho(X, \hat{X}) \geqslant KN^{-\alpha/n}$, where $K$ is a constant. As an example to compare this result with the distortion-rate theory, the block coding rate of the above quantizer is $R = n^{-1} \log N$ and the DRF for a Gaussian source and MSE distortion measure is $\sigma^2 e^{-2R} = \sigma^2 N^{-2/n}$, so that $K = \sigma^2$ yields the OPTA. We note that P. L. Zador derived similar but more precise such bounds for block quantizers in a lengthy unpublished Bell Telephone Laboratories Technical Memorandum in 1966.

Dunn and Berger (Papers 27 and 28) considered block quantization and permutation codes, a technique based on D. Slepian's permutation codes for channels. The two classes are shown to be essentially equivalent and their performance compares favorably with rate-distortion bounds. Furthermore, the permutation codes appear to be implementable with reasonable complexity.

Papers 29 through 32, by Pratt, Habibi and Wintz, Campanella and Robinson, and Atal and Hanauer, respectively, all involve performing a block transformation on the data and then one-dimensional quantizing in the transform domain. The various transformations include Fourier, Hadamard, Karhunen–Loeve, and the more complicated processing of Atal and Hanauer to perform a system identification of a short-term vocal tract model. In each case these coefficients are quantized for digital communications. All but the transformations of Atal and Hanauer are themselves invertible, or nearly so, and hence cannot affect the OPTA, although the nonstationarity of images and speech must be replaced by assumptions of local stationarity to make probabilistic approaches relevant.

Papers 33, 34, and 35 also involve predictive or interpolative approaches that send information only about those samples differing from their prediction by some threshold. As a result, these schemes map source blocks of varying size into code blocks of varying size and hence require elaborate synchronization. As with noiseless variable-length schemes, these algorithms are highly sensitive to occasional channel errors. As fixed-length block codes are special cases of variable-length block codes, and as the distortion-rate theory converse coding theorem does not require a fixed block structure, the distortion-rate function still yields the OPTA for these sytems. The analysis of these papers, however, is concerned with various compression coefficients relating the average number of symbols into the channel buffer per source symbol. These systems are sometimes called *predictive–comparison techniques,* because a threshold comparison is required to determine the transmitted information.

# 26



Reprinted from *Inform. Control,* **1,** 153–158 (1958)

## On The Quantization of Finite Dimensional Messages[1]

Marcel P. Schützenberger[2]

*Research Laboratory of Electronics, Massachusetts Institute of Technology, Cambridge, Massachusetts*

Let $L$ be the average value of a measure of quantization noise, and let $H$ be the negentropy of the quantized signal. Some reciprocal relationship exists between these quantities, since, for example, increasing the number of possible quantized values reduces $L$ but increases $H$. We give a lower bound to $L$ as a function of $H$ and show that it may be realized up to a constant factor. Roughly speaking, this shows that every bit added to $H$ multiplies $L$ by a factor depending on the dimensionality of the message and the measure of quantization noise used.

### I. INTRODUCTION

Let the message $\xi$ be an $n$-dimensional continuous variate with *a priori* probability density $f(\xi)$. Before it can be transmitted through a discrete channel it has to be replaced by a quantized signal $[\xi]$, that is, by some approximate quantity taking only a finite number of distinct values.

We assume here that the channel is perfectly noiseless so that the only source of error lies in the quantization $\xi \to [\xi]$. The accuracy is usually measured by the average $L$ of some given nondecreasing function $\ell(\mid \xi - [\xi] \mid)$ over the *a priori* distribution of $\xi$. We shall consider only those functions $\ell$ which are of the form $c \mid \xi - [\xi] \mid^{\alpha} (\alpha > 0)$ and our results will consequently cover the case of the so-called rms criterion ($\alpha = 2$).

Shannon's theory of noiseless communication indicates that the natural measure of the cost of transmission is the negentropy $H$ of the quantized signal $[\xi]$. With these conventions, the optimum is obtained when, for a given value of $H$ (or of $L$), the other quantity is as small as possible. Intuitively, some general relationship must presumably exist between $H$ and $L$, since any action which tends to decrease one of them (for in-

[1] This work was supported in part by the U. S. Army (Signal Corps), the U. S. Air Force (Office of Scientific Research, Air Research and Development Command), and the U. S. Navy (Office of Naval Research).

[2] Present address: Faculté des Sciences de Poitiers, France.

stance the multiplication of the number of different values of $[\xi]$) has exactly the opposite effect on the other.

Under some broad conditions we give here a lower bound to the value of $L$ as a function of $H$ and we show that this bound may be reached up to a constant proportionality factor. Loosely speaking, these two results mean that every bit of information allows on the average a reduction of $L$ by a factor no more but not less than $2^{-\alpha/n}$, whatever be the density function $f(\xi)$. In particular, $L \geqq KN^{-\alpha/n}$ with $K$, a constant, for every quantization with $N$ different quantized values $[\xi]$.

## II. HYPOTHESES

We state first our hypotheses:

A. The message is an $n$-dimensional variate ($n < \infty$) admitting a continuous, bounded density $f(\xi)$ in its domain of variation $E = \{\xi : f(\xi) > 0\}$

Further,

$$\left| \int_E f(\xi) \log f(\xi)\, d\xi \right| < \infty.$$

B. There exists a finite $\theta$ for which

$$\int_E |\xi|^{\alpha+\theta} f(\xi)\, d\xi < \infty.$$

A quantization $\xi \to [\xi]$ will be identified with a partition $W = \{E_i\}$ of $E$; each $E_i$ is the set of the $\xi$'s admitting the same quantized value $[\xi] = a_i$. For any $W$ we define:

$$H(W) = -\sum P_i \log P_i$$

where

$$P_i = \int_{E_i} f(\xi)\, d\xi$$

and

$$L(W) = \int_E c\, |\xi - [\xi]|^\alpha f(\xi)\, d\xi = \sum P_i L_i'$$

where

$$L_i' = P_i^{-1} \int_{E_i} c\, |\xi - [\xi]|^\alpha f(\xi)\, d\xi.$$

Finally, we say that a sequence of quantizations $W_1 = \{E_{1i}\}$, $W_2 =$

$\{E_{2i}\} \cdots, W_j = \{E_{ji}\} \cdots$, is *systematically convergent* if, for all $j$, every $E_{j+1,i}$ is entirely contained in some $E_{ji'}$ and if $\overline{\lim}_{j\to\infty} L(W_j) = 0$.

*First inequality.* If $f(\xi)$ satisfies $A$, there exists a constant $K$ with the property that $L(W) \geqq K(\exp -\alpha/n)\, H(W)$ for all possible quantizations of $\xi$.

*Second inequality.* If $f(\xi)$ satisfies $A$ and $B$, there exists a constant $K'$ and a systematically convergent sequence $\{W_j\}$ with the property that $L(W_j) \leqq K'(\exp -\alpha/n)\, H(W_j)$ for all $j$.

## III. PROOF OF THE INEQUALITIES

In what follows $g_1, g_2, \cdots$ denote geometric constants which are functions of $\alpha$ and $n$ only; $k_1, k_2, \cdots$ denote nonzero finite constants whose values depend upon $f(\xi)$ but not upon the quantization considered.

We shall use twice the fact that for any partition $W = \{E_i\}$ the sum $|-\sum P_i \log f_i|$, where $f_i$ is the value of $f(\xi)$ at some inner point of $E_i$, is uniformly bounded. This results immediately from the hypotheses by the following inequalities

$$|\sum P_i \log 1/f_i| = |\sum P_i \log f^*/f_i - \sum P_i \log f^*|$$

$$\leqq \sum P_i |\log f^*/f_i| + |\log f^*| < \int_E f(\xi)\, |\log f^*/f(\xi)|\, d\xi + |\log f^*|$$

$$\leqq \int_E f(\xi) \log 1/f(\xi)\, d\xi + 2\,|\log f^*|$$

where

$$f^* = \sup_{\xi\epsilon E} f(\xi).$$

### First Inequality

We take a fixed arbitrary number $p$ $(0 < p < 1)$ and, for each $E_i$ of $W$ we define a value $f_i$ and a subset $E_i'$ of $E_i$ by the relations:

$$E_i' = \{\xi\epsilon E_i\,;\, f(\xi) \geqq f_i\}; \qquad \int_{E_i'} f(\xi)\, d\xi = p \int_{E_i} f(\xi)\, d\xi = pP_i\,.$$

We have

$$P_iL_i' \geqq \inf_x \int_{E_i} c\,|\xi - x|^\alpha f(\xi)\, d\xi = c\int_{E_i} |\xi - x_i|^\alpha f(\xi)\, d\xi$$

$$\geqq c\int_{E_i'} |\xi - x_i|^\alpha f(\xi)\, d\xi \geqq cf_i \int_{E_i} |\xi - x_i|^\alpha\, d\xi = cf_iL_i''.$$

It is a classical result that for a fixed value of meas($E_i'$), the sum $L_i''$ is a minimum when $E_i'$ is an $n$-dimensional sphere with radius $\rho_i$ centered at $x_i$. Consequently, $P_i L_i' \geqq c g_1 f_i \rho_i^{n+\alpha}$ where $\rho_i$ is defined by $\text{meas}(E_i') = g_2 \rho_i^n$ and where $g_1$ and $g_2$ are geometric constants. If we now define $\bar{f}_i$ by the equality $\bar{f}_i \, \text{meas}(E_i') = pP_i = \int_{E_i'} f(\xi)\, d\xi$, we can eliminate $\rho_i$ and meas($E_i'$). Thus we obtain

$$P_i L_i' \geqq P_i^{1+\alpha/n} c g_3 p^{1+\alpha/n} f_i \bar{f}_i^{-1-\alpha/n}.$$

Taking into account the remark made at the beginning of this section, we find that

$$L_i' \geqq c g_3 (p/f^*)^{1+\alpha/n} p_i^{\alpha/n} f_i$$

and

$$-\sum P_i \log L_i' \leqq \left(\frac{\alpha}{n}\right) H(W) + \log k_1 - \sum P_i \log f_i$$

$$\leqq \left(\frac{\alpha}{n}\right) H(W) - \log K.$$

This concludes the proof, since we have

$$L(W) = \sum P_i L_i' \geqq \exp - \sum P_i \log L_i' \quad [= K \exp - \alpha/n H(W)]$$

because of the convexity of the function $\log 1/x$.

SECOND INEQUALITY

The construction of a systematically convergent sequence can be carried out in many ways. We indicate here one method which is probably among the simplest ones. In the first place we observe that the classical inequality on the absolute moments

$$\left[\int_{E'} |\xi|^{\alpha} f(\xi)\, d\xi\right]^{1/\alpha} \leqq \left[\int_{E'} |\xi|^{\alpha+\theta} f(\xi)\, d\xi\right]^{(\alpha+\theta)^{-1}} \left[\int_{E'} f(\xi)\, d\xi\right]^{\theta(\alpha+\theta)^{-1}}$$

gives under the hypothesis $B$

$$\int_{E'} |\xi^{\alpha}|\, f(\xi)\, d\xi \leqq \left[\int_{E'} |\xi|^{\alpha+\theta} f(\xi)\, d\xi\right]^{\alpha(\alpha+\theta)^{-1}} \left[\int_{E'} f(\xi)\, d\xi\right]^{\theta(\alpha+\theta)^{-1}}$$

$$= k_2 \left[\int_{E'} f(\xi)\, d\xi\right]^{\theta(\alpha+\theta)^{-1}}$$

for any subset $E'$ of $E$.

Let us take now an arbitrary length $d$ and construct a connected domain $F$ around the origin made up of the juxtaposition of $n$-dimensional cubes $C_i$, with $d$ the length of the side of each cube. We can make $F$ big enough so that

$$e = \int_{E-F} f(\xi)\, d\xi$$

satisfies the relation $e^{\theta/\alpha+\theta} \leqq d^\alpha$. We consider the quantization $W$ in which, $[\xi] = x_i$, the center of $C_i$, when $\xi \epsilon C_i$ and $[\xi] = 0$ when $\xi \epsilon E - F$. We have

$$H(W) = -\sum P_i \log P_i - e \log e - P_i \log f_i + n \log 1/d - e \log e$$

(where, again, $f_i$ is the value of $f(\xi)$ at some inner point of $C_i$), that is,

$$n \log 1/d \geqq H(W) - k_3 + e \log e.$$

Had we considered instead of $F$ some domain $F'$ for which

$$e' = \int_{E-F'} f(\xi)\, d\xi \leqq \int_{E-F} f(\xi)\, d\xi = e$$

the last inequality would still have been valid, for $x \log 1/x$ is a decreasing function of $x$. Consequently $d^n \leqq K'' \exp - H(W)$ for some $K''$. We compute now $L(W)$.

$$\sum P_i L_i' = c \int_{E-F} |\, \xi \,|^\alpha f(\xi)\, d\xi + \sum c \int_{C_i} |\, \xi - x_i \,|^\alpha f(\xi)\, d\xi$$

but, for any $C_i$:

$$\int_{C_i} |\, \xi - x_i \,|^\alpha f(\xi)\, d\xi \leqq \int_{C_i} \left| \sup_{\xi \epsilon C_i} |\, \xi - x_i \,| \right|^\alpha f(\xi)\, d\xi$$

$$\leqq g_4\, d^\alpha \int_{C_i} f(\xi)\, d\xi = g_4\, d^\alpha P_i$$

and

$$\int_{E-F} |\, \xi \,|^\alpha f(\xi)\, d\xi \leqq k_2 e^{\theta(\alpha+\theta)^{-1}} \leqq k_2\, d^\alpha.$$

Thus

$$L(W) = \sum P_i L_i' \leqq K''' d^\alpha \leqq K' \exp - \alpha/n H(W).$$

By construction the constant $K'$ can be chosen such that it does not depend upon $W$. We consider now the partition $W = W_1$ as the first term of the sequence $\{W_j\}$ and we take a second value $d'$ such that $d$ is equal to some multiple of $d'$.

We subdivide every $C_i$ into smaller cubes $C_i'$ with length of the side $d'$ and we add new cubes of the same size around $F$ so as to obtain a domain $F'$ for which, as above,

$$\int_{E-F'} f(\xi)\, d\xi \leqq d'^{(\alpha+\theta)\alpha\theta^{-1}}.$$

Obviously the partition $W_2 = W'$ satisfies $L(W') \leqq L(W)$; $L(W') \leqq K' \exp - \alpha/nH(W')$, and this concludes the proof since we can choose, by iterating the same method, a sequence $d, d', \cdots$ converging to zero.

## IV. REMARKS

i. The hypotheses $A$ and $B$ are sufficient but obviously not necessary for the validity of the results. In the same manner, the assumption that the "loss function" $\ell(r)$, $(r = |\xi - [\xi]|)$, has the form $cr^\alpha$ could be weakened and the results would hold substantially, in an asymptotic fashion, for any $\ell(r)$ with $\lim_{r\to 0} rd/dr \log \ell(r) = \alpha > 0$. But this would definitely not be true for arbitrary $\ell(r)$ (as, for example, $\exp -1/r$ or $r \log 1/r$) and the normalization function $H(W)$ does not seem then to play the same natural role.

ii. A more detailed computation allows one to get closer estimates of the constants $K$ and $K'$. However, they remain different and their ratio tends to infinity with $n$. For $n = 2$, a better "second inequality" can be obtained by use of a covering of the plane with hexagons instead of squares. Our present ignorance concerning the most elementary properties of the coverings of the space for $n \geqq 3$ seems to lie at the root of the discrepancy between $K$ and $K'$.

RECEIVED: September 6, 1957.

# 27

Reprinted from *Proc. Columbia Symp. Signal Transmission Processing,* IEEE Circuit Theory Group and the Department of Electrical Engineering, Columbia University, New York, 1965, pp. 76–81

## THE PERFORMANCE OF A CLASS OF n DIMENSIONAL QUANTIZERS FOR A GAUSSIAN SOURCE*

James G. Dunn

Department of Electrical Engineering, Columbia University
New York, N. Y.
and
ITT Federal Laboratories
Nutley, N. J.

Summary

The performance in terms of information rate and mean square distortion is computed for a class of n dimensional quantizers, whose inputs are random vectors with a spherically symmetrical Gaussian distribution, for n up to 399. This class has the property that the output vectors are equiprobable, equal energy, and are essentially equivalent to the Variant I permutation codes described by Slepian. The quantizing regions are combinations of the fundamental regions of the symmetry group of a regular simplex and the output vectors are the centroids of the quantizing regions.

The performance is calculated for varying rates and dimension n with the aid of Gaussian order statistics. The results are compared with the Shannon bound and several quantizers are found which are within a fraction of a bit of this bound.

### I. Introduction

The performance of a class of quantizers for a source with a n dimensional spherically symmetrical Gaussian distribution is computed for values of n up to 399. These quantizers have the property that their output vectors are equiprobable, have equal energy, and are essentially equivalent to the Variant I permutation codes described by Slepian.[11,12]

In section II, the quantizing regions are defined as the fundamental regions [4] of the symmetry group of a regular simplex. It is then shown that, if the quantizer outputs are chosen as the centroids of these quantizing regions, then the output vectors are equiprobable and have equal energy. In section III, the method of computing the quantizer performance using Gaussian order statistics is described. This method is derived in detail in the Appendix.

In section IV, the quantizing regions are allowed to include a number of fundamental regions in order to permit a more flexible relation between M, the number of regions, and n. In terms of n+1 dimensional coordinates of the points (defined in the Appendix), the quantizer outputs are shown to be the Variant I permutation codes.

The quantizer performance is evaluated in terms of the information rate per dimension of the output, R, and the mean square distortion, D. It is desired to make the rate, R, as small as possible for a fixed distortion, D. The results are compared with Shannon's greatest lower bound on this rate, $R_{min}$. It was found that if a large number of fundamental regions are combined to form a quantizing region, then quantizers can be found whose rate is within a fraction of a bit of $R_{min}$. On the other hand, if the fundamental regions are themselves the quantizing regions, then the rate can be several bits higher than $R_{min}$.

### II. Operation Of The Quantizer

Every finite group of order g of orthogonal transformations on a n dimensional Euclidean space, $E_n$, partitions the space into g congruent fundamental regions.[4,9] These regions, which are permuted by the operations of the group, can be taken as unbounded, convex pyramidal cones whose boundaries are hyperplanes through the origin and which overlap only on these boundaries.[3] The use of such regions will be considered for the particular case, of the symmetry group, $A_n$, of a regular simplex.

The vertices of the regular simplex (assumed to be inscribed in a sphere centered at the origin) will be denoted by the vectors $\underline{v}_1$, $\underline{v}_2$, ..., $\underline{v}_{n+1}$, all of equal length. The group $A_n$, for any n, is one of the three general classes of groups which can be generated by reflections (Coxeter [4], sec. 11.5). The fundamental regions associated with $A_n$ are completely defined by the regular simplex. The boundaries of these regions are portions of the reflecting hyperplanes which generate the group. The operations of $A_n$ correspond to the $g = (n+1)!$ distinct permutations of the vertices, and the $n(n+1)/2$ reflections correspond to the transpositions which interchange just two vertices.[13,4] The type of reflection under consideration is an orthogonal

*This paper forms a portion of a dissertation to be submitted to Columbia University in partial fulfillment of requirements for the Sc. d. degree.

transformation which reflects the points of $E_n$ in a hyperplane through the origin. We will denote a typical reflection in $A_n$ by $(ij)$, where the corresponding reflecting hyperplane perpendicularly bisects the edge of the regular simplex which joins the vertices $\underline{v}_i$ and $\underline{v}_j$ and contains all the other vertices.

We will denote a general permutation in $S_{n+1}$, the symmetric group of degree $(n+1)$[1], by s:

$$s = \begin{pmatrix} 1 & 2 & \cdots & n+1 \\ i_1 & i_2 & \cdots & i_{n+1} \end{pmatrix} \tag{1}$$

It is well known [1] that $S_{n+1}$ can be generated by the n transpositions (we use here the shortened cyclic notation for s):

$$(12),\ (23),\ \cdots,\ (n,n+1) \tag{2}$$

and the corresponding reflecting hyperplanes form the boundaries of one of the fundamental regions (Coxeter [4], sec. 7.9), which we will denote by $F_0$. If $\underline{x}$ is a general point in $E_n$, we can define $F_0$, using the usual scalar product between vectors, as:

$$F_0 = \left[\underline{x} \mid \underline{x} \cdot \underline{v}_1 \geq \underline{x} \cdot \underline{v}_2 \geq \cdots \geq \underline{x} \cdot \underline{v}_{n+1}\right] \tag{3}$$

The general fundamental region is defined by:

$$F(s) = \left[\underline{x} \mid \underline{x} \cdot \underline{v}_{i_1} \geq \underline{x} \cdot \underline{v}_{i_2} \geq \cdots \geq \underline{x} \cdot \underline{v}_{i_{n+1}}\right] \tag{4}$$

Figure 1 illustrates $F_0$ for the case n=3.

The input to the quantizer will be a random vector, $\underline{x}$, which is assumed to have a spherically symmetrical Gaussian distribution:

$$dG(\underline{x}) = \frac{1}{(2\pi Q)^{n/2}} e^{-\frac{1}{2}\frac{\|\underline{x}\|^2}{Q}} d\underline{x} \tag{5}$$

The probability that $\underline{x}$ lies on one of the boundaries between fundamental regions is zero, so that such an event can be ignored in computing the performance of the quantizer. Let:

$$P(s) = \text{Prob}\left[\underline{x} \in F(s)\right] = \int_{F(s)} dG(\underline{x}) \tag{6}$$

and let $U(s)$ be the orthogonal transformation in $A_n$ which carries $F_0$ into $F(s)$. In (6), we can make the change of variable $\underline{x} = U(s)\,\underline{q}$:

$$P(s) = \int_{F_0} dG(U(s)\underline{q}) = \int_{F_0} dG(\underline{q}) = P_0$$

since, from (5), $G(\underline{x})$ is seen to be invariant under an orthogonal change of variable. Since the sum of all the $P(s)$ is unity:

$$P(s) = \frac{1}{g}, \quad s \in S_{n+1} \tag{7}$$

The operation of the quantizer is that if $\underline{x}$ falls in $F(s)$, the quantizer provides an output, $\underline{y}(s)$, to be regarded as an approximation to the input, $\underline{x}$. The performance of the quantizer will be measured by the information rate per dimension of the output, R:

$$R = \frac{1}{n} \log_2 g \tag{8}$$

and by the mean square distortion per dimension, D:

$$D = \frac{1}{n} E \|\underline{x} - \underline{y}(s)\|^2 \tag{9}$$

The quantizer output, $\underline{y}(s)$, which minimizes D is the conditional expectation of $\underline{x}$ given that $\underline{x} \in F(s)$ (Doob [5], Chap. II, Eq. 3.13'), or, in other words, $\underline{y}(s)$ is the centroid of that portion of the probability distribution $G(\underline{x})$ which lies in $F(s)$. This truncated distribution will be denoted by $I_{F(s)}(\underline{x})G(\underline{x})$, where $I_{F(s)}(\underline{x})$ is the indicator function of the set $F(s)$.

$$\underline{y}(s) = g \int_{F(s)} \underline{x}\, dG(\underline{x}) \tag{10}$$

By making the same change of variable used before, we find:

$$\underline{y}(s) = U(s)\, \underline{y}_0 \tag{11}$$

where $\underline{y}_0$ is the centroid of $F_0$.

With this choice for $\underline{y}(s)$, (9) simplifies to:

$$D = \frac{1}{n} E \|\underline{x}\|^2 - \frac{1}{n} E \|\underline{y}(s)\|^2$$

or, using (11):

$$D = Q - \frac{1}{n} \|\underline{y}_0\|^2 \tag{12}$$

Thus, to calculate the quantizer performance, it is only necessary to calculate the length of the centroid for $F_0$. This will be done in the following section. We will then compare the performance of these quantizers with the greatest lower bound on the rate for a given distortion given by Shannon ([10], Th. 22):

$$R_{min} = \frac{1}{2} \log_2 \frac{Q}{D} \tag{13}$$

## III. Centroid Of The Fundamental Region

The method of calculating the length of the centroid of the fundamental region is derived in the Appendix. This method depends on considering the n dimensional space, $E_n$, as a subspace of a n+1 dimensional space, $E_{n+1}$. An orthonormal coordinate system, $\underline{a}_i$, i = 1, 2, ···, n+1, can be defined in $E_{n+1}$ such that the group, $\Delta(s)$, of all coordinate permutations with respect to this basis induces the symmetry group $A_n$ in the subspace $E_n$.

It is shown in the Appendix that the centroid of the fundamental region, $F_0'$, of the group $\Delta(s)$ with respect to a spherically symmetrical Gaussian distribution in $E_{n+1}$ is the same as the centroid of $F_0$ in $E_n$. It is also shown that the n+1 dimensional coordinates of the centroid are the expected values, $\bar{\xi}_i$, of the Gaussian order statistics.[6] The $\bar{\xi}_i$ are tabulated [7] for n+1 up to 400 and can thus be used to compute the length of the centroid. Using Harter's table [7], $||\underline{y}_0||^2$ was calculated for n=9, 49, 99, and 399, and, using (8) and (12), the corresponding rate and distortion were obtained.

The results are shown in Figure 2, along with some other results obtained in the next section. The performance of the quantizers just described for the four values of n correspond to those points with the highest rate for each n. It can be seen that for the higher values of n, the rate is several bits greater than Shannon's lower bound, $R_{min}$:

For comparison, Figure 2 also shows the performance of two classes of one dimensional quantizers. These one dimensional quantizers could be used to quantize the n dimensional source by quantizing each coordinate separately. Curve A shows the performance of Max's [8], minimum distortion quantizers for between 11 and 36 output levels. These quantizers have minimum distortion for a fixed number of output levels, without regard to rate. Curve B shows the performance of one dimensional quantizers whose output levels are equiprobable and are the centroids of their corresponding quantizing regions. The number of output levels varies from 5 to 100.

## IV. Combinations of Fundamental Regions

Let:

$$n_1+n_2 + \cdots + n_r = n+1 \tag{14}$$

be an arbitrary partition of n+1 into positive integers. Then we can define a corresponding subgroup of $S_{n+1}$:

$$H = S_{n_1} \times S_{n_2} \times \cdots \times S_{n_r} \tag{15}$$

as the direct product of subgroups $S_{n_i}$, symmetric groups of degree $n_i$. $S_{n_1}$ is the symmetric group on the first $n_1$ integers and is generated by the first $n_1$ - 1 transpositions in (2). $S_{n_2}$ is the symmetric group on the next $n_2$ integers, and so on. The order, h, of H is then:

$$h = n_1!\, n_2! \cdots n_r! \tag{16}$$

Under the operations of $A_n$ which correspond to elements in H, the fundamental region $F_0$ is permuted among h of the F(s); let:

$$\Gamma_0 = \bigcup_{s\in H} F(s) \tag{17}$$

and let $\underline{w}_0$ be its centroid:

$$\underline{w}_0 = \frac{1}{h} \sum_{s\in H} \underline{y}(s) \tag{18}$$

$\underline{w}_0$ is invariant under the operations of $A_n$ for which s∈H, since these only permute the terms in the summation. Thus, $\underline{w}_0$ lies on all the reflecting hyperplanes corresponding to those transpositions in (2) which generate H.

All of the operations of $A_n$ generate the points:

$$\underline{w}(s) = U(s)\, \underline{w}_0 = \Delta(s)\, \underline{w}_0 \quad , \ s\in S_{n+1} \tag{19}$$

Let M be the number of distinct points defined by (19). As operations on the points $\underline{w}(s)$, $A_n$ can be considered as a transitive permutation representation of $S_{n+1}$ of degree M in which H leaves one point, $\underline{w}_0$, fixed. By Burnside [1], sec. 133:

$$M = \frac{g}{h} = \frac{(n+1)!}{n_1!\, n_2! \cdots n_r!} \tag{20}$$

and the distinct points $\underline{w}(s)$ correspond to the distinct left cosets sH of H in $S_{n+1}$. Corresponding to these points we have M distinct regions $\Gamma(s)$ obtained from $\Gamma_0$ by the operations of $A_n$. If the quantizer uses the $\Gamma(s)$ for its quantizing regions instead of the F(s), and the corresponding centroids $\underline{w}(s)$ as outputs, it is possible to obtain a large variation in rate, $R = \frac{1}{n} \log_2 M$, for a fixed n.

In terms of the n+1 dimensional coordinates introduced in the Appendix, (19) shows that the points $\underline{w}(s)$ are Variant I permutation codes given by Slepian.[11,12] The quantizer performs the same operations as a decoder for a continuous channel. Slepian has pointed out that minimum distance decoding can be performed simply by ordering the n+1 dimensional coordinates. The quantizer also performs minimum distance decoding in that it must choose which $\underline{w}(s)$ is closest to the input $\underline{x}$. The only difference in implementation is that the quantizer must first perform the n+1 cross-correlations $\underline{x}\cdot\underline{v}_1 = \underline{x}\cdot\underline{a}_i$ in order to obtain the n+1 dimensional coordinates.

The question arises as to what constitutes a good choice for the subgroup H. It has been found that the distortion can vary considerably for different subgroups whose order h is essentially the same. No answer to this question has been found: Table I and Figure 2 show the best results which were obtained by trial and error for several different classes of subgroups. It can be seen that it is possible to obtain quantizers with much better performance than those of the previous section. For a fixed n, this better performance (lower R) is obtained at a somewhat greater distortion value than before. It is believed that this better performance is due to a better arrangement of the output points which are immediate neighbors of $\underline{w}_0$. Most of the subgroups used to obtain Table I were chosen by a method which will now be described briefly.

We can define the nearest neighbors of $\underline{w}_0$ as those points obtained from $\underline{w}_0$ by a single reflection in one of the bounding hyperplanes of $\Gamma_0$. If all the points $\underline{w}(s)$ are considered vertices of a convex polytope, then the nearest neighbors of $\underline{w}_0$ are those points connected to $\underline{w}_0$ by an edge. If all the edges are equal (i.e., if the nearest neighbor distance is maximized), then the figure becomes a uniform polytope.[2] Slepian [11] has shown that in terms of the n+1 dimensional coordinates, this occurs when the values which these coordinates can take are equally spaced.

Inspection of the means of the order statistics, $\xi_i$, shows that these are far from being uniformly spaced. However, we can make them approximately uniform by certain selections of the subgroup H, or, in other words, by appropriate choices of the partition (14). The n+1 dimensional coordinates of $\underline{w}_0$, for a given partition (14), will have the form, using (18):

$$\underline{w}_0 = \mathrm{col}\left[\zeta_1, \zeta_1, \cdots, \zeta_1, \zeta_2, \zeta_2, \cdots, \zeta_2, \cdots, \zeta_r, \zeta_r, \cdots \zeta_r\right] \quad (21)$$

where:

$$\zeta_i = \frac{1}{n_i} \sum_j \xi_j \ , \quad i = 1, 2, \cdots, r \quad (22)$$

and where j extends over those coordinates permuted by $S_{n_i}$.

## V. Acknowledgement

The author is indebted to a great many persons who made possible the research on which the present paper is based. I am particularly grateful for the advice given by Professor T.E. Stern of Columbia University, who supervised this research.* The work was supported by ITT Federal Laboratories, who gave permission to publish the results. Dr. D. Slepian kindly provided copies of his unpublished memorandum.

## Appendix

The purpose of this appendix is to compute $\|\underline{v}_0\|^2$. It will be convenient to use n+1 dimensional coordinates; thus, let $\underline{a}_i$, $i = 1, \cdots$, n+1, be a set of orthonormal basis vectors for $E_{n+1}$ and let $\underline{z}$ denote a general point in $E_{n+1}$ with coordinates $z_i = \underline{z}\cdot\underline{a}_i$. Let:

$$\underline{z}_0 = \frac{1}{n+1} \sum_{i=1}^{n+1} \underline{a}_i \quad (23)$$

and:

$$\underline{v}_i = \underline{a}_i - \underline{z}_0 \ , \quad i = 1, \cdots, n+1 \quad (24)$$

It is readily verified that $\underline{v}_i\cdot\underline{z}_0 = 0$ for all i; that $\|\underline{v}_i - \underline{v}_j\|^2 = \|\underline{a}_i - \underline{a}_j\|^2 = 2$ for $i \neq j$; and that all $\underline{v}_i$ have the same length. Let L denote the one dimensional subspace determined by $\underline{z}_0$; then the $\underline{v}_i$ are the vertices of a regular simplex which lies in the n dimensional subspace, which we take as $E_n$, completely orthogonal to L. Figure 3 illustrates this for n=2.

Let $\Delta(s)$, $s \in S_{n+1}$, be the group of all coordinate permutations on the basis vectors $\underline{a}_i$ in $E_{n+1}$. Because of the one to one correspondence (24) between the vertices, $\underline{v}_i$, and basis vectors, $\underline{a}_i$, $\Delta(s)$ induces the symmetry operation $\underline{U}(s)$ of $A_n$ in the subspace $E_n$. The set:

$$F'_0 = \left[ \underline{z} \mid z_1 \geq z_2 \geq \cdots \geq z_{n+1} \right] \quad (25)$$

is evidently a fundamental region for the group $\Delta(s)$. F'(s) is defined in a similar manner.

---

*Research supervision was supported by the Office of Naval Research under contract NONR 4259 (04) and by the National Science Foundation under grant GP-2789.

Every point $\underline{z}$ in $E_{n+1}$ can be written in the form:

$$\underline{z} = \underline{x} + \underline{p} \tag{26}$$

where $\underline{x}$ lies in $E_n$, i.e., $\underline{x}'\underline{z}_0 = 0$, and $\underline{p}$ lies in L. Then:

$$z_i = \underline{z}'\underline{a}_i = \underline{x}'\underline{v}_i + \underline{p}'\underline{z}_0 \tag{27}$$

The orthogonal projection (along L) of $\underline{z}$ into $E_n$ is thus obtained by subtracting a constant, independent of i, from each coordinate $z_i$. Since this will not change the order in (25), we see that the projection of $F'_0$ into $E_n$ is the $F_0$ defined by (3).

Let:

$$dG'(\underline{z}) = \frac{1}{(2\pi Q)^{\frac{n+1}{2}}} e^{-\frac{1}{2}\frac{\|\underline{z}\|^2}{Q}} d\underline{z} \tag{28}$$

so that $G(\underline{x})$ is just the marginal distribution of $G'(\underline{z})$ on the subspace $E_n$. By the same argument used to obtain (7), we see that Prob $\left[\underline{z} \in F'(s)\right]$ = 1/g. The centroid of $F'_0$ is:

$$\underline{y}'_0 = g\int_{F'_0} \underline{z}\, dG'(\underline{z}) = g\int_{F_0} dG(\underline{x}) \frac{1}{\sqrt{2\pi Q}} \int_L (\underline{x}+\underline{p})\, e^{-\frac{1}{2}\frac{\|\underline{p}\|^2}{Q}} d\underline{p} = g\int_{F_0} \underline{x}\, dG(\underline{x}) = \underline{y}_0 \tag{29}$$

Define a mapping $\underline{z} \to \underline{\xi}$ of the space $E_{n+1}$ onto the fundamental region $F'_0$ such that $\xi_1$ is the largest of the $z_i$, $\xi_2$ is the next largest, etc., and finally, $\xi_{n+1}$ is the smallest of the $z_i$. If we ignore what happens at the boundaries of the F'(s), this mapping may be defined by:

$$\underline{\xi} = \sum_{s\in S_{n+1}} I_{F'(s)}(\underline{z})\ \Delta^{-1}(s)\,\underline{z} \tag{30}$$

Let $H(\underline{\xi})$ be the distribution function for $\underline{\xi}$, then:

$$dH(\underline{\xi}) = \sum_{s\in S_{n+1}} I_{F'(s)}(\Delta(s)\,\underline{\xi})\ dG'(\Delta(s)\underline{\xi})$$

Since $G'(\underline{z})$ is invariant under an orthogonal change of variables:

$$H(\underline{\xi}) = g\, I_{F'_0}(\underline{\xi})\ G'(\underline{\xi}) \tag{31}$$

so that (29) becomes:

$$\underline{y}_0 = g\int_{E_{n+1}} \underline{z}\, I_{F'_0}(\underline{z})\, dG'(\underline{z}) = \int_{E_{n+1}} \underline{\xi}\, dH(\underline{\xi}) = \overline{\underline{\xi}} \tag{32}$$

Normalizing Q to unity in (28), the $\xi_i$ are seen to be the Gaussian order statistics[6] so that $\overline{\xi}_i$ can be obtained from available tables.[7] Finally, $\|\underline{y}_0\|^2$ is the sum of the squares of the $\overline{\xi}_i$.

## References


1.) W. Burnside, "Theory of Groups of Finite Order" (2nd. Ed.), Dover, New York, 1955.

2.) H.S.M. Coxeter, "The polytopes with regular-prismatic vertex figures." Phil. Trans., Royal Society of London, ser. A, vol. 229, pp. 329-425; 1930.

3.) H.S.M. Coxeter, "Discrete groups generated by reflections," Annals of Math., vol. 35, pp. 588-621; July, 1934.

4.) H.S.M. Coxeter, "Regular Polytopes" (2nd. Ed.), MacMillan, New York, 1963.

5.) J.L. Doob, "Stochastic Processes," Wiley, New York, 1953.

6.) S.S. Gupta, "Bibliography on the multivariate normal integrals and related topics," Ann. Math. Stat., vol. 34, pp. 829-838; 1963.

7.) H.L. Harter, "Expected values of normal order statistics," Biometrika, vol. 48, pp. 151-165; 1961.

8.) J. Max, "Quantizing for minimum distortion," IEEE TRANSACTIONS ON INFORMATION THEORY, vol. IT-6, pp. 7-12; March, 1960.

9.) G. de B. Robinson, "On the fundamental region of an orthogonal representation of a finite group," Proc. London Math. Soc. ser. 2, vol. 43, pp. 289-301; 1937.

10.) C. E. Shannon, "A mathematical theory of communication," Bell System Tech. Jour., vol. 27, pp. 623-656; October, 1948.

11.) D. Slepian, "Several new families of alphabets for signalling," Unpublished memorandum; April 12, 1951.

12.) D. Slepian, "Permutation modulation," presented at ICMCI, Tokyo, Japan, September 4-7, 1964.

13.) J. A. Todd, "The groups of symmetries of the regular polytopes," Proc. Cambridge Phil. Soc., vol. 27, pp. 212-231; 1931.

Table I

Summary of Performance of quantizers for Gaussian Source

| n | Partition of n+1 | $(Q/D)_{db}$ | R-bits |
|---|---|---|---|
| 9 | 1,1,···,1 | 9.18 | 2.18 |
| | 1,1,1,1,2,1,1,1,1, | 9.07 | 2.08 |
| | 1,2,4,2,1 | 7.72 | 1.69 |
| | 2,6,2 | 5.48 | 1.04 |
| 49 | 1,1, ···,1 | 15.08 | 4.36 |
| | 1,1,5,4,11,6,11,4, 5,1,1 | 12.60 | 2.68 |
| | 1,5,11,6,11,5,1 | 10.92 | 2.16 |
| | 2,13,20,13,2 | 8.93 | 1.75 |
| | 1,12,24,12,1 | 8.02 | 2.11 |
| 99 | 1,1, ···,1 | 17.96 | 5.29 |
| | 1,2,3,···, 9,10, 9, ···,1 | 16.48 | 3.64 |
| | 1,2,8,10,20,18,20, 10,8,2,1 | 13.95 | 2.77 |
| | 1,8,24,34,24,8,1 | 10.97 | 2.11 |
| 399 | 1,1, ···,1 | 22.98 | 7.23 |
| | 1,2,3, ···,19,20, 19, ···,1 | 21.94 | 4.78 |
| | 1,1,3,5,9,16,22, 33,40,40,50,40,40, 33, ···, 1 | 18.94 | 3.78 |
| | 5,5,35,40,65,100, 65,40,35,5,5 | 14.68 | 2.87 |

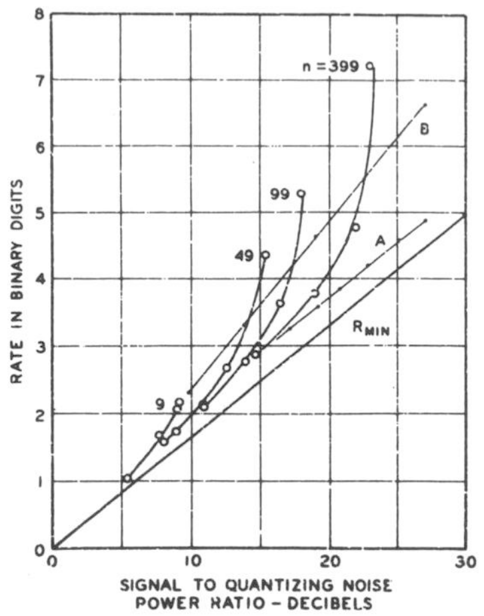


Fig. 2. Performance of n dimensional quantizers for a Gaussian source. For comparison, curve A shows the performance of Max's[8] one dimensional minimum distortion quantizers and curve B is for one dimensional quantizers with equiprobable levels.

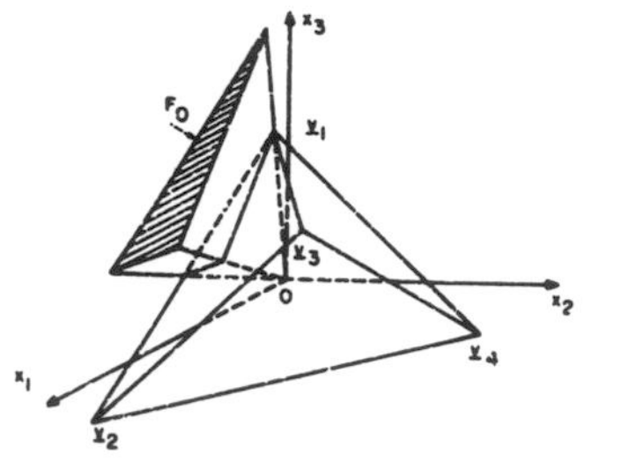

Fig. 1. Fundamental region, $\Gamma_0$, for the symmetry group $A_3$.

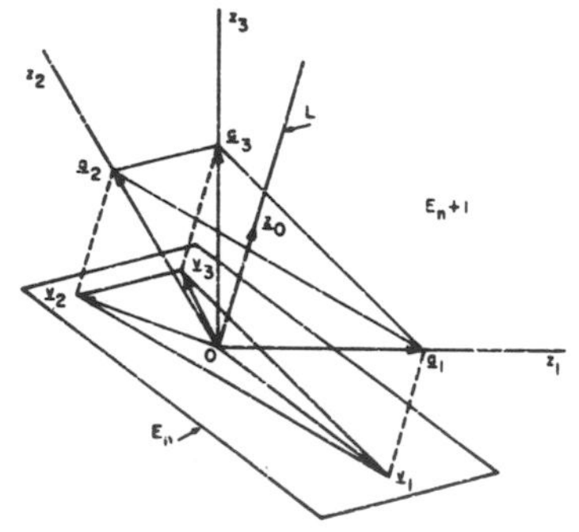


Fig. 3. Illustrating n + 1 dimensional coordinates for n = 2.

# 28



Reprinted from *IEEE Trans. Inform. Theory,* **IT-18**(6), 759–765 (1972)

# Optimum Quantizers and Permutation Codes

TOBY BERGER, MEMBER, IEEE

***Abstract*—Amplitude quantization and permutation encoding are two of the many approaches to efficient digitization of analog data. It is shown in this paper that these seemingly different approaches actually are equivalent in the sense that their optimum rate versus distortion performances are identical. Although this equivalence becomes exact only when the quantizer output is perfectly entropy coded and the permutation code block length is infinite, it nonetheless has practical consequences both for quantization and for permutation encoding. In particular, this equivalence permits us to deduce that permutation codes provide a readily implementable block-coding alternative to buffer-instrumented variable-length codes. Moreover, the abundance of methods in the literature for optimizing quantizers with respect to various criteria can be translated directly into algorithms for generating source permutation codes that are optimum for the same purposes.**

**The optimum performance attainable with quantizers (hence, permutation codes) of a fixed entropy rate is explored too. The investigation reveals that quantizers with uniformly spaced thresholds are quasi-optimum with considerable generality, and are truly optimum in the mean-squared sense for data having either an exponential or a Laplacian distribution. An attempt is made to provide some analytical insight into why simple uniform quantization is so good so generally.**

Manuscript received January 3, 1972; revised February 25, 1972.
The author is with the School of Electrical Engineering, Cornell University, Ithaca, N.Y. 14850.

## I. Introduction and Synopsis

ALTHOUGH communication and information theorists have suggested many novel digitization techniques, simple quantization continues to be used almost universally in practice. The widespread preference for quantization has a sound basis. Quantizers are relatively easy to implement and, moreover, their encoding performance usually is nearly optimum. For example, in the case of minimum-mean-square digitization of a Gaussian sequence, quantizers with uniformly spaced levels have entropies that exceed the rate-distortion function lower bound by only one fourth of a bit [1].

The main drawback to quantization is that a variable-length code must be employed if one wishes to ensure that the actual bit rate only barely exceeds the quantizer entropy. Moreover, if very accurate reproduction is required, the quantizer must have many levels, some of which are much more probable than others.[1] This means that certain words in the variable-length code have to be much longer than others, which leads to difficult buffering problems [2].

Permutation codes for sources [3], [4] provide a synchronous alternative to buffer-instrumented variable-length encoding. In this paper we show that, given any quantizer, there exists a permutation code whose entropy rate $R$ and average distortion $D$ approximate those of the quantizer as closely as desired. When $D$ is very small, the block length $n$ of the permutation code in question has to be very large. Intuition notwithstanding, however, we show that the principal task in permutation encoding, that of partially ordering the $n$ source outputs, actually becomes easier to perform as $n$ gets large. As a result, permutation codes become so easy to implement for large $n$ that they offer an attractive alternative to buffer-instrumented variable-length encoding in those applications in which the associated block-coding delay is tolerable.

The optimum $R$ versus $D$ performance attainable with quantizers (hence, permutation codes) is explored too. In the case of the squared-error distortion measure, the optimum quantizer is specified by a set of simultaneous nonlinear equations that can be solved recursively. Investigation reveals that quantizers with uniformly spaced thresholds perform effectively as well as do the optimum quantizers generated by the recursive solution procedure. This result holds not only in the limit as $D \to 0$, when the optimum quantizer itself is known to have threshold spacings that tend toward uniformity [5], but also for moderate and large values of $D$. Moreover, if the source outputs are governed by either an exponential density or a Laplacian density, then the optimum quantizer is shown to be characterized by threshold spacings that are exactly uniform. Some analytical insight into why uniform quantization is so good so generally is provided by an examination of optimum quantizers for piecewise-constant probability densities and $r$th-power distortion measures.

## II. Basic Equations of Quantization

Let $X$ denote the real random variable to be digitized and let $F(\cdot)$ denote its cumulative distribution function. A device with input $X$ and output $Y$ will be called a quantizer if $a_{i-1} < X \leq a_i$ implies $Y = y_i$. The $a_i$ are called the quantization thresholds and the $y_i$ are called the reconstruction levels. We shall assume without any loss of generality that for all $i$

$$p_i = F(a_i) - F(a_{i-1}) > 0. \tag{1}$$

Although in practice there are only finitely many levels $\{y_i\}$ and thresholds $\{a_i\}$, we shall allow for the possibility of a countable infinity of levels and thresholds.

With each quantizer we associate two quantities called the entropy rate $R$ and the average distortion $D$. These are defined by

$$R = -\sum_i p_i \log p_i \tag{2}$$

and

$$D = E|Y - X|^r = \sum_i \int_{a_{i-1}}^{a_i} |x - y_i|^r \, dF(x). \tag{3}$$

Here, and in all that follows, it is assumed that $E|X|^r < \infty$.[2] An optimum quantizer is one that minimizes $D$ for fixed $R$. Optimization of quantizers is discussed in Sections VI and VII.

## III. Basic Equations of Permutation Codes

A permutation code of block length $n$ is a collection of real $n$-vectors, called codewords, with the following structure. For some set $\{n_i\}$ of nonnegative[3] integers satisfying

$$\sum_i n_i = n \tag{4}$$

and some strictly increasing set $\{\mu_i\}$ of real numbers, the code consists of all $n$-vectors that have $n_i$ of their components equal to $\mu_i$ for each $i$. Clearly, the codewords all are permutations of one another and the number of words in the code is

$$N = \frac{n!}{\prod_i n_i!}. \tag{5}$$

Let $B = \{y_1, \cdots, y_N\}$ be a permutation code of block length $n$ with parameters $\{n_i\}$ and $\{\mu_i\}$, and define

$$S_i = \sum_{j \leq i} n_j. \tag{6}$$

*Theorem 1:* Given any real $n$-vector $\boldsymbol{x} = (x_1, \cdots, x_n)$, the codeword $\boldsymbol{y} = (y_1, \cdots, y_n) \in B$ that minimizes

$$d(\boldsymbol{x}, \boldsymbol{y}) = \sum_{k=1}^{n} |x_k - y_k|^r, \qquad r \geq 1, \tag{7}$$

is obtained by replacing the $S_{i-1} + 1$ through $S_i$ smallest components of $\boldsymbol{x}$ by $\mu_i$ for all $i$.

*Proof:* This is a special case of Theorem 1 of Berger *et al.* [4].

Now consider a random $n$-vector $\boldsymbol{X} = (X_1, \cdots, X_n)$ with

[1] For a broad and interesting class of distortion measures, the thresholds of the quantizer whose entropy is minimum for a specified average distortion $D$ become uniformly spaced as $D \to 0$ (cf. Section VII). This phenomenon accounts for the highly nonequiprobable nature of the output levels when an accurate reproduction is required.

[2] Although $E|Y - X|^r$ can be made to be finite even when $E|X|^r$ does not exist by employing an appropriate infinite-level quantizer, such cases are of limited interest.

[3] Obviously, at most $n$ of the $n_i$ are nonzero. Allowing the $n_i$ to be zero is notationally convenient in what follows because it avoids explicit reindexing of the $n_i$ as $n$ varies; in general, we have countably many $n_i$ indexed both negatively and positively even for finite $n$.

statistically independent components each of which is distributed as the random variable $X$ of Section II. It should be clear that, if the permutation code $B$ is used to encode the value $x$ assumed by $X$, then each of the codewords has probability $1/N$ of being used. The number of bits per component needed to encode $X$ with $B$ (i.e., to specify the index of the resulting codeword) therefore is

$$R = n^{-1} \log_2 N = n^{-1} \left( \log_2 n! - \sum_i \log_2 n_i! \right). \quad (8)$$

The average distortion per component that results from encoding $X$ with $B$ is

$$D = E \left[ n^{-1} \sum_i \sum_{j=S_{i-1}+1}^{S_i} |X_n{}^j - \mu_i|^r \right], \quad (9)$$

where $X_n{}^j$ is the $j$th smallest component of $X$.

## IV. EQUIVALENCE OF QUANTIZERS AND PERMUTATION CODES

Although quantization and permutation encoding are two seemingly different approaches to source digitization, the following theorem establishes that they actually are equivalent in the sense that their optimum $R$ versus $D$ performances are identical.

*Theorem 2:* Let $X$ be a random variable with cumulative distribution function $F(\cdot)$, and let $\{X_k\}$ be a sequence of independent random variables identically distributed as $X$. Given any quantizer $(\{a_i\}, \{\gamma_i\})$ that encodes $X$ with finite rate $R$ and finite distortion $D$, there exists a sequence of permutation codes $B_n$ of block length $n$, $n = 1,2,\cdots$, that encode $(X_1, \cdots, X_n)$ with respective rates $R_n$ and per-component average distortions $D_n$ that satisfy both $\lim_{n \to \infty} R_n = R$ and $\lim_{n \to \infty} D_n = D$.

*Proof:* For all $n$ let the parameter set $\{\mu_i\}$ of the code $B_n$ equal the set $\{\gamma_i\}$ of output levels of the quantizer. Let the other parameter set $\{n_i\}$ of the code $B_n$ vary with $n$ in such a way that

$$\lim_{n \to \infty} n^{-1} S_i = F(a_i) \quad (10a)$$

or equivalently in such a way that

$$\lim_{n \to \infty} n_i/n = \lim_{n \to \infty} n^{-1}(S_i - S_{i-1}) = F(a_i) - F(a_{i-1}) = p_i. \quad (10b)$$

Since $n_i$ grows linearly with $n$ because $p_i > 0$, we know that $\log_2 n_i! \sim n_i \log_2 n_i - n_i \log_2 e + o(n)$, so from (4), (8), (10b), and the fact that $R$ is finite, we have

$$R_n \sim \log_2 n - \sum_i (n_i/n) \log_2 n_i + \left( 1 - n^{-1} \sum_i n_i \right) \log_2 e$$

$$= \sum_i p_i \log_2 n - \sum_i (n_i/n) \log_2 n_i \to -\sum_i p_i \log p_i = R.$$

Upon comparing (3) and (9), we see that the proof will be complete if we can show that

$$\lim_{n \to \infty} E \left[ n^{-1} \sum_i \sum_{j=S_{i-1}+1}^{S_i} |X_n{}^j - \gamma_i|^r \right]$$

$$= \sum_i \int_{a_{i-1}}^{a_i} |x - \gamma_i|^r \, dF(x). \quad (11)$$

We do this in the Appendix by establishing both that the limit on the left side of (11) is finite and that the desired convergence in fact holds with probability one, namely

$$n^{-1} \sum_i \sum_{j=S_{i-1}+1}^{S_i} |X_n{}^j - \gamma_i|^r$$

$$\xrightarrow[\substack{\text{with} \\ \text{probability 1}}]{} \sum_i \int_{a_{i-1}}^{a_i} |x - \gamma_i|^r \, dF(x). \quad (12)$$

These two results together imply the validity of (11), thereby completing the proof.

We see from Theorem 2 that the best permutation code is at least as good as the best quantizer in the $(R,D)$ sense. Conversely, Theorems 1 and 2 together imply that the performance of the best permutation code for $r \geq 1$ is no better in the limit of infinite block length than is that of the best quantizer. Although a proof is lacking, it seems reasonable to conjecture that the performance of the optimum permutation code of block length $n$ and rate $R$ or less can only improve with increasing $n$; this indeed has been the case in all examples investigated to date. The validity of this conjecture would imply that, at least for $r \geq 1$, the best quantizer is as good as the best permutation code, too. The source coding significance of the intimate relationship between quantizers and permutation codes is explored further in the next section.

## V. PERMUTATION CODES VERSUS VARIABLE-LENGTH CODES

Since we now know that the $R$ versus $D$ performance of an optimum quantizer and variable-length code is also attainable via permutation coding, we must address the question of which of the two techniques is better suited to a given application. If a small value of $D$ is required, then $n$ must be made very large in order for the rate of the permutation code to approach that of the entropy-coded quantizer (cf. [4]). In certain applications the concomitant coding delay may become intolerable, in which case buffer-instrumented variable-length coding of the quantizer outputs is probably the more desirable alternative. We say "probably" rather than "certainly" because buffer overflows usually occur after $|X|$ has assumed large improbable values on several successive samples. The average distortion incurred per sample lost because of a buffer overflow is therefore inordinately large compared to $E|X|^r$. This means that a very long buffer must be employed in order truly to realize a small required value of $D$. This, in turn, results in a large average coding delay, especially if the probability of buffer underflow must be kept very small also in order to ensure operation at a rate that only barely exceeds the quantizer output entropy. Since detailed analytical investigation of the average distortion and average coding delay associated with buffer-instrumented variable-length encoding of quantizer outputs is lacking at present, it is not entirely clear that this technique is superior to permutation coding even from the standpoint of coding delay.

For applications in which large coding delays are tolerable, we submit that permutation codes are preferable to variable-length codes. Since permutation codes are a subclass of block codes, they operate synchronously and thereby avoid all the buffering problems discussed above. Perhaps even more important, and certainly more surprising, is the fact that permutation codes become increasingly simpler to implement as the block length $n$ increases. In this regard it has been shown [4] that the effort required for (noiseless) channel encoding and decoding of the index of the selected permutation grows only linearly with block length. The potentially troublesome operation is that of partially ordering the source outputs in the manner prescribed by Theorem 1 in order to effect optimum source encoding. A complete ordering would require a number of comparisons that grows as $n \log n$ [6], but this difficulty can be circumvented in the case of the desired partial ordering.[4] In particular, for large $n$ we can capitalize on the law of large numbers as follows. Instead of partially ordering the source outputs in the prescribed manner, we simply quantize them individually with the quantizer that corresponds in the sense of Theorem 2 to the permutation code being employed. Although the random number $N_i$ of outputs that fall in the $i$th quantization bin $[a_{i-1},a_i)$ usually will not be exactly $n_i$, $|N_i - n_i|$ will be $0(\sqrt{n})$ in the limit of large $n$ with probability 1. Hence, we can closely approximate the codeword that corresponds to the desired partial ordering simply by replacing the $S_{i-1} + 1$ through $S_i$ smallest quantized source outputs by $\mu_i$. Ties may be broken according to any scheme whatever when ordering the quantizer outputs, so no additional ordering need be done beyond the partial ordering already effected by the quantization itself. In other words, we force the desired composition $\{n_i\}$ by a procedure, which in effect removes certain of the quantized samples from their actual quantization bins and places them in neighboring bins. This results in an average distortion $D_n$ that of course exceeds the average distortion $D$ between the source outputs and the quantizer outputs. However, since the number $M$ of quantized samples that have to be moved out of their bins satisfies $n^{-1}M \to 0$ with probability 1, we have $D_n \to D$ with probability 1. Asymptotically in $n$, then, the scheme in question circumvents the partial-ordering problem entirely with no degradation in performance. For moderately large values of $n$, it may prove advisable to establish guard bands $(a_i - \delta, a_i + \delta)$ around the quantization thresholds and then to move the samples that fall in these bands first when breaking ties, thereby yielding a $D_n$ somewhat closer to $D$.

The preceding discussion strongly suggests that permutation coding is a very promising technique for source digitization when large coding delays are tolerable because the encoding effort per source output does not increase with the block length. Additional light has been shed on the intimate relationship between permutation codes and quantizers, with particular emphasis on the sense in which permutation coding provides a possible replacement not for the quantizer itself, but rather solely for the variable-length coding of the quantizer outputs.

[4] If the number of nonzero $n_i$ remains bounded as $n \to \infty$, which corresponds in the sense of Theorem 2 to a finite-level quantizer, then effecting the desired partial ordering consists of locating the positions of a fixed number of prescribed quantiles in a sample of size $n$. The number of comparisons needed to accomplish this is known to grow only linearly with $n$ [7].

## VI. Optimum Quantizers

Since optimization of a permutation code is tantamount to optimization of the quantizer that corresponds to it in the sense of Theorem 2, it is of interest to be able to determine the parameters of an optimum quantizer. In this regard the reconstruction levels $\{\gamma_i\}$ have no effect on the entropy rate $R$, so they always should be chosen to minimize $D$. A simple calculation reveals that the optimum $\gamma_i$ is specified uniquely in terms of $a_{i-1}$, $a_i$, and $r$ by the requirement

$$\int_{a_{i-1}}^{\gamma_i} (\gamma_i - x)^{r-1}\, dF(x) = \int_{\gamma_i}^{a_i} (x - \gamma_i)^{r-1}\, dF(x). \quad (13)$$

Since it usually is very difficult to solve (13) for $\gamma_i$ explicitly for general $r$, we shall specialize to the important case $r = 2$. In this case (13) reduces to the well-known result that $\gamma_i$ is the mean of $X$ conditional on the fact that $a_{i-1} < X \le a_i$, namely

$$\gamma_i = \int_{a_{i-1}}^{a_i} x\, dF(x) \Big/ \int_{a_{i-1}}^{a_i} dF(x) = (1/p_i) \int_{a_{i-1}}^{a_i} x\, dF(x). \quad (14)$$

For $r = 2$, then, the task of designing an optimum quantizer of rate $R$ reduces to that of choosing the thresholds $\{a_i\}$ so as to minimize $D$ of (3) subject to (14) and to the fact that $-\sum p_i \log p_i$ must equal the specified value of $R$. Toward this end we use (14) and (1)–(3) to express the quantity $J = D + \lambda^{-1}R$ solely in terms of the $\{a_i\}$, and then set $dJ/da_i = 0$. This yields a set of simultaneous nonlinear equations indexed by $i$ that can be put in the form

$$p_{i+1} = p_i \exp\left[\lambda(\gamma_{i+1} - \gamma_i)(\gamma_{i+1} + \gamma_i - 2a_i)\right], \quad (15)$$

where the Lagrange multiplier $\lambda$ must be selected to achieve the desired value of $R$. It is very difficult to solve (15) for the $\{a_i\}$ because $p_i$ and $\gamma_i$ are themselves rather complicated functions of $a_{i-1}$ and $a_i$ via (1) and (14), respectively. This probably explains why optimum quantizers of a fixed entropy rate were not determined long ago. It turns out, however, that (15) can be solved recursively as follows. If it is assumed that $a_{i-1}$, $a_i$, and $\lambda$ are known, then $p_i$ and $\gamma_i$ can be computed from (1) and (14). The only unknowns that then remain in (15) are $p_{i+1}$ and $\gamma_{i+1}$, both of which are increasing functions of $a_{i+1}$. It follows that, by gradually increasing our guess of the amount by which $a_{i+1}$ exceeds $a_i$, we eventually reach the value of $a_{i+1}$ for which the two sides of (15) are equal. With $a_{i+1}$ now known, the same procedure can be used to determine $a_{i+2}$, and so forth.

The recursive procedure previously described yields a three-parameter family of quantizers that satisfy (15), the parameters being $a_0$, $a_1$, and $\lambda$. (It should be clear how $a_{-1}, a_{-2}, \cdots$ can be determined recursively in a manner similar to that just described for determining $a_2, a_3, \cdots$.)

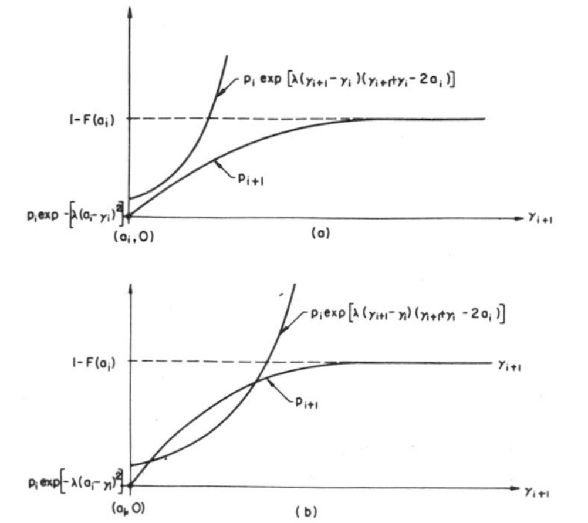


Fig. 1. Graphical solution of (15). (a) No solution. (b) Two solutions.

However, since (15) is only a necessary condition for optimality, not all the quantizers in this three-parameter family are optimum. Thus, it is necessary to determine which of the many quantizers in this family that have the desired rate $R$ has the least average distortion. Fortunately, in many cases of interest the situation is not quite this desperate. If, for example, $F(\cdot)$ possesses a density $f = F'$ that is symmetric about its mean, then it is clear that either the interval $(a_0,a_1)$ should be centered about the mean or $a_0$ should equal the mean. This reduces the problem to investigation of a pair of two-parameter families of quantizers. If there is a finite number $c$ such that $F(x) = 0$ for $x < c$ and $F(x) > 0$ for $x > c$, then it is clear that we may take $a_0 = c$ and need determine the $a_i$ only for $i$ positive; again, we obtain a two-parameter family of quantizers indexed by $a_1$ and $\lambda$. Similarly, if there exists $d$ such that $F(x) = 1$ for $x \geq d$ and $F(x) < 1$ for $x < d$, then we may set $a_0 = d$ without loss of generality, thereby obtaining a two-parameter family of quantizers $\{a_i, i \leq 0\}$ indexed by $a_{-1}$ and $\lambda$. Finally, if both $c$ and $d$ exist with the above properties, then all quantizers of interest have only finitely many thresholds of the form $c = a_0 < a_1 < a_2 < \cdots < a_K = d$ for some $K$. It follows that only certain choices of the pair $(a_1,\lambda)$ will yield a recursively determined set of $\{a_i\}$, one of which equals $d$ exactly. Hence, in such an instance there are only a finite number of quantizers that satisfy (15) for each value of $\lambda$, but we have to solve a two-point boundary value problem in order to determine them.

To make matters worse, the solution of (15) for $a_{i+1}$ in terms of $a_{i-1}$, $a_i$, and $\lambda$ is unique only if $F(\cdot)$ is continuous and $\lambda$ is negative, whereas the best quantizers we have been able to find in the examples we have studied to date all correspond to positive values of $\lambda$. For $\lambda > 0$, (15) can have several solutions $a_{i+1}(a_{i-1},a_i,\lambda)$. Usually, however, one of the two situations sketched in Fig. 1 prevails. In Fig. 1(a) there are no solutions, which means that $a_{i+1} = \infty$, i.e., $a_i$ is the last finite threshold. In Fig. 1(b) there are two solutions, the smaller of which seems to have yielded somewhat better quantizers in the examples that we have studied. Moreover, it even is not entirely clear at present whether the same solution should be used for all $i$ or the smaller solution should be used for some values of $i$ and the larger one for others.

## VII. Uniform Quantizers

Study of (15), despite the myriad difficulties chronicled above, has proved to be rewarding. Perhaps the most surprising discovery was that, although (15) produced quantizers with rather nonuniform threshold separations $a_i - a_{i-1}$, in none of the cases we explored were their rates ever found to be more than 0.005 bits lower than those of uniform quantizers that achieved the same $D$. We knew that the optimum quantizers would tend toward uniformity in the limit of small $D$ (large $R$), since Gish and Pierce [5] already had established that uniform quantizers are asymptotically optimum in this limit for all $r > 0$.[5] The unexpected phenomenon was that, even at moderate and large values of $D$, uniform quantizers had rates that for all intents and purposes were as low as those of the nonuniform quantizers that actually satisfied (15).[6] Moreover, in the special case of the exponential probability density $f(x) = \alpha \exp(-\alpha|x|)$, $x > 0$, and the Laplacian probability density $f(x) = (\alpha/2)\exp(-\alpha|x|)$, the computer solution indicated that quantizers with uniformly spaced thresholds $a_i = i\Delta$ satisfied (15) exactly. An analytical check immediately verified this fact. Further analysis then yielded the following parametric expression for the $R$ versus $D$ performance curve of the optimized quantizers in the exponential case:

$$R = (1-\theta)^{-1}[-\theta \log \theta - (1-\theta)\log(1-\theta)] \quad (16a)$$

$$D = \alpha^{-2}[1 - \theta(1-\theta)^{-2}\log^2 \theta]. \quad (16b)$$

As the parameter $\theta = e^{-\alpha\Delta}$ runs from 0 to 1, $D$ runs from $\alpha^{-2}$ to 0 and $R$ runs from 0 to $\infty$. In the Laplacian case, $R$ is greater than in the exponential case by log 2, while $D$ remains unchanged. It is of interest to note that in the limit of small $D$ (i.e., $\theta \to 1$), the asymptotic behavior of (16) is $R \sim \log(e/\sqrt{12\alpha^2 D})$, whereas the absolute lower limit on all source-encoding systems set by the asymptotic behavior of the rate-distortion function $R(D) \sim \log\sqrt{e/2\pi\alpha^2 D}$ is only $\log\sqrt{\pi e/6} \approx 0.51$ bits lower [9, sect. 4.3.4].

Some appreciation for why uniform quantization is so good so generally can be gleaned from considering the following problem. Suppose that $F$ possesses a density $f = F'$ that is piecewise constant, say $f(x) = c_k$ for all $x$ in the interval $I_k$, $k = 1,2,\cdots$. Further suppose that our

[5] The Gish–Pierce result implies that uniform quantizers should satisfy (15) in the limit as the interthreshold width $\delta \to 0$. In this regard asymptotic analysis reveals that for $\lambda = 6/\delta^2$ the difference between the two sides of (15) for a uniform quantizer with threshold spacing $\delta$ vanishes like $\delta^5$ at all points at which $F(\cdot)$ is twice differentiable.

[6] The near optimality of uniform quantization for all $D$ had been observed previously by Wood [8] in the case of Gaussian signals, but the phenomenon apparently prevails quite generally.

task is to choose the number $N_k$ of quantization bins to be assigned to $I_k$ in such a way as to minimize $D = E|Y - X|^r$ subject to the requirement that the quantizer entropy may not exceed $R$. Although intuition may suggest that the density with which we should pack quantization levels into $I_k$ should be an increasing function of $c_k$, the following analysis reveals that the same density of levels should be used everywhere. Since (15) is satisfied by uniformly spaced levels when $X$ is uniformly distributed, the reconstruction levels of the bins assigned to $I_k$ should be equally spaced within $I_k$. Hence, if we let $L_k$ denote the length of $I_k$,

$$J \triangleq D + \mu R = \sum_k c_k L_k \left[ \frac{L_k^{r+1}}{(r+1)2^r N_k^{r+1}} - \mu \log \frac{c_k L_k}{N_k} \right].$$

Setting $dJ/dN_k = 0$ yields $(L_k/N_k)^{r+1} = 2^r \mu$, so the width $L_k/N_k$ of the quantization bins in $I_k$ is independent of $k$. That is, the optimum quantizer has uniformly spaced thresholds. Of course, a truly uniform quantizer cannot be constructed if the $L_k$ are incommensurate and can be constructed only for certain values of $R$ and $D$ if the $L_k$ are commensurate. In the limit as $D \to 0$, however, the thresholds have to crowd together, so the uniform solution can be approximated as closely as desired even if the $L_k$ are incommensurate. Since any $f(\cdot)$ can be expressed as the limit of a sequence of piecewise-constant density functions, the present analysis can be extended to provide an alternative derivation of the result of Gish and Pierce [5] that uniform quantization is asymptotically optimum as $D \to 0$ for arbitrary $f(\cdot)$ and arbitrary $r > 0$.

## APPENDIX

### PROOF OF (11)

We follow the approach outlined in the discussion embodying (12). Since the left side of (11) clearly is nonnegative, we can establish its finiteness by bounding it from above. For this purpose we employ the inequality [10]

$$|a + b|^r \le c_r |a|^r + c_r |b|^r, \qquad r > 0,$$

where $c_r = 1$ if $r \le 1$ and $c_r = 2^{r-1}$ if $r \ge 1$. It follows that

$$E\left[ n^{-1} \sum_i \sum_{j=S_{i-1}+1}^{S_i} |X_n^j - \gamma_i|^r \right]$$

$$\le c_r E\left[ n^{-1} \sum_i \sum_{j=S_{i-1}+1}^{S_i} |X_n^j|^r + |\gamma_i|^r \right]$$

$$= c_r E\left[ n^{-1} \sum_{j=1}^n |X_n^j|^r \right] + c_r n^{-1} \sum_i (S_i - S_{i-1})|\gamma_i|^r$$

$$= c_r E\left[ n^{-1} \sum_{j=1}^n |X_j|^r \right] + c_r n^{-1} \sum_i n_i |\gamma_i|^r$$

$$= c_r E|X|^r + c_r \sum_i (n_i/n)|\gamma_i|^r.$$

Now $E|X|^r < \infty$ by assumption, while (10b) implies that

$$\sum_i (n_i/n)|\gamma_i|^r \to \sum_i p_i |\gamma_i|^r = E|Y|^r,$$

where $Y$ is the quantized version of $X$. Since

$$E|Y|^r \le c_r E|X|^r + c_r E|Y - X|^r = c_r E|X|^r + c_r D < \infty$$

the desired finiteness has been established.

It remains only to establish (12), which is of the form

$$n^{-1} \sum_i \sum_{j=S_{i-1}+1}^{S_i} |X_n^j - \gamma_i|^r \xrightarrow[\text{with probability 1}]{} E[|X - g(X)|^r], \quad \text{(A-1)}$$

where $g$ is the quantizer function $g(x) = \gamma_i$, $a_{i-1} < x \le a_i$. Toward this end, introduce the empirical cumulative distribution functions $F_n$, $n = 1, 2, \cdots$, according to the usual definition

$$F_n(x) = N(x)/n, \qquad \text{(A-2)}$$

where $N(x)$ is the number of values of $j$ between 1 and $n$ inclusive for which $X_j \le x$. Let $F_i$ and $F_{n,i}$ denote $F(a_i)$ and $F_n(a_i)$, respectively. Also, select the parameters $\{n_i\}$ (equivalently $\{S_i\}$) of the permutation code $B_n$ according to the prescription $S_i = [nF_i]$, where $[y]$ denotes the integral part of $y$. Note that this choice of the $\{S_i\}$ is consistent with (10a). Next write

$$n^{-1} \sum_{j=S_{i-1}+1}^{S_i} |X_n^j - \gamma_i|^r$$

$$= n^{-1} \sum_{j=[nF_i]+1}^{nF_{n,i}-1} |X_n^j - \gamma_i|^r + n^{-1} \sum_{j=nF_{n,i-1}+1}^{nF_{n,i}} |X_n^j - \gamma_i|^r$$

$$+ n^{-1} \sum_{j=nF_{n,i}+1}^{[nF_i]} |X_n^j - \gamma_i|^r. \quad \text{(A-3)}$$

Since $F_{n,i} \to F_i$ with probability 1 by the Borel strong law, the number of terms in the first and third sums on the right side of (A-3) is $o(n)$ with probability 1 for each $i$. Were the terms bounded, it would follow that both of these terms approach 0 with probability 1. The potential difficulty stemming from the unboundedness of $|X_n^j - \gamma_i|^r$ is circumvented easily, however. The third sum, for example, is devoid of terms with probability 1 if $F_i = 0$ or 1. If $0 < F_i < 1$, then we can find a finite $\delta > 0$ such that $F(a_i - \delta) < F_i < F(a_i + \delta)$. The Borel strong law then implies that $X_n^{[nF_i]} \in (a_i - \delta, a_i + \delta)$ for $n$ sufficiently large with probability 1. It follows therefrom that $X_n^j \in (a_i - \delta, a_i + \delta)$ for all $j$ between $nF_{n,i} + 1$ and $[nF_i]$ for all but finitely many $n$ with probability 1. Since the number of such $j$ is $o(n)$ with probability 1 and $|X_n^j - \gamma_i|^r \le |a_i + \delta - \gamma_i|^r < \infty$ for each of them, the third term approaches 0 with probability 1. Similar arguments imply that the first term approaches 0 with probability 1. The task of establishing (A-1) therefore has been reduced to showing that

$$n^{-1} \sum_i \sum_{j=nF_{n,i-1}+1}^{nF_{n,i}} |X_n^j - \gamma_i|^r \xrightarrow[\text{with probability 1}]{} E[|X - g(X)|^r]. \quad \text{(A-4)}$$

From the definition of $F_{n,i}$, we know that $X_n^j \in (a_{i-1}, a_i]$ for $nF_{n,i-1} + 1 \le j \le nF_{n,i}$, so an alternative way of expressing (A-4) is

$$n^{-1} \sum_i \sum_{j=nF_{n,i-1}+1}^{nF_{n,i}} |X_n^j - g(X_n^j)|^r \xrightarrow[\text{with probability 1}]{} E[|X - g(X)|^r]. \quad \text{(A-5)}$$

Since each value of $j = 1, \cdots, n$ appears in one and only one of the ranges $nF_{n,i-1} + 1 \le j \le nF_{n,i}$, (A-5) reduces to

$$n^{-1} \sum_{j=1}^{n} |X_j - g(X_j)|^r \xrightarrow[\text{probability 1}]{\text{with}} E[|X - g(X)|^r]$$

the validity of which is a direct consequence of the pointwise ergodic theorem.

## References

[1] T. J. Goblick, Jr., and J. L. Holsinger, "Analog source digitization: A comparison of theory and practice," *IEEE Trans. Inform. Theory*, vol. IT-13, pp. 323–326, Apr. 1967.
[2] F. Jelinek, "Buffer overflow in variable length coding of fixed rate sources," *IEEE Trans. Inform. Theory*, vol. IT-14, pp. 490–501, May 1968.
[3] J. G. Dunn, "The performance of a class of $n$-dimensional quantizers for a Gaussian source," in *Proc. Columbia Symp. Signal Transmission and Processing*, Columbia Univ., New York, N.Y., pp. 76–81, May 1965.
[4] T. Berger, F. Jelinek, and J. K. Wolf, "Permutation codes for sources," *IEEE Trans. Inform. Theory*, vol. IT-18, pp. 160–169, Jan. 1972.
[5] H. Gish and J. N. Pierce, "Asymptotically efficient quantizing," *IEEE Trans. Inform. Theory*, vol. IT-14, pp. 676–683, Sept. 1968.
[6] C. A. R. Hoare, "Quicksort," *Comput. J.*, vol. 5, pp. 10–15, 1962.
[7] M. Blum, "Computational complexity," presented at the 1972 IEEE Int. Symp. Information Theory, Asilomar, Calif., Jan. 31–Feb. 3, 1972.
[8] R. C. Wood, "On optimum quantization," *IEEE Trans. Inform. Theory*, vol. IT-15, pp. 248–252, Mar. 1969.
[9] T. Berger, *Rate Distortion Theory: A Mathematical Basis for Data Compression*. Englewood Cliffs, N.J.: Prentice-Hall, 1971.
[10] M. Loève, *Probability Theory*, 3rd ed. Princeton, N.J.: Van Nostrand, 1963, p. 155.

# 29



Reprinted from *Proc. Mervin J. Kelly Commun. Conf.*, 1970, pp. 17-4-1–17-4-5

# A COMPARISON OF DIGITAL IMAGE TRANSFORMS

William K. Pratt
University of Southern California
Los Angeles, California 90007

## I. INTRODUCTION

Digital image transforms, as a means of achieving a bandwidth reduction and a tolerance for channel errors, have received widespread interest in the past few years [1,2]. This paper provides a comparison of the bandwidth reduction capabilities of the three image transforms - Fourier, Hadamard, and Karhunen-Loeve - that have shown the most promise for this application.

## II. IMAGE TRANSFORMS

### Formulation

An image may be represented by an array of intensity components or samples over the image surface by two dimensional sampling. For the present discussion an image array will be considered to be a square array of $N^2$ intensity samples described by the function $f(x,y)$ over the image coordinates $(x,y)$. An image transform maps the image array into a two dimensional array of the same dimension defined by

$$F(u,v) = \sum_{x=0}^{N-1} \sum_{y=0}^{N-1} f(x,y)\, a(x,y,u,v) \tag{1}$$

for $u,v = 0,1,2,\ldots, N-1$, where $a(x,y,u,v)$ is the forward transform kernel. The corresponding reverse transformation is given by

$$\hat{f}(x,y) = \sum_{u=0}^{N-1} \sum_{v=0}^{N-1} F(u,v)\, b(x,y,u,v) \tag{2}$$

for $x,y = 0,1,2,\ldots, N-1$, where $b(x,y,u,v)$ is the reverse transform kernel. When the function $\hat{f}(x,y)$ resulting from the reverse transform operation is equivalent to the original image, $f(x,y)$, the reverse transform is called an inverse transform.

### Fourier Transform [3]

The two dimensional Fourier transform of an image field, $f(x,y)$, may be expressed as

$$F(u,v) = \frac{1}{N} \sum_{x=0}^{N-1} \sum_{y=0}^{N-1} f(x,y) \exp\left\{-\frac{2\pi i}{N}(ux + vy)\right\} \tag{3}$$

---

This project was supported in part by NASA under Grant NGR-05-018-044 and Contract NAS 12-2240.

The inverse Fourier transform which reconstructs the original image is given by

$$f(x,y) = \frac{1}{N} \sum_{u=0}^{N-1} \sum_{y=0}^{N-1} F(u,v) \exp\left\{\frac{2\pi i}{N}(ux + vy)\right\} \qquad (4)$$

Since the transform kernels are separable and symmetric the two dimensional transform can be computed as two sequential one dimensional transforms. The terms u and v are called the spatial frequencies of the image in analogy with time series analysis.

Even though F(x,y) is a real positive function, its transform, F(u,v), is in general complex. Thus, while the image contains $N^2$ components, the transform contains $2N^2$ components, the real and imaginary, or magnitude and phase components of each spatial frequency. However, since f(x,y) is a real positive function, F(u,v) exhibits a property of conjugate symmetry. As a result, it is only necessary to transmit the samples of one half of the transform plane; the other half can be reconstructed from the half plane samples transmitted. Hence the Fourier transform of an image can be described by $N^2$ data components.

<u>Hadamard Transform</u> [4]

The Hadamard transform, also known as the Walsh transform, is based upon the Hadamard matrix which is a square array of plus and minus ones whose rows and columns are orthogonal to one another. Consideration will be given here only to Hadamard transforms of order $N=2^n$ where n is an integer. Transforms of this type can be expressed as

$$F(u,v) = \frac{1}{N} \sum_{x=0}^{N-1} \sum_{y=0}^{N-1} f(x,y)\,(-1)^{q(x,y,u,v)} \qquad (5)$$

where the function q(x,y,u,v) [4] defines an "ordered" Hadamard transform in which the number of zero crossings, called the sequency, of the orthogonal rectangular waveforms of the expansion is increasing sequentially with u and v. The Hadamard transform is separable symmetric.

<u>Karhunen-Loeve Transform</u> [2,5]

The two dimensional Karhunen-Loeve transform of an image as expressed in Eq.1 utilizes a transform kernel that satisfies the equation

$$\lambda(u,v)a(x,y,u,v) = \sum_{x'=0}^{N-1} \sum_{y'=0}^{N-1} C\{x,x',y,y'\}\, a(x',y',u,v) \qquad (6)$$

The $\lambda(u,v)$ are the eigenvalues of the covariance function $C\{x,x',y,y'\}$ of the class of images to be coded. The kernel a(x,y,u,v) therefore represents the matrix of the eigenvectors of the covariance function. If the covariance function can be expressed as

$$C\{x,x',y,y'\} = C_1\{x,x'\}\, C_2\{y,y'\} \qquad (7)$$

then the transform kernel $a(x,y,u,v)$ can be separated and the resulting two dimensional transform can then be computed sequentially along each row and column of the image array. The inverse Karhunen-Loeve transform is given by Eq. 2, where the kernel $b(x,y,u,v)$ represents the transpose of the eigenvector matrix of the covariance function.

## III. STATISTICAL ANALYSIS OF IMAGE TRANSFORMS

The statistical analysis of image transforms is predicated on the representation of an original image as a two dimensional stochastic process, $f(x,y)$, with a spatial mean $\overline{f(x,y)}$ and covariance function $C\{x_1,x_2,y_1,y_2\}$. From Eq. 1 and the linearity of the expectation operator

$$\overline{F(u,v)} = \sum_{x=0}^{N-1} \sum_{y=0}^{N-1} \overline{f(x,y)}\, a(x,y,u,v) = N\, \overline{f(x,y)}\, \delta(u,v) \qquad (8)$$

The general expression for the variance of transform domain samples can be shown to be

$$\sigma^2(u,v) = \sum_{x_1=0}^{N-1} \sum_{x_2=0}^{N-1} \sum_{y_1=0}^{N-1} \sum_{y_2=0}^{N-1} C\{x_1,x_2,y_1,y_2\}\, a(x_1,y_1,u,v)\, a^*(x_2,y_2,u,v) \qquad (9)$$

## IV. GENERALIZED TRANSFORM CODING

The basic premise of image transform coding is that the two dimensional transform of an image has an energy distribution more amenable to coding than the spatial domain representation. As a result of the inherent element-to-element correlation of natural images, for many image transforms, the energy in the transform domain tends to be clustered in a relatively few number of transform samples. This property can be exploited to achieve a sample reduction compared to conventional spatial domain coding.

There are two methods of obtaining a sample reduction by transform coding -- zonal sampling and threshold sampling. In zonal sampling the image reconstruction is made with a subset, usually the lowest spatial coefficients, of the transform domain samples. Those samples which are employed in the reconstruction are chosen before the transformation on the basis of expected energy. With threshold sampling the reconstruction is made with a subset of the largest magnitude transform domain samples.

### Zonal Sampling

With zonal sampling the image is reconstructed with M of the $N^2$ transform samples determined by a mask function $M(u,v)$. The reconstructed image is

$$\hat{f}(x,y) = \sum_{u=0}^{N-1} \sum_{v=0}^{N-1} F(u,v)\, b(x,y,u,v) \qquad u,v \in M(u,v) \qquad (10)$$

As a fidelity criterion consider the mean square error defined as

$$\mathcal{E}_s \equiv \frac{1}{N^2} E\left\{ \sum_{x=0}^{N-1} \sum_{y=0}^{N-1} \left[ f(x,y) - \hat{f}(x,y) \right] \right\} \tag{11}$$

It can be shown that

$$\mathcal{E}_s = C(0,0,0,0) - \frac{1}{N^2} \sum_{u=0}^{N-1} \sum_{v=0}^{N-1} \sigma^2(u,v) \qquad u,v \in M(u,v) \tag{12}$$

The transform which minimizes the mean square error therefore is the transform which accumulates the maximum amount of variance (image energy) in the M transform samples determined by the mask function M(u,v). If the mask function is chosen by ordering the eigenvalues of the image covariance function it can be shown that the Karhunen-Loeve is the optimum of all linear transformations.

Threshold Sampling

Zonal sampling in the transform domain will provide small mean square error reconstructions of good subjective quality if the actual magnitude of a transform domain sample does not differ greatly from the standard deviation $\sigma(u,v)$. The difficulty with zonal sampling is that in most natural images there are many high spatial frequency samples lying outside the sampling zone that are of significatn magnitude. In threshold sampling rather than determining a priori which transform domain samples are to be coded, the selection is made after the transform has been taken on a particular image. A threshold level is established either a priori, or perhaps adaptively, and only those samples whose magnitudes are greater than the threshold are coded.

## V. EXPERIMENTAL COMPARISON OF IMAGE TRANSFORMS

A series of experiments has been conducted to determine the image coding performance of the Fourier, Hadamard, and Karhunen-Loeve transforms for natural images. As a result of the computational requirements of the Karhunen-Loeve transform, the image block size was limited to 16 by 16 elements. Larger block sizes provide only marginly greater bandwidth reduction factors for the same mean square error, but the subjectively objectionable "grid" effect noticeable at high bandwidth reduction factors is not present if the transform is taken over the full image.

Figure 1 illustrates the forward transforms of a 256 by 256 element image containing 64 grey levels. The Karhunen-Loeve transform was based upon a covariance function modeled by a Gauss-Markov process with an adjacent element correlation of 0.9. Reconstructions of the image for zonal and threshold sampling are also shown in figure 1. For the Karhunen-Loeve transform the zonal sampling mask was determined by the eigenvalues of the image covariance function. A hyperbolic shaped zonal sampling mask was employed for the Fourier and Hadamard transforms. The sample reduction factors for zonal sampling are 4:1 and for threshold sampling 7:1. If the position code bits required for threshold sampling are included, the bandwidth reduction factors for both types of transform domain sampling are nearly equivalent.

## VI. SUMMARY

On the basis of the predicted mean square error the best transform for bandwidth reduction is the Karhunen-Loeve followed by the Fourier followed by the Hadamard. In terms of ease of implementation the ordering is reversed.

Experimentally it has been found that the measured mean square error orders the transforms as does the predicted error. Subjectively, the Fourier and Hadamard transforms provide about equal quality reconstructions, while the Karhunen-Loeve is somewhat better. Threshold sampling provides better results than zonal sampling for an equivalent bandwidth reduction factor.

## REFERENCES

1. W.K. Pratt and H.C. Andrews, "Application of Fourier-Hadamard Transformation to Bandwidth Compression," MIT Symposium on Picture Bandwidth Compression, April 1969.

2. A. Habibi and P. Wintz, "Optimum Linear Transformations for Encoding 2-Dimensional Data," MIT Symposium on Picture Bandwidth Compression, April 1969.

3. H.C. Andrews and W.K. Pratt, "Television Bandwidth Reduction by Encoding Spatial Frequencies," Journal Society of Motion Picture and Television Engineers, Vol.77 (December 1968), pp. 1270-1281.

4. W.K. Pratt, J. Kane, and H.C. Andrews, "Hadamard Transform Image Coding," Proceedings IEEE, Vol. 57, No.1 (January 1969).

5. W.K. Pratt, "Karhunen-Loeve Transform Coding of Images," 1970 IEEE International Symposium on Information Theory, June 1970.

# 30



Reprinted from *IEEE Trans. Commun. Tech.*, **Com-19**(1), 50–62 (1971)

# Image Coding by Linear Transformation and Block Quantization

ALI HABIBI, MEMBER, IEEE, AND PAUL A. WINTZ, MEMBER, IEEE

***Abstract*—The feasibility of coding two-dimensional data arrays by first performing a two-dimensional linear transformation on the data and then block quantizing the transformed data is investigated. The Fourier, Hadamard, and Karhunen–Loève transformations are considered. Theoretical results for Markov data and experimental results for four pictures comparing these transform methods to the standard method of raster scanning, sampling, and pulse-count modulation code are presented.**

## I. Introduction

THE PROBLEM of transforming an image into binary digits and the problem of transforming the binary digits back into a replica of the original image are considered. Both continuous and discrete monochromatic two-dimensional data sources are considered. We refer to a particular digitizing and reconstruction strategy as a code. Different codes are compared on the basis of their rate versus distortion functions, i.e., the total number of bits required to achieve a particular fidelity criterion. Fidelity criteria considered are the mean square error between the original and reconstructed images, and the subjective quality of the reconstructed images relative to the original.

One method for digitizing an image is to perform a sequence of two transformations on the image. The first transforms the image into a finite number of samples and is called sampling; the second rounds off each sample to one of a finite number of preset values and is called quantization.

Four sampling transformations are considered. These are the zero-order hold (ZOH), Fourier (F), Hadamard (H), and Karhunen–Loève (KL) transformations.

The quantization strategy takes into account possible unequal average energies in the samples. Since the amount of information contained in each sample is proportional to its energy, more quantization levels are allotted to the high-energy samples.

Finally, each code requires a reconstruction transformation for transforming the digitized samples into a replica of the original image. The reconstruction transformations are the inverses of the sampling transformations. In addition, we include first-order hold (FOH) reconstruction, used with ZOH sampling.

The idea of applying optimum and suboptimum linear transformations and block quantization to picture bandwidth reduction was proposed by Huang and Woods [1], [2]. Fourier and Hadamard transform image coding has been reported by Andrews, Kane, and Pratt [3]–[5]. Anderson and Huang [6] used the Fourier transform in an adaptive image coding system.

In this paper we present a method for optimizing the Fourier and Hadamard techniques with respect to their bandwidth reduction capabilities. We also present a direct comparison of their performances to the performance of the standard technique of raster scanning an image and time sampling the resulting waveform. We also derive the optimum linear sampling transformation (KL) in order to make a direct performance comparison of ZOH (standard raster scanning), F, H, and KL (the optimum system).

In Section II we present a mathematical framework for modeling images and the image coding technique consisting of sampling, quantization, and reconstruction. These theoretical results are then used to optimize the design of the codes incorporating ZOH, F, H, and KL samples and to compare their performances (mean-square error) for the Markov random field data model to Shannon's rate distortion function for this data source.

In Section III we describe the results of an experimental program in which these codes were used to code four photographs. Since the theoretically designed codes are based on the mean-square error criterion and the assumptions of Markov data and Gaussian samples, a second optimization procedure was used to adjust the system parameters to achieve the best subjective effect. The resulting codes are compared on the basis of their mean-square error and reconstructed picture quality.

## II. Theoretical Results

### *A. Image Model*

Any particular monochromatic image can be modeled by specifying its value (gray level) $u(x,y)$ at each spatial coordinate $(x,y)$. Continuous, discrete, and digitized images can be modeled by allowing $u$, $x$, and $y$ to be continuous and/or discrete parameters. An ensemble of such images can be modeled by interpreting $u(x,y)$ as a random field. For convenience we assume that the random field

Paper approved for publication by the Communication Theory Committee of the IEEE Communication Technology Group for publication without oral presentation. This research was supported by NASA under Research Grant NGR 15-005-106. Manuscript received August 10, 1970; revised October 5, 1970.

A. Habibi was with the School of Electrical Engineering, Purdue University, Lafayette, Ind. He is now with the Bell Telephone Laboratories, Inc., Holmdel, N. J.

P. A. Wintz is with the School of Electrical Engineering, Purdue University, Lafayette, Ind.

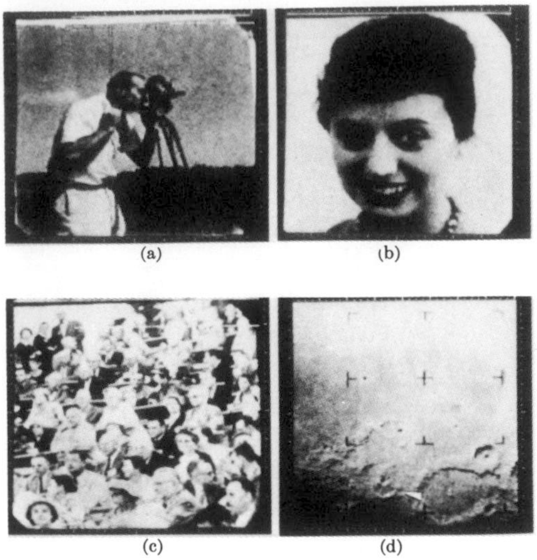

Fig. 1. Original copies of digital pictures. Each picture is an array of 256 × 256 picture elements quantized to $2^8$ levels except the moon shot which is quantized to $2^6$ levels.

$u(x,y)$ has zero mean, i.e.,

$$E\{u(x,y)\} = 0. \qquad (1)$$

This is equivalent to assuming knowledge of the mean intensity and setting the scale on $u$ accordingly. To keep the notation as simple as possible we consider only square images, i.e., $0 \leq x,\ y \leq A$. The generalization to other shapes is straightforward.

Experimental evidence [7]–[9] indicates that a reasonable autocorrelation function for a large variety of pictorial data is given by

$$R(x,x',y,y') = \exp\left[-\alpha \mid x - x' \mid - \beta \mid y - y' \mid\right]. \qquad (2)$$

Random fields having autocorrelation functions invariant to all translations are said to be homogeneous (wide sense stationary). Since (2) depends only on $\Delta x = x - x'$ and $\Delta y = y - y'$ it has this property and can be written in the form

$$R(\Delta x,\Delta y) = \exp\left[-\alpha \mid \Delta x \mid - \beta \mid \Delta y \mid\right]. \qquad (3)$$

This autocorrelation function can be used to model images with different amounts of correlation in the horizontal and vertical directions by choosing different values for $\alpha$ and $\beta$. Contours of equal correlation are obviously parallelograms.

Four images are presented in Fig. 1. Each was reconstructed (photographed from a cathode-ray tube) from a digital array of 256 × 256 picture elements. Each picture element for the cameraman, face, and crowd was quantized to 256 gray levels; the moon was quantized to 64 gray levels. We refer to these pictures as originals. The cameraman, face, and crowd were chosen because

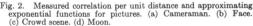

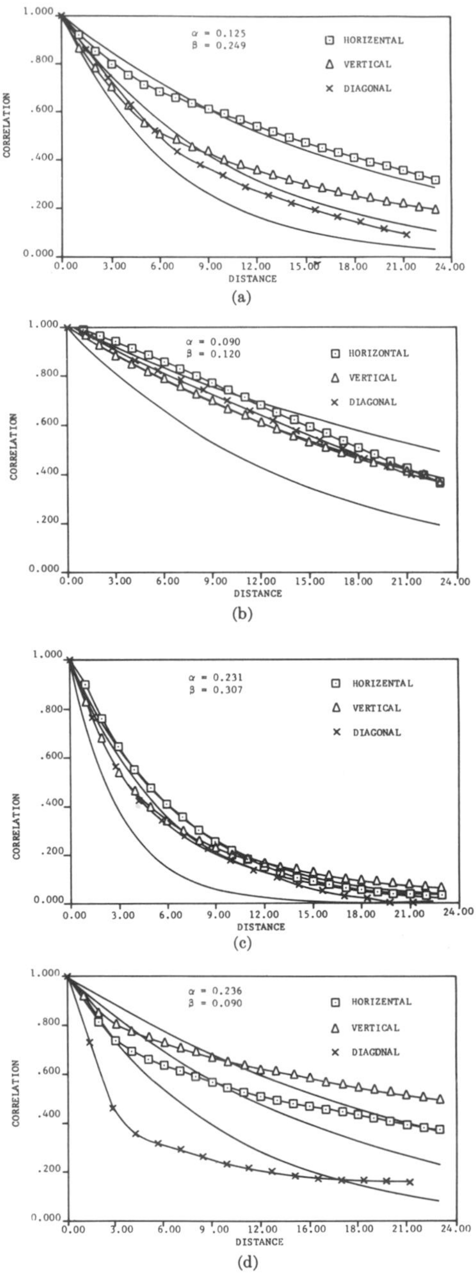


Fig. 2. Measured correlation per unit distance and approximating exponential functions for pictures. (a) Cameraman. (b) Face. (c) Crowd scene. (d) Moon.

they contain moderate, small, and large amounts of detail, respectively. The measured autocorrelation functions for these images are presented in Fig. 2. Curves resulting from the model (2) are also presented in Fig. 2 along with their $\alpha$ and $\beta$. Note the relationship between $\alpha$ and $\beta$ and the amount of detail in the image. Although the match between these data and the Markov assumption is not perfect, the model is reasonable for our purposes.

*B. Image Sampling and Reconstruction*

Any linear transformation that maps a continuous image into an $n \times n$ array of samples can be modeled by writing the image $u(x,y)$ as a linear combination of continuous orthonormal basis images $\varphi_{ij}(x,y)$ (two-dimensional basis functions)

$$u(x,y) = \sum_{i=1}^{\infty} \sum_{j=1}^{\infty} u_{ij}\varphi_{ij}(x,y) \approx \sum_{i=1}^{n} \sum_{j=1}^{n} u_{ij}\varphi_{ij}(x,y) = u^*(x,y), \qquad 0 \leq x, y \leq A \tag{4}$$

where the $u_{ij}$ are given by

$$u_{ij} = \int_0^A \int_0^A u(x,y)\varphi_{ij}(x,y)\, dx\, dy, \qquad i,j = 1,2,\cdots,n. \tag{5}$$

Here, (5) defines the transformation that transforms the image $u(x,y)$ into the $n^2$ samples $u_{ij}$, $i,j = 1,2,\cdots,n$. The right-hand side of (4) defines the transformation for forming the reconstructed image $u^*(x,y)$ from the $n^2$ samples.

We define the normalized mean-integral-square sampling error between the original image $u(x,y)$ and the reconstructed image $u^*(x,y)$ by

$$\epsilon_s^2 = E\left\{\frac{1}{A^2}\int_0^A \int_0^A [u(x,y) - u^*(x,y)]^2\, dx\, dy\right\} = R(0,0) - \frac{1}{A^2}\sum_{i=1}^{n}\sum_{j=1}^{n} \sigma_{ij}^2. \tag{6}$$

When considering a particular image, we omit the expectation operator and interpret $R(0,0)$ as the image energy per unit area, the $\sigma_{ij}^2$ as the energies in the samples $u_{ij}$, and $\epsilon_s^2$ as the error between the images $u(x,y)$ and $u^*(x,y)$. When considering an ensemble of images, we interpret $u(x,y)$ and $u^*(x,y)$ as random processes, $R(0,0)$ as the average energy per unit area, the $u_{ij}$ as random variables, and the $\sigma_{ij}^2$ as the variances of the samples, i.e.,

$$\sigma_{ij}^2 = E\{u_{ij}^2\} = \int_0^A \int_0^A \int_0^A \int_0^A R(x,x',y,y')\varphi_{ij}(x,y) \cdot \varphi_{ij}(x',y')\, dx\, dy\, dx'\, dy', \qquad i,j = 1,2,\cdots,n. \tag{7}$$

For discrete data, say an $N \times N$ array $u(x,y)$, $x,y = 1,2,\cdots,N$, we write the image as a linear combination of orthonormal discrete basis images $\varphi_{ij}(x,y)$ ($N \times N$ matrices), i.e.,

$$u(x,y) = \sum_{i=1}^{N} \sum_{j=1}^{N} u_{ij}\varphi_{ij}(x,y) \approx \sum_{i=1}^{n} \sum_{j=1}^{n} u_{ij}\varphi_{ij}(x,y) = u_{ij}^*(x,y), \qquad x,y = 1,2,\cdots,N. \tag{8}$$

Here

$$u_{ij} = \sum_{x=1}^{N} \sum_{y=1}^{N} u(x,y)\varphi_{ij}(x,y), \qquad i,j = 1,2,\cdots,n,\ n \leq N. \tag{9}$$

Hence (9) defines the linear transformation that transforms the original discrete image $u(x,y)$, an $N \times N$ array, into the $n^2$ samples, an $n \times n$ array. Note that each sample $u_{ij}$ is a linear combination of all the picture elements $u(x,y)$, $x,y = 1,2,\cdots,N$, of the original image. The right-hand side of (8) defines the transformation for forming the reconstructed image $u_{ij}^*(x,y)$ from the $n^2$ samples. Each element of the reconstructed array is a linear combination of all the samples. For discrete data we define the normalized mean-sum-square error between the original image $u(x,y)$ and the reconstructed image $u^*(x,y)$

$$\epsilon_s^2 = E\left\{\frac{1}{N^2}\sum_{i=1}^{N}\sum_{j=1}^{N} [u(x,y) - u^*(x,y)]^2\right\} = R(0,0) - \frac{1}{N^2}\sum_{i=1}^{n}\sum_{j=1}^{n} \sigma_{ij}^2. \tag{10}$$

Comments analogous to those made for continuous data following (6) also hold here, where

$$\sigma_{ij}^2 = E\{u_{ij}^2\} = \sum_{x=1}^{N}\sum_{y=1}^{N}\sum_{x'=1}^{N}\sum_{y'=1}^{N} R(x,x',y,y')\varphi_{ij}(x,y)\varphi_{ij}(x',y'). \tag{11}$$

Finally, we point out that for the continuous data case the error (6) approaches zero as $n^2 \rightarrow \infty$ for any set of complete basis images. On the other hand, for discrete data the error (10) is zero for any set of $n^2 = N^2$ basis images that span the space of the data. We also point out that both continuous and discrete images can be mapped into $n^2 \times 1$ arrays (vectors), the difference being simply a matter of notation.

Each of the four transformations described in Section I, ZOH, F, H, and KL, can be modeled by (4) and (5) or (8) and (9) by making the appropriate choice of basis images.

1) *Zero-Order Hold (ZOH)*: Perhaps the most common method for transforming a continuous image into an array

of samples is to raster scan the image and then time sample the resulting waveform. This amounts to transforming a continuous image into an $n \times n$ array of samples such that each sample has the same value as the original image at that coordinate. This sampling technique can be modeled by (5) by choosing basis images of the form

$$\varphi_{ij}(x,y) = \begin{cases} (n/A)^2, & (i-1)A/n \le x \le iA/n, \\ & (j-1)A/n \le y \le jA/n \\ 0, & \text{elsewhere.} \end{cases} \quad (12)$$

These basis functions are best illustrated by dividing the image domain into $n^2$ square regions. Then each basis function is zero everywhere except over one of these regions where it has constant value $(n/A)^2$. According to (5) the samples $u_{ij}$ are now given by

$$u_{ij} = \left(\frac{n}{A}\right)^2 \int_{(i-1)A/n}^{iA/n} \int_{(j-1)A/n}^{jA/n} u(x,y)\, dx\, dy. \quad (13)$$

Hence, each sample is the average value of the image over that region. The reconstruction transformation (4) for these basis images corresponds to a two-dimensional zero-order hold device.

The technique of raster scanning followed by time sampling can also be modeled by choosing basis images of the form

$$\varphi_{ij}(x,y) = \frac{\sin[(4\pi n/A)(x + A/2n - i)]}{(4\pi n/A)(x + A/2n - i)} \cdot \frac{\sin(4\pi n/A)(y + A/2n - j)}{(4\pi n/A)(y + A/2n - j)}. \quad (14)$$

Each basis image now consists of a two dimensional sinc function ($\text{sinc}\, x = \sin x/x$) centered over one of the square regions. For these basis images the samples $u_{ij}$ given by (5) turn out to be the values of the original image at the peaks of the sinc functions, i.e., at the centers of the square regions. The reconstruction transformation (4) now corresponds to an ideal two-dimensional low-pass filter.

Neither of these sets of basis images provide a precise model for the raster scan sampling and reconstruction technique. The sinc functions provide a good model for the sampling process but not for the reconstruction process. On the other hand, the average value functions provide a good model for the standard ZOH reconstruction process but not for sampling process since the values of the samples are the average value of the image over each square region rather than the value at the center of the region. Furthermore, the sinc functions are spatial frequency limited whereas images are space limited. Hence (4)–(6) are not valid for the sinc functions because they do not exhibit the required properties of completeness, orthonormality, etc. Since the average value functions appear to provide a reasonable model for the raster scan process, have a less complicated mathematical form, and avoid the mathematical subtleties associated with the sinc functions, we choose to use these basis images to model raster scan sampling.

Substituting (2) and (12) into (7) we find that the variances of the ZOH samples for Markov data are given by

$$\sigma_{ij}^2 = \frac{4}{\alpha\beta}\left[1 + \frac{n}{\alpha A}(e^{-\alpha A/n} - 1)\right]\left[1 + \frac{n}{\beta A}(e^{-\beta A/n} - 1)\right], \quad i,j = 1,2,\cdots,n. \quad (15)$$

Note that the $\sigma_{ij}^2$ do not depend on $i$ and $j$. (All $n^2$ samples have the same variance.) We now substitute (2) and (15) into (6) to obtain the ZOH sampling error, which is

$$\epsilon_s^2 = 1 - \frac{4n^2}{\alpha\beta A^2}\left[1 + \frac{n}{\alpha A}(e^{-\alpha A/n} - 1)\right] \cdot \left[1 + \frac{n}{\beta A}(e^{-\beta A/n} - 1)\right]. \quad (16)$$

Note that the ZOH sampling error depends on only the three parameters $\alpha A$, $\beta A$, and $n$. $\epsilon_s^2$ is plotted as a function of $n$, for $\alpha A = \beta A = 1$, in Fig. 3.

For discrete random fields the ZOH sampling transformation again corresponds to dividing the image into $n^2$ square regions. This time we average all the picture elements in each region to obtain each of the $n^2$ samples. Here we assume that $N^2$ is an integer multiple of $n^2$. Hence each sample is the average of a $1 \times 1$, $2 \times 2$, $3 \times 3$, etc., array of picture elements.

2) *Fourier (F)*: By choosing basis images of the form

$$\varphi_{ij}(x,y) = \exp\left[-\frac{2\pi(-1)^{1/2}}{A}(ix + jy)\right], \quad i,j = 1,2,\cdots,n \quad (17)$$

we obtain an $n \times n$ array of samples that are the first $n^2$ coefficients of the two-dimensional F series expansion of the continuous image $u(x,y)$. The variances of these samples for Markov data are obtained by substituting (2) and (17) into (7). We obtain

$$\sigma_{ij}^2 = \frac{2\alpha A + 2(e^{-\alpha A} - 1)[(\alpha A)^2 - (2\pi i)^2]/[(\alpha A)^2 + (2\pi i)^2]}{(\alpha A)^2 + (2\pi i)^2} \cdot \frac{2\beta A + 2(e^{-\beta A} - 1)[(\beta A)^2 - (2\pi j)^2]/[(\beta A)^2 + (2\pi j)^2]}{(\beta A)^2 + (2\pi j)^2}. \quad (18)$$

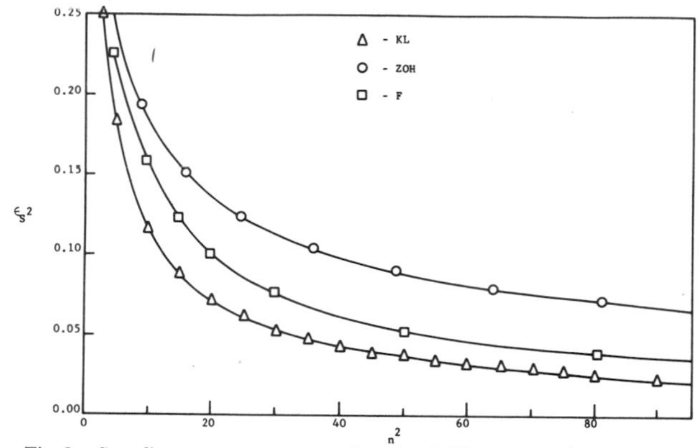


Fig. 3. Sampling mean-square error of random field versus number of samples.

The variances of the F samples depend on the three parameters $\alpha A$, $\beta A$, and $n$ but also on $i$ and $j$. The error corresponding to this choice of basis functions is easily computed by substituting $R(0,0) = 1$ and (18) into (6). The sampling error depends only on $\alpha A$, $\beta A$, and $n^2$ and is presented graphically in Fig. 3 for $\alpha A = \beta A = 1$.

For discrete data the discrete two-dimensional F transformation corresponds to choosing basis images of the form

$$\varphi_{ij}(x,y) = \frac{1}{N} \exp\left[ - \frac{2\pi(-1)^{1/2}}{N} (ix + jy) \right],$$

$$i,j = 1,2,\cdots,n, \quad x,y = 1,2,\cdots,N. \qquad (19)$$

The variances of these samples were computed by substituting (2) and (19) into (11) and the mean-square error was computed from (10). The resulting equations are somewhat unwieldy, and therefore we do not present them here. (See [10], [11]). These variances, ordered according to their magnitudes, are presented graphically in Fig. 4 for $\alpha N = \beta N = 1$. The sampling error for $\alpha N = \beta N = 1$ is presented in Fig. 5 as a function of $n^2$.

3) *Hadamard (H)*: The H transformation is a matrix transformation and is applicable only to discrete data. Here the basis images are defined by

$$\varphi_{ij}(x,y) = \frac{1}{N} (-1)^{\sum_{l=0}^{\log_2 N-1}[g_l^b(i)x_l^b + g_l^b(j)y_l^b]},$$

$$i,j = 1,2,\cdots,n, \quad x,y = 1,2,\cdots,N \qquad (20)$$

where $g_l^b(i)$, $x_l^b$, $g_l^b(j)$, and $y_l^b$ are the $l$th bit in the binary representations of $g(i)$, $x$, $g(j)$, and $y$, respectively. The variances of the samples for this choice of basis images were computed by substituting (2) and (20) into (11), and the corresponding sampling error was computed from (10). Again, the equations are somewhat unwieldy and can be found in [10], [11]. The sample variances, arranged in order of decreasing magnitudes, are presented in Fig. 4 for $\alpha N = \beta N = 1$. The corresponding sampling error is shown in Fig. 5.

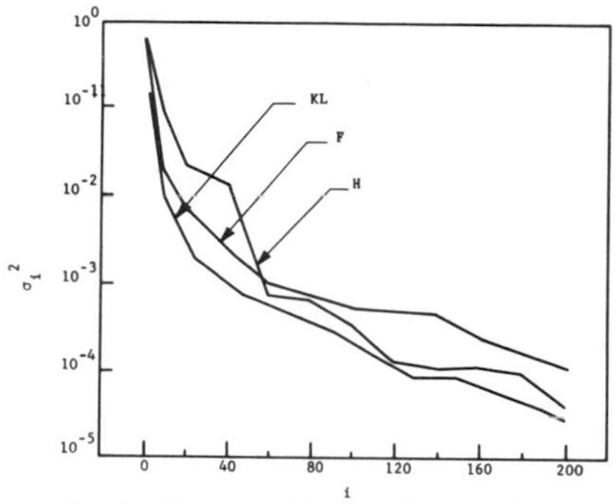


Fig. 4. Variances of F, H, and KL samples.

A set of basis images for continuous data analogous to the H transformations could be constructed from the Walsh functions [12], but we did not pursue this approach.

4) *Karhunen–Loève (KL)*: The basis images that achieve the minimum sampling error for a given number of samples $n^2$ are given by the $n^2$ eigenfunctions corresponding to the $n^2$ largest eigenvalues of the integral equation:

$$\lambda\varphi(x,y) = \int_0^A \int_0^A R(x,x',y,y')\varphi(x,y)\varphi(x',y')\,dx'\,dy'. \qquad (21)$$

This is a straightforward generalization of the solution for one-dimensional data obtained by Koschman [13] and Brown [14]. For a separable kernel (autocorrelation function) such as (2) the eigenfunctions and eigenvalues are separable[1] so that the double integral (21) can be separated into two single integral equations that can be

[1] That is, $\varphi_{kl}(x,y) = \phi_k(\alpha,x)\phi_l(\beta,y)$, and $\lambda_{kl} = \Psi_k(\alpha)\Psi_l(\beta)$. Here we first compute the eigenvalues $\Psi_k(\alpha)$ and $\Psi_l(\beta)$ in order to rank the $\lambda_{ij}$. In general, this does not result in using the first $n$ of the $\Psi_k(\alpha)$, $k = 1,2,\cdots$, and the first $n$ of the $\Psi_l(\beta)$, $l = 1,2,\cdots$, but rather, more of one and fewer of the other. See [11].

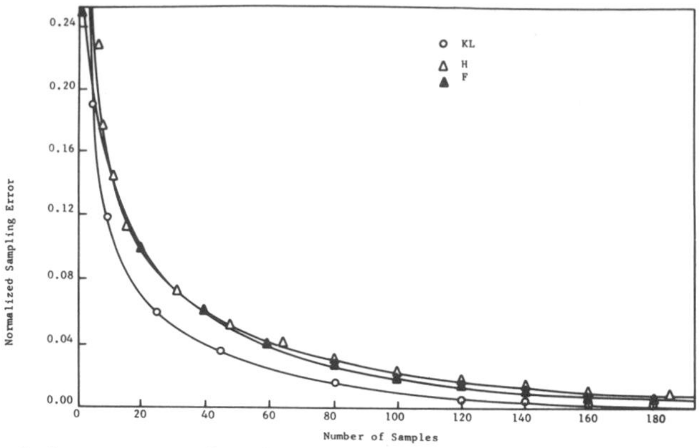


Fig. 5. Normalized mean-sum-squared sampling error versus number of samples for various discrete samplers.

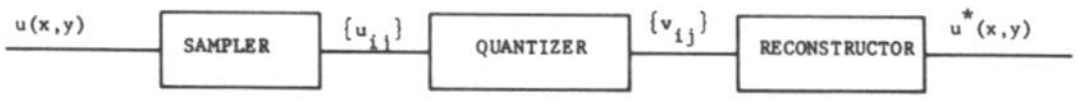


Fig. 6. Coding–decoding system.

solved separately. Furthermore, the solutions to

$$\Psi(\gamma)\phi(\gamma,x) = \int_0^A \exp(-\gamma \mid x - x' \mid)\phi(x')\,dx'$$

are well known [15], [16], and the variances of the samples are given by the eigenvalues, i.e.,

$$\sigma_{ij}^2 = \lambda_{ij}. \tag{22}$$

Hence the resulting sampling error is given by

$$\epsilon_s^2 = 1 - \frac{1}{A^2}\sum_{i=1}^{n}\sum_{j=1}^{n}\lambda_{ij}. \tag{23}$$

$\epsilon_s^2$ is presented graphically in Fig. 3 as a function of $n^2$ for $\alpha A = \beta A = 1$. We also point out that the KL samples are uncorrelated.

For discrete data the development is the same except that the integrals are replaced by summations and the functionals by matrices. This is a generalization of Hotelling's method of principal components [17]. For separable covariances, the basis images are also separable, i.e.,

$$\varphi_{kl}(x,y) = \phi_k(\alpha,x)\phi_l(\beta,y). \tag{24}$$

The vectors $\varphi_k(\alpha,x)$ are the first eigenvectors of the covariance matrix of any row of the original data array, i.e., the eigenvectors of the $N \times N$ matrix with entries $\exp[-\alpha \mid x - x' \mid]$, $x,x' = 1,2,\cdots,N$, corresponding to the largest eigenvalues. The vectors $\phi_l(\beta,y)$ are the first eigenvectors of the covariance matrix of any column of the data array, i.e., the eigenvectors of the matrix with entries $\exp[-\beta \mid y - y' \mid]$, $y,y' = 1,2,\cdots,N$, corresponding to the largest eigenvalues. As for the continuous-data case, these samples are uncorrelated and their variances are given by the eigenvalues, i.e.,

$$\sigma_{ij}^2 = \lambda_{ij} = \Psi_k(\alpha)\Psi_l(\beta) \tag{25}$$

where the $\Psi_k(\alpha)$ and $\Psi_l(\beta)$ are the eigenvalues of the covariance matrices with entries $\exp[-\alpha \mid x - x' \mid]$ and $\exp[-\beta \mid y - y' \mid]$, respectively. Finally, the mean-square error is obtained by substituting the variances into (10). The sampling error for the KL transformation is presented graphically in Fig. 5 for $\alpha N = \beta N = 1$. The 256 basis images for $\alpha = 0.125$, $\beta = 0.249$, and $N = 16$ are presented and discussed in more detail in Section III.

### *C. Block Quantization of Samples*

In theory, any set of $n$ samples can be uniquely mapped into a single sample on (0,1) [18], [19]. However, this concept has no utility in practical systems because the resolution to which the resulting sample must be known also increases by a factor of $n$. Hence we consider the problem of quantizing the $n^2$ samples produced by the sampling transformation.

Consider the image coding–decoding system presented in Fig. 6. The sampling and reconstruction transformations were considered in the preceding section. The only difference is the addition of the quantizer which rounds off each sample $u_{ij}$ to $v_{ij}$. Hence the samples $u_{ij}$ are given by (5) or (9) as before, but the reconstruction transformation is now governed by

$$u^*(x,y) = \sum_{i=1}^{n}\sum_{j=1}^{n} v_{ij}\varphi_{ij}(x,y). \tag{26}$$

That is, the quantized samples are used to form the reconstructed image. The mean-square error between the input and output images of the system of Fig. 6 can be decomposed into the sum [20]

$$\epsilon^2 = \epsilon_s^2 + \epsilon_q^2. \tag{27}$$

Here $\epsilon_s^2$ is the sampling error defined by (6) for continuous data and (10) for discrete data, and $\epsilon_q^2$ is the mean-sum-square error between the quantizer input and output

$$\epsilon_q^2 = \begin{cases} \dfrac{1}{A^2} E\{\sum_{i=1}^{n} \sum_{j=1}^{n} (u_{ij} - v_{ij})^2\} & \text{continuous data} \\ \dfrac{1}{N^2} E\{\sum_{i=1}^{n} \sum_{j=1}^{n} (u_{ij} - v_{ij})^2\} & \text{discrete data.} \end{cases} \tag{28}$$

The quantization error depends on the quantizer structure (the number of quantization levels, the transition levels, and the quantization values) and the statistics of the samples. The design and performance evaluation of optimum quantizers has received considerable attention [21], [22]. From [23, fig. 12] the quantization error for the optimum uniform quantizer for the sample $u_{ij}$ is given by

$$E\{(u_{ij} - v_{ij})^2\} = \begin{cases} \sigma_{ij}^2(16)^{-m_{ij}/2} & \text{uniform samples} \\ \sigma_{ij}^2(10)^{-m_{ij}/2} & \text{Gaussian samples} \end{cases} \tag{29}$$

where $\sigma_{ij}^2$ is the variance of the sample $u_{ij}$, and $2^{m_{ij}}$ is the number of quantization levels assigned to sample $u_{ij}$. Since all of the sampling transformations, except ZOH, produce samples that result from filtering the entire image (continuous data) or are a linear combination of all image elements (discrete data), we expect these samples to be approximately Gaussian. (For the continuous data case we invoke the uniform mixing condition and for discrete data the central limit theorem.) Substitution of (6), (10), (28), and (29) into (27) yields an expression for the error for the system of Fig. 6

$$\epsilon^2 = \begin{cases} R(0,0) - \dfrac{1}{A^2} \sum_{i=1}^{n} \sum_{j=1}^{n} \sigma_{ij}^2(1 - 10^{-m_{ij}/2}) & \text{continuous data} \\ R(0,0) - \dfrac{1}{N^2} \sum_{i=1}^{n} \sum_{j=1}^{n} \sigma_{ij}^2(1 - 10^{-m_{ij}/2}) & \text{discrete data.} \end{cases} \tag{30}$$

We can now optimize the system of Fig. 6 with respect to the number of samples $n$ and the number of bits per sample $m_{ij}$ by minimizing (30) with respect to the $n^2 + 1$ parameters $n, m_{11}, m_{12}, m_{21}, \cdots, m_{nn}$.

For ZOH the variances of all the samples are equal (15) and so the obvious solution is to assign an equal number of bits (quantization levels) to each sample. Let

$$M = \sum_{i=1}^{n} \sum_{i=1}^{n} m_{ij} \tag{31}$$

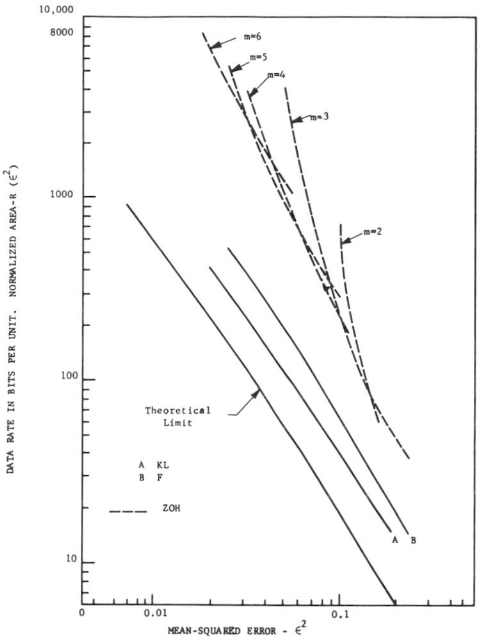


Fig. 7. Comparison of data rate versus $\epsilon^2$ for continuous random fields.

be the total number of bits available for coding the image. Then we assign $m_{ij} = M/n = m$ bits for each sample and the problem reduces to finding the pair $n,m$ for a given $M$ that minimizes (30). Fig. 7 shows $M/A^2$ (the rate per unit image area) versus $\epsilon^2$ for various choices of $m$ for continuous images with autocorrelation function (2) and $\alpha A = \beta A = 1$. The choice for $m$ (and, therefore, $n$ since specifying $M$ and $m$ uniquely determines $n$) for every $M$ that yields minimum $\epsilon^2$ is obvious from the figure.

The F, H, and KL transformations produce samples with monotonically decreasing variances as illustrated in Fig. 4. The problem of assigning $M$ bits to $n$ samples with unequal variances was first considered by Huang and Schultheiss [24]. Wintz and Kurtenbach [25] suggested the following rule[2] for assigning $M$ bits to $n^2$ samples with variances $\sigma_{ij}^2$, $i,j = 1,2,\cdots,n$.

1) Compute the $n^2$ numbers

$$\hat{m}_{ij} = \frac{M}{n^2} + 2 \log \sigma_{ij}^2 - \frac{1}{n^2} \sum_{i=1}^{n} \sum_{j=1}^{n} \log \sigma_{ij}^2. \tag{32}$$

[2] This rule is based on curves developed in [23] while the rule given by Huang and Schultheiss [24] was based on some curves of Max [21]. There is some discrepancy between these curves and, therefore, in the resulting bit assignment algorithms. It appears that Huang and Schultheiss use the optimum nonuniform quantizer while Kurtenbach and Wintz used the optimum uniform quantizer. The optimum uniform quantizer is much easier to implement and its performance, for Gaussian data, is almost as good as that of the nonuniform quantizer.

2) Round off each $\hat{m}_{ij}$ to the nearest integer $m_{ij}$.
3) If

$$\sum_{i=1}^{n} \sum_{j=1}^{n} m_{ij} \neq M$$

arbitrarily adjust some of the $m_{ij}$ until they sum to $M$.

This rule was used for the F, H, and KL transformations for various values of $M$. For each $M$, a value for $n^2$ was chosen, the rule applied, and the resulting $\epsilon^2$ computed. This was repeated for various $n^2$ to determine the optimum value for $n^2$. The resulting rate versus $\epsilon^2$ for the F and KL transformations followed by the optimum block quantization transformation is presented in Fig. 7 for continuous data with $\alpha A = \beta B = 1$. Analogous results for discrete data with $\alpha N = \beta N = 1$ are presented in Fig. 8.

Also presented in Figs. 7 and 8 are the rate distortion functions for the respective random fields. These are theoretical limits below which it is impossible to operate.[3] These rate distortion functions are for the Gaussian Markov field, but also serve as upper bounds for all non-Gaussian Markov fields. For example, refer to Fig. 7 and suppose that we can tolerate an error of 0.1. No coding scheme can achieve this error with less than 18 bits. The KL method requires 40 bits, the F method 62 bits, and ZOH (optimized raster scanning and pulse-code modulation (PCM) coding) requires 190 bits. For the discrete data example of Fig. 8, the numbers for an error of 0.1 are 30 for the theoretical limit, 36 for KL, 44 for F, and 59 for H.

## III. Experimental Results

Each of the four techniques, ZOH, F, H, and KL, were used to code each of the four pictures of Fig. 1. Because the original 256 × 256 arrays are too large for convenient computer processing, each array was first divided into 256 smaller arrays of 16 × 16 picture elements each. Each 16 × 16 array was then transformed, block quantized, reconstructed, and inserted back into its proper place in the reconstructed image. After viewing the reconstructed images, the bit assignments were varied by a trial and error procedure in order to determine bit assignments more suitable for visual data. After a number of iterations we found that for the KL transformation the quality of the reconstructed image was improved slightly by assigning more bits to the samples with the larger variances and proportionally fewer bits to the samples with the smaller variances. The bit assignments dictated by the theory as well as those that gave the best subjective results are presented in Table I. Note that the subjective assignment has the added advantage of reducing the number of samples that must be computed by 20 percent or more. The modified bit allocation also resulted in a slightly smaller mean-square error. Variations in the

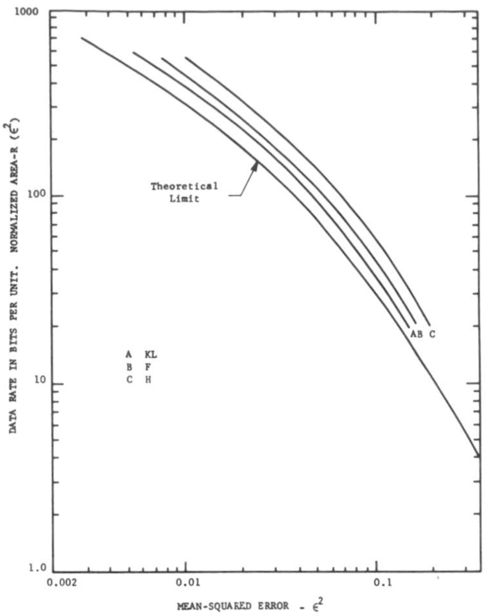


Fig. 8. Comparison of data rate versus mean-squared error for discrete random fields.

bit assignments for the F and H transformations were also tried, but no assignments that yielded consistently better results were found. Hence the bit assignments suggested by the theory were used for the F and H transformations.

The experimental results are presented in Figs. 9–11 for bit rates of 2.0, 1.0, and 0.5 bits per picture element. Here we have divided the total number of bits used to code each picture by $(256)^2$ (the number of picture elements in the original picture) in order to obtain numbers of convenient sizes. Recall that the original cameraman, face, and crowd had 8 bits per picture element while the moon original had 6 bits per picture element.

The mean-square error between each of these reconstructed pictures and their originals were also computed. The results for the cameraman are graphed with solid lines in Fig. 12. Each solid symbol (triangle, square, circle, diamond) corresponds to one of the pictures of Figs. 9(a), 10(a), and 11(a). The dashed curves in Fig. 12 were computed with the theoretical results of Section II and give the average performance of each of the four transformations for Markov data with the same $\alpha$ and $\beta$ as the cameraman picture. The rate distortion function for the Gaussian Markov random field with this $\alpha$ and $\beta$ is also presented and labeled theoretical limit. This also serves as an upper bound for non-Gaussian Markov data. The performance of the KL system is better than the limit for high mean-square errors. Apparently, the cameraman picture is not a valid sample function of the Gaussian

[3] These curves were derived in [10], [11] by generalizing the procedure used by McDonald and Schultheiss [26] to compute the rate distortion function for the analogous one-dimensional data case. See also [29].

TABLE I
BIT ASSIGNMENT FOR KL TRANSFORMATION FOR 2, 1, AND 0.5 BITS PER PICTURE ELEMENT; $\alpha = 0.125$, $\beta = 0.249$

| Binary Digits | 2 Bits per Picture Element | | 1 Bit per Picture Element | | 0.5 Bit per Picture Element | |
|---|---|---|---|---|---|---|
| | Theoretical | Subjective | Theoretical | Subjective | Theoretical | Subjective |
| 8 | | 1–3 | | | | |
| 7 | 1–3 | 4–9 | | 1–2 | | |
| 6 | 4–9 | 10–21 | 1–2 | 3–6 | | 1–2 |
| 5 | 10–21 | 22–47 | 3–6 | 7–15 | 1–2 | 3–6 |
| 4 | 22–47 | 44–88 | 7–15 | 16–38 | 3–6 | 7–14 |
| 3 | 48–90 | 89–90 | 16–38 | 39–56 | 7–14 | 15–25 |
| 2 | 91–139 | 91–115 | 39–73 | 57–66 | 15–35 | 26–35 |
| 1 | 140–203 | 116–139 | 74–122 | 67–73 | 36–71 | 36–46 |

The samples listed in columns two through seven are assigned the number of bits listed in column 1. For example, at 2 bits per picture element (32) assigns 7 bits each to samples 1, 2, 3; 6 bits each to samples 4, 5, 6, 7, 8, 9, etc.

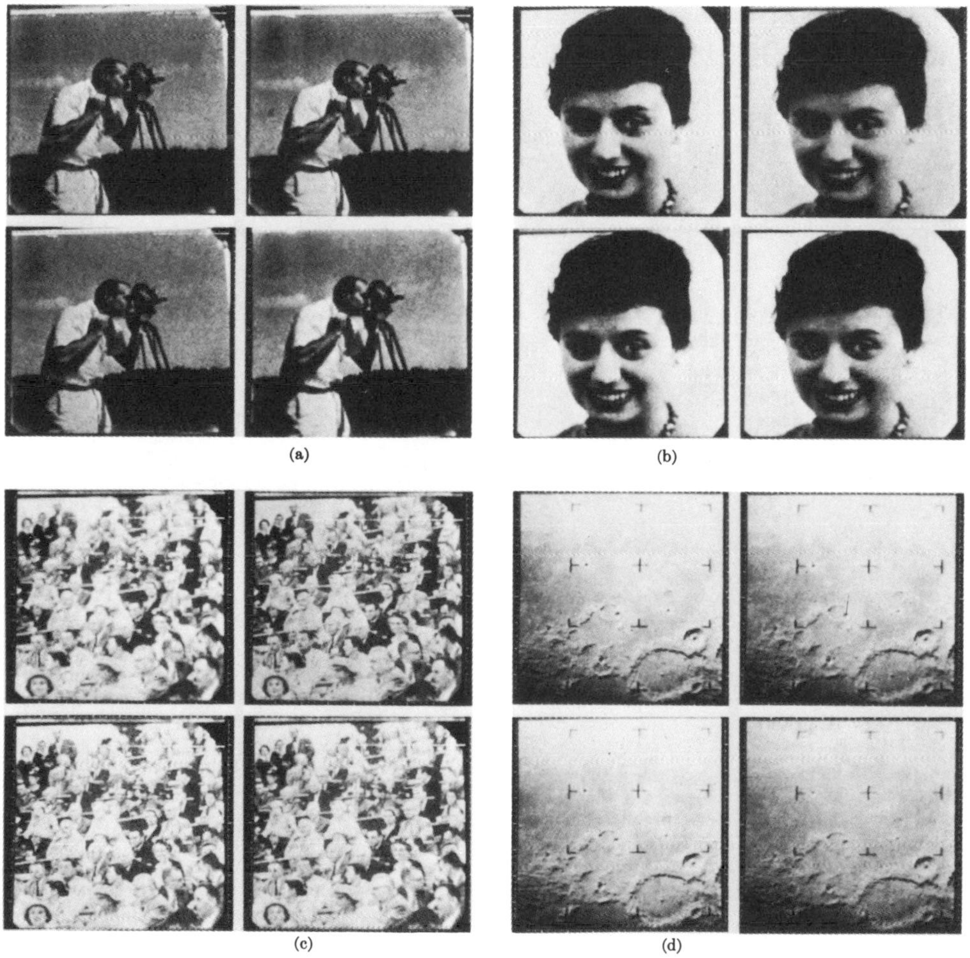

Fig. 9. Encoded pictures by various transformations using 2 bits per picture element. (a) Cameraman. (b) Face. (c) Crowd scene. (d) Moon.

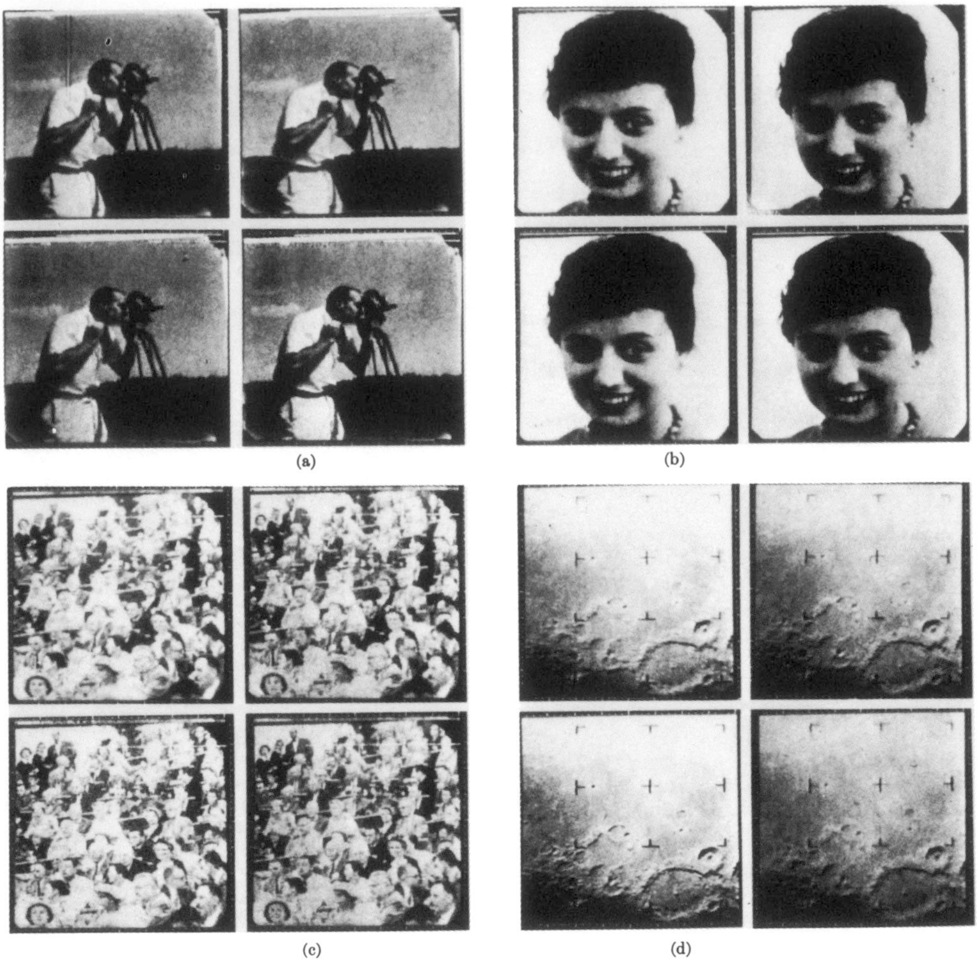


Fig. 10. Encoded pictures by various transformations using 1 bit per picture element. (a) Cameraman. (b) Face. (c) Crowd scene. (d) Moon.

Markov process, or at least, not a typical one. Note that there is considerable correlation between the mean-square errors of Fig. 12 and the quality of the pictures of Figs. 9(a), 10(a), and 11(a).

Fig. 13 shows the reconstructed cameraman pictures for ZOH sampling and FOH reconstruction. FOH reconstruction produces pictures with somewhat better subjective quality, but they have larger mean-square errors.

Recall that the F, H, and KL transformations were optimized (matched to the picture statistics) through the parameters $\alpha$ and $\beta$. For KL both the sampling and quantization transformations depend on $\alpha$ and $\beta$ while for F and H only the quantizer depends on $\alpha$ and $\beta$. To determine the sensitivity of the code performances on the values chosen for $\alpha$ and $\beta$ we used the cameraman parameters ($\alpha = 0.125$, $\beta = 0.249$) to code the girl and crowd. The results show negligible degradation relative to the results obtained using the girl and crowd parameters (see [11]). A theoretical investigation of performance sensitivity to mismatch between the values of $\alpha$ and $\beta$ used in the coding system and the actual values of $\alpha$ and $\beta$ of the Markov data can be found in [11, appendix F]. The theoretical results also indicate that system performance is quite insensitive to moderate mismatch between the design statistics and the statistics of the image processed.

The KL basis images for $\alpha = 0.125$ and $\beta = 0.249$ are presented in Fig. 14. These $16 \times 16$ arrays have been ordered according to the magnitudes of their eigenvalues starting in the upper left-hand corner across the first row, then from left to right across the second row, etc.

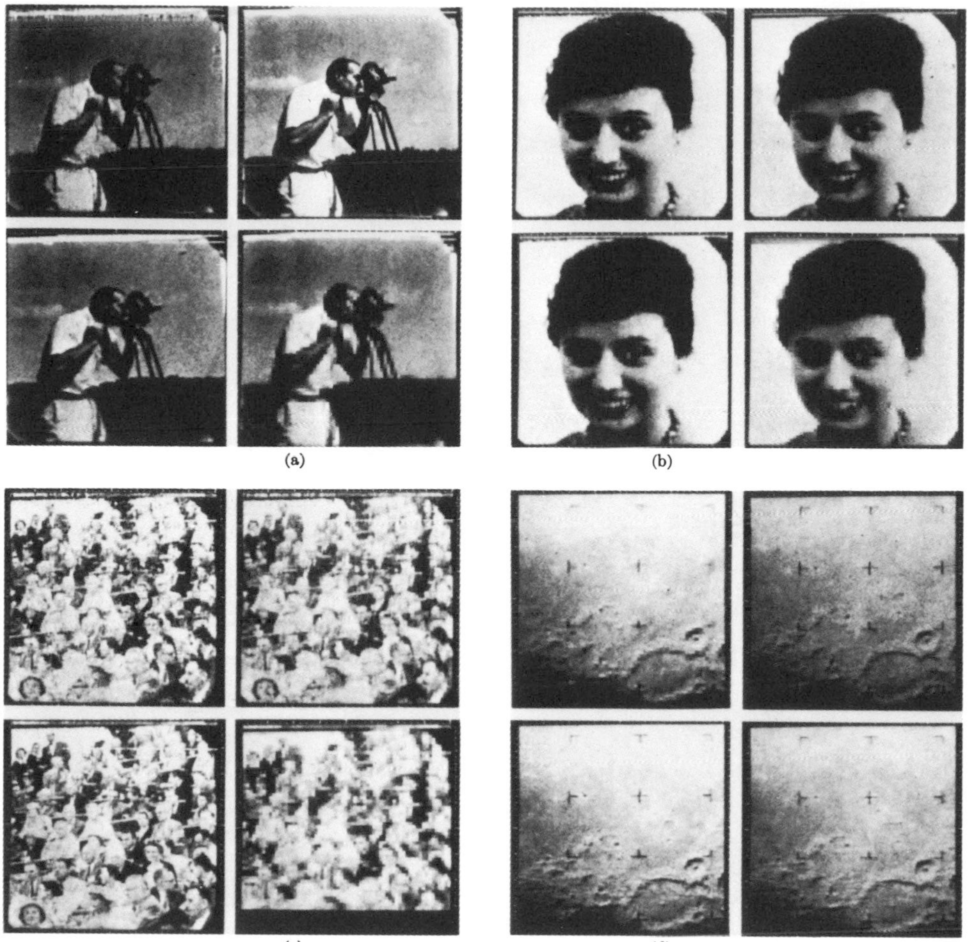

Fig. 11. Encoded pictures by various transformations using 0.5 bit per picture element. (a) Cameraman. (b) Face. (c) Crowd scene. (d) Moon.

Note that the first basis image has uniform gray level so that the first KL sample (coefficient) is the average gray level. The second basis image corresponds to the first harmonic in the vertical direction so that the second sample (coefficient) is a measure of the amount of vertical first harmonic in sampled image. The third basis image appears to correspond approximately to the first harmonic in the horizontal direction, etc.

Some experiments with an adaptive coding system were also made. In the adaptive system $\alpha$ and $\beta$ were estimated for each $16 \times 16$ array of picture elements and quantized to one of the 16 pairs $(\alpha_i,\beta_j)$, $i,j = 1,2,3,4$. Then the transformation and block quantizer for that $(\alpha_i,\beta_j)$ were used to code that block. Four additional bits per block are required to code any $\alpha,\beta$ pair used in order that the decoder can use the same pair in the reconstruction process. The system is adaptive since the number of bits used to code each block depends on the estimated value for $\alpha$ and $\beta$ for that block. Since $\alpha$ and $\beta$ are a measure of the amount of detail (correlation) in that block, the number of bits used to code each block is proportional to the amount of detail in that block. The performances for all three transformations F, H, and KL were only marginally better than the performances of the corresponding non-adaptive systems. Details can be found in [11].

A different adaptive system based on the KL transformation and block quantization, but using pattern recognition techniques to classify blocks, is presently

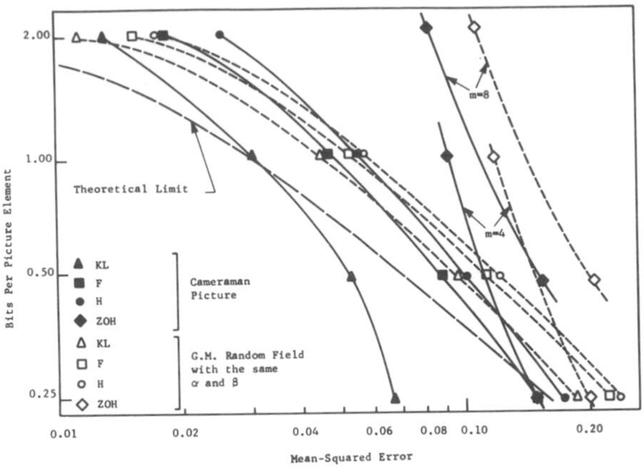


Fig. 12. Bit rate versus mean-square error for various two-dimensional transformations.

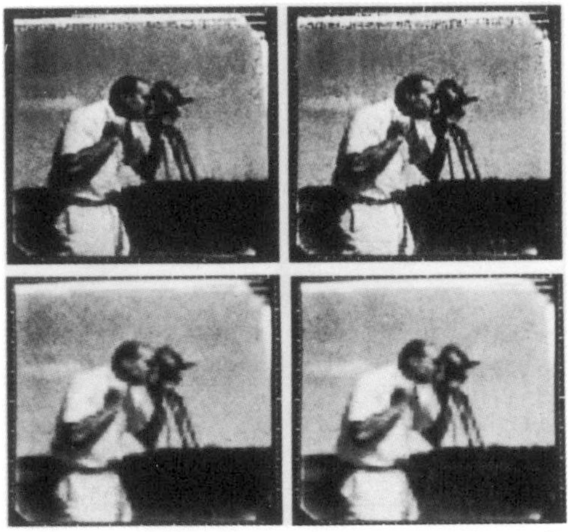

Fig. 13. Encoded pictures of cameraman using ZOH sampling and FOH reconstructor.

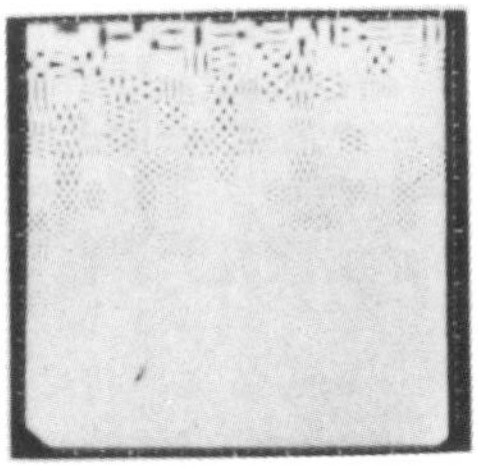

Fig. 14. KL basis images for cameraman picture.

under investigation [27]. This system produces pictures at 1 bit per picture element that are comparable in quality to the pictures produced by the nonadaptive systems described in this paper at 2 bits per picture element.

## IV. Conclusions

Image coding strategies based on the F, H, and KL transformations were optimized and used to code several pictures. These performances were then compared to the performance of the standard raster scan method. The KL transformation gave the best performance but was followed closely by the F and H transformations. All three performed significantly better than the raster scan method.

The amount of computation required to implement each of the four coding schemes is roughly proportional to their performances. For an original image consisting of an $N \times N$ array of picture elements, the KL transformation requires $N^2$ multiplications and $N^2$ additions to compute all of the $N^2$ KL samples. However, with the modified bit assignment, only about one third of these samples need be computed for good quality pictures. The F transformation requires $N \log N$ multiplications and $N \log N$ additions with the fast Fourier transform algorithm. The H transformation requires $N \log N$ additions with the fast Hadamard transform. When the fast Fourier or fast Hadamard transform are used, all $N^2$ samples must be computed, even though only about one half need be retained for good performance.

Recall that the F, H, and KL systems require a different quantizer for each sample. The implementation of such a block quantizer requires only one analog-to-digital converter but it must be preceded by an amplifier whose gain is different for each sample. Another quantization scheme that achieves approximately the same performance and does not require the variable gain amplifier has been proposed by Hayes and Bobilin [28]. However, this scheme requires a variable length (Huffman) code.

In summary, the H transformation appears to present the best tradeoff between system performance and complexity. For the types of pictures investigated here the H system requires approximately one third as many bits as the standard raster scan system to achieve pictures of comparable quality.


## Acknowledgment

The authors wish to thank Dr. T. Huang of the Massachussetts Institute of Technology for supplying the digitized pictures of the cameraman, face, and crowd, and F. Billingsley of NASA/JPL for the moon picture. The coding and reconstruction digital processing was done on Purdue University's CDC 6500 system. The pictures were produced with a CRT display system by W. Robey of the Department of Electrical Engineering at Purdue University.


## References


[1] T. S. Huang and J. W. Woods, "Picture bandwidth compression by block quantization," presented at the 1969 Int. Symp. Inform. Theory, Ellenville, N. Y.

[2] J. W. Woods and T. S. Huang, "Picture bandwidth compression by linear transformation and block quantization," presented at the 1969 Symp. Picture Bandwidth Compression, M.I.T., Cambridge, Mass.

[3] W. K. Pratt and H. C. Andrews, "Two-dimensional transform coding of images," presented at the 1969 Int. Symp. Inform. Theory, Ellenville, N. Y.

[4] ——, "Application of Fourier–Hadamard transformation to bandwidth compression," presented at the 1969 Symp. Picture Bandwidth Compression, M.I.T., Cambridge, Mass.

[5] W. K. Pratt, J. Kane, and H. C. Andrews, "Hadamard transform image coding," *Proc. IEEE*, vol. 57, Jan. 1969, pp. 58–68.

[6] G. B. Anderson and T. S. Huang, "Picture bandwidth compression by piecewise Fourier transformation," in *Proc. Purdue Centennial Year Symp. Inform. Processing*, 1969.

[7] E. R. Kretzmer, "Statistics of television signals," *Bell Syst. Tech. J.*, July 1952, pp. 751–763.

[8] L. E. Franks, "A model for the random video process," *Bell Syst. Tech. J.*, Apr. 1966.

[9] T. S. Huang, "The subjective effect of two-dimensional pictorial noise," *IEEE Trans. Inform. Theory*, vol. IT-11, Jan. 1965, pp. 43–53.

[10] A. Habibi and P. A. Wintz, "Optimum linear transformations for encoding two-dimensional data," School of Elec. Eng., Purdue Univ., Lafayette, Ind., Tech. Rep. TR-EE69-15, May 1969.

[11] ——, "Linear transformations for encoding 2-dimensional sources," School of Elec. Eng., Purdue Univ., Lafayette, Ind., Tech. Rep. TR-EE70-2, June 1970.

[12] H. F. Harmuth, "Applications of Walsh functions in communications," *IEEE Spectrum*, vol. 6, Nov. 1969, pp. 82–91.

[13] A. Koschman, "On the filtering of nonstationary time series," in *Proc. 1954 Nat. Electron. Conf.*, p. 126.

[14] J. L. Brown, Jr., "Mean-square truncation error in series expansions of random functions," *J. SIAM*, vol. 8, Mar. 1960, pp. 18–32.

[15] W. B. Davenport, Jr., and W. L. Root, *An Introduction to the Theory of Random Signals and Noise.* New York: McGraw-Hill, 1958.

[16] H. L. VanTrees, *Detection, Estimation, and Modulation Theory.* New York: Wiley, 1963.

[17] H. Hotelling, "Analysis of a complex of statistical variables into principal components," *J. Educ. Psychol.*, vol. 24, 1933, pp. 417–441, 498–520.

[18] A. E. Laemmel, "Dimension reducing mapping for signal compression," Microwave Res. Inst., Polytechnic Inst. of Brooklyn, Brooklyn, N. Y., Rep. R-632-57, PIB560, 1967.

[19] T. Bially, "Space-filling curves: their generation and their application to bandwidth reduction," *IEEE Trans. Inform. Theory*, vol. IT-15, Nov. 1969, pp. 658–664.

[20] R. E. Totty and G. C. Clark, "Reconstruction error in waveform transmission," *IEEE Trans. Inform. Theory*, vol. IT-13, Apr. 1967, pp. 336–338.

[21] J. Max, "Quantizing for minimum distortion," *IRE Trans. Inform. Theory*, vol. IT-6, Mar. 1960, pp. 7–12.

[22] R. C. Wood, "On optimum quantization," *IEEE Trans. Inform. Theory*, vol. IT-15, Mar. 1969, pp. 248–252.

[23] A. J. Kurtenbach and P. A. Wintz, "Quantizing for noisy channels," *IEEE Trans. Commun. Technol.*, vol. COM-17, Apr. 1969, pp. 291–302.

[24] J. J. Y. Huang and P. M. Schultheiss, "Block quantization of correlated Gaussian random variables," *IEEE Trans. Commun. Syst.*, vol. CS-11, Sept. 1963, pp. 289–296.

[25] P. A. Wintz and A. J. Kurtenbach, "Waveform error control in PCM telemetry," *IEEE Trans. Inform. Theory*, vol. IT-14, Sept. 1968, pp. 650–661.

[26] R. A. McDonald and P. M. Schultheiss, "Information rates of Gaussian signals under criteria constraining the error spectrum," *Proc. IEEE* (Corresp.), vol. 52, Apr. 1964, pp. 415–416.

[27] M. Tasto and P. A. Wintz, "Picture bandwidth compression by adaptive block quantization," School of Elec. Eng., Purdue Univ., Lafayette, Ind., Tech. Rep. TR-EE-70-14, May 1969.

[28] J. F. Hayes and R. Bobilin, "Efficient waveform encoding," School of Elec. Eng., Purdue Univ., Lafayette, Ind., Tech. Rep. TR-EE69-4, Feb. 1969.

[29] J. F. Hayes, A. Habibi, and P. A. Wintz, "Rate distortion function for a Gaussian source model of images," *IEEE Trans. Inform. Theory*, vol. IT-16, July 1970, pp. 507–509.


**Ali Habibi** (S'64–M'70) was born in Hamadan, Iran, on March 14, 1942. He received the B.S. degree from West Virginia University, Morgantown, the M.S. degree from Cornell University, Ithaca, N. Y., and the Ph.D. degree from Purdue University, Lafayette, Ind., in 1965, 1967, and 1970, respectively, all in electrical engineering.

While at Cornell University he was a Research Assistant in the System Theory Group, and from 1967 to 1970 he was a Research Instructor at Purdue University. Since 1970 he has been employed at Bell Telephone Laboratories, Holmdel, N. J., working in the Telephone and Picturephone Planning Center.

Dr. Habibi is a member of Eta Kappa Nu, Tau Beta Pi, Sigma Tau Sigma, and Sigma Xi.

**Paul A. Wintz** (S'61–M'64) was born in Batesville, Ind., on March 7, 1935. He received the B.S., M.S., and Ph.D. degrees in electrical engineering from Purdue University, Lafayette, Ind., in 1959, 1961, and 1964, respectively.

While attending Purdue University, he was employed for three years as an Engineer by Duncan Electric Company, Lafayette. Since 1961 he has been on the faculty of Purdue University, first as an Instructor of Electrical Engineering, and from 1964 to 1967 as an Assistant Professor. He is currently an Associate Professor of Electrical Engineering, and along with his teaching duties, he directs several research activities in the area of statistical communication theory. His current interests involve adaptive telemetry systems, data compression, and image coding and transmission. He has also served as Consultant for a number of corporations and government agencies.

Dr. Wintz is a member of Sigma Xi.

# 31



Reprinted from *IEEE Trans. Commun. Tech.*, **Com-19**(6), 1045–1049 (1971)

# A Comparison of Orthogonal Transformations for Digital Speech Processing

S. J. CAMPANELLA AND GUNER S. ROBINSON

*Abstract*—Discrete forms of the Fourier, Hadamard, and Karhunen–Loève transforms are examined for their capacity to reduce the bit rate necessary to transmit speech signals. To rate their effectiveness in accomplishing this goal the quantizing error (or noise) resulting for each transformation method at various bit rates is computed and compared with that for conventional companded PCM processing. Based on this comparison, it is found that Karhunen–Loève provides a reduction in bit rate of 13.5 kbits/s, Fourier 10 kbits/s, and Hadamard 7.5 kbits/s as compared with the bit rate required for companded PCM. These bit-rate reductions are shown to be somewhat independent of the transmission bit rate.

## I. Introduction

ORTHOGONAL transformations of signals offer a means for reduction of the bit rate necessary for the transmission of signals. In this paper, applications of Fourier [1], [2], Walsh [2], [3], and Karhunen–Loève [4]–[7] orthogonal transformations to speech are discussed. The opportunity to reduce bit rate resides in the fact that the variances of the orthogonal function coefficients are different for different coefficients. If this property indeed exists for a signal of interest, then the bit rate needed to transmit the signal can be significantly reduced as compared to that needed for conventional PCM transmission.

Orthogonal transformation techniques have been suggested and explored to various degrees by a number of investigators. A large body of references on applications to image processing are given by Habibi and Wintz [8]. Kramer and Mathews suggested the use of a linear transformation (based on the eigenvectors of the covariance matrix of a set of signals, i.e., Karhunen–Loève transformation) for transmitting a set of correlated signals, with specific application to information rate reduction of a channel vocoder [9]. Kulya applied such a technique to vocoder parametric control signals in his orthogonal vocoder [10]. Crowther and Rader have applied the Hadamard transformation to the information rate reduction of vocoder signals [11]. Huang and Schultheiss [12] gave a development of the discrete version of the linear transformation technique that was used as the basis for the Karhunen–Loève transform method used in the investigation reported in this paper.

Other techniques are available for accomplishing information rate reduction of speech. Differential coded PCM at 40 kbits/s has been shown by McDonald [13] to produce a $S/N$ ratio equal to that of 56 kbit/s PCM speech. Greefkes [14] has shown that delta modulation using digital feedback to accomplish optimized companding exhibits a performance equivalent to 56 kbit/s PCM at a rate of 40 kbit/s. A comparison of the linear transformation and predictive coding methods, which is relevant to the topic under discussion, is given in a paper by Nitadori [15].

In the following discussion, it is shown that data rate reductions of 13.5, 10, and 7.5 kbits/s are possible using discrete Karhunen–Loève, Fourier, and Walsh representations, respectively, as compared with 56 kbit/s PCM. These values of reduction tend to be independent of the bit rate.

It should be explained that discrete forms of the transformations are necessarily employed in digital signal processing. The discrete form of the Walsh transformation is known as the Hadamard transformation. Thus, in the following, the term Hadamard refers to the discrete Walsh transformation.

## II. Information Rate Reduction Using Orthogonal Transforms

A discrete time series $f(nT)$ possessing a total signal power $\sigma^2$ may be expressed in terms of a set of orthogonal coefficients $\{C_i\}$ and orthogonal functions $\{F_i(nT)\}$ by the transformation

$$f(nT) = \sum_{i=0}^{N-1} C_i F_i(nT). \tag{1}$$

In this expression, $T$ is the time between samples, $n$ is the sample index, and $N$ is the number of samples per processing window. The window size $NT$ is not related to any specific feature of the signal, such as the pitch period or formant structure of speech. Rather it is based on the effective spectral resolution needed to represent the characteristics of the spectrum of speech over an ensemble of talkers and words. The choice of window size is discussed in greater detail at the end of Section II. The set of orthogonal functions may be any one of many different types. The types of transforms used are the discrete forms of the Fourier, Hadamard (Walsh), and Karhunen–Loève. In the Fourier case, the orthogonal functions are discrete sampled sines and cosines as illustrated in the first column l of Fig. 1, for $N = 16$. In the Hadamard case, the orthogonal functions are discrete sampled Walsh functions as shown in the second column

Manuscript received April 12, 1971; revised August 12, 1971. This work was supported in part by NASA.

The authors are with the Communications Satellite Corporation, COMSAT Laboratories, Clarksburg, Md. 20734.

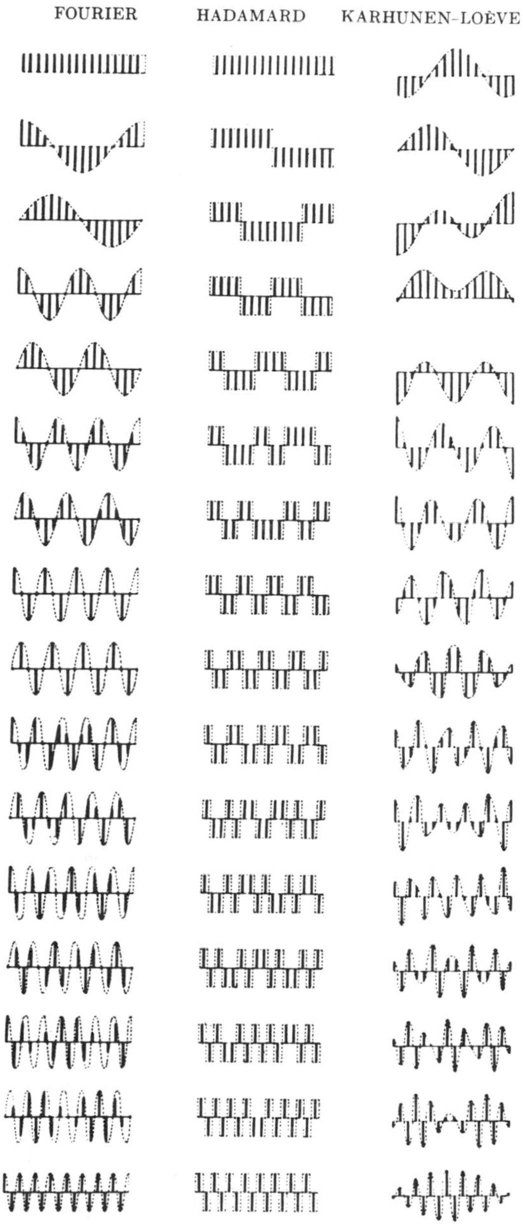


Fig. 1. Discrete orthogonal functions $N = 16$.

of Fig. 1 for $N = 16$. For the Karhunen–Loève, the orthogonal functions used are a special set determined from the autocorrelation function computed over an ensemble of talkers and utterances typical of those to be processed. The orthogonal functions are the eigenfunctions of the covariance matrix

$$C = R(0)\begin{bmatrix} 1 & \rho(1) & \rho(2) & \rho(3) & \cdots & \rho(15) \\ \rho(1) & 1 & \rho(1) & \rho(2) & & \rho(14) \\ \rho(2) & \rho(1) & 1 & \rho(1) & & \rho(13) \\ \rho(3) & \rho(2) & \rho(1) & 1 & & \rho(12) \\ \vdots & & & & & \vdots \\ \cdot & & & & & \rho(1) \\ \rho(15) & \rho(14) & \rho(13) & \rho(12) & \cdots & 1 \end{bmatrix}$$

where $R(0)$ is the variance of the ensemble of samples and $\rho(k)$ is autocorrelation coefficient at delay time $kT$. The autocorrelation functions for the speech of male and female talkers used to demonstrate the method are shown in Fig. 2. These were obtained by averaging over the entire speech sample (of 16 samples) for each talker. It should be noted that 16 autocorrelation values, taken $T = 125$ μs apart, are needed to compose the covariance matrix for $N = 16$. The discrete eigenfunctions, which constitute the set of orthogonal functions in terms of which the speech is processed, are shown in the third column of Fig. 1. Note that there is no eigenfunction that is simply constant over the entire window.

It is the aim now to determine a general expression for the information rate needed for transmission of the coefficients so that the time series may be reconstructed with the same signal-to-quantizing-noise ratio as that achieved by conventional PCM transmission of the same time series. This can be done in terms of the set of variances $\{\sigma_i^2\}$ associated in one-for-one correspondence with the set of coefficients $\{C_i\}$. Consider that coefficient $C_i$ with variance $\sigma_i^2$ is quantized using $n_i$ binary digits. Then the quantizing error or noise attending coded transmission of this coefficient is [1], [16]

$$\overline{\epsilon_i^2} = \frac{K_i}{N^2}\frac{\sigma_i^2}{2^{2n_i}}. \tag{2}$$

$K_i$ is a constant that expresses the consequence of the scaling and companding associated with quantizing the coefficient. $N^2$ is a normalizing factor where $N$ is the number of samples in the time series set involved in determining the coefficients. $N$ is also the number of orthogonal coefficients required to represent a set of time series samples of size $N$. The total quantizing noise contributed by quantized transmission of orthogonal coefficients is then

$$\overline{\epsilon_O^2} = \frac{1}{N^2}\sum_{i=0}^{N-1} K_i \frac{\sigma_i^2}{2^{2n_i}}. \tag{3}$$

If the same information were transmitted using PCM [16], the quantizing error or noise would be

$$\overline{\epsilon_{PCM}^2} = K_{PCM}\frac{\sigma^2}{2^{2M}} \tag{4}$$

where $M$ is the total number of bits used to quantize

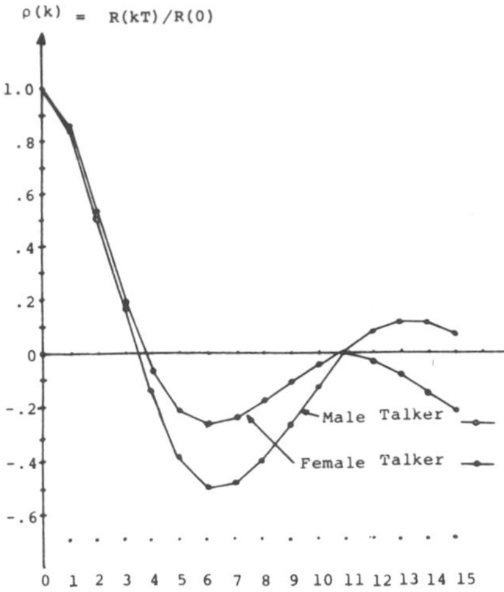


Fig. 2. Normalized autocorrelation functions.

each sample, $\sigma^2$ is the signal power, which is also the signal variance since bias is assumed to be removed, and $K_{PCM}$ is a constant that expresses the consequence of scaling and companding.

The quantizing noise given by (3) is minimized when the contributions are all equal [12]. This can be shown by equating all partial derivatives of (3) with respect to the variables $\{n_i\}$ to zero, observing the constraint that

$$\sum_{0}^{N-1} n_i = NM$$

where $NM$ is the total number of bits assigned to each window. Thus, if the sum of $N$ contributions is to equal the quantizing noise for the PCM case, then each must equal $\overline{\epsilon^2}_{PCM}/N$ and the following equality must be satisfied for each coefficient:

$$\overline{\epsilon^2}_i = \overline{\epsilon^2}_{PCM}/N. \tag{5}$$

Using (3) and (4), the above relation yields the following expression for the number of bits required for each coefficient to fulfill the condition of quantization noise equality:

$$n_i = M + \tfrac{1}{2}\log_2\left(N\frac{K_i}{K_{PCM}}\right) + \log_2\left(\frac{\sigma_i}{N\sigma}\right). \tag{6}$$

The total bit rate for the transmission of the quantized and coded coefficients is thus

$$R_0 = \frac{1}{NT}\sum_{i=0}^{N-1} n_i, \qquad \text{bits/s} \tag{7}$$

where $T$ is the time between speech samples. The bit rate for transmitting the same signal with the same quantizing noise by conventional PCM is

$$R_{PCM} = M/T. \tag{8}$$

If the orthogonal representation is to reduce the bit rate, it is necessary that the average bit assignment be less than $M$. Thus

$$\frac{1}{N}\sum_{i=0}^{N-1} n_i < M.$$

The spectral distribution of the quantizing noise generated when coefficients are quantized using the bit assignments given by (6) is very nearly white. This follows from the spectral distributions of the orthogonal functions and the fact that the number of quantizing levels is adjusted to produce an equal value of quantizing error for all of the orthogonal functions.

The size of the analysis window is determined by the number of signal samples $N$ entering into the computation of the orthogonal coefficients. If these samples are taken at intervals of $T$ seconds, then the analysis window has a time duration of $NT$. For Fourier analysis, it is well known that the frequency resolution of this window is given by $(NT)^{-1}$. If the spectral distribution property of the signal is to be responsible for causing the differences in the coefficient variances that are responsible for the information rate reduction, then the resolution provided by the window must be sufficient to resolve these differences.

In the analysis that follows, $N$ has been assigned a value of 16. One reason for this assignment was that it is an integral power of 2, a condition that permits the use of the fast processing form of the orthogonal transformations. Also, this value provides a frequency resolution of 500 Hz for $T = 125$ μs, which is sufficient to resolve the long-term spectral distribution of speech in terms of the variances of the Fourier coefficients.

The value of $N = 64$, providing a frequency resolution of 125 Hz, has also been examined and found to improve the efficiency of the representation by a small amount. Higher values of $N$ will provide greater resolution capacity, easily capable of resolving the short-term formant spectrum structure of speech; however, beneficial use of this short-term spectrum structure to reduce information rate requires frequent recomputation of coefficient variance and reassignment of quantizing levels. This latter form of orthogonal signal processing, referred to as adaptive, is not discussed further in this paper.

The rationale used above for determination of the sample window size for the Fourier case also applies approximately for the Hadamard and Karhunen–Loève transformations. This follows from the fact that the spectral distributions of the orthogonal functions of these latter transforms bear a strong similarity to those of the Fourier set.

## III. Results Obtained for Fourier, Hadamard, and Karhunen–Loève Transformations

Fourier, Hadamard, and Karhunen–Loève representations of speech have been studied experimentally and the results are discussed in the following.

The speech used for the processing had a duration of 65 s and consisted of five test sentences spoken by two men and two women. This speech was sampled at a rate of 8000 samples per second, corresponding to a sampling interval of $T = 125\ \mu s$. Sets of 16 samples were used for computing a corresponding number of orthogonal function coefficients for each transform. Coefficient variances were determined by computing the average of the squared deviations of the coefficients over the 65-s speech event.

The resulting normalized standard deviations of the coefficients are given in the second column of Tables I–III for the Fourier, Hadamard, and Karhunen–Loève transforms, respectively. The ratios of the normalized standard deviations to the total signal standard deviation for each transform are given in the third column of each table, and the corresponding values of bits per coefficient as determined from (6), rounded off to the nearest integer, for an equivalent PCM bit rate of $R_{PCM} = 56$ kbits/s, i.e., a value of $M = 7$ bits, are given in the fourth column of each table. A $\mu = 100$ logarithmic companding law was used for coding of the PCM samples and also the orthogonal transform coefficients. In view of the fact that the same companding law has been used for the PCM samples and the orthogonal transform coefficients it has been assumed that $K_i = K_{PCM}$. The resulting bit rates for transmission of the signal information in orthogonal coefficient form for each case are given at the bottom of each table.

It is seen that the bit rate required to give a signal-to-quantizing-noise performance equal to that of conventional 56 kbit/s PCM is 46 kbit/s for the Fourier processing, 48.5 kbit/s for the Hadamard processing, and 42.5 kbit/s for the Karhunen–Loève processing. These represent reductions of 10 kbit/s, 7.5 kbit/s, and 13.5 kbit/s, respectively.

Experiments have also been performed, using optimized bit assignments, which yield bit rates of 56, 28, and 14 kbit/s. The results expressed in terms of computed signal-to-quantizing-noise ratio $S/N_Q$ for each case are given in the second column of Table IV. The computed $S/N_Q$ for PCM processing is given in the third column. These values were obtained from a plot of $S/N_Q$ versus bit rate computed for the same speech samples used for orthogonal processing. The bit rates for which the points on the plot were originally computed were 16, 32, and 56 kbit/s. The improvement in the $S/N_Q$ achieved by use of the orthogonal processing is given in the fourth column. It is seen that the improvement averages about 5 dB for the Fourier processing, 3 dB for the Hadamard processing, and 9 dB for the Karhunen–Loève processing.

With regard to the Karhunen–Loève transform, it should be recognized that since speech is not a stationary process, and since the speech covariance matrix (which is used in computing the Karhunen–Loève transform matrix) is different from one person to another, an adaptive scheme would be expected to produce better results. A continuously adaptive scheme requiring recomputation of the Karhunen–Loève transform matrix during the processing of speech, may be impractical. Therefore, this route was not taken. Rather, a speaker-adaptive Karhunen–Loève processing system requiring the use of different transformation matrices for different speakers was used. For some applications this may be practical. The results given in Table III are accordingly for a single male talker. The transform matrix computed for the male voice was used to process the speech of a female to test its capacity to accommodate a signal significantly different from that for which it was computed. At a bit rate of 28 kbit/s the resulting $S/N_Q$ was computed as 20.7 dB for the female voice. This represents an improvement of 8.6 dB with respect to the conventional PCM at the same

TABLE I

FOURIER TRANSFORM ($N = 16$) $\sigma = 1024$, $R_{PCM} = 56$ kbit/s

| $i$ | $\frac{\sigma_i}{N}$ | $\frac{\sigma_i}{N\sigma}$ | $n_i$ |
|---|---|---|---|
| 0 | 336 | 0.328 | 7 |
| 1 | 544 | 0.530 | 8 |
| 2 | 548 | 0.540 | 8 |
| 3 | 306 | 0.298 | 7 |
| 4 | 352 | 0.343 | 7 |
| 5 | 162 | 0.158 | 6 |
| 6 | 181 | 0.176 | 6 |
| 7 | 118 | 0.115 | 6 |
| 8 | 119 | 0.116 | 6 |
| 9 | 106 | 0.103 | 5 |
| 10 | 90 | 0.088 | 5 |
| 11 | 81 | 0.079 | 5 |
| 12 | 46 | 0.045 | 4 |
| 13 | 76 | 0.074 | 4 |
| 14 | 23 | 0.023 | 4 |
| 15 | 51 | 0.050 | 4 |
| Total bits → | | | 92 |
| $R_0$ kbit/s | | | 46.0 |
| Bit rate reduction = 10 kbit/s | | | |

TABLE II

HADAMARD TRANSFORM ($N = 16$) $\sigma = 1024$, $R_{PCM} = 56$ kbit/s

| $i$ | $\frac{\sigma_i}{N}$ | $\frac{\sigma_i}{N\sigma}$ | $n_i$ |
|---|---|---|---|
| 0 | 336 | 0.328 | 7 |
| 1 | 485 | 0.474 | 8 |
| 2 | 471 | 0.460 | 8 |
| 3 | 342 | 0.333 | 7 |
| 4 | 267 | 0.261 | 7 |
| 5 | 279 | 0.272 | 7 |
| 6 | 216 | 0.211 | 6 |
| 7 | 137 | 0.134 | 6 |
| 8 | 95 | 0.093 | 5 |
| 9 | 101 | 0.099 | 5 |
| 10 | 111 | 0.109 | 5 |
| 11 | 112 | 0.109 | 5 |
| 12 | 119 | 0.117 | 6 |
| 13 | 126 | 0.123 | 6 |
| 14 | 97 | 0.095 | 5 |
| 15 | 51 | 0.050 | 4 |
| Total bits → | | | 97 |
| $R_0$ kbit/s | | | 48.5 |
| Bit rate reduction = 7.5 kbit/s | | | |

TABLE III

KARHUNEN–LOÈVE TRANSFORM ($N = 16$) FOR ONE MALE TALKER $\sigma = 1842$, $R_{PCM} = 56$ kbit/s

| $i$ | $\frac{\sigma_i}{N}$ | $\frac{\sigma_i}{N\sigma}$ | $n_i$ |
|---|---|---|---|
| 0 | 1070 | 0.581 | 8 |
| 1 | 1044 | 0.567 | 8 |
| 2 | 678 | 0.368 | 8 |
| 3 | 587 | 0.319 | 7 |
| 4 | 399 | 0.217 | 7 |
| 5 | 275 | 0.149 | 6 |
| 6 | 182 | 0.099 | 6 |
| 7 | 149 | 0.081 | 5 |
| 8 | 144 | 0.078 | 5 |
| 9 | 140 | 0.076 | 5 |
| 10 | 104 | 0.056 | 5 |
| 11 | 68 | 0.037 | 4 |
| 12 | 50 | 0.027 | 4 |
| 13 | 39 | 0.021 | 3 |
| 14 | 15 | 0.008 | 2 |
| 15 | 10 | 0.006 | 2 |
| Total bits → | | | 85 |
| $R_0$ kbit/s | | | 42.5 |
| Bit rate reduction = 13.5 kbit/s | | | |

TABLE IV

SIGNAL-TO-QUANTIZING-NOISE RATIOS FOR FOURIER, HADAMARD AND KARHUNEN-LOÈVE TRANSFORMS

| | Bit Rate (kbit/s) | Orthogonal Transform $S/N_Q$ (dB) | PCM $S/N_Q$ (dB) | Improvement in $S/N_Q$ (dB) |
|---|---|---|---|---|
| | 56 | 37.9 | 33.3 | 4.6 |
| Fourier | 28 | 17.6 | 12.1 | 5.5 |
| | 14 | 8.9 | 2.9 | 6.0 |
| | 56 | 36.1 | 33.3 | 2.8 |
| Hadamard | 28 | 15.6 | 12.1 | 3.5 |
| | 14 | 5.4 | 2.9 | 2.5 |
| | 56 | 41 | 33.3 | 7.7 |
| Karhunen–Loève | 28 | 21.9 | 12.1 | 9.8 |
| | 14 | 12.6 | 2.9 | 9.7 |

bit rate. This is a greater gain than that achieved by either the Fourier or Hadamard processing of the same signal.

## IV. CONCLUSIONS

As compared with 56 kbit/s logarithmically companded PCM, bit-rate savings of 13.5, 10.0, and 7.5 kbit/s have been achieved for speech signals using discrete Karhunen–Loève, Fourier, and Hadamard orthogonal transformations, respectively. The processing in each case is based on a sample window size of $N = 16$, the samples being taken at intervals of $T = 125\ \mu s$.

The performance of these orthogonal transformations has also been investigated in terms of improvement in signal-to-quantizing noise relative to that accomplished using logarithmically companded PCM at bit rates of 56, 28, and 14 kbit/s. This has demonstrated that the improvement achieved tends to be somewhat independent of bit rate. The improvements in signal to quantizing noise achieved by each form of processing averaged over the three bit-rate values are as follows: Karhunen–Loève 9 dB, Fourier 5 dB, and Hadamard 3 dB.

## REFERENCES


[1] G. S. Robinson and R. L. Granger, "Fast Fourier transform speech compression," *Proc. 1970 IEEE Int. Conf. Communications*, paper 26-5, June 1970.

[2] S. J. Campanella and G. S. Robinson, "A comparison of Walsh and Fourier transformations for application to speech," *Proc. 1971 Symp. Walsh Functions*, Washington, D. C., pp. 199–205.

[3] G. S. Robinson, "Walsh-Hadamard transform speech compression," *Proc. 4th Hawaii Int. Conf. System Sciences*, pp. 411–413, Jan. 1971.

[4] W. B. Davenport and W. L. Root, *Random Signals and Noise*. New York: McGraw-Hill, 1958, pp. 96–101.

[5] A. Papoulis, *Probability, Random Variables and Stochastic Processes*. New York: McGraw-Hill, 1965, pp. 457–461.

[6] S. Watanabe, "Karhunen-Loève expansion and factor analysis," *Trans. Prague Conf. Information Theory*, 1965, pp. 635–660.

[7] H. L. Van Trees, *Detection, Estimation and Modulation Theory, Part I*. New York: Wiley, 1968, p. 178.

[8] A. Habibi and P. A. Wintz, "Image coding by linear transformation and block quantization," *IEEE Trans. Commun. Technol.*, vol. COM-19, pp. 50–62, Feb. 1971.

[9] H. P. Kramer and M. V. Mathews, "A linear coding for transmitting a set of correlated signals," *IRE Trans. Inform. Theory*, vol. IT-2, pp. 41–46, Sept. 1956.

[10] V. I. Kulya, "Experimental investigation of the correlation relations in the speech spectrum and a comparison of some variants of orthogonal vocoder," *Telecommunications*, vol. 18, no. 4, pp. 39–50, 1964.

[11] W. R. Crowther and C. M. Rader, "Efficient coding of vocoder channel signals using linear transformation," *Proc. IEEE* (Lett.), vol. 54, pp. 1594–1595, Nov. 1966.

[12] J. J. Y. Huang and P. M. Schultheiss, "Block quantization of correlated Gaussian random variables," *IEEE Trans. Commun. Syst.*, vol. CS-11, pp. 289–296, Sept. 1963.

[13] R. A. McDonald, "Signal-to-noise and idle channel performance of differential pulse code modulation systems—particular applications to voice signals," *Bell Syst. Tech. J.*, pp. 1123–1151, Sept. 1966.

[14] J. A. Greefkes, "A digitally controlled delta codec for speech transmission," *Proc. 1970 Int. Conf. Communications*, paper 7-5, June 1970.

[15] K. Nitadori, "Linear transformation coding and predictive coding—two methods of digital encoding for continuous sources with discrete parameters," *Electron. Commun. Japan*, vol. 53-A, no. 2, pp. 37–45, 1970.

[16] W. R. Bennett, "Spectra of quantized signals," *Bell Syst. Tech. J.*, vol. 27, pp. 446–472, July 1948.


[*Editors' Note:* Author biographies have been omitted owing to lack of space.]

# 32


*Reprinted from J. Acoust. Soc. Amer.*, **50**(2), 637–650, 655 (1971)

# Speech Analysis and Synthesis by Linear Prediction of the Speech Wave

B. S. Atal and Suzanne L. Hanauer

*Bell Telephone Laboratories, Incorporated, Murray Hill, New Jersey 07974*

We describe a procedure for efficient encoding of the speech wave by representing it in terms of time-varying parameters related to the transfer function of the vocal tract and the characteristics of the excitation. The speech wave, sampled at 10 kHz, is analyzed by predicting the present speech sample as a linear combination of the 12 previous samples. The 12 predictor coefficients are determined by minimizing the mean-squared error between the actual and the predicted values of the speech samples. Fifteen parameters—namely, the 12 predictor coefficients, the pitch period, a binary parameter indicating whether the speech is voiced or unvoiced, and the rms value of the speech samples—are derived by analysis of the speech wave, encoded and transmitted to the synthesizer. The speech wave is synthesized as the output of a linear recursive filter excited by either a sequence of quasiperiodic pulses or a white-noise source. Application of this method for efficient transmission and storage of speech signals as well as procedures for determining other speech characteristics, such as formant frequencies and bandwidths, the spectral envelope, and the autocorrelation function, are discussed.

## INTRODUCTION

Efficient representation of speech signals in terms of a small number of slowly varying parameters is a problem of considerable importance in speech research. Most methods for analyzing speech start by transforming the acoustic data into spectral form by performing a short-time Fourier analysis of the speech wave.[1] Although spectral analysis is a well-known technique for studying signals, its application to speech signals suffers from a number of serious limitations arising from the nonstationary as well as the quasiperiodic properties of the speech wave.[2] As a result, methods based on spectral analysis often do not provide a sufficiently accurate description of speech articulation. We present in this paper a new approach to speech analysis and synthesis in which we represent the speech waveform directly in terms of time-varying parameters related to the transfer function of the vocal tract and the characteristics of the source function.[3–5] By modeling the speech wave itself, rather than its spectrum, we avoid the problems inherent in frequency-domain methods. For instance, the traditional Fourier analysis methods require a relatively long speech segment to provide adequate spectral resolution. As a result, rapidly changing speech events cannot be accurately followed. Furthermore, because of the periodic nature of voiced speech, little information about the spectrum between pitch harmonics is available; consequently, the frequency-domain techniques do not perform satisfactorily for high-pitched voices such as the voices of women and children. Although pitch-synchronous analysis-by-synthesis techniques can provide a partial solution to the above difficulties, such techniques are extremely cumbersome and time consuming even for modern digital computers and are therefore unsuitable for automatic processing of large amounts of speech data.[6,7] In contrast, the techniques presented in this paper are shown to avoid these problems completely.

The speech analysis–synthesis technique described in this paper is applicable to a wide range of research problems in speech production and perception. One of the main objectives of our method is the synthesis of speech which is indistinguishable from normal human speech. Much can be learned about the information-carrying structure of speech by selectively altering the properties of the speech signal. These techniques can thus serve as a tool for modifying the acoustic properties of a given speech signal without degrading the speech quality. Some other potential applications of these techniques are in the areas of efficient storage and transmission of speech, automatic formant and pitch extraction, and speaker and speech recognition.

In the rest of the paper, we describe a parametric model for representing the speech signal in the time

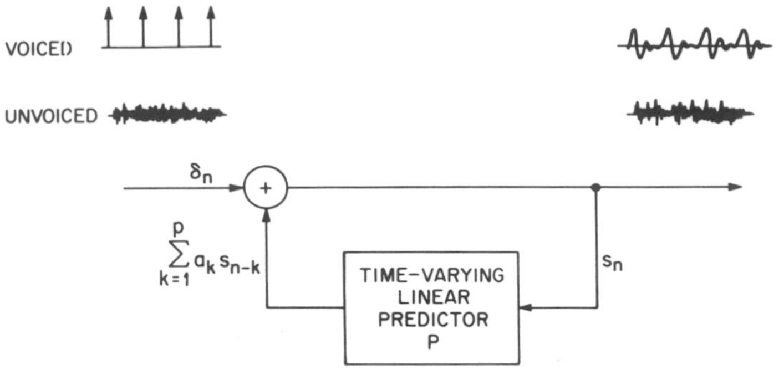


FIG. 1. Block diagram of a functional model of speech production based on the linear prediction representation of the speech wave.

domain; we discuss methods for analyzing the speech wave to obtain these parameters and for synthesizing the speech wave from them. Finally, we discuss applications for efficient coding of speech, estimation of the spectral envelope, formant analysis, and for modifying the acoustic properties of the speech signal.

The paper is organized such that most of the mathematical details are discussed in a set of appendixes. The main body of the paper is nearly complete in itself, and those readers who are not interested in the mathematical or computational aspects may skip the appendixes.

## I. MODEL FOR PARAMETRIC REPRESENTATION OF THE SPEECH WAVE

In modern signal-processing techniques, the procedures for analyzing a signal make use of all the information that can be obtained in advance about the structure of that signal. The first step in signal analysis is thus to make a model of the signal.

Speech sounds are produced as a result of acoustical excitation of the human vocal tract. During the production of voiced sounds, the vocal tract is excited by a series of nearly periodic pulses generated by the vocal cords. In the case of unvoiced sounds, the excitation is provided by air passing turbulently through constrictions in the tract. A simple model of the vocal tract can be made by representing it as a discrete time-varying linear filter. If we assume that the variations with time of the vocal-tract shape can be approximated with sufficient accuracy by a succession of stationary shapes, it is possible to define a transfer function in the complex $z$ domain for the vocal tract. The transfer function of a linear network can always be represented by its poles and zeros. It is well known that for nonnasal voiced speech sounds the transfer function of the vocal tract has no zeros.[8] For these sounds, the vocal tract can therefore be adequately represented by an all-pole (recursive) filter. A representation of the vocal tract for unvoiced and nasal sounds usually includes the antiresonances (zeros) as well as the resonances (poles) of the vocal tract. Since the zeros of the transfer function of the vocal tract for unvoiced and nasal sounds lie within the unit circle in the $z$ plane,[9] each factor in the numerator of the transfer function can be approximated by multiple poles in the denominator of the transfer function.[10] In addition, the location of a pole is considerably more important perceptually than the location of a zero; the zeros in most cases contribute only to the spectral balance. Thus, an explicit representation of the antiresonances by zeros of the linear filter is not necessary. An all-pole model of the vocal tract can approximate the effect of antiresonances on the speech wave in the frequency range of interest to any desired accuracy.

The $z$ transform of the glottal volume flow during a single pitch period can also be assumed to have poles only and no zeros. With this approximation, the $z$ transform of the glottal flow can be represented by

$$U_g(z)=\frac{K_1}{(1-z_az^{-1})(1-z_bz^{-1})}, \tag{1}$$

where $K_1$ is a constant related to the amplitude of the glottal flow and $z_a$, $z_b$ are poles on the real axis inside the unit circle. In most cases, one of the poles is very close to the unit circle. If the radiation of sound from the mouth is approximated as radiation from a simple spherical source, then the ratio between the sound pressure at the microphone and the volume velocity at the lips is represented in the $z$-transform notation as $K_2(1-z^{-1})$, where $K_2$ is a constant related to the amplitude of the volume flow at the lips and the distance from the lips to the microphone.[11] The contribution of the glottal volume flow, together with the radiation, can thus be represented in the transfer function by the factor

$$\frac{K_1K_2(1-z^{-1})}{(1-z_az^{-1})(1-z_bz^{-1})},$$

which, in turn, can be approximated as

$$\frac{K_1K_2}{[1+(1-z_a)z^{-1}](1-z_bz^{-1})}. \tag{2}$$

The error introduced by this approximation is given by

$$-\frac{K_1K_2z^{-2}(1-z_a)}{(1-z_az^{-1})[1+(1-z_a)z^{-1}](1-z_bz^{-1})}.$$

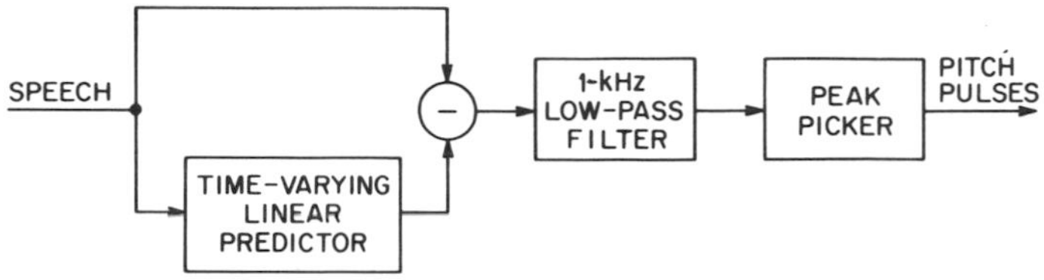


FIG. 2. Block diagram of the pitch pulse detector.

The contribution of this error to the transfer function in the frequency range of interest can be assumed to be small, since $z_a \approx 1$.

One of the important features of our model is that the combined contributions of the glottal flow, the vocal tract, and the radiation are represented by a single recursive filter. The difficult problem of separating the contribution of the source function from that of the vocal tract is thus completely avoided.

This representation of the speech signal is illustrated in sampled-data form in Fig. 1. The vocal-cord excitation for voiced sounds is produced by a pulse generator with adjustable period and amplitude. The noise-like excitation of unvoiced sounds is produced by a white-noise source. The linear predictor $P$, a transversal filter with $p$ delays of one sample interval each, forms a weighted sum of the past $p$ samples at the input of the predictor. The output of the linear filter at the $n$th sampling instant is given by

$$s_n = \sum_{k=1}^{p} a_k s_{n-k} + \delta_n, \tag{3}$$

where the "predictor coefficients" $a_k$ account for the filtering action of the vocal tract, the radiation, and the glottal flow; and $\delta_n$ represents the $n$th sample of the excitation.

The transfer function of the linear filter of Fig. 1 is given by

$$T(z) = 1/(1 - \sum_{k=1}^{p} a_k z^{-k}). \tag{4}$$

The poles of $T(z)$ are the (reciprocal) zeros of the polynomial (in $z^{-1}$) in the denominator on the right side of Eq. 4. The linear filter thus has a total of $p$ poles which are either real or occur in conjugate pairs. Moreover, for the linear filter to be stable, the poles must be inside the unit circle.

The number of coefficients $p$ required to represent any speech segment adequately is determined by the number of resonances and antiresonances of the vocal tract in the frequency range of interest, the nature of the glottal volume flow function, and the radiation. As discussed earlier, two poles are usually adequate to represent the influence of the glottal flow and the radiation on the speech wave. It is shown in Appendix B that, in order to represent the poles of the vocal-tract transfer function adequately, the linear predictor memory must be equal to twice the time required for sound waves to travel from the glottis to the lips (nasal opening for nasal sounds). For example, if the vocal tract is 17 cm in length, the memory of the predictor should be roughly 1 msec in order to represent the poles of transfer function of the vocal tract. The corresponding value of $p$ is then 10 for a sampling interval of 0.1 msec. With the two poles required for the glottal flow and the radiation added, $p$ should be approximately 12. These calculations are meant to provide only a rough estimate of $p$ and will depend to some extent on the speaker as well as on the spoken material. The results based on speech synthesis experiments (see Sec. IV) indicate that, in most cases, a value of $p$ equal to 12 is adequate at a sampling frequency of 10 kHz. $p$ is, naturally, a function of the sampling frequency $f_s$ and is roughly proportional to $f_s$.

The predictor coefficients $a_k$, together with the pitch period, the rms value of the speech samples, and a binary parameter indicating whether the speech is voiced or unvoiced, provide a complete representation of the speech wave over a time interval during which the vocal-tract shape is assumed to be constant. During speech production, of course, the vocal-tract shape changes continuously in time. In most cases, it is sufficient to readjust these parameters periodically, for example, once every 5 or 10 msec.

## II. SPEECH ANALYSIS

### A. Determination of the Predictor Parameters

Going back to Fig. 1, we see that, except for one sample at the beginning of every pitch period, samples of voiced speech are linearly predictable in terms of the past $p$ speech samples. We now use this property of the speech wave to determine the predictor coefficients. Let us define the prediction error $E_n$ as the difference between the speech sample $s_n$ and its predicted value $\hat{s}_n$ given by

$$\hat{s}_n = \sum_{k=1}^{p} a_k s_{n-k}. \tag{5}$$

$E_n$ is then given by

$$E_n = s_n - \hat{s}_n = s_n - \sum_{k=1}^{p} a_k s_{n-k}. \tag{6}$$

We define the mean-squared prediction error $\langle E_n^2 \rangle_{av}$ as the average of $E_n^2$ over all the sampling instances $n$ in the speech segment to be analyzed except those at the

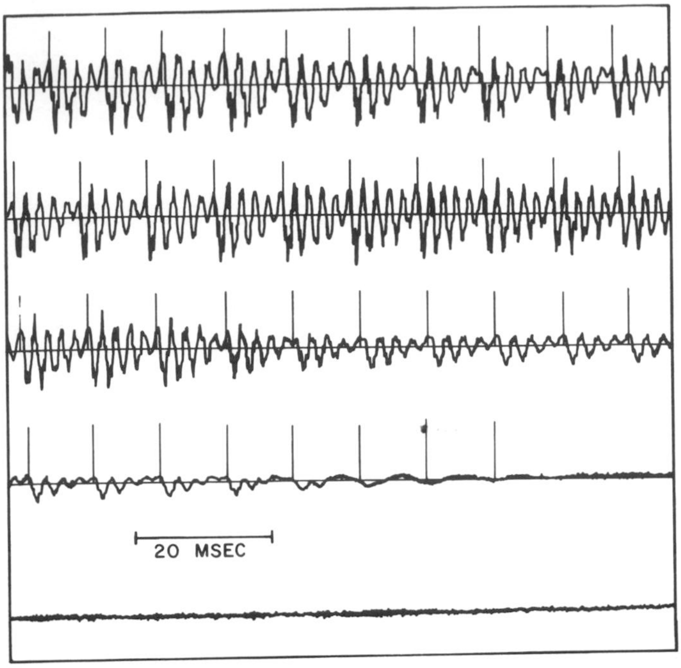


FIG. 3. Waveform of the speech signal together with the positions of the pitch pulses (shown by vertical lines).

beginning of each pitch period, i.e.,

$$\langle E_n^2\rangle_{\text{av}} = \langle (s_n - \sum_{k=1}^{p} a_k s_{n-k})^2\rangle_{\text{av}}. \tag{7}$$

The predictor coefficients $a_k$ of Eq. 3 are chosen so as to minimize the mean-squared prediction error $\langle E_n^2\rangle_{\text{av}}$. The same procedure is used to determine the predictor parameters for unvoiced sounds, too.

The coefficients $a_k$ which minimize the mean-squared prediction error are obtained by setting the partial derivative of $\langle E_n^2\rangle_{\text{av}}$ with respect to each $a_k$ equal to zero. It can then be shown[3] that the coefficients $a_k$ are obtained as solutions of the set of equations

$$\sum_{k=1}^{p} \varphi_{jk} a_k = \varphi_{j0}, \quad j=1, 2, \cdots, p, \tag{8}$$

where

$$\varphi_{jk} = \langle s_{n-j} s_{n-k}\rangle_{\text{av}}. \tag{9}$$

In general, the solution of a set of simultaneous linear equations requires a great deal of computation. However, the set of linear equations given by Eq. 8 is a special one, since the matrix of coefficients is symmetric and positive definite. There are several methods of solving such equations.[12,13] A computationally efficient method of solving Eq. 8 is outlined in Appendix C.

Occasionally, the coefficients $a_k$ obtained by solving Eq. 8 produce poles in the transfer function which are outside the unit circle. This can happen whenever a pole of the transfer function near the unit circle appears outside the unit circle, owing to approximations in the model. The locations of all such poles must be corrected. A simple computational procedure to determine if any pole of the transfer function is outside the unit circle and a method for correcting the predictor coefficients are described in Appendix D.

### B. Pitch Analysis

Although any reliable pitch-analysis method can be used to determine the pitch of the speech signal, we outline here briefly two methods of pitch analysis which are sufficiently reliable and accurate for our purpose.

In the first method,[14] the speech wave is filtered through a 1-kHz low-pass filter and each filtered speech sample is raised to the third power to emphasize the high-amplitude portions of the speech waveform. The duration of the pitch period is obtained by performing a pitch-synchronous correlation analysis of the cubed speech. The voiced–unvoiced decision is based on two factors, the density of zero crossings in the speech wave and the peak value of the correlation function. This method of pitch analysis is described in detail in Ref. 14.

The second method of pitch analysis is based on the linear prediction representation of the speech wave.[15] It follows from Fig. 1 that, except for a sample at the beginning of each pitch period, every sample of the voiced speech waveform can be predicted from the past sample values. Therefore, the positions of individual pitch pulses can be determined by computing the prediction error $E_n$ given by Eq. 6 and then locating the

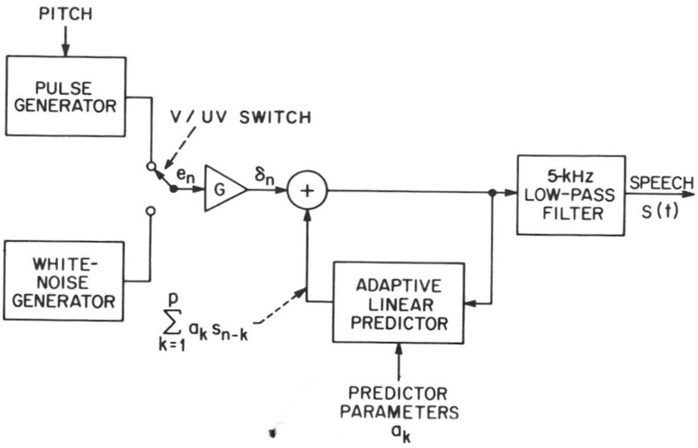


FIG. 4. Block diagram of the speech synthesizer.

samples for which the prediction error is large. The latter function is easily accomplished by a suitable peak-picking procedure. This procedure is illustrated in Fig. 2. In practice, the prediction error was found to be large at the beginning of the pitch periods and a relatively simple peak-picking procedure was found to be effective. The voiced–unvoiced decision is based on the ratio of the mean-squared value of the speech samples to the mean-squared value of the prediction error samples. This ratio is considerably smaller for unvoiced speech sounds than for voiced speech sounds—typically, by a factor of 10. The result of the pitch analysis on a short segment of the speech wave is illustrated in Fig. 3. The positions of the individual pitch pulses, shown by vertical lines, are superimposed on the speech waveform for easy comparison.

## III. SPEECH SYNTHESIS

The speech signal is synthesized by means of the same parametric representation as was used in the analysis. A block diagram of the speech synthesizer is shown in Fig. 4. The control parameters supplied to the synthesizer are the pitch period, a binary voiced–unvoiced parameter, the rms value of the speech samples, and the $p$ predictor coefficients. The pulse generator produces a pulse of unit amplitude at the beginning of each pitch period. The white-noise generator produces uncorrelated uniformly distributed random samples with standard deviation equal to 1 at each sampling instant. The selection between the pulse generator and the white-noise generator is made by the voiced–unvoiced switch. The amplitude of the excitation signal is adjusted by the amplifier $G$. The linearly predicted value $\hat{s}_n$ of the speech signal is combined with the excitation signal $\delta_n$ to form the $n$th sample of the synthesized speech signal. The speech samples are finally low-pass filtered to provide the continuous speech wave $s(t)$.

It may be pointed out here that, although for time-invariant networks the synthesizer of Fig. 4 will be equivalent to a traditional formant synthesizer with variable formant bandwidths, its operation for the time-varying case (which is true in speech synthesis) differs significantly from that of a formant synthesizer. For instance, a formant synthesizer has separate filters for each formant and, thus, a correct labeling of formant frequencies is essential for the proper functioning of a formant synthesizer. This is not necessary for the synthesizer of Fig. 4, since the formants are synthesized together by one recursive filter. Moreover, the amplitude of the pitch pulses as well as the white noise is adjusted to provide the correct rms value of the synthetic speech samples.

The synthesizer control parameters are reset to their new values at the beginning of every pitch period for voiced speech and once every 10 msec for unvoiced speech. If the control parameters are not determined pitch-synchronously in the analysis, new parameters are computed by suitable interpolation of the original parameters to allow pitch-synchronous resetting of the synthesizer. The pitch period and the rms value are interpolated "geometrically" (linear interpolation on a logarithmic scale). In interpolating the predictor coefficients, it is necessary to ensure the stability of the recursive filter in the synthesizer. The stability cannot, in general, be ensured by direct linear interpolation of the predictor parameters. One suitable method is to interpolate the first $p$ samples of the autocorrelation function of the impulse response of the recursive filter. The autocorrelation function has the important advantage of having a one-to-one relationship with the predictor coefficients. Therefore, the predictor coefficients can be recomputed from the autocorrelation function. Moreover, the predictor coefficients derived from the autocorrelation function always result in a stable filter in the synthesizer.[16] The relationship between the predictor coefficients and the autocorrelation function can be derived as follows:

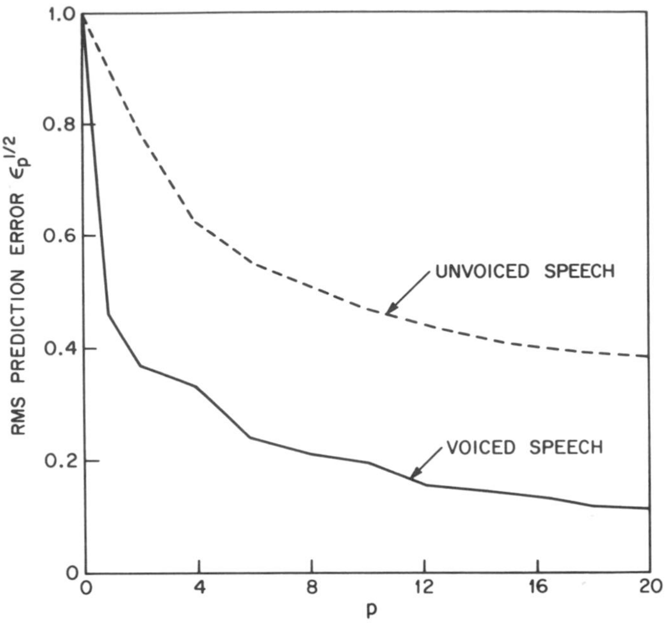


FIG. 5. Variation of the minimum value of the rms prediction error with $p$, the number of predictor coefficients. Solid line shows the curve for voiced speech. Dotted line shows the curve for unvoiced speech.

From Eq. 3, the impulse response of the linear recursive filter of Fig. 1 satisfies the equation

$$s_n = \sum_{k=1}^{p} a_k s_{n-k}, \quad n \geq 1, \tag{10}$$

with the initial conditions $s_0 = 1$ and $s_n = 0$ for $n < 0$. The autocorrelation function of the impulse response is, by definition, given by

$$r_{|i|} = \sum_{n=0}^{\infty} s_n s_{n+|i|}. \tag{11}$$

Let us multiply both sides of Eq. 10 by $s_{n+i}$ and perform a sum over $n$ from 0 to $\infty$. We then obtain

$$r_i = \sum_{k=1}^{p} a_k r_{|i-k|}, \quad i \geq 1, \tag{12}$$

and

$$r_0 = \sum_{k=1}^{p} a_k r_k + 1. \tag{13}$$

Equations 12 and 13 enable us to compute the samples of the autocorrelation function from the predictor coefficients, and the predictor coefficients from the autocorrelation function. A computational procedure for performing the above operations is outlined in Appendix E.

The gain of the amplifier G is adjusted to provide the correct power in the synthesized speech signal. In any speech segment, the amplitude of the $n$th synthesized speech sample $s_n$ can be decomposed into two parts: one part $q_n$ contributed by the memory of the linear predictor carried over from the previous speech segments and the other part $v_n$ contributed by the excitation from the current speech segment. Thus, $s_n = q_n + v_n = q_n + g u_n$, where $g$ is the gain of the amplifier G. Let us assume that $n = 1$ is the first sample and $n = M$ the last sample of the current speech segment. The first part $q_n$ is given by

$$q_n = \sum_{k=1}^{p} a_k q_{n-k}, \quad 1 \leq n \leq M, \tag{14}$$

where $q_0, q_{-1}, \cdots, q_{1-p}$ represent the memory of the predictor carried over from the previous synthesized speech segments. In addition, $u_n$ is given by

$$u_n = \sum_{k=1}^{p} a_k u_{n-k} + e_n, \quad 1 \leq n \leq M, \tag{15}$$

where $u_n = 0$ for nonpositive values of $n$, and $e_n$ is the $n$th sample at the output of the voiced–unvoiced switch as shown in Fig. 4. Let $P_s$ be the mean-squared value of the speech samples. Then $P_s$ is given by

$$P_s = \frac{1}{M} \sum_{n=1}^{M} (q_n + g u_n)^2 = \overline{(q_n + g u_n)^2}. \tag{16}$$

On further rearrangement of terms, Eq. 16 is rewritten as

$$g^2 \overline{u_n^2} + 2g \overline{q_n u_n} + \overline{q_n^2} - P_s = 0. \tag{17}$$

Equation 17 is solved for $g$ such that $g$ is real and non-

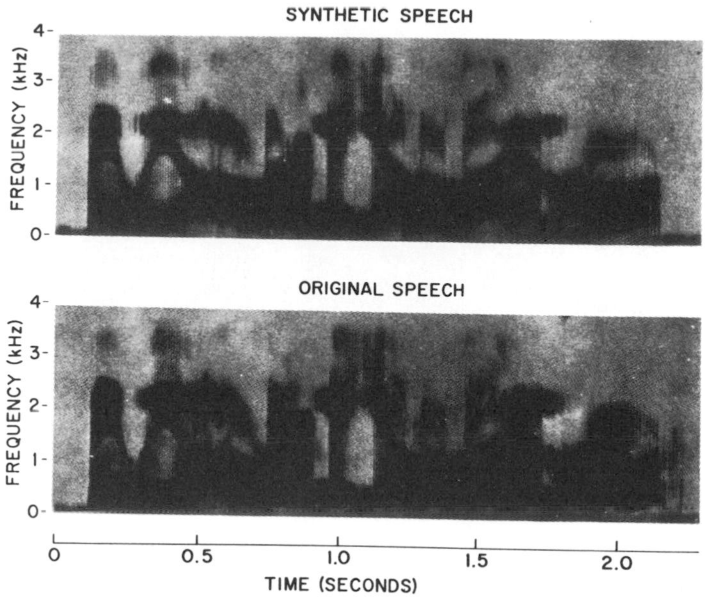


FIG. 6. Comparison of wide-band sound spectrograms for synthetic and original speech signals for the utterance "May we all learn a yellow lion roar," spoken by a male speaker: (a) synthetic speech, and (b) original speech.

negative. In case such a solution does not exist, $g$ is set to zero. The $n$th sample of the synthesized wave is finally obtained by adding $q_n$ to $gu_n$.

## IV. COMPUTER SIMULATION OF THE ANALYSIS–SYNTHESIS SYSTEM

In order to assess the subjective quality of the synthesized speech, the speech analysis and synthesis system described above was simulated on a digital computer. The speech wave was first low-pass filtered to 5 kHz and then sampled at a frequency of 10 kHz. The analysis segment was set equal to a pitch period for voiced speech and equal to 10 msec for unvoiced speech. The various parameters were then determined for each analysis segment according to the procedure described in Sec. II. These parameters were finally used to control the speech synthesizer shown in Fig. 4.

The optimum value for the number of predictor parameters $p$ was determined as follows: The speech wave was synthesized for various values of $p$ between 2 and 18. Informal listening tests revealed no significant differences between synthetic speech samples for $p$ larger than 12. There was slight degradation in speech quality at $p$ equal to 8. However, even for $p$ as low as 2, the synthetic speech was intelligible although poor in quality. The influence of decreasing $p$ to values less than 10 was most noticeable on nasal consonants. Furthermore, the effect of decreasing $p$ was less noticeable on female voices than on male voices. This could be expected in view of the fact that the length of the vocal tract for female speakers is generally shorter than for male speakers and that the nasal tract is slightly longer than the oral tract. From these results, it was concluded that a value of $p$ equal to 12 was required to provide an adequate representation of the speech signal. It may be worthwhile at this point to compare these results with the objective results based on an examination of the variation of the prediction error as a function of $p$. In Fig. 5, we have plotted the minimum value of the rms prediction error as a function of several values of $p$. The speech power in each case was normalized to unity. The results are presented separately for voiced and unvoiced speech. As can be seen in the figure, the prediction error curve is relatively flat for values of $p$ greater than 12 for voiced speech and for $p$ greater than 6 for unvoiced speech. These results suggest again that $p$ equal to 12 is adequate for voiced speech. For unvoiced speech, a lower value of $p$, e.g., $p$ equal to 6, should be adequate. For those readers who wish to listen to the quality of synthesized speech at various values of $p$, a recording accompanies this article. Appendix A gives the contents of the record. The reader should listen at this point to the first section of the record.

In informal listening tests, the quality of the synthetic speech was found to be very close to that of the original speech for a wide range of speakers and spoken material. No significant differences were observed between the synthetic speech samples of male and female speakers. The second section of the record includes examples of synthesized speech for several utterances of different speakers. In each case, $p$ was set to equal to 12. The spectrograms of the synthetic and the original speech for two of these utterances are compared in Figs. 6 and 7. As can be seen, the spectrogram of the synthetic speech closely resembles that of the original speech.

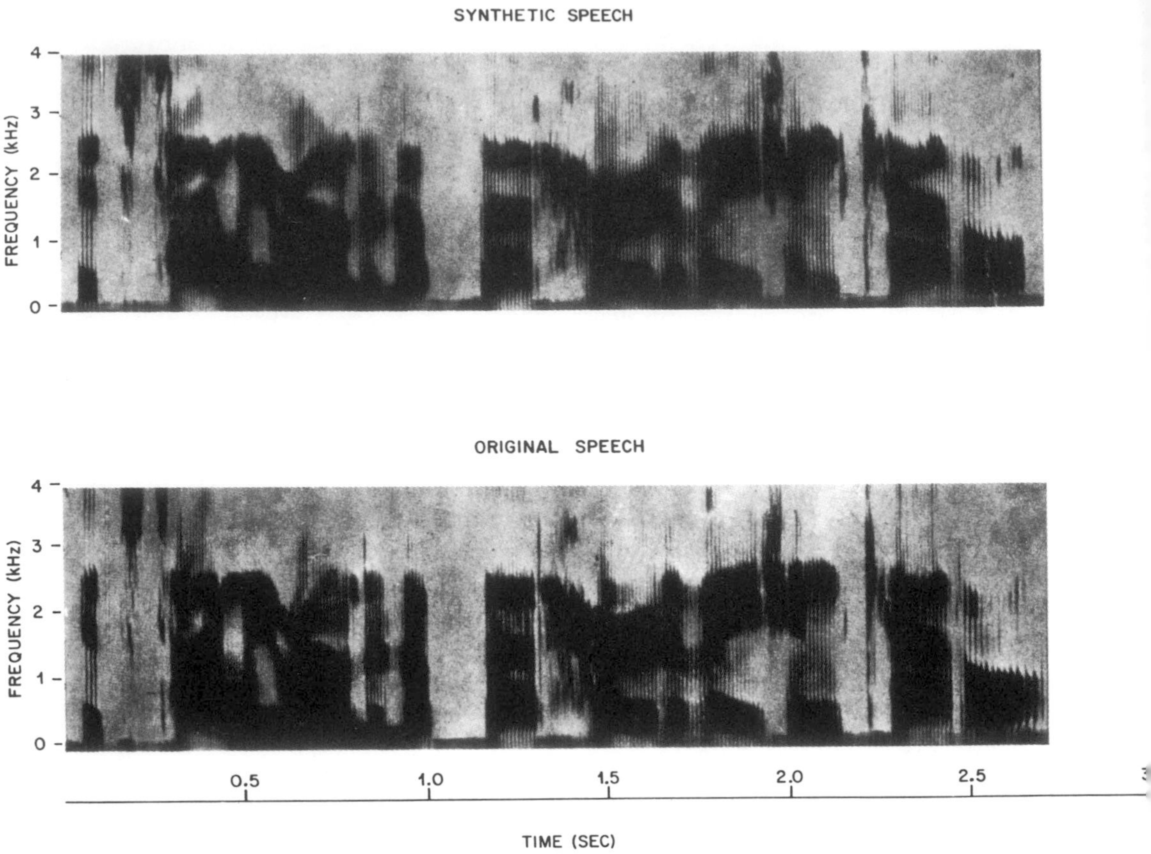


FIG. 7. Comparison of wide-band sound spectrograms for synthetic and original speech signals for the utterance "It's time we rounded up that herd of Asian cattle," spoken by a male speaker: (a) synthetic speech, and (b) original speech.

## V. APPLICATIONS

### A. Digital Storage and Transmission of Speech

Methods for encoding speech at data rates considerably smaller than those needed for PCM encoding are important in many practical applications. For example, automatic answerback services can be practical if a sufficiently large vocabulary of words and phrases can be stored economically in a digital computer. Efficient speech coding methods can reduce, by a factor of 30 or more, the space needed for storing the vocabulary. We discuss in this section several procedures for efficient coding of the synthesizer control information.

The synthesizer control information includes 15 parameters for every analysis interval, i.e., the twelve predictor coefficients, the pitch period, the voiced–unvoiced parameter, and the rms value. The methods for proper encoding of this information, except the predictor coefficients, are relatively well understood.[17] On the other hand, the procedure for encoding the predictor coefficients must include provision for ensuring the stability of the linear filter in the synthesizer. In general, to ensure stability, relatively high accuracy (about 8–10 bits per coefficient) is required if the predictor coefficients are quantized directly. Moreover, the predictor coefficients are samples of the inverse Fourier transform of the reciprocal of the transfer function. The reciprocal of the transfer function has zeros precisely where the transfer function has poles. Therefore, small errors in the predictor coefficients often can result in large errors in the poles. The direct quantization of the predictor coefficients is thus not efficient. One suitable method is to convert the 12 predictor coefficients to another equivalent set of parameters which possess well-defined constraints for achieving the desired stability. For example, the poles of the linear filter can be computed from the predictor coefficients. For stability of the filter, it is sufficient that the poles be inside the unit circle. The stability is therefore easily ensured by quantizing the frequencies and the bandwidths of the poles. The poles of the transfer function are by definition the

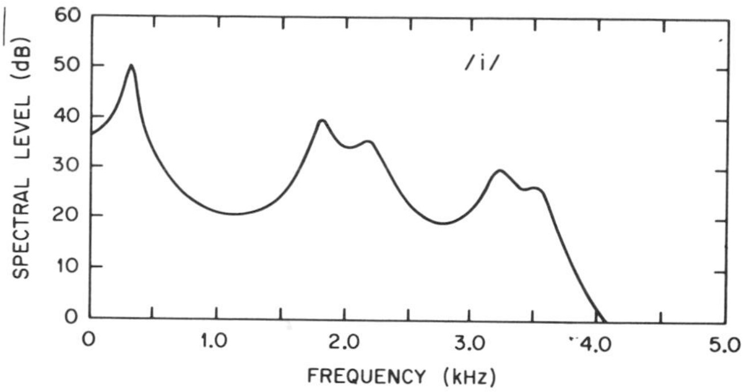


Fig. 8. Spectral envelope for the vowel /i/ in "we," spoken by a male speaker ($F_0 = 120$ Hz).

roots of the polynomial equation

$$\sum_{k=1}^{p} a_k z^{-k} = 1, \tag{18}$$

where, as before, $a_k$ are the predictor coefficients. Table I shows the precision with which each of the parameters is quantized. It was found that the frequencies and the bandwidths of the poles can be quantized within 60 bits without producing any perceptible effect on the synthesized speech. Adding this value to the bits needed for the pitch (6 bits), the rms value (5 bits), and the voiced–unvoiced parameter (1 bit), one arrives at a value of 72 bits (60+6+5+1) for each frame of analyzed data. The data rate in bits/sec is obtained by multiplying the number of bits used to encode each frame of data by the number of frames of data stored or transmitted per second. Thus, a bit rate of 7200 bits/sec is achieved if the parameters are sampled at a rate of 100/sec. The bit rate is lowered to 2400 bits/sec at a sampling rate of 33/sec.

At this point, the reader can listen to recorded examples of synthesized speech encoded at three different data rates, namely, 7200, 4800, and 2400 bits/sec, respectively, in the third section of the enclosed record.

The quantizing of the frequencies and the bandwidths of the poles is not the only method of encoding the predictor coefficients. For example, it can be shown (see Appendix F) that a transfer function with $p$ poles is always realizable as the transfer function of an acoustic tube consisting of $p$ cylindrical sections of equal length

Table I. Quantization of synthesizer control information.

| Parameter | Number of levels | Bits |
|---|---|---|
| Pitch | 64 | 6 |
| $V/UV$ | 2 | 1 |
| rms | 32 | 5 |
| Frequencies and bandwidths of the poles | | 60 |
| | Total | 72 |

with the last section terminated by a unit acoustic resistance. Moreover, the poles are always inside the unit circle if the cross-sectional area of each cylindrical section is positive. Thus, the stability of the synthesizer filter is easily achieved by quantizing the areas of the sections or any other suitable function of the areas.

No significant difference in speech quality was observed for the different quantizing methods outlined above at various bit rates above 2400 bits/sec. It is quite possible that at very low bit rates these different methods of coding may show appreciable differences. An example of speech synthesized using area quantization is presented in the fourth section of the record.

The data rates discussed in this paper are suitable for speech-transmission applications where large buffer storage is to be avoided. The efficiency of speech coding naturally can vary considerably from one application to another. For example, it has been assumed so far that the speech signal is analyzed at uniform time intervals. However, it may be more efficient to vary the analysis interval so that it is short during fast articulatory transitions and long during steady-state segments. Furthermore, in applications such as disk storage of voice messages, additional savings can be realized by choosing the quantization levels for each parameter around its mean value determined in advance over short time intervals. The mean value itself can be quantized separately.

### B. Separation of Spectral Envelope and Fine Structure

It is often desirable to separate the envelope of the speech spectrum from its fine structure.[18] The representation of the speech signal shown in Fig. 1 is very suitable for achieving this decomposition. In this representation, the fine structure of the spectrum is contributed by the source while the envelope is contributed by the linear filter. Thus, the two are easily separated.[19] The spectral envelope is the power spectrum of the impulse response of the linear filter. In mathematical notation, the relationship between the spectral envelope $G(f)$ at the frequency $f$ and the predictor coefficients is expressed by

$$G(f) = 1 / \left| 1 - \sum_{k=1}^{p} a_k e^{-2\pi j f k / f_s} \right|^2, \tag{19}$$

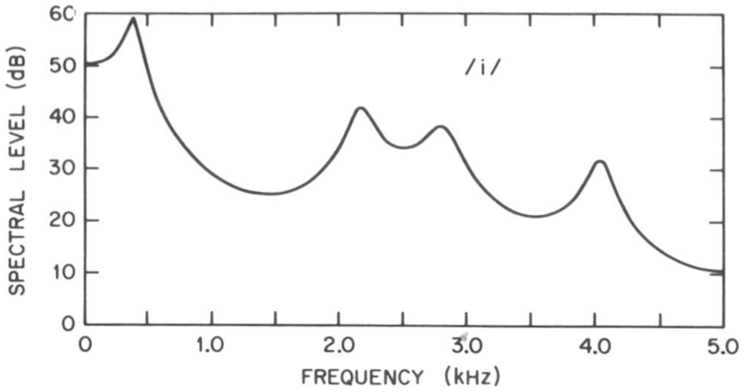


FIG. 9. Spectral envelope for the vowel /i/ in "we," spoken by a female speaker ($F_0$=200 Hz).

where $a_k$, as before, are the predictor coefficients and $f_s$ is the sampling frequency. Two examples of the spectral envelope obtained in the above manner for the vowel /i/ belonging to the word "we" in the utterance "May we all learn a yellow lion roar" spoken by a male and a female speaker are illustrated in Figs. 8 and 9, respectively. We would like to add here that a spectral section obtained on a sound spectrograph failed to separate the third formant from the second formant for the female speaker both in the wide-band and the narrow-band analysis. The spectral section showed one broad peak for the two formants. On the other hand, the spectral envelope of Fig. 9 shows the two formants without any ambiguity. Of course, it is difficult to evaluate the accuracy of this method from results based on real speech alone. Results with synthetic speech, where the spectral envelope is known precisely, indicate that the spectral envelope is accurately determined over a wide range of pitch values (from 50 to 300 Hz).

It also follows from Eq. 19 that, although the Fourier transform of $G(f)$ is not time limited, the Fourier transform of $1/G(f)$ is time limited to $2p/f_s$ sec. Thus, spectral samples of $G(f)$, spaced $f_s/2p$ Hz apart, are sufficient for reconstruction of the spectral envelope. For $p=12$ and $f_s=10$ kHz, this means that a spacing of roughly 400 Hz between spectral samples is adequate.

In some applications, it may be desired to compute the Fourier transform of $G(f)$, namely, the autocorrelation function. The autocorrelation function can be determined directly from the predictor coefficients without computing $G(f)$. The relationship between the predictor coefficients and the autocorrelation function is given in Eqs. 12 and 13, and a computational method for performing these operations is outlined in Appendix E.

### C. Formant Analysis

The objective of formant analysis is to determine the complex natural frequencies of the vocal tract as they change during speech production. If the vocal-tract configuration were known, these natural frequencies could be computed. However, the speech signal is influenced both by the properties of the source and by the vocal tract. For example, if the source spectrum has a zero close to one of the natural frequencies of the vocal tract, it will be extremely difficult, if not impossible, to determine the frequency or the bandwidth of that particular formant. A side-branch element such as the nasal cavity creates a similar problem. In determining formant frequencies and bandwidths from the speech signal, one can at best hope to obtain such information which is not obscured or lost owing to the influence of the source.

Present methods of formant analysis usually start by transforming the speech signal into a short-time Fourier spectrum, and consequently suffer from many additional problems which are inherent in short-time Fourier transform techniques.[5,6,20,21] Such problems, of course, can be completely avoided by determining the formant frequencies and bandwidths directly from the speech wave.[2]

In the representation of the speech wave shown in Fig. 1, the linear filter represents the combined contributions of the vocal tract and the source to the spectral envelope. Thus, the poles of the transfer function of the filter include the poles of the vocal tract as well as the source. So far, we have made no attempt to separate these two contributions. For formant analysis, however, it is necessary that the poles of the vocal tract be separated out from the transfer function. In general, it is our experience that the poles contributed by the source either fall on the real axis in the unit circle or produce a relatively small peak in the spectral envelope. The magnitude of the spectral peak produced by a pole can easily be computed and compared with a threshold to determine whether a pole of the transfer function is indeed a natural frequency of the vocal tract. This is accomplished as follows:

From Eq. 4, the poles of the transfer function are the roots of the polynomial equation

$$\sum_{k=1}^{p} a_k z^{-k} = 1. \tag{20}$$

Let there be $n$ complex conjugate pairs of roots $z_1, z_1^*$; $z_2, z_2^*$; $\cdots$; $z_n, z_n^*$. The transfer function due to these

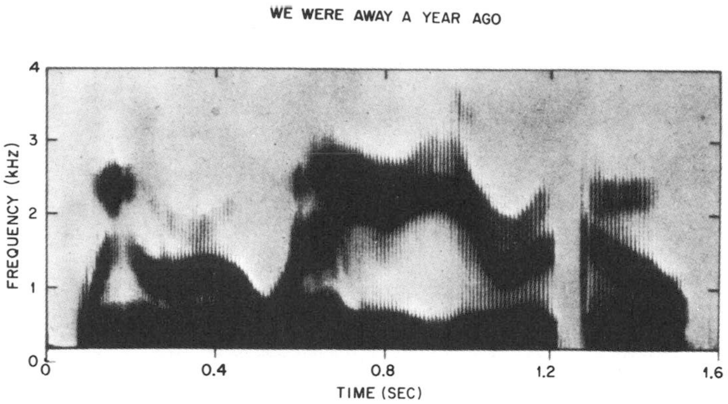


(a)

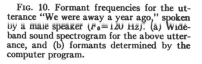

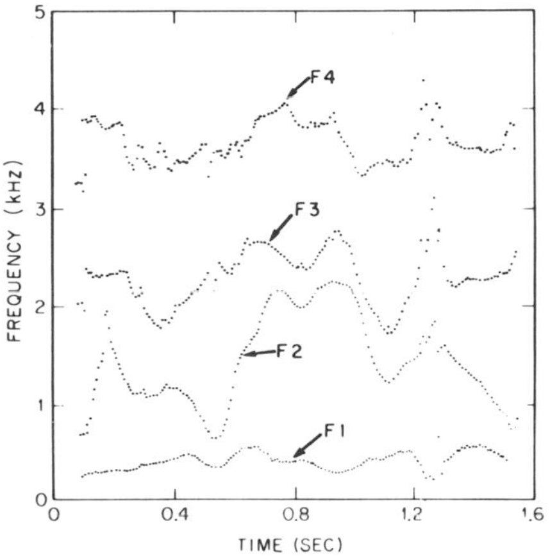


(b)

FIG. 10. Formant frequencies for the utterance "We were away a year ago," spoken by a male speaker ($F_0=120$ Hz). (a) Wide-band sound spectrogram for the above utterance, and (b) formants determined by the computer program.

roots is given by

$$V(z)=\prod_{i=1}^{n}(1-z_i)(1-z_i^*)/\prod_{i=1}^{n}(z-z_i)(z-z_i^*),\quad (21)$$

where the additional factors in the numerator set the transfer function at dc ($z=1$) equal to 1. The spectral peak produced by the $k$th complex conjugate pole pair is given by

$$A_k=\left|\frac{(1-z_k)(1-z_k^*)}{(z-z_k)(z-z_k^*)}\right|^2,\quad (22)$$

where $z=\exp(2\pi jf_kT)$, $z_k=|z_k|\exp(2\pi jf_kT)$, and $T$ is the sampling interval. The threshold value of $A_k$ was set equal to 1.7. Finally, the formant frequency $F_k$ and the bandwidth (two-sided) $B_k$ are related to the $z$-plane root $z_k$ by

$$F_k=(1/2\pi T)\ \mathrm{Im}(\ln z_k),\quad (23)$$

and

$$B_k=(1/\pi T)\ \mathrm{Re}\left(\frac{1}{\ln z_k}\right).\quad (24)$$

Examples of the formant frequencies determined according to the above procedure are illustrated in Figs. 10–12. Each figure consists of (a) a wide-band sound spectrogram of the utterance, and (b) formant data as determined by the above method. The results are presented for three different utterances. The first utterance, "We were away a year ago," was spoken by a male speaker (average fundamental frequency $F_0=120$ Hz).

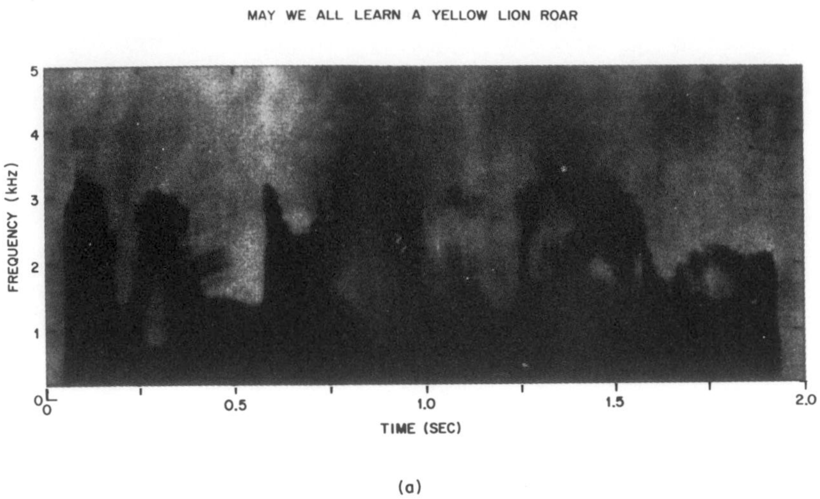


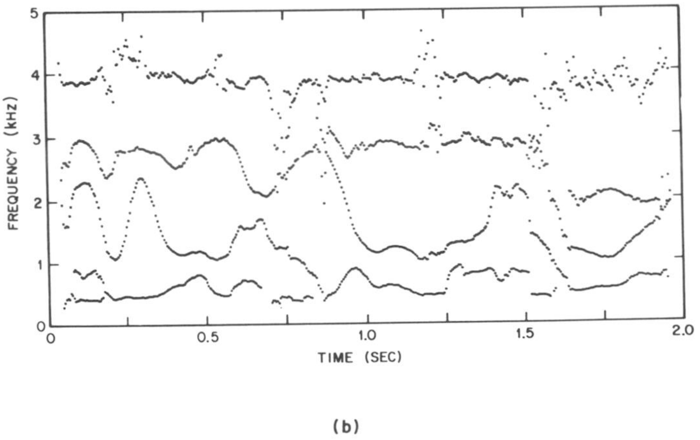


FIG. 11. Formant frequencies for the utterance "May we all learn a yellow lion roar," spoken by a female speaker ($F_0=200$ Hz). (a) Wide-band sound spectrogram for the above utterance, and (b) formants determined by the computer program.

The second utterance, "May we all learn a yellow lion roar," was spoken by a female speaker ($F_0=200$ Hz). The third utterance, "Why do I owe you a letter?" was spoken by a male speaker ($F_0=125$ Hz). Each point in these plots represents the results from a single frame of the speech signal which was equal to a pitch period in Figs. 10 and 11 and equal to 10 msec in Fig. 12. No smoothing of the formant data over adjacent frames was done.

TABLE II. Factor by which each parameter was scaled for simulating a female voice from parameters derived from a male voice.

| Parameter | Scaling factor |
|---|---|
| Pitch period $T$ | 0.58 |
| Formant frequencies $F_i$ | 1.14 |
| Formant bandwidths $B_i$ | $2-F_i/5000$ |

Again, in order to obtain a better estimate of the accuracy of this method of formant analysis, speech was synthesized with a known formant structure. The correspondence between the actual formant frequencies and bandwidths and the computed ones was found to be extremely close.

### D. Re-forming the Speech Signals

The ability to modify the acoustical characteristics of a speech signal without degrading its quality is important for a wide variety of applications. For example, information regarding the relative importance of various acoustic variables in speech perception can be obtained by listening to speech in which some particular

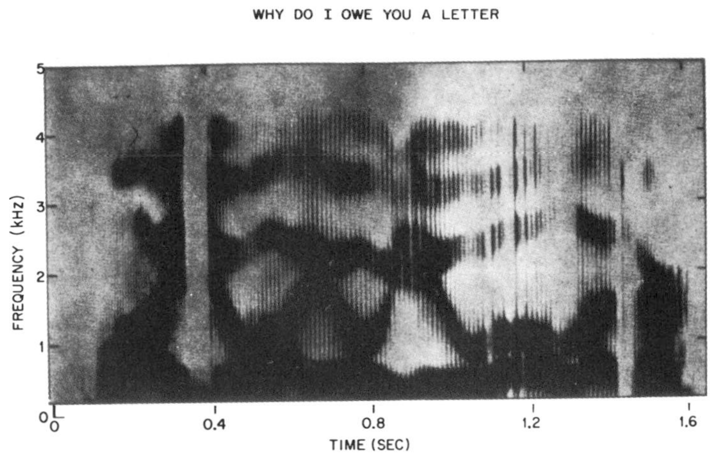


(a)

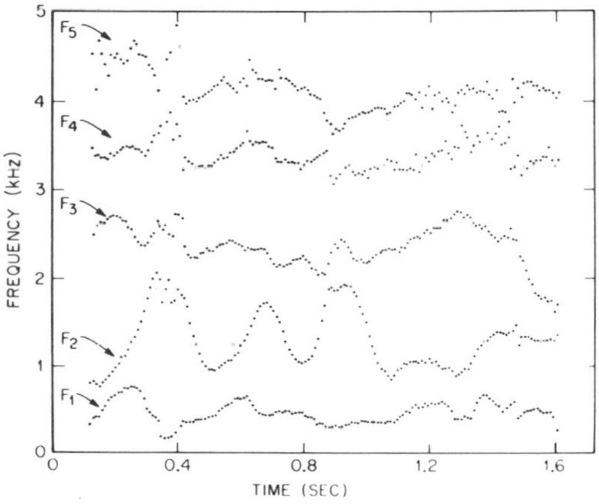


(b)

FIG. 12. Formant frequencies for the utterance "Why do I owe you a letter?" spoken by a male speaker ($F_0=125$ Hz). (a) Wide-band sound spectrogram for the above utterance, and (b) formants determined by the computer program.

acoustic variables have been altered in a controlled manner. The speech analysis and synthesis techniques described in this paper can be used as a flexible and convenient method for conducting such speech-perception experiments. We would like to point out here that the synthesis procedure allows independent control of such speech characteristics as spectral envelope, relative durations, pitch, and intensity. Thus, the speaking rate of a given speech signal may be altered, e.g., for producing fast speech for blind persons or for producing slow speech for learning foreign languages. Or, in an application such as the recovery of "helium speech," the frequencies of the spectral envelope can be scaled, leaving the fundamental frequency unchanged. Moreover, in synthesizing sentence-length utterances from stored data about individual words, the method can be used to reshape the intonation and stress contours so that the speech sounds natural.

Examples of speech in which selected acoustical characteristics have been altered are presented in the fifth section of the enclosed record. First, the listener can hear the utterance at the normal speaking rate. Next, the speaking rate is increased by a factor of 1.5. As the third item, the same utterance with the speaking rate reduced by a factor of 1.5 is presented. Finally, an example of a speech signal in which the pitch, the formant frequencies, and their bandwidths were changed from their original values, obtained from a male voice, to

TABLE III. Computation times needed to perform various operations discussed in the paper on the GE 635 ($p=10$, $f_s=10$ kHz).

| Operation | Computation time |
|---|---|
| Predictor coefficients from speech samples (No. of samples=100) | 75 msec/frame |
| Spectral envelope (500 spectral samples) from predictor coefficients | 250 msec/frame |
| Formant frequencies and bandwidths from predictor coefficients | 60 msec/frame |
| $p$ samples of autocorrelation function from predictor coefficients | 10 msec/frame |
| Speech from predictor coefficients | 8 times real time |
| Pitch analysis | 10 times real time |

simulate a "female" voice is presented. The factor by which each parameter was changed from its original value is shown in Table II.

## VI. COMPUTATIONAL EFFICIENCY

The computation times needed to perform several of the operations described in this paper are summarized in Table III. The programs were run on a GE 635 computer having a cycle time of 1 μsec. As can be seen, this method of speech analysis and synthesis is computationally efficient. In fact, the techniques are about five to 10 times faster than the ones needed to perform equivalent operations by fast-Fourier-transform methods. For instance, both the formant frequencies and their bandwidths are determined in 135 msec for each frame of the speech wave 10 msec long. Assuming that the formants are analyzed once every 10 msec, the program will run in about 13 times real time; by comparison, fast-Fourier-transform techniques need about 100 times real time. Even for computing the spectral envelope, the method based on predictor coefficients is at least three times faster than the fast-Fourier-transform methods. The complete analysis and synthesis procedure was found to run in approximately 25 times real time. Real-time operation could easily be achieved by using special hardware to perform some of the functions.

## VII. CONCLUSIONS

We have presented a method for automatic analysis and synthesis of speech signals by representing them in terms of time-varying parameters related to the transfer function of the vocal tract and the characteristics of the excitation. An important property of the speech wave, namely, its linear predictability, forms the basis of both the analysis and synthesis procedures. Unlike past speech analysis methods based on Fourier analysis, the method described here derives the speech parameters from a direct analysis of the speech wave. Consequently, various problems encountered when Fourier analysis is applied to nonstationary and quasiperiodic signals like speech are avoided. One of the main advantages of this method is that the analysis procedure requires only a short segment of the speech wave to yield accurate results. This method is therefore very suitable for following rapidly changing speech events. It is also suitable for analyzing the speech of speakers with high-pitched voices, such as women or children. As an additional advantage, the analyzed parameters are rigorously related to other well-known speech characteristics. Thus, by first representing the speech signal in terms of the predictor coefficients, other speech characteristics can be determined as desired without much additional computation.

The speech signal is synthesized by a single recursive filter. The synthesizer, thus, does not require any information about the individual formants and the formants need not be determined explicitly during analysis. Moreover, the synthesizer makes use of the formant bandwidths of real speech, in contrast to formant synthesizers, which use fixed bandwidths for each formant. Informal listening tests show very little or no perceptible degradation in the quality of the synthesized speech. These results suggest that the analyzed parameters retain all the perceptually important features of the speech signal. Furthermore, the various parameters used for the synthesis can be encoded efficiently. It was found possible to reduce the data rate to approximately 2400 bits/sec without producing significant degradation in the speech quality. The above bit rate is smaller by a factor of about 30 than that for direct PCM encoding of the speech waveform. The latter bit rate is approximately 70 000 bits (70 000 bits=7 bits/sample×10 000 samples/sec).

In addition to providing an efficient and accurate description of the speech signal, the method is computationally very fast. The entire analysis and synthesis procedure runs at about 25 times real time on a GE 635 digital computer. The method is thus well suited for analyzing large amounts of speech data automatically on the computer.

[*Editors' Note:* Material has been omitted at this point.]

[1] J. L. Flanagan, *Speech Analysis Synthesis and Perception* (Academic, New York, 1965), p. 119.
[2] E. N. Pinson, "Pitch-Synchronous Time-Domain Estimation of Formant Frequencies and Bandwidths," J. Acoust. Soc. Amer. **35**, 1264–1273 (1963).
[3] B. S. Atal and M. R. Schroeder, "Adaptive Predictive Coding of Speech Signals," Bell System Tech. J. **49**, 1973–1986 (1970).
[4] B. S. Atal, "Speech Analysis and Synthesis by Linear Prediction of the Speech Wave," J. Acoust. Soc. Amer. **47**, 65(A) (1970).
[5] B. S. Atal, "Characterization of Speech Signals by Linear Prediction of the Speech Wave," Proc. IEEE Symp. on Feature Extraction and Selection in Pattern Recognition, Argonne, Ill. (Oct. 1970), pp. 202–209.
[6] M. V. Mathews, J. E. Miller, and E. E. David, Jr., "Pitch Synchronous Analysis of Voiced Sounds," J. Acoust. Soc. Amer. **33**, 179–186 (1961).
[7] C. G. Bell, H. Fujisaki, J. M. Heinz, K. N. Stevens, and A. S. House, "Reduction of Speech Spectra by Analysis-by-Synthesis Techniques," J. Acoust. Soc. Amer. **33**, 1725–1736 (1961).
[8] G. Fant, *Acoustic Theory of Speech Production* (Mouton, The Hague, 1960), p. 42.
[9] B. S. Atal, "Sound Transmission in the Vocal Tract with Applications to Speech Analysis and Synthesis," Proc. Int. Congr. Acoust., 7th, Budapest, Hungary (Aug. 1971).
[10] Each factor of the form $(1-az^{-1})$ can be approximated by $[1/(1+az^{-1}+a^2z^{-2}+\cdots)]$ if $|a|<1$, which is the case if the zeros are inside the unit circle.
[11] Ref. 1, p. 33.
[12] C. E. Fröberg, *Introduction to Numerical Analysis* (Addison-Wesley, Reading, Mass., 1969), 2nd ed., pp. 81–101.
[13] J. P. Ellington and H. McCallion, "The Determination of Control System Characteristics from a Transient Response," Proc. IEE **105**, Part C, 370–373 (1958).
[14] B. S. Atal, "Automatic Speaker Recognition Based on Pitch Contours," PhD thesis, Polytech. Inst. Brooklyn (1968).
[15] B. S. Atal, "Pitch-Period Analysis by Inverse Filtering" (to be published).
[16] U. Grenander and G. Szegö, *Toeplitz Forms and Their Applications* (Univ. California Press, Berkeley, 1958), p. 40.
[17] L. G. Stead and R. C. Weston, "Sampling and Quantizing the Parameters of a Formant-Tracking Vocoder System," Proc. Speech Commun. Seminar, R.I.T., Stockholm (29 Aug.–1 Sept. 1962).
[18] M. R. Schroeder, "Vocoders: Analysis and Synthesis of Speech," Proc. IEEE **54**, 720–734 (1966).
[19] The problem of separating the spectral envelope from the fine structure of the speech spectrum should be distinguished from the problem of separating the influence of the source from the speech spectrum. The latter problem is far more difficult and is discussed partially in the next subsection.
[20] R. W. Schafer and L. R. Rabiner, "System for Automatic Formant Analysis of Voiced Speech," J. Acoust. Soc. Amer. **47**, 634–648 (1970).
[21] J. P. Olive, "Automatic Formant Tracking by a Newton–Raphson Technique," J. Acoust. Soc. Amer. **50**, 661–670 (1971).
[B1] I. Malecki, *Physical Foundations of Technical Acoustics*, English transl. by I. Bellert (Pergamon, Oxford, England, 1969), p. 475.
[C1] D. K. Faddeev and V. N. Faddeeva, *Computational Methods of Linear Algebra*, English transl. by R. C. Williams (W. H. Freeman, San Francisco, 1963), pp. 144 147.
[D1] Ref. 16, pp. 40–41. See also L. Ya. Geronimus, *Orthogonal Polynomials* (Consultants Bureau, New York, 1961), p. 156.
[D2] Ref. 12, pp. 21–28.

# 33



Reprinted from *Proc. IEEE,* **56**(2), 176–186 (1968)

# The Theoretical Analysis of Data Compression Systems

LEE D. DAVISSON, MEMBER, IEEE

***Abstract*—The concept of reducing the required transmission rate for a given system through prediction, interpolation, or other such techniques loosely labeled as "data compression" is now well known. The problems in analyzing such systems by theoretical means are formidable in even the simplest situations due to the inherent nonlinear nature of the operations performed. This paper discusses these difficulties, presents some approximate and exact solutions, and suggests areas where further work is needed.**

## I. Introduction

THE characterization "data compression" has been loosely used to describe any method of data transfer which decreases the amount of transmission energy required for messages from a given source for a given received data quality relative to some norm. Usually the source is incompletely described (who knows the probability distribution in a space experiment performed for the first time?) and possibly nonstationary, one result of which is that the compression system is seldom optimal in any sense, although it may be "good." Synonyms are occasionally used (which may tend to be more restrictive in meaning) such as "redundancy reduction," "bandwidth reduction," and, more rarely in this context at least, "source encoding." The methods used can vary from sending periodically a few data parameters[1]–[3] such as sample mean, variance, etc. (so-called "entropy reducing transformations," from which the original source signal can not be reconstructed), to heuristic coding methods whereby "good" codes are constructed for the generated data (from which the source signal can be reconstructed subject to some error fidelity criterion). This paper will concentrate on the latter, essentially digital, techniques. Certain of these can be further classified as special methods designed for a specific data source, e.g., voice and TV systems (as described in the literature[4]–[17]) with little generality or use elsewhere. These methods will not be mentioned specifically, but will be considered to be possible applications of the ensuing theory.

For a given source and a given error fidelity criterion, the minimum possible transmission rate is found in the rate distortion function of Shannon.[18]–[19] Data compression techniques are generally suboptimal in that this rate is almost always exceeded. This is true, among other reasons, because the methods are proposed for those situations where the knowledge of the source characteristics is limited at best, where the optimum system is hopelessly complex (requiring, perhaps, a code book of mammoth dimensions), or where the optimum is theoretically intractable. One only hopes to make a significant improvement on the average over some standard technique and, in doing so, hopefully approach the optimum. The particular coding idea used for a given source may vary considerably in complexity and ingenuity. It may be "fixed" in nature or "adaptive" (a somewhat overused word). In the former case, the compression algorithm is of a relatively simple nature and does not change with time as the source properties change. An example of this is where the data are fitted or approximated to within some maximum error magnitude by a series of

Manuscript received December 22, 1967. The work reported here was supported by NASA Grant NGR-31-001-068. *This invited paper is one of a series planned on topics of general interest.—The Editor.*

The author is with the School of Engineering and Applied Science, Princeton University, Princeton, N. J.

polynomial segments, usually straight lines (sometimes called a "fan" method or interpolator). The line end points and lengths are sent in place of the data, resulting in many cases in a net transmission rate reduction as compared to sending periodic data sample values. No allowance is made, however, for any curve shape other than that which is a priori determined. An *adaptive* system of this class, on the other hand, would typically allow the curve shape to vary depending on the data encountered by optimizing, over the immediate past, some sample cost function. The border line between fixed and adaptive systems is somewhat subject to the viewpoint of the observer. In the example cited, a variable curve shape is said to be adaptive, even though the *method* of determining the best curve shape may be fixed. Thus adaptivity is a relative quality for which various levels are distinguishable. Indeed, some authors have called "adaptive" such fixed methods as exemplified by the straight-line fitting scheme described above. Generally speaking, it seems that the less one knows regarding the source, the more "adaptive" (perhaps flexible or complex would be better descriptors) must the compression system be if good performance is to be obtained under a wide range of operating conditions.

The choice of a specific technique for a given application is not an easy one because no algorithm is clearly superior for all possible conditions within the statistical definitions of a given source. Thus there is no unique "best" way and the ultimate decision must be based on such things as the generality of a method relative to the source knowledge, the philosophical ideas of the user, and relative equipment complexities. The goal of theoretical analysis can only be to suggest the comparative merits of competitive methods for a given form of statistics, channel characteristics, and data requirements, indicating in some way under which conditions one technique is superior to another.

Some analysis as to the effectiveness of a given scheme for a given data model has appeared in the literature although many problems remain. Particular attention has been devoted to the approximate signal-to-noise ratio for methods such as delta modulation and differential pulse code modulation (DPCM)[20]–[43] and to empirical results[33]–[43] have appeared. Readers may also be interested in some of the published theoretical work which considers transmission energy reduction for various other compression algorithms.[44]–[57] This paper is of a review nature, presenting a quantitative and qualitative discussion of certain aspects of the work with specific application to fixed and adaptive methods of data compression involving prediction or interpolation on sampled data. The aim is to present only a framework within which other techniques can be approached because, as indicated above, an exhaustive unifying theory for all possible suboptimal schemes relative to all possible sources is not feasible (at this time at least). It is intended to indicate some of the approaches, solutions, and approximate solutions that have been tried, while future problem areas. The results and their interpretation are presented in preference to detailed calculations.

System design is divided into two categories. The first is the noiseless encoding of the source and the second is channel encoding. It is the first problem to which data compression is primarily directed, it being assumed that the complexity of the algorithm justifies an equally complex channel coder so that channel errors are negligible. For the most part, the paper is directed to the first problem. However, the effect of channel errors is also covered briefly. The first part of the paper describes in detail the data statistical models and compression techniques to be considered. This is followed by a discussion of some figures of merit which might be applied to a system. Obviously, if some ordering of systems is to be attempted, some cost function or figure of merit must be defined. Three figures of merit, called compression ratios, for comparing systems are used in this paper and are defined in Section IV. Next the analysis of the compression algorithms is considered relative to these figures of merit. Finally the effects of an imperfect channel are discussed.

## II. Data Model

For the purposes of theoretical analysis, it is necessary to choose a data model. This may be more or less general, depending upon how quantitative a result is desired. In this paper it is assumed that the compression algorithms are applied to data which are sampled at an a priori fixed periodic rate. This is not as restrictive as it may seem since one can sample very rapidly to approximate the results for continuous time. Digital transmission is assumed. Thus the sample values must be quantized. In the ensuing sections, in *some* cases, the data is assumed to be so finely quantized prior to compression that the effects are negligible (referred to as being unquantized or continuous). As will be seen, assumptions in regard to quantization affect the choice of a compression technique.

The generated sampled source signal is denoted by the sequence $\cdots, s_n, s_{n+1}, s_{n+2}, \cdots$, or more compactly, $\{s_n\}$. Thus, $s_n$ is the $n$th signal sample value. At the receiver the reconstructed sequence is denoted by $\{y_n\}$, where $s_n \neq y_n$ in general because of the compression algorithm and possibly because of channel errors.

To evaluate system effectiveness numerically, the precise statistical nature of the source must be specified. The most natural choice for unquantized data is the stationary Gaussian time sequence. By this it is meant that any finite set of sample values is describable statistically by a joint Gaussian distribution which is independent of time shifts. This model is used because of its frequent occurrence in nature (at least approximately) as well as the comparative ease of analytical manipulation. Let $E[\cdot]$ be the statistical expectation operator. The mean or average value of the signal is taken to be zero.

$$E[s_n] = 0, \qquad \text{for every } n.$$

The results can be modified to allow for a nonzero mean, but for simplicity this will not be done. The correlation function which then completely specifies the source probability distribution is denoted as

$$R(k) = E[s_n s_{n-k}]. \tag{1}$$

This is real and symmetric since $\{s_n\}$ is taken to be real. It is assumed that the correlation function is square summable so that its Fourier series, the spectral density, is

$$p(\lambda) = \sum_{k=-\infty}^{\infty} R(k)e^{ik\lambda}, \tag{2}$$

so that

$$R(k) = \frac{1}{2\pi}\int_{-\pi}^{\pi} e^{-ik\lambda}p(\lambda)d\lambda \tag{3}$$

and

$$\frac{1}{2\pi}\int_{-\pi}^{\pi} p^2(\lambda)d\lambda = \sum_{k=-\infty}^{\infty} R^2(k) < \infty. \tag{4}$$

This is a very weak restriction implying in particular the convergence of sample averages to the expectation (ergodicity). In some cases the data is taken to be *Markov* in addition to the preceding, which means that data conditional probabilities depend on only the *finite* past. That is, the data is said to be $m$th-order Markov if the probability functions of sample value $s_n$ conditioned on the infinite past can be terminated with $m$ preceding values:

$$f(s_n|s_{n-1}, s_{n-2}, \cdots) = f(s_n|s_{n-1}, s_{n-2}, \cdots, s_{n-m}).$$

For continuous Gaussian data, this implies that for some set of $m+1$ values $\{\rho_n\}$

$$p(\lambda) = \left| \sum_{j=0}^{m} \rho_j e^{ij\lambda} \right|^{-2}. \tag{5}$$

Particular interest is focused on $m=1$ where

$$p(\lambda) = |1 - \rho e^{i\lambda}|^2$$

$$R(k) = \rho^{|k|}. \tag{5a}$$

For a detailed discussion of this and other properties of Gaussian sequences the reader should consult the appropriate literature.

For quantized data the Gaussian model is not adequate since it applies only to continuous variables. Here it is assumed that the sample values take on one of the $L$ values (levels) $1, 2, \cdots, L$. The quantity of interest is then the transition or conditional probability of a given level being generated conditioned on the immediate past:

$$P(s_n|s_{n-1}, s_{n-2}, \cdots) \tag{6}$$

for all possible values of the arguments. This probability is always assumed to have the *Markov* property by which it is assumed that the conditioning is only on the finite past as defined above for continuous data. In many cases $m=1$.

As in the unquantized case, the data is assumed stationary (which means that the conditional probability is independent of $n$). Under this assumption the joint probability can be found from the conditional probability. For details the reader can consult the literature on Markov chains.

It must be emphasized again that the assumption of a data model does *not* mean that this is known in system design. It is merely chosen so that numerical results can be derived for analytical purposes. In addition the assumption of stationarity does not severely restrict the generality of the results since they really only depend upon local properties. Hence the results apply as well to nonstationary data except in regions where the source *probabilities* (not the data) are changing more rapidly than the time spanned by the compression algorithm.

## III. Data Compression Techniques

The purpose of this section is to describe the nature of the data compression algorithms. At this point it is assumed that no channel errors occur so that the transmitter can monitor the data quality at the receiver. Thus receiver errors are due solely to the compression method. Normally the algorithm is required to keep these errors below some threshold in magnitude.

Two wide classes of techniques are considered in this paper. These classes include most of the techniques that have been proposed to date for data compression when the object is to reconstruct the generated signal at the receiver subject to a fidelity criterion. The classes are called "prediction" and "interpolation." In a prediction method an estimate $\hat{s}_n$ is formed at the compressor of each succeeding sample value based upon the past values as *seen by the receiver* $y_{n-1}, y_{n-2}, \cdots$ (in the absence of channel errors the transmitter knows the reconstructed received sequence). If the prediction error magnitude $|\hat{s}_n - s_n|$ is less than some preset threshold $\gamma$, the value is not transmitted but is replaced by its predicted value. Otherwise, the value itself is sent along with some information regarding its proper time slot, this information taking the form, typically, of the number of samples until the next transmitted value (a form of run length coding). Additional compression could be attained by taking further advantage of the prediction error distribution entropy rather than inserting the data samples themselves as in "entropy reducing" DPCM.[28],[29] However, the usual philosophy is that too little is known of this distribution to generate an optimum code, that at any rate most of the possible compression is gotten by the method described, and that furthermore, the presence of "raw" data samples occasionally is valuable in combating noise. The theoretical tools which follow are not, however, restricted to this case and could readily be applied to other techniques.

In the interpolation techniques, estimates $\hat{s}_{n+1}, \hat{s}_{n+2}, \cdots, \hat{s}_{n+j-1}$ are made of all values between a given transmitted value $s_n$ and the most distant possible point in the future $s_{n+j}$, such that the maximum interpolation error is below the preset threshold $\gamma$:

$$\max_{1 \le i \le j-1} |\hat{s}_{n+i} - s_{n+i}| \le \gamma. \tag{7}$$

$s_{n+m+1}$ is then transmitted. The estimates in general can depend upon the past history of the (reconstructed) sequence as well as the most recent transmitted value, the future value and its time of occurrence, and the particular intermediate value estimated.

In a way the prediction idea is just a special case of interpolation without the future value, although it is convenient to treat them separately. This does *not* mean, however, that interpolation is *always* superior to prediction because of the necessity in the former of either encoding two sample values with each transmission (the end points $s_n$ and $s_{n+j}$) rather than one as in the prediction method, or constraining the beginning point of each interpolation interval to equal the last transmitted end point. This latter idea suffers qualitatively from the fact that the point after the last end point ($s_{n+j+1}$ above) could not *itself* be used as the end point of the preceding interval, suggesting that an irregular statistical change has occurred between samples $s_{n+j}$ and $s_{n+j+1}$. Thus interpolation may suffer from the attempt to estimate $s_{n+j+1}$ from the end value $s_{n+j}$ (the last transmitted value)

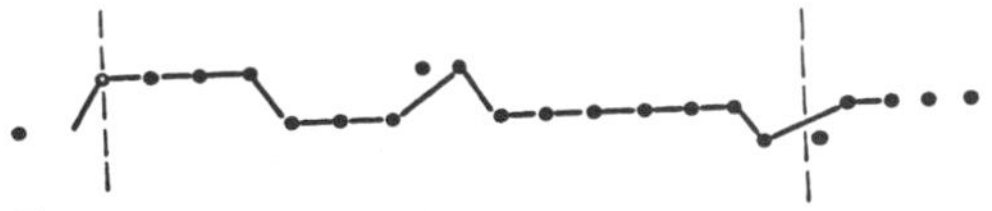

Fig. 1. A qualitative comparison of prediction and interpolation on quantized data. The dots represent data points as a function of time and the lines are the interpolation fit. $\gamma=0$.

and some future point. This is illustrated in Fig. 1 for a straight-line interpolation scheme. For the segment of data shown, eight sample values must be transmitted for quantized data with no error (intermediate interpolations are rounded off in reconstruction) whereas the simple predictor which predicts the next value to be the same as the last requires only five. If the sample location reconstruction code is the same in both cases, the predictor is better. Hence the relative superiority of interpolation versus prediction depends on the situation. This is shown more quantitatively later. It must be stated as a final remark on this subject for now, however, that in some applications[36]-[38] interpolation is found empirically to be superior.

It has not been stated yet exactly how the form of the predictor or interpolator is to be chosen. This is left to the sections on analysis.

## IV. Figures of Merit

Shannon[18],[19] defines the rate distortion function as the minimum information rate required to attain a given average distortion for a given source probability distribution. This provides an ultimate basis for system evaluation. However, except for simple cases such as the mean square error fidelity criterion, the mathematics are intractable. The usual basis of comparison in data compression is the system where the sample values are separately encoded using a fixed word length [pulse code modulation (PCM)]. As described in Section III, a compression system of the type considered in this paper operates to define those sample values (sometimes called nonredundant) which are necessary for the accurate reconstruction of the generated source time series at the receiver with a maximum error constraint. These values, together with associated parameters such as time of occurrence and possibly other reconstruction information, are sent to the receiver. The most commonly quoted figure of merit for such a system is the "sample" or *data compression ratio* defined as the ratio of generated sample values to the transmitted values. Thus a high compression ratio is associated with a "good" system. Since, however, this definition does not include the effect on overall efficiency of the transmission of timing information, it is only meaningful in comparing systems within the class of those requiring the same information rate per transmitted sample. A more adequate figure of merit is the *bit compression ratio* which is the ratio of the information bits for transmission of the original sample values to those required in the system with data compression including all reconstruction information in addition to the transmitted sample values. The calculation of this figure of merit requires one to be more specific since coding is included. Thus computations are somewhat more involved.

The bit compression ratio is still not an adequate quantity for all applications. Because the compressed message data rate is smaller, the effect of channel transmission errors is to make the received reconstructed data of generally lower quality than in the straight transmission of the sample values. Only in virtually noiseless cases such as in information retrieval applications or when elaborate channel codes are employed is the bit compression ratio completely meaningful. To include the effect of channel errors, the *energy compression ratio* has been defined[50] as the energy required per sample to transmit the data uncompressed divided by the energy when compressed under the same noise conditions and transmission scheme for the same received reconstructed data "quality." Here quality is determined by some such value as mean square error or probability of sample error. This definition is of course more restrictive since a data quality criterion and a noise and transmitter model must be chosen. The noise is normally assumed to be white Gaussian and transmission to be coherent, although other models could be used. Thus energy compression can be gained by using better channel coding as well as by compression. This is reasonable since one should compare entire systems rather than just portions. Unfortunately, the energy compression is much more difficult to compute. Basically the difficulty revolves around the dependence of accurate reconstruction at a given time at the receiver on the accuracy of all preceding received reconstruction information.

In the following material, reference to "compression ratio" means any of the three. If one of these is meant specifically, it is so stated.

## V. Analysis of Prediction Techniques

In this section several prediction methods, some fixed

and some adaptive, for quantized and unquantized data are presented and a discussion of some approaches and pitfalls in their analysis is given. As will be seen, it is usually not possible or else not computationally feasible to get exact answers for a given predictor because of the inherent nonlinear operations performed by the compression algorithm.

*A. Continuous Valued Samples—Fixed Prediction*

Consider first prediction for unquantized data. At time $n-1$ an estimate $\hat{s}_n$ of the next value is formed based on $y_{n-1}, y_{n-2}, \cdots$, where $y_n$ is either $s_n$ or $\hat{s}_n$ depending on the error $\hat{s}_n - s_n$ as described in Section III and below. The prediction is taken to be a linear weighting of the past $m$ values for further simplification (this class contains the minimum mean square error predictor for prediction on Gaussian $m$th-order Markov sequences; however, see the next paragraph):

$$\hat{s}_n = \sum_{j=1}^{m} \alpha_j y_{n-j}. \quad (8)$$

The coefficients $\{\alpha_j\}$ can be learned adaptively as is discussed in more detail in Section V-B, chosen a priori to minimize the mean square error if the source statistics are known well enough, or fixed at some intuitively pleasing value (in one commonly described method[33],[41] the prediction is the extrapolated $(m-1)$th-degree polynomial in time which passes through the preceding $m$ points; e.g., for $m=1$, $\alpha_i=1$). If the prediction error $z_n = \hat{s}_n - s_n$ is less than some threshold $\gamma$ in magnitude, the value is not transmitted but instead is replaced by its prediction. This is done at the transmitter as well as at the receiver to maintain proper error control at the latter. Hence there is *nonlinear* prediction error *feedback*. This is where the analytical problems arise.

It is well known that if *linear* operations are performed on a Gaussian sequence, the resulting sequence is Gaussian. Unfortunately, the sequence of values $\{y_n\}$ is *not* Gaussian because it results from *nonlinear* data operations on the Gaussian sequence $\{s_n\}$. One result of this is that the optimum predictor is not linear and should, in fact, depend on which of the values $y_{n-1}, y_{n-2}, \cdots, y_{n-m}$ are predicted values and which are exact data points. This is a subject for future research. For now, the linear predictor of (8) is considered.

Suppose now that the predictor weights mentioned above are fixed somehow and it is desired to calculate the data compression ratio for the assumed Gaussian mean zero model for some spectral density $p(\lambda)$, as defined in (8). Take as a first approximation the case where the threshold is very small relative to the signal power, i.e., $\gamma \approx 0$. This is the approach used by O'Neal[28],[29] in analyzing DPCM. Then prediction is on the data itself ($s_{n-j} \approx y_{n-j}$), and the error

$$z_n = \sum_{j=1}^{m} \alpha_j s_{n-j} - s_n \quad (9)$$

is Gaussian (being a linear combination of Gaussians) with mean zero and variance

$$\sigma^2 = E[z_n^2]. \quad (10)$$

This is most conveniently expressed in spectral form as

$$\sigma^2 = \frac{1}{2\pi} \int_{-\pi}^{\pi} \left| 1 - \sum_{j=1}^{m} \alpha_j e^{ij\lambda} \right|^2 p(\lambda) d\lambda. \quad (11)$$

Then the data compression ratio is given by the reciprocal of the prediction probability complement:

$$C_d = \left[ 1 - \int_{-\gamma/\sigma}^{\gamma/\sigma} \frac{e^{-u^2/2}}{\sqrt{2\pi}} du \right]^{-1}. \quad (12)$$

Unfortunately, as shown elsewhere,[47] this can be a very poor approximation for reasonable compression ratios (say greater than 1.5). A more accurate approximation results if it is assumed that the $y_n$ and $z_n$ sequences are Gaussian but have different correlation functions and spectral densities than when $\gamma=0$. Then[47] the error variance satisfies an integral equation similar to (11) with a correction factor dependent on $\sigma$:

$$\sigma^2 = \frac{1}{2\pi} \int_{-\pi}^{\pi} F\left[ \sum_{j=1}^{m} \alpha_j e^{ij\lambda}, \frac{\gamma}{\sigma} \right] \left| 1 - \sum_{j=1}^{m} \alpha_j e^{ij\lambda} \right|^2 p(\lambda) d\lambda \quad (13)$$

where $F \geq 1$ is a correction factor which results in a higher variance than that of (11). When this equation is solved (numerically) for $\sigma^2$ and used in (12) for the data compression ratio, relatively good agreement is found with computer simulations.[47] In one numerical example, the compression ratio was found to be 37.9 under the first approximation as compared with 2.08 and 2.40 for the second approximation and computer simulations, respectively. Another interesting result[47] is that the predictor which minimizes (13) can perform quite a bit better than that which minimizes (11) and still better than an $(m-1)$th-degree polynomial extrapolator which has often been suggested for data compression.[33]–[41]

The above analysis is approximate. An exact solution for the compression ratio is somewhat more involved. To illustrate the difficulties, consider first a simple case, $m=1$, so that $\hat{s}_n = \alpha y_{n-1}$. Taking a somewhat different approach than before, suppose $s_n$ is not predicted (to within the threshold $\gamma$, that is, $|z_n| > \gamma$). Let the probability, conditioned on this event and the value of $s_n$, that the next $j$ predicted values are within the threshold for any fixed value of $s_n$ be

$$P(j \mid s_n, |s_n - \alpha y_{n-1}| > \gamma) = \text{Prob}\left[ |s_{n+1} - \alpha s_n| \leq \gamma, \cdots, |s_{n+j} - \alpha s_{n+j-1}| \leq \gamma \mid s_n, |s_n - \alpha y_{n-1}| > \gamma \right]. \quad (14)$$

Unfortunately, this probability depends on the fact that $s_n$ is a transmitted point *as well as* its value. Hence it can not be evaluated generally. However, if the signal is first-order Markov (see Section III), the conditional probability does not depend on the event $|s_n - \alpha y_{n-1}| > \gamma$ which can be dropped, but *only on* $s_n$, and can be evaluated using the usual Gaussian conditional density. Then the marginal probability of $j$ predicted values (from which the compression can be calculated) is given by

$$\int_{-\infty}^{\infty} P(j|s_n) f(s_n||s_n - \alpha y_{n-1}| > \gamma) ds_n \tag{15}$$

where $f(\cdot|\cdot)$ is the probability density of $s_n$ *conditioned* on its being an unpredicted value. Unfortunately, this is not easily found, so one is generally faced with the problem of knowing only the conditional probability of $j$ even for this simple data model. This problem was faced by Ehrman[54] who set $\alpha = 1$ throughout and whose solution was to evaluate $P(j|s_n)$ for several values of $s_n$. However, if in addition to the above restrictions, one chooses $\alpha$ = correlation coefficient of $(s_n, s_{n+1}) = \rho$ [see (5a)], then it can be shown that $P(j|s_n)$ is independent of $s_n$. This was indirectly noted by Ehrman[54] who found that a solution was possible (for $\alpha = 1$ through the Fokker-Plank equation) for a Weiner process [which is (nonstationary) Markov so the independence of $s_n$ results]. Note then that only for the first-order Markov process with $m = 1$ and $\alpha = \rho$ is a solution possible by this direct method.

Starting with still another approach to the exact analysis, the following integral equation can be derived[51] which describes exactly the conditional probability density $p(\cdot|\cdot)$ of the prediction error $z_n$ given $s_n$ for arbitrary $\alpha$ (where the source is still first-order Markov):

$$p(z_n|s_n) = \int_{-\infty}^{\infty} \frac{g\left(\frac{s_n + z_n}{\alpha} - z_{n-1}r(z_{n-1})|s_n\right)}{\alpha} \cdot p\left(z_{n-1}\middle|\frac{s_n + z_n}{\alpha} - z_{n-1}r(z_{n-1})\right) dz_{n-1} \tag{16}$$

where

$$r(z_{n-1}) = \begin{cases} 1 & |z_{n-1}| \le \gamma \\ 0 & |z_{n-1}| > \gamma \end{cases}$$

$g(s_n|s_{n-1})$ = Gaussian conditional density of $s_n$ given $s_{n-1}$.

This can be evaluated numerically on a digital computer. A similar equation results for $m > 1$ and higher-order Markov processes. Unfortunately a practical method of solution for the more complicated cases has not been found yet due to the excessive computation time involved. Possibly some sort of orthogonal expansion can be found.

*B. Continuous Valued Samples—Adaptive Prediction*

In the preceding section it is assumed that the predictor weights $\alpha_1, \alpha_2, \cdots, \alpha_m$ are fixed. However, in applications a sufficiently detailed knowledge of the source may not be available to specify a predictor which even approaches the optimum. In other situations only time-averaged statistical values may be known which do not properly account for intermediate nonstationarities. The purpose of this section is to show how the weights can be determined adaptively and to indicate their performance relative to the optimal weights.

In the context of the compression coding scheme described in the foregoing, it would be desirable to determine that predictor which locally maximizes the probability of prediction. This could be done, for example, by maximizing the number of predictions that are within the threshold over the immediate past. If $N$ predictions are used in this procedure, and a prediction of $s_n$ is looked for, the predictor would be determined by

$$\max_{\{\alpha_j\}} \frac{1}{N} \sum_{i=1}^{N} r\left(y_{n-i} - \sum_{j=1}^{m} \alpha_j y_{n-i-j}\right) \tag{17}$$

where $r(\cdot)$ is as in (16).

Unfortunately the maximization is difficult to perform, requiring a procedure such as a randomized search. In addition, for finite $N$, the solution is not usually unique. Thus one is led to consider adaptive techniques which, while more readily implemented, perform equally well over some wide class of data and reasonably well elsewhere. The obvious choice is the minimization of sample mean square error (least squares) which is equivalent (at least as $N \to \infty$) to the maximization of the prediction probability for many distributions including in particular the Gaussian. Thus one determines the predictor by finding the minimum average squared error:

$$S_{m,N}^2 = \min_{\{\alpha_j\}} \frac{1}{N} \sum_{i=1}^{N} \left(y_{n-i} - \sum_{j=1}^{m} \alpha_j y_{n-i-j}\right)^2. \tag{18}$$

The minimization can be performed numerically by any of several methods such as steepest descent.[44] Details will not be given here. Another approach to the least squared error predictor design is through stochastic approximation.[62]

Supposing that the predictor is determined by (18), it is natural to ask how large $N$ must be to get reasonable performance and how $m$ should be chosen. Clearly it is desirable to make $N$ small so that changes in the data statistical structure are accommodated rapidly. On the other hand, $N$ must be large enough so that accurate "learning" of the predictor results. A partial answer is given in another paper[52] where it is shown that for large $N$, the prediction error variance as a function of $N$ (for Gaussian data, $\{y_n\} = \{s_n\}$) is given by

$$\sigma_{m,N}^2 = \sigma_{m,\infty}^2\left(1 + \frac{m}{N}\right). \tag{19}$$

This provides a measure of the loss in using a finite value of $N$ for fixed $m$. Although this strictly applies only for operations on the original signal sequence, it is found empirically[53] that the same factor of $1 + m/N$ is a good approximation for closed loop operation.

It has been shown[46] how the degrees of predictor freedom $m$ can be chosen based on the sample error variance $S_{m,N}^2$ of (18) for fixed $N$. Clearly it is desirable to make $m$ large enough so that "most" of the predictability of $s_n$ is used but not to the point of diminishing returns where there are too many degrees of freedom in minimizing (18) for accurate "learning." It has also been shown[46] that the average value of the sample prediction variance (for $\{y_n\}=\{s_n\}$) is, for large $N$,

$$E[S_{m,N}^2] = \sigma_{m,\infty}^2\left(1 - \frac{m}{N}\right). \tag{20}$$

That is, for fixed $N$ the sample error variance decreases *on the average* at the same rate as the actual prediction variance increases. Thus

$$S_{m,N}^2 \frac{\left(1 + \frac{m}{N}\right)}{\left(1 - \frac{m}{N}\right)} \tag{21}$$

can be used to estimate the effect of varying $m$ and $N$ on the actual prediction error variance. It is not yet known how close the estimated value of $m$ is to the optimum for fixed $N$ when this procedure is used, although empirical results look promising.[46]

### C. Discrete Valued Samples—Fixed Prediction

Consider now the prediction of quantized data. If the transition probabilities are known, then the best predictor (for the coding scheme described) for prediction to within $\gamma$ levels of accuracy is clearly that which maximizes the probability of this prediction—a form of maximum likelihood or modal prediction:

$$\sum_{k=-\gamma}^{\gamma} P(\hat{s}_n + k|y_{n-1}, y_{n-2}, \dots, y_{n-m}) = \max_j \sum_{k=-\gamma}^{\gamma} P(j + k|y_{n-1}, \dots, y_{n-m}). \tag{22}$$

This is a form of predictive coding as described by Elias.[59] Note however, that the conditioning is on the $\{y_n\}$ sequence and ideally is dependent on which are predictions and which are not. In general the predictor does not depend in a linear way on the preceding $m$ values although a prediction of the form of (8) may work well in some cases. The analysis of such prediction methods presents many of the same problems as presented in part A of this section except that here, in the discrete case, it is sometimes reasonable to let $\gamma=0$, in which case the analysis is trivial; i.e., the probability of prediction is simply

$$E\left[\max_k P(k|s_{n-1}, s_{n-2}, \dots, s_{n-m}\right] \tag{23}$$

where the expectation is over the sample values and is readily evaluated for any transition probability.

If, however, $\gamma\neq 0$, the same difficulty as before arises; namely, errors in previous predictions result in a lowering of the prediction probability from that with no errors and can not be evaluated directly. For the special case where the data is first-order Markov and the run probabilities are independent of the initial value, equations result analogous to (14)–(15), which can be evaluated. For any other situation, a different idea must be used. One attack for $m=1$ is to solve the following equation satisfied by the conditional probability of the prediction error sequence $\{z_n\}$ given the level $s_n$:

$$P(z_n|s_n) = \sum_{z_{n-1}, s_{n-1}} P(z_n|s_n, z_{n-1}, s_{n-1})P(s_{n-1}|s_n) \cdot P(z_{n-1}|s_{n-1}). \tag{24}$$

This is analogous to (16). Note that $z_n$ is determined exactly by $s_n, z_{n-1}, s_{n-1}$, so that

$$P(z_n|s_n, z_{n-1}, s_{n-1}) = \begin{cases} 1 & z_n = \hat{s}_n - s_n \\ 0 & \text{otherwise} \end{cases}$$

and $p(s_{n-1}|s_n)$ is the known data transition probability.

If the data are coarsely quantized so that the number of signal levels is not large, the above equation is readily solved. A similar equation results for larger values of $m$. Unfortunately, the number of dimensions and hence computations increases exponentially with $m$.

### D. Discrete Valued Samples—Adaptive Prediction

If little is known of the source or if the transition probability of (22) can not be calculated with the prediction error feedback, it may be useful to use an adaptive technique which estimates the predictor of (22). The most reasonable way to do this is by simply keeping track of the relative frequencies of occurrence of the various signal levels conditioned on the past (a conditional histogram) and choosing as a prediction that value which maximizes (22) with the probability replaced by its estimate.[48] If there are $L$ levels, $L^m$ histograms and $L^{m+1}$ storage locations must be provided, placing a practical limitation on $m$. A reduction in the storage requirement by a factor of $L-1$ can be achieved by using a conditional *mean* predictor[44] rather than a conditional mode predictor at some possible loss in prediction probability.

Little theoretical analysis has been done on these predictors. Some empirical results for television data appear elsewhere.[39],[48]

## VI. Analysis of Interpolation Techniques

In Section V some approaches to the analysis of prediction techniques are outlined. Difficulties similar to those encountered there are involved in the analysis of interpolation methods. Considerably fewer results have been obtained however. The calculation of the compression ratios under open loop conditions ($\{y_n\}\approx\{s_n\}$) as in (11)–(12) for the predictor is straightforward. Unfortunately the effects of nonlinear interpolation error feedback must be considered here as well as in the previous discussion. For the predictor it is possible to obtain the approximate result of (13) by assuming that the feedback affects the correlation function of the data but not the Gaussian property. So far no result has been found for interpolation based on this approximation.

A second analytical approach is based on the calculation of the probability of interpolating $j-1$ values *conditioned* on $s_n$ and $s_{n+j}$ as fixed *end points* (as defined in Section III).

This conditional quantity, which is analogous to (14) for prediction, is readily evaluated only when the data are first-order Markov. However, the difficulty discussed after (15) in evaluating the unconditional probability arises here, when an arbitrary interpolating polynomial is used. The joint probability of $s_n$ and $s_{n+j}$ as end points is *not* Gaussian nor readily evaluated. However, if the interpolator is the maximum likelihood estimate for the intermediate points $s_{n+i}$ conditioned on $s_n$ and $s_{n+j}$, then the conditional probability is independent of the end points and the difficulty is avoided as it was for prediction. This was noted empirically by Ehrman[54] for interpolation on a Weiner process using straight-line segments which *are* maximum likelihood for this process (see Section V-A for a comparison with prediction on a Weiner process). More generally, for a Gaussian first-order Markov process with correlation coefficient $\rho$ [see (5a)], the maximum likelihood estimate of $s_{n+i}$ is

$$\hat{s}_{n+i} = \tfrac{1}{2}[\rho^i s_n + \rho^{j-i} s_{n+j}]. \quad (25)$$

Thus the best interpolator has some curvature to it. However, if $\rho$ is close to unity (as would be the case if much compression is to be gained), a straight line should do well.

As in the prediction method, if the data are not first-order Markov, if the maximum likelihood interpolator is not used, or if the past values $y_{n-1}, y_{n-2}, \cdots$ are also used in addition to $s_n$ and $s_{n+j}$, the technique of analysis in the preceding paragraph fails. Instead equations similar to (16) and (24) must be derived for the interpolation probabilities involving either an integral equation or a summation, depending on whether the data are continuous or discrete valued. In another paper[49] such a result is derived, specifically for straight-line interpolation on discrete data with no allowable error in reconstruction. However, the method of analysis can be generalized. Basically the idea is to calculate the probability of the interpolating polynomial connecting a sequence of values after a transmitted value *conditioned on* the sequence of values interpolated by the preceding line segment:

$$P_{\text{Int}}(s_n, s_{n+1}, \cdots, s_{n+j} | s_n, s_{n-1}, \cdots, s_{n-k}). \quad (26)$$

The Int subscript is to emphasize that this is not the usual data conditional probability but the probability that the sequence $s_n, s_{n+1}, \cdots, s_{n+j}$ is the interpolated sequence following the interpolated sequence $s_n, s_{n-1}, \cdots, s_{n-i}$ (either $s_n$ or $s_{n-1}$ may be the end point of that sequence depending on the coding used as indicated in Section III). That is, for the interpolator used on the past (conditioned) sequence, $P_{\text{Int}}$ in (26) is only defined when

$$\max_{1 \le i \le k-1} |s_{n-i} - \hat{s}_{n-i}| \le \gamma \quad (27)$$

*and* on the next (conditional) sequence in (26) the probability is only defined for

$$\max_{1 \le i \le j-1} |s_{n+i} - \hat{s}_{n+i}| \le \gamma.$$

The key to evaluating (26) is to note that the effect of the compression *procedure* is to assign (conditional) probability zero to any sequence of future values for which it would have been possible to extend the previous interpolator. All other values of the conditional probability are the same as the usual data conditional probability except for a normalizing factor.

Once the set of conditional probabilities is determined, the marginal probabilities of the various sequences are found from the set of equations

$$P(s_n, s_{n+1}, \cdots, s_{n+j}) = \sum P_{\text{Int}}(s_n, s_{n+1}, \cdots, s_{n+j} | s_n, s_{n-1}, \cdots, s_{n-k}) \cdot P(s_n, s_{n-1}, \cdots, s_{n-k}), \quad (28)$$

where the values on the left-hand side and the summation are over all possible values of the sequences and all values of $j$ and $k$. In the case of continuous valued variables, summation is replaced by integration. Once the marginal probabilities are known, the interpolation probabilities are known and the compression ratio can be calculated.

Obviously the solution to the set of equations (28) becomes impractical computationally when there are too many possible values. For example, if the sample values are encoded into $L$ levels, the interpolator segments have a common end point in $s_n$ and are constrained to be smaller in time length than $T$ sampling intervals, and if $\gamma = 0$, then there are $L^3T^2$ conditional probabilities and $L^2T$ marginal probabilities which soon become unwieldy. Hopefully an approximate method of solving (28) or possibly another analytical approach can be developed.

Still to be investigated are adaptive methods of interpolation analogous to (18) for prediction.

## VII. A Comparison of Prediction and Interpolation

It should be apparent from the multitude of possibilities discussed in the preceding sections that it is not feasible to compare all possible techniques on all possible sources. In this section a comparison is made between a simple fixed predictor and a simple fixed interpolator for two quantized data models, an example taken from another paper.[49] In one case the predictor is superior. In the other, the interpolator is superior. The prediction of sample $s_n$ is taken to be the last value $y_{n-1}$ [in (8), $m=1$, $\alpha_1$, $\alpha_1 = 1$] (sometimes called "zero order hold" prediction) and the interpolation is straight-line (sometimes called "fan" interpolation) where the starting value of one line is the end of the last. The data is quantized to 8 levels and no reconstruction error is allowed. Equations (23) and (28) are solved for the prediction and interpolation probabilities from which the average number of samples between transmissions (average run length) is calculated. The data are encoded as a sequence of sample-run length pairs, using 3 bits for the level and 4 bits for the run length, allowing a maximum of 16 run lengths.

Figs. 2 and 3 taken from the aforementioned paper[49] where more details are found, present the bit compression ratios with respect to PCM transmission of the 3 bit samples for the predictor and the interpolator with first- and second-order Markov processes, respectively. Note that for useful compression ratios the predictor is better in Fig. 2, whereas in Fig. 3 the interpolator is preferred. Unfortunately, neither comes close to the optimum based on the source entropy.

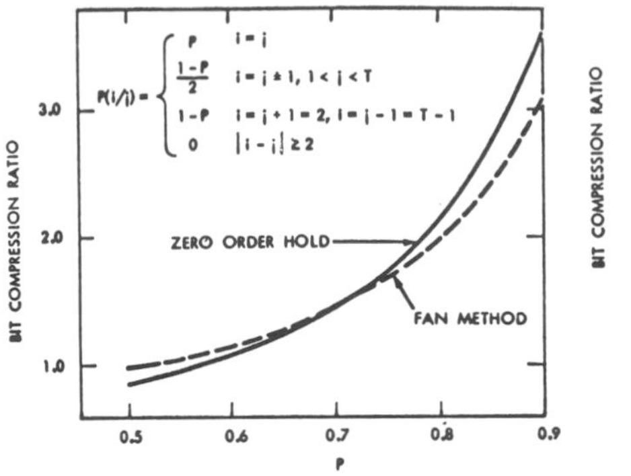


Fig. 2. Compression ratios for prediction (zero-order hold) and interpolation (fan method) for a first-order Markov process with transition probability $p(i\,|\,j)$.

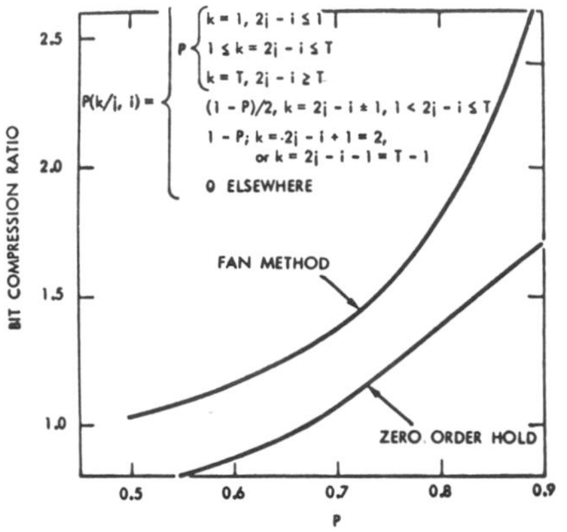


Fig. 3. Compression ratios for prediction (zero-order hold) and interpolation (fan method) for a second-order Markov process with transition probability $p(k\,|\,j, i)$.

These results indicate the need to examine the data model carefully before selecting a compression algorithm. It is expected that equivalent results would be obtained for the analysis of any fixed algorithm. That is, there is no clearly superior method for all sources under all conditions. If insufficient knowledge of the source is available, an adaptive method as described in Section V may become useful in spite of the greatly increased complexity required. As shown elsewhere,[39],[48] an adaptive algorithm is never worse in compression ratio than a comparable fixed algorithm and it may be quite a bit better. For television data, it is apparently true, however, that the statistics are well enough known and the problem has been studied empirically to the extent where a fixed algorithm performs almost as well as an adaptive one,[39] and of the possible methods, interpolation is the best.[36],[38]

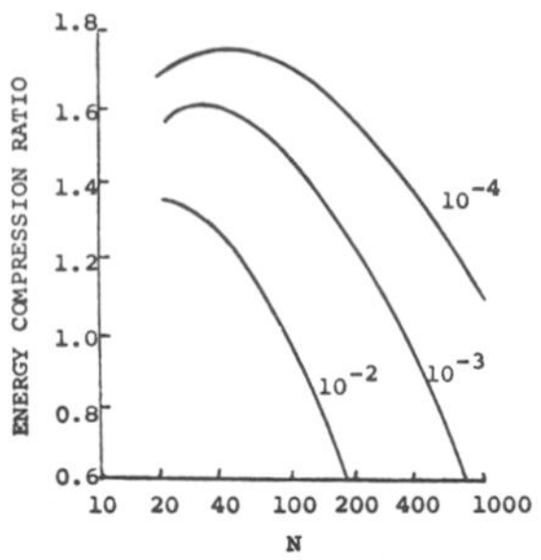


Fig. 4. Energy compression ratio as a function of $N$, the number of samples between synchronization for bit error rates of $10^{-2}$, $10^{-3}$, $10^{-4}$. Data compression ratio = 4.96 and bit compression ratio = 2.43.

## VIII. The Effect of Channel Errors

Up to this point it has been assumed that transmission is made essentially error-free through the use of sufficiently complex channel codes (which insert controlled redundancy in place of the uncontrolled redundancy in the source data). The purpose of this section is to show that advantages gained from compression can be lost or at least degraded through the increased noise sensitivity. Raga[61] obtained approximate theoretical and empirical results using a mean square fidelity criterion for video data with perfect line synchronization. Another paper[50] contains exact theoretical results for a first-order Markov process. Wolf[31] considered the problem for delta modulation.

The following example is taken from the second work.[50] The predictor is that of the example in Section VII ($m=1$, $\alpha_1=1$), the data is first-order Markov in 16 levels, 16 run lengths are used, and the level-run length pairs are transmitted in blocks separated by synchronization words $N$ samples apart (a form of controlled redundancy). Although this number of samples in each block is fixed, the number of code words in each block varies with the data. It is assumed that *synchronization* is error-free so that errors do not accumulate from block to block. Within each block, however, an error in one of the timing words shifts all succeeding data in location. A binary symmetric channel is assumed, thus timing errors are additive and independent so that the location error variance increases linearly with distance from synchronization. Thus from this point of view, synchronization words should appear frequently. On the other hand, the insertion of a synchronization word in the data causes the last run in the block to be truncated, resulting in two transmissions in place of one. Thus there is a tradeoff between error propagation and run truncation.

Fig. 4 presents the energy compression ratio as a function of the number of samples in a block for various bit error probabilities. Note that for each error rate there is a value of $N$ which maximizes the energy compression. In each case this is significantly below the data and bit compression ratios with no synchronization. It is also seen that an energy compression ratio smaller than unity results if the block length is too large. As shown elsewhere[50] considerable improvement is made if channel coding is employed.

## IX. Conclusions

In the preceding sections considerations in the analysis of data compression systems have been discussed together with some of the exact and approximate results which have been obtained. Many problems still remain to be solved. Some of these are indicated. Certainly if an understanding of the possible ways of communicating data from an imperfectly known source is to be gained, the solution to these problems is of interest.

## References


[1] T. O. Anderson *et al.*, "Demonstration of a quantile system for compression of data from deep space probes," Conf. on Adaptive Telemetry, NASA Goddard Spaceflight Center Rept. X-731-67-7, pp. 55–73, January 1967.

[2] I. Eisenberger and E. C. Posner, "Systematic statistics used for data compression of space telemetry," *Am. Stat. Assoc.*, vol. 60, pp. 97–113, March 1965.

[3] J. W. Snively, Jr., "A parameter extraction technique," Conf. on Adaptive Telemetry, NASA Goddard Spaceflight Center Rept. X-731-67-7, pp. 117–127, January 1967.

[4] M. P. Beddoes, "Two channel method for compressing bandwidth of television signals," *Proc. IEE (London)*, vol. 110, pp. 369–374, February 1963.

[5] W. T. Bisignani, G. P. Richards, and J. W. Whelan, "The improved gray scale and the coarse-fine PCM systems, two new digital TV bandwidth reduction techniques," *Proc. IEEE*, vol. 54, pp. 376–390, March 1966.

[6] N. G. Deryugin, "Theoretical possibilities of compressing bandwidth of TV channel," *Telecommun.*, no. 8, pp. 805–810, 1958.

[7] D. Gabor and P. C. J. Hill, "Television bandwidth compression by contour interpolation," *Proc. IEE (London)*, vol. 108, pt. B, pp. 303–315, 634, May 1961.

[8] T. S. Huang, "PCM picture transmission," *IEEE Spectrum*, vol. 2, pp. 57–63, December 1965.

[9] T. S. Huang and M. Chikhaoui, "The effect of BSC on PCM picture quality," *IEEE Trans. Information Theory*, vol. IT-13, pp. 270–273, April 1967.

[10] B. Julesz, "A method of coding TV signals based on edge detection," *Bell Sys. Tech. J.*, vol. 38, pp. 1001–1020, July 1959.

[11] E. R. Kretzmer, "Statistics of television signals," *Bell Sys. Tech. J.*, vol. 31, pp. 751–763, July 1952.

[12] W. K. Pratt, "A bibliography on television bandwidth reduction studies," *IEEE Trans. Information Theory*, vol. IT-13, pp. 114–115, January 1967.

[13] G. P. Richards and W. T. Bisignani, "Redundancy reduction applied to coarse-fine encoded video," *Proc. IEEE*, vol. 55, pp. 1707–1717, October 1967.

[14] L. G. Roberts, "Picture coding using pseudo-random noise," *IRE Trans. Information Theory*, vol. IT-8, pp. 145–154, February 1962.

[15] W. F. Schreiber, "The measurement of third order probability distributions of television signals," *IRE Trans. Information Theory*, vol. IT-2, pp. 94–105, September 1956.

[16] W. F. Schreiber, C. F. Knapp, and N. D. Kay, "Synthetic highs, an experimental TV bandwidth reduction system," *J. Soc. Motion Picture and TV Engrs.*, vol. 68, pp. 525–537, August 1959.

[17] M. R. Schroeder, J. L. Flanagan, and E. A. Lundry, "Bandwidth compression of speech by analytic-signal rooting," *Proc. IEEE*, vol. 55, pp. 396–401, March 1967.

[18] C. E. Shannon, "Coding theorems for a discrete source with a fidelity criterion," *IRE Nat'l Conv. Rec.*, pt. 4, pp. 142–163, 1959.

[19] C. E. Shannon and W. Weaver, *The Mathematical Theory of Communication*. Urbana, Ill.: University of Illinois Press, 1949.

[20] J. E. Abate, "Linear and adaptive delta modulation," *Proc. IEEE*, vol. 55, pp. 298–308, March 1967.

[21] F. W. Arter, "Simple delta modulation system," *Proc. IRE (Australia)*, vol. 23, pp. 517–523, September 1962.

[22] P. A. Bello, R. N. Lincoln, and H. Gish, "Statistical delta modulation," *Proc. IEEE*, vol. 55, pp. 308–319, March 1967.

[23] F. deJager, "Delta modulation, a method of PCM transmission using a one-unit code," *Philips Research Repts.*, vol. 7, pp. 442–466, 1952.

[24] T. Fine, "Properties of an optimum digital system and applications," *IEEE Trans. Information Theory*, vol. IT-10, pp. 287–296, October 1964.

[25] T. J. Goblick, Jr., "Theoretical limitations on the transmission of data from analog sources," *IEEE Trans. Information Theory*, vol. IT-11, pp. 558–567, October 1965.

[26] R. E. Graham, "Predictive quantizing of television signals," *IRE WESCON Conv. Rec.*, pt. 4, pp. 147–157, 1958.

[27] R. A. McDonald, "Signal-to-noise performance and idle channel performance of differential pulse code modulation systems, with particular applications to voice signals," *Bell Sys. Tech. J.*, vol. 45, September 1966.

[28] J. B. O'Neal, Jr., "A bound on signal-to-quantizing noise ratios for digital encoding systems," *Proc. IEEE*, vol. 55, pp. 287–292, March 1967.

[29] ——, "Predictive quantizing systems (differential pulse code modulation) for the transmission of television signals," *Bell Sys. Tech. J.*, vol. 45, pp. 689–721, May–June 1966.

[30] J. W. Schwartz and R. C. Barker, "Bit-plane encoding: A technique for source encoding," *IEEE Trans. Aerospace and Electronic Systems*, vol. AES-2, pp. 385–392, July 1966.

[31] J. K. Wolf, "Effects of channel errors on delta modulation," *IEEE Trans. Communication Technology*, vol. COM-14, pp. 2–7, February 1966.

[32] C. C. Cutler, "Differential PCM," U. S. Patent 2 605 361, July 29, 1952.

[33] C. A. Andrews, J. M. Davies, and G. R. Schwarz, "Adaptive data compression," *Proc. IEEE*, vol. 55, pp. 267–277, March 1967.

[34] A. V. Balakrishnan, R. L. Kutz, and R. A. Stampfl, "Adaptive data compression for video signals," NASA Goddard Spaceflight Center, Rept. X-730-66-110.

[35] L. W. Gardenhire, "Redundancy reduction—The key to adaptive telemetry," *Proc. Nat'l Telemetering Conf.*, paper 6-5, 1964.

[36] D. Hochman, H. Katzman, and D. R. Weber, "Application of redundancy reduction to television bandwidth compression," *Proc. IEEE*, vol. 55, pp. 263–266, March 1967.

[37] J. R. Hulme and R. A. Schomburg, "A data bandwidth compressor for space-vehicle telemetry," *Proc. Nat'l Telemetering Conf.*, vol. 2, paper 3-2, 1962.

[38] C. M. Kortman, "Redundancy reduction—A practical method of data compression," *Proc. IEEE*, vol. 55, pp. 253–263, March 1967.

[39] R. L. Kutz and J. A. Sciulli, "An adaptive image compression system and its performance in a noisy channel," presented at the Internatl Information Theory Symp., 1967; to be published in *IEEE Trans. Information Theory*, vol. IT-14, March 1968.

[40] H. N. Massey, "An experimental telemetry data compressor," *Proc. Nat'l Telemetering Conf.*, pp. 25–28, 1965.

[41] J. E. Medlin, "Sampled-data prediction for telemetry bandwidth compression," *IEEE Trans. Space Electronics and Telemetry*, vol. SET-11, pp. 29–36, March 1965.

[42] R. A. Schomburg, "Computer simulation of a data compressor for aerospace telemetry systems," *IRE Nat'l Symp. Space Electronics and Telemetry*, paper 4.2, 1962.

[43] D. R. Weber and F. J. Wynhoff, "The concept of self-adaptive data compression," *IRE Nat'l Symp. Space Electronics and Telemetry*, paper 4.1, 1962.

[44] A. V. Balakrishnan, "An adaptive nonlinear data predictor," *Proc. Nat'l Telemetering Conf.*, vol. 2, paper 6-5, 1962.

[45] ——, "Effect of signal processing, linear and non-linear, on signal statistics," *J. Research NBS*, vol. 68D, pp. 953–965, September 1964.

[46] L. D. Davisson, "The adaptive prediction of time-series," *Proc. Nat'l Electronics Conf.*, 1966.

[47] ——, "An approximate theory of prediction for data compression," *IEEE Trans. Information Theory*, vol. IT-13, pp. 274–278, April 1967.

[48] ——, "Data compression and its application to video signals," (Summer Workshop Program in Analysis of Space Data and Measurement of Space Environments.) NASA Goddard Spaceflight Center, Final Rept., pp. A-35–A-56, 1965.

[49] ——, "Data compression using straight line interpolation," to be published in *IEEE Trans. Information Theory*, May 1968.

[50] ——, "The effect of channel errors on data compression," *WESCON Conf. (Session 6, Data Compression)*, 1967.

[51] ——, "On the theoretical analysis of data compression tech-

niques," to be published in *Proc. Hawaii Internat'l Conf. of System Sciences*, 1968.

[52] ——, "The prediction error of stationary Gaussian time series of unknown covariance," *IEEE Trans. Information Theory*, vol. IT-11, pp. 527–532, October 1965.

[53] ——, "Theory of adaptive data compression," in *Advances in Communication Systems*, vol. 2. New York: Academic Press, 1966.

[54] L. Ehrman, "Analysis of some redundancy removal bandwidth compression techniques," *Proc. IEEE*, vol. 55, pp. 278–287, March 1967.

[55] T. J. Lynch, "Performance measures for compressed and coded space telemetry systems," *IEEE Trans. Aerospace and Electronic Systems*, vol. AES-3, pp. 784–795, September 1967.

[56] M. Kanefsky, "Data compression using bit plane encoding," Summer Workshop, NASA Goddard Spaceflight Center, Final Rept. X-700-67-94, pp. 1–21, 1966.

[57] R. B. Kelley, "The effect of channel errors on a sample compression system employing binary sequence time encoding," Summer Workshop, NASA Goddard Spaceflight Center, Final Rept. X-700-67-94, pp. 45–64, 1966.

[58] H. Blasbalg and R. Van Blerkom, "Message compression," *IRE Trans. Space Electronics and Telemetry*, vol. SET-8, pp. 228–238, September 1962.

[59] P. Elias, "Predictive coding—Part I," *IRE Trans. Information Theory*, vol. IT-1, pp. 16–33, March 1955.

[60] D. Gabor, W. P. L. Wilby, and R. Woodcock, "A universal non-linear filter predictor and simulator which optimizes itself by a learning process," *Proc. IEE (London)*, vol. 108, pp. 422–438, July 1961.

[61] G. L. Raga, "Wideband video data transmission," *IEEE Trans. Communication Technology*, vol. COM-15, pp. 124–129, February 1967.

[62] D. J. Sakrison, "Stochastic approximation: A recursive method for solving regression problems," in *Advances in Communication Systems*. New York: Academic Press, 1966, pp. 51–106.

# 34



Reprinted from *Proc. IEEE*, **55**(3), 278–287 (1967)

# Analysis of Some Redundancy Removal Bandwidth Compression Techniques

L. EHRMAN, MEMBER, IEEE

*Abstract*—**Three redundancy removal bandwidth compression algorithms —the floating-aperture predictor, the zero-order interpolator, and the fan interpolator—are analyzed. Theoretical expressions are found for the mean and mean-square times between output samples of these devices when the input signal is a Markov process. These expressions are evaluated for the case in which the input is a first-order Gaussian Markov process, and the resulting output sampling rates and transmission bandwidths are compared to those required by a PCM system using uniform sampling and optimum linear filter interpolation. It is shown that, given sufficient a priori knowledge of the signal process, there is little to be gained by using these redundancy removal techniques in place of the PCM system. However, if the signal statistics are unknown, the use of these algorithms instead of PCM may provide a considerable bandwidth reduction.**

## I. Introduction

CURRENT INTEREST in the telemetry field has centered about a class of redundancy removal bandwidth compression algorithms which operate by fitting the longest straight line to the signal data and transmitting signal information only when the signal deviates by more than a fixed limit from the straight line. The signal is reconstructed at the receiving terminal by means of a straight-line interpolation of the received data, with the resulting sample point error always being less than the fixed limit [1]–[3]. The rationale behind these techniques is that the average transmission rate need not be chosen beforehand. The input sampling rate is allowed to be very high and the algorithm is then applied to remove the redundant samples and transmit at the minimum rate necessary to reconstruct the original signal. The nonredundant samples are selected according to the error criterion of the algorithm, and, through the use of buffer storage, transmitted at a uniform rate.

In this paper we develop the theoretical performances of three of the most commonly used algorithms—the floating-aperture predictor, the zero-order interpolator, and the fan interpolator. Analytical expressions are found for the mean and mean-square time between output samples for each algorithm. These expressions are then numerically evaluated for the case in which the signal is a first-order Gaussian Markov process.

The sampling rate is then compared with that required for uniformly sampled PCM, utilizing an optimum time-invariant filter interpolation. Finally, by taking into account the signal timing requirements, the transmission bandwidth required for each algorithm is compared with that required with uniform sampling. To our knowledge, all of the analytic results of this paper pertaining to the redundancy reduction algorithms are new, with the exception of (58); this equation was derived by Goldstein et al. [4] using a different analytic technique. Related results derived by means of digital simulations can be found, e.g., in [5] and [6]. In addition, relevant theoretical concepts can be found in the literature on random walks [12].

Manuscript received November 3, 1966; revised January 10, 1967. This paper is based on a Ph.D. dissertation which the author expects to present to the Department of Electrical Engineering, Northeastern University, Boston, Mass. The author was supported in part, during the research reported in this paper, by the National Science Foundation under an NSF Cooperative Graduate Fellowship. Computation facilities were made available by the M.I.T. Computation Center, Cambridge, Mass.

The author is with SIGNATRON, Inc., Lexington, Mass.

## II. Description of the Bandwidth Compression Algorithms

### *Floating-Aperture Predictor*

The floating-aperture predictor system is illustrated in Fig. 1. The continuous input signal $x(t)$ is sampled at uniform time intervals of $\Delta T$ with the value of the sample taken at time $t_n = t_0 + n\Delta T$, $n = 0, \pm 1, \pm 2, \cdots$, being denoted by $X_n$. The sample value $X_0$ and its time of occurrence $t_0$ are placed in a buffer for future transmission, and two boundaries, defining an aperture, are placed at $X_0 + \Delta X$ and $X_0 - \Delta X$. The quantity $\Delta X$ is the prediction tolerance. As long as subsequent sample values $X_1, X_2, \cdots$, fall within the aperture, no action is taken. The first time, say at $t_i$, that a sample falls out of the aperture, $X_i$ and $t_i$ are placed in the buffer for future transmission, the aperture boundaries are moved to $X_i + \Delta X$, $X_i - \Delta X$, and the sampling is continued. The time $T = i\Delta T$ that it took for the signal samples to first leave the aperture is a random variable. We denote its conditional mean by $E[T|X_0]$ and its conditional mean square by $E[T^2|X_0]$, where $X_0$ is the initial sample value. The unconditional mean and mean-square times between output samples are given by

$$E[T] = \int_{-\infty}^{\infty} E[T|x_0]p(x_0)\,dx_0 \quad (1)$$

$$E[T^2] = \int_{-\infty}^{\infty} E[T^2|x_0]p(x_0)\,dx_0 \quad (2)$$

where $p(x_0)$ is the probability density function of the initial sample values.

The quantity $\mu\Delta X$ is defined as the peak signal excursion away from $X_0$ in the direction opposite to the exit boundary. The signal occupies $(1+\mu)\Delta X$ of the $2\Delta X$-wide aperture space.

The reconstructed signal $\hat{x}(t)$ is given by a stair-step approximation. For example, for the signal shown in Fig. 1,

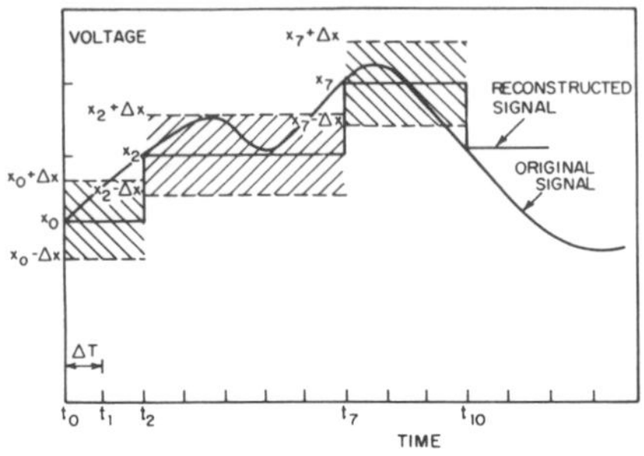


Fig. 1. Operation of the floating-aperture predictor.

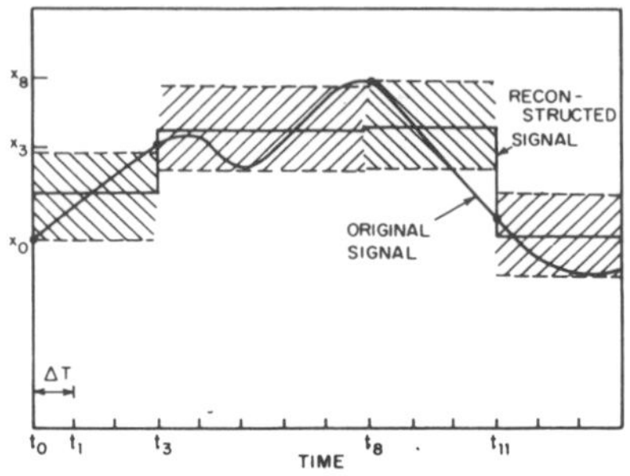


Fig. 2. Operation of the zero-order interpolator.

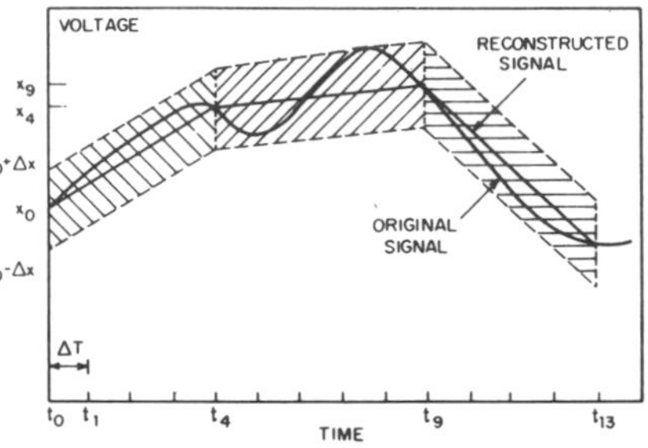


Fig. 3. Operation of the fan interpolator.

$$\hat{x}(t) = \begin{cases} x_0 & 0 \le t \le t_2 \\ x_2 & t_2 \le t \le t_7 \\ x_7 & t_7 \le t \le t_{10}. \end{cases}$$

As long as the input sampling rate is high enough that the original signal does not go out of the aperture and return within it during the interval between two samples, the interpolation error is less than $\Delta X$ in absolute value for all sample intervals except the last. This condition is essentially the same as saying that the interpolation error is much greater than the aliasing error; neglecting the "excess over the boundary," then, $\Delta X$ is the maximum reconstruction error possible for the floating-aperture predictor.

*Zero-Order Interpolator*

The zero-order interpolator, like the floating-aperture predictor, is a horizontal aperture device with a stair-step reconstruction. However, where the floating-aperture predictor utilized only the a priori knowledge of the initial sample value in centering the aperture, the zero-order interpolator operates by maximizing the length of time that the signal, starting at a given point in the aperture space, will stay in the aperture space. This is accomplished by moving the aperture vertically after each signal sample is taken and adjusting the aperture so that the signal samples stay in the aperture for the longest possible time. Figure 2 shows the zero-order interpolator fitted to the same signal as Fig. 1. The aperture is centered at $X_0+\mu\Delta X$, where in general $0 \le \mu \le 1$, and the signal occupies the entire aperture space of $2\Delta X$. The time, say $t_i$, at which the aperture can no longer be adjusted so that all previous samples fall within the aperture, is placed in a buffer for future transmission along with the position of the center of the aperture. The sampling is then continued, with the first sample being $X_i$.

An examination of the signal and aperture geometry shows that the mean time between output samples is lower-bounded by the mean time between output samples of a floating-aperture predictor with the same size aperture, and upper-bounded by the mean time between output samples of a floating-aperture predictor with an aperture twice the size.

*Fan Interpolator*

The fan interpolator operates by fitting the longest straight line between two sample points, say $X_0$ and $X_n$, such that all the intermediate sample points fall within the slanting aperture defined by the two straight lines between $X_0+\Delta X$ and $X_n+\Delta X$, and $X_0-\Delta X$ and $X_n-\Delta X$. Figure 3 shows the fan interpolator operating on the same signal as in Figs. 1 and 2. The values $X_0$ and $t_0$ are placed in a buffer for future transmission, and at times $t_0+n\Delta T$, $n=2, 3, \cdots$, apertures of width $2\Delta X$ are drawn, centered on the line joining $X_0$ and $X_n$. As long as all the intermediate samples $X_2 \cdots X_{n-1}$ fall within the aperture, no action is taken. The first time, say $t_i$, that any intermediate sample falls out of the aperture, the values $X_{i-1}$ and $t_{i-1}$ are placed in the buffer for future transmission, and the sampling is continued using $X_{i-1}$ as the starting point.

The signal is reconstructed at the receiving terminal by drawing straight lines between the received points $\{X_i, t_i\}$. As all the sample points fall within the aperture space, there is no excess over the boundary as exists with the two previous algorithms described. The maximum excursion on the direction opposite to the exit boundary is $\mu\Delta X$, and the signal occupies $(1+\mu)\Delta X$ of the $2\Delta X$-wide aperture space.

## III. Principles of Markov Processes

The Markov process will play a central role in the analysis of the bandwidth compression algorithms, and we now summarize some of its important properties [7]. A discrete parameter stochastic process $\{x(n\Delta T), n=0, 1, \cdots\}$ or a continuous parameter stochastic process $\{x(t), t \ge 0\}$ is said to be a (first-order) Markov process if, for any set of $n$ time points $t_1 < t_2 < \cdots < t_n$ in the index set of the process, the conditional distribution of $x(t_n)$ for given values of $x(t_1)$,

$x(t_2) \cdots x(t_{n-1})$ depends only on $x(t_{n-1})$, the most recent known value; more precisely for every $n=1, 2, \cdots$, any real numbers $X_1 \cdots X_n$, $t_1 < t_2 < \cdots < t_n$,

$$P\{x(t_n) \le X_n | x(t_1) = X_1, \cdots, x(t_{n-1}) = X_{n-1}\} = P\{x(t_n) < X_n | x(t_{n-1}) = X_{n-1}\}. \quad (3)$$

The same relation holds for the probability density function of the process, i.e.,

$$p\{x(t_n)|x(t_1) \cdots x(t_{n-1})\} = p\{x(t_n)|x(t_{n-1})\}. \quad (4)$$

It therefore follows that the $n$th-order conditional probability density function of the process can be factored as follows:

$$p\{x(t_n) \cdots x(t_1)|x(t_0)\} = p\{x(t_n)|x(t_{n-1})\} \cdots p(x(t_1)|x(t_0)\}. \quad (5)$$

By considering the $x$'s to be a **k** component vector random variable,

$$\mathbf{x}(t_n) = \{x_1(t_n), \cdots, x_k(t_n)\} \quad (6)$$

one can similarly define a **k** component vector Markov process for which

$$p\{\mathbf{x}(t_n)|\mathbf{x}(t_{n-1}), \cdots, \mathbf{x}(t_1)\} = p\{\mathbf{x}(t_n)|\mathbf{x}(t_{n-1})\}. \quad (7)$$

The vector Markov process is of practical engineering importance, since the result of filtering white Gaussian noise through a $k$-pole RLC network is a **k** component Gaussian Markov process; the voltage across the capacitor of a RC network which is driven by white Gaussian noise is, in fact, the familiar first-order stationary Gaussian Markov process.

The conditional probability density function of a first-order Markov process varies with time as described by two partial differential equations first derived by Kolmogorov, and known as the forward Kolmogorov, or Fokker-Planck equation, and the backward Kolmogorov equation [8]. The backward Kolmogorov equation is

$$-\frac{\partial p\{x(t)|x(t_0)\}}{\partial t_0} = \frac{A_2\{x(t_0)\}}{2}\frac{\partial^2 p\{x(t)|x(t_0)\}}{\partial x(t_0)^2} + A_1\{x(t_0)\}\frac{\partial p\{x(t)|x(t_0)\}}{\partial x(t_0)} \quad (8)$$

where

$$A_n = \lim_{t-t_0 \to 0} \frac{1}{t-t_0}\int_{-\infty}^{\infty} \{x(t) - x(t_0)\}^n p\{x(t)|x(t_0)\}\, dx(t).$$

The backward equation will be used later to solve for the mean and mean-square times between output samples of the floating-aperture predictor.

## IV. Mean and Mean Square Time Between Output Samples

*Floating-Aperture Predictor*

1) *Sampled Inputs:* In order to find the mean and mean-square times between output samples of the floating-aperture predictor, we consider a quantity $P(n|X_0)$, the probability that the first crossing of either the upper or lower aperture boundary occurred at step $n$, given that $x(t_0) = X_0$:

$$P(n|X_0) = \text{Prob}\,\{[X_0 - \Delta X < x(t_i) < X_0 + \Delta X,\ 1 \le i \le n-1] \text{ and } [(x(t_n) \ge X_0 + \Delta X] \text{ or } (x(t_n) \le X_0 - \Delta X)]|x(_0) = X_0\}. \quad (9)$$

The mean and mean-square times between output samples are then

$$E[T|X_0] = \Delta T \sum_{n=1}^{\infty} nP(n|X_0) \quad (10)$$

$$E[T^2|X_0] = \Delta T^2 \sum_{n=1}^{\infty} n^2 P(n|X_0). \quad (11)$$

First we will examine the events in (9). For the floating-aperture predictor, $Q_1(X_0)$, the probability that the signal sample at $t_1$ falls in the aperture space, is

$$Q_1(X_0) = \int_{X_0-\Delta X}^{X_0+\Delta X} dx_1 p(x_1|X_0). \quad (12)$$

In general, $Q_n(X_0)$, the probability that the signals at times $t_1 \cdots t_n$ all fall in the aperture space, is

$$Q_n(X_0) = \int_{X_0-\Delta X}^{X_0+\Delta X} \cdots \int dx_n \cdots dx_1 p(x_n, \cdots, x_1|X_0). \quad (13)$$

For the case in which the signal is a time-homogeneous Markov process, the use of (5) in (13) results in simplifications, and $Q_n(X_0)$ can be then written recursively as

$$Q_n(X_0) = \int_{X_0-\Delta X}^{X_0+\Delta X} dy q_n(y, X_0) \quad (14)$$

where

$$q_n(y, X_0) = \int_{X_0-\Delta X}^{X_0+\Delta X} dz p(y|z) q_{n-1}(z, X_0) \quad (15)$$

and

$$q_1(y, X_0) = p(y|X_0), \qquad Q_0(X_0) = 1.$$

From the definition of $Q_n(X_0)$ and $P(n|X_0)$ in (9), it follows that

$$P(n|X_0) = Q_{n-1}(X_0) - Q_n(X_0). \quad (16)$$

Therefore,

$$E[T|X_0] = \Delta T \sum_{n=1}^{\infty} n\{Q_{n-1}(X_0) - Q_n(X_0)\} \quad (17)$$

$$= \Delta T \sum_{n=1}^{\infty} Q_n(X_0) \quad (18)$$

and similarly,

$$E[T^2|X_0] = \Delta T^2 \sum_{n=0}^{\infty} (2n+1) Q_n(X_0). \quad (19)$$

Equation (15) is of the same form as the iterated kernel of a Fredholm integral equation, which leads us to suspect that (18) and (19) may correspond to the solutions of two integral equations. In fact, it can be shown [9] that if we consider the two Fredholm equations of the second kind,

$$\overline{t(x_0)} = \int_{X_0-\Delta X}^{X_0+\Delta X} p(y|x_0)\,\overline{t(y)}\,dy + \Delta T \tag{20}$$

$$\overline{t^2(x_0)} = \int_{X_0-\Delta X}^{X_0+\Delta X} p(y|x_0)\,\overline{t^2(y)}\,dy + 2\Delta T\,\overline{t(x_0)} - \Delta T^2 \tag{21}$$

then

$$E[T|X_0] = \overline{t(X_0)} \tag{22}$$

and

$$E[T^2|X_0] = \overline{t^2(X_0)}. \tag{23}$$

The proof of this consists of finding the Neumann series solutions to (20) and (21), and showing that they are equal to (18) and (19) evaluated at $X_0$. Since, if the Neumann series solution of a Fredholm integral equation exists, it is the unique solution to the equation [10], this completes the proof.

Similarly, if the signal into the predictor is the component $x_1(t)$ of a **k** component vector Markov process, and we define the **k**-dimensional aperture space $S$ as

$$S = \begin{cases} [X_0 - \Delta X, X_0 + \Delta X] & \text{for } x_1(t) \\ [-\infty, \infty] & \text{for } x_2(t), \cdots, x_k(t) \end{cases}$$

then it can be shown [9] that

$$E[T|\mathbf{X}_0] = \overline{t(\mathbf{X}_0)} \tag{24}$$

$$E[T^2|\mathbf{X}_0] = \overline{t^2(\mathbf{X}_0)} \tag{25}$$

where

$$\overline{t(\mathbf{x}_0)} = \int \cdot \underset{S}{\cdot} \cdot \int p(\mathbf{y}|\mathbf{x}_0)\,\overline{t(\mathbf{y})}\,d\mathbf{y} + \Delta T \tag{26}$$

$$\overline{t^2(\mathbf{x}_0)} = \int \cdot \underset{S}{\cdot} \cdot \int p(\mathbf{y}|\mathbf{x}_0)\,\overline{t^2(\mathbf{y})}\,d\mathbf{y} + 2\Delta T\,\overline{t(\mathbf{x}_0)} - \Delta T^2. \tag{27}$$

2) *Continuous Input:* As the input sampling rate increases, the mean time between output samples of a floating-aperture predictor should approach the mean absorption time of the signal process considered as a continuous parameter random walk on an absorbing barrier aperture space; for a first-order, time-homogeneous Markov process, this can be found from the backward Kolmogorov equation (8) [11]. Let $p\{x(t)|x(t_0)\}$ be a solution to (8) which satisfies the boundary conditions at $x_1$ and $x_2$, with $x_1 < x_2$:

$$\left.\begin{aligned} p\{x_1|x(t_0)\} &= 0 \\ p\{x_2|x(t_0)\} &= 0 \end{aligned}\right\} \quad t > t_0$$

and the initial condition

$$p\{x(t_0)|X_0\} = \delta\{x(t_0) - X_0\}.$$

The probability that the boundary is not reached during a time interval $\tau = t - t_0$, $P(\tau|x_0)$, is

$$P(\tau|x_0) = \int_{x_1}^{x_2} p\{x(t)|x_0\}\,dx(t). \tag{28}$$

The mean time to absorption is then

$$E[T|x_0] = \int_0^\infty \tau \frac{d}{d\tau}[1 - P(\tau|x_0)]\,d\tau \tag{29}$$

$$= -\int_0^\infty \tau\,dP(\tau|x_0). \tag{30}$$

Integrating (30) by parts and using the boundary conditions $P(0|x_0)=1$, $P(\infty|x_0)=0$, then:

$$E[T|x_0] = \int_0^\infty P(\tau|x_0)\,d\tau. \tag{31}$$

Integrating (8) with respect to $x(t_0)$ from $x_1$ to $x_2$ and with respect to $\tau$ from 0 to $\infty$, and then using (31), results in the differential equation

$$-1 = A_1(x_0)\frac{d}{dx_0}E[T|x_0] + \frac{1}{2}A_2(x_0)\frac{d^2}{dx_0^2}E[T|x_0] \tag{32}$$

with the boundary conditions

$$E[T|x_1] = E[T|x_2] = 0.$$

Similarly, it can be shown [9] that $E[T^2|x_0]$ satisfies the differential equation

$$-2E[T|x_0] = A_1(x_0)\frac{d}{dx_2}E[T^2|x_0] + \frac{1}{2}A_2(x_0)\frac{d^2}{dx_0^2}E[T^2|x_0] \tag{33}$$

with the boundary conditions

$$E[T^2|x_1] = E[T^2|x_2] = 0.$$

*Zero-Order Interpolator*

The mean and mean-square times between output samples from a zero-order interpolator can be expressed in terms of the random variable known as the range of the process [9]. Given the sequence of sample values $\{x(t_0+i\Delta T), i=0, 1, \cdots\}$, and defining

$$M_n = \max\{x(t_0 + i\Delta T),\ 0 \le i \le n\}$$
$$m_n = \min\{x(t_0 + i\Delta T),\ 0 \le i \le n\}$$

then $R_n$, the range of the signal over the $n+1$ samples, is

$$R_n = M_n - m_n.$$

The zero-order interpolator can be characterized as the device which measures the length of time that it takes for the range to first exceed the aperture width of $2\Delta X$, given that the signal has the value $X_0$ at $t_0$. The probability density function of the range of a sampled sequence is difficult to find in analytic form. However, the probability density function of a continuous parameter first-order Markov process can be found in terms of the Laplace transform of the backward Kolmogorov equation by a method of Darling and Siegert [12]. If we consider that the input sampling rate is arbitrarily high, then the time between output samples of a zero-order interpolator approaches the time that it takes for the range $r(t) = \max \{x(\tau)\} - \min \{x(\tau)\}$, $t_0 \leq \tau \leq t$, of the underlying continuous process, to first exceed $2\Delta X$. If $p(r; t|X_0)$ is the probability density function of the range of the underlying continuous process, at time $t_0 + t$, given that the initial sample value at $t_0$ was $X_0$, then

$$\text{Prob} \{r(t) < 2\Delta X | x(t_0) = X_0\} = \int_0^{2\Delta X} p(r; t|X_0)\, dr. \quad (34)$$

The mean time that it takes for the range to exceed the aperture width is then

$$E[T|X_0] = -\int_0^\infty t \left\{ \frac{d}{dt} \int_0^{2\Delta X} p(r; t|X_0)\, dr \right\} dt. \quad (35)$$

Integrating (35) by parts results in

$$E[T|X_0] = -t \int_0^{2\Delta X} dr\, p(r; t|X_0) \Big|_0^\infty$$
$$+ \int_0^\infty dt \int_0^{2\Delta X} p(r; t|X_0)\, dr. \quad (36)$$

If $E[T|X_0]$ is to be finite, then

$$\int_0^{2\Delta X} p(r; t|X_0)\, dr$$

must approach zero faster than $1/t$ as $t$ approaches infinity.

Therefore, (36) reduces to

$$E[T|X_0] = \int_0^\infty dt \int_0^{2\Delta X} p(r; t|X_0)\, dr \quad (37)$$

Similarly, it can be shown [9] that if $E[T^2|X_0]$ is finite, then

$$E[T^2|X_0] = 2 \int_0^\infty t\, dt \int_0^{2\Delta X} p(r; t|X_0)\, dr. \quad (38)$$

*Fan Interpolator*

The mean and mean-square times between output samples of the fan interpolator can be found by a modification of the method used of the floating-aperture predictor [9]. Assume that the slope of the aperture connecting the initial sample $X_0$ and the $(n+1)$st sample $X_n$ is $m$ volts per sample interval. Then $Q_n(X_0, m)$, the probability that samples $x(t_1), \cdots, x(t_{n-1})$ are all in the aperture of slope $m$ and width $2\Delta X$, is

$$Q_n(X_0, m) = \int_{X_0+(n-1)m-\Delta X}^{X_0+(n-1)m+\Delta X} dx(t_{n-1}) \cdots \int_{X_0+m-\Delta X}^{X_0+m+\Delta X} dx(t_1)$$
$$\cdot p\{x(t_{n-1}), \cdots, x(t_1)|x(t_0) = X_0, x(t_n) = X_0 + nm\}. \quad (39)$$

From the properties of conditional probabilities, $Q_n(X_0, m)$ can also be written as

$$Q_n(X_0, m) = \frac{\int_{X_0+(n-1)m-\Delta X}^{X_0+(n-1)m+\Delta X} dx(t_{n-1}) \cdots \int_{X_0+m-\Delta X}^{X_0+m+\Delta X} dx(t_1) p\{x(t_n) = X_0 + nm, x(t_{n-1}) \cdots x(t_1)|x(t_0) = X_0\}}{p\{x(t_n) = X_0 + nm|x(t_0) = X_0\}}. \quad (40)$$

Then $P(n|X_0, m)$, the probability that at least one of the intermediate samples falls out of the aperture at time $t_n$ for the first time, given the initial sample value $X_0$ and slope $m$, is

$$P(n|X_0, m) = Q_{n-1}(X_0, m) - Q_n(X_0, m). \quad (41)$$

The mean and mean-square times between output samples of the fan interpolator are, therefore,

$$E[T|X_0, m]$$
$$= \Delta T \sum_{n=2}^\infty (n-1)\{Q_{n-1}(X_0, m) - Q_n(X_0, m)\} \quad (42)$$

$$E[T^2|X_0, m]$$
$$= \Delta T^2 \sum_{n=2}^\infty (n-1)^2 \{Q_{n-1}(X_0, m) - Q_n(X_0, m)\}. \quad (43)$$

For the case in which the signal is a $k$ component vector Markov process, the $Q_n$ can be determined as a set of iterated kth-order integrals. Consider the case $k=1$, the first-order Markov process. Then, using (5) in (41) results in

$$Q_n(X_0, m)$$
$$= \frac{\int_{X_0+(n-1)m-\Delta X}^{X_0+(n-1)m+\Delta X} dx(t_{n-1}) \cdots \int_{X_0+m-\Delta X}^{X_0+m+\Delta X} dx(t_1) p\{x(t_n) = X_0 + nm|x(t_{n-1})\} p\{x(t_{n-1})|x(t_{n-2})\} \cdots p\{x(t_1)|x(t_0) = X_0\}}{p\{x(t_n) = X_0 + nm|x(t_0) = X_0\}}. \quad (44)$$

For computational purposes, (44) can be more easily written in the recursive form

$$Q_n(X_0, m) = \frac{q_n\{x(t_n) = X_0 + nm, x(t_0) = X_0\}}{p\{x(t_n) = X_0 + nm|x(t_0) = X_0\}} \quad (45)$$

where [see (15)]

$$q_n\{x(t_n), x(t_0) = X_0\} = \int_{X_0+(n-1)m-\Delta X}^{X_0+(n-1)m+\Delta X}$$
$$\cdot p\{x(t_n)|x(t_{n-1})\} q_{n-1}\{x(t_{n-1}), x(t_0) = X_0\}\, dx(t_{n-1}). \quad (46)$$

The extension to **k** greater than one is evident. The basic equations are (42) through (46), with vector variables taking the place of first-order variables. The integration is performed on a **k**-dimensional space $S_n$ defined as

$$S_n = \begin{cases} [X_0 + nm - \Delta X,\ X_1 + nm + \Delta X] & \text{for } x_1(t_n) \\ [-\infty, \infty] & \text{for } x_2(t_n) \cdots x_k(t_n). \end{cases}$$

## V. Results

We now present the results obtained by applying the foregoing theory to first-order Gaussian Markov processes.

*Floating-Aperture Predictor*

The first-order stationary Gaussian Markov process which results from passing white Gaussian noise of spectral density $N_0$ volts²/Hz through an $RC$ filter satisfies the Kolmogorov equations with coefficients [15]:

$$A_1(x_0) = -x_0/(RC) \quad (47a)$$

$$A_2(x_0) = N_0/(RC)^2. \quad (47b)$$

The conditional probability density function is

$$p(x(\Delta T)|x(0)) = \frac{\exp -\left(\dfrac{(x(\Delta T) - \rho x(0))^2}{2\sigma^2(1-\rho^2)}\right)}{\sqrt{2\pi\sigma^2(1-\rho^2)}} \quad (48)$$

where

$$\rho = \exp(-\Delta T/(RC))$$
$$\sigma^2 = N_0/(2RC) = \text{mean-square signal value.} \quad (49)$$

The solutions of the differential equations (32) and (33) are:

$$E[T|x_0] = -\frac{RC}{\sigma^2}\int_{X_0-\Delta X}^{x_0} dv e^{v^2/2\sigma^2}\int_{X_0-\Delta X}^{v} e^{-(u^2/2\sigma^2)}du + \frac{RC}{\sigma^2}\frac{\int_{X_0-\Delta X}^{X_0+\Delta X} dv e^{v^2/2\sigma^2}\int_{X_0-\Delta X}^{v} e^{-(u^2/2\sigma^2)}du}{\int_{X_0-\Delta X}^{X_0+\Delta X} e^{v^2/2\sigma^2}dv} \cdot \int_{X_0-\Delta X}^{x_0} e^{v^2/2\sigma^2}dv \quad (50)$$

$$E[T^2|x_0] = -\frac{RC}{\sigma^2}\int_{X_0-\Delta X}^{x_0} dv e^{v^2/2\sigma^2}\int_{X_0-\Delta X}^{v} E[T|u]e^{-(u^2/2\sigma^2)}du + \frac{RC}{\sigma^2}\frac{\int_{X_0-\Delta X}^{X_0+\Delta X} dv e^{v^2/2\sigma^2}\int_{X_0-\Delta X}^{v} E[T|u]e^{-(u^2/2\sigma^2)}du}{\int_{X_0-\Delta X}^{X_0+\Delta X} e^{v^2/2\sigma^2}dv} \cdot \int_{X_0-\Delta X}^{x_0} e^{v^2/2\sigma^2}dv. \quad (51)$$

Equations (50) and (51) have been evaluated on a digital computer. Figure 4 shows the normalized solution of (50) as a function of the half-aperture width for the four initial sample values 0, $\sigma$, $2\sigma$, and $3\sigma$. It is seen that the mean time between output samples is basically independent of $X_0$, the initial sample value, for half-aperture widths less than about $0.25\sigma$. Futhermore, for small aperture widths, the mean time between output samples is asymptotic to the straight line $E[T|X_0]=0.5\ RC(\Delta X/\sigma)^2$, regardless of the value of $X_0$. A simple series solution can be found for (50) in the special case of $X_0=0$. For this value, (50) reduces to

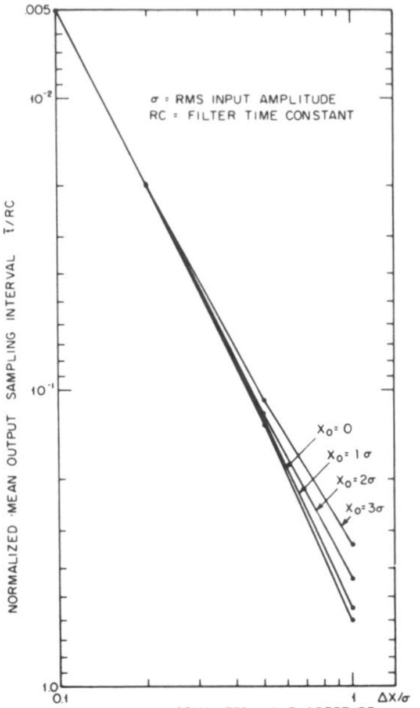


Fig. 4. The effect of initial sample value on the output sampling interval. Continuous $RC$ Gaussian process, floating-aperture predictor.

$$E[T|0] = 2RC\int_0^{\Delta X/\sqrt{2}\sigma} dv e^{v^2}\int_0^v e^{-u^2}du. \quad (52)$$

The solution of (52) is

$$E[T|0] = RC\sum_{m=0}^{\infty}\sum_{n=0}^{\infty}\frac{(-)^n\left(\dfrac{\Delta X}{\sigma}\right)^{2(n+m+1)}}{2^{(n+m)}(n+m+1)(2n+1)m!n!} \quad (53)$$

the first three terms of which are

$$E[T|0] = RC\left[\frac{1}{2}\left(\frac{\Delta X}{\sigma}\right)^2 + \frac{1}{12}\left(\frac{\Delta X}{\sigma}\right)^4 + \frac{1}{90}\left(\frac{\Delta X}{\sigma}\right)^6 \cdots\right]. \quad (54)$$

The asymptotic solution noted above is simply the first term of (54). The integral equations (20) and (21) with (48) as a kernel have also been solved on a digital computer. Figures 5 and 6 show the means and standard deviation, respectively, of the time between output samples for three different input sampling rates,

$\Delta T = 0.05\ RC(\Delta X/\sigma)^2$, $0.1\ RC(\Delta X/\sigma)^2$ and $0.5\ RC(\Delta X/\sigma)^2$.

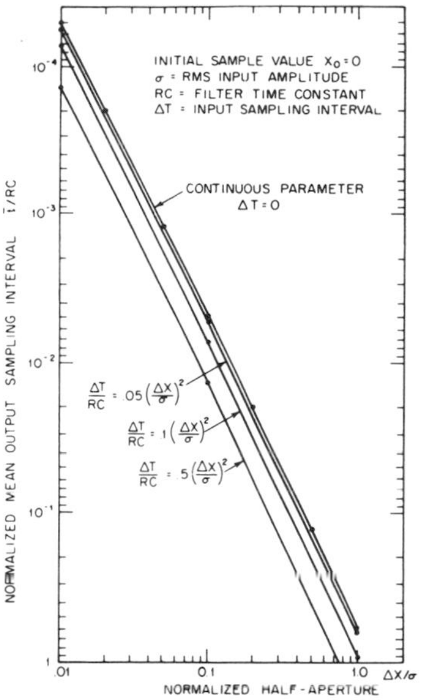


Fig. 5. The effect of input sampling interval on the output sampling interval. *RC* Gaussian process, floating-aperture predictor.

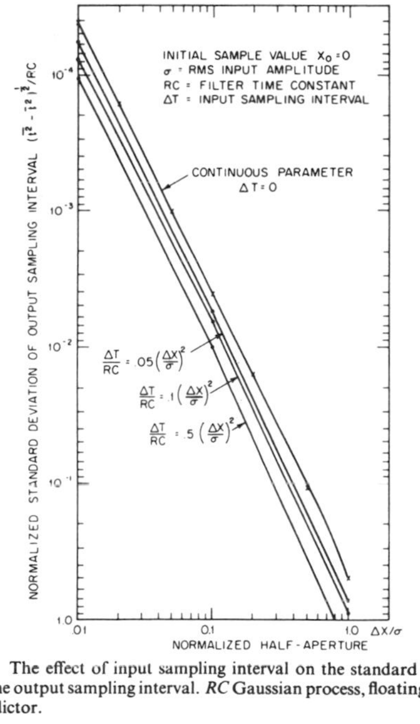


Fig. 6. The effect of input sampling interval on the standard deviation of the output sampling interval. *RC* Gaussian process, floating-aperture predictor.

Also shown in Figs. 5 and 6 are the means and standard deviations of the time between output samples given by the solutions of the differential equations (50) and (51), denoted by $\Delta T = 0$. It is seen that as the input sampling rate increases, the means and standard deviations of the time between output samples approach that of the continuous case. For small aperture widths, $\sigma_T$, the standard deviation of the sample time is asymptotic to the straight line $\sigma_T = 0.41\ RC(\Delta X/\sigma)^2$.

Insight into the meaning of the solutions for the *RC* Gaussian Markov case, as well as a degree of mathematical simplification, can be achieved, if we consider the Wiener process as an alternate signal process [15]. The Wiener process, a zero-mean, nonstationary Gaussian Markov process, corresponds to a random walk with no restoring force and results from integrating white Gaussian noise in a perfect integrator. It satisfies the Kolmogorov equations with coefficients

$$A_1(x_0) = 0 \tag{55a}$$

$$A_2(x_0) = 2D \tag{55b}$$

where $D$ is a diffusion constant which defines the Wiener process. The conditional probability density function is

$$p[x(\Delta T)|x(0)] = \frac{\exp\left(-\dfrac{(x(\Delta T) - x(0))^2}{4D\Delta T}\right)}{\sqrt{4\pi D\Delta T}}. \tag{56}$$

Using (55), the solutions to the differential equations (32) and (33) are

$$E[T|X_0] = \Delta X^2/(2D) \tag{57}$$

$$E[T^2|X_0] = 5\Delta X^4/(12D^2). \tag{58}$$

Thus, for the Wiener process, the means and standard deviations of the time between output samples from a floating-aperture predictor are both independent of the initial sample value for any size aperture; the conditioning of (57) and (58) is therefore unnecessary.

Returning to (49) for a moment, we see that for time intervals $\Delta T$ which are short compared with the time constant *RC* the correlation coefficient $\rho$ is approximately 1, while $1-\rho^2$ is approximately $2\Delta T/RC$. The conditional probability density function of the *RC* Gaussian Markov process is then approximately

$$p(x(\Delta T)|x(0)) \simeq \frac{\exp -\left[\dfrac{[x(\Delta T) - x(0)]^2}{4\sigma^2\Delta T/RC}\right]}{\sqrt{4\pi\sigma^2\Delta T/RC}}; \quad \Delta T \ll RC. \tag{59}$$

Comparing (59) and (56), we see that for short time intervals the conditional probability density function of the *RC* Gaussian Markov process behaves approximately in the same manner as that of a Wiener process, with the diffusion constant $D$ equal to $\sigma^2/RC$. Thus, for aperture widths such that the mean time between output samples is small compared to the time constant *RC* of the Gaussian Markov process, the integral equations (20) and (21) and the differential equations (32) and (33) give approximately the same solutions when the input signal is either the $RC$ Gaussian Markov process or the Wiener process with $D=\sigma^2/RC$. For example, setting $D=\sigma^2/RC$ in (57) and (58) and defining the standard deviation of the time between output samples as $\sigma_T$ results in

$$E[T] = 0.5\, RC(\Delta X/\sigma)^2 \tag{60}$$

$$\sigma_T = 0.82\, E[T]. \tag{61}$$

Equations (60) and (61) are the small aperture asymptotes of $E[T|X_0]$ and $\sigma_T$ for the $RC$ Gaussian Markov process in the floating-aperture predictor. Thus, for aperture widths less than the RMS value of the process, one can validly study the behavior of the simpler Wiener process in the floating aperture predictor, with the results being asymptotically those which would be found if the more complicated $RC$ Gaussian Markov process were used. For larger apertures the approximation is not valid and the exact $RC$ Gaussian Markov distribution must be studied. In the remainder of this paper, however, numerical calculations will be based on the Wiener process, with the understanding that, for small apertures, the results are essentially the same as would be found for the $RC$ Gaussian Markov process.

Since the samples are buffered before transmission at a uniform rate, the transmission rate of the floating aperture predictor is $E[T]^{-1}$ samples per second.

*Zero-Order Interpolator*

The probability density function of the range of a Wiener process is [16]

$$p(r;t|X_0) = \frac{2}{\pi} r^{-1} L'(r/(2\sqrt{2Dt}) \tag{62}$$

where

$$L(u) = \frac{\sqrt{2\pi}}{u} \sum_{k=1}^{\infty} \exp\left(-\frac{(2k-1)^2\pi^2}{8u^2}\right).$$

Using (62) in (37) and (38) results, after considerable manipulation, in

$$E[T|X_0] = \Delta X^2/D \tag{63}$$

$$E[T^2|X_0] = 4\Delta X^4/(3D^2). \tag{64}$$

As $p(r;t|X_0)$ is, for the Wiener process, independent of $X_0$, (63) and (64) are equal to $E[T]$ and $E[T^2]$, respectively. The standard deviation of the output sample interval is

$$\sigma_T = 0.58\, E(T). \tag{65}$$

Comparing (63) with (57) and (65) with (61) shows the mean time between output samples for the zero-order interpolator to be twice that of the floating-aperture predictor, while the relative standard deviation, $\sigma_T/E[T]$, is smaller by a factor of $\sqrt{2}$.

Thus it follows that the transmission rate of the zero-order interpolator is half that of the floating-aperture predictor when used on the Wiener process.

*Fan Interpolator*

Equations (42) and (43) were evaluated on a digital computer for the case in which the signal is a Wiener process. For an input sampling interval of 0.05 $RC(\Delta X/\sigma)^2$, the mean and standard deviations of the time between output samples were found to be

$$E[T] = 1.2\, RC(\Delta X/\sigma)^2 \tag{66}$$

$$= 1.2\, \Delta X^2/D \tag{67}$$

$$\sigma_T = 0.6\, E[T]. \tag{68}$$

The means and standard deviation were both found to be independent of the initial sample value and the aperture slope. Thus, the transmission rate of the fan interpolator is approximately a factor of 2.4 lower than that of the floating-aperture predictor [see (57)], when used on the Wiener process.

## VI. Comparison with Uniform Sampling

We have shown the relative effectiveness of the three redundancy removal bandwidth compression algorithms in the previous section. In order to allow a comparison against a more commonly used standard, we now summarize known results from sampling theory and compare the transmission rates required by the redundancy removal algorithms to those required by an optimum PCM system.

*Interpolation of Uniformly Sampled Signals*

If a random process with power spectral density $\Phi_{xx}(\omega)$ is uniformly sampled and subsequently reconstructed from the samples by the use of the optimum time-invariant linear filter, then $\overline{\varepsilon_{\text{OPT}}^2}$, the resulting mean-square interpolation error, is [13]

$$\overline{\varepsilon_{\text{OPT}}^2} = \frac{1}{2\pi}\int_{-\infty}^{\infty} \Phi_{xx}(\omega)\left[1 - \frac{\Phi_{xx}(\omega)}{\sum_{n=-\infty}^{\infty} \Phi_{xx}(\omega + 2\pi n/\Delta T)}\right] d\omega. \tag{69}$$

For the $RC$ Gaussian Markov process,

$$\Phi_{xx}(\omega) = \frac{2\sigma^2/(RC)^2}{\left(\frac{1}{RC}\right)^2 + \omega^2}. \tag{70}$$

Using (70) in (69) results in

$$\overline{\varepsilon_{\text{OPT}}^2} = \left[\sigma^2 \coth\frac{\Delta T}{RC} - \frac{RC}{\Delta T}\right]. \tag{71}$$

Similarly, for the Wiener process with the same high-frequency power density spectrum as the $RC$ Gaussian Markov process,

$$\Phi_{xx}(\omega) = 2\left(\frac{\sigma^2}{\omega RC}\right)^2. \tag{72}$$

Using (72) in (69) results in

$$\overline{\varepsilon_{\text{OPT}}^2} = \sigma^2\Delta T/(3RC). \tag{73}$$

For sampling, i.e., $\Delta T << RC$, the Taylor's series expansion of (71) reduces to (73) with an error of the order of $(\Delta T/RC)^3$. Thus, for high sampling rates, we again see the approximate interchangeability of the $RC$ Gaussian Markov and Wiener processes.

A second result which we now use comes from quantization theory. When an analog signal is to be transmitted in digital form, some type of quantizer is required. If a uniform quantizer of step width $2\Delta X$ is used, i.e., the same size aperture as we have been considering for the redundancy removal devices, then the mean-square reconstruction error due to quantization is approximately equal to $\Delta X^2/3$ [17].

It is good system design to have the error due to quantization nominally equal to that due to interpolation. Equating (73) to $\Delta X^2/3$, we then find that the sampling rate $\Delta T_{PCM}$ for a PCM system with a quantization size equal to the aperture width of the redundancy removal algorithms is

$$\Delta T_{PCM} = RC\left(\frac{\Delta X}{\sigma}\right)^2 \quad (74)$$

$$= \Delta X^2/D. \quad (75)$$

One way to compare the performance of the compaction systems considered here with the uniformly sampled and optimally filtered PCM is to examine the ratio $E[T]/\Delta T_{PCM}$. Table I summarizes the sampling rates required for the three redundancy removal algorithms relative to optimum PCM for the same size aperture and the first-order Gaussian Markov process.

TABLE I

RELATIVE MEAN OUTPUT SAMPLING RATES FOR SEVERAL SYSTEMS

| System | Mean Output Sampling Rate / Optimum Filter PCM Sampling Rate |
|---|---|
| Floating-Aperture Predictor | 2.0 |
| Zero-Order Interpolator | 1.0 |
| Fan Interpolator | 0.83 |

It is seen that, using sampling rate as a criterion, the floating-aperture predictor system is not as efficient as is uniform sampling and optimum linear filter interpolation. On the other hand, the zero-order interpolator is as good as, and the fan interpolator is better than uniform sampling and optimum linear filter interpolation. It should be further pointed out that, given the desired interpolation error, a redundancy removal algorithm will always adjust its transmission rate to the input signal, while a system which uses uniform sampling will, due to a lack of sufficient a priori knowledge, usually sample at either too high a rate, resulting in unneeded accuracy, or too low a rate, resulting in a loss of accuracy.

In order to make bandwidth comparisons, it is necessary to recall that the redundancy removal algorithms require the transmission of sample timing information, which is not needed in the uniform sampling case, along with each sample amplitude value. Defining $\rho$ as the ratio of the timing word length to the sample amplitude word length, the bandwidth required for each of the redundancy removal algorithms would be a factor of $(1+\rho)$ greater than that indicated by sampling rate considerations alone. As an example, if the amplitude word were six bits in length and the timing word were four bits in length, then $\rho = 2/3$ and the floating aperture predictor would require 2.0 times as much bandwidth as would uniform sampling and optimum linear filter interpolation; the zero-order interpolator would require 1.7 times as much bandwidth, and the fan interpolator 1.3 times as much bandwidth, as would optimum uniform sampling.

We have, throughout this paper, referred to the existence of a buffer as an integral part of a redundancy removal system. A parameter of importance in buffer design is the relative standard deviation of the time between buffer input samples; in our notation this would be $\sigma_T/E[T]$. The implication of this quantity is that the smaller the relative standard deviation, the less stringent the buffer requirements. The limiting case of this is uniform sampling which requires no buffer at all for correct operation. From (61), (65), and (68), we see that the floating-aperture predictor has a relative standard deviation approximately 1.4 times as great as either the zero-order interpolator or the fan interpolator. Thus, it would be expected that the floating-aperture predictor would require a larger buffer than the other systems.

## VII. Summary and Conclusions

In this paper we have shown how three redundancy removal bandwidth compression techniques can be analyzed, and have computed their performance for the case of the first-order Gaussian Markov input signal. We have shown that the best of these three systems, the fan interpolator, will require about the same transmission bandwidth as an optimum uniform sampling system, while the other two algorithms will require wider transmission bandwidths than will the optimum uniform sampling systems. In view of this, it is proper to ask if these algorithms actually deserve to be called bandwidth compression techniques. The answer to the question depends on the information known about the signal. If the signal process were a well defined stationary random process, then uniform sampling and optimum interpolation would probably be simpler to instrument and require a narrower transmission bandwidth than would these algorithms. On the other hand, if, as is usually the case, the signal statistics were unknown or time-varying, in order to use uniform sampling it would be necessary to estimate the signal spectrum at the transmitter, sample at the proper uniform rate, and then reconstruct with the proper interpolation filter at the receiver. The instrumentation requirements implied by this at the transmitter would in most cases tend to be sufficiently unreasonable so that the system designer would simply sample at a rate consistent with the widest spectrum that is expected, with the result that the data would be oversampled most of the time. It is in these cases that the redundancy removal algorithms can be expected to result in a substantial savings in transmission bandwidth.

## ACKNOWLEDGMENT

The author wishes to thank his associates at both SIGNATRON, Inc., and Northeastern University, particularly Dr. J. J. Bussgang and Prof. W. H. Lob, for suggestions during the course of this research.

## REFERENCES

[1] D. R. Weber, "A synopsis on data compression," *Proc. Nat'l Telemetering Conf.*, pp. 9–16, 1965.
[2] L. W. Gardenhire, "Redundancy reduction—The key to adaptive telemetry," *Proc. Nat'l Telemetering Conf.*, 1964.
[3] J. E. Medlin, "Sampled data prediction for telemetry bandwidth compression," *IEEE Trans. on Space Electronics and Telemetry*, vol. SET-11, p. 29, March 1965.
[4] R. M. Goldstein, E. C. Posner, H. C. Rumsey, and A. J. Viterbi, "A Fokker-Planck equation arising in data compression," Jet Propulsion Labs., California Institute of Technology, Pasadena, Space Programs Summary 37-19, vol. IV, p. 172, February 28, 1963.
[5] A. Bostrom, R. Goldstein, and E. C. Posner, "The floating-aperture data compression system applied to Gaussian inputs," Jet Propulsion Labs., California Institute of Technology, Pasadena, Space Programs Summary 37-17, vol. IV, p. 81, October 30, 1962.
[6] C. J. Palermo, R. V. Palermo, and H. Horwitz, "The use of data omission for redundancy removal," presented at the 1965 Internat'l Space Electronics and Telemetry Symp., Miami Beach, Fla.
[7] E. Parzen, *Stochastic Processes*. San Francisco: Holden-Day, 1962, p. 188.
[8] A. T. Bharucha-Reid, *Elements of the Theory of Markov Processes and Their Applications*. New York: McGraw-Hill, 1960, p. 102.
[9] L. Ehrman, "A study of adaptive bandwidth compression," Ph.D. dissertation, Northeastern University, Boston, Mass., to be submitted.
[10] E. Goursat, *A Course in Mathematical Analysis*, vol. III, pt. 2. New York: Dover, 1964, p. 29.
[11] R. L. Stratonovitch, *Topics in the Theory of Random Noise*, vol. 1. New York: Gordon and Breach, Inc., 1963, p. 79.
[12] D. A. Darling and A. J. F. Siegert, "The first passage problem for a continuous Markov process," *Ann. Math. Stat.*, vol. 24, pp. 624–639, 1953.
[13] D. W. Tufts, "A sampling theorem for stationary random processes," M.I.T. Research Lab. of Electronics, Cambridge, Mass., Quarterly Progress Rept. 53, pp. 87–93, April 15, 1959.
[14] K. L. Jordan, Jr., "Discrete representation of random signals," M.I.T. Research Lab. of Electronics, Cambridge, Mass., Tech. Rept. 378, p. 78, July 14, 1961.
[15] D. Middleton, *An Introduction to Statistical Communication Theory*. New York: McGraw-Hill, 1960, p. 445.
[16] W. Feller, "The asymptotic distribution of the range of sums of independent random variables," *Ann. Math. Stat.*, vol. 22, pp. 427–432, 1951.
[17] W. R. Bennett, "Spectra of quantized signals," *Bell Sys. Tech. J.*, vol. 27, pp. 446–472, July 1948.

Reprinted from *IEEE Trans. Inform. Theory,* **IT-14**(3) 390–394 (1968)

# Data Compression Using Straight Line Interpolation

LEE D. DAVISSON, MEMBER, IEEE

*Abstract*—**One simple method of data compression relies on the approximation of the source output by polynomial segments or "interpolators." The parameters of each polynomial are transmitted in place of the original data. This paper presents a method of theoretically analyzing such techniques. Straight line interpolation is considered specifically although the ideas can be readily generalized. It is shown that the class of compression methods considered may or may not perform well depending on the data and, thus, that in some cases more complex techniques, including possibly adaptive methods, might be used, depending on the knowledge of the data statistical model.**

## I. Introduction

ONE METHOD which has been suggested for data compression relies on the approximation of the source time series by straight line segments.[1]-[4] Starting from some initial point, the line which minimizes the maximum error magnitude between the line and the data over the length of the line is found as a function of the length. The longest line for which the maximum error is below a given threshold is found and used to approximate the data. This procedure may be performed directly on the source data or on the sampled and quantized data. The encoded message contains information about the length of the line and its starting and ending points. As the average line length increases, a net transmission rate reduction is achieved. The starting point may be chosen to be either the final end point of the previous interval, in which case only one sample value per line is transmitted, or, alternately, the first sample after that is used. If the preceding end point is used to start the next segment, the transmitted code word length is reduced at the expense of decreased flexibility (i.e., degrees of freedom) in the interpolation scheme, which may or may not result in a net compression ratio decrease. A scheme of the general class just described is sometimes called a "fan" method. Obviously, other methods could be described using more complicated interpolators than straight lines; however, the analysis presented here concentrates on the latter. Generalization to any other proposed scheme of this class is possible.

Because of the fixed nature of the method, it may or may not closely approximate the "optimum" (i.e., a transmission rate close to the source entropy). The purpose of this paper is to present a method of analysis, and to explore the advantages and limitations of the technique in terms of the compression ratio defined as the transmission rate in the absence of the algorithm, to that which results when it is applied. As will be seen here, the value of the technique relative to another method, such as run length encoding (sometimes called zero order hold prediction), where the number of consecutive samples at a given level is transmitted, depends on the data source distribution. It will be shown that for the specific fan method chosen the scheme is inferior to run length coding for some types of data, in particular the type found when TV signals are coarsely quantized with no further error allowed in the compression algorithm. For other data models, the fan method is shown to be better than run length encoding, as verified in certain of the references.[3],[4] Thus, the relative advantage of one algorithm over another depends on the data source probability distributions. If these are sufficiently well known, either empirically or from physical considerations, the intelligent choice of an algorithm of a fixed simple type can be made. In other cases, an adaptive algorithm, such as described in other work,[6]-[9] may be warranted.

An analysis of several compression algorithms appeared recently (Ehrman[3]). In contrast to the work presented here, Ehrman's results do not consider quantization errors and, in fact, can apply exactly only to a Wiener process. Apparently, generalization is not possible. On the other hand, in this paper, the method of analysis can be applied to any polynomial interpolation scheme for data with any probability model subject only to such computational time limits as the investigator wishes to impose.

## II. Data Compression Technique

Specifically, the straight line interpolation method analyzed in detail here is as follows.

1) The data are sampled and quantized.

2) No error is acceptable in the reconstructed data due to the compression algorithm. If the line fitting the data does not go through one of the quantization levels, the data are reconstructed by rounding off to the nearest level, as illustrated in Fig. 1. If the line is halfway between levels, the higher level is chosen, i.e., 2.5 → 3. Thus, no error results between the reconstructed and original quantized values.

3) The starting point for a given line is the same as the final end point of the previous line.

4) The message is encoded as a level-run length pair. The level is the final end point of the line, one of $L$ levels, and the run length, or timing word, is one of $T$ possible "runs" between line end points. For simplicity, the level is encoded into a $\log_2 L$-bit word and the run length is

Manuscript received April 28, 1967; revised October 29, 1967. This work was supported by the NASA Goddard Spaceflight Center Summer Workshop Program and NASA Contract NGR-31-001-068. An initial version appeared in NASA Report X-700-67-94.[1]

The author is with Princeton University, Princeton, N. J.

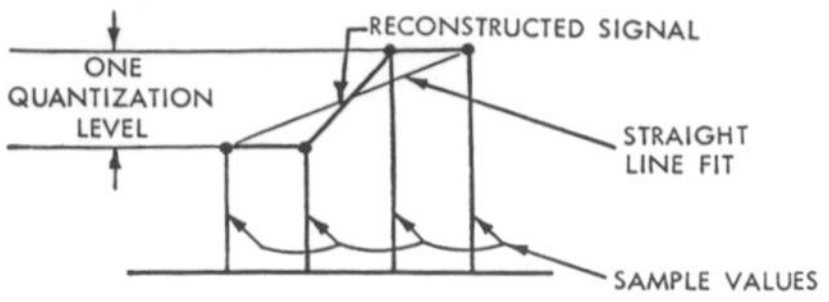


Fig. 1. Illustration of the straight line compression algorithm.

encoded into a $\log_2 T$-bit word. Further compression could be obtained by variable word length encoding.

It will be clear that the analytical techniques presented in the remainder of the paper can be generalized to include other methods of coding and interpolation.

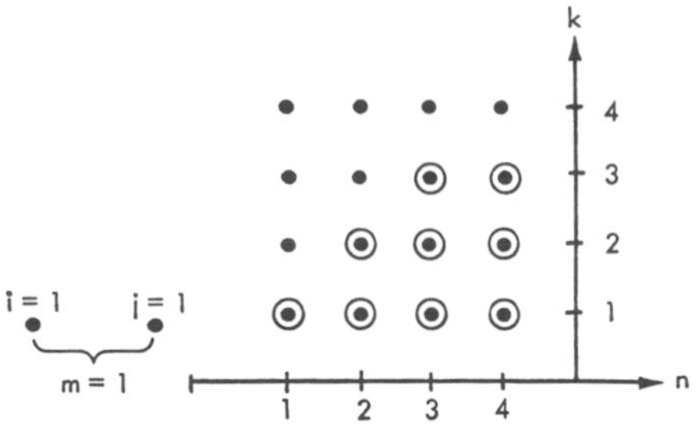


Fig. 2. End points of probability zero (encircled) after line of length one from level one to level one.

## III. Analysis

It is assumed in the following that the data are a stationary stochastic sequence. In order to find the compression ratio, the probability distribution of the line run lengths in terms of given data probability distribution is required. Suppose the $(q+1)$th line segment has as its initial end point the level $j$, and as its final end point the level $k$ located $n$ samples away. The probability of this occurrence is denoted by $p_q(j, k, n)$, which is read "the probability that the $(q+1)$th line from the beginning of the compression procedure goes from level $j$ to level $k$ in $n$ steps." The reason for the dependence on $q$ even though the data are stationary will be mentioned shortly. Suffice it to say that, in general, as $q \to \infty$, the probability approaches a steady-state value

$$p(j, k, n).$$

The average run length in terms of this probability is given by

$$\bar{n} = \sum_{j,k,n} np(j, k, n).$$

Then, the compression ratio for the coding scheme described above is

$$\frac{\bar{n} \log_2 L}{\log_2 T + \log_2 L}.$$

It is important to note that, with the exception of the first line segment which has no predecessors, the probability $p_q(j, k, n)$ depends on the procedure as used on the data preceding the line starting point, as well as the data source probability distribution and the procedure used on the succeeding data. That is, the probability of starting at level $j$ and proceeding along a straight line to level $k$ and no further in $n$ steps is affected by the fact that the $j$th level is the end point of the last line segment and, thus, that the preceding line segment could be extended no further. To illustrate this, consider the conditional probability of this event denoted as $(j, k, n)$ given that the previous starting point was $i$ and the previous run length was $m$ denoted by $p(j, k, n \mid i, j, m)$, which is read as "the probability of going from level $j$ to level $k$ in $n$ steps given that the previous line was from level $i$ to level $j$ in $m$ steps." Unlike the marginal probability, the conditional probability (for stationary data) does not depend on $q$ for reasons which will be seen shortly. Certain values of the conditional probability are zero independent of the data source distributions. For example,

$$p(l, l, n \mid l, l, m) = 0 \qquad \text{for} \qquad m < T.$$

This probability is zero because the occurrence of level $l$ after $(l, l, m)$ implies that the line connecting level $l$ with level $l$ in $m$ steps could have been extended further, violating the algorithm. Thus, the effect of the fan procedure on the line distribution is to assign zero to certain values of the conditional probability independent of the source statistics. To further illustrate this idea, in Fig. 2 where $L = T = 4$, those end points (values of $(k, n)$) which have probability zero are circled for $i = j = m = 1$. Note that for every path from $j$ to one of the encircled end points $(k, n)$, it is possible to make the line which starts at $i$ longer. Let the set of points $(k, n)$ where the conditional probability is zero for a given value $(i, j, m)$ be denoted by $S_{ijm}$ (the circled values in the preceding example), and the complement of this set, the remaining points, be denoted by $S^c_{ijm}$. Then, in terms of the conditional probability of the data $p_d(j, k, n \mid i, j, m)$ (which has nothing to do with the compression algorithm, but is determined solely by the source distributions), the desired line conditional probability can be specified as

$$p(j, k, n|i, j, m) = \begin{cases} 0 \text{ if } (k, n) \varepsilon S_{ijm} \\ \dfrac{p_d(j, k, n|i, j, m)}{P_d(S^c_{ijm})} \text{ if } (k, n) \varepsilon S^c_{ijm} \end{cases} \tag{1}$$

where $P_d(S^c_{ijm})$ is the data probability of occurrence of the set $S^c_{ijm}$ given $(i, j, m)$ has occurred

$$P_d(S^c_{ijm}) = \sum_{(k,n)\varepsilon S^c_{ijm}} p_d(j, k, n|i, j, m). \tag{2}$$

It is emphasized again that the data conditional probability does not depend on the compression procedure, as contrasted with the "fan" conditional probability.

The conditional probabilities of (1) can be calculated by straightforward (although, as will be seen, usually lengthy) calculations. Note that they are independent of $q$. It is clear that the desired unconditional probabilities are then given by the equations

$$p_q(j, k, n) = \sum_{i,m} p(j, k, n|i, j, m)p_{(q-1)}(i, j, m) \quad (3)$$

$$j, k = 1, \cdots, L$$

$$n = 1, \cdots, T.$$

These equations can be solved for the probability desired as a function of the interval number $q$ subject to the constraint that the initial value is determined only by the data, i.e., for $q = 0$,

$$p_0(j, k, n) = p_d(j, k, n). \quad (4)$$

Let the conditional probability matrix be denoted by $\Pi$ and the desired probability column vector be given by $\pi_q$. Then, (3) can be put in the matrix form

$$\pi_q = \Pi \, \pi_{q-1}. \quad (5)$$

Proceeding recursively and using (1), this becomes

$$\pi_q = \Pi^q \, \pi_0.$$

As $q \rightarrow \infty$, it can be shown that under very general conditions[1] $\pi_q$ approaches a limit $\pi_\infty$ which is independent of $\pi_0$ and satisfies the equation

$$\pi_\infty = \Pi \, \pi_\infty. \quad (6)$$

## IV. Computer Results

Unfortunately, it is not practical to solve (6) directly. Note that the matrix $\Pi$ contains $L^3T^2$ elements. Typically for $L = 16$, $T = 16$, this is $16^5 \approx 10^6$ elements. However, a recursive solution based on (5) is possible. Since $\pi_q \rightarrow \pi_\infty$, the compression ratio $C_q \rightarrow C_\infty$. Thus, one can obtain an approximate solution by calculating enough steps so that $|C_q - C_{q-1}|$ is less than some threshold.

Even with this recursive solution, the computations are lengthy since the $L^3T^2$ conditional probabilities can not be stored in core memory for problems of reasonable dimensionality and, therefore, must be either recalculated after every step or stored on a disk where seek times are a significant factor. It is difficult to estimate precisely how many machine cycles are required to find each probability vector $\pi_q$ due to the complexity of the logic required.

One economy possible in the programming is the bypass of most of the calculations when the data probability $p_d(i, j, m)$ is sufficiently small. The following table gives representative running times on an IBM 7094 for the first-order Markov process which accompanies the table. $p_1(\cdot \mid \cdot)$ is the process one-step transition probability.

[1] Roughly speaking, the conditions are satisfied if all line sequences $(j, k, n)$ of nonzero probability occur infinitely often in an infinite sequence of values. This is always true in practice. See any reference on Markov chains for a more precise statement.

| $L$ | $T$ | Time (minutes) |
|---|---|---|
| 4 | 8 | 1 |
| 4 | 16 | 2 |
| 8 | 8 | 3 |
| 8 | 16 | 10 |
| 16 | 16 | 73 |

$$p_1(i \mid j) = \begin{cases} 0; & |i - j| \geq 2 \\ p; & i = j \\ 1 - p; & i = j + 1 = 2 \\ & \text{or} \quad i = j - 1 = T - 1 \\ \dfrac{1 - p}{2}; & i = j \pm 1, \; 1 < j < T. \end{cases}$$

As suspected, the amount of running time goes up sharply with $L^3T^2$. Because of this, the numerical results given shortly are confined to $L = 8$.

The Markov process chosen for the example is a simplified model for coarsely quantized TV data which has been found empirically to be approximately first order Markov with the highest transition probability being from the present level to the same level in one step.[5],[7] The rest of the probability weight is primarily on the neighboring levels. Presumably the model might apply to other types of data sources as well. For the first-order Markov process, the conditional probability of (1) follows from

$$p_d(j, k, n \mid i, j, m) = p_1(i_1 \mid j)p_1(i_2 \mid i_1) \cdots p_1(k \mid i_{n-1})$$

where $i_1, i_2, \cdots, i_{n-1}$ are the reconstructed levels for the starting value $j$ and the end point $k$.

The data generated by this model for "large" values of $p$, say $p > 0.7$, are dominated by a sequence of straight level lines of average length given by

$$(1 - p) \sum_{n=0} np^n = \frac{1}{1 - p}$$

with occasional rising and falling sequences of isolated points forming nonlevel lines. For these values of $p$, the simple zero-order hold or run length method of encoding can be expected to be superior to the fan method. The reason for this is illustrated in Fig. 3 where a "typical" sequence generated by the above source is shown. Between the dashed lines, the fan method requires 8 lines whereas simple run length coding requires only 5 messages.

On the other hand, if $p$ is "small", say less than 0.5, rising and falling sequences tend to dominate the data and the fan method is superior to the zero-order hold predictor. Unfortunately, the advantage in this case is of no use, since the resulting compression ratio over straight PCM encoding is small.

Fig. 4 illustrates this reasoning. Fig. 4(a) is the bit compression ratio as a function of $p$ for 8 quantization

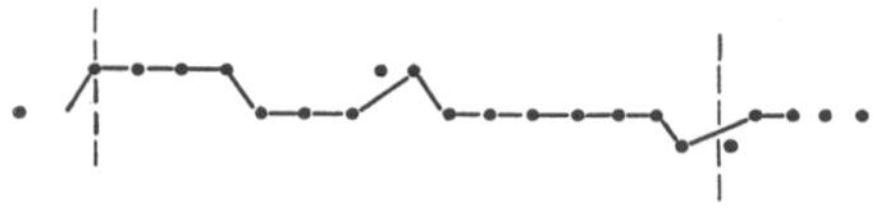

Fig. 3. Typical sequence generated by the first-order Markov source.

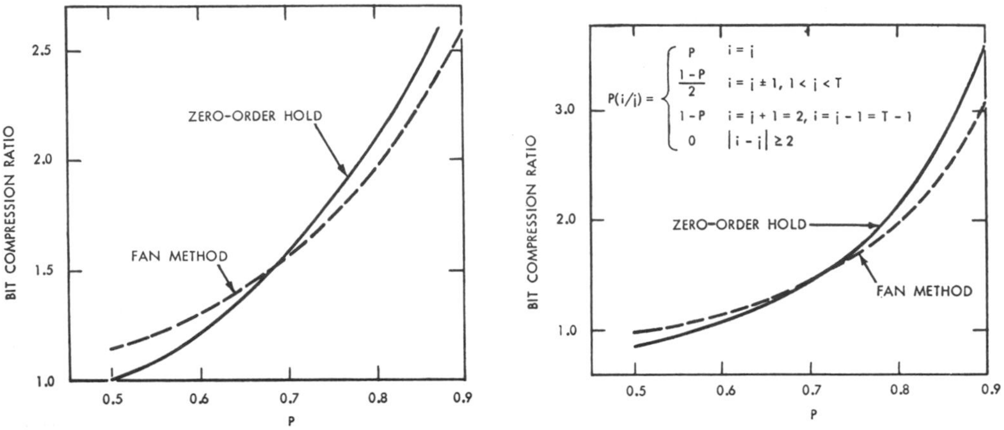


(a) (b)

Fig. 4. Compression ratios for first-order Markov process. (a) $L = 8$, $T = 8$; (b) $L = 8$, $T = 16$.

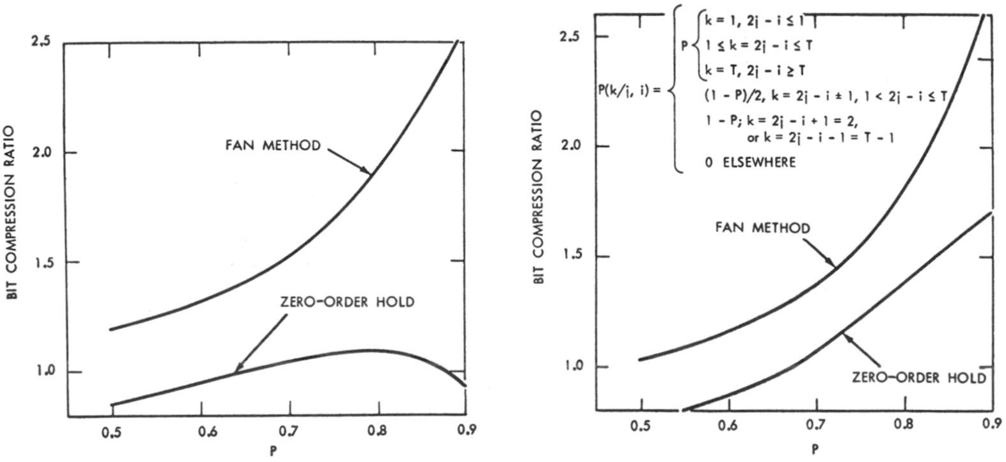


(a) (b)

Fig. 5. Compression ratios for a second-order Markov process. (a) $L = 8$, $T = 8$; (b) $L = 8$, $T = 16$.

levels (3 level bits) and 8 timing words (3 run length bits), where Fig. 4(b) is for 8 levels and 16 run lengths. Note that for reasonable compression ratios, one would favor the zero-order hold system. In both cases, the compression ratio curves cross at about $p = 0.7$. Thus, one can tentatively conclude that for first-order Markov data such as this, where no error is allowed in the algorithm, this fan method should not be used.

Of course, if the algorithm is applied to more finely quantized data where several quantization levels of error are allowed in fitting the interpolating line, the results may be different, as found empirically in Hochman *et al.*[4] and theoretically in Ehrman.[3]

It is also true that this fan algorithm is not inferior for data probabilities other than the first-order Markov. Consider the following second-order Markov process, where the most probable level based on the immediate past is the extrapolation of the last two points if this is one of the $L$ levels, and the closest of the top or bottom levels if this is not so:

$$p_d(k \mid j, i) \begin{cases} p; \begin{cases} k = 1, \; 2j - i \leq 1 \\ 1 \leq k, 2j - i \leq T \\ k = T, \; 2j - i \geq T \end{cases} \\ \dfrac{1-p}{2}; k = 2j - i \pm 1, 1 < 2j - i < T \\ 1 - p; k = 2j - i + 1 = 2 \\ \qquad \text{or} \quad k = 2j - i - 1 = T - 1 \\ 0 \text{ elsewhere.} \end{cases}$$

For these data, there tend to be many nonlevel straight line runs so that one would expect the fan method to have the advantage. Analytical results bear out this expectation. Fig. 5 illustrates the bit compression ratios for each system as a function of $p$ for 8 quantizing levels, and 8 and 16 run length words. Note that the fan method is, indeed, the better performer.

## V. Some Final Comments

The analysis of Section IV indicates the need to examine the data model carefully before selecting a compression algorithm. It is expected that equivalent results would be obtained for the analysis of any algorithm of a fixed nature. That is, there is no clearly superior method for all data. If insufficient knowledge about the source is available, the choice between algorithms of this class then becomes somewhat arbitrary. At some point, an adaptive algorithm, such as those described in other work,[6]-[9] may become usful in spite of the greatly increased complexity required. As shown in Kutz and Sciulli[6] and Davisson,[7] an adaptive algorithm is never worse in terms of compression ratio than a comparable algorithm of a fixed nature, and, in some cases, may be quite a bit better. If the data source probabilities are completely characterized, a straight line is not generally the best interpolator. In fact, the best polynomial (of the same degree of freedom) passes through the mode of the conditional probability (the "maximum likelihood" line) at those sample locations between each possible set of end points. If this method is used, the analysis is considerably simplified, at least for a first-order Markov process. For unquantized data, the analysis is accomplished as in Ehrman,[3] where the author was able to obtain his results for the special case of a Weiner process because a straight line is the maximum likelihood line for a Weiner process.

It is interesting to consider the extension of the analysis of Section III to finely quantized data. The analytical technique is impractical as the number of quantization levels and/or run lengths increases, due to the amount of computer time required. For no quantization, the equation satisfied by the set of run probabilities is

$$p_q(y, z, n) = \int_{-\infty}^{\infty} \sum_m p_d(y, z, n \mid x, y, m) p_{q-1}(x, y, m) \, dx$$
$$- \infty \leq y, z \leq \infty .$$

This equation can not be solved analytically. However, it can be approximated and solved on a digital computer by choosing a discrete set of values for $y$ and $z$. Although this may seem at first glance to be equivalent to the analysis of Section III which dealt directly with quantized data, it is not, because the conditional probability $p_d$ is determined for continuous deviations from the interpolating line, rather than the discrete set chosen for the computations.

## References

[1] L. D. Davisson, "The fan method of data compression," 1966 Goddard Summer Workshop, Final Rept., NASA Rept. X-700-67-94, pp. 23–30.

[2] W. A. Youngblood, "Estimation of the channel capacity required for picture transmission," Sc.D. dissertation, Dept. of Elec. Engrg., Massachusetts Institute of Technology, Cambridge, Mass., May 1958.

[3] L. Ehrman, "Analysis of some redundancy removal bandwidth compression techniques," *Proc. IEEE*, vol. 55, pp. 278–287, March 1967.

[4] D. Hochman, H. Katzman, and D. R. Weber, "Application of redundancy reduction to television bandwidth compression," *Proc. IEEE*, vol. 55, pp. 263–266, March 1967.

[5] W. F. Schreiber, "The measurement of third-order probability distributions of TV signals," *IRE Trans. Information Theory*, pp. 94–105, September 1956.

[6] R. L. Kutz and J. A. Sciulli, "An adaptive image compression system and its performance in a noisy channel," presented at the Internat'l Symp. on Information Theory, San Remo, Italy, September 1967.

[7] L. D. Davisson, "Data compression and its application to video signals," 1965 Goddard Summer Workshop, Final Rept., NASA Rept. X-100-65-407, pp. A-35–A-55.

[8] A. V. Balakrishnan, "An adaptive non-linear data predictor," *Proc. Nat'l Telemetering Conf.* (Washington, D. C., 1962), Paper 6-5.

[9] L. D. Davisson, "Theory of adaptive data compression," in *Advances in Communications Systems*. New York: Academic Press, 1966, pp. 173–192.

# Part VI

# NONBLOCK DATA COMPRESSION

# Editors' Comments on Papers 36 Through 46



Most of the previous algorithms for data compression have involved the separate processing of nonoverlapping blocks of source data. Such schemes require fairly elaborate synchronization and can be quite complex. In addition, they do not take full advantage of past redundancy since they only view the current source block to obtain a reproduction block. In Part VI we consider systems that process overlapping segments of data and hence are not block codes in the usual sense, but instead are usually nonlinear discrete-time filters.

Such data compressors fall basically into two classes: (1) specific nonlinear filters, such as delta modulators or predictive quantizers, and (2) nonblock structures, such as convolutional codes, usually used for channel decoding in information theory but applied instead to encode sources. Codes of the second type are usually viewed as very long block codes, but they are included in this grouping as they perform locally in a nonblock manner, that is, as a time-varying nonlinear filter.

When a nonblock structure is used, the Shannon theory is not directly applicable. Much recent work, however, has extended the Shannon theory to such structures, as reported by the Gray and Davisson in Paper 2. These results will be included in our forthcoming Benchmark volume *Ergodic and Information Theory*.

In Paper 36, Fine describes the general approach of optimal nonlinear filtering, presents an iterative optimization procedure, and uses his techniques to analyze quantization and delta modulation. He considers alphabet-constrained rather than entropy-constrained OPTA. In Paper 37, Bello, Lincoln, and Gish further develop Fine's approach to delta modulation and present simulation results. Abate (Paper 38) and Song, Garodnick, and Schilling (Paper 39) study fixed and adaptive delta modulation by both approximate analysis and simulation.

Balakrishnan (Paper 40) and Lucky (Paper 41) use the predictive philosophy of Elias to first remove the redundancy (or obtain the innovations sequence) of the source via filtering, and then to quantize the errors rather than the original sequence. Although a natural application of Elias's techniques, error propagation may occur in the reconstruction, since small errors in the innovations may produce large errors in the reconstructed source. Both Balakrishnan and Lucky consider adaptive predictors so that the system need not have precise a priori knowledge of source statistics and is relatively insensitive to slowly varying nonstationarities.

In Paper 42, Curry, Vander Velde, and Potter study the effect on predictive quantization and PCM of using quantized samples for nonlinear estimation with Kalman-type estimators, various approximations, and simulation. They also consider the variable-length block prediction–comparison schemes of Part V.

An excellent tutorial on applications of predictive quantization and delta modulation to speech digitization may be found in N. S. Jayant

[''Digital Coding of Speech Waveforms: PCM, DPCM, and DM Quantizers,'' *Proc. IEEE,* **62,** 611–632 (1974)].

Papers 43 through 46 are data-compression algorithms derived from the channel coding theory. Basically, they involve using a convolutional channel encoder or a causal, nonlinear filter (trellis code) as a source decoder and a tree-search algorithm, such as a channel sequential or stack decoder or the Viterbi algorithm. The decoder, being a filter, operates in a nonblock fashion. The encoder can operate in a block fashion by searching the decoder tree to a fixed depth $n$ to find the best code word and then transmitting the entire word, or it can operate as a nonblock structure by transmitting only the first channel symbol and then searching the next $n$ nodes, that is, getting a good, long-run fit before producing each symbol. Unlike the delta modulator, this allows the encoder to print out the next channel symbol by finding the best immediate step available knowing the ''future'' source outputs for $n$ time units. This avoids the peril of good local steps leading to bad long-term behavior.

This incremental approach to tree codes is described and experimentally studied for speech applications by Anderson and Bodie (Paper 46). They show that tree coding can be viewed as a natural generalization of predictive quantization, and they experimentally obtain surprisingly good compression on real speech with only moderately complex equipment. Their preliminary results suggest a hopeful future for techniques from information theory in real data compression systems.

Reprinted from *IEEE Trans. Inform. Theory,* **IT-10**(4), 287–296 (1964)

# Properties of an Optimum Digital System and Applications

TERRENCE FINE, MEMBER, IEEE

***Summary***—**A model representative of any time-sampled, real-valued input and output digital system without feedback from system input to output (there may be internal feedback loops) is presented, and properties that are necessary for an optimum (nonlinear) digital system are developed. The model itself consists of a cascade of three mapping operations that successively transform the real-valued input sequence into an *M*-ary valued digital sequence, thence into an *N*-ary valued digital sequence, and finally into a real-valued output sequence. The operating routine and optimality criterion function chosen permit us to consider the problems of prediction, interpolation or synchronous operation as well as a wide variety of loss functions.**

**The derived properties are discussed with particular regard to the quadratic loss function and synchronous or interpolatory operation and then applied to the determination of several optimum systems. Optimum nonlinear amplitude quantizers, pulse code and delta modulation systems, and stepped controllers are described. In particular, conditions are given under which delta modulation is superior to pulse code modulation and some remarks are made concerning suboptimal delta modulation systems and their relation to previous work.**

Manuscript received September 30, 1963; revised May 12, 1964. This work, which is based on part of a Ph.D. dissertation, Division of Engineering and Applied Physics, Harvard University, Cambridge, Massachusetts, June, 1963, was supported in part by the National Science Foundation and the Office of Naval Research.

The author is with the Division of Engineering and Applied Physics, Harvard University, Cambridge, Mass.

## I. Introduction to the Digital System and Formulation of the Optimization Problem

THIS PAPER, derived from earlier work of the author [1], is concerned with systems operating at times $\{t_i, \cdots, t_n\}$ on input sample sequences $\{I_i, \cdots, I_n\}$ and internally generating discrete valued digital sequences $\{s_i, \cdots, s_n\}$ and $\{s'_i, \cdots, s'_n\}$ as well as a real-valued output sequence $\{R_i, \cdots, R_n\}$. The initial time $t_i$ is representative of the system start-up time, or in a system with memory truncation, how far the memory extends into the past (the difference between $t_n$ and $t_i$ being constant). For convenience, the notation for sequences is abbreviated by placing a superscript bar over the most recent element in the sequence, *e.g.*, $\{I_i, \cdots, I_n\}$ is denoted by $\bar{I}_n$. The mappings between sequences are generically denoted by $M_i$. In particular, $M_1$ maps the real-valued sequence $\bar{I}_n$ into the $M$-ary valued sequence $\bar{s}_n$ (elements drawn from an alphabet $a_1, \cdots, a_M$); $M_2$ maps the $M$-ary valued sequence $\bar{s}_n$ into the $N$-ary valued sequence $\bar{s}'_n$; and $M_3$ maps the $N$-ary valued sequence $\bar{s}'_n$ into the real-valued sequence $\bar{R}_n$.

Fig. 1 schematically represents the class of digital

system under consideration. The mappings $M_1$ and $M_3$ are deterministic functions of an input sequence yielding an output sequence and are what we wish to design. The optimum design is subject to the constraint that $M_2$ can accept only $M$-ary sequences and generate only $N$-ary sequences at the sampling times $t_n$. Furthermore, while the operation of $M_2$ is assumed to be initially specified, it may either be a probabilistic or deterministic mapping. The specification of $M_2$ in either eventuality may be accomplished by providing the conditional probability of obtaining an $M_2$ output sequence $\bar{s}'_n$ given an $M_2$ input sequence $\bar{s}_n$, $Pr\ (\bar{s}'_n \mid \bar{s}_n)$. If $M_2$ is deterministic, then $Pr\ (\bar{s}'_n \mid \bar{s}_n)$ is constrained to attain only the values 0 and 1.

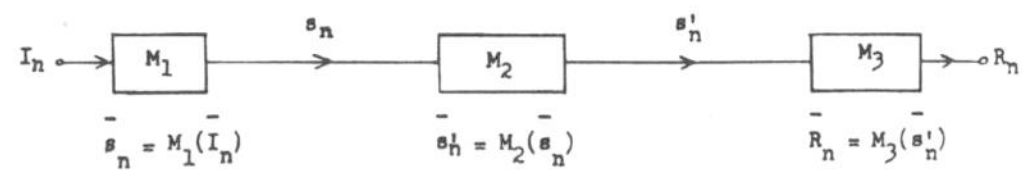


Fig. 1—Digital system model.

In order to further our subsequent objectives, it is necessary to emphasize the operation of the system as it appears at the time $t_n$. For example, upon receipt of the input $I_n$ a deterministic mapping $M_1$, chosen in accordance with the past of the input sequence, $\bar{I}_{n-1}$, is effected to yield the $M$-ary element $s_n$. The past will be considered to play an implicit role in the system operation and only the present will be explicitly treated. The design of the system for all time can be developed from this point of view if we start calculating at the initial time $t_i$ and iterate forward in time.

Now consider the choice of a system error criterion by means of which to compare various digital systems in the class outlined above, in order to settle upon a system not worse than any other in the class. The system error criterion adopted is generated from the commonly useful class of mean $\phi$ criteria $E[\phi(I_{n+k} - R_n)]$. The basic error variable is formed from the difference between the system input $I_{n+k}$ at a time $t_{n+k}$ and the system output $R_n$ at a possibly different time $t_n$; the error variable is then distorted by a criterion function $\phi$ and the result statistically averaged over the possible inputs and outputs. The presence of the anticipation $k$ permits simultaneous treatment of problems of interpolation ($k < 0$), prediction ($k > 0$) and synchronous ($k = 0$) reconstruction. The criterion function $\phi$ will generally be assumed to be bounded away from minus infinity, continuous, and nondecreasing for positive argument and nonincreasing for negative argument. (The properties required of $\phi$ will be stated more specifically in the course of the development.)

To complete the specification of an optimization problem, it is necessary to consider an appropriate system operating routine in addition to the above described "instantaneous" error criterion. The idea behind the operating routine is akin to that of realizability; an output at a time $t_n$ must make use of all the information available at the input up to but not beyond $t_n$, and furthermore, events occurring in the past cannot be influenced by future events. These two conditions make it necessary to discriminate between $k$ positive and $k$ nonpositive, insofar as the optimum design of $M_1$ is concerned. If $k$ is nonpositive, then the mapping $M_1$ attempts to select that value of $s_{n+k}$ that minimizes the error criterion conditioned upon the available information $E[\phi(I_{n+k}-R_n) \mid s_{n+k}, \bar{I}_{n+k}]$. This is a reasonable choice since all of the information up to $t_{m+k}$ is being used, and in addition, $t_{n+k}$ being less than $t_n$, this choice of $s_{n+k}$ is able to influence the future system output $R_n$. However, if $k$ is positive then, although the requirement of using all of the information available to $M_1$ at time $t_{n+k}$ is satisfied, this choice of $s_{n+k}$ cannot influence the system output $R_n$ at an earlier time $t_n$. Thus if $k$ is positive the operating procedure is modified to require that $M_1$ select $s_n$ at time $t_n$ to minimize $E[\phi(I_{n+k} - R_n) \mid s_n, \bar{I}_n]$, and this choice maintains the predictive nature of the system output as well as satisfying our operating routine. The mapping $M_3$ is easily treated by claiming that it selects the $R_n$ which minimizes $E[\phi(I_{n+k} - R_n) \mid \bar{s}'_n]$. Notice that this choice satisfies our operating routine no matter what $k$ is.

The pairs of conditions given above for $M_1$ and $M_3$ serve to establish a reasonable optimization problem within the class of digital systems initially described. In subsequent sections, properties of the optimum system are obtained for a wide class of criterion functions $\phi$, stochastic inputs $\bar{I}_n$, general mapping $M_2$, and arbitrary anticipation $k$. The important special cases of a quadratic criterion, zero anticipation, and $M_2$ the identity are examined in greater detail. Before proceeding, though, it is necessary to add that the model discussed oversimplifies the actual situation. Problems of appropriate signalling waveforms, deterministic distortion, transmitter and receiver synchronization, and so forth are neglected.

## II. Solution to the Optimization Problem

The determination of the necessary conditions that an optimum system must satisfy proceeds in three stages: 1) assume that $M_3$ is specified and find the optimum $M_1$ corresponding to this $M_3$, 2) assume that $M_1$ is specified and find the optimum $M_3$ corresponding to this $M_1$, 3) solve the interrelated design equations of stages 1) and 2) simultaneously to find the jointly optimum design. This general procedure is quite analogous to the minimization of a function of two variables in the calculus. The optimum value of each variable, assuming that the other is held constant, is found, and then both of the conditions are simultaneously solved for the actual minimum or stationary point.

The properties that will be discovered using the three stage procedure will only be necessary for an optimum but not sufficient. Lack of sufficiency arises in practice not from the nonexistence of a minimum for the system error but from the possibility of relative extrema or several solutions to the necessary conditions. Sufficiency is obtained by checking all of the solutions to the necessary conditions by means of the magnitude of system error that they give rise to, and then choosing that solution yielding the absolute minimum over-all error. An attempt to employ dynamic programming in the determination of the system yielding the absolute minimum error is being made by J. D. Bruce [2]. However, this author does not follow Bruce's approach since Bruce's work is restricted to quantization and requires assumptions this author does not wish to make.

Treating prediction problems first ($k > 0$), it is seen that the optimum mapping $M_1$ must be such that, upon receipt of $I_n$ and previous knowledge of $\bar{I}_{n-1}$, it selects one of the $M$ possible values $a_i$ from the $M$-ary alphabet for $s_n$ so that the value of the system error, $E[\phi(I_{n+k} - R_n) \mid \bar{I}_n, s_n]$, for this choice is not greater than the system error that would result from any of the remaining $(M - 1)$ choices for $s_n$. This is a necessary and sufficient condition that $M_1$ be optimum for initially specified mappings $M_2$ and $M_3$ and given source statistics.

The point sets $p_n(a_1, \bar{I}_{n-1}), \cdots, p_n(a_M, \bar{I}_{n-1})$ are introduced as a means of describing the optimum mapping $M_1$. The set $p_n(a_i, \bar{I}_{n-1})$ is a subset of the real numbers and the inverse image of the optimum mapping $M_1$ from $I_n$ (the particular past $\bar{I}_{n-1}$ being considered fixed) to the $s_n$ value of $a_i$. The set $p_n(a_i, \bar{I}_{n-1})$ is then the set of values of $I_n$ that are optimally mapped into the $s_n$ value of $a_i$, given the past of the input, $\bar{I}_{n-1}$. Using set notation,

$$p_n(a_i, \bar{I}_{n-1}) = \{I_n: M_1(\bar{I}_n) = a_i\}. \tag{1}$$

The $M$ sets, $p_n(a_i, \bar{I}_{n-1})$, provide an exhaustive subdivision of the $I_n$ space of the real numbers, and in most cases of practical interest they will be mutually disjoint except at a finite number of points. Implicit in (1) is the functional dependence of $p_n(a_i, \bar{I}_{n-1})$ upon the past of the input, $\bar{I}_{n-1}$. Corresponding to each possible distinct sequence $\bar{I}_{n-1}$, (there are $(n - i)^M$ possibilities), there will be some group of sets $p_n(a_1, \bar{I}_{n-1}), \cdots, p_n(a_M, \bar{I}_{n-1})$. At the time $t_n$, we assume a particular past $\bar{I}_{n-1}$ has occurred, and we wish to select just that group of sets corresponding to $\bar{I}_{n-1}$. In what follows we prefer to leave this dependence upon $\bar{I}_{n-1}$ as implicit rather than explicit. To this end we suppress $\bar{I}_{n-1}$ and write only $p_n(a_1), \cdots, p_n(a_M)$, where the various point sets share the same past. Furthermore, in all that follows the sets $p_n(a_1), \cdots, p_n(a_M)$ all share the same particular past $\bar{I}_{n-1}$.

The necessary and sufficient condition that $M_1$ be optimum can now be phrased in the following manner: For all $j = 1, \cdots, M$

$$p_n(a_j) = \{I_n: E[\phi(I_{n+k} - R_n) \mid s_n = a_j, \bar{I}_n] \leq E[\phi(I_{n+k} - R_n) \mid s_n \neq a_j, \bar{I}_n]\}. \tag{2}$$

The set $p_n(a_j)$ is the set of input values $I_n$ that yield an error when mapped into a value of $s_n$ equal to $a_j$ which is not greater than the error when $I_n$ is mapped into any of the remaining $(M - 1)$ choices of the alphabet.

To simplify subsequent discussion concerning the reversal of the inequality in (2) as $I_n$ shifts from one set $p_n(a_j)$ to another set $p_n(a_r)$, we define a function $f_{jr}(I_n)$ which, when $I_n$ is in $p_n(a_j)$, will be non-negative for all $r$

$$f_{jr}(I_n) = E[\phi(I_{n+k} - R_n) \mid s_n = a_r, \bar{I}_n] - E[\phi(I_{n+k} - R_n) \mid s_n = a_j, \bar{I}_n]. \tag{3}$$

Thus we see that $f_{jr}(I_n)$ being non-negative for all $r$ is equivalent to $I_n$ being in $p_n(a_j)$, and that if $f_{jr}(I_n)$ is negative for some $r$, then $I_n$ is not in $p_n(a_j)$. The operation of statistical expectation in (3) is taken with respect to the distribution of the random variable $I_{n+k} - R_n$ conditioned upon the events $s_n$ and $\bar{I}_n$. From our previous formulation of the system model we observe that $R_n$ is a random variable when conditioned upon $\bar{I}_n$ only if $M_2$ is a probabilistic mapping, and $I_{n+k}$ is random when conditioned upon $\bar{I}_n$ only if $k$ is positive.

Throughout this paper the functions $f_{jr}(I_n)$ will be assumed to be continuous functions for all values of the argument $I_n$. A sufficient condition that $f_{jr}(I_n)$ be a continuous function is that $E[\phi(I_{n+k} - R_n) \mid I_n, \bar{I}_{n-1}, s_n]$ is a continuous function of $I_n$ no matter what choice we make for $s_n$. Writing the conditional expectation as an integral with respect to the conditional density function of the random variable $I_{n+k} - R_n$, we have

$$E[\phi(I_{n+k} - R_n) \mid I_n, \bar{I}_{n-1}, s_n] = \int_{-\infty}^{+\infty} \phi(x) p_{I_{n+k}-R_n}(x \mid \bar{I}_n, s_n)\, dx. \tag{4}$$

If it is assumed that the integrand above is bounded for all $x$ by an integrable function independent of $I_n$ and that $p_{I_{n+k}-R_n}$ is an almost everywhere continuous function of $I_n$, then the dominated convergence theorem (Loeve [3]) assures us that $E[\phi \mid \bar{I}_n, s_n]$ is a continuous function of $I_n$. Thus the boundedness of the integrand in (4) by an appropriate integrable function and its continuity almost everywhere in $I_n$ provide a sufficient condition that $f_{jr}$ be continuous in $I_n$. These assumptions do not appear to be particularly restrictive but must be verified in applications or replaced with more suitable ones.

With the definition of $f_{jr}$ given by (3) we see that the set $p_n(a_j)$ given by (2) consists of those points $I_n$ for which $f_{jr}$ is non-negative for each $r$. Therefore, $p_n(a_j)$ is given by the following logical intersection of sets

$$p_n(a_j) = \bigcap_{r=1}^{M} \{I_n: f_{jr}(I_n) \geq 0\}. \tag{5}$$

In the Appendix we prove that, if $f_{jr}$ is continuous, it follows from (5) that $p_n(a_j)$ can be uniquely represented as at most a denumerable union of disjoint, closed intervals having lower endpoints $L_{ln}^k(a_j)$ and upper endpoints $L_{un}^k(a_j)$

$$p_n(a_j) = \bigcup_{k=1}^{\infty} [L_{ln}^k(a_j), L_{un}^k(a_j)]. \tag{6}$$

The design problem of determining the optimum $M_1$ given a particular past $\bar{I}_{n-1}$ is thus equivalent to determining the optimum sets $p_n(a_i)$ and this, in turn, is equivalent to finding at most a denumerable number of endpoints $L_{ln}^k$ and $L_{un}^k$.

The next step in the optimization procedure is to argue that the endpoints described above are solutions of the equations $f_{ir}(x)$ equal to zero. The $M$ sets $p_n(a_1), \cdots, p_n(a_M)$ are exhaustive of the real line since every real number $I_n$ is mapped into some digital output $a_i$. Therefore, immediately above the finite upper endpoint (there is a similar argument for lower end points) of one of the disjoint intervals in the set $p_n(a_i)$ we must be in some other set, say $p_n(a_r)$. Now $p_n(a_r)$ is also a union of closed intervals so that it must possess a closed interval with lower endpoint equal to the upper endpoint of the interval in $p_n(a_i)$. Let us generically denote endpoints common to two sets $p_n(a_i)$ and $p_n(a_r)$ by $L_n(a_i, a_r)$. The point $L_n(a_i, a_r)$ being in $p_n(a_i)$ implies that for any $r f_{ir}(L_n(a_i, a_r))$ is non-negative, while its membership in $p_n(a_r)$ implies that for any $j$ $f_{rj}(L_n(a_i, a_r))$ is also non-negative. However, (3) tells us that $f_{ri}$ is the negative of $f_{ir}$ so we must conclude that $f_{ir}(L_n(a_i, a_r))$ is zero. If $f_{ir}$ were positive, then $f_{ri}$ would be negative, and this would contradict the fact that $L_n(a_i, a_r)$ is in both sets $p_n(a_i)$ and $p_n(a_r)$. Thus we find, as claimed, that any finite endpoint $L_n(a_i, a_r)$ belonging to one set $p_n(a_i)$, and therefore also to some other set $p_n(a_r)$, must satisfy the equation obtained by setting (3) equal to zero

$$E[\phi(I_{n+k} - R_n) \mid s_n = a_i, I_n = L_n(a_i, a_r), \bar{I}_{n-1}]$$
$$= E[\phi(I_{n+k} - R_n) \mid s_n = a_r, I_n = L_n(a_i, a_r), \bar{I}_{n-1}]. \quad (7)$$

There will also exist two infinite endpoints, plus and minus infinity, for which the above argument is inapplicable. It is easy to see, though, that minus infinity is assigned to that set having the smallest finite upper endpoint and plus infinity to the set having the largest finite lower endpoint.

Eq. (7) is the sought for characterization of the optimum mapping $M_1$ when $M_2$ and $M_3$ are specified and $k$ is positive. Although (2) was a necessary and sufficient condition for optimality, the result given by (7) is only a necessary condition. There may exist solutions to (7) for $L_n$ which do not correspond to points of transition of the direction of the inequality in (2). Sufficiency was lost in going from (2) to (7), for in (7) we do not require that $f_{ir}$ actually change sign about zero, as is required for a true transition point, but only that it become zero. The number of solutions to (7) cannot usually be determined in advance, but we will be particularly interested in those instances where the solution is unique.

Proceeding to the second stage of the optimization procedure we assume that $M_1$ and $M_2$ are specified and attempt to determine the corresponding optimum $M_3$ so as to minimize $E[\phi(I_{n+k} - R_n) \mid \bar{s}_n']$. Remembering that $M_3$ is a deterministic mapping from $\bar{s}_n'$ to $R_n$ completely at our disposal, informs us that the optimum $M_3$ is the one that provides that real number $R_n$ which minimizes the system error. The minimization can be affected by means of the usual calculus of a single variable. Thus a necessary condition for an optimum $M_3$ is the following:

$$\frac{dE[\phi(I_{n+k} - R_n) \mid \bar{s}_n']}{dR_n} = 0. \quad (8)$$

Interchanging orders of differentiation and integration (expectation) as can be justified by assumptions of continuous differentiability for $\phi$, $I_{n+k}$ continuity for $p(I_{n+k} \mid \bar{s}_n')$ and uniform convergence (Brand [4]),[1] we obtain

$$E\left[\frac{d\phi(I_{n+k} - R_n)}{dR_n} \,\middle|\, \bar{s}_n'\right] = 0. \quad (9)$$

Eq. (9) is the desired necessary condition yielding a property characteristic of the optimum $M_3$ given $M_1$ and $M_2$.

The final stage in the optimization procedure is to search through the solutions provided by the optimization equations (7) and (9) for that pair of solutions yielding the minimum over-all error. We notice that the equations are not independent. The solutions to (7) depend upon $M_3$, which is given by (9), while the solutions to (9) depend upon $M_1$, which is given by (7). It is possible to solve this problem in closed analytic fashion in special cases, but we would more commonly be driven to employ an iterative search procedure.

To summarize, we note that the mappings $M_1$ and $M_3$ were assumed to be completely at our disposal except for the important constraints that $M_1$ mapped sequences of real numbers into sequences of $M$-ary elements with the same number of members, and $M_3$ mapped sequences of $N$-ary elements into sequences of real numbers with the same number of members. The mapping $M_2$ from $M$-ary sequences to $N$-ary sequences with the same number of members was assumed to be beyond our ability to control. We then adopted a system error criterion $E[\phi(I_{n+k} - R_n)]$, and found the relation of (7) between the optimum $M_1$ and a given $M_2$ and $M_3$ and the relation of (9) between the optimum $M_3$ and a given $M_1$ and $M_2$.

We now consider the problems of interpolation and synchronous operation ($k \leq 0$). The procedure in this phase of the investigation is so analogous to that just employed that we shall not present it in as full detail and shall use indexed equation numbers to facilitate comparisons with the preceding work. The optimum mapping $M_1$ must now be such that upon receipt of $I_{n+k}$ and previous knowledge of $\bar{I}_{n+k-1}$ it selects one of the $M$ possible values $a_i$ from the $M$-ary alphabet for $s_{n+k}$ so that the value of the system error $E[\phi(I_{n+k} - R_n) \mid \bar{I}_{n+k}, s_{n+k} = a_i]$ for this choice is not greater than the system error that would result from any of the remaining $(M - 1)$ choices for $s_{n+k}$.

The point sets $p_{n+k}(a_i)$ of values of the input $I_{n+k}$ that are optimally mapped by $M_1$ into the $s_{n+k}$ value of $a_i$

[1] Other minimization procedures might require less restrictive assumptions concerning $\phi$ and $p(I_n|\bar{s}'_{n-k})$.

are given by

$$p_{n+k}(a_j) = \{I_{n+k}: E[\phi(I_{n+k} - R_n) \mid \bar{I}_{n+k}, s_{n+k} = a_j] \le E[\phi(I_{n+k} - R_n) \mid \bar{I}_{n+k}, s_{n+k} \neq a_j]\}. \quad (2a)$$

The representation of $p_{n+k}(a_j)$ as a union of intervals as in (6) is again introduced, and the continuous function $f_{jr}(I_{n+k})$ is defined by

$$f_{jr}(I_{n+k}) = E[\phi(I_{n+k} - R_n) \mid \bar{I}_{n+k}, s_{n+k} = a_r] - E[\phi(I_{n+k} - R_n) \mid \bar{I}_{n+k}, s_{n+k} = a_j]. \quad (3a)$$

By means of the continuity and closure arguments following (6) we again conclude that a necessary condition that an endpoint $L_{n+k}(a_j, a_r)$ separating $p_{n+k}(a_j)$ and $p_{n+k}(a_r)$ must satisfy is

$$E[\phi(I_{n+k} - R_n) \mid I_{n+k} = L_{n+k}(a_j, a_r), \bar{I}_{n+k-1}, s_{n+k} = a_j] = E[\phi(I_{n+k} - R_n) \mid I_{n+k} = L_{n+k}(a_j, a_r), \bar{I}_{n+k-1}, s_{n+k} = a_r]. \quad (7a)$$

However, we are now in a position to further simplify (7a) by means of the observation that $I_{n+k}$ is no longer a random variable in (7a); it is constrained by the conditioning to be equal to $L_{n+k}$. In addition, insofar as the output random variable $R_n$ is concerned, knowledge of the sequence $\bar{s}_{n+k}$ is a sufficient statistic with respect to the apparently more extensive information contained in $\bar{I}_{n+k}$. Applying these observations to (7a) yields the reduced equation

$$E[\phi(L_{n+k} - R_n) \mid s_{n+k} = a_j, \bar{s}_{n+k-1}] = E[\phi(L_{n+k} - R_n) \mid s_{n+k} = a_r, \bar{s}_{n+k-1}]. \quad (7b)$$

Eq. (7b) is the desired necessary condition that the optimum mapping $M_1$ must satisfy when $M_2$ and $M_3$ are specified and $k$ is nonpositive; it is a somewhat simpler result than (7).

The second stage of the optimization procedure in which we find the optimum mapping $M_3$ given specified mappings $M_1$ and $M_2$ is entirely analogous to that culminating in (9), and there is no need to reproduce it here. This conclusion follows from the fact that the operating routine for the mapping $M_3$ is the same for all values of the anticipation $k$. Finally, the remarks concerning the necessity for the simultaneous solution of (7) and (9) apply here also for (7b) and (9).

## III. The Quadratic Loss Function

The quadratic loss function is probably the most important choice for $\phi$, judging from the extent of its favor in the literature. Fortunately, the results embodied in (7b) and (9) simplify when $\phi$ is quadratic. Eq. (7b) for $\phi$ quadratic becomes:

$$E[(L_{n+k}(a_j, a_r) - R_n)^2 \mid s_{n+k} = a_j, \bar{s}_{n+k-1}] = E[(L_{n+k}(a_j, a_r) - R_n)^2 \mid s_{n+k} = a_r, \bar{s}_{n+k-1}]. \quad (10)$$

After simple algebraic rearrangement and recognition that $L_{n+k}$, being a nonrandom number, can commute with the conditional expectation we obtain:

$$L_{n+k}(a_j, a_r) = \frac{E[R_n^2 \mid s_{n+k} = a_r, \bar{s}_{n+k-1}] - E[R_n^2 \mid s_{n+k} = a_j, \bar{s}_{n+k-1}]}{2E[R_n \mid s_{n+k} = a_r, \bar{s}_{n+k-1}] - 2E[R_n \mid s_{n+k} = a_j, \bar{s}_{n+k-1}]}. \quad (11)$$

Eq. (9) becomes, after differentiation and recognition that $R_n$ can commute with expectations conditional upon $\bar{s}_n'$,

$$R_n = E[I_{n+k} \mid \bar{s}_n']. \quad (12)$$

Eq. (11) implies that there exists a unique solution satisfying (7b) for each pair of values taken on by $s_{n+k}$. This statement is still too broad, and it is not true that the points $L_{n+k}(a_j, a_r)$ corresponding to every pair of $s_{n+k}$ values $a_j$ and $a_r$ actually correspond to transition points in the optimum design. In order to sort out the significant solutions we return to the necessary and sufficient condition given by (2a).

For all $j = 1, \cdots, M$; for all $r \neq j$

$$p_{n+k}(a_j) = \{I_{n+k}: I_{n+k}^2 - 2I_{n+k}E[R_n \mid s_{n+k} = a_j, \bar{s}_{n+k-1}] + E[R_n^2 \mid s_{n+k} = a_j, \bar{s}_{n+k-1}] \le I_{n+k}^2 - 2I_{n+k}E[R_n \mid s_{n+k} = a_r, \bar{s}_{n+k-1}] + E[R_n^2 \mid s_{n+k} = a_r, \bar{s}_{n+k-1}]\}. \quad (13)$$

Rearranging (13) we find that the set $p_{n+k}(a_j)$ is such that, for all $r$ unequal to $j$, $I_{n+k}$ must satisfy:

$$p_{n+k}(a_j) = \begin{cases} \{I_{n+k}: I_{n+k} \ge L_{n+k}(a_j, a_r)\} & \text{if } E[R_n \mid s_{n+k} = a_j, \bar{s}_{n+k-1}] \ge E[R_n \mid s_{n+k} = a_r, \bar{s}_{n+k-1}] \\ \{I_{n+k}: I_{n+k} \le L_{n+k}(a_j, a_r)\} & \text{if } E[R_n \mid s_{n+k} = a_j, \bar{s}_{n+k-1}] \le E[R_n \mid s_{n+k} = a_r, \bar{s}_{n+k-1}]. \end{cases} \quad (14)$$

For convenience we denote those $s_{n+k}$ values for which the upper condition in (14) holds by $a_{x_i}$ and those $s_{n+k}$ values for which the lower condition in (14) holds by $a_{y_i}$. The only manner in which $I_{n+k}$ can satisfy (14) for all $r$ unequal to $j$ is for $I_{n+k}$ to be not greater than the least $L_{n+k}(a_j, a_{y_i})$ and not less than the greatest $L_{n+k}(a_j, a_{x_i})$. Thus we find:

$$p_{n+k}(a_j) = \{I_{n+k}: \max_{x_i} L_{n+k}(a_j, a_{x_i}) \le I_{n+k} \le \min_{y_i} L_{n+k}(a_j, a_{y_i})\}. \quad (15)$$

The interesting conclusion to be drawn from (15) is that for a quadratic loss function $\phi$ and $k$ nonpositive, $p_{n+k}(a_j)$ is a single interval with endpoints of the form of (11) selected according to (15). The simple form found for $p_{n+k}(a_j)$ is not expected to hold for a great variety of loss functions when $M_2$ is not deterministic. Indeed it is possible to find cases for the absolute value loss function for which $p_{n+k}$ is a union of more than one disjoint interval.

As an illustration of the application of the results of this section, we consider the following relatively simple design problem. The input process makes independent transitions every other sampling time and is otherwise constant and distributed with density function $p_I(x)$. The channel $M_2$ accepts only a binary valued input $(a_1, a_2)$ and is otherwise the identity mapping; while a noisy channel example would have been preferable, the increased number of alternatives to be considered make it unfit for compact presentation though not difficult to carry out. The system error criterion taken is that for quadratic loss and no anticipation, $E[(I_n - R_n)^2]$.

We observe that because of the independent transitions of the input at every other sampling time and the lack of channel memory we gain nothing by building a system with a memory greater than one sampling time. Therefore, the design is complete if we present it only for a transition time $t_1$ and the subsequent sampling time $t_2$ during which the input is held constant. Turning to time $t_1$ first (11) and (12) become

$$L_1(a_1, a_2) = L_1$$

$$= \frac{R_1^2(s_1 = a_1) - R_1^2(s_2 = a_2)}{2R_1(s_1 = a_1) - 2R_1(s_2 = a_2)} = \frac{R_1(a_1) + R_2(a_2)}{2}, \quad (16)$$

and

$$R_1(s_1) = E[I_1 \mid s_1]. \quad (17)$$

In the binary quadratic case, there is only one solution for $L_1$, and the sets $p_1(a_1)$ and $p_1(a_2)$ just correspond to the intervals $(-\infty, L_1)$ and $(L_1, \infty)$, respectively. Therefore, we may write the conditional expectation in (17) as an integration with respect to $p_I$ over an interval dependent upon $L_1$ as follows:

$$R_1(a_1) = \frac{\int_{-\infty}^{L_1} x p_I(x)\,dx}{\int_{-\infty}^{L_1} p_I(x)\,dx}; \qquad R_1(a_2) = \frac{\int_{L_1}^{\infty} x p_I(x)\,dx}{\int_{L_1}^{\infty} p_I(x)\,dx}. \quad (18)$$

Eqs. (16) and (18) then yield a single, generally transcendental, equation to be solved for $L_1$. In particular if $p_I(x)$ is Gaussian with mean $m$ and variance $\sigma^2$ then it can be easily verified that $L_1$ is equal to $m$, $R_1(a_1)$ equals $m - \sigma\sqrt{2/\pi}$ and $R_1(a_2)$ equals $m + \sigma\sqrt{2/\pi}$. This completes the system design at $t_1$, and we now turn to $t_2$.

At time $t_2$ there are two cases to be considered and they correspond to the two possible transmissions $a_1$ or $a_2$ at time $t_1$. For convenience we assume that $a_1$ was transmitted at $t_1$. Eqs. (11) and (12) become

$$L_2(a_1, a_2 \mid s_1 = a_1) = L_2^-$$

$$= \frac{R_2^2(s_1 = a_1, s_2 = a_2) - R_2^2(s_1 = a_1, s_2 = a_1)}{2R_2(s_1 = a_1, s_2 = a_2) - 2R_2(s_1 = a_1, s_2 = a_1)}$$

or

$$L_2^- = \frac{R_2(s_1 = a_1, s_2 = a_2) + R_2(s_1 = a_1, s_2 = a_1)}{2}, \quad (19)$$

and

$$R_2(s_1 = a_1, s_2) = E(I_2 \mid s_1 = a_1, s_2). \quad (20)$$

As before we express $R_2$ as an integration with respect to $p_I(x)$, making use of the observation that $p_2(a_1)$ and $p_2(a_2)$ are semi-infinite intervals,

$$R_2(s_1 = a_1, s_2 = a_1) = \frac{\int_{-\infty}^{L_2^-} x p_I(x)\,dx}{\int_{-\infty}^{L_2^-} p_I(x)\,dx};$$

$$R_2(s_1 = a_1, s_2 = a_2) = \frac{\int_{L_2^-}^{L_1} x p_I(x)\,dx}{\int_{L_2^-}^{L_1} p_I(x)\,dx}. \quad (21)$$

If we now combine (19) and (21) and use the fact that $L_1$ is known from our design at $t_1$, we find a simple equation for $L_2^-$. In the particular case that $p_I(x)$ is Gaussian with mean $m$ and variance $\sigma^2$, it can be verified that the solution for $L_2^-$ is $m - 0.982\sigma$. Substituting this value of $L_2^-$ in (20) yields the result that $R_2(s_1 = a_1, s_2 = a_1)$ equals $m - 1.5100$ and $R_2(s_1 = a_1, s_2 = a_2)$ equals $m - 0.4530$. Had we assumed that $s_1 = a_2$ we would have correspondingly concluded that $L_2^+$ equalled $m + 0.982\sigma$, $R_2(s_1 = a_2, s_2 = a_1)$ equalled $m + 0.453\sigma$ and $R_2(s_1 = a_2, s_2 = a_2)$ equalled $m + 1.510\sigma$. These results are tabulated below and complete the system design.

Optimum Mean Square System for $I_1 = I_2 = I$ Normally Distributed $(m, \sigma^2)$

| | If $I_1$ is: | then $s_1$ is: | and if $I_2$ is: | then $s_2$ is: |
|---|---|---|---|---|
| $M_1$: | $I_1 \geq m$ | $a_2$ | $I_2 \geq m + 0.982\sigma$ | $a_2$ |
| | | | $I_2 < m + 0.982\sigma$ | $a_1$ |
| | $I_1 < m$ | $a_1$ | $I_2 \geq m - 0.982\sigma$ | $a_2$ |
| | | | $I_2 < m - 0.982\sigma$ | $a_1$ |
| | If $s_1$ is: | then $R_1$ is: | and if $s_2$ is: | then $R_2$ is: |
| $M_3$: | $a_2$ | $m + 0.982\sigma$ | $a_2$ | $m + 1.510\sigma$ |
| | | | $a_1$ | $m + 0.453\sigma$ |
| | $a_1$ | $m - 0.982\sigma$ | $a_2$ | $m - 0.453\sigma$ |
| | | | $a_1$ | $m - 1.510\sigma$ |

## IV. Amplitude Quantization

The quantization problem is one of subdividing the range of a random variable into a preassigned, finite number of regions such that the error, judged according to a given criterion function, that obtains when the value of the random variable is optimally estimated, given only the information as to which region the variable lies in, is a minimum. As an alternative statement of the quantization problem in terms of our digital system model we take $I_n$ to be the random variable to be quantized, $M_1$ the assignment of the quantizing regions,

$M_2$ the digital identity mapping, and $M_3$ the mapping to the reconstruction $R_n$; $k$ is taken to be zero. Although we allow for the possibility of a quantization scheme dependent upon the past, $\bar{I}_{n-1}$, it is more common to consider memoryless quantization. Using $I_i$, the initial element, in place of $I_n$ would specialize our results to the memoryless case. The problem of reconstruction from noisy samples can also be formally treated in terms of $M_2$ as a random mapping, but we do not do so here. (See Section V.)

As in our previous work we take $E[\phi(I_n - R_n)]$ as the criterion function. Let $R_n(a_j)$ denote the reconstruction $R_n$ generated by the selection of $a_j$ for $s_n$. The expectation sign in (7b) can be removed because, for $k$ zero and $M_2$ deterministic, $R_n$ is deterministically given by $M_3M_2M_1(\bar{I}_n)$. The finite point $L_n(a_j, a_r)$ was defined in Section II as simultaneously the endpoint of a component interval of $p_n(a_j)$ and of $p_n(a_r)$. Eqs. (7b) and (9) then become:

$$\phi(L_n(a_j, a_r) - R_n(a_j)) = \phi(L_n(a_j, a_r) - R_n(a_r)) \tag{22}$$

and

$$E[\phi'(I_n - R_n] | \bar{s}_n] = 0. \tag{23}$$

We observe that if we make the hypothesis that $\phi$ is strictly monotonically increasing with increasing absolute value of its argument, it implies that $\phi$ is an even function. To see this we need only assume to the contrary that $\phi(z)$ is greater than $\phi(-z)$. The equality of the absolute values of $z$ and its negative when coupled with the strict monotonicity of $\phi$ yields the desired conclusion. Since $\phi$ is even, under the monotonicity assumption a solution to (22) exists for all selections of $a_r$, and the solution is given by:

$$L_n(a_j, a_r) = \tfrac{1}{2}R_n(a_j) + \tfrac{1}{2}R_n(a_r). \tag{24}$$

Eq. (24) can be verified by direct substitution in (22).

The solution given by (24) is also the unique solution to (22) if $R_n(a_j)$ is unequal to $R_n(a_r)$. In an optimum quantizer $R_n(a_j)$ and $R_n(a_r)$ are unequal, and even in a suboptimal quantizer this is a reasonable hypothesis. To verify uniqueness we need only add an arbitrary increment $d$ to the solution given in (24) and substitute in (22):

$$\phi(d - \tfrac{1}{2}(R_n(a_j) - R_n(a_r))) \stackrel{?}{=} \phi(d + \tfrac{1}{2}(R_n(a_j) - R_n(a_r))). \tag{25}$$

The absolute value of $d$ minus a constant cannot equal the absolute value of $d$ plus the same constant when $d$ and the constant are both nonzero. Therefore, by the strict monotonicity of $\phi$ the solution given by (24) is unique. We may further observe that $\phi$ distorts the magnitude of distances but not their relative order.

The necessary condition expressed by (24) allows for many irrelevant solutions. In order to select the relevant solutions we specialize (2) for the quantization problem.

$$p_n(a_j) = \{I_n : \phi(I_n - R_n(a_j)) \le \phi(I_n - R_n(a_r)) \quad \text{all} \quad r \neq j\}. \tag{26}$$

The points $I_n$ at which equality obtains in (25) are given by (24). For convenience, and without loss of generality, we order the system outputs $R_n$ as follows:

$$R_n(a_j) \ge R_n(a_r) \quad \text{if and only if} \quad j \ge r. \tag{27}$$

From (24) for the possible endpoints $L_n(a_j, a_r)$ of component intervals of $p_n(a_j)$, we have that closest end point below the point $R_n(a_j)$ corresponds to the midpoint between $R_n(a_j)$ and $R_n(a_{j-1})$ while the closest endpoint above $R_n(a_j)$ is the midpoint between it and $R_n(a_{j+1})$. Furthermore it is readily verified that the points $I_n$ lying in this interval about the point $R_n(a_j)$ are closer to $R_n(a_j)$ than to any other $R_n$, and they belong to $p_n(a_j)$ by the distance order preservation property of $\phi$. Finally we demonstrate that any $I_n$ not in this one interval about $R_n(a_j)$ does not belong to $p_n(a_j)$. Assume, for example, that $I_n$ lies below $L_n(a_j, a_{j-1})$, the midpoint between $R_n(a_j)$ and $R_n(a_{j-1})$. Since the distance between $I_n$ and $R_n(a_j)$ is greater than that between $I_n$ and $R_n(a_{j-1})$, it follows that $\phi(I_n - R_n(a_{j-1}))$ must be less than $\phi(I_n - R_n(a_j))$. This contradicts the inequality in (25) and proves that $I_n$ less than $L_n(a_j, a_{j-1})$ does not lie in the set $p_n(a_j)$. A similar argument suffices to show that if $I_n$ lies above $L_n(a_j, a_{j+1})$, the midpoint between $R_n(a_j)$ and $R_n(a_{j+1})$, it is not a member of $p_n(a_j)$. For completeness we note that $L_{1n}(a_1)$ is minus infinity and $L_{un}(a_m)$ is plus infinity. The conclusion we obtain for the optimum quantizer is that for each $j$, $p_n(a_j)$ is a single interval containing the point $R_n(a_j)$, with a lower endpoint that bisects the interval between $R_n(a_j)$ and $R_n(a_{j-1})$ and an upper end point that bisects the interval between $R_n(a_j)$ and $R_n(a_{j+1})$. As an illustration, we consider the binary quantizer with the two system outputs $R_n(a_1)$ and $R_n(a_2)$. The sets $p_n(a_1)$ and $p_n(a_2)$ are given by:

$$p_n(a_1) = (-\infty, L_n]; \qquad p_n(a_2) = [L_n, +\infty) \tag{28}$$

where $L_n = \tfrac{1}{2}R_n(a_1) + \tfrac{1}{2}R_n(a_2)$.

The condition to determine the optimum reconstruction mapping $M_3$, given $M_1$, is provided by (23) and is not reducible in general. If the loss function $\phi$ is taken to be quadratic, then (12) indicates that the solution for $R_n$ is the conditional expectation of the input $E(I_n \mid \bar{s}_n)$. As another example of the application of (23) we take the absolute value loss function. For positive arguments the derivative of the absolute value is plus one, and for negative arguments the derivative is minus one. Eq. (23) is rewritten by employing the subconditioning property of conditional expectations.[2]

$$E[\phi'(I_n - R_n) \mid \bar{s}_n]$$
$$= Pr\,(I_n \ge R_n \mid \bar{s}_n)E[\phi'(I_n - R_n) \mid I_n \ge R_n, \bar{s}_n]$$
$$+ Pr\,(I_n < R_n \mid \bar{s}_n)E[\phi'(I_n - R_n) \mid I_n < R_n, \bar{s}_n] = 0. \tag{29}$$

Employing our remarks concerning $\phi'$ in (29) we find:

$$Pr\,(I_n \ge R_n \mid \bar{s}_n) = Pr\,(I_n < R_n \mid \bar{s}_n). \tag{30}$$

[2] See Loeve [5], p. 350.

Therefore for an absolute value loss function, $R_n$ is optimally given by the conditional median of the $I_n$ distribution given $\bar{s}_n$, a well-known result.

Essentially these conclusions concerning optimum quantization were previously obtained by Lloyd [5], Bluestein [6], and to a lesser extent by Max [7]. Our treatment is like Lloyd's and we have learned from Lloyd's work The additional conclusion available from Section III, that optimum quantization for noisy channels, with respect to a quadratic criterion, can be effected in terms of single intervals for $p_n(a_i)$, seems to be new.

## V. Pulse Code and Delta Modulation

Pulse code modulation is a system of communication with the usual elements of transmitter, channel, and receiver. The transmitter samples the input waveform, or message, at preassigned times and then quantizes the amplitude of the input samples. The information concerning the quantization region that the input amplitude lies in is then transmitted. The channel linking the transmitter and receiver may be either noisy or noiseless. The receiver accepts the information about the location of the input and uses it to reconstruct the original input message. If we only consider the time sampled input and its reconstruction, then in our digital system model the transmitter is $M_1$, the channel $M_2$, the receiver $M_3$, and we assume $M$ equals $N$ and $k$ is zero. A final point to consider is that in common pulse code modulation systems the quantization procedure is time invariant, and in particular, the quantization regions are not dependent upon the past of the input process $\bar{I}_{n-1}$. The independence of the past implies, in our formulation, that the initial parameter $t_i$ is equal to $t_n$ so that $\bar{I}_n$ is replaced by $I_n$.

For the noiseless channel ($M_2$ the identity mapping) this problem is identical with the quantization problem discussed in Section IV. If the channel is noisy ($M_2$ a random mapping) then the results are more complex. Eqs. (7b) and (9) become:

$$E[\phi(L_n(a_j, a_r) - R_n) \mid s_n = a_j] = E[\phi(L_n(a_j, a_r) - R_n) \mid s_n = a_r] \quad (31)$$

and

$$E[\phi'(I_n - R_n) \mid s_n'] = 0. \quad (32)$$

If $\phi$ is the quadratic loss function, then the results of Section III would enable us to further simplify (31) and (32).

A delta modulation communication system is a digital system for which we may interpret $M_1$ as the transmitter, $M_2$ as the channel, and $M_3$ as the receiver. In the delta modulation system provision is made for a time varying quantization scheme (unlike PCM) by the insertion of a feedback loop from the transmitter output to its input. (See Fig. 2.) In the common binary delta modulation system ($M$ and $N$ equal to 2, *e.g.*, $a_1 = 1$, $a_2 = -1$) the transmitter quantizes the input $I_n$ by means

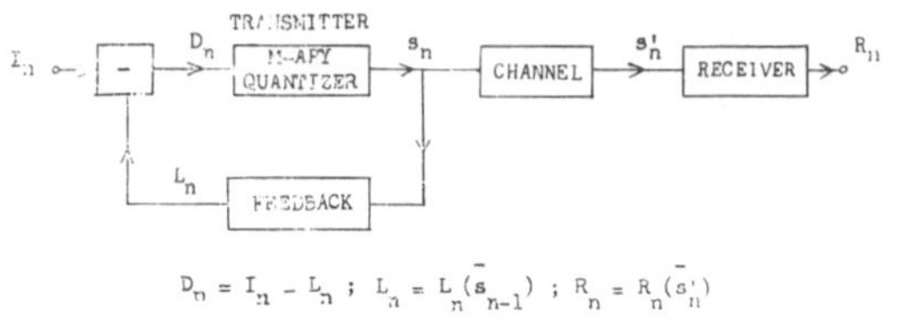


Fig. 2—Delta modulation system.

of a binary quantization of the difference between $I_n$ and the output of the feedback loop $L_n$. The mapping $M_1$ can then be described in terms of two sets $p_n(a_1)$ and $p_n(a_2)$ given by:

$$p_n(a_1) = \{I_n : I_n \geq L_n\}, \qquad p_n(a_2) = \{I_n : I_n \leq L_n\}. \quad (33)$$

The results of Section III for $M$ equal to 2 show that a semi-infinite interval is indeed the optimum form for $p_n$ when the loss function is quadratic, $k$ is nonpositive and the channel arbitrary. Furthermore, if the channel is noiseless and $k$ is zero, then the results of Section IV show that again the semi-infinite interval is the optimum form for $p_n$ for a wide class of loss functions. When $k$ is nonpositive we have pointed out that conditioning upon $\bar{I}_n$ can be replaced by conditioning upon $\bar{s}_n$. The analog of (31) becomes:

$$E[\phi(L_n - R_n) \mid s_n = a_1, \bar{s}_{n-1}] = E[\phi(L_n - R_n) \mid s_n = a_2, \bar{s}_{n-1}]. \quad (34)$$

Eq. (34) indicates that $L_n$, and thus the optimum sets $p_n$, are only functions of $\bar{s}_{n-1}$. Therefore the feedback arrangement of the delta modulation transmitter provides precisely the correct data for the generation of the optimum $L_n$.

The above discussion demonstrates that the delta modulation system is an allowable representation of the optimum binary digital system under the operating conditions discussed above. Furthermore it is observed that the delta modulation system provides a time varying quantization pattern unlike ordinary binary pulse code modulation. We conclude that binary delta modulation is in principle superior to binary pulse code modulation. (Practical PCM systems generally employ binary transmissions and thus are binary systems.)

It is possible to make additional observations concerning binary delta modulation systems if we restrict ourselves to the case of a noiseless channel and $k$ zero. For the noiseless channel the optimum feedback loop has an output $L_n$ given by:

$$L_n = \tfrac{1}{2}R_n(a_1) + \tfrac{1}{2}R_n(a_2) \quad \text{where} \quad a_1 = 1, \quad a_2 = -1. \quad (35)$$

The optimum receiver output $R_n$ satisfies:

$$E[\phi'(I_n - R_n) \mid \bar{s}_n] = 0. \quad (36)$$

If for various reasons, including engineering practicality, the receiver is constrained to be a linear function of the received binary-valued symbols $\bar{s}_n$ given by:

$$R_n(a_j) = \sum_m^{n-1} h_{nm}s_m + h_{nn}(s_n = a_j), \tag{37}$$

then from (35) we find for $L_n$:

$$L_n = \sum_m^{n-1} h_{nm}s_m. \tag{38}$$

Thus the feedback loop is directly related to the linear receiver. This intimate relationship between the linear receiver and the optimum feedback loop corresponding to it was tacitly assumed in the intuitive investigations pursued by the early delta modulation system designers. Our work provides a justification, for example, for using integrator feedback with an integrating receiver, as was done by de Jager [8], Zetterberg [9], and others.

An interesting approximation to (35) is based upon the hypothesis that at the time $t_n$ a positive transmission is as likely as a negative one, and therefore both have a conditional probability of $\frac{1}{2}$ of occurring. This assumption permits us to rewrite (35) to find:

$$L_n = E[R_n \mid \bar{s}_{n-1}]. \tag{39}$$

If, in addition, we assume a quadratic loss function then the optimum receiver is given by a conditional expectation, and the subconditioning property applied to (39) yields

$$L_n = E[I_n \mid \bar{s}_{n-1}]. \tag{40}$$

The significance of (40) is that the transmitter design equation is no longer implicitly dependent upon the receiver design. The joint optimization problem has been approximately reduced to two direct calculations, and this is a substantial calculational simplification. The approximation just indicated can be interpreted as claiming that the noiseless channel, quadratically optimum, binary communication system transmits at the maximum information rate.

The maximum information rate approximation implies a very special structure for the input stochastic process if it is the hold exactly. The approximation assumes that $L_n$, which is given by (40) as the conditional mean of the input distribution, is also approximately the conditional median of the input distribution ($I_n$ is as likely to be above $L_n$ as below it). If the probability distribution function for $I_n$ conditional upon $\bar{s}_{n-1}$ is symmetric, then the conditions are met, and the approximation is exact.

## VI. Compensation of a Stepped Controller

A problem of some interest in control engineering is that of the compensation of a fixed element to achieve improved system performance [10]. If we restrict ourselves to the case of time-sampled inputs then the results of Section II can be readily specialized to treat the compensation problem. We assume that the mapping $M_3$ represents the fixed element or plant whose output $R_n$ is to be a reconstruction of an input stochastic or deterministic process $I_n$; the reconstruction fidelity is assumed measurable by the conditional expectation $E[\phi(I_n - R_n) \mid \bar{s}_n']$. The presence of the stepped controller in the plant is implicitly provided by the constraint that the input to $M_3$ be $N$-ary. A representation for the system under consideration is provided in Fig. 3. The mapping $M_2$, being superfluous, is omitted in effect by taking it to be the digital identity mapping.

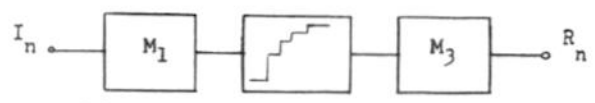

Fig. 3—Series plant compensation.

For the problem posed above, series and feedback compensation are entirely identical in their capabilities. Nothing is learned by observing $R_n$ that is not known from $\bar{I}_n$. Therefore our choice of determining the optimum series compensator is made without loss of generality. This problem is now completely equivalent to the $N$-ary quantization problem discussed in Section IV or the communication problems discussed in Section V, with the additional simplification that we need only find the optimum mapping $M_1$ for a given mapping $M_3$.

## Appendix

Our objective is to prove that if $f_{jr}(I_n)$ is a real, single-valued continuous function defined on the real line $R$, then the set $p_n(a_j)$ given by (5) can be represented by at most a denumerable union of disjoint, closed intervals. We first apply de Morgan's rule,[3] which states that the intersection of sets $A_t$ is equal to the complement of the union of the complements of $A_t$, to (5) to obtain

$$p_n(a_j) = \left(\bigcup_{r=1}^{M} (\{I_n : f_{jr}(I_n) \geq 0\})^c\right)^c. \tag{41}$$

Since $f_{jr}$ is a single-valued function defined on the whole real line, the complement of the set $\{I_n : f_{jr}(I_n) \geq 0\}$ must be the set $\{I_n : f_{jr}(I_n) < 0\}$. (It suffices to verify that the two sets are disjoint and their union is the real line.)

From the topological definition of a continuous function,[4] which is equivalent to the ordinary definition when the topological space is the real line $R$, we see that for a continuous function the inverse image of an open set in $R$ is an open set in $R$. Now the set $\{I_n : f_{jr}(I_n) < 0\}$ is indeed the inverse image of the open set $(-\infty, 0)$ and thus must also be an open set in $R$. Furthermore, as the union of open sets is open (and here we are only dealing with finite unions) we see that $p_n$ is the complement of an open set.

There is a theorem characterizing open sets in $R$ [11] which states that every open set in $R$ can be represented

[3] See Loeve [3], p. 57.
[4] See Loeve [3], p. 67.

by at most a denumerable union of disjoint, open intervals in $R$. Therefore the set $p_n$ can be represented by

$$p_n = \left(\bigcup_{k=1}^{\infty} (a_k, b_k)\right)^c \quad \text{where} \quad a_k < b_k < a_{k+1}. \tag{42}$$

Finally, since the open intervals in (42) are disjoint, $p_n$ can also be given as the union of closed intervals.

$$p_n = \bigcup_{k=1}^{\infty} [b_k, a_{k+1}], \tag{43}$$

when the endpoints are arranged so that $a_{k+1}$ is greater than $a_k$.

Eq. (43) is the desired conclusion permitting us to write (6).

## Acknowledgment

The author wishes to thank Prof. D. W. Tufts of Harvard University for his encouragement and criticism and the reviewers for their comments.

## References

[1] T. Fine, "Properties of an Optimum Digital System," Ph.D. dissertation, Harvard University, Cambridge, Mass.; 1963.

[2] J. D. Bruce, "Optimum quantization of a signal contaminated by noise," *Quarterly Progress Report*, Research Lab. of Electronics, Mass. Inst. Tech., Cambridge, Mass., vol. 70, pp. 206–213; July, 1963.

[3] M. Loeve, "Probability Theory," D. Van Nostrand Co., Inc., New York, N. Y., p. 125; 1955.

[4] L. Brand, "Advanced Calculus," John Wiley and Sons, Inc., New York, N. Y., p. 434; 1955.

[5] S. P. Lloyd, "Least Squares Quantization in PCM," Bell Telephone Labs., Murray Hill, N. J. Also, "The Quantization Problem," Private Communication.

[6] L. I. Bluestein, "The Quantization of Noisy and Noise-Free Data for Minimum Error," based upon, "A Hierarchy of Quantizers," Ph.D. dissertation, Dept. of Elec. Engrg., Columbia University, New York, N. Y.; 1962.

[7] J. Max, "Quantizing for minimum distortion," IRE Trans. on Information Theory, vol. IT-6, pp. 7–12; March, 1960.

[8] F. de Jager, "Delta Modulation, A Method of PCM Transmission Using the 1-Unit Code," Phillips Research Report R-203, vol. 7, pp. 442–466; 1957.

[9] L. H. Zetterberg, "A comparison between delta and pulse code modulation," *Ericsson Technics*, vol. 2, pp. 95–154; 1955.

[10] H. Van Trees, "Synthesis of Optimum Nonlinear Control Systems," The M. I. T. Press Research Monograph, M. I. T. Press, Cambridge, Mass.; 1962.

[11] T. Apostol, "Mathematical Analysis," Addison-Wesley Co., Inc., Reading, Mass., p. 43; 1957.

# 37



Reprinted from *Proc. IEEE*, **55**(3), 308–316, 319 (1967)

# Statistical Delta Modulation

PHILLIP A. BELLO, SENIOR MEMBER, IEEE, RICHARD N. LINCOLN, MEMBER, IEEE, AND HERBERT GISH

***Abstract*—This report describes the results of a study of Statistical Delta Modulation (SDM), a new method of digital transmission of analog information.[1] In this method the system design is tailored to the statistical properties of the input data so as to provide analog reconstruction values with a minimum mean squared error. The method of system design is an iterative procedure in which conditional means are evaluated based upon actual input data. The report presents the theory of operation of the system and describes the results of a computer simulation in which such questions as the effects of sampling rate, channel noise, system memory, and mismatched input processes are discussed. At the present time only a brief comparison has been made with conventional techniques. It was found that at low sampling rates and for a particular non-Gaussian process, sampling rate reductions of 38 percent could be achieved relative to a conventional delta modulation system at the same SNR performance.**

## I. Introduction

THE PROBLEM of effective conversion of analog information to digital data and the reconversion process has received considerable attention in recent times and is currently a field of active interest [1]–[5], [9]. This paper is a summary of some results of a program which has investigated a new system of digital transmission of analog data proposed by SIGNATRON[1] under the name "Statistical Delta Modulation" (SDM). This technique was discovered by T. Fine and is based on the theoretical development reported in [6].

In SDM the system design is tailored to the statistical properties of the input data so as to provide analog reconstruction values with a minimum mean squared error. The design of the SDM device can, in principle, be performed analytically if the statistics of the input process are known. However, even for a first-order Markov process, the calculations are very complex. A general analytic procedure that can be used in the case of $n$th-order Markov processes is presented in the Appendix.

Notwithstanding the analytic difficulties, a typical realization of the input process may be used to design the device by the computation of appropriate conditional means, and this is the type of procedure that has been used to design SDM devices during the study, both the input process and device being simulated on a digital computer.

In Section II we present a brief analysis showing the evolution of the SDM device as an optimum means of digital transmission of analog data. Although Fine's theory applies to $M$-ary as well as binary transmission (see [6]), the derivations and results in this study apply to the binary case only.

Section III briefly discusses the iterative procedures used to design the SDM devices.

The various computer results are presented in Section IV. Most of the performance data concerns devices designed for a second-order Markov process. The effects of memory

Manuscript received December 1, 1966; revised January 6, 1967; final revision January 10, 1967. The work reported herein was carried out under Contract AF 19(628)-5539 for the Air Force Cambridge Research Laboratories, Office of Aerospace Research, Bedford, Mass.

H. Gish is with SIGNATRON, Inc., Lexington, Mass., and Harvard University, Cambridge, Mass.

R. N. Lincoln is with the RCA David Sarnoff Research Laboratory, Princeton, N. J. He was formerly with SIGNATRON, Inc., Lexington, Mass.

[1] Patent application pending.

length, sampling rate, and an imperfect channel on the performance of the devices are shown by various graphs. If an optimum device is designed for a given input process and a slightly different input process is used, performance will be less than optimum. This type of degradation is investigated with respect to gain and bandwidth variations of the input signals.

Section V is a summary section and presents conclusions and recommendations for further research. The Appendix extends Fine's [6] infinite memory analysis and shows how, in principle, the performance of SDM systems with finite memory may be computed when sufficient statistical knowledge of the input process is available. Particular attention is given to a vector Markov input process for which it is shown that a set of simultaneous integral equations arise whose solution will yield the desired SDM performance.

## II. Description of SDM

In this section we shall present a brief derivation of the equations satisfied by the SDM device for the case of binary transmission and a noiseless channel. The system we wish to consider is presented in its most general form in Fig. 1. In Fig. 1(a) we show the analog-sample-to-binary-symbol-conversion operation and in Fig. 1(b), the binary-symbol-to-analog-sample reconstruction device. The analog process $y(t)$ is sampled periodically and converted to the sequence $\{y_n\}$, which is then transformed into the binary sequence $\{b_n\}$, where for simplicity we take

$$b_n = \pm 1. \tag{1}$$

We initially leave the form of the A-B converter unspecified because, as we shall see below, its form is determined by constraints on the B-A converter.[2]

A modulation operation (not shown) converts the binary sequence into a waveform suitable for transmission.

After (noiseless) demodulation at the receiver the restored binary sequence is processed by a B-A converter which reconstructs samples $\{r_n\}$ from the binary input sequence. Finally, the reconstructed analog samples must be fed to an interpolator to provide the final continuous analog waveform. The optimization procedure to be described does not include the interpolation filter in order to simplify the devices under consideration, although, in principle, the interpolation filter may be included.

It may be noted from Fig. 1(b) that we have expressed the analog reconstruction value at the $n$th sample as

$$r_n = f_n(b_n, b_{n-1}, \cdots, b_{n-m}). \tag{2}$$

There are three constraints implied by (2) that are worth setting down:

[2] We use the symbols A-B (Analog-to-Binary) and B-A (Binary-to-Analog) rather than A-D and D-A to specifically point out that we are considering an optimization problem in which each analog sample is transformed into a binary number and vice versa, so that the number of samples per second equals the number of bits per second transmitted. The conventional PCM systems do not fall in this class, but all delta modulation systems do. The optimization has been extended to include $M$'ary transmissions (see Fine [6]) and in this latter, more general optimization, the PCM device is included in the class of systems studied.

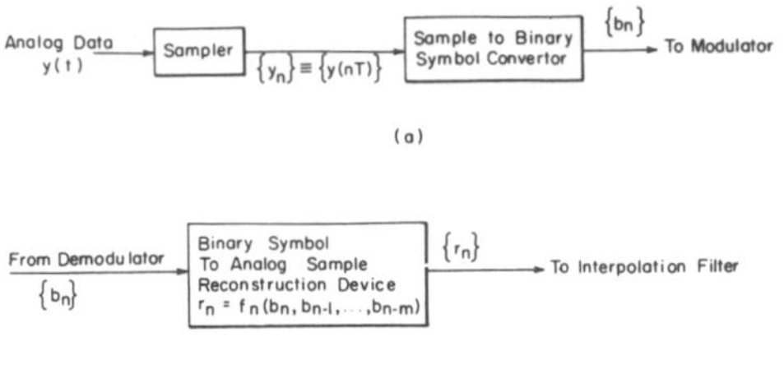


Fig. 1. System definition.

1) the reconstructed value is to depend *only* upon the received binary values
2) there is a finite memory $m$, i.e., the reconstructed value depends on the present binary symbol and the past $m$ binary symbols
3) the B-A converter can change with time ($n$).

In order to find an optimum system, i.e., simultaneously optimum B-A and A-B converters, we shall proceed in two steps, following Fine [6]. First we shall find an optimum A-B converter given a B-A converter. Then we shall find the optimum B-A converter given an A-B converter. We obtain simultaneous optimization by requiring the equations defining the conditionally optimum A-B converter and conditionally optimum B-A converter to be both satisfied.

Thus let us assume that a particular B-A converter has been selected and it is desired to determine the A-B converter that is optimum for that B-A converter. The problem faced by the A-B converter is simply this: shall the particular sample $y_n$ be transformed into a $+1$ or a $-1$? To answer this question we may determine the two possible reconstruction values corresponding to $b_n = \pm 1$ and simply select that value ($+1$ or $-1$) which yields the error

$$\varepsilon_n = |r_n - y_n| \tag{3}$$

which is smallest.

It may readily be seen that if $b_n$ is chosen $+1$ when it is nearer to $f_n(+1, b_{n-1}, \cdots, b_{n-m})$ and $-1$ when it is nearer to $f_n(-1, b_{n-1}, \cdots, b_{n-m})$, then the smallest error will occur. A simple way of implementing this decision is to compare $y_n$ with a level set $l_n$ equal to the arithmetic mean,

$$l_n = \tfrac{1}{2}[f_n(-1, b_{n-1}, \cdots, b_{n-m}) + f_n(+1, b_{n-1}, \cdots, b_{n-m})] \tag{4}$$

and to transmit a $+1$ when $y_n$ exceeds $l_n$ and a $-1$ when it is less than $l_n$. Thus the configuration of the optimum A-B converter is as shown in Fig. 2. A threshold level is generated from (4) which is a function of the $m$ previous transmissions and time ($n$). Then the difference between the input sample and this level set is fed to a quantizer to generate the current binary output.

Consider now the complementary problem, that of finding the optimum B-A converter for a given A-B converter. If we adopt minimum mean squared error as our optimization criterion, then, as is well known, the value of $r_n$ to

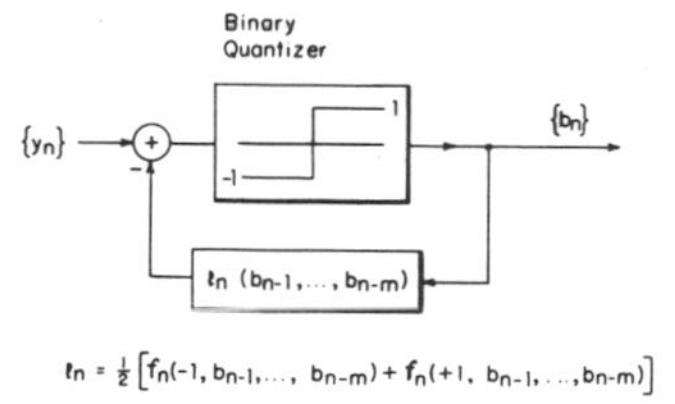


Fig. 2. Optimum A-B converter for given B-A converter.

choose is the conditional mean of the input $y_n$, given the set of values $b_n, b_{n-1}, \cdots, b_{n-m}$. Thus the optimum B-A converter is

$$r_n = E[y_n | b_n, b_{n-1}, \cdots, b_{n-m}]. \tag{5}$$

Simultaneous optimization thus requires that (4) and (5) both be satisfied. Combining these equations, we have

$$l_n(\bar{B}_{n-1}) = \tfrac{1}{2}[E(y_n | b_n = +1, \bar{B}_{n-1}) + E(y_n | b_n = -1, \bar{B}_{n-1})] \tag{6}$$

where we have used the notation

$$\bar{B}_{n-1} = (b_{n-1}, b_{n-2}, \cdots, b_{n-m}). \tag{7}$$

It should be realized that (6) is an implicit equation in the quantity $l_n(\bar{B}_{n-1})$ since the determination of the expectations in (6) required knowledge of $l_n(\bar{B}_{n-1})$.

The level sets and reconstruction values arising from the above optimization are a function of time $n$. Due to the assumed stationarity of the input process it may be expected that if this transient development is carried far enough in time, a steady state will be reached in which level sets and mapping functions $f_n(\cdot)$ approach asymptotically fixed functions.

While it is possible to carry out the above transient development by simulating the device and input on a computer and forming appropriate conditional means, it appears quite impractical in terms of computer time. The procedure actually used in the study is a direct solution of the steady-state device with the aid of an appropriate iterative procedure as described briefly in the following section.

This iterative procedure is due to Gish [8] who reconsidered Fine's problem under the constraint that the A-B and B-A converters be time-invariant devices, and who has shown that the procedure can be used to obtain optimum devices.

## III. Iterative Procedure for Solution of Steady-State Device

As the previous section has indicated, a strictly analytic approach to solution of steady-state SDM devices for an arbitrarily selected process is virtually impossible. Fortunately, however, an iterative or "guess and test" procedure may be used in which the necessary conditional means in (6) are computed by direct measurement after simulation of the input process and trial SDM devices.

The procedure is as follows. An initial B-A converter (alternately referred to as demodulator or receiver in subsequent sections) is assumed. That is, an initial mapping is made between all possible binary words of length $m+1$ and the $2^{m+1}$ reconstruction values. Let this initial mapping be denoted by

$$R_0(\bar{B}'_n) \tag{8}$$

where

$$\bar{B}'_n = (b_n, b_{n-1}, \cdots, b_{n-m}). \tag{9}$$

Equation (4) is then applied to determine an A-B converter. That is, level sets are determined by

$$L_0(\bar{B}_{n-1} = \bar{\gamma}) = \tfrac{1}{2}[R_0(\bar{B}'_n = 1, \bar{\gamma}) + R_0(\bar{B}'_n = -1, \bar{\gamma})]. \tag{10}$$

Once the A-B converter is determined the simulated input process is fed into the simulated initial A-B converter to produce a stream of binary numbers. A new receiver mapping is determined by evaluating conditional means according to (5) which yields reconstruction values that minimize the mean squared reconstruction error for that initial A-B converter. Let this new B-A converter be denoted by $R_1(\bar{B}'_n)$. Then a new A-B converter is determined from

$$L_1(\bar{B}_{n-1} = \bar{\gamma}) = \tfrac{1}{2}[R_1(\bar{B}'_n = 1, \bar{\gamma}) + R_1(\bar{B}'_n = -1, \bar{\gamma})]. \tag{11}$$

The above procedure is iterated until the reconstruction values and level sets reproduce themselves within a prescribed accuracy, i,e., until

$$R_{n+1}(\bar{B}'_n) \approx R_n(\bar{B}'_n) \tag{12}$$

$$L_{n+1}(\bar{B}_{n-1}) \approx L_n(\bar{B}_{n-1}). \tag{13}$$

It should be noted that in order to evaluate a particular conditional mean as in (5) one can only use what may be a very small subset of the total input sample set $\{y_n\}$, since there are $2^{m+1}$ possible different binary numbers in storage at the receiver at any time and a particular conditional mean requires only those inputs to be considered which yield a particular one of the $2^{m+1}$ binary numbers at the receiver. In the simulation procedure used we have required that each conditional mean be computed using a subset of input samples containing at least 10 000 input samples. Since the sequences $\bar{B}'_n$ are not of equal probability of occurrence, the time required to compute all conditional means with at least 10 000 samples is determined by the least probable sequence. The running time for the design of the SDM devices far exceeds the available continuous time allotment of the computer used (AFCRL's M-460 built by Univac) and software interfaces were included in various programs to store necessary working registers so that the programs could be dumped onto magnetic tape in the form of a core image.

## IV. Results of Computation

Much of the insight into the structure and performance of steady-state SDM Finite Memory devices (subsequently referred to simply as SDM devices) has been obtained empirically on the M-460 computer. The optimization algorithms for SDM devices are sufficiently complex that, in general, no analytic solution for the optimum SDM for a given input process and given device parameters can be found (see the Appendix). Thus, as mentioned previously, a direct simulation approach has been programmed to derive and test SDM devices. The results of this empirical work are presented in this section.

*A. Processes Simulated*

The initial contract requirement was the study of SDM devices for simple Gaussian correlated input processes. Therefore, the capability for the direct simulation of particular first-, second-, and third-order Gaussian vector Markov processes was developed. An arbitrary selection was made of correlated random processes equivalent to the output of white noise energized, repeated real root, linear filters. For computational convenience, it was decided to constrain the standard deviation of all signal processes to be one, and the mean to be zero. Intermediate empirical results showed the desirability of a capability of non-Gaussian signal processes as well, and as a result, an arbitrarily selected no-memory nonlinearity was developed to operate on the output of the second-order Gaussian Markov process.

1) *Second-Order Gaussian Markov Signal:* Most of the performance data has been taken on a second-order Gaussian Markov signal. The general second-order Markov relationship of a discrete process $y_n$ can be stated as

$$y_n = a_0\mu_n + a_1\mu_{n-1} + b_1 y_{n-1} + b_2 y_{n-2} \tag{14}$$

where the process $\mu_n$ is Gaussian, stationary, and uncorrelated. By suitable choice of the coefficients in (14) (e.g., using the methods of Levin [7]), the sequence $y_n$ can be made to represent a set of samples of the output of a two-pole linear filter when energized by white noise. These coefficients were chosen so that the resulting filter had the transfer function

$$H(s) = \frac{A}{(1 + \tau s)^2} \tag{15}$$

where the gain constant $A$ is chosen so that the variance of the output samples are unity. The autocorrelation function of the output samples is readily found to be

$$\phi(n) = (1 + |n|/R)\exp(-|n|/R) \tag{16}$$

where

$$R \triangleq \tau/T = \text{the number of signal samples per time constant of } H(s) \tag{17}$$

$$T \triangleq \text{time between adjacent samples.} \tag{18}$$

The quantity $R$ is used as a basic signal parameter for all the signals in the program.

2) *Non-Gaussian Signal:* To destroy the Gaussian statistics of the signal process, a no-memory nonlinearity was arbitrarily selected to operate on the output of the signal described in Section IV-A-1). This nonlinearity is essentially a cubing operation, with peak amplitude saturation that truncates the extremes of the range of the output process to reduce the tails of the output amplitude probability density function. In particular, if $y(t)$ is the continuous process which is sampled in Section IV-A-1), then the non-Gaussian process $z(t)$ satisfies the equation

$$z(t) = \begin{cases} Ky^3(t); & |y|^3 \leq 4 \\ 0; & |y|^3 > 4. \end{cases} \tag{19}$$

The odd symmetric property of $z(t)$ preserves the zero mean of the process, thus only a normalizing amplifier $K$ is required to return the output signal statistics to the (0, 1) convention. This value of $K$ was found to be 0.5816. The amplitude probability density function of the continuous output process, $y(t)$, is

$$P_y(y) = \left\{ \frac{\exp\left[-\frac{1}{2}\left(\frac{y}{K}\right)^{2/3}\right]}{3k\sqrt{2\pi}\left(\frac{y}{K}\right)^{2/3}} + 0.05547 \cdot \left[\delta(y - 4K) + \delta(y + 4K)\right] \right\}, \quad |y| \leq 4K+ \tag{20}$$

and is even symmetric. This process is henceforth referred to as the truncated cubic signal.

*B. Convergence Phenomena of Iteration Procedure*

Optimum SDM devices with various parameters for the signals described in Section IV-A were developed by direct simulation techniques. The basic device parameters are $m$ and $R$ where

$$m \triangleq \text{the bit memory length of the device} \tag{21}$$

and $R$ is defined by (17).

Some theoretical analysis carried out during the study demonstrates the existence of solutions and the convergence of the iterative procedure under mild conditions. However, no uniqueness conditions were demonstrated. That is, more than one solution may exist to the iteration procedure. Our results show that this is indeed the case, since the repeated application of optimization algorithms during the development of the optimum SDM device for given parameters usually yields two solutions. Both of these solutions can be considered to be "steady-state" in the sense that changes in performance and structure of the devices created at each iteration stage are relatively minimum in the neighborhoods of the solutions. However, only one of the solutions is "stable" in terms of the computational algorithm itself, in the sense that only one of the solutions becomes a constant point of device performance and structure, i.e., it is essentially unchanged as further iterations are completed. Unfortunately the first solution usually performs best. This fact underlies the necessity of secondary storage of the best performing device in all development programs.

These interesting phenomena are best presented graphically. Figure 3 shows the performance figure and a structural factor as a function of iteration number, of each new device in the development of the optimum SDM device with $m=5$, for the second-order Gaussian Markov signal with $R=2.5$. The performance figure is displayed as the ratio of signal variance to mean square reconstruction error of the device, expressed in decibels. The initial device was purposely chosen to perform poorly. As the iteration proceeds, the $2^{m+1}$ reconstruction values change, with some changing more than others. The structural factor is the magnitude of the maximum change in any reconstruction value of the new demodulator created by the present iteration, from the corresponding reconstruction value of the optimum device to date in secondary storage, the maximum being taken over the $2^{m+1}$ possible reconstruction values.

The stable state is reached when the device performance figure starts to oscillate about an apparent mean value. The curve exhibits an unavoidable simulation measurement error due to the finite time used to measure conditional means. In fact, the instability of the first solution achieved at iteration step 10 may be caused by measurement error. It is possible that this solution may represent an unstable equilibrium analogous to a ball balanced on a wand, where the structural factor curve would drop to zero and remain unchanged if the measurement error could be eliminated.

For the situations we have studied, the iteration step number at which the best device is achieved seems to depend only on $m$ and $R$, and not on the initial device. The front part of both curves appears to behave like the discharge of an RC circuit. These curves are typical of the convergence phenomena of the SDM optimization algorithm.

### C. *Results for Second-Order Gaussian Markov Process*

In this section we present some simulation results for the second-order Gaussian Markov process. The effects of memory length and sampling rate upon the performance of optimum SDM are presented, along with the performance of optimized SDM devices under the conditions of mismatch in input signal parameters and imperfect transmission channels.

1) *Effects of Memory Length:* Figure 4 shows a graph of the performance figures of optimum SDM devices as a function of memory length $m$, with the normalized sampling rate of $R$ of the signal held constant at the value 2.5. The performance figure at $m=0$ has been shown analytically to be 4.405 dB. The agreement with empirical results at this point is exceptionally good (within 0.05 dB).

The curve rises sharply from $m=0$ to $m=1$ and continues rather uniformly at a reduced slope until saturation begins approximately at $m=8$. This shows that there is a limit to the "useful" memory length of an SDM device for this signal (scarcely a surprising result, in light of the finite correlation time of the input). Thus when the ratio of $m/R$ exceeds 3.2 or so, the small return in performance for the cost of longer memory seems prohibitive.

This argument holds with this signal at or near the same $m/R$ ratio for any $R$. The particular $R$ in Fig. 4 was chosen to show saturation effects within the memory length limit ($M \leqq 10$) of the SDM device development computer program for this signal.

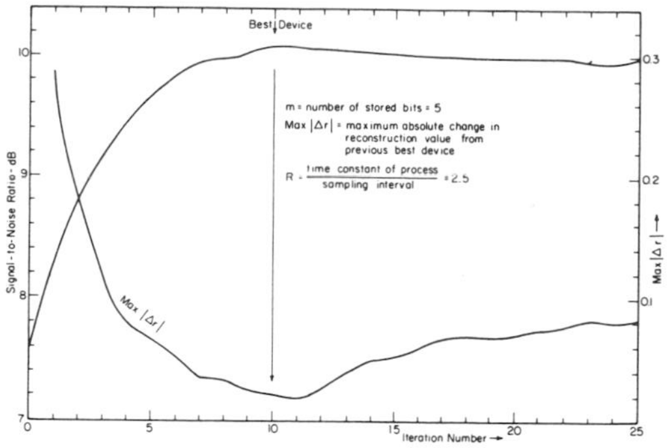


Fig. 3. SNR performance versus iteration number.

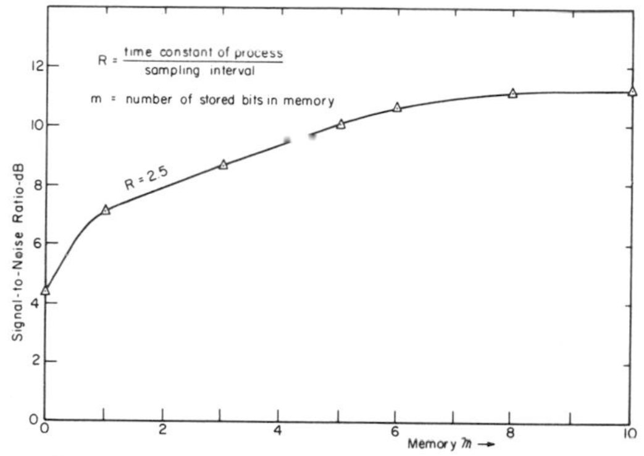


Fig. 4. Signal-to-noise ratio as a function of memory length for a fixed sampling rate; second-order Gaussian Markov process.

2) *Effects of Sampling Rate with Fixed Memory:* Figure 5 shows a graph of the performance figures of optimum SDM devices as a function of normalized sampling rate $R$, with the memory length $m$ of the devices held constant at 5. The wave has an effective breakpoint at $R \approx 2$ in that for $R<2$, the slope is much steeper than in the region $R>2$.

When the memory length is fixed and the sampling rate increases, the performance improves but gradually saturates. This saturation occurs because at sufficiently high sampling rates the input process will become essentially a random constant for the time interval covered by the given system memory. In order to remove the saturation and have performance improve continually with sampling rate the system memory must be continually increased as the sampling rate increases so that the time span covered by the stored samples equals a time constant or more of the input process.

The beginning of saturation is just discernible at $R=40$, where the devices start to take on their random constant input signal form. The fact that the performance of optimized SDM devices with fixed memory is maximum under the conditions of asymptotically high sampling rates is clearly demonstrated.

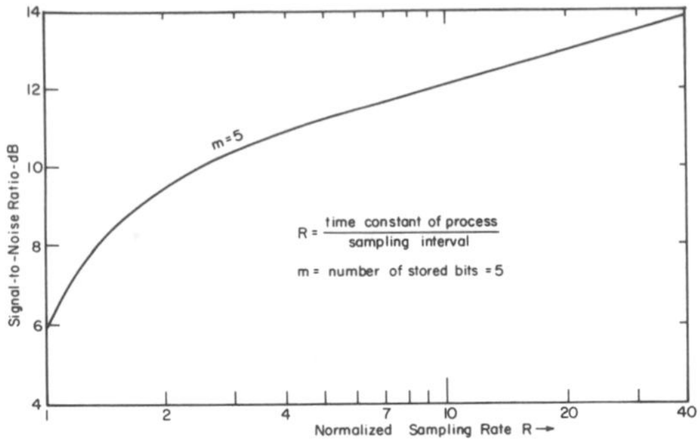


Fig. 5. Signal-to-noise ratio versus sampling rate for fixed memory; second-order Gaussian Markov process.

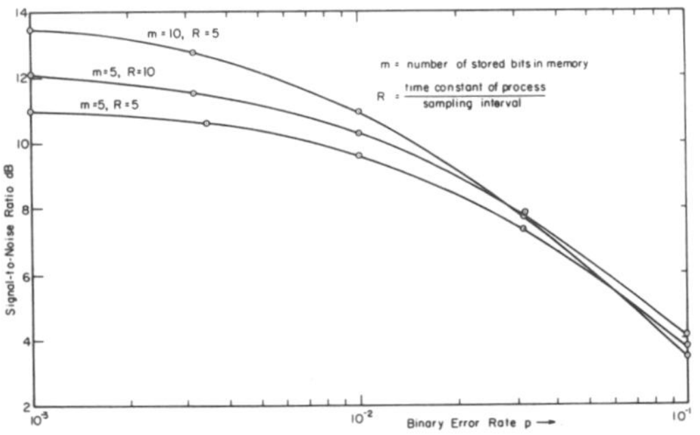


Fig. 6. Signal-to-noise ratio as a function of error rate at receiver for SDM device optimized in absence of errors; second-order Gaussian Markov process.

A similar saturation effect would be exhibited for any $m$. This value was chosen to permit reasonable running times for the computer SDM device development program.

3) *Effects of Imperfect Channels:* The programs written to test the effect of an imperfect channel on optimum SDM devices measure SNR performance of a device optimized in the absence of noise[3] under conditions of an imperfect channel where random uncorrelated binary errors are made at the receiver. Figure 6 shows SNR performance versus error rate for three cases, ($m=10$, $R=5$), ($m=5$, $R=10$), ($m=5$, $R=5$).

A direct comparison of the ($m=10$, $R=5$) and ($m=5$, $R=5$) in Fig. 5 shows that while on a perfect channel one may expect to improve performance significantly by increasing memory length until a saturation ratio of $m/R$ is reached [see Section IV-C-1)], this becomes less true over an imperfect channel since the extra memory length is more susceptible to errors by retaining incorrect bits longer. For example, with a channel bit error probability of $10^{-3}$, for ($m=10$, $R=5$) Fig. 6 shows a performance approximately 1.5 dB superior to that of the ($m=5$, $R=5$) case while at an error rate of $10^{-1}$, the two performance figures are virtually the same. It appears that an optimum SDM device with given $m$ and $R$ parameters should never give significantly worse performance over an imperfect channel than an optimum SDM device with the same $R$ and shorter memory, even if the longer memory device exhibits a saturated $m/R$ ratio. This can be seen by considering the fact that if the longer memory device exhibits saturation, the retained bits in memory corresponding to the extreme past of the transmission history become uncorrelated with the input signal, and hence an error in this portion of bit memory has little effect on performance. If the longer memory device is not yet saturated, it will exhibit a significant improvement in performance over a perfect channel in comparison to its shorter memory counterpart; and this advantage is not likely to be reversed as channel quality degrades. If the performance of two optimum devices is compared where one has an $m/R$ ratio on the point of saturation and the other has larger memory ($R$ being constant, of course), the performance curves should be virtually identical throughout. Thus a memory length on the verge of saturation appears to be the best choice for a given sampling rate, unless the channel used for transmission is poor enough that a shorter memory device will perform equally well.

4) *System Performance with Mismatched Inputs:* Results were obtained showing the performance of optimum SDM devices over perfect channels with signal inputs other than those for which the devices were optimized. These data show the sensitivity of the optimization technique and device performance to changes in input statistics. The variance and the sampling rate of the input signal process were varied considerably from the optimization specifications of the tested device. Figure 7 shows a typical performance figure of an optimum device ($m=5$, $R=2.5$) as a function of the decibel mismatch in gain. The devices appear relatively insensitive to gain mismatch. No doubt if we had the computer capability of generating sufficiently high performance devices, more gain sensitivity would have been observed.

Figure 8 shows the performance figure of the optimum $m=5$, $R=10$ device as a function of sampling rate $R$. While it is obvious that performance of any optimum SDM device increases as $R$ is increased from the development matched point, it should be noted that the performance shown in Fig. 8 could be improved at all values of $R \neq 10$ by developing the optimum device at those points. Subtraction of the performance curve in Fig. 8 from the optimum $m=5$ performance of Fig. 5 yields the decibel performance degradation of Fig. 7 from optimum for those parameters. The results are plotted in Fig. 9 which shows the sensitivity of the general device to changes in sampling rate.

5) *Observed Linear Structure in SDM Device:* Fine [6] has discussed the possibility of optimum transmitter and receiver mappings which are constrained to be linear. The general problem of the optimization of the performance of time-invariant SDM devices with the linear constraint has been studied by Gish [8], who demonstrates an iterative procedure for designing such devices which is considerably simpler than that which must be used to design general SDM devices.

[3] The optimization technique can be readily applied to a noisy channel if desired.

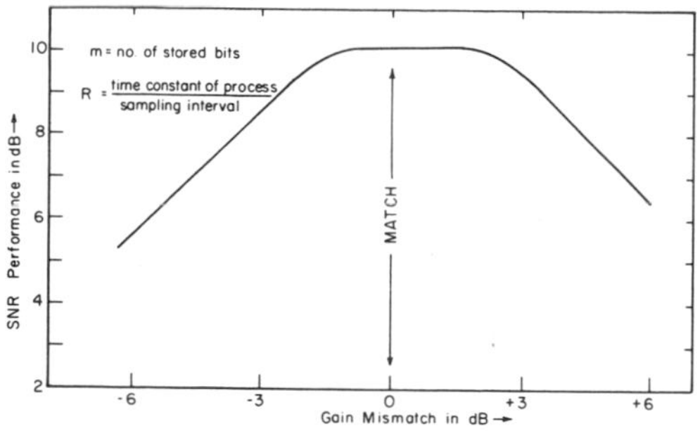

Fig. 7. Sensitivity of an optimum SDM device to gain mismatch ($m=5$, $R=2.5$); second-order Gaussian Markov process.

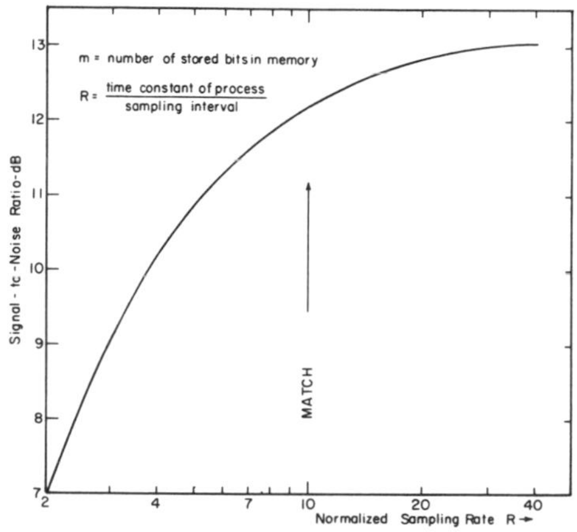


Fig. 8. Signal-to-noise ratio as a function of sampling rates for optimum SDM ($m=5$, $R=10$); second-order Gaussian Markov process.

During the course of the present study the question arose as to the degree of nonlinearity of the receiver and level set mappings of the optimum SDM devices designed in the study without a linear constraint. Linear mappings were chosen in a systematic way to approximate the nonlinear mappings of the SDM devices for the second-order Markov process. It was discovered that the apparently nonlinear mappings were in fact very nearly linear. In addition, comparative performance testing of these linearized approximations showed insignificant difference in performance from the original SDM devices as is shown in Table I.

It remains to be seen whether the level of performance of these devices can be obtained by the linear optimization algorithm as well. Linear development of SDM devices for a few of the parameter sets in Table I would produce the answer, and the undertaking of this task is planned. An equality of performance between a few well-chosen generally optimized and linearly optimized devices would show a constrained linearity of the general algorithm for this signal.

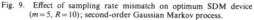

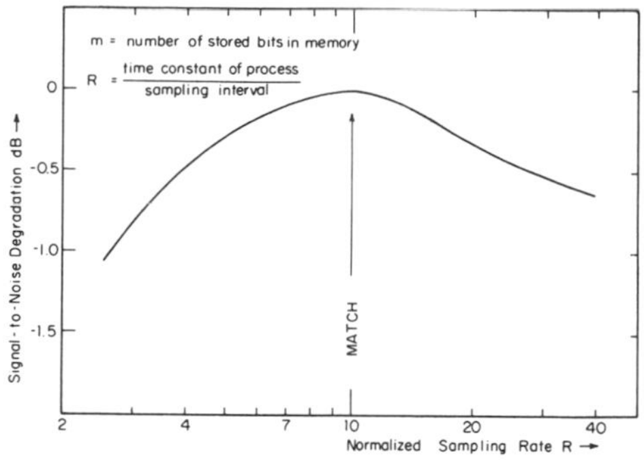


Fig. 9. Effect of sampling rate mismatch on optimum SDM device ($m=5$, $R=10$); second-order Gaussian Markov process.

TABLE I

Differential Performance between Generally Optimized SDM Devices and Linearized Equivalents

| Parameters | dB Differential = S/N Opt/S/N Linearized |
|---|---|
| $m=5$, $R=5$ | −.01 |
| $m=5$, $R=2.5$ | +.02 |
| $m=5$, $R=1.25$ | .00 |
| $m=3$, $R=2.5$ | +.03 |
| $m=6$, $R=2.5$ | +.02 |

The near-linearity of the optimum SDM devices for the second-order Gaussian process may possibly be traceable to the fact that the minimum mean squared estimation for a Gaussian process is linear. However, due to the gross nonlinearity of the binary quantizer the quantizer output is decidedly non-Gaussian and the analogy is not too clear.

### D. Results for a Non-Gaussian Process

The press of time prevented any generally optimized SDM device development for a non-Gaussian process. However, a series of direct comparisons between optimized quasi-infinite memory SDM devices with a *linear* constraint[4] and optimum conventional delta modulation[5] (CD) devices was made as a function of sampling rate $R$. The SDM devices were chosen to be linear because it was desired to use memories larger than 10, the limit of computer capability for devices optimized without a linear constraint. The chosen SDM devices were quasi-infinite in the following sense. An $m/R$ saturation ratio [see Section IV-C-1)] for this signal was found empirically. Then an upper bound on memory length of 20 was chosen to be compatible with the core size of the computer. The SDM device memory length

[4] The simplified procedure of Gish [8] was used to derive the parameters of the linear SDM devices.

[5] The delta modulation device was allowed to have infinite memory (perfect integrator in feedback loop) and the step size for maximum output SNR was determined by simulating the conventional delta modulation system with different step sizes and using the non-Gaussian noise as input.

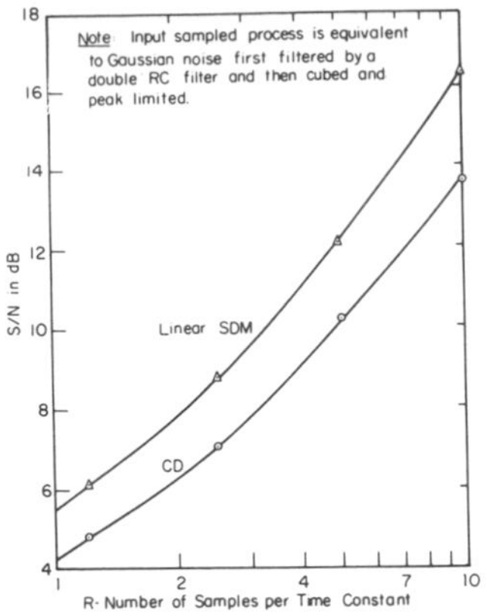


Fig. 10. Signal-to-quantizing-noise ratio (S/N) in decibels of linear SDM and conventional delta modulation versus normal sampling rate ($R$).

was thus absolutely limited to 20, but was well within the $m/R$ saturation region for all $R$ if the value of $m$ required was not greater than 20. The results of this effort are shown in Fig. 10 as a comparison of linear[6] SDM and CD performance. It can be seen from Fig. 10 that the sampling rate of linear SDM can be reduced by a factor of 1.5 and still match CD performance at the original sampling rate. It follows that a generally optimized SDM must do as well and may do better.

It would be of interest to carry out the nonlinear to linear comparisons described in Section IV-C-5) in order to determine the linearity of the general optimization algorithm for this highly non-Gaussian process.

## V. Conclusions and Recommendations

The study reported here concerns a new method of digital transmission of analog signals called Statistical Delta Modulation (SDM). The study consisted both of analysis and computer simulation of a Statistical Delta Modulation system with a statistically known input signal.

This system accepts as input a sequence of sampled values of an analog signal, transmits binary signals, and delivers at the receiver output a sequence of values approximating the sampled sequence at the transmitter input in a minimum mean squared error sense.

An optimally selected level or threshold set dependent upon a finite number $m$ of past input sample values (called the memory) is used to convert sampled analog values to binary digits.

The approach used to design the SDM devices involves an iterative procedure in which an initial transmitter mapping between analog samples and binary transmissions is assumed. Using the specified input process and the initial transmitter, the conditional means of the received signals were obtained to derive a receiver which was optimum for the initial transmitter. An algorithm is used to generate a new transmitter for the optimized receiver. This iterative procedure is repeated until the transmitter and receiver mappings change by sufficiently small amounts. This design procedure is rather time-consuming for large memories. Thus our present limitation using the M-460 computer appears to be around a memory of ten.

Several conclusions may be made about SDM devices based upon observation of the computer simulation results and theoretical understanding of SDM operation. Consider first the effect of memory length. The calculations show that system performance improves as the memory increases but eventually saturates for sufficiently large memory. This shows that there is a limit to the "useful" memory length of an SDM device, a conclusion to be expected because of the finite correlation time of the input process. It was found that very little performance improvement occurs when the memory spans a time exceeding around three time constants of the input second-order Gaussian Markov process.

When the memory length is fixed and the sampling rate increases the performance improves but gradually saturates. This saturation occurs because, at sufficiently high sampling rates, the input process will become essentially a random constant for the time interval covered by the given system memory.

The effect of an imperfect channel (i.e., errors in the received binary stream) is to cause a degradation which generally is more harmful at the longer memories. Thus while longer memory provides performance improvement (except for saturation conditions), the degree of performance improvement decreases as the channel error rate increases. For example, in the case of a second-order Gaussian Markov process sampled at the rate of 5 samples per time constant, there exists a 1.5-dB improvement of performance with a memory of 10 samples relative to that with a memory of five samples for a channel error rate of $10^{-3}$. By the time the channel error rate reaches $10^{-1}$ the performance of the two systems is essentially the same.

The SDM device is designed to be optimum for a given input process sampled at a given rate. A question of interest is the degree of sensitivity of the device performance to changes in the input process, i.e., to mismatching the input process. Results were obtained for sensitivity to gain mismatch and sampling rate mismatch (this latter mismatch can be interpreted as a bandwidth change for fixed sampling rate). The curves indicate that the devices considered are not markedly sensitive to mismatch. However, for the memory capability allowed by the digital computer, devices with very high performance could not be designed and this may have some bearing on the noticed insensitivity to mismatch.

Due to the general lack of available performance data on PCM and conventional delta modulation (CD) systems for different types of input processes and due to the time limitations of the contract which did not allow the collection of such data, no extensive comparison of SDM with PCM and

[6] By "linear" SDM we mean an SDM device optimized with linear mapping constraints.

CD was carried out. However, one comparative performance run of SDM and CD for an arbitrarily selected input process showed the possibility of reducing the required sampling rate in SDM by 38 percent and yet having the same SNR performance as CD, at least for the region of lower sampling rates. With regard to PCM, we note that experimental data and theoretical comparisons of CD relative to PCM [4] have shown that CD is superior at the low sampling rates. Even the very latest approach in PCM [5], Differential Pulse Code Modulation, shows no better performance than CD modulation at low sampling rates. It follows that since we have demonstrated that for the input process considered SDM is superior to CD at low sampling rates, it also is superior to PCM and DPCM at low sampling rates. It is important to note that this result applies only to a particular, arbitrarily selected, input process and cannot be said to represent either the best or worst that can be done with SDM relative to conventional techniques. Study to date has strongly indicated that the statistics of the input process do influence the degree of improvement attainable with SDM. Thus to obtain an adequate theoretical understanding of the benefits attainable with SDM, a range of input statistics should be considered.

For all the generally optimized SDM devices designed for Gaussian input processes it has been found that an optimum SDM device of the same memory but with linear mapping constraint provides essentially the same mean squared reconstruction error. This result may be connected with the fact that the optimum estimator (or predictor) of a Gaussian process is a linear device. However, the analogy is not too clear since the binary quantizer obviously makes the transmitted process drastically non-Gaussian.

*[Editors' Note:* Material has been omitted at this point.]

## References

[1] F. DeJager, "Delta modulation. A method of PCM transmission using a 1-unit code," *Philips Res. Rept.*, vol. 7, pp. 442–466, 1952.

[2] H. Van de Weg, "Quantizing noise of a single integration delta modulation system with an *n*-digit code," *Philips Res. Rept.*, vol. 8, pp. 367–385, 1953.

[3] L. A. Zetterberg, "A comparison between delta and pulse code modulation," *Ericsson Tech.*, vol. 2, no. 1, pp. 95–154, 1955.

[4] J. B. O'Neal, Jr., "Delta modulation quantizing noise, analytical and computer simulation results for Gaussian and television inputs," *Bell Sys. Tech. J.*, vol. 45, pp. 117–141, January 1966.

[5] ——, "Predictive quantizing systems for the transmission of television signals," *Bell Sys. Tech. J.*, vol. 45, pp. 689–721, May–June 1966.

[6] T. Fine, "Properties of an optimum digital system and applications," *IEEE Trans. on Information Theory*, vol. IT-10, pp. 287–296, October 1964.

[7] M. J. Levin, "Generation of a sampled Gaussian time series having a specified correlation function," *IRE Trans. on Information Theory*, vol. IT-6, pp. 545–548, December 1960.

[8] H. Gish, "Optimum quantization of random sequences," Ph.D. dissertation, Division of Engrg. and Appl. Phys., Harvard University, Cambridge, Mass., in preparation.

[9] R. A. McDonald, "Signal-to-noise and idle channel performance of differential pulse code modulation systems—Particular applications to voice signals," *Bell Sys. Tech. J.*, vol. 45, September 1966.

# 38



Reprinted from *Proc. IEEE,* **55**(3), 298–308 (1967)

# Linear and Adaptive Delta Modulation

J. E. ABATE, MEMBER, IEEE

***Abstract*—New results are presented, offering insight into the performance and optimization of linear and adaptive delta modulation, together with a comparison with pulse code modulation. The results are applied to three cases of practical interest: television, speech, and broadband signals.**

**The results are presented as follows: first, a characterization of the quantization noise of linear delta modulation (DM) is given; second, an adaptive DM system which seems promising for television and speech is evaluated; and third, a comparison between PCM and adaptive DM is made for speech, television, and broadband signals.**

**It is concluded that 1) the adaptive system provides DM with a companding capability, 2) adaptive DM offers a bit rate or channel bandwidth reduction capability in comparison with PCM for television signals, 3) adaptive DM appears better suited to television and speech signals than linear DM, 4) the maximum *S/N* performance of adaptive DM is the same as that of linear DM, 5) the companding improvement offered by adaptive DM is not limited by the same practical considerations as those of PCM, and 6) the *S/N* performance of adaptive DM is the same for both Gaussian and exponential signal densities.**

## I. Introduction

The purpose of this paper is threefold: first, to provide insight into the behavior and optimization of delta modulation (DM) by characterizing its performance by relatively simple closed-form approximate solutions; second, to discuss an adaptive DM system which seems promising for television and speech application; and third, to compare the performance of linear and adaptive DM with that of pulse code modulation (PCM). The fidelity criterion used to define optimum performance is that of minimum mean square error or noise power.

Delta modulation is a simple type of predictive quantizing system and is essentially a one-digit differential pulse code modulation system [23]. Such systems are based primarily on an invention by Cutler [1] and de Jager [2] who used one or more integrators to perform the prediction function. The invention is based on transmission of the quantized difference between successive sample values rather than the samples themselves. When the quantizer contains only two levels, the system is reduced to its simplest form and is referred to as delta modulation, or simply DM. Both the encoder and decoder make an estimate or prediction of the signal's value, based on the previously transmitted signal. In linear DM, the value of the signal at each sample time is predicted to be a particular linear function of the past values of the quantized signal [6]. Redundant signals (e.g., television and speech) are well suited for predictive quantizing because of the accuracy possible in their prediction.

In adaptive DM, the value of the signal at each sample time is predicted to be a nonlinear function of the past values of the quantized signal [35]. Introducing nonlinear prediction into DM by forcing the system to respond adaptively to changes in the slope of the input signal provides a useful means of extending the range over which the delta system yields its optimum performance. This would not be necessary if the message signal ensemble were stationary. However, ensembles of many communication signals are nonstationary. These include speech, television, facsimile signals, and the like. It is, therefore, useful to consider a means of incorporating adaptive techniques into the delta process, enabling the system to encode nonstationary ensembles in an optimal way.

For problems concerning the performance and optimization of DM, it is convenient to have a model, involving only a few essential parameters, which will satisfactorily characterize the noise performance of the DM system. Present formulations of DM are complex and unwieldy. In Section II, the description of DM performance will be simplified by employing useful approximations and observations of computer simulation results. Using simple closed-form expressions to describe DM noise performance, we hope to gain insight into the operation of linear DM, especially with an eye toward characterizing adaptive systems. These simple formulations do suggest adaptive systems.

In Section III, an adaptive system which seems promising for television and speech application will be presented. From the simple closed-form approximations of Section II, the expected performance of the adaptive system will be presented. Computer simulations are used to verify the predictions of performance and aid in system optimization. The amount of companding improvement achieved by the adaptive system will be given, along with expressions relating to the optimum selection of linear and adaptive system parameters.

Since encoding a continuous message by DM may be much simpler and cheaper than by PCM, there is considerable interest in determining how the performance of DM relates to that of PCM. In Section IV, a performance comparison will be made between PCM and linear and adaptive DM. The performance of the adaptive DM system will be compared with companded PCM for speech application. A characterization of PCM granular and overload noises with Gaussian and exponentially distributed inputs will be given. The optimum performance of PCM for television and broadband signal application will be compared with that of DM.

This paper will deal mainly with three signals of practical importance: television, speech, and broadband signals. The first two will be approximated by a signal having an integrated power spectrum and an exponential probability density function. The integrated spectrum is defined as one

Manuscript received December 5, 1966; revised January 11, 1967. This paper represents a portion of a doctoral dissertation written at Newark College of Engineering, Newark, N. J., 1967. The research reported herein was supported by Bell Telephone Laboratories, Inc., Holmdel, N. J.

The author is with Bell Telephone Laboratories, Inc., Holmdel, N. J.

having an asymptote of negative six decibels per octave of increasing frequency starting at $\omega_3$ and band-limited to some maximum frequency $\omega_m$. The suitability of the integrated spectrum and exponential density for describing television and speech signals can be established by examining the results of Kretzmer [41], O'Neal [23], Davenport [15], and Fletcher [34]. The broadband signal (e.g., frequency division multiplexed signals) will be approximated by one having a uniform or white spectrum band-limited to $\omega_m$, and a Gaussian probability density function. The results reported in this paper can be applied directly to other communication or stochastic signals which have the spectrum and density characteristics described above.

The following assumptions and restrictions will be used in this paper:

1) error-free transmission in the digital channel
2) constant sampling or bit rate in the encoder
3) single ideal integrator in the encoder and decoder.

It can be shown [35] that the principal results reported apply equally well if a small amount of loss is incorporated in the integrator, or if a small amount of second integration is used in both the encoder and decoder.

The synthesis of optimal filters so as to minimize the subjective effects of quantizing noise in a feedback quantizing system has been reported by Kimme and Kuo [40]. In this paper, we will not deal with subjective effects, but will confine our attention to the mean square error criterion of system performance.

## II. Linear Delta Modulation

O'Neal [6] has given a good description of linear DM and was the first to compare the results of digital computer simulation with those of analysis. Van De Weg [3] has provided an expression for granular noise power, and Protonotarios [30] has described slope overload noise in detail. In addition to the above, the literature abounds with discussion, modification, and application of linear DM [2]–[14], [16]–[22], [25]–[28].

In this section, granular and overload noise powers are characterized by simple closed-form approximate solutions. These solutions were obtained with the aid of empirical observations made from computer simulation results which were obtained from an IBM 7094 program reported by O'Neal [6], who used random numbers to represent sample values of the input signal.

We begin by defining a new term called the slope loading factor. In order to avoid slope overload, the slope capability of the DM system must be greater than the slope of the input signal. Since the former is given by the product of step size $k$ and sampling rate $f_s$, then, in order that the system not be overloaded, the following condition must be satisfied:

$$kf_s > |f'(t)| \qquad (1)$$

where $|f'(t)|$ represents the magnitude of the input signal derivative with respect to time. If we denote the mean power of the derivative of the stationary stochastic signal by $D$, then we shall define a term, denoted by $\mathbf{s}$ and called the slope loading factor, as follows:

$$\mathbf{s} \equiv (kf_s)/\sqrt{D}. \qquad (2)$$

The slope loading factor given by (2) represents the ratio of the slope capability of the system to the effective value of the slope of the stationary signal. It is, therefore, a dimensionless quantity and a measure of the degree by which the input is loading the capability of the DM system. In terms of the one-sided power spectrum $F(\omega)$ of the signal, the mean power of the signal derivative is given by

$$D = \int_0^{\omega_m} \omega^2 F(\omega)\, d\omega \qquad (3)$$

where $\omega_m = 2\pi f_m$ is the maximum angular frequency to which the signal is band-limited prior to encoding.

In Table I, the values of $F(\omega)$ and $\mathbf{s}$ are given for the types of signals to be considered in this paper. For television and speech, the integrated power spectrum as given in Table I will be used with values of $\omega_3/\omega_m$ of 0.011 and 0.23, respectively. These values will be used throughout this paper. The slope loading factor is expressed in Table I in terms of the bandwidth expansion factor $B$, which is the ratio of the bandwidth required of the digital channel to that of the signal. For DM systems, $B$ is simply one-half the ratio of sampling rate to signal bandwidth, or $f_s/2f_m$.

It can be shown [35] that granular noise power $N_G$ as a function of $\mathbf{s}$ can be given with reasonable accuracy by two asymptotes. The first of these has a slope of six decibels per octave, that is, granular nose power increases by six decibels per octave increase of $\mathbf{s}$, and exists in the region $\mathbf{s}<8$. The second asymptote has a slope of nine decibels per octave, and exists in the region $\mathbf{s}>8$. The asymptotes are

$$N_G = \frac{\pi^2}{6}\left(\frac{D}{\omega_m^2}\right)\frac{\mathbf{s}^2}{B^3} \quad \text{for } \mathbf{s} < 8, \qquad (4)$$

and

$$N_G = \frac{\pi^2}{48}\left(\frac{D}{\omega_m^2}\right)\frac{\mathbf{s}^3}{B^3} \quad \text{for } \mathbf{s} > 8. \qquad (5)$$

For uniform and integrated spectra, these expressions are given in Table I, where for convenience the mean signal power $S$ and all impedances are assumed to be unity. When $S$ is not unity, it is, of course, simply necessary to include it in the numerator of $F(\omega)$ and the denominator of noise power, and to include $\sqrt{S}$ in the denominator of $\mathbf{s}$ (i.e., divide $k$ by $\sqrt{S}$, the standard deviation of the signal). Noise power is of course expressed in watts.

In DM systems, granular noise predominates for large values of $\mathbf{s}$, and overload noise predominates for small values of $\mathbf{s}$. From computer simulation results [35], it has been observed that minimum quantization noise power occurs at a value of the slope loading factor given approximately by

TABLE I

LINEAR DM RESULTS WITH UNIFORM AND INTEGRATED SIGNAL SPECTRA

| | From Equation | Uniform Spectrum | Integrated Spectrum |
|---|---|---|---|
| $F(\omega)$ | from given data | $\frac{1}{\omega_m}$ | $\frac{1}{\omega_3 \tan \frac{\omega_m}{\omega_3}}\left[\frac{1}{1+\left(\frac{\omega}{\omega_3}\right)^2}\right]$ |
| s | (2) | $\frac{\sqrt{3}}{\pi} kB$ | $\frac{Bk}{\pi\sqrt{\frac{\omega_3/\omega_m}{\tan^{-1}\omega_m/\omega_3}-\left(\frac{\omega_3}{\omega_m}\right)^2}}$ |
| $N_G$, s < 8 | (4) | $\frac{\pi^2}{18}\frac{s^2}{B^3}$ | $\frac{\pi^2 s^2}{6B^3}\left[\frac{\frac{\omega_3}{\omega_m}}{\tan^{-1}\frac{\omega_m}{\omega_3}}-\left(\frac{\omega_3}{\omega_m}\right)^2\right]$ |
| $N_G$, s > 8 | (5) | $\frac{\pi^2}{144}\frac{s^3}{B^3}$ | $\frac{\pi^2 s^3}{48B^3}\left[\frac{\frac{\omega_3}{\omega_m}}{\tan^{-1}\frac{\omega_m}{\omega_3}}-\left(\frac{\omega_3}{\omega_m}\right)^2\right]$ |
| $N_O$ | (7) | $\frac{8\pi^2}{81} e^{-3s}(3s+1)$ | $\frac{8\pi^2}{27}\left[\frac{\frac{\omega_3}{\omega_m}}{\tan^{-1}\frac{\omega_m}{\omega_3}}-\left(\frac{\omega_3}{\omega_m}\right)^2\right] e^{-3s}(3s+1)$ |
| Minimum $N_Q$ | (8) | $\frac{\pi^2}{18}\left[\frac{(\ln B)^2+2.06\ln B+1.17}{B^3}\right]$ | $\frac{\pi^2}{6}\left[\frac{\frac{\omega_3}{\omega_m}}{\tan^{-1}\frac{\omega_m}{\omega_3}}-\left(\frac{\omega_3}{\omega_m}\right)^2\right]\left[\frac{(\ln B)^2+2.06\ln B+1.17}{B^3}\right]$ |

$$\mathbf{s} = \ln 2B. \qquad (6)$$

This relationship is illustrated in Fig. 1, along with points obtained by computer simulation for the cases of uniform, television, and speech spectra. In the computer simulation, both Gaussian and exponential signal amplitude distributions were used with each of the three spectra cited. It was found [35] that the results were substantially the same, that is, neither minimum quantization noise nor the points illustrated in Fig. 1 changed significantly when the amplitude distribution of the signal was changed. More will be said about this in Section III.

Using (6) and the fact that at its minimum the derivative of quantization noise with respect to slope loading factor must vanish, closed-form empirical expressions for overload noise power $N_O$ and minimum quantization noise power $N_Q$ can be obtained. The result can be shown [35] to be as follows:

$$N_O = \frac{8\pi^2}{27}\left(\frac{D}{\omega_m^2}\right) e^{-3\mathbf{s}}(3\mathbf{s}+1) \qquad (7)$$

$$\text{minimum } N_Q = \frac{\pi^2}{6}\left(\frac{D}{\omega_m^2}\right)\left[\frac{(\ln B)^2+2.06\ln B+1.17}{B^3}\right]. \qquad (8)$$

For uniform and integrated spectra, (7) and (8) are given in Table I. The optimum performance (i.e., maximum $S/N_Q$) for uniform, television, and speech spectra are illustrated in Fig. 2, where the ordinate expressed in decibels is the ratio of mean signal power to minimum $N_Q$, or simply

$$\text{maximum } S/N_Q = -10 \log_{10}(\text{minimum } N_Q) \qquad (9)$$

and where $S$ has been assumed unity for convenience, as stated earlier.

The $S/N_Q$ performance as a function of the slope loading factor is illustrated in Fig. 3 for the uniform signal spectrum case at several values of $B$. For the integrated spectrum case, the performance curves are identical to those of Fig. 3, the only change required being a shifting of the ordinate scale. It is clear that this is so from (4), (5), and (7), since noise power at some specified value of s is proportional only to derivative power $D$. Similarly, for a specified value of $B$, the minimum quantization noise power given by (8) is proportional to the derivative power. For example, to obtain the $S/N_Q$ performance of television or speech, it is simply necessary to add 16.9 dB or 4.5 dB, respectively, to the $S/N_Q$ values that appear on the ordinate scale in Fig. 3. The computer points shown in Fig. 3 were first reported by

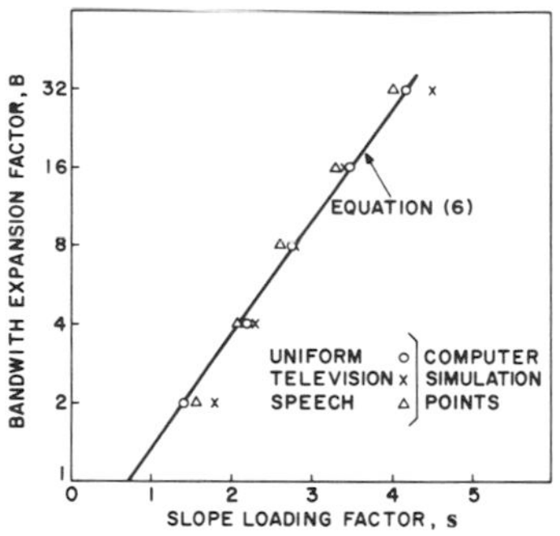


Fig. 1. Relationship between $B$ and $\mathbf{s}$ in linear DM at minimum quantization noise.

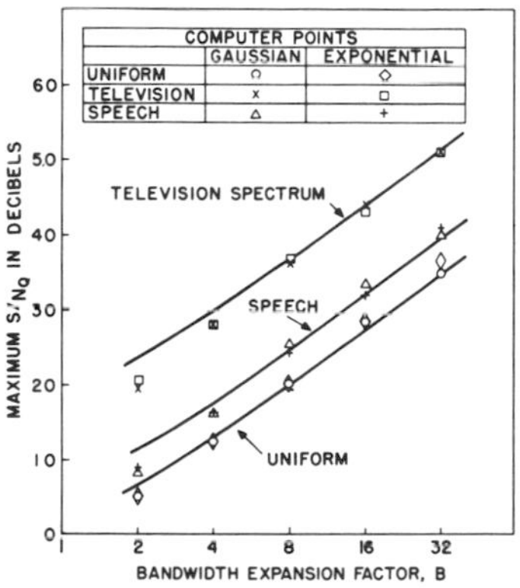


Fig. 2. Optimum performance of linear DM; curves obtained from (8), (9), and Table I; points from computer simulation.

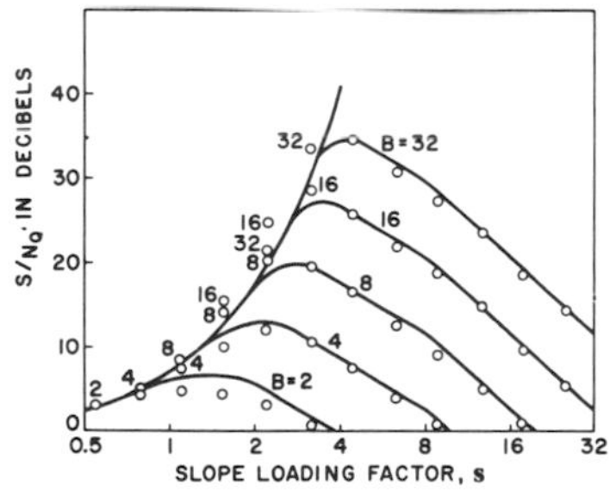


Fig. 3. $S/N_Q$ performance of linear DM with uniform signal spectrum; curves obtained from (4), (5), and (7); points from computer simulation, Gaussian signal distribution.

O'Neal [6]; his normalized step size can be shown to be related to the slope loading factor.

Unfortunately, in the linear DM system the quantization noise is sensitive to small changes in the mean power of the signal. As a result, the range of $\mathbf{s}$ over which $S/N_Q$ is near maximum is small. From (2) it is clear that a change in signal power produces a change in slope loading factor $\mathbf{s}$. If $\mathbf{s}$ is substantially different in value from that given by (6), then $N_Q$ will not be close to its minimum value and the DM system is suboptimum. As an example, for the case of $B=8$ in Fig. 3, if the quantization noise is to be held to less than twice its minimum value (i.e., $S/N_Q \geq 17$ dB), the slope loading factor must be constrained such that $2<\mathbf{s}<4.5$. This in turn requires that the effective value of the signal must be constrained to a variation of less than approximately $\pm 40$ percent. This is indeed a severe restriction for signals of practical importance such as television and speech. Forcing the DM system to respond adaptively to changes in the input signal, by changing the slope loading factor with time, overcomes the restriction of a narrow optimum performance range. This adaptation of linear DM will be the subject of the next section.

## III. Adaptive Delta Modulation

The objective of this section is to discuss an adaptive DM system which seems promising for television and speech application. The simple expressions presented in the previous section will be modified to describe the expected system performance. Results of computer simulations are presented which verify the performance, provide the sets of conditions for which it is applicable, and aid in establishing the conditions for optimization.

In order to give the DM system the capability of encoding nonstationary signals in an optimal way, the restraint that exists in linear delta (i.e., slope loading factor is fixed) must be removed. That is, the system should be permitted to become self-regulating or adaptive so that optimum performance (i.e., maximum $S/N_Q$) is achieved over a broad range of input signal variation. If the signal is stationary, then the DM system is optimally loaded when the slope loading factor is made to satisfy (6). If the signal is nonstationary, the DM system will be optimally loaded if and only if the slope loading factor is changed in accordance with the changing signal parameter. The objective of the adaptive DM system discussed herein is to maintain optimal loading and performance (i.e., maximum $S/N_Q$) by controlling the value of the slope loading factor. Since the sampling rate is assumed constant for a given system, it is clear from (2) that by controlling the step size, the slope loading factor may be assigned any specified value.

The problem is to decide how to measure the nonstationarity of the signal and, hence, the changing slope loading factor. That is, what measurement should be made and how should it be accomplished so that signal variations can bring about a reassignment of the value of $k$. Undoubtedly there are many approaches to this problem. In this section, one solution that appears promising is presented. It involves monitoring the instantaneous derivative of the encoded signal, determining if the condition specified by (1) is satisfied, and changing the step size if necessary in a discrete manner to prevent slope overload.

Essentially, there can be both a discrete and a continuous method of adapting the system to changes in the signal derivative. The former, called "discrete adaptive DM," observes the binary pulse sequence at the quantizer output and changes the step size in finite increments; it is illustrated in Fig. 4. The latter, called "continuous adaptive DM," observes the continuous input signal and changes the step in a continuous manner; it is illustrated in Fig. 5. In this paper, only the discrete adaptive system will be quantitatively discussed.

In the discrete adaptive system, the switch control chooses, in effect, a gain $K_i$ by which to increase the quantum step size. The choice made by the control is dictated by a logical decision process based on observations of the sequence of pulses leaving the quantizer. For example, when slope overload occurs, causing suboptimal performance, the quantizer output is a series of pulses of the same polarity (i.e., a series of plus one's or minus one's). In response to this series of consecutive pulses, the switch control selects a gain $K_i$ greater than $K_{i-1}$, such that the new larger step size is $K_i$ multiplied by the smallest step size $k$, or simply $K_i k$. If the pulse polarity remains unchanged, the step size is incrementally increased to $K_{i+1}k$, $K_{i+2}k$, etc., until the largest value of $K_n k$ is reached. The step size incrementally decreases when a polarity reversal occurs. In the decoder, the same pulse sequences are sensed by a switch control identical to that in the encoder, and thus the step size changes are made synchronously and identically. Since the step size is changed at a rate equal to that of the sampling rate, the discrete adaptive DM system may be viewed as a linear DM into which instantaneous companding has been introduced.

In the continuous adaptive system illustrated in Fig. 5, the control signal is the continuous derivative of the input signal. Because the control signal must use some of the transmission channel capacity, it must of necessity require only a fraction of the input signal bandwidth. As a result, the rate at which the step size is varied is very much smaller than the sampling rate. Thus, the continuous adaptive DM system may be viewed as a linear DM into which syllabic companding has been introduced.

Several configurations similar to those illustrated in Figs. 4 and 5 appear in the literature [16], [29], [31]–[33]. Brown and Brolin [31] have discussed a continuous adaptive DM system for speech application. Their conclusions agree with those presented here. Winkler [16], [29] has given a qualitative description of a system similar to that of discrete adaptive DM. Cutler [38] has patented an adaptive system which differs from those presented here in that quantizer input and output rather than step size are the regulating functions.

The discrete adaptive DM system, as illustrated in Fig. 4, was simulated on an IBM 7094 digital computer with a program which is a modification of that first written by O'Neal [6]. A résumé of the results [35] relevant to this paper are illustrated in Figs. 6 through 11. A bandwidth expansion factor value of eight is illustrated; other values produce similar results. The curves illustrated are obtained from (13), (8), (14), (15), and (16), providing the asymptotes $S/N_O'$, maximum $S/N_Q$, $S/N_G'(\mathbf{s}<8K_n)$, and $S/N_G'(\mathbf{s}>8K_n)$, respectively. A discussion of these figures follows.

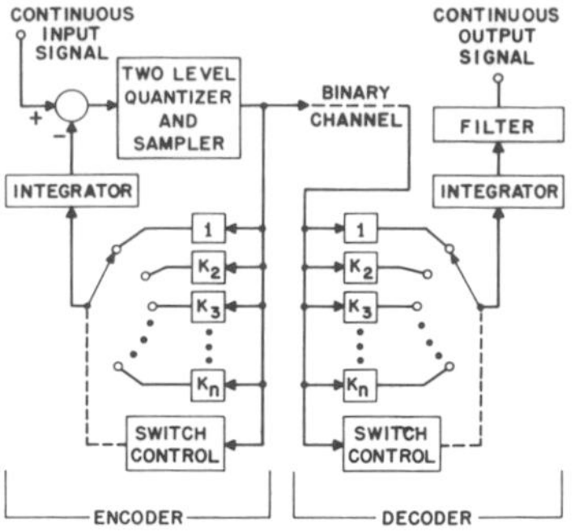

Fig. 4. Discrete adaptive DM system.

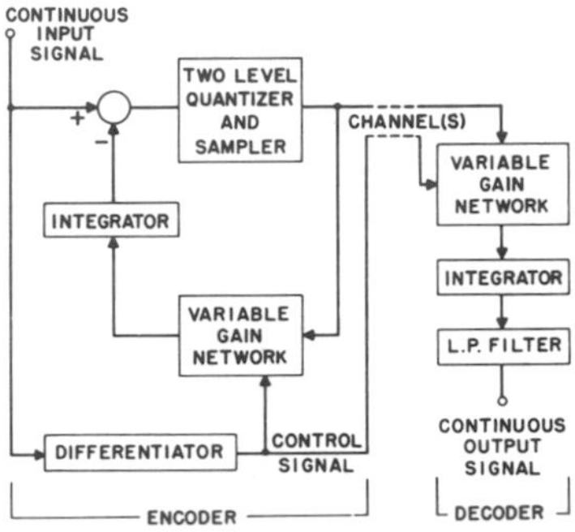

Fig. 5. Continuous adaptive DM system.

Because the discrete adaptive DM system is able to increase its step size in an instantaneous manner at the sampling rate from the smallest value $k$ to $K_2 k, \cdots, K_n k$ in sequential increments, slope overload is not the controlling degradation until the derivative of the signal $f'(t)$ is greater than the maximum slope capability of the system, that is, when

$$|f'(t)| > K_n k f_s. \tag{10}$$

As a result, the maximum value of the slope loading factor for adaptive DM is greater than that given by (2) for linear DM by the factor $K_n$, and is, therefore,

$$\text{maximum } \mathbf{s} \text{ (adaptive DM)} = (K_n k f_s)/\sqrt{D}. \tag{11}$$

It is somewhat more convenient, for purposes of comparison with linear DM, to use a slope loading factor definition consistent with that of (2). We therefore define what will be called the "normalized slope loading factor" ($\mathbf{s}'$) for adaptive DM. It is given by

$$\mathbf{s}' \equiv (k' f_s)/\sqrt{D} \tag{12}$$

where $k'$ is the product of $K_n$ and $k$. The normalized slope loading factor thus has a value at each sampling instant given by one member of the sequence $(1/K_n)\mathbf{s}'$, $(K_2/K_n)\mathbf{s}', \cdots, (K_{n-1}/K_n)\mathbf{s}', \mathbf{s}'$. It can easily be shown [35] that the asymptotic bounds for discrete adaptive DM over-

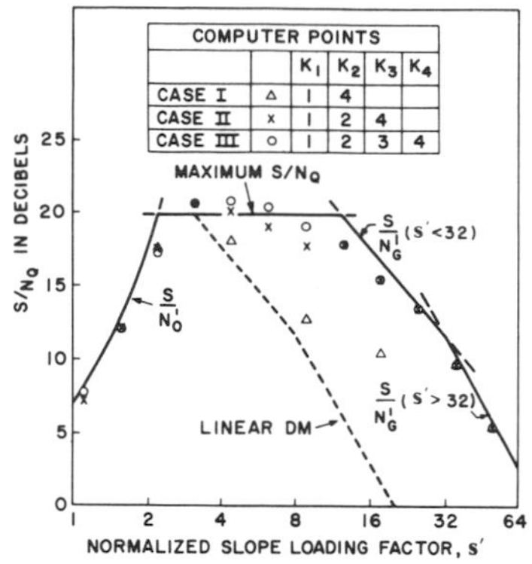


Fig. 6. $S/N_Q$ performance of discrete adaptive DM, with uniform signal spectrum, $B=8$, $K_n=4$, and various computer-simulated values of $K_i$, Gaussian distribution.

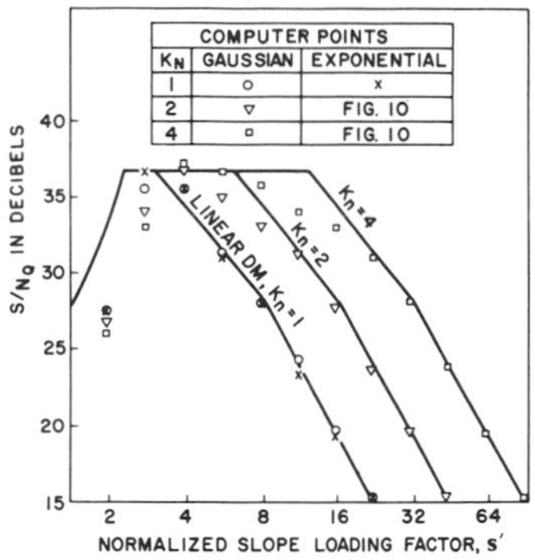


Fig. 9. $S/N_Q$ performance of discrete adaptive DM, with television signal spectrum; curves obtained from (13), (8), (14), and (15); points from computer simulation. $B=8$, $K_i=i$.

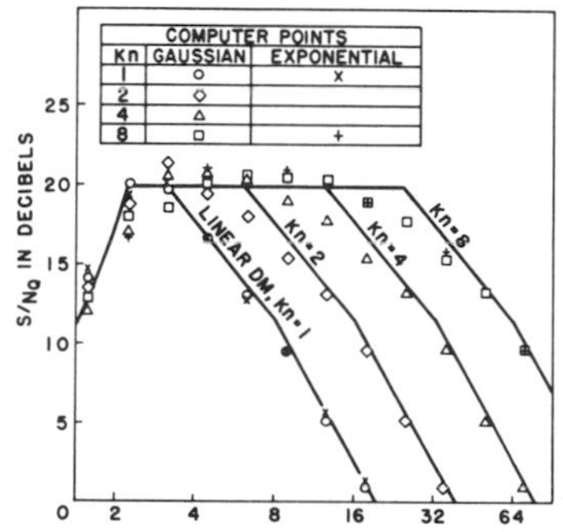


Fig. 7. $S/N_Q$ performance of discrete adaptive DM, with uniform signal spectrum; curves obtained from (13), (8), (14), and (15); points from computer simulation. $B=8$, $K_i=i$.

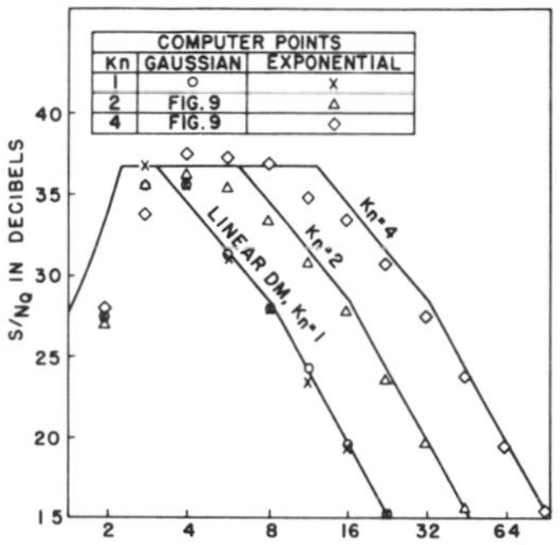


Fig. 10. $S/N_Q$ performance of discrete adaptive DM, with television signal spectrum; curves obtained from (13), (8), (14), and (15); points from computer simulation. $B=8$, $K_i=i$.

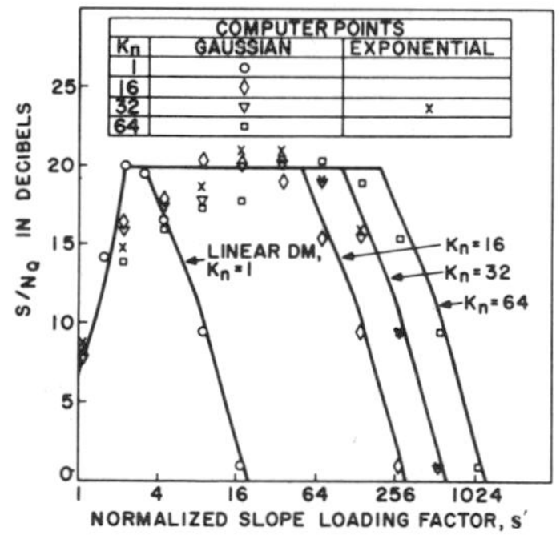


Fig. 8. $S/N_Q$ performance of discrete adaptive DM, with uniform signal spectrum; curves obtained from (13), (8), (14), and (15); points from computer simulation. $B=8$, $K_i=i$.

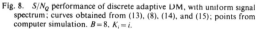

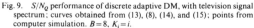

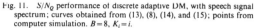

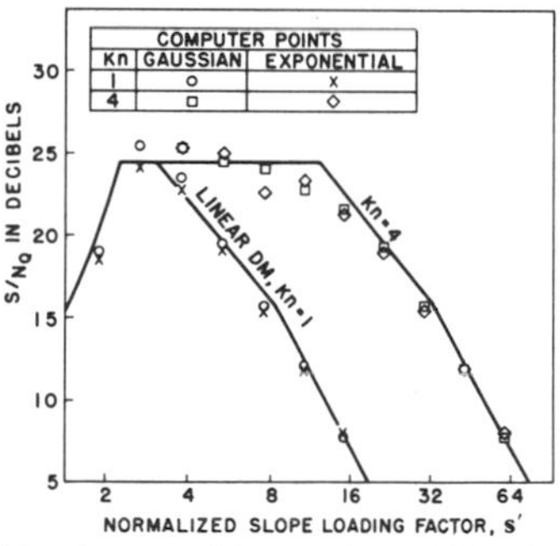


Fig. 11. $S/N_Q$ performance of discrete adaptive DM, with speech signal spectrum; curves obtained from (13), (8), (14), and (15); points from computer simulation. $B=8$, $K_i=i$.

load noise $N_O'$ and granular noise $N_G'$ as functions of $s'$ are given by

$$N_O' = \frac{8\pi^2}{27}\left(\frac{D}{\omega_m^2}\right)e^{-3s'}(3s+1), \quad \text{for } s' < \ln 2B \tag{13}$$

$$N_G' = \frac{\pi^2}{6B^3K_n^2}\left(\frac{D}{\omega_m^2}\right)(s')^2, \quad \text{for } \ln 2B < s' < 8K_n \tag{14}$$

$$N_G' = \frac{\pi^2}{48B^3K_n^3}\left(\frac{D}{\omega_m^2}\right)(s')^3, \quad \text{for } s' > 8K_n. \tag{15}$$

It was expected, and computer simulation has verified [35], that the minimum quantization noise power as given by (8) is not decreased in the adaptive system. This is reasonable inasmuch as optimum DM performance depends essentially upon the signal power spectrum and bandwidth expansion factor. It was unexpected, however, that minimum quantization noise did not increase when large values of $K_n$ were used in an effort to achieve large amounts of companding. Companding in a quantizing system refers to the process of signal compression and later expansion, the former in the encoder and the latter in the decoder. The purpose of companding is to allow weak signals (i.e., small signal power) to be encoded with approximately the same quantizing noise as strong signals (i.e., large signal power). In PCM, companding can be obtained by using a nonuniform quantizer. In the discrete adaptive DM system, computer simulation has shown that companding is achieved without an increase of minimum quantization noise power. This was indeed an unexpected but gratifying result. A quantitative comparison of this result with that of PCM is given in Section IV. Thus, the expression given in (8) for linear DM minimum quantization noise may be used as a good approximation for the adaptive case.

An important problem in discrete adaptive DM is the selection of the final gain factor $K_n$. It is clear from (14), (15), (4), and (5), and from Figs. 7 to 11, that the amount of signal power variation that the adaptive system tolerates, before performance falls substantially below that of maximum $S/N_Q$, has been increased by $[K_n]^2$. In the communication literature [31], [36], such an increase has been referred to as companding improvement or simply the amount of companding and is usually expressed in decibels. For discrete adaptive DM, the approximate companding improvement $C$ is simply

$$C = (20 \log K_n) \text{ dB}. \tag{16}$$

At $K_n = 1$, linear DM results and optimum performance occurs at only one value of mean signal power, or, in other words, one value of the slope loading factor [i.e., that value given by (6)].

If the power of a given signal varies from some smallest value $S_1$ to some largest value $S_2$, it is a simple matter to select the appropriate values of step size $k$ and multiplier $K_n$ to achieve the desired companding. From (2) and (6), it is clear that the step size should be

$$k = \left(\frac{\sqrt{D}}{f_s} \ln 2B\right)\sqrt{S_1} \tag{17}$$

where $D$ is the derivative power calculated on the basis of unity mean signal power, and $\sqrt{S_1}$ is the smallest standard deviation of the signal. The gain multiplier $K_n$ is simply the ratio of the standard deviations of the largest and smallest values of the signal, or

$$K_n = \sqrt{S_2/S_1}. \tag{18}$$

For example, for a television signal characterized by the integrated spectrum of Table I where $\omega_3/\omega_m$ is 0.011, the step size $k$ becomes:

$$k(\text{television}) = 0.26\left(\frac{\ln 2B}{B}\right)\sqrt{S_1}. \tag{19}$$

The power of a video signal varies considerably from line to line in a raster-scanned field, as well as from picture to picture over long periods of time. Since one would like to make $K_n$ as large as possible to encompass as many different picture types as possible, but since equipment complexity increases as $K_n$ increases, it can be shown [35] that a reasonable compromise is obtained by letting $K_n = 4$. Figures 9 and 10 illustrate this case. Although television signals may be characterized by an exponential density as illustrated in Fig. 10, the results are essentially unchanged for a Gaussian density as illustrated in Fig. 9. From the computer simulation results given in Fig. 10 for $K_n = 4$, it can be seen that the $S/N_Q$ remains within three decibels of maximum $S/N_Q$ over a range of variation of approximately four to one for the normalized slope loading factor or the signal standard deviation. In linear DM, the same variation would have produced a decrease of at least nine decibels, and possibly as much as thirteen decibels from maximum $S/N_Q$.

Another problem in discrete adaptive DM is the selection of intermediate gain factors $K_2, K_3, \cdots, K_{n-1}$. The choice of final gain factor $K_n$ is dictated by the amount of desired companding as discussed above. The effect of intermediate gain factors on $S/N_Q$ performance was investigated by computer simulation [35], and typical results are illustrated in Fig. 6, where $K_n = 4$ (i.e., the largest step size is four times that of the smallest step). Three cases are illustrated. Case I represents a two-level (i.e., $n = 2$) adaptive system; that is, a sequence of two consecutive pulses of the same sign causes the step size to increase from the smallest value $k$ to its largest value $K_2k = 4k$, with no intermediate values. The performance of this method falls considerably below the predicted asymptotes illustrated. Case II represents exponential gain factor increments, that is, $K_i = 2^{i-1}$, and is a three-level adaptive system (i.e., $n = 3$). The sequence $k, K_2k, \cdots, K_nk$ becomes $k, 2k, 4k$. Although the results of Case II are significantly better than those of Case I, they still are somewhat less than expected. Winkler [16] has proposed a scheme similar to Case II, suggesting that the system contained more information per pulse than linear DM. He therefore has termed such a system "High Information Delta Modulation."

Case III represents linear gain factor increments, that is, $K_i = i$, and is in this instance a four-level adaptive system (i.e., $n = 4$). The results using linear increments show approximately a three-decibel increase over exponential increments in companding improvement near maximum $S/N_Q$, and are closer to the asymptotes predicted by (13), (14), and (15). Computer simulation results using linear increments as in Case III are given in Figs. 7 to 11, illustrating the performances of discrete adaptive DM for the cases of uniform and integrated signal spectra as applied to television and speech.

Figures 7 and 8 illustrate uniform signal spectrum performance, the former for $K_n = 1, 2, 4, 8$ and the latter for $K_n = 1, 16, 32, 64$. In general, computer results for the spectra considered show that both Gaussian and exponential signal amplitude distributions yield substantially the same performance. For large values of $K_n$(i.e., $K_n \geq 16$), the results indicate that $S/N_Q$ performance falls below that predicted by (13) and (8), especially in the region $2 < s' < 8$, as shown in Fig. 8. The companding improvement for large $K_n$, however, is not greatly decreased. For example, when $K_n = 64$ as in Fig. 8, the companding improvement realized, such that $S/N_Q$ remains within 3 dB of maximum $S/N_Q$, as shown by computer results, is approximately 32 dB. This result differs from that predicted by (16) by 4 dB.

Figures 9 and 10 illustrate television signal spectrum performance, the former with Gaussian, the latter with exponential distribution of signal amplitudes given for comparison. The results are seen to be almost identical, the largest difference in $S/N_Q$ being approximately one decibel. Figure 11 illustrates one case for speech; a more realistic one is given in Section IV, where a comparison with PCM is made.

## IV. Comparison with PCM

In this section it will be shown 1) how discrete adaptive DM compares with companded PCM for speech application, 2) that discrete adaptive DM may be better suited to television signals than PCM, and 3) that the PCM quantization noise characteristic is similar to that of linear DM illustrated in Fig. 3.

Smith [36] has proposed a logarithmic nonuniform quantizer which has been found desirable when the message is speech. McDonald [24] computer-simulated the case of a speech message signal and a four-digit nonuniform (i.e., companded) quantizer having the logarithmic characteristic recommended by Smith [36]. His results are illustrated in Fig. 12, along with that for comparison of the discrete adaptive DM system described in Section III, having the same bandwidth expansion factor (i.e., for four-digit PCM, $B = 4$), using linear increments $K_i = i$, and a $K_n$ of eight. This particular value of $K_n$ was used because it yields approximately the same amount of companding as the logarithmic quantizer of Smith [36] with $\mu = 100$. The abscissa of Fig. 12 corresponds to that given by McDonald [24], and for the case of adaptive DM is related to the normalized slope loading factor of (12) by the expression

$$\{\text{Input Relative to Full Load}\} = \left[20 \log_{10} \frac{\ln 2B}{s'}\right] \text{dB} \quad (20)$$

where the factor $\ln 2B$ represents the value of the slope loading factor given by (6) at which maximum $S/N_Q$ is achieved by linear DM. Zero decibels on the abscissa of Fig. 12 correspond to that value of the slope loading factor given by (6). For PCM, a higher degree of companding (i.e., $\mu > 100$) is in practice very difficult to achieve for reasons explained by Mann et al. [37]. For discrete adaptive DM, on the other hand, there appears to be no difficulty for either theoretical or practical reasons in extending the companding improvement to values much larger than that illustrated in Fig. 12. Whether the additional companding capability that discrete adaptive DM offers could in fact improve speech communication is not known at this time. Because of the subjective nature of speech communication, further tests would be required before more conclusions regarding the possible benefits of discrete adaptive DM over PCM could be reached.

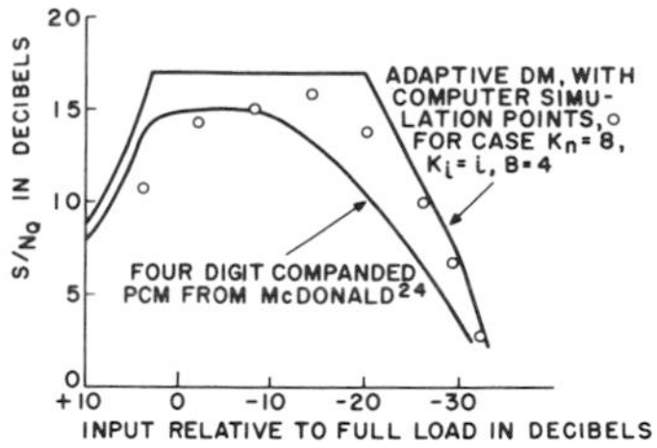

Fig. 12. Comparison of companded PCM and discrete adaptive DM with speech signal.

Quantization in PCM is a memoryless operation of converting the continuous message signal into a discrete signal that assumes only a finite number of levels. As in DM, the quantization noise in PCM manifests itself in two forms. The first is that resulting from the discrete quantization process, and will be called granular noise so as to draw an analogy with its DM counterpart. In the literature, however, this is commonly known as quantizing noise, since the second form of noise is usually ignored. This second form of PCM quantization noise is caused by the limiting of the message signal to the maximum and minimum levels of the quantizer. This noise is similar to that produced by a linear device with saturation (i.e., an ideal limiter), and will be called overload noise. As opposed to DM overload noise, which is produced when the message signal *slope* exceeds the slope capability of the DM quantizer, PCM overload noise is produced when the message signal *amplitude* exceeds the maximum level of the PCM quantizer. Exact analytical expressions for both PCM granular and overload noise powers can be derived as a function of the bandwidth expansion factor (which for PCM equals the number of digits of encoding), and a defined quantity called herein the "amplitude loading factor."

Given that the PCM quantizer sorts the input into a finite number of ranges and produces uniformly spaced output or representative levels whose upper and lower saturation levels are $\alpha$ times the standard deviation of the signal, then it can be shown [35] that the granular noise power $N_G$ and overload noise power $N_O$ for Gaussian and exponentially distributed stationary signals are those given in Table II. The quantity $\alpha$ will be called the amplitude loading

TABLE II

PCM PERFORMANCE WITH GAUSSIAN AND EXPONENTIAL (STATIONARY) SIGNAL PROBABILITY DENSITY FUNCTIONS

| | Gaussian Density | Exponential Density |
|---|---|---|
| Probability Density Function $p(x)$ | $\frac{1}{\sqrt{2\pi}} e^{-\frac{1}{2}x^2}$ | $\frac{1}{\sqrt{2}} e^{-\sqrt{2}\lvert x\rvert}$ |
| Granular Noise Power $N_G$ | $\frac{1}{3} \frac{\alpha^2}{2^{2B}}$ | $\frac{1}{3} \frac{\alpha^2}{2^{2B}}$ |
| Overload Noise Power $N_O$ | $(1+\alpha^2)\left[2\int_\alpha^\infty \frac{1}{\sqrt{2\pi}} e^{-\frac{1}{2}x^2}\,dx\right] - \sqrt{\frac{2}{\pi}}\,\alpha e^{-\frac{1}{2}\alpha^2}$ | $e^{-\sqrt{2}\alpha}$ |

factor for PCM. It is analogous to the slope loading factor of linear DM. The distributions given in Table II represent the two cases of practical importance mentioned earlier, namely, 1) broadband signals characterized by a uniform spectrum and Gaussian probability density function, and 2) television signals characterized by an integrated spectrum and exponential probability density function. The results are illustrated for the Gaussian case in Fig. 13, and the exponential case in Fig. 14. The characteristic curves illustrated are seen to be similar to those of linear DM illustrated in Fig. 3. The difference between the two is that, whereas DM performance is limited by slope overload, PCM performance is limited by amplitude overload. The dashed lines in Figs. 13 and 14 illustrate the asymptotic bounds of overload noise power.

The optimum performances (i.e., maximum $S/N_Q$) realized by the PCM system for the stationary Gaussian and exponential densities are illustrated in Fig. 15, along with that of the DM system for comparison. For PCM, the bandwidth expansion factor is identical with the number of digits of encoding. The performance of PCM with Gaussian signals is superior to that with exponential signals because the overload noise power in the Gaussian case is somewhat less, the decay of the exponential density with amplitude being more gradual. For broadband signals having a uniform spectral density and Gaussian amplitude density, it is clear that for stationary signals PCM provides superior performance to that of DM.

For television signals, DM provides a greater maximum $S/N_Q$ than PCM for values of $B$ less than eight (i.e., eight digits of PCM encoding). For entertainment television, approximately six or seven digits of PCM encoding have been found to produce pictures of good quality [39]. Although the $S/N_Q$ performance is not the only important criterion in characterizing picture quality, it provides a sound basis upon which to objectively compare and optimize promising encoding systems. A final comparison rests, of course, with a subjective test. Because of the nonstationary nature of television signals, adaptive DM appears better suited than linear DM to such signals.

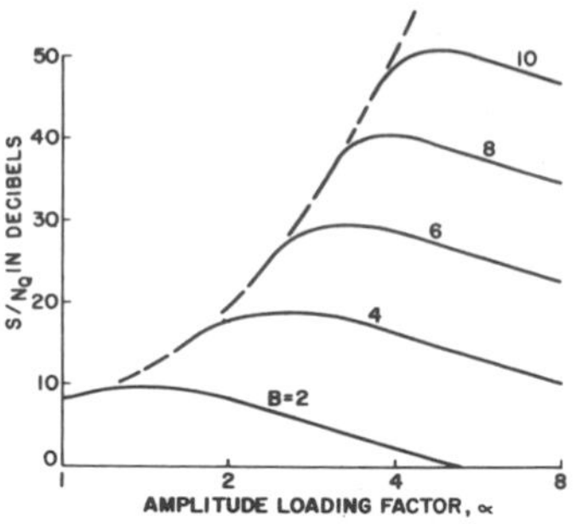


Fig. 13. PCM performance with Gaussian signal distribution.

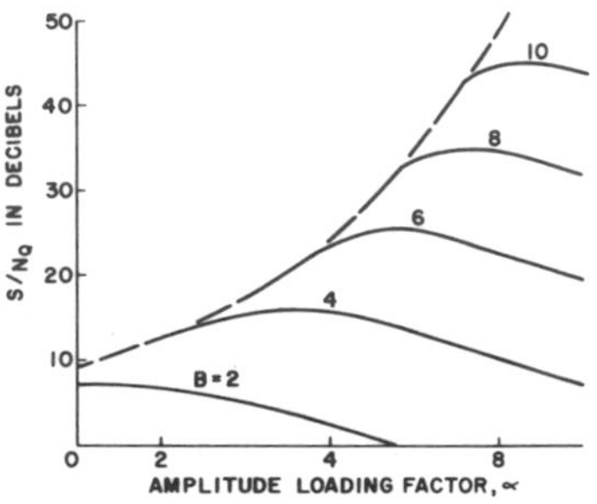


Fig. 14. PCM performance with exponential signal distribution.

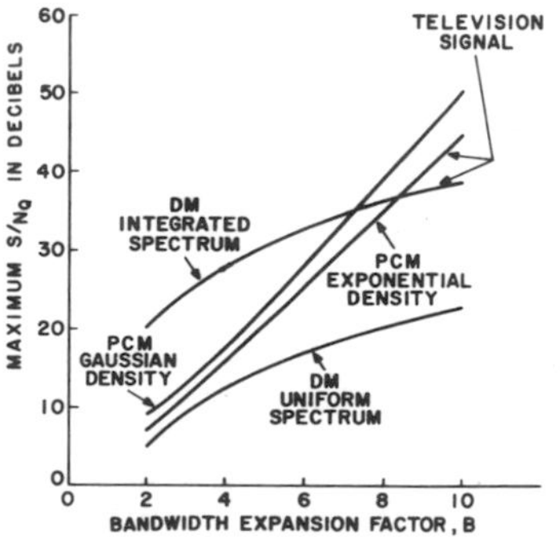


Fig. 15. Comparison of DM and PCM optimum performance with stationary signals.

## V. CONCLUSIONS

The $S/N$ performance and optimization of linear DM, adaptive DM, and PCM have been presented, together with the results of computer simulations. The three important cases of television, speech, and broadband signals are treated in detail.

The results presented fall into three groups. First, linear DM granular, overload, and minimum quantization noise powers are described by simple closed-form solutions. From these expressions, and from computer simulations, the following have been found for linear DM.

1) It is possible to predict with a simple expression the optimum performance obtainable from DM at various bandwidth expansion factor values.

2) Minimum quantization noise power is proportional to the mean power of the signal derivative; as a result, $S/N_Q$ performance with an integrated spectrum, such as television or speech, exceeds that with a uniform spectrum, such as a broadband signal.

3) A quantity defined as the slope loading factor is a useful parameter in characterizing DM performance.

4) The $S/N_Q$ performance with a Gaussian signal density is approximately the same as that with an exponential signal density.

5) If the mean power of the signal changes by a relatively small amount, $S/N_Q$ performance decreases; as a result, for nonstationary signals such as speech and television, companding is desirable.

Second, an adaptive DM system which seems promising for television and speech is evaluated. The linear DM noise power solutions were modified to describe the expected performance of the adaptive system. From these results, and from those of computer simulations, the following findings were made.

1) The adaptive system provides DM with a companding capability.

2) The maximum $S/N_Q$ performance of adaptive DM remains approximately the same as that of linear DM.

3) The companding improvement offered by adaptive DM does not appear to be limited by the same practical considerations as in a PCM system.

4) The $S/N_Q$ performance of adaptive DM is the same for both Gaussian and exponential signal densities. In a PCM system, the maximum $S/N_Q$ performance with a stationary exponential signal density is shown to be from two to six decibels below that of a Gaussian density.

5) The largest step size gain multiplier $K_n$ determines for adaptive DM the amount of companding improvement, and the intermediate multipliers $K_2, \cdots, K_{n-1}$ determine how well the companded $S/N_Q$ performance meets the predicted asymptotes.

Third, a comparison is made between PCM and linear and adaptive DM with speech, television, and broadband signals, with the following conclusions being reached.

1) For speech with $B=4$, the $S/N_Q$ performance of the adaptive DM system with $K_n=8$, $K_i=i$ is approximately the same as that of a companded PCM system using a logarithmic quantizer with $\mu=100$.

2) For television, DM provides a greater maximum $S/N_Q$ than PCM for values of $B$ less than eight. Alternatively, it could be stated that for the same $S/N_Q$ performance, DM offers a bit rate or channel bandwidth reduction capability in comparison with PCM in the region $B<8$. Because of the nonstationary nature of television and speech signals, adaptive DM appears better suited than linear DM to such signals.

3) For broadband signals, the $S/N_Q$ performance of PCM is superior to that of either linear or adaptive DM.

4) Because of the subjective nature of speech and television communication, further tests are required before more conclusions regarding the possible benefits of discrete adaptive DM can be reached.

## Acknowledgment

The author wishes to thank Dr. J. J. Padalino, Professor in Electrical Engineering, Newark College of Engineering, for his encouragement and helpful comments and suggestions. The author also wishes to thank his many associates at Bell Telephone Laboratories, Inc., who during the past four years have provided numerous stimulating discussions and suggestions. Particular thanks are given to J. B. O'Neal, Jr., W. H. Jules, P. Gevas, and G. Gulbenkian.

## References

[1] C. C. Cutler, "Differential quantization of communication signals," U. S. Patent 2 605 361, July 29, 1952.
[2] F. de Jager, "Delta modulation, a method of PCM transmission using a one-unit code," *Philips Research Rept.*, vol. 7, 1952.
[3] H. Van De Weg, "Quantizing noise of a single integration delta modulation system with an *N*-digit code," *Philips Research Rept.*, vol. 8, 1953.
[4] L. Zetterberg, "A comparison between delta and pulse code modulation," *Ericsson Tech.*, vol. 2, no. 1, 1955.
[5] C. A. Halijak and J. S. Tripp, "A deterministic study of delta modulation," *IRE Internat'l Conv. Rec.*, pt. 8, pp. 247–259, 1963.
[6] J. B. O'Neal, "Delta modulation quantizing noise analytical and computer simulation results for Gaussian and television input signals," *Bell Sys. Tech. J.*, vol. 45, January 1966.
[7] J. F. Schouten et al., "Delta modulation, a new modulation system for telecommunication," *Philips Tech. Rev.*, vol. 13, no. 9, March 1952.
[8] F. W. Arter, "Simple delta modulation system," *Proc. IRE* (*Australia*), vol. 23, pp. 517–523, September 1962.
[9] J. C. Balder and C. Kramer, "Video transmission by delta modulation using tunnel diodes," *Proc. IRE*, vol. 50, pp. 428–431, April 1962.
[10] H. Inose and Y. Yasuda, "A unity bit coding method by negative feedback," *Proc. IEEE*, vol. 51, pp. 1524–1535, November 1963.
[11] H. Inose et al., "New modulation technique simplifies circuits," *Electronics*, vol. 36, January 25, 1963.
[12] H. Inose, Y. Yasuda, and J. Murakami, "A telemetering system by code modulation—delta-sigma modulation," *IRE Trans. on Space Electronics and Telemetry*, vol. SET-8, pp. 204–209, September 1962.
[13] A. Lender and M. Kozuch, "Single bit delta modulating systems," *Electronics*, vol. 34, November 17, 1961.
[14] ——, "Experimental delta modulator," *Nat'l Symp. on Global Commun.*, pp. 95–98, 1961.
[15] W. B. Davenport, Jr., "An experimental study of speech-wave probability distributions," *J. Acoust. Soc. Am.*, vol. 24, pp. 390–399, July 1952.
[16] M. R. Winkler, "High information delta modulation," *IEEE Internat'l Conv. Rec.*, pt. 8, pp. 260–265, 1963.
[17] J. C. Balder and C. Kramer, "Analog-to-digital conversion by means of delta modulation," *IEEE Trans. on Space Electronics and Telemetry*, vol. SET-10, pp. 87–90, September 1964.
[18] I. Habara, "Delta modulator using Esaki diodes," *J. IECE* (*Japan*), vol. 46, p. 835, 1963.
[19] K. Nitadori, "Statistical analysis of delta PCM," *J. IECE* (*Japan*), vol. 48, February 1965.
[20] T. Fine, "Properties of an optimum digital system and applications," *IEEE Trans. on Information Theory*, vol. IT-10, pp. 287–296, October 1964.
[21] H. Debart, "Study of delta modulation system from the information theory viewpoint" (in French), *Cables et Transm.* (*Paris*), vol. 15, pp. 198–204, 1961.
[22] L. J. Libois, "A novel method of code modulation—delta modulation" (in French), *Ondé Élec.*, vol. 32, pp. 26–31, January 1952.

[23] J. B. O'Neal, "Predictive quantizing systems (differential pulse code modulation) for the transmission of television signals," *Bell Sys. Tech. J.*, vol. 45, May–June 1966.

[24] R. A. McDonald, "Signal-to-noise performance and idle channel performance of differential pulse code modulation systems, with particular applications to voice signals," *Bell Sys. Tech. J.*, vol. 45, September 1966.

[25] G. J. Murphy and G. Shuraym, "Delta modulation in feedback control systems," *Proc. Nat'l Electronics Conf.*, October 1965.

[26] R. L. Remm et al., "Analysis and implementation of a delta modulation pictorial encoding system," *Proc. Nat'l Telemetering Conf.*, 1966.

[27] P. F. Panter, *Modulation, Noise, and Spectral Analysis*. New York: McGraw-Hill, 1965.

[28] F. K. Bowers, "What use is delta modulation to the transmission engineer?" *Proc. AIEE*, vol. 76, pt. I, pp. 142–147, May 1957.

[29] M. R. Winkler, "Pictorial Transmission with HIDM," *IEEE Internat'l Conv. Rec.*, pt. 1, pp. 285–290, 1965.

[30] E. N. Protonotarios, "Overload noise in delta modulation," to be published.

[31] J. M. Brown and S. J. Brolin, "Companded delta modulation for telephony," *NEREM Rec.*, 1966.

[32] A. Tomozawa and H. Kaneko, "Companded delta modulation for telephone transmission," *Proc. NEC*, 1966.

[33] F. de Jager and J. A. Greefkes, "Continuous delta modulation," *GLOBECOM VI*, 1964.

[34] H. Fletcher, *Speech and Hearing in Communication*. Princeton, N. J.: Van Nostrand, 1953.

[35] J. E. Abate, "Linear and adaptive delta modulation," D.Eng.Sc. dissertation, Newark College of Engineering, Newark, N. J., April 1967.

[36] B. Smith, "Instantaneous companding of quantized signals," *Bell Sys. Tech. J.*, vol. 27, pp. 446–472, July 1948.

[37] H. M. Mann et al., "A companded coder for an experimental PCM terminal," Bell Telephone System Mono. 4085, pp. 55–108.

[38] C. C. Cutler, "Quantized transmission with variable quanta," U. S. Patent 2 724 740, November 22, 1955.

[39] W. M. Goodall, "Television by pulse code modulation," *Bell Sys. Tech. J.*, vol. 30, pp. 33–49, January 1951.

[40] E. G. Kimme and F. F. Kuo, "Synthesis of optimal filters for a feedback quantization system," *IEEE Internat'l Conv. Rec.*, pt. 2, pp. 16–26, 1963.

[41] E. R. Kretzmer, "Statistics of television signals," *Bell Sys. Tech. J.*, vol. 31, pp. 751–763, July 1952.

# 39



Reprinted from *IEEE Trans. Commun. Tech.*, **Com-19**(6), 1033–1042, 1044 (1971)

# A Variable-Step-Size Robust Delta Modulator

CHING-LONG SONG, MEMBER, IEEE, JOSEPH GARODNICK, AND DONALD L. SCHILLING, SENIOR MEMBER, IEEE

**_Abstract_—An optimum adaptive delta modulator–demodulator configuration is derived. This device utilizes two past samples to obtain a step size which minimizes the mean square error for a Markov Gaussian source. The optimum system is compared using computer simulations with the linear delta modulator and an enhanced Abate delta modulator. In addition the performance is compared to the rate distortion bound for a Markov source. It is shown that the optimum delta modulator is neither quantization nor slope-overload limited.**

**The highly nonlinear equations obtained for the optimum transmitter and receiver are approximated by piecewise-linear equations in order to obtain system equations which can be transformed into hardware. The derivation of the experimental system is presented.**

**The experimental "optimum" system, an enhanced version of the Abate delta modulator and a linear delta modulator were tested and compared using sinusoidal, square-wave, and pseudorandom binary sequence inputs. The results show that the output signal-to-noise (SNR) ratio is approximately independent of the input signal power and is subject only to the limitations of the hardware employed. In addition, voice was recorded using these systems. The demodulated voice indicates negligible degradation is caused by the optimum system and by the enhanced Abate system while the linear delta modulator suffers significant degradation at a sampling frequency of 56 k/s. The systems were also tested at 19.2 k/s. At this bit rate, speech recognition, using the experimental "optimum" system, remained completely intelligible.**

## I. Introduction

DELTA MODULATION has received widespread attention recently due to the increased information rate possible, as compared to conventional source encoding schemes. However, the commonly studied linear delta modulator has severe limitations. The disadvantages and limited performance of the linear delta modulator have been described by O'Neal [1], Tomozawa and Kaneko [2], Brolin and Brown [3], and Abate [4]. The basic limitations are due to the narrow dynamic range produced by two inherent characteristics. The first is the granular or quantization noise produced by the finite step size of the system. The second is slope overload noise introduced when the system cannot follow the input signal. Hence the delta modulator has only one optimum point; i.e., where the output signal-to-noise ratio (SNR) is a maximum for a given input power. To overcome these basic problems, it is possible to vary the step size of the system to cope with the changing input signal. Hence an adaptive scheme.

Manuscript received May 28, 1971; revised August 13, 1971. This paper represents portions of Ph. D. dissertations submitted to the Polytechnic Institute of Brooklyn and the City College of New York. This research was partially supported by NASA under Grants NGR 33-013-063 and NGR 33-013-048.

The authors are with the Department of Electrical Engineering, City College of New York, New York, N. Y. 10031.

Several different adaptive delta modulators, both continuous and discrete, have been presented in the recent past [2]–[7]. However, instead of obtaining an adaptive procedure empirically, as did the previous investigators, this paper presents an analytical approach to obtain an adaptive scheme which produces a least mean square error for a Markov–Gaussian source when the transmitter and the receiver are each optimized separately.

The nonlinear equations obtained for the theoretically optimum system are reduced to piecewise-linear equations and implemented using digital integrated circuits. To do this, the incoming analog signal is first sampled and then converted to a digital format using an A/D converter. All processing is then performed digitally. The output signal is then D/A converted to obtain the processed analog signal.

An 8-bit A/D converter and internal arithmetic accuracy of 8 bits were used, for simplicity, in the experimental unit. However, this limited the dynamic range and response of the system. In practice one would use a 12-bit A/D converter and 12- to 16-bit accuracy in the internal arithmetic.

## II. Digital Linear Delta Modulator

The encoder and decoder of a linear digital delta modulator are shown in Fig. 1. The input consists of samples of a continuous input waveform, normally a highly correlated sequence $\{s_k\}$. The difference between $s_k$ and $x_k$, called $d_k$, is quantized into one of two levels to produce a sequence of positive and negative 1's denoted by $\{e_k\}$. The accumulator is used as a predictor, estimating the value of the next source sample. In the case of a noiseless channel, the decoder receives the sample $e_k$ and then adds the estimate $x_k$ from the accumulator to form an output sample $r_k$.

A digital computer simulation of the digital delta modulator with a first-order Markov sequence having a Gaussian amplitude distribution as an input, results in the performance curve shown in Fig. 2. This curve has the same general shape as the performance curve of the continuous linear delta modulator. Note that the system is optimum for a very narrow range of input signal power, and the SNR ratio decreases on both sides of the optimum point. The slope for low-input power is due to the granular noise produced by the finite step size fed to the accumulator. The downward slope for high-input signal power is accounted for by the inability of the accumulator to follow the input. This condition is commonly called slope overload [1]. In a practical applica-

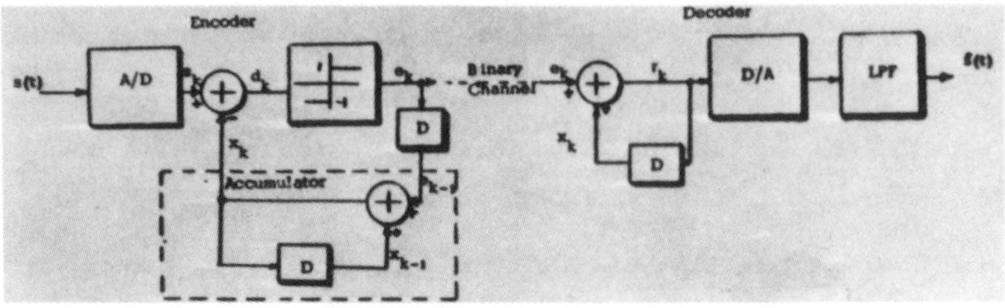


Fig. 1. Block diagram of a digital linear delta modulator.

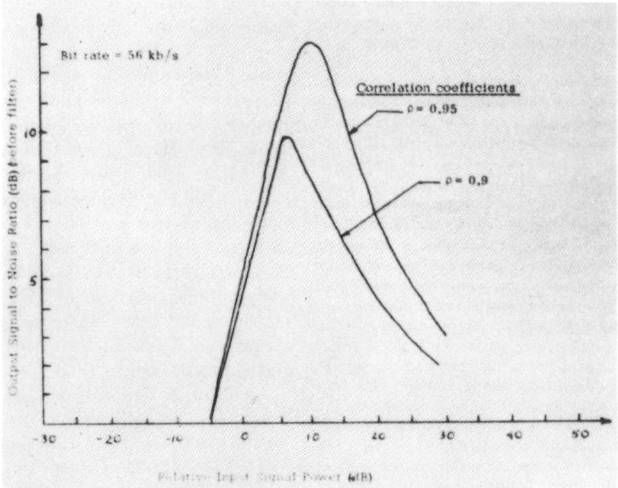


Fig. 2. Performance curves of a linear digital delta modulator.

tion, these two detrimental factors severely limit the usefulness of the linear delta modulation scheme.

## III. Digital Song Variable Step Size Delta Modulator [8]

Fig. 3 shows the general structure of the optimum adaptive delta modulation system studied in this paper. Note that in general the optimum predictor and estimator differ. This was initially pointed out by Fine [9]. The reason for this difference is that the predictor can only use the past output sequence

$$e^{k-1} \equiv e_{k-1}, e_{k-2}, \cdots, e_1 \tag{1}$$

and the past predicted sequence

$$x^{k-1} \equiv x_{k-1}, x_{k-2}, \cdots, x_1 \tag{2}$$

to predict the future sample of the source $s_k$, while the estimator can utilize $e^k$ and $x^k$ to estimate $s_k$. Thus additional information is employed by the estimator.

To find the optimum predictor using a mean square cost function, we minimize the expression:

$$E\{s_k - x_k(e^{k-1}, x^{k-1})\}^2. \tag{3}$$

The system discussed in this paper employs only the two past samples. Thus we minimize

$$E\{s_k - x_k(e_{k-1}, e_{k-2}, x_{k-1}, x_{k-2})\}^2. \tag{4}$$

Similarly, the optimum estimator using a mean square cost function, is obtained by minimizing the expression

$$E\{s_k - r_k(e_k, e_{k-1}, x_k, x_{k-1})\}^2. \tag{5}$$

The results obtained by minimizing (4) and (5) are well known

$$x_k = E\{s_k \mid x_{k-1}, x_{k-2}, e_{k-1}, e_{k-2}\} \tag{6}$$

and

$$r_k = E\{s_k \mid x_k, x_{k-1}, e_k, e_{k-1}\}. \tag{7}$$

Assuming that the input signal is Markov, with samples generated from the difference equation

$$s_k = \rho s_{k-1} + \lambda_{k-1} \tag{8}$$

where each $\lambda_{k-1}$ is uncorrelated, normal, zero mean, with standard deviation $\sigma_{\lambda_{k-1}}$, it is easily shown that

$$x_{k+1} = \rho r_k. \tag{9}$$

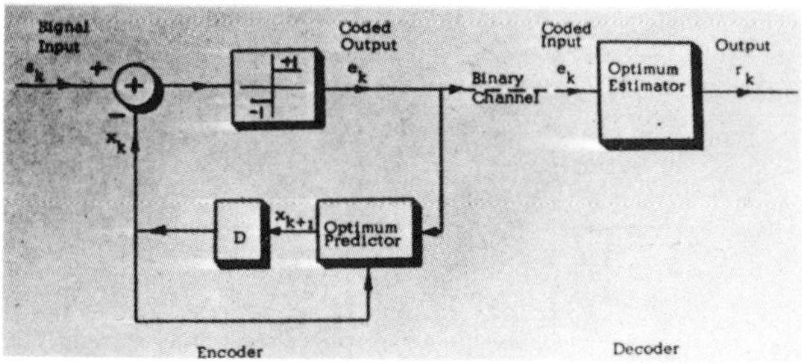


Fig. 3. Optimum adaptive delta modulation system.

Equation (9) follows directly from (6) and (7). Since

$$x_{k+1} = E\{s_{k+1} \mid x_k, x_{k-1}, e_{k-1}, e_{k-2}\} \tag{10}$$

and

$$s_{k+1} = \rho s_k + \lambda_k \tag{11}$$

substituting (11) into (10) yields

$$\begin{aligned} x_{k+1} &= \rho E\{s_k \mid x_k, x_{k-1}, e_{k-1}, e_{k-2}\} \\ &= \rho r_k. \end{aligned} \tag{12}$$

Equations (6), (7), and (12) suggest that the structure of the optimum adaptive delta modulation system is as shown in Fig. 4.

## IV. Two-Past-Sample Case

For a system employing two past sample observations, the estimator equation is

$$r_k = \int_{-\infty}^{\infty} s_k P(s_k \mid x_{k-1}{}^k, e_{k-1}{}^k)\, ds_k.$$

In Appendix I, $r_k$ is shown to be

$$r_k = \begin{cases} \dfrac{\displaystyle\int_{-\infty}^{x_{k-1}} \left[\rho q'(z_{k-1}) s_{k-1} + \frac{\sigma_{\lambda_{k-1}}}{\sqrt{2\pi}} \exp\left(-\tfrac{1}{2} z_{k-1}{}^2\right)\right] P(s_{k-1})\, ds_{k-1}}{\displaystyle\int_{-\infty}^{x_{k-1}} q'(z_{k-1}) P(s_{k-1})\, ds_{k-1}}, & e_{k-1} = -1,\ e_k = +1 \quad (13a) \\[2ex] \dfrac{\displaystyle\int_{x_{k-1}}^{\infty} \left[\rho q'(z_{k-1}) s_{k-1} + \frac{\sigma_{\lambda_{k-1}}}{\sqrt{2\pi}} \exp\left(-\tfrac{1}{2} z_{k-1}{}^2\right)\right] P(s_{k-1})\, ds_{k-1}}{\displaystyle\int_{x_{k-1}}^{\infty} q'(z_{k-1}) P(s_{k-1})\, ds_{k-1}}, & e_{k-1} = +1,\ e_k = +1 \quad (13b) \\[2ex] \dfrac{\displaystyle\int_{x_{k-1}}^{\infty} \left[\rho s_{k-1} q(z_{k-1}) - \frac{\sigma_{\lambda_{k-1}}}{\sqrt{2\pi}} \exp\left(-\tfrac{1}{2} z_{k-1}{}^2\right)\right] P(s_{k-1})\, ds_{k-1}}{\displaystyle\int_{x_{k-1}}^{\infty} q(z_{k-1}) P(s_{k-1})\, ds_{k-1}}, & e_{k-1} = +1,\ e_k = -1 \quad (13c) \\[2ex] \dfrac{\displaystyle\int_{-\infty}^{x_{k-1}} \left[\rho s_{k-1} q(z_{k-1}) - \frac{\sigma_{\lambda_{k-1}}}{\sqrt{2\pi}} \exp\left(-\tfrac{1}{2} z_{k-1}{}^2\right)\right] P(s_{k-1})\, ds_{k-1}}{\displaystyle\int_{-\infty}^{x_{k-1}} q(z_{k-1}) P(s_{k-1})\, ds_{k-1}}, & e_{k-1} = -1,\ e_k = -1 \quad (13d) \end{cases}$$

where

$$z_{k-1} = \frac{x_k - \rho s_{k-1}}{\sigma_{\lambda_{k-1}}} \tag{13e}$$

and

$$q'(z) \equiv \frac{1}{\sqrt{2\pi}} \int_z^{\infty} \exp\left(-u^2/2\right) du \tag{13f}$$

$$q(z) \equiv 1 - q'(z). \tag{13g}$$

## V. Approximate System

Equation (13) involves integrals with the random variable $x_{k-1}$ in the limits. The functional relationship between the estimator $r_k$ and the estimates $x_k$ and $x_{k-1}$ are not apparent by simply considering these integral relations. To simplify the results and make the results more useful the following approximations are made:

$$q'(y) \approx \begin{cases} \tfrac{1}{2} e^{-ay^2}, & y > 0 \\ 1 - \tfrac{1}{2} e^{-ay^2}, & y < 0 \end{cases} \tag{14a}$$

and

$$q(y) = 1 - q'(y). \tag{14b}$$

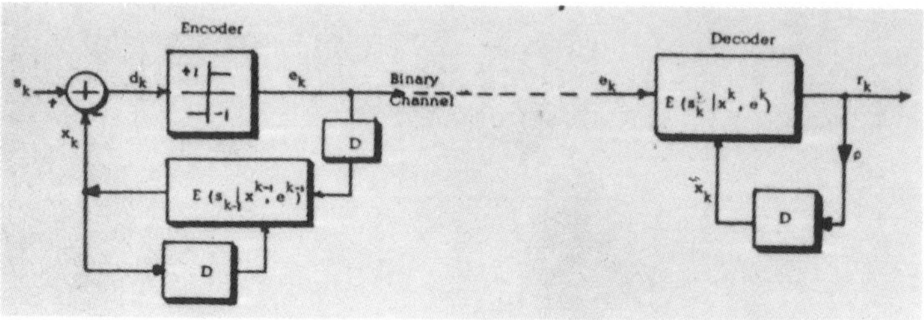


Fig. 4. Equivalent optimum step size adaptive delta modulation system.

The value of $a$ which minimizes the mean square error between $q'(x)$ and the approximate relation given by (14) is $a = 1.23$. However, by trial and error, we have found that the value of $a$ which results in the greatest simplification of (13) is $a = 0.5$. A comparison of these two results is shown in Fig. 5.

For the examples of interest, the input samples are highly correlated ($0.9 \le \rho < 1$) and Appendix II shows that (13) can be reduced to the following:

$$r_k = \begin{cases} \dfrac{2}{\sqrt{2\pi}}\sigma_{\lambda_{k-1}} + \left\{x_k - \dfrac{\sigma_{\lambda_{k-1}}}{\sqrt{2\pi}} \dfrac{\exp(-\frac{1}{2}y_k^2)}{q(y_k)}\right\}, & e_{k-1} = -1,\ e_k = +1 \quad (15a) \\ \dfrac{2}{\sqrt{2\pi}}\sigma_{\lambda_{k-1}} + \left\{x_k + \dfrac{\sigma_{\lambda_{k-1}}}{\sqrt{2\pi}} \dfrac{\exp(-\frac{1}{2}y_k^2)}{q'(y_k)}\right\}, & e_{k-1} = +1,\ e_k = +1 \quad (15b) \\ -\dfrac{2}{\sqrt{2\pi}}\sigma_{\lambda_{k-1}} + \left\{x_k + \dfrac{\sigma_{\lambda_{k-1}}}{\sqrt{2\pi}} \dfrac{\exp(-\frac{1}{2}y_k^2)}{q'(y_k)}\right\}, & e_{k-1} = +1,\ e_k = -1 \quad (15c) \\ -\dfrac{2}{\sqrt{2\pi}}\sigma_{\lambda_{k-1}} + \left\{x_k - \dfrac{\sigma_{\lambda_{k-1}}}{\sqrt{2\pi}} \dfrac{\exp(-\frac{1}{2}y_k^2)}{q(y_k)}\right\}, & e_{k-1} = -1,\ e_k = -1 \quad (15d) \end{cases}$$

where

$$y_k = \frac{\rho x_{k-1} - x_k}{\sigma_{\lambda_{k-1}}}. \quad (15e)$$

To obtain some insight into the variation of the output SNR ratio of this system due to changes in input signal power level, it is interesting to note that since $\rho$ is approximately equal to $1\,(\rho \ge 0.9)$

$$r_k = \rho x_{k+1} \simeq x_{k+1}.$$

Also

$$y_k \simeq (x_{k-1} - x_k)/\sigma_{\lambda_{k-1}}.$$

Thus (15) can be written as

$$-y_{k+1} = \pm\sqrt{\frac{2}{\pi}} + \frac{1}{\sqrt{2\pi}} \frac{\exp(-\frac{1}{2}y_k^2)}{q'(y_k)} \qquad \text{(15b) and (15c)} \quad (16a)$$

or

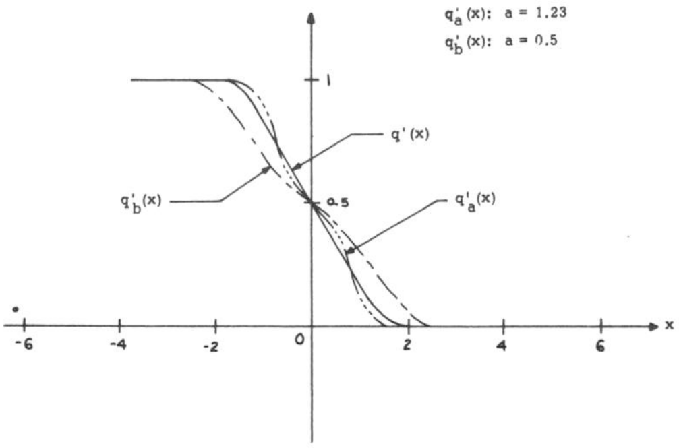


Fig. 5. Approximations of the $q$ function.

$$-y_{k+1} = \pm\sqrt{\frac{2}{\pi}} - \frac{1}{\sqrt{2\pi}} \frac{\exp(-\frac{1}{2}y_k^2)}{q(y_k)} \qquad \text{(15a) and (15d)}. \quad (16b)$$

If we further assume that $y_{k+1} \simeq y_k$ we see that $y_k$ is a function only of $e_k$ and $e_{k-1}$

$$y_k \simeq \frac{x_{k-1} - x_k}{\sigma_{\lambda_{k-1}}} = f(e_k, e_{k-1}). \quad (16c)$$

The output SNR, when measured before a baseband filter, can be defined as

$$\frac{S}{N} \equiv \frac{E(x_k^2)}{E(x_k - x_{k-1})^2} = \frac{E\left(\dfrac{x_k}{\sigma_{\lambda_{k-1}}}\right)^2}{E(y_k^2)}. \quad (17)$$

Thus the output SNR is independent of $\sigma_{\lambda_{k-1}}$ and hence independent of the input signal power level. The system described by (15), therefore, is seen to behave like a linear delta modulator providing the linear DM always operates with an optimum step size.

## VI. Simulation Performance

The performance of the approximate Song system, described by (9) and (15) and with $q(y)$ and $q'(y)$ replaced by (14), was observed using computer simulations. The ratio of the signal power to the total mean square error (no baseband filtering was employed) was determined as a function of input signal power. The responses of the Song system and of the linear system were each simulated by operating on 1000 consecutive stationary first-order Markov, Gaussian amplitude distributed samples. The simulation performance is shown in Fig. 6.

The results show that, for $\rho = 0.9$ and $\rho = 0.95$ (the values of $\rho$ employed in the simulation), the output SNR of the Song delta modulator (DM) is indeed independent of input level. The output SNR was found to be the same as the peak output SNR obtained for the linear DM. The measurements were taken over on 80 dB variation in input signal level.

The performance using three or more past samples increases the $S/N$ level above that of the two past sample case. However, a study of the three past sample case yields extremely complicated estimator equations and the simplification to obtain a practical system implementation is not feasible. Furthermore, comparison of the performance of the two sample case to that of the rate distortion bound shows that not much more improvement can be gained by using three past samples.

The rate distortion bounds for a first-order Markov, Gaussian source for $\rho$ (correlation coefficient) = 0.95 and for $\rho = 0.9$ are derived in Appendix III. The results show that the SNR for the two past sample case is only 3.1 dB less than the rate distortion bound for $\rho = 0.95$, and only 3.2 dB less than the rate distortion bound for $\rho =$ 0.9.

## VII. Design of the Experimental Digital System

Equation (15) is the basis for the design of the experimental system. However, $r_k$ requires the knowledge of $\sigma_{\lambda_{k-1}}$ and $\rho$. Furthermore (15) is highly nonlinear. The approximations made to reduce (15) to a form which was easily constructed using digital integrated circuits are as follows.

1) Assume $\rho = 1$. Since $\rho$ is unknown, but close to unity, this assumption eliminates the need for estimation and multiplication, which is a time consuming process.

2) With $\rho \equiv 1$, (15e) becomes

$$y_k = \frac{x_{k-1} - x_k}{\sigma_{\lambda_{k-1}}} \quad (18a)$$

where, from (8),

$$\sigma_{\lambda_{k-1}}{}^2 = E(s_k - \rho s_{k-1})^2 \simeq E(s_k - s_{k-1})^2. \quad (18b)$$

Since $x_k$ is the estimate of $s_k$, and $x_{k-1}$ the estimate of $s_{k-1}$

$$\sigma_{\lambda_{k-1}}{}^2 \simeq E(x_k - x_{k-1})^2. \quad (18c)$$

Even this result is difficult to transform to hardware. However, by letting

$$\sigma_{\lambda_{k-1}}{}^2 \equiv (x_k - x_{k-1})^2. \quad (19)$$

Equation (18a) simplifies to

$$y_k \simeq \operatorname{sgn}(x_{k-1} - x_k). \quad (20)$$

Using (20) and (13f) and (13g), (15) simplify dramatically to a set of linear equations. The results are for

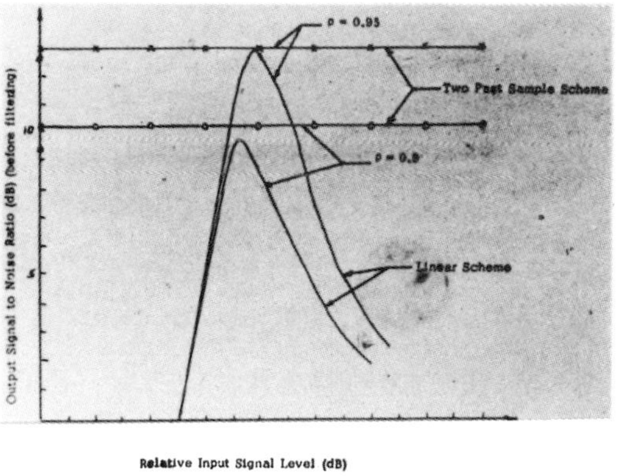


Fig. 6. Approximated two-past-sample scheme compared to the linear delta modulator assuming $\sigma_\lambda$ is known.

$$x_k - x_{k-1} > 0$$

$$r_k = x_{k+1} = \begin{cases} x_k + 0.51(x_k - x_{k-1}), & e_{k-1} = -1, \; e_k = 1 \quad (21a) \\ x_k + 1.15(x_k - x_{k-1}), & e_{k-1} = 1, \; e_k = 1 \quad (21b) \\ x_k - 0.51(x_k - x_{k-1}), & e_{k-1} = 1, \; e_k = -1 \quad (21c) \\ x_k - 1.15(x_k - x_{k-1}), & e_{k-1} = -1, \; e_k = -1 \quad (21d) \end{cases}$$

and for

$$x_k - x_{k-1} < 0$$

$$r_k = x_{k+1} = \begin{cases} x_k - 0.15(x_k - x_{k-1}), & e_{k-1} = -1, \; e_k = 1 \quad (22a) \\ x_k - 1.15(x_k - x_{k-1}), & e_{k-1} = 1, \; e_k = 1 \quad (22b) \\ x_k + 0.51(x_k - x_{k-1}), & e_{k-1} = 1, \; e_k = -1 \quad (22c) \\ x_k + 1.15(x_k - x_{k-1}), & e_{k-1} = -1, \; e_k = -1. \quad (22d) \end{cases}$$

Equations (21) and (22) can also be simplified. Consider $e_k = +1$. Then (21a) and (21b) show that $x_{k+1} - x_k \geq 0$. Similarly, (22a) and (22b) show that $x_{k+1} - x_k > 0$. Now let $k = n - 1$. Then when $e_{n-1} = +1$, $x_n - x_{n-1} \geq 0$. Hence (22b) and (22c) cannot arise since they require $x_k - x_{k-1} < 0$ for $e_{k-1} = +1$ (here we have replaced $n$ by $k$). Using a similar argument one can show that (21a) and (21d) can be disregarded. We are, therefore, left with (21b), (21c), (22a), and (22d) which are identical to Jayant's scheme [7]. In Jayant's notation $P = 1.15$ and $Q = 0.51$.[1]

In the design of the Song system, no attempt is made to rigorously adhere to (21) and (22) since they result from a large number of approximations. Instead these equations are used as a guide. As such, all eight equations are employed and none are discarded.

To construct $r_k$, knowing $x_k$, $x_k - x_{k-1}$, $e_k$ and $e_{k-1}$ it is convenient to rewrite (21) and (22) as

$$r_k = x_{k+1} = \begin{cases} x_k + 0.815\,|x_k - x_{k-1}| - 0.3\,|x_k - x_{k-1}|, & e_{k-1} = -1,\; e_k = 1 \quad \text{(23a)} \\ x_k + 0.815\,|x_k - x_{k-1}| + 0.3\,|x_k - x_{k-1}|, & e_{k-1} = 1,\; e_k = 1 \quad \text{(23b)} \\ x_k - 0.815\,|x_k - x_{k-1}| + 0.3\,|x_k - x_{k-1}|, & e_{k-1} = 1,\; e_k = -1 \quad \text{(23c)} \\ x_k - 0.815\,|x_k - x_{k-1}| - 0.3\,|x_k - x_{k-1}|, & e_{k-1} = -1,\; e_k = -1 \quad \text{(23d)} \end{cases}$$

$r_k$ can then be written as

$$r_k = x_{k+1} = x_k + g_1 + g_2 \qquad (24)$$

where

$$g_1 = g_1(e_k, x_k - x_{k-1})$$
$$g_2 = g_2(e_{k-1}, x_k - x_{k-1})$$

the function $g_1$ and $g_2$ are shown in Fig. 7.

## VIII. Experimental Results

The system shown in Fig. 8 was constructed using DTL integrated circuits. An 8-bit A/D converter was employed which limited the system performance. The minimum quantization step was 40 mV and the maximum voltage was limited to ±5V.

Due to the finite word length present in the implemented system, we must fix a minimum step size to ensure that a dead zone will not occur near the origin. Also the derivation of (24) indicated that the slopes for $g_1$ and $g_2$ may depend upon the statistics of the incoming signal. Hence $g_1$ and $g_2$ in Fig. 7 are modified as shown in Fig. 9 where $g_1$ and $g_2$ have slopes $\alpha$ and $\beta$, respectively.

The resulting equations for $g_1$ and $g_2$ obtained from Fig. 9 are for

$$x_k - x_{k-1} > 0$$

$$g_1(e_k = +1) = 0.08 + \alpha(x_k - x_{k-1} - 0.08) \cdot U(x_k - x_{k-1} - 0.08) \qquad (25a)$$

$$g_1(e_k = -1) = -0.08 - \alpha(x_k - x_{k-1} - 0.08) \cdot U(x_k - x_{k-1} - 0.08) \qquad (25b)$$

[1] This was pointed out to the authors by D. Goodman.

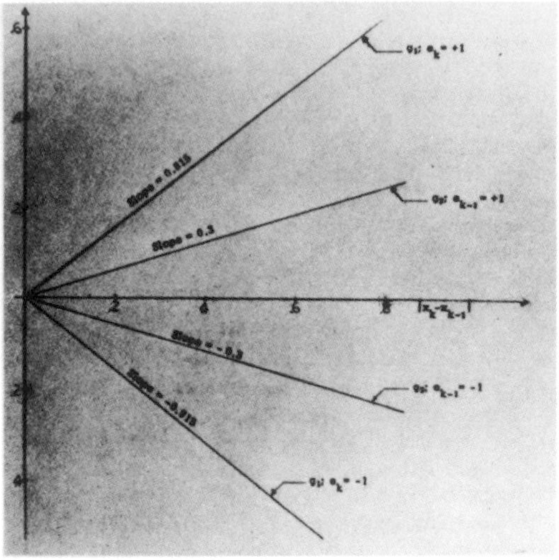


Fig. 7. Calculated function generators for the two-past-sample scheme.

$$g_2(e_k = +1) = [0.04 + \beta(x_k - x_{k-1} - 0.08)] \cdot U(x_k - x_{k-1} - 0.08) \qquad (25c)$$

$$g_2(e_k = -1) = -[0.04 + \beta(x_k - x_{k-1} - 0.08)] \cdot U(x_k - x_{k-1} - 0.08) \qquad (25d)$$

and for

$$x_k - x_{k-1} < 0$$

$$g_1(e_k = +1) = 0.08 - \alpha(x_k - x_{k-1} + 0.08) \cdot U(-[x_k - x_{k-1}] - 0.08) \qquad (26a)$$

$$g_1(e_k = -1) = -0.08 + \alpha(x_k - x_{k-1} + 0.08) \cdot U(-[x_k - x_{k-1}] - 0.08) \qquad (26b)$$

$$g_2(e_k = +1) = [0.04 - \beta(x_k - x_{k-1} + 0.08)] \cdot U(-[x_k - x_{k-1}] - 0.08) \qquad (26c)$$

$$g_2(e_k = -1) = -[0.04 - \beta(x_k - x_{k-1} + 0.08)] \cdot U(-[x_k - x_{k-1}] - 0.08) \qquad (26d)$$

where

$$U(z) = \begin{cases} 1, & z \geq 0 \\ 0, & z < 0. \end{cases} \qquad (27)$$

The data rate was adjustable although results were obtained at 56 kbit/s and 19.2 kbit/s. The quantitative results presented in this paper, (Figs. 11–13), were all obtained at 56 kbit/s.

### *$\alpha$ and $\beta$*

The slopes $\alpha$ and $\beta$ were each adjusted to take on only the values $\frac{1}{4}$, $\frac{1}{2}$, 1, and 2 for ease of implementation. It

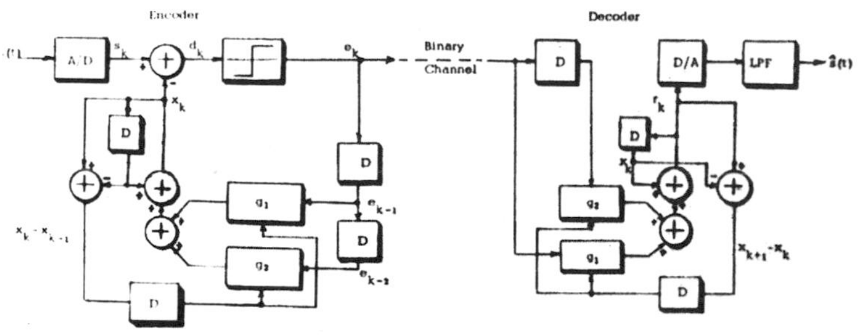


Fig. 8. Implemented structure of the variable step robust delta modulator-demodulator.

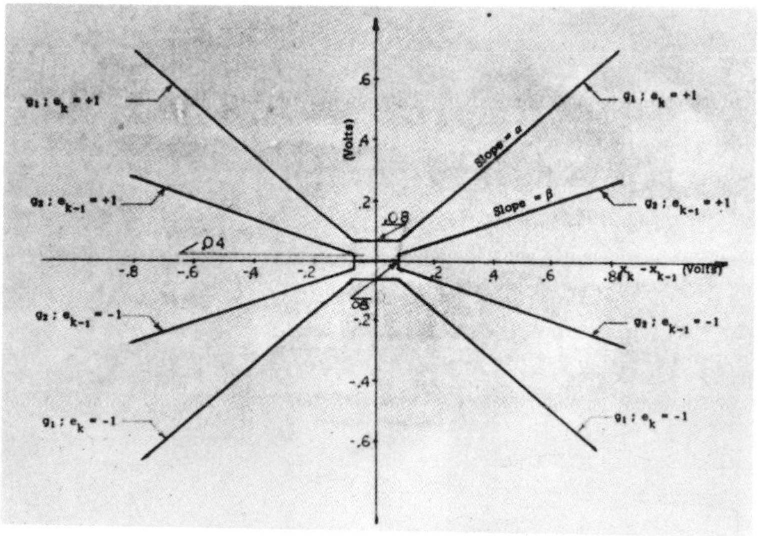


Fig. 9. Function generators for the two-past-sample scheme.

was found that speech had greater clarity when $\alpha = 1$ and $\beta = 0$, while video information had greater clarity for $\alpha = 1$ and $\beta = \frac{1}{2}$.

When $\alpha = 1$ and $\beta = 0$, the step-size increases and decreases linearly, which is equivalent to an *enhanced Abate adaptive scheme* with 128 control switches. To see this, assume that the system is in slope overload, $x_1 = 0.2$ V and $x_1 - x_0 = 0.1$ V. Then using either Fig. 9 or (25), (26), and (23), we have

$$x_2 = 0.2 + (0.08 + 0.02 + 0.04) = 0.34.$$

Now $x_2 - x_1 = 0.14$ and therefore

$$x_3 = 0.34 + (0.08 + 0.06 + 0.04) = 0.52.$$

Now $x_3 - x_2 = 0.18$. Note that the step size continually increases by 0.04 as long as we are in slope overload. As soon as the overload condition ends, the step size decreases by 0.04. Since 8-bit logic is employed, the step-size can be increased 128 times.

When $\alpha = 1$ and $\beta = 0.5$, the step size increases and decreases in a nonlinear manner. In the slope overload region, for example, the system operates as Jayant's scheme with $P = 1.15$ and $Q = 0.5$.

It is also interesting to note that for $\alpha = 1, \beta = 0$, the system can have different steady-state quantization steps, while the $\alpha = 1, \beta = \frac{1}{2}$ system, always has a minimum quantization step, 0.04, in steady state.

A computer simulation was performed for a Markov input and the performance of the approximated system with $\alpha = 1$ and $\beta = 0$ is shown in Fig. 10. The results from this figure indicate that a flat response is possible with sufficient arithmetic accuracy when using the course estimate of signal power. A minimum step size of 0.04 was used in the simulation. Hence the output SNR falls off for the low-input signal power.

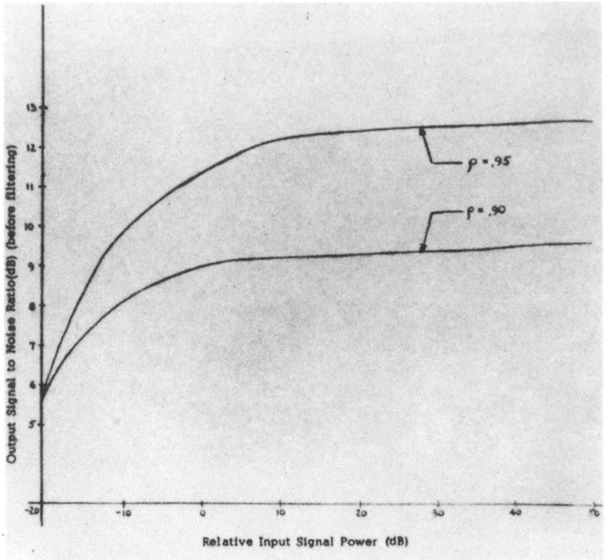


Fig. 10. Performance of the approximated delta modulation scheme to a Markov input assuming $\sigma_\lambda$ is unknown.

500 Hz Square Wave Input

Adaptive Delta Modulator $\alpha=1$, $\beta=0$

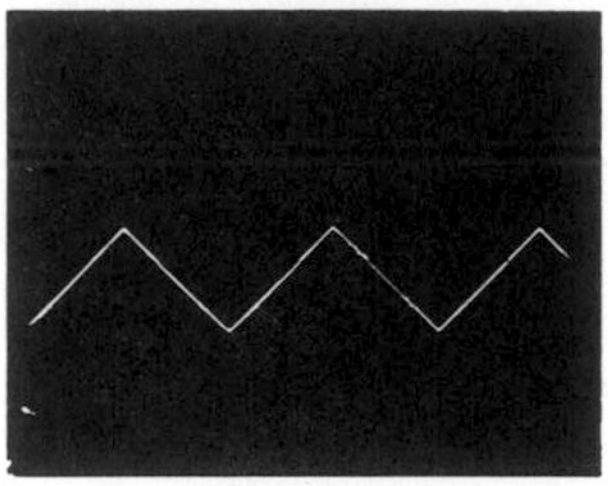

Linear Delta Modulator

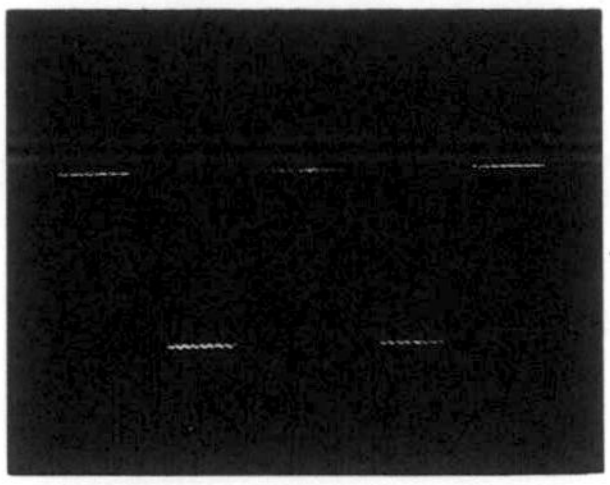

Adaptive Delta Modulator $\alpha=1$, $\beta=0.5$

Fig. 11. Responses to a 500-Hz square wave.

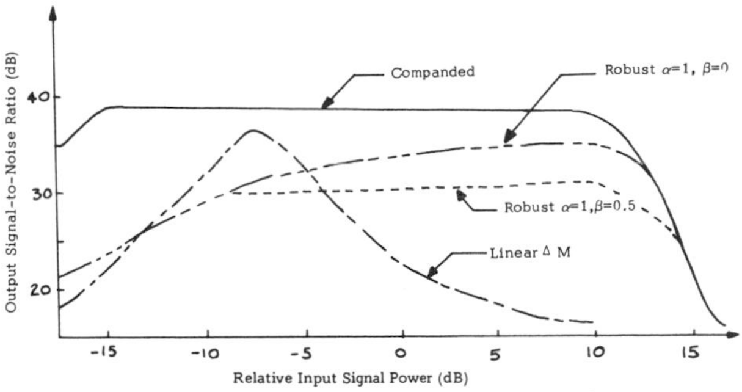


Fig. 12. Response of the variable step size robust delta modulator to sinusoidal signals compared with the linear delta modulator and an existing companded scheme.

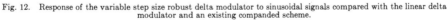

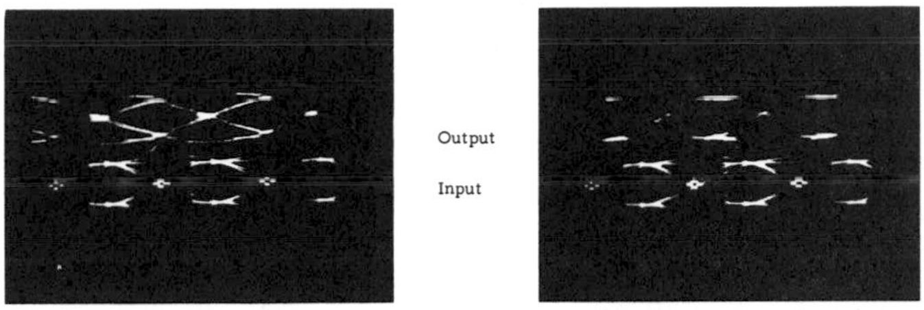


Fig. 13. (a) Eye pattern of the linear delta modulator. (b) Eye pattern of the adaptive delta modulator ($\alpha = 1, \beta = 0.5$).

The performance of the actual real-time system is demonstrated in the following sections.

*Response to a Square Wave Input*

The response of the system to a 500-Hz square-wave input is shown in Fig. 11 for $\alpha = 1$, $\beta = 0.5$, $\alpha = 1$, $\beta = 0$; and the linear delta modulator. The square-wave responses show that the system performs best with $\alpha = 1$, and $\beta = 0.5$.

*Response to Sinusoidal Inputs*

The output SNR versus the input-signal power curve shown in Fig. 12 was measured for an input frequency of 800 Hz and sampling rate of 56 kbit/s. The slopes of the curves in the small-signal region are caused by the quantizing noise of the A/D and D/A converters. If the logic would be extended to 10-bit words, the flat portion would be extended 12 dB in the low-signal direction. Thus the number of bits could be increased significantly to enable the system to operate at signal levels as small as desired. The upper limit of the input signal power is due to the ±5 V limitation of A/D and D/A converters. For sinusoidal inputs the resulting curves show that for $\alpha = 1$ and $\beta = 0$, the system performs the best.

Note that using an 8-bit system results in a degraded performance compared to that of an analog companded delta modulator described by Schindler [10] whose performance is given by the uppermost curve in Fig. 12.

*Response to Random Data Sequences*

The oscillograms shown in Fig. 13(a) and (b) show the eye patterns of the system responses to random data sequences. The input was obtained by passing the output of the pseudo-random sequence generator through a low-pass filter. Fig. 13(a) shows the eye pattern of the linear delta modulator while Fig. 13(b) shows the eye pattern of the adaptive delta modulator with $\alpha = 1$ and $\beta = 0.5$. The results clearly show that the adaptive systems have much better ability in reconstructing the data.

## IX. Conclusions

The general structure of the variable step-size digital adaptive delta modulator was derived from the optimum adaptive DM system. The special case of the two past sample observation was found to be comparatively simple to construct and useful for practical applications. The structure was derived by assuming known statistics of a first-order Markov process. However, in the implemented system, the design included continuous estimation of the parameters of the input signal. Hence the signal statistics were not needed *a priori*.

The system was designed and constructed for real-time operation using all digital hardware. It was tested for several deterministic signals as well as pseudo-random data sequences. The experimental results show that the system performance was quite good for all types of input signals. With extended hardware the output SNR can be made relatively independent of the input signal power.

[*Editors' Note:* Material has been omitted at this point.]

## References


[1] J. B. O'Neal, Jr., "Delta modulation quantizing noise analytical and computer simulation results for Gaussian and television input signals," *Bell Syst. Tech. J.*, Jan. 1966.

[2] A. Tomozawa and H. Kaneko, "Companded delta modulation for telephone transmission," *IEEE Trans. Commun. Technol.*, vol. COM-16, pp. 149–157, Feb. 1968.

[3] S. J. Brolin and J. M. Brown, "Companded delta modulation for telephone," *IEEE Trans. Commun. Technol.*, vol. COM-16, pp. 157–162, Feb. 1968.

[4] J. E. Abate, "Linear and adaptive delta modulation," *Proc. IEEE*, vol. 55, pp. 298–308, Mar. 1967.

[5] M. R. Winkler, "High information delta modulation," *IEEE Int. Conv. Rec.*, pt. 1, pp. 285–290, 1965.

[6] J. A. Greefkes and F. de Jager, "Continuous delta modulation," *Philips Res. Rep.*, vol. 23, pp. 233–246, Apr. 1968.

[7] N. S. Jayant, "Adaptive delta modulation with a one-bit memory," *Bell Syst. Tech. J.*, vol. 49, pp. 321–342, Mar. 1970.

[8] C. L. Song, "Adaptive delta modulation," Ph. D. dissertation, Polytechnic Inst. Brooklyn, New York, 1971.

[9] T. Fine, "Properties of an optimum digital system and applications," *IEEE Trans. Inform. Theory*, vol. IT-10, pp. 287–296, Oct. 1964.

[10] H. R. Schindler, "Delta modulation," *IEEE Spectrum*, vol. 7, pp. 69–78, Oct. 1970.

[11] H. Gish, "Optimum quantization of random sequences," Ph.D. dissertation, Harvard University, Cambridge, Mass., 1967.

# 40



Reprinted from *Proc. Natl. Telemetry Conf.*, 1962, pp. 6.5-1–6.5-15

# AN ADAPTIVE NONLINEAR DATA PREDICTOR

A. V. Balakrishnan
University of California
Los Angeles, California

## SUMMARY

Data prediction and/or extrapolation methods are of utility in several phases of telemetry and data processing systems. For instance, they are applicable to the problem of filling in 'drop-out' areas in telemetry data. More importantly, however, such methods provide a direct means of exploiting data redundancy for the purpose of band-width or power reduction. This paper describes a prediction method which, because of its adaptive (or self-learning) and nonlinear nature, is particularly suited to the latter application. The significance of the adaptive feature lies in the fact that since the prediction is determined by a self-learning process, no a priori assumptions concerning the data need to be made, and thus, for instance, the bandwidth reduction is initiated only if the data redundancy warrants it. The nonlinear feature allows the predictor to be as complex as necessary, avoiding any degradation due to linearity restrictions.

The method consists essentially of training the operator on the date immediately prior to the prediction point. If the data can be described as a stationary stochastic process and the time length of the data is large enough, the method automatically yields the optimal prediction. Moreover, an estimate of the error to be expected is furnished so that optimal selection of operator parameters is possible.

Results obtained using this method on typical data are presented. Applications to adaptive communication systems are discussed.

* * *

The main purpose of this paper is to outline a method and philosophy of prediction and/or extrapolation for use with telemetry data. As an 'adaptive' or 'learning' method, it is closest to the work of Gabor[1] although different in rationale and implementation. Gabor pursues a broader aim, while the current work is concerned with 'pure' prediction only. The applications we intend are to filling in 'drop-out' areas in telemetry data and more importantly to band-width and/or power conservation systems. Gabor[1] and Bose-Wiener[2] assume that the observed data is one 'long' sample of an 'ergodic' process. Gabor[1] himself assumes 'band-limitedness' in addition. In our view the need for such ad hoc assumptions is disconcerting and in the kinds of data we deal with, even questionable. In this paper we introduce a philosophy of prediction which does not require any such assumptions and at the same time yields a concrete notion of the 'optimality' of the prediction. Like the Gabor work, the prediction is not limited to linear operations and can be as complex as necessary.

The basic prediction philosophy is discussed in Section 2. Various means of instrumenting the prediction operator are described in Section 3. Some numerical results are presented in Section 4, and finally some applications in Section 5.

## 2. Basic Prediction Philosophy

The data prediction problem that concerns us is that of 'pure' prediction (that is, the data is assumed free from noise) and can be stated quite simply: we are given a 'wave-form' of duration T, a function x(t), $o \leq t \leq T$, in other words, and we are required to 'predict' the value at time $T + \Delta$. The parameter t can be discrete or continuous and $\Delta$ is a small fraction of T. Any operation is to be based on this data alone, no other additional a priori knowledge being available. This is, of course, an ancient problem and here we wish to treat it strictly in the telemetry data processing context, and note two major points of view in dealing with it. One which may be considered the "numerical analysis" point of view consists in assuming that certainly any physically realized wave form must be analytic and can thus be approximated by polynomials. The data may thus be 'fitted' to a polynomial of high enough degree and we then simply use this polynomial to 'predict' the future values. The other and more recent view is the statistical view in which we assume (perhaps with good reason) that the data is a finite sample of a stationary stochastic process whose average properties such as moments and/or distributions are known or calculable from the data. For a process of given description we can apply the well-developed mean square prediction theory. Perhaps the main advantage with this view is that it gives us a quantitative, albeit theoretical, notion of the error in prediction. The problem of measuring the average statistics from a finite sample can be quite delicate, however. (For example see Grenander and Rosenblatt's work[3] on evaluation of the spectrum from finite data for prediction.) In the polynomial fitting method, the interpretation of the prediction error - which is, after all, the crucial point - is more nebulous, bound up with what degree polynomial to use and what portion of the data is to be fitted. Moreover, as ordinarily used, the fitting operations on the data are linear.

In the present work we adopt a rationale for prediction which is free from a priori assumptions concerning the 'model'. In a general sense what is involved in both the above methods is first 'model-making' consistent with the data and as a second step using the numbers derived therefrom to perform some optimal operations. If an understanding of the mechanism generating the model is desired, the first step is essential. If what we want is prediction, then we shall show that it is possible to proceed directly (and hence more optimally) to the best prediction without the intermediate step of model-making. It may be, of course, that several philosophies lead to the same operations on the data. Even here, the present method offers some practical advantages. Moreover, it is only natural to use the philosophy that requires the least prior assumptions.

We note first that any prediction is an operation or operator on the part of the data, and in our case the finite part is all that is available. The main point of departure in our view is that if we have a prediction operator, which based on all the available input data, functions optimally in the immediate past of the point where the prediction is required, this is all that we can ask for meaningfully as a solution to the prediction problem. Thus the only basis on which we can a priori judge any prediction method is to 'back off' slightly from the present and compare the actual available data with the predicted value using the given prediction operator. Let us see how this can be formulated analytically. Let the total available data be described as a function $x(t)$, $o \le t \le T$, and let it be required to predict the value at $T + \Delta$, $\Delta > o$, being a small fraction of T. Let us next consider the data in the interval $o < t < T - \Delta$. If for any $t_o$ in this interval we should choose to make a 'prediction' of the function value $\Delta$ ahead from the past values up to $t_o$ denoting the predicted value by

$$x^*(t_o + \Delta)$$

we can explicitly observe the error

$$x^*(t_o + \Delta) - x(t_o + \Delta)$$

Let us next note that the general prediction operator will be a 'function' of a finite segment of the past. Let us denote the length at this segment by S. Then of course

$$x^*(t_o + \Delta) = O\left( x(\sigma) : t_o - S < \sigma < t_o \right) \qquad (2.1)$$

O representing the prediction operator. Next we have to specify the error criterion. Here we choose the mean square error, first because it is simpler analytically and is almost universally used, making comparison with other methods possible. The kind of solution presented being definitely not 'analytic', based rather on successive approximation, other measures of error can be used at the risk of greater complexity. As far as the rationale of the method is concerned, this is largely a matter of detail, than principle. We thus use to determine optimality:

$$\frac{1}{T-\Delta-L} \int_L^{T-\Delta} \left[ x^*(t+\Delta) - x(t+\Delta) \right]^2 dt = \epsilon^2 \qquad (2.2)$$

where $L \ge S$, and we proceed on the basis that the operator O is best which minimizes (2.2). We can of course, generalize (2.2) as:

$$\frac{1}{T-\Delta-L} \int_L^{T-\Delta} \rho(t)\, C\left( x^*(t+\Delta) - x(t+\Delta) \right) dt \qquad (2.3)$$

where $\rho(t)$ is a positive weight function and $C(\cdot)$ is, say, a symmetric positive cost function. Before considering the problem of determining the optimal operator O, let us note an important consistency principle. Suppose the data is regarded as one long sample of an ergodic process. Then (2.2) yields exactly the optimal operator in the statistical sense. However, we have not needed to make any such assumption concerning the data; nor have to compute average statistics first. The point is that while the data may not be enough for determining let us say the spectrum, it may be quite adequate for the prediction itself. Unlike the polynomial fitting, the operations on the data can be as nonlinear as necessary, and at the same time (2.2) normalized to

$$\epsilon^2 \Big/ \frac{1}{T-\Delta-L} \int_L^{T-\Delta} x(t+\Delta)^2 dt \qquad (2.4)$$

yields a quantitative measure of the prediction error on which to judge how good the prediction will be.

## 3. Determination of Optimal Predictor - I

By determination of the optimal predictor what we mean here is the determination of a computer algorithm based on a successive iteration or similar method which is shown to converge to the optimum. We shall first consider what we shall call the 'continuous' or 'analogue' method even though the program itself is best suited (at present at any rate) for a digital computer. This method is closest in principle to the one proposed by Gabor[2], although not restricted by any band-limitedness or ergodicity assumption. The general mathematical notions involved in the method may be found in (4), and we shall not go into details here. We begin by considering the Hilbert ($L_2$) space of square integrable functions over $(L, T-\Delta)$. Then the operator O is seen to be a nonlinear operator or function, mapping $L_2(O, S)$ into $L_2(L, T-\Delta)$. Confining ourselves only to (Frechet) analytic functions[4], such a function has the following 'Taylor Series' expansion:

$$x^*(t+\Delta) = \sum_1^\infty \frac{1}{n!}\int_0^S \cdots \int_0^S K_n(t_1, \dots t_n)\, x(t-t_1)\dots x(t-t_n)\, dt_1 \dots dt_n \qquad (3\text{-}1)$$

This is an infinite series, and for any finite term approximation (or an approximation of given complexity) we have the representation

$$x_N^*(t+\Delta) = \sum_1^N \int_0^S \cdots \int_0^S K_n(t_1, \dots t_n)\, x(t-t_1)\dots x(t-t_n)\, dt_1 \dots dt_n \qquad (3.2)$$

and we have to determine the 'weight functions' $K_n(t_1, \dots t_n)$ that minimize the error

$$\frac{1}{T-\Delta-L}\int_L^{T-\Delta}\left[x_N^*(t+\Delta) - x(t+\Delta)\right]^2 dt \qquad (3.3)$$

We may do this by the method of steepest descent, details of convergence on which are given in (4). In this approximation, as noted in (4), it is important to notice that there may be no optimal weight function of the form in (3.2) but there will always be a sequence of such functions which approximate the minimal operator. In other words, an approximation is all that we can hope to achieve at best, and the usual solutions to 'integral equations' must be interpreted in this light. To indicate the steepest descent method, let us note that each term in (3.2) is a linear continuous mapping from $(L_2(S^n)$ into $L_2(L, T-\Delta)$ so that we can denote (3.2) by:

$$x_N^* = \sum_1^N L_i(K_i) \qquad (3.4)$$

Let us next consider the product Hilbert Space $\prod_1^N L_2(S^n)$ denoting it by H. Then (3.4) is a mapping from H into $L_2(L, T-\Delta)$, and let it be denoted:

$$x_N^* = LK$$

where L is now a linear bounded operator, K is in H. It is actually a compact operator. In any case (3.3) can now be written as, using $\|\ \|$ to denote the norm in $L_2(L, T-\Delta)$,

$$\|x_N^* - L_k\|^2 = \|x_N^*\|^2 - 2\left[L_k, x_N^*\right] + \left[L_k, L_k\right]$$

where [, ] denotes the inner product. Let $L^*$ denote the adjoint of L, so that we can write

$$\|x_N^* - L_k\|^2 = \|x_N^*\|^2 + \left[L^*LK, K\right] - 2\left[K, L^*x_N^*\right] \qquad (3.5)$$

the inner products [, ] now denoting the inner products in H. Let us denote:

$$L^* x_N^* = g$$

$$L^* L = R$$

Then we have only to minimize the quadratic form

$$Q(K) = \left[RK, K\right] - 2\left[K, g\right]$$

over K in H. There is (as shown in (4)) always a sequence of elements $K_n$ in H such that

$$\operatorname*{Inf}_K Q(K) = \lim_n Q(K_n) \qquad (3.6)$$

where

$$\lim_n R K_n = g \qquad (3.7)$$

so that formally we are 'solving' the 'integral equation'

$$RK = g$$

A sequence as in (3.6) can be obtained by the method of steepest descent, where $K_n$ is determined from the iteration

$$K_{n+1} = K_n - \epsilon_n\left[Rx_n - g\right]$$

where

$$\epsilon_n = \frac{\|Rx_n - g\|^2}{\left[R^2x_n - Rg,\ Rx_n - g\right]}$$

With this choice,

$$Q\left(K_{n+1}\right) - Q\left(K_n\right) = -\epsilon_n^2$$

It should also be noted that

$$\left[RK, K\right] = \sum_i \sum_j \left[L_i K_i, L_j K_j\right]$$

$$RK = \text{col.}\left[\sum_{j=i}^{N} L_i^* L_j K_j\right]$$

As is evident, the complexity of the method increases as N increases. This is particularly true in the digital computer programs, the increase in dimensionality requiring a corresponding increase in storage. It would be nice to have methods of estimating magnitude of error as a function of N but this does not appear to be available at present. Of course, it would also be nice not to have to rely on the series expansion (3.1), but again at present there does not appear to be any direct way of synthesizing the optimal operator. In the next section we shall consider a method which goes somewhat in this direction, but is in turn itself beset with difficulties of convergence to the optimum.

### 3.2 Determination of the Prediction Operator II: Digital Method

In a sense, part of the trouble with the previous method is that we determine the optimal operator, while what we need is really only the optimal operation on the present. In other words we determine a function for all values of its argument, while we actually use its value only at one point. We shall now describe a method which is free from this, and at the same time, as pointed out above, does not require an increasingly complex hierarchy of representations. This method is essentially a modification of the method of Bose-Wiener.[2] For this, we assume that the data is sampled, so that S is now an integer and the optimal operator thus is simply a function of S real variables. What we need is a way of determining this function. Specifically, let $\Delta$ also be the sampling interval so that say

$$T = N\Delta$$

and let

$$x(m\Delta) = x_m$$

we want to determine a function O of S variables so as to minimize for fixed K, $1 \le K << N$,

$$\sum_{L}^{N-K} \left(x_{n+k} - O\left[x_n, x_{n-1}, \ldots x_{n-S}\right]\right)^2$$

Actually we need only the value

$$O\left(x_N, x_{N-1}, \ldots x_{N-S}\right) \qquad (3.8)$$

Let a, b be such that

$$a = \min x_n$$

$$b = \max x_n$$

Subdivide the interval (a, b) into equal intervals of length q and let us correspondingly subdivide the S-dimensional cube of edge (a, b) into (half-open) elementary cubes of width q. Let M be the number of such cubes, and define step functions $\{\Phi_i\}$ such that $\Phi_i$ is equal to one on the ith cube and zero otherwise. This amounts essentially to quantitizing the amplitudes. Then the $\Phi_i$ are orthogonal functions in S variables. We now limit ourselves to the best mean square representation of O(·) in terms of these functions, or in other words, the projection of O(·) on the subspace generated by these orthogonal functions. This projection is then of course given by

$$\sum a_i \Phi_i$$

where

$$a_i = \frac{\sum_{L}^{N-K} x_{n+k} \Phi_i\left(x_n, x_{n-1}, \ldots x_{n-S}\right)}{\sum_{L}^{N-K} \Phi_i^2\left(x_n, \ldots x_{n-S}\right)} \qquad (3.10)$$

and the best prediction operation itself is given by

$$x_{N+k}^* = \sum a_i \Phi_1\left(x_N, \ldots x_{N-S}\right) \qquad (3.11)$$

The interpretation of (3.11) is quite simple. Determine the cube in which the point $(x_N, \ldots x_{N-S})$ lies. For each occupancy of this cube or cell by S-dimensional points $(x_n, \ldots x_{n-S})$ in the past (with $N \le N-k$), determine the average of the corresponding $k^{th}$ successor $x_{N+k}$. This average is the prediction. In other words the predicted value is of the form:

$$x_{N+k}^* = \frac{\sum_{1=1}^{m} x_{n_1} + k}{m}$$

for those $n_i$ such that $\left(x_{n_i}, \ldots x_{n_{i-S}}\right)$ falls in the cell occupied by $\left(x_N, \ldots x_{N-S}\right)$

This method does not distinguish between linear or nonlinear operations and goes directly to the prediction for the specific point. The complexity does increase with S however, as is only to be expected. It has one major drawback, namely that the coefficients $\{a_i\}$ may be undefined so that no prediction is possible. This will happen if (and only if) the cell occupied by $(x_N, x_{N-1}, \ldots x_{N-S})$ is never occupied by any past points $(x_n, x_{n-1}, x_{n-S})$ for $n \leq N-K$. In this case there is an integer m such that

$$\Phi_i \left(x_N, \ldots x_{N-S}\right) = \delta_i^m$$

and

$$\Phi_m \left(x_n, \ldots x_{n-S}\right) = 0 \text{ for } n \leq N-K$$

Hence in (3.11) all $a_i$ vanish except for i=m, and for i=m on the other hand, both numerator and denominator are zero, so that $a_m$ is undefined, so that the prediction itself is undefined. Such a situation can occur, for example, with data that is monotone increasing or decreasing.

Suppose now that we assume that the data is a long sample of an ergodic process. Then (3.12) is seen to coincide with the sample conditional expectation of $x_{N+k}$, conditioned on the past values $x_n$, $n \leq N$, being quantitized. This is of course, the correct solution given by statistical theory. If the assumption of ergodic series holds, and T is large enough, then the singular case of undetermined prediction of the previous paragraph is an impossible event, since in that case the probability of $(x_N, \ldots x_{N-S})$ occupying the previously unoccupied cell is zero. In practice, in applying this method, it means that the data should be 'edited' for trend removal such as monotonicity - perform as many restorable operations as necessary to make the data as nearly 'stationary' as possible. It may also be noted that the difficulty of lack of determination of prediction does not occur in the previous method. In the case of linearly monotonic data, for instance, the first term (linear operator) will already provide the optimum predictor.

There is also a moderate increase in complexity of the method on the computer with decrease in q although not as great as that due to increase in S. For a given finite length of data, it is clear that as q is decreased indefinitely, the singular case of indeterminate prediction will be eventually reached.

### 3.3 Determination of Optimal Predictor III

The main difficulty with method II is that as we decrease q in an effort to reduce prediction error, the prediction may become indeterminate. We shall now describe a final method which by combining method II with method I may be used to offset this difficulty. The basic idea here is that instead of determining the whole operator or function as in method I, or at the other extreme determining it only at one point as in method II, we determine it in the immediate neighbourhood of the point where prediction is required. Thus in this method we again assume sampling and digitizing. Having chosen a quantum size q, we center the 'present' point $(x_N, \ldots x_{N-S})$ in a q-cell. The quantum size should be large enough so that a sufficient number of 'past' points $(x_n, \ldots x_{n-S})$, $n \leq N-S$, fall in this cell. The notion of sufficiency will be made precise in a moment. We now use the method I and determine the optimal operator O from:

$$\sum_n \left[x_{n+k} - O\left(x_n, \ldots x_{n-S}\right)\right]^2 \qquad (3.12)$$

where the summation is only over those n such that the corresponding 'past' points fall in the q-cell about the present value. The minimization of (3.12) is carried out using the same procedure as in method I. Thus we assume a finite expansion for the O (...) function as in (3.2), and determine the corresponding weight functions by the method of steepest descent. The procedure is somewhat simplified by the fact that the parameter 't' is now discrete. The number of occupancies must, however, be large enough so that unique determination is possible; for N=2 in (3.2) for instance we must have at least

$$S + S(S+1)/2$$

occupancies such that we have that many linearly independent forms in the unknown weights. It should be noted that for q sufficiently large this method of course, reverts to method I for the case where the parameter t is discrete. As in any method, the proper choice of quantum size has to be based on the minimum obtainable observed prediction error.

## 4. Results

Mainly to illustrate the type of results that may be expected, we shall now present some computer studies on some actual data using the methods of the previous section. The data is not intended to be typical, since we cannot presume to say what is typical. Nor are the results intended to be construed as conclusive or exhaustive. Rather than make up any artificial data such as sums of sine waves or polynomials, we have used some actual telemetry data chosen solely on the basis of availability. It happens to be some radar velocity data which was edited to remove trends and sampled at the rate of ten samples a second. All three methods were tried on the same portion of the data. Comparative studies on different kinds of data must await further work.

Results Using Method I

The section of the data which was used in prediction is plotted in Figure 1.1. The learning mode used fifty samples. The prediction inverval was the sampling interval, and the prediction was based on the past five samples (S=5/10 sec in (2.1)). To study the improvement in prediction with complexity of the prediction operator, a linear predictor and a nonlinear predictor of order two (that is, with N=2 in (3.2)) were optimized. The magnitude of the prediction error (as a function of time) is plotted in Figure 1.2. No attempt was made to reset the prediction operator at each point, and the same predictor was used at all the points shown. This would be one possible mode of operation in adaptive schemes where the prediction error is monitored and a new prediction operator is tried only if the error exceeds a suitable threshold. In Figure 1.3 we have plotted the actual predicted values for comparison with Figure 1.1. The improvement of the 'nonlinear' predictor over the linear is noticeable at the large excursions of the data. The number of iterations required for the nonlinear predictor was about thirty, and the initial step used the best linear filter.

Results Using Method II

In method II we have an additional parameter to adjust namely the quantum size q. In Figures 2.1 through 2.6 we have plotted the squared magnitude of the error as a function of q at various data points. The circles indicate the observed error (averaged in accordance with (3.3)) and the triangles the actual error. The prediction interval is again the sampling interval, the prediction being based on the past two data samples. The learning mode again used fifty samples. The prediction operator was optimized anew at each point, thus allowing it to be 'time-varying'. The points where the prediction errors are plotted are not the same as in the previous case, and were picked to indicate the variation in behaviour from point to point. The dependence on quantum size for a given point is, it may be noticed, negligible. Only quantum sizes for which at least two occupancies were available are included, hence the abrupt cessation of data below a minimal size.

Results Using Method III

Some results obtained using method III are summarized in Figures 2.7 and 2.8. A second order predictor was used (with N=2 in (3.2)). Instead of individual prediction errors, here we have plotted the root mean square error averaged over several points, as a function of quantum size. In both figures the prediction was based on two past points. The first successor was predicted in Figure 2.7 and the second successor in Figure 2.8. The main noticeable fact is that the observed error decreases until a critical quantum size is reached and increases thereafter. This appears to be characteristic, and may be explained by the fact that for finite run the number of data cell-occupancies eventually decrease and become too small for good prediction. The q values in these figures are of course larger than in the previous ones in order to have enough occupancies to solve for the optimal predictor. While our results are still preliminary and no exhaustive studies of the dependence of prediction on the various parameters can yet be presented, we have included the results of some runs using three past samples in Figures 2.9 and 2.10, and with five past samples in Figures 2.11 and 2.12. With increase in number of past samples used, the number of occupancies again decreases. In these latter figures we have used only the first order term in the expansion (N=1 in (3.2)) and predict the first successor in 2.9 and 2.11, and the second successor in 2.10 and 2.12. The curves are similar to the previous ones, and prediction ceases now (as is to be expected) at a higher cut-off q value.

The final choice among these various methods may well be made on considerations other than the quality of prediction alone. The increase in complexity with increase in the length of data on which prediction is based is common to all methods, being perhaps least in method II. The computation time is about the same for methods I and III somewhat less again for method II. While data variability will make any conclusive statements difficult, it is hoped that the continuing studies will shed light on many of the as yet unanswered questions.

5. Applications

We shall now indicate briefly some applications which motivated for the most part the current work. The immediate or direct applications of the kind of methods espoused are to data extrapolation such as filling in drop out areas in telemetry data or to input-adaptive control systems where the control is based on predicted input behaviour. In these applications we are interested in prediction per se, and a priori assumptions concerning the data are not sensible. The choice of parameters such as S and q will now be governed by the observed error.

Perhaps less direct but more important applications are to communications systems where one wishes to exploit data redundancy for the purpose of band-width or power conservation. Since predictability is a measure of this redundancy, the methods advocated here are applicable to such systems especially where adaptive features are necessary. Thus, for example, data at any instant need be transmitted only if it is not predictable based on the transmitted data in the past, the predictability being determined by a preset threshold on the error. The maximal complexity of the predictor may also be predetermined so that that the receiver will use the same predictor as the transmitter. A quantitative analysis of how much saving is possible is complex even after assumptions concerning the data sources are made for the purpose of analysis. It is characteristic of adaptive systems of this type that little analytical theory can be developed to yield quantitative answers, and we can at best assure ourselves that enough adaptivity has been incorporated to take maximum advantage of any saving possible.

It may be worth pointing out that in these schemes for band-width or power conservation, the overall system fidelity - from source to final destination - has to be evaluated as well as the conservation feature. As an example we may consider a band-width reduction system for PCM transmission of analogue data. Let $\{x_n\}$ represent the sampled analogue data (which in the first instance we will assume to be stationary stochastic) which is digitized to N levels such that

$$x_n = \zeta_i \text{ for } a_i \leq x_n < a_{i+1}$$

each level being transmitted in a binary code, and thus requiring $\log_2 N$ bits. If $p_{ij}$ is the (joint) probability of transmitting the word corresponding to $\zeta_i$ and receiving $\zeta_j$, the mean square error between the source data and the received analogue data is given by:

$$\epsilon^2 = \sigma^2 - \sum\sum m_i^2 p_{ij} + \sum\sum \left(m_i - \zeta_j\right)^2 p_{ij}$$

$$= \left[\sigma^2 - \sum\sum m_i^2 p_{ij} + \sum_L \left(m_i - \zeta_L\right)^2 p_{ii}\right] +$$

$$+ \sum_{L\neq j}\sum \left(m_i - \zeta_j\right)^2 p_{ij}$$

where

$$\sigma^2 = E\left(x_n^2\right) \text{ E denoting expected value}$$

$$m_i = \int_{a_i}^{a_{i+1}} x\, p(x)\, dx \Big/ \int_{a_i}^{a_{i+1}} p(x)\, dx$$

the density function corresponding to $x_n$ being denoted by $p(\cdot)$. Here in (5.1) the first group of terms represent the contribution of quantization noise and the final term to the channel noise. The optimal choice of the levels $\zeta_i$ will now minimize (5.1). Ordinarily in PCM transmission, the error due to channel noise can be omitted. Thus, we note that we have

$$\epsilon^2 = \sigma^2 Q_n, \quad Q_n \geq Q_{n+1} \tag{5.2}$$

where $Q_n$ is the minimal error for n levels for signal of unit variance. Hence, a reduction in variance means that we can use a smaller number of levels for the same mean square error. Now such a reduction is possible by removal of the redundancy or the predictable part. Thus let

$$z_n = x_n - E\left[x_n / x_{n-k}, K\geq 0\right] = x_n - x_n^*$$

where the second term on the stochastic basis is the best mean square prediction of the present based on the past. Then

$$E\left(z_n^2\right) = \sigma_z^2 = \sigma^2 - E\left(x_n^{*2}\right)$$

and the variance of $z_n$ is thus smaller so that a reduction in quantization levels and hence in transmission band-width is possible. However, it must be borne in mind that the receiver must reconstruct the original data from the received quantized $z_n$, and the overall error has to be evaluated. Let $y_n$ represent the reconstructed signal, and let the fidelity criterion be the mean square error. Then it is possible to show in general that

$$E\left[\left(x_n - y_n\right)^2\right] = \sigma^2 Q'_m$$

where $Q'_m$ is the quantization error in quantizing to m levels of $[z_n/\sigma_z]$. Thus if $x_n$ and $z_n$, normalized to unit variance, have the same distribution, we see that we may just as well have quantized the source $x_n$ itself to the smaller number of levels, with the same fidelity. Such a case occurs when the signal $x_n$ is Gaussian. When the distributions are different, it is possible that the quantization error in $z_n$ is smaller, so that the scheme of redundancy removal is more efficient. Also we have used the fidelity criterion of mean square error and this may not be the right criterion and for other criteria the prediction system may be better.

Among other applications similar in principle we may mention one involving data display compression in telemetry where only those portions of the data where there is activity based on excedent of prediction error are displayed.

ACKNOWLEDGMENT

We would like to acknowledge the generous help of D. Brown of Space Technology Laboratories and H. Hsieh of UCLA, Department of Engineering, in programming for the digital computer. Thanks are also due to J. F. Ormsby for similar assistance in the earlier phases of this work.

REFERENCES

1. D. Gabor, W. P. L. Wilby, and R. Woodcock, "A Universal Nonlinear Filter Predictor and Simulator Which Optimizes Itself by a Learning Process", The Institution of Electrical Engineers, July, 1960.

2. A. G. Bose, "A Theory of Nonlinear Systems", M I T Research Lab. of Electronics, Report Number 309, 1956.

3. U. Grenander and M. Rosenblatt, "Statistical Analysis of Stationary Time Series", John Wiley and Sons, New York, 1957.

4. A. V. Balakrishnan, "A General Theory of Nonlinear Estimation Problems in Control Systems", Siam Symposium on Mathematical Problems in Control Systems, Washington, D. C., 1961; to be published in the SIAM Journal on Control, September, 1962.

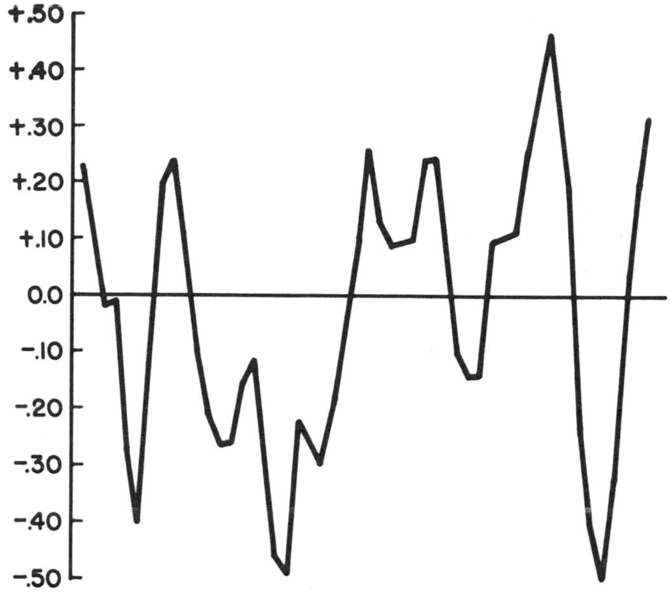


ACTUAL DATA (SAMPLES)

FIGURE 1.1

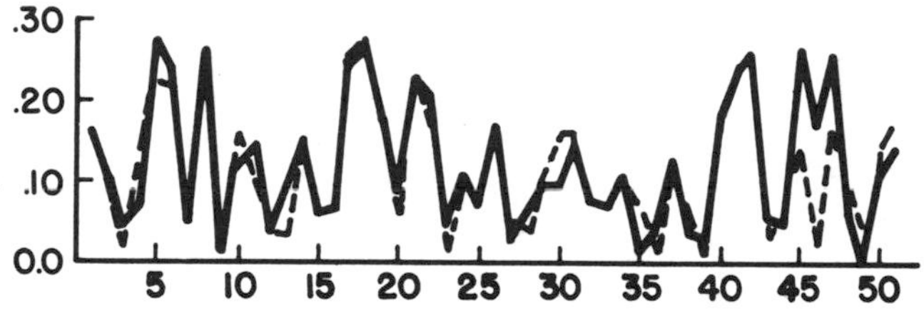


MAGNITUDE OF PREDICTION ERROR

{LINEAR ——— / NON-LINEAR - - -}

FIGURE 1.2

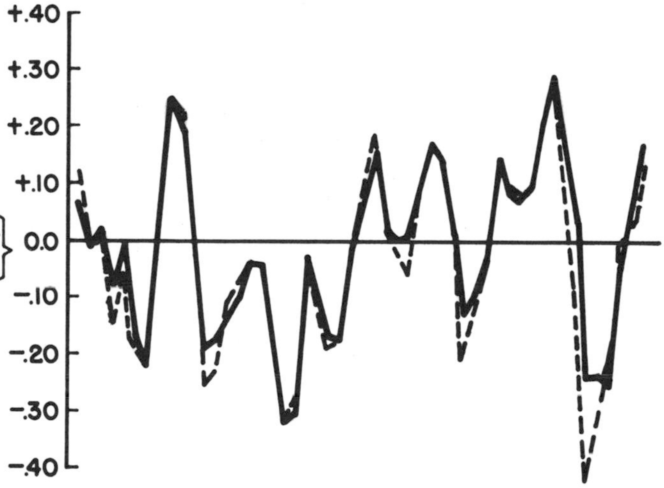


PREDICTION DATA

{LINEAR ——— / NON-LINEAR - - -}

FIGURE 1.3

FIGURE 2.1

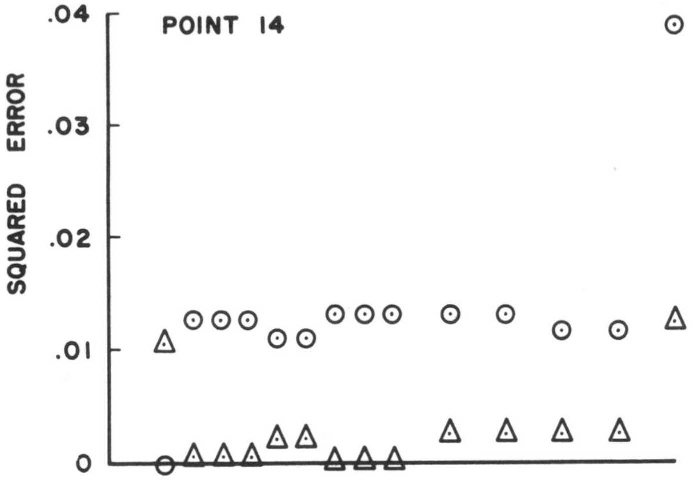


FIGURE 2.2

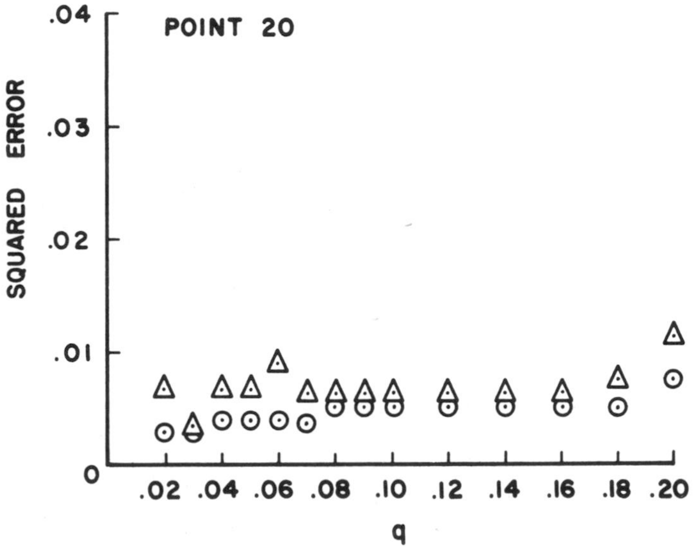

FIGURE 2.3

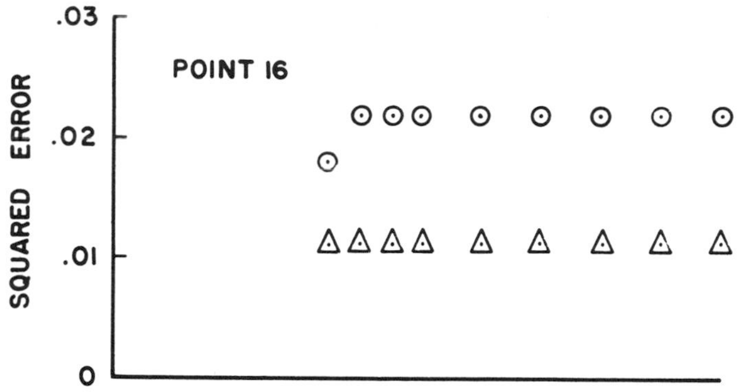


FIGURE 2.4

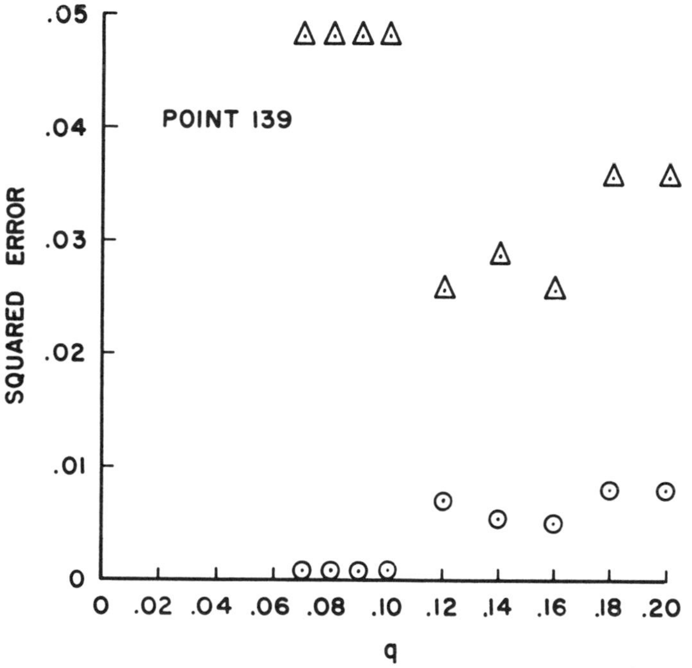

FIGURE 2.5

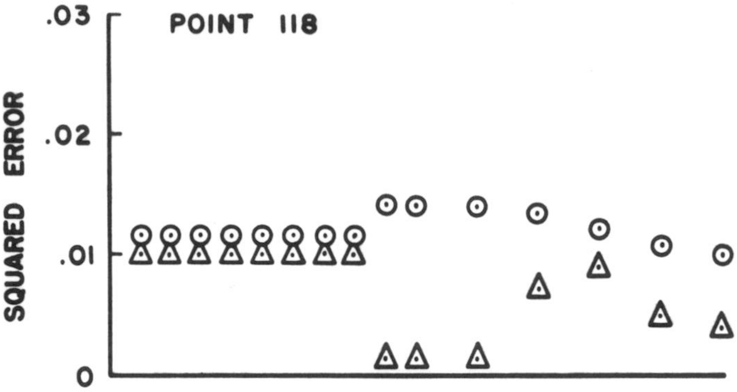


FIGURE 2.6

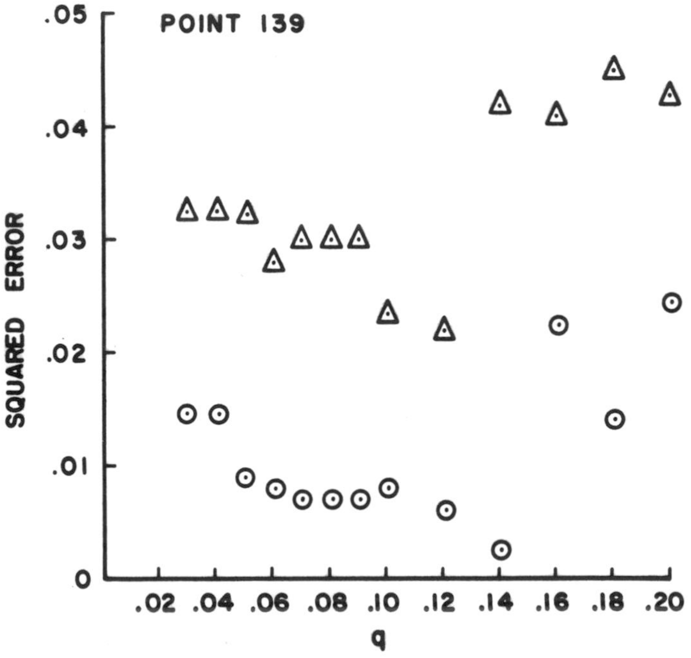

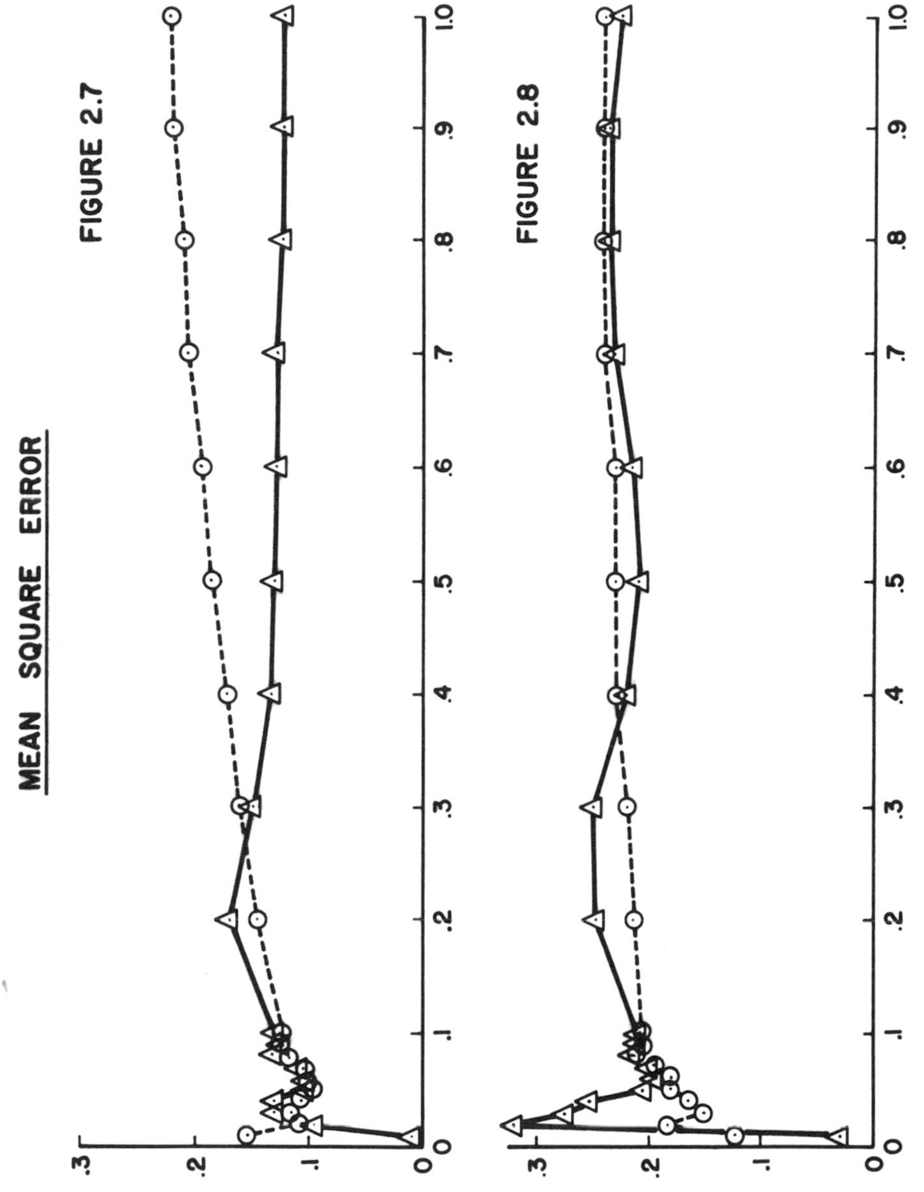
MEAN SQUARE ERROR
FIGURE 2.7
FIGURE 2.8
.3
.2
.1
0
.1
.2
.3
.4
.5
.6
.7
.8
.9
1.0

MEAN SQUARE ERROR

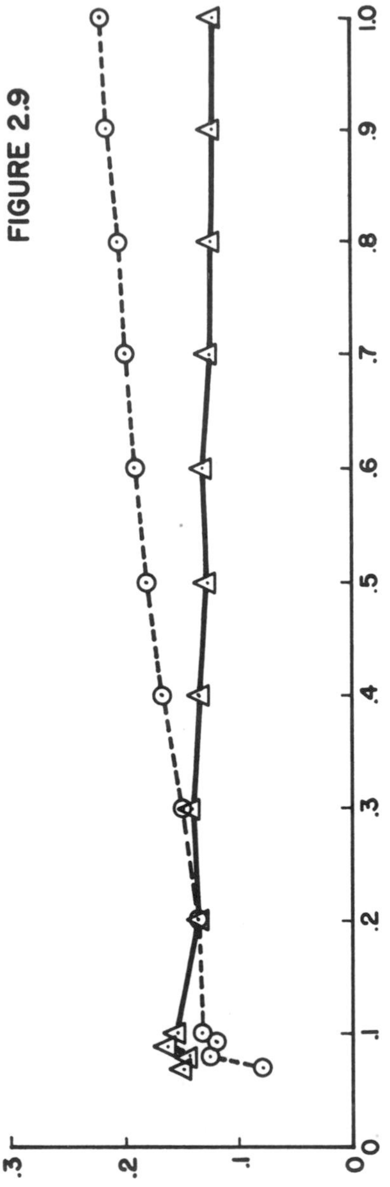


FIGURE 2.9

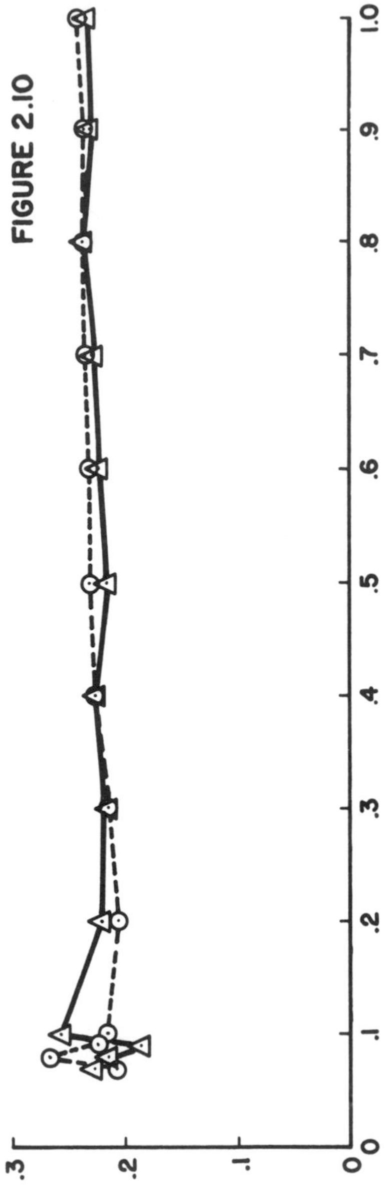


FIGURE 2.10

MEAN SQUARE ERROR

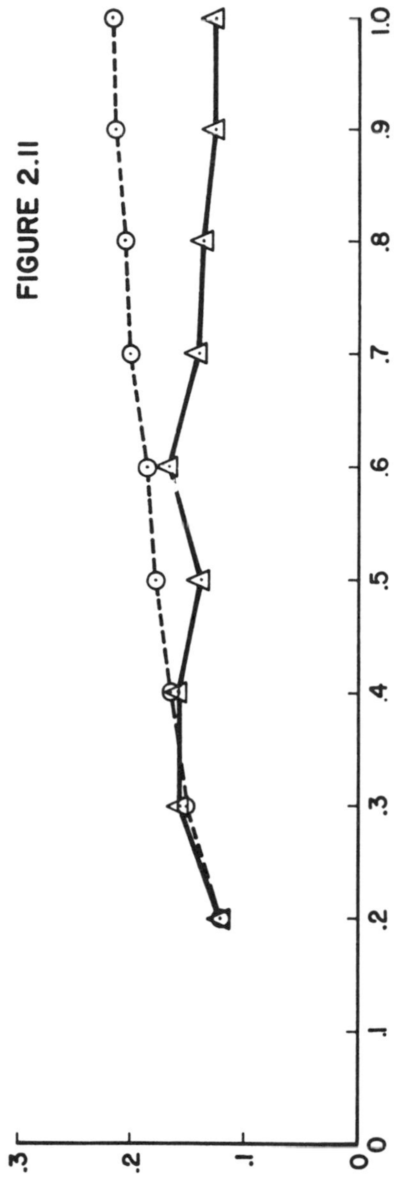


FIGURE 2.11

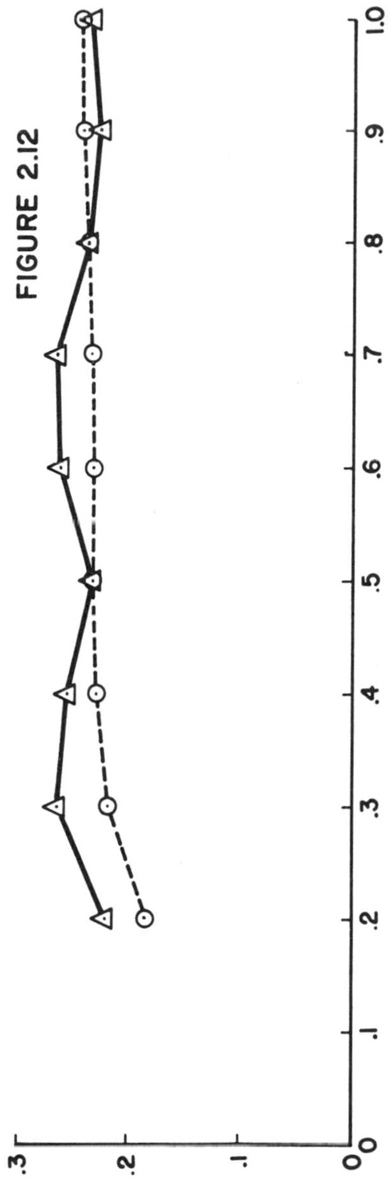


FIGURE 2.12

# 41



Reprinted from *Bell System Tech. J.*, **47**(4), 549–573 (1968)

# Adaptive Redundancy Removal in Data Transmission

By R. W. LUCKY

*This paper suggests an adaptive filter, similar to that used in automatic equalization, for use as a predictor in data compression systems. It discusses some of the applications of this adaptive predictor in digital data transmission. In the event of redundant data input to the system the predictor could be used to lower the transmitted power output required for a given error rate or to decrease the error rate while maintaining constant transmitted power. The action of these redundancy-removal and restoration systems is analyzed in simple cases involving Markov inputs.*

## I. INTRODUCTION

In the design, analysis, and testing of data transmission systems it is invariably assumed that the input digits are identically distributed, independent random variables. However, in many actual systems the input digits may arise from a physical source which imposes significant correlations in the data train. In these cases we know that the entropy of the source is less than when independent digits are presented. Accordingly, we should be able to use the redundancy in the input message to provide, in some sense, more efficient transmission. For example, we could imagine the redundancy being used to decrease bandwidth, to increase speed, to lower probability of error, or to lower average signal power.

Redundancy removal in analog transmission systems was investigated in the early 1950's by Oliver, Kretzmer, Harrison, and Elias[1–4]. Each of these papers relied on the theory of linear prediction as developed by Wiener in the early 1940's.[5] Figure 1 shows the basic idea. It is assumed that the input samples are taken from a stationary time series $\{x_n\}$. These samples are passed through a linear filter whose output $\hat{x}_n$ at time $t_n$ forms a linear prediction of the sample $x_n$ based on all preceding samples. The prediction $\hat{x}_n$ is subtracted from the actual sample $x_n$ and only the error $e_n$ is passed on for further processing and

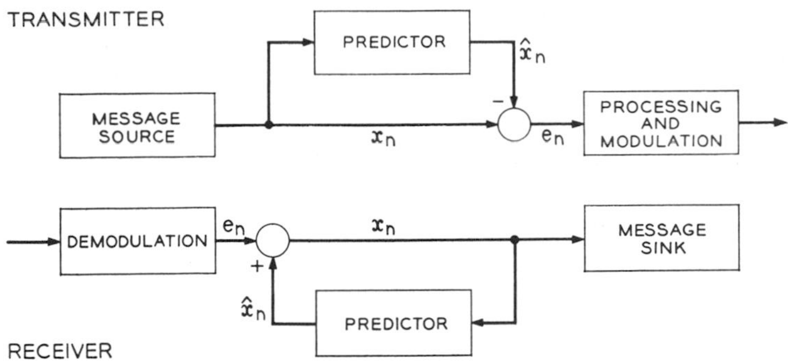


Fig. 1 — Predictive system.

transmission. Since the portion $\{\hat{x}_n\}$ "removed" from the input sequence is a deterministic function of the error sequence, no information has been lost and the original sequence can be reconstructed at the receiver by the feedback loop shown in the figure.

The philosophy of predictive systems has been widely studied for its application in bandwidth compression of telemetry data and of television; for example, see Kortman, Davisson, and O'Neal.[6–8] In these examples the error samples $e_k$ are quantized and transmitted by pcm. Because of redundancy, that is, predictability, in the source data, fewer digits per sample (and consequently less bandwidth) are required for transmitting the error samples than for transmitting the original samples for a given fidelity of reconstruction.

One of the difficulties with these data compression systems is in determining the predictor filter. Although the theory of linear prediction for stationary time series is well known, the practical determination of the statistical properties of the input data and the realization of the corresponding optimum filter are nearly impossible. Generally, an approximate average statistical description is used for the input data and a considerably simplified version of the optimum filter is constructed. Most existing compression schemes appear to use only linear or zero-order extrapolation of the previous sample to form the prediction of the succeeding sample. More complicated and adaptive prediction techniques have been confined to computer-processed data.

In this paper we describe a simply-instrumented adaptive filter for use as a predictor. This filter uses a finite tapped delay line whose coefficients are continually adjusted to provide a least squares prediction of incoming data. The coefficient settings are based on the statistics of a finite section of the past data (the learning period). As the statistics of the data during this learning period change, the coefficients are changed to provide an updated version of the predictor filter.

Although the most obvious applications of this adaptive predictor would be in the transmission of television or some other very redundant analog signal, we choose here to explore its application in digital data transmission. In the past, little attention seems to have been focused on the use of prediction in digital transmission. Presumably this is because the most effective use of prediction would be in the compression of the analog wave from which the digits are taken.

However, there do exist situations in which the input digital signal is not under the control of the transmission systems designer. This occurs notably in the design of data communications equipment. Although it has been common practice to use redundancy in speech signals to ease transmission system requirements (the TASI system is a dramatic example), nothing similar has been attempted with digital data signals. There would seem to be no compelling reason why any redundancy in digital signals should not be taken advantage of, as long as the error statistics of the output data were not adversely affected by the procedure. After describing a digital redundancy removal and restoration system we shall discuss its possible benefits to the customer and to the transmission plant.

## II. SYSTEM DESCRIPTION

Figure 2 shows a digital redundancy removal and restoration scheme. For simplicity we assume that the input digits $a_n$ are binary, although the technique obviously extends to multilevel transmission. The input sequence is passed through a shift-register transversal filter whose tap gains $c_k$ have been adjusted so that the filter output $\hat{a}_n$, where

$$\hat{a}_n = \sum_{k=1}^{N} c_k a_{n-k} , \tag{1}$$

is a linear least squares prediction of $a_n$. This prediction is subtracted from the actual sample $a_n$ and only the difference $e_n$ is passed to the modulator for transmission. Notice that, although $a_n$ is a binary variable taking on the values $\pm 1$, both $\hat{a}_n$ and $e_n$ are analog. Unless the digits $a_n$ are uncorrelated, the error samples $e_n$ will have smaller variance than the unit variance of the input data. Consequently, a linear modulator

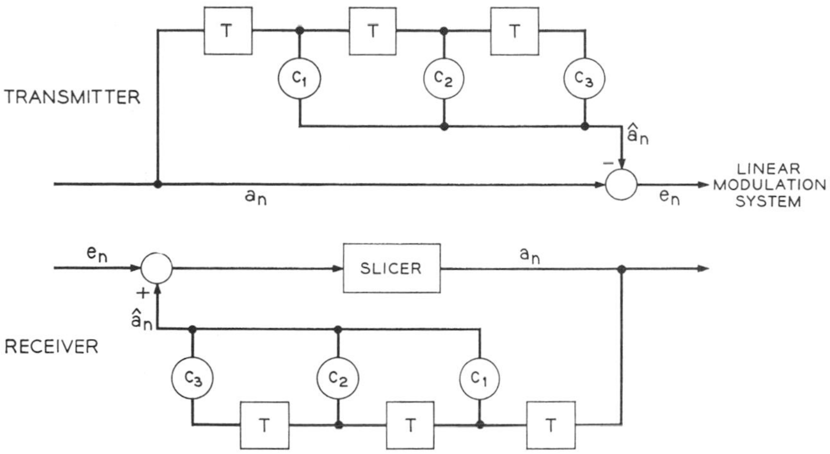


Fig. 2 — Digital redundancy removal and restoration.

will put out less line power in transmitting the error samples than in transmitting the original data.

After demodulation at the receiver, the missing, predictable, component $\hat{a}_n$ must be added to the error sample $e_n$ before slicing, in order to recover $a_n$. This component is obtained by a bootstrap arrangement wherein the detected symbols are passed through a transversal filter identical to that at the transmitter in order to form the predictions $\hat{a}_n$. The receiver is similar in arrangement to the circuitry used in dc restoration.

There are two relatively simple ways in which this system could be used to improve transmission efficiency. As shown in Figure 2 the system lowers the average transmitted power without appreciably affecting the output data error rate. In this mode of operation any benefit from the data redundancy is used to lower the load requirements on the transmission plant. If many data sets were equipped with such circuitry, the average power handled by the plant would be lowered in a statistical fashion. Some sets, transmitting entirely random data, would require their normal power complement. Others, transmitting redundant data, would require considerably less. Notice that this is exactly the type of effect which now takes place for voice transmission.

As the input data becomes entirely redundant in the limit, the transmitted power goes to zero. In this case the input data consists of a periodic pattern. In spite of the zero-level line signal, the pattern is reconstructed exactly at the receiver (in the absence of noise). Such an eventuality would alleviate the problems now encountered with the transmission of periodic data. These data patterns normally lead to tones, that is, line spectra, in the transmission channel which cause certain overloading and other system malfunctions.

Currently the problem is being treated in wideband transmission by the introduction of digital scramblers.[9] In practice the zero-level transmitted signal would not be a satisfactory solution to the tone problem since some signal strength would be required for synchronizing and timing maintenance. However, proper design of the system could ensure that some minimum signal strength was maintained under all circumstances. For example, a nonlinear element in each predictor could be used to keep the predictions smaller than unity. As long as the same nonlinearity were used in both transmitter and receiver, the data signal would be reconstructed perfectly at the receiver.

The other simple way to use redundancy removal to aid transmission would be to keep the level of transmitted power constant while lowering the probability of error. In this case, compensating gain controls would be placed at the transmitter output and at the receiver input. These controls would be adjusted to keep the transmitted power constant regardless of signal redundancy. During periods of redundancy most of the voltage presented to the slicer at the receiver would come via the feedback predictor and therefore would be noiseless (in the absence of errors). Since the small error signal transmitted would be greatly amplified to keep line power constant, the total noise presented to the slicer after complementary deamplification would be much smaller than in normal transmission. Consequently, the error rate would be diminished during periods of redundant data transmission.

Complementary amplification and deamplification surrounding channel noise introduction are automatically accomplished in transmission over compandored facilities. Normally for these channels we would expect that the error rate would be independent of transmitted power level. In the redundancy removal system, however, this mechanism is defeated by using the noiseless feedback in the detection process.

There are further uses of redundancy removal in data transmission, but they appear to involve more complicated system arrangements. For example, the bit rate and bandwidth of the data signal could be lowered for redundant data. This could be accomplished by slicing the prediction $\hat{a}_n$ to obtain a closest *digital* prediction and then subtracting $\hat{a}_n$ from $a_n$ in digital form. The resulting error digits could then be processed by run-length encoding to achieve message compression. Of course we would then need a buffer to ensure a constant channel bit rate. We will not discuss this type of system further here.

Thus far we have alluded to the possible benefits of redundancy removal in data transmission. There is also one major drawback—that of error propagation. Since the estimate $\hat{a}_n$ at the receiver depends on the correct reception of all previous data, the compensation at the receiver is perfect only in the absence of errors. When an error occurs, the probability of error in succeeding bits tends to be larger and an error propagating effect occurs. Notice that this effect does not depend on the particular circuit configuration for its existence, but is a philosophical necessity in any redundancy removal operation. We analyze the effect of error propagation in a simple example in Section V. Normally we would not expect the error propagation to increase the entire error rate by more than a small algebraic factor.

## III. THE ADAPTIVE PREDICTION FILTER

In the theory of linear prediction developed by Wiener[5] and others it is assumed that the input samples $a_n$ are taken from a stationary time series with known covariance function $R(n)$, where

$$E[a_m a_n] = R(m - n). \tag{2}$$

The power output, which is the mean square prediction error, is

$$P = E[e_n^2] = E\left\{\left(a_n - \sum_{k=1}^{N} c_k a_{n-k}\right)^2\right\}. \tag{3}$$

The coefficients $c_k$; $k = 1, \ldots N$, which minimize this prediction error, can be obtained by the solution of the $N$ simultaneous equations

$$\sum_{k=1}^{N} c_k R(n - k) = R(n); \qquad n = 1, 2, \cdots, N. \tag{4}$$

In case of an infinite filter ($N = \infty$) the coefficients $c_k$ and the prediction error are given by a method involving factoring of the spectral density $G(f)$ of the input process. Under proper conditions the prediction error $P$ can be expressed in the form

$$P = \exp\left[\int_{-\frac{1}{2}}^{\frac{1}{2}} \log G(f)\, df\right] \tag{5}$$

(See Doob for the mathematical niceties of this result.[10]) Notice that if the input symbols are independent, $G(f) = 1$, $|f| \leq 1/2$, and $P = 1$. Since the input power is also unity no gain is achieved by the prediction process. If, on the other hand, $G(f)$ is not flat the prediction error, $P$ is less than unity and power is saved.

While the mathematics of linear prediction for stationary time series serve as a guide to actual system performance, it is clear that the assumptions are philosophically inadmissible. Furthermore, since the data source is outside the designer's control, it would be extremely unlikely that the covariance function would be known in advance. For these reasons, Balakrishnan[11] in 1961 developed a mathematical formulation for a learning or adaptive predictor wherein the form of the prediction operator was dependent solely on the past data and not on any assumptions of stationarity or of prior knowledge of data statistics.

In Balakrishnan's formulation that prediction operator is chosen as optimum at time $t_n$ which works best when applied at times $t_{n-1}, \ldots, t_{n-L}$. Since all past information is available, we could "try out" all possible prediction operators on the previous data and select the operator for which

$$E_n = \sum_{j=1}^{L} [a_{n-j} - \hat{a}_{n-j}]^2 w_j \tag{6}$$

is minimum. The weights $w_j$ could be used to assign a relative importance to each past trial of the predictor.

For our finite linear predictor we have

$$E_n = \sum_{j=1}^{L} \left[ a_{n-j} - \sum_{k=1}^{N} c_k a_{n-j-k} \right]^2 w_j \, . \tag{7}$$

In order to develop a physical implementation for this adaptive filter we use a motivation based on a steepest descent approach. The derivatives of the error $E_n$ with respect to the coefficients $c_m$ are

$$\frac{\partial E_n}{\partial c_m} = - \sum_{j=1}^{L} 2w_j \left[ a_{n-j} - \sum_{k=1}^{N} c_k a_{n-j-k} \right] a_{n-j-m} \tag{8}$$

$$\frac{\partial E_n}{\partial c_m} = - \sum_{j=1}^{L} 2w_j e_{n-j} a_{n-j-m} \, . \tag{9}$$

Notice that these derivatives can be obtained by passing the product of sample $a_{n-m}$ and the error voltage $e_n$ through a filter with impulse response $\{w_j\}$. Thus we are led to the adaptive filter configuration shown in Figure 3. This configuration is entirely similar to that currently being used for equalization[12] and for echo suppression.[13, 14]

When the input samples $a_n$ are digital, the circuitry of Figure 3 is quite simple. The delay line becomes a shift register and the multipliers become simple polarity switches. However, the circuit is not limited to digital applications, but could be used in such analog functions as telemetry or television compression systems.

In any event, the response of the system, involving accuracy and settling time as well as stability, is controlled by selection of the smoothing filters $W(\omega)$. Basically these filters must perform an averaging followed by an integration. If the data were stationary and the memory $L$ sufficiently long, the result of averaging the product of the error and sample voltages for the $m^{\text{th}}$ tap coefficient would give (see equation 8)

$$y_m(t) \cong E[a_{n-m}e_n] = R(m) - \sum_{k=1}^{N} c_k(t)R(m-k). \tag{10}$$

Then these voltages would be integrated for use as tap coefficients, so that the governing system equations would be

$$\dot{c}_m(t) = A\left[R(m) - \sum_{k=1}^{N} c_k(t)R(m-k)\right] \quad \text{for} \quad m = 1, \cdots, N. \tag{11}$$

This system would be stable for all $A$, since the covariance matrix, whose $nm^{\text{th}}$ entry is $R(n\text{-}m)$, must be positive definite (see Davenport and Root[15]). All voltages $y_m(t)$ would be asymptotically reduced to

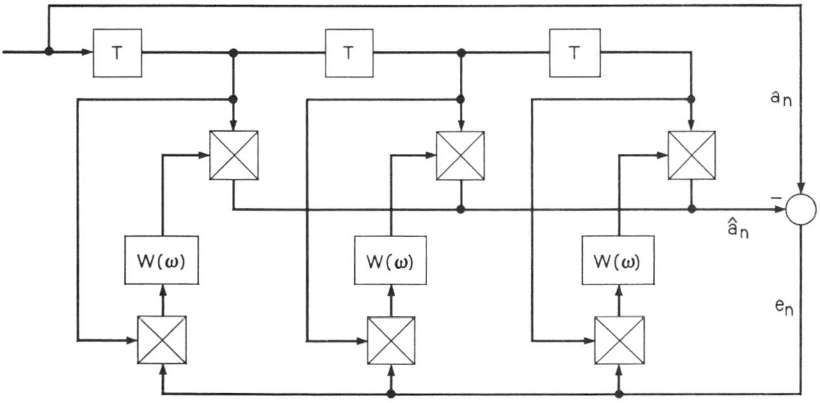


Fig. 3 — Adaptive prediction filter.

zero and the filter coefficients would asymptotically approach those of the optimum (least squares) linear predictor of equation (4).

For nonstationary data and realistic filters $W(\omega)$ the analysis of the nonlinear, multidimensional control system is extremely complicated. Let us study the dynamics of the one-dimensional system formed by using a one-tap predictor as a guide to the behavior of the system.

In order to put this analysis into proper perspective with regard to the system of Figure 2 we should observe that when the input data statistics change abruptly, both transmitter and receiver predictors undergo the same transients. If the predictors are identical, these transients cancel exactly at the receiver summer and no loss in noise margin is suffered. However, the statistics of the transmitted signal are affected by only the transmitter predictor. Therefore, the proper design of the adaptive predictor is crucial to obtaining desirable line power statistics, but not to the performance of the entire system.

## IV. THE ONE-TAP TRANSMITTER FOR BINARY DATA

Figure 4 shows a one-tap transmitter with a binary input signal of the form

$$\begin{aligned} s(t) &= \sum_{n=0}^{\infty} a_n r(t - nT) \\ a_n &= \pm 1 \\ r(t) &= \begin{cases} 1 & 0 \leqq t < T \\ 0 & \text{elsewhere} \end{cases}. \end{aligned} \tag{12}$$

The transmitted voltage is given by

$$e(t) = s(t) - c(t)s(t - T) \tag{13}$$

where

$$c(t) = Aw(t)*[s(t - T)e(t)]. \tag{14}$$

Because of the binary nature of the input $s^2(t) = 1$ and thus

$$c(t) = Aw(t)*[s(t)s(t - T) - c(t)]. \tag{15}$$

Let $m(t) = s(t)s(t-T)$; then the Laplace transform solution for $C(s)$ is*

* Some liberty has been taken with the shift-register starting state.

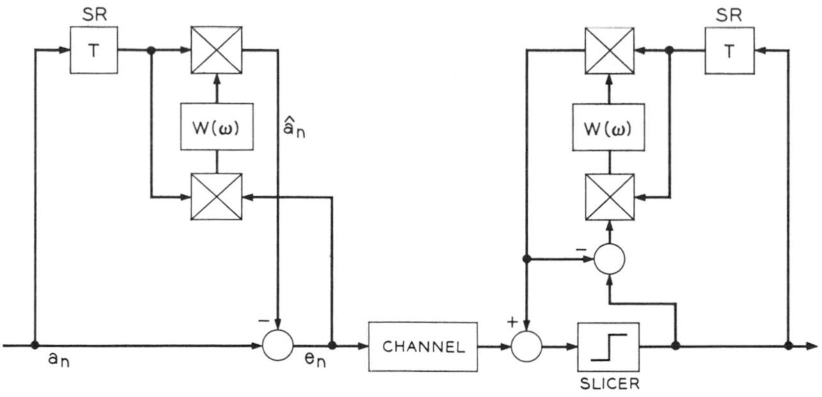


Fig. 4 — One-tap digital system.

$$C(s) = \frac{AW(s)M(s)}{1 + AW(s)}. \tag{16}$$

Now returning to equation (13) we multiply both sides by $s(t-T)$ to obtain

$$e(t)s(t - T) = m(t) - c(t). \tag{17}$$

Combining equations (16) and (17) gives

$$e(t)s(t - T) = m(t)*h(t) \tag{18}$$

where

$$H(s) = \frac{1}{1 + AW(s)}. \tag{19}$$

The output signal itself can be written by again multiplying equation (18) by $s(t-T)$

$$e(t) = s(t - T)[m(t)*h(t)]. \tag{20}$$

Notice that the special properties of binary sequences have been used in arriving at this solution, so that equation (20) does not hold for multilevel or analog input.

Figure 5(a) shows the mathematically equivalent transmitter given by equation (20) as well as its corresponding receiver. Since the second multiplier does not affect the transmitted power in any way, both transmitter and receiver can be simplified by its removal to result in the equivalent represented by Figure 5(b).* This final

* The systems differ in their noise performance, however.

equivalent system is amazingly simple and appears to bear little resemblance to the initial system of Figure 4. It is interesting to observe that, while the initial system was termed "adaptive," no one would seriously consider its equivalent in Figure 5(b) as being adaptive in any sense.

Figure 5(b) has an intriguing interpretation. The input data is first subjected to the nonlinear operation of delay and multiplication. The output of the multiplier is

$$m(t) = \sum_n a_n a_{n-1} r(t - nT). \tag{21}$$

This voltage has a mean value given by $R(1)$ in the stationary case. If the filter $W(\omega)$ has been designed as a low pass filter, then the filter $1/[1 + AW(\omega)]$ in the equivalent circuit is a high pass filter. Thus the dc component of $m(t)$ is removed before transmission and reinserted via a dc restorer at the receiver. In other words, a nonlinear operation on the input signal has converted the correlation into a spectral line which can then be removed by a time invariant linear filter. It would seem that some generalization of this concept should be possible, but as yet none has been found.

The equivalent circuit can be used for design purposes in selecting

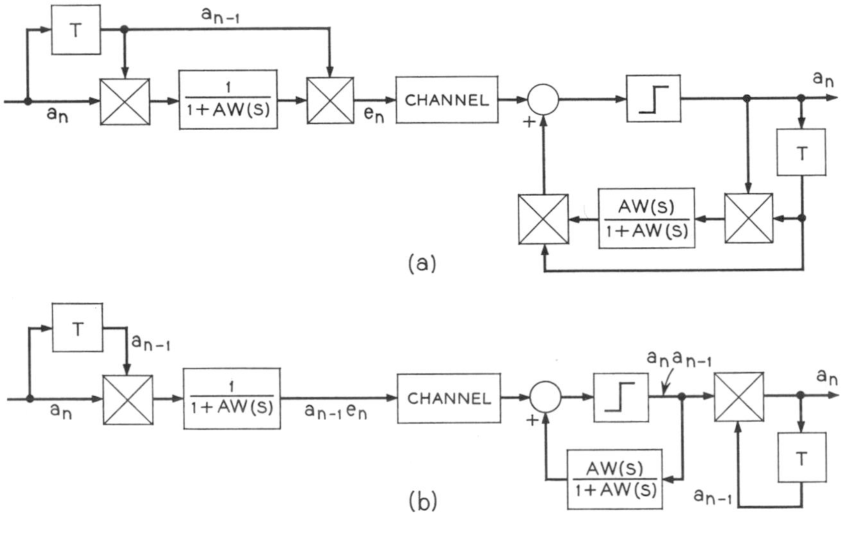


Fig. 5 — Equivalent binary one-tap systems. (a) Equivalent system. (b) Simplified equivalent.

$W(\omega)$, or for calculating line power or transient response. Here are the results of a few straightforward examples.

*Example 1*

Simple RC filter, dotting pattern input applied at time zero:

$$W(s) = \frac{\alpha}{s + \alpha}; \qquad \alpha = \frac{1}{RC}$$

$$a_n = \begin{cases} +1, & n \text{ even} \\ -1, & n \text{ odd} \end{cases}. \tag{22}$$

A deterministic sequence is to be transmitted. We find that the output of the equivalent circuit is

$$e(t)s(t - T) = -\left[\frac{1}{A + 1} u(t) + \frac{A}{A + 1} e^{-\alpha(A+1)t}\right]. \tag{23}$$

Thus the error voltage transmitted in the original circuit becomes

$$e(t) = \left[\sum_{n=0}^{\infty} (-1)^n r(t - nT)\right]\left[\frac{1}{A + 1} u(t) + \frac{A}{A + 1} e^{-\alpha(A+1)t}\right]. \tag{24}$$

The error voltage does not approach zero because of the lack of an integration in the smoothing filter.

*Example 2*

Simple RC filter, markov input:

If the input is a first order Markov process the one-tap predictor becomes the optimum linear predictor. (We study this case more thoroughly in the next section.) The covariance function of the input time series is taken to be

$$R(n) = R^{|n|}. \tag{25}$$

Since we now are dealing with a random input, our concern is with the transmitted power level rather than the exact waveform as in the previous example. The transmitted power is the same in Figures 4 and 5b, so we use the simpler structure of the latter diagram for analysis.

When the input Markov process is subjected to delay and multiplication, it can be shown that the resultant symbols $(a_n a_{n-1})$ have mean value $R$ and are uncorrelated. The spectral density of the multiplier output $m(t)$ is given by

$$S_M(\omega) = R^2\,\delta(\omega) + (1 - R^2)T\,\frac{\sin^2 \frac{\omega T}{2}}{\left(\frac{\omega T}{2}\right)^2}. \tag{26}$$

This spectral density can be multiplied by $|H(\omega)|^2$ and integrated to give the transmitted power. The power becomes

$$P = \frac{R^2}{(1 + A)^2} + (1 - R^2) \cdot \left\{ \frac{1}{(1 + A)^2} + \left[1 - \frac{1}{(1 + A)^2}\right]\left[\frac{1 - e^{-\alpha(1+A)T}}{\alpha(1 + A)T}\right]\right\}. \tag{27}$$

Ideally, of course, this power should be $(1-R^2)$, but the crude RC filter is unable to approximate this result unless the gain is high and the time constant $(1/\alpha)$ is large.

Better results in both examples could be achieved by an improved selection of the filter characteristic $W(\omega)$. We can see from the equivalent circuit that the best choice of $W(\omega)$ makes $1/[1 + AW(\omega)]$ an efficient high pass filter with a transmission zero at $\omega = 0$. Of course this must be compromised with any requirement on the filter response time.

In this section we stress the use of the equivalent circuit as a method of analysis rather than as an implementable system. Clearly, if one were to build a one-tap binary predictor, the circuit of Figure 5(b) would be preferred to that of the original system. However we believe that such a restricted system would not be of great practical interest.

While the implementation of the simple equivalent circuit cannot be extended to wider application, it is hoped that the easy analysis of the simple system conveys some insight into the performance of multiloop systems. This would be particularly true if there were small interaction between taps on the multiloop system. Such a situation would occur if the covariance $R(n)$ decreased rapidly with $n$.

## V. ERROR PROPAGATION

When noise is added in the transmission channel there is some probability of the received digits being incorrectly detected by the slicer. Even though the transmitted power might have been substantially reduced by the redundancy removal, the probability of an initial error is identical to that of a full power system. Once an error has been made, however, the probability of making subsequent errors is increased because of the incorrect symbol being used in redundancy restoration. Thus, errors tend to bunch together in the received data. Besides increasing the average probability of error this error propagation considerably complicates the problems of error control in the entire system.

Error propagation in dc restoration circuits has been examined by Zador, Aaron, and Simon.[16, 17] It appears to be a very complicated problem, in general, which is even more confused by the presence of the adaptive, pattern sensitive filters in the redundancy removal system we are considering here. Therefore, we shall attempt the analysis of only the simplest meaningful theoretical model. Both transmitter and receiver will have one-tap transversal filters as shown in Figure 4. The input data is taken to be a binary first order Markov process, with zero mean and covariance

$$R(n) = R^{|n|}.$$

The transition matrix for this process is:

| | | $a_{n+1}$: $+1$ | $a_{n+1}$: $-1$ |
|---|---|---|---|
| $a_n$ | $+1$ | $\frac{1+R}{2}$ | $\frac{1-R}{2}$ |
| | $-1$ | $\frac{1-R}{2}$ | $\frac{1+R}{2}$ |

The ideal linear predictor for this time series is simply $\hat{a}_n = Ra_{n-1}$ and the average transmitted power using this predictor is $1 - R^2$. Since the ideal predictor uses only a single tap filter, the assumption of single tap filters in the actual system is not particularly restrictive. If additional taps were used, their gains would be small and their effect on error propagation would not be significant.

We will assume that noise samples $\xi_k$, uncorrelated Gaussian random variables with zero mean and variance $\sigma^2$, are added to the transmitted symbols in the channel. We further assume that sufficient smoothing is done at the transmitter so that the tap gain may be fixed at its optimum value, $R$. Thus the transmitted samples are

$$e_k = a_k - Ra_{k-1}\,. \tag{28}$$

Now at the receiver we shall write the received symbols as $\beta_k a_k$. The parameter $\beta_k = \pm 1$ indicates the absence $(+1)$ or the presence $(-1)$ of an error at time $t_k$. If the tap gain at the receiver is denoted by the parameter $c$, the detected symbols can be written

$$\beta_k a_k = \operatorname{sgn}\,[a_k - a_{k-1}(R - c\beta_{k-1}) + \xi_k]. \tag{29}$$

Thus the error parameter $\beta_k$ is

$$\beta_k = \operatorname{sgn}\,[1 - a_k a_{k-1}(R - c\beta_{k-1}) + \eta_k] \tag{30}$$

where $\eta_k = \xi_k a_k$ has the same statistical properties as $\xi_k$. The probability of error at time $t_k$ is the probability that $\beta_k = -1$, which is the probability that $\eta_k$ is such that the term in brackets is negative.

Now we must turn our attention to the behavior of the receiver tap gain $c$. If no errors are made, then this gain is identical to the transmitter gain and as $k \to \infty$, $c \to R$. However, because of the presence of errors, the receiver tap gain tends to be different from the transmitter tap gain. At time $t_k$ the output voltage of the multiplier at the receiver is

$$v_k = \beta_k a_k \beta_{k-1} a_{k-1} - c. \tag{31}$$

The random variables $v_k$ are averaged to determine the movement of $c$. Notice that, since $|\,\beta_k a_k \beta_{k-1} a_{k-1}\,| = 1$, the magnitude of $c$ cannot exceed unity except as a transient starting state. This eliminates any possibility of a runaway in $c$ resulting from unusual error patterns.

We assume that the action of the loop at the receiver is to reduce to zero the expectation of the multiplier output voltage at time infinity. Thus

$$E[v_\infty] = 0 = \lim_{k\to\infty} E[\beta_k a_k \beta_{k-1} a_{k-1}] - c_\infty\,. \tag{32}$$

This type of final behavior would be exhibited by systems in which $W(\omega)$ consisted of a long term averaging followed by an integration. The expectation of the term in brackets in equation (32) depends on $c_\infty$ itself, so in general we end with a fairly complicated equation requiring a trial and error solution for $c_\infty$. By taking the limit as $k \to \infty$ of the expectation we eliminate the dependence on time and on the initial probability distributions for the random variables involved.

Define a vector random variable $\bar{\alpha}_k = (a_k\,,\, \beta_k)$ taking on the four possible states (+1, +1), (+1, −1), (−1, +1) and (−1, −1), denoted by states 1 through 4, respectively. Because $a_k$ is Markov and since the expression for $\beta_k$ in equation (30) involves only $a_k$, $a_{k-1}$, $\beta_{k-1}$, and $\eta_k$, we conclude that $\bar{\alpha}$ is also Markov. The four-by-four transition matrix $\pi$ for $\bar{\alpha}$ has entries $p_{ij}$ which may be calculated from the original transition matrix for the input symbols $a_k$ and from equation (30) for the probabilities of error in various states. Table I lists these transition probabilities. If the 4-entry row vector $\bar{w}^{(k)}$ gives the probabilities of $\bar{\alpha}_k$ assuming each of the four possible states, then

$$\bar{w}^{(k)} = \bar{w}^{(k-1)}\pi. \tag{33}$$

In terms of the initial state distribution $\bar{w}^{(0)}$

$$\bar{w}^{(n)} = \bar{w}^{(0)}\pi^n. \tag{34}$$

For $|R| < 1$ it is clear from standard Markov chain theory (see, for example, Reference 18) that steady-state probabilities exist for

Table I—Transition Probabilities for $\bar{\alpha}_k = (a_k, \beta_k)$

$$Q(x) = \int_x^\infty \frac{e^{-y^2/2}}{\sqrt{2\pi}}\,dy$$

$$p_{11} = p_{33} = \left(\frac{1+R}{2}\right)\left[1 - Q\left(\frac{1-R+c}{\sigma}\right)\right]$$

$$p_{12} = p_{34} = \left(\frac{1+R}{2}\right)Q\left(\frac{1-R+c}{\sigma}\right)$$

$$p_{13} = p_{31} = \left(\frac{1-R}{2}\right)\left[1 - Q\left(\frac{1+R-c}{\sigma}\right)\right]$$

$$p_{14} = p_{32} = \left(\frac{1-R}{2}\right)Q\left(\frac{1+R-c}{\sigma}\right)$$

$$p_{21} = p_{43} = \left(\frac{1+R}{2}\right)\left[1 - Q\left(\frac{1-R-c}{\sigma}\right)\right]$$

$$p_{22} = p_{44} = \left(\frac{1+R}{2}\right)Q\left(\frac{1-R-c}{\sigma}\right)$$

$$p_{23} = p_{41} = \left(\frac{1-R}{2}\right)\left[1 - Q\left(\frac{1+R+c}{\sigma}\right)\right]$$

$$p_{24} = p_{42} = \left(\frac{1-R}{2}\right)Q\left(\frac{1+R+c}{\sigma}\right)$$

the transition matrix $\pi$, that is, $\bar{w}^{(n)}$ approaches a constant vector $\bar{w}$ as $n \to \infty$ independent of $\bar{w}^{(0)}$. The steady-state probabilities of the four possible states can be obtained by the solution of the equations given by

$$\bar{w}\pi = \bar{w}. \tag{35}$$

Some algebraic manipulation yields the probabilities

$$w_1 = P(a_\infty = +1, \beta_\infty = +1) = \frac{\frac{1}{2}(1 - p_{22} - p_{24})}{1 - p_{22} + p_{12} - p_{24} + p_{14}} \tag{36}$$

$$w_2 = P(a_\infty = +1, \beta_\infty = -1) = \tfrac{1}{2} - w_1 \tag{37}$$

$$w_3 = P(a_\infty = -1, \beta_\infty = +1) = w_1 \tag{38}$$

$$w_4 = P(a_\infty = -1, \beta_\infty = -1) = \tfrac{1}{2} - w_1 \tag{39}$$

where the transition probabilities $p_{12}$, $p_{14}$, $p_{22}$, and $p_{24}$ are given in Table I as functions of $c$, $R$, and $\sigma$.

The expected value of the multiplier output at time infinity can now be written in terms of the steady-state probabilities $w_i$ and the transition probabilities $p_{ij}$.

$$E[v_\infty] = w_1[p_{11} - p_{12} - p_{13} + p_{14}] + w_2[p_{22} + p_{23} - p_{21} - p_{24}]$$
$$+ w_3[p_{32} + p_{33} - p_{31} - p_{34}] + w_4[p_{41} + p_{44} - p_{42} - p_{43}] - c. \tag{40}$$

Again some algebraic manipulation yields the result

$$E[v_\infty] = \frac{R[1-p_{14}-p_{24}-p_{22}-p_{12}]+2[p_{14}-p_{12}]+4[p_{22}p_{12}-p_{24}p_{14}]}{1-p_{22}+p_{12}-p_{24}+p_{14}} - c. \tag{41}$$

The value of the tap gain at time infinity can be found by trial and error. A value of $c$ is assumed, the transition probabilities are computed and $E[v_\infty]$ is found. The value of $c$ for which $E[v_\infty] = 0$ is $c_\infty$. Notice that under suitable assumptions $E[v_\infty]$ gives the rate of change of the coefficient $c$ in the dynamic action of the system.

The probability of error after the system has settled is simply the probability that $\bar{a}_\infty$ is in a state where $\beta_\infty = -1$, which is simply $(w_2 + w_4)$.

$$P_e = \frac{p_{12} + p_{14}}{1 - p_{22} + p_{12} - p_{24} + p_{14}}. \tag{42}$$

The transition probabilities here must be computed using $c_\infty$.

Expressions (41) and (42) have been written in terms of only those transition probabilities which involve errors. Thus, as $\sigma \to 0$, each of the transition probabilities in (41) and (42) approaches zero,

$c_\infty \to R$, and $P_e \to 0$. Each of these probabilities can be visualized as the probability that the noise (zero mean, variance $\sigma^2$) is greater than the one of these four thresholds:

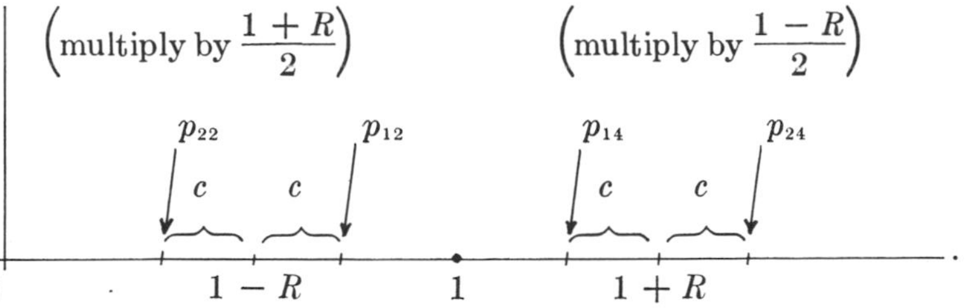


Thus $p_{24}$ is the smallest transition probability, while $p_{22}$ is the largest.

If the transition probabilities are small, it can be seen from equation (42) that $P_e$ is principally determined by $(p_{12} + p_{14})$, which is minimized by $c = R$. Also we notice from equation (42) that the tap gain $c$ approaches $R$ very closely for small transition probabilities. In general, however, $c = R$ will not be the best setting to minimize the error probability in equation (42), nor is it the setting to which the loop settles. Unfortunately it appears that these are not compensating offsets. For example, in Figure 6 we have plotted $P_e$ and $E[v_\infty]$ against $c$, for a case in which $R = 0.4$ and $\sigma = 0.4$. Although neither

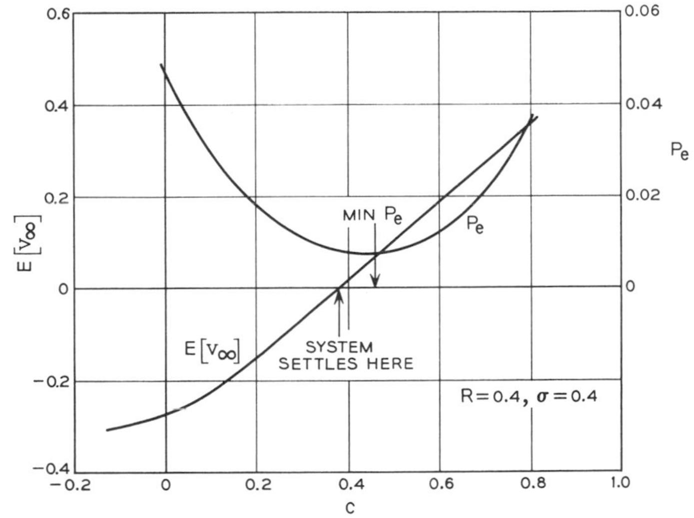


Fig. 6 — Probability of error and $E[v_\infty]$ vs receiver tap gain $c$.

effect is very significant, it can be seen that the system settles ($E[v_\infty] = 0$) for a value of $c$ somewhat smaller than $R$, while the minimum error probability is obtained at a value of $c$ somewhat larger than $R$.

In all but the most severe noise conditions the approximation of $c_\infty = R$ would be satisfactory and we would have

$$P_e|_{c=R} = \frac{Q\left(\frac{1}{\sigma}\right)}{1 - \left(\frac{1+R}{2}\right)Q\left(\frac{1-2R}{\sigma}\right) - \left(\frac{1-R}{2}\right)Q\left(\frac{1+2R}{\sigma}\right) + Q\left(\frac{1}{\sigma}\right)}. \tag{43}$$

But $Q(1/\sigma)$ is the probability of error in the original system (no redundancy removal). If this probability, called $P_{e0}$, is small, then $Q(1 + 2R/\sigma)$ is much smaller and we have the very good approximation

$$P_e|_{P_{e0}\text{ small}} \cong \frac{P_{e0}}{\left[1 - \left(\frac{1+R}{2}\right)Q\left(\frac{1-2R}{\sigma}\right)\right]} \tag{44}$$

The factor in the denominator gives the amplification of the original error rate due to error propagation. Finally if $R > 1/2$, then $Q(1 - 2R/\sigma)$ approaches unity and we get the severe dependence upon $R$

$$P_e|_{\substack{P_{e0}\text{ small}\\ R>\frac{1}{2}}} \cong \frac{2P_{e0}}{1-R}. \tag{45}$$

The most significant aspect of the error propagation behavior of the circuit is that the redundancy removal and restoration system has impressed the statistics of the input data (Markov here) upon the error statistics of the output. It is clear that this philosophy would hold in general. In the case of highly correlated input we would end with highly correlated errors. The problems of error control could be made quite severe in this manner.

## VI. EXPERIMENTAL RESULTS

A three-tap, adaptive transmitter and a similar receiver were designed and constructed by V. G. Koll. The system was designed for binary data transmission so that the multipliers in Figure 3 became polarity switches, while the delay line took the form of a shift register. The filters $W(s)$ consisted of simple RC low pass sections followed by integrators, that is,

$$W(s) = \frac{\alpha}{s(s + \alpha)}. \tag{46}$$

With this choice of smoothing, the steady-state error for a periodic input (period 3 or less here) was zero. It was in fact observed that during the transmission of periodic data the transmitter could be disconnected with no effect on the received data pattern.

The input data for the system was obtained by passing white Gaussian noise through a variable cutoff, low pass filter. If we assume an ideal low pass filter, with cutoff frequency $W$ Hz, then the autocorrelation function of the filter output is

$$R_1(\tau) = 2N_0W\left[\frac{\sin 2\pi W\tau}{2\pi W\tau}\right]. \tag{47}$$

This voltage is then sampled at rate $(1/T)$ and subjected to infinite clipping so as to produce the correlated input bits. Van Vleck and Middleton[19] show that the resulting autocorrelation is

$$R(n) = \frac{2}{\pi}\sin^{-1}\left[\frac{\sin 2\pi nWT}{2\pi nWT}\right]. \tag{48}$$

For a filter cutoff of $1/2T$ Hz the data is uncorrelated. By decreasing the filter cutoff frequency the redundancy in the data can be increased.

The action of the adaptive redundancy remover is shown in Figure 7 for two different values of filter cutoff. Notice that as the redundancy is increased the transmitted waveform has longer periods of near zero voltage where predictability is good and occasional peaks where the predictor is "surprised." Except for a few minor discontinuities the reconstructed signal before slicing at the receiver is the same as the original input waveform at the transmitter. The relative power saving as a function of filter cutoff is shown in Figure 8.

In order to predict system performance in Gaussian noise we make the crude approximation that the input process is Markov with $R(1)$ as given in equation (48). According to this approximation the transmitted power should be $1 - R(1)^2$. This value is also shown in Figure 8 in comparison with the actual measured power output. Since the exact correlation function is known, the theoretical signal power output could be computed precisely through equation (4). However, we have no corresponding means of computing the degree of error propagation

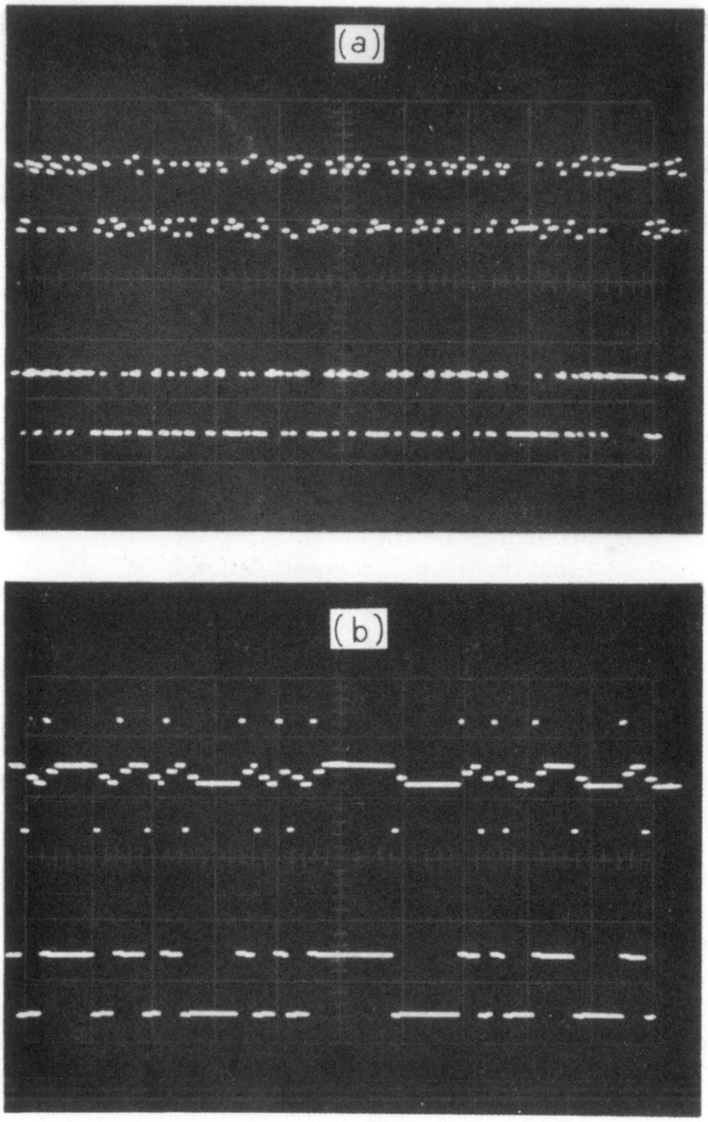


Fig. 7 — Transmitted and reconstructed signals. (a) Filter cutoff $\omega T = 0.4$ [little redundancy, $R(1) = 0.15$]. (b) Filter cutoff $\omega T = 0.1$ [moderate redundancy, $R(1) = 0.77$].

for the non-Markov source. The approximate curve of signal power in Figure 8 is shown only as a way of evaluating the Markov approximation for later use in predicting error propagation values.

Bandlimited white Gaussian noise was added to the transmitted signal, and error rates were experimentally determined by V. G. Koll at a number of filter cutoff (redundancy) positions. The results of these tests are shown in Figure 9 in curves of probability of error versus signal-to-noise ratio. Beside these measured curves have been plotted theoretically computed curves which are based on the Markov approximation and on the use of equation (43) for $P_e$.

Although all necessary information for performance determination is contained in Figure 9, it is instructive to plot two additional curves of probability of error versus filter cutoff. These curves are shown in Figure 10. In one curve the transmitter and receiver gains are held constant so that the line power decreases according to the curve of Figure 8 while the probability of error increases with increasing redundancy because of the effects of error propagation. In the other curve of Figure 10 the transmitter and receiver gains have been adjusted with increasing redundancy so as to hold line power constant. In this case the probability of error decreases with increasing redundancy.

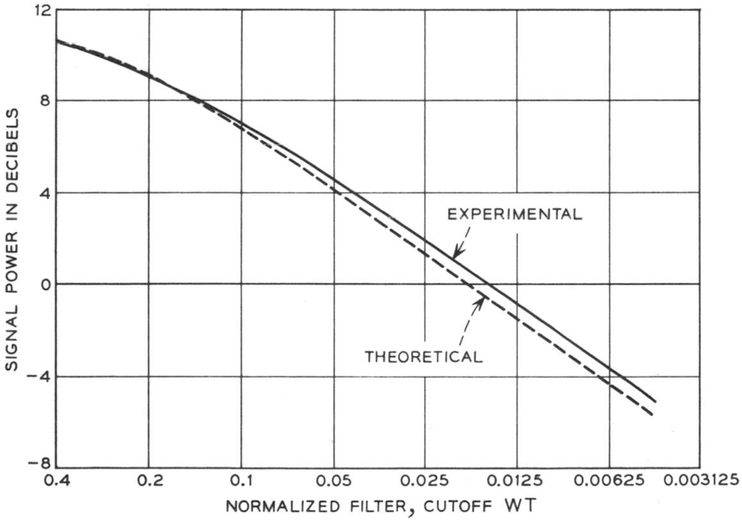


Fig. 8 — Signal power saving by redundancy removal.

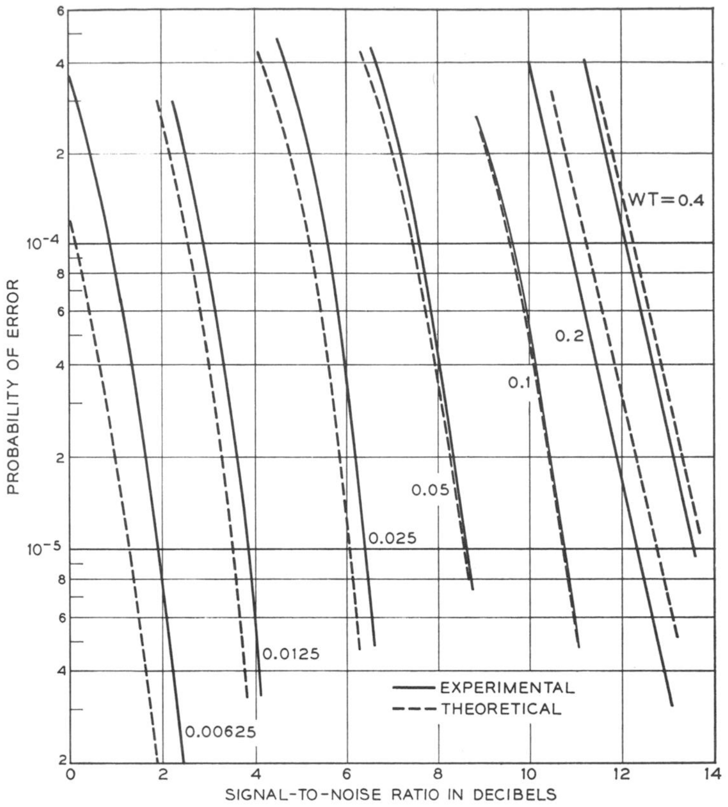


Fig. 9 — Performance of redundancy removal system at various values of normalized filter cutoff $\omega T$.

## VII. CONCLUSION

We have advanced two main points. First we suggest the possibility of using an easily-implemented adaptive predictor for data compression systems. Second, we investigated the use of this adaptive predictor in digital transmission.

We have seen that the predictor can be used to increase transmission efficiency for redundant data either by decreasing signal power for a given error rate or by decreasing probability of error for a given signal power. Although the required circuitry for the digital application is quite simple, it is nearly impossible to make an economic evaluation of the system because of the complete lack of knowledge of the prevalence and degree of redundancy in customer input data.

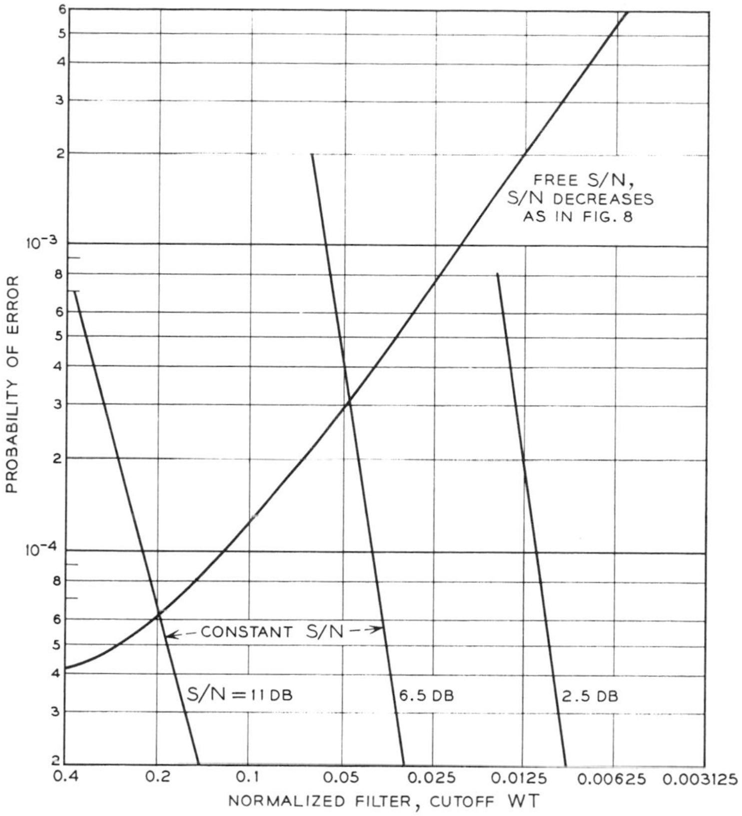


Fig. 10 — Probability of error vs filter cutoff for constant and for free S/N.

## VIII. ACKNOWLEDGEMENT

The author is indebted to V. G. Koll who designed, constructed, and tested the three-tap experimental ssytem. Mr. Koll also made the photos and the experimental performance curves in Figures 7 through 10.

## REFERENCES

1. Oliver, B. N., "Efficient Coding," B.S.T.J., *31,* No. 4 (July 1952), pp. 724–750.
2. Kretzmer, E. R., "Statistics of Television Signals," B.S.T.J., *31,* No. 4 (July 1952), pp. 751–763.
3. Harrison, C. W., "Experiments with Linear Prediction in Television," B.S.T.J., *31,* No. 4 (July 1952), pp. 764–783.
4. Elias, P., "Predictive Coding," IRE Trans. Inform. Theory, *IT*-1, No. 1 (March 1955), pp. 16–33.

5. Wiener, N., *Extrapolation, Interpolation and Smoothing of Stationary Time Series,* Cambridge, Mass.: MIT Press, 1949.
6. Kortman, C. M., "Redundancy Reduction—A Practical Method of Data Compression," Proc. IEEE, *55,* No. 3 (March 1967), pp. 253–263.
7. Davison, L. D., "Theory of Adaptive Data Compression," in *Recent Advances in Communication Systems,* vol. 2, ed. A. V. Balakrishnan, New York: Academic Press, 1966.
8. O'Neal, J. B., "Predictive Quantizing Systems," B.S.T.J., *45,* No. 5 (May-June 1966), pp. 689–721.
9. Savage, J. E., "Some Simple Self-Synchronizing Digital Data Scramblers," B.S.T.J., *46,* No. 2 (February 1967), pp. 449–487.
10. Doob, J. L., *Stochastic Processes,* Chapter 12, New York: John Wiley and Sons, Inc., 1953.
11. Balakrishnan, A. V., "An Adaptive Non-Linear Data Predictor," 1962 Nat. Telemetering Conf. Proc.
12. Lucky, R. W. and Rudin, H. R., "An Automatic Equalizer for General-Purpose Communication Channels," B.S.T.J., *46,* No. 9 (November 1967), pp. 2179–2208.
13. Becker, F. K. and Rudin, H. R., "Application of Automatic Transversal Filters to the Problem of Echo Suppression," B.S.T.J., *45,* No. 10 (December 1966), pp. 1847–1850.
14. Sondhi, M. M. and Presti, A. J., "A Self-Adaptive Echo Canceller," B.S.T.J., *45,* No. 10 (December 1966), pp. 1851–1853.
15. Davenport, W. B. and Root, W. L., *An Introduction to the Theory of Random Signals and Noise,* New York: McGraw-Hill Book Co., Inc., 1958, p. 105.
16. Zador, P. L., "Error Probabilities in Data System Pulse Regenerator with DC Restoration," B.S.T.J., *45,* No. 6 (July-August 1966), pp. 979–984.
17. Aaron, M. R. and Simon, M. K., "Approximation of the Error Probability in a Regenerative Repeater with Quantized Feedback," B.S.T.J., *45,* No. 10 (December 1966), pp. 1845–1847.
18. Kemeny, J. G. and Snell, J. L., *Finite Markov Chains,* New York: D. Van Nostrand Co., Inc., 1959.
19. Van Vleck, J. H. and Middleton, D., "The Spectrum of Clipped Noise," Proc. IEEE, *54,* No. 1 (January 1966), pp. 2–19 (reprint).

# 42



Reprinted from *IEEE Trans. Inform. Theory,* **IT-16**(2), 152–159, 161 (1970)

# Nonlinear Estimation With Quantized Measurements—PCM, Predictive Quantization, and Data Compression

RENWICK E. CURRY, MEMBER, IEEE, WALLACE E. VANDER VELDE, MEMBER, IEEE, AND JAMES E. POTTER, MEMBER, IEEE

***Abstract*—Statistics conditioned on quantized measurements are considered in the general case. These results are specialized to Gaussian parameters and then extended to discrete-time linear systems. The conditional mean of the system's state vector may be found by passing the conditional mean of the measurement history through the Kalman filter that would be used had the measurements been linear. Repetitive use of Bayes' rule is not required. Because the implementation of this result requires lengthy numerical quadrature, two approximations are considered: the first is a power-series expansion of the probablity-density function; the second is a discrete-time version of a previously proposed algorithm that assumes the conditional distribution is normal. Both algorithms may be used with any memory length on stationary or nonstationary data. The two algorithms are applied to the noiseless-channel versions of the PCM, predictive quantization, and predictive-comparison data compression systems; ensemble-average performance estimates of the nonlinear filters are derived. Simulation results show that the performance estimates are quite accurate for most of the cases tested.**

Manuscript received August 16, 1968; revised June 18, 1969. A major portion of this work was presented at the IEEE International Symp. on Information Theory, Ellenville, N. Y., January 28–31, 1969. The research was sponsored by NASA Grant NsG 254-62, and is based in part on a Ph.D. dissertation submitted to the Dept. of Aeron. and Astron., Massachusetts Institute of Technology, Cambridge.

The authors are with the Department of Aeronautics and Astronautics, Massachusetts Institute of Technology, Cambridge, Mass., 02139.

## I. Introduction and Summary

THE increasing demand on existing digital facilities (e.g., communication channels and data storage) can be alleviated by representing the same amount of information with fewer bits at the expense of more sophisticated data processing. The current interest in this area [1] goes by the various names of "redundancy reduction," "data compression," and others. Common to the great majority of these approaches is the problem of computing estimates from quantized data. This paper considers the analysis and implementation of nonlinear estimation with quantized measurements, and these techniques are applied to three types of digital systems—PCM, predictive quantization, and predictive-comparison data compression.

*Relevant Work*

Much work has been done in the area of linear filtering of quantized measurements [2]–[4], and some has been done on the general nonlinear filtering problem [5]–[7]. Unfortunately, these latter treatments require either the repetitive use of Bayes' rule, or the power-series expansion of the nonlinear measurement function, a technique that is not applicable to the quantizer's staircase input–output graph. Balikrishnan [9] presents an adaptive nonlinear predictor, but to the best of the authors' knowledge, only Meier *et al.* [8] have specifically considered nonlinear estimation with quantized measurements using a priori information. They derive some nonlinear estimates including the conditional mean and covariance of a scalar state based on one quantized measurement. The a priori distribution for both scalars is assumed to be Gaussian, and they indicate that subsequent estimates must be found by repetitive use of Bayes' rule, since the posterior distribution is no longer normal.

The PCM problem is considered by Ruchkin [2], Steiglitz [3], and Kellog [4] who use linear filtering to reconstruct the system's input. Fine [10] gives a theoretical treatment of optimum digital systems with an example of predictive quantization (feedback around a binary quantizer). Bello *et al.* [11] have computed Fine's nonlinear feedback function by Monte Carlo techniques and give some simulation results. Gish [12], O'Neal [13], and Irwin and O'Neal [14] consider the problem of designing linear-feedback functions. Predictive-comparison data compression systems are in the class of predictive-quantization systems. In [15] Davisson finds the (approximate) optimum linear-feedback operation for small thresholds; in [16] he considers an adaptive system. A review of many theoretical analyses is contained in [17].

*Summary*

Linear estimation uses the quantizer's staircase input–output graph. Nonlinear estimation uses the information that the quantized measurements $z$ lie in a hypercube $A$. In Section II, it is shown that moments conditioned on quantized measurements can be computed in two steps: 1) find the expectation conditioned on a measurement $z$ (the usual estimation problem); 2) average this function of $z$ conditioned on the event $z \in A$. These results are specialized to Gaussian distributions and then extended to linear dynamical systems; the conditional mean of the state vector is found by passing the conditional mean of the measurement history through the Kalman filter that would be used had the measurements been linear. Thus, the conditional mean can be computed without the repetitive use of Bayes' rule.

Section III considers two approximate nonlinear filters to compute the conditional mean of stationary and nonstationary data. The first involves a power-series expansion to find the conditional probability-density function. The second is a recursive computation that approximates the conditional distribution just prior to a quantized measurement by a normal distribution. Section IV applies these approximations to the noiseless-channel versions of the PCM, predictive quantization, and predictive-comparison data-compression systems. Estimates of the ensemble performance are derived for each system. This is extremely important in design work since it allows evaluation of system performance without Monte Carlo simulation.

The three systems have been simulated on a digital computer, and the actual performance is compared to the ensemble estimates in Section V; agreement is quite good for most of the cases tested. Section VI closes with a summary of the major conclusions of the results.

## II. Conditional Statistics

*Preliminaries*

Let $x$ be an $n$-component parameter vector and $z$ an $m$-component measurement vector. They are related through a (perhaps nonlinear) measurement equation that may or may not include noisy observations. It is assumed that the joint probability-density function of $x$ and $z$, $p_{x,z}(\xi, \zeta)$, exists and is known. Let the individual components of $z$ be quantized, and thus $z \in A$ implies $\{a^i \leq z^i < b^i,\ i = 1, \cdots, m\}$. The majority of the following results do not depend on the fact that $A$ is a hypercube.

*Conditional Expectations*

It is well known (e.g., [18], p. 37) that if $\mathfrak{F}_1$ and $\mathfrak{F}_2$ are Borel fields and $\mathfrak{F}_1 \subset \mathfrak{F}_2$, then for the random variable $y$

$$\mathcal{E}[\mathcal{E}(y|\mathfrak{F}_2)|\mathfrak{F}_1) = \mathcal{E}(y|\mathfrak{F}_1]. \tag{1}$$

For the purposes of estimation with quantized measurements, let $y$ be $f(x)$, $\mathfrak{F}_1$ be generated by $z \in A$, and $\mathfrak{F}_2$ be generated by $z$. The equality (1) is now reversed, i.e., the unknown quantity becomes the known quantity, with the result that

$$\mathcal{E}[f(x) \mid z \in A] = \mathcal{E}[\mathcal{E}(f(x) \mid z) \mid z \in A]. \tag{2}$$

Observe that the expectation of $f(x)$ conditioned on quantized measurements can be performed in two steps: 1) find $\mathcal{E}(f(x) \mid z)$; this is the usual goal of estimation with unquantized measurements; 2) find the expectation of $\mathcal{E}(f(x) \mid z)$ conditioned on $z \in A$. For step 2) one must use the probability-density function for $z$ conditioned on $z \in A$.

$$p_{z|z\in A}(\zeta) = \begin{cases} \dfrac{p_z(\zeta)}{P(z \in A)} = \dfrac{p_z(\zeta)}{\displaystyle\int_A p_z(\zeta)\, d\zeta} & \zeta \in A \\ 0 & \zeta \notin A \end{cases} \tag{3}$$

where $p_z(\zeta)$ is the a priori probability density of the measurement vector.

*Gaussian Parameters*

Let the distribution of the parameter vector $x$ be normal with mean $\bar{x}$ and covariance $M$: $N[\bar{x}, M]$. Let the measurements be linearly related to $x$ with additive independent observation noise.

$$z = Hx + v \tag{4}$$

where $H$ is an $m \times n$ matrix and $v$ is the noise vector $N[0, R]$. To find the mean of $x$ conditioned on quantized measurements let $f(x) = x$. The results of executing the first step in the procedure are well known.

$$\mathcal{E}(x \mid z) = \bar{x} + K[z - H\bar{x}] \tag{5}$$

where

$$K = MH^T(HMH^T + R)^{-1}. \tag{6}$$

The second step in the procedure is to take the expectation of (5) conditioned on $z \in A$ to find the mean of $x$ conditioned on $z \in A$.

$$\mathcal{E}(x \mid z \in A) = \bar{x} + K[\mathcal{E}(z \mid z \in A) - H\bar{x}]. \tag{7}$$

Note the importance of the weighting $K$, which is optimum for linear measurements, in this nonlinear estimate. It is easily shown [19] that the covariance in the estimate conditioned on $z \in A$ is given by

$$\text{cov}\,(x \mid z \in A) = P + K\,\text{cov}\,(z \mid z \in A)K^T \tag{8}$$

where $P$ is the covariance of $x$ that would be obtained had the measurements been linear:

$$P = \text{cov}\,(x \mid z) = M - MH^T(HMH^T + R)^{-1}HM. \tag{9}$$

Both the conditional mean and covariance reduce to the proper form when the measurements are unquantized since the probability-density function of $z$ conditioned on $z \in A$ approaches an impulse. Interestingly enough, (8) shows that quantization increases the (minimum) variance as though it were uncertainty added *after* a linear measurement had been processed. This is in sharp distinction to the point of view that treats quantization as observation noise added *before* the linear measurement.

*Extension to Linear Systems*

Assume that a Gauss–Markov process is described by the following equations. Here, as elsewhere, we use subscripts to denote the time index and superscripts to denote elements of an array.

$$x_{i+1} = \Phi_i x_i + w_i, \qquad i = 0, \cdots, K \tag{10}$$

$$z_i = H_i x_i + v_i, \qquad i = 1, \cdots, K \tag{11}$$

$$x_0 = N[\bar{x}_0, P_0], \tag{12}$$

$$\mathcal{E}(w_i) = 0, \qquad \mathcal{E}(w_i w_j^T) = Q_i \delta_{ij} \tag{13}$$

$$\mathcal{E}(v_i) = 0, \qquad \mathcal{E}(v_i v_j^T) = R_i \delta_{ij} \tag{14}$$

$$\mathcal{E}(w_i v_j^T) = \mathcal{E}(w_i x_0^T) = \mathcal{E}(v_i x_0^T) = 0 \tag{15}$$

where

$x_i$ = system state vector at time $t_i$,
$\Phi_i$ = system transition matrix from time $t_i$ to $t_{i+1}$,
$w_i$ = Gaussian process noise at time $t_i$,
$z_i$ = measurement vector at time $t_i$,
$H_i$ = measurement matrix at time $t_i$,
$v_i$ = Gaussian observation noise at time $t_i$.

The solutions to filtering, smoothing, and prediction problems can be found by using the results of the Gaussian parameter estimation problem considered earlier since the a priori distribution of all random variables is normal.

1) Let $x$ be the state vector(s) under consideration, $z$ be the collection of all measurement vectors, and $A$ be the region in which they fall.
2) Compute the mean of $z$ conditioned on $z \in A$.
3) Solve (7) for the mean of the state vector(s) conditioned on $z \in A$.

*Remarks*

The prediction solution is directly obtained from the filtering solution because of the independence of the process-noise vectors $\{w_i\}$. Only the conditional mean of the state vector is considered in the sequel, since the mean of a linear function of the state is the same linear function of the mean.

Equation (7) now represents the "batch-processing" solution to the estimation problem. These equations may be solved recursively via the Kalman filter using $\mathcal{E}(z_i \mid z \in A)$ as the filter input at time $t_i$. Additional computations on these filter inputs are required for the smoothing problem [20].

This formulation yields the conditional mean of the state vector for nonstationary data and arbitrary quantization schemes. Note that repeated use of Bayes' rule is not required.

If $z$ is a scalar, then the conditional mean and covariance can be found in terms of exponential and error functions. For a vector with two or more components, numerical quadrature is required to obtain a precise computation of $\mathcal{E}(z \mid z \in A)$. Despite this difficulty, this approach does provide one common point of departure for design purposes, and approximations can be made that depend on the specific method of quantization.

## III. Approximate Nonlinear Estimation

*Power-Series Expansion*

Here we describe a power-series method to approximate the mean and covariance of an $m$-component zero-mean Gaussian vector conditioned on quantized measurements. Its use is restricted to cases where the quantum-interval-to-standard-deviation ratio is small, since fourth and higher order terms are neglected.

Let the vector inequality define the quantum region $A$

$$a \leq z < b, \tag{16}$$

i.e., $\{a^i \leq z^i < b^i, i = 1, \cdots, m\}$. The geometric center of $A$ is the vector $\gamma$

$$\gamma = \tfrac{1}{2}(b + a), \tag{17}$$

and the vector of quantum-interval halfwidths is $\{\alpha^i\}$

$$\alpha = \tfrac{1}{2}(b - a). \tag{18}$$

The Gaussian probability-density function is expanded in a power series about $\gamma$ and fourth and higher order terms are neglected. The details of this straightforward but lengthy procedure have been carried out in [19] with the result that

$$\mathcal{E}(z \mid z \in A) = (I - C\Gamma^{-1})\gamma \tag{19}$$

$$\text{cov}\,(z \mid z \in A) = C \qquad C^{ij} = \begin{cases} (\alpha^i)^2/3 & i = j \\ 0 & i \neq j \end{cases} \tag{20}$$

where

$$\Gamma = \mathcal{E}(zz^T).$$

The conditional mean is given by the geometric center of $A$ plus a second-order correction term. This approximation, given by (19), looks deceptively linear, but it is nonlinear because both $\gamma$ and $\alpha$ are part of the measurement. Both (19) and (20) may be used in (7) and (8) to give estimates of the mean and covariance of $x$ conditioned on quantized measurements.

Since this case involves small quantum intervals, it is instructive to compare the commonly used method of assuming that the quantization noise (quantizer output minus input) is uncorrelated observation noise with covariance $C$ given by (20). *After* the observations are made and the $\{\alpha^i\}$ are known, the minimum variance linear estimate $\tilde{x}$ and its covariance $\tilde{P}$ are

$$\tilde{x} = \bar{x} + \tilde{K}[\gamma - H\bar{x}] \tag{21}$$

$$\tilde{P} = M - MH^T(HMH^T + R + C)^{-1}HM \tag{22}$$

where

$$\tilde{K} = MH^T(HMH^T + R + C)^{-1}. \tag{23}$$

Interestingly enough, it can be verified [19] that (21) and (22) agree with the optimal estimate found by substituting (19) and (20) into (7) and (8) if fourth and higher order terms are negligible. The primary significance is that the difference between the covariance of the estimate (21) and the minimum covariance is only of fourth order. Furthermore, (21) can be solved recursively quite easily if it is the batch-processing estimate for a system described by (10)–(15). It is still a nonlinear estimate since the $\{\alpha^i\}$ are functions of the observations; filter weights and covariances cannot be computed in advance unless the $\{\alpha^i\}$ are all equal.

### *Gaussian-Fit Algorithm*

The Gaussian-fit algorithm is the name given in [19] for a discrete-time nonlinear filter that recursively fits a Gaussian distribution to the first two moments of the conditional distribution of a system's state vector. It is analogous to the suggestion of Jazwinski [21], who had discrete measurements of a continuous-time nonlinear state equation. Bass and Schwartz [22] present a version having both continuous-time measurements and dynamics; they expand the nonlinear measurement function in a power series, a procedure that is inapplicable to quantization. Fisher [23] apparently matches more generalized moments of the conditional distribution. Davisson [15] makes similar assumptions concerning the distribution over the ensemble of measurements. Here, we present some heuristic justification for the technique and derive (in the Appendix) an ensemble-average performance estimate for stationary or nonstationary data.

Consider the system described by (10)–(15) and make the following assumption.

A1: The conditional distribution of the state just prior to the $i$th measurement is $N[\hat{x}_{i|i-1}, M_i]$.

Then we know from Section II and (10)–(15) that

$$\hat{x}_{i|i} = \hat{x}_{i|i-1} + K_i[\mathcal{E}(z_i \mid z_i \in A_i) - H_i\hat{x}_{i|i-1}] \tag{24}$$

$$K_i = M_iH_i^T(H_iM_iH_i^T + R_i)^{-1} \tag{25}$$

$$P_i = M_i - M_iH_i^T(H_iM_iH_i^T + R_i)^{-1}H_iM_i \tag{26}$$

$$E_i = P_i + K_i\,\text{cov}\,(z_i \mid z_i \in A_i)K_i^T \tag{27}$$

$$\hat{x}_{i+1|i} = \Phi_i\hat{x}_{i|i} \tag{28}$$

$$M_{i+1} = \Phi_iE_i\Phi_i^T + Q_i \tag{29}$$

where the newly introduced symbols are

- $\hat{x}_{i|i}$ = conditional mean (under A1) of $x_i$ given quantized measurements up to and including $t_i$,
- $\hat{x}_{i|i-1}$ = conditional mean (under A1) of $x_i$ given quantized measurements up to and including $t_{i-1}$,
- $A_i$ = quantum region for $z_i$,
- $M_i$ = conditional covariance (under A1) of $x_i$ given quantized measurements up to and including $t_{i-1}$,
- $K_i$ = Kalman filter gain matrix at $t_i$,
- $P_i$ = conditional covariance (under A1) of the estimate had the $i$th measurement been linear,
- $E_i$ = conditional covariance (under A1) of $x_i$ given quantized measurements up to and including $t_i$.

Under assumption A1, (28) and (29) correctly describe the propagation of the first two moments of the conditional distribution although it is no longer Gaussian. The Gaussian-fit algorithm assumes that A1 is again true at time $t_{i+1}$, i.e., it "fits" a Gaussian distribution to the moments given by (28) and (29). To give some justification for this procedure, let $e = x - \hat{x}$ and subtract (28) from (10)

$$e_{i+1|i} = \Phi_ie_{i|i} + w_i. \tag{30}$$

Neither $e_{i|i}$ nor $e_{i+1|i}$ is Gaussian, although $e_{i+1|i}$ should tend toward a Gaussian distribution because of the addition of Gaussian-process noise $w_i$, and the mixing of the components of $e_{i|i}$ by the state transition matrix.

Assumption A1 is not precisely true so the Gaussian-fit algorithm described by the recursion relations (24)–(29) yields only approximations to the conditional moments. These recursion relations are very much like the Kalman filter with two important differences.

1) The conditional mean of the measurement vector at $t_i$ is used as the filter input. This conditional mean is computed on the assumption that the distribution of the measurement is $N[H_i\hat{x}_{i|i-1}, H_iM_iH_i^T + R_i]$.
2) The conditional covariance equation (27) is being forced by the random variable cov $(z_i \mid z_i \in A_i)$. In general, there is no steady-state mean-square error for stationary input processes, and filter weights are unknown until the previous measurement has been taken.

The primary advantages of the Gaussian-fit algorithm are 1) it is relatively easy to compute, 2) it can handle nonstationary data as easily as stationary data, and 3) its general operation is independent of the quantization scheme used. The primary disadvantages are 1) it requries more computation than the optimum linear filter, and 2) it can be applied with some justification only to Gauss–Markov processes. A recursive smoothing algorithm, which combines the output of two Gaussian-fit filters, is described in [19]. Like the Gaussian-fit algorithm itself, the use of the smoothing technique is not limited to quantized measurements, but may be used with other nonlinearities.

## IV. PCM, Predictive Quantization, and Data Compression

### PCM

The noiseless-channel version of the PCM problem is shown in Fig. 1. Note that the quantizer output is the interval $A_n$ in which the scalar sample $z_n$ falls.

When the quantum intervals are small enough, the conditional mean receiver for Gaussian variables is of the form (7) with the conditional mean of the measurement history (approximately) given by (19). In these equations, $z$ is that portion of $\{z_n\}$ upon which the estimate is based. If $\{z_n\}$ is given by (10)–(15), the alternative form (21)–(23) may be solved recursively using the augmented observation-noise variance, which depends on the intervals in which the measurements lie. For arbitrarily large quantum intervals, the Gaussian-fit algorithm may be applied in a straightforward manner to approximate the conditional mean receiver for the filtering and prediction problems. The smoothing problem is more complex and is considered in [19].

An estimate of the ensemble performance of the Gaussian-fit algorithm in the PCM mode is given in the Appendix.

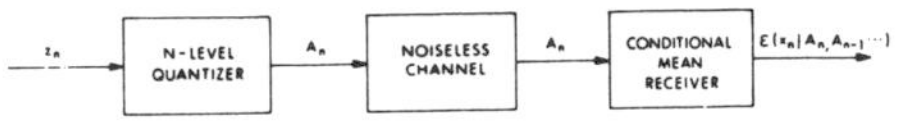


Fig. 1. Noiseless-channel PCM.

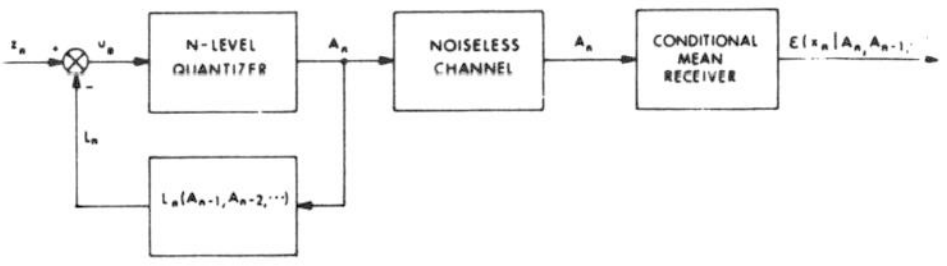


Fig. 2. Noiseless-channel predictive quantization.

### Predictive Quantization

*System Description:* Fig. 2 shows the noiseless-channel version of the predictive quantization problem for a mean-square-error criterion. This system configuration is not as general as the one considered by Fine [10] since the quantizer is time invariant. The scalar random process $\{z_n\}$ is assumed to be the output of a system described by (10)–(15). The $N$-level quantizer is chosen beforehand, but is fixed once the system is in operation. The scalar feedback function $L_n(A_{n-1}, A_{n-2}, \cdots)$ is subtracted from the incoming sample $z_n$ to minimize the mean-square-reconstruction error. The determination of $L_n$ and the design of the quantizer are considered then in the following section.

*System Optimization:* Fine [10] outlines the system design procedure in three steps. 1) Find the optimum receiver for a given transmitter. 2) Find the optimum transmitter for a given receiver. 3) Solve the simultaneous conditions of 1) and 2) for the optimum system. These are necessary, but not sufficient conditions [10]. Here we have already performed step 1) for the quadratic criterion since the conditional mean receiver is indicated in Fig. 2. Steps 2) and 3) are performed by choosing the optimum feedback quantity $L_n^0$ such that

$$\mathcal{E}[\text{cov}\,(x_n|\,L_n, A_n, A_{n-1}, \cdots)\,|A_{n-1}, \cdots] - \mathcal{E}[\text{cov}\,(x_n|\,L_n^0, A_n, A_{n-1}, \cdots)\,|A_{n-1}, \cdots] \geq 0 \quad (31)$$

where cov $(x_n|\cdot)$ is the conditional covariance of the estimate. This equation is difficult to solve because it requires knowledge of the conditional distribution. An approximate solution can be found with the aid of the Gaussian-fit algorithm. Under assumption A1, the conditional moments are given in recursive form by (24)–(29), and the conditional covariance by (27) with the index $i$ replaced by $n$. Let the quantized variable be $u_n$ (see Fig. 2) and, furthermore, let

$$\begin{aligned} u_n &= z_n - L_n(A_{n-1}, \cdots) \\ u_n^0 &= z_n - L_n^0(A_{n-1}, \cdots). \end{aligned} \quad (32)$$

Note that in (27) we may use cov $(u_n|\cdot)$ in place of

cov $(z_n|\cdot)$ since the expectation is conditioned on $\{A_{n-1}, A_{n-2}, \cdots\}$, and thus, $z_n$ and $u_n$ differ only by the constant $L_n$. If the $N$ quantum intervals are denoted by $\{A^j, j = 1, \cdots, N\}$, then substituting (27) into (31) and simplifying produces the scalar equation

$$\sum_{j=1}^{N} \operatorname{cov}(u_n \mid u_n \in A^j)P(u_n \in A^j) - \sum_{j=1}^{N} \operatorname{cov}(u_n^0 \mid u_n^0 \in A^j)P(u_n^0 \in A^j) \geq 0 \qquad (33)$$

where these quantities are computed under the assumption that $z_n$ (hence, $u_n$ and $u_n^0$) are normally distributed. But (33) is no more than a statement that $L_n$ should be chosen to minimize the distortion in quantizing the normal random variable $z_n$. Thus by symmetry arguments, it can be concluded that for a well-designed quantizer $L_n^0$ should be the (approximate) conditional mean of $z_n$,

$$L_n^0(A_{n-1}, \cdots) = \mathcal{E}(z_n \mid A_{n-1}, \cdots) = H_n\hat{x}_{n|n-1} \qquad (34)$$

which is generated by the Gaussian-fit algorithm in the prediction mode. To show that (34) is not always optimum, even with the Gaussian assumption, consider the case when the standard deviation of the prediction of $z_n$ is very much smaller than the quantum interval widths. Then the quantizer appears to be $N - 1$ binary quantizers placed end to end, and $L_n^0$ will be chosen to place the mean of $u_n^0$ at one of these quantizer switch points. The quantum intervals can be chosen to avoid this difficulty and this problem is treated in the Appendix.

*Data Compression*

*System Description:* Fig. 3 shows the block diagram of the predictive-comparison type of data compression system. The analysis contained here is concerned only with the prediction and filtering aspects, and such important problems as buffer control, timing information, and channel noise are not considered.

The threshold device in Fig. 3 is a quantizer (one large quantum interval, many small quantum intervals), and the linear slope indicates that quantization during encoding can be neglected. The quantizer output is fed back through $L_n(A_{n-1}, \cdots)$ and subtracted from the input $z_n$. If the magnitude of the difference $u_n$ is less than $\alpha$ (a known parameter) then nothing is sent to the receiver; if $|u_n| > \alpha$, then $u_n$ is sent to the receiver. If the receiver does a parallel computation of $L_n(A_{n-1}, \cdots)$, then the system input $z_n$ is calculated by adding $u_n$ and $L_n$. The estimate of $z_n$ when $u_n$ is not sent may be performed under a variety of criteria; in all cases the error in the estimate is known to be less than $\alpha$.

*System Optimization:* The criterion considered here for system optimization will not contain data fidelity since this can be controlled through the choice of the threshold width. (In fact, choosing $L_n$ to minimize distortion would yield the obvious result $L_n^0 = \pm \infty$.) Instead, $L_n(A_{n-1}, \cdots)$ is chosen solely on the basis that it minimizes the (conditional) probability that $u_n$ is sent to the receiver. This is not necessarily the same as minimizing the average number of samples sent out of the total number processed. This latter task may be formulated as an optimal stochastic control problem requiring a dynamic programming solution. The solution would hardly be worth the effort.

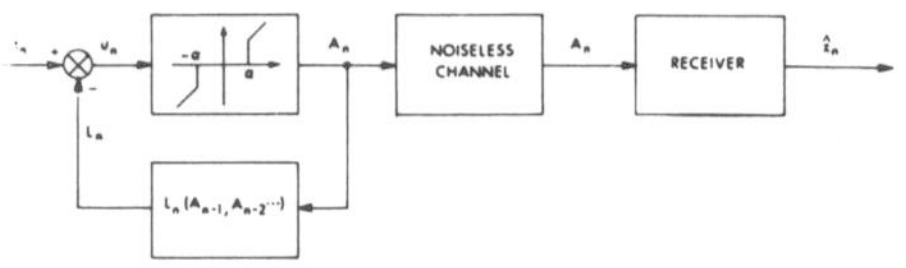


Fig. 3. Noiseless-channel predictive-comparison data compression.

When the $\{z_n\}$ process is generated by (10)–(15), the Gaussian-fit algorithm may be used in the feedback path for arbitrarily wide thresholds. Regardless of the number of samples that have been rejected or sent, the distribution of $z_n$ conditioned on quantized measurements at times $\{t_{n-1}, \cdots\}$ is assumed to be normal. Thus, the conditional probability of rejecting $z_n$ is maximized by choosing $L_n$ to be the (approximate) conditional mean $H_n\hat{x}_{n|n-1}$. The ensemble performance estimate of this system using the Gaussian-fit algorithm is derived in the Appendix.

Alternative approaches to system design rely on feeding back the prediction (in some sense) of the next sample $z_n$ [14], [15], and [24]. Davisson [15] considers a stationary Gaussian input sequence and small threshold widths; he finds the optimum linear predictor for $z_n$ based on the most recent $M$ samples, and uses it in the feedback path. Drawing on the results of Sections II and III, the optimum nonlinear predictor is found from (7) with $x$ replaced by $z_n$, and $z$ replaced by $\{z_{n-1}, \cdots, z_{n-M}\}$, and $\mathcal{E}(z \mid z \in A)$ given by (19). The net result is a set of filter weights for $\{z_{n-1}, \cdots, z_{n-M}\}$, each of which takes on one of $2^M$ values, depending on which samples have been quantized.

## V. Simulation Results

This section describes the results of digital computer simulations of the Gaussian-fit algorithm as applied to the PCM, predictive quantization, and data compression systems described in Section IV. Bello *et al.* [11] present simulation results for predictive quantization with a binary quantizer. Their approach is a numerical approximation (by Monte Carlo techniques) to the optimum feedback function, whereas an analytical approximation (the Gaussian-fit algorithm) is used here. They consider various memory lengths and a binary quantizer, and here, because of the recursive nature of the computations, we use a growing memory (but finite storage) and arbitrary quantizers. Although the Gaussian-fit algorithm and its performance estimate may be used on nonstationary data, only stationary data have been simulated as yet.

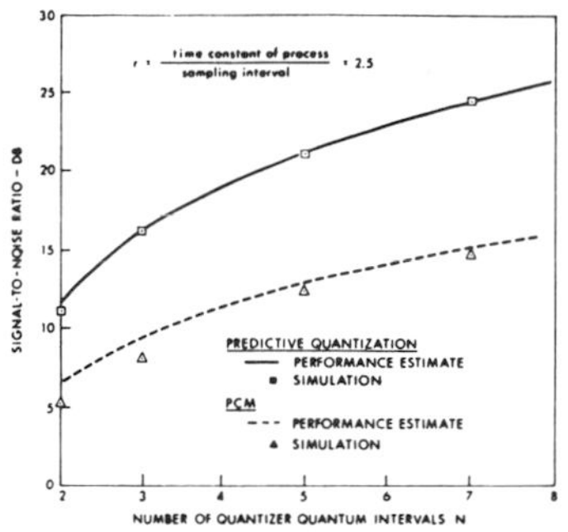


Fig. 4. SNR for the Gaussian-fit algorithm PCM and predictive quantization.

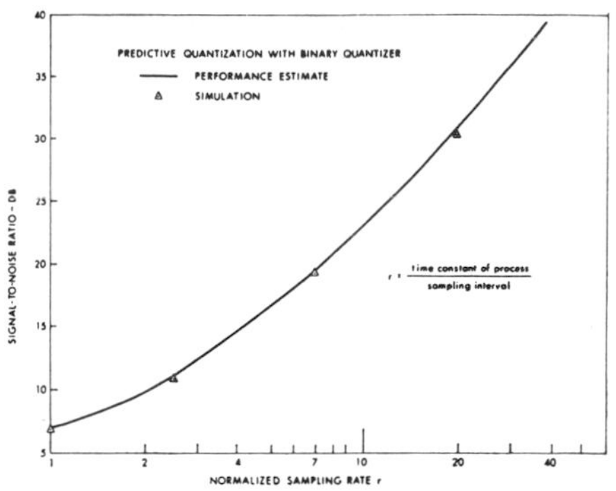


Fig. 5. SNR for the Gaussian-fit algorithm, predictive quantization binary quantizer.

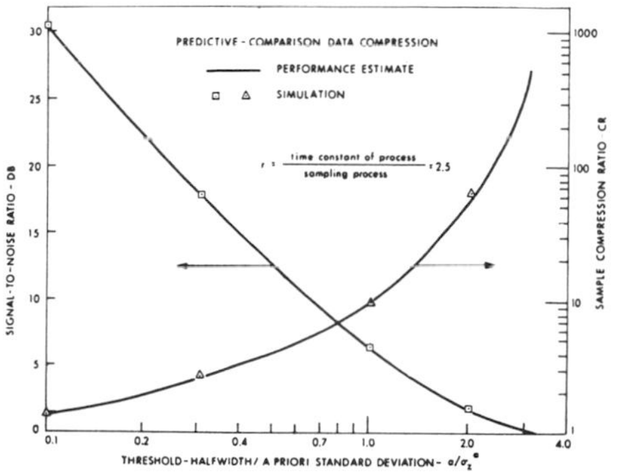


Fig. 6. SNR and sample compression ratio for the Gaussian-fit algorithm, predictive-comparison data compression.

*Simulation Description*

*Input Process:* The simulated second-order Gauss–Markov input process is the sampled output of a linear system driven by Gaussian white noise. The transfer function of the shaping filter is the same as used in [11],

$$H(s) = \frac{c}{(1 + \tau s)^2} \tag{35}$$

where the gain $c$ is chosen to provide the proper variance at the output. Observation noise was not used here, but is considered in [19]. Thus the autocorrelation of the input process is

$$\phi_{zz}(n) = \mathcal{E}(z_i z_{i+n}) = (1 + |n|/r) \exp(-|n|/r) \tag{36}$$

where

$r = \tau/T$ = number of samples per time constant $\tau$
$T$ = time between samples.

*Error Measurement:* Each system was simulated by operating on 5000 consecutive samples. The estimation errors were squared and averaged to give an estimate of the ensemble mean-square error of the system. The autocorrelation of the estimation errors were measured, and from this the confidence limits have been assessed as being greater than a 90-percent probability that the measured error variance lies within 10 percent of its true value.

*PCM and Predictive Quantization*

Fig. 4 displays the ratio of signal variance to ensemble mean-square estimation error (expressed in decibels) as a function of the number of quantizer quantum intervals. Both the PCM and predictive quantization systems are shown with the input process parameter $r = 2.5$. The lines are the performance estimates (as derived in the Appendix) and the data points are the simulation results. The predictive quantization system performs significantly better than the PCM system, as is to be expected. The performance estimate is quite accurate except for PCM with a small number of quantum intervals (less than 5). Here, the estimate is optimistic, a characteristic that has been noted in other simulations [19]. The quantizer quantum intervals have been chosen to minimize the ensemble mean-square error (see Appendix).

Fig. 5 shows how the predictive quantization system with a binary quantizer reacts to different signal correlations. The performance estimate and the simulation results are exhibited as a function of the input-process parameter $r$. (As a point of reference, the adjacent sample correlation is 0.736 for $r = 1$, 0.938, for $r = 2.5$, and 0.9988 for $r = 20$.) Again, the performance estimate is quite accurate.

*Data Compression*

Fig. 6 contains the outcomes for the predictive-comparison data compression system. Performance estimates and simulation results of the mean-square-error and sample-compression ratio are shown as a function of $(\alpha/\sigma_s^*)$, the ratio of threshold halfwidth to a priori standard deviation. Note the excellent agreement between performance estimates and simulation results.

## VI. Conclusions

Expectations conditioned on quantized measurements $(z \in A)$ can be found in two steps. 1) Find the expectation conditioned on $z$. 2) Average this (conditional) expectation conditioned on $z \in A$. When applied to discrete-time linear Gaussian systems, it was shown that the conditional mean of the system's state vector can be found without Bayes' rule by passing the conditional mean of the measurement history through the Kalman filter. This result provides one common point of departure for system design.

Two nonlinear approximations are considered for Gaussian variables. The first uses a power-series expansion and neglects fourth and higher order powers of the quantum-interval-to-standard-deviation ratio, and is equivalent to treating quantization as additional observation noise. The second approach, called the Gaussian-fit algorithm, assumes that the conditional distribution is normal. It is a recursive computation for arbitrarily wide quantum intervals, but can be applied with some justification only to $n$th-order Gauss–Markov processes.

The approximations are applied to the noiseless channel versions of three digital systems—PCM, predictive quantization, and predictive-comparison data compression. Both methods can be used on stationary and nonstationary data, and in the feedback path without additional calculations, e.g., Monte Carlo. The Gaussian-fit algorithm uses a growing memory (but finite storage) for these computations. Estimates of the ensemble mean-square reconstruction error are derived for the Gaussian-fit algorithm when used in each of the three systems. Simulation results indicate that these ensemble performance estimates are quite accurate (except for very coarse PCM), so that parametric studies with Monte Carlo techniques are not required to evaluate the system's ensemble mean-square error.

[*Editors' Note:* Material has been omitted at this point.]

## References


[1] *Proc. IEEE, Special Issue on Redundancy Reduction*, vol. 55, March 1967.
[2] D. Ruchkin, "Linear reconstruction of quantized and sampled signals," *IRE Trans. Communications Systems*, vol. CS-9, pp. 350–355, December 1961.
[3] K. Steiglitz, "Transmission of an analog signal over a fixed bit-rate channel," *IEEE Trans. Information Theory*, vol. IT-12, pp. 469–474, October 1966.
[4] W. Kellog, "Information rates in sampling and quantization," *IEEE Trans. Information Theory*, vol. IT-13, pp. 506–511, July 1967.
[5] Y. C. Ho and R. C. K. Lee, "A Bayesian approach to problems in stochastic estimation and control," *Proc. JACC*, pp. 382–387, 1964.
[6] R. Bucy, "Nonlinear filtering theory," *IEEE Trans. Automatic Control* (Correspondence), vol. AC-10, p. 198, April 1965.
[7] W. M. Wonham, "Some applications of stochastic differential equations to nonlinear filtering," *J. SIAM Control*, ser. A, vol. 2, pp. 347–369, 1964.
[8] L. Meier, A. Korsak, and R. Larson, "Effect of data quantization on tracker performance," Stanford Research Institute, Menlo Park, Calif., Tech. Memo. 3, Project 6642, October 1967.
[9] A. Balakrishnan, "An adaptive nonlinear data predictor," *Proc. Natl. Telemetry Conf.*, 1962.
[10] T. Fine, "Properties of an optimum digital system and applications," *IEEE Trans. Information Theory*, vol. IT-10, pp. 287–296, October 1964.
[11] P. Bello, R. Lincoln, and H. Gish, "Statistical delta modulation," *Proc. IEEE*, vol. 55, pp. 308–319, March 1967.
[12] H. Gish, "Optimum quantization of random sequences," Div. of Engrg. and Appl. Phys., Harvard University, Cambridge, Mass., Rept. 529, May 1967.
[13] J. O'Neal, "Predictive quantizing systems (differential pulse code modulation) for the transmission of television signals," *Bell Sys. Tech. J.*, vol. 45, pp. 689–720, 1966.
[14] J. Irwin and J. O'Neal, "The design of optimum DPCM (differential pulse code modulation) encoding systems via the Kalman predictor," *Preprints JACC*, pp. 130–136, June 1968.
[15] L. Davisson, "An approximate theory of prediction for data compression," *IEEE Trans. Information Theory*, vol. IT-13, pp. 274–278, April 1967.
[16] L. Davisson, "Theory of adaptive data compression," in *Advances in Communication Systems*, A. Balakrishnan, Ed. New York: Academic Press, 1966.
[17] L. Davisson, "The theoretical analysis of data compression systems," *Proc. IEEE*, vol. 56, pp. 176–186, February 1968.
[18] J. Doob, *Stochastic Processes*. New York: Wiley, 1953.
[19] R. Curry, *Estimation and Control with Quantized Measurements*. Cambridge, Mass.: M.I.T. Press (to be published).
[20] D. Fraser, "A new technique for the optimal smoothing of data," Sc.D. thesis, Dept. of Aeron. and Astron., Massachusetts Institute of Technology, Cambridge, Mass., January 1967.
[21] A. Jazwinski, "Filtering for nonlinear dynamical systems," *IEEE Trans. Automatic Control* (Correspondence), vol. AC-11, p. 765, October 1966.
[22] R. Bass and L. Schwartz, "Extensions to multichannel nonlinear filtering," Hughes Rept. SSD 60220R, February 1966.
[23] J. Fisher, "Conditional probability density functions and optimal nonlinear estimation," Ph.D. dissertation, University of California, Los Angeles, 1966.
[24] L. Ehrman, "Analysis of some redundancy removal bandwidth compression techniques," *Proc. IEEE*, vol. 55, pp. 278–287, March 1967.
[25] J. Max, "Quantizing for minimum distortion," *IRE Trans. Information Theory*, vol. IT-6, pp. 7–12, March 1960.

# 43



Reprinted from *IEEE Trans. Inform. Theory,* **IT-17,** 118–119 (1971)

## Instrumentable Tree Encoding of Information Sources

***Abstract*—We study here the use of tree codes to encode time-discrete memoryless sources with respect to a fidelity criterion. An easily instrumented scheme is proposed for use with binary sources and the Hamming distortion metric. Results of simulation with random and convolutional codes are given.**

In this correspondence, we study the encoding of time-discrete memoryless sources with respect to a fidelity criterion by the use of tree codes. Recently, it has been proven by Jelinek [1] that tree codes used with sources have the same rate-distortion function $R(D)$ as block codes. We seek here an instrumentable encoding scheme whose performance is near $R(D)$.

A particular encoding algorithm is investigated by computer simulation. We assume a binary source with independent and equiprobable letters. Binary convolutional codes [3] whose words have a tree structure with two branches stemming from each node are used to encode with respect to the Hamming distance measure, $d(z, \hat{z}) = 1 - \delta(z, \hat{z})$. More general convolutional codes are available for use with arbitrary sources and distance measures ([2], sec. 10.12).

Schematically, a source encoder can be divided into a tree generator and a searching algorithm to find a codeword in the tree sufficiently close to the source output. We depend on convolutional coding apparatus for tree generation and concentrate attention in this correspondence on the search problem. Our search algorithm is governed by two parameters, $M$ and $L$. Initially, it investigates all tree-code paths to a depth $l$, where $l = \log_2 M$ for some $M$. Thereafter it progresses through the code tree one level at a time, keeping a constant stock of $M$ paths that are best in the sense of the fidelity measure. At each level, the $2M$ extensions of these $M$ paths are judged, and the poorer $M$ eliminated. After waiting a certain memory length $L$, the search algorithm releases to the user, as it advances to a new tree level, a single digit. The totality of these, one per search algorithm iteration, comprises a map through the tree of the most accurate path found. At the same time, they form the compressed source data.

Fig. 1 shows our algorithm deciding an $L$-delayed output digit on the left (decide 0 for the upward tending branch, 1 for the downward tending branch), before advancing to a new level on the right. The decision may eliminate some of the $M$ best paths in the whole tree, in which case enough paths are included from the chosen half of the tree to total $M$ altogether. For the sake of brevity, we forego further subtleties of operation.

Convolutional trees are characterized by a constraint length $\nu$ that is equal to the number of most recent map digits influencing the present branch. It turns out that for a given number $M$ of paths kept by the search algorithm as it progresses, the constraint length of the average code need not be longer than some function of $M$. For $M \leq 10$, $\nu$ need not be longer than 10, and for $10 < M \leq 100$, constraint lengths in excess of 15 will not yield lower distortion. Of course, $\nu \leq L$.

Given available storage size $ML$, we have apportioned it between $M$, the number of paths kept, and $L$, the memory length, so as to minimize the distortion obtainable from codes of sufficiently long constraint length (see preceding paragraph). The best experimental balance for an average convolutional code seems to be $L \approx M + 10$. As $L$ and $M$ grow larger, this becomes simply $L \approx M \approx \sqrt{\text{Storage}}$. Table I relates storage to performance for codes chosen at random from a convolutional ensemble so restricted that the corresponding digits on the two branches stemming from each node are complementary. ($\Delta(\ )$ is the inverse rate-distortion function [2].)

Since the foregoing results apply only to codes picked at random from our convolutional ensembles, particular codes were chosen and simulated. For all choices of $\nu$, $M$, and $L$, specific codes were found that performed 20–30 percent closer than their ensemble averages to the optimal distortion given by the inverse rate-

Manuscript received March 16, 1970.

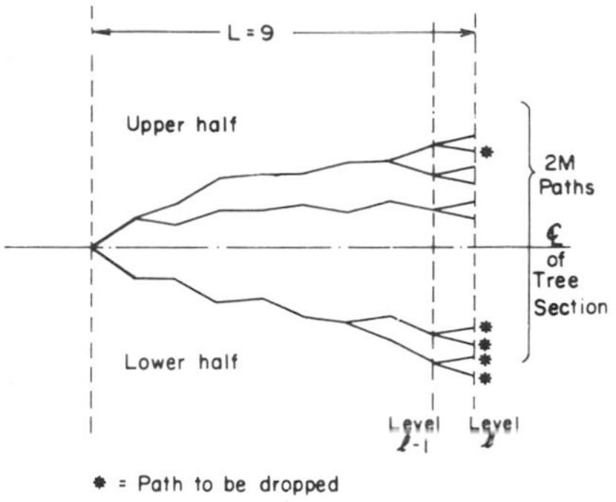


Fig. 1. Encoder tree paths: $M = 5$, $L = 9$ (only 10 of $2^7$ paths shown).

TABLE I
AVERAGE DISTORTION PER SOURCE DIGIT OF CONVOLUTIONAL ENSEMBLE*

| Storage | Distortion |
|---|---|
| 3000 | 0.1265 |
| 1000 | 0.1315 |
| 100 | 0.150 |

* $\nu = 15$, $M + 10 = L$, Rate $= \frac{1}{2}$, $\Delta(\frac{1}{2}) = 0.110$.

TABLE II
EXPERIMENTAL ENSEMBLE AVERAGES AND BEST RATE ½ CODES FOR VARIOUS SIMULATION PARAMETERS*

| $L$ | $M$ | $\nu$† | Code† | Best Code Distribution† | Convolutional Ensemble Average† | Complementary Ensemble Average | Random Ensemble Average |
|---|---|---|---|---|---|---|---|
| 25 | 10 | 10 | 1) | 1.141 | 0.149 | 0.148 | 0.166 |
| 25 | 25 | 10 | 2) | 0.139 | 0.1445 | 0.144 | 0.156 |
| 50 | 50 | 25 | 3) | 0.1295 | 0.1335 | 0.134 | 0.1405 |

Code Generators

1) $G_1$ = 10000 00000    2) $G_1$ = 10000 00000
$G_2$ = 11010 11010    $G_2$ = 11101 10111

3) $G_1$ = 10101 11111 10001 00010 00110
$G_2$ = 11101 00010 11010 01010 00101

* All distortion averages taken at level $L$.
† Applies only to convolutional codes.

distortion function [2] $\Delta(R)$. Some of these are listed in Table II, along with various ensemble averages for comparison. The generator notations $G_1$ and $G_2$ are those used by Bussgang in his classic paper on convolutional codes [3].

Exactly which codes perform well seems to depend on search algorithm parameters and seems particularly affected by $M$. The first code shown in Table II does not improve materially for $M$ larger than 10, even though it was the best code found for this $M$, and indeed its behavior becomes worse than the experimental ensemble average for $\nu = 10$ and large enough $M$.

It is instructive to compare our algorithm's effects on convolutional codes, which may or may not be optimal, with its use on an optimal class of codes. Accordingly, we conclude with the results of simulating the algorithm on code trees chosen both entirely at random and with the single restriction that the two branches from

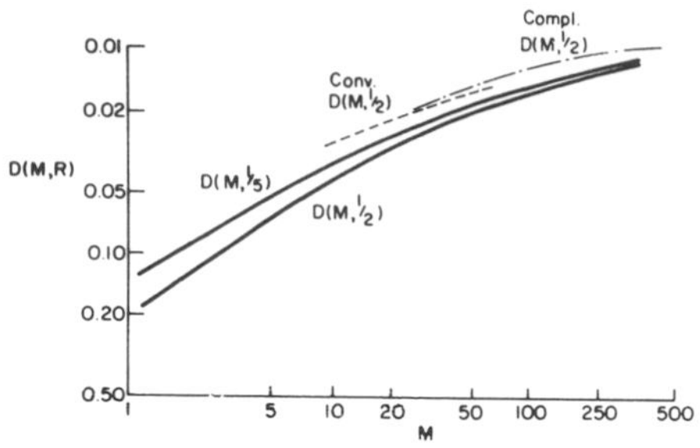


Fig. 2. Disparity $D(M, R)$ versus $M$. ($\Delta(1/2) = 0.110$) ($\Delta(1/5) = 0.243$).

each node be complementary. This latter property was possessed by all our convolutional codes as well. If for a fixed $M$ and rate $R$, $D(M, R)$ is defined as the disparity between the inverse rate-distortion function $\Delta(R)$ and the ultimate performance of our encoder as $L$ becomes large, Fig. 2 shows $D(M, R)$ approaches zero quickly (it follows from Jelinek [1] that for the former ensemble at least, $D(\infty, R) = 0$). A four-way comparison between the random ensemble, the random complementary branch ensemble, the convolutional (complementary) ensemble, and good convolutional codes, all with the same parameters, is listed in Table II. Significantly, it appears that an average tree chosen purely at random (i.e., without complementariness) performs worse than an average tree chosen at random from our complementary branch convolutional ensemble. However, the performances of the complementary random and convolutional ensembles were about the same for $M = 10, 25$, and 50. Particular convolutional codes, of course, are better than their ensemble average.

F. Jelinek
J. B. Anderson
School of Elec. Eng. and
Ctr. for Radiophys.
and Space Res.
Cornell University
Ithaca, N.Y. 14850

## References

[1] F. Jelinek, "Tree encoding of memoryless time-discrete sources with a fidelity criterion," *IEEE Trans. Inform. Theory*, vol. IT-15, pp. 584–590, September 1969.
[2] —, *Probabilistic Information Theory*. New York: McGraw-Hill, 1968.
[3] J. J. Bussgang, "Some properties of binary convolutional code generators," *IEEE Trans. Inform. Theory*, vol. IT-11, pp. 90–100, January 1965.

# 44



Reprinted from *IEEE Trans. Inform. Theory,* **IT-20**(3), 332–336 (1974)

# Tree Encoding of Gaussian Sources

ROBERT J. DICK, TOBY BERGER, MEMBER, IEEE, AND FREDERICK JELINEK, FELLOW, IEEE

***Abstract*—Tree codes are known to be capable of performing arbitrarily close to the rate-distortion function for any memoryless source and single-letter fidelity criterion. Tree coding and tree search strategies are investigated for the discrete-time memoryless Gaussian source encoded for a signal-power-to-mean-squared-error ratio of about 30 dB (about 5 binary digits per source output). Also, a theoretical lower bound on average search effort is derived. Two code search strategies (the Viterbi algorithm and the stack algorithm) were simulated in assembly language on a large digital computer. After suitable modifications, both strategies yielded encoding with a signal-to-distortion ratio about 1 dB below the limit set by the rate-distortion function. Although this performance is better than that of any previously known instrumentable scheme, it unfortunately requires search computation of the order of $10^5$ machine cycles per source output encoded.**

## I. Introduction

THIS PAPER addresses the problem of data compression coding for the discrete-time memoryless Gaussian source and the mean-squared-error criterion. The source generates independent $N(0,1)$ outputs at uniformly spaced time instants, where $N(m,v)$ denotes the normal, or Gaussian, distribution with mean $m$ and variance $v$.

A reproduction of the source output sequence is to be given to a user. Distortion is measured by the average of the square of the difference between each source output and its reproduction for the user. Implicit in this distortion measure is the rule that any (finite) constant amount of delay in the transmission does not reduce the fidelity. The coding rate for a transmission of $n$ source outputs is the log of the number of possible reproducing sequences divided by $n$. The problem then is to minimize the tradeoff of rate $R$ versus distortion $D$. The lowest possible $R$ for a given $D$ prescribed by rate-distortion theory is $R(D) = -\frac{1}{2}\log D$, for $0 \leq D \leq 1$ [1].

Goblick and Holsinger [2] have analyzed the performance of the procedure of encoding with a quantizer having $M$ uniformly spaced output levels $\{v_i\}$, $i = 1,2,\cdots,M$. Each source output is mapped into the nearest quantizer output level and the set of output levels is symmetrical about (centered at) zero. The quantizer outputs will have entropy

$$H(V) = -\sum_{i=1}^{M} p_i \log p_i < \log M \qquad (1)$$

where $p_i$ is the probability of the output $v_i$. The quantizer outputs theoretically could be coded at rate $H(V)$ to achieve arbitrarily small probability of erroneous reconstruction. Such an *entropy-coded quantizer* has a rate $R^*(D)$ given by

$$R^*(D) = K - \tfrac{1}{2}\log_2 D \qquad (2)$$

bits per source output, where $K \simeq \frac{1}{4}$ [2].

However, if the rate of digit transmission is fixed at $R^*(D)$ bits per source output, then entropy coding of the quantizer is quite difficult. In fact, for variable-length coding, the probability is one that sooner or later any given transmission delay will be exceeded [3]. Fixing the maximum coding delay then results in loss of information about source outputs. Further, since the long coding delays usually are caused by the improbable large-magnitude source outputs, the lost information may result in severe distortion.

Berger *et al.* [4] have presented and analyzed a coding scheme called *permutation coding*, which is an alternative to quantization followed by entropy coding. It has the same optimum coding rate of $R^*(D)$ as the entropy-coded quantizer [5].

Manuscript received May 23, 1973; revised December 17, 1973. This work was supported in part by NASA under Contract NAS-2-5643 and in part by the National Science Foundation under Grant GK-32240.

R. J. Dick and T. Berger are with the School of Electrical Engineering, Cornell University, Ithaca, N.Y. 14850.
F. Jelinek is with IBM Thomas J. Watson Research Center, Yorktown Heights, N.Y. 10598, on leave from the School of Electrical Engineering, Cornell University, Ithaca, N.Y. 14850.

For $R$ such that $2^R$ is an integer, a source code of rate $R$ and block length $n$ is obtained by assigning a real number to each of $n \times 2^{nR}$ positions, thereby producing $2^{nR}$ sequences of length $n$ called codewords. Jelinek has established that a particular technique known as tree coding possesses the potential to perform arbitrarily close to $R(D)$ [6].

Numbers are assigned to the positions of a tree code of rate $R$ as follows. The codewords are numbered from 0 to $2^{nR} - 1$ ($2^R$ an integer) by means of $2^R$-ary sequences of length $n$. Prior to the actual assignment of real numbers, the codeword positions first are assigned *states* by shifting the corresponding $2^R$-ary sequence from right to left into a $\nu$-stage shift register initially filled with zeros; position $k$ is assigned state $(k,S)$ where $S$ is the content of the shift register after $k$ shifts.[1] Each state then is labeled by a real number, and finally each position is assigned the real number that labels its state.

We define a parameter

$$s = (\nu - 1)R$$

which we call the state freedom. Strictly speaking, a true tree code results only for $s \geq (n - 1)R$. However, in what follows we shall always have $s < (n - 1)R$ which results in what often is called a trellis code.

In the simplest form of tree encoding of the above Gaussian source, each state is assigned a random number independently, each distributed as $N(0,\sigma_y^2)$, whereupon each position is assigned the real number assigned to its state. For $D$ such that $R = R(D)$ and for $\sigma_y^2 = 1 - D$, the resulting code ensemble is optimal in the limit of large $s$ and $n$ in the following sense. The expectation over all codes and source output sequences of the average distortion of the best codeword for each source sequence is arbitrarily close to $D$ [6]. In our simulations we modified this coding as described in Section III.

We shall consider two methods for searching a tree code to find good codewords. One, called the Viterbi algorithm, consists of keeping $s$ small and performing successive stages of path elimination equivalent to exhaustive search of the code. The other, called the stack algorithm, uses large $s$. Define a path of length $l$ to be a sequence of the first $l$ states of any codeword. Define the distortion of a path to be the sum of the squares of the differences between the real numbers assigned to the states of the path and the corresponding source outputs. Then the stack algorithm forms a *path metric* by subtracting from the distortion of each path under consideration a *par value* of distortion which for a path of length $l$ is a function only of the first $l$ source outputs. The algorithm keeps a stack of paths ordered by path metric. It proceeds by removing from the stack that path with the smallest metric, computing the metrics of all the one-state extensions of that path, and then inserting the extensions into the stack. It then takes the new smallest-metric path, and so on.

[1] In compact mathematical notation position $k(1 \leq k \leq n)$ of codeword $l(0 \leq l \leq 2^{nR} - 1)$ has $S = \lfloor l2^{(k-n)R} \rfloor \pmod{2^{R\nu}}$, where $\lfloor x \rfloor$ denotes the integral part of $x$.

Results obtained by simulations of the Viterbi and stack algorithms are presented in Section III. Since the simulations were performed, Anderson and Jelinek [7] have presented and analyzed a variation of the stack algorithm called the two-cycle algorithm, and Gallager [8] has analyzed a related algorithm.

Before discussing the simulations, we present a lower bound to search effort that is applicable to any algorithm for searching any randomly generated code.

## II. A Lower Bound to Code Search

The following lower bound will apply to the expected value of average search required by any fixed algorithm for searching a randomly generated code, the expectation being taken over the random generation both of the code and of the source outputs.

We are assuming that the encoding algorithm is fixed without regard to the particular code actually generated. Hence, as far as expected encoder search is concerned, each number assigned to each state could just as well be generated independently at random just before the encoder investigates it. Arguments based on supply from these hypothetical random trials versus demand due to the required joint distribution of source outputs and their approximations will prove the following theorem.

*Theorem 1:* Let an encoder operate by searching a random code according to a fixed algorithm. Let the source be time discrete and memoryless with each output distributed as a random variable $X$. Let the code states be assigned numbers generated independently at random with each distributed as a random variable $Y$. Let the decoder be required to produce outputs (not necessarily memoryless) so that the expected relative frequency of each source output-decoder output pair has the joint distribution of $X$ and another random variable $Z$. Let $S(x)$ be the expected average number of code states searched to encode source outputs of value $x$. Then

$$S(x) \geq \sup_y \frac{f_{X,Z}(x,y)}{f_X(x)f_Y(y)}, \qquad \text{for all } x. \tag{3}$$

It follows from this that

$$E[S(X)] \geq \int dx \sup_y \frac{f_{X,Z}(x,y)}{f_Y(y)}. \tag{4}$$

*Proof:* Formula (4) follows from (3) by taking the expectation of both sides over $X$. The argument for proving (3) is as follows. Consider an interval $I$ to which the required decoder output conditional distribution assigns probability $p$. Then a fraction $p$ of the decoder outputs are required to be within $I$. Let $W$ denote the expected waiting time in the hypothetical independent trials required before the encoder can find a state assigned a number inside the interval $I$. Then the expected average search is at least $pW$.

The expected waiting time $W$ in successive independent trials for an event of probability $q$ in each trial is

$$W = \sum_{t=1}^{\infty} t(1 - q)^{t-1}q = \frac{1}{q}. \tag{5}$$

Now the event $y \le Y < y + dy$ has probability $f_Y(y)dy$. Given that $x$ was the source output, the event $y \le Z < y + dy$ must have relative frequency

$$p = f_{Z|X}(y \mid x)dy = \frac{f_{X,Z}(x,y)dy}{f_X(x)}, \qquad \text{for all } x. \quad (6)$$

Thus with relative frequency $f_{Z|X}(y \mid x)dy$ an event is required which takes an expected amount of search $[f_Y(y)dy]^{-1}$ to find. Even if no search is necessary when this event is not required, still the expected average amount of search is at least

$$S(x) \ge \frac{f_{Z|X}(y \mid x)dy}{f_Y(y)dy} = \frac{f_{X,Z}(x,y)}{f_X(x)f_Y(y)}, \qquad \text{for all } x,y. \quad (7)$$

Taking the supremum of the right side of (7) over $y$ gives (3). Q.E.D.

For optimal encoding with distortion $D$ of the Gaussian source previously described, it is known that $Z$ must be $N(0, 1 - D)$ and $X - Z$ must be independent of $Z$ and must be $N(0,D)$ [1]. The usual method for generating a code is to have $Y$ be $N(0, 1 - D)$, also. By applying Theorem 1 to the Gaussian case, we shall show that such coding must have infinite average search.

*Theorem 2:* Under the conditions of Theorem 1, let $X$ be $N(0,1)$, $Y$ be $N(0,\sigma_y^2)$, $Z$ be $N(0,\sigma_z^2)$ and let $(X,Z)$ be jointly Gaussian with correlation coefficient $\rho = E[XZ]/\sigma_z > 0$. Then if $\sigma_y^2 \le \sigma_z^2$, $E[S(X)] = \infty$.

*Proof:* The argument is simply a substitution into (4) of Theorem 1. When this is done and the supremum is taken, we find that if $\sigma_y^2 \le (1 - \rho^2)\sigma_z^2$, then $S(x) = \infty$ for all $x$. If $\sigma_y^2 > (1 - \rho^2)\sigma_z^2$, then

$$E[S(X)] \ge \int dx \sqrt{\frac{\sigma_y^2}{2\pi\sigma_z^2(1 - \rho^2)}} \exp\left\{-\frac{x^2}{2}\left[\frac{\sigma_y^2 - \sigma_z^2}{\sigma_y^2 - (1 - \rho^2)\sigma_z^2}\right]\right\}. \quad (8)$$

This integral is infinite if $\sigma_y^2 \le \sigma_z^2$. Q.E.D.

The reason the search is infinite for $\sigma_y^2 \le \sigma_z^2$ is that the very rare source outputs become very troublesome. $S(x)$ becomes inversely proportional to $f_X(x)$ and $E[S(X)] = \infty$.

The search underbound of Theorem 1 is easy to compute for a variety of sources and distortion measures but is generally extremely loose. Consider, for example, the binary symmetric source with the average-Hamming-distance distortion measure encoded at rate of $\frac{1}{2}$ bit per source output. Then the optimal $X$, $Z$ are given by

$$P_{X,Z}(0,0) = P_{X,Z}(1,1) = 0.445$$

$$P_{X,Z}(0,1) = P_{X,Z}(1,0) = 0.055$$

and $D = 0.110$. Applying Theorem 1 to this case with $Y$ distributed as $Z$ gives $E(S(X)) \ge 1.78$ branches per source output. Anderson [9] applied a tree search algorithm to this case and found that even for better than average codes a search of at least 70 branches per source output was required to get within 20 percent of the optimal $D$. Later we shall calculate the search lower bound for the truncated Gaussian source described in the following.

## III. A Coding Simulation

It was decided to investigate the performance of tree coding for $D^{-1} = 2^{10}$, the signal-to-noise ratio necessary for good reproduction of speech. This requires a rate of about 5 bits per source sample. A number of modifications to the coding previously described were found necessary.

The first was due to the finding that a source output of large magnitude occurring right at the start of coding usually resulted in extremely large distortion. This problem was answered, at the cost of a slight increase in rate, by starting the coding one position late. That is, the first source output was matched against the second letter of each codeword, the second against the third, and so on. At 5 bits per sample this start-up procedure gave 1024 chances to find a good match to the first source letter.

Another, more serious, problem had two sides. The theoretical side, predicated on Theorem 2, was that very large outputs, so rare as not to occur in the simulation, might prove so troublesome to the coding that they would ruin its effectiveness. The practical side was that source outputs larger than three standard deviations in magnitude did indeed prove to be extremely difficult to handle. Our approach to this problem was to encode separately those source outputs whose magnitudes exceeded 3.5. This cutoff was selected because it was found experimentally to be better than cutoffs $2\frac{7}{8}$ and $3\frac{3}{16}$ [10], chosen for comparison.

Three problems associated with using a cutoff are as follows:

a) how to indicate which source outputs have magnitude beyond the cutoff;
b) how to encode source outputs beyond the cutoff;
c) how to encode source outputs falling between the cutoffs.

Problem a) may be handled by using 120 extra bits per 15 000 source outputs. There is a coding scheme which is easy to implement which can indicate up to 15 extreme source outputs and their signs with these 120 extra bits. If more should occur, only the 15 most extreme are indicated. This reduces the expected number of extreme source outputs from 6.98 per 15 000 to less than $4 \times 10^{-3}$ per 15 000 [10].

Problem b) may be handled by quantizing output $x > c$ into $E[X \mid X > c]$.

Problem c) was dealt with by applying an algorithm of Blahut [11] to find the optimal probability distribution (in the rate-distortion sense) to fill a tree for coding the truncated Gaussian distribution. This was done by dividing the interval $[-3.5,3.5]$ into subintervals each of width $2^{-7}$ and treating the resulting discrete source.

A number of modifications were also made to the basic stack algorithm. One is that the stack was made to contain path groups instead of individual paths. A path group is defined as all paths which are one-branch extensions of a given path and which have not yet been extended. Each path group is given the metric of the lowest metric path it contains. Stack size is then the upper limit on the number of path groups the stack may contain. Whenever the stack is about to contain more path groups, the path group with the largest metric is eliminated.

Another modification was that whenever there were paths of negative metric, the longest such path was extended, instead of the lowest metric path. This speeds the search forward when it is progressing well.

Another modification was that whenever any multiple of 100 000 path extensions had taken place in coding a single block of 250 samples, all but the 32 longest paths were eliminated and all path metrics were reduced by a constant which just made them all nonpositive. This was done to force the algorithm past difficult data in order to make it finish coding each block in a reasonable amount of time.

Except in one run, all the stack runs had a par value function equal to a constant times the optimal distortion as a function of the source outputs given by the results of the Blahut iterations. The distortion goal of such a run is defined to be the expected value of the constant times the par value. The exceptional run was one in which the par value function was $2^{-10}(1 + 0.25\,x^2)$, where $x$ represents the source output, a function which allowed much more distortion for large source outputs than the usual one did.

In order better to study the effect of large source outputs, most runs had a larger proportion of blocks containing such outputs than that which would occur naturally. This was done as follows. Each block was classified small, medium, or large according to whether the maximum magnitude sample remaining in it after truncation was less than $2\frac{7}{8}$, between $2\frac{7}{8}$ and $3\frac{3}{16}$, or between $3\frac{3}{16}$ and $3\frac{1}{2}$, respectively. For block length 250, such blocks have probability of 0.408, 0.376, and 0.215, respectively. Block mean-squared error, block code search, and their variances were computed for each type of block separately, then averaged according to the probabilities just given. The average variance was then divided by the total number of blocks coded and the square root of the result taken to give an estimate of the standard deviation of each measurement.

The performance of the coding was evaluated by means of the *performance index* $I$ given by

$$I = D \times 2^{2R}. \tag{8}$$

The expectation of $I$ is always $\geq 1$ and the smaller it is the better is the coding. This is a convenient measure because the optimal expected performance index of permutation codes and entropy-coded quantizers is always about $I = 1.41$.

For the tree coding just described, let $H_s$ be the number of bits of startup and $N_c$ the length of a block. Let $p$ be the probability of each tail, that is of each interval $(-\infty, -3.5)$ and $(3.5, \infty)$, and let $D_t$ be the average expected distortion for source outputs in the tails. Let $R_c$ and $D_c$ be the rate and distortion, respectively, in the coding of the truncated source. Let $R_t$ be the rate of the coding indicating for each source output which of the three intervals it is in.

TABLE I
RESULTS OF THE SIMULATION RUNS

| type | stack size | distortion goal x $2^{10}$ | nodes per datum | performance index $\pm\,\sigma$ |
|---|---|---|---|---|
| stack | 3000 | 1.05 | 727±28 | 1.243±.013 |
| stack | 3000 | 1.10 | 639±58 | 1.258±.018 |
| stack | 3000 | 1.15 | 498±54 | 1.276±.020 |
| Viterbi | / | / | 512 | 1.308±.018 |
| stack | 3000 | * | 330±54 | 1.326±.014 |
| stack | 300 | 1.25 | 170±26 | 1.365±.024 |
| stack | 300 | 1.15 | 274±34 | 1.366±.036 |
| stack | 300 | 1.10 | 320±37 | 1.375±.043 |
| stack | 300 | 1.20 | 262±34 | 1.382±.036 |

* distortion goal for each datum was $2^{-10}(1 + .25\,|\text{datum}|^2)$

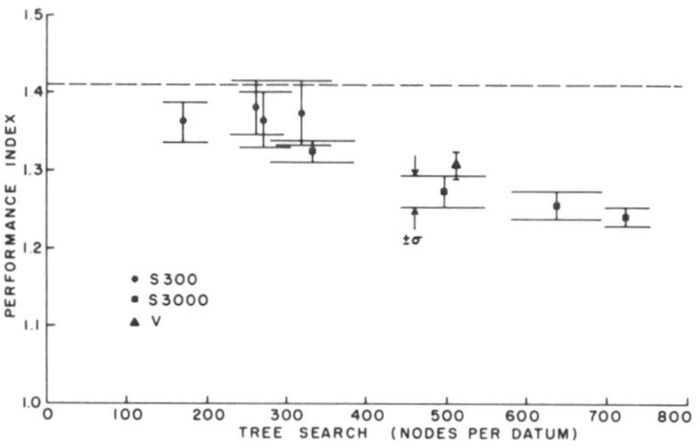


Fig. 1. Results of the simulation runs.

Then the overall rate of the coding is

$$R = R_t + (1 - 2p)R_c + H_s/N_c$$

and the overall distortion $D$ is

$$D = 2pD_t + (1 - 2p)D_c.$$

Here $H_s = 5$, $N_c = 250$, $2p = 0.466 \times 10^{-3}$, $2pD_t \times 2^{10} = 0.271 \times 10^{-1}$, $R_c = 5$, and $R_t = 0.628 \times 10^{-2}$. Hence $R = 5.02395$, $2^{2R} = 1059$, and hence

$$I = \frac{1059}{1024}(0.0271 + 0.999534 D_c \times 2^{10}). \tag{9}$$

This is for ideal coding to indicate extreme source outputs. For the practical coding of [10], $I$ is increased above this by 0.56 percent.

Table I and Fig. 1 give the simulation results. One node per datum equals 32 code states per source output. The Viterbi algorithm search does not vary because it is fixed by the state freedom of the code. In the figure, $S$ indicates the stack algorithm and is followed by the stack size. $V$ indicates the result due to the Viterbi algorithm.

An approximation of the lower bound to search effort for the truncated Gaussian source may be obtained by letting the integral of (8) be limited to the interval $-3.5$ to 3.5 for $D = 2^{-10}$. We let $Z$ be jointly distributed with $X$ in the optimal way and let $Y$ have the marginal distribution of $Z$. The resulting approximation says $E(S(X)) \geq 89$ branches per source output, or in the terms of Table I, 2.8 nodes per datum. Table I shows that to get within 30 percent of the optimal $D$ a search hundreds of times this is required. Thus the lower bound to search effort is about two orders of magnitude smaller than the search required by algorithms investigated to date. This underscores the importance of the search lower bound being infinity for the untruncated Gaussian source.

There are both positive and negative sides to the simulation results. On the positive side it has been demonstrated that tree coding algorithms which surpass the performance of coded quantizers and permutation codes can be implemented with today's machines. On the negative side, however, the simulations reveal that the algorithms require enormous computational effort at a rate of 5 bits per source output. Hence real-time tree encoding of practical analog sources at high rates in not instrumentable at present.

## References

[1] T. Berger, *Rate Distortion Theory: A Mathematical Basis for Data Compression.* Englewood Cliffs, N.J.: Prentice-Hall, 1971.

[2] T. J. Goblick, Jr., and J. L. Holsinger, "Analog source digitization: A comparison of theory and practice," *IEEE Trans. Inform. Theory* (Corresp.), vol. IT-13, pp. 323–326, Apr. 1967.

[3] F. Jelinek, "Buffer overflow in variable length coding of fixed rate sources," *IEEE Trans. Inform. Theory*, vol. IT-14, pp. 490–501, May 1968.

[4] T. Berger, F. Jelinek, and J. K. Wolf, "Permutation codes for sources," *IEEE Trans. Inform. Theory*, vol. IT-18, pp. 160–169, Jan. 1972.

[5] T. Berger, "Optimum quantizers and permutation codes," *IEEE Trans. Inform. Theory*, vol. IT-18, pp. 759–765, Nov. 1972.

[6] F. Jelinek, "Tree encoding of memoryless time-discrete sources with a fidelity criterion," *IEEE Trans. Inform. Theory*, vol. IT-15, pp. 584–590, Sept. 1969.

[7] J. B. Anderson and F. Jelinek, "A 2-cycle algorithm for source coding with a fidelity criterion," *IEEE Trans. Inform. Theory*, vol. IT-19, pp. 77–92, Jan. 1973.

[8] R. G. Gallager, "Tree encoding for symmetric sources with a distortion measure," presented at the 1973 IEEE Int. Symp. on Information Theory, Ashkelon, Israel, June 25–29.

[9] J. B. Anderson, "Instrumentable tree encoding of information sources," M.S. thesis, Cornell Univ., Ithaca, N.Y., 1969.

[10] R. J. Dick, "Tree coding for Gaussian sources," Ph.D. dissertation, Cornell Univ., Ithaca, N.Y., 1973.

[11] R. E. Blahut, "Computation of channel capacity and rate-distortion functions," *IEEE Trans. Inform. Theory*, vol. IT-18, pp. 460–473, July 1972.

# 45



Reprinted from *IEEE Trans. Inform. Theory,* **IT-20**(3), 325–332 (1974)

# Trellis Encoding of Memoryless Discrete-Time Sources with a Fidelity Criterion

ANDREW J. VITERBI, FELLOW, IEEE, AND JIM K. OMURA, MEMBER, IEEE

***Abstract*—For memoryless discrete-time sources and bounded single-letter distortion measures, we derive a bound on the average per-letter distortion achievable by a trellis source code of fixed constraint length. For any fixed code rate greater than $R(D^*)$, the rate-distortion function at $D^*$, this bound decreases toward $D^*$ exponentially with constraint length.**

## I. Introduction

THE SOURCE coding theorem, first proved for block codes by Shannon [1], was conjectured for tree codes by Goblick [2] and proved by Jelinek [3] for memoryless sources. Jelinek also conjectured that for finite-constraint-length trellis codes the average distortion converges to the rate-distortion limit as constraint length increases, in a manner similar to block codes. He performed simulations [4] with memoryless sources which appeared to substantiate this conjecture. Both Jelinek [4] and Omura [5] also demonstrated that optimal (minimum-distortion) source encoding, using a finite-constraint-length trellis code, can be performed by the Viterbi algorithm [6], which was first proposed for decoding convolutional codes transmitted over a noisy channel.

In this paper, we prove the following source coding theorem for discrete-time memoryless sources with a bounded single-letter distortion measure using trellis[1] codes.

*Theorem:* For any memoryless source with bounded distortion measure, there exists a time-varying trellis code with $q$-ary inputs and constraint length $K$ for which the average per-letter distortion $\bar{D}$ is bounded by

$$\bar{D} \leq D^* + \frac{d_b q^{-KE(R)}}{[1 - q^{-\varepsilon E(R)}]^2}$$

where $d_b$ is a constant and $E(R)$ and $\varepsilon$ are positive for code rates $R$ greater than $R(D^*)$, the rate-distortion function of the source.

Besides demonstrating the applicability of trellis codes to source encoding, this theorem also represents a more precise version of Jelinek's theorem [3] for tree codes.

The techniques used in proving the main result are structurally reminiscent of the channel coding bounds [6] for decoding convolutional codes, while analytically they resemble closely the proof of a similar result for block codes [7]. In Section II we recall the basic definitions and terminology of rate-distortion theory, and we proceed briefly to review the basic lemma in the block coding proof [7], in order to set the stage for the corresponding trellis source coding result which we prove in Section III.

## II. Preliminaries and Basic Lemma

We review the definitions and basic framework of rate-distortion theory in the context of block codes; we shall introduce the modifications necessary for trellis codes in the next section.

Let a memoryless source generate the sequence of source symbols $\boldsymbol{x} = x_1,x_2,\cdots,x_N$ from an alphabet $X$ with source symbol probability distribution $q(x)$. Consider the ensemble of block codes of $M$ codewords whose destination sequences $\boldsymbol{y}_m = y_{m1},y_{m2},\cdots,y_{mN}$; $m = 1,2,\cdots,M$ are taken from an alphabet $Y$. Let the bounded distortion measure between source and destination sequences be

$$d(\boldsymbol{x},\boldsymbol{y}_m) = \sum_{n=1}^{N} d(x_n, y_{mn}),$$

and for each $x \in X, y \in Y$ suppose the single-letter distortion measure is bounded by $d(x,y) \leq d_b$. Let the probability measure on the ensemble of code destination sequences be a product measure, with the distribution on the destination symbols being chosen according to

$$w(y) = \sum_{x \in X} q(x)p(y \mid x) \tag{1}$$

where $p(y \mid x)$ is for the moment an arbitrary conditional distribution. Bayes' rule establishes also the "backward" conditional distribution

$$p(x \mid y) = \frac{q(x)p(y \mid x)}{w(y)}. \tag{2}$$

Thus each codeword of the ensemble of codes has the product measure

$$w_N(\boldsymbol{y}_m) = \prod_{n=1}^{N} w(y_{mn}). \tag{3}$$

To this ensemble let us adjoin the "forbidden" codeword $\boldsymbol{y}_0 = y_{01}y_{02},\cdots,y_{0N}$, which is statistically dependent on

Manuscript received April 30, 1973; revised November 1, 1973. This work was supported in part by the Army Research Office (Durham) under Grant DA-ARO-D-31-124-71-G89 and in part by the National Science Foundation under Grant GK-23982.

A. J. Viterbi is with the LINKABIT Corporation, San Diego, Calif. 92121, on leave from the Department of System Science, University of California, Los Angeles, Calif.

J. K. Omura is with the Department of System Science, University of California, Los Angeles, Calif.

[1] The class of convolutional codes, fixed or time varying, is of course contained in the class of trellis codes. In fact, the most general trellis code may be generated by the same shift register encoder as a time-varying convolutional code, but with the linear combinational logic replaced by nonlinear operations.

the source sequence $x$ according to the product distribution

$$p_N(y_0 \mid x) = \prod_{n=1}^{N} p(y_{0n} \mid x_n) \tag{4}$$

where $p(y \mid x)$ is chosen the same as in definition (1). Since it is clearly impossible to select a codeword *a posteriori* according to the source sequence to be encoded, we can never use this "forbidden" codeword, but rather we shall use it as a standard of comparison against the distortion of the available codewords. In fact, the average per-letter distortion, if the forbidden codeword destination sequence were used, would be

$$\begin{aligned}\overline{d(x,y_0)} &= \sum_{n=1}^{N} \overline{d(x_n, y_{0n})}\\ &= N \sum_x \sum_y q(x)p(y \mid x)\, d(x,y)\\ &\triangleq ND_0. \end{aligned} \tag{5}$$

Equation (5) defines in terms of the conditional distribution chosen in (1).

For each source sequence $x$ the block encoder assigns the destination sequence $y_{m'}$, and hence the corresponding codeword, if

$$d(x,y_{m'}) = \min_{m \geq 1} d(x,y_m). \tag{6}$$

As we have assumed, for each $x$ there is also a forbidden destination $y_0$ related to $x$ by the conditional distribution (4). Now for the destination sequence selected we *may* have

$$d(x,y_{m'}) \leq d(x,y_0)$$

but if this condition is *not* met, then at least we always have

$$d(x,y_{m'}) \leq Nd_b$$

since the single-letter distortion measure is assumed to be bounded by $d_b$. Thus the ensemble average sequence distortion is bounded by

$$\overline{\min_{m \geq 1} d(x,y_m)} \leq \overline{d(x,y_0)} + Nd_b \Pr\{\min_{m \geq 1} d(x,y_m) > d(x,y_0)\} \tag{7}$$

and consequently the average per-letter distortion $\bar{D}$ is bounded by

$$\begin{aligned}\bar{D} &\triangleq \frac{1}{N}\overline{\min_{m \geq 1} d(x,y_m)}\\ &\leq D_0 + d_b \Pr\{\min_{m \geq 1} d(x,y_m) > d(x,y_0)\}.\end{aligned} \tag{8}$$

The crucial step then is to bound this probability. The result is given by the following lemma, due to Omura [7].

*Lemma (Block Source Encoding):* Over the ensembles defined

$$\Pr\{\min_{m \geq 1} d(x,y_m) > d(x,y_0)\} \leq 2^{-N[E_0(\rho) - \rho R]}$$

where

$$R = (\log_2 M)/N, \qquad \text{bits}$$

and

$$E_0(\rho) = -\log_2 \sum_x \left[\sum_y w(y)p(x \mid y)^{1/(1+\rho)}\right]^{1+\rho}, \qquad -1 \leq \rho \leq 0. \tag{9}$$

*Discussion:* Using arguments essentially identical to those used by Gallager [8] in the proof of the channel coding theorem, it can be shown that the negative exponent $\max_{-1 \leq \rho \leq 0} [E_0(\rho) - \rho R]$ is positive for all $R > I(q,p)$, where

$$I(q,p) \triangleq \sum_x \sum_y q(x)p(y \mid x) \log_2 \left(\frac{p(y \mid x)}{w(y)}\right).$$

Consequently,

$$\bar{D} \leq D_0 + d_b 2^{-NE(R)} \tag{10}$$

where $E(R) > 0$, for all $R > I(q,p)$. Finally, choosing the conditional distribution $p(y \mid x)$ of (1) so as to minimize the mutual information under the condition $D_0 \leq D^*$, we may replace (10) by

$$\bar{D} \leq D^* + d_b 2^{-NE(R)} \tag{11}$$

where $E(R) > 0$, for all $R > R(D^*) = \min_{p(y|x):D_0 \leq D^*} I(q,p)$, which is of course the rate-distortion source coding theorem for block codes. The proof of the lemma is of particular interest, since we shall require essentially the same techniques to prove the corresponding theorem for trellis codes. We therefore briefly summarize it here.

*Proof of lemma:* Suppose initially we fix the code $Y \triangleq y_1, y_2, \cdots, y_M$. Then, defining the indicator function

$$\Phi(x,Y,y_0) = \begin{cases} 1, & \text{if } \min_{m \geq 1} d(x,y_m) > d(x,y_0)\\ 0, & \text{otherwise}\end{cases} \tag{12}$$

and letting

$$\begin{aligned} q_N(x) &= \prod_{n=1}^{N} q(x_n)\\ w_N(y) &= \prod_{n=1}^{N} w(y_n)\\ p_N(y \mid x) &= \prod_{n=1}^{N} p(y_n \mid x_n)\\ p_N(x \mid y) &= \prod_{n=1}^{N} p(x_n \mid y_n) \end{aligned} \tag{13}$$

we have over the source and forbidden codeword ensembles

$$\begin{aligned} \Pr\{&\min_{m \geq 1} d(x,y_m) > d(x,y_0) \mid Y\}\\ &= E_{x,y_0}[\Phi(x,Y,y_0)]\\ &= \sum_x \sum_{y_0} q_N(x) p_N(y_0 \mid x)\Phi(x,Y,y_0)\\ &= \sum_x \sum_{y_0} w_N(y_0) p_N(x \mid y_0)\Phi(x,Y,y_0)\\ &\leq \sum_x \left[\sum_{y_0} w_N(y_0) p_N(x \mid y_0)^{1/\beta}\right]^{\beta} \left[\sum_{y_0} w_N(y_0)\Phi(x,Y,y_0)\right]^{1-\beta} \end{aligned} \tag{14}$$

where $0 \leq \beta \leq 1$ and the last step follows from Hölder's inequality and the fact that $\Phi^{1/(1-\beta)} = \Phi$.

Finally, averaging over the code ensemble of $Y = y_1,y_2,\cdots,y_M$ and using the moment inequality for convex functions, we obtain

$$\Pr\{\min_{m\geq 1} d(x,y_m) > d(x,y_0)\}$$

$$\leq \sum_x \left[\sum_{y_0} w_N(y_0)p_N(x \mid y_0)^{1/\beta}\right]^\beta \cdot E_Y\left[\sum_{y_0} w_N(y_0)\Phi(x,Y,y_0)\right]^{1-\beta}$$

$$\leq \sum_x \left[\sum_{y_0} w_N(y_0)p_N(x \mid y_0)^{1/\beta}\right]^\beta \cdot \left[\sum_{y_0}\sum_{y_1}\cdots\sum_{y_M}\prod_{m=0}^{M} w_N(y_m)\Phi(x,Y,y_0)\right]^{1-\beta}. \quad (15)$$

However, note that the sum within the second brackets just equals $\Pr\{\min_{m\geq 1} d(x,y_m) > d(x,y_0)\}$, but with *identical* (unconditional) *measures* on each codeword $y_1,y_2,\cdots,y_M$ and the forbidden codeword $y_0$. Thus it follows that this summation must equal $1/(M+1)$. Then bounding this term by $1/M$, letting $\rho = \beta - 1$, and using the memoryless properties (13) in the first term, we have

$$\Pr\{\min_{m\geq 1} d(x,y_m) > d(x,y_0)\}$$

$$\leq \frac{1}{M^{-\rho}}\left\{\sum_x\left[\sum_y w(y)P(x \mid y)^{1/(1+\rho)}\right]^{1+\rho}\right\}^N$$

$$= 2^{-N[E_0(\rho)-\rho R]}, \qquad -1 \leq \rho \leq 0.$$

where $R \triangleq \log_2 M/N$ and $E_0(\rho)$ is defined in (9).

We shall utilize very similar techniques in proving the corresponding trellis source coding theorem in the next section.

## III. Trellis Source Coding Theorem

Trellis codes, whether fixed or time varying, can most conveniently be described and analyzed by means of a trellis diagram [9], [10]. Fig. 1 shows the shift-register source decoder and the corresponding trellis for a binary trellis code. We assume for the present a binary trellis code with $n$ destination symbols per branch, resulting in a code rate $R = 1/n$ bits per source symbol. We shall generalize later. For analysis purposes, we assume also a time-varying code which may be implemented by varying the tap positions, according to a predetermined pattern, after each new code bit is received. This allows us to consider a broader ensemble of codes than would be possible with a fixed decoder. Each branch of the diagram is labelled with the corresponding destination $n$-dimensional vector and the states or contents of the decoder register are denoted by the vertical position in the diagram, also shown at the left of the diagram. The trellis is assumed to be initiated in any of the $2^{K-1}$ states but terminated in the **0** state, and no encoding or decoding is performed during the final merging; this will be called the tail of the trellis. Thus the total code length is $L$ branches, while the tail requires $K - 1$ branches. The encoder, analogous to a channel decoder, searches for that path in the trellis whose destination sequence $y$ most closely resembles (in the sense of the distortion measure) the source sequence $x$. It is readily shown [4], [5] that this minimum-distortion path can be found with minimal complexity by the same Viterbi algorithm which searches for the most likely path for a convolutionally coded channel [6], [9], [10].

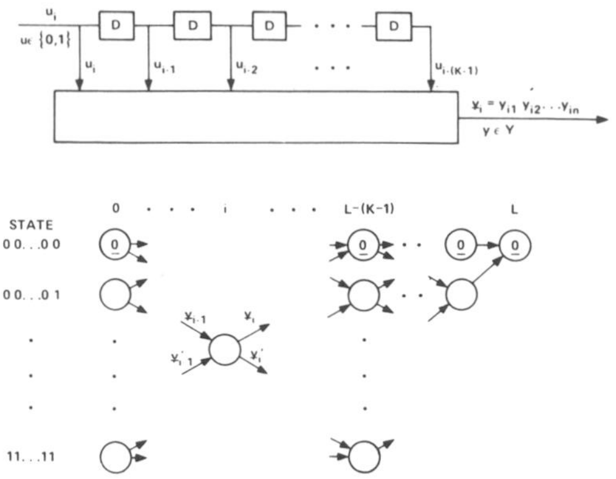


Fig. 1. Shift-register source decoder and trellis.

We now proceed to determine the ensemble average distortion of the minimum-distortion path. The major complicating factor here, compared to block codes, is the elaborate and labyrinthine structure of the trellis. Thus, in particular, while for block codes we could compare performance with an arbitrarily adjoined "forbidden codeword," it will be readily apparent that adjoining a structurally disjoint "forbidden path" to the trellis cannot provide a comparison because of the lack of structural homogeneity in the resultant structure.

Fortunately, we are provided with an alternative, which amounts to treating the top path of the trellis, which corresponds to the all-zero sequence entering the decoder, as the forbidden path. We begin by choosing the trellis code according to the measure $\omega(y)$. That is, each branch is selected independently according to the product measure $\omega_n(y) = \prod_{i=1}^n \omega(y_i)$ and, of course, this code is known to both encoder and decoder. Now suppose that in the *encoder only* we replace the branch code vectors of the all-**0** path by code vectors chosen according to the conditional product measure $p_n(y_0 \mid x) = \prod_{i=1}^n p(y_{0i} \mid x_i)$. The encoder then proceeds to code the source according to this modified trellis, and transmits only the branch decisions to the decoder. The shift-register decoder reconstructs the destination sequence $y$, which is an approximation to the original source sequence $x$ according to the original code which was chosen according to the measure $\omega(y)$ for all paths. Thus whenever the encoder indicates a branch on the all-**0** path, the decoder may put out a destination sequence with greater distortion than chosen by the encoder, but at all times the per-branch distortion is bounded by $nd_b$, since $d_b$ is the per-symbol distortion bound. This strategem thus allows us to encode the forbidden (top) path with the same conditional distribution as we used for the forbidden codeword in the block coding theorem, and use this for comparison purposes.

We should note, however, that the forbidden path plays a somewhat different role here than that of the forbidden codeword of the previous section. In particular, it is not sufficient to determine the probability that the entire forbidden path has lower distortion than any other path, for this will not decrease asymptotically with constraint length. In fact, it is quite likely (asymptotically with probability one) that the minimum-distortion path will merge over some finite segment or segments with the forbidden path. Rather, we must recognize that a temporary merger, say for $k$ branches, with the forbidden path is by no means disastrous. In fact, it merely causes the decoder to emit arbitrary destination symbols over the $k$ merged branches, with a total distortion no greater than $knd_b$.

We now consider the ensemble of all possible time-varying trellis codes defined previously. That is, all symbols at the decoder are endowed with measure $\omega_n(y)$, as are all branches at the encoder except those on the forbidden path, which are endowed with measure $p_n(y_0 \mid x)$. We begin by establishing the following result.

*Lemma 1:* Over the code ensemble defined, the average distortion of the $L$-branch minimum-distortion path reconstructed at the decoder is bounded by

$$\overline{\min_{\boldsymbol{y}} d(\boldsymbol{x},\boldsymbol{y})} \le LnD_0 + nd_b \sum_{j=1}^{L} \sum_{k=1}^{L-j} kP_{jk} \qquad (16)$$

where

$$P_{jk} = \Pr\left\{\begin{array}{l}\text{minimum-distortion path merges with the}\\ \text{forbidden path at node } j \text{ and remains}\\ \text{merged for exactly } k \text{ branches.}\end{array}\right\} \qquad (17)$$

and

$$D_0 = \sum_x \sum_y q(x)p(y \mid x)\, d(x,y) \qquad (18)$$

$$d_b = \max_{x,y} d(x,y).$$

*Proof:* Over the entire $L$-branch span, the minimum-distortion path selected must have average distortion no greater than that of the forbidden path whenever it is unmerged with the forbidden path, for otherwise the latter would be selected. When the selected path is merged with the forbidden path for a length of exactly $k$ branches, the average distortion of the selected path is no greater than $knd_b$ over the $k$ merged branches. Any such merger can begin at any node[2] ($j = 1,2,\cdots,L$) and will occur with probability $P_{jk}$ as defined by (17), and $k$ may be any integer up to $L - j$ (see Fig. 1). Hence the average distortion of the minimum distortion path is upperbounded by

$$\overline{\min_{\boldsymbol{y}} d(\boldsymbol{x},\boldsymbol{y})} \le LnD_0 + nd_b \sum_{j=1}^{L} \sum_{k=1}^{L-j} kP_{jk}.$$

[2] We begin encoding at the point at which the trellis becomes complete; the initial tail which would result if we began in the **0** state, is not used in the encoding procedure, since the reduced alternatives would result in higher distortion.

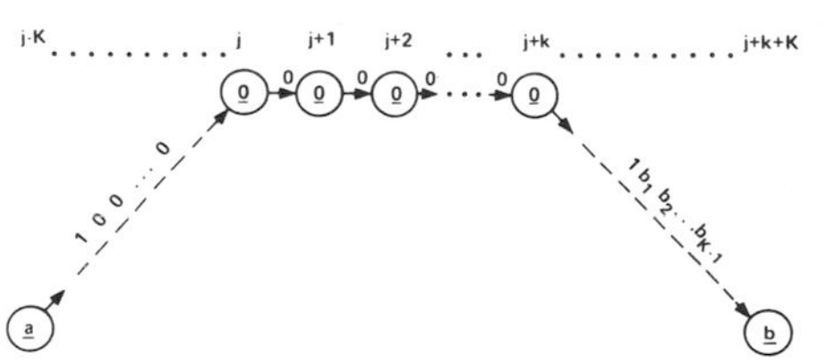


Fig. 2. Merger with forbidden path.

Thus there remains only to evaluate the probability of merged segments, as defined in (17), over the given code ensemble. By arguments similar to those used in the basic lemma for block source coding, but applied to the more delicate trellis structure, we now prove the following.

*Lemma 2 (Trellis Source Coding):* Over the ensemble defined

$$P_{jk} \le 2^{(K-1)\rho} 2^{-k\{[E_0(\rho)/R]-\rho\}} \qquad (19)$$

where

$$E_0(\rho) = -\log_2 \sum_x \left[\sum_y w(y)p(x \mid y)^{1/(1+\rho)}\right]^{1+\rho}, \qquad -1 \le \rho \le 0.$$

*Proof:* If the path selected is merged with the forbidden path for exactly $k$ branches, starting with the $j$th node, it must correspond to a binary sequence (at the decoder input) of the form

$$\underset{\substack{\uparrow\\ \text{node } j-K}}{a_1a_2\cdots a_{K-1}\,1\,0\,0}\cdots \underset{\substack{\uparrow\\ \text{node } j}}{0\,0\,0}\cdots \underset{\substack{\uparrow\\ \text{node } j+k}}{0\,1}\, b_1b_2\cdots \underset{\substack{\uparrow\\ \text{node } j+k+K}}{b_{K-1}}$$

At node $j - K$ we take the decoder to be in state $\boldsymbol{a} \triangleq a_1a_2\cdots a_{K-1}$ and at node $j + k + K$ to be in state $\boldsymbol{b} \triangleq b_1b_2\cdots b_{K-1}$. The "1" immediately following node $j - K$ is required, for otherwise merging would occur within $K - 1$ branches prior to node $j$, thus eliminating the possibility of merging at exactly node $j$. Similarly a "1" must follow node $j + k$, for otherwise the merged span would be longer than exactly $k$, as assumed. The merged span is shown in Fig. 2. Note also that states $\boldsymbol{a}$ and $\boldsymbol{b}$ are unrestricted and either or both may possibly be $\boldsymbol{0}$.

Now for the moment, let us assume that states $\boldsymbol{a}$ and $\boldsymbol{b}$ are fixed (that is, the selected path is assumed to have passed through $\boldsymbol{a}$ at node $j - K$ and $\boldsymbol{b}$ at node $j + k + K$). Then we seek the probability that the path

$$\boldsymbol{a}\ \underbrace{1\ 0\ 0\cdots 0\ 0\ 1}_{\longleftarrow K-1+k \longrightarrow}\ \boldsymbol{b}$$

merged over a span of $k$ branches with the forbidden path, is the minimum-distortion path from state $\boldsymbol{a}$ to state $\boldsymbol{b}$. Denote this probability by $P_{jk}(\boldsymbol{a},\boldsymbol{b})$. Let $\boldsymbol{u} = u_{j-(K-1)}\cdots u_{j+k-1}$ and let $\boldsymbol{0}$ denote $\boldsymbol{u} = \boldsymbol{0}$. Then

$$P_{jk}(\boldsymbol{a},\boldsymbol{b}) = \Pr\left[\boldsymbol{a}\ 1\ \boldsymbol{0}\ 1\ \boldsymbol{b} \text{ best in } \{\boldsymbol{a}\ u_{j-K}\ \boldsymbol{u}\ u_{j+k}\ \boldsymbol{b}\}\right]$$

$$\le \Pr\left[\boldsymbol{a}\ 1\ \boldsymbol{0}\ 1\ \boldsymbol{b} \text{ best in } \{\boldsymbol{a}\ 1\ \boldsymbol{u}\ 1\ \boldsymbol{b}\}\right]$$

where "best" signifies the minimum-distortion path in the given set; the inequality follows from the fact that the latter set is contained in the former. Since $\boldsymbol{u}$ is an arbitrary binary sequence of length $K - 1 + k$, there are clearly $2^{K-1-k}$ distinct paths in this set. Expressed in terms of distortion, this becomes

$$P_{jk}(\boldsymbol{a},\boldsymbol{b}) \leq \Pr\{d(\boldsymbol{x},\boldsymbol{y}_0) < \min_{\boldsymbol{u}\neq 0} d(\boldsymbol{x},\boldsymbol{y}_{\boldsymbol{u}}) \mid \boldsymbol{a},\boldsymbol{b}\} \tag{20}$$

where $\boldsymbol{y}_{\boldsymbol{u}}$ is the destination sequence corresponding to the segment $\boldsymbol{u}$ of the decoder input sequence $\boldsymbol{a}\ 1\ \boldsymbol{u}\ 1\ \boldsymbol{b}$. Note that many of these paths will be merged with the forbidden path $\boldsymbol{a}\ 1\ \boldsymbol{0}\ 1\ \boldsymbol{b}$ over some span, but in all cases this span will be less than $k$ branches long and hence already accounted for by a $P_{jk}$ term of lower index $k$, which corresponds to a forbidden path segment of shorter length (cf. (16) and (17)).

As in the proof of the basic lemma for block codes, let us fix for the moment the trellis code (destination sequences) for all branches except those on the forbidden path. Then note, as shown in Fig. 2, that even the path $\boldsymbol{y}_0$ is merged with the forbidden path over only $k$ branches, so for its initial $K$ and final $K$ branches the sequences are fixed. We now require the following notation.

$\boldsymbol{x}^t,\boldsymbol{y}_{\boldsymbol{u}}^t$ denote source and destination sequences over the first $K$ and final $K$ branches. (The tails of the subtrellis under consideration. See Fig. 2.)

$\boldsymbol{x}^c$ denotes the source sequence over the central $k$ branches.

$\boldsymbol{y}_{\boldsymbol{u}}^c$ denotes those central portions of each destination sequence which are *not* merged with the forbidden path.

$\boldsymbol{y}_0^c$ denotes the destination sequence of the forbidden path over the central $k$ branches. Note also that $\boldsymbol{y}_0^c$ is the only segment of $\boldsymbol{y}_0$, that is relevant here because the forbidden path exists only over the central portion of the subtrellis.

Then, proceeding in the same manner as in the proof of the block coding lemma, with the indicator function we have

$$\Phi(\boldsymbol{x},\boldsymbol{Y},\boldsymbol{y}_0^c) = \begin{cases} 1, & \text{if } \min_{\boldsymbol{u}\neq 0} d(\boldsymbol{x},\boldsymbol{y}_{\boldsymbol{u}}) > d(\boldsymbol{x},\boldsymbol{y}_0) \\ 0, & \text{otherwise} \end{cases}$$

where in this case $\boldsymbol{Y} = \{\boldsymbol{y}_{\boldsymbol{u}}^c, \boldsymbol{y}_{\boldsymbol{u}}^t : \boldsymbol{u} \neq 0\}$, we have

$$\begin{aligned}
&\Pr\{d(\boldsymbol{x},\boldsymbol{y}_0) < \min_{\boldsymbol{u}\neq 0} d(\boldsymbol{x},\boldsymbol{y}_{\boldsymbol{u}}) \mid \boldsymbol{a},\boldsymbol{b},\boldsymbol{Y}\} \\
&= E_{\boldsymbol{x},\boldsymbol{y}_0^c}\{\Phi(\boldsymbol{x},\boldsymbol{Y},\boldsymbol{y}_0^c) \mid \boldsymbol{a},\boldsymbol{b},\boldsymbol{Y}\} \\
&= \sum_{\boldsymbol{x}^t} q(\boldsymbol{x}^t) \sum_{\boldsymbol{x}^c} \sum_{\boldsymbol{y}_0^c} q(\boldsymbol{x}^c) p(\boldsymbol{y}_0^c \mid \boldsymbol{x}^c) \Phi(\boldsymbol{x},\boldsymbol{Y},\boldsymbol{y}_0^c) \\
&= \sum_{\boldsymbol{x}^t} q(\boldsymbol{x}^t) \sum_{\boldsymbol{x}^c} \sum_{\boldsymbol{y}_0^c} w(\boldsymbol{y}_0^c) p(\boldsymbol{x}^c \mid \boldsymbol{y}_0^c) \Phi(\boldsymbol{x},\boldsymbol{Y},\boldsymbol{y}_0^c) \\
&\leq \sum_{\boldsymbol{x}^t} q(\boldsymbol{x}^t) \sum_{\boldsymbol{x}^c} \left[\sum_{\boldsymbol{y}_0^c} w(\boldsymbol{y}_0^c) p(\boldsymbol{x}^c \mid \boldsymbol{y}_0^c)^{1/\beta}\right]^{\beta} \\
&\quad \cdot \left[\sum_{\boldsymbol{y}_0^c} w(\boldsymbol{y}_0^c) \Phi(\boldsymbol{x},\boldsymbol{Y},\boldsymbol{y}_0^c)\right]^{1-\beta}
\end{aligned} \tag{21}$$

for $0 < \beta \leq 1$. We now remove the condition on $\boldsymbol{Y} = \{\boldsymbol{y}_{\boldsymbol{u}}^c,\boldsymbol{y}_{\boldsymbol{u}}^t : \boldsymbol{u} \neq \boldsymbol{0}\}$ by averaging on all branches *not* on the forbidden path. However, this affects only the last bracketed term, and using the moment inequality for convex functions, we obtain

$$\begin{aligned}
&\Pr\{d(\boldsymbol{x},\boldsymbol{y}_0) < \min_{\boldsymbol{u}\neq 0} d(\boldsymbol{x},\boldsymbol{y}_{\boldsymbol{u}}) \mid \boldsymbol{a},\boldsymbol{b}\} \\
&\leq \sum_{\boldsymbol{x}^t} q(\boldsymbol{x}^t) \sum_{\boldsymbol{x}^c} \left[\sum_{\boldsymbol{y}_0^c} w(\boldsymbol{y}_0^c) p(\boldsymbol{x}^c \mid \boldsymbol{y}_0^c)^{1/\beta}\right]^{\beta} \\
&\quad \cdot E_{\boldsymbol{Y}} \left[\sum_{\boldsymbol{y}_0^c} w(\boldsymbol{y}_0^c) \Phi(\boldsymbol{x},\boldsymbol{Y},\boldsymbol{y}_0^c)\right]^{1-\beta} \\
&\leq \sum_{\boldsymbol{x}^t} q(\boldsymbol{x}^t) \sum_{\boldsymbol{x}^c} \left[\sum_{\boldsymbol{y}_0^c} w(\boldsymbol{y}_0^c) p(\boldsymbol{x}^c \mid \boldsymbol{y}_0^c)^{1/\beta}\right]^{\beta} \\
&\quad \cdot \left[\sum_{\boldsymbol{y}_0^c} w(\boldsymbol{y}_0^c) E_{\boldsymbol{Y}} \Phi(\boldsymbol{x},\boldsymbol{Y},\boldsymbol{y}_0^c)\right]^{1-\beta}.
\end{aligned} \tag{22}$$

In the last bracketed term the expectation is with respect to only the unmerged branches of the trellis and its tails; each such branch has measure $\prod_{i=1}^{n} w(y_i)$ where the $\{y_i\}_{i=1}^{n}$ are the distinct symbols of the given branch, and this is exactly the same measure as the marginal distribution for each branch of the forbidden path $\boldsymbol{y}_0^c$, as given by (1). Hence the last term in brackets becomes

$$\sum_{\boldsymbol{y}_0^c} w(\boldsymbol{y}_0^c) E_{\boldsymbol{Y}} \Phi(\boldsymbol{x},\boldsymbol{Y},\boldsymbol{y}_{\boldsymbol{u}}^c) = \frac{1}{2^{K-1+k}} \tag{23}$$

for now all paths in the trellis have the *same measure*, and they are structurally symmetric; thus this probability is just the inverse of the total number of paths in the subtrellis, which is exactly $2^{K-1+k}$. Substitution of (23) into (22) yields

$$\begin{aligned}
P_{jk}(\boldsymbol{a},\boldsymbol{b}) &\leq \Pr\{d(\boldsymbol{x},\boldsymbol{y}_0^c) < \min_{\boldsymbol{u}\neq 0} d(\boldsymbol{x},\boldsymbol{y}_{\boldsymbol{u}}) \mid \boldsymbol{a},\boldsymbol{b}\} \\
&\leq \sum_{\boldsymbol{x}^t} q(\boldsymbol{x}^t) \sum_{\boldsymbol{x}^c} \left[\sum_{\boldsymbol{y}_0^c} w(\boldsymbol{y}_0^c) p(\boldsymbol{x}^c \mid \boldsymbol{y}_0^c)^{1/\beta}\right]^{\beta} 2^{-(K-1+k)(1-\beta)} \\
&= 2^{-(K-1+k)(1-\beta)} \sum_{\boldsymbol{x}^c} \left[\sum_{\boldsymbol{y}_0^c} w(\boldsymbol{y}_0^c) p(\boldsymbol{x}^c \mid \boldsymbol{y}_0^c)^{1/\beta}\right]^{\beta}, \\
&\qquad 0 \leq \beta \leq 1.
\end{aligned}$$

Then, letting $\rho = \beta - 1$ and using the fact that both measures in the bracket are products of identical measures over $kn$ symbols, we have

$$P_{jk}(\boldsymbol{a},\boldsymbol{b}) \leq 2^{(K-1+k)\rho} \left\{\sum_{x} \left[\sum_{y} w(y) p(x \mid y)^{1/(1+\rho)}\right]^{1+\rho}\right\}^{kn}, \quad -1 \leq \rho \leq 0. \tag{24}$$

Finally, recognizing that the result is invariant to the choice of initial and final states $\boldsymbol{a}$ and $\boldsymbol{b}$ and using the definition of $E_0(\rho)$ in (9) and $R \triangleq 1/n$, we obtain

$$P_{jk} \leq 2^{(K-1)\rho} 2^{k[\rho - E_0(\rho)/R]}, \qquad -1 < \rho \leq 0$$

which establishes the desired bound.

Combining Lemmas 1 and 2 we readily prove the trellis source coding theorem. For from (16) and (19), we have the

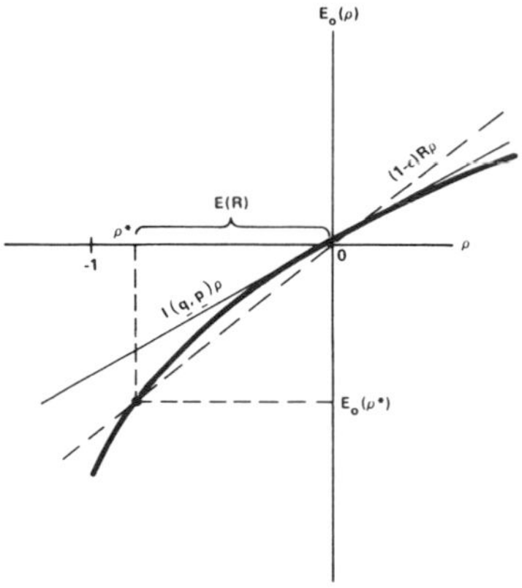

Fig. 3. Properties of $E_0(\rho)$.

average per-symbol distortion

$$\begin{aligned}\bar{D} &= \frac{1}{Ln} \overline{\min_{y} d(x,y)} \\ &\leq D_0 + \frac{d_b}{L} \sum_{j=1}^{L} \sum_{k=1}^{L-j} kP_{jk} \\ &< D_0 + d_b \sum_{k=0}^{\infty} kP_{jk} \\ &\leq D_0 + d_b 2^{(K-1)\rho} \sum_{k=0}^{\infty} k 2^{-k\{[E_0(\rho)/R]-\rho\}} \\ &\leq D_0 + \frac{d_b 2^{(K-1)\rho}}{[1 - 2^{-\{[E_0(\rho)/R]-\rho\}}]^2}, \qquad -1 \leq \rho \leq 0. \end{aligned} \tag{25}$$

However, $E_0(\rho)$ as defined in (19) is just the Gallager function [8], which plays the same key role in the proof of the channel coding theorem. In the interval $-1 \leq \rho \leq 0$ it is characterized by the following properties.

a) $$E_0(\rho) \leq 0.$$

b) $E_0(\rho)$ is monotonically increasing.

c) $$\lim_{\rho \to 0} \frac{\partial E_0(\rho)}{\partial \rho} = I(\boldsymbol{q},\boldsymbol{p}).$$

d) $$\frac{\partial^2 E_0(\rho)}{\partial \rho^2} \leq 0.$$

Clearly $\rho$ must be chosen such that the exponent $[E_0(\rho)/R] - \rho$ will be positive, for otherwise the summation in (25) does not converge. The aforementioned properties are demonstrated in Fig. 3, which also suggests the geometric construction which minimizes the numerator exponent subject to a fixed positive constraint on the denominator exponent in the second term of (25). Thus suppose we choose $R$ to satisfy the relation

$$R = \frac{E_0(p)}{\rho(1 - \varepsilon)}, \qquad \varepsilon > 0. \tag{26}$$

Then the bound (25) can be expressed as

$$\bar{D} \leq D_0 + \frac{d_b 2^{-(K-1)E(R)}}{[1 - 2^{-\varepsilon E(R)}]^2}$$

where $E(R)$ is established by the parametric equations

$$E(R) = -\rho$$

$$R = \frac{E_0(\rho)}{\rho(1 - \varepsilon)}, \qquad -1 \leq \rho \leq 0. \tag{27}$$

From the properties of $E(\rho)$ (see Fig. 3) it follows that the exponent $E(R)$ is positive for all $\rho < 0$. Now suppose we consider the limit as $\rho \to 0$

$$\lim_{\rho \uparrow 0} \frac{E_0(\rho)}{\rho} = \lim_{\rho \uparrow 0} \frac{\partial E_0(\rho)}{\partial \rho} = I(\boldsymbol{p},\boldsymbol{q}) \tag{28}$$

where $I(\boldsymbol{p},\boldsymbol{q})$ is defined immediately following (9). Thus it follows that

$$\bar{D} \leq D_0 + \frac{d_b 2^{-(K-1)E(R)}}{[1 - 2^{-\varepsilon E(R)}]^2} \tag{29}$$

where $\varepsilon > 0$ and $E(R) > 0$ for $R > I(\boldsymbol{q},\boldsymbol{p})/(1 - \varepsilon)$. Since (29) is an average over the entire ensemble, there exists at least one code over the given ensemble whose per-symbol distortion is no greater than $\bar{D}$ in (29). Recall that the distribution $p(y \mid x)$ was arbitrary, and so if we choose it to minimize $I(\boldsymbol{q},\boldsymbol{p})$ subject to the constraint $D_0 \leq D^*$, as in (11), we obtain the following theorem.

*Trellis Source Coding Theorem:* For a memoryless source with single letter distortion measure bounded by $d_b$, and any $\varepsilon > 0$, there exists a trellis code of rate $R = 1/n > R(D^*)/(1 - \varepsilon)$ and constraint length $K$ for which the per-letter distortion $D$ is bounded by

$$D \leq D^* + \frac{d_b 2^{(K-1)\rho}}{[1 - 2^{\varepsilon\rho}]^2} \tag{30}$$

where $\rho \in (-1,0)$ satisfies

$$R = \frac{E_0(\rho)}{\rho(1 - \varepsilon)} = \frac{1}{n} \tag{31}$$

and

$$E_0(\rho) = -\log_2 \sum_{x} \left[ \sum_{y} w^*(y) p^*(x \mid y)^{1/(1+\rho)} \right]^{1+\rho} \tag{32}$$

where the asterisks signify that the probability distributions are derived from the conditional probability $p^*(y \mid x)$ that satisfies $I(\boldsymbol{q},\boldsymbol{p}) = R(D^*)$. A $\rho$ satisfying (31) always exists whenever

$$R > \frac{R(D^*)}{1 - \varepsilon}$$

where

$$R(D^*) = \min_{p(y|x): D_0 \leq D^*} I(\boldsymbol{q},\boldsymbol{p})$$

with

$$D_0 = \sum_{x} \sum_{y} q(x) p(y \mid x) \, d(x,y)$$

and

$$I(\boldsymbol{q},\boldsymbol{p}) = \sum_x \sum_y q(x)p(y \mid x) \log_2 \frac{p(y \mid x)}{w(y)}.$$

Alternately, we may express the bound (30) in the form (which parallels the standard channel coding bounds)

$$D \leq D^* + \frac{d_b 2^{-(K-1)E(R)}}{[1 - 2^{-\varepsilon E(R)}]^2} \tag{33}$$

where $E(R)$ is determined by the parametric equations (27) with $E_0(\rho)$ as defined in (32).

Up to this point we have considered only decoders with binary inputs, which corresponds to a trellis diagram where only two branches leave each node. We now generalize the theorem to the case where the decoder has one of $q$ inputs so that the corresponding trellis diagram has $q$ branches leaving each node. For these codes the rate is

$$R = \frac{\log_2 q}{n}, \quad \text{bits/symbol.} \tag{34}$$

The proof is essentially the same as for the binary case where $q = 2$, but it requires conditioning on $\boldsymbol{a},\boldsymbol{b}$ and the two nonzero symbols that follow $\boldsymbol{a}$ and precede $\boldsymbol{b}$. For arbitrary integer $q$, (16), (17), and (18) are the same, but now $P_{jk}$ is bounded by

$$P_{jk} \leq q^{(K-1)} q^{-k\{[E_0(\rho)/R]-\rho\}}. \tag{35}$$

Hence, for this more general case, we have the same source coding theorem with (33) replaced by

$$D \leq D^* + \frac{d_b q^{-(K-1)E(R)}}{[1 - q^{-\varepsilon E(R)}]^2} \tag{36}$$

where $R$ is defined in (34).

For this case, we examine the convergence to the rate-distortion bound $(D^*,R(D^*))$ as constraint length $K$ increases. For sufficiently large $K$, $\varepsilon$ can be made as small as desired. Thus in the neighborhood of $R = R(D^*)$, the behavior of the distortion bound (36) can be evaluated by the following bound, which is useful for large $K$.

*Corollary:* There exists a $q$-ary input trellis code of rate $R = (\log_2 q)/n$ and constraint length $K$ for which the per-letter distortion $D$ is bounded by

$$D - D^* \leq \frac{d_b q^{-(K-1)[R-R(D^*)]/B}}{[1 - q^{-[R-R(D^*)]^2/2RB}]^2} \tag{37}$$

where $0 < R - R(D^*) < \frac{1}{2}B$ and $B$ satisfies

$$\left|\frac{\partial^2 E_0(\rho)}{\partial \rho^2}\right| \leq B, \quad \text{for all } \rho \in [-\tfrac{1}{2},0]. \tag{38}$$

*Proof:* The trellis source coding theorem yields

$$D - D^* \leq \frac{d_b q^{(K-1)\rho}}{[1 - q^{-\{[E_0(\rho)/R]-\rho\}}]^2}$$

where we require

$$\varepsilon = 1 + \frac{E_0(\rho)/R}{-\rho} > 0$$

and

$$-1 \leq \rho \leq 0.$$

$E_0(\rho)$ is defined in (32) in terms of the conditional distribution $p^*(y \mid x)$ which minimizes $I(\boldsymbol{q},\boldsymbol{p})$ subject to $D_0 \leq D^*$, so the $I(\boldsymbol{q},\boldsymbol{p}^*) = R(D^*)$. Then, expanding $E_0(\rho)$ about $\rho = 0$ and utilizing its properties, we have

$$E_0(\rho) = E_0(0) + \rho E_0'(0) + \int_0^\rho \int_0^w E_0''(\alpha)\, d\alpha\, dw$$

$$\geq \rho R(D^*) - \frac{\rho^2}{2} B, \quad -\tfrac{1}{2} \leq \rho \leq 0.$$

Hence

$$\varepsilon \geq 1 + \frac{\rho R(D^*) - \rho^2 B/2}{-\rho R}$$

$$= \frac{R - R(D^*) + \rho B/2}{R}.$$

Assume $R - R(D^*) \leq \frac{1}{2}B$, so we can choose

$$\rho = -\frac{R - R(D^*)}{B} < 0.$$

Then

$$\varepsilon \geq \frac{R - R(D^*)}{2R}$$

and

$$D - D^* \leq \frac{d_b q^{-(K-1)[R-R(D^*)]/B}}{[1 - q^{-[R-R(D^*)]^2/2RB}]^2}.$$

As an example, suppose that for large $K$ and any $\gamma > 0$ we choose $R$ as a function of $K$ to satisfy

$$R - R(D^*) \sim (\gamma + 4)B\left(\frac{\log_q K}{K}\right). \tag{39}$$

Then from this corollary we have

$$D - D^* \lesssim \frac{A}{(\gamma + 4)^4} \frac{K^{-\gamma}}{(\log_q K)^4} \tag{40}$$

where $A$ is a constant.

## IV. Conclusions

We have obtained a trellis source coding theorem for memoryless sources and bounded single-letter distortion measures in the form of a bound which bears the same duality to the convolutional channel coding error bound [6] that the recent block source coding bound of Omura [7] bears to the block channel coding bound [8]. This represents an alternate and more direct proof of the source tree coding theorem of Jelinek [3]. In addition, we have shown convergence to the rate-distortion bound with $R - R(D^*) \sim 0(\log K/K)$ and $D - D^* \lesssim 0(K^{-\gamma})$, which is a stronger result in terms of constraint length than has been shown for block source code convergence in terms of block length.

## References

[1] C. E. Shannon, "Coding theorems for a discrete source with a fidelity criterion," in *IRE Nat. Conv. Rec.*, pt. 4, pp. 142–163, 1959; also in *Information and Decision Processes*, R. E. Machol

Ed. New York: McGraw-Hill, 1960, pp. 93–126.

[2] T. J. Goblick, Jr., "Coding for a discrete information source with a distortion measure," Ph.D. dissertation, Dep. Elec. Eng., M.I.T., Cambridge, Mass., 1962.

[3] F. Jelinek, "Tree encoding of memoryless time-discrete sources with a fidelity criterion," *IEEE Trans. Inform. Theory*, vol. IT-15, pp. 584–590, Sept. 1969.

[4] ——, "Study of sequential decoding," Cornell Univ., Ithaca, N.Y., Progress Rep. to NASA under Contract NAS 2-5643, Aug. 1970, pp. 70–110.

[5] J. K. Omura, "On the Viterbi algorithm for source coding" (Abstract), in *Proc. 1972 IEEE Int. Symp. on Information Theory*, Pacific Grove, Calif., Jan., p. 21.

[6] A. J. Viterbi, "Error bounds for convolutional codes and an asymptotically optimum decoding algorithm," *IEEE Trans. Inform. Theory*, vol. IT-13, pp 260–269, Apr. 1967.

[7] J. K. Omura, "A source coding theorem for discrete-time sources," *IEEE Trans. Inform. Theory*, vol. IT-19, pp. 490–498, July 1973.

[8] R. G. Gallager, "A simple derivation of the coding theorem and some applications," *IEEE Trans. Inform. Theory*, vol. IT-11, pp. 3–18, Jan. 1965.

[9] G. D. Forney, Jr., "The Viterbi algorithm," *Proc. IEEE* (Invited Paper), vol. 61, pp. 268–278, Mar. 1973.

[10] A. J. Viterbi, "Convolutional codes and their performance in communication systems," *IEEE Trans. Commun. Technol.*, vol. COM-19, pp. 751–772, Oct. 1971.

# 46



Reprinted from *IEEE Trans. Inform. Theory,* **IT-21**(4), 379–387 (1975)

# Tree Encoding of Speech

JOHN B. ANDERSON, MEMBER, IEEE, AND JOHN B. BODIE

***Abstract*—Recently developed methods of tree source coding with a fidelity criterion are applied to speech coding. We first demonstrate that tree codes are inherent in A–D speech convertors of the waveform following type and point to ordinary and adaptive delta modulation and differential pulse code modulation (DPCM) as examples. Insights of coding theory improve these trees at low rates; we offer two new code classes, one obtained by smoothing the DPCM tree and one using the rate-distortion theory of autoregressive sources. Using these codes, we study the performance of a simple synchronous tree searching algorithm called the *M*-algorithm that maintains a small fixed number of paths in contention. 1 and 2 bit/sample code trees, used to encode actual speech at 8, 10, and 16 kbits/s, yield improved dynamic range and channel error resistance, and 4–8 dB improvement in mean-square error (mse) over ordinary single-path searched DPCM. These improvements in excess of analytical estimates suggest that tree coding methods perform better with real-life sources than previously thought.**

## I. Introduction

SPURRED ON by hardware advances, schemes for digitizing speech have advanced rapidly. Beyond the rudimentary schemes of pulse code modulation (PCM) and delta modulation have appeared differential pulse code modulation (DPCM), which quantizes the deviation from a least mean squared (LMS) prediction, and various adaptive schemes, which can change their own circuit parameters. A second group, the vocoders, analyze waveforms and release only certain characteristics like spectral energy. Interest here is only with the former group, all of which attempt to track a waveform.

In a parallel development the technique of tree coding has developed from the early sequential channel decoders of Wozencraft and Fano to sequential source encoders for conversion of analogue (or digital) data to reduced digital form. Design of such a source encoder comprises two distinct parts—choice of an effective tree code and choice of an algorithm to search the tree. Recent advances have involved the latter [1]–[4]. Among these search algorithms a second distinction can be made between single-path searches, which develop only one line of decisions, and multipath approaches, which pursue several lines and choose among them at a later point. As we show in Section II, the waveform-following schemes in the preceding are in reality single-path searched tree encoders. From the point of view of coding, this is their clearest shortcoming. Section V describes encoding actual speech by a multipath search that keeps a fixed number *M* of paths in consideration. It turns out that the multipath search for this "real-life" source actually exceeds predictions based on analytical sources.

Effective codes have received less attention. Once in the context of coding, however, the simple schemes point directly to improved codes based on both heuristic and rate-distortion grounds. Code generators are best looked upon as digital filters. We discuss this and efficient instrumentation in Sections III and IV. That simple hardware and relatively constrained searches significantly improve performance point to an encouraging future for information-theoretic designs.

The rate-distortion viewpoint requires a source model and a fidelity criterion. Although speech intelligibility is both frequency sensitive and nearly phase insensitive, we have chosen the mean-squared error (mse) criterion. Without such a well-defined measure, informative comparisons among codes and algorithms are difficult to make and the gap between theory and practice too wide to bridge. Of course, articulation index and psychometric measures may still be taken for the encoder as a unit. Appropriate source models are proposed in Section III.

## II. Tree Codes of Conventional Single-Path Encoders

Virtually all waveform encoders function sequentially. In sequential coding, a sequence of decisions are made uniformly in time and according to the same rules. A PCM encoder, for instance, quantizes each analogue sample in an unchanging manner while DPCM predicts according to a

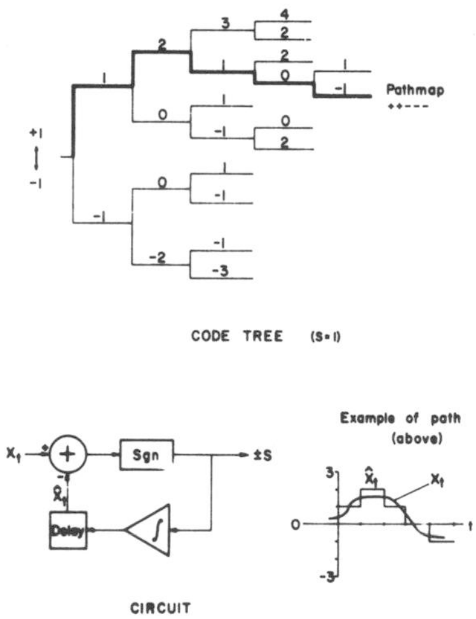


Fig. 1. Circuit, code tree, and example for linear delta modulation.

Manuscript received August 21, 1974; revised January 22, 1975. This work was supported in part by the Defense Research Board under Grant 9540-40.

J. B. Anderson is with the Department of Electrical Engineering and the Communications Research Laboratory, McMaster University, Hamilton, Ont., Canada.

J. B. Bodie is with the Avionics Division, Computing Devices Company, Ottawa, Ont., Canada.

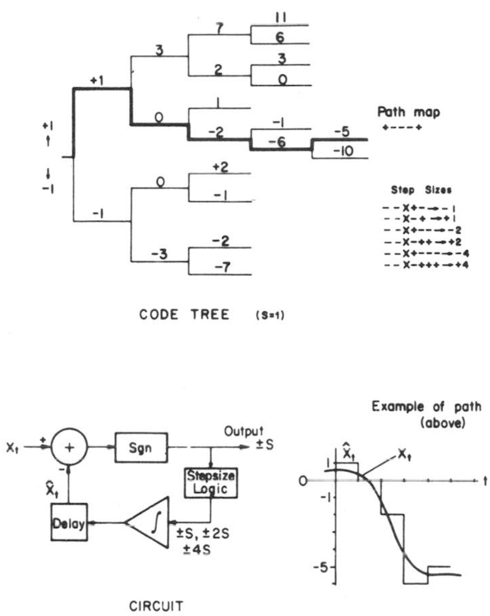


Fig. 2. Circuit, code tree, and example for adaptive delta modulation.

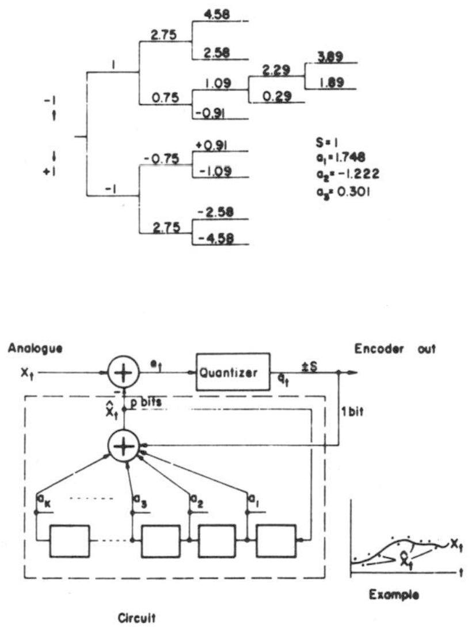


Fig. 3. Circuit, code tree, and example for DPCM. Recursive realization of McDonald model.

fixed rule and then quantizes the prediction error. As such, the possible decision outcomes of a waveform encoder can be graphically listed on a code tree like that of Fig. 1. On each branch lies a letter $\hat{x}$ representing a decision outcome. Since all decisions are made identically, a fixed number $b$ of branches stem from each node. One sample $x_t$ arrives for each tree level.

One of the earliest and simplest encoders used for speech was the delta modulator. After each sample, the modulator (see Fig. 1) augments a staircase approximation with a positive or negative step of fixed size. Thus two branches stem from each node in the code tree of Fig. 1, one for each decision. As the example in the figure shows, which tree path is followed depends on the input samples, and the path is located by a binary sequence called a *path map* $(+1,+1,-1,-1,-1$ in the example). By knowing the tree, the decoder uses the sequence to recreate the approximation in a process that amounts to integrating the map sequence.

The character of delta modulation is clear from its code tree. Having a fixed step size $s$, the code cannot follow transients rising faster than $s$ per sample time. No codeword is appropriate for slowly varying signals. These shortcomings are commonly known as slope overload and quantization noise. On a more subtle level, the code seems to lack the structureless quality that good codes usually have.

The fact that delta modulation performs poorly for its bit rate has motivated searches for improved modifications. Fig. 2 shows an adaptive delta modulator that doubles its step size after each path map $+1$ and halves it after each $-1$. Adaptivity is accomplished in the "step size logic"; many logics have been proposed. The code tree that results is somewhat less structured, and tests show that it performs better.

Adaptive delta modulation still does not take into account source statistics. One scheme to do this is DPCM in which the object is a LMS estimation $\bar{x}$ of the next input sample based on the previous $K$ samples. By a standard derivation (see [5]) the mse of estimation is minimized if $\bar{x} = \sum_{i=1}^{K} a_i x_{t-i}$ where

$$\boldsymbol{a}_{\text{opt}} = \boldsymbol{R}^{-1}\boldsymbol{r} \tag{1}$$

at an estimation mse of

$$\sigma_{\min}^2 = 1 - \boldsymbol{a}_{\text{opt}}^T\boldsymbol{r} = 1 - \boldsymbol{r}^T\boldsymbol{R}^{-1}\boldsymbol{r}. \tag{2}$$

$X_t$ is assumed to be a stationary zero-mean process with variance 1 and autocorrelation function $r(\tau)$, $\tau = 0,1,\cdots$. In (1), $\boldsymbol{r}$ is the column vector of these coefficients beginning with $r(1)$, $\boldsymbol{R}$ is a matrix of these

$$\boldsymbol{R} = \begin{bmatrix} 1 & r(1) & r(2) & \cdots & r(K-1) \\ r(1) & 1 & r(1) & \cdots & r(K-2) \\ r(2) & r(1) & 1 & \cdots & r(K-3) \\ \vdots & \vdots & \vdots & \cdots & \vdots \\ r(K-1) & r(K-2) & r(K-3) & \cdots & 1 \end{bmatrix}$$

and $\boldsymbol{a}$ is the column vector of $\{a_i\}$.

In actual practice, DPCM approximates LMS prediction by quantizing the estimation error $e_t$, as shown in the circuit of Fig. 3. The result of an $l$-bit quantization $q_t$ of $e_t$ is added to the estimate $\bar{x}_t$ to form $\hat{x}_t$, a decision appearing on the appropriate tree branch. $2^l$ branches stem from each node of the DPCM code tree.

One must carefully distinguish $x_t$ and $\hat{x}_t$. If the $x_t$ are used in the delay line of Fig. 3, the encoder and decoder (which does see the $x_t$) do not use the same code, and overall performance can only be degraded. (Some authors restate this as loss of feedback). Therefore, successive $\hat{x}_t$ are actually related by

$$\hat{x}_t = \sum_{i=1}^{K} a_i \hat{x}_{t-i} + q_t \tag{3}$$

and not by the standard mse relation. All the $\hat{x}_t$ producible through (3) make up the A–D code tree of Fig. 3.

Fig. 3 is a typical code tree of DPCM, derived using the source model of the next section. It is much less tightly structured than the earlier trees, and without (3) a pattern is difficult to trace. DPCM trees encode at up to half the rate of simpler trees for the same fidelity but may still be improved. In replacing $x_t$ with $\hat{x}_t$, quantization is introduced into the LMS optimization, but more importantly, sequential prediction is a single-path procedure, and multipath searches lead to a different code class.

In the figure, the encoder contains a comparator, certain logic, and a recursive digital filter whose output is a high precision $\hat{x}_t$ and whose input is low precision, actually a path map sequence $\boldsymbol{q}$. (Henceforth, we identify quantizer levels with path map symbols and use the symbol $\boldsymbol{q}$ for both). At the filter input the path maps appear digit-by-digit; whichever map is chosen by the encoder will also be the encoder output. The filter effect is characterized by the $z$ transform $1/(1 - A)$, with $A(z) = a_1 z^{-1} + a_2 z^{-2} + \cdots + a_K z^{-K}$. Since its output is a branch letter $\hat{x}_t$, the filter is actually the *code tree generator*.

We have not drawn trees for the adaptive schemes such as adaptive PCM [7] and adaptive DPCM [8]. The latter in particular has an exceedingly complicated code tree.

## III. Speech Source and Optimal Code Classes

With Flanagan [9], we view speech as a *quasi-stationary* source whose short-time behavior is stationary but whose modes of stationarity occasionally change. In theory, one could enumerate all the modes and their frequency of occurrence, arriving at an ensemble of sources. Several schemes, such as adaptive DPCM and the predictive vocoder, try to identify and adapt to these modes. Most schemes, including DPCM, pursue the simpler procedure of working with long term averages of mode parameters, taking a nonadaptive point of view. To avoid the complexities of adaptive trees, we shall adopt the latter approach.

Since the DPCM code generator filter plays a basic role in later code classes, we return to the calculation of the $\{a_i\}$. Fig. 4 shows the variation across modes in early terms of the autocorrelation function $r(\tau)$, for a typical male speaker. (Data were taken with a high-speed Hewlett-Packard 3721A correlator that recalculated a new autocorrelation every 0.1 s). If one uses (1)–(3) to design a one-step predictor at $f_s = 8000$/s, there is little difficulty, since $r(1)$ varies little. The same is more so at higher sampling rates. For longer term predictors, $r(2)$ and $r(3)$ vary significantly among modes. Previous authors have

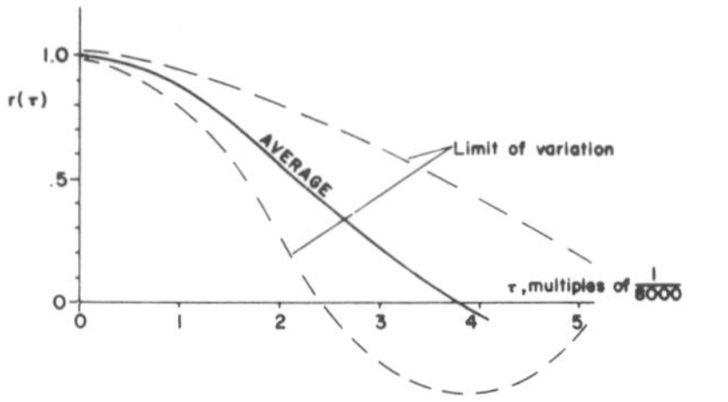


Fig. 4. Variation in short-term speech autocorrelation (approx.). Male speaker; $f_s$ = 8 kHz.

taken a long term average of the autocorrelation (see O'Neal and Stroh [5] or McDonald [6]), i.e., the heavy line of Fig. 4. One can in fact prove this is the optimal course for *single-path* searched DPCM when quantization effects are ignored, a reasonable assumption for high-quality DPCM.

*Lemma 1:* If $X_t$ is a quasi-stationary source whose modes vary with some distribution, the LMS prediction of $X_t$ is given by

$$\boldsymbol{a}_{\text{opt}} = E[\boldsymbol{R}]^{-1} E[\boldsymbol{r}] \tag{4}$$

$$E[\sigma^2]_{\min} = 1 - \boldsymbol{a}_{\text{opt}}^T E[\boldsymbol{r}] \tag{5}$$

where $E[\boldsymbol{R}]$ and $E[\boldsymbol{r}]$ are the matrix and column of expected values of $r(\tau)$.

*Proof:* For each mode of stationarity and fixed $\boldsymbol{a}$, the mse of estimation is

$$\sigma^2 = 1 - 2\boldsymbol{a}^T \boldsymbol{r} + \boldsymbol{a}^T \boldsymbol{R} \boldsymbol{a}.$$

Averaging over the ensemble of modes, one gets the same expression with $E[\sigma^2]$, $E[\boldsymbol{R}]$, and $E[\boldsymbol{r}]$ using the linearity in $\boldsymbol{r}$ and $\boldsymbol{R}$ to interchange expectations. Minimizing $E[\sigma^2]$ over the choice of $\boldsymbol{a}$ gives (4) and (5) instead of (1) and (2).

For multipath searches, choice of $\boldsymbol{a}_{\text{opt}}$ is an open question, partially answered in the succeeding paragraphs.

### *Heuristic Class of Good Codes*

One code class is easily derived on heuristic grounds and is important because its design and effect closely resemble a class derived from rate-distortion theory. Qualitatively, a primary effect of quantizing $x_t$ as some $\hat{x}_t$ is to superpose on the sample stream a "jitter" or $f_s/2$ note. This is clear from Fig. 5(a), which shows a waveform encoded by the algorithm described in Section V. Other effects concentrate at high frequencies; for multipath searches, slope overload is a minor problem. In short, one would like to filter out high-frequency components in the code tree, particularly the note at $f_s/2$.

We can accomplish this with minimally increased complexity if the following *smoother filter* is cascaded with the code generator filter $1/(1 - A)$:

1) zeroes at $f_s/2$;
2) some attenuation near $f_s/2$;

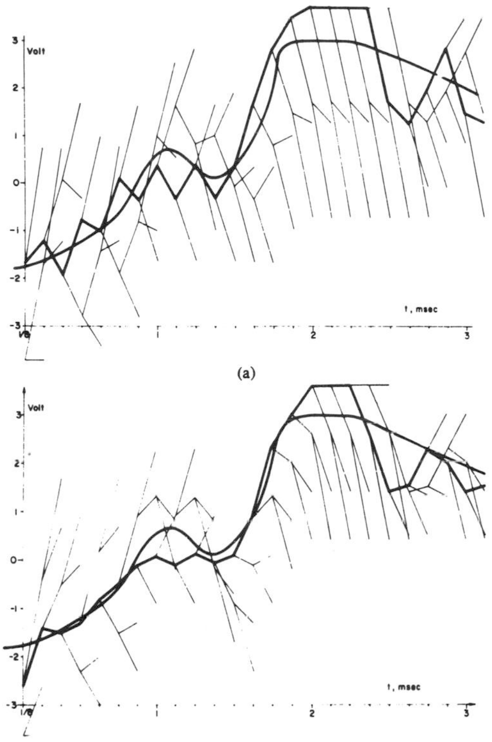


(b)

Fig. 5. Multipath encoding ($M = 2$) of an analog waveform. Heavy lines are waveform and final encoding, light lines are tree paths dropped. Butterworth predictor with $s = 1$ and $f_s = 8$ kHz. (a) No smoothing. (b) Smoothing filter $F$.

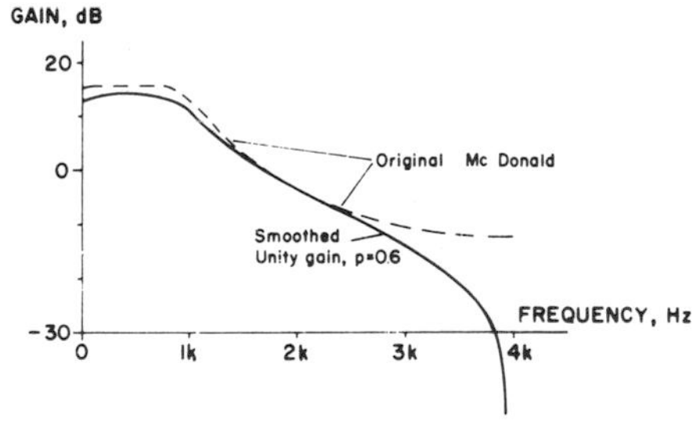


Fig. 6. Gain vs. frequency of McDonald predictor filter before and after smoothing with $F(z) = 1 + 0.6z^{-1} - 0.4z^{-2}$ normalized to unity peak gain.

3) short impulse response (to avoid lengthening the total predictor filter and to keep its impulse response short),
4) minimal delay (so the encoder will tend to make decisions near the point of best fit rather than "ahead" of it).

1)–4) are easily met with a short transversal filter having $z$ transform $F(z) = f_0 + f_0 z^{-1}$ or $f_0 + pf_0 z^{-1} + (p - 1)f_0 z^{-2}$, where $\frac{1}{2} \leq p \leq 1$ is a free parameter. Fig. 6 shows the gain of a total code generator filter $F/(1 - A)$, before and after smoothing with the $p = 0.6$ filter normalized to unity peak gain, while Fig. 5(b) shows the search of Fig. 5(a) using the smoothed code. For choice of $p$ and other details, see [10].

When these *smoothed LMS predictor* codes are used, noise is lessened and the $f_s/2$ note disappears, but a more subtle effect occurs. A multipath search algorithm continually makes decisions based on its path distortion measure, and artificial perturbations in this due to quantization noise make these decisions less meaningful. Even for single-path schemes, smoothing should be done at encoding rather than at decoding as in earlier schemes so that both ends use the same code. Perhaps the most interesting aspect of smoothed LMS codes is their relation to the next class.

*Rate-Distortion Derived Codes*

Thus far we have not derived a code class from the viewpoint of a multipath search. Recent work in rate-distribution theory has studied the autoregressive source coupled with the mse distortion measure. Using assumptions similar to those made for DPCM, one can find $R(D)$ for a given autoregressive model, determine near-optimal instrumentable codes, and compare practice with theory.

An *autoregressive* source produces a sequence $\{X_t\}$ according to

$$X_t = \sum_{i=1}^{K} a_i X_{t-i} + Z_t \tag{6}$$

where $\{Z_t\}$ are independent identically distributed (i.i.d.) zero-mean Gaussians with variance $\sigma^2$. The source bears a dual relation to an LMS predictor—given a source of order $K$, an LMS predictor of the same order predicts the next source output to an irreducible i.i.d. Gaussian error. The rate-distortion function of $X$, $R_X(D)$, the least number of bits per source letter needed to reproduce $X$ to an average mse $D$, was found parametrically by Gray [17] (in [12, theorem 6.3.2]):

$$R(D_\theta) = \frac{1}{2\pi} \int_{-\pi}^{\pi} \max\left[0, \frac{1}{2} \log \frac{1}{\theta g(\omega)}\right] d\omega \tag{7}$$

where

$$D_\theta = \frac{1}{2\pi} \int_{-\pi}^{\pi} \min\left[\theta, \frac{1}{g(\omega)}\right] d\omega \tag{8}$$

and

$$g(\omega) = \frac{1}{\sigma^2} \left|1 - \sum_{k=1}^{K} a_k e^{-jk\omega}\right|^2, \qquad \sigma^2 = \mathrm{var}\,(Z) \tag{9}$$

$g(\omega)$ follows directly from the autoregressive coefficients $\{a_i\}$; $1/g(\omega)$ is the spectrum square-magnitude of the recursive filter $1/(1 - A)$. If $D_0 = \inf 1/g(\omega)$, a remarkable theorem of Gray and Berger holds.

TABLE I
DPCM PERFORMANCE AND RATE-DISTORTION LIMITS FOR MATCHING AUTOREGRESSIVE SOURCE MODELS, COMPARED WITH ACTUAL SPEECH PERFORMANCE; ALL FIGURES dB SNR; $\Delta = R^{-1}(\cdot)$

| | | MARS Model | | | | Actual Speech | | | |
|---|---|---|---|---|---|---|---|---|---|
| | | LMS Pred/ Quant* | | R(D) Limit | | LMS Pred/ Quant | | Multi-Path Search (M=8) | |
| McDonald | | 2bit | 3bit | Δ(2) | Δ(3) | 1bit | 2bit | 1bit | 2bit |
| 3 tap | $D_0$=0.055 | 19.3 | 24.7 | <22.0 | 28.1dB | 7.9 | 14.0 | >12.5 | >21dB |
| 2 tap | 0.094 | 18.9 | 24.2 | 21.6 | 27.7 | . . . | | . . . | |
| 1 tap | 0.288 | 15.3 | 20.6 | 18.0 | 24.1 | . . . | | . . . | |
| Butterworth | | | | | | | | | |
| 3 tap | 0.113 | 14.8 | 20.1 | 17.5 | 23.6 | 6.3 | 16.1 | >12 | >20 |

*Approximate
<Indicates Overbound
>Indicates Underbound

*Theorem* [*12, theorem 6.3.3*]*:* For mse distortion measure,

$$R_X(D) = R_z(D), \qquad 0 < D < D_0$$

$$R_X(D) \geq R_z(D), \qquad \text{otherwise.} \tag{10}$$

That is, despite the fact that $X$ has a larger variance than does $Z$, $R(D)$ for $X$ is simply $R(D)$ for $Z$ (which is $\frac{1}{2}\log \sigma^2/D$), when $D < D_0$. var $(X)$ can be shown to be $\sigma^2/\sigma^2_{\min}$, where $\sigma^2_{\min}$ is the solution of (2) with $\boldsymbol{a}_{\text{opt}}$ equal to the autoregression coefficients.

A random ensemble of tree codes that actually achieves (10) was found by Gray and Berger as well (Theorem 6.3.4). A codeword (that is, tree path) in this optimal class can be generated by passing i.i.d. $\mathcal{N}(0,\sigma^2)$ variates through the filter with transform $B(z)/(1 - A(z))$, where $B$ is the solution of

$$|B(z)|^2 = \sigma^2 - D|A(z)|^2. \tag{11}$$

If this autoregressive source was encoded by ordinary DPCM, the code generator filter would be simply $1/(1 - A)$, since the autocorrelation function $r(\tau)$ for this source and its $\{a_i\}$ are related by (1). Apparently, $B$ is the modification to LMS prediction required for true optimality in the sense of squared error for a fixed bit rate.

Near $R_X(D)$, Berger interprets the process $X$ spectrally as the coding process plus white noise of power $D$. Specifically,

$$D + \left|\frac{B(z)}{1 - A(z)}\right|^2 = \left|\frac{\sigma}{1 - A(z)}\right|^2 \tag{12}$$

from which (11) follows. This helps support the attitude that code generator filters seek to attain certain magnitude spectra. Unfortunately, no coding theorem for $D > D_0$ has been shown, and it is easy to see that (12) cannot hold. However, for the autoregressive speech source model, $D_0$ occurs at 2–3 bits/sample. Thus theory is often applicable and at least suggestive where it is not.

The optimal class is not instrumentable, there being a variate to store for every tree branch. A reasonable means to an instrumentable class is simply to quantize the filter input Gaussians to the same number of levels as there are branches out of a node. Suppose, as is the custom in tree coding, increments to branches out of the same node are also complementary; that is, if the $\hat{x}_t$ on a branch exceeds the previous $\hat{x}_{t-1}$ along the path, then $\hat{x}_t$ on a sister branch falls short by the same amount. Then $B/(1 - A)$ is simply fed by path map sequences. For the binary branching tree, with 1-bit quantization of the filter input, any choice of variates once quantized and complemented leads to the same tree. For a $2^l$-branching tree, with $l$-bit quantization, one places a different level on each branch since there would be no point in having the same $\hat{x}$ on two branches out of the same node. In any case, generating the tree now amounts to recalling path maps and applying them to a digital filter.

The foregoing suggests encoding of speech by codes based on an autoregressive source with similar correlation. Define the *matching autoregressive source* (MARS) of order $K$ to be that autoregressive source having the same autocorrelation $r(\tau)$ at $\tau = 0, 1/f_s, \cdots, K/f_s$ as a given zero-mean time-discrete stationary source. Then $\{a_i\}$ and $r(\tau)$ are related by (1)–(2) for both. For large enough $K$, the second-order cumulative distribution functions of both processes agree to within any $\varepsilon$ if the original process is well behaved. A complicated enough autoregressive model accurately represents the correlation of a stationary mode of speech.

There is a close relation between LMS prediction of a stationary source and its MARS. Both circuits have identical coefficients. The first predicts $X_t$ from $K$ earlier $x_j$ to an error $e_t$, while the second generates a process $X_t$ from earlier $x_j$ and an i.i.d. Gaussian. Out to $K$ time units, the autocorrelations for both processes $X_t$ are the same. Both $E_t$ and $Z_t$ have the same variance. Successive $e_t$, however, need to be neither Gaussian nor independent (although $e_t$ is always uncorrelated with the prediction $\hat{x}_t$), and are so if and only if the process to be predicted is autoregressive of order $\leq K$.

We call codes obtained through the MARS procedure *rate-distortion derived* codes. Shown in Table I are MARS's for correlations suggested by McDonald [6] and for the correlation induced by a two-pole Butterworth filter with breakpoint $f_0 = 1$ kHz acting on an i.i.d. input. ($f_0$ is chosen so the resulting spectrum closely matches the long-term spectrum of speech; the Butterworth code generator often performs better than the McDonald). Assuming a Gaussian $Z$ with var $(Z) = 1$, $D_0$ is the largest mse in $Z$ (or in the autoregressive $X$) to which the theory applies.

From Max [13], the mse of a 2-bit and a 3-bit optimal quantizer for Gaussians is 0.1174, and 0.0345, respectively. For these $D$, the table gives the mse expressed as signal-to-noise ratio (SNR) for LMS prediction of the autoregressive $X$ followed by optimal mse quantization of the Gaussian error $e_t$, (that is, DPCM). Using the well-known "SNR Improvement" relation (see O'Neal and Stroh [5]) of DPCM, this SNR is approximately $-10 \log D\sigma^2_{\min}$. Next in the table are SNR for optimal codes, the solutions of $R_X(D) = 2$ and 3 expressed as SNR. (The theory for tree codes does not yet apply to 1 bit/sample).

Finally, SNR are given for actual speech, both LMS predicted/quantized (DPCM), and multipath encoded as

TABLE II
AUTOCORRELATIONS, PREDICTOR COEFFICIENTS, AND *B*-FILTER COEFFICIENTS FOR MCDONALD AND BUTTERWORTH SOURCE MODELS; $\sigma = 1$

| Auto-Correlation | $\{a_i\}$ | Coefficients of B Filter D = 0.1 | D = 0.05 | D = 0.01 |
|---|---|---|---|---|
| Butterworth | | | | |
| r(1)=0.790 | $a_1$= 1.231 | $b_0$= 0.894 | 0.990 | |
| r(2)=0.441 | $a_2$=-0.625 | $b_1$= 0.096 | 0.0085 | . . . |
| r(3)=0.170 | $a_3$= 0.119 | $b_2$=-0.0164 | -0.0015 | |
| McDonald | | | | |
| 0.864 | 1.748 | | 0.87 | 0.976 |
| 0.557 | -1.222 | . . . . | 0.15 | 0.0255 |
| 0.227 | 0.301 | | -0.030 | -0.0054 |

in Section V. A smoothed code is used, either heuristic or rate distortion, whichever performs better. Although the figures for MARS models and speech are roughly comparable, optimal multipath searching improves MARS models by 3–4 dB, while relatively simple multipath improves speech by at least 4–7 dB.

The filter $B(z)$ defined by (11) is a transversal filter of the order of one less than $A(z)$. Using a procedure outlined in [10], one can calculate the $B(z)$ given in Table II. From the magnitude plot of Fig. 7, it is clear that $B$ is basically a low-pass filter, with some passband attenuation, the severity of which increases with $D$. This is not unreasonable, since quantization effects center at high frequencies, and rate-distortion theory trades off high-frequency signal components against reduction of this noise. Also, a code intended for a multipath search can afford the luxury of words more condensed in amplitude.

Surprisingly, the two modifications to the DPCM filter $1/(1 - A)$, $B$ and the heuristic smoother $F$, are similar in effect. In the range 1–2 bits/sample intended for $F$ where present-day theory does not apply, future work may point to a far more severe low-pass than the filters of Fig. 7, perhaps as severe as $F$.

## IV. INSTRUMENTATION OF CODE GENERATORS

Traditionally, DPCM encoders have generated their codes by what amounts to a recursive filter whose input is the path map sequence. We now explore several generator circuits, list their storage and arithmetical requirements, and conclude that a transversal realization is usually more efficient for multipath algorithms. (Readers not familiar with such algorithms should turn to Section V for a description of a typical algorithm).

Consider the transversal generator filter in the box of Fig. 8, which receives the same path map inputs as the boxed filter in Fig. 3. By an elementary lemma of digital filtering, the two filters' outputs are also the same $\hat{x}_t$.

*Lemma 2:* If $\hat{x}_t$ satisfies (3), then it also satisfies

$$\hat{x}_t = \sum_{i=1}^{t} c_i q_{t-i} + q_t$$

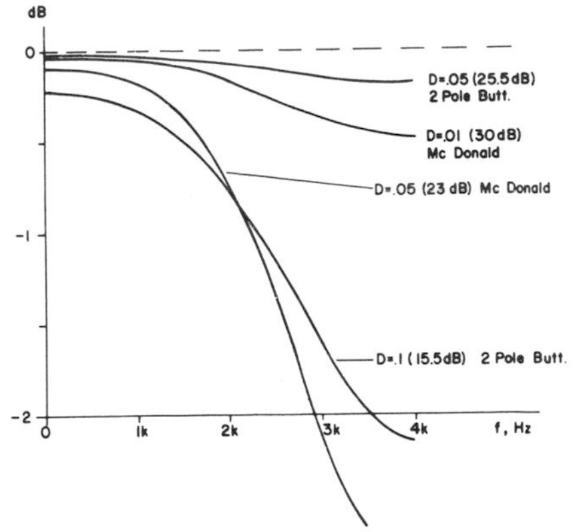


Fig. 7. Gain vs. frequency for rate-distortion derived filters $B$. $D$ is mse at (SNR) corresponding for encoding of matching autoregressive source.

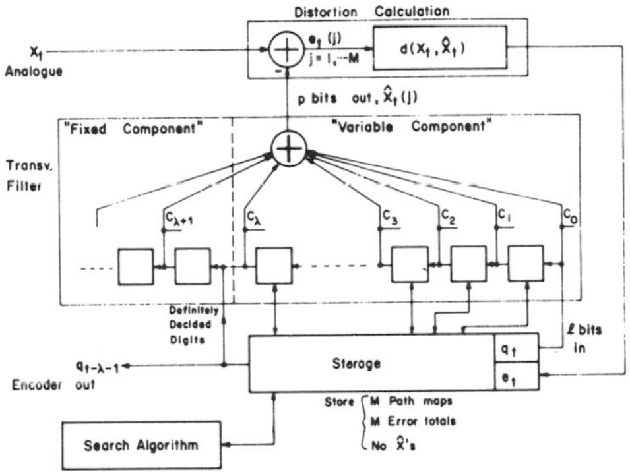


Fig. 8. General multipath encoder using transversal code generator.

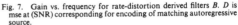

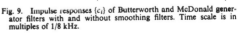

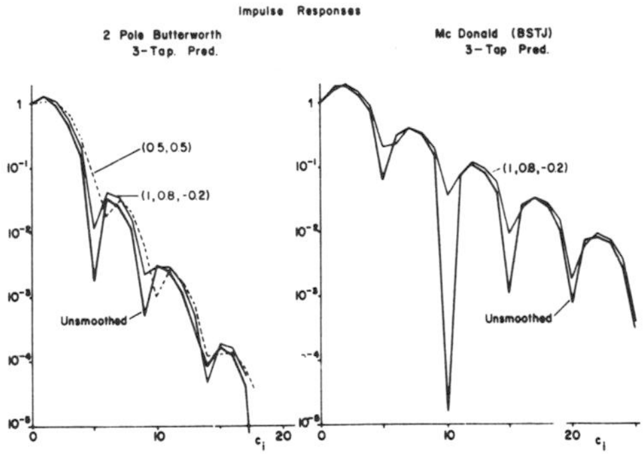


Fig. 9. Impulse responses $\{c_i\}$ of Butterworth and McDonald generator filters with and without smoothing filters. Time scale is in multiples of 1/8 kHz.

so long as

$$c_i = \sum_{j=1}^{i} a_j c_{i-j} \qquad c_0 = 1 \qquad c_i = 0, \qquad i < 0.$$

*Proof:* See [10].

The $\{c_i\}$ are in fact the impulse response of $1/(1 - A)$. Note that $q_t$ is a $b$-level quantity, but its levels may not be related in multiples of two, or any other number base. No essential change in instrumentation comes of this.

To be instrumentable, this equivalent circuit needs several length constraints. The *filter order* $v$, though generally infinite, is not so in practical terms, since for any stable filter $1/(1 - A)$, $|c_i| \downarrow 0$, as $i \to \infty$. As is clear from the impulse responses of Fig. 9, the $\{c_i\}$ may be truncated when they fall below the filter precision. For example, 6-bit plus sign precision implies only 17 and 7 coefficients for the McDonald and Butterworth generators. A second length constraint is $\lambda$, the *memory length*, the path map length over which digits may *vary* among path maps in storage. Though actually a function of the search algorithm, $\lambda$ affects the code generator organization. One can view $\hat{x}_t$ as having two components: A variable component depends on which path map is chosen from storage and is computed from the most recent $\lambda$ digits; a fixed component is calculated from decided digits. Fig. 8 reflects this. Time $(t - \lambda)$ is the point of decision among path alternatives, after which map digits are simply moved through a $b$-level shift register. $\lambda$ is also the encoder delay.

Used by a multipath search, Fig. 8 has the significant advantage that map digits may be parallel-inserted into the filter; the recursive realization requires serial insertion, usually impractical, or parallel-insertion of high precision $\hat{x}_{t-1}, \cdots, \hat{x}_{t-K}$ for each path. To this shortcoming in storage is added a requirement for $K$ high precision multipliers. Table III shows this in detail. If $\hat{x}$ and $q$ are of $p$ and $l$-bit precision (customarily $p = 7$ or $8$, $l = 1 - 3$) an encoder using Fig. 3 stores $MK$ high precision $\hat{x}$ and the $\{a_i\}$, totaling $(M + 1)Kp$ bits, while Fig. 8 requires $M$ low precision path maps for $M\lambda l + p\lambda$ bits. Fig. 3 must also execute $MK$ $p - x - p$ multiplications followed by additions to accomplish what Fig. 8 does in $M\lambda l$ additions only. Only a long $\lambda$ could reverse the balance and this has not proven true for speech.

Also listed in Table III is a modification to Fig. 8 in which all $\hat{x}$ are precalculated and stored in a read-only memory. Path maps are simply addresses to this storage. Almost all arithmetic is eliminated at a modest increase in storage provided the number of different path maps $2^{l\lambda}$ is relatively small. Actually, a range of circuits exists between these two in which arithmetic is traded off against varying degrees of read-only memory (see, for instance, Little [14]). Roughly speaking, Fig. 8 over Fig. 3 eliminates multiplication while the modification eliminates arithmetic altogether. Both Fig. 8 and its modification place storage into the cheaper read-only category.

TABLE III
STORAGE, ARITHMETIC, AND SHIFT REGISTER REQUIREMENTS FOR TRANSVERSAL AND RECURSIVE CODE GENERATOR REALIZATIONS

| | Fig. 3 (Recursive) | Fig. 8 (Transversal) |
|---|---|---|
| Storage, bits | | |
| Read-Only ([] = Modif.) | (K+1)p | (ν+1)p<br>[(ν+1)p + b^λ p] |
| Read-Write | MKp | λMℓ |
| Arithmetic, p-adders ([] = Modif.) | M(K+1)p + MK | Mλℓ + (ν−λ)<br>[(ν−λ)ℓ + M] |
| Shift Register Length | Kp | νℓ |

Assumptions: $M$ full paths of length $K$ or $\lambda$ stored (reducible by chained storage); $p - x - p$ multiplier made up of $p$ $p$-bit adders; search logic and distortion increment calculation not included.

When the table is dominated either by the precisions $p$ and $l$, or by large $M$, the comparison is clearer. For either, the recursive exceeds the transversal realization by the factor $p/l$ in both storage and arithmetic.

For a long impulse response or a very short recursive filter order $K$, a compromise realization may be advantageous. For instance, the variable component may be generated transversally, preserving the advantages of this form, while the fixed component is generated by a special recursive section. For details, see [10].

Thus far, we have designed the transversal LMS predictor filter $1/(1 - A)$, but extension to other classes is not difficult. Both classes simply cascade a transversal section, $F$ or $B$, into $1/(1 - A)$. The $i$th coefficient of the total transversal equivalent is given by $\sum_{j=0}^{I} f_j c_{i-j}$, where $I$ is the order of $F$ (or $B$). New coefficients appear alongside the old in Fig. 9. They differ only slightly; in particular, the point of truncation is not materially changed. Gains of the latter code classes are purchased at no cost of circuitry.

An important quantity stemming from the $\{c_i\}$ is the *impulse response energy* $\varepsilon^2$ of a code generator filter. Since each isolated channel error superposes an impulse response replica on the true decoder output, one can easily show that (see [10])

$$\text{SNR (due to channel noise)} = 1/\varepsilon^2 p \sigma_{\min}^2 \tag{13}$$

for var $(X) = 1$ and error rates $p \leq 0.01$. At 8 kHz, $\varepsilon^2$ is 14.12 for the Butterworth $1/(1 - A)$ and 40.10 for the McDonald. Thus when channel noise dominates, the short-response Butterworth filter has higher SNR, despite its poorer $\sigma_{\min}$.

## V. ENCODING OF SPEECH

Now we describe results of encoding speech with these codes using a simple search algorithm called the $M$-algorithm (see Berger [12, sec. 6.2], [1], or [11]). Briefly, the algorithm pursues a fixed number $M$ of paths at each level throughout the code tree. At each level, all $bM$ branches are extended out of the $M$ saved paths and only the best $M$ of these is saved for the next level. To insure finite storage, only $\lambda$ (the memory length) path map digits are retained.

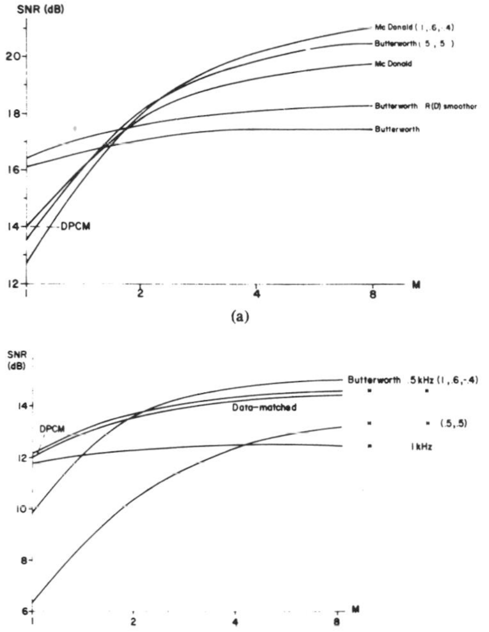


Fig. 10. $M$-algorithm performance; SNR vs. $M$. Parenthesized expressions are coefficients of $F$; data-matched code uses correlation of actual speech sample. (a) $R = 2$, $f_s = 8$ kHz. (b) $R = 2$, $f_s = 5$ kHz.

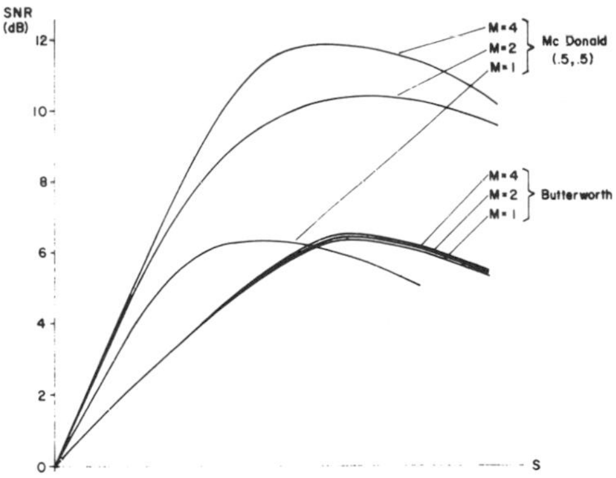


Fig. 11. $M$-algorithm performance; SNR vs. step size $s$ for $M = 1,2,4$. $R = 1, f_s = 8$ kHz.

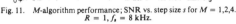

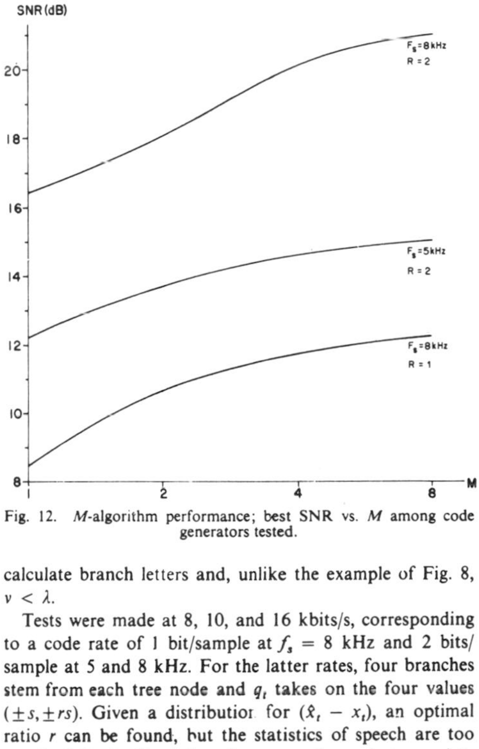


Fig. 12. $M$-algorithm performance; best SNR vs. $M$ among code generators tested.

The algorithm amounts to a highly truncated Viterbi approach.

The $M$-algorithm was chosen for the fundamental nature of its procedure and its simple practical instrumentation. Although other algorithms have proven more efficient asymptotically close to the rate-distortion limit, the $M$-algorithm appears better in the low computation-medium performance region (see [4]). Also, it attains synchronism without buffers and achieves most of its performance with small $M$ (2–10) and $\lambda$ (5–20).

Several 2-s speech samples were taken from a standard test tape [15] (although all plots are based on the same sample) and processed by an encoder–decoder software implemented on a CDC 1700 computer. Ordinarily, the speech was bandlimited prior to 8 kHz sampling, using 24 dB/octave Butterworth filters with cutoffs at 30 and 3000 Hz. For tests at the 5 kHz sampling rate, the upper limit was changed to 2500 Hz at 96 dB/octave. A modified-transversal code generator was employed, consisting of a filter output table of 1024 words, so that the filter order $\nu$ was always 10. (From Fig. 9, this will compromise only the McDonald $f_s = 5$ kHz curves). It was convenient to set the memory length $\lambda$ to 16 bits; thus bits 11–16 do not help calculate branch letters and, unlike the example of Fig. 8, $\nu < \lambda$.

Tests were made at 8, 10, and 16 kbits/s, corresponding to a code rate of 1 bit/sample at $f_s = 8$ kHz and 2 bits/sample at 5 and 8 kHz. For the latter rates, four branches stem from each tree node and $q_t$ takes on the four values $(\pm s, \pm rs)$. Given a distribution for $(\hat{x}_t - x_t)$, an optimal ratio $r$ can be found, but the statistics of speech are too poorly defined. Simulation, however, shows that a variety of codes and search parameters all lead to the empirical value 0.23. This is close to $r$ for the exponential density function. For further details, see [11].

At the 16 kbit rate ($R = 2, f_s = 8$K), Fig. 10(a) plots mse expressed as SNR versus $M$, for several code generators. Here the rate obtained for ordinary DPCM ($M = 1$) is about 14 dB. Codes from the heuristic smoother class do generally better than others, adding several dB to their unsmoothed counterparts. Surprisingly, the Butterworth and Butterworth $R(D)$ codes improve on DPCM at its own game at $M = 1$. The plot shows what will be a typical pattern, that good codes demand a larger $M$ to find their better paths while poorer codes can perform well at $M = 1$ or 2 but do not improve with a larger search.

Fig. 10(b) gives the same data for the 10 kbit rate ($R = 2$, $f_s = 5$K). Again, the smoothed-LMS codes offer improvement with the less severe $(1, 0.6, -0.4)$ smoother offering most.

Fig. 11 which expresses the data for the 8 kbit rate ($R = 1$, $f_s = 8$K) is a different form, showing SNR versus $s$, the fundamental step size of the code generator. This plot shows the *dynamic range* of encoding, the range over which the encoder input variance—or equivalently the step size—may change while the SNR remains within a certain bound. Since the $s$ axis is relative, no scale is shown; only percentage deviations are significant. Dynamic range was occasionally increased by both smoothers and a larger $M$, but in no consistent pattern.

As $M$ increases, SNR for the Butterworth class and for the McDonald class (not shown) show almost no change, but when the severe smoother (0.5,0.5) is added, the situation dramatically reverses. Apparently, some type of smoothing is mandatory at this low bit rate. DPCM performance is 7.9 dB.

From the figures it is clear that multipath searching can allow a short impulse response generator to perform well where it would not otherwise, thus gaining the increased noise immunity of these filters. Calculations show these filters can sustain channel error rates as high as 0.01 (at $R = 2$) before total SNR suffers.

Choice of a code generator depends critically on $M$. Fig. 12 thus gives a composite picture of the best SNR attained by any generator tested for each $M$. It shows that the performance increase due solely to an $M = 8$ multipath tree search lies in the range 3–5 dB. (Another 0.5–2.5 dB are added by using more sophisticated codes than the DPCM class.) This performance is in the range of adaptive DPCM—but tree encoding provides adaptivity through its tree searching rather than the complexities of adaptive DPCM.

## VI. Conclusions

We have shown that tree encoding applied to speech yields significantly improved encoders both through multipath searching and more subtly designed codes. In addition, one can gain wider dynamic range, and, paradoxically, more resistance to channel errors. Subjectively, one hears decorrelated instead of correlated noise and no $f_s/2$ note.

The improved SNR of tree encoding probably centers in the higher frequencies, not necessarily in the range of speech intelligibility. For better speech recognition, then, a frequency-sensitive distortion measure for the search algorithm is needed.

The most far-reaching implication of this work is the magnitude of the SNR improvement. It is commonly believed (see, for instance, Berger, [12, sec. 5.1]) that rate-distortion optimal coding can do no more than 1–3 dB better than DPCM, for a probabilistic source with given autocorrelation. Actual tree encoding of the Gaussian i.i.d. source, either by the $M$-algorithm [11] or the stack algorithm [16], has borne this out. (Optimal DPCM coding of the autoregressive source amounts to decorrelation followed by the Gaussian i.i.d. problem). Yet we have found gains for speech as large as 7 dB. Perhaps what is missing from the theoretical calculations is the changeable disposition of real-life sources, and the ability of simple, but not too simple, information-theoretic schemes to adapt with them.

## Acknowledgment

The authors are grateful for two careful reviews, and for the comments of G. D. Forney, T. Berger, R. Gray, and A. Viterbi, among others.

## References

[1] F. Jelinek and J. B. Anderson, "Instrumentable tree encoding of information sources," *IEEE Trans. Inform. Theory*, vol. IT-17, pp. 118–119, Jan. 1971.
[2] J. B. Anderson and F. Jelinek, "A 2-cycle algorithm for source coding with a fidelity criterion," *IEEE Trans. Inform. Theory*, vol. IT-19, pp. 77–92, Jan. 1973.
[3] R. G. Gallager, "Tree encoding for sources with a distortion measure," *IEEE Trans. Inform. Theory*, vol. IT-20, pp. 65–76, Jan. 1974.
[4] J. B. Anderson, "A stack algorithm for source coding with a fidelity criterion," *IEEE Trans. Inform. Theory*, vol. IT-20, pp. 211–226, Mar. 1974.
[5] J. B. O'Neal, Jr., and R. W. Stroh, "Differential PCM for speech and data signals," *IEEE Trans. Commun. Technol.*, vol. COM-20, pp. 900–912, Oct. 1972.
[6] R. A. McDonald, "Signal-to-noise and idle channel performance of differential pulse code modulation systems—particular applications to voice signals," *Bell Syst. Tech. J.*, vol. 45, pp. 1123–1151, Sept. 1966.
[7] P. Cummisky, N. S. Jayant, and J. D. Flanagan, "Adaptive quantization in differential PCM coding of speech," in *Conf. Rec., 1973 IEEE Int. Conf. Communications*, pp. 46/17–46/22.
[8] J. G. Dunn, "Experimental 9600-bits/s voice digitizer employing adaptive prediction," *IEEE Trans. Commun. Technol.*, vol. COM-19, pp. 1021–1032, Dec. 1971.
[9] J. S. Flanagan, *Speech Analysis, Synthesis, and Perception*, 2nd ed. New York: Springer-Verlag, 1972.
[10] J. B. Anderson, "Tree coding for $A$-to-$D$ conversion of speech," Commun. Res. Lab., McMaster Univ., Hamilton, Ont., Canada, CRL Internal Rep. Series CRL-9, Nov. 1973.
[11] J. B. Bodie, "Multi-path tree encoding for analog data sources," Commun. Res. Lab., McMaster Univ., Hamilton, Ont., Canada, CRL Internal Rep. Series CRL-20, June 1974.
[12] T. Berger, *Rate Distortion Theory, A Mathematical Basis for Data Compression*. Englewood Cliffs, N.J.: Prentice-Hall, 1971.
[13] J. Max, "Quantizing for minimum distortion," *IRE Trans. Inform. Theory*, vol. IT-6, pp. 7–12, Mar. 1960.
[14] W. D. Little, "An algorithm for high-speed digital filters," *IEEE Trans. Comput.*, vol. C-23, pp. 466–469, May 1974.
[15] "Speech analysis/synthesis survey test tape," *Int. Conf. Speech Communication and Processing*, Boston, Mass., 1972.
[16] R. J. Dick, T. Berger, and F. Jelinek, "Tree encoding of Gaussian sources," *IEEE Trans. Inform. Theory*, vol. IT-20, pp. 332–336, May 1974.
[17] R. T. Gray, "Information rates of autoregressive sources," *IEEE Trans. Inform. Theory*, vol. IT-16, pp. 412–421, July 1970.

# AUTHOR CITATION INDEX

# SUBJECT INDEX

# About the Editors

LEE D. DAVISSON received his B.S.E. degree from Princeton University in 1958, and the M.S.E. and Ph.D. degrees from the University of California at Los Angeles in 1961 and 1964, respectively. From 1964 to 1969 he was an Associate Professor of Electrical Engineering at Princeton University. Since 1969 he has been Professor of Electrical Engineering at the University of Southern California. Dr. Davisson has published a number of papers in data compression over the past ten years.

ROBERT M. GRAY is an Associate Professor of Electrical Engineering at Stanford University, where he teaches courses on random processes, communications and information theory, and data compression, and performs research on the mathematical theory of data compression and reliable communication. Professor Gray received his B.S. and M.S. in electrical engineering from the Massachusetts Institute of Technology in 1966 and the Ph.D. from the University of Southern California in 1969. Professor Gray has worked as an electrical engineer at the Jet Propulsion Laboratory, Pasadena, California, and the U.S. Naval Ordnance Laboratory, Silver Springs, Maryland, and as a consultant to several companies. He is a member of IEEE, SIAM, IMS, AAAS, ICF, Sigma Xi, and Eta Kappa Nu.